THE ROUTLEDGE HANDBOOK OF KOREAN AS A SECOND LANGUAGE

The Routledge Handbook of Korean as a Second Language aims to define the field and to present the latest research in Korean as a second language (KSL).

It comprises a detailed overview of the field of KSL teaching and learning, discusses its development, and captures critical cutting-edge research within its major subfields. As the first handbook of KSL published in English, this book will be of particular interest to advanced undergraduates, graduate students, language teachers, curriculum developers, and researchers in the fields of KSL and applied linguistics.

While each chapter will be authored by internationally renowned scholars in its major subfields, the handbook aims to maintain accessibility so that it can also be of value to non-specialists.

Andrew Sangpil Byon is Associate Professor in the Department of East Asian Studies at the University at Albany, State University of New York.

Danielle Ooyoung Pyun is Associate Professor in the Department of East Asian Languages and Literatures at The Ohio State University, Columbus, Ohio.

Cover image: Sean Pavone/Alamy Stock Photo

First published 2022
by Routledge
4 Park Square, Milton Park, Abingdon, Oxon OX14 4RN

and by Routledge
605 Third Avenue, New York, NY 10158

Routledge is an imprint of the Taylor & Francis Group, an informa business

© 2022 selection and editorial matter, Andrew Sangpil Byon and Danielle Ooyoung Pyun; individual chapters, the contributors

The right of Andrew Sangpil Byon and Danielle Ooyoung Pyun to be identified as the authors of the editorial material, and of the authors for their individual chapters, has been asserted in accordance with sections 77 and 78 of the Copyright, Designs and Patents Act 1988.

All rights reserved. No part of this book may be reprinted or reproduced or utilised in any form or by any electronic, mechanical, or other means, now known or hereafter invented, including photocopying and recording, or in any information storage or retrieval system, without permission in writing from the publishers.

Trademark notice: Product or corporate names may be trademarks or registered trademarks, and are used only for identification and explanation without intent to infringe.

British Library Cataloguing-in-Publication Data
A catalogue record for this book is available from the British Library

Library of Congress Cataloging-in-Publication Data
Names: Byon, Andrew Sangpil, editor. | Pyun, Danielle Ooyoung, editor.
Title: The Routledge handbook of Korean as a second language / edited by Andrew S. Byon and Danielle O. Pyun.
Description: London ; New York : Routledge, 2022. | Includes bibliographical references and index.
Identifiers: LCCN 2021047313 (print) | LCCN 2021047314 (ebook) | ISBN 9780367472894 (hardback) | ISBN 9781032219059 (paperback) | ISBN 9781003034704 (ebook)
Subjects: LCSH: Korean language—Study and teaching—Foreign speakers. | Second language acquisition—Methodology. | LCGFT: Essays.
Classification: LCC PL907 .R68 2022 (print) | LCC PL907 (ebook) | DDC 495.780071—dc23/eng/20211228
LC record available at https://lccn.loc.gov/2021047313
LC ebook record available at https://lccn.loc.gov/2021047314

ISBN: 978-0-367-47289-4 (hbk)
ISBN: 978-1-032-21905-9 (pbk)
ISBN: 978-1-003-03470-4 (ebk)

DOI: 10.4324/9781003034704

Typeset in Times New Roman
by Apex CoVantage, LLC

THE ROUTLEDGE HANDBOOK OF KOREAN AS A SECOND LANGUAGE

Edited by Andrew Sangpil Byon and Danielle Ooyoung Pyun

LONDON AND NEW YORK

8	Task-based language teaching in Korean classroom contexts: promoting learner engagement during task performance *YouJin Kim and Sanghee Kang*	129
9	Instructional technology in KSL settings *Jayoung Song*	149
10	Culture in Korean language teaching: focusing on a dynamic view of culture *Kyung-Eun Yoon*	176
11	Korean for specific purposes *Ji-Young Jung*	194
12	Content-based instruction in KSL settings *Sang-Keun Shin*	222
13	Community service-learning in Korean *Sung-Ock S. Sohn and Soyeon Kim*	235

PART III
Approaches to Korean as a second language — **255**

14	Corpus-based research and KSL *Sun-Hee Lee*	257
15	Conversation analysis for KSL: teaching and learning sequence organization *Mary Shin Kim*	277
16	The intersection of discourse, grammar, register, pragmatics, and culture *Susan Strauss and Jongoh Eun*	298
17	Error analysis *Seong-Chul Shin*	319
18	Social interactions in KSL settings *Hakyoon Lee*	346
19	National standards and Korean as a second language *Young-mee Yu Cho*	364

CONTENTS

List of contributors   *viii*

1 Korean as a second/foreign language (KSL): an overview   1
   Andrew Sangpil Byon and Danielle Ooyoung Pyun

PART I
The acquisition of Korean as a second language   **9**

2 Second language learning of polysemous Korean words   11
   Ebru Türker

3 Phonological acquisition   32
   Jeffrey J. Holliday

4 Linguistic politeness   51
   Lucien Brown

5 KSL syntax and semantics   68
   EunHee Lee

6 Relative clauses in Korean as a second language: old and new findings   89
   William O'Grady and Chae-Eun Kim

PART II
Teaching and learning Korean as a second language   **109**

7 Pragmatic teaching and learning   111
   Jieun Kiaer, Jiyoung Shin, and Derek Driggs

20 Usage-based approach to grammar in Korean language teaching
    and learning 386
    Hyo Sang Lee

PART IV
Individual differences and social factors **415**

21 Individual learner differences in learning Korean as a second language 417
    Danielle Ooyoung Pyun and Andrew Sangpil Byon

22 Korean as a heritage language 437
    Samantha Harris and Jin Sook Lee

23 Language ideologies and identity formation among KSL learners 454
    Mi Yung Park

24 Instructor individual characteristics in a KSL/KFL setting: a research
    perspective 473
    Hye-Sook Wang

PART V
Assessment **491**

25 KSL assessment: the TOPIK, achievement tests, and research trends 493
    *Chungsook Kim, Jung Hee Lee, Danielle Ooyoung Pyun, and
    Andrew Sangpil Byon*

26 Integrated performance assessment and KSL 518
    Sahie Kang

27 Interactional competence in Korean and its assessment 540
    Hyo Sang Lee, Kyung-Eun Yoon, and Sang-Seok Yoon

Index 568

CONTRIBUTORS

Lucien Brown (Ph.D. in Korean Language Research, SOAS, University of London, 2008) is Senior Lecturer of Korean Studies at Monash University. He has published extensively on Korean politeness and honorifics, both in native-speaker and language-learner contexts.

Andrew Sangpil Byon (Ph.D. in Korean Linguistics, University of Hawai'i at Mānoa, 2001) is Associate Professor of Korean Studies in the Department of East Asian Studies at the University at Albany, State University of New York. His research areas are Korean as a foreign/second language pedagogy, second language acquisition (L2 pragmatics), and sociolinguistics.

Young-mee Yu Cho (Ph.D. in Linguistics, Stanford University, 1990) is Associate Professor in the Department of Asian Languages and Cultures at Rutgers, The State University of New Jersey. She is one of the five authors of the first four volumes of the definitive textbook series, *Integrated Korean* (2000–2020) as well as a new series for heritage learners, *Integrated Korean: Accelerated 1 & 2* (2020). She spearheaded the publication of the *National Standards for Korean Language Learning* in 2012 and produced the *College Korean Curriculum Inspired by National Standards for Korean* as Chair of the AATK Curriculum Development Project in 2015.

Derek Driggs is a DPhil candidate in Oriental Studies at the University of Oxford. He researches pragmatics and the relationship between honorifics, hierarchy, and intimacy in East Asian languages. He is an experienced teacher of the Korean language and is interested in effective methods of teaching pragmatic skills.

Jongoh Eun (Ph.D. in Applied Linguistics, The Pennsylvania State University, 2003) is Professor at the Defense Language Institute Foreign Language Center. He has extensive experience with teaching, developing teaching materials/curriculum and supervising at all levels of Korean programs from Basic to Intermediate and Advanced Courses at DLIFLC. His research interests include all aspects of Korean L2 pedagogy, including discourse-based grammar, approaches to the teaching of culture in L2 settings, authentic materials development, and curriculum development.

Contributors

Samantha Harris (M.A. TESOL, Georgetown University, 2016) is a Ph.D. candidate in the Department of Education at the University of California, Santa Barbara. Her research focuses on the intersections of language, race, and education, with a specific focus on heritage language learners and students classified as English Learners.

Jeffrey J. Holliday (Ph.D. in Linguistics, The Ohio State University, 2012) is Assistant Professor of Korean Linguistics at Korea University. He is interested in second language phonological acquisition, speech perception, sociophonetics, and Korean language variation and change.

Ji-Young Jung (Ed.D. in Applied Linguistics, Teachers College, Columbia University, 2009) is Lecturer in Korean at Columbia University. Her research areas are foreign language pedagogy, second language acquisition, discourse analysis, and heritage language education.

Sahie Kang (Ph.D. in Linguistics, University of Florida, 1990) is Professor and Director of School of Korean at Middlebury College and serves as a facilitator of ACTFL Assessment and Professional Development Workshops. She served as Dean of Arabic, Korean, and other language schools at Defense Language Institute and as President of AATK and Vice President of IAKLE. Kang specializes in second language pedagogy and assessment, curriculum design, learner language analysis, and discourse analysis.

Sanghee Kang (M.A. Applied Linguistics, Georgia State University, 2016) is a doctoral student in the Department of Applied Linguistics & ESL at Georgia State University. Her research interests include second language acquisition, task-based language teaching, computer-assisted language learning, and L2 writing.

Jieun Kiaer (Ph.D. in Linguistics, University of London, 2007) is YBM-KF Associate Professor in Korean Language and Linguistics at the University of Oxford. Her research areas include pragmatics, syntax-phonology interface, translanguaging, Korean English, and non-verbal honorifics.

Chae-Eun Kim (Ph.D. in Linguistics, University of Hawai'i at Mānoa, 2013) is Assistant Professor in the Department of English at Chosun University in Gwangju, Korea. Her research areas include morphological syntax, pedagogical grammar, and second language acquisition.

Chungsook Kim (Ph.D. in Korean Linguistics, Korea University) is Professor in the Department of Korean Language and Literature at Korea University. Her research areas are Korean language curriculum, Korean language material development, and Korean language assessment as a foreign language.

Mary Shin Kim (Ph.D. in Korean Linguistics, University of California, Los Angeles, 2006) is Associate Professor in the Department of East Asian Languages and Literatures at the University of Hawai'i at Mānoa. Her research focuses on interactional linguistics, conversation analysis, and second language pedagogy.

Soyeon Kim (Ph.D. in Applied Linguistics, University of California, Los Angeles, 2016) is Director of the Korean Language Program in the Department of Asian Languages and Cultures at the University of Michigan. Her research areas include interactional linguistics, discourse analysis, and second language pedagogy.

Contributors

YouJin Kim (Ph.D. in Applied Linguistics, Northern Arizona University, 2009) is Professor in the Department of Applied Linguistics and ESL, Georgia State University. Her research specializes in second language acquisition (SLA), second language pedagogy, and task-based language teaching and assessment in applied linguistics.

EunHee Lee (Ph.D. in Linguistics, University at Groningen, the Netherlands, 2000) is Professor in the Linguistics Department at the University at Buffalo. Her research areas are Korean linguistics, semantics, and second language acquisition.

Hakyoon Lee (Ph.D. in Second Language Studies, The University of Hawai'i at Mānoa, 2014) is Assistant Professor in the Department of World Languages and Cultures at Georgia State University. She has been teaching Korean at GSU since the fall semester of 2013. Her research interests lie at the intersection of language and identity, sociolinguistics, bilingualism, multilingualism, and immigrant education.

Hyo Sang Lee (Ph.D. in Linguistics, University of California, Los Angeles, 1991) is Associate Professor of Korean Language and Linguistics in the Department of East Asian Languages and Cultures at Indiana University. His research areas are discourse-pragmatic approach to grammar, grammaticalization, language change and synchronic variation, linguistic typology, and Korean as a foreign/second language pedagogy.

Jin Sook Lee (Ph.D. in Education, Stanford University, 2000) is Professor of Education and affiliate faculty member of Linguistics and Asian American Studies at the University of California, Santa Barbara. Her research areas are heritage language maintenance, bilingual education, and English as a second language development and pedagogy.

Jung Hee Lee (Ph.D. in Korean Language and Literature, Kyung Hee University) is Professor in the Graduate School of Education at Kyung Hee University. She specializes in KSL (Korean as a second/foreign language) and her research focuses on KSL pedagogy, Korean language curriculum, and material development.

Sun-Hee Lee (Ph.D. in Korean Linguistics at Yonsei University, 2000 and Ph.D. in Linguistics at The Ohio State University, 2004) is Professor of East Asian Languages and Cultures at Wellesley College. Her research areas are corpus linguistics, learner corpora, and Korean grammar. She has been publishing books and articles on anaphora, argument structure, particles, and learner language as well as the corpus-based discourse analysis of news media.

William O'Grady (Ph.D. in Linguistics, University of Chicago, 1978) is Professor of Linguistics at the University of Hawai'i at Mānoa. His interests include syntax, language acquisition, heritage languages, Korean, and Jejueo.

Mi Yung Park (Ph.D. in Korean Linguistics, University of Hawai'i at Mānoa, 2014) is Senior Lecturer in Korean at the University of Auckland. Her research areas are language and identity, heritage language education, and multilingualism.

Danielle Ooyoung Pyun (Ph.D. in Foreign and Second Language Education, The Ohio State University, 2003) is Associate Professor in the Department of East Asian Languages and Literatures at The Ohio State University, where she teaches Korean language and culture courses and directs the Korean language program. She specializes in Korean language pedagogy, and her research interests include classroom L2 (second/foreign) acquisition, L2 assessment, learner variables, and instructional materials development.

Jiyoung Shin (Ph.D. in Linguistics, University of London, 1997) is Professor of Korean Linguistics at Korea University. Her research areas are phonology and phonetics, particularly socio-phonetics of Korean, the interface of syntax/semantics and phonology, and spoken grammar for Korean.

Sang-Keun Shin (Ph.D. in Applied Linguistics, University of California, Los Angeles, 2004) is Professor in the Department of English Language Education at Ewha Womans University. He is the director of Ewha Womans University Korean Language Education Center. His research interests include language assessment, second language pedagogy, and second language teacher education.

Seong-Chul Shin (Ph.D. in Linguistics, University of New South Wales, Sydney, 2006) is Senior Lecturer/Associate Professor in Korean Studies at the School of Humanities and Languages, UNSW. He teaches both undergraduate and postgraduate Korean courses and conducts research in the areas of Korean as a foreign, second, or heritage language with a particular focus on error analysis, pedagogy, curriculum planning, and language policy issues.

Sung-Ock S. Sohn (Ph.D. in Linguistics, University of Hawaiʻi at Mānoa, 1988) is Professor of Korean language and linguistics in the Department of Asian Languages and Cultures at the University of California, Los Angeles (UCLA). Her research areas are discourse-functional linguistics in Korean, Asian language pedagogy, and grammaticalization.

Jayoung Song (Ph.D. in Foreign Language Education, the University of Texas at Austin, 2015) is Assistant Professor of Korean in the Department of Asian Studies at Pennsylvania State University. Her research focuses on Korean applied linguistics, computer-assisted language learning, intercultural communication, and second language reading, all of which she incorporates in her teaching.

Susan Strauss (Ph.D. in Applied Linguistics, UCLA, 1998) is Associate Professor of Applied Linguistics and Asian Studies at Penn State. Her research centers on the analysis of discourse and its application to culture, semantics, pragmatics, grammar, and cognition. She is co-author of *Discourse Analysis: Putting Our Worlds Into Words* (with Parastou Feiz) and *Grammar, Meaning, and Concepts: A Discourse-Based Approach to English Grammar* (with Parastou Feiz and Xuehua Xiang), has co-edited four volumes of *Japanese-Korean Linguistics* (CSLI, Stanford), and served as editor-in-chief for *The Korean Language in America*, Penn State University Press.

Ebru Türker (Ph.D. in Korean Linguistics, University of Hawaiʻi at Mānoa, 2006) is Associate Professor of Korean Studies in the School of International Letters and Cultures at Arizona State University. Her research areas are second language acquisition of Korean, psycholinguistic experimental methods for studying the bilingual lexicon, figurative language, and corpus linguistics.

Contributors

Hye-Sook Wang (Ph.D. in English Language and Linguistics, University of Wisconsin at Madison, 1993) is Associate Professor of Korean Studies in the Department of East Asian Studies at Brown University. Her main research interests are in sociolinguistics, cross-cultural communication/intercultural pragmatics, and teaching Korean as a second or foreign language.

Kyung-Eun Yoon (Ph.D. in Educational Psychology, University of Illinois at Urbana-Champaign, 2006) is Senior Lecturer in the Department of Modern Languages, Linguistics and Intercultural Communication at the University of Maryland, Baltimore County. Her research interests are conversation analysis, discourse analysis, and language pedagogy, related to the Korean language and culture.

Sang-Seok Yoon (Ph.D. in Korean Linguistics, University of Hawai'i at Mānoa, 2010) is Assistant Professor of Korean Linguistics in the Department of Asian & Slavic Languages and Literatures at the University of Iowa. His research area includes politeness, interlanguage pragmatics, and teaching Korean as a foreign/second language.

1
KOREAN AS A SECOND/FOREIGN LANGUAGE (KSL)

An overview

Andrew Sangpil Byon and Danielle Ooyoung Pyun

Introduction

Korean as a second/foreign language (KSL) is an academic endeavor, and it is based on a rigorous and scientific process of accumulating knowledge about KSL teaching and learning either inside or outside of classroom settings.[1] Within the field of second/foreign language (L2) studies, KSL has expanded and gained ground as an independent academic discipline in the past two to three decades. Accordingly, there has been a growing number of Korean reference materials published in English and available to the general population and international market in recent years. For example, as for Korean linguistics, there have been two handbooks published: Brown and Yeon (2015) and Cho and Whitman (in press). Both handbooks provide an overview of the field of Korean linguistics as it currently stands, serving as a comprehensive guide to a wide range of topics in Korean linguistics. These books have a section on language acquisition. However, the primary target readers are researchers and advanced students in Korean linguistics.

As for Korean as a foreign language, Byon and Pyun (2012) and Cho (2021) are noteworthy. The edited volume by Byon and Pyun (2012) is a collection of both theoretical and empirical studies that support the development of instructional strategies and enhancement of student learning and performance of Korean as a foreign language in the US educational college setting. While each article in the volume is of significant value, offering a number of pedagogical implications, the scope and focus of the book is not comprehensive enough to be used as a handbook for KSL. Meanwhile, Cho (2021) is a welcome addition to the field, as this addresses several key topics and findings of KSL research. However, its main focus is on Korean as a foreign language (KFL) in the US college setting, and it is primarily designed and intended as a textbook for graduate programs in KFL, rather than a comprehensive reference guide.

Despite the increasing number of Korean reference publications for English-speaking readers, there has not yet been one that presents state-of-the-art overviews of KSL research in English.

This handbook fills this void as the first authoritative body of work written and published in English to serve as a comprehensive reference guide for the rapidly expanding field of KSL. The volume aims to define the field, providing a wide range of topics in KSL, discussing the development within the topic areas, surveying the latest research in KSL, capturing critical accounts of cutting-edge research within its major subfields, and suggesting a path for future research.

The handbook consists of 27 chapters (including the current chapter) written by 35 world-renowned experts and prominently emerging researchers in the field. The contributors come from diverse research backgrounds precisely due to KSL's cross-disciplinary nature (e.g., linguistics, conversational analysis, corpus linguistics, discourse analysis, language testing, multilingualism, pragmatics, sociolinguistics, psycholinguistics, foreign language pedagogy, and so forth). They were requested to provide an informed, but not necessarily exhaustive, introduction to the topic under consideration. We believe that each chapter serves four purposes: (1) providing key findings and issues of updated literature, (2) sharing the contributors' understanding of and approaches to the issues, (3) providing direct links between research and practice, and (4) suggesting directions for future research.

Components of the handbook

To achieve the goal of surveying state-of-the-art research in the multifaceted disciplines of KSL, we divided the handbook into the following five parts, and each part covers varying topics of KSL:

Part I: The acquisition of Korean as a second language
(vocabulary, phonology, linguistic politeness, syntax, and semantics)

Part II: Teaching and learning Korean as a second language
(pragmatics, task-based language teaching, instructional technology, culture, Korean for specific purposes, content-based instruction, and community-service learning)

Part III: Approaches to Korean as a second language
(corpus-based research, conversational analysis, discourse analysis, error analysis, social interactions, national standards, and usage-based approach)

Part IV: Individual differences and social factors
(psychological and cognitive factors, Korean as a heritage language, language ideologies and identity formations, and instructor variables)

Part V: Assessment
(assessment methods, integrated performance assessment, and interactional competence assessment)

It should be noted that, in reality, there is sometimes considerable and inevitable overlap between chapters. For instance, the subject of Korean honorifics is covered not only in Chapter 4, "Linguistics politeness," but also in Chapter 7, "Pragmatics teaching and learning," and Chapter 10, "Culture in Korean language teaching: focusing on a dynamic view of culture." Issues related to heritage language learners are extensively discussed in Chapter 22, "Korean as a heritage language," but it is also discussed in Chapter 23, "Language ideologies and identity formation among KSL learners." However, many of these same topics and variables are covered in multiple chapters from different but complementary perspectives.

Part I: The acquisition of Korean as a second language

Part 1 (Chapters 2–6) concerns different aspects of KSL from language-acquisition perspectives. The first chapter of this section discusses KSL learners' vocabulary acquisition. One most common cause for KSL lexical errors is L1 interference. The meaning of the target word, for instance, rarely overlaps in its entirety with that of learners' L1. However, learners often directly translate the target word from their L1 to L2. When a target word has multiple meanings and usage, the error is more prone to occur.

Chapter 2, by Ebru Türker, looks into L2 lexical acquisition in KSL contents with a focus on teaching and learning of polysemous Korean words in KSL contexts. The author provides a survey of empirical and theoretical works related to L2 polysemous words acquisition and explores how the current L2 theoretical and instructional approaches of L2 polysemous acquisition studies can be applied to KSL settings. As pedagogical implications, the author suggests that the frequency of occurrences of polysemous meanings in both written and spoken speech modes should be considered when prioritizing target words to teach. In addition, she advocates for consciousness-raising activities that aim to raise learners' awareness regarding the differences in L1 and L2 word meanings.

Understanding how KSL learners acquire phonological segments is crucial for pronunciation teaching. In Chapter 3, Jeffrey J. Holliday reviews key research findings and issues related to the segmental phonology of Korean. With an introduction to the phonetic properties of Korean phonological contrasts and its relevant theoretical frameworks, the author focuses on phonological acquisition patterns of stops, affricates, fricatives, sonorants, and vowels by KSL learners with different L1s (e.g., Chinese and English).

KSL learners' communicative success depends to a large extent on their ability to understand and express "politeness." Traditionally, the description of politeness in Korean linguistics and KSL literature tends to focus on its intricate honorifics. However, an increasing number of recent studies point out that politeness is communicated not only through linguistic levels but also multimodality. Chapter 4, by Lucien Brown, provides a comprehensive overview regarding how Korean politeness (or impoliteness) is achieved not only through its intricate honorifics system but also through various communicative acts, formulaic expressions, and multimodal cues. In addition, the author surveys up-to-date research on KSL learners' acquisition of politeness, both inside and outside of the classroom setting. He remarks that even highly advanced learners may not display appropriate use of honorifics, and learners can intentionally defy the norm in order to highlight their "foreigner" or "L2 learner" identity. For future research direction, the author calls for more extensive research that covers not only fixed linguistic politeness but also other aspects, such as address terms, speech acts, impoliteness, and multimodality.

The last two chapters of this section tackle the issues related to the L2 acquisition of Korean syntax in KSL settings. In Chapter 5, EunHee Lee overviews unique syntactic and semantic features of Korean that include clause types, case, number, topic markings on nominals, relative clauses, honorifics, tense, aspect marking on verbs, and *wh*-questions. Then, Lee introduces several key linguistic hypotheses to investigate whether/if/how these hypotheses can be applicable in describing KSL acquisition.

Korean is one of the most difficult languages to acquire, especially for learners with English as their first language, and this is partly attributed to the vast morphosyntactic differences in English and Korean. Chapter 6, by William O'Grady and Chae-Eun Kim, focuses on the acquisition of Korean relative clauses, presenting two case studies involving the acquisition of relative clauses by American adult KSL learners. Their two case studies, though separated by a span of two decades, reveal that the difficulty of relativization follows the relational hierarchy: Subject > Direct Object > Indirect Object/Oblique.

Part II: Teaching and learning Korean as a second language

Part II (Chapters 7–13) covers a number of central issues related to KSL pedagogy. The chapters in this section explore different types of instruction that have been theoretically and empirically supported, presenting overarching themes of past and present pedagogy with implications for future practice.

Chapter 7, by Jieun Kiaer, Jiyoung Shin, and Derek Driggs, discusses several instructional issues pertaining to pragmatic features in KSL settings. The authors offer an overview of multifaceted pragmatics features of Korean that include address terms, speech styles, speech acts, and appropriate nonverbal behaviors. Examining how pragmatic elements have been taught and assessed in KSL instructional contexts, the authors reveal that current educational practices often have overlooked the pragmatic features, and teaching materials often fail to reflect sociopragmatic complexity, embedded in the language, correctly. For future endeavors, the authors urge for more innovative and explicit instruction of pragmatic elements in contexts.

In the last few decades, task-based language teaching (TBLT) has emerged as a major teaching method in the field of instructional second language acquisition. Chapter 8, by YouJin Kim and Sanghee Kang, looks into the TBLT for KSL. The authors first introduce major concepts and terminologies related to TBLT, then summarize core findings and research issues of past and present studies on TBLT, and finally discuss its key issues related to its task design, implementation factors, and assessment. After which, they explore instructional implications and applications for KSL settings.

Beside TBLT, another fast-growing topic that has received increasing attention among L2 pedagogy is computer-assisted language learning (CALL). As coinciding technology advancements and positive empirical findings from CALL studies accumulate, the use of technology in KSL has also become more autonomous, convenient, and frequent in this digital world.

Chapter 9, by Jayoung Song, focuses on instructional technology in KSL settings. With an aim to review and explore what, why, how, and to what extent the instructional technology can benefit KSL teaching and learning, the author narrates a historical overview on the KSL instructional technology; discusses theories pertinent to L2 teaching and learning with technology; and introduces the past, present, and emerging technological tools for KSL pedagogy.

In Chapter 10, Kyung-Eun Yoon concerns L2 culture teaching and learning in the KSL curriculum. The author provides an overview of existing L2, as well as KSL studies on teaching culture. The author discusses how target cultural values are embedded and reflected in the Korean language – its intricate honorific system and major communicative acts, such as apologies, complaints, and requests – and discusses challenges faced by KSL teachers with suggestions for future research directions.

With the increasing number of KSL learners who intend to learn the target language for a specific use or purpose, the research interest in Korean for a specific purpose (KSP) and the need to develop KSL curricular of interdisciplinary and of a student-oriented nature that can meet different demands of learners, has been growing. Chapter 11, by Ji-Young Jung, examines the current status and possibilities for future research on KSP. Jung points out key trends, findings, and issues in KSP research and practice in the United States, as well as in South Korea. Different forms of KSP reviewed include Korean for occupational purposes (e.g., business Korean, Korean for healthcare professions, Korean for translation/interpretation, Korean for missionaries, etc.), Korean for tourism, and Korean for female marriage immigrants (although specific to Korean as a second language context). The author takes the chapter further by finding ways of teaching and learning KSP in the digitally advanced era. Also included in the chapter are instructions as to how to design the curriculum and assess KSP, including high-stakes tests.

Content-based instruction (CBI) is a teaching method that combines content study and target language study, designed to correspond to the needs of learners (Brinton, Snow, & Wesche, 2004). The focus of Chapter 12, by Sang-Keun Shin, is content-based instruction (CBI) and KSL. Shin summarizes the definitions and characteristics of various CBI models, introduces major CBI courses in KSL settings, discusses the challenges faced with CBI, and gives suggestions for future direction.

The physical classroom is not the only context of interest for KSL, as considerable L2 learning can occur outside of the classroom. In Chapter 13, Sung-Ock S. Sohn and Soyeon Kim introduce community service learning as an effective pedagogical tool for delivering KSL language curricula. The authors report two case studies of advanced-level Korean classes at higher institutions in North America, where learners put their language skills into authentic practice and at the same time provide service to a number of community sectors, such as hospitals, public schools, and local community centers. Demonstrating how service-learning opportunities enable learners to make connections between their language skills and real-life settings, the authors assert that these community engagements enhance learners' language learning further and raise their sociocultural awareness.

Part III: approaches to Korean as a second language

The chapters in this section (Chapters 14–20) examine different approaches to KSL. First, the advancement in technology makes it possible for L2 researchers and educators to assess large bodies of both written and spoken digital data and apply the corpus analysis to L2 classroom settings. The topic of Chapter 14, by Sun-Hee Lee, is the application of the corpus linguistic analysis approach to KSL. By focusing on a specific type of corpus, that of KSL learner corpus data that has the potential to provide valuable information regarding language use patterns and frequency information of learners, the author introduces diverse KSL learner corpora resources and looks into a number of ways learner corpora can be designed, annotated, accessed, analyzed, and applied to KSL instruction.

Conversational analysis (CA) studies have broadened our understanding of how people talk and interact by describing the overall structure and infrastructure of interaction. Mary Shin Kim, in Chapter 15, overviews central findings of CA studies and considers how the CA framework can be applied to KSL teaching. She focuses on illustrating how turns, actions, and activities are in sequences and discusses how the structures and resources of turn-taking and sequences can be adapted to KSL instruction.

In Chapter 16, Susan Strauss and Jongoh Eun discuss the application of discourse-based analytic techniques in developing KSL teaching materials with authentic texts. The authors survey main issues and research findings pertinent to the use of authentic texts in L2 and introduce a number of discourse analytic techniques involving multiple scopes of analysis. Then they demonstrate how to analyze the authentic texts and develop them into more student-centered and culture-focused real-life teaching materials.

Chapter 17, by Seong-Chul Shin, provides a detailed, descriptive, and informative overview of primary findings and issues of KSL error analysis research. The author categorizes learner errors into categories: orthographic errors, lexical errors, and grammatical errors. Then he further analyzes and identifies their types, occurrence rate, and possible sources or causes. The author also takes an in-depth look into how to improve instruction to minimize such errors.

The topic of Chapter 18, by Hakyoon Lee, is social interaction and KSL. The author reviews the fundamental constructs for L2 social interactions and overviews the key findings and issues of major L2, as well as KSL social interaction studies. She examines L2 social interactions in varying contexts, such as classroom interactions, family interactions, and community settings, such as churches and schools.

In the past decade, significant progress has been made in KSL in the US educational setting with the establishment of National Standards for Korean. Korean Standards offers a scheme for designing, implementing, and assessing the extended sequence of KSL study for K–16 students. Young-mee Yu Cho, in Chapter 19, gives an overview of Korean Standards and discusses a number of substantial contributions Korean Standards have made in the KSL field. In addition, she presents Standards-based KSL teaching materials and suggests future works to be done.

In Chapter 20, Hyo Sang Lee presents a usage-based approach to grammar for KSL teaching and learning. After reviewing the main tenets of the usage-based theory of language, the author examines how grammatical descriptions are presented in major KSL textbooks to assess whether they appropriately and correctly reflect the actual usage patterns of Korean. The author reports that the Korean-language examples used in the books are not authentic discourse and that their grammatical descriptions are mostly prescriptive and rule-based, hence they do not reflect the actual usage patterns of Korean. The author advocates the use of the usage-based approach to KSL grammar teaching, calling for increasing awareness among KSL teachers regarding the importance of teaching what Koreans actually speak, not what linguists consider correct grammar.

Part IV: individual differences and social factors

Individual learner variables influence L2 learning processes and outcomes, and thus they have long received much attention in SLA (second language acquisition). Part IV (Chapters 21–24) covers issues related to individual differences and social factors in KSL settings. In Chapter 21, Danielle Ooyoung Pyun and Andrew Sangpil Byon focus on a number of KSL learner variables, such as motivation, anxiety, and linguistic confidence. They first go over the central constructs of the individual learner variables reviewed in SLA. Then they take a step further by examining key findings and issues from relevant KSL literature and suggesting directions for future research.

Chapter 22, by Samantha Harris and Jin Sook Lee, concerns Korean as a heritage language learner issue. Reviewing literature critically, Harris and Lee discuss the expanding profiles of Korean as heritage language speakers and offer a more inclusive definition of who should make up Korean as a heritage language (KHL) learner. That is, the definition of KHL learners and speakers should include not only those who have ethnic ties but also those who have cultural and/or linguistic connections to Korean. The authors also discuss the varying language practices of KHL speakers, often characterized by frequent code-switching and mixing. With this growing diversity of Korean as a heritage language learner population in mind, the chapter calls for a reevaluation of the goals of KHL education.

In Chapter 23, Mi Yung Park surveys the key research findings and issues in the study of language ideologies and identity among KSL learners of different backgrounds. Focusing on three groups of KSL learners, namely, heritage learners, study abroad learners, and migrant learners (including marriage-migrant women, and North Korean refugees), the author discusses how these groups of KSL learners form their identities in varying sociocultural settings and how their identities and language ideologies affect their language-learning experiences. As a pedagogical implication, the chapter calls for a need to develop KSL curricula that reflect these KSL learners' multifaceted and multilayered identities, language ideologies, and their diverse sociocultural and socioeconomic backgrounds. It also raises teachers and learners' awareness of linguistic and cultural diversities that exist in the current multilingual and multicultural contexts.

Chapter 24 by Hye-Sook Wang discusses the main research findings and issues related to a necessary, yet relatively under-explored component of KSL, that of individual characteristics of KSL teachers. The chapter reviews a number of instructor variables, such as teacher talk, educational backgrounds, teaching experiences, gender, and teachers' perceptions, and suggests research topics for future development.

Part V: assessment

Part V (Chapters 25–27) concerns a number of core issues related to KSL assessment. The goal of Chapter 25 by Chungsook Kim, Jung Hee Lee, Danielle Ooyoung Pyun, and Andrew Sang-pil Byon is fourfold. First, it provides a comprehensive overview of the Test of Proficiency in Korean (TOPIK), the most widely used KSL proficiency test. Second, the chapter reviews current practices of achievement tests amongst KSL institutions in Korea. Third, it delineates the research trends in KSL assessment fields, providing a general overview of the KSL assessment studies published in the last four decades. Lastly, the chapter discusses future directions for research on KSL assessment.

The topic of Chapter 26 by Sahie Kang is Integrated Performance Assessment (IPA), which is an approach that aims to evaluate learners' in-class language-performance progress and, at the same time, coach them to achieve proficiency goals. The author summarizes the L2 as well as KSL research on IPA and explores their pedagogical implications for KSL settings.

In Chapter 27, Hyo Sang Lee, Kyung-Eun Yoon, and Sang-Seok Yoon set out to explore the assessment issues related to interactional competence in KSL contexts. Noting that linguistic competence is still the major focus of KSL education and assessment, the authors argue for the need to measure learners' interactional competence. Then, drawing from conversation analysis–based studies on interactional competence, the authors demonstrate how, compared to native speakers, learners of different proficiency levels manifest varying strategic components of interactional competence, such as listeners' responses, self- or other-repairs, turn-taking, etc. In addition, they propose a set of criteria for assessing KSL learners' level-appropriate interactional competence.

Concluding remarks

As the first handbook of KSL published in English, this volume would be of particular interest to advanced undergraduates, graduate students, language teachers, curriculum developers, and researchers in the fields of KSL and applied linguistics. It is hoped that the readers find this book helpful and useful in defining this rapidly growing field, understanding the key findings and issues in the latest KSL research, gaining insightful pedagogical implications, and exploring innovative and productive ideas for future research.

Acknowledgement

While working toward the completion of this volume, we are indebted to many individuals. First and foremost, our gratitude extends to the contributors in this volume for their commitment, patience, and understanding from the initial stage of submitting abstracts to the final production phase. It has been truly an honor and a privilege to collaborate with all of them. We also express our special appreciation to anonymous reviewers for their thorough reviews and valuable feedback on the earlier manuscripts. Our sincere acknowledgement also goes to the patience and professional support of the editorial and production team of Routledge, including Andrea Hartill, Iola Ashby, and Ellie Auton. Lastly, our heartfelt thanks go to our respective families for their encouragement and support.

Note

1 Here we define KSL as the term that encapsulates Korean learning in all contexts, i.e., both Korean as a foreign language (KFL) settings and Korean as a second language (KSL) settings. We are aware that some Korean language educators, especially in the United States, maintain this strong KFL/KSL distinction. However, in the broader field of second language acquisition, this foreign language (FL)/second language (SL) dichotomy has been much criticized, and the universal use of SL has prevailed. By using KSL in a broader sense, we feel that readers can understand and interpret the findings of our chapters in a more comprehensive and holistic manner.

References

Brinton, D. M., Snow, M. A., & Wesche, M. B. (2004). *Content-based second language instruction*. Ann Arbor, MI: University of Michigan Press.

Brown, L., & Yeon, J. (Eds.). (2015). *The handbook of Korean linguistics*. Oxford: Wiley-Blackwell.

Byon, A., & Pyun, D. (Eds.). (2012). *Teaching and learning Korean as a foreign language: A collection of empirical studies*. Columbus, OH: National Foreign Language Resource Center, The Ohio State University.

Cho, S., & Whitman, J. (Eds.). (in press). *The Cambridge handbook of Korean linguistics*. Cambridge: Cambridge University Press.

Cho, Y. (Ed.). (2021). *Teaching Korean as a foreign language: Theories and practices*. Oxon and New York: Routledge.

PART I

The acquisition of Korean as a second language

2
SECOND LANGUAGE LEARNING OF POLYSEMOUS KOREAN WORDS

Ebru Türker

Introduction

This chapter provides an overview of recent empirical findings on the acquisition of polysemous words from the perspective of second language acquisition (SLA), focusing on Korean as a second language (KSL). It examines prior studies on learners' development of knowledge of polysemous words to provide improved and more nuanced, research-based pedagogical approaches to teaching them.

Lexical knowledge development is an essential part of acquiring second language (L2) proficiency (Schmitt, 2008). Research on this topic provides insights into how L2 learners internalize and acquire lexical items cognitively and how they process, comprehend, and produce lexical items in the target language. Studies addressing lexical proficiency and its development have examined lexical accuracy (Crossley, Salsbury, & McNamara, 2010; De La Fuente, 2002; Ellis, 1995; Schmitt, 1998), lexical richness (Broeder, Extra, & van Hout, 1993; Daller, van Hout, & Treffers-Daller, 2003; Laufer & Nation, 1995), lexical frequency (Ellis, 2002; Madlener, 2016; Nation, 2001b; Vilkaitė-Lozdienė & Schmitt, 2020), and lexical diversity (Greidanus & Nienhuis, 2001; Polio, 2001). There is far less research on the development of word senses or lexical networks (Meara, 2002; Schmitt, 1998), although there is evidence that one way to improve vocabulary knowledge is to make use of the sense relations of polysemous words (Wesche & Paribakht, 1996).

In learning a second language, achieving lexical proficiency requires gaining a richness and depth of word knowledge beyond single meanings. Previous research has shown that learning multiple meanings of polysemous words is difficult for L2 learners. For instance, Laufer (1997, p. 26) observed that, for L2 learners, polysemous words will often be "words you think you know" but do not; that is, learners can be familiar with only a word's most frequent uses and therefore misinterpret it when they encounter it used in a different sense.

Both breadth and depth of vocabulary knowledge are widely used to improve and determine lexical proficiency.[1] Breadth refers to the size of a learner's vocabulary. Depth concerns all aspects of lexical knowledge beyond the basic form-meaning mapping and is also described as the richness, quality, or "depth" of understanding (Anderson & Freebody, 1981); it includes words' polysemous senses along with their concepts and referents, collocations, associations, constraints, morphological and pragmatic features, and even registers (Daller, van Hout, & Treffers-Daller, 2007; Henriksen, 1999; Nation, 2001a; Qian & Schedl, 2004; Read, 2004; Yanagisawa & Webb, 2020). A considerable number of studies have investigated the relationship between breadth and depth of vocabulary knowledge (Meara & Wolter, 2004; Qian, 1999; Vermeer, 2001). While attention to both dimensions is crucial, in general, it is the depth of vocabulary knowledge that enables L2 learners to integrate and organize entries in their L2 lexicon (Meara, 2006; Milton & Fitzpatrick, 2014; Qian, 1999, 2002; Read, 2004; Sarvenaz & Mansoor, 2012; Vermeer, 2001; Wesche & Paribakht, 1996; Zareva, 2007).

This study deals with depth of vocabulary knowledge and, specifically, the L2 acquisition of Korean polysemous words. In Section 2, I will introduce empirical studies and theoretical models on the L2 learning of polysemous words that propose alternative approaches to how L1 and L2 lexical knowledge is integrated, as well as to how L2 learners' interlanguage develops as they gain L2 proficiency. In Section 3, I will provide an overview of the KSL research on polysemous word acquisition. In Section 4, I will present suggestions on how to improve pedagogical methods that can be adopted both in research and in classroom instruction. Section 5 concludes the chapter.

L2 acquisition of polysemous words

In L2 research, the acquisition of polysemous words has been examined from two different vantage points. One strand of research focuses on developmental progress or the incremental acquisition of multiple senses of a polysemous word in the target language. Schmitt's (1998) longitudinal study is an early example. He investigated the incremental acquisition of 11 English polysemous words by 3 advanced L2 learners. Using a survey, he collected data three times over the course of a year, asking the learners to explicitly produce their knowledge of the words. He observed an initial stage of growth and then a plateau in both their knowledge and their retention of the words' multiple senses. He also found that the L2 learners were unable to establish associations among a word's multiple senses if they had not acquired the senses. Schmitt's study, as the first to look at the incremental progress of the acquisition of multiple senses of polysemous words, made a significant contribution to the field of vocabulary research, but it was a very small-scale exploratory investigation and deserves to be updated with a replication study (Pellicer-Sánchez, 2019).

In the same strand, Verspoor and Lowie (2003) took a cognitive-linguistic approach, conceiving of polysemous words in terms of radial networks of senses. They found that providing L2 learners with the core meaning of a polysemous English word was effective in helping them guess at peripheral meanings, as well as in improving the learners' long-term retention of meanings, while providing non-core meanings was less effective at helping learners guess other meanings and did not improve retention.[2] Crossley et al. (2010) examined the development of English word polysemy and frequency use in the spoken production of six L2 learners over a year of English study in the United States. They found the learners to use more of the meanings of the more frequent words over time, which provides evidence that the growth of L2 knowledge of words used with multiple senses correlates with variations in word frequency, indicating close relations between frequency and polysemy effects. Furthermore, by separately tracking the learners' development of knowledge of the senses of six English polysemous words, they found significant growth in the learners' production of multiple word senses during the first four months. They showed it was only after the learners acquired the core meanings of these polysemous words that they acquired and were able to produce the peripheral senses. However, they did not observe that word sense acquisition continued to develop after the fourth month; rather, the expansion of the learners' knowledge was contingent on the word senses that were available to the learners for a given lexical entry.

In a more recent study, Crossley and Skalicky (2019) investigated semantic priming effects for polysemous words using a lexical decision task and employing two types of polysemy: dominant polysemy (i.e., closely related senses) and subordinate polysemy (i.e., distantly related senses). They compared an L1 population and an advanced L2 population to understand differences between L1 and L2 lexicons and also, by proxy, how an L2 lexicon develops. They found a processing advantage for the L1 group only with dominant polysemes, not subordinate polysemes. They interpreted these results as an indication that L2 speakers have weaker lexical associations than L1 speakers. Studies in this line of research have made a crucial contribution to the advancement of vocabulary research, increasing understanding of the development of the L2 acquisition of polysemous words, as well as the expansion and organization of an L2 lexicon. Yet this type of research could be further improved by considering the L1 lexical knowledge of L2 learners. In the majority of these studies, the participants have a variety of L1 backgrounds, but study design rarely controls this variation; however, a few recent studies have suggested that L2 learners' word knowledge differs depending on L1 background (Greidanus, Beks, & Wakely, 2005; Horiba, 2012).

The second strand of research investigates cases in which an L1 polysemous word is realized as multiple independent words in the L2. Theoretical studies have proposed two views on the organization of the bilingual mental lexicon; either the L1 and L2 are kept separate or the L1 and L2 can interfere with each other in processing. In support of an interference model, L2 learners have often been found to produce and understand L2 words based on the meanings of their L1 translations, which can lead to lexical errors, as when the L1 translation of a word corresponds to two L2 words. Levelt (1989) explained the occurrence of such errors in terms of a three-stage process. In the first stage, semantic and syntactic information, or lemma information, in the L1 translation facilitates L2 word use; constant exposure and productive use of L2 words facilitates coactivation of an L2 word along with the lemma structure of its L1 translation. In the second stage, lemma information in the L1 translation is copied or mapped onto the corresponding L2 word. In the third stage, lexical development leads to full integration for specific lexical knowledge of the L2 word along with the elimination of L1 information. As an outcome, the L2 word is used with more automaticity and little effect from the L1. Some research, however, has indicated that lexical development can stop before reaching the third stage. Thus, even for proficient L2 learners, L1 lemma mediation may be a regular and continuing lexical processing state (Jiang, 2000). The semantic transfer hypothesis, namely, that the semantic content of L2 words is transferred from their L1 translations, has been supported by some empirical studies (Elston-Güttler, Paulmann, & Kotz, 2005; Jiang, 2002, 2004; Kroll & Steward, 1994), but at the same time, findings of other studies are consistent with the view that it is possible to make direct connections from L2 words to semantic and conceptual representations, without the influence of the L1, through the gradual increase of proficiency (Hernandez, Li, & MacWhinney, 2005; Kroll & Tokowicz, 2001).

Regarding the L1 effect in the learning of polysemous words, Elston-Güttler and Williams (2008) examined cases in which an L1 polysemous word is realized by two independent L2 words (e.g., German *Blase* and English *bubble, blister*). Their participants were L1-German advanced L2 learners of English. The study's goal was to determine whether interference effects result from L1 translation or are related to independent form-meaning mappings. They used an anomaly detection task in which participants were asked whether a target word formed an acceptable completion to a sentence. They also took into consideration factors of word type (noun vs. verb) and degree of relatedness of L1 senses (high vs. moderate). The results showed that the L2 learners, but not a native control group, made more errors and had longer correct response times in the anomaly sentence condition ("His shoes were uncomfortable due to a bubble") than in the control condition. The study suggests that L1 lexicalization patterns influence the semantic processing of L2 words and continue to have an effect even after the learners have made direct form-meaning connections for L2 words.

Few studies have examined the effects of differing lexicalization patterns when different L2 words correspond to polysemous meanings of an L1 word. For example, the Chinese word *wenti* can be translated into English as *problem* or *question*. Jiang (2002) demonstrated that Chinese–English bilinguals judged English word pairs like *problem–question* as more highly semantically related (relative to unrelated control pairs) than English monolinguals did and also demonstrated faster response times. Jiang argued that these results are in accord with the predictions of the L1 lemma mediation hypothesis: After the initial stage of learning L2 words through association with L1 translations, L2 learners do actually manage to access lexical information automatically and directly from L2 words. However, according to Jiang, the L1 effect continues to influence their processing, which can present challenges to obtaining native-like form-meaning mappings, partly because the semantic differences may be less salient or non-existent in the learner's vocabulary.

Another factor in the L2 acquisition of polysemous words is diversity of multiple meanings in both L1 and L2 when a word is polysemous in both languages. In fact, most basic words fall into this category: While a core meaning may be the same in L1 and L2, the words will vary widely in their other (closely and remotely related) senses. In a recent study, Cañizares-Álvarez and Gathercole (2020) examined learners' use of words that had the same or similar forms but differing meaning extensions in their L1 (Spanish) and L2 (English). Specifically, they looked at the influence of factors such as frequency in each language and how the polysemy of a word in the L1 affects the L2 learners' use of such words. They controlled the stimuli for L1 polysemy (high vs. low), frequency in Spanish, frequency of the English cognate form, and frequency of the English non-cognate translations. Participants were asked to translate words in context from Spanish to English. The results revealed that both L2 input frequency and L1–L2 similarity affect L2 lexical acquisition; but more importantly, the complexity of the polysemous meanings of an L1 word as well as the frequency of that L1 word also greatly contribute to L2 lexical acquisition. While complexity in polysemous structure may hinder the construction of possible meaning mappings between L1 and L2 words, infrequent L1 meanings can be less accessible than frequent ones. They suggested that it is beneficial for learners to pay close attention to the complexity of meaning extensions in both first and second languages.

In L2 vocabulary learning, input frequency is considered one of the most important factors in facilitating acquisition. Usage-based approaches assume that more frequent exposure to a word leads to more likely acquisition of that word (Ellis, 2002; Nation, 2001b; Schmitt, 2008, 2010, 2014). Corpus analysis is the most common method of determining word frequency; however, frequency counts in an L1 corpus do not necessarily translate directly to amount of input for L2 learners (Schmitt, 2014; Zhang & Mai, 2018). This is because corpora vary in size, discourse types, genres, and registers, and because L2 learners vary in age, social and educational background, environments in which they receive L2 instruction, and out-of-class exposure (reading, films, TV, etc.). Yet the common consensus in vocabulary teaching is that the more frequent a word is in use in the target language, the more likely it is to be useful to L2 learners (Gilquin, 2006), based on the assumption that L2 learners will encounter these words often and be in frequent need of them. In L2 vocabulary studies, word frequency in the target language is considered essential information for both research and L2 teaching, but it is important to remember that it is by no means the sole factor in learning.

L2 acquisition of Korean polysemous words

Within the field of KSL, there is limited research on the L2 acquisition of polysemous words. The existing studies discuss the meaning variations of common vocabulary and the challenges KSL learners experience in acquiring and producing these extended meanings (Eom, 2017; Kang, M. J. & Chang, S. M., 2014; Kim, E. H., 2011; Lee, S. Y. & Lee, Y. K., 2020; Lee, Y. K., 2007). The majority of these studies discuss the semantics, contextual nuances, and cultural underpinnings of polysemous words and remark that KSL learners should be taught these aspects to be able to use them appropriately. E. H. Kim (2011), for instance, focused on the word *mekta* 'to eat' and described its primary and extended meanings within a frame semantics model and a cultural model. In frame semantics theory, words are defined by a semantic set of essential features and the features are considered necessary and sufficient to define and understand a word. Therefore, Kim suggested frame structures for various polysemous meanings of *mekta* to describe and differentiate essential knowledge information of extended senses as well as their cultural underpinnings relating to those primary and extended meanings. Introducing over 30 different meanings of the word *mekta*, including in serial verb constructions and multiword sequences, she highlighted the importance of L1–L2 mapping differences. She demonstrated that the majority of form-meaning pairs and their extended meanings in Korean had no corresponding form in the L1s of many Korean learners (e.g., Chinese, Burmese, Vietnamese, Mongolian, Kazakh). Where there is an equivalent form-meaning pair in the L1, the extended meanings differ, especially in the case of idiomatic expressions. For example, the Korean expression *maum mekta* 'to set one's mind on something' translated into Kazakh means 'to be worried, concerned'; and when the Korean expression *kwukswu mekta* 'to get married' is rendered in Chinese, it is a way of asking 'how was your birthday?' In learning polysemous meanings, Kim argued, L2 learners not only experience difficulties due to their different cultural backgrounds but also make erroneous predictions when they try to use contextual clues for meaning interpretation.

In another study, Y. K. Lee (2007) investigated KSL learners' ability to use the various polysemous meanings of the Korean word *pota* 'to see, to look'. To do so, she compared the uses of *pota* by advanced KSL learners to the uses of *pota* reported in a Korean lexical frequency dictionary. The learner data were from Korea University's learner corpus and comprised KSL learners' essays written for midterm and final exams between the years 2003 and 2005. Comparing raw frequencies and percentages between the two datasets,[3] she indicated that while the Korean lexical frequency dictionary identified 71 different meanings of *pota*, the advanced KSL learners produced fewer than 20 different meanings. Her analysis showed that the learners employed the two most frequently used meanings, that is, the primary meaning of *pota* 'to see' and one of its extended meanings, 'to perceive; to be aware of; to recognize'. Lee argued that one of the main reasons KSL learners use notably fewer polysemous meanings than L1 speakers is that textbooks do not provide learners exposure to more than a few of the various extended meanings.[4]

Along the same lines, Eom (2017) compared the polysemous uses and frequencies of the Korean word *johta* 'to be good' in the written production of intermediate Korean language learners, advanced Korean language learners, and native speakers of Korean. She found the intermediate learners to use the word *johta* more frequently than the native speakers, but no difference between the advanced learners and the native speakers. Eom explained these results as due to differences in vocabulary knowledge: Native speakers naturally have a larger vocabulary than intermediate L2 learners, and thus are able to alternate among synonyms. The finding that the advanced learners' production frequency was similar to that of the native speakers indicates the learners' appropriate development of vocabulary knowledge. As for the various meanings of *johta* (one primary and six peripheral meanings), Eom indicated that all the groups used the primary meaning most frequently and the peripheral meanings at the same relative rates.[5]

More recently, S. Y. Lee and Y. K. Lee (2020) investigated KSL learners' production of the Korean word *kata* 'to go'. Using the Korean Learners' Corpus compiled by the National Institute of Korean Language, they collected data from beginning, intermediate, and advanced learners.[6] They analyzed the retrieved data to look for uses of 43 polysemous meanings of *kata* identified in Korean dictionaries. The beginning learners adopted 12 different meanings, but 71% of occurrences used only one: the basic meaning of *kata*, which is 'to move from one place to another'. At the intermediate level, the occurrences of this basic meaning decreased to 54% of all uses, and the learners produced a total of 20 different meanings, including 'abstract movement' (9%) and 'change of affiliation' (5%). At the advanced level, the learners adopted 31 different meanings of *kata*, including meanings related to abstract concepts, such as 'shift of belief, value, and perspective of an individual or a society'. These results indicate that KSL learners are able to acquire multiple meanings of *kata*, from basic to extended, gradually as their proficiency increases. Lee and Lee's findings are in accord with the results of another earlier study focusing on intermediate and advanced KSL learners' ability to make the correct choice between *kata* 'to go' and *ota* 'to come' in lexical decision tasks with sentences that varied the vantage points of speaker versus hearer; concrete versus abstract motion; and subjective, objective, or mental motion. E. J. Park (2015) found that advanced KSL learners, regardless of their L1, are able to use *kata* 'to go' and *ota* 'to come' correctly at similar rates to L1-Korean speakers.

Within the field of Korean linguistics, polysemous words or units are often analyzed within the framework of cognitive linguistics (henceforth CL). While there are numerous studies within this framework, with or without the use of corpus methods, the research on the L2 acquisition of Korean polysemous words by KSL learners is limited. There is a need for more empirical research exploring how KSL learners acquire polysemous words and whether they do so similarly or differently from L2 learners of other languages.

A more purposeful approach to the teaching of polysemous words

Previous studies in the field of KSL have proposed several useful pedagogical methods for the teaching of Korean polysemous words. Here, I review studies that provide teaching methods for formal classroom instruction and propose a number of ways to facilitate teaching effectiveness.

Prioritizing core meanings and applying CL-inspired teaching approaches

Both within the field of KSL and L2 studies in general, there has been a consensus on teaching polysemous words with their *primary* or *core* meaning first, followed by their secondary meanings. This is because the primary sense serves to define a word by the concept that *connects* all its senses (Nation, 2001a) and is often the underlying component of semantic extensions (McCarthy, 2001). The core meaning has a key role in the activation of extended meanings, as it triggers conceptual priming as a means of assisting L2 learners to discover the relationship between core and extended meanings (Verspoor & Lowie, 2003). This concept of core meanings comes from a CL-inspired usage-based approach (Littlemore, 2009; Tyler, 2012; Tyler & Evans, 2004; Verspoor & Lowie, 2003).

The core-meaning approach has been acknowledged and applied in pedagogical studies on teaching Korean polysemous words, such as the verb *pota* 'to see, look' (Koh, K. T., 2008; Lee, Y. K., 2007; Moon, K. H., 2006; Shim & Mun, 2015); the verb *mekta* 'to eat' (Kim, E. H., 2011), and the adjective *johta* 'to be good' (Eom, 2017; Lee, K. M., 2015). In these studies, dictionary definitions and/or corpus usages are often employed to determine the primary and extended meanings of polysemous words. The most commonly suggested vocabulary teaching activities are introducing the meaning of a word with or without context, constructing sentences using provided vocabulary items, and identifying appropriate vocabulary with fill-in-the-blank or multiple-choice methods. While these resources are essential and certainly useful, they do not provide pedagogical information on making the connection among the primary meaning and extended meanings or how they are related to each other. Existing linguistic studies analyzing and describing polysemous structures of words are a useful resource for language instructors to some extent, but the majority of them are heavily theoretical, and they can be too complicated and obscure to apply to classroom materials.

L2 studies of polysemous items have explored the effectiveness of these CL-inspired approaches to teaching, and ways to improve them (e.g., Beréndi, Csábi, & Kövecses, 2008; Boers, De Rycker, & De Knop, 2010; Buescher & Strauss, 2015; Cho, 2010; Csábi, 2004; Masuda & Labarca, 2015, 2018; Mitsugi, 2017; Morimoto & Loewen, 2007; Tyler, 2012; Tyler, Mueller, & Ho, 2010; White, 2012; Wong, Zhao, & MacWhinney, 2018; Zao, Huang, Zhou, & Wang, 2020). The basic assumption of these approaches is that awareness of the underlying core meaning of a polysemous word or unit will assist learners in better comprehending figurative usages (Morimoto & Loewen, 2007), as well as allow them to more efficiently incorporate extended senses into a semantic network, leading, in turn, to better retention (Masuda, 2013; Masuda & Labarca, 2015, 2018; Verspoor & Lowie, 2003).

Image schemas are one of the most prominent CL concepts that have been used as an alternative way to teach polysemous units to L2 learners.[7] Image schemas are abstract visual images used to depict conceptual representations of spatial relations, movements, complex concepts, and events. They are often used to demonstrate the conceptualization of spatial relations between entities and their extended meanings. Image schema–based instruction has been defined as "a form of vocabulary instruction in which the process of learning a word is mediated by the use of image-schema" (Morimoto & Loewen, 2007, p. 351). The purpose of this approach is not to teach the many meanings of a polysemous word exhaustively but, rather, to provide "learners with a basis on which they can effectively process the various meanings in subsequent input" (p. 351). There are a few empirical studies investigating the effectiveness of image schema–based instruction or feedback, some of which provide support for the method and some of which do not. For example, in a much-cited study, Morimoto and Loewen (2007) compared two instructional treatments for the acquisition of L2 polysemous words. Their participants were L1-Japanese high school learners of English. The treatments were 20 minutes of instruction on two polysemous words, the verb *break* and the preposition *over*. The first treatment group received instruction with a diagram-based method, the second group's instruction used a translation-based method, and a control group received no instruction on the polysemous target words. All participants took a processing-based acceptability judgment test and three production-based picture description tests: a pretest, posttest 1 (two days after the instructional treatment), and posttest 2 (two weeks after the instructional treatment). While both treatment groups outperformed the control group, no significant difference was found between the two treatment groups. The authors attributed the lack of difference to the treatments being single, short, and teacher-centered sessions.

In another study using a CL-inspired teaching method, Masuda and Labarca (2018) explored the effectiveness of either schematic or pictorial aids when teaching polysemous meanings of the Japanese particles *ni* and *de*. The experimental group was taught with schematic diagrams and accounts of prototypicality, while the control group was taught with pictorial aids and descriptive rules from a textbook. Both groups then completed three pair-work activities. The prototypicality account suggests teaching the prototypical meaning first and then teaching the less-prototypical uses by linking them with the prototypical meaning (Langacker, 2008, p. 83). The study aimed to teach four prototypical functions ('existential' and 'goal' for *ni*; 'location' and 'instrument' for *de*) and four less-prototypical uses ('time' and 'purpose' for *ni*; 'manner' and 'range' for *de*). The findings showed no difference between the experimental and the control groups on their gain scores between pretest and posttest (the experimental group received higher scores than the control group, but the difference was not statistically significant). However, only the experimental group maintained their gains on the three-week-delayed posttest, which shows better retention from instruction using schematic diagrams and accounts of prototypicality. Masuda and Labarca suggested that both teaching methods could have been improved by presenting various meanings to learners in connected discourse with more communicative intention (153). In this approach, the design of communicative tasks should stimulate cognitive involvement to facilitate learning by giving learners the opportunity to direct their attention to various polysemous uses with different discourse activities, such as common, recursive conversations, and communicative tasks related to real-life contexts. This type of method, known as *task-induced involvement* (Laufer & Hulstijn, 2001), contributes to the teaching of polysemous meanings by raising learners' awareness of certain L2 polysemous elements (isolated vocabulary items, phrases, multi-word sequences, etc.), and is also suited to CL-inspired teaching approaches (Boers et al., 2010).

Wong et al.'s (2018) study was the first to implement diagram-based instruction in a computer-based tutorial system. The participants were L1-Cantonese high school learners of English. Three treatment groups received instruction on English prepositions, while a control group did not. The participants were randomly selected to receive one of three types of feedback: schematic diagram feedback, metalinguistic rule feedback, or correctness feedback (only indicating correct or incorrect performance). Only the first experimental group received diagram-based feedback and was exposed to chaining between spatial and nonspatial polysemes. The participants then took a translation test and a cloze test. The control group showed no change. The cloze test results showed no significant differences between the three treatment groups. In the translation test, however, the schematic diagram feedback group outperformed the correctness feedback group. In addition, for nonspatial polysemes, the schematic diagram feedback group showed a much larger accuracy gain (20%) than the metalinguistic feedback group (6%) or the correctness feedback group (3%). The study concluded that learners can develop a better understanding of prepositions, and particularly of nonspatial polysemous prepositions, through schematic diagram feedback. In the same line of research, more recently, a study by Zao et al. (2020) provided strong neurolinguistic evidence for the effectiveness of schematic diagram feedback, as opposed to correctness feedback. L1-Chinese learners of English received computer-based preposition instruction and training with a sentence–picture matching task (e.g., *The frog hopped <u>over</u> the pebbles* vs. *The frog hopped <u>toward</u> the pebbles*.), followed by immediate feedback. The experimental group received the feedback through schematic diagram representations and verbal explanations. The control group received the same instruction and training but only correctness feedback. The results of a production task and electrophysiological (ERP)[8] measures showed that the schematic diagram feedback led to significant improvement in the production of prepositions and increased brain activity and that the treatment was more effective for lower L2 proficiency learners.

Image schema–based instruction is still an under-researched area in applied linguistics in general as well as in the field of KSL. To my knowledge, only two KSL studies have suggested teaching approaches using image schema–based instruction for polysemous units; one is on the Korean postpositions -*ey* and -*eyse* (Türker, 2013), and the other is on the Korean verb *kelta* 'to hang (up)' (Oh, 2010). Türker's study presented the primary and extended meanings of the Korean postpositions within the framework of cognitive linguistics, described the motivations of their meaning extensions, and provided semantic networks to be used for formal classroom teaching. A semantic network is a representation of the semantic relations of polysemous meanings. The study argued that employing the semantic network model and indicating the importance of the primary meaning and its effects on further extended meanings would assist learners' understanding of their usages. Elsewhere, the same author provided more detailed image schemas of the postpositions -*ey* and -*eyse*, depicting their various spatial location uses, which could also be used in instructional materials (Türker, 2005).

In Oh's (2010) study, she presented basic and extended meanings of the verb *kelta* 'to hang (up)' as they are explained in a Korean dictionary. She provided several visual figures displaying similar and different aspects of these meanings, such as image schemas and pictures to be applied and used in Korean language classes to help learners recognize meaning extensions through metaphorical processes. While such studies are very limited in number, this area of research in the field of KSL, on teaching methods of polysemous words, requires more attention, both for creating teaching materials and for developing empirical studies to determine and improve the effectiveness of image schema–based instruction. Here, the important point is to provide learners contexts that enable them to recognize both core and extended meanings to understand how they are related to each other. Because polysemous meanings are motivated and therefore can be explained, the rote memorization of lists of extended meanings is insufficient. Instead, teaching materials need to contain semantic information with necessary contexts, which can be provided with relevant examples, images, instances of discourse, events, and social and/or cultural understandings that capture and reflect polysemous words' figurative extensions. Even though there is a consensus on prioritizing the core meaning in the initial stage of instruction for teaching polysemous words, communicative pedagogical approaches and instructional methods would be improved by awareness-raising techniques that draw on the insights of cognitive linguistics and sociocultural theory to develop innovative methods for the classroom. There is also a need for research on the appropriate pedagogical sequencing of tasks eliciting multiple meanings of polysemous items so that they can be presented to learners in conditions that gradually increase the level of challenge. While these types of classroom activities can heighten learners' awareness of polysemous elements by manipulating task types in various contexts and with discourse activities, it is continuous exposure and language use over time that enables learners to acquire polysemous meanings and the ability to retrieve the meanings with automaticity and produce them accurately and fluently in real-time communication.

Word frequency across different speech modes

Teaching the most frequently used words first, as determined by corpus analysis, is a common practice in L2 vocabulary teaching. This approach has been extended to the teaching of polysemous words, as the primary meaning of a word is usually the most frequently used one, whereas the peripheral meanings are used with much less frequency. While this is a general tendency, it is not always the case; sometimes one of the peripheral meanings of a polysemous word is more frequently used than its primary meaning. For instance, the primary meaning of the Korean verb *nolta* is 'to play'; however, its extended meaning 'to hang out' is the one that is used most frequently, particularly in spoken language. Likewise, for the Korean adjective *sellenghata*, it is the extended meaning 'to be fluffy' that is most commonly used in colloquial speech to denote a joke or an atmosphere, while the primary meaning, 'to be somewhat chilly, cold', referring to the temperature, is much less frequently used. Therefore, when deciding on which of the multiple meanings of a polysemous word should be taught, I argue that the meaning that is most frequently used in spoken language should be taught first, even if it is not the primary meaning. This is because it is in the spoken mode that language change often occurs, and such language developments should be reflected in vocabulary instruction as well as in textbooks.

While a corpus is an important tool for determining frequency, "frequency counts are least useful when they are based on a general corpus covering the range of the language; they are more useful if they are differentiated for region and register" (Leech, 2011, p. 13). This is mainly because word frequencies and word usages vary depending on register and genre. Traditionally, Korean linguistic research and Korean language instruction were based on formal written language, and language education was prescriptive. However, with the influence of usage-based approaches, there has been a shift of focus from written to spoken language (Koo, H. J., 2005; Kwon, J. I., 2002, 2003; Mok, J. S., 2010). Accordingly, studies often highlight the divergent practices of spoken language (Koo, H. J., 2005) and argue that it, like written language, has its own distinct grammatical features[9] (Kwon, J. I., 2003). J. S. Mok (2010) remarked that because the traditional Korean grammar was determined and analyzed based on written language, there is a need for more exploration of the features of spontaneous spoken language and that this form of pedagogical instruction, particularly for speaking and listening, should be the focus of L2 Korean education. Analyzing Korean-language textbooks and Korean grammar books for L2 learners of Korean, H. S. Jee (2009) demonstrated that the spoken forms and features of the Korean language are not adequately introduced in these materials and suggested that pedagogical materials for KSL learners should be redesigned for the purpose of transmitting the skills of natural speaking production. In regard to lexical matters, corpus studies have revealed differences in lexical use and frequency between the spoken and written discourse of Korean speakers (Kim, H. S., 2012; Lee, P. Y. & Kim, J. S., 2008). More recently, An (2018) compared aspects of verb usage in spoken and written Korean language by employing the Sejong Corpus, demonstrating a discrepancy in verb frequencies between its spoken and written corpora. Table 2.1 shows the most frequently occurring verbs in the spoken corpus, along with their rank in the written corpus, while Table 2.2 shows the most frequently occurring verbs in the written corpus and their ranks in the spoken corpus. As can be observed from the two tables, the type and frequency of verbs are different in spoken and written discourse. An (2018) argued that the differences in the uses and frequencies of verbs between spoken and written language can be attributed to the different contexts of language use in spoken and written discourse.

To my knowledge, no study to date on Korean polysemous words has compared the frequency of the occurrences of multiple senses across different speech modes or genres, yet there is a need to explore this variation for developing research and pedagogical materials. Studies often determine polysemous structures by utilizing dictionaries and retrieved data from a corpus. One typical example of this type of study is Bak's (2014), in which he explored polysemous meanings of the verb *chacta* 'to find; to look for' by using a written corpus and dictionary sources developed by the National Institute of Korean Language. Based on the

Table 2.1 High-frequency verbs in the spoken corpus

Verb	Spoken Corpus			Written Corpus		
	Ranking	Freq.	%	Ranking	Freq.	%
ileta 'to do this way'	22	998	7.58	334	965	0.36
sikhita 'to order'	35	482	3.66	173	2118	0.79
tulita 'to give'	40	446	3.39	233	1488	0.56
nolta 'to play'	44	395	3.00	165	2245	0.84
ccikta 'to take a photo'	51	361	2.74	200	1756	0.66
ppayta 'to take away'	55	337	2.56	223	1567	0.58
wuskita 'to make laugh'	64	256	1.94	817	242	0.09
sakwita 'to date'	75	210	1.59	584	423	0.16
ppopta 'to pull out'	76	208	1.58	225	1560	0.58
nemekata 'to cross'	83	192	1.46	286	1206	0.45
pelta 'to make money'	87	177	1.34	251	1364	0.51
ssawuta 'to fight'	89	173	1.31	198	1775	0.66
kkayta 'to wake up'	95	158	1.20	252	1362	0.51
Total		4393	33.35		18071	6.75

Source: Adapted from An (2018, p. 218)

Table 2.2 High-frequency verbs in the written corpus

Verb	Written Corpus			Spoken Corpus		
	Ranking	Freq.	%	Ranking	Freq.	%
palkhita 'to reveal'	27	9891	3.69	226	38	0.29
cista 'to make'	44	7128	2.66	155	86	0.65
iluta 'to arrive'	57	5776	2.16	437	17	0.13
yellita 'to open'	68	4954	1.85	295	33	0.25
naseta 'to come out'	72	4743	1.77	571	10	0.08
oluta 'to climb'	76	4481	1.67	222	51	0.39
hyanghata 'to head for'	77	4439	1.66	321	28	0.21
palapota 'to watch'	81	4322	1.61	231	48	0.36
pelita 'to start'	93	3589	1.34	616	9	0.07
cinita 'to keep'	94	3427	1.28	405	19	0.14
Total		52750	19.69		339	2.57

Source: Adapted from An (2018, p. 219)

data retrieved from the written corpus, he determined nine meanings of the verb *chacta* along with their frequency of occurrence, as shown in Table 2.3, and he explained and illustrated each meaning with an example sentence. One way to improve studies in this strand would be to collect and analyze data from spoken as well as written corpora. This is crucial because, as seen in An's (2018) study, relying on a single source is insufficient and can be misleading in regard to frequency. In addition, compiling data from different modes enables us to determine and compare the usage of polysemous forms' multiple senses in spoken versus written discourse. Furthermore, within the field of Korean linguistics, there are numerous studies analyzing the extended senses of Korean polysemous words with or without utilizing written corpora, and, more recently, with the availability of frequency-based dictionaries, more studies

Table 2.3 Frequency of occurrence of meanings of *chacta*

Concept Meaning	Frequency (#)	%	Ranking
thamsayk 'to look for'	1596	55.1	1
kyumyeng 'to investigate'	492	17	2
pangmwun 'to visit; to stop by'	465	16	3
chwituk 'to get, to obtain'	127	4.4	4
kemsayk 'to search'	62	2.1	5
hoypok 'to recover'	55	1.9	6
hoyswu 'to collect; to withdraw'	47	1.6	7
yocheng 'to request; to demand'	31	1.1	8
pwulum 'to call out'	24	0.8	9
Total	2899	100	

Source: Adapted from Bak (2014, p. 97)

based on spoken corpora are being conducted. Türker (in press), for example, examined extended meanings of the polysemous word *nwun* 'eye' by obtaining data from the *Spoken Korean Frequency Dictionary*[10] to investigate extended meanings and their mapping mechanisms as well as their motivations. These research articles and frequency-based dictionaries[11] focusing on a particular speech mode are valuable resources, not only for teaching particular lexical items, for instance, polysemous words and their extended senses that most commonly occur in colloquial language, but also for obtaining additional information on their frequency of occurrence. Instructional materials prepared with particular attention to the speech mode would be more beneficial for language instructors as well as L2 learners.

Studies employing data-driven methods for both research and pedagogical materials often fail to provide information about the structure of the corpora they use. However, corpus structure is important, as it has a direct impact on the outcomes of any frequency-related analysis. To conduct a precise analysis on the frequency of polysemous words in any dataset (e.g., a corpus of the target language, a learner corpus, textbooks, etc.), it is crucial to select the appropriate sampling method. Even though corpora are ideally maximally representative of (a particular variety of) a language, this is usually not the case, as genre and source year distributions are often not equally distributed in existing corpora. For example, in the Sejong Corpus, the written corpus comprises approximately 95% of the data, and the spoken corpus only about 5%. The written corpus includes varying proportions of nonfiction books, newspapers, novels, essays, magazines, and other types of source texts.[12] The corpus data can be reorganized prior to data retrieval, for instance, by degree of formality, year of publication, or by selecting equal proportions from genre sets. These modified data-analysis approaches can assist us to conduct more fine-grained analysis on the type and frequency of occurrence of multiple senses of polysemous words and thus to provide more reliable resources for researchers, language instructors, and L2 learners.

In sum, it is crucial for L2 learners to obtain an understanding of the multiple meanings and uses of polysemous words primarily in spoken language, which is in accord with the communicative approach often used for Korean language classroom instruction. Determining the frequency of polysemous uses in the ways discussed in this section would guide language instructors as well as textbook writers to regulate and select which extended meanings are to be taught to L2 learners. The more frequently used meanings should be introduced in the lower proficiency levels, and the less frequent uses in the upper proficiency levels. While knowledge of alternative frequency uses between spoken and written discourse might be intuitive for native speakers of Korean to some extent, in the case of KSL learners, such knowledge can only be gained through sufficient exposure to appropriate input.

Further notes on pedagogical approaches to teaching polysemous words

A survey conducted by K. H. Moon (2005) revealed that Korean language instructors consider the teaching of polysemous meanings to be a secondary concern within overall vocabulary instruction. According to participants' responses, this is because polysemous structure is considered to be rather theoretical by the instructors, and thus they assume it to be difficult for learners. The survey also showed more focus on synonyms and antonyms and less focus on homonyms and polysemous word instruction. With respect to teaching methods for polysemous words, the instructors considered that the primary meaning of a polysemous word should be taught first, followed by derived meanings along with meaning change mechanisms. They noted that to enhance learners' understanding, using the word within context denoting the intended meaning, identifying or comparing polysemous words with synonyms, and providing other forms of phrasal or sentential patterns or multiword sequences may increase the effectiveness of instruction. As revealed in this survey, teaching polysemous words is a thorny process, especially considering the amount of vocabulary with multiple meanings.

In addition to the points already discussed, I suggest that language instructors may be able to utilize L2 learners' L1 knowledge, if the instructors have linguistic knowledge of the learners' L1, when teaching secondary meanings of polysemous words. The facilitative effect of L1 influence has been studied and recommended in L2 studies (Jarvis, 2000, 2011; Kellerman, 1986, 1995; Pavlenko & Jarvis, 2001), and it can be employed in Korean language classrooms to provide more effective instruction. From the learners' point of view, the difficulty or easiness of the secondary meanings of a polysemous word is not completely related to the polysemous complexity of the word but, rather, is more affected by degree of transferability (Seol & Inagaki, 2016). If L1 and L2 show similarity in a polysemous structure and meaning extensions, it is easier for learners to access both semantic and conceptual content and thus the procedure is less effortful. Alternatively, extended meanings in one language may be partially or completely nonexistent in the other, which requires more elaborate instruction and more effort for acquisition.

Moreover, as shown by Cañizares-Álvarez and Gathercole (2020; see Section 2), L1 frequency plays an important role when learners access their L1 lexicon for polysemous words that show similarity in L1 and L2. In addition, instruction on polysemous words requires further information on the cultural aspects and underpinnings of meaning extensions. For example, the expression *papul mekesseyo* is not the same as its literal translation, 'I ate rice', in English. To understand the polysemous meanings of the Korean word *pap*, L2 learners need to be informed about Korean food culture. Another condition in which Korean language instructors could support L2 learners through their L1 is in cases where an L1 polysemous word is realized by two independent words in the L2, as discussed in Section 2. For instance, the English phrase *to be annoyed* corresponds to two lexical items in Korean, *ccacungnata* and *kwichanhta*. The word *memory* in English corresponds to *chwuek* and *kiek*, which cannot be used interchangeably, in Korean. Similarly, *sayonghata* and *iyonghata* are both translated into English as 'to use' but are required in different contexts in Korean. Furthermore, some Korean words that correspond to one English word denote more detailed semantic or pragmatic connotations (e.g., *yachay*, *chayso*, and *namwul* for 'vegetable'; *palta* and *phanmayhata* for 'to sell'; *ipta*, *sinta*, *kkita*, *mayta*, *phwulta*, *chakyonghata*, *chata*, and *hata* for 'wear'). English L1 speakers often experience difficulty differentiating these types of words. Such differences can be addressed during instruction by utilizing awareness-raising techniques in the classroom setting. The native-like use of knowledge of multiple senses of polysemous words can be fostered by having learners compare their own L1 with target language information.

The following types of activity may assist KSL learners to refine their understanding of Korean polysemous words that they are not yet able to use or interpret appropriately.

A. For KSL classrooms sharing the same L1

1. Divide the students into two groups. One group produces multiple uses of a polysemous word in L2 Korean, whereas the other group produces multiple uses of the same polysemous word in their L1.
2. Linguistic utterances, semantic differences, and concepts are presented and compared. The instructor follows up with further discussion with respect to contextual and pragmatic uses depending on alternative speech modes.
3. Using sources such as dictionary entries or search engines such as Google or Naver, students examine polysemous uses and identify and interpret individual polysemous meanings. They can report if they come up with any uses or situations where a meaning is different or has no equivalent in their L1.

B. For KSL classrooms with multiple L1s

1. Divide the students into groups with the same L1. Each group produces multiple uses of a polysemous word in L2 Korean. Then, in the second step, they produce multiple uses of the same polysemous word in their L1.
2. Each group presents linguistic utterances, semantic differences, and concepts in a comparative manner with the L2. Then, students explore and identify cross-lingual and cross-cultural similarities and differences among the different L1 groups. Students evaluate how close or distant their L1 and Korean are and discuss degrees of disparity in pragmatic, social, or cultural aspects.
3. The same activity in 3 of the previous exercise can be applied.

Another point that needs to be brought up with respect to the view that "more frequent = more important to learn" when teaching polysemous words is that it may lead to *overuse*. As mentioned earlier, Eom's (2017) study on the polysemous uses and frequency of the adjective *johta* 'to be good' found relative overuse by the intermediate L2 Korean learners. Likewise, a few studies have discussed how "learners from a wide variety of (unrelated) mother tongue backgrounds display a common tendency to overuse common, non-specific words such as *important . . .* or *big* or *nice*" (De Cock & Granger, 2004, p. 78). In the case of Eom's study, part of the reason for this outcome, according to my view, might be that *johta* 'to be good' is one of the first adjectives L2 Korean learners learn in formal classroom instruction. Another reason may be due to limitations on learners' word choices in writing production. However, on the other hand, a more general reason for such overuse is that it is likely to be one of the most frequent words they encounter and use. Leech (2011, p. 14) remarked that "it is important to make a distinction between frequency in past experience for the learners, and frequency in projected future experience." The key point is that, as the proficiency level increases over time, the direction of teaching input should move toward "less frequent = more important to learn," both in regard to less frequently used words in general and less commonly used meanings of polysemous words in particular. Including only high-frequency uses may simply not be sufficient for intermediate and advanced learners. Implementing less frequent meanings, step by step and over time, will allow learners to be able to use polysemous words in their multiple meanings, including collocational patterns and idiomatic expressions relevant to secondary meanings, and thus improve the depth of their vocabulary knowledge. Acquiring polysemous meanings of words and less frequent words will allow learners to produce language with more discrimination as they develop, which will help them in evaluations of their lexical proficiency. While polysemy can be described at different levels of granularity and from different angles (Gries, 2015, p. 482), language instructors should be prepared to carefully select sets of polysemous meanings depending on the proficiency levels of the learners as well as on the time constraints associated with classroom-based language instruction.

Conclusion

In this chapter, I have provided an overview of empirical and pedagogical studies on polysemous word acquisition both in applied linguistics in general and in the field of KSL. Polysemous word acquisition should be integrated into vocabulary teaching properly to improve the depth of vocabulary knowledge of L2 learners. Given that it may be impossible to exhaustively teach the extended meanings of polysemous words in classroom contexts, crucial questions are what should be taught and what teaching methods can be most effective. I have argued that both in compiling research materials and in preparing pedagogical tools for teaching Korean polysemous words, usage-based approaches need to be adopted to understand the frequency of polysemous meanings. More specifically, I suggested that rather than using a general corpus as a data source, it is more appropriate and more useful to gather data from the speech mode because frequency varies in written and spoken modes. In Korean classroom settings, I have argued that the frequency of occurrence of polysemous meanings should be based on the spoken mode as it correlates with the communicative teaching method better, particularly for teaching lower-proficiency learners.

While the complexity of L2 polysemous words is expected to pose special challenges to L2 learners, lexical errors may indeed be influenced by the L1 lexicon and concepts. Oftentimes, extended meanings or concepts that differ between L1 and L2, and even subtle differences between the two languages, are difficult for L2 learners to detect. Therefore, teaching tools and instructional materials should be designed by paying special attention to differences between L1 and L2. To remedy L1 interference and to develop awareness-raising instruction, alternative teaching approaches, such as image schema–based instruction, can be adopted to reinforce learners' noticing of the differences between L1 and L2. Furthermore, polysemous uses that are prevalent in the L2 and different in the L1 can be exploited for purposes of cross-cultural embeddedness. Assisting learners to actively produce various meanings of Korean polysemous words in both their spoken and written production should help learners approximate Korean native speakers' language uses.

With respect to future research on L2 acquisition of Korean polysemous units, there is a significant need for empirical analyses in the field of KSL to investigate the effectiveness of suggested pedagogical methods. Future studies in this regard will enable us to improve existing pedagogical approaches and lead to the development of new teaching methods. Also, considering the frequency variation of lexical items in different speech modes and inevitable language change over time, more linguistic research targeted at different Korean polysemous words is called for. It is also necessary to conduct further research that explores the developmental progress or the incremental acquisition of multiple senses of Korean polysemous words for learners with the same and different L1 backgrounds. This will assist us to better recognize and understand whether learning challenges are related to mismatches between L1 and L2 lexicons or due to the structural complexity of polysemous words. Additionally, adjustments to the design of future studies, for example, selecting appropriate corpora, whether spoken or written, for comparing L2 data or textbook content, could provide better analysis. Furthermore, while KSL studies on polysemous words typically accept dictionary entries as standard, it is important to remember that not all native speakers of Korean will actively use or even know or distinguish all the extended senses of a given word. Using data collected from L1-Korean participants would allow more nuanced comparisons between L1 and L2 usage.

This chapter has reviewed major theoretical and pedagogical studies in the fields of SLA and KSL to provide a better understanding of Korean polysemous items, and it has discussed many of the features predicted and applied in the existing literature on the topic. We hope that the discussion and the suggestions we have provided, along with other similar studies, offer useful insights to researchers and language instructors with regard to the teaching of polysemy.

Notes

1. For an overview of work on vocabulary breadth and vocabulary depth, see Gyllstad (2013).
2. The core meaning denotes neither the oldest meaning, as meanings change over time, nor the most frequent meaning because some extended meanings may be the most frequent. Rather, it is a meaning that is considered literal and central by native speakers.
3. The study should have used normalized frequencies rather than raw frequencies and percentages because the two datasets it compared were of different sizes.
4. The comparison would have been more useful if it had determined the meanings of *pota* most commonly used by native speakers and analyzed the learners' use of those, rather than all 71 meanings listed in the dictionary. It is also worth noting that it is not realistic to expect textbooks to include as many polysemous meanings as a dictionary.
5. The study reported only percentages, and it is therefore unclear whether there were statistically significant differences between any of the groups.
6. The Korean Learners' Corpus consists of 1,891,031 words (1,510,004 words of written data and 381,027 words of spoken data) collected from KSL learners who are native speakers of 81 different languages coming from 124 countries, and it is available at: https://kcorpus.korean.go.kr/.
7. See Mandler and Cánovas (2014) for further information on image schemas.
8. The event-related potentials (ERPs) method tracks real-time scalp-recorded electrophysiological brain activity.
9. Several studies in Korean linguistics (e.g., Bae, Son, & Kim, 2011; Jang, G. H., 2003; Kim, M. H., 2004; Min, H. S., 2007) have described the characteristic features of spoken versus written language.
10. *Hankwuke kwue pinto sacen* (Spoken Korean frequency dictionary), by Seo (2014), is based on the Yonsei Spoken Corpus.
11. *Haksupyong kipon myengsa yene pinto sacen* (Basic noun and collocation frequency dictionary for learning) by Y. K. Han (2016), is based on the *Hyentaykwuke sayong pinto khophesu* [Modern Korean frequency usage corpus]. Korean idiom dictionaries, such as *Wuli mal swuke 1000kaci* (1,000 words of our idioms; Lee, J. W., Ra, G. M., & Lee, I. O., 2008) and *500 Common Korean Idioms* (Pyun, D. O., 2018), are also available sources.
12. According to Türker (forthcoming), the Sejong Corpus written data consists of 39% nonfiction books, 24% newspapers, 16% novels, 11% magazines, 5% essays, and 5% other genres from the period 1980–2004, but with significant fluctuations in these percentages across the years.

References

An, C. W. (2018). A comparative study on the attributes of verb uses in spoken and written language environments. *Korean Literature & Language Education, 24*, 213–243.

Anderson, R. C., & Freebody, P. (1981). Vocabulary knowledge. In J. T. Guthrie (Ed.), *Comprehension and teaching: Research reviews* (pp. 77–117). Newark, DE: International Reading Association.

Bae, J. Y., Son, H. O., & Kim, M. G. (2011). A study on an integrated grammar of spoken and written language in contemporary Korean and the problem with building corpus. *Journal of Human Studies, 27*, 141–200.

Bak, J. H. (2014). A study of establishing for semantic network of verb '*chacta*': Focus on corpus example analysis. *Hanminjok Emunhak, 67*, 87–113.

Beréndi, M., Csábi, S., & Kövecses, Z. (2008). Using conceptual metaphors and metonymies in vocabulary teaching. In F. Boers & S. Lindstromberg (Eds.), *Cognitive linguistic approaches to teaching vocabulary and phraseology* (pp. 65–100). Berlin and New York: Mouton de Gruyter.

Boers, F., De Rycker, A., & De Knop, S. (2010). Fostering language teaching efficiency through cognitive linguistics: Introduction. In S. De Knop, F. Boers, & A. De Rycker (Eds.), *Fostering language teaching efficiency through cognitive linguistics* (pp. 1–26). Berlin and New York: Mouton de Gruyter.

Broeder, P., Extra, G., & van Hout, R. (1993). Richness and variety in the developing lexicon. In C. Perdue (Ed.), *Adult language acquisition: Vol. 2. The results* (pp. 145–163). Cambridge: Cambridge University Press.

Buescher, K., & Strauss, S. (2015). Cognitive linguistic analysis of French prepositions *à*, *dans*, and *en* and a sociocultural theoretical approach to teaching them. In K. Masuda, C. Arnett, & A. Labarca (Eds.), *Cognitive linguistics and sociocultural theory: Applications to foreign/second language teaching* (pp. 155–181). Berlin and Boston: Mouton de Gruyter.

Cañizares-Álvarez, C., & Gathercole, V. C. M. (2020). The influence of first language polysemy and first language and second language lexical frequencies on second language learners' use of false cognates. *International Journal of Bilingualism, 24*(3), 530–541.

Cho, K. (2010). Fostering the acquisition of English prepositions by Japanese learners with networks and prototypes. In S. De Knop, F. Boers, & A. De Rycker (Eds.), *Fostering language teaching efficiency through cognitive linguistics* (pp. 259–275). Berlin and New York: Mouton de Gruyter.

Crossley, S. A., Salsbury, T., & McNamara, D. S. (2010). The role of lexical cohesive devices in triggering negotiations for meaning. *Issues in Applied Linguistics, 18*(1), 55–80.

Crossley, S. A., & Skalicky, S. (2019). Making sense of polysemy relations in first and second language speakers of English. *International Journal of Bilingualism, 23*(2), 400–416.

Csábi, S. (2004). A cognitive linguistic view of polysemy in English and its implications for teaching. In M. Achard & S. Niemeier (Eds.), *Cognitive linguistics, second language acquisition, and foreign language teaching* (pp. 233–256). Berlin: Mouton de Gruyter.

Daller, H., van Hout, R., & Treffers-Daller, J. (2003). Lexical richness in the spontaneous speech of bilinguals. *Applied Linguistics, 24*(2), 197–222.

Daller, H., van Hout, R., & Treffers-Daller, J. (2007). Editors' introduction: Conventions, terminology and an overview of the book. In H. Daller, J. Multon, & J. Treffers-Daller (Eds.), *Modelling and assessing vocabulary knowledge* (pp. 1–32). Cambridge: Cambridge University Press.

De Cock, S., & Granger, S. (2004). Computer learner corpora and monolingual learners' dictionaries: The perfect match. In W. Teubert & M. Mahlberg (Eds.), *The corpus approach to lexicography* [Special issue]. *Lexicographica, 20*, 72–86.

De La Fuente, M. J. (2002). Negotiation and oral acquisition of L2 vocabulary: The roles of input and output in the receptive and productive acquisition of words. *Studies in Second Language Acquisition, 24*, 81–112.

Ellis, N. C. (2002). Frequency effects in language processing: A review with implications for theories of implicit and explicit language acquisition. *Studies in Second Language Acquisition, 24*(2), 143–188.

Ellis, R. (1995). Modified oral input and the acquisition of word meanings. *Applied Linguistics, 16*, 409–435.

Elston-Güttler, K. E., Paulmann, S., & Kotz, S. A. (2005). Who's in control? Proficiency and L1 influence on L2 processing. *Journal of Cognitive Neuroscience, 17*, 1593–1610.

Elston-Güttler, K. E., & Williams, J. N. (2008). First language polysemy affects second language meaning interpretation: Evidence for activation of first language concepts during second language reading. *Second Language Research, 24*(2), 167–187.

Eom, J. S. (2017). A study on the use of polysemous word by KSL: Focusing on the adjective 'johta'. *Hanminjok Emunhak, 78*, 37–63.

Gilquin, G. (2006). Highly polysemous words in foreign language teaching: How to give learners a flying start. In *Proceedings of the seventh conference on teaching and language corpora* (pp. 58–60). Université Paris 7 – Denis Diderot, 1–4 July 2006.

Greidanus, T., Beks, B., & Wakely, R. (2005). Testing the development of French word knowledge by advanced Dutch- and English-speaking learners and native speakers. *Modern Language Journal, 89*, 221–233.

Greidanus, T., & Nienhuis, L. (2001). Testing the quality of word knowledge in a second language by means of word associations: Types of distractors and types of associations. *The Modern Language Journal, 85*(4), 567–577.

Gries, S. Th. (2015). Polysemy. In E. Dabrowska & D. S. Divjak (Eds.), *Handbook of cognitive linguistics* (pp. 472–490). Berlin and Boston: de Gruyter Mouton.

Gyllstad, H. (2013). Looking at L2 vocabulary knowledge dimensions from an assessment perspective: Challenges and potential solutions. In C. Bardel, C. Lindqvist, & B. Laufer (Eds.), *L2 vocabulary acquisition, knowledge and use* (pp. 11–28). Amsterdam: EuroSLA.

Han, Y. K. (2016). *Haksupyong kipon myengsa yene pinto sacen [Basic noun and collocation frequency dictionary for learning]*. Seoul: Hankookmunhwasa.

Henriksen, B. (1999). Three dimensions of vocabulary development. *Studies in Second Language Acquisition, 21*(2), 303–317.

Hernandez, A., Li, P., & MacWhinney, B. (2005). The emergence of competing modules in bilingualism. *Trends in Cognitive Sciences, 9,* 220–225.

Horiba, Y. (2012). Word knowledge and its relation to text comprehension: A comparative study of Chinese- and Korean-speaking L2 learners and L1 speakers of Japanese. *The Modern Language Journal, 96*(1), 108–121.

Jang, G. H. (2003). A trial on restruction of written language/spoken language and their styles. *Korean Semantics, 13,* 143–165.

Jarvis, S. (2000). Methodological rigor in the study of transfer: Identifying L1 influence on the interlanguage lexicon. *Language Learning, 50,* 245–309.

Jarvis, S. (2011). Conceptual transfer: Crosslinguistic effects in categorization and construal. *Bilingualism: Language and Cognition, 14*(1), 1–8.

Jee, H. S. (2009). How to write Korean spoken grammar from a pedagogical perspective. *Korean Linguistics, 45,* 113–139.

Jiang, N. (2000). Lexical representation and development in a second language. *Applied Linguistics, 21,* 47–77.

Jiang, N. (2002). Form-meaning mapping in vocabulary acquisition in a second language. *Studies in Second Language Acquisition, 24,* 617–637.

Jiang, N. (2004). Semantic transfer and its implications for vocabulary teaching in a second language. *The Modern Language Journal, 88*(4), 416–432.

Kang, M. J., & Chang, S. M. (2014). An analysis of lexical errors of Korean language learners: Some American college learners' case. *Journal of Pan-Pacific Association of Applied Linguistics, 18*(2), 93–110.

Kellerman, E. (1986). An eye for an eye: Crosslinguistic constraints on the development of the L2 lexicon. In M. Sharwood Smith & E. Kellerman (Eds.), *Crosslinguistic influence in second language acquisition* (pp. 35–48). Oxford, UK: Pergamon Press.

Kellerman, E. (1995). Crosslinguistic influence: Transfer to nowhere? *Annual Review of Applied Linguistics, 15,* 125–150.

Kim, E. H. (2011). A study of how advanced Korean learners recognize multiple meanings of verb 'mekta'. *Korean Language Education Research, 41,* 311–338.

Kim, H. S. (2012). Research of word usage for vocabulary education based on vocabulary survey of primary school students. *Journal of Korean National Language and Literature, 48,* 493–516.

Kim, M. H. (2004). A study on the characteristics of spoken and written Korean. *Korean Language Research, 15,* 23–73.

Koh, K. T. (2008). On the teaching Korean verbs as polysemous verb 'po' (to see). *Journal of Korean Language, 19*(2), 1–21.

Koo, H. J. (2005). On corpus-based studies of spoken language. *Journal of Linguistic Science, 32,* 1–32.

Kroll, J. F., & Steward, E. (1994). Category interference in translation and picture naming: Evidence for asymmetric connections between bilingual memory representations. *Journal of Memory and Language, 33,* 149–174.

Kroll, J. F., & Tokowicz, N. (2001). The development of conceptual representation for words in a second language. In J. L. Nicol & T. Langendoen (Eds.), *One mind, two languages: Bilingual language processing* (pp. 49–71). Cambridge, MA: Blackwell.

Kwon, J. I. (2002). Korean interrogative sentences in spoken discourse. *Hangeul, 257,* 167–200.

Kwon, J. I. (2003). The synchrony and diachrony of Korean declarative sentences in spoken discourse. *Eoneohag: Journal of the Linguistic Society of Korea, 37,* 25–46.

Langacker, R. W. (2008). Cognitive grammar as a basis for language instruction. In P. Robinson & N. C. Ellis (Eds.), *Handbook of cognitive linguistics and second language acquisition* (pp. 66–88). Oxon and New York: Routledge.

Laufer, B. (1997). The lexical plight in second language reading: Words you don't know, words you think you know, and words you can't guess. In J. Coady & T. Huckin (Eds.), *Second language vocabulary acquisition* (pp. 20–34). Cambridge: Cambridge University Press.

Laufer, B., & Hulstijn, J. (2001). Incidental vocabulary acquisition in a second language: The construct of task-induced involvement. *Applied Linguistics, 22*, 1–26.

Laufer, B., & Nation, P. (1995). Vocabulary size and use: Lexical richness in L2 written production. *Applied Linguistics, 16*(3), 307–322.

Lee, J. W., Ra, G. M., & Lee, I. O. (2008). *Ttus to moluko cacwu ssunun wuli mal swuke 1000kaci [1,000 words of our idioms]*. Seoul: Yedam.

Lee, K. M. (2015). Educational information and characteristics of the constructions of the adjective 'johta' for Korean language learners. *Journal of the Research Society of Language and Literature, 86*, 3–36.

Lee, P. Y., & Kim, J. S. (2008). A study on the vocabulary frequency and distribution in spoken language of elementary school students. *Korean Language Education Research, 28*(2), 557–595.

Lee, S. Y., & Lee, Y. K. (2020). Research on Korean language learners' use of Korean polysemy: Focusing on the locomotive verb '*kata*'. *The Journal of the Study of Korean Language and Literature, 67*, 399–432.

Lee, Y. K. (2007). Corpus-based study in polysemy used by learners of Korean: The case of the verb *pota*. *Bilingual Research, 35*, 281–301.

Leech, G. (2011). Frequency, corpora and language learning. In F. Meunier, S. De Cock, G. Gilquin, & M. Paquot (Eds.), *A taste for corpora: In honour of Sylviane Granger* (pp. 7–32). Amsterdam and Philadelphia: John Benjamins Publishing Company.

Levelt, W. J. M. (1989). *Speaking: From intention to articulation*. Cambridge, MA: MIT Press.

Littlemore, J. (2009). *Applying cognitive linguistics to second language learning and teaching*. New York: Palgrave Macmillan.

Madlener, K. (2016). Input optimization: Effects of type and token frequency manipulations in instructed second language learning. In H. Behrens & S. Pfänder (Eds.), *Experience counts: Frequency effects in language* (pp. 133–173). Berlin: Mouton de Gruyter.

Mandler, J. M., & Cánovas, C. P. (2014). On defining image schemas. *Language and Cognition, 6*(4), 510–532.

Masuda, K. (2013). Applying cognitive linguistics to teaching Japanese polysemous particles. *Sophia Linguistica, 60*, 105–122.

Masuda, K., & Labarca, A. (2015). Schematic diagram use and languaging quality in learning Japanese polysemous particles 'ni' and 'de'. In K. Masuda, C. Arnett, & A. Labarca (Eds.), *Cognitive linguistics and sociocultural theory: Applications to foreign/second language teaching* (pp. 203–232). Berlin and Boston: Mouton de Gruyter.

Masuda, K., & Labarca, A. (2018). Students' perception and different performance in a combined usage-based and sociocultural theory approach to learning Japanese polysemous particles. In A. Tyler, L. Ortega, M. Uno, & H. I. Park (Eds.), *Usage-inspired L2 instruction: Researched pedagogy* (pp. 117–142). Amsterdam and Philadelphia: John Benjamins Publishing Company.

McCarthy, M. (2001). *Vocabulary*. Oxford: Oxford University Press.

Meara, P. (2002). The rediscovery of vocabulary. *Second Language Research, 18*(4), 393–407.

Meara, P. (2006). Emergent properties of multilingual lexicons. *Applied Linguistics, 27*(4), 620–644.

Meara, P., & Wolter, B. (2004). V_Links: Beyond vocabulary depth. In D. Albrechtsen, K. Haastrup, & B. Henriksen (Eds.), *Angles on the English-speaking world* (Vol. 4, pp. 85–96). Copenhagen: Museum Tusculanum Press.

Milton, J., & Fitzpatrick, T. (2014). Introduction: Deconstructing vocabulary knowledge. In J. Milton & T. Fitzpatrick (Eds.), *Dimensions of vocabulary knowledge* (pp. 1–13). London: Palgrave Macmillan.

Min, H. S. (2007). Colloquial use and literary misuse. *Grammar Education, 6*, 53–113.

Mitsugi, M. (2017). Effect of schema-based instruction on learning polysemous English prepositions: Analyzing through learners' perceptions. *Journal of Pan-Pacific Association of Applied Linguistics, 22*(1), 43–63.

Mok, J. S. (2010). Modeling for a spoken Korean grammar. *Korean Linguistics, 46*, 81–122.

Moon, K. H. (2005). The present condition and prospect of Korean polysemic words education for foreigners. *Korean Education, 71*, 67–89.

Moon, K. H. (2006). Teaching methods of polysemic word for Korean vocabulary education verb 'boda (to see)'. *Bilingual Research, 30*, 143–177.

Morimoto, S., & Loewen, S. (2007). A comparison of the effects of image-schema-based instruction and translation-based instruction on the acquisition of L2 polysemous words. *Language Teaching Research, 11*(3), 347–372.

Nation, I. S. P. (2001a). *Learning vocabulary in another language*. Cambridge: Cambridge University Press.
Nation, I. S. P. (2001b). How many high frequency words are there in English? *Language, Learning and Literature: Studies Presented to Hakan Ringbom, Abo Akademi University, Abo, English Department Publications, 4*, 167–181.
Oh, H. J. (2010). A study on the Korean verb *geol-da*'s cognitive meaning. *Korean Semantics, 32*, 141–168.
Park, E. J. (2015). A study aspect of cognition on *kata/ota* of Korean learners. *Korean Language and Literature, 93*, 387–406.
Pavlenko, A., & Jarvis, S. (2001). Conceptual transfer: New perspectives on the study of cross linguistic influence. In E. Németh (Ed.), *Cognition in language use: Selected papers from the Seventh International Pragmatics Conference* (Vol. 1, pp. 288–301). Antwerp: International Pragmatics Association.
Pellicer-Sánchez, A. (2019). Examining second language vocabulary growth: Replications of Schmitt (1998) and Webb & Chang (2012). *Language Teaching, 52*(4), 512–523.
Polio, C. (2001). Research methodology in second language writing research: The case of text-based studies. In T. Silva & P. K. Matsuda (Eds.), *On second language writing* (pp. 91–115). Mahwah, NJ: Lawrence Erlbaum.
Pyun, D. O. (2018). *500 common Korean idioms*. Oxon and New York: Routledge.
Qian, D. D. (1999). Assessing the roles of depth and breadth of vocabulary knowledge in reading comprehension. *Canadian Modern Language Review, 56*(2), 282–308.
Qian, D. D. (2002). Investigating the relationship between vocabulary knowledge and academic reading performance: An assessment perspective. *Language Learning, 53*, 513–536.
Qian, D. D., & Schedl, M. (2004). Evaluation of an in-depth vocabulary knowledge measure for assessing reading performance. *Language Testing, 21*(1), 28–52.
Read, J. (2004). Plumbing the depths: How should the construct of vocabulary knowledge be defined? In P. Bogaards & B. Laufer (Eds.), *Vocabulary in a second language* (pp. 209–227). Amsterdam and Philadelphia: John Benjamins Publishing Company.
Sarvenaz, H., & Mansoor, T. (2012). The role of depth versus breadth of vocabulary knowledge in success and ease in L2 lexical inferencing. *TESL Canada Journal, 30*(1), 1–21.
Schmitt, N. (1998). Tracking the incremental acquisition of second language vocabulary: A longitudinal study. *Language Learning, 48*(2), 281–317.
Schmitt, N. (2008). Review article: Instructed second language vocabulary learning. *Language Teaching Research, 12*(3), 329–363.
Schmitt, N. (2010). *Researching vocabulary: A vocabulary research manual*. London: Palgrave Macmillan.
Schmitt, N. (2014). Size and depth of vocabulary knowledge: What the research shows. *Language Learning, 64*, 913–951.
Seo, S. (2014). *Hankwuke kwue pinto sacen* [*Spoken Korean frequency dictionary*]. Seoul: Hankook munhwasa.
Seol, H. S., & Inagaki, S. (2016). Transferability of the L1 polysemous verbs *yalta* and *pota* in Korean learners' acquisition of Japanese: Effects of L1 prototypes, presence/absence of L1 uses in the L2, and L2 proficiency. *The Korean Journal of Japanology, 106*, 115–127.
Shim, H. R., & Mun, J. H. (2015). A study on categorizing the meanings of Korean polysemy: Focusing on the verb *pota*. *Grammar Education, 23*, 125–148.
Türker, E. (2005). *The locative expressions in Korean and Turkish: A cognitive grammar approach* [Unpublished doctoral dissertation]. University of Hawai'i at Mānoa, Honolulu.
Türker, E. (2013). Second language acquisition of Korean postpositions *-ey* and *-eyse*: A cognitive pedagogical approach. In S. Sohn, S. Cho, & P. You (Eds.), *Studies in Korean linguistics and language pedagogy* (pp. 346–383). Seoul: Korea University Press.
Türker, E. (in press). Metaphoric and metonymic patterns with the body-part term *nwun* 'eye(s)' in Korean. In S. Cho & J. Whitman (Eds.), *The Cambridge handbook of Korean language and linguistics* (pp. 554–580). Cambridge: Cambridge University Press.
Türker, E. (forthcoming). A quantitative analysis of Korean emotion metaphors across modern written genres.
Tyler, A. (2012). *Cognitive linguistics and second language learning: Theoretical basics and experimental evidence*. Oxon and New York: Routledge.
Tyler, A., & Evans, V. (2004). Applying cognitive linguistics to pedagogical grammar: The case of *over*. In M. Achard & S. Niemeier (Eds.), *Cognitive linguistics, second language acquisition, and foreign language teaching* (pp. 257–280). Berlin: Mouton de Gruyter.
Tyler, A., Mueller, C., & Ho, V. (2010). Applying cognitive linguistics to instructed L2 learning. *AILA Review, 23*, 30–49.

Vermeer, A. (2001). Breadth and depth of vocabulary in relation to L1/L2 acquisition and frequency of input. *Applied Psycholinguistics*, *22*(2), 217–235.

Verspoor, M., & Lowie, W. (2003). Making sense of polysemous words. *Language Learning*, *53*(3), 547–586.

Vilkaitė-Lozdienė, L., & Schmitt, N. (2020). Frequency as a guide for vocabulary usefulness: Hi-, mid-, and low-frequency words. In S. Webb (Ed.), *The Routledge handbook of vocabulary studies* (pp. 81–96). Oxon and New York: Routledge.

Wesche, M., & Paribakht, T. S. (1996). Assessing second language vocabulary knowledge: Depth versus breadth. *The Canadian Modern Language Review*, *53*, 13–40.

White, B. (2012). A conceptual approach to the instruction of phrasal verbs. *The Modern Language Journal*, *96*(3), 419–433.

Wong, M. H. I., Zhao, H., & MacWhinney, B. (2018). A cognitive linguistics application for second language pedagogy: The English preposition tutor. *Language Learning*, *68*, 438–468.

Yanagisawa, A., & Webb, S. (2020). Measuring depth of vocabulary knowledge. In S. Webb (Ed.), *The Routledge handbook of vocabulary studies*. Oxon and New York: Routledge.

Zao, H., Huang, S., Zhou, Y., & Wang, R. (2020). Schematic diagrams in second language learning of English prepositions: A behavioral and event-related potential study. *Studies in Second Language Acquisition*, *42*(4), 721–748.

Zareva, A. (2007). Structure of the second language mental lexicon: How does it compare to native speakers' lexical organization? *Second Language Research*, *23*, 123–153.

Zhang, X., & Mai, C. (2018). Effects of entrenchment and preemption in second language learners' acceptance of English denominal verbs. *Applied Psycholinguistics*, *39*, 413–436.

3
PHONOLOGICAL ACQUISITION

Jeffrey J. Holliday

Introduction

Over the past 50 years, research on second language (L2) phonological acquisition has expanded immensely. And while the vast majority of it has focused on L2 English, in the past 20 years there has been a steadily growing literature on L2 Korean, as well. The goals of this chapter are to introduce the reader to the segmental phonology of Korean, to review some studies of the L2 acquisition of this system, and to suggest some directions for future research. It would be impossible to provide a thorough treatment of all potential issues in just this one chapter, so we will focus specifically on issues for which the most empirical data has been reported: the acquisition of stops, affricates, fricatives, and vowels.

The Korean phonological inventory

Across studies of Korean L2 phonological acquisition, there exists some variation in terminology, choice of phonetic symbols, and both the phonetic and phonological characterization of the sounds of Korean. This variation can complicate attempts to synthesize the results of such studies. In this section, we will therefore provide an overview of the Korean segmental phonological inventory and describe some unresolved issues that should be borne in mind when interpreting the findings of studies on the L2 phonological acquisition of Korean.

Consonants

The phonological inventory of Modern Seoul Korean (hereafter, Korean) contains 19 consonants, listed in Table 3.1. As is typical in spoken languages, the consonants can be classified according to their manner and place of articulation. Manner of articulation refers to the way in which the sound is produced (e.g., by stopping the airflow and then releasing it with a burst, as in a stop), whereas the place of articulation refers to the location along the vocal tract at which the primary articulation is made (e.g., with both lips, as in bilabial place).

The Hangul letter given for each consonant represents the most typical letter used to write that sound (i.e., in syllable-initial position, except for /ŋ/, which only occurs in syllable-final position). But these same sounds can also be the result of phonetic or phonological processes

Table 3.1 The Korean consonant inventory

Manner	Phonation type[1]	Place of articulation				
		Bilabial	Denti-alveolar	Alveolopalatal	Velar	Glottal
Stop	Fortis (Tense)	/p*/ <ㅃ>	/t*/ <ㄸ>		/k*/ <ㄲ>	
	Lenis (Lax)	/p/ <ㅂ>	/t/ <ㄷ>		/k/ <ㄱ>	
	Aspirated	/pʰ/ <ㅍ>	/tʰ/ <ㅌ>		/kʰ/ <ㅋ>	
Affricate	Fortis (Tense)			/tɕ*/ <ㅉ>		
	Lenis (Lax)			/tɕ/ <ㅈ>		
	Aspirated			/tɕʰ/ <ㅊ>		
Fricative	Fortis (Tense)		/s*/ <ㅆ>			/h/ <ㅎ>
	Non-fortis		/s/ <ㅅ>			
Nasal		/m/ <ㅁ>	/n/ <ㄴ>		/ŋ/ <ㅇ>	
Liquid			/l/ <ㄹ>			

that arise from certain sequences of sounds. For example, regressive nasal assimilation can cause the letter <ㄱ> /k/ to be pronounced as the homorganic nasal [ŋ] when it is followed by another nasal, as in the word <악마> [aŋma].[2] What is important to bear in mind here is simply that the Hangul spelling of a word does not always reflect its phonetic realization and that these variations are also part of the phonological knowledge that L2 learners of Korean acquire.

While more detailed information about the phonetic properties of Korean consonants will be discussed as relevant in subsequent sections, the Korean three-way contrast among fortis, lenis, and aspirated stops (and affricates) will be preemptively explained here given its centrality to many other issues. In brief, these three phonation types are phonetically cued in word-initial position by differences in both voice onset time (VOT) and the fundamental frequency (f0) of the following vowel. The VOT of a stop, typically measured in milliseconds (ms), is the temporal difference between the release of the stop closure and the onset of voicing in the following vowel, and f0 is the number of vocal fold vibrations per second, typically measured in hertz (Hz). The perceptual correlate of f0 is pitch, e.g., a sound with a higher f0 is perceived has having a higher pitch. Generally, word-initial fortis stops are produced with short lag VOT and a high f0, lenis stops with long lag VOT and a low f0, and aspirated stops with long lag VOT and a high f0. Thus, the lenis-aspirated contrast is cued primarily by f0, the fortis-aspirated contrast primarily by VOT, and the fortis-lenis contrast by both. Although these f0 differences are somewhat attenuated in word-medial position, the contrast is nonetheless maintained as lenis stops become phonetically voiced when appearing between two voiced sounds (e.g., intervocalically). More detailed discussion of the phonetic and phonological properties of this contrast can be found in Shin, Kiaer, and Cha (2013, pp. 57–68) and Lee, Holliday, and Kong (2020).

The contrast between the fricatives /s/ and /s*/, known as sibilant fricatives, has some parallels with the three-way stop contrast, but there is not yet a consensus on its phonological characterization. While the fricative /s*/ is widely classified as fortis, as it shares many of the acoustic and articulatory properties of other fortis consonants and is subject to the same set of phonological processes, the fricative /s/ shares some properties with lenis obstruents and other properties with aspirated obstruents. A more thorough discussion of this issue can be found in Chang (2013). For the remainder of this chapter, we will refer to /s/ simply as "non-fortis".

Vowels

The inventory of Korean vowels is given in Table 3.2. Because descriptions of Korean vowels differ across references and textbooks, a few points of clarification are warranted. First, the inventory in Table 3.2 reflects Modern Seoul Korean as it is spoken by people born after approximately 1970. While some Korean grammars depict the vowel inventory as including the front round vowels /y/ (for <ㅟ>) and /ø/ (for <ㅚ>), the reality is that nearly all speakers of Modern Seoul Korean produce these as unrounded vowels with on-glides, [wi] and [wɛ] (Kwak, 2003). Furthermore, while Hangul preserves an orthographic distinction between /e/ <ㅔ> and /ɛ/ <ㅐ>, most speakers have completely neutralized this phonological contrast (Kwak, 2003; Kang & Kong, 2016). Second, among the diphthongs in Table 3.2, we make a subdivision between "complex vowels" and "palatalized vowels". The complex vowels are those written as combinations of two other vowel letters and comprise four glide-vowel sequences (i.e., [wa, wʌ, wɛ, wi]) and one true diphthong (i.e., [ɨi]). The palatalized vowels are also phonetically realized as glide-vowel sequences (i.e., [ja, jʌ, jo, ju, jɛ]) but are written in Hangul as individual letters, not as combinations of two vowel letters. Third, vowel length is completely ignored in the current chapter, as it has also disappeared as a contrastive feature in the speech of most speakers of Modern Seoul Korean.

Theoretical frameworks in L2 segmental perception and production

Because studies of Korean L2 segmental acquisition often reference theoretical models such as PAM, PAM-L2, or SLM, we will provide a brief overview of these models here. First, the Perceptual Assimilation Model, commonly referred to as PAM, is laid out in detail in Best (1995). The purpose of PAM is to model how naïve listeners perceptually assimilate non-native speech sounds. Perceptual assimilation is the process of perceiving a non-native speech sound as a member of a native category. For example, when a native English listener hears the Korean sound /i/, they are likely to perceive it as a good example of their English /i/ category. On the other hand, the Korean sound /p*/ may be perceived as a good example of their English /b/ category. Thus, perceptual assimilation is essentially the mapping of non-native speech sounds onto native phonological categories.

PAM makes several predictions related to this process. First, non-native speech sounds can be assimilated in one of three ways: assimilated to a native category, not assimilated to any native category, or not perceived as speech. Second, when a speech sound is assimilated, its goodness of assimilation can vary from excellent to poor. Third, the way in which members of a non-native phonological contrast assimilate to native categories is predictive of how well

Table 3.2 The Korean vowel inventory

Monophthongs	*Diphthongs*	
	Complex vowels	*Palatalized vowels*
/a/ <ㅏ>	/wa/ <ㅘ>	/ja/ <ㅑ>
/ʌ/ <ㅓ>	/wʌ/ <ㅝ>	/jʌ/ <ㅕ>
/o/ <ㅗ>	/wɛ/ <ㅙ,ㅞ,ㅚ>	/jo/ <ㅛ>
/u/ <ㅜ>	/wi/ <ㅟ>	/ju/ <ㅠ>
/ɨ/ <ㅡ>[3]	/ɨi/ <ㅢ>	/jɛ/ <ㅒ, ㅖ>
/i/ <ㅣ>		
/ɛ/ <ㅐ, ㅔ>		

listeners will be able to discriminate between those sounds, which is the ability to judge two sounds as "the same" or "different". Discrimination is often tested through an AX discrimination task, in which two sounds are played with a short interceding pause (e.g., 500 ms), and the listener has to determine whether the sounds were the same or different.

One important aspect of PAM, as discussed in both Best (1995) and Best and Tyler (2007), is that its predictions were only intended to apply to naïve non-native perception – that is, perception by listeners who have no experience with or exposure to the language. Thus, PAM was not intended to be used to make predictions about the perception of L2 learners. To address this, Best and Tyler (2007) offered the PAM-L2 model, which was designed as an extension of PAM to the L2 learning environment. While the reader is referred to Best and Tyler (2007) for a more thorough description, an important point raised therein and relevant to the current discussion of L2 Korean is the fact that (naïve) non-native perception and L2 perception are fundamentally different phenomena. In the case of non-native perception, the listener has no knowledge about the phonological system of the foreign language and can only perceive incoming speech sounds in terms of the phonetic similarity to L1 sounds and categories. But in L2 perception, the listener has knowledge of the phonological system of the L2 and may have developed perceptual mappings between the L1 and L2 that rely on more than just phonetic similarity. While this distinction may seem minute, it is important to bear in mind when reviewing the literature on L2 Korean phonological acquisition.

Whereas PAM and PAM-L2 are models of non-native and L2 speech sound *perception*, the Speech Learning Model (SLM; Flege, 1995) is a model of L2 speech sound *acquisition*. It seeks to explain the production and perception of L2 speech sounds by L2 learners. One of its main claims is that an L2 sound that is similar – but not identical – to an L1 sound will be harder to acquire than an L2 sound that is totally different from any L1 sound. Although it may seem counterintuitive at first, this claim rests on the idea of perceptual equivalence: if an L2 sound is too similar to an L1 sound, it will be perceived by the learner as simply "the same" as the L1 sound, and it will be difficult to produce any difference between them. For a more detailed explanation, the reader is referred to Flege (1987) and Flege (1995).

Overview of this chapter

Research on the L2 acquisition of Korean segments began in earnest only in the late 1990s, presumably motivated in part by an increase in students learning Korean as a second or foreign language. It should also be noted that the volume of research published in Korean, either in Korean scholarly journals or graduate theses, has always been far greater than that published in English or other languages, and the English-language literature should therefore be viewed as only part of the extant research record. Accordingly, one goal of this chapter is to highlight some important studies that have been published in Korean but may have remained unknown to a wider international community.

While the main focus of this chapter (and book) is on L2 learners of Korean, in this chapter we will also look at some studies that have investigated the perception of Korean sounds by naïve non-native listeners. The term "naïve" refers to listeners who have not studied Korean and have had no meaningful exposure to it. The primary reason for looking at such studies is that the naïve listener represents the "pre-learner state". Up until the moment an L2 learner stepped into their first Korean classroom, they were themselves "naïve", and understanding how such listeners perceive Korean sounds can help us understand more about the process by which L2 speech sounds are learned. There are also good reasons to suspect that even a little bit of L2 experience can affect how L2 sounds are perceived (Best & Tyler, 2007), but it is hard to understand what the effect of L2 experience is without comparing results to those from listeners without such experience. Thus, in each of the main sections of this chapter, which focus on stops, affricates, fricatives, and vowels, we will first review any relevant findings on naïve listeners and then move on to studies of L2 learners.

Finally, it should be noted that the range of L1s investigated is naturally limited. Research on L2 phonological acquisition requires access to a population of L2 learners large enough to draw meaningful conclusions about, and so the L1s that get investigated end up being those with enough L2 learners that researchers have access to. As a result, by far the most commonly investigated L1 population is Mandarin, especially among studies carried out in Korea, with the next most frequently studied L1s being English, Japanese, and, in more recent years, Vietnamese. Thus, when reviewing the literature, we must always bear in mind that what is known about L2 Korean phonological acquisition is constrained by this set of L1s, and some generalizations may not hold as more research is carried out in the future.

Stops

Research on the stop contrast comprises a large share of the literature on L2 Korean phonological acquisition, and virtually all of it concerns the three-way laryngeal stop contrast (discussed above). There may be several reasons for this. First, the most important phonetic cues to the contrast, VOT and f0, are well understood and are relatively easy to measure. Second, almost all research on L2 Korean phonology has examined L1 speakers of languages with a two-way contrast (e.g., voiced–voiceless, as in Japanese, or unaspirated–aspirated, as in English or Mandarin), and the acquisition of Korean's three-way voiceless contrast poses a genuine challenge for many of these L2 learners. And third, stop sounds are very frequent in Korean, raising the stakes for intelligible pronunciation.

Stop perception

For many novice L2 learners of Korean, their first encounter with the three-way contrast is characterized by wonder – how do listeners tell the three sounds apart? Studies examining the perception of Korean stops by naïve listeners have shown, at least for the L1s that have been tested, that perceiving at least two of the members of the contrast as "the same" is typical. The specific pattern of perception has been shown to depend on the phonetic properties of the stop contrast in the L1: for languages with a two-way stop contrast, the contrast can usually be characterized as one of voicing (contrasting voiced [b, d, g] with voiceless [p, t, k]) or one of aspiration (unaspirated [p, t, k] with aspirated [p^h, t^h, k^h]). For example, among the listener L1s that have been tested, the stop contrast in Spanish and Dutch is one of voicing, in English and Mandarin one of aspiration, and in Japanese it seems to be undergoing a change from voicing to aspiration.

It has been reported that L1 English (Schmidt, 2007) and Mandarin (Holliday, 2014a) naïve listeners assimilate both lenis and aspirated stops to English and Mandarin aspirated stop categories [p^h, t^h, k^h] (i.e., those written as <p, t, k> in English and pinyin), and fortis stops to unaspirated stop categories [p, t, k] (i.e., <b, d, g>). The simplest explanation for this finding is that L1 English and Mandarin naïve listeners assimilate Korean stops based on VOT: Korean long-lag lenis and aspirated stops assimilate to L1 long-lag aspirated stops, and Korean short-lag fortis stops to L1 short-lag unaspirated stops. Thus, while f0 is an important cue that L1 Korean listeners use to help identify a stop as lenis or aspirated (Lee, Politzer-Ahles, & Jongman, 2013), it does not affect which L1 stop category L1 English and Mandarin naïve listeners perceive the Korean stops as being most similar to. Similar results have also been reported for L1 Japanese listeners (Yasuta, 2004; Holliday, 2019). Although Japanese historically contrasted voiced and voiceless stops, recent data indicates that Japanese voiced stops may be produced with short-lag VOT and voiceless stops with intermediate-lag VOT (Riney, Takagi, Ota, & Uchida, 2007; Takada, 2008), rendering the Japanese contrast somewhat similar to that of English and Mandarin.

In the case of Spanish, Martínez García and Holliday (2019) found that naïve listeners assimilated all Korean stops – fortis, lenis, and aspirated – to their Spanish voiceless category, although fortis stops were perceived as voiced some of the time as well. This result suggests that L1 listeners of a language with a stop voicing contrast may perceive all three Korean stop phonation types as more similar to each other than L1 listeners of a language with a stop aspiration contrast. Studies that have tested naïve listeners on discrimination have confirmed this. Martínez García and Holliday (2019) and Choi (2015) tested the discrimination of L1 Spanish and Dutch naïve listeners, and found that discrimination on all three contrasts ranged from roughly 40% to 65%. But in a smaller study on L1 listeners of English, a language with a stop aspiration contrast, Kang and Lee (2002) reported that only the discrimination of the lenis-aspirated contrast was very poor, and performance on the fortis-lenis and fortis-aspirated contrasts was at ceiling.

In summary, studies on the perceptual assimilation and discrimination of word-initial Korean stops by naïve listeners from a range of L1s indicate that listeners typically perceive at least two of the three Korean stop types as the same: either the lenis and aspirated stops are perceived as similar to each other with the fortis stop perceived as distinct, or all three stop types are perceived as similar to each other, with none of them perceived as particularly distinct. But what have studies of actual L2 learners revealed? One of the few investigations of Korean stop perceptual assimilation by L2 learners was Kim (2006), who tested L1 Mandarin novice learners studying in Daegu. Although they consistently assimilated fortis and aspirated stops to their Mandarin unaspirated and aspirated categories, like the naïve listeners in Holliday (2014a), lenis stops were variably perceived as both unaspirated and aspirated.

This finding raises the question of whether it was the listeners' L2 experience that led them to perceive lenis stops differently from naïve listeners. And while it may be the case, we cannot rule out the possibility that the acoustic properties of the stimuli had an effect. The stimuli used in Kim (2006) were produced by native Korean speakers from Daegu, who (along with speakers from the larger Gyeongsang region) have been shown to produce lenis stops with shorter VOT than speakers from other regions, especially Seoul (Lee & Jongman, 2012). A smaller-scale but similar study run on L2 Korean learners in China using stimuli produced by a native speaker of Seoul Korean reported that word-initial lenis stops assimilated much more consistently to Mandarin aspirated categories (Ren & Mok, 2015).

In any case, while L2 learners' perceptual assimilation patterns may be useful in predicting the ability to discriminate between or identify the members of L2 contrasts, other tasks are needed to directly measure such abilities. In terms of discrimination, both Oh (2013) and Ryu (2016) reported that while novice L2 learners were about 80% accurate, about half of the errors on "same trials" involved lenis stops, and 91% (Oh, 2013) and 63% (Ryu, 2016) of errors on "different trials" involved the lenis-aspirated contrast. Jung and Kwon (2010) tested very novice L2 learners from a range of L1 backgrounds using a similar task in their study as well, although overall accuracy was 61% and lenis-aspirated trials comprised 64% of errors. Oh (2013) further tested L1 Mandarin learners' AX discrimination ability in intervocalic position (e.g., 아다-아타), and found that not only was accuracy significantly lower, at 73%, but that 100% of the errors were on lenis-fortis trials. Thus, while the lenis and aspirated stops are the most difficult for L1 Mandarin L2 learners to perceive the difference between in word-initial position, in intervocalic word-medial position the difficulty shifts to the lenis-fortis contrast.

Discrimination tasks require the listener to tell whether two sounds are different from each other, but they do not require the listener to identify what either of the sounds are. In other words, a listener may be able to tell that the two sounds 다-타 are not the same, but they may not be able to tell which is lenis and which is aspirated, and in real-life speech perception it is the ability to correctly identify a phonetic target that is ultimately needed for lexical access and comprehension. To probe this ability, researchers use identification tasks in which a listener is presented with stimuli one at a time and asked to identify the target. One interesting aspect of this method is that it allows the researcher to observe the direction of misperception. That is, lenis and aspirated stops may be perceptually confusable, but is it because lenis stops are misperceived as aspirated, aspirated stops are misperceived as lenis, or both?

Studies using this method with word-initial Korean stops have found, unsurprisingly, that the majority of L1 Mandarin learners' perceptual errors involve lenis stops. Both T.-K. Kim (2014) and Ryu (2016) showed not only that the majority of errors were between lenis and aspirated stops but that it was much more likely for a lenis stop to be misperceived as aspirated than vice versa. Furthermore, among the errors involving lenis and fortis stops, it was rarely the case that a lenis stop was perceived as fortis; instead, it was more likely that a fortis stop was perceived as lenis. The directionality of these errors is interesting because it suggests that the difficulty L2 learners have in accurately identifying word-initial Korean stops is not just due to general confusion but, rather, an incorrect perceptual target for lenis stops. In other words, it may not be that they are guessing randomly but that they actually do have a well-defined mental representation of what a lenis stop should be. The results of T.-K. Kim (2014) and Ryu (2016) suggest that the listeners in those studies had a lenis stop perceptual target closer to an actual fortis stop, which would explain why actual lenis stops were incorrectly perceived as aspirated, and actual fortis stops were incorrectly perceived as lenis.

Not all studies report such asymmetric results, however, so we cannot take the results of T.-K. Kim (2014) and Ryu (2016) to be necessary outcomes. Yang (2017) reported that word-initial lenis and aspirated stops were often misperceived as each other, but the strength of directionality was weaker than in T.-K. Kim (2014) and Ryu (2016), and there was no directionality at all observed in misperceptions of lenis and fortis stops. There were many other methodological differences among these studies, however, and so a more controlled and targeted investigation of directionality in perception errors may be needed.

Stop production

In summary, studies on L2 perception of Korean stops have generally shown that most difficulties faced by L2 learners involve lenis stops: they are most often confused with aspirated stops in word-initial position, and with fortis stops in word-medial intervocalic position. Findings on L2 production, on the other hand, cannot be summarized so succinctly. While L2 production studies have focused mostly on word-initial position, and mostly on L1 speakers of languages with a voiceless unaspirated–aspirated stop contrast, the results reported across studies vary widely.

Chang (2010) reported longitudinal stop productions data from L1 English novice learners (n = 26) who had just arrived in Seoul for a six-week intensive Korean language program. After five weeks of study, a wide variety of production patterns were observed, despite participants having the same L1 background and being enrolled in the same intensive course. While some of the learners did produce a three-way contrast, none seemed to do it in a native-like way:

some used only VOT, others used only f0, and others used both VOT and f0 but in a novel way (e.g., producing aspirated stops with long-lag VOT but low f0, and lenis stops with low f0 but short-lag VOT). Other learners produced only a two-way contrast in production, totally merging lenis and aspirated stops or lenis and fortis stops, and other learners produced no distinction among the stops whatsoever. Holliday (2015) collected similar data on L1 Mandarin novice learners (n = 12) after six weeks of instruction, and then half of the learners were re-recorded both 6 and 12 months later. In the recordings done after six weeks, just as in Chang (2010), wide variation in production strategies was observed, with some learners making clear two-way contrasts, and others making no contrast at all. The longitudinal data showed improvement with three of the six learners who exhibited near-native-like productions after one year of instruction. Yet another learner seemed to produce native-like VOT but with no contrast at all in f0, while the remaining two learners showed no improvement whatsoever despite being enrolled in the same intensive course as everyone else.

The finding in common between these two studies seems to be that when L1 speakers of a language with a two-way stop contrast try to learn Korean's three-way contrast, they do not all follow the same path. Holliday (2019), on the other hand, presented analogous data from L1 Japanese learners and found virtually no variation among learners whatsoever. Other studies have suggested that learners' production errors are at least partially predicted by their L1 (e.g., Chang, Burge, & Choi, 2011; Han & Kim, 2014), but because these studies reported only group-level statistics, it is unclear how much variation existed among learners. Chang et al. (2011) suggested that L1 Mandarin learners (n = 8) were able to use f0 and H1-H2 in ways that L1 English and Spanish learners were not, whereas Han and Kim (2014) reported that even novice L1 Mandarin learners (n = 6) produced what was essentially a three-way VOT contrast, with distinct VOT ranges for each phonation type. Lastly, Oh (2018) reported that even novice L1 Mandarin learners (n = 16) with roughly two to three months of in-country L2 instruction produced all three Korean stop types with VOT and f0 values that did not significantly deviate from L1 Korean norms.

What, then, can be concluded from these studies? First, it is probably true that a range of production patterns can be observed even among L2 learners from the same L1 background. Two of the three studies that actually reported acoustic measurements for each individual learner did report wide variation. A fair amount of variation has been observed even in studies of the L2 acquisition of a single acoustic cue (VOT) in a two-way stop contrast, as in L2 Spanish (e.g., Nagle, 2017; Casillas, 2020). Second, while it is difficult to say which of the three stop types poses the greatest difficulty for L2 learners (especially given the narrow range of L1s that have been investigated), one point of agreement among studies seems to be that the aspirated stops are the least challenging. Third, learners seem to learn how to use VOT to signal the contrast before they learn how to use f0. Indeed, some of the studies that reported on L1 Mandarin learners found that even after an entire year of in-country intensive L2 instruction, some learners were unable to manipulate f0 in a native-like way.

Affricates

The L2 acquisition of Korean affricates has been investigated mostly in two domains: the three-way laryngeal contrast and place of articulation. In the case of the laryngeal contrast, among fortis <ㅉ> /tɕ*/, lenis <ㅈ> /tɕ/, and aspirated <ㅊ> /tɕʰ/, there may not be much reason to presume the error patterns and difficulties would significantly differ from what has been observed in research on the three-way stop laryngeal contrast, given that the laryngeal mechanism underlying both is ostensibly the same. With respect to place of articulation, on the other hand, there exists a range of potential difficulties for L2 learners. For example, while Korean affricates are alveolopalatal and can occur with any vowel, Mandarin affricates are articulated at three different places of articulation and subject to vowel co-occurrence restrictions (Ren & Mok, 2015), which could pose a difficulty for L1 Mandarin learners of Korean (Jung, 2008). To date, however, most published research dealing with the L2 perception or production of Korean affricates has focused on the laryngeal contrast, with very little discussion of place of articulation.

Affricate perception

We begin this section again by looking at the perceptual assimilation of Korean affricates by naïve listeners, the results of which touch on both of these domains. In Schmidt (2007), L1 English listeners assimilated Korean affricates to both affricate and stop categories, with Korean /tɕʰ/ almost always assimilating to an aspirated category (either /tʃʰ/ or /t/), Korean /tɕ/ to an aspirated category nearly 85% of the time (with the remainder to the unaspirated affricate /dʒ/), and Korean /tɕ*/ assimilating to an unaspirated category (either /dʒ/, /z/, or /d/) a little over 85% of the time. Thus, much like the results for stops, L1 English listeners usually assimilate lenis and aspirated affricates to an aspirated category and fortis affricates to an unaspirated category. With respect to place of articulation, the question raised by the results of Schmidt (2007) is whether the assimilation of Korean affricates to stop categories (/t/ or /d/) is driven by the perception of place or the perception of manner, e.g., Korean /tʃʰ/ could be perceived as English /t/ because it is perceived a stop (and not an affricate), or it could be because it is perceived as alveolar (and not postalveolar, as English affricates are). While this question remains open, it helps exemplify that the more difficult aspect of Korean affricate perception to explain is not the perception of the laryngeal contrast but of the place of articulation.

As for naïve L1 Mandarin listeners, the perception of the laryngeal contrast in affricates again seems to be quite similar to that of stops. Mandarin contrasts aspirated and unaspirated affricates at three places of articulation: denti-alveolar /ts, tsʰ/, alveolopalatal /tɕ, tɕʰ/, and postalveolar or retroflex /tʃ, tʃʰ/. The listeners in Holliday (2014a) almost always assimilated Korean /tɕʰ/ to an aspirated Mandarin category (usually an affricate, but sometimes a stop), and Korean /tɕ*/ almost always to an unaspirated category. Lenis /tɕ/ again patterned with aspirated /tɕʰ/, usually assimilating to an aspirated category but also sometimes to an unaspirated category. Just as with the stops, this result can be mostly predicted by VOT alone. The potentially more interesting question, alluded to earlier, is how L1 Mandarin listeners would perceive the place of articulation. Mandarin has both aspirated and unaspirated alveolopalatal affricates, just like Korean, so why do listeners not always assimilate to those categories? One reason is that Mandarin alveolopalatal affricates can only be followed by the vowels /i/ or /y/, or a palatal onglide. Thus, the sequence of /tɕ/ + /a/ would only be possible if a glide were inserted, resulting in a pronunciation like [tɕia] or [tɕja], and written as <jia> in pinyin. Therefore, the Korean syllable /tɕa/ <자>, with no palatal on-glide, may be difficult for an L1 Mandarin listener to assimilate to a native category: although the affricate is alveolopalatal, the lack of an on-glide may make the listener hesitant to respond that it sounds similar to a Mandarin alveolopalatal. The listeners in Holliday (2014a) indeed displayed such a tendency. When the vowel in the stimulus was /a/, the affricates were assimilated to Mandarin affricate categories at all three places of articulation – denti-alveolar, alveolopalatal, and postalveolar – at roughly equal rates. But when the vowel was /i/, the affricates were almost always assimilated to a Mandarin alveolopalatal affricate category, and when the vowel was /u/ they were assimilated mostly to Mandarin postalveolar categories.

Very few studies have investigated the perception of affricates by actual L2 learners. One example, Kim and Kim (2013), tested the identification of Korean affricates by L1 Vietnamese listeners. The acquisition of Korean affricates by L1 Vietnamese learners is potentially interesting because Vietnamese, unlike other L1s common among L2 Korean learners, has no affricates at all, which raises questions like: Do they perceive them as stops? Or fricatives? And when they produce them, do they produce true affricates, or do they substitute a stop or fricative? And at what place of articulation? Unfortunately, studies that have investigated affricate acquisition by L1 Vietnamese learners have left these questions for future work and have instead focused on the laryngeal contrast. Using an identification task, Kim and Kim (2013) found that listeners confused all three affricate phonation types with each other, with accuracy in word-initial position hovering around 40% and in word-medial position around 47%.

Affricate production

Affricate productions recorded from the same group of L1 Vietnamese learners in Kim and Kim (2013) also revealed no significant phonetic differences among the three affricate types, with all three most closely resembling a fortis affricate. Jang (2018) analyzed the affricate productions of another group of L1 Vietnamese learners and found a wide range of production patterns, with some learners producing a three-way contrast, others only a two-way, and many of them producing no contrast among the three affricates at all. Like some of the studies on L2 stop production discussed earlier, by reporting the production pattern of each individual participant in the study, Jang (2018) shows us that while the learners as a whole do not produce the contrast correctly, they are not all making the same errors.

Again, however, the acoustic analyses in Kim and Kim (2013) and Jang (2018), are focused on the three-way laryngeal contrast and not place or manner of articulation. Studies of L1 Mandarin learners' affricate productions share this focus, reporting many of the same difficulties reported for stops. For example, Lei and Kim (2010) and Jo (2017) report difficulties by L1 Mandarin learners manipulating f0, and Jo (2017) found that novice learners' lenis affricates were often perceived by native Korean listeners as fortis. These error patterns are quite similar to those found in L2 stop productions and are, perhaps, to be expected. There remain virtually no studies that have investigated place of articulation in L2 Korean affricate production.

Fricatives

Like the three-way laryngeal contrast in stops and affricates, the contrast between the Korean sibilant fricatives, non-fortis <ㅅ> /s/ and fortis <ㅆ> /s*/, is typologically uncommon. It is not just the fortis quality of /s*/ that marks the contrast, however. As many studies have pointed out, non-fortis /s/ is produced with aspiration in non-high vowel contexts, resulting in syllables like <사> /sa/ and <새> /sɛ/ being phonetically realized like [sʰa] and [sʰɛ]. Aspiration is minimal or absent in high-vowel contexts like <수> /su/ or <시> /si/, and totally absent in fortis fricatives. As aspirated fricatives are cross-linguistically quite rare (Jacques, 2011), the largest L2 Korean learner population whose L1 contains aspirated fricatives is most likely Burmese. Another wrinkle in the Korean sibilant fricative contrast concerns palatalization. While the non-fortis /s/ becomes alveolopalatal [ɕ] when followed by /i/ or /j/, there is disagreement about whether the fortis fricative /s*/ also palatalizes in the same environment. Some texts claim it is always palatalized and others that it is never palatalized. The truth is probably somewhere in between, and there has yet to be any in-depth investigation of the issue.

Fricative perception

In terms of perceptual assimilation by naïve listeners, L1 English (Schmidt, 2007) and Japanese (Holliday, 2012) listeners have been reported to assimilate Korean fricatives in a similar way, with both /s/ and /s*/ assimilating to their L1 /s/ category when the following vowel was /a/ or /u/, and to their L1 /ʃ/ (English) or /ɕ/ (Japanese) category when the following vowel was /i/. In a cross-language discrimination task, Cheon and Anderson (2008) further showed that L1 English naïve listeners perceived both Korean 사 /sa/ and 싸 /s*a/ as quite similar – but not identical – to English /sa/. Korean 시 /si/, on the other hand, was perceived as a much closer fit to English /ʃ/, and Korean 씨 /s*i/ as split between English /s/ and /ʃ/.

L1 Mandarin listeners (Holliday, 2014a, 2016) have been shown to be similar to L1 English and Japanese listeners in the /u/ and /i/ contexts: both 수 /su/ and 쑤 /s*u/ were assimilated to Mandarin /su/, and both 시 /si/ and 씨 /s*i/ (when palatalized) were assimilated to Mandarin /ɕi/. In the /a/ context, however, L1 Mandarin listeners consistently assimilate Korean 싸 /s*a/ to Mandarin /sa/, but Korean 사 /sa/ to Mandarin /sa/ and /tsʰa/.[4] In other words, in the /a/ context, and only the /a/ context, the Korean non-fortis fricative /s/ is perceived by L1 Mandarin listeners as an aspirated affricate roughly half the time.

To date, research on the L2 perception of the Korean sibilant fricative contrast is limited. One consistent finding is that L1 English, Japanese, and Mandarin listeners struggle to correctly identify /s/ and /s*/ in any vowel context (Holliday, 2014b, 2016). In Cheon (2005), even L2 Korean learners with more than five years of experience only identified Korean fricatives with 67% accuracy, even when the experimental stimuli were isolated CVs from a single talker. But this finding for L1 English and Japanese is not surprising: if naïve listeners perceptually assimilate both Korean /s/ and /s*/ to a single L1 category, PAM (Best, 1995) predicts that discrimination accuracy should be poor. And if the perceptual assimilation patterns of L1 English and Japanese L2 learners remain unchanged, we should expect discrimination and identification accuracy to be poor as well.

Despite the somewhat different perceptual assimilation results from naïve listeners, L1 Mandarin L2 learners of Korean have roughly the same difficulties as their L1 English and Japanese counterparts. Because naïve L1 Mandarin listeners often perceive Korean 사 /sa/ as an affricate and 싸 /s*a/ as a fricative, one might expect L1 Mandarin learners of Korean to perceive them differently as well, but results from both Ren and Mok (2015) and Holliday (2016) show that both novice and advanced L2 learners perceptually assimilate both 사 /sa/ and 싸 /s*a/ to a Mandarin fricative category (usually /s/), and that their discrimination of the contrast is poor. It was shown in Holliday (2016) that even naïve listeners were more accurate at discriminating between 사 /sa/ and 싸 /s*a/ than L2 learners. Because these discrimination results are predicted by how the Korean fricatives are perceptually assimilated (see Best, 1995; Best & Tyler, 2007), perhaps the next question to investigate with respect to L2 Korean fricatives is why the perceptual assimilation of L2 learners might differ from naïve listeners.

Fricative production

Lastly, the production of Korean /s/ and /s*/ by L2 learners seems to generally reflect how they are perceptually assimilated. In her study of L1 English learners, Cheon (2006) found that no contrast was produced between /s/ and /s*/ by novice learners, and only minimal contrast by advanced learners. In their study of L1 Mandarin novice learners, Kallay and Holliday (2012) also found virtually no distinction between /s/ and /s*/ in any vowel context: Korean 사 /sa/ and 싸 /s*a/ were produced identically to Mandarin /sa/, and Korean 시 /si/ and 씨 /s*i/ identically to Mandarin /ɕi/.

These findings from Cheon (2006) and Kallay and Holliday (2012) suggest the possibility that L2 learners' production targets are tied to perception. If learners perceive /s/ and /s*/ to be more or less identical, as has been shown, then it would be surprising to observe significant differences in their production. Holliday and Hong (2020) tested this question explicitly by asking L1 Mandarin naïve listeners and L2 learners to listen to Korean fricative productions and imitate them as accurately as possible. Their repetitions were then played to another group of L1 Korean listeners, who were asked to identify the sound they heard. Across vowel contexts, the L2 learners' productions were perceived variably, as both /s/ and /s*/, lending further support to the idea that accurate fricative production remains challenging, even for more advanced L2 learners.

Vowels

There are two issues to bear in mind when reviewing the literature on vowel acquisition. First, as alluded to above, language instructors (and researchers) may hold different views regarding what the vowels of Korean are and which ones should be taught. As explained earlier, the Korean vowel system has undergone changes in the past few decades, most notably in the neutralization of /e-ɛ/ and the diphthongization of /y/ and /ø/ into /wi/ and /we/, respectively. A survey of studies over the past 20 years reveals some that do not acknowledge these changes at all and others that suggest teaching such distinctions is not worth the effort when not even the instructors themselves pronounce them (e.g., Jang, 2002).

Second, in addition to these phonological changes that have resulted in the total loss of certain monophthongs, there have also been phonetic changes that have shifted the articulatory targets of vowels in ways that native speakers themselves may not be aware of. Specifically, acoustic studies of Korean monophthongs even as recently as Yang (1996) showed that the contrast between /o/ and /u/ was primarily one of height: in the vowel space, /u/ occupied the high back corner, with /o/ almost directly below it. But more recent studies of native Korean monophthong production have shown that /o/ has raised to a position that nearly coincides with where /u/ used to be, while /u/ has moved forward a bit (Kim, J., 2014, Fig. 1; Kang & Kong, 2016, Fig. 1; Lee, Shin, & Shin, 2017, Fig. 1). The high-back quadrant of the Korean vowel space is already the most crowded, with /o/, /u/, /ɨ/, and /ʌ/, and has long been identified as the source of most difficulties for L2 learners of Korean (e.g., Jang, 2002; Kwon, 2007).

Vowel perception

One of the few studies of Korean vowel perception by naïve listeners was Kim (2018), who tested the perceptual assimilation of Korean monophthongs by L1 Mandarin and Vietnamese naïve listeners. Among the L1 Mandarin listeners, it was found that while Korean /u/ assimilated clearly to Mandarin /u/, Korean /o/ was also often (70%) assimilated to Mandarin /u/, and less often (30%) to Mandarin /o/. Korean /ʌ/, on the other hand, did not assimilate clearly to any single Mandarin category, being perceived as /ɤ/, /o/, or something else. The L1 Vietnamese listeners exhibited similar patterns, with Korean /o/ assimilating mostly to Vietnamese /o/ but also sometimes /u/, and Korean /u/ assimilating mostly to Vietnamese /u/ but also sometimes to /o/. And in two studies of the discrimination ability of L1 Arabic naïve listeners, Hong and Jun (2013) and Hong (2018) reported the most difficulty in discriminating between Korean /o/ and /u/.

Although we have seen other cases in which the perception of naïve listeners does not straightforwardly predict that of L2 learners, the perceptual confusability of the Korean high back vowels among L2 learners has been demonstrated in several different studies. In an identification task, Ryu (2018) reported similar confusion patterns in L1 English and L1 Mandarin L2 learners, who misperceived /ʌ/ and /u/ as /o/, and /o/ as /ʌ/. L1 English (but not Mandarin) learners also occasionally misperceived /ɨ/ as /u/. In another study of L1 Mandarin learners, Park (2010) also found that both /ʌ/ and /u/ were misperceived as /o/, and vice versa. The confusion between /o/ and /u/ may also extend to palatalized vowels, as Kim and Kwon (2019) show that L1 Mongolian novice L2 learners often misperceived /jo/ and /ju/ for each other.

Kim and Kwon (2019) further demonstrate the complexity involved in understanding the perception of Korean diphthongs. While many L2 perception tasks involve playing a stimulus and asking the listener to choose from a closed set of categories, Kim and Kwon (2019) allowed the L1 Mongolian listeners to write their responses freely any way they chose. As a result, some diphthongs were perceived as not diphthongs at all, but monophthongs (e.g., /jɛ/ as /ɛ/), or even a sequence of two monophthongs (e.g., /wɛ/ as /uɛ/). Kim (2020) applied this free response method to perceptual assimilation of the entire inventory of Korean monophthongs and diphthongs: L1 Mandarin novice and advanced L2 learners listened to Korean vowels and wrote in pinyin what it sounded like in Mandarin. While the results revealed once again that both Korean /o/ is often assimilated to Mandarin <u>, the free response style also revealed that Korean /ʌ/ assimilates most often not to a single Mandarin vowel, but rather <ao>, followed by <o>, <ou>, and <e>. Thus, some studies may actually underestimate perceptual variability both within and across listeners by restricting their responses to only a few options.

Vowel production

Confusion between Korean /o/ and /u/ has been observed in L2 production as well. Han and Kim (2011) recorded six L1 Mandarin learners every two months over their first year of L2 Korean instruction and had L1 Korean listeners identify and rate their productions of the vowels /a, ɛ, i, o, u/. The learners' vowels were almost always correctly identified with the exception of /u/, which was misperceived as /o/ roughly 20–35% of the time at all time points. This asymmetric misperception is likely a consequence of the raising of /o/ in Seoul in Korean discussed earlier. It is possible that learners' /o/ or /u/ productions could also be misperceived as /ʌ/ or /ɨ/, but these options were not given to the listeners.

In another longitudinal study, J. Kim (2014) recorded the entire set of Korean monophthongs produced by 23 L1 Mandarin learners after one month and 12 months of L2 instruction, and compared the acoustic properties to those of Korean vowels produced by native speakers. The results suggested an improvement in /o/ over the course of the year, indicated by an overall raising to the high back corner of the vowel space. The learners' productions of /u/, however, moved further *back*, and after 12 months were almost entirely overlapping with their /o/ productions. What could explain this apparent decrease in vowel production accuracy? L2 learners with more canonical /o/ and /u/ targets in their L1 are likely to be very aware that Korean /o/ is raised, but they may not realize that Korean /u/ is fronted if they do not have a separate high central vowel category. The difficulty in establishing an L2 category very close to an already existing L1 category (Flege, 1995) could then lead learners to simply merge the two, resulting in overlapping distributions of /o/ and /u/.

Other issues

Coda consonants

With respect to Korean coda consonants, there are two main issues that L2 learners must grapple with. First, there is the existence and inventory of coda consonants itself, as all Korean consonant phonemes other than /p*/ and /t*/ may appear in syllable-final position. Second, among these, the obstruents (i.e., stops, affricates, and fricatives) become neutralized to homorganic unreleased stops. In other words, all bilabial and velar stops are phonetically realized as [p̚] and [k̚], respectively, and all denti-alveolar stops, affricates, and fricatives are realized as [t̚]. The only consonants permitted in coda position in Mandarin are [n] and [ŋ], while Japanese has only a single coda nasal whose place of articulation is underspecified. Thus, for L1 speakers of these languages, the very existence of coda stops or liquids would be new, and even among coda nasals it may difficult to differentiate among them. English, on the other hand, permits many consonants in coda position, but it is also common for them to be released (i.e., the slight burst or puff of air at the end of a word like "kick"). In Korean, coda stops must be produced without any audible release.

Yoon (2013) identifies several areas of difficulty for L2 learners relating to coda consonants. For example, when the following syllable has an empty onset, a coda consonant will resyllabify instead of neutralize. Additionally, because neutralized coda consonants are unreleased, they may be harder to distinguish perceptually, especially when not in word-final position and followed by another obstruent. Thus, while L2 learners are not prone to misperceive stop place of articulation in syllable-initial position, evidence suggests that they may struggle in syllable-final position (Kim, T.-K., 2014). Learners may also struggle with lexical access, as orthographically distinct words may be phonetically indistinguishable (e.g., [it*a] could be *exist* <있다> /is*ta/ or *forget* <잊다> /itɛta/).

Other phonological processes

Due to its automatic, predictable nature, coda neutralization is viewed as a phonological (or phonetic) process in Korean. But there are many others, and as they operate at the segmental level, the acquisition of these processes is not independent from the acquisition of segments themselves. One such process is post-obstruent tensification, in which a lenis obstruent or non-fortis fricative is realized as fortis when directly preceded by another obstruent, e.g., *block* <막다> /makta/ is realized as [makt*a]. To complicate matters further, although tensification always occurs in post-obstruent position, it can also occur in other positions for historical or morphological reasons, such as in the word *flour* <밀가루> /milkalu/, pronounced as [milk*aru]. The L2 learner therefore must master not only the pronunciation of fortis obstruents but also the rules that govern when underlying lenis obstruents should be pronounced as fortis. Work by Lee and Park (2018) suggests that accuracy of word-initial fortis stop pronunciation is not related to accuracy in tensified fortis stop pronunciation and that the former is not a prerequisite for the latter. Thus, while the current chapter focused on the acquisition of underlying segments, and a more thorough exploration of the acquisition of phonological processes is left for future work, it should not be assumed that mastery of phonological processes follows directly from the mastery of individual segments.

Global properties

Although some research on L2 Korean segmental acquisition is of purely theoretical interest, it is safe to say that much of it is, ultimately, pedagogically motivated. Many researchers want to understand the problems that L2 learners of Korean face in order to help them improve their pronunciation. But how is their pronunciation evaluated? Many of the studies cited in this chapter use laboratory methods to measure acoustic differences between the productions of L1 and L2 speakers, or psycholinguistic methods to measure accuracy on some perception task. But does good performance on these tasks correlate with good pronunciation evaluation by native Korean listeners? In other words, just because an L2 speaker fails to produce an L2 sound in a completely native-like way does not mean that a listener will notice, or that it will negatively affect intelligibility.

Thus, there is a need for more research that bridges the gap between the laboratory analysis of L2 Korean segmental production and the evaluation of L2 learners' speech in terms of intelligibility, comprehensibility, or foreign accent.[5] For example, Jung (2020) investigated whether larger deviations from L1 Korean acoustic norms in the isolated word productions of L2 Korean learners were correlated with stronger foreign accent. Some correlations were found, but more research is needed to better understand the contributions of segmental and suprasegmental properties of L2 Korean to not only foreign accent, but also the sociolinguistic perception of other talker attributes.

Conclusion

In tandem with the increase in research on L2 Korean phonology in the early 2000s, it became clear that more empirically informed pronunciation teaching methods were needed. According to Jang (2002), both instructors and students would benefit from deeper knowledge about the phonetic differences between the L1 and L2 and that having students merely listen to and repeat the instructor's pronunciation has its limits. To this end, the primary goal of the current chapter was to provide an empirical basis for understanding phenomena in the L2 acquisition of Korean segmental phonology. It is our hope that the evidence offered herein may not only motivate more research in this area but also inform the teaching practices of Korean language instructors.

In the preceding sections, we summarized some of the issues faced by L2 learners in the acquisition of Korean stops, affricates, fricatives, and vowels. Conspicuously absent from this chapter was any discussion of suprasegmental issues. While this omission is regrettable, the scope of the chapter was already so vast that it was judged better to leave for future work. In the space that remains, some suggestions for directions and methods in future research are offered.

In terms of methodology, studies of perceptual assimilation in L2 learners may help shed light on why certain Korean sounds are difficult for some learners. According to Flege (1995), one reason a learner may produce an L2 sound incorrectly is that the learner perceives it to be equivalent to an already existing L1 sound. To explore whether this is the case, it is necessary to probe the perceptual mappings between L1 and L2 categories, and perceptual assimilation is one task that can do exactly that. Relatedly, more work is also needed to offer a more unified account of the acquisition of individual phonemes. For example, in the case of stops, while there are many studies that have investigated production and perception in word-initial position, there are far fewer that have looked at word-medial position, and even fewer that have speculated how the two may be related. L2 learners of Korean probably do not start out thinking that lenis stops should be pronounced differently in different syllabic environments. How and when is that knowledge acquired?

Another promising – and needed – area of future research concerns the relationship between specific pronunciation teaching methods and learner outcomes. So-called classroom studies that implement a pronunciation teaching technique in one classroom while withholding it in a comparable control classroom are the only truly ecologically valid way to test whether a particular teaching technique is effective (Derwing & Munro, 2015, p. 83). For example, it was observed above that learners from various L1 backgrounds struggle to manipulate f0 correctly in their L2 production of Korean stops. But how many of these learners were explicitly aware of how the f0 of the following vowel correlates with stop phonation type? Did their instructors ever point this out to them or provide any contrastive examples or training? We may speculate that such instruction would be helpful, but it could only be empirically demonstrated through a controlled classroom study, which would also give a sense of how effective (and therefore worthwhile) such instruction would be. In one study in this vein, Isbell, Park, and Lee (2019) conducted a classroom-based study on the effect of specialized pronunciation instruction on the comprehensibility, accentedness, and segmental error rates of L2 Korean learners' speech. While the results were mixed, the study represents an important step in connecting classroom instruction to actual learner outcomes in L2 Korean pronunciation.

In terms of analysis and interpretation, not many of the studies cited in this chapter looked closely at individual differences. When accuracy is high, this may be fine since mathematically there is little room for variation. But when the mean accuracy rate on a task hovers around 50%, it raises questions about what the errors are, whether they are distributed across learners or concentrated within a few, and whether they occur across the stimulus set or are caused only by a subset of difficult stimuli. This issue can be partly addressed by using statistical methods that take both intra- and inter-subject and -item variability into account, but it can also be addressed by simply providing data visualizations or appendices that show performance across subjects and items.

Lastly, with the exception of those that investigated L1 English learners, many (if not all) of the studies cited in this chapter were actually investigating the production and perception of L3 Korean, since most of the participants in the studies studied English as an L2 to at least some degree. While the level of English proficiency or experience would play a role, we feel compelled to point out that this issue has been virtually ignored in every study cited here. And while there is growing interest in L3 phonological acquisition, to our knowledge there has been no systematic or large-scale investigation of L2 effects – especially L2 English – on L3 Korean phonological acquisition (although see Hong and Jun [2013] for an example of a study that explicitly examines the effect of L2 English experience, albeit among a population of naïve listeners). This issue is inextricably linked to questions about perceptual equivalence: if a learner of Korean already has phonological categories for both their L1 and English, it is reasonable to expect that their pronunciation or perception of Korean could be connected to both the structure of and mappings between these categories.

Notes

1 While the terms "fortis" and "lenis" are used in the current chapter, the terms "tense" and "lax" are also common.
2 A thorough discussion of Korean phonetic and phonological process can be found in chapters 8 and 9 of Shin, Kiaer, and Cha (2013, pp. 178–215) and chapter 7 of Sohn (2013, pp. 163–177).
3 Other references may transcribe this vowel with the IPA symbol /ɯ/.
4 Some listeners in Holliday (2014a) and Holliday (2016) assimilated Korean /s/ and /s*/ in the /a/ and /u/ contexts to a Mandarin postalveolar/retroflex, such as /ʃ/ or /tʃʰ/, but it was speculated that this was due to L1 dialectal variation in which the contrast between Mandarin denti-alveolars and postalveolars (e.g., /s/ and /ʃ/) has been neutralized.
5 For a review of these concepts, please see Chapter 1 of Derwing and Munro (2015).

References

Best, C. T. (1995). A direct realist view of cross-language speech perception. In W. Strange (Ed.), *Speech perception and linguistic experience: Issues in cross-language research* (pp. 171–204). Timonium: York Press.

Best, C. T., & Tyler, M. D. (2007). Nonnative and second-language speech perception: Commonalities and complementarities. In O. S. Bohn & M. Munro (Eds.), *Language experience in second language speech learning: In honor of James Emil Flege* (pp. 13–34). Amsterdam and Philadelphia: John Benjamins Publishing Company.

Casillas, J. V. (2020). The longitudinal development of fine-phonetic detail: Stop production in a domestic immersion program. *Language Learning, 70*(3), 768–806.

Chang, C. B. (2010). The implementation of laryngeal contrast in Korean as a second language. In Susumu Kuno, Ik-Hwan Lee, John Whitman, Joan Maling, Young-Se Kang, Peter Sells, Hyang-Sook Sohn, & Youngjun Jang (Eds.), *Harvard studies in Korean linguistics XIII* (pp. 91–104). Seoul, South Korea: Hanshin.

Chang, C. B. (2013). The production and perception of coronal fricatives in Seoul Korean: The case for a fourth laryngeal category. *Korean Linguistics, 15*(1), 7–49.

Chang, S.-E., Burge, M., & Choi, Y. (2011). A cross-linguistic study of Korean laryngeal stops by the native speakers of Chinese, English, Korean, and Spanish. In *Proceedings of the 17th international congress of phonetic sciences* (pp. 432–435). City University of Hong Kong, Hong Kong.

Cheon, S. Y. (2005). *Production and perception of phonological contrasts in second language acquisition: Korean and English fricatives* [Unpublished doctoral dissertation]. University of Hawai'i.

Cheon, S. Y. (2006). Production of Korean fricatives in second language acquisition. *Korean Linguistics, 13*, 17–48.

Cheon, S. Y., & Anderson, V. B. (2008). Acoustic and perceptual similarities between English and Korean sibilants: Implications for second language acquisition. *Korean Linguistics, 14*, 41–64.

Choi, J. (2015). Dutch listeners' perception of Korean stop consonants. *Phonetics and Speech Sciences, 7*(1), 89–95.

Derwing, T. M., & Munro, M. J. (2015). *Pronunciation fundamentals: Evidence-based perspectives for L2 teaching and research*. Amsterdam and Philadelphia: John Benjamins Publishing Company.

Flege, J. E. (1987). The production of "new" and "similar" phones in a foreign language: Evidence for the effect of equivalence classification. *Journal of Phonetics, 15*(1), 47–65.

Flege, J. E. (1995). Second language speech learning: Theory, findings, and problems. In W. Strange (Ed.), *Speech perception and linguistic experience: Issues in cross-language research* (pp. 233–277). Timonium: York Press.

Han, J.-I., & Kim, J.-Y. (2011). A one-year longitudinal study of Korean vowel productions by Chinese learners. *Korean Journal of Linguistics (언어), 36*(4), 1101–1115.

Han, J.-I., & Kim, J.-Y. (2014). Acquisition of Korean stops by native speakers of Mandarin Chinese: A one-year longitudinal study. *Korean Journal of Linguistics (언어), 39*(2), 377–403.

Holliday, J. J. (2012). *The emergence of L2 phonological contrast in perception: The case of Korean sibilant fricatives* [Unpublished doctoral dissertation]. The Ohio State University.

Holliday, J. J. (2014a). The perceptual assimilation of Korean obstruents by native Mandarin listeners. *Journal of the Acoustical Society of America, 135*(3), 1585–1595.

Holliday, J. J. (2014b). The perception of Seoul Korean fricatives by listeners from five different native dialect and language groups. *Korean Linguistics, 16*(2), 91–108.

Holliday, J. J. (2015). A longitudinal study of the second language acquisition of a three-way stop contrast. *Journal of Phonetics, 50*, 1–14.

Holliday, J. J. (2016). Second language experience can hinder the discrimination of nonnative phonological contrasts. *Phonetica, 73*(1), 33–51.

Holliday, J. J. (2019). The perception and production of word-initial Korean stops by native speakers of Japanese. *Language and Speech, 62*(3), 494–508.

Holliday, J. J., & Hong, M. (2020). Non-word repetition may reveal different errors in naïve listeners and second language learners. *Phonetics and Speech Sciences (말소리와 음성과학), 12*(1), 1–9.

Hong, S.-A. (2018). Perception of Korean vowel contrasts by Maghrebi Arabic and French bilinguals: A preliminary study for classification of Arabic-speaking Korean learners. *Bilingual Research (이중언어학), 71*, 361–384.

Hong, S.-A., & Jun, J. (2013). Does bilingualism help trilingualism in phonetic perception? *Linguistic Research (언어 연구), 30*(1), 33–49.

Isbell, D. R., Park, O.-S., & Lee, K. (2019). Learning Korean pronunciation: Effects of instruction, proficiency, and L1. *Journal of Second Language Pronunciation, 5*(1), 13–48.

Jacques, G. (2011). A panchronic study of aspirated fricatives, with new evidence from Pumi. *Lingua, 121*(9), 1518–1538.

Jang, H. (2002). The study on pronunciation error made by Chinese native speaker in learning Korean (중국어 모국어 화자의 한국어 학습시 나타나는 발음상의 오류와 그 교육 방안). *Korean Linguistics* (한국어학), *15*, 211–227.

Jang, H.-J. (2018). Analysis of pronunciation types and acoustic properties in Korean word-initial affricate of Vietnamese Korean learners (베트남인 학습자의 한국어 어두 파찰음 발음 유형과 음향적 특성). *Journal of Korean National Language and Literature* (겨레어문학), *61*, 363–385.

Jo, M.-H. (2017). Phonological and phonetic study of affricative pronunciation errors by Chinese learners of Korean. *Journal of Korean Culture*, *37*, 903–128.

Jung, H. (2020). 한국어 학습자의 단어 발화에서 인식된 외국 어투에 대한 연구 *[An investigation of foreign accent in the word productions of non-native speakers of Korean]* [Unpublished doctoral dissertation]. Korea University.

Jung, M. (2008). Strategic pronunciation instruction for learners of Korean: A case with Chinese learners of Korean. *Korean Linguistics*, *38*, 345–369.

Jung, M., & Kwon, S. (2010). A study on the phonetic discrimination and acquisition ability of Korean language learners. *Phonetics and Speech Sciences*, *2*(1), 23–32.

Kallay, J., & Holliday, J. J. (2012). Using spectral measures to differentiate Mandarin and Korean sibilant fricatives. In *Proceedings of INTERSPEECH 2012* (pp. 118–121). International Speech Communication Association.

Kang, J., & Kong, E. J. (2016). Static and dynamic spectral properties of the monophthong vowels in Seoul Korean: Implication on sound change. *Phonetics and Speech Sciences*, *8*(4), 39–47.

Kang, S.-J., & Lee, S.-D. (2002). Acoustic properties of word-initial Korean stops in speech perception. *Journal of Language Science* (언어과학), *9*(2), 1–20.

Kim, J. (2014). A comparative study of second language acquisition models: Focusing on vowel acquisition by Chinese learners of Korean. *Phonetics and Speech Sciences*, *6*(4), 27–36.

Kim, J. Y. (2018). 중국인과 베트남인의 한국어 단순모음 습득 연구 *[A study on the acquisition of Korean monophthongs by native speakers of Chinese and Vietnamese]* [Unpublished doctoral dissertation]. Kunsan National University.

Kim, S. (2006). 한국어 평음/경음/기음에 대한 중국인의 지각적 범주 연구 [Chinese adults' perceptual categorization of Korean lenis, fortis, aspirated]. *Bilingual Research* (이중언어학), *32*, 57–79.

Kim, S., & Kwon, S. (2019). Perception and production of Korean diphthongs by Mongolian learners of Korean. *Studies in Phonetics, Phonology and Morphology* (음성음운형태론연구), *25*(3), 415–437.

Kim, S.-H., & Kim, Y.-J. (2013). A study on Korean affricates produced by Vietnamese speakers (베트남인 화자의 한국어 파찰음 발음 연구). *Korean Linguistics* (한국어학), *59*, 145–168.

Kim, T.-K. (2014). Phonemic discrimination of Korean by native Chinese speakers (중국어 모어 화자의 한국어 음소 변별에 대한 연구). *Korean Language and Literature in International Context* (국제어문), *62*, 405–425.

Kim, Y. (2020). 중국인 학습자의 한국어 모음 지각 동화 및 식별 양상 *[The perceptual assimilation and discrimination of Korean vowels by native Chinese learners of Korean]* [Unpublished master's thesis]. Korea University.

Kwak, C.-G. (2003). The vowel system of contemporary Korean and direction of change (현대국어의 모음체계와 그 변화의 방향). *Journal of Korean Linguistics*, *41*, 59–91.

Kwon, S. (2007). *An experimental study of Korean simple vowel acquisition focused on Japanese learners [*한국어 단모음 습득에 대한 실험음성학적 연구: 일본어권 학습자를 중심으로*]* [Unpublished doctoral dissertation]. Ewha Womans University.

Lee, H., & Jongman, A. (2012). Effects of tone on the three-way laryngeal distinction in Korean: An acoustic and aerodynamic comparison of the Seoul and South Kyungsang dialects. *Journal of the International Phonetic Association*, *42*(2), 145–169.

Lee, H., Holliday, J. J., & Kong, E. J. (2020). Diachronic change and synchronic variation in the Korean stop laryngeal contrast. *Language and Linguistics Compass*, *14*(7), e12374.

Lee, H., Politzer-Ahles, S., & Jongman, A. (2013). Speakers of tonal and non-tonal Korean dialects use different cue weightings in the perception of the three-way laryngeal stop contrast. *Journal of Phonetics*, *41*(2), 117–132.

Lee, H., Shin, W., & Shin, J. (2017). A sociophonetic study on high/mid back vowels in Korean. *Phonetics and Speech Sciences*, *9*(2), 39–51.

Lee, J., & Park, K. (2018). A study on the Korean learners' realization aspect and teaching methods of glottalization after obstruent (한국어 학습자의 평폐쇄음 뒤 경음화 실현 양상 및 교육 방안에 대한 일고찰). *Bilingual Research* (이중언어학), *71*, 223–248.

Lei, L., & Kim, Y. (2010). The acoustic and phonetic study of Korean affricates produced by Chinese speakers. *Studies in Phonetics, Phonology and Morphology, 16*(3), 383–400.

Martínez García, M. T., & Holliday, J. J. (2019). The perception of Korean stops by native speakers of Spanish. In *Proceedings of the 19th international congress of phonetic sciences* (pp. 2585–2589). Australasian Speech Science and Technology Association Inc., Canberra.

Nagle, C. L. (2017). A longitudinal study of voice onset time development in L2 Spanish stops. *Applied Linguistics, 40*(1), 86–107.

Oh, E. (2018). Effects of L2 experience on the production of Korean stop contrasts by Mandarin Chinese learners. *Linguistic Research, 35*(1), 233–251.

Oh, J. (2013). Distinctive perceptual aspect of Korean stop by phonation type on Chinese learners beginning to study Korean (중국인 한국어 학습자의 발성 유형에 따른 한국어 폐쇄음의 변별 지각 양상). *Journal of the International Network of Korean Language and Culture (*한국언어문화학*), 10*(1), 57–73.

Park, J.-Y. (2010). 중국인 한국어 학습자의 한국어 단모음 지각과 산출 관계 연구 *[The perception and production of Korean monophthongs by native Chinese learners of Korean]* [Unpublished master's thesis]. Korea University.

Ren, X., & Mok, P. (2015). Mandarin L2 learners' perception of Korean obstruents in different contexts. In *Proceedings of the 2015 Seoul international conference on speech sciences* (pp. 101–102). The Korean Society of Speech Sciences, Seoul.

Riney, T. J., Takagi, N., Ota, K., & Uchida, Y. (2007). The intermediate degree of VOT in Japanese initial voiceless stops. *Journal of Phonetics, 35*(3), 439–443.

Ryu, N.-Y. (2016). Effects of L2 proficiency on Mandarin speakers' perception of Korean stops and affricates (중국인 학습자의 한국어 숙련도에 따른 한국어 파열음과 파찰음의 변별 지각 양상). *Journal of Korean Language Education (*한국어 교육*), 27*(4), 35–56.

Ryu, N.-Y. (2018). Perception of Korean vowels by English and Mandarin learners of Korean: Effects of acoustic similarity between L1 and L2 sounds and L2 experience. *Journal of Korean Language Education (*한국어 교육*), 29*(1), 1–23.

Schmidt, A. M. (2007). Cross-language consonant identification: English and Korean. In O.-S. Bohn & M. J. Munro (Eds.), *Language experience in second language speech learning: In honor of James Emil Flege* (pp. 185–200). Amsterdam and Philadelphia: John Benjamins Publishing Company.

Shin, J., Kiaer, J., & Cha, J. (2013). *The sounds of Korean*. Cambridge: Cambridge University Press.

Sohn, H.-M. (2013). *The Korean language*. Seoul: Korea University Press.

Takada, M. (2008). VOT variation in Japanese word-initial stops. In B. Heselwood & C. Upton (Eds.), *Proceedings of methods XIII: Papers from the Thirteenth International Conference on Methods in Dialectology* (pp. 372–382). Frankfurt/Main: Peter Lang.

Yang, B. (1996). A comparative study of American English and Korean vowels produced by male and female speakers. *Journal of Phonetics, 24*(2), 245–261.

Yang, X. (2017). 중국인 한국어 학습자의 한국어 폐쇄음 산출과 지각에 대한 연구 *[An investigation of the production and perception of Korean stops by native Chinese learners of Korean]* [Unpublished master's thesis]. Korea University.

Yasuta, T. (2004). *Stop perception in second language phonology: Perception of English and Korean stops by Japanese speakers* [Unpublished doctoral dissertation]. University of Hawai'i.

Yoon, E. K. (2013). A phonetic/phonological approach to teaching pronunciation of Korean syllable-final consonants (한국어 종성의 습득 연구를 위한 음성음운적 접근). *Journal of Dong-ak Language and Literature (*동악어문학*), 61*, 421–442.

4
LINGUISTIC POLITENESS

Lucien Brown

Introduction

Acquiring a second language (L2) is not merely a process of learning new vocabulary items, grammatical structures and phonological rules. Take the example of a Korean learner addressing their Korean teacher with 안녕, 선생! *annyeng, sensayng!* 'Hi teacher!'. There is nothing necessarily incorrect about this utterance in terms of grammar or lexicon. Yet it seems certain that the Korean teacher (and other Korean speakers) would see this utterance as being "wrong" in the sense that it is inappropriate and fails to consider the context, specifically the relationship that the speaker has with the addressee. Despite not containing any grammatical errors, the utterance would likely be taken as evidence that the learner is not a proficient speaker of Korean and therefore is lacking in some area of Korean language acquisition.

Effective communication not only requires that the grammar is "right" but also that the speaker is saying the "right" thing at the "right" time in the "right" place and in the "right" way (Gee, 2015, p. 147). This area of language, the ability to use language appropriately in context with due regard for your relationship with others, is referred to as *linguistic politeness*, which sits within the field of *pragmatics*. The need to modulate language use according to the context is particularly keenly felt in an honorific language such as Korean.

In this chapter, I begin by introducing the concept of linguistic politeness and introduce some key areas of politeness in the Korean language. I then look at how politeness is acquired by L2 learners, focussing on research done on Korean. The chapter concludes with pedagogical implications and future directions.

Defining linguistic politeness

Politeness is a vital aspect of everyday life and involves the speaker's ability to use socially appropriate language. In this chapter, I follow the definition of linguistic politeness offered by Brown (2015, p. 11620): "Politeness is essentially a matter of taking into account the feelings of others as to how they should be treated, including behaving in a manner that demonstrates appropriate concern for interactors' social status and their social relationship." The academic study of politeness dates back to the 1970s and the works of language philosophers such as Geoffrey Leech (2016), Robin Lakoff (1977) and the co-authored works by Penelope Brown and Stephen Levinson (1978, 1987).

According to the definition given in the previous paragraph, politeness is to do with how we treat other people, with this treatment being dependent on the type of relationship with the other party, as well as the context. Politeness research generally assumes that the type of politeness required is sensitive to power (i.e. relative social status) and distance (i.e. degree of intimacy) (Brown & Levinson, 1987), as well as other contextual factors. Since politeness always depends on the context, no single word or expression will always be considered polite. Even honorifics may sound impolite when used out of context.

Whether an utterance is judged as polite or not does not depend only on the intentions of the speaker but also on the interpretation of the hearer. Indeed, recent models of linguistic politeness argue that the reactions of the hearer can be used as a source of evidence for researchers to judge whether politeness has occurred. Kim and Brown (2019), following Mitchell and Haugh (2015), show that recipients may exercise their own agency in deciding whether an utterance is polite (or impolite) or not.

Politeness is not just about using deferential language but also language that is friendly and promotes comity. In Brown and Levinson's (1987) traditional framework, these two modes of politeness were captured under the concepts of "negative politeness" (politeness strategies that emphasize avoidance of imposition to the hearer) and "positive politeness" (politeness strategies used to make the hearer feel good about themselves), respectively. Politeness is also not just something that speakers perform for the benefit of others but also a way for speakers to display an appropriate image of themselves. In the terminology of Erving Goffman (1956), polite language is not just a marker of deference (i.e., the individual's relationship to others) but also of demeanour (i.e. the individual's own qualities) (cf. Dunn, 2013, p. 239). In addition, politeness research has also expanded into the field of impoliteness. Although impoliteness was traditionally seen as the inverse or opposite of politeness, more recent accounts see impoliteness as a social practice in its own right that is pragmatically governed and which is performed for various context-specific reasons (see Culpeper, 2011).

The definition given earlier mentions that politeness is a phenomenon that involves "taking into account the feelings of others." As such, one factor that regulates the application of polite language is emotional attunement and, more specifically, using language that augments, or at least does not threaten, the emotional states of others and also preserves the emotional wellbeing of the speaker themselves. Starting with Brown and Levinson (1987), this aspect of politeness has been captured under the notion of "face". This term, introduced into academia in the work of Erving Goffman (see Goffman, 2005) refers to the individual's emotional desire to have their public self-image respected and maintained.

Research increasingly shows that politeness does not only reside in linguistic behaviour but is an embodied and multimodal phenomenon. As pointed out by Brown and Prieto (2017), the evaluation of an utterance as polite or impolite will depend not just on the verbal content but also on the prosodic delivery and accompanying nonverbal behaviours. Polite linguistic behaviour may be delivered with distinct prosody (e.g. a clearer voice, with less animated pitch contours) and also with nonverbal behaviour that appears calmer and more constrained (e.g. fewer gestures, smaller postures, more erect and constrained body position).

Whereas traditional research on politeness attempted to establish cross-linguistic politeness universals, more recent studies focus on the culture-specific ways in which politeness is understood. As part of this, researchers have problematized the use of the term "politeness" itself as a universal term that can be applied to the study of different languages. Even though many languages may have different lexemes that are somewhat similar to "politeness", the nuances of such terms may only partially map onto the English concept. For example, Pizziconi's (2007) comparative study of British English and Japanese found that "friendliness" patterned closely with politeness in British English, whereas Japanese speakers associated *tenei* "politeness" with modesty and restraint. Contemporary politeness theory places increasing importance on looking at the culture-specific ways that speakers understand the linguistic and embodied practices through which they manage interpersonal relationships.

Linguistic politeness in Korean

Concepts of politeness in Korean

Politeness is generally assumed to have an important position in Korean culture, with one of the traditional nicknames for Korea being 동방예의지국 *Tongpang Yeyuy Cikwuk*, "the nation of propriety in the East" (Kim, E., 2018). Despite this, scholars have struggled to establish the closest lexical equivalent to "politeness" in the Korean language. Some studies have listed 공손 *kongson* as the Korean term for "politeness" (see Brown, L., 2011b, p. 111). But as pointed out by Brown (2013c), although this term may be the closest literal translation, it is fairly infrequent in everyday conversation. In this section, I will introduce three concepts that appear to be more frequently used: 존중 *concwung*, 예의 *yeyuy* and 친절 *chincel*.

Concwung, which corresponds most closely to the English concept "respect", encapsulates two aspects: (1) general respect for others as human beings and (2) respect for elders and status superiors due to their increased age and/or status. Previous research has stressed the importance of elder respect (Brown, L., 2011a), with Yoon (2004) noting that Korean social relationships are broadly based on distinguishing 윗사람 *wis-salam* 'people above (the speaker)' from 아랫사람 *alays-salam* 'people below'. Status superiors are shown deference not just through the ritualized use of honorifics but also though the avoidance of disagreeing with them or causing them discomfort (Yoon, K.-J., 2004). However, as pointed out by Kim and Brown (2019), even outside of clear social hierarchies, Koreans tend to be concerned with whether their position is acknowledged with a certain minimum level of respect. If someone perceives that their position is not properly acknowledged, they may feel they are being looked down upon (무시하다 *mwusihata* or 깔보다 *kkalpota*).

Yeyuy refer to civility or courtesy. This concept tends to be understood in a non-hierarchical sense in that *yeyuy* can be performed both by a status inferior and also by a status superior. As discussed in Kim (2018), the concept of politeness as public civility and horizontal social ideals of morality emerged in Korea in the late 19th century with the rise of modern education and adoption of Western discourses on self-cultivation. The term *yeyuy* captures the idea of politeness as decorum (Jung, 2005), whereby both seniors and juniors contribute to the upkeep of socially desirable norms of interaction.

Finally, *chincel* refers to politeness as kindness, friendliness or hospitableness. Unlike *concwung* and *yeyuy*, which can be performed towards someone you already have an established relationship with, *chincel* may be performed by total strangers, including in the commodified production of politeness performed by service personnel. According to Yang, Seo, and Kang (2013), *chincel* is a multimodal phenomenon comprising of the control of speech, facial expression, behaviour and appearance. The improvement of this public face of politeness has been encouraged on the national level by public campaigns, such as the 2015 친절한 대한민국 캠페인 *Chincelhan Tayhanminkwuk Campaign* (Han, K., 2015), which utilized the slogan "Korean smiles on you."

Honorifics

Korean has an intricate honorifics system, the exploration of which has dominated existent studies of Korean politeness. The system consists of two main parts: hearer honorifics (also known

Table 4.1 Korean speech styles

English name	Korean name	Declarative ending†	Formal/Informal	Honorific category
deferential	합쇼체 *hapsyo-chey*	−(스)ㅂ니다 *−(su)pnita*	Formal	Honorific
polite	해요체 *hayyo-chey*	−아/어요 *−a/eyo*	Informal	Honorific
semiformal	하오체 *hao-chey*	−오/소 *−(s)o*	Formal	Authoritative
familiar	하게체 *hakey-chey*	−네 *−ney*	Formal	Authoritative
intimate	해체 *hay-chey*	−아/어 *−a/e*	Informal	Non-honorific
plain	해라체 *hayla-chey*	−다 *−ta*	Formal	Non-honorific

† "Formal" styles have separate interrogative, imperative and hortative endings.

as speech styles) and referent honorifics. Hearer honorification features a system of six different speech styles (Table 4.1). As shown in the rightmost column, the six styles can roughly be classified into three categories according to their prototypical usage: honorific, non-honorific and authoritative (Brown, L., 2011a; Chang, 1996). Broadly speaking, the honorific styles are used when addressing strangers, non-intimates and superiors, whereas the non-honorific styles are reserved for intimates of similar or inferior age rank as well as children. Finally, the authoritative styles are used non-reciprocally by adults of middle age and above towards younger adults. They are rarely used by younger speakers and are not frequently taught in Korean language classes. This means that the speech style system taught to L2 learners tends to be limited to honorific and non-honorific styles, thereby following the most basic binary division recognized by Korean speakers between 존댓말 *contaymal* 'respect speech' and 반말 *panmal* 'half-speech' (Brown, L., 2011a, pp. 25–30; Lee, I. & Ramsey, 2000, pp. 249–262).

As shown in the second column from the right in Table 4.1, the speech styles can be further classified depending on whether they are formal or informal (Suh, C., 1984; Sung, 1985). Within the honorific styles, there is one formal style (deferential) and one informal style (polite). Likewise, non-honorific styles also feature one formal style (plain) and one informal style (intimate). The distinction between formal and informal should be understood as a grammatical distinction rather than a pragmatic one. As shown in Table 4.2, formal styles explicitly encode sentence type in their morphology, which is not the case for informal styles. On the other hand, whereas informal style can occur with affect particles (i.e. verb endings marking speaker emotion and stance), this is not the case with formal styles. The following sentences have no direct equivalents in formal styles:

1 a. 커피가 진하**네**(요)!
      *khephi-ka cinha-**ney** -yo*
      'My, this coffee is strong!'
  b. 난 어제 했**거든**(요).
      *Na-n ecey ha-yss-**ketun** (-yo).*
      'I did it yesterday, you know.'

Table 4.2 Speech styles and sentence type in formal styles

	Declarative	Interrogative	Imperative	Hortative
deferential	–습니다	–습니까	–(으)ㅂ시오	–십시다
	–(su)pnita	–(su)pnikka	–(u)psio	–sipsita
plain	–다	–니/(느)냐	–(아/어)라	–자
	–ta	–ni/(nu)nya	–(a/e)la	–ca

   c. 누구나 실수하<u>지</u>(요).
     *Nwukwu-na silswuha-**ci** -(yo).*
     'Everyone makes mistakes, you know.'

With their propensity to communicate modal and affective meanings, informal styles are applied more freely in colloquial conversation, although formal styles are also used for certain pragmatic functions.

Contrary to the fairly widespread misconception that speech styles are used in a very uniform way, Korean speakers actually frequently switch between different styles. In public speech (lectures, sermons, TV talk shows), speakers use deferential style to mark their utterances as important, factual information that is being delivered in their onstage role but polite style for personal asides and other non-factual comments (Brown, L., 2015b). In situations where honorific speech would be the norm, speakers may also downgrade to non-honorific speech to be strategically rude or to promote intimacy, although this would rarely happen towards elders (Brown, L., 2015a). Meanwhile, in non-honorific speech, intimate style is used as the main style, whereas plain style is reserved for specific pragmatic functions, namely the conveyance of newly perceived or retrieved information. In intimate speech, speakers may also switch to honorific styles in order to be sarcastic (Brown, L., 2013c).

The second part of the Korean honorifics system is referent honorifics, which include a range of lexical substitutions and the subject honorific marker (–*(u)si*–). This –*(u)si*– form occurs prototypically in sentences such as the following when the grammatical subject of the sentence is a status superior:

2   선생님께서 오셨습니다.
    *sensayng-nim-kkeyse o-**si** -ess-(su)pnita*
    'Esteemed teacher has come.'

Traditionally, the appearance of –*(u)si*– in sentences such as the previous one was described as a form of agreement: When the subject noun is marked for honorification (e.g. when it contains the honorific suffix –님 –*nim*), –*(u)si*– should obligatorily appear on the predicate (see Kim, T., 2007; Sung, 1985). However, this "agreement" claim has a number of issues (Choe, 2004), not least that corpus studies show that less than 50% of sentences featuring a status superior as the subject noun actually include –*(u)si*– (Song, S., Choe, & Oh, 2019). However, since use of –*(u)si*– with a noun referring to a status inferior (or non-human) referent is very uncommon, the inclusion of –*(u)si*– is still a strong cue for listeners that the sentence subject is a status superior human referent (Kim, L. K. & Kaiser, 2009).

Address terms

Korean has an intricate system of address and reference terms that work alongside honorifics in marking respect and politeness. In interactions with elders, superiors and adult strangers, titles and kinship terms are used instead of pronouns and personal names. In the workplace, various professional titles are employed (e.g. 사장님 *sacangnim* 'company president', 부장님 *pwucangnim* 'department head', etc.). Elsewhere, kinship terms are widely used not just for family members of senior age but also in interpersonal relationships with people of similar relative age to that depicted by the kinship term. Elders may be addressed as 할아버지 *halapeci* 'grandfather' or 할머니 *halmeni* 'grandmother'. Meanwhile, more marginal age superiors may be addressed using terms that translate as "elder sibling": 언니 *enni*, 누나 *nwuna*, 오빠 *oppa* and 형 *hyeng*. Those with children may sometimes be addressed with teknonymic terms (i.e. terms such as 민호 엄마 *Minho emma* 'Minho's mom'). When personal names are used, they are often suffixed with –씨 *–ssi* (a suffix marking social distance used towards non-intimates of equal or younger age) or –아/야 *–(y)a* (a vocative used towards intimates). Kim (2003) refers to the cultural preference for using titles, kinship terms and teknonymics over personal names as part of a "taboo of name calling avoidance".

Speech acts

The term "speech acts" refers to actions performed through speaking, including requests, refusals, compliments and apologies. Korean speech acts have their own culture-specific characteristics that render them challenging for L2 learners, particularly in the way they interact with honorifics.

A tendency has been noted in many languages for indirect **requests** (e.g. "Can you pass the salt?") to be more polite than direct requests ("Pass the salt!"). Korean also contains linguistic devices for making requests indirect, including the use of incomplete sentences where the clause containing the request head act has been deleted, such as the following when a student asking for a recommendation letter may ask (Byon, A. S., 2006b, p. 250):

3 추천서 좀 필요해서요 . . . [여쭈어 보려고 왔습니다].
   chuchense-ka com philyohayse-yo . . . [yeccwue polyeko wa-ss-(su)pnita].
   'I need a recommendation letter so . . . (I came here to ask you).'

However, Byon's (2006b) data show that in some situations Koreans tend to prefer basic directives, even when addressing status superiors and/or strangers:

4 교수님! 써 주십시오, 네?
   Kyoswu-nim! Sse cwu-si-psio, ney?
   'Professor, please write (a letter) for me, yes?'

One of the reasons for this is that, in Korean, even direct speech-act forms can carry high honorific meaning through the use of honorifics, thus negating the need (to some extent) for using indirect language. M. S. Kim (2020) shows that direct forms tend to occur in situations in which both participants are engaged in the same pre-established activity, and where the requester anticipates the requestee to comply with the request, even when the requestee is socially distant.

In the case of **refusals**, Korean speakers prefer more indirect formulations than may be the case in other languages. Kwon (2004) showed that Korean speakers used direct refusal formulas less frequently than American English speakers but used more hesitation markers. Meanwhile, Lyuh (1994) found that whereas American respondents tended to give detailed explanations for their refusals, Koreans often cited unspecified "problems" or "things to do". In addition, Korean respondents avoided giving reasons that could be viewed as under their control (e.g. "I'm on a diet" as a reason for refusing a cookie) and instead preferred to cite factors that were outside their control (e.g. "I have an upset stomach"). Korean speakers also showed more sensitivity to the relative status of the interlocutor (Kwon, 2004).

Compliments are speech acts that involve the statement of a positive evaluation of the interlocutor (and/or their possessions, behaviours, achievements and in-group). Topics of compliments are culture-specific in that they tend to reflect what is valued or considered noteworthy in a particular culture. After receiving a compliment, responding to it may also not be easy due to conflicting pragmatic constraints. Accepting a compliment contradicts a general preference for modesty ("modesty maxim" – Leech, 2016), whereas rejecting it may violate the desire to be agreeable ("agreement maxim" – Leech, 2016). Research shows that Koreans prefer to reject or deflect compliments rather than accepting them (Han, C., 1992; Lee, W., 2001; Suh, K. H., 2010). W. Lee (2001) showed that the strategies used by the respondents changed markedly depending on their social relationship with the interlocutor. When addressing a teacher, students tended to reject (28.2%) or simply accept the apology with a deferential expression of thanks (34.2%), such as 고맙습니다 *komap-supnita* 'thank you'. When addressing friends, on the other hand, the most common strategy was to reply with a joke (22.6%), for example, 뭐 먹고 싶어? *mwe mek-ko siph-e?* 'what do you want to eat?' (i.e. 'what do you want me to buy you for lunch?').

Apologies are speech acts that involve the speaker recognizing an offence towards the interlocutor, for which the speaker takes some degree of responsibility. Korean has two commonly used apology terms: 미안하다 *mianhata* and 죄송하다 *coysonghata* '(I am) sorry'. Whereas *mianhata* is used towards age/rank equals and subordinates (and may occur in any speech style), *coysonghata* is reserved for status superiors and/or formal settings and appears only with honorific styles (Hatfield & Hahn, 2011). Kim (2008) notes that *mianhata* and *coysonghata* are distinct from English '(I am) sorry' in that they include the meaning of "taking on responsibility" and therefore tend not to occur alongside other expressions of responsibility (e.g. 'It was my fault'). In addition, Korean speakers disprefer the inclusion of detailed explanations since these run the risk of sounding like you are blaming something or somebody else, which decreases the sincerity of the apology. Instead, Korean speakers have an increased preference for "compensatory utterances": offers to repair the damage or make up for the misdemeanour in other ways, such as treating the other party to a meal.

Impoliteness

The expression of impoliteness in the Korean language also features characteristics that are specific to Korean language and culture. Perhaps somewhat surprisingly, one language-specific resource for impoliteness in Korean is the honorifics system itself. Brown (2013c) demonstrates how honorifics are frequently depicted in Korean TV dramas in relationships between intimates, where they become markers of sarcasm. Utterances that feature honorific features juxtaposed with non-honorific features are particularly open to sarcastic interpretations, such as when referent honorific marker (*–(u)si–*) is used alongside non-honorific speech styles:

5   댁의 일이나 신경 쓰셔.
    *tayk-uy il-ina sinkyeng ssu-**s**i-e*
    'Mind your own business!'

These sarcastic honorific utterances may be applied for "genuine impoliteness" (i.e. to cause offense to the interlocutor) but are more frequently used in "mock impoliteness" (i.e. jokes and banter).

Impoliteness can also be communicated by the strategic dropping of honorifics or by using inappropriate address terms. J. Lee (1999) illustrates the omission of honorifics for deliberate rudeness with the example of a taxi driver using non-honorific *panmal* to a female driver after a collision on the freeway:

6   야! 운전 똑바로 못해?
    Ya! Wuncen ttokpalo mos hay?
    'Hey! Can't you drive properly-intimate?'

Meanwhile, Lee and Ramsey (2000, p. 226) point out that the second-person pronoun 당신 *tangsin* 'you' is highly marked for disrespect and insult when used outside of certain close relationships.

One linguistic category that is closely related to impoliteness is the use of swearing, which refers to the use of taboo language for expressive rather than referential meanings (Jay & Janschewitz, 2008, p. 268). Swearing communicates emotional meanings which may range from distain, disagreement and shock through to passion, sincerity, solidarity and jocularity (Beers Fägersten, & Stapleton, 2017). In contrast to English, where high-frequency swear words tend to derive from bodily effluvia, sex and religion, common Korean swear words often literally denote animals (e.g. 새끼 *saykki* 'son of a bitch', lit. 'offspring') and mental incapacity (e.g. 지랄 *cilal* 'go crazy', originally 'epileptic fit') in addition to sex (e.g. 좆 *coc* lit. 'penis'). Korean swear words often occur in compounds or combinations; for instance, 놈 *nom* 'bastard' and 년 *nyen* 'bitch' more often occur in combinations, such as in *michin nom/nyen* 'crazy bastard/bitch' (Kim, S., 2002).

Multimodality

Korean speakers use important prosodic and nonverbal cues to differentiate between honorific and non-honorific language. In terms of the acoustic modality, honorific speech tends to have lower pitch and is quieter, clearer, more monotonous, more careful and pronounced with a more tensed voice (Winter & Grawunder, 2012). Brown, Winter, Idemaru, and Grawunder (2014) furthermore demonstrated that Korean speakers can use these prosodic cues to tell the difference between utterances spoken to a superior and those spoken to a status-equal intimate, even in the absence of explicit honorific marking. When interacting with status superiors, Korean speakers are more likely to maintain direct bodily orientation and gaze on the line of sight, whereas they suppress manual and facial gestures, as well as touch (Brown, L. & Winter, 2019). When manual gestures are used, they tend to be smaller, less animated and less informative (Brown, L., Kim, Hübscher, & Winter, forthcoming).

As in any language, Korean also features the inclusion of ritualized polite gestures and the avoidance of gestures that are considered impolite. Ritualized polite gestures in Korean include bowing and the use of two hands when performing actions, such as giving material objects to or pouring drinks for another person (Brown, L. et al., forthcoming; Brown, L. & Winter, 2019; Dennison & Bergen, 2010). Meanwhile, gestures to avoid (particularly when addressing superiors) include index finger points (which are replaced with open palm points) and beckoning gestures with the fingers raised upwards (the fingers should be pointed downwards for the gesture to be considered polite).

Second language acquisition of politeness

Learning to be polite in an L2 involves the development of two main kinds of knowledge.

First, it involves structural knowledge of the linguistic (and nonverbal) resources needed for conveying politeness-related meanings. This falls under what has traditionally been described as **pragmalinguistic competence** (Leech, 2016; Thomas, 1983). To take Korean verbal honorific morphology as an example, in order for an L2 learner to use these forms appropriately across a range of settings, they will need to have knowledge of how to conjugate verbs into at least four speech styles, plus how to conjugate verbs using the subject honorific *–(u)si–*.

Second, learning to be polite involves developing cultural knowledge of the contexts in which politeness-related linguistic (and nonverbal) resources are used and the ability to vary language usage in accordance with these factors. In the terms of Leech (2016) and Thomas (1983), this is referred to as **sociopragmatic competence**. This knowledge of contexts and the linguistic and nonverbal behaviour that is typically used within them has been conceptualized in previous research as "frames" (Brown, L., 2011a; Pizziconi, 2006), "scripts" (Schank & Abelson, 2013) and "Mental Event Representations" or MERs (Nelson, 1986, 1996). Bialystok (1993, p. 51) describes acquisition of pragmatics as "mapping . . . between form and social context."

An important point to make here is that the ability to map form onto context does not only require that L2 learners acquire knowledge of the forms but also that they acquire knowledge of the contexts as well. The reason why contexts need to be learned is that they may be culture specific. For instance, consider Korean ceremonies such as 제사 *ceysa*, 환갑 *hwankap* or a Korean funeral, or even age/rank-based interactions within the workplace or school. It is not enough for learners to simply know honorific forms or the rules of thumb that underpin their usage to participate successfully in contexts such as these if they lack knowledge of the contexts themselves. As pointed out by Kramsch and Andersen (1999), context is something that cannot be learned easily in an explicit or abstracted way but which requires considerable apprenticeship. The process of learning different social routines and the language use that occurs within them is referred to as **language socialization** (Duff, 2003; Ochs & Schieffelin, 2009).

The process of learning politeness in an L2 is fundamentally different to learning politeness in the L1. As pointed out by Brown (2011b, p. 89), L2 learners already possess detailed "frames" of knowledge regarding contexts and the kind of language use that typically occurs within them, meaning that L2 sociopragmatic learning is best seen as re-analysing and enriching existing frames, rather than creating this knowledge from scratch. Knowledge of how politeness works in the L1 can actually be an important and useful resource for L2 learners since some fundamental aspects of how politeness works may be universal. However, it can also result in learners incorrectly transferring pragmatic forms and their contextual meanings into the second language. To take a simple example, native speakers of Korean sometimes transfer usage of Korean titles and kinship terms into English and, for instance, address educators as "teacher" (i.e. the direct translation of 선생님 *sensayngnim*). This does not work well in English since "teacher" is merely the name of a profession (rather than a professional title) and does not typically occur as an address term. L2 learners may draw on a wide variety of information sources when developing their pragmatic knowledge beyond the L1, including explicit classroom instruction, print and media sources, their own interactions and observations in the target language and things they have learned while acquiring other languages (Brown, L., 2011a, p. 90).

The L2 learning of politeness may also differ from L1 politeness in the sequence that it follows, at least for learners in instructed settings. Whereas children learning their L1(s) start with learning casual and informal language and then gradually learn more formal language as they enter school (and ultimately the workplace) and are socialized into different contexts of interaction, instructed L2 learning tends to begin with language that already contains a certain level of formality. This difference is felt particularly keenly in Korean due to the developed system of honorifics. Whereas L1 children learn non-honorific language first in the home and pick up honorifics as they interact with the extended family and then with teachers at school (Park, S., Nam, &

Seo, 2003), L2 learners tend to be taught honorific language (or at least semi-honorific language) from the start and then typically learn non-honorific language as their learning branches out into authentic contexts (e.g. interacting with Korean friends). This process may well be different for naturalistic learners who might learn non-honorific language first from friends and/or Korean media and then learn honorifics in the classroom. The same applies to heritage learners, who may lack knowledge of honorifics even if their spoken Korean is fairly fluent.

The learning of politeness in the L2 may be complicated by the lack of socialization into the contexts and identities that would typically be available to L1 speakers. To apply Korean politeness norms in their entirety would require, to some extent, that the learner "becomes Korean" and adopts the roles and responsibilities of Korean speakers (Brown, L., 2011a, pp. 97–98). However, even when learners spend an extended time in the target culture, this does not necessarily mean that L2 speakers are able to gain access to the same contexts and subjectivities as L1 speakers, since this may not be expected or valued either by the learners themselves or the local community. Building on Lave and Wenger's (1991) concept of "legitimate peripheral participation", Norton (2013) claims that L2 speakers who are not granted enough "legitimacy" (i.e. who are not positioned as "potential members" of the community) are not afforded the same opportunities to participate in the community and develop linguistic competence, including politeness routines. For example, although we might expect learners who study abroad in Korea to be immersed in the target language and culture, Brown (Brown, L., 2011a, p. 101) points out that the identity of "exchange student" does not necessarily allow learners to develop the identities that would be needed to learn native-like politeness norms. Exchange students are often sequestered into foreigner-only accommodation and spend most of their time taking classes and socializing with other exchange students. Moreover, they do not have a 학년 *haknyen* 'university year' or 학번 *hakpen* 'student number' and thus exist outside the relational and hierarchical structure of the university, meaning they lack the contexts for developing the same usage of honorifics, address terms and other politeness features that are available to native-speaker students.

Opportunities for language socialization may differ somewhat depending on ethnicity-related factors. As noted by Brown (2011a, p. 103), Korean ideologies of racial homogeneity mean that heritage learners (and also those who appear to be ethnically Korean) may be expected to adopt native-like subject positions, whereas non-heritage learners may be expected to maintain their foreigner identities. For both groups, this is a double-edged sword when it comes to politeness learning. Heritage learners enjoy advantages in being socialized into Korean modes of social interaction but also suffer harsh censure for flouting native-speaker norms. Conversely, non-heritage learners enjoy the privilege of being able to flout politeness norms without social censure, but on the other hand are deprived of the contexts for immersion into native-like interaction.

Compared to L1 children, L2 learners possess more agency to resist politeness norms to which they ideologically disapprove of or which do not sit comfortably with their pre-existing identities. In other words, L2 learners may explicitly and consciously choose *not* to follow L1 politeness norms. Choosing not to follow the norms is, however, a privilege that may be available more to some learners than others. Notably, elective language learners (i.e. those who learn a language out of choice from a position of equal or superior power) have more freedom to flout norms than circumstantial learners (i.e. minority language speakers who have little choice but to learn the majority language). Thus, in the Korean context, Caucasian learners from Western countries visiting Korea as exchange students may be able to flout the norms, whereas marriage migrants from South East Asia may not (Park, M. Y., 2017). As noted earlier, heritage learners may also have less leeway to "break the rules" due to ethnicity-based expectations.

Acquisition of honorifics

Given the complexity of the Korean honorifics system, unsurprisingly the acquisition of these forms has been found to pose acquisitional issues to L2 learners of Korean. Korean learners even at more advanced stages of acquisition may lack pragmalinguistic and sociopragmatic knowledge of honorifics forms. Brown (2011a, 2013b) found that advanced learners of Korean from Western backgrounds who were residing in Korea tended to vary their use of honorific levels less than native speakers. Specifically, learners would tend to stick to honorific speech styles (particularly the polite style), but lacked knowledge of referent honorifics such as *–(u)si–*. This lack of knowledge of referent honorifics even among advanced learners of Korean is also seen in Mueller and Jiang (2013), whose experimental data showed that advanced L1 English learners of Korean did not display the same sensitivity as native speakers to infelicitous usages of *–(u)si–* (see also Lee, M., 1997). Heritage learners (Park, K., 1998), as well as learners with L1 Chinese (Sun & Kim, 2012) and L1 Vietnamese (Phan & Kwon, 2018), also display lower levels of knowledge of referent honorifics. Although these difficulties may be experienced by learners of all language backgrounds to various extents, Japanese L1 learners may enjoy an advantage thanks to positive transfer from Japanese, which has a similar honorifics system (Wang, 2019).

The simplified honorifics systems of L2 learners appear to somewhat match the depiction of these forms in teaching materials, as well as the opportunities for learners to be socialized into the use of these forms outside the classroom. Brown (2010) noted that Korean textbooks provide an impoverished depiction of honorifics whereby most dialogues feature honorific speech styles (without referent honorifics) being used in horizontal relationships. Non-honorific language between intimates is underrepresented, as are high honorific forms used in interactions with status superiors. Outside the classroom, learners who visit Korea as exchange students or temporary workers may also struggle to gain socialization into the contexts and subject positions in which more varied use of honorifics may be applied. In Brown (Brown, L., 2011a, p. 253), Canadian graduate student Matthew noted that "the fact that I am a foreigner to a certain extent controls my social position" and therefore the types of honorific language that were afforded to him.

Brown's (2011a, 2013b) studies showed that learners were caught in a struggle to establish how the usage of honorifics applied to them as "foreigners" and "L2 learners". Whereas some learners attempted to use correct honorifics to mark their alignment with Korean cultural values and rejection of the "foreigner" tag, others intentionally negotiated patterns of honorifics usage that departed from L1 norms. UK exchange student Richard attempted to negotiate non-honorific language in many of his interactions, even with speakers who were several years older than him. During interviews, he claimed that it was possible for him in his position as a foreigner to "get to a stage where we would use *panmal* [non-honorific language], which he claimed was "possible to almost any age" (Brown, L., 2013b, p. 286). "I feel that Koreans would object less to me suggesting it", opined Richard.

Whereas classroom learners who are exposed to honorific forms in the classroom tend to overuse honorific speech styles, the opposite pattern may apply to heritage learners who learn non-honorific speech in the family setting and then acquire honorifics later with formal Korean language education and/or socialization into language usage in more formal settings. Byon (2003) looked at how teachers in Saturday Korean language schools in Honolulu used the polite ending – 요 – *yo* to socialize learners into sociocultural norms regarding respect to those of higher status and speaking politely in public.

Acquisition of address terms

Similar to the use of honorifics, previous studies show that language learners use a limited range of address terms due to a lack of socialization into the contexts where these forms are used and ideological resistance to adopting hierarchical patterns of language usage. Brown (2011a) showed that learners overgeneralize the use of personal names appended with the – 씨 – *ssi* suffix, which is also the pattern that is overemphasized in Korean teaching materials (Brown, L., 2010). This pattern may be suitable for addressing a distant acquaintance of similar age/rank but is neither intimate enough to use with a friend nor respectful enough to use with a superior.

Learners sometimes inappropriately use 당신 *tangsin* due to perceived similarities with a universal second-person pronoun (Brown, L., 2011a for L1 English learners; Yang et al., 2013 for L1 Turkish learners). Whereas some female learners use the address term 오빠 *oppa* 'older brother of a woman' due to positive connotations with Korean popular culture, others avoid the term due to its gendered nature (Brown, L., 2013a). Learners also display varied usage of the first-person pronouns 저 *ce* 'humble' and 나 *na* 'plain', as noted in Turkozu's (2011) study of Turkish L1 learners.

Learners are able to refine their understanding and usage of address terms through participating in CMC (computer-mediated communication). In Kim and Brown (2014), American MA student Grace learned that her use of 언니 *enni* 'older sister of a woman' for addressing a former teacher was not considered appropriate by the teacher and thus upgraded to 선생님 *sensayngnim*. Meanwhile, British MA student Jane negotiated the usage of 이모 *imo* '(maternal) auntie' with her former homestay "host mother."

Heritage learners use address terms in complex ways to negotiate their identities. J. Song (2009) showed that Korean parents rigorously attempted to socialize their children into using appropriate kinship terms but that children skilfully applied different strategies to avoid what the author refers to as "Korean status-charged address terms". When the parents of Greg and Joonho encouraged them to refer to an older boy named Sicheol as *hyeng* 'older brother of a man', Greg code-switched to English to avoid the term. Meanwhile, Joonho used an Anglicized pronunciation of Sicheol's name, which he claimed was "an English name" and which, according to him, did not require the addition of a kinship term. Conversely, Kang (2004) showed that in other instances heritage learners may switch from English to Korean specifically to use kinship terms and enact Korean-style modes of sociality.

Acquisition of speech acts

A number of studies have shown that the acquisition of speech acts by Korean L2 learners follows a different path to that of native speakers.

Looking first at requests, Byon (2002, 2004b) found that American learners of Korean showed decreased sensitivity to power factors than Korean native speakers. Whereas Korean native speakers would preface their requests to status superiors with ritualized self-introductions and apologies, L2 learners did not use these patterns. They also did not follow the L1 Korean preference for leading up to the request head act by giving reasons for it first and instead jumped straight into the request. This made their requests appear more direct, as did their failure to apply down-graders, such as the understater 좀 *com* 'a little' and the suggester – (으)ㄹ까 *-(u)l kka(yo)?* 'do you think?' Byon (2004a) showed through a listening task that Korean learners experienced difficulties in judging the appropriateness of audio-taped requests. The reasons for incorrect responses included unfamiliarity with euphemistic honorific verbs (such as 드리다 *tulita* 'to give' and 여쭤다

'to ask') and other difficulties with honorifics, as well as different perceptions regarding the directness levels of speech acts.

Byon (2005) conducted a cross-cultural study of apologies performed by three groups: American learners of Korean, native speakers of Korean and native speakers of American English. The results showed that the three groups all used similar apology formulae, which speaks to the universality of apology strategies and also shows how L1 pragmatic knowledge can become an important source of knowledge for the L2. However, as in the case of requests, the American learners of Korean showed weaker power sensitivity than the Korean native speakers and diverged from native speaker norms in the use of address terms and by not providing self-introductory remarks when addressing a superior.

Acquisition of multimodal politeness

The development of multimodal aspects of Korean politeness have yet to be investigated in detail. However, Oh, Brown, and Idemaru (forthcoming) found that L1 Chinese learners of Korean (intermediate to advanced proficiency, living in Seoul for 3.5 years) could distinguish Korean honorific speech from non-honorific speech in the absence of verbal honorifics and just from the sound of the speaker's voice at an accuracy rate of 62.5%, which was marginally better than Chinese listeners who had never learned Korean. This result suggests that exposure to Korean led to some level of increased sensitivity to the sound of politeness. Furthermore, Oh and Cui (2020) showed that intermediate/advanced Chinese learners of Korean successfully produced the acoustic distinction between honorific and non-honorific speech in Korean, recruiting features that they did not use in Chinese, such as decreased pitch variability and a greater control of vocal fold vibration (jitter).

Pedagogical applications

In the area of syntax, debates continue as to whether explicit treatment of grammar in the language classroom is facilitative to L2 acquisition. However, in areas such as pragmatics, politeness and the teaching of sociocultural aspects of language, there are no such controversies regarding learnability and teachability. It is accepted and widely empirically supported that the language classroom is a venue where learners can fruitfully learn about politeness.

Despite the potential for politeness to be explicitly taught in the language classroom (and despite the widespread agreement that politeness constitutes an important part of learning Korean), it is perhaps surprising that the teaching of politeness does not take a central position in most Korean language curricula. This situation is evinced by the simplified and stilted version of honorifics that is presented in Korean language textbooks (Brown, L., 2010; Choo, 1999). Brown's (2010) analysis of three popular series of Korean language textbooks shows that they tend to downplay the importance of honorifics and instead encourage learners just to stick to a simplified honorific style. The idea that L2 learners do not need to learn non-honorific speech is indeed explicitly articulated in some Korean language education manuals (Brown, L., 2011b, p. 96).

The underrepresentation of politeness elements in language textbooks means that Korean language practitioners increasingly look to use media materials for teaching honorifics and other politeness-related language. Byon (2007) followed by Brown (2013d) used consciousness-raising tasks, including the use of cloze-style activities, based on content from talk shows and TV dramas to teach the distinction between the deferential and polite styles, and the intimate and plain styles, respectively.

Since the use of politeness features rich variation and involves questions of speaker identity, educators should avoid teaching pragmatics in a way that is strictly rule based. Rather, materials should encourage learners to explore speech variation and uncover pragmatic meanings for themselves. In Byon (2006a), learners designed and implemented a DCT ("discourse completion task" – a tool used by researchers to elicit speech-act data) on requests and compared and discussed results collected from native speakers of English and of Korean. Through this process, students uncovered the politeness norms for themselves and came to think critically about cultural differences. For instance, Korean respondents frequently prefaced their requests to professors with apologies for causing inconvenience, whereas Americans' request style suggested they saw such requests as their legitimate right. In this way, Korean language educators can use various projects to enhance learner knowledge of politeness.

The teaching of politeness can also involve explicit discussion of what politeness means for individual learners and the individual intentions of whether learners plan to apply Korean politeness forms in native-like ways. In Yoon and Brown (2018), the authors used a series of activities that involved the learners discussing the multimodal features of Korean politeness as manifest in media materials. During these discussions, learners were explicitly encouraged to talk about the ways in which they would employ (or not employ) multimodal resources for politeness. Learners were also given an activity that involved them critiquing and revising a booklet that gave information for foreigners in Korea regarding politeness, thus giving them agency in the process of learning politeness.

Future directions

The ability to use language at an appropriate degree of politeness is a key skill in L2 learning, and essential to the establishment and maintenance of various forms of social relationships. It also represents a challenging area of language acquisition since it involves not only knowledge of linguistic forms but also knowledge of culture and context. In addition, the learning of politeness in an L2 involves questions of learner identity and agency in a way not seen in other areas of language acquisition. The issue of learning politeness should be particularly keenly felt for Korean, given the existence of the complex honorific system that is often touted as one of the major characteristics of the language.

Still, it is fair to say that research on politeness in the Korean language is in a relatively underdeveloped state, particularly in L2 contexts. Going forward, more extensive research in areas including different speech acts, impoliteness and multimodality will be needed to give a more complete picture of how politeness is achieved in Korean speech. In addition, researchers working in L2 acquisition will need to explore how language learners acquire more varied forms of politeness in Korean beyond the fixation on honorifics that has dominated the field to date. Going forward, politeness needs to be established as an integral and central component of the learning and teaching of Korean as a second language.

References

Beers Fägersten, K., & Stapleton, K. (2017). *Advances in swearing research: New languages and new contexts*. Amsterdam and Philadelphia: John Benjamins Publishing Company.

Bialystok, E. (1993). Symbolic representation and attentional control in pragmatic competence. In G. Kasper & S. Blum-Kulka (Eds.), *Interlanguage pragmatics* (pp. 43–57). New York: Oxford University Press.

Brown, L. (2010). Questions of appropriateness and authenticity in the representation of Korean honorifics in textbooks for second language learners. *Language, Culture and Curriculum, 23*(1), 35–50.

Brown, L. (2011a). *Korean honorifics and politeness in second language learning*. Amsterdam and Philadelphia: John Benjamins Publishing Company.

Brown, L. (2011b). Korean honorifics and "revealed," "ignored" and "suppressed" aspects of Korean culture and politeness. In F. Bargiela-Chiappini and D. Kádár (Eds.), *Politeness across cultures* (pp. 106–127). London: Palgrave Macmillan.

Brown, L. (2013a). "Oppa, hold my purse:" A sociocultural study of identity and indexicality in the perception and use of oppa 'older brother' by second language learners. *Korean Language in America*, 1–22.

Brown, L. (2013b). Identity and honorifics use in Korean study abroad. In C. Kinginger (Ed.), *Social and cultural aspects of language learning in study abroad* (pp. 269–298). Amsterdam and Philadelphia: John Benjamins Publishing Company.

Brown, L. (2013c). "Mind your own esteemed business": Sarcastic honorifics use and impoliteness in Korean TV dramas. *Journal of Politeness Research*, *9*(2), 159–186.

Brown, L. (2013d). Teaching 'casual' and/or 'impolite' language through multimedia: The case of non-honorific panmal speech styles in Korean. *Language, Culture and Curriculum*, *26*(1), 1–18.

Brown, L. (2015a). Honorifics and politeness. *The Handbook of Korean Linguistics*, 303–319.

Brown, L. (2015b). Revisiting "polite" – yo and "deferential" – supnita speech style shifting in Korean from the viewpoint of indexicality. *Journal of Pragmatics*, *79*, 43–59.

Brown, L., Kim, H., Hübscher, I., & Winter, B. (forthcoming). Gestures are modulated by social context: A study of multimodal politeness in two cultures. *TBA*.

Brown, L., & Prieto, P. (2017). (Im) politeness: Prosody and gesture. In J. Culpeper, M. Haugh, & D. Kádár (Eds.), *The Palgrave handbook of linguistic (im) politeness* (pp. 357–379). New York: Springer.

Brown, L., & Winter, B. (2019). Multimodal indexicality in Korean: "Doing deference" and "performing intimacy" through nonverbal behavior. *Journal of Politeness Research*, *15*(1), 25–54.

Brown, L., Winter, B., Idemaru, K., & Grawunder, S. (2014). Phonetics and politeness: Perceiving Korean honorific and non-honorific speech through phonetic cues. *Journal of Pragmatics*, *66*, 45–60.

Brown, P. (2015). Politeness and language. In *The international encyclopedia of the social and behavioural sciences (IESBS)* (2nd ed., pp. 326–330). Amsterdam: Elsevier.

Brown, P., & Levinson, S. C. (1978). Universals in language usage: Politeness phenomena. In *Questions and politeness: Strategies in social interaction* (pp. 56–311). Cambridge: Cambridge University Press.

Brown, P., & Levinson, S. C. (1987). *Politeness: Some universals in language usage* (Vol. 4). Cambridge: Cambridge University Press.

Byon, A. S. (2002). Pragmalinguistic features of KFL learners in the speech act of request. *Korean Linguistics*, *11*(1), 151–182.

Byon, A. S. (2003). Language socialisation and Korean as a heritage language: A study of Hawaiian classrooms. *Language Culture and Curriculum*, *16*(3), 269–283.

Byon, A. S. (2004a). Learning linguistic politeness. *Applied Language Learning*, *14*(1), 37–62.

Byon, A. S. (2004b). Sociopragmatic analysis of Korean requests: Pedagogical settings. *Journal of Pragmatics*, *36*(9), 1673–1704.

Byon, A. S. (2005). Apologizing in Korean: Cross-cultural analysis in classroom settings. *Korean Studies*, 137–166.

Byon, A. S. (2006a). Developing KFL students' pragmatic awareness of Korean speech acts: The use of discourse completion tasks. *Language Awareness*, *15*(4), 244–263.

Byon, A. S. (2006b). The role of linguistic indirectness and honorifics in achieving linguistic politeness in Korean requests. *Journal of Politeness Research*, *2*(2), 247–276.

Byon, A. S. (2007). Teaching the polite and the deferential speech levels, using media materials: Advanced KFL classroom settings. In D. Yoshimi & H. Wang (Eds.), *Selected papers from pragmatics in the CJK classroom: The state of the art* (pp. 21–64). Honolulu, HI: University of Hawaii Press.

Chang, S.-J. (1996). *Korean* (Vol. 4). Amsterdam and Philadelphia: John Benjamins Publishing Company.

Choe, J. (2004). Obligatory honorification and the honorific feature. *Sayngsengmwunpepyenkwu [Studies in Generative Grammar]*, *14*(4), 545–559.

Choo, M. (1999). Teaching language styles of Korean. *The Korean Language in America*, *3*, 77–95.

Culpeper, J. (2011). *Impoliteness: Using language to cause offence* (Vol. 28). Cambridge: Cambridge University Press.

Dennison, H. Y., & Bergen, B. K. (2010). Language-driven motor simulation is sensitive to social context. *Proceedings of the Annual Meeting of the Cognitive Science Society*, *32*(32).

Duff, P. A. (2003). Intertextuality and hybrid discourses: The infusion of pop culture in educational discourse. *Linguistics and Education*, *14*(3–4), 231–276.

Dunn, C. D. (2013). Speaking politely, kindly, and beautifully: Ideologies of politeness in Japanese business etiquette training. *Multilingua: Journal of Cross-Cultural and Interlanguage Communication, 32*(2), 225.

Gee, J. (2015). *Social linguistics and literacies: Ideology in discourses*. Oxon and New York: Routledge.

Goffman, E. (1956). The nature of deference and demeanor. *American Anthropologist, 58*(3), 473–502.

Goffman, E. (2005). *Interaction ritual: Essays in face to face behavior*. New Brunswick, NJ: AldineTransaction.

Han, C. (1992). A comparative study of compliment responses: Korean females in Korean interactions and in English interactions. *Working Papers in Educational Linguistics, 8*(2), 17–31.

Han, K. (2015). Korea smiles on you, Tasi chac-ko siph-un tayhanminkwuk-ul mantu-nun "chincelhan tayhanminkwuk khaympheyn" [Korea smiles on you, the "Kind Korea Campaign" remaking South Korea]. *Hankwukkwankwangcengchayk [Korea Tourism Policy], 60*, 94–97.

Hatfield, H., & Hahn, J.-W. (2011). What Korean apologies require of politeness theory. *Journal of Pragmatics, 43*(5), 1303–1317.

Jay, T., & Janschewitz, K. (2008). The pragmatics of swearing. *Journal of Politeness Research, 4*(2), 267–288.

Jung, Y. (2005). Power and politeness in Korean business correspondence. *Asian Business Discourse(s), 29*, 291.

Kang, M. A. (2004). Constructing ethnic identity through discourse: Self-categorization among Korean American camp counselors. *Pragmatics, 14*, 217–233.

Kim, A., & Brown, L. (2019). Agency and impoliteness in Korean online interactions. *Internet Pragmatics, 2*(2), 233–259.

Kim, E. (2018). *Language and politeness in the 'Nation of Propriety in the East': A history of linguistic ideologies of Korean honorification* [Ph.D. thesis]. University of British Columbia.

Kim, E. Y. A., & Brown, L. (2014). Negotiating pragmatic competence in computer mediated communication: The case of Korean address terms. *Calico Journal, 31*(3), 264–282.

Kim, H. (2003). Hyentay hankuke hochinge-uy yeksel: 2-cha sahoy nay nulena-nun chincoke sayong [The paradox of address term usage in modern Korean: The increase of kinship term usage in secondary society]. *Sahoyenehak [The Sociolinguistic Journal of Korea], 11*(1), 55–93.

Kim, H. (2008). The semantic and pragmatic analysis of South Korean and Australian English apologetic speech acts. *Journal of Pragmatics, 40*(2), 257–278.

Kim, L. K., & Kaiser, E. (2009). Effects of honorific agreement on null subject interpretation in Korean. In *Proceedings of 2009 Seoul international conference on linguistic interfaces*. Yonsei University, Seoul.

Kim, M. S. (2020). Imperative requests in Korean interaction. *Japanese/Korean Linguistics, 26*.

Kim, S. (2002). Yoksel-uy thukcil-ey kwanhan yenkwu [A study on the characteristics of abuse in Korean]. *Hwapepyenkwu [Discourse Analysis], 4*, 271–290.

Kim, T. (2007). *Hankuke taywupep [Korean honorifics]*. Seoul: Yeklak.

Kramsch, C., & Andersen, R. W. (1999). Teaching text and context through multimedia. *Language Learning & Technology, 2*(2), 31–42.

Kwon, J. (2004). Expressing refusals in Korean and in American English. *Multilingua, 23*(4), 339–364.

Lakoff, R. (1977). What you can do with words: Politeness, pragmatics and performatives. In A. Rogers, B. Wall, & J. Murphy (Eds.), *Proceedings of the Texas conference on performatives, presuppositions and implicatures* (pp. 79–106). Arlington, TX: Center of Applied Linguistics.

Lave, J., & Wenger, E. (1991). *Situated learning: Legitimate peripheral participation*. Cambridge: Cambridge University Press.

Lee, I., & Ramsey, S. R. (2000). *The Korean language*. New York: SUNY Press.

Lee, J. (1999). Kwukekyengepep-uy cenlyakcek yongpep-ey tayhaye [On the strategic usage of Korean honorifics]. *Ehakyenkwu [Language Research], 35*(1), 91–122.

Lee, M. (1997). Acquisition of Korean referent honorifics by adult learners of Korean as a second language. *Korean Language in America*, 99–110.

Lee, W. (2001). *Tamhwa pwunsek [Discourse analysis]*. Seoul: Hankook Munhwasa.

Leech, G. N. (2016). *Principles of pragmatics*. Oxon and New York: Routledge.

Lyuh, I. (1994). *The art of refusal: Comparison of Korean and American cultures* [Ph.D. dissertation]. Indiana University.

Mitchell, N., & Haugh, M. (2015). Agency, accountability and evaluations of impoliteness. *Journal of Politeness Research, 11*(2), 207–238.

Mueller, J., & Jiang, N. (2013). The acquisition of the Korean honorific affix (u) si by advanced L2 learners. *The Modern Language Journal, 97*(2), 318–339.

Nelson, K. (1986). Event knowledge and cognitive development. In K. Nelson (Ed.), *Event knowledge: Structure and function in development* (pp. 1–20). Mahwah, NJ: Lawrence Erlbaum.

Nelson, K. (1996). *Language in cognitive development: Emergence of the mediated mind*. Cambridge: Cambridge University Press.

Norton, B. (2013). *Identity and language learning: Extending the conversation*. Clevedon, UK: Multilingual Matters.

Ochs, E., & Schieffelin, B. B. (2009). Language acquisition and socialization: Three developmental stories and their implications. In *Linguistic anthropology: A reader* (pp. 263–301). Malden, MA: Wiley.

Oh, E., & Cui, M. (2020). The acquisition of acoustic correlates of politeness by native Chinese speakers. *Linguistic Research*, *37*, 113–134.

Oh, G. E., Brown, L., Idemaru, K., & Cui, M. (forthcoming). Effects of L2 experience on Mandarin listeners' perception of Korean politeness. *Language and Speech*.

Park, K. (1998). The characteristics of Korean American learners' use of speech levels and honorifics in Korean. *Mincokmunhwayenkwu [Korean Classics Studies]*, *29*, 349–377.

Park, M. Y. (2017). Resisting linguistic and ethnic marginalization: Voices of Southeast Asian marriage-migrant women in Korea. *Language and Intercultural Communication*, *17*(2), 118–134.

Park, S., Nam, K., & Seo, S. (2003). Tayhaksaeng kwue theyksuthu-eyse-uy cosa emi-uy pwunpho-wa sayong yangsang-ey taeha-n yenkwu [Research into the use of verb ending particles in university students' spoken texts]. *Theyksuthu Enehak [Text Linguistics]*, *15*, 139–188.

Phan, H., & Kwon, S. (2018). Peythunam haksupca-uy hankwuke kyengepep olyu yangsang yenkwu [Errors in use of Korean honorifics by Korean learners in Vietnam]. *Kwukekyoyukhakyenkwu [Korean Language Education Research]*, *53*(2), 290–329.

Pizziconi, B. (2006). Learning to reframe: Japanese benefactives, metalinguistic beliefs and the identities of L2 users. In Y. Asako, U. Tae, & N. Masashi (Eds.), *Readings in second language pedagogy and second language acquisition: In Japanese context* (pp. 119–154). Amsterdam and Philadelphia: John Benjamins Publishing Company.

Pizziconi, B. (2007). The lexical mapping of politeness in British English and Japanese. *Journal of Politeness Research*, *3*(2), 207–241.

Schank, R. C., & Abelson, R. P. (2013). *Scripts, plans, goals, and understanding: An inquiry into human knowledge structures*. Hove: Psychology Press.

Song, J. (2009). Bilingual creativity and self-negotiation. In A. Reyes & A. Lo (Eds.), *Beyond Yellow English: Toward a linguistic anthropology of Asian Pacific America* (pp. 309–324). Oxford: Oxford University Press.

Song, S., Choe, J.-W., & Oh, E. (2019). An empirical study of honorific mismatches in Korean. *Language Sciences*, *75*, 47–71.

Suh, C. (1984). *Contaypep yenkwu [Honorifics research]*. Seoul: Hanshin.

Suh, K. H. (2010). A contrastive study of compliment responses of Korean, Chinese, and English speakers. *Yengmiyenkwu [English and American Studies]*, *22*, 131–162.

Sun, L., & Kim, Y. (2012). Hyengtaycipcwung-ul hwalyonghan kyengepep kyoyuk yenkwu – chungkwukin hankwuke haksupca-lul taysang-ulo [A study on the Korean honorific education for Chinese learners based on form-focused instruction]. *Saykwukekyoyuk [Korean Language Education Research]*, *29*, 57–92.

Sung, K. (1985). *Hyentay taywupep yenkwu [Research on contemporary honorifics]*. Seoul: Gaemunsa.

Thomas, J. (1983). Cross-cultural pragmatic failure. *Applied Linguistics*, *4*(2), 91–112.

Turkozu, G. (2011). Thekhiin haksupca-lul wihan hankwuke taywupep kyoyuk – phyencikul-ey nathananun olyupwunsek-ul pathang-ulo [Korean language honorifics education for Turkish learners of Korean: Based on error analysis of letter writing]. In *2011-Nyen Kwukceyhankwukekyoyukhakhoy Palphyo Nonmwuncip [Proceedings of 2011 annual conference of the international association of Korean language education]* (pp. 514–524). Kyung Hee University, Seoul.

Wang, H.-S. (2019). Comprehension of the honorifics system by learners of Korean. *The Korean Language in America*, *23*(1), 53–84.

Winter, B., & Grawunder, S. (2012). The phonetic profile of Korean formal and informal speech registers. *Journal of Phonetics*, *40*(6), 808–815.

Yang, S., Seo, W., & Kang, B. (2013). Chincel yoso-wa chincelinsik-uy kwankeypwunsek tosi nay sepisu iyongca-wa congsaca-lul cwungsim-ulo [Comparative analysis between kindness factors and perception: Focused on customers and providers in service industry of city]. *Tosihayngcenghakpo [Journal of The Korean Urban Management Association]*, *24*(2), 205–231.

Yoon, K.-J. (2004). Not just words: Korean social models and the use of honorifics. *Intercultural Pragmatics*, *1*(2), 189–210.

Yoon, S. Y., & Brown, L. (2018). A multiliteracies approach to teaching Korean multimodal (im) politeness. *The Korean Language in America*, *21*(2), 154–185.

5
KSL SYNTAX AND SEMANTICS

EunHee Lee

Introduction

This chapter discusses the acquisition of syntax and semantics of Korean as a second language mostly by L1 English speakers and Korean heritage speakers. The reason why we focus on these particular L1 groups is not only because most research has examined these populations but also because L2 learning is so heavily influenced by features of L1 that it is practically impossible to build a model of L2 learning that does not take the structure of the L1 into account. Recently, interest in the L1 influence on the L2 system has received renewed attention. Scholars used to think that learning a second language simply involved moving from the L1 system to the L2 system, predicting a full transfer of L1 features and blaming every error on the differences between the source and the target languages. This position was proven wrong as research discovered not only that many errors cannot be attributed to either L1 or L2 but that some universal acquisition patterns also exist across different L1 backgrounds. However, with the technological progress which permits big corpus data analyses, along with advances in neurolinguistics using sophisticated brain imaging techniques and computational methods, the way in which the existing form–meaning mapping in L1 influences further learning has once again come to the forefront of language-learning theories.[1] A systematic and scientific comparison between L1 and L2 can only facilitate learning, rather than approaching language learning as a one-size-fits-all kind of method.

Languages not only use different structures to encode the same meaning, but similar structures are often mapped to different meanings across languages. Such form–meaning mismatch between L1 and L2 poses a significant challenge to L2 learners, especially when the L1 and L2 are typologically different, as in the case of Korean and English. The relationship of form–meaning mapping is said to be arbitrary. Once the strongest and most salient cue, i.e., the form, is associated with a response, i.e., the meaning, other cues are often ignored, making a new mapping extremely difficult, if not impossible. Contra common belief, repetition only makes things worse for cues that are hard to notice, like the third-person singular suffix *-s* or the past tense suffix *-ed* on the English verbs when there are stronger and more obvious functional cues, such as third-person singular pronoun subjects like *she* or past time adverbs like *yesterday* (Ellis, 2006). The situation can be even worse for Korean learners, as Korean is morphologically so rich. This is the reason why people who learn Korean (or any other language for that matter) in a non-instructional setting often fail to use these tiny grammatical affixes. Assuming that grammar is nothing but a complex set of weighted form–function/meaning mappings, retrieval of the weighted cues will be crucial for successful mastery of the structural knowledge for L2 learners and bilinguals (Bates & MacWhinney, 1989).

Much language teaching, in particular grammar instruction, however, still relies on conventional ideas about language learning, e.g., rote memorization of irregularities and mechanical drill exercises for endless grammatical paradigms, instead of relying on more recent scientific discoveries. Such methods are not conducive to learning at all because they easily sap the motivation of even the most motivated learners. In this chapter, we will approach the grammar from a functional perspective, explaining why the grammar is the way it is. We assume, in line with mainstream linguistic theories, that grammatical operations are universal and that there is only one simple operation, namely, putting two words together to form the predicate–argument structure (Chomsky, 1995; Heim & Kratzer, 1998; Jackendoff, 2002). Experienced bilinguals are known to have a single abstract grammatical structure regardless of word order or case marking (Kantola & van Gompel, 2011). If this is true, then grammatical features on lexical items and functional morphology will constitute the bulk of L2 grammar acquisition (Slavakova, 2016), which deserves particular attention when the L2 is, like Korean, morphologically very rich.

This chapter is organized as follows. Section 2 presents an overview of Korean grammar, highlighting its unique structural and semantic features and the syntax–semantics mismatch between L1 English and L2 Korean. Section 3 surveys recent KSL literature, investigating topics such as clause types, case, number, and topic markings on nominals, relative clauses, honorifics, tense and aspect marking on verbs, and *wh*-questions. The research discussed is by no means exhaustive, but it is representative of the current state of the field. A number of influential hypotheses have been proposed with regard to the form–meaning (re)mapping in L2 acquisition, the subset hypothesis, the shared-structure hypothesis, the interface hypothesis, and the feature-assembly hypothesis, to name just a few. We will explore whether these hypotheses have any explanatory power in describing L2 Korean acquisition patterns. Section 4 concludes with a summary and implications for instructional treatments.

Korean clause structure

If you just blurt out a bunch of words, you might be able to get your message across to a patient listener, but you won't be conveying your message very clearly or elegantly. You need a grammar to put the words together to form a coherent sentence. Bates and MacWhinney (1989) view grammars as a class of solutions to the problem of mapping nonlinear meanings/thoughts onto a linear medium, which is highly constrained, only relying on word order, morphological marking, and prosody. According to this view, universal aspects of human grammar inevitably reveal themselves whenever universal categories of thought have to be mapped onto a limited channel. The basic categories they cite include principles of motion, space, time, and principles of human actions and intentions. This section will lay down the fundamental linguistic similarities and differences between Korean and English in the framework of Bates and MacWhinney's (1989) **competition model**. Instead of viewing L1 as a roadblock to the L2 acquisition, and in order to use it as a shortcut, we have to have a relatively sophisticated understanding of the grammatical systems of the L1 and L2 from a comparative perspective, as well as the language-learning mechanisms discovered through scientific research. The most noticeable difference between Korean and English concerns the division of labor between morphology and syntax: Korean is morphologically complex, whereas English is syntax heavy. However, the meaning conveyed by different ways of putting words and morphemes together, we argue, is the same as it derives from the universal need to express fundamental concepts and states of affairs important to all of us.

Central grammatical roles

Lexical items with various built-in concepts must be connected to one another through **grammatical roles**. Predicates (verbs and modifiers) open up the positions for grammatical roles, which are filled by arguments (nominals). This basic combinatorial process is called **saturation**, which is operative in every language. For example, an intransitive verb like *run* or 달리다 [tɑlli.tɑ] 'run' requires one participant in the event described, the runner, while a transitive verb like *eat* or 먹다 [mʌk.tɑ] 'eat' needs two arguments, the eater and the eaten. These unsaturated verbs are saturated when they are given their required argument(s) to express a full proposition, which can then be judged as true or false. The word-order pattern and morphological markings cue particular grammatical relations. In English, word order signifies these different roles, whereas in Korean, morphological marking on lexical items does the same thing.

The central argument roles of the verb are common in English and Korean, which are **subject**, **object**, **indirect**, **oblique**, and **result**. If there is only one argument, the argument is the subject. Subject is the argument from whose point of view the clause is interpreted, serving the **perspective** role. We will use subject and perspective interchangeably from now on. In the Korean sentence in (1), the topic marker 는 [nɯn] on the subject brings out the perspective role more explicitly.

1 김은 걸었다.[2]
 Kim-un kel-ess-ta.
 'Kim walked.'

If there are two arguments, one is the subject and the other is the object. Object is the argument that is maximally involved in or changed by the action of the verb, performing the **affected** role. This does not mean the object must be physically or visibly changed.

2 김은 밥을 먹었다.
 Kim-un pap-ul mek-ess-ta.
 'Kim ate rice/a meal.'

Verbs can take up to three central arguments, which are subject, object, and indirect, as in (3a); subject, object, and oblique, as in (3b); or subject, object, and result, as in (3c). Indirect argument serves the **secondary perspective** role, by engaging in a secondary action as a beneficiary or recipient. Oblique is the argument of a preposition, carrying out the **circumstantial** role, such as location. Result is the end result or goal, performing the **outcome** role. These verbs describe a change of location, possession, or state.

3 a. 김은 리를/에게 책을 주었다.
 Kim-un li-lul/eykey chayk-ul cwu-ess-ta.
 'Kim gave Lee a book' (with the accusative *lul*) or 'Kim gave a book to Lee' (with the dative *eykey*).
 b. 김은 책을 책상 위에 놓았다.
 Kim-un chayk-ul chayksang wi-ey noh-ass-ta.
 'Kim put the book on the table.'

c. 김은 벽을 빨갛게 칠했다.
   Kim-un pyek-ul ppalkah-key chilha-yss-ta.
   'Kim painted the wall red.'

The basic clause structures are schematically represented as follows. **V** stands for verb, **Sub** abbreviates subject, **Obl** abbreviates oblique, **Obj** abbreviates object, **Ind** means indirect, and **Resl** means Result. E stands for English, K stands for Korean.

4 a. **Subj V [E/K]**
      'X moves'
      Intransitive motion (Ex. (1))
   b. **Subj V Obj [E]** or **Subj Obj V [K]**
      'X affects Y'
      Transitive motion (Ex. (2))
   c. **Subj V Obj Ind [E]** or **Subj Ind Obj V [K]**
      'X causes Y to receive/be located at Z'
      Ditransitive (Ex. (3a))
   d. **Subj V Obj Obl [E]** or **Subj Obj Obl V [K]**
      'X causes Y to move $Z_{path/location}$'
      Caused motion (Ex. (3b))
   e. **Subj V Obj Resl [E]** or **Subj Obj Resl V [K]**
      'X causes Y to become Z_{state}'
      Resultative (Ex. (3c))

It is important to recognize that many [verb + object] combinations are subject to varying relations derived from the nature of semantic composition. Semantic composition is not limited to the literal combination; extended and more abstract relations can be formed when the contributions of the verb and the object are not mechanical. The basic multipurpose verbs in English, such as *take*, *give*, *get*, *put*, *see*, *stand*, etc., describe physical events or states central to human experience but can undergo **metonymic or metaphoric sense extensions** of their core physical meanings when they combine with non-referential or abstract arguments. For example, *give* can describe a physical transfer of possession (literal, as in *give a present*), abstract transfer of allocation (as in *give time*), convey or conduct an action in light verb construction where the object has the predicate meaning (as in *give a bath, give a shout, make a decision*), and idiomatic expression (as in *give the slip*). Similarly, the Korean verb 먹다 [mʌk.ta] 'to eat' has a literal meaning of consuming food with an object referring to food, like 밥 [pap] 'rice', but has derived meanings with other object nouns, such as 나이 [nai] 'age', 욕 [jok] 'criticism', 더위 [tʌwi] 'heat', and 벌점 [pʌltɕʌm] 'penalty'. 나이를 먹다 [nai.lul mʌk.ta], which literally means 'to eat age', means 'to get older'. Language learners often try to memorize these phrases just like they memorize individual words. It is important, however, to understand why language works this way. Form–function mapping is not one to one but many to many, and such flexibility makes language an economical yet productive communicative system.

Competition for argument slots and cues

According to the competition model (Bates & MacWhinney, 1989), while a clause has, at most, three or four central argument slots, there are dozens of possible **semantic roles** that compete for the limited argument slots. Bates and MacWhinney (1989) assume that the connection between the role and the candidate argument is not hard-wired in the lexicon but is formed dynamically during processing. For example, the subject/perspective role of the verb *hit* can be an agent, as in (5a), an instrument, as in (5b), or a patient, as in (5c). Korean does not normally allow an inanimate subject in the passive verb; since the lexical (derivational) passive in Korean is an **adversative passive**, there is no corresponding sentence for (5c).[3] While clause-initial position, third-person singular subject agreement, and the nominal status are the cues for the subject/perspective role in English, the (honorific) case marker, **honorific agreement** 시 [si] (allomorph 으시 [ɯsi] after a consonant]), and the **nominal status** of the argument cue the subject/perspective in Korean. The honorific suffix is used only when the subject is higher in social status than the speaker, which will be discussed in more detail in Section 2.3.2. Because nominative and accusative markers are often omitted in casual speech, **pre-object position**, **definiteness**, and **animacy** also serve as secondary cues for the subjecthood in Korean. Prototypical subjects are definite and animate, while prototypical objects are indefinite and inanimate (Aissen, 2003; Lee, H., 2006). Since animacy, which entails volition, intention, and sentience, is a stronger cue for the subject in Korean than in English, instrument subjects are rare in Korean.

5   a.   공이 울타리를 때렸다.
        Kong-i wulthali-lul ttayly-ess-ta.
        'The ball hit the fence.'
   b.   아버지께서 울타리를 때리셨다.
        Apeci-kkeyse wulthali-lul ttayli-sy-ess-ta.
        'My father hit the fence.'
   c.   *The fence* was hit by the ball/by Father.

When predicates combine with arguments, the dependency relation is marked either on the selected argument (using case) or on the selecting predicate (using agreement). Thus, languages are broadly divided into **dependent-marking** and **head-marking** languages (Nichols, 1986). Both English and Korean have relatively impoverished agreements, so they can be categorized as dependent-marking languages. While case is only discernable on pronouns in English (e.g., *I, me*), all Korean nouns carry case suffixes to mark their structural relations to the predicate. Korean 가 [ka] (allomorph 이 [i] after a consonant) marks the subject, 을 [ɯl] (allomorph 를 [lɯl] after a vowel) marks the object, and 의 [ɯj] is the possessive suffix. Suffixes can be stacked in the order of **discourse suffixes** (e.g., 만 [man] 'only', 도 [to] 'also', 조차 [tɕotɕʰa], 마저 [matɕʌ] 'even') followed by case suffixes. In English, these discourse markers are all independent words (free morphemes). **Postposition suffixes**, such as locative 에서 [esʌ] 'at', directive 에 [e] 'to', dative 에게 [eke] (or 한테 [hantʰe]), goal 까지 [k'atɕi], instrument 로 [lo] (allmorph 으로 [ɯlo] after a consonant), which correspond to English prepositions, precede case suffixes or the topic suffix, as (6) illustrates. A strict order of postposition suffix-discourse suffix-case or topic suffix must be observed in Korean nominal inflection.[4]

6   김에게만을/은 주었다.
    Kim-eykey-man-ul/un cwu-ess-ta.
    'I gave it only to Kim.'

In Korean, verbs and objects can be separated by adverbs, as in (7), which is not acceptable in English. This means that morphological cues are so well-developed that they need not be supplemented by positional cues.

7   김이 책을 열심히 읽었다.
    Kim-i chayk-ul yelsimhi ilk-ess-ta.
    '*Kim read diligently the book.'

Intransitive verbs come in two different types: the single argument of unergative verbs is an agent, as in (1), while the sole argument of unaccusative verbs is a theme or patient, as (8) exemplifies (Burzio, 1986; Perlmutter, 1978). The agent of a transitive/unergative verb and the patient of an unaccusative verb occupy the subject position in both Korean and English.

8   김이 넘어졌다.
    Kim-i nemecy-ess-ta.
    'Kim fell.'

Cues for indirect/secondary perspective are the first post-verbal position in English and both the animacy and accusative case marker 를 [lul] in Korean, as shown in (9a). In both Korean and English, the case marking on the indirect can alternate between accusative and dative *to* and 에게 [eke]. In this case, the preposition or the postposition cues indirect case role, as in (9b).[5]

9 a. 김이 리를 책을 주었다.
      Kim-i li-lul chayk-ul cwu-ess-ta.
      'Kim gave Lee the book.'
   b. 김이 리에게 책을 주었다.
      Kim-i li-eykey chayk-ul cwu-ess-ta.
      'Kim gave the book to Lee.'

As in the case of transitive motion events, the subject case role in the dative motion of transfer can be filled with an agent or an instrument, where animacy is the cue for the former. The object role, on the other hand, is filled by a patient, whose cues are **inanimate**, **indefinite**, and **nominal status**. As shown in (10b), when the subject is an instrument, the indirect role cannot take the accusative marker but is dative-marked in Korean.

10 a. 아버지께서 김을/에게 책을 주셨다.
      Apeci-kkeyse kim-ul/-eykey chayk-ul cwu-sy-ess-ta.
      'Her father gave Kim a book.'
    b. 그의 방문이 김에게/*을 희망을 주었다.
      Ku-uy pangmwun-i kim-eykey/*-ul huymang-ul cwu-ess-ta.
      'His visit gave Kim hope.'

Verbs taking oblique arguments are typically change of location or posture verbs, such as *put*, *stand*, *sit*, *lie*, etc. Cues for oblique are prepositions in English and postpositions in Korean. Both agent and instrument can occupy the subject position, as (11) shows.

11 a. 김이 책을 책상 위에 놓았다.
      Kim-i chayk-ul chayksang wiey noh-ass-ta.
      'Kim put the book on the table.'
    b. 그녀의 재능이 김을 정상에 올려놓았다.
      Kunye-uy caynung-i kim-ul cengsang-ey ollyenoh-ass-ta.
      'Her talent put Kim on top.'

Cues for result are the position after the object in English, and the result suffix 게 [ke] (or 도록 [tolok]) in Korean. Any action verb can take an optional result phrase to describe the outcome of the action.

12   김이 발이 아프게 춤추었다.
     Kim-i pal-i aphu-key chwumchwu-ess-ta.
     'Kim danced her feet sore.'

In English, of the five central roles (subject, object, indirect, oblique, and result), only the subject is fully obligatory. English requires a dummy subject *it*, which does not contribute a referent, as in (13a). Korean lacks a dummy subject, as shown in (13b), which suggests that the syntax–semantics mapping is more transparent in Korean than in English (Lee, E., 2019).

13   a.   It is raining.
     b.   비가 온다
          Pi-ka o-n-ta
          'The rain is coming.'

There are no verbs for which the indirect is obligatory, while it is harder to omit the required object (Bates & MacWhinney, 1989). Omitting arguments is much easier in Korean than in English.[6] **Null pronouns** pick out a salient entity in the utterance or discourse context. In (14), the subject (*Kim*) and the object (*the car*) of the first sentence are referred back to using pronouns in English but null pronouns in Korean. We will discuss null/zero pronouns in greater detail in Section 2.3.1.

14   김이 어제 차를 샀다. 오늘 나한테 보여 주었다.
     Kim-i ecey cha-lul s-ass-ta. onul na-hanthey poye cwu-ess-ta.
     'Kim bought a car yesterday. She showed it to me today.'

Information structure

Information structure is an independent layer from the grammatical argument structure that affects the clause structure. Since Korean word order is flexible, informational structural concerns heavily influence its clause structure. An utterance expresses a complete thought embedded in a common ground and a concrete utterance context shared by the speaker and the hearer. It is packaged in such a way that it will convey its intended meaning clearly and efficiently. Listing simple short sentences may add to clarity but is not very efficient. Like other human activities, we want speaking to be economical, limiting the redundancy, and going for maximal informativity. Each utterance in a discourse also must hang together if you don't want to sound mentally deficient. Utterances must be informative, meaning that they must contain new information. However, to be relevant, they also must relate to something that is already known. Organizing utterances in terms of old and new information coherently is as important as speaking grammatically. Well-packaged utterances with balanced old and new information is a high-level distinction that even native speakers need practice to achieve. Languages have a lot of devices to help us achieve this. We use pro-forms or ellipses for already mentioned things or events, use expressions that presuppose mutually known facts, and take advantage of grammatical means, such as the main and subordinate clause distinction, nominalization, and relative clauses, to highlight the main message. Some expressions carry presupposed information. For example, the definite article *the* in English and the topic suffix 는 [nun] in Korean presuppose that the entity in question is already familiar to the speaker and the hearer. Also, subordinate clauses, complex nominals, and relative clauses are typically employed to indicate subsidiary information, which help make the main assertion comprehensible. It is not a matter of grammatical rules when to end an utterance and begin a new one but a strategic plan. Often, however, such information structural features have an impact on grammar, too.

It is often said that English is a **subject prominent (SP) language** and Korean is a **topic prominent (TP) language** (Li & Thompson, 1976). The basic sentence structure of SP languages is the predicate and argument structure of a proposition. On the other hand, the structure of TP languages is the information partition between topic, which is given and what the rest of the sentence is about, and focus, which provides new information about the topic. TP languages are often characterized by frequent omission of arguments retrievable from context (zero pronoun), grammatical means of marking the topic-comment structure (morphological topic marking and/or word order), impoverished subject–verb agreement, and absence of obligatory definite and indefinite determiners (bare nouns) (Li & Thompson, 1976). Topic is a free argument of the verb assigned to the clause-initial nominals. The most common central role for the topic is that of subject/perspective. English uses word order to express non-canonical topics (e.g., *Kim, I like* [*but Lee, I don't*]). In Korean, a topic and a subject can be assigned to different nominals. In (15), 수박 [supɑk] 'watermelon' is the topic of the utterance, indicated by the topic suffix 은 [ɯn] (allomorph 는 [nɯn] after a vowel), and 김 [kim] 'Kim' is the subject of the predicate 먹다 [mʌk.tɑ] 'eat', marked by the nominative marker 이 [i].

15 수박은 김이 먹었다.
    swupak-un kim-i meket-ta.
    'Speaking of watermelon, Kim ate it.'

Focus is also optional and conveys **contrastive presupposition**. In English, focus is typically marked by stress (e.g., *I like KIM* [*not Lee*]). Association of focus with the object is the default. Focus is the element that can be directly questioned. Therefore, indirect objects, which are secondary perspective, excluding them from being focused, cannot normally be directly questioned (**Who was given the book?*) (Bates & MacWhinney, 1989). *Wh*-elements in questions correspond to a new and prominent entity. In Korean, the 이/가 [i]/[kɑ] suffix serves a dual function of nominative and focus case roles. Likewise, the 을/를 [ɯl]/[lɯl] suffix serves the dual role of the accusative and focus case roles in Korean. Focus meaning becomes salient with high pitch. It also additionally indicates a marked combination of object with definite and/or animate nominals (Kwon & Zribi-Hertz, 2007).

To specify topics, we assume that structural descriptions of sentences include **focus structures** (F-structure henceforth) where foci are paired up with topics (Erteschik-Shir, 2007). F-structure is largely determined by what kind of questions are being asked in the given context. The most basic F-structure, among a variety of types, is the one where the topic is paired up with a predication focus. In Korean, the topic-marked NP typically expresses such a structure.

16 버스는 오고 있다.
    Pesu-nun o-ko iss-ta.
    (What about the bus?) 'The bus, it is coming.'
    [the bus/it]$_{TOP}$ [is coming]$_{FOC}$

Topics typically appear in the initial position of an utterance. If a topic-marked NP occurs in a subordinate clause, it is almost always contrastive.

17 김이 버스는 왔다고 말했다.
    Kim-i pesu-nun w-ass-ta-ko malha-yss-ta.
    'Kim said the bus came (but not the taxi).'

The nominative marked NP, on the other hand, is ambiguous between an event focus reading, in which the topic position is occupied by a **null stage topic** denoting a spatiotemporal discourse referent and a **narrow focus reading**, in which the referent is the answer to the *wh*-question, marking a contrastive choice among alternatives. The NP can be either definite or indefinite and refers to topics embedded in predicate focus.

18 버스가 오고 있다.
    Pesu-ka o-ko iss-ta.
    a. (What's happening?) 'A bus coming.'
        [Ø]$_{TOP1}$ [[a bus]$_{TOP2}$ [is coming]$_{FOC2}$]$_{FOC1}$
    b. (What is coming?) 'What is coming is a bus.'
        [[a bus]$_{FOC}$]$_{TOP}$ is coming

Zero pronouns indicate **active topics**. Active topics are "freshly lit-up" topic entities that get represented in the F-structure. In English, active topics are realized as pronouns. In Korean discourse, zero pronouns typically refer to a salient and continuous referent, often the topic in the subject position in an immediately preceding clause (Gundel, Nancy Hedeberg, & Zacharski, 1993). That is, the zero pronoun in the subject position maintains the same subject as the previous utterance, whereas an overt subject tends to shift it to newly introduced discourse entities in the previous utterance in Korean (Han, 2006).

Case ellipsis is possible when an NP is neither the active topic nor the focus and thus invisible to F-structure (Kwon & Zribi-Hertz, 2007). Moreover, the prototypical or unmarked combinations, namely, the subject with a definite and animate referent, on the one hand, and the object with an indefinite and inanimate referent, on the other, need not be marked overtly and thus permit case ellipsis (Lee, H., 2006). Object case ellipsis occurs when the [verb + object] is event-denoting complex predicate and the object nominal is not narrowly focused, as in (19).

19 김이 공부했다.
    Kim-i kongpwuhay-ss-ta.
    'Kim studied.'

Caseless subject NPs are the most salient **discourse topics**, an entity that the current discourse is about.

20 버스 온다!
    Pesu o-n-ta.
    'Here comes the bus!'

Nominative-case marked NPs in non-canonical word order and embedded subject position in (21a), (21b), and (21c) cannot be omitted, and the same constraint holds for an indefinite subject in (21d) and a question word in (21e). In these contexts, they do not have a discourse topic status but are instead either focused (for indefinite and question) or backgrounded (non-canonical word order, embedded subject).

21 a. 김을 리*(가) 만났다.
 Kim-ul li*(ka) mann-ass-ta.
 'It was Kim whom Lee met.'
 b. 리는 김*(이) 떠난 것을 몰랐다.
 Li-nun kim*(-i) ttena-n kes-ul moll-ass-ta.
 'Lee did not know that Kim left.'
 c. 리는 김*(이) 좋아하는 남자를 만났다.
 Li-nun kim*(-i) cohaha-nun namca-lul mann-ass-ta.
 'Lee met the man whom Kim likes.'
 d. 한 남자*(가) 살았다.
 Han namca*(-ka) sal-ass-ta.
 'There lived a man.'
 e. 누구*(가) 책을 샀니?
 Nwukwu*(-ka) chayk-ul s-ass-ni?
 'Who bought a book?'

Relative clause and background

Relative head is the most complex grammatical role, serving a dual function (Bates & MacWhinney, 1989). In the main clause, it serves as an argument or an adjunct of the verb. In the relative clause, it also serves as an argument of the verb by filling a **gap** in the argument structure of the verb. Instead of a relative pronoun, as in English, Korean uses an adnominal suffix, carrying a tense feature such as the past 은 [un], the present 는 [nun], and the future 을 [ul]. We can still link the head noun with one of the arguments of the verb in the relative clause in most cases. For example, 남자 [namtɕa] 'man' in (22) is the direct object complement of the verb 좋아하다 [tɕoahada] 'to like'.

22 a. 김이 좋아한 남자
 Kim-i cohaha-n namca
 'the man whom Kim liked'
 b. 김이 좋아하는 남자
 Kim-i cohaha-nun namca
 'the man whom Kim likes'
 c. 김이 좋아할 남자
 Kim-i cohaha-l namca
 'the man whom Kim will like'

The head noun cannot be related to an element that is more deeply embedded in a relative clause, as shown in (23). This constraint is called **island constraint** in linguistics because islands are not connected to the mainland, and the residents of the island cannot freely communicate with the residents in the mainland. Such constraints seem to follow from information structural considerations. Relative clauses often mark **backgrounded information** that is not essential to the main point of a clause. The head noun in a relative clause, as opposed to the content of the relative clause, is prominent in discourse and thus cannot be related to the material inside the relative clause, which is backgrounded. It is pragmatically anomalous to treat an element as simultaneously backgrounded and discourse prominent.[7]

23 a. *리가 ___ 사귀는 여자를 만난 남자
 *Li-ka ___ sakwi-nun yeca-lul manna-n namca
 '*The man [whom1 [Lee met [the woman [who dates e1]]]'
 b. ?리가 ___ 먹은 것이 김을 짜증나게 하는 음식
 ?Li-ka ___ mek-un kes-i kim-ul ccacungnakey ha-nun umsik
 '*The food1 [which [that Lee ate t1] annoys Kim]]'

Relative clauses can be **gapless** in Korean, that is, sentences do not contain a syntactic gap corresponding to the displaced element, as in (24). In this case, relative clauses are not necessarily backgrounded. Head nouns in gapless relative clauses are closely related to the event described by the adnominal clause.[8]

24 a. 머리가 좋아지는 약
 Meli-ka cohaci-nun yak
 'medicine that one becomes smart by taking'
 b. 물이 떨어지는 소리
 Mwul-i tteleci-nun soli
 'sound created by water's dripping'

Honorifics and politeness

Korean is an honorific language, which has a rich grammatical marking for the social relationship among discourse participants. **Hearer honorifics** signal the relationship between the speaker and the addressee, which include a system of inflectional endings encoding different speech styles that attach to the predicate, as shown in (25). Different honorific forms and their combinations index degrees of separation and connection (Brown, 2011). In contemporary Korean, the deferential and polite speech levels are used to index separation, whereas intimate and plain speech levels index connection.

25 a. deferential style (습)니다 [(sɯ)pnidɑ]
 b. polite style 아/어요 [ɑjo]/[ʌjo]
 c. intimate style 아/어 [ɑ]/[ʌ]
 d. plain style 다 [tɑ]

The former two levels are considered honorific speech styles and the latter two are non-honorific speech styles (Chang, 1996). Honorific speech styles are used exclusively by status inferiors to status superiors and mutually between the unacquainted or unfamiliar. Non-honorific styles, on the other hand, are exclusively used by status superiors to status inferiors and mutually between friends and the well-acquainted. The **intimate style**, which frequently alternates with the **plain style**, is the most commonly used non-honorific speech style. The **polite style** represents the most common speech styles that can be used both with superiors and with those of similar or younger age (with low intimacy). Simply by suffixing [jo] to the intimate ending, the honorific speech level can be formed. The **deferential style** indexes the greatest degree of separation. Although the polite style is polite enough in most situations, the deferential style is preferred in highly formal situations.

Referent honorifics are another important component of the honorifics system that marks the relationship between the speaker and the grammatical referents or between different grammatical referents within the utterance. They comprised subject honorifics and object honorifics.

Subject honorifics indicate the relationship between the speaker and the grammatical subject of the sentence. It is achieved through the application of (1) the honorific suffix (으)시 [(ɯ)si] and (2) vocabulary substitutions (e.g., 사람 [sɑlɑm] 'person' vs. 분 [pun] 'person (hon)'), and (3) the substitution of 께서 [k'esʌ] for the subject case suffix 이/가 [i]/[kɑ]. In contemporary Korean, whether (으)시 [(ɯ)si] is included when talking about a third person relies on other contextual factors, e.g., whether or not the subject being referred to is physically present at the speech situation and whether an imperative speech act is performed (Brown, 2011). Korean object honorifics involve the use of the honorific dative suffix 께 [k'e] instead of 에게/한테 [eke]/[hantʰe] and the lexical substitutions (e.g., 주다 [tɕu.tɑ] 'give' vs. 드리다 [tɯli.tɑ] 'give (hon)'). Example (26) from Brown (2011) graphically displays the elaborate honorific system in Korean.

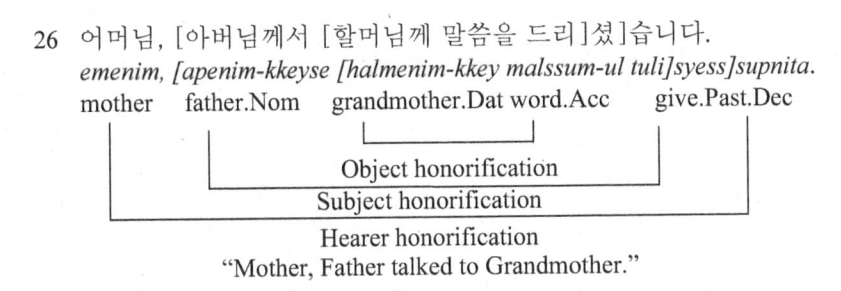

26 어머님, [아버님께서 [할머님께 말씀을 드리]셨]습니다.
    emenim, [apenim-kkeyse [halmenim-kkey malssum-ul tuli]syess]supnita.
    mother   father.Nom   grandmother.Dat word.Acc   give.Past.Dec

    Object honorification
    Subject honorification
    Hearer honorification
    "Mother, Father talked to Grandmother."

To summarize, this section described major grammatical features of Korean and provided a functional analysis of them based on Bates and MacWhinney's (1989) competition model, focusing on the basic clause structure, case marking and postpositions on nouns, honorifics, and information structure. In the next section, we will examine acquisition studies on these grammatical properties.

A survey of KSL literature

Clause types

Figuring out the basic clause types in L2 constitutes one of the foundational tasks in language learning. In this section, we will discuss the acquisition of basic clause types in L2 Korean, including transitive, causative, unaccusative, unergative, and dative clauses. Although Korean transitive structures have a different word order (Subject-Object-Verb [SOV]) from English transitives (SVO), they are structurally alike since they share functional relations and semantic role orders. In an active sentence, the agent is realized as the subject, while the patient occupies the object position, and the former entirely precedes the latter. The **shared-syntax hypothesis** states that syntactic processes and representations become integrated for similar structures in L1 and L2 as L2 proficiency increases (Bernolet, Hartsuiker, & Pickering, 2007; Hartsuiker & Bernolet, 2017). Hwang, Shin, and Hartsuiker (2018) conducted two experiments to test this hypothesis. They found that proficient Korean–English bilinguals displayed a stronger between-language priming effect in the similar transitive clause than less-proficient bilinguals.[9] The significant priming effect regardless of word-order differences in Korean and English supports the shared-syntax hypothesis. Korean and English, however, show a difference in causatives. English causative constructions are often expressed using a simple transitive clause in Korean. Unlike English, Korean has derivational causative suffixes (as well as passives), resulting in a more marginal role for structural causatives.

27 a. Kim had his computer fixed.
    b. 김이 컴퓨터를 고쳤다. (?고치게 했다.)
        Kim-i khemphyuthe-lul kochy-ess-ta. (?kochi-key hay-ss-ta.)

Hwang et al.'s (2018) picture-sentence verification task revealed that Korean–English speakers made more syntactic **transfer errors** as their proficiency increased. Despite their successful understanding of a causative structure, more proficient bilinguals were more likely to accept an active transitive structure as appropriate in describing a causative event. The result is equally predicted by the shared-syntax account. According to this model, a causative event activates both an active transitive structure and a causative structure in proficient bilinguals because Korean does not distinguish between the two. As syntax is shared in Korean and English, a strong link between a causative event and an active transitive structure in Korean leads to a greater activation of an active transitive structure in English, resulting in more transfer errors. In sum, their study suggests that Korean–English bilinguals share syntactic representations for both similar and different constructions, indicating that the bilingual grammatical system is highly integrated.

Turning next to intransitive verbs, the argument of unergative verbs do not license floating quantifiers, whereas that of unaccusative verbs do (Ahn, 1991). Assuming that the subject argument of the unaccusative verb originated in VP, the mutual c-command requirement between the head noun and the quantifier is satisfied, explaining the acceptability of (28b) (Miyagawa, 1989).

28 a. *아기가 크게 세 명 울었다.
        Aki-ka khukey sey myeng wul-ess-ta.
        [Intended] 'Three babies cried loudly.'
    b. 아기가$_1$ 병원에서 e$_1$ 세 명 태어났다.
        Aki-ka pyengwen-eyse sey myeng thayen-ass-ta.
        'Three babies were born at the hospital.'

English does not allow Korean-type floating quantifiers, as its quantifiers (or determiners in general) do not have the phrasal structure of numeral followed by classifiers that functions as a syntactic constituent and can move independently. In English, floating quantifiers are not restricted to unaccusative clauses. Note that *all* in (29) is an adverbial that is not necessarily c-commanded by the subject.

29 a. The children have *all* slept.
    b. The children have *all* come.

Lee (2011) examined the acquisition of unaccusativity by Korean heritage learners using a written acceptability judgment task, and she found that early Korean–English bilinguals showed different patterns from late bilinguals and Korean native speakers in terms of their acceptance of floating quantifiers in unaccusative and unergative clauses. Early bilinguals accepted floating quantifiers on both unaccusative and unergative clauses in Korean, whereas late bilinguals showed a native-like pattern. That is, early onset of exposure to the socially dominant language, English, negatively influenced the grammatical knowledge of L2 Korean, which can be attributed to the **poverty of stimulus** (as they get less Korean input) compounded by a **lack of negative evidence** (English allows floating quantifier adverbs in all clause types, and sentences like [28a] do not appear in Korean speech). Korean grammar in this domain is more conservative (subset) than English: the **subset principle** states that learners can only move to less conservative (superset) grammar on the basis of positive evidence. Also, L1 English speakers of L2 Korean learners transfer their supersets form L1, needing negative evidence, which cannot be provided in the Korean input.

Shin and Christianson (2009), using a sentence-recall experiment, provided evidence of shared representations for dative alternation structures in English and Korean, which we observed in (6). They reported cross-linguistic argument-order-independent structural priming in canonical Korean postpositional and English prepositional dative structures, providing evidence for shared bilingual syntactic processing. Importantly, they argue that the observed priming occurs at the functional level, rather than at the positional level, because these constructions display a high degree of structural similarity across the two languages, except for the argument order.

In sum, the literature on clause type in L2 Korean and Korean–English bilinguals in general supports the shared syntax hypothesis and the subset principle. Implications for instruction include explicit instructions of important cues and negative evidence (for the ungrammaticality of quantifier floating for unergative verbs).

Nominal inflection: case, number and topic marking

Kim, O'Grady, and Schwartz (2018) used a picture-selection task to examine the acquisition of case marking by heritage learners. The result showed that while the students successfully matched pictures with their corresponding descriptions in the canonical SOV sentence, they had significant difficulty with non-canonical OSV sentences, reflecting a reliance on word order rather than the case marking. In their corrective production task, however, they were much more accurate in offering the correct case markers, particularly in a contrastive focus context. The authors attribute this finding to the task complexity.

Number or quantity is expressed via numeral classifiers in Korean, which poses significant challenges to English speakers as they have to learn which nouns go with which classifiers. The English plural marker -s is obligatory when the number of the count noun argument is plural, whereas the Korean plural marker 들 [tul] is optional and marks not only nouns but also attaches to other constituents, adding the meaning of distributivity.

30 아이들이 운동장에서들 놀았다.
    Aitul-i wuntongcang-eyse-tul nol-ass-ta.
    'The children each played in (possibly different) playgrounds.'

Hwang and Lardiere (2013) conducted preference/acceptability, truth-value judgment, and translation tasks and found that features associated with the intrinsic plural, which is more similar to the English plural in terms of grammatical function, were more easily acquired than those of the extrinsic (distributive) plural.

As discussed previously, in Korean, nouns are followed by postpositions and then either a case marker or a discourse marker. That is, Korean case markers compete with discourse markers, traditionally called delimiters, for their position. Rigid templatic order in nominal (as well as verbal) inflection can pose a significant challenge to L2 Korean learners. Kim et al. (2018) and Laleko and Polinsky (2016) report that the heritage learners showed relatively poor performance on the use of the topic marker (in an obligatory context). They attribute the problems heritage learners have with topic marking to a more general difficulty claimed by the **interface hypothesis** (Sorace, 2011), which suggests that syntactic phenomena requiring pragmatics/discourse knowledge is more difficult to acquire fully or is more susceptible to attrition.

Choosing between the nominative marker and the topic marker requires interface knowledge of semantics and discourse, placing additional demands on processing resources. In E. Lee (2018), which examined narratives elicited via a picture description task, I argued that while the concept of topic may be universal and thus is acquired naturally, the morphological topic marking posed a considerable challenge to L2 Korean speakers of L1 English (and L1 Chinese). I explained the results by appealing to the universal acquisition path based on pragmatic-lexical-morphosyntactic cline: while the concept of the topic is (arguably) universal, its morphological marking is influenced by L1 as well as learning experience. The results are also in line with the **bottleneck hypothesis** (Slavakova, 2016), which claims that inflectional morphology is the bottleneck of L2 acquisition.

In sum, inflectional morphology on nominals poses a significant problem to KSL learners, which is explained by the interface hypothesis and the bottleneck hypothesis. Korean inflection not only marks grammatical relations but also pertains to discourse functional relations, requiring interface knowledge and extra processing costs. **Over-analysis** occurs when L2 speakers pick out lexical items at the expense of grammatical morphemes, which is very common among L2 speakers in non-instructional settings. MacWhinney (2017) argues that, in overcoming over-analysis, **noticing** adds accuracy and **chunking** adds fluency by turning explicit knowledge into procedural knowledge. Instructional treatment should include activities that allow the learners to notice the inflectional morphology and contextualized production practices of complex NPs as units to increase fluency. By associating definiteness (marked by *the* in English) with topic-hood and focus (marked by high pitch and prominence in English) with a sub-unit of comment, L2 speakers will eventually be able to more naturally use topic marking, focus marking, zero pronoun, and case ellipsis (Lee, E., 2020). It is important to recognize that information structure plays a more determining role than propositional content in Korean utterance structure.

Relative clause

O'Grady, Lee, and Choo (2003) examined whether the subject or the object relative clause (RC) is easier to acquire in L2 Korean, testing the **linear distance** vs. **the structural distance hypotheses**. These hypotheses concern the question of whether the linear distance or the depth of embedding causes difficulty recognizing the filler-gap dependency. Both hypotheses predict that the subject relative will be easier in English. In Korean, on the other hand, RC precedes the head noun, as shown in (30), and the subject relative gap is structurally closer to the head noun than to the object relative gap but is linearly more distant.

30 a. 김이 만난 사람
   Kim-i manna-n salam
   'the person whom Kim met ___'
 b. 김을 만난 사람
   Kim-ul manna-n salam
   'the person who ___ met Kim'

O'Grady et al. (2003) found a strong preference for subject RC, as predicted by the structural distance hypothesis. Jeon and Kim (2007) also showed that subject RC is easier to acquire, in line with Keenan and Comrie's (1977) **noun phrase accessibility hierarchy**. They also tested the acquisition of head-internal RC (= gapless RCs) and discovered that it is acquired later than the head-external RC, due to the different mechanism than to linking the head and the gap.

They conclude that head-external RCs are not RCs but, rather, attributive clauses (Comrie, 2002). Comrie (2007) argues that East Asian RCs are connected to the head noun loosely based on pragmatic co-reference and thus are not subject to the noun phrase accessibility hierarchy. If this is correct, then subject advantage is not predicted, contra empirical evidence. Along these lines, Lee-Ellis (2011) takes a more nuanced approach, arguing that various factors (animacy, topicality of the head noun, proficiency, task effect) other than the subject vs. object asymmetry influence RC acquisition among heritage speakers. Kwon, Polinsky, and Kluender (2006) show that there is a processing advantage for both the subject gap in Korean RCs and subject pro-drop in Korean adjunct clauses. See Chapter 6 of this volume for more detailed discussion of RC acquisition.

Verbal inflection: honorific, tense, and aspect

The Korean honorifics system constitutes one of the most complex but indispensable areas of L2 Korean acquisition. The acquisition of honorifics does not only constitute the learning of a grammatical system but the negotiation of socio-pragmatic knowledge. Brown (2011) argues that L2 Korean speakers are significantly influenced by ideologies regarding what counts as being polite or respectful, as well as the differences between Korean and American modes of politeness and social norms. He also claims that as honorifics explicitly signal expected social roles and relationships, the use of honorifics plays a determining role in the process of identity negotiation. He found that L2 Korean speakers overgeneralized the application of honorific speech styles at the expense of non-honorific styles. On the other hand, they used referent honorifics significantly less than native speakers did, overusing proper names, instead of more natural titles and/or kinship terms. This can be explained by the **optionality** of referent honorifics and **frequency** of addressee honorifics. It is virtually impossible not to think of the social relationship between the speaker and the hearer when producing even a very simple sentence in Korean because polite or nonpolite speech style suffixes are obligatory.

Moving onto tense and aspect morphology, Kim and Lee (2006) confirmed the **aspect hypothesis** in L2 Korean. The aspect hypothesis (Andersen & Shirai, 1996; Bardovi-Harlig, 2000; Li & Shirai, 2000) states that the initial tense-aspect morphology in interlanguage redundantly marks the inherent lexical aspect of the verb. In Lee and Kim (2007), we conducted a picture description task and cloze test to investigate the acquisition of imperfective markers in L2 Korean in greater depth. We found that the progressive marker is acquired before the resultative marker due to L1 influence. In E. Lee (2018), I examined tense and aspect morphology in oral narrative data elicited through a film retelling task from L1 English L2 learners and heritage speakers of Korean, comparing the predictions of **discourse hypothesis** and aspect hypothesis. The discourse hypothesis (Bardovi-Harlig, 1998) states that interlanguage tense–aspect morphology initially marks the foreground and background distinction in the narrative. I examined heritage speakers' acquisition to discover whether an early age of acquisition, despite significant attrition later in life, leads to more native-like attainment of Korean. Unlike previous studies, the results suggested that discursive factors play a more significant role than lexical factors in determining the tense/aspect choice, and that temporal categories are interpreted indexically in the early stage of development. The results are consistent with the **concept-oriented approach** to language development, which assumes that it proceeds from basic universal concepts expressed using pragmatic resources (gesture, world knowledge, features in the immediate utterance context) to lexical means (content words) and finally to more complex morphosyntactic formal manifestations of a target language (Bardovi-Harlig, 2014). The pragmatic-lexical-grammatical cline model assumes that language acquisition begins with basic semantic and cognitive categories at the language-cognition interface, which are often presumed to be biologically determined and universal, to an increasingly complex grammatical system, which is subject to wide variations due to different lexical and phonological feature selection and assembly by different languages from the universal feature set. Assuming this model, the pragmatic/discursive feature of grounding is expected to have a stronger influence than lexical features at an earlier stage, which I found in the study. This result also showed that grammatical tense develops from an egocentric category to a perspective shift marker over time as its meaning becomes more abstract.

In sum, verbal inflection in Korean is highly complex, and it is easy to transfer simpler L1 English grammatical categories to L2 Korean. Using L1 cues to process L2 is known as transfer, and when it is inappropriate it is called **negative transfer**. To overcome L1 negative transfers, MacWhinney (2017) suggests that **decoupling** aligns L2 forms with analogous L1 forms, while promoting accessing words, meanings, and syntactic structures more directly without always relying on L1. Using a concept-oriented approach, instructional treatment can enhance the learner's awareness of common communicative and universal needs while drawing their attention to unfamiliar grammatical categories, such as honorifics.

Wh-questions

Korean is a *wh-in-situ* language, meaning that questions are formed without moving the wh-word to the front. In Korean, wh-words do not have quantificational force but act more like indefinites. For example, 누구 [nuku] means 'who' and 'someone'. A certain group of expressions, such as negative polarity items (NPIs) like 아무도 [amuto] 'anyone', universal and existential NPs, focused NP-[to/man] 'NP also/only,' and disjunctive NPs, are prohibited from c-commanding *wh*-phrases, as shown in (31) (Beck, 2006; Beck & Kim, 1997). This phenomenon is called the **intervention effect** (IE).

31 a. *아무도 무엇을 사지 않았니?
      Amwu-to mwues-ul sa-ci anh-ass-ni?
      'What did no one buy?'
  b. *누구나가 무엇을 샀니?
      Nwukwuna-ka mwues-ul s-ass-ni?
      'What did everyone buy?'

In this context, Korean objects are scrambled out to the front to avoid the IE.

32 무엇을 아무도 사지 않았니?
    Mwues-ul amwu-to sa-ci anh-ass-ni?
    'What didn't anyone buy?'

Song and Schwartz (2009) used a picture narration task and an elicited production task to examine three groups of language learners – L2 adults, L2 children, and L1 children – in the development of Korean *wh*-constructions with NPIs, focusing in particular on the L2 child– L2 adult comparison to test the **fundamental differential hypothesis**. This hypothesis claims that child L1 and adult L2 acquisitions are fundamentally different as the access to UG is absent or limited in the case of adult L2 acquisition. They point out that the constructions present poverty of stimulus context. Their results showed that some adult and child L2 had knowledge about *wh* and intervention and showed the same developmental pattern, which goes against fundamental differential hypothesis but lends support to the assertion that universal grammar (UG) constrains adult SLA.

In sum, the acquisition of *wh*-questions in Korean revealed that L2 speakers' grammatical representation is not fundamentally different from native speakers'. Together with the shared-structure hypothesis, this means that L2 Korean learners can overcome the remapping difficulty and utilize the universal structure motivated by semantic and pragmatic factors to achieve the desired competency outcome.

Conclusion

This chapter provided a functional approach to Korean grammar and surveyed recent KSL acquisition literature with regard to various hypotheses. In many cases, Korean makes more grammatical distinctions using overt morphology than English does, while the flexible word order and complex clauses add subtle discourse structural information. The interface hypothesis and the bottleneck hypothesis predict the learning difficulty of pragmatically laden inflectional morphology. Giving explicit instruction on relevant cues, negative evidence, as well as providing ample opportunity to observe positive evidence seems necessary to overcome the difficulty. At the same time, emphasizing the universal communicative needs of languages common to Korean and English will be conducive to speed up the acquisition process. L2 Korean learners can eventually achieve high competency in Korean, predicted by the concept-oriented language acquisition model and the shared structure hypothesis.

Notes

1 See the publications of Nick Ellis and Brian MacWhinney, among others.
2 The abbreviations in the glosses are as follows. Top: topic, Nom: nominative, Acc: accusative, Dat: dative, Loc: locative, Pl: plural, Cl: classifier, Neg: negation, Cau: causative, Pres: present, Past: past, Fut: future, Res: resultative, Rel: relative clause, Prog: progressive, Dec: declarative, Int: interrogative, Imp: imperative.
3 Korean has various types of passives, including lexical, morphological, and analytic (Oshima, 2006; Hong, 1990; Yeon, 2003). Morphological passives are formed using different allomorphs: *-i, -hi, -li,* and *-ki*. Lexical passives with *tanghata* 'suffer' and morphological passives imply that the subject is adversely affected by the described event (Oshima, 2006).
4 Assuming that postposition suffixes are case suffixes, the case-stacking phenomenon in Korean has been much discussed (Gerdts & Youn, 1988, 1990; Schütze, 1996; Lee, in press; Levin, 2016).
5 See Rappaport and Levin (2008) for the dative alternation. It is assumed that the double object construction implies that the recipient is a possessor and that the dative construction lacks such implication (Goldberg, 1992, 1995; Harley, 2002).
6 "Omitting" is intended to mean that an argument may not be overtly expressed, not that an argument slot is not saturated at all.
7 As pointed out by an anonymous reviewer, other island constraints cannot be easily explained away by information structural considerations and pragmatics.
    (i)   *김을 리가 [좋아하는 친구를] 만났다.
         *Kim-ul$_1$ Li-ka [t$_2$ t$_1$ cohaha-nun] chinkwu-lul$_2$]-ul mann-ass-ta.
         'Lee met the friend who likes Kim.'

Although relative clauses often mark backgrounded (not at issue) information, it is not always the case. In (ii), the relative clause is focused, providing an answer to a wh-question.
    (ii) A: 리가 어떤 친구를 만났니?
            Li-ka etten chinkwu-lul-ul mann-ass-ni
            'What kind of friend did Lee meet?'
       B: 리가 [김을 좋아하는 친구를] 만났어.
            Li-ka Kim-ul cohaha-nun chinkwu-lul-ul mann-ass-e.
            'Lee met the friend who likes Kim.'

8 Head-internal relative clauses have been argued to exist in English as well (Collins & Radford, 2015).
9 The priming effect refers to the phenomenon where an exposure to a prior stimulus affects the response to a subsequent stimulus without being consciously aware of it.

References

Ahn, H. (1991). *Light verbs and VP-movement, negation and clausal architecture in Korean and Japanese* [Ph.D. dissertation].University of Wisconsin, Madison.

Aissen, J. (2003). Differential object marking: Iconicity vs. economy. *Natural Language and Linguistic Theory, 21*, 435–483.

Andersen, R., & Shirai, Y. (1996). The primacy of aspect in first and second language acquisition: The pidgin-creole connection. In W. Ritchie & T. Bhatia (Eds.), *Handbook of second language acquisition* (pp. 527–570). Cambridge: Academic Press.

Bardovi-Harlig, K. (1998). Narrative structure and lexical aspect: Conspiring factors in second language acquisition of tense-aspect morphology. *Studies in Second Language Acquisition, 20*, 471–508.

Bardovi-Harlig, K. (2000). *Tense and aspect in second language acquisition: Form, meaning, and use*. Oxford: Blackwell.

Bardovi-Harlig, K. (2014). One functional approach to SLA: The concept-oriented approach. In B. VanPatten & J. Williams (Eds.), *Theories in second language acquisition*. Oxon and New York: Routledge.

Bates, E., & MacWhinney, B. (1989). Functionalism and the competition model. In E. Bates & B. MacWhinney (Eds.), *The crosslinguistic study of sentence processing* (pp. 3–76). Cambridge: Cambridge University Press.

Beck, S. (2006). Intervention effects follow from focus interpretation. *Natural Language Semantics, 14*, 1–56.

Beck, S., & Kim, S. (1997). On wh- and operator scope in Korean. *Journal of East Asian Linguistics, 6*, 339–384.

Bernolet, S., Hartsuiker, R., & Pickering, M. (2007). Shared syntactic representations in bilinguals: Evidence for the role of word-order repetition. *Journal of Experimental Psychology: Learning, Memory, and Cognition, 33*, 931–949.

Brown, L. (2011). *Korean honorifics and politeness in second language learning*. Amsterdam and Philadelphia: John Benjamins Publishing Company.

Burzio, L. (1986). *Italian syntax: A government-binding approach*. Berlin: Springer.

Chang, S. (1996). *Korean*. Amsterdam and Philadelphia: John Benjamins Publishing Company.

Chomsky, N. (1995). *The minimalist program*. Cambridge: The MIT Press.

Collins, C., & Radford, A. (2015). Gaps, ghosts and gapless relatives in spoken English. *Studia Linguistica, 69*, 191–235.

Comrie, B. (2002). Typology and language acquisition: The case of relative clauses. In A. Ramat (Ed.), *Typology and second language acquisition* (pp. 19–37). Berlin: Mouton de Gruyter.

Comrie, B. (2007). Acquisition of relative clauses in relation to language typology. *Studies in Second Language Acquisition, 29*, 301–309.

Ellis, N. (2006). Selective attention and transfer phenomena in L2 acquisition: Contingency, cue competition, salience, interference, overshadowing, blocking, and perceptual learning. *Applied Linguistics, 27*, 164–194.

Erteschik-Shir, N. (2007). *Information structure: The syntax-discourse interface*. Oxford: Oxford University Press.

Gerdts, D., & Youn, C. (1988). Korean psych constructions: Advancement or retreat? *Chicago Linguistics Society, 24*, 155–175.

Gerdts, D., & Youn, C. (1990). Non-nominative subjects in Korean. *Harvard Studies in Korean Linguistics*, III, 235–248.

Goldberg, A. (1992). The inherent semantics of argument structure: The case of the English ditransitive construction. *Cognitive Linguistics, 3*, 37–74.

Goldberg, A. (1995). *Constructions: A construction grammar approach to argument structure*. Chicago: The University of Chicago Press.

Gundel, J., Nancy Hedeberg, N., & Zacharski, R. (1993). Cognitive status and the form of referring expressions in discourse. *Language, 69*, 274–307.

Han, N. (2006). *Korean zero pronouns: Analysis and resolution* [Ph.D. dissertation]. University of Pennsylvania.

Harley, H. (2002). Possession and the double object construction. *Linguistic Variation Yearbook*, *2*, 31–70.
Hartsuiker, R., & Bernolet, S. (2017). The development of shared syntax in second language learning. *Bilingualism: Language and Cognition*, *20*, 219–234.
Heim, I., & Kratzer, A. (1998). *Semantics in generative grammar*. Oxford: Blackwell.
Hong, K. (1990). *Korean syntax and universal grammar* [Ph.D. dissertation]. Harvard University.
Hwang, H., Shin, J., & Hartsuiker, R. (2018). Late bilinguals share syntax unsparingly between L1 and L2: Evidence from crosslinguistically similar and different constructions. *Language Learning*, *68*, 177–205.
Hwang, S., & Lardiere, D. (2013). Plural-marking in L2 Korean: A feature-based approach. *Second Language Research*, *29*, 57–86.
Jackendoff, R. (2002). *Foundations of language*. Oxford: Oxford University Press.
Jeon, K., & Kim, H. (2007). Development of relativization in Korean as a foreign language: The noun phrase accessibility hierarchy in head-internal and head-external relative clauses. *Studies in Second Language Acquisition*, *29*, 253–276.
Kantola, L., & van Gompel, R. (2011). Between- and within-language priming is the same: Evidence for shared bilingual syntactic representations. *Memory and Cognition*, *39*, 276- 290.
Keenan, E., & Comrie, B. (1977). Noun phrase accessibility and universal grammar. *Linguistic Inquiry*, *8*, 63–99.
Kim, H., & Lee, E. (2006). The development of tense and aspect morphology in L2 Korean. In J. Song (Ed.), *Frontiers of Korean language acquisition* (pp. 91–126). London: The Saffron Book, Eastern Art Publishing.
Kim, K., O'Grady, W., & Schwartz, B. (2018). Case in heritage Korean. *Linguistic Approaches to Bilingualism*, *8*, 252–282.
Kwon, S., Polinsky, M., & Kluender, R. (2006). Subject preference in Korean. In *Proceedings of the 25th West Coast Conference on Formal Linguistics* (pp. 1–14). Somerville: Cascadilla Press.
Kwon, S., & Zribi-Hertz, A. (2007). Differential function marking, case, and information structure: Evidence from Korean. *Language*, *84*, 258–299.
Laleko, O., & Polinsky, M. (2016). Between syntax and discourse: Topic and case marking in heritage speakers and L2 learners of Japanese and Korean. *Linguistic Approaches to Bilingualism*, *6*, 396–439.
Lee, E. (2018). L2 and heritage Korean tense morphology in discourse: Interplay between lexical and discursive meaning. *Heritage Language Journal*, *15*, 173–202.
Lee, E. (2019). *Korean syntax and semantics*. Cambridge: Cambridge University Press.
Lee, E. (2020). The universal topic prominence stage hypothesis and L1 transfer: A study of L2 Korean written narratives by L1 English and L1 Chinese speakers. *Linguistic Approach to Bilingualism*, *10*, 184–215.
Lee, E. (in press). Case (stacking) in Korean: Argument structure or information structure? In J. Whitman & S. Cho (Eds.), *Handbook of Korean linguistics*. Cambridge: Cambridge University Press.
Lee, E., & Kim, H. (2007). On cross-linguistic variations in imperfective aspect: The case of L2 Korean. *Language Learning*, *57*, 651–685.
Lee, H. (2006). Parallel optimization in case systems: Evidence from case ellipsis in Korean. *Journal of East Asian Linguistics*, *15*, 69–96.
Lee, T. (2011). Grammatical knowledge of Korean heritage speakers: Early vs. late bilinguals. *Linguistic Approaches to Bilingualism*, *1*, 149–174.
Lee-Ellis, S. (2011). The elicited production of Korean relative clauses by heritage speakers. *Studies in Second Language Acquisition*, *33*, 57–89.
Levin, T. (2016). Successive-cyclic case assignment: Korean nominative-nominative case- stacking. *Natural Language and Linguistic Theory*, *35*, 447–498.
Li, C., & Thompson, S. (1976). Subject and topic: A new typology of language. In C. Li (Ed.), *Subject and topic* (pp. 458–489). Cambridge: Academic Press.
Li, P., & Shirai, Y. (2000). *The acquisition of lexical and grammatical aspect*. Berlin: Mouton de Gruyter.
MacWhinney, B. (2017). Entrenchment in second-language learning. In H.-J. Schmid (Ed.), *Entrenchment and the psychology of language learning: How we reorganize and adapt linguistic knowledge* (pp. 343–366). Berlin: Mouton de Gruyter.
Miyagawa, S. (1989). *Syntax and semantics: Structure and case marking in Japanese*. Cambridge: Academic Press.
Nichols, J. (1986). Head-marking and dependent-marking grammar. *Language*, *62*, 56–119.
O'Grady, W., Lee, M., & Choo, M. (2003). A subject-object asymmetry in the acquisition of relative clauses in Korean as a second language. *Studies in Second Language Acquisition*, *25*, 433–448.

Oshima, D. (2006). Adversity and Korean/Japanese passives: Constructional analogy. *Journal of East Asian Linguistics, 15*, 137–166.

Perlmutter, D. (1978). Impersonal passives and the unaccusative hypothesis. In *Proceedings from the 4th regional meeting of the Berkeley Linguistic Society* (pp. 157–189). Berkeley: UC Berkeley.

Rappaport Hovav, M., & Levin, B. (2008). The English dative alternation: The case for verb sensitivity. *Journal of Linguistics, 44*, 129–167.

Schütze, C. (1996). Korean "case stacking" isn't: Unifying noncase uses of case particles. In K. Kusumoto (Ed.), *North East Linguistic Society (NELS)* (Vol. 26, pp. 351–365). Amherst: GLSA.

Shin, J., & Christianson, K. (2009). Syntactic processing in Korean-English bilingual production: Evidence from cross-linguistic structural priming. *Cognition, 112*, 175–180.

Slavakova, R. (2016). *Second language acquisition*. Oxford: Oxford University Press.

Song, H., & Schwartz, B. (2009). Testing the fundamental difference hypothesis: L2 adult, L2 child, and L1 child comparisons in the acquisition of Korean wh-constructions with negative polarity items. *Studies in Second Language Acquisition, 31*, 323–361.

Sorace, A. (2011). Pinning down the concept of "interface" in bilingualism. *Linguistic Approaches to Bilingualism, 1*, 1–33.

Yeon, J. (2003). *Korean grammatical constructions: Their form and meaning* (Vol. 1). Saffron Korean Linguistics Series. London: Saffron Books.

6
RELATIVE CLAUSES IN KOREAN AS A SECOND LANGUAGE
Old and new findings*

William O'Grady and Chae-Eun Kim

Introduction

The last three decades have seen a surge of Korean language programs in America and around the world. This development, unparalleled in the recent history of second language pedagogy, has been accompanied by the need to create an infrastructure to support every aspect of teaching – from textbooks to professional conferences to training programs for teachers. An important part of this infrastructure consists of research that focuses on the acquisition of Korean as a second language by native speakers of European languages, especially English.

It is hard to imagine two languages that are typologically more distinct than English and Korean. Korean has an agglutinating morphology, case marking for its arguments, a default SOV order that allows for both scrambling and argument drop, and a phonology that includes unusual contrasts among its stops, affricates and fricatives. English has none of these things.

As noted by O'Grady and Choi (2015), these differences make Korean an almost ideal object of study for research on second language acquisition (SLA). Since there are relatively few opportunities for direct or indirect similarity-motivated transfer from English to Korean, parallels in the way in which the two languages are acquired could provide valuable clues about the internal mechanisms and forces that drive second language learning. Thanks to the current availability of a substantial number of learners of Korean as a second language, this line of inquiry can now be pursued in a way that would previously not have been practical.

A pattern that has proven particularly relevant to comparative studies of SLA involves relative clauses (RCs), which manifest strikingly different morphosyntactic properties in Korean and English, as the following examples help show.[1]

1   Korean:
    [$_{RC}$ Mary-ka   ecey   _ manna-n]   namca
       Mary-NOM   yesterday _ meet-PST.ADN   man
    'the man Mary met yesterday'

2   English:
    the man [$_{RC}$ that/who Mary met _ yesterday]

As illustrated here, Korean RCs differ from their English counterparts in at least three ways: they occur to the left rather than the right of the noun they modify, their internal order is verb-final rather than verb-medial, and they rely on case rather than word order to distinguish between subject and direct object NPs.

It has long been known that the difficulty of particular relative clause patterns reflects the well-known relational hierarchy first put forward by Keenan and Comrie (1977) and presented here in the modified format proposed by J. Hawkins (1999, p. 253, 2004, p. 177).

3   The relational hierarchy
      Subject > Direct Object > Indirect Object/Oblique

This hierarchy, which originated as a generalization about linguistic typology, has come to play a major role in the study of language acquisition, including second language acquisition. Data from L2 Korean has been important to this endeavor, as we will see shortly.

We will focus here on two studies of the acquisition of Korean relative clauses (RCs) by adult second language learners. The first study, to be discussed in Sections 2 and 3, examines the relevance of Korean to an understanding of why subject RCs appear to be preferred over direct object RCs, both by native speakers and by second language learners, in a broad range of languages. Sections 4 and 5 focus on the much less studied question of how learners deal with indirect object and oblique RCs. We consider the joint implications of the findings from these two studies in section 6.

Subject and direct object relative clauses

One of the more robust findings in the field of second language syntax is that English subject relative clauses such as (4) are easier for second language learners to produce and understand than are direct object relatives such as (5) – a fact that has been well documented thanks to a series of pioneering studies (e.g., Gass, 1979; Eckman, Bell, & Nelson, 1988; Doughty, 1991; Wolfe-Quintero, 1992; Hamilton, 1994, 1995; Sadighi, 1994; Izumi, 2003).

4   Subject relative clause:
      the girl [that _ helped the boy]

5   Direct object relative clause:
      the girl [that the boy helped _]

This finding raises an obvious question: What makes direct object relative clauses more difficult than their subject counterparts?

One possibility, put forward by Tarallo and Myhill (1983) and R. Hawkins (1989), is that the difficulty of relative clauses can be predicted by the linear distance between the "filler" (the NP modified by the RC) and the gap created by the relativization operation.

6   a.   Subject relative clause:
          the man [that _ likes the woman]
          |_____|
          distance between the filler and the gap = 1 word

b. Direct object relative clause:
   the man [that the woman likes _]
   distance between the filler and the gap = 4 words

There are other ways to calculate the effect of distance. Instead of simply counting the number of words that occur between the filler and the gap, Gibson (1998) tracks the number of intervening words that have 'discourse referents' – e.g., nouns and verbs, but not determiners. Moreover, Friedmann, Belletti, and Rizzi (2009) suggest that distance effects are compounded when the gap is separated from the filler NP by a phrase with the same structural and semantic properties. This happens in (6b), where an animate NP (*the woman*) intervenes between the gap and the head of the relative clause (the animate NP *the man*). Regardless of the calculus, however, the end result is the same: the distance between filler and gap in English is greater in direct object RCs than in their subject counterparts.

A quite different hypothesis about the preference for subject RCs, put forward by Diessel and Tomasello (2005), focuses on canonical word order. The key insight underlying this proposal is that subject relative clauses bear a strong resemblance to the canonical SVO pattern of English, in which the subject occurs to the left of a verb (*likes* in the following example) and the direct object to its right. In contrast, in the more difficult direct object pattern, the positioning of the two NPs does not exhibit this alignment, thereby complicating the structure's interpretation.

7 a. Subject relative clause:
      the man that [_ likes the woman]
                    S   V   O
   b. Direct object relative clause:
      the man that [the woman likes _]
                    O   S   V

Although the linear distance hypothesis and the canonical word order hypothesis were initially proposed for English, they are intended as general explanations – valid in all languages – for why certain types of relative clauses are more difficult to learn and use than others. They can and should therefore be tested in as many languages as possible, especially languages whose relative clauses differ from those of English in crucial ways. Korean is a case in point for two reasons.

First, the distance between the filler and the gap in Korean relative clauses is longer in subject RCs than in direct object RCs – the reverse of what we find in English.

8 a. Subject relative clause:
      여자를 좋아하는 남자
      [_ **yeca-lul   cohaha-nun]** namca
       _ woman-Acc   like-Prs.Adn   man
      distance between the gap and the filler = 2 words
   b. Direct object relative clause:
      여자가 좋아하는 남자
      [**yeca-ka   _   cohaha-nun]** namca
       woman-Nom _   like-Prs.Adn   man
      distance between the gap and the filler = 1 word

If the distance hypothesis is correct, learners of Korean as a second language should be better at interpreting direct object RCs than subject RCs.

A second difference relates to canonical word order. Whereas English subject RCs differ from object RCs in manifesting a word order that resembles the language's canonical SVO pattern, there is no such isomorphism in Korean. Neither subject RCs nor direct object RCs manifest the canonical SOV word order of that language.

9   a.   Subject relative clause:
여자를 좋아하는 남자
[_ **yeca-lul**   **cohaha-nun**]   namca
_ woman-Acc love-Prs.Adn   man
     O   V   S

    b.   Direct object relative clause:
여자가 좋아하는 남자
[**yeca-ka**   _ **cohaha-nun**]   namca
woman-Nom _ love-Prs.Adn   man
   S   V   O

The canonical word order hypothesis therefore does not predict a subject advantage for Korean.

An experiment by O'Grady, Lee, and Choo (2003) provided a way to test and evaluate the validity of the linear order hypothesis and the canonical word order hypothesis for the acquisition of Korean as a second language.

A first experiment

Participants

A total of 53 native English speakers participated in the experiment – 25 second-semester students and 28 fourth-semester students at two separate American universities. All the participants were non-heritage learners in that they grew up in homes where Korean was not spoken. Moreover, the second-semester participants had been exposed to relative clauses only a week before the experiment, leaving them with little time to have been affected by input or instruction.

Materials and method

The experiment focuses on the contrast been the subject and direct RC patterns exemplified next.

10 a.   Subject relative clause:
여자를 좋아하는 남자
[_ **yeca-lul**   **cohaha-nun**]   namca
_ woman-Acc love-Prs.Adn   man
'the man who loves the woman'

    b.   Direct object relative clause:
여자가 좋아하는 남자
[**yeca-ka**   _ **cohaha-nun**]   namca
woman-Nom _ love-Prs.Adn man
'the man who the woman loves'

The test items consisted of five subject relative clauses and five direct object relative clauses, all randomly interspersed.

Participants heard the test items one by one and were instructed to circle the right person from among the choices illustrated in an accompanying figure designed specifically for that test item. The choices for the test items in (10) are illustrated in Figure 6.1. In this example, the subject RC in (10a) picks out the man in the picture on the upper right, whereas the direct object RC in (10b) describes the man in the picture on the bottom.

Results

The participants did far better on subject RCs than on direct object RCs, with scores of 73.2% correct on the former pattern, compared to only 22.6% for the latter (F $(1,52) = 30.59$, p = .0001).[2] Comparable results were subsequently reported for comprehension by Kim (2005) and for production by Jeon and Kim (2007).

Equally revealing is an asymmetry in reversal errors (i.e., the number of times a pattern of one type was misanalyzed as a pattern of the other type): direct object RCs were misunderstood as subject RCs 115 times, while subject RCs were misanalyzed as direct objects RCs only 26 times – a clear indication that subject relative clauses are favored. The performance of individual participants also revealed a strong preference for subject relative clauses: 34 of the 53 learners responded correctly to at least four of the five subject RCs in the experiment, but only ten did that well on direct object RCs.

Figure 6.1 Sample pictures from the O'Grady et al. study

Table 6.1 Comprehension scores (number of subjects = 53)

	Correct	Reversals	Other
Subject RCs	194 (73.2%)	26 (9.8%)	45 (17%)
Direct Object. RCs	60 (22.6%)	115 (43.4%)	90 (34%)

```
        S
       / \
     Subj  VP
          / \
         V  Dir Obj
```

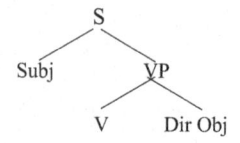

Figure 6.2 The structural prominence of subjects and direct objects

Discussion

Overall, then, it seems clear that learners of Korean as a second language have a strong preference for subject RCs over direct object RCs, just as learners of English do, despite very substantial differences between the two languages with respect to the structure of their relative clauses. This is not the result predicted by either the linear distance hypothesis or the canonical word order hypothesis: as noted previously, the first hypothesis predicts that direct object RCs should be easier than subject RCs in Korean, and the second hypothesis predicts no difference between the two relative clause types. How, then, can we explain the very strong preference for subject RCs in Korean?[3]

One possibility, put forward by O'Grady et al. (2003) is that relativization favors the more structurally prominent argument in a clause – that is, as illustrated in Figure 6.2, the NP that occurs in the higher position in syntactic structure, namely, the subject.

This proposal fits well with the results obtained from a wide range of languages, all of which show a preference for subject relative clauses over their direct object counterparts. However, a largely unexplored issue places this hypothesis in jeopardy. As we will see next, the key data also comes from the acquisition of Korean as a second language.

Indirect object and oblique relative clauses

For many years and for many languages, work on the L2 acquisition of relative clauses has focused on subject and direct object RCs, essentially ignoring patterns in which relativization targets the indirect object or an oblique argument, as in the following examples.

11 a. Sentence containing an indirect object:
        A girl gave a bag to **the boy**.
    b. Indirect object RC:
        the boy [that a girl gave a bag to _]

12 a. Sentence containing an oblique RC:
        The boy put the book on **a box**.
    b. Oblique RC:
        the box [that the boy put a book on _]

According to traditional assumptions about English phrase structure, subjects are higher than direct objects, which in turn are higher than indirect objects and obliques (e.g., Hawkins, J., 2004, p. 178), as illustrated in the following tree structure, based loosely on Larson (1988).

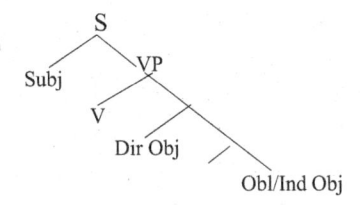

Figure 6.3 The place of indirect objects and obliques in syntactic structure (English)

The fact that English indirect objects and obliques occupy a lower position in syntactic structure than subjects and direct objects predicts that they should also be more difficult. Kim and O'Grady (2016) report just such a result for child learners of English as a first language, and Chae-Eun Kim (pers. comm.) has found a similar asymmetry for adult learners of English as a second language. These are promising results, but SOV languages such as Korean present a different picture. Consider in this regard the following two sentences:

13 Sentence containing an indirect object:
    소녀가 소년에게 가방을 주었다.
    Sonye-ka **sonyen-eykey** kapang-ul cwu-ess-ta.
    girl-Nom boy-Dat bag-Acc give-Pst-SE
    'The girl gave a bag to the boy.'

14 Sentence containing an oblique argument:
    소년이 상자에 책을 놓았다.
    Sonyen-i **sangca-ey** chayk-ul noh-ass-ta.
    boy-Nom box-Loc book-Acc put-Pst-SE
    'The boy put the book on the box.'

As illustrated next, the most widely adopted syntactic structure for these patterns in SOV languages such as Korean places the indirect object and the oblique in a higher position than the direct object – the reverse of what has been proposed for English (e.g., Aoshima, Phillips, & Weinberg, 2004, p. 26 and the references cited there).

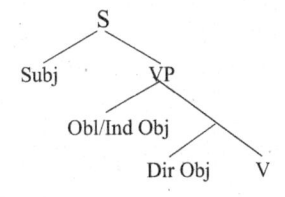

Figure 6.4 The place of indirect objects and obliques in syntactic structure (Korean)

All other things being equal, a theory of RC learning based on structural prominence therefore makes the following two predictions for a language like Korean:

- Since the subject is the most structurally prominent NP in a sentence, subject RCs should be easier than all other RC types.
- Based on their structural position, indirect object and oblique RCs should be easier than direct object RCs.

The first prediction aligns well with the results from our earlier experiment and from other experiments that have examined that contrast. In contrast, the second prediction projects a major difference in RC preferences for L2 learners of SVO languages versus learners of SOV languages. In particular, based on structural prominence, direct object RCs should be easier than indirect object and oblique RCs in SVO languages, but the reverse should be true in SOV languages.

Once again, Korean is an ideal language to test this hypothesis, since (a) it allows relativization of both indirect objects and obliques (unlike many languages; see Keenan & Comrie, 1977), and (b) thanks to its SOV word order, it places indirect objects and obliques in a higher position in syntactic structure than direct objects. We turn next to an experiment that we conducted to test the two predictions outlined earlier.

A second experiment

Participants

Twenty-six learners of Korean as a second language (mean age = 22.23) participated in the KSL portion of the study. All were native speakers of English who were enrolled either in a Korean language program at a U.S. university or were studying at a university in Korea as international students, where their length of residence ranged from six months to two years.

A Korean C-test consisting of 125 items (Lee-Ellis, 2011) was used to divide the participants into a higher-proficiency group consisting of ten males and three females (mean score = 169.07) and a lower-proficiency group of three males and ten females (mean score = 49.69). A control group of 22 adult native speakers of Korean (14 female and 8 male; mean age = 21.5) also participated in the experiment.

Materials and method/procedure

RCs were elicited with the help of a production task based on the one employed in various forms by Cho (1999), Goodluck and Stojanovic (1996), Hsu, Hermon, and Zukowski (2009), Zukowski (2009) and Kim and O'Grady (2016). Our decision to employ an elicited production task rather than a comprehension task was motivated by the greater demands it places on the participants, who have to design and build relative clauses from scratch. This opens the door for the emergence of informative morphosyntactic errors and avoidance strategies that would not otherwise be evident.

Four types of RC patterns were elicited, instantiating a contrast between subject and indirect object RCs and a contrast between direct object and oblique RCs, as illustrated next.

15 a. Subject RC:
        소녀에게 가방을 주는 소년
        [_   sonye-eykey   kapang-ul   cwu-nun]   sonyen
          _   girl-Dat   bag-Acc   give-Adn.Prs boy
        'the boy that is giving a bag to the girl'
    b. Indirect object RC:
        소녀가 가방을 주는 소년
        [sonye-ka   _   kapang-ul   cwu-nun]   sonyen
        girl-Nom   _   bag-Acc   give-Adn.Prs boy
        'the boy that the girl is giving a bag to _'

16 a. Direct object RC:
        소년이 상자에 놓는 책
        [sonyen-i sangca-ey   _   noh-nun]   chayk
        boy-Nom   box-on   _   put-Adn.Prs book
        'the book that the boy is putting _ on the box'
    b. Oblique RC:
        소년이 책을 놓는 상자
        [sonyen-i _   chayk-ul   noh-nun]   sangca
        boy-Nom   _   book-Acc   put-Adn.Prs box
        'the box that the boy is putting the book on _'

In creating the test items, we were careful to select words that were frequently used in textbooks and in instructional settings to ensure their familiarity even to members of the lower-proficiency group. In addition, care was taken to ensure that production of the test items required attention to morphosyntactic details. In the first set of test items, both the subjects and the indirect objects had animate referents that could, in principle, have corresponded to either an agent or a recipient; case marking and/or word order was required to express their actual role in the sentence. Similarly, in the second set of test items, both the direct objects and the obliques were inanimate and therefore capable of functioning as either a patient or a location – depending on morphosyntactic cues.

All participants were tested individually in a quiet setting, first on subject and indirect object relative clauses and then a week later on direct object and oblique relative clauses.[4] Half of the participants in the first experiment were tested on the subject RCs first, and the other half on the indirect object RCs first. Items within each block were randomized. The entire task took approximately 30 minutes to finish.

Testing on the direct object and oblique RCs followed a similar procedure, with half the participants tested on randomly ordered direct object RC items first and the other half on oblique RC items first. At the end of this session, the participants filled out a background information questionnaire and were given a C-test to measure their proficiency. The entire session lasted approximately 40 minutes.

At the beginning of the experiment, the participants heard the following instructions:

> After listening to what [the woman in the recording] says, you will hear a beep sound and see an arrow mark. I would like you to describe the person (or thing) that has the arrow mark. Can you do it?

The following is an illustration of the protocol used to elicit subject relative clauses.

Indirect objects were elicited in a parallel way, except that in this case, an arrow (with an accompanying beep) appeared over the boy on the right in the second set of pictures.

Step 1: Recorded description of the first set of pictures: "In the first picture, a boy is giving a bag to a girl. In the second picture, a girl is giving a bag to a boy".

Step 2: An arrow appears over the boy in the picture on the left.

Figure 6.5 Sample protocol used to elicit a subject RC. Targeted response: "the boy [that _ is giving a bag to the girl]." (In Korean: [_ sonye-eykey kapang-ul cwu-nun] sonyen)

The materials used to elicit direct object RCs are exemplified in Figure 6.7.

The elicitation of oblique RCs proceeded in a parallel way, except that this time the arrow picked out one of the boxes, as illustrated in Figure 6.8.

Before proceeding, it is important to note an important difference between comprehension tasks and production tasks with respect to the type of information they can be expected to yield in the case of relative clauses. Comprehension tasks, such as the one discussed in Section

Step 1: Recorded description of the first set of pictures: "In the first picture, a boy is giving a bag to a girl. In the second picture, a girl is giving a bag to a boy".

Step 2: An arrow appears over the boy in the picture on the left.

Figure 6.6 Sample protocol used to elicit an indirect object RC. Targeted response: "the boy [that the girl is giving a bag to _]." (In Korean: [sonye-ka _ kapang-ul cwu-nun] sonyen)

3, typically produce a clear-cut result – a test item is either correctly understood or not. In contrast, the data from RC production tasks commonly include signs of avoidance strategies, which are reflected in a reluctance to produce particular patterns and/or their replacement by other constructions. Although avoidance cannot be interpreted as a failure to acquire a particular pattern, it does offer clues about the pattern's degree of difficulty. This is precisely the sort of information our experiment is designed to uncover.

Step 1: Recorded description of the first set of pictures: "In the first picture, a boy is putting a book on a box. In the second picture, a girl is putting a book on a box".

Step 2: An arrow indicates the book in the picture on the left, to which the experimenter also points.

Figure 6.7 Sample protocol used to elicit a direct object RC. Targeted response: "the book [that the boy put _ on a box]." (In Korean: [sonyen-i sangca-ey _ noh-nun] chayk)

Results

Data were recorded in Audacity, transcribed by one of the authors, and entered onto a spreadsheet for coding and analysis. If more than one answer was given for a particular test item, only the first one was considered. In scoring our results, we counted a pattern as correct if its word order and case marking were consistent with the targeted RC pattern, regardless of possible errors in the verbal morphology.

Step 1: Recorded description of the first set of pictures: "In the first picture, a boy is putting a book on a box. In the second picture, a girl is putting a book on a box".

Step 2: An arrow indicates the book in the picture on the left, to which the experimenter also points.

Figure 6.8 Sample protocol used to elicit an oblique RC. Targeted response: "the box [that the boy put a book on _]." (In Korean: [sonyen-i _ chayk-ul noh-nun] sangca)

Subject and indirect object RCs

Table 6.2 summarizes our results for the conditions that targeted subject and indirect objects RCs.

What is particularly striking here is the huge asymmetry in the production of the two RC types in the conditions designed to elicit them. Whereas all three groups were highly successful on the test items that elicited subject RCs, the second language learners produced no indirect

Table 6.2 Percentage of target-like responses in the subject and indirect object RC conditions

Group	Subject RCs	Indirect object RCs
Lower proficiency	93.85%	0%
Higher proficiency	100.00%	0%
Native speakers	100.00%	7.6%

object RCs at all. Even more surprising, native speakers also showed a great reluctance to produce patterns of this type. This finding obviously does not indicate that adult native speakers of Korean have not acquired indirect object RCs. Nor do we believe that it is an artifact of our experimental design; as we will see shortly, an avoidance of indirect object RCs is also characteristic of naturalistic speech.

The most common strategy for avoiding indirect object RCs (75.38% for the lower-proficiency group, 89.2% for the higher-proficiency group, and 75.3% for the native speakers) involved modification of the lexical items in the experimenter's lead-in sentences in ways that allowed the production of a subject RC instead of an indirect object RC. This strategy is illustrated in the following example, in which the verb *cwu-ta* 'give' is replaced by *pat-ta* 'receive' so that the relativized element (*sonyen* 'boy') can be encoded as a subject rather than an indirect object.

17 a. Targeted indirect object RC
   소녀가 가방을 주는 소년
   [sonye-ka _ kapang-ul cwu-nun] sonyen
   girl-Nom _ bag-Acc give-Asp-Adn.Prs boy
   'the boy that the girl is giving a bag to _'
  b. Actual response (subject RC)
   가방을 받고 있는 소년
   [_ kapang-ul pat-koiss-nun] sonyen
   _ bag-Acc receive-Asp-Adn.Prs boy
   'the boy that _ is receiving a bag'

In sum, as predicted, subject RCs are favored over their indirect object counterparts – by a very wide margin. Native speakers and second language learners produce subject RCs in virtually all situations calling for them and go to considerable lengths, through the use of lexical substitution, to avoid use of indirect object RCs. Crucially, the asymmetry seems to be linked entirely to RC type, as the pictures and discourse contexts used to elicit the two patterns were identical in every respect.

Direct object and oblique RCs

Table 6.3 summarizes our results for the contrast between direct object and oblique RCs.

All three groups of participants produced targeted direct object RCs at a significantly higher rate than oblique RCs. In the case of both patterns, the most common avoidance strategy (43.08% for direct object RCs and 76.93% for oblique RCs) involved the production of a structure other than a relative clause. For example:

Table 6.3 Percentage of target-like responses in the direct object and oblique RC conditions

Group	Direct Object RCs	Oblique RCs	
Lower proficiency	44.61%	6.15%	$t(12) = 5.57, p < .000$
Higher proficiency	84.62%	46.15%	$t(12) = 5, p < .000$
Native speakers	83.7%	70.0%	$t(21) = 2.854, p = .009$

Table 6.4 Percentage of target-like responses in all four conditions

Group	Subject RCs	Direct Object RCs	Ind. Object RCs	Oblique RCs
L-P KSL learners	93.85%	44.61%	0%	6.15%
H-P KSL learners	100%	84.62%	0%	46.15%
Native speakers	100%	83.7%	7.6%	70%

18 a. Targetted oblique RC:
  소년이 책을 놓는 상자
  [sonyen-i _ chayk-ul noh-nun] sangca
  boy-NOM _ book-ACC put-ADN.PST box
  'the box that the boy is putting the book on _'

    b. Actual response (declarative sentence):
  소년이 상자에 책을 놓고 있어요.
  Sonyen-i sangca-ey chayk-ul noh-koiss-eyo
  boy-NOM box-on book-ACC put-ASP-SE
  'The boy is putting a book on the box.'

Discussion

Table 6.4 summarizes the success rates of the participants on the four types of relative clauses that were elicited in the production task

A key finding here lies in the better performance of all three groups of participants on direct object RCs compared to indirect object and oblique RCs. This result offers a direct challenge to theories of relative clause difficulty based on structural prominence. Although both indirect objects and obliques occupy higher positions in Korean syntactic structure (see Figure 6.4), our results show substantially higher success on direct object relative clauses. Once again, the study of Korean has revealed a finding of importance to the understanding of second language acquisition in general: structural prominence does not determine the difficulty of Korean relative clauses for second language learners.

Concluding remarks

The results from our two studies, separated by a span of almost 20 years, point toward three asymmetries in the acquisition and use of relative clauses by KSL learners.

19 a. subject > direct object
    b. subject > indirect object
    c. direct object > indirect object/oblique

The interest of these findings stems in large part from the light they shed on deeper theoretical issues pertaining both to the nature of relative clauses and the challenges associated with second language acquisition.

The first study (O'Grady et al., 2003), reported in Section 3, demonstrates that neither linear distance nor canonical word order can explain the degree of difficulty associated with different types of Korean relative clauses. The second and newer study, summarized in Section 5, undermines a third major hypothesis, refuting the idea that a relative clause's degree of difficulty can be explained by reference to structural prominence. These findings emphasize the value and importance of comparative studies of second language acquisition, making it possible to tease apart and test hypotheses that would otherwise be confounded. But they also raise an obvious question: why are some relative clauses more difficult than others for learners of Korean as a second language?

One explanation worth pursuing involves the amount of exposure learners receive to different types of relative clause patterns. The contrasts here are suggestive. For example, Kang (2014, p. 18) has uncovered a frequency continuum for Korean relative clauses that exactly mirrors the relational hierarchy; see Table 6.5. (Kang's data comes from newspaper stories that make up one part of the Sejong Corpus.)

We have found similar asymmetries in the Child Language Data Exchange System (CHILDES) database for maternal speech to four monolingual children aged 2–6 who were learning Korean as a first language; see Table 6.6. Not surprisingly, as illustrated in Table 6.7, the same asymmetry shows up in the speech of four Korean children whose interaction with caregivers is documented in the CHILDES database. Huh (2015, p. 858) reports similar contrasts in speech samples from adult learners of Korean as a second language.

These findings appear to make sense: learners acquire what they hear, and their speech resembles the input they receive. However, it is important to note in closing that the existence

Table 6.5 Frequency of relative clause types in a portion of the Sejong corpus

Relative clause type	Number of instances
Subject	521
Direct object	136
Indirect object/Oblique	58

Table 6.6 Frequency of relative clause types in Korean maternal speech

Relative clause type	Number of instances
Subject	483
Direct object	205
Indirect object/Oblique	80

Table 6.7 Frequency of relative clause types in the speech of four children aged 2–6

Relative clause type	Number of instances
Subject	28
Direct object	7
Indirect object/Oblique	0

of frequency contrasts itself raises a new and perhaps more difficult question: why are some relative clause patterns more commonly used than others? The answer, for now at least, is that we do not yet know, although a variety of possibilities have been suggested (for a review, see Kim & O'Grady, 2016).

The research program required to resolve this issue will, of necessity, require attention to a broad sampling of patterns in a varied set of languages as well as the study of different populations of speakers, ranging from child first language learners to adult second language learners. Nonetheless, there is every reason to believe that the study of Korean and of its acquisition by second language learners will have an important role to play in the investigation of these matters.

Notes

* We thank Miho Choo, Gyu-Ho Shin, an anonymous reviewer and the editors for their assistance and advice.
1 We use the following abbreviations: A$_{DN}$ = adnominal, P$_{RS}$ = present, P$_{ST}$ = past, N$_{OM}$ = nominative, A$_{CC}$ = accusative, D$_{AT}$ = dative, SE = sentence ender.
2 Because there was no significant difference in the performance of the second-semester and fourth-semester students, their scores were collapsed.
3 We focus here exclusively on relative clauses in second language acquisition. However, the question is actually considerably broader since a similar preference arises in the acquisition of Korean as a first language and in the processing of relative clauses by adult native speakers (e.g., Kwon, Polinsky, & Kluender, 2006; Kwon, Lee, Gordon, & Kluender, 2010; Kim & O'Grady, 2016).
4 One member of the native speaker control group who participated in the first experiment was absent from the second experiment.

References

Aoshima, S., Phillips, C., & Weinberg, A. (2004). Processing filler-gap dependencies in a head-final language. *Journal of Memory and Language, 51*, 23–54.
Cho, S. (1999). *The acquisition of relative clauses: Experimental studies on Korean* [Ph.D. dissertation]. Department of Linguistics, University of Hawaii at Manoa.
Diessel, H., & Tomasello, M. (2005). A new look at the acquisition of relative clauses. *Language, 81*, 1–25.
Doughty, C. (1991). Second language instruction does make a difference. *Studies in Second Language Acquisitio, 13*, 431–469.
Eckman, F., Bell, L., & Nelson, D. (1988). On the generalization of relative clause instruction in the acquisition of English as a second language. *Applied Linguistics, 9*, 1–20.
Friedmann, N., Belletti, A., & Rizzi, L. (2009). Relativized relatives: Types of intervention in the acquisition of A-bar dependencies. *Lingua, 119*, 67–88.
Gass, S. (1979). Language transfer and universal grammatical relations. *Language Learning, 29*, 327–344.
Gibson, E. (1998). Linguistics complexity: Locality of syntactic dependencies. *Cognition, 69*, 1–76.
Goodluck, H., & Stojanovic, D. (1996). The structure and acquisition of relative clauses in Serbo-Croatian. *Language Acquisition, 5*, 285–315.
Hamilton, R. (1994). Is implicational generalization unidirectional and maximal? Evidence from relativization instruction in a second language. *Language Learning, 44*, 123–157.
Hamilton, R. (1995). The noun phrase accessibility hierarchy in SLA: Determining the basis for its developmental effects. In F. Eckman, D. Highland, P. Lee, J. Mileham, & R. Weber (Eds.), *Second language acquisition: Theory and pedagogy* (pp. 101–114). Mahwah, NJ: Erlbaum.
Hawkins, J. (1999). Processing complexity and filler-gap dependencies. *Language, 75*, 244–285.
Hawkins, J. (2004). *Efficiency and complexity in grammars*. Oxford: Oxford University Press.
Hawkins, R. (1989). Do second language learners acquire restrictive relative clauses on the basis of relational or configurational information? The acquisition of French subject, direct object, and genitive restrictive clauses by second language learners. *Second Language Research, 5*, 156–188.

Hsu, C.-C., Hermon, G., & Zukowski, A. (2009). Young children's production of head-final relative clauses: Elicited production data from Chinese children. *Journal of East Asian Linguistics, 18*, 323–360.

Huh, S. (2015). A corpus study of L2 Korean relative clause development. *Language Research, 51*, 845–868.

Izumi, S. (2003). Processing difficulty in comprehension and production of relative clauses by learners of English as a second language. *Language Learning, 53*(2), 285–323.

Jeon, K., & Kim, H.-Y. (2007). Development of relativization in Korean as a foreign language: The noun phrase accessibility hierarchy in head-internal and head-external relative clauses. *Studies in Second Language Acquisition, 29*, 253–276.

Kang, S. (2014). The role and syntactic and semantic information in the frequency distribution of relative clauses in Korean: A corpus-based analysis. *Language Information, 19*, 5–32.

Keenan, E., & Comrie, B. (1977). Noun phrase accessibility and universal grammar. *Linguistic Inquiry, 8*, 63–99.

Kim, C.-E., & O'Grady, W. (2016). Asymmetries in children's production of relative clauses: Data from English and Korean. *Journal of Child Language, 42*, 1038–1071.

Kim, H.-S. (2005). *Processing strategies and transfer of heritage and non-heritage learners of Korean* [Unpublished Ph.D. dissertation]. Department of East Asian Languages and Literatures, University of Hawaii at Manoa.

Kwon, N., Lee, Y., Gordon, P., & Kluender, R. (2010). Cognitive and linguistic factors affecting subject/object asymmetry: An eye-tracking study of prenominal relative clauses in Korean. *Language, 86*, 546–582.

Kwon, N., Polinsky, M., & Kluender, R. (2006). Subject preference in Korean. In D. Baumer, D. Montero & M. Scanlon (Eds.), *Proceedings of the 25th West Coast Conference on formal linguistics* (pp. 1–14). Somerville, MA: Cascadilla Proceedings Project.

Larson, R. (1988). On the double object construction. *Linguistic Inquiry, 19*, 335–392.

Lee-Ellis, S. (2011). The elicited production of Korean relative clauses by heritage speakers. *Studies in Second Language Acquisition, 33*, 57–89.

O'Grady, W., & Choi, M. (2015). The acquisition of Korean syntax by second language learners. In L. Brown & J. Kim (Eds.), *The handbook of Korean linguistics* (pp. 355–372). Boston, MA: Wiley-Blackwell.

O'Grady, W., Lee, M., & Choo, M. (2003). A subject–object asymmetry in the acquisition of relative clauses in Korean as a second language. *Studies in Second Language Acquisition, 25*, 433–448.

Sadighi, F. (1994). The acquisition of English restrictive relative clauses by Chinese, Japanese, and Korean adult native speakers. *IRAL: International Review of Applied Linguistics in Language Teaching, 32*(2), 141.

Tarallo, F., & Myhill, J. (1983). Interference and natural language processing in second language acquisition. *Language Learning, 33*, 55–76.

Wolfe-Quintero, K. (1992). Learnability and the acquisition of extraction in relative clauses and *wh* questions. *Studies in Second Language Acquisition, 14*, 39–70.

Zukowski, A. (2009). Elicited production of relative clauses in children with Williams syndrome. *Language and Cognition Processes, 24*, 1–42.

APPENDIX
Full list of target test items

Experiment 1

1. In the first picture, a boy is giving a bag to a girl. In the second picture, a girl is giving a bag to a boy.
2. In the first picture, a boy is showing a hat to a girl. In the second picture, a girl is showing a hat to a boy.
3. In the first picture, a boy is throwing a ball to a girl. In the second picture, a girl is throwing a ball to a boy.
4. In the first picture, a boy is passing a box to a girl. In the second picture, a girl is passing a box to a boy.
5. In the first picture, a boy is handing a cup to a girl. In the second picture, a girl is handing a cup to a boy.
6. In the first picture, a girl is bringing a chair to a boy. In the second picture, a boy is bringing a chair to a girl.
7. In the first picture, a girl is reading a book to a boy. In the second picture, a boy is reading a book to a girl.
8. In the first picture, a girl is pushing a bicycle to a boy. In the second picture, a boy is pushing a bicycle to a girl.
9. In the first picture, a girl is lending an umbrella to a boy. In the second picture, a boy is lending an umbrella to a girl.
10. In the first picture, a girl is kicking a ball to a boy. In the second picture, a boy is kicking a ball to a girl.

Experiment 2

1. In the first picture, a boy is putting a book on a box. In the second picture, a girl is putting a book on a box.
2. In the first picture, a boy is dropping a sock into a basket. In the second picture, a girl is dropping a sock into a basket.
3. In the first picture, a boy is placing a bag on a notebook. In the second picture, a girl is placing a bag on a notebook.

4. In the first picture, a boy is setting a napkin on a dish. In the second picture, a girl is setting a napkin on a dish.
5. In the first picture, a boy is laying a sweater on a blanket. In the second picture, a girl is laying a sweater on a blanket.
6. In the first picture, a boy is throwing a bag onto a cushion. In the second picture, a girl is throwing a bag onto a cushion.
7. In the first picture, a boy is pouring water into juice. In the second picture, a girl is pouring water into juice.
8. In the first picture, a boy is pushing a table toward a couch. In the second picture, a girl is pushing a table toward a couch.
9. In the first picture, a boy is hiding a photo under a letter. In the second picture, a girl is hiding a photo under a letter.
10. In the first picture, a boy is tossing a hat onto a cushion. In the second picture, a girl is tossing a hat onto a cushion.

PART II

Teaching and learning Korean as a second language

7
PRAGMATIC TEACHING AND LEARNING

Jieun Kiaer, Jiyoung Shin, and Derek Driggs

Introduction

This chapter discusses how Korean pragmatics are taught and learned within the tenet of Korean as a second language (KSL) teaching and learning. Study of Korean as a foreign language (KFL) has surged in recent years, driven by the popularity of South Korean popular culture, e.g., K-pop, K-drama, and K-film. This phenomenon of booming international interest in Korean culture is commonly referred to as the 'Korean Wave' (*hallyu*). Despite overall decreases in enrolment in second language classes, numbers of foreign students enrolled in Korean classes in the US rose by 14% between 2013 and 2016. This trend is continuing to rise globally as K-pop and other Korean media increase in popularity (Pickles, 2018). However, new learners of Korean soon come up against the challenge of the language's pragmatic elements. Pragmatic competence is an important skill for speakers of Korean, especially for learners who study the language to help their cultural engagement. This is because pragmatic factors play an essential role in forming intimacy and hierarchy in real-world relationships.

According to the Foreign Service Institute (2019), an organ of the US Federal Government, Korean is classed as a Category IV language. This is the highest possible ranking, meaning the language is exceptionally difficult for native English-speaking learners. A major obstacle for students of Korean as an additional language is the degree of socio-pragmatic complexity embedded in language use. For instance, Korean pragmatics are arguably much more extensive than even other Category IV languages, like Japanese or Chinese. Although complex pragmatic patterns are found in all languages in some limited speech situations, the pervasive Korean system is notorious for the difficulty it poses for foreign learners. The process of making one's linguistic input pragmatically adequate is one of the most challenging features for learners of Korean and cannot be ignored. However, pragmatic elements of language use have thus far been overlooked in materials for learners of KFL and also for learners of KSL. A brief examination of TOPIK, CEFR, and ACTFL measures of language proficiency reveals that, though pragmatic skills are considered an important part of fluency, skills specific to Korean which are vital to appropriate linguistic performance cannot be measured by the criteria currently being examined, as we will discuss later in this chapter.

This is partly due to the nature of teaching and learning pragmatics. The decision of whether to employ casual or polite speech styles is challenging for L2 learners of Korean. Correctly deducing the optimal speech style to use in a given conversation requires interpersonal skills and application of knowledge about Korean society to judge the status relationship between interlocutors. It is possible for L2 learners to acquire tact in employing Korean politeness through exposure to real situations, engaging with speakers in a process of trial and error. However, it is exceptionally difficult to acquire such interpersonal skills through written materials, like grammar textbooks (Kiaer, 2017). The problem is compounded by the fact that many written materials, like books and newspapers, overwhelmingly use the plain style, giving little exposure to the other speech levels. Even a face-to-face classroom environment typically does not provide exposure to the broad range of social situations necessary for the acquisition of socio-pragmatic features in Korean. To solve the problems caused by classroom-bound teaching based on written textbook materials, innovative methods of teaching pragmatics need to be introduced.

Korean is becoming more relevant to non-Korean populations. Korea has traditionally been a largely homogeneous society, with relatively few residents or citizens of foreign background and with very few non-Koreans learning Korean outside of Korea. However, this is changing rapidly today. Both the number of foreigners learning Korean and the amount of people of foreign background living in Korea are rapidly growing. As of 2018, 5% of children born in Korea were multi-ethnic. As of 2030, it is predicted that 10% of the population will be either foreign-born or multi-ethnic (Larmer, 2018). Though still a tiny minority of the overall population, this number is vastly different from previous demographic statistics. As more people of various cultural and linguistic backgrounds become a part of Korean society, it becomes important to consider how they will integrate and become contributing members of their communities, rather than existing separately from native Koreans. In addition to the increase of foreign presence in Korea, more people around the world are learning Korean as a second language. Because of the increasing relevance of Korean to non-Korean people, it is important to examine Korean pragmatics and how they can better be taught to KFL learners.

In the following, we provide a general investigation of and illustrate the importance of several areas which may be considered central to Korean pragmatics. Specifically, in this chapter, we review types of honorifics, Korean speech styles, address terms, and non-verbal honorifics, among other areas. We then briefly examine existing KFL curricula and assessment measures to see if these pragmatic elements are being addressed. This will serve as a starting point for future research regarding how to more effectively teach pragmatic skills to learners of Korean, as well as other Asian languages which show similar socio-pragmatic complexity (Kiaer, 2020a).

Korean pragmatics

Korean is a socio-pragmatically rich language. It is sensitive to the relationship between the speaker and hearer at every moment of interaction. Most expressions in Korean have a dimension that encodes the hierarchical relationship between the interlocutors and the speaker's relationship and attitude towards the addressee. In English such relationships are not consequential in deciding the composition of an utterance. A speaker can say 'It is raining', 'It is 2 O'clock' without knowing who the hearer is. This is not the case in Korean. Almost every aspect of speech is attuned to the speaker's relationship with the speech partner. The first hurdle arises from the question of what one should call or how one should address the hearer. Koreans almost never call each other by first name alone. Instead, they use an appropriate address term. Finding the right term matters even with a stranger, right from the beginning of an interaction. This is the reason why Koreans often ask each other's age even just a few minutes after meeting. Sometimes, the questions can continue and may cover somewhat personal things, like whether the other person is married or has children. These are questions that people unfamiliar with this culture can find quite imposing and overwhelming, but they are necessary for finding the right address terms and making the conversation flow smoothly.

Though a simple list of address terms for various relationships, as can be found in various grammar books, may be useful to learners, finding the proper address term for an interaction is a complex, context-driven matter. Using address terms properly is important because if wrongly used, they could seriously offend or upset someone. Yet, despite textbook explanations, there are not any set rules for which address terms should be used at a given time. In each instance, one must calculate and juggle various factors to find the right terms to reflect the intended relational dynamics. Hence, it is not only learners of Korean who find this difficult – native Korean speakers equally struggle to choose the right address terms for each situation. One has to consider multiple factors, such as the age and social status of the person to whom one is speaking. In addition, one needs to consider the environment – whether it is a private or public space. On a very basic level, one can perhaps compare this to choosing clothes to suit an occasion and expected company. The social hierarchy determined by age or position, however, does not always dictate the choice of address terms.

Politeness theorists Brown and Levinson (1987) created an equation to represent what happens in a person's mind (regardless of language) when calculating what level of politeness is required in any specific interaction. The three major variables that must be incorporated into those mental calculations are distance, power, and degree of imposition. Distance can be with respect to age or social hierarchy. Power is in reference to the relative positions of the conversational participants within an existing power structure. Degree of imposition refers to how imposing the listener will find an utterance. For example, when talking to a best friend (low distance, low power), polite language wouldn't be needed to comment on the weather or complain about a teacher (low degrees of imposition). However, when asking this same friend to give up her weekend to watch a little brother or complete another favour (high degree of imposition), more politeness strategies will be employed. Some researchers feel that speakers of Korean and many other Asian languages tend to calculate the requisite politeness higher than is common in many Western cultures, particularly with reference to the variables of distance. While an American might calculate a lower amount of distance in an attempt to be kind, a Korean could calculate a higher level of distance to be respectful and polite. This often leads to faux pas in intercultural communication.

Therefore, when one is deciding what to say in Korean, one must decide whether to put more emphasis on respect or intimacy. In Korean, unlike many other languages, it is impossible to hide one's attitude towards his/her addressee. That is, the choice of address terms directly reflects one's attitude towards the person whom he/she is talking to or about. For instance, the use of honorific suffixes or particles such as -님(*nim*) or -께서(*kkeyse*) reflect the speaker's respectful attitude towards the addressee.

The pragmatic system of Korean includes many varied attributes and characteristics which do not appear in Western languages but are similar to those found in other East Asian languages. Most of these characteristics are related to honorifics. The Korean honorifics system has been described as "differences in speech that depend upon relative social rank" (Lee & Ramsey, 2000, p. 224), but it is much more complicated than a formulaic ranking system. Much research has been done about this system, and it has been said that "it may well be that no language on earth has a more finely differentiated system of honorifics" (Lee & Ramsey, 2000, p. 224). The fine differentiation described here plays a pragmatic role; it sends messages about relationships and the way interlocutors see them, thus establishing in-groups and out-groups, hierarchical boundaries, and interpersonal intimacy or the lack thereof. Here, we examine a few of the characteristics related to honorifics which are essential for successful linguistic interactions. We have chosen to focus on types of honorifics, speech styles, address terms, and non-verbal honorifics. Each of these elements plays into the complex honorific system of Korean.

Types of honorifics

The Korean speaker employs different words and grammar forms depending on his or her relationship with the hearer, as well as the setting in which the interaction occurs. Different aspects of this relationship are taken into consideration. Yeon and Brown describe both hearer or addressee honorifics and referent honorifics, the former being based on the speaker's calculation of his or her relationship with the hearer, and the second being decided by the speaker and hearer's respective relationships with the person being spoken about (Yeon & Brown, 2011, p. 171). The address term, which is another central part of the honorific system, plays a role in both kinds of honorifics (Lee & Ramsey, 2000, p. 238). We will be discussing the address term more later in this chapter. Subject honorifics are also commonly referred to.

In referent honorifics, we typically deal with the exaltation of the subject, accomplished by attaching special particles to nouns, or the exaltation of the object, which is accomplished by adding pre-final endings to verbs (Lee & Ramsey, 2000, p. 239). Examples of referent honorifics are shown next. The underlined expressions are honorific expressions:

Example of Referent honorifics:

1 오늘 선생님<u>께</u> 전화 <u>드렸</u>어요.
  onul sensayng-nim-kkey cenhwa tulyesseyo
  Today teacher-dear-DAT$_{HON}$ call gave$_{HON.POL}$
  I called my teacher today. (showing respect)

Hearer honorifics are more constantly present in speech, as they concern the interlocutors themselves, in the present. These are accomplished through different sentence endings, which combine to create different speech levels, or styles. "The 'style' expresses linguistically the relative social rank of the person to whom the speaker is talking . . . [and is] determined by something outside the sentence, namely, the rank of the listener" (Lee & Ramsey, 2000, p. 239). The first- and second-person pronouns and address terms used are also a part of the hearer honorific system. An example of hearer honorifics is shown in bold next, with the first showing a modified verb ending along with a polite speech style and the second showing an honorific verb along with a formal speech style. We also show an example of subject honorifics.

Example of Hearer/addressee honorifics:

2 선생님, 오늘 저녁 어디 가**세**요?
  sensayng-nim, onul cenyek eti ka-sey-yo?
  Teacher-dear today evening where go-$_{HON.POL}$

Teacher, where are you going this evening? (showing respect and deference to the hearer)

Example of Subject honorifics:

3 선생님이 학교에 오<u>시</u>었어요.
  sensayng-nim-i, hakkyio-ey o-si-esseyo?
  Teacher-dear school-at come-HON-PAST.POL
  Teacher came to school (showing respect and deference to the subject of the sentence)

In the following, we will be dealing more with hearer honorifics.

Speech styles in Korean

Most scholars agree that there are six main speech levels, or styles, in Korean (Yeon & Brown, 2011, p. 17; Lee & Ramsey, 2000, p. 250):

Formal styles (a-d)

a   formal style/*hapsyo-chey*
b   semiformal style/*hao-chey*
c   familiar style/*hakey-chey*
d   plain style/*hayla-chey*

Informal styles (e-f)

e   polite style/*hayyo-chey*
f   half-talk or intimate style/*panmal*/*hey-chey*

The formal style is used by speakers to those of superior status or age in circumstances where great respect or decorum are needed. These situations include settings like public speeches, presentations, or reports to superiors. This style is also used to show extra respect to elders in settings which otherwise wouldn't be considered formal. Members of the military often use this form when speaking to those of higher rank. The polite style is also used to those of superior status or age and is much more commonly used than the formal style. This is the typical style used in discourse between strangers and is also used with close friends, acquaintances, or family members of greater age than the speaker. The semiformal style and the familiar style are used much less commonly in modern Korea but both can be heard in specific settings. Specifically, these forms are used by adults with lower-ranking adults with low intimacy. They allow a measure of distance to be maintained and show less superiority than lower styles. Half-talk is used between very close intimates regardless of age, as well as by superiors to inferiors or adults to children. Plain style is similar, but it is typically only used with inferiors or children.

The six-style system is actually much more complex than this explanation suggests, and the pragmatic meanings and implications of each form are varied and subtle. However, most Koreans conceptualize their language in terms of formal and informal, or high and low, rather than by six different categories. According to Lee and Ramsey, "Today . . . when Koreans talk about speech styles, the most common . . . contrast is between *panmal*, 'informal, intimate speech' and *contaysmal*, which, roughly translated means 'polite speech'" (Lee & Ramsey, 2000, p. 251). Thus, the informal half-talk (we will refer to this style as 반말 [*panmal*] and 'half-talk' interchangeably) and polite – 요 (*yo*) form "have come to be the twin pillars of the speech-style system of modern Korean" (Lee & Ramsey, 2000, p. 260). This difference between high form and low form, or formal and informal styles, is a sensitive one that is frequently discussed by native speakers of Korean. We will deal primarily with these two categories in this chapter.

Speech style shift: a complex endeavour to balance intimacy and respect

The choice of speech style (the varieties of which we will discuss later) shifts as the interpersonal relationship changes. For instance, when two people first meet, they will typically use the politeness ending – 요 (*yo*) with each other, even if they are the same age, as a courtesy.

Yet, once they become closer to each other, they will often start dropping – 요 (*yo*) to create a more intimate, close relationship. This shift will happen on the part of either the senior party or both parties, depending on the level of intimacy they want to achieve. This process is subtle and requires mutual agreement and negotiation. Sudden shifts towards casual speech styles can create tension and conflict. In fact, this is an oft-reported conflict, at times even resulting in violence (Kiaer, Park, Choi, & Driggs, 2019). This process of tuning into the right style is not straightforward. Dropping – 요 (*yo*) and choosing a half-talk style can be seen as a sign of solidarity and intimacy but can be misunderstood as a lack of respect. Importantly, the tuning process to measure the interpersonal relations and subsequently following efforts to find the appropriate expressions are not one-off decisions that happen in the course of interaction. Instead, these procedures must continue at every meaningful utterance unit during the interaction. For instance, the effort to balance intimacy and respect is found in finding the right interjections, personal pronouns, address terms, endings, and non-verbal gestures.

In the following examples the propositional meaning is exactly the same, but each proposes a different interpersonal dynamic.

4   어머나, 너도 그거 알아?
    emena, ne-to ku-ke al-a?
    oh, you-also that-thing know$_{CASUAL}$
    Oh, do you know that too?

In this example, the expression 어머나 (*emena*) is most likely used by a female. The use of the second-person pronoun 너 (*ne*) means the two are close and the speaker is either equal to or superior to the hearer. The verb 알아 (*ala*) is in a casual style and shows the intimacy and superiority of the speaker.

5   어머, 선생님도 그거 아십니까?
    e-me, sen-sayng-nim-to ku-ke a-sip-ni-kka?
    Oh, teacher-dear-also that-thing know$_{HON\text{-}FORMAL}$
    Oh, do you know that too?

In this example, the expression 어머 (*eme*) is most likely used gender neutrally. 선생님 (*sensayngnim*) is used not only as a title but as a place holder for an honorific subject. The honorific suffix -시 (*-ssi*) is added to honour the subject. The ending -ㅂ니까 (*-pnikka*) is added to signify formality.

Because varied styles or levels of speech exist, speakers of Korean are constantly faced with the decision of which style to use in a given situation or relationship. There are also many instances when a speaker has to switch styles to show a change in situation or dynamic. As would be expected, this can be sensitive and difficult to work through on many levels. Despite the complexity of these decisions, most scholars have treated them as being primarily based on age and social hierarchy (Lee & Ramsey, 2000, p. 224). Lee and others describe this power balance as the "primary factor" in determining speech style. Power in a Korean context is usually defined as being "represented by age, status, social class, etc." (Lee, 2012, p. 272).

However, a brief examination of speech styles in use suggests that power cannot be the sole factor at play. For instance, young children are likely to use half-talk with their parents and grandparents and other older family members. In fact, they may use half-talk with other close adults who are not members of the family because of a certain level of familiarity or closeness. Even adults are likely to continue to use half-talk with their parents and other family members in their private conversations. However, when these conversations are had in the presence of others, often the more polite – 요 (-yo) form is used. In these instances, and others, half-talk seems to be used more freely than a prescriptive approach to speech styles would suggest, and formal forms seem to be less a matter of showing respect than of fitting an image of social appropriateness. But just because there is a level of freedom in the use of informal styles doesn't mean they can be used indiscriminately or in every relationship of a certain type.

Many of the diverse pragmatic meanings of each speech style, and the reasons behind a choice to change speech styles, have been explored in previous research. Strauss and Eun, for example, have explored the variations which exist just in formal styles. Specifically, they found that the difference in the polite – 요 (-yo) ending and the deferential -습니다 (-supnita) ending is greater than a simply hierarchical one: "Rather than relating to social status and hierarchy, honorific speech level choice is actually motivated quite strongly by information status with respect to both speaker and interlocutor" (Oh Eun & Strauss, 2004, p. 271). The information status they describe refers to the difference between the sharing of information that was previously unknown and information that was already known. Further research by the same authors found that in-groups and out-groups are more important than other factors related to speech styles (Strauss & Eun, 2005).

Brown examines the formal styles even further. His analysis is complex on a different level; he says that "The difference between -요 *(-yo)* and -습니다 *(-supnita)* is that the former lacks the presentational qualities of the latter" (Brown, 2015, p. 57). The presentational quality he refers to is an issue of role; utterances made in a specific role are likely to be said in a different style than those made outside of that role. In actuality, these styles are probably used in all these ways at different times and in different circumstances to communicate pragmatic meanings.

As mentioned, even native speakers are not always consciously aware of the various meanings of speech styles they use. Often, Koreans identify politeness as the main feature of the speech styles and decisions to shift (Kim, 2011, p. 177). Intimacy is often described as a "secondary factor" (Lee, 2012, p. 272) when compared to power or hierarchy, but it is also recognized that it can override differences in age when speech style is being determined (Lee, 2012, p. 319). Generally, though, both native Korean speakers and researchers point to power as the main factor in speech-style delineation. Lee (2012) quoted Park (1995), who described that "Unlike English and other Western languages, where [honorifics] and address terms are distinguished according to the level of intimacy, in Korean . . . honorifics continue to be used in accordance with the degree of . . . power . . . regardless of intimacy level" (Lee, 2012, p. 321). Lee (2012) clarified that sometimes the influence of intimacy can outbalance that of power, explaining that "In situations where the two factors collide, one factor does not take precedence over the other, but rather, according to conversation or linguistic usage context, and . . . relationship, the [impact] of the two factors will be different" (Lee, 2012, p. 332).

Recent research has suggested that intimacy in relationships may be more important than power in determination of speech style. Park (2017), for example, analysed reality TV shows to show that the shift to half-talk itself is a way to establish further intimacy in a relationship. She looked specifically at couples' use of this shift, but the principle can be extended to other relationships as well. In Korean, there is often a point reached in a relationship where the interlocutors will have a discussion about speech styles, essentially establishing their level of closeness by asking to or requesting that the other speaker 'drop' the level of speech being used. Alan Hyun-Oak Kim agreed about the weight of the intimacy variable. He described relationships where interlocutors use higher levels of speech as 'H-fields' and explained that, "when two people become intimate, their H-field dissolves" (Kim, 2011, pp. 194–195). Kim elaborated on the idea that speech level could be more related to intimacy than hierarchical power, explaining that this H-field – either its presence or dissolution – is used to show in-group and out-group relationships (Kim, 2011, p. 195). He also showed, importantly, that the use of 'respectful' language is not always a good thing; when used to an intimate in place of a less formal form it may cause serious offence (Kim, 2011, p. 195). He reiterated the fact that a shift to a lower speech style, in proper context, often symbolizes a new level of closeness in a relationship rather than some kind of disrespect or lack of politeness (Kim, 2011, p. 197).

The following are examples of proposals for shifts in speech style which happen in different kinds of situations, possibly as the result of different variables.

6 교수님, 말씀 편하게 낮추셔도 됩니다!
   kyoswu-nim, malssum phyen-ha-key nac-chwu-sye-to toyp-ni-ta!
   Professor, you can lower your words comfortably!
   The speaker is inviting the hearer to shift from the formal style to half-talk, indicating a desire to be thought of as a 'comfortable junior'.

7 형 저 한테 말 편하게 놔주세요!
   hyeng mal phyen-ha-key ha-sey-yo!
   Brother, please lower your speech comfortably to me!
   The speaker is inviting the hearer to shift from the formal style to half-talk, indicating a desire to be thought of as a 'comfortable junior'.

8 나 말을 편하게 해도 되지?
   na mal-ul phyen-ha-key hay-to toy-ci?
   I can speak comfortably, right?
   The speaker is confirming that the hearer is all right with his/her use of half-talk, showing that the hearer is seen as a 'comfortable junior'.

9 너도 말 놔!
   ne-to mal nwa!
   You lower your speech, too!
   The speaker is inviting the hearer to also shift from the formal to half-talk, indicating a desire to be thought of as a 'comfortable senior'.

In each of the previous examples, the speaker and hearer have to follow cues to understand each other's attitudes and intents. For native speakers and non-native speakers of Korean alike, acting in a pragmatically appropriate way in these situations is key to establishing the proper balance of power, intimacy, and other elements in the relationship. As shown earlier, expressing intimacy and respect are important aspects of speech styles. Yet, the meanings of speech styles are complex and multi-faceted. For instance, Lee and Yu Cho (2015) show that shifting between honorific and non-honorific language is sometimes the result of the speaker's intentional manipulation of social meanings and can reset the relationship between the interlocutors. Kim (2020) shows how speech-style shifts in web-toons create a new meaning of sarcasm being associated with formal speech styles, which are generally known to be used in expressing respect.

The following statement from mother to son is an example of the formal style and honorifics being used to express sarcasm.

10 식사하시고 게임하시지요??
   sik-sa-ha-si-ko key-im-ha-si-ci-yo?
   Why don't you eat your meal and then play your game?

How to address people: address terms and second-person pronouns

The address term, which is linked to but different from speech styles, plays an equally important pragmatic role. Korean address terms are varied and, like speech styles, convey important information about the context of a given utterance. In fact, speech styles are rendered meaningless if used with improper address terms. Like speech styles, whether an address term is proper or not depends on many variables, including the power and intimacy factors discussed previously. Here we will summarize the basic rules of address terms in Korean. For the purposes of this chapter, second-person pronouns and all terms with a vocative function will be considered address terms, including names, titles, and kinship terms.

The first category to discuss is the second-person pronoun, the equivalent of the English 'you'. Korean, unlike English, does not have a universally acceptable second-person pronoun (Yeon & Brown, 2011, p. 76). The second-person pronouns in Korean, like speech styles, serve mainly to denote levels of intimacy and power. Which pronoun is used often depends on the speech style being used (Lee & Ramsey, 2000, p. 225). Second-person pronouns can be generally divided into the same categories as the speech styles summarized previously:

As shown earlier, more formal styles of speech do not allow for the usage of any second-person pronouns; titles are used instead (Yeon & Brown, 2011, p. 78). This seems to indicate a feeling that in Korean, referring directly to the person one is talking to is very personal and intimate and is therefore reserved for situations where such interaction is socially appropriate. Names are therefore not used nearly as often as is typical in English (Kiaer et al., submitted; Kim, H., 2003).

There are other second-person pronouns or address terms used within the styles which are perhaps less common or are used with more specificity. The variance in terms used is interesting; each term avoids a direct reference to the person (through the use of 'you' or a name), suggesting complex feelings around address. In English, the most commonly used vocative address term is the personal name. Koreans do not use names nearly as liberally as English speakers. This being the case, middle-aged and older Koreans, who naturally spend less time with parents and intimate superiors, often report that they rarely hear their own given names used at all.

Second-person pronouns are very difficult to translate from English to Korean, but according to Kim Hyeyeong (2008) second-person pronouns are usually translated to 당신 (*tangsin*). This creates pragmatic inconsistency, displaying the core pragmatic differences in the two languages, and illustrates how even a simple pronoun like 'you' poses pragmatic difficulty to learners of Korean.

Titles are also used as address terms in the vocative sense. These titles can include occupational titles, such as 교수님 (*kyoswunim*, professor), 기사님 (*kisanim*, driver), or 목사님 (*moksanim*, preacher), but such titles are extended to more generic use as well. For example,

Table 7.1 Speech styles and second-person pronouns

Speech Style	Correlating Second-Person Pronoun (Subject)
formal style/*hapsyo-chey*	None (or gesture, often using two hands)/title
polite style/*hayyo-chey*	None (or gesture, often using two hands)/title
semiformal style/*hao-chey*	*tangsin* (당신)
familiar style/*hakey-chey*	*caney* (자네)
half-talk or intimate style/*panmal*/*hay-chey*	*ne* (너)/name+vocative particle (*a*/아, *ya*/야, *i*/이)
plain style/*hayla-chey*	*ne* (너)/name+vocative particle (*a*/아, *ya*/야, *i*/이)

Table 7.2 Kinship terms in Korean

	Father	Mother	Older Brother	Older Sister	Younger Brother/Sister	Aunt	In-Laws
Male	아버지 *Apeci* 'father' 아빠 *appa* 'daddy'	어머니 *emeni* 'mother' 엄마 *emma* 'mother'	형 *hyeong*	누나 *nwuna*	Name + -아/-야-*a/ya*	고모 *komo* (dad's sisters) 이모 *imo* (mum's sisters)	아버님 *apenim* 'father-in-law'
Female	아버지 *Apeci* 'father' 아빠 *appa* 'daddy'	어머니 *emeni* 'mother' 엄마 *emma* 'mother'	오빠 *oppa*	언니 *enni*	Name + -아/-야-*a/ya*	고모 *komo* (dad's sisters) 이모 *imo* (mum's sisters)	어머님 *emenim* 'mother-in-law'

the term 선생님 (*sensayngnim*), which means teacher, can be used to address socially superior strangers of any position, as can the term 사장님 (*sacangnim*), which means manager. Each of the titles listed here also includes the -님 (*nim*) honorific suffix, used deferentially to superiors or strangers. To people of similar or lower social position, -씨 (*ssi*) – similar to Mr or Ms in English – can be added to the full, family, or given name; each combination expresses a different level of respect or lack thereof (Kiaer et al., submitted; Lee & Ramsey, 2000, pp. 230–238).

Within families, a strict and complicated system of kinship terms is used. Like in English, fathers and mothers are referred to as such, but each other family member has an assigned title as well. Family members only use the names of those in the family they are older than. Such kinship terms depend on age and gender (Yeon & Brown, 2011, p. 36). The following table shows how kinship terms in Korean are gender and age sensitive.

Often, the kinship terms for older siblings are used along with names. For example, a younger brother may say '철수 형 (Chelswu *hyeng*)', or '민희 누나 (Minhui *nwuna*)'. When parents or older siblings call the names of their children or younger siblings, they almost always add the vocative particles 아/야/이 (*a/ya/i*) after the name, depending on whether the name ends with a consonant or a vowel and what the context is. Even twins address each other with these kinship terms, depending on who was born first (Yeon & Brown, 2011, pp. 38–39).

Kinship terms are hugely important in Korean society; they are extended for use outside the family as well. Given names are only used by close friends who were born in the same year as each other or with close friends who are younger. When names are used in this way, the vocative particles mentioned earlier are almost always added.

To close friends who are even just one year older, the same titles are used as with older siblings. For example, if 김철수 (Kim Chelswu) was born in 1993 and was very close to 신정우 (Sin Cengwu), who was born in 1992, he would call him 형 (*hyeng*) or 정우 형 (Cengwu *hyeng*). This would hold true even if the two were close enough and in a setting where it was permissible to use half-talk (Kiaer et al., submitted). Other kinship terms, like 아저씨 (*acessi*, uncle) and 이모 (*imo*, aunt) are extended to adults who are not family as well. These adults can range from servers in restaurants to adult intimates (Yeon & Brown, 2011, p. 39). The usage of kinship terms creates a feeling of belonging, differentiates between in-groups and out-groups, and increases feelings of intimacy.

Non-verbal honorifics

In addition to speech styles and address terms, there are also very important non-verbal aspects of the Korean honorific system which form an essential part of Korean pragmatics. Though these have not been explored or defined in as much detail as verbal honorifics, such as speech styles and address terms, they cannot be overlooked in an examination of the Korean honorific system.

The field of non-verbal communication in a linguistic context, and specifically in the context of Asian languages, has rarely been discussed. Kendon (1988) explains how words have to follow a standard set of rules according to syntactic norms, whereas gesture can be used in a much more general and less regulated sense (Kendon, 1988, p. 132). McNeill (1992) agrees that gestures are fundamentally different from language (McNeill, 1992, p. 19), for similar reasons to those presented by Kendon. Wharton (2009) addresses many of the previously mentioned descriptions of gesture in relation to language. He seems to refute the claim that gesture is not communicative, stating that it can be as long as it is both salient and relevant (Wharton, 2009, p. 153).

Knapp et al. (Knapp, Hall, & Horgan, 2014, pp. 448–456) describes non-verbal communication in terms of communicating intimacy and dominance, assuming that showing dominance rather than subordinance in social situations is always desirable. While this may be true in a Western context, East Asian culture often requires interlocutors to take a position of deference, which is different from both dominance and subordinance. For interlocutors in an East Asian context, non-verbally communicating deference is often an important face-saving act (Brown & Levinson, 1987).

In a Korean context specifically, deferential gesture is used almost inseparably from the honorific system, making it an essential part of pragmatics in any Korean interaction. Some of the main features of the deferential gesture system include bowing, nodding, posture, and gaze, among others. Though these gestures are certainly not defined or standardized, they virtually always accompany honorific and deferential interactions to the extent that their absence may undermine the honorific function of verbal honorifics. To learners of Korean and other Asian languages, the presence of these gestural honorifics may pose challenges in becoming pragmatically effective communicators. The problem of cultural differences in sending and understanding gestural cues accurately has been discussed by various researchers. Even examining one type of gesture, like bowing and nodding, reveals the complex nature of gestural honorifics in a Korean context. In the following, we will briefly explore nodding in an East Asian context.

Nodding and bowing

Maynard (1987) suggests that the main purpose of head movement (i.e. nodding and bowing) in Japanese is related to turn-taking. She concludes that turn-taking head movement is prominent in Japanese conversation. Kita and Ide (2007) discuss the functions of nodding (along with *aizuchi*, the Japanese term for affirmative sounds made intermittently throughout conversation) in conversation in the context of social relationships. They examine previous studies and use some corpus data to explore the usage and occurrence of nodding and *aizuchi*. The authors point out that, unlike English, Japanese allows for nodding and *aizuchi* in much more versatile places, often not related to turn-taking, by both the speaker and the hearer. They theorize that this is in part due to the Japanese cultural emphasis on consideration to the needs of others and that nodding and *aizuchi* are used to create a sense of community and harmony between speaker and hearer.

Other researchers have also examined the role of head movement in conversational dynamics. Kim (2015) breaks away from traditional notions of back-channelling and turn-taking and points out some of the pragmatic roles of movement, specifically in Korean. He notes that head movement most often occurs with expressions of emotion and is used to sympathize or empathize. Kim (2012) shows how nodding in conversation allows the interlocutor to feel the speaker's engagement in the conversation without a need to be interrupted, and Kogure (2007) shows how in a Japanese context, nodding allows speakers to feel more harmony in their conversations. McClave (2000) points out how speakers are exceptionally sensitive to head movement and what it signals during conversation.

As discussed, nodding and bowing in East Asian contexts can be complicated and multi-layered. In Korea, however, it must accompany all types of greetings, as well as expressions of thanks, apology, appreciation, humility, and deference. A given conversation may include dozens of small bows in addition to deeper or longer bows at the beginning and end of the conversation. Bows send an important message about seniority in terms of social hierarchy, but even the senior in a given relationship will often bow slightly in most interactions. This can certainly be seen as an intentional and meaningful communication, but it is often involuntary as well; Korean people are sometimes seen bowing in phone conversations where their bows can certainly not be seen by the recipient.

This complex type of gesture forms an essential part of Korean honorifics and removing it will likely impede interlocutors' ability to socially to navigate a given conversation. This is only one example of non-verbal honorific skills unique to Korean. These skills are diverse and complicated and can pose extra challenges to learners, but they are essential to pragmatic consistency. Further research is needed in this important area.

Multimodal modulation hypothesis

Our consideration here of non-verbal honorifics is completely linked to other aspects of the honorific system and cannot be examined effectively outside that context. Honorific expressions of every type need to be selected in every level of discourse to present attitudinal meanings, such as respect, in a consistent and enhanced way. If the attitudinal expressions in the utterance show contrasting attitudes, the utterance can become less sincere. For instance, the expressions in (A) are those used to show respect from a junior's perspective, while the expressions in (B) are those used by equals, such as same-age friends and family members. If the expressions in two groups are mixed, the utterance becomes socio-pragmatically less coherent and adequate, as in (11) and (12). In (11), the vocative particle -야 (-*ya*) indicates the speaker's seniority over the hearer, yet -세요 (-*seyo*) contradicts that pragmatic expectation. Hence, the entire utterance becomes pragmatically odd. In (12), contrary to (iii), the respectful suffix -님 (-*nim*) indicates the hearer's seniority over the speaker, yet the verb 와 (*wa*) is a casual, non-honorific form and contradicts the pragmatic expectation. Hence, this utterance also becomes pragmatically odd.

A Expressions used by a junior to a senior
  i   Honorific suffixes: -님 (-*nim*) (dear), -시 (-*si*) (the subject honorific suffix).
  ii Formal or polite speech styles.
  iii Non-verbal expressions: nodding, bowing or slight bending, clasping hands, indirect gestures such as hedging expressions (e.g. scratching the head).
B Expressions used by equals (same-age friends and family members)
  i   Vocative particles – 아/-야 (*a/-ya*).
  ii Address terms and second-person pronouns: Second-person pronouns are quite difficult to choose unless the two parties have a close relationship, as in family.
  iii Casual or half-talk speech styles (when negotiation is made).
  iv Non-verbal expressions: patting, straight back, nodding, bowing, or slight bending.

11 ???¹ 지나야 여기 오세요.
    Jina-ya, yeki o-sey-yo.
    J-VOC here come-HON-POL
    'Jina, please come here'.

12 ??? 지나님 여기 와.
    Jina-nim, yeki wa.
    J-respect here come
    'Jina, please come here'

Kiaer proposed the multimodal modulation hypothesis, which states the following:

> The core linguistic ability found in human communication is to be able to modulate or attune/orchestrate different levels/modes of information in a harmonious way, sensitive to the socio-pragmatic needs of each situation. If conflicting or inconsistent meanings are communicated, the communication will become socio-pragmatically inappropriate, insincere or unreliable, or convey humor or sarcasm.
>
> *(Kiaer, 2020a, p. 93)*

This multimodal modulation hypothesis suggests that honorifics are multifaceted and involve a huge range of variables, of which non-verbal honorifics are just one. All these variables, including speech styles, address terms, and non-verbal honorifics, have to show consistency. For instance, if one begins with an honorific attitude which postulates a relationship where hearer is superior to speaker, the speaker needs to maintain this attitude throughout. Otherwise, the utterance appears unnatural or even sarcastic due to semantic and pragmatic inconsistency.

Pragmatics in Korean language education

With a better understanding of important pragmatic aspects of Korean, the next step is to evaluate existing language curricula and assessment tools to see if these aspects are being addressed. In the following, we comment on some commonly used Korean language curricula and assessment measures.

Pragmatic skills in Korean language curricula

Brown points out that, often, "L2 pedagogy has a tendency to ignore a sizeable area of language use, not just verbal strategies that are deliberately rude, but also language that is simply casual and informal or even just intimate and affectionate" (Brown, 2013, p. 2). It seems very likely that many pragmatic aspects of Korean, like half-talk, address terms, and non-verbal honorifics, are not being prioritized in most Korean as a foreign language (KFL) curricula.² This would follow the trend of ignoring lower speech styles in Korean education in favour of higher, more respectful ones (Brown, 2013). In Brown's study, three textbook series published in Korea are examined. It is determined that in these textbooks, the dialogues included use *contaysmal* a vast majority of the time, with very few examples of half-talk usage (Brown, 2010).

Another recent study looks specifically at address term usage in major KFL textbooks and finds that kinship terms as used by Koreans to express intimacy outside of the family setting are not taught to foreign learners (Kiaer et al., 2020). Specifically, the study shows how dialogues consistently ignore the potentiality of using address terms outside the generic -씨 (-*ssi*) term. Despite a very large number of dialogues about a huge variety of subjects, relationships are simplified to include only friendly acquaintances, with no attempt to portray address terms in a realistic sense. The very few times kinship terms are used in a realistic way, they are shown with no explanation, as if this is a point which doesn't need to be taught explicitly. Half-talk is typically used along with the use of names or the 너 (*ne*) pronoun, as if all interlocutors were the same age.[3]

Clearly, pragmatic aspects of Korean, including speech styles, address terms, and non-verbal honorifics, are not being treated as a priority in KFL education. It is unclear whether this originates with Korean textbook writers' assumption that foreigners do not need to use kinship terms. This may be the case; Brown comments on the tendency of some textbook writers to claim that foreigners will rarely be in social situations which require the use of intimate language (Brown, 2013, p. 5). It may also stem from the foreigners' exclusion of themselves from in-groups where such language would be needed. This will require further research to understand better.

Assessment of pragmatic skills

Methods for properly assessing pragmatics have been explored for many years. Most assessment has tended to focus on "polite and impolite speech, complimenting, use of discourse markers" (Tsutagawa, 2015, p. 1), and other similar skills. While such skills are certainly important, they fail to encompass the breadth of pragmatic functionality required to navigate the Korean honorific system.

A brief examination of CEFR (Common European Framework of Reference), ACTFL (American Council of Teachers of Foreign Languages), and TOPIK (Test for Proficiency in Korean) measures of language proficiency reveals that, though pragmatic skills are considered an important part of fluency, skills specific to Korean which are vital to appropriate linguistic performance (some of which we have discussed here) cannot be measured – and are not being measured – by the criteria currently being examined.

In terms of pragmatic skills, the CEFR levels describe areas such as flexibility, turn-taking, coherence, and propositional precision. None of these include skills which could be applied to Korean speech styles or address terms. The CEFR levels also include a section about sociolinguistic skills, which describes an ability to navigate "idiomatic expressions and colloquialisms with awareness of connotative levels of meaning" and to understand "the sociolinguistic and sociocultural implications of language used by native speakers" (CEFR, 2001). These are only a few of many criteria used within this system to assess competence in speaking a language, but they are the only ones which are pragmatic in nature. Though these pragmatic skills are certainly an important part of being an effective communicator, they have little to say about whether a person can modify speech to express deference, intimacy, or power in a socially appropriate way. In Korean, as has been mentioned, not even a single utterance can be made without making a decision about these pragmatic issues, but the CEFR provides no way to assess them.

Among other identifiers, the ACTFL levels describe a speaker at the highest proficiency level (distinguished) as having the ability to "tailor language to a variety of audiences by adapting . . . speech and register in ways that are culturally authentic" (ACTFL, 2012). This would seem to encompass honorifics, but it is odd that such a skill would be described as particularly advanced in an almost unusual sense. Even a low-level speaker of Korean still has to use honorifics correctly, whether he or she is talking about something elementary or advanced, formal or informal. Other pragmatic aspects which are essential to becoming a communicative speaker of Korean, such as address terms and non-verbal honorifics, are not examined by the ACTFL's indicators.

The TOPIK levels describe that a speaker at the second highest level (5) will be "Able to use the expressions properly, depending on formal, informal, spoken/written context," while a speaker at the highest level (6) will "Experience no difficulty in performing the functions or conveying the meaning" (Won, 2016). Though informal and formal contexts are mentioned, clearly the focus here is on conveying meaning, rather than on pragmatic skills; it is unclear whether the descriptions of formal and informal are referring to honorifics or simply to setting.

By the standards set forth by the CEFR, ACTFL, and TOPIK, then, a learner of Korean with a large vocabulary and grammatical understanding who hasn't learned to use honorifics appropriately could still be seen as a high-level speaker. Not only do they fail to treat pragmatic skills unique to Korean as essential linguistic features, these and other measures currently provide no way to measure whether a learner of Korean can use these pragmatic skills effectively.

Suggestions

This chapter provides a detailed look at the pragmatic elements of Korean, illustrating how central a role they play in the language. We have also provided an examination of current educational practices in KFL teaching. Not only do textbooks fail to address these issues, current assessment norms provide no means for measuring proficiency in these important areas. The reasons for these problems are surely deep rooted and varied and may be based in a belief on the part of Korean native speakers that they are simply too difficult for foreigners to learn (Kiaer et al., submitted) or that foreigners have no reason to learn to integrate themselves into social hierarchies and intimacy groups. Whatever the reasons might be, it is clear that teaching pragmatics must become a much greater priority in KFL learning spaces.

We feel that diversification is needed in the teaching of pragmatics. Specifically, improving in this area will require diversification of methods used, diversification of the range in which learning takes place, and diversification of subjects covered.

As we seek to diversify teaching methods, the first step is to broaden definitions of pragmatic skills in assessments to include East Asian–typical pragmatics. In addition to changes which must be made to assessment tools, textbooks must be modified as well. The dialogues in most KSL textbooks fail to provide accurate context about how Korean speakers use pragmatic skills. Dialogues in textbooks should be redesigned at each level to help learners understand how to realistically and effectively use various speech styles, address terms, and non-verbal honorific skills. These dialogues must recognize that pragmatics like those present in honorifics are not specific to advanced levels of Korean but must be present at every level for communication to happen effectively.

Textbooks are just one tool used in teaching. Research about teaching pragmatics has generally agreed that it is more effective when done explicitly than implicitly (Moody, 2014, p. 40). This explicit teaching can take a variety of forms, but in order to be successful, honorifics must be taught in context because of the complex role they play. It is often assumed that face-to-face teaching is more effective in discussions of pragmatics, but in fact it may be limited; the student–teacher relationship is very specific and doesn't provide learners with contexts needed to explore diverse pragmatic skills. The same can be said for classmate relationships. Face-to-face teaching must be complemented by more contextual, diverse interactions. Kambara (2011) suggests that because context is required to effectively teach pragmatics, in this case in Japanese, film clips can be used in the classroom (Kambara, 2011, p. 147). Brown (2013) proposes teaching Korean pragmatics in a similar way, using multimedia, like clips from dramas, to demonstrate principles in a way where "contextual factors are expected to be more complex than those encountered in fabricated dialogues" (Brown, 2013, p. 7). A recent study presented by the authors in conference found that drama clips are successful in treating even obscure pragmatic elements like dialect and regional identity (Kiaer et al., 2019). Using multimedia effectively to present the context in which speech styles, address terms, and non-verbal honorifics are used in Korean could be an effective way to teach KFL learners explicitly to use pragmatic strategies.

Diversification is also needed in range of learning. Immersion has generally been pointed to as the failsafe method for learning pragmatics. In the wake of crises like COVID-19, however, opportunities for study abroad and immersive learning are sometimes less available than they were before. Rather than letting these limitations keep all learning in the classroom, however, educators can take advantage of virtual opportunities to increase range. Studies on the use of social media in language education to date show that it can be a powerful resource in increasing range. An understanding of the differences between individual features of social media and how they are perceived by learners and teachers is fundamental to creating successful teaching strategies based on social media resources. Combining previous analyses of disparities between teachers' and learners' perceptions of social media inside and outside education (Lambton-Howard, Kiaer, & Kharrufa, 2020), previous research stresses the importance of simple and realistic engagements with social media. According to these studies, most learners engage with digital technologies in "fairly simplistic" and "pragmatic" ways (Sharpe & Beetham, 2007). It is thus essential to create student-led, authentic models for social media integration and reflect this in assessment exercises. One priority in the deployment of social media recognized here is modelling an authentic communication flow. For example, AI-based social media, such as app technology, can be efficiently adapted to supplement classroom resources for the teaching and learning of pragmatics. In this case, especially in a world in which social media is increasingly ubiquitous in the lives of learners, an online learning approach combining social media interactions with chatbots and AI technology could provide optimal conditions for L2 learners to develop a working understanding of Korean pragmatics because it would allow them to examine natural language use in context.

Diversification is also needed in content being taught. Very often what has been taught in the classroom fails to represent diversity among interlocutors and their linguistic and cultural backgrounds. For instance, most interactions found in the textbooks focus on standard Korean (close to Seoul Korean) if interlocutors are Koreans (Kiaer, 2020b). Research shows that teaching about regional differences and non-standard varieties of Korean increases learners' confidence in pragmatic interactions (Kiaer et al., 2019). The textbooks frequently used rarely show this kind of diversity. They also rarely show how speech styles are shifted through negotiation to reflect intimacy or respect, even though this competence comprises an important part of pragmatic knowledge for KFL and KSL learners. As educators diversify the methods they use, the range in which language learning takes place, and the variety of content taught, learners can be better equipped with pragmatic competencies.

Conclusion

A brief examination of pragmatic features of Korean reveals that they form an essential part of any linguistic interaction in a Korean context. Some of these features include speech styles and skilfully switching between them, the proper use of address and kinship terms, and appropriate non-verbal signalling. Without these pragmatic features, a person cannot hope to communicate effectively or in a culturally appropriate way. However, pragmatic features such as speech styles, address terms, and non-verbal honorifics continue to go unaddressed in KFL curricula and are not measured by current assessment tools – even assessment tools designed specifically for Korean. The reason behind this is complex; it may result from the assumption of Koreans that foreigners do not need to integrate into Korean society, or it may come from the difficulty of teaching pragmatics for language educators. Further research is needed to better understand how these pragmatic aspects of the Korean language can effectively be taught to KFL/KSL learners in a way that enables them to navigate Korean social structures effectively.

Notes

1 Indicates pragmatic inconsistency.
2 Interestingly, early textbooks (from 1800 missionaries) tended to focus on pragmatic aspects, but language education has continued to trend more towards morphosyntactic aspects of the language.
3 A preliminary examination by the authors of other textbooks from Yonsei University, Ewha University, Hankuk University of Foreign Studies, and Seoul National University revealed very similar results.

References

ACTFL. (2012). *The ACTFL proficiency guidelines 2012*. Retrieved from www.actfl.org/sites/default/files/pdfs/public/ACTFLProficiencyGuidelines2012_FINAL.pdf

Brown, L. (2010). Questions of appropriateness and authenticity in the representation of Korean honorifics in textbooks for second language learners. *Language, Culture and Curriculum, 23*(1), 35–50.

Brown, L. (2013). Teaching 'casual' and/or 'impolite' language through multimedia: The case of non-honorific panmal speech styles in Korean. *Language, Culture and Curriculum, 26*, 1–18.

Brown, L. (2015). Revisiting "polite"-yo and "deferential" – Supnita speech style shifting in Korean from the viewpoint of indexicality. *Journal of Pragmatics, 79*, 43–59.

Brown, P., & Levinson, S. (1987). *Politeness: Some universals in language usage*. Cambridge: Cambridge University Press.

CEFR. (2001). *Common European Framework of Reference for languages: Learning, teaching, assessment*. Retrieved from www.coe.int/en/web/common-european-framework-reference-languages/the-cefr-descriptors

Kambara, W. (2011). Teaching Japanese pragmatic competence using film clips. *L2 Journal, 3*(2). http://doi.org/10.5070/L23210001

Kendon, A. (1988). How gestures can become like words. In. Fernando Poyatos (Ed.), *Cross cultural perspectives in nonverbal communication* (pp. 131–141). Toronto: C.J. Hugrele.

Kiaer, J. (2017). Korean drama and variety shows in teaching pragmatics and intercultural communicative competence: A case study from KFL learners' interviews. *International Korean Language Education, 3*(1), 109–142.

Kiaer, J. (2020a). *Pragmatic particles*. London: Bloomsbury.

Kiaer, J. (2020b). *Study abroad in Korea: Korean language and culture* (1st ed.). London: Routledge.

Kiaer, J., & Driggs, D. (2019). Exposing KFL learners to varieties of Korean through multimedia: Effects on perception and implications for teaching. In *Presented at 24th annual American Association of Teachers of Korean conference and workshop*. University of Minnesota Twin Cities, Minneapolis, Minnesota.

Kiaer, J., Driggs, D., Choi, N., & Brown, L. (submitted). Why don't' you call me hyung? *Journal of Language, Identity & Education*.

Kiaer, J., Park, M., Choi, N., & Driggs, D. (2019). The roles of age, gender and setting in Korean half-talk shift. *Discourse and Cognition, 26*, 279–308.

Kim, A. H. (2011). Korean politeness. In S. Mills & D. Kadar (Eds.), *Politeness in East Asia: Theory and practice* (pp. 176–207). Cambridge: Cambridge University Press.

Kim, H. (2003). *Hyentay hankuke hochinge-uy yeksel: 2-cha sahoy nay nulena-nun chincoke sayong* [The paradox of address term usage in modern Korean: The increase of kinship term usage in secondary society]. *Sahoyenehak [The Sociolinguistic Journal of Korea], 11*(1), 55–93.

Kim, H. (2008). Hyengtay pwunsek khophesuey kipanhan penyekmwunui nophim phyohyen yenkwu [Research on honorific expression in translation, from the form analysis corpus]. *Penyekhak yenkwu, 9*(4), 41–76.

Kim, H. (2012). Interactional functions of nodding in conversation. *The Sociolinguistic Journal of Korea, 20*(1), 1–26.

Kim, H. (2015). Hankwuke hwacaui piene hayngwi yenkwu- Kamthansaey tongpanhanun momcisul cwungsimulo [Research on non-verbal behaviour of Korean-focused on gestures accompanied by interjection]. *Journal of Bangyo Language and Literature, 40*, 157–181.

Kim, J. (2003). Young couples' communication in changing Korea. *Modern English and English Literature [hyentay yenge yengmwunhak], 47*(3), 197–217.

Kim, J. (2020). *Speech level shift in Korean as rhetorical device: Sarcasm, teasing, seriousness*. Talk presented at the Korean Studies Workshop at Oxford University.

Kita, S., & Ide, S. (2007). Nodding, *aizuchi*, and final particles in Japanese conversation: How conversation reflects the ideology of communication and social relationships. *Journal of Pragmatics, 39*, 1242–1254.

Knapp, M. L., Hall, J. A., & Horgan, T. G. (2014). *Nonverbal communication in human interaction*. Belmont: Wadsworth/Cengage learning.

Kogure, M. (2007). Nodding and smiling in silence during the loop sequence of backchannels in Japanese conversation. *Journal of Pragmatics, 39*, 1275–1289.

Lambton-Howard, D., Kiaer, J., & Kharrufa, A. (2020). 'Social media is their space': Student and teacher use and perception of features of social media in language education, *Behaviour & Information Technology*. https://doi.org/10.1080/0144929X.2020.1774653

Larmer, B. (2018). *South Korea's most dangerous enemy: Demographics*. Retrieved from www.nytimes.com/2018/02/20/magazine/south-koreas-most-dangerous-enemy-demographics.html

Lee, I., & Ramsey, S. (2000). *The Korean language*. Albany, NY: State University of New York Press.

Lee, J. (2012). *Principles of the function and usage of Korean honorifics [Hankwuke kyengepepei kinungkwa sayong wenli]*. Seoul: Sotong.

Lee, K., & Yu Cho, Y. (2015). Social meanings of honorific/non-honorific alternations in Korean and Japanese. *Korean Linguistics, 17*(2), 207–241.

Maynard, S. K. (1987). Interactional functions of a nonverbal sign. *Journal of Pragmatics, 11*, 589–606.

McClave, Z. (2000). Linguistic functions of head movements in the context of speech. *Journal of Pragmatics, 32*, 855–878.

McNeill, D. (1992). *Hand and mind: What gestures reveal about thought*. Chicago: University of Chicago Press.

Moody, S. (2014). Should we teach rules for pragmatics? Explicit instruction and emergent awareness of Japanese plain and polite forms. *Japanese Language and Literature, 48*(1), 39–69.

Oh Eun, J., & Strauss, S. (2004). The primacy of information status in the alternation between deferential and polite forms in Korean public discourse. *Language Sciences* (Oxford), *26*(3), 251–272.

Park, M. (2017). Negotiating solidarity and politeness in Korean interaction. *International Journal of Korean Language Education, 3*(1), 197–237.

Park, Y. (1995). The sociolinguistics of hearer honorifics [*Sangtay nophimpepei sahoi enehak*], *Emwun Noncip, 34*, 549–570. Mincoke mwunhakhoi.

Pickles, M. (2018). *K-pop drives boom in Korean language lessons*. Retrieved from www.bbc.co.uk/news/business-44770777

Sharpe, R., & Beetham, H. (2007). *Rethinking pedagogy for a digital age: Designing and delivering e-learning*. New York: Taylor & Francis [CAM].

Strauss, S., & Eun, J. (2005). Indexicality and honorific speech level choice in Korean. *Linguistics, 43*(3), 611–651.

Tsutagawa, F. (2015). Future directions in pragmatics assessment. *Working Papers in Applied Linguistics and TESOL, 12*(2), 43–45.

Wharton, T. (2009). *Pragmatics and non-verbal communication*. Cambridge: Cambridge University Press.

Won, Y. (2016). Common European Framework of Reference for Language (CEFR) and Test of Proficiency in Korean (TOPIK). *International Journal of Area Studies, 11*(1), 39–58.

Yeon, J., & Brown, L. (2011). *Korean: A comprehensive grammar*. Oxon and New York: Routledge.

8
TASK-BASED LANGUAGE TEACHING IN KOREAN CLASSROOM CONTEXTS
Promoting learner engagement during task performance

YouJin Kim and Sanghee Kang

Introduction

Over the last few decades, task-based language teaching (TBLT) has received an increasing amount of attention in the field of second language acquisition (SLA) and pedagogy (e.g., Ellis, 2003; Kim, 2015; Long, 2015, 2016; Samuda & Bygate, 2008). Since task design is based on learners' real-world needs and interests, it is expected that such task characteristics will motivate learners to be involved in interaction and to produce target-language output while completing tasks. Additionally, tasks offer contexts where learners can provide support to each other while solving linguistic problems. Due to strong empirical support for the benefits of tasks in language learning, today TBLT is widely considered an effective language-teaching approach (Ellis, 2018; Long, 2015).

The purpose of this chapter is to review previous research on TBLT and address pedagogical implications for second language (L2) Korean language instruction, particularly focusing on peer interaction during task performance. Situated within the research domain of TBLT, the chapter focuses on promoting learner engagement in tasks. We do so by reviewing previous task research that has examined task design and task implementation factors in Korean as a foreign or second language (KSL hereafter) contexts. The first section will start with a review of important terms and concepts, such as task, and different approaches to TBLT (task-based vs. task-referenced vs. task-supported). The next section reviews empirical classroom-based research focusing on task design and implementation factors while interpreting the results from learner engagement perspectives. The final two sections address the pedagogical implications of previous research in KSL contexts and directions for future research.

Tasks and task-based language teaching

What are tasks?

In the field of TBLT, one of the most widely discussed topics is what qualifies to be called a "task." Over the last three decades, as the field of TBLT has expanded, a task has been defined in a number of ways. Table 8.1 presents examples of definitions of a task provided by researchers and L2 practitioners. As shown in Table 8.1, even though there is some overlap among definitions, it has been pointed out that "there is no complete agreement as to what constitutes a task" (Ellis, 2003, p. 2). For example, while Long's (1985) definition of a task includes both activities that involve language use (e.g., filling out a form) and those that do not require the use of language (e.g., painting a fence), Ellis (2003) defines a task as an activity in which learners engage in language use which resembles a real-world communicative activity.

Ellis, Skehan, Li, Shintani, and Lambert (2020) argue that the proliferation of definitions of a task results in a need for a definition that can be applied in various contexts and for diverse purposes. Ellis et al. (2020, p. 10) attribute a lack of agreement in definitions to the failure to distinguish two senses of task (Breen, 1989) – task-as-workplan (i.e., "the design materials that will create a context for the communicative use of the L2") and task-as-process (i.e., "the language use resulting from the performance of the task"). They then suggest that a task should be defined in terms of the task-as-workplan as it creates a fruitful site for communicative language use. Ellis and his colleagues (Ellis et al., 2020, p. 10) further propose four criteria to determine the qualification of a given task as a task-as-workplan based on Ellis and Shintani (2014):

1 The primary focus is on meaning.
2 There is some kind of gap.

Table 8.1 Definitions of a task

Source	Definition
Long (1985)	A task is "a piece of work undertaken for oneself or for others, freely or for some reward. Thus, examples of tasks include painting a fence, dressing a child, filling out a form . . . In other words, by 'task' is meant the hundred and one things people do in everyday life, at work, at play, and in between. 'Tasks' are the things people will tell you they do if you ask them and they are not applied linguists."
Prabhu (1987)	An activity which required learners to arrive at an outcome from given information through some process of thought and which allowed teachers to control and regulate that process.
Nunan (1989)	A communicative task is a "piece of classroom work which involves learners in comprehending, manipulating, producing, or interacting in the target language while their attention is principally focused on meaning rather than form. The task should also have a sense of completeness, being able to stand alone as a communicative act in its own right."
Skehan (1996)	A task is "an activity in which meaning is primary; there is some sort of relationship to the real world; task completion has some priority; and the assessment of task performance is in terms of task outcome."
Ellis (2003)	A task is intended to result in language use that bears a resemblance, direct or indirect, to the way language is used in the real world. Like other language activities, a task can engage productive or receptive and oral or written skills and also various cognitive processes.
Van den Branden (2006)	A task is an educational activity which is designed and organized to stimulate and support learners in reaching their language-learning goals.
Samuda and Bygate (2008)	A task is a holistic activity which engages language use to achieve some non-linguistic outcome while meeting a linguistic challenge, with the overall aim of promoting language learning, through process or product or both.

Source: Adapted from Kim, 2015, p. 164

3   Learners rely mainly on their own linguistic and non-linguistic resources.
4   There is a clearly defined communicative outcome.

Similar to the definition of tasks, task classifications have been discussed considerably. Ellis (2003) categorizes tasks in terms of task features, such as information exchange, expected task outcome, and convergence. According to Ellis (2003), when a task requires learners to exchange information for the task to be completed (e.g., information gap tasks), the information can be split either one way or two ways. In one-way tasks, a single person holds the information that is needed for task completion, while in two-way tasks, information is split between two learners and both learners are obliged to share information to achieve the task outcome. For example, if a learner holds a map and describes the map to another learner who needs to draw a similar map based on what he or she hears, this task can be described as a one-way task. If two learners have two different schedules and need to figure out when to meet to study the following week, this would be an example of a two-way task. Researchers have compared one-way and two-way tasks, but the results have not reached similar conclusions (Ellis, 2003; Samuda & Bygate, 2008). For example, while Long (1980) showed that two-way tasks elicited more negotiation for meaning than one-way tasks, other studies, such as Gass and Varonis (1985), have reported that one-way tasks were more effective in producing more negotiation for meaning.

Another distinction that can be made with tasks is between open and closed tasks. Ellis (2003) describes open tasks as those that do not have a pre-determined solution; thus, various solutions can be drawn from task performance (e.g., discuss what events should be included in the graduation ceremony), whereas closed tasks are those with a definite number of solutions decided in advance (e.g., between options A and B, decide which event you and your partner want to host together at the graduation ceremony). Long (1989) states that closed tasks will be more likely to produce more negotiated talk and more useful negotiation work, which can result in L2 acquisition because closed tasks elicit more topics, more language reformulations, and more feedback as learners are required to find the correct answer. However, for open tasks such as free conversation, Long maintains that learners tend to discuss topics briefly or even give up when a difficult topic is presented and to offer less feedback and fewer resources.

A distinction of convergent tasks and divergent tasks has also received attention (Duff, 1986; Pica, Young, & Doughty, 1987). Convergent tasks are tasks in which all learners need to jointly agree on a task outcome (e.g., problem-solving tasks), while in divergent tasks, such as debates, learners can reach different outcomes or conclusions by pursuing independent goals (Pica et al., 1987). Convergent tasks have been found to elicit more comprehensible input (more turns per task, more questions, and more confirmation checks) than divergent tasks, which result in more output, with learners producing more words and more complex utterances (Duff, 1986).

To help conceptualize what a task looks like, Figure 8.1 presents a sample task ("Text a Friend about Spring Break" from the task-based Korean language textbook *Learning Korean Through Tasks: High Beginner to Low Intermediate* [Kim, Choi, Yun, Kim, & Kang, 2021, pp. 62–65]). Targeting high beginner to low intermediate-level learners, this task was designed to provide a context for meaningful communicative language use in a task-supported language curriculum. Thus, each task was developed with target features in mind. The example task is a collaborative speaking and writing task, in which two learners work together toward a goal. As shown in Figure 8.1, each learner is given a different information sheet. After reviewing their own given information, learners exchange information orally to accomplish the first goal (i.e., to make a plan for the upcoming weekend during spring break). Then, based on the shared information, learners write text messages in Korean to talk about their spring break trip and to discuss plans for the weekend. Even though some information about what they are doing during spring break was provided in the task input, there is also missing information that students need to come up with. Thus, this task can be considered to have characteristics of both open and closed tasks. Also, in this task, information is split two ways, and the two learners are required to exchange information to complete the task. These aspects make the given task a two-way information gap task. Regarding the final outcome, as students need to jointly agree on the output, this task is a convergent task.

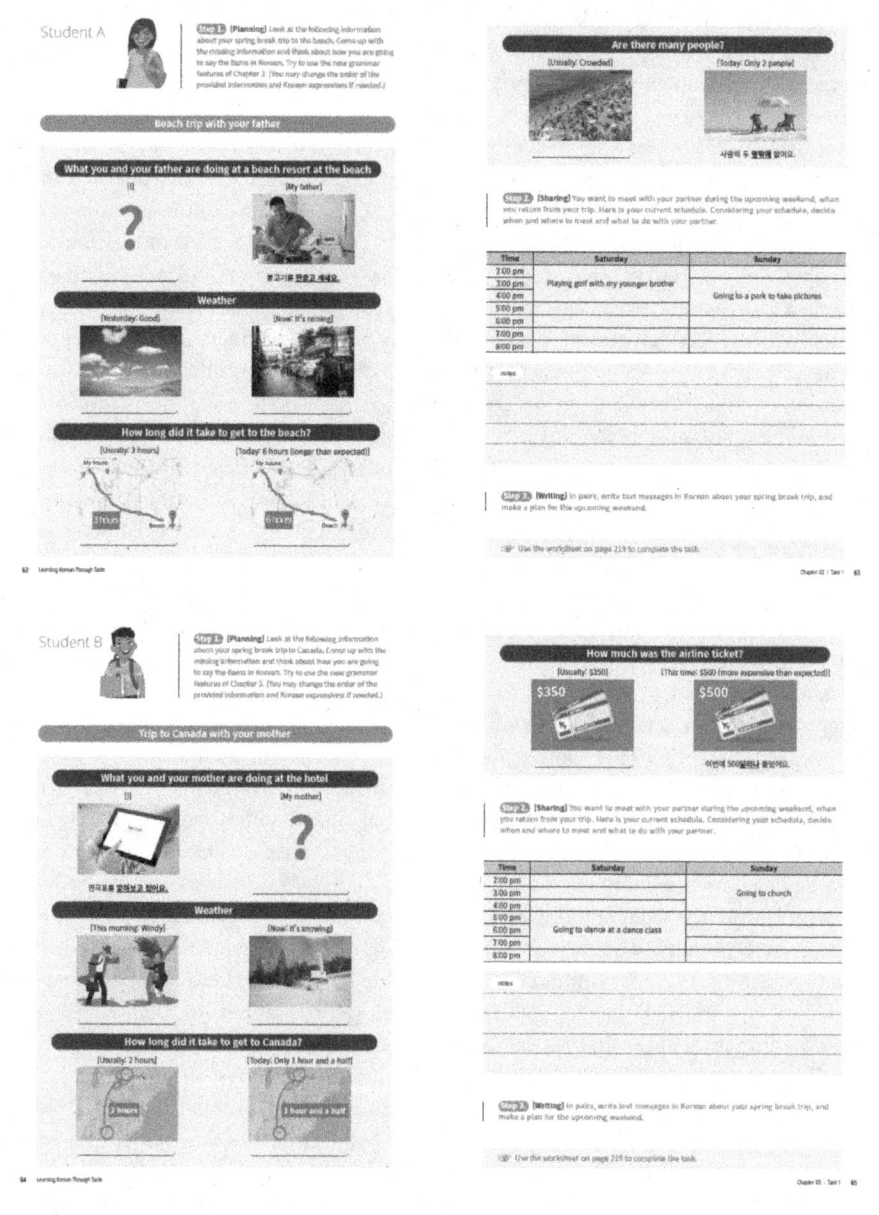

Figure 8.1 A sample task ("Text a Friend about Spring Break")

Source: from Kim et al. (2021)

This sample task meets Ellis et al.'s (2020) four task criteria. More specifically, it provides a site where learners can engage in language use which is similar to the way the equivalent real-world communicative activity is done. Clearly, it has a real-world relationship in that what students are asked to do – asking about what friends are currently doing or making a spring break plan – are tasks that are commonly done in the real world, particularly in the US context. Based on Ellis et al.'s (2020) criteria for defining a task, the primary focus of this task is on meaning since learners are concerned with comprehending and producing messages to talk about their trip and make a plan for the weekend. In terms of a gap, this task is designed in a way that learners need to exchange information by asking about how spring break is going and asking about each other's schedules and share their opinions to plan what they want to do for the weekend. In this task, learners need to draw on their existing linguistic knowledge (i.e., vocabulary, grammar) and may use non-linguistic resources (e.g., gestures) to negotiate for meaning. Finally, this task specifies a clear communicative outcome – text messages.

What is TBLT?

TBLT has been developed based on various theories of language acquisition and L2 pedagogy as an alternative approach to structure-based approaches that are characterized by synthetic syllabi which divide language into discrete parts and involve form-oriented language practices (Ellis, 2017; Long, 2015; Long & Norris, 2000). According to Van den Branden (2006), TBLT is "an approach to language education in which students are given functional tasks that invite them to focus primarily on meaning exchange and to use language for real-world, non-linguistic purposes" (p. 1). Thus, in TBLT pedagogy, meaning is prioritized; however, form is not disregarded (Ellis et al., 2020). Tasks are used as the defining unit in structuring a language curriculum and a syllabus; that is, the TBLT curriculum centers around tasks. Furthermore, TBLT highlights learning the L2 through using the language during task performance (Bygate, Norris, & Van den Branden, 2015). As such, the aims of TBLT are ultimately to help the learner develop L2 fluency by providing meaningful communicative contexts where learners can draw on their existing linguistic knowledge, gain new linguistic knowledge, and develop interactional competence through input, interactions, and attention to form while performing tasks (Ellis, 2017).

Bygate (2016) introduces four main elements of a task-based approach (pp. 388–390), which L2 practitioners and programs can draw upon in adopting task-based teaching in language education:

1. TBLT as a needs-based approach
2. The three-phase procedure
3. A discovery-based element to TBLT
4. TBLT as a project-based approach

When designing a language curriculum based on TBLT, Bygate (2016) emphasizes that identifying the target tasks – tasks that learners will need to perform in the target language – should be the first step (i.e., needs analysis); then, the identified tasks are sequenced in terms of task complexity and difficulty in order to structure the curriculum. The second element proposed by Bygate is implementing a three-phase procedure, which means that tasks consist of a pre-task phase, an on-task phase (or during-task phase), and a post-task phase. The functions of each phase and the teacher's and students' roles during each phase are described in Table 8.2.

The third element Bygate suggests is a discovery-based aspect, which entails that "the task is deliberately used as a way of leading students into discovering something they are not quite able to

Table 8.2 Three-phase procedure

Phase	Description	
	Teacher	*Students*
Pre-task	• Providing general information about the task (purpose, the conceptual content, expected outcome) • Presenting the input material	• Getting ready for task performance
On-task	• Monitoring students to offer support and clarification	• Engaging in the task
Post-task	• Providing form-focused language practice	• Reviewing task outcomes in terms of language use through teacher feedback or self-correction • Sharing task outcomes with the class

Source: Bygate, 2016; taken from Kim et al., 2021, p. 10

perform" (p. 389). By performing a task, learners are first driven to focus on meaning for communication, and while attempting to convey and comprehend meaning, they gradually come to realize that they do not have all the linguistic resources necessary to complete the task, which may result in learning new language. The last element which Bygate highlights is that TBLT is a project-based approach, in which a task is used to create a communicative space for contextualized language work (e.g., a consumer report, an environmental study, a webpage). According to Bygate, tasks as projects can be incorporated within the context of a classroom as individual work, group work, or a whole-class project; they can also be implemented as an inter-school web-based project.

Different approaches to the use of tasks in syllabus design

In TBLT literature, different approaches to incorporating tasks in course syllabi or curricula have been discussed. Table 8.3 presents three types of syllabi with different approaches to the use of tasks (Samuda & Bygate, 2008, pp. 58–60; Bygate, 2016).

As displayed in Table 8.3, Samuda and Bygate (2008) and Bygate (2016) argue that the biggest difference in the three approaches lies in the role of tasks. In TBLT, tasks define the curriculum, the syllabus, and the assessment, and instruction center around tasks. In task-referenced language teaching (TRLT), the role of tasks is limited to assessment. Tasks are used as a reference (i.e., achievement targets) to evaluate language-learning outcomes. Task-supported language teaching (TSLT) incorporates tasks in existing structural syllabi to provide more opportunities in which learners can engage in additional communicative language use (Bygate, 2016). In terms of assessment in TSLT, tasks can be employed as an assessing component, but unlike TBLT and TRLT, tasks do not define assessment. One might wonder which approach is most effective in promoting second language learning. There has not been much research that compared the effects of different pedagogic positions except for Li, Ellis, and Zhu (2016). They compared the effectiveness of TBLT and TSLT in promoting L2 learners' acquisition of the English passive structure and found that TSLT was more effective than pure TBLT in acquiring new grammatical features in a foreign language context. Because such a finding was based on one study, to understand the effectiveness of both approaches in language learning, more research comparing the two conditions is warranted.

So far, we have reviewed the key concepts and rationale of TBLT. TBLT has been widely accepted by L2 practitioners and extensively researched in the field of second language learning. Researchers in Korean language pedagogy have also shown an interest in TBLT as a pedagogical approach. Recently, Park, Choi, and Ko (2020) discussed pedagogical approaches

Table 8.3 Approaches to the use of tasks in the syllabus

	Task-based language teaching (TBLT)	Task-referenced language teaching (TRLT)	Task-supported language teaching (TSLT)
The role of tasks for instruction	• The basic unit of instruction • A defining element in curriculum and syllabuses	• No explicit proposal about the use of tasks in instruction	• An important but not the only component in teaching • Used with other activities
The role of tasks for assessment	• Defining component of assessment (i.e., task-based assessment)	• Setting achievement targets • Evaluating language-learning outcomes	• A potential element of assessment but not necessarily the defining element
Examples	• Van den Branden (2006) • Chaudron et al. (2001) • Kong (2012)	• Brindley and Slatyer (2002)	• East (2012) • Kim, Kang, Yun, Kim, and Choi (2020)

and practices in Korean instruction and described three approaches that have been most widely adopted and researched, which include TBLT. Researchers and teachers at the University of Hawai'i have played a particularly important role in promoting TBLT projects in Korean instructional contexts. For instance, Chaudron et al. (2001) describe a task-based needs analysis of a Korean language program in the United States, and Kim, Kong, Lee, and Lee (2001) report the process of implementing and evaluating TBLT modules. Afterward, Kong (2012) implemented task-based pedagogy in the Korean Language Flagship Center MA program at the University of Hawai'i and presented how seven stages of TBLT implementation were carried in the MA program (i.e., needs analysis, target task types, pedagogic tasks, sequencing tasks, appropriate methodology and pedagogy, assessments, and program evaluation). Some researchers have investigated how learners perceive TBLT implemented in a Korean program. For example, Pyun (2013) surveyed the attitudes toward TBLT of Korean language learners who received task-based instruction and further investigated how learners' attitudes were related to learner characteristics (e.g., anxiety, motivation, self-efficacy).

Overall, although little task-based research has been done at the curriculum level in the Korean classroom, there has been an increasing amount of research focusing on to what extent task-based instruction facilitates Korean language learning. To address this question, researchers have conducted classroom-based task research motivated by the theories of SLA. In particular, researchers within the research domain of instructed SLA (ISLA), whose research primarily focuses on examining how learning conditions can be manipulated to facilitate L2 development (Loewen, 2020), have examined different aspects of task design and task implementation in an attempt to find evidence for the ultimate language instruction environment using pedagogic tasks. In the following sections, we review Korean classroom–based ISLA research in which tasks are the main tool in a Korean classroom and pedagogical implications are offered. We interpret previous task design and implementation research findings from task-engagement perspectives.

Task design, task implementation, and task engagement

Engagement with tasks in the language classroom

According to Philp and Duchesne (2016, p. 51), engagement refers to, "a state of heightened attention and involvement, in which participation is reflected not only in the cognitive dimension, but in social, behavioral, and affective dimensions as well." Based on the work of educational psychology, Philp and Duchesne claim that engagement is a multifaceted construct that incorporates multiple dimensions (i.e., cognitive, behavior, emotional, and social) and that "the interdependence of the dimensions of engagement is a vital characteristic of the construct" (p. 52).

Cognitive engagement is associated with mental effort and the process of maintaining cognitive conscious attention. Previous research identified cognitive engagement through the presence of verbal forms during interactions, including phrases such as "I think" and "because." Additionally, students' cognitive engagement with language during task performance has been identified in analysis units such as form-focused episodes and language-related episodes (LREs) (Kim & McDonough, 2008). LREs refer to "any part of a dialogue where the students talk about the language they are producing, question their language use, or correct themselves or others" (Swain & Lapkin, 1998, p. 326). For instance, Example 1 shows two KSL learners' discussion on the use of the past tense morpheme during a dictogloss task. Both learners were cognitively engaged with the grammar choice during the task.

Example 1:[1] Grammatical LREs (taken from Kim & McDonough, 2008, pp. 217–218)

1   S1: 아버지가 선생님이다?
    (a-bu-ji-ga sun-saeng-nim-i-da?)
    [Father is a teacher?]
2   S2: 아버지는 선생님 이었다. 현재 아니고 과거
    (a-bu-ji-nun sun-saeng-nim-i-et-da. hyun-jae a-ni-go, gwa-guh)
    [Father was a teacher, not present, past]

According to Philp and Duchesne (2016), behavioral engagement can be described in terms of time on task or participation, and thus being on-task is considered the same as being behaviorally engaged. They note that behavioral engagement has been perceived as a dichotomy (engaged vs. disengaged) or a continuum depending on the degree and quality of participation, using amount of effort, persistence, and active involvement as components to consider.

Emotional engagement has been defined in various ways. In terms of emotional engagement during task performance, Skinner, Kindermann, and Furrer (2009) define it as motivated involvement during task performance, which can be indicated through enthusiasm, interest, enjoyment, purposefulness, and autonomy. Philp and Duchesne (2016) further mention that emotional engagement may "include students' feeling of connection or disconnection with their peers in the class and, particularly, their task interlocutors" (p. 56).

Philp and Duchesne (2016) introduce the idea of social engagement, which, according to them, is closely related to emotional engagement. Social engagement is particularly relevant to peer interaction when peers create their own learning environment through interaction. Students' pair dynamics (Storch, 2002) are suggested as a way to describe social engagement. Thus, social engagement needs to be interpreted as a context-specific construct.

Recently, these different dimensions of task engagement have received growing interest. In particular, researchers have tried to show the interdependence of these characteristics. For instance, Baralt, Gurzynski-Weiss, and Kim (2016) compared the degree of learner engagement in terms of cognitive, affective, and social dimensions in face-to-face and computer-mediated communication contexts. They found that learners who established social relationships with their peers, which was found more in face-to-face settings, were more likely to engage with and deploy attentional resources to a language task compared to those who did not. In a more tightly controlled intervention study, Phung (2017) examined behavioral, cognitive, and social measures of learners' engagement in L2 use and compared ESL learners' performance during a task that they preferred more and a task that they preferred less. The findings suggest that the learners showed a higher level of cognitive engagement in L2 use (i.e., greater negotiation of meaning and form) when performing their preferred task, and their preference was impacted by several factors, such as topic and opportunities to create ideas and address a genuine communicative need.

In sum, although the concept of task engagement is an important one that has a direct impact on classroom language pedagogy, the scope of the research domain on this topic is rather limited. In the subsequent sections, we offer a brief overview of task research focusing on classroom interaction and review previous Korean classroom-based task research that examined task design and implementation factors. We interpret these results from learner-engagement perspectives.

Task design and task implementation factors and their associations with task engagement

In her overview article, Kim (2015) discusses previous research focusing on the use of tasks in language classrooms, particularly highlighting task design and implementation variables examined in classroom interaction studies. As shown in Figure 8.2 (from Kim, 2015, p. 167), the role of different task design variables (e.g., task characteristics, task types, task complexity) and task implementation variables (e.g., interlocutor characteristics, task planning, task modeling, task repetition) were often found to impact interactional features during task performance, linguistic performance, and the subsequent task-based language learning.

As mentioned earlier, one of the reasons for a surge in the amount of classroom-based task research is because of the convergence of the two fields, that is, SLA and TBLT. As the importance of learner–learner interaction in language learning from various theoretical

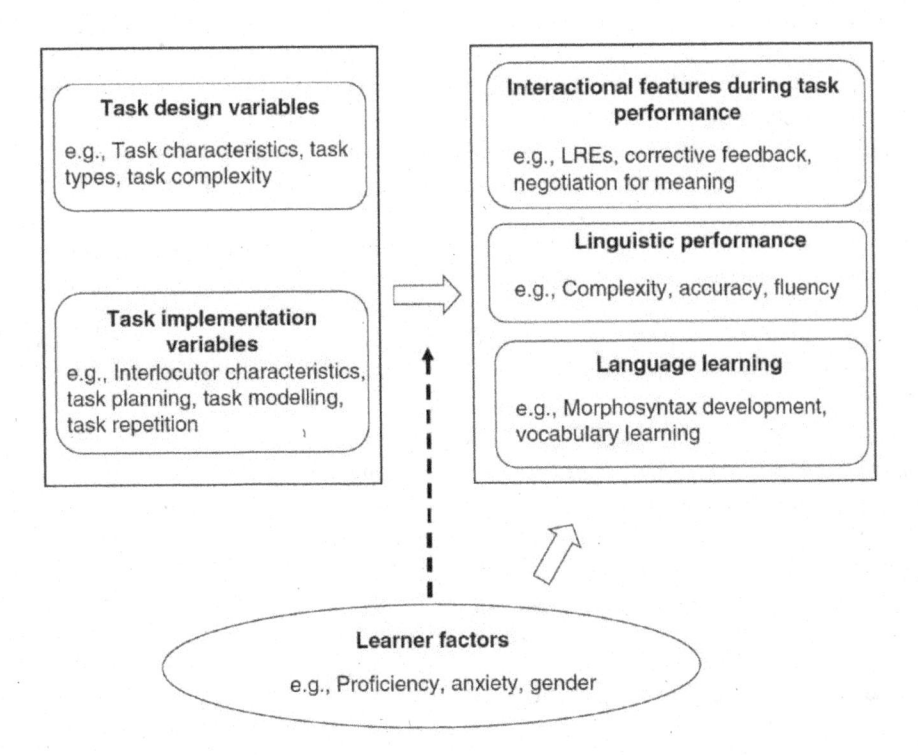

Figure 8.2 Task design and implementation variables investigated in classroom interaction studies

perspectives (e.g., sociocultural theory, interaction approaches to language teaching) has been highlighted, collaborative tasks in particular have been suggested as useful teaching tools to facilitate exposure to the target language and to promote meaningful language-use opportunities. As a result, both SLA and TBLT researchers have begun to examine various aspects of the design and implementation of collaborative tasks with the common goal of finding the ultimate language-learning site. Although the majority of studies to date have targeted English language learning, recently, increasing attention has been paid to Korean language acquisition.

In terms of task engagement and its association with other task design and implementation factors, the majority of the variables that are presented in Figure 8.2 either directly or indirectly impact different dimensions of task engagement (cognitive, behavioral, emotional, social). We chose the following three factors for our discussion on how to promote different aspects of task engagement, as these topics were increasingly examined in previous KSL task-oriented classroom-based studies, and previous findings are relevant to different aspects of task engagement: (1) comparing individual and collaborative tasks, (2) investigating the role of interlocutor variables (e.g., proficiency level and heritage vs. non-heritage status), and (3) examining the effects of task repetition. Finally, we also introduce synchronous corrective feedback as a way to promote engagement with language during task performance. Representative sample studies are reviewed in Table 8.4.

Comparing individual and collaborative task performance and associated learning outcomes

Researchers have compared individual tasks and collaborative tasks in terms of task performance and the subsequent task-supported learning. For instance, using a dictogloss task, Kim (2008) compared individual and collaborative task performance among 32 KSL university learners in Korea. She analyzed students' attention to target vocabulary words using LREs. The findings showed that learners produced a similar number of LREs; however, the collaborative task condition allowed learners to be exposed to twice as many LREs as in the individual task performance condition. As a result, the collaborative task group outperformed the individual task group on the vocabulary posttest.

In a follow-up study, Cho and Kim (in press) used an email writing task and compared individual and collaborative writing conditions in learning honorifics. Students performed two tasks which followed the same procedure but had different content. The novel aspect of this study was to incorporate synchronous written corrective feedback (SWCF) while students were performing collaborative writing tasks either individually or in pairs. While the individual group was asked to think aloud during task performance, the collaborative group interactions were recorded (see Examples 2 and 3 taken from Cho & Kim, in press). As shown in Example 2, receiving the indirect SWCF (i.e., circling errors without offering the correct form) allowed students working individually to notice an interlanguage gap and encouraged them to correct their errors, which seemed to offer learning opportunities. On the other hand, when two students worked together, they were able to discuss and solve language issues together (i.e., the occurrence of LREs), and indirect SWCF particularly facilitated this process. Overall, Cho and Kim report no significant difference between the individual and collaborative writing conditions in terms of the suppliance and accuracy of target honorific forms and the subsequent learning of honorific features measured by production tests. Cho and Kim claim that with SWCF, individual task performance could be as beneficial as collaborative writing tasks.

Table 8.4 Classroom-based Korean task-based research

Study	Participants	Tasks	Goals (or main variables)	Findings
Kim and McDonough (2008)	24 KSL university learners in Korea	Dictogloss task	• To compare effects of interlocutor proficiency (intermediate vs. advanced) on the occurrence of LREs and pair dynamics	• Working with advanced interlocutors resulted in significantly more lexical LREs and correctly resolved LREs. • Pair dynamics changed depending on interlocutor proficiency levels.
Kim (2008)	32 KSL university learners in Korea	Dictogloss task	• To compare the impact of individual vs. collaborative task performance on vocabulary learning	• Learners produced a similar number of LREs for both individual and collaborative tasks. • Collaborative tasks promoted a greater degree of vocabulary learning than individual tasks.
Kim, Lee, and Kim (2018)	14 heritage language and 32 foreign language university learners in the US (high beginner level)	Collaborative writing task (drama script writing task)	• To examine the development of receptive and productive knowledge of Korean honorifics by comparing learning outcomes of heritage language learners (HLLs) and foreign language learners (FLLs) on collaborative writing tasks • To examine students' perceptions of collaborative writing tasks and pair work	• Both HLLs and FLLs showed development of receptive and productive knowledge of Korean honorifics. • HLLs in HLL–FLL dyads outperformed FLLs in FLL–FLL dyads in the immediate learning of productive knowledge of Korean honorifics but not delayed learning. • Both HLL–FLL and FLL–FLL dyads paid more attention to honorific nouns and honorific verb suffixes than to honorific verbs or honorific subject particles. • HLLs and FLLs both showed positive attitudes toward their partners during collaborative tasks.
Kim, Choi, Kang, Kim, and Yun (2020)	53 foreign language university learners in the US (high beginner level)	Collaborative writing tasks (e-mail writing, postcard writing, blog post writing tasks)	• To compare the effect of direct and indirect synchronous written corrective feedback (SWCF) during collaborative writing on learning grammar • To examine learners' perceptions of SWCF	• Direct SWCF promoted greater accuracy in writing than indirect SWCF. • Both SWCF types led to the learning of new linguistic features through collaborative writing. • No difference was observed in learners' perceptions of SWCF between the two types of SWCF.

(Continued)

Table 8.4 (Continued)

Study	Participants	Tasks	Goals (or main variables)	Findings
Kim, Kang et al. (2020)	38 foreign language university learners in the US (high beginner level)	Collaborative writing task (shopping blog entry)	• To compare the impact of exact task repetition and procedural task repetition on the complexity and accuracy of task output, learners' attention to linguistic features, and the subsequent learning of grammar	• Exact task repetition benefited syntactic complexity and accuracy of target grammar features, but little evidence of benefits for global accuracy was gathered. • The exact task repetition condition showed a noticeable decrease in learners' attention to target features from Task 1 to Task 2, while a similar amount of attention was given by learners during Tasks 1 and 2 in the procedural task repetition condition. • The procedural task repetition group outperformed the exact task repetition group on the posttest.
Cho and Kim (in press)	32 foreign language university learners in the US (high beginner level)	Collaborative writing task (e-mail-writing task)	• To compare the effectiveness of individual and collaborative writing tasks in learning honorifics • To examine students' perceptions of individual and collaborative writing tasks	• No difference was found in the learning of Korean honorifics between the individual task and collaborative writing task conditions. • Students from both groups had generally positive perceptions of their task performance, but the collaborative group showed a higher degree of task enjoyment.
Kim, Choi, Yun, Kim, and Choi (in press)	54 foreign language university learners in the US (high beginner level)	Collaborative writing task (online journal entry)	• To examine the effects of task repetition and indirect SWCF on the quality of written task outcome and the subsequent learning of grammar	• Task repetition improved writing fluency. • SWCF facilitated accuracy in students' writing. • No significant benefit of SWCF on grammar learning was found.

Example 2: Think-aloud data from the individual group (taken from Cho & Kim, in press)[2]

1   Learner A: Ah (receiving WCF)
2   Learner A: not possession but existence, it's going to be . . .
3   Learner A: So the honorific ending for 있다 (to be) for existence is 계세요 (the honorific form of to be)

Example 3: Interaction data from the collaborative group (taken from Cho & Kim, in press)

4   Learner B: So, it would be 남편 (husband) . . .
5   Learner C: Would you use, would you use, would you use 께서는 (kkey-se; honorific particle)?
6   Learner B: To honor her husband?
7   Learner C: 께서는 (kkey-se; honorific particle)

Additionally, Cho and Kim (in press) examined students' perceptions of task performance. Both groups found Task 2 (the procedure repetition of Task 1) to be more interesting (enjoyment) and to provide more learning opportunities than Task 1 (the first time they performed the task). The collaborative group considered Task 1 more difficult than Task 2. By repeating the same task procedure with different content, the level of task difficulty that students perceived was lower. Moreover, the students felt more relaxed while completing Task 2 than Task 1 and were more willing to do similar tasks later. On the other hand, the individual group considered Task 2 more difficult than Task 1. They reported being less relaxed while completing Task 2 than Task 1 and less willing to perform similar tasks later.

    The aforementioned studies that compared individual and collaborative tasks can provide insights into the extent to which learners engage with tasks either working individually or in pairs/groups. In terms of cognitive engagement, these two studies suggest that with the same task design, there might not be a significantly different degree of cognitive engagement (as operationalized by the number of LREs), especially if the individual group receives SWCF. In terms of social engagement, without a doubt, pair work offers more social engagement opportunities than an individual task. Furthermore, the student perception survey results from Cho and Kim shed light on students' emotional engagement. Students seemed to become more comfortable and more motivated to perform tasks as they repeated similar tasks when working with peers compared to working individually.

The role of interlocutor effects in collaborative task performance

When implementing collaborative tasks, one of the most challenging jobs for teachers is making pairing/grouping decisions. Researchers have investigated the role of interlocutors' backgrounds in task performance. For instance, Kim and McDonough (2008) compared how intermediate-level learners (core participants) differed in terms of pair dynamics and the amount of attention that they paid to language (LREs) depending on whether they worked with other intermediate-level learners or advanced-level learners. The occurrence of LREs indicates students' cognitive engagement, and pair dynamics were representative of social engagement. Kim and McDonough also asked students about their perceptions of pair work, which can shed light on their emotional engagement with the task. The findings showed that working with advanced interlocutors elicited more lexical LREs and correctly resolved LREs than working with intermediate-level learners. In terms of pair dynamics, interlocutor proficiency levels were associated with patterns of pair work. For instance, learners who showed a dominant pattern when working with a fellow intermediate-level learner changed their dynamic to a collaborative pattern when working with an advanced learner. The core intermediate-level learners preferred working with an advanced learner who provided scaffolding during task performance. This is one of the first studies on collaborative tasks targeting KSL; the findings suggest that interlocutor proficiency impacts students' attention to language form and pair dynamics.

Another interlocutor-related topic in collaborative task research is learners' heritage background in the target language. This is also a concern for language policy in foreign language programs at colleges and universities. Kim et al. (2018) compared pairing/grouping between heritage language learners and foreign language learners (HLL–FLL vs. FLL–FLL). They examined the development of receptive and productive knowledge of Korean honorifics by HLLs and FLLs. Building on previous LRE research, they used pragmatic-related episodes (PREs) to identify learners' attention to discussion of sociopragmatics and pragmalinguistics (i.e., cognitive engagement). The findings showed that both HLLs and FLLs developed receptive and productive knowledge of Korean honorifics through collaborative writing tasks (drama script writing tasks). In terms of the subsequent learning, HLLs in HLL–FLL dyads outperformed FLLs in FLL–FLL dyads on the immediate learning of productive knowledge of Korean honorifics but not on the delayed learning. Furthermore, with regard to the occurrence of PREs (i.e., cognitive engagement with pragmatic features), HLLs resolved PREs at a higher rate than FLLs. Kim, Lee, and Kim claim that heritage learners served as resourceful interlocutors, probably thanks to their superior understanding of Korean honorifics culture.

Interlocutor effects are critical in collaborative task research. Task design and implementation factors are often mediated by who learners work with during task performance. As shown in these two previous Korean classroom studies, learners' proficiency levels and heritage backgrounds could impact cognitive engagement with language as observed in LREs and PREs as well as social and emotional engagement in tasks. In particular, Kim et al. (2018) provided evidence for emotional engagement in tasks. They reported that both HLLs and FLLs agreed that collaborative tasks were helpful in learning Korean honorifics. They further explained that having learners work with familiar classmates during pair work resulted in positive attitudes toward their partners and pair work.

The effects of task repetition in task performance and language learning

The next important task implementation topic that is directly related to task engagement is task repetition. For instance, from a pedagogical perspective, repeating the same task may boost learners' confidence and can free up cognitive resources that can be used to focus on linguistic features. On the other hand, repeating a task can negatively impact students' emotional engagement, as students may find it rather boring.

Based on Levelt's speech production model (1989), SLA researchers claim that repeating tasks would allow L2 speakers to focus more attention on language, which would impact the quality of language production. Since Bygate's (1996, 1999, 2001, 2018) empirical research on the relationship between task repetition and the quality of oral performance (i.e., complexity, accuracy, and fluency), task repetition has been of major interest among TBLT researchers. Researchers have identified three types of task repetition: repeating the content, repeating the procedure, and repeating the exact task. Traditionally, task repetition studies have focused on repeating the exact same task and the ways exact task repetition impacts the quality of language output, particularly using oral production tasks (Bygate, 1999, 2001). Content repetition allows learners to become familiar with the content of task input and/or expected task output, which can help students to be naturally exposed to the same vocabulary multiple times as they repeat the content (Carver & Kim, 2020). Finally, procedural repetition allows students to become familiar with the procedure of a task so that while performing the same procedure with different content, they can focus more on language production (Kim & Tracy-Ventura, 2013).

Due to the increasing interest in collaborative tasks, we review task repetition studies that examined learner-learner interaction during collaborative task performance. Recent classroom-based studies have asked students to repeat different aspects of collaborative tasks and have analyzed students' attention to language (i.e., cognitive engagement), the occurrence of interaction patterns (i.e., social engagement), and the quality of language production (e.g., fluency, accuracy). So far only a handful of task repetition research has been conducted in Korean classrooms; thus, it is premature to make any conclusive recommendations. However, similar to other task repetition research in English instruction contexts, the research seems to suggest that different characteristics of task repetition may be beneficial for different dimensions of Korean language production and learning. For instance, as shown in Table 8.4, Kim, Kang, et al. (2020) compared the influence of exact task repetition and procedural task repetition on the complexity and accuracy of written task outcomes and the subsequent learning of Korean grammar (i.e., -(으)ㄹ 수 있/없다 *(-(u)l swu iss/eps-ta*; can/cannot), -(으)면서 *(-(u)myense*; while), -고 나서 *(-ko nase*; after), -(으)ㄹ *(-(u)l*; the noun-modifying form)) by Korean language learners who were enrolled in a second-semester Korean class at a US university. The findings showed that the exact task repetition condition was beneficial for eliciting structures that were more syntactically complex and more accurate use of target grammatical features. However, no benefit was found for global accuracy. In terms of the subsequent learning, the procedural task repetition group outperformed the exact task repetition group.

From a pedagogical perspective, when teachers ask students to repeat different aspects of tasks, one might wonder whether teacher feedback should be provided to facilitate language learning through repeating different aspects of collaborative tasks. Kim et al. (in press) addressed this concern (see Table 8.4). They asked 54 Korean language learners who were enrolled in a university-level Korean language class to perform the same collaborative writing task twice. One group repeated the task without any feedback, whereas the other group received indirect SWCF while performing the task. The findings showed that exact task repetition improved writing fluency for all learners, and SWCF facilitated accuracy in students' writing. However, SWCF did not facilitate the subsequent learning of grammar (particles, honorifics, noun modifiers).

To further examine the role of SWCF in the quality of written task output and the subsequent learning of Korean grammar, Kim, Choi et al. (2020) implemented a series of tasks in three instructional units and implemented procedural repetition (see Table 8.4). Two forms of SWCF were compared for their effectiveness: direct and indirect. For the direct SWCF condition, teachers provided the correct form of an error while students were completing collaborative writing, whereas they just circled errors, without giving an explanation, for the indirect SWCF condition. The findings showed that direct SWCF was helpful in promoting accuracy of task outcome. However, both feedback types were found to be helpful for Korean grammar learning. When the teacher provided SWCF, learners could cognitively engage with the language, particularly with task-induced features (cognitive engagement). In particular, indirect SWCF helped students to be socially engaged with their peers while discussing how to fix errors after the teacher circled them. In general, students were satisfied with receiving SWCF while completing the collaborative writing task (emotional engagement).

In sum, although to date no empirical study targeting learner engagement in Korean tasks has been conducted, we argue that many task design and implementation factors are associated with task engagement. Compared to task research conducted in English language contexts, task research in Korean language instruction is scarce. However, as reviewed earlier, an increasing amount of research has shed light on the benefits of tasks in learning Korean and the importance of considering different task design and implementation factors. In the following sections, we discuss pedagogical implications of these studies and directions for future research.

Pedagogical implications

TBLT has been recognized as one of the most effective teaching approaches based on previous empirical evidence. In this chapter, we reviewed a range of definitions of tasks and different versions of designing task-based syllabi and curricula (task-based, task-referenced, and task-supported). As claimed in previous research (Kim, Jung, & Tracy-Ventura, 2017; McDonough, 2015), task-based instruction needs to be developed and modified within specific instructional contexts (i.e., localized TBLT). Thus, it is important to draw more contextualized pedagogical implications from KSL research.

Overall, because the different aspects of task engagement are interdependent, it is pertinent to consider how to promote learner engagement across all four dimensions. So, how can teachers constructively improve task engagement in Korean language instruction? First, collaborative tasks can provide a beneficial space where emotional and social engagement can occur among learners. While performing collaborative tasks, which are socially situated, learners have opportunities to interact with an interlocutor for a communicative purpose, which can take the form of different types of pair dynamics. Positive emotional engagement can be boosted through collaborative work, as evidenced in Cho and Kim (in press), which showed that learners who worked collaboratively had a more positive attitude toward tasks than learners who worked individually. Collaborative tasks have also been found to be beneficial in promoting cognitive engagement (e.g., Kim & McDonough, 2008), as they help learners talk more about their language use during task performance.

In the current chapter, only two learner factors were discussed: interlocutor proficiency and heritage status. In low-level Korean classes, learners' heritage status did not seem to play a significant role, except that heritage learners resolved LREs more accurately compared to foreign language learners. However, interlocutor proficiency seemed to be an important factor, as students benefitted from working with more advanced learners, and they also preferred to do so.

Previous research has also suggested important roles for different types of task repetition. Although exact task repetition might be useful for promoting more accurate use of target features during task performance, the subsequent learning outcomes of procedural task repetition seem to be greater than of exact task repetition. In TBLT curricula, task repetition is essential as it provides practice opportunities that are necessary for language learning (DeKeyser, 2007), but the critical question is what aspects of tasks need to be repeated. We would argue that it depends on the learning objectives (accuracy of task performance vs. long-term learning of target grammar). Also, to avoid boredom, teachers need to provide a clear rationale for task repetition and help learners to be aware of the quality of task outcomes and associated language use.

Much of previous task research has been learner-centered, analyzing learning outcomes or learner-learner interaction during task performance. However, the teacher's role and what they can do to promote task-based learning while learners carry out tasks is also an important question. Previous studies have indicated that SWCF has a positive impact on heightening students' cognitive engagement (e.g., Cho & Kim, in press), serving as scaffolding. As discussed earlier, the teacher's corrective feedback is known to encourage learners to engage in more dialogues about language use and to reach more correct conclusions in their language-related discussions. Also, lower-level students seem to appreciate synchronous teacher feedback while completing tasks. As different types of corrective feedback are available (e.g., indirect vs. direct), teachers will need to be aware of how different types of feedback impact learners' cognitive engagement and result in language learning. For example, in Kim, Choi et al. (2020), it was found that direct SWCF was more helpful in improving accuracy in writing than indirect corrective feedback. SWCF may also be beneficial in enhancing cognitive engagement during individual tasks by stimulating learners to pay attention to linguistic forms, to notice an interlanguage gap, and to stretch their linguistic resources.

Nonetheless, teachers will need to be cautious in interpreting learners' engagement displayed during task performance because higher levels of engagement do not necessarily lead to greater language gains. For example, a greater number of language-related discussions might not always have a positive relationship with better task performance (Kim & Kang, 2020).

Suggestions for future research

Over the last three decades, the field of TBLT has expanded in terms of its range of theoretical support, methodological advancements, and the inclusion of different instructional contexts. As previous research (Ellis, 2017; Long, 2016) claims, some of the criticisms of TBLT have been responded to empirically, and future research is warranted in order to connect research and practice. In this section, we would like to suggest four areas that deserve further investigation.

First, to promote synergistic research-practice effects in TBLT, the important area in need of growth is teacher development. As Kim (2018) states, the majority of TBLT research to date has focused on students – their task performance, learning outcomes, and perceptions of TBLT. However, without teachers' knowledge of up-to-date teaching pedagogy, their intention to implement tasks in their classes, and hands-on experience with task design, task-based Korean language teaching might not be sustainable. As teachers put TBLT into action, TBLT research should focus more on teacher development. Also, teacher training programs should be designed to address the issues that hinder teachers, particularly in-service teachers, from properly implementing task-based instruction and to provide adequate opportunities in which teachers can engage in task design, development, and evaluation. Many studies reviewed in the previous section were fruitful outcomes of an SLA researcher–Korean program director–Korean instructor collaboration (e.g., Kim, Choi et al., 2020; Kim et al., in press). To promote evidence-driven, task-based instruction in Korean language teaching, it is very important to invest in teacher development, and one way to do so is through researcher–teacher collaborations during teacher training.

A second research topic that needs further attention is integrated skills development though task performance. Previous Korean TBLT studies have focused primarily on production skills (i.e., speaking and writing), and they mainly examined students of lower proficiency levels. Recently, however, Korean language learners' needs have become more diversified; thus, instruction and research should address these emerging needs by expanding their scope. For example, for more advanced learners, reading-to-write would offer a good platform for language use and advanced language exposure. Also, given the surge of content-based language instruction in KSL context (Park et al., 2020), tasks that integrate different skills might benefit language learners in such classrooms.

Thirdly, with the potential pedagogical value of new technology and the recent shift to online learning, the role of technology-mediated language teaching and learning is becoming significantly more important. In particular, technology-mediated TBLT (González-Lloret & Ortega,

2014) is receiving growing attention from practitioners and researchers. The fusion of technology and task-based instruction can bring situational authenticity to the classroom and create socially situated contexts more easily. Also, the use of technological tools (e.g., YouTube, virtual reality, artificial intelligence) would allow more freedom for teachers and learners by removing spatial and temporal constraints. Despite the pedagogical possibilities that technology-mediated TBLT can bring to language learning, little research related to technology has been conducted in task-based Korean language teaching. Thus, further work needs to be done to establish evidence of the impact of technology-mediated TBLT on Korean language pedagogy.

Lastly, future research should examine task-based Korean language teaching that goes beyond grammar and vocabulary. Overall, the scope of previous task-based research has been limited to Korean grammar, pragmatics, and vocabulary learning. To expand the research domain of TBLT in Korean language teaching, it is pertinent to expand the target linguistic areas by examining diverse linguistic aspects of task performance, such as pronunciation and intercultural competence, and by targeting different language skills as well as integrated skills.

Conclusion

To conclude, the field of TBLT has expanded noticeably within a short period of time. A large number of monographs, edited volumes, and research articles have moved the field forward, and as a result, there is now an international organization dedicated to promoting TBLT (www.iatblt.org/), which also organizes biannual conferences and a new academic journal, namely, *TASK* (https://benjamins.com/catalog/task). Additionally, Gurzynski-Weiss and her colleagues recently launched the Language Learning Task Bank (https://tblt.indiana.edu/), where L2 practitioners and researchers share their instructional tasks. Learning to design effective tasks and successful task-based syllabi does not happen overnight, and sharing language learning tasks through databases is an excellent way to promote TBLT and such databases are a great resource for teacher training. The current review paper demonstrates how important task design and task implementation factors are for promoting successful task-based language teaching, particularly from learner-engagement perspectives. TBLT research in Korean language instruction is still in its infancy, and it is our hope that there will be more researcher–teacher collaboration, which would result in evidence-driven course materials designed through research-practice connections in Korean language classroom contexts.

Notes

1 Since examples 1, 2, and 3 presented here are directly taken from the published articles, we kept the Korean data presentation of the original sources.
2 Romanization for three Korean expressions: Line 3 있다 *issta* (to be); Line 3 계세요 *kyeyseyyo* (the honorific form of to be); Line 4 남편 *namphyen* (husband) in Examples 2 and 3.

References

Baralt, M., Gurzynski-Weiss, L., & Kim, Y. (2016). Engagement with the language: How examining learners' affective and social engagement explains successful learner-generated attention to form. In M. Sato & S. Ballinger (Eds.), *Peer interaction and second language learning: Pedagogical potential and research agenda* (pp. 209–239). Amsterdam and Philadelphia: John Benjamins Publishing Company.
Breen, M. (1989). The evaluation cycle for language learning tasks. In R. K. Johnson (Ed.), *The second language curriculum* (pp. 187–206). Cambridge: Cambridge University Press.
Brindley, G., & Slatyer, H. (2002). Exploring task difficulty in ESL listening assessment. *Language Testing*, *19*(4), 369–394.
Bygate, M. (1996). Effects of task repetition: Appraising the developing language of learners. In J. Willis & D. Willis (Eds.), *Challenge and change in language teaching* (pp. 136–146). Oxford: Heinemann.

Bygate, M. (1999). Task as context for the framing, re-framing, and un-framing of language. *System, 27*, 33–48.

Bygate, M. (2001). Effects of task repetition on the structure and control of oral language. In M. Bygate, P. Skehan, & M. Swain (Eds.), *Researching pedagogic tasks: Second language learning, teaching and testing* (pp. 23–48). London: Longman.

Bygate, M. (2016). Sources, developments and directions of task-based language teaching. *The Language Learning Journal, 44*(4), 381–400.

Bygate, M. (2018). *Learning language through task repetition* (Vol. 11). Amsterdam and Philadelphia: John Benjamins Publishing Company.

Bygate, M., Norris, J. M., & Van den Branden, K. (2015). Task-based language teaching. In C. Chapelle (Ed.), *Encyclopedia of applied linguistics* (pp. 1–8). Oxford: Wiley-Blackwell.

Carver, J., & Kim, Y. (2020). French learners' past tense development through collaborative writing tasks: The role of procedural and content repetition. *Canadian Modern Language Review, 76*(2), 114–138.

Chaudron, C., Doughty, C., Kim, Y., Kong, D., Lee, J., Lee, Y., . . . & Urano, K. (2001). A task-based needs analysis of a tertiary Korean as a foreign language program. In M. H. Long (Ed.), *Second language needs analysis*. Cambridge: Cambridge University Press.

Cho, H., & Kim, Y. (in press, online first). Learning Korean honorifics through individual and collaborative writing tasks and written corrective feedback. *Applied Linguistics Review*.

DeKeyser, R. (2007). Skill acquisition theory. In B. VanPatten & J. Williams (Eds.), *Theories in second language acquisition* (pp. 97–114). Mahwah, NJ: Erlbaum.

Duff, P. (1986). Another look at interlanguage talk: Taking task to task. In R. Day (Ed.), *Talking to learn: Conversation in second language acquisition*. Rowley, MA: Newbury House.

East, M. (2012). *Task-based language teaching from the teachers' perspective: Insights from New Zealand* (Vol. 3). Amsterdam and Philadelphia: John Benjamins Publishing Company.

Ellis, R. (2003). *Task-based language learning and teaching*. Oxford: Oxford University Press.

Ellis, R. (2017). Position paper: Moving task-based language teaching forward. *Language Teaching, 50*(4), 507–526.

Ellis, R. (2018). *Reflections on task-based language teaching*. Clevedon, UK: Multilingual Matters.

Ellis, R., & Shintani, N. (2014). *Exploring language pedagogy through second language acquisition research*. Oxon and New York: Routledge.

Ellis, R., Skehan, P., Li, S., Shintani, N., & Lambert, C. (2020). *Task-based language teaching: Theory and practice*. Cambridge: Cambridge University Press.

Gass, S., & Varonis, E. (1985). Task variation and nonnative/nonnative negotiations of meaning. In S. Gass & C. Madden (Eds.), *Input in second language acquisition* (pp. 149–161). Rowley, MA: Newbury House.

González-Lloret, M., & Ortega, L. (2014). *Technology-mediated TBLT: Researching technology and tasks*. Amsterdam and Philadelphia: John Benjamins Publishing Company.

Gurzynski-Weiss, L., & IATBLT. (n.d.). *The TBLT language learning task bank*. Retrieved from https://tblt.indiana.edu

Kim, M., Lee, H., & Kim, Y. (2018). Learning of Korean honorifics through collaborative tasks: Comparing heritage and non-heritage speakers. In N. Taguchi & Y. Kim (Eds.), *Task- based approaches to teaching and assessing pragmatics* (pp. 28–54). Amsterdam and Philadelphia: John Benjamins Publishing Company.

Kim, Y. (2008). The contribution of collaborative and individual tasks to the acquisition of L2 vocabulary. *The Modern Language Journal, 92*(1), 114–130.

Kim, Y. (2015). The role of tasks as vehicles for learning in classroom interaction. In N. Markee (Ed.), *Handbook of classroom discourse and interaction* (pp. 163–181). Oxford: Wiley-Blackwell.

Kim, Y. (2018). Moving localized TBLT in Korea forward: Real issues and future directions. *Studies in English Education, 23*, 859–889.

Kim, Y., Choi, B., Kang, S., Kim, B., & Yun, H. (2020). Comparing the effects of direct and indirect synchronous written corrective feedback: Learning outcomes and students' perceptions. *Foreign Language Annals, 53*(1), 176–199.

Kim, Y., Choi, B., Yun, H., Kim, B., & Choi, S. (in press). Task repetition, synchronous written corrective feedback and the learning of Korean: A classroom-based study. *Language Teaching Research*.

Kim, Y., Choi, B., Yun, H., Kim, B., & Kang, S. (2021). *Learning Korean through tasks*. Seoul: Kong and Park.

Kim, Y., Jung, Y., & Tracy-Ventura, N. (2017). Implementation of a localized task-based course in an EFL context: A study of students' evolving perceptions. *TESOL Quarterly, 51*(3), 632–660.

Kim, Y., & Kang, S. (2020). Writing to make meaning through collaborative multimodal composing among Korean EFL learners: Writing processes, writing quality and student perception. *Computers and Composition, 58*.

Kim, Y., Kang, S., Yun, H., Kim, B., & Choi, B. (2020). The effects of task repetition on writing quality, peer interaction, and learning of Korean grammar. *Foreign Language Annals, 53*(4), 827–849.

Kim, Y., Kong, D. K., Lee, J. H., & Lee, Y. (2001). Implementation and evaluation of an approach to task-based Korean language teaching. *Korean Language in America, 6*, 45–51.

Kim, Y., & McDonough, K. (2008). The effect of interlocutor proficiency on the collaborative dialogue between Korean as a second language learners. *Language Teaching Research, 12*(2), 211–234.

Kim, Y., & Tracy-Ventura, N. (2013). The role of task repetition in L2 performance development: What needs to be repeated during task-based interaction? *System, 41*, 829–840.

Kong, D. (2012). Task-based language teaching in an advanced Korean language learning program. *Korean Language in America, 17*, 32–48.

Levelt, W. (1989). *Speaking: From intention to articulation*. Cambridge: Cambridge University Press.

Li, S., Ellis, R., & Zhu, Y. (2016). Task-based versus task-supported language instruction: An experimental study. *Annual Review of Applied Linguistics, 36*, 205.

Loewen, S. (2020). *Introduction to instructed second language acquisition*. Oxon and New York: Routledge.

Long, M. H. (1980). *Input, interaction, and second language acquisition* [Unpublished doctoral dissertation]. University of California, Los Angeles.

Long, M. H. (1985). A role for instruction in second language acquisition: Task-based language teaching. In K. Hyltenstam & M. Pienemann (Eds.), *Modelling and assessing second language acquisition* (pp. 77–99). Clevedon, UK: Multilingual Matters.

Long, M. H. (1989). Task, group, and task-group interactions. *University of Hawaii Working Papers in ESL, 8*, 1–26.

Long, M. H. (2015). *Second language acquisition and task-based language teaching*. Oxford: Wiley-Blackwell.

Long, M. H. (2016). In defense of tasks and TBLT: Nonissues and real issues. *Annual Review of Applied Linguistics, 36*, 5–33.

Long, M. H., & Norris, J. M. (2000). Task-based teaching and assessment. In C. Chapelle (Ed.), *Encyclopedia of applied linguistics* (pp. 597–603). Oxford: Wiley-Blackwell.

McDonough, K. (2015). Perceived benefits and challenges with the use of collaborative tasks in EFL contexts. In M. Bygate (Ed.), *Domains and directions in the development of TBLT* (pp. 225–246). Amsterdam and Philadelphia: John Benjamins Publishing Company.

Nunan, D. (1989). *Designing tasks for the communicative classroom*. Cambridge: Cambridge University Press.

Park, M., Choi, B., & Ko, S. (2020). Pedagogical approaches and practices in teaching Korean. In Y. Y. Cho (Ed.), *Teaching Korean as a foreign language* (pp. 24–53). Oxon and New York: Routledge.

Philp, J., & Duchesne, S. (2016). Exploring engagement in tasks in the language classroom. *Annual Review of Applied Linguistics, 36*, 50–72.

Phung, L. (2017). Task preference, affective response, and engagement in L2 use in a US university context. *Language Teaching Research, 21*(6), 751–766.

Pica, T., Young, R., & Doughty, C. (1987). The impact of interaction on comprehension. *TESOL Quarterly, 21*(4), 737–758.

Prabhu, N. S. (1987). *Second language pedagogy*. Oxford: Oxford University Press.

Pyun, D. O. (2013). Attitudes toward task-based language learning: A study of college Korean language learners. *Foreign Language Annals, 46*(1), 108–121.

Samuda, V., & Bygate, M. (2008). *Tasks in second language learning*. New York: Palgrave Macmillan.

Skehan, P. (1996). A framework for the implementation of task-based instruction. *Applied Linguistics, 17*, 38–62.

Skinner, E. A., Kindermann, T. A., & Furrer, C. J. (2009). A motivational perspective on engagement and disaffection: Conceptualization and assessment of children's behavioral and emotional participation in academic activities in the classroom. *Educational and Psychological Measurement, 69*(3), 493–525.

Storch, N. (2002). Patterns of interaction in ESL pair work. *Language Learning, 52*(1), 119–158.

Swain, M., & Lapkin, S. (1998). Interaction and second language learning: Two adolescent French immersion students working together. *The Modern Language Journal, 82*(3), 320–337.

Van den Branden, K. (2006). *Task-based language education: From theory to practice*. Cambridge: Cambridge University Press.

9
INSTRUCTIONAL TECHNOLOGY IN KSL SETTINGS

Jayoung Song

Introduction

In all aspects of language learning, educators and students are increasingly using instructional technology. Instructional technology provides a significant extension of the types of language experiences learners engage in. Therefore, it is crucial for language practitioners and researchers to grasp the extent to which instructional technology can contribute to language learning.

Up until recently, the field of Korean as a second language (KSL) had been challenged, as had other less commonly taught languages, by fundamental issues such as lack of teaching resources (including instructional technology) due to limited funding and enrollment in Korean programs (Cho, 2000; Kim, N., 1994; Kim, Y., 1994). As a result, the development of instructional technology in Korean language instruction got underway relatively late. Even now, there are relatively few studies concerning this area (Godwin-Jones, 2013; Jeon, 2004). Nevertheless, this chapter represents an attempt to include as many relevant research findings as possible to understand what, why, how, and to what end instructional technology leads to successful language learning and how it can be used to create optimal instructional practices in KSL settings. The chapter starts with a historical overview on language learning via technology in other foreign language education, followed by specific use of instructional technology in KSL teaching and learning. Then, the chapter discusses core issues, including technologies for the teaching and learning of specific competence (e.g., grammar and vocabulary, reading, writing, and speaking, and intercultural competence), theories and pedagogies related to online language teaching, and emerging technologies (e.g., virtual reality, mobile-based language learning). The chapter concludes by suggesting future directions for teachers and researchers.

Historical discussion

Behavioristic phase of CALL

Many second language teachers may think the use of technology in language instruction started in the mid-1990s with the advent of the internet and the widespread use of personal computers (Heift & Chapelle, 2013). However, the idea of incorporating technology in second/foreign language learning goes back to the late 1960s and early 1970s. This is when computers evolved to support interaction between a learner and computer (Otto, 2017). This opened the pathway to computer assisted language learning (CALL), which started with a "search for any study of application of the computer in language teaching and learning" (Levy, 1997). Early CALL researchers were interested in the benefits of using computers to practice forms of language, especially grammar and vocabulary, through self-paced learning with immediate performance feedback.

One of the early CALL projects, developed at the University of Illinois at Urbana-Champaign, was the Programmed Logic for Automated Teaching Operations (PLATO) project (Otto et al., 2017). The PLATO system featured a number of capabilities, including those of tutorials and practice exercises. The custom-designed screen allowed touch-screen input and audio playback and could display complex international characters, including Chinese, Russian, Hindi, and Hebrew. Given that CALL was generally not available for languages with non-Roman characters at that time, language practitioners welcomed the advent of PLATO for a variety of foreign languages (Hart, 1995). This pioneering work occurred during the behavioristic phase of CALL, where computers were used as a medium to offer repetitive drills and quizzes as practice (Da & Zheng, 2018; Warschauer, 1996). CALL applications at this time provided minimal interaction between learners and computers and among students; feedback to learners was mostly in the form of the application marking answers correct or incorrect (Bax, 2003).

Communicative phase of CALL

The next period of CALL is referred to as the communicative phase. It was based on communicative approaches to language teaching, the pedagogical emphasis at that time (Warschauer, 1996). One of the main approaches was to build intrinsic motivation and foster interactivity both between learner and computer and learner and learner, all of which was missing from the behavioristic CALL model (Stevens, 1989). In an attempt to escape from the drill-and-practice model of CALL, some developers designed games and simulations, such as Sanders and Sanders's (1995) Spion, a German spy game (Otto, 2017). These games provided a relaxed context for communicative language use. Another promising technology of the 1980s was the interactive videodisc (Otto et al., 2017). While there was a flourishing of software programs for commonly taught languages, for the less commonly taught ones (including Korean) there began to appear videodisc-based software (Rubin, Ediger, Coffin, Van Handle, & Whiskeyman, 1990). One of the early reported uses of computers in Korean language teaching was the Korean interactive videodisc (KIVE) project. KIVE, which was initiated by the Defense Language Institute Foreign Language Center, was capable of presenting visual information. This capability made possible rich input for practice, including vocabulary, grammar, useful phrases, speaking practice, reading, and listening practice, along with immediate feedback (Kim, 1995).

Integrative phase of CALL

With the arrival of the 21st century came a social turn in CALL, as well as in the field of second language acquisition. Emerging as one of the anchoring theories in language instruction was sociocultural theory. This theory held that language learners are social beings whose linguistic development occurs through social interaction mediated by language (Lantolf, 2000). This trend of thought led to CALL entering an integrative phase that put emphasis on the internet and the principal use of computers for authentic discourse and agency (Warschauer, 1996). The integrative use of CALL was facilitated by the advent of Web 2.0, which allowed users to take part in creating and designing their own place, such as wikis, blogs, and podcasts, and social media platforms such as Facebook, Twitter, and so forth. Changes in language acquisition theory and the mode of CALL brought about changes in instructional models in KSL. Instruction models shifted away from teacher-centered toward student-oriented and collaborative learning environments where students played an active role as creator of digital texts, media, and constructors of knowledge in and out of the classroom (Otto et al., 2017). KSL educators experimented with Web 2.0 tools and social media tools, as they were motivated by these tools' accessibility and capacity for collaborative learning and interaction. Some examples include groupware for online group work (Yoshida, Tani, Uchida, Masui, & Nakayama, 2014), digital storytelling (Cho, 2013; Park, 2014), video projects (Huilin Zhang, 2019; Roh, 2011), and social media tools (Ahn & Shim, 2018; Cho, 2014; Jin, 2015; Kwon, 2012; Jee, 2015; Park, 2012).

A couple of decades of experimentation and investigation has yielded all manner of technology for use in KSL classrooms. KSL educators use the tools to improve linguistic skills as well as the cultural understanding of KSL learners at all proficiency levels. These technologies include not only the fundamental media used in instruction, such as text, audio, video, and multimedia materials, but also advanced technologies. Hence, today the acronym CALL refers to "any environment in which a learner, alone or collaboratively with peers, uses technology in a second or other language" (Heift & Chapelle, 2013, p. 556). While various combinations of CALL are used in language classrooms, their role in language learning has, over time, changed drastically. It has gone from serving an auxiliary role in the curriculum to a core source of authentic learning materials and a conduit for collaborative language-learning experiences (Heift & Chapelle, 2013). Throughout all the substantial changes in technological capabilities and teaching practices, some core issues have endured concerning how technology can help facilitate language learning.

Core issues

Technologies for teaching and learning grammar and vocabulary

There has been ongoing debate regarding the two main approaches to teaching grammar – the explicit and the implicit. Explicit grammar teaching focuses on systematically teaching isolated linguistic forms by following a structural syllabus (Hulstijn, 2005). Implicit approaches focus on meaning and/or communication rather than linguistic form (Krashen, 1981). These two approaches are reflected in the way technology is used for L2 grammar (Heift & Vyatkina, 2017). In KSL settings for L2 grammar, there are three technology-based pedagogies – tutorial CALL, intelligent CALL (ICALL), and corpus-based CALL.

Tutorial CALL

In tutorial CALL, the computer plays a role as a tutor by evaluating learner responses and presenting learning materials in one-on-one interactions (Heift & Vyatkina, 2017). Tutorial CALL, based on a deductive teaching approach to grammar, offers explicit explanations of grammatical concepts. Its activities include fill-in-the-blank, multiple choice, and match or translate small pieces of text items (Hubbard & Siskin, 2004). A good example of tutorial CALL is the interactive videodisc. In a study of interactive videodisc projects, Kim (1987) introduced computer-controlled video lessons in which students were presented with videos selected from TV drama series. The courseware was designed to enable students to watch selected videos with access to the HELP OPTION, which provided grammar and vocabulary notes as well as translation of the scenes. The videos are followed by lesson activities such as cloze exercises, vocabulary building, listening comprehension, and translation exercises with immediate feedback. Similarly, the interactive videodisc developed by the Defense Language Institute incorporates videos with the scripts of the segment followed by grammar and vocabulary exercises, as shown in Figure 9.1 (Kim, 1995).

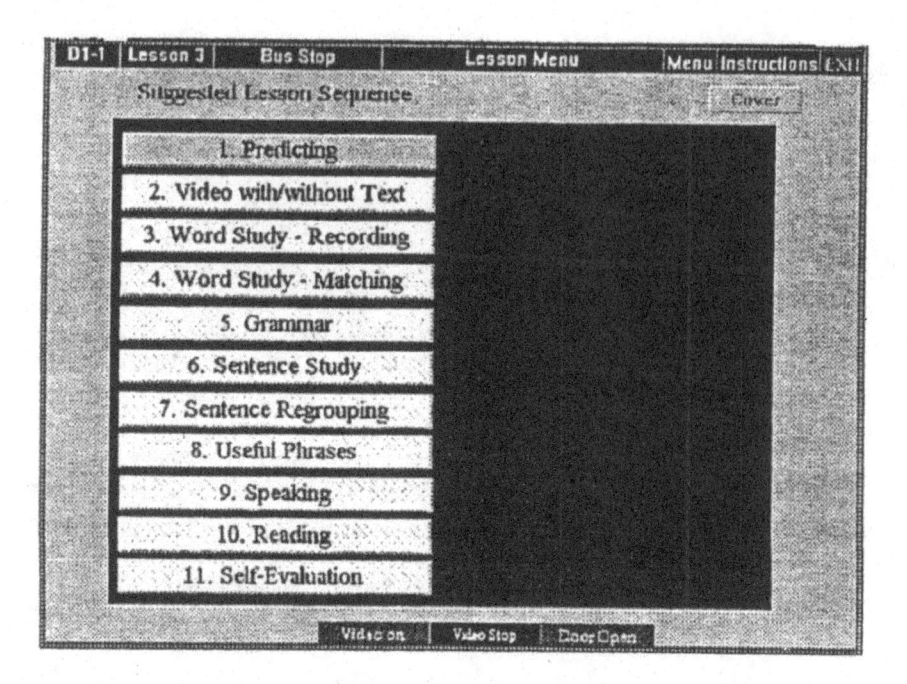

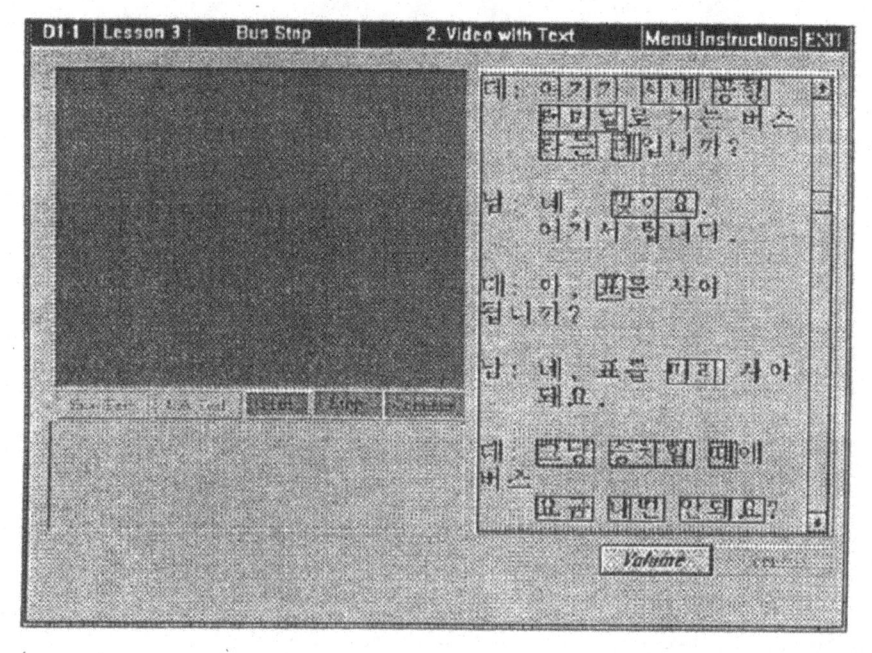

Figure 9.1 Design of the lesson

    The major advantage of the interactive videodisc lies in its capacity to present authentic target language input for practice and to provide a venue for individualized learning in which students can work at their own pace. Its major limitations include an absence of drill-based practice and its limited feedback (i.e., mostly right or wrong response).

Intelligent CALL (ICALL)

To compensate for the limitations of tutorial CALL, ICALL provides a more sophisticated analysis of students' input and offers contextual learner feedback based on natural language processing, student modeling, and expert system (Heift & Vyatkina, 2017). ICALL programs are not only used for learner–computer interactions but also for learner–learner interactions in a goal-oriented CALL activity. For example, Dickinson, Eom, Kang, Lee, and Sachs (2008) developed an ICALL system that could teach L2 Korean learners how to use particles. Learners engage in an information-gap activity in which they must identify similarities and differences in a spot-the-difference task, in which students construct Korean sentences by dragging words from a word bank. Before submitting their answers to their peers in a chat box, they receive corrective feedback from the ICALL application. When embedded in a computer-mediated communication (CMC) environment, the ICALL program serves as a tool for implicit grammar teaching. The user interface is shown in Figure 9.2.

Corpus-based CALL

As informatization has become common in every field of study, there has, in recent years, been a large increase in the variety of studies and projects concerning computerization of the Korean language (Seo, 2005). The focus of the early Korean corpus lies in the computerization of the written language. With the development of speech-processing technology, a variety of corpora have evolved, including spontaneous speech called Seoul corpus, a learner's corpus inclusive of the writing and speech of learners of the Korean language, and a regional dialect corpus (Seo, 2005; Yun et al., 2015). Sejong Corpora, one of the long-term corpus projects (1998–present),

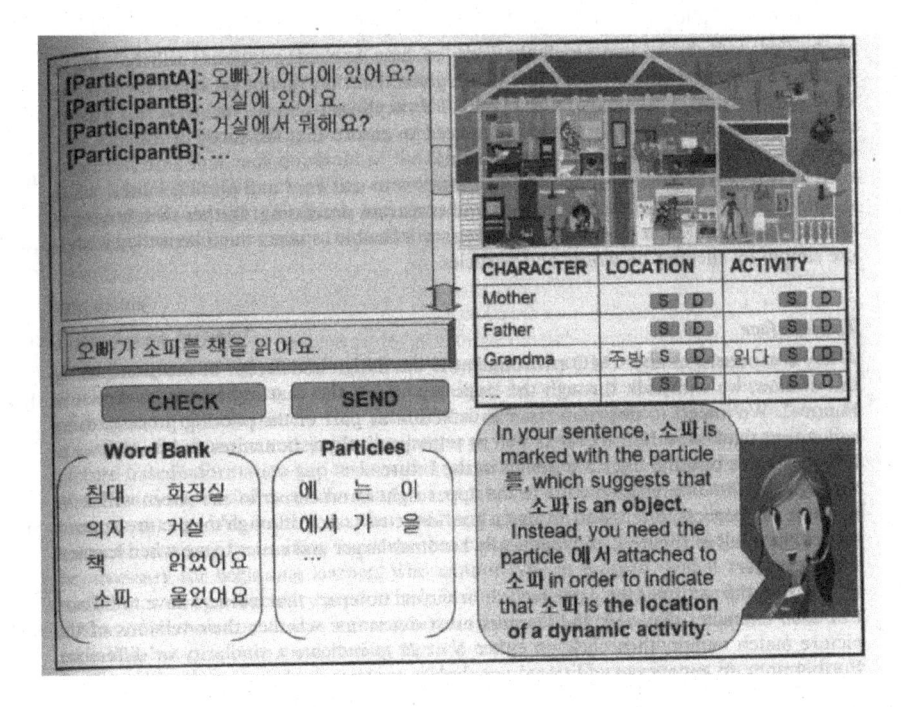

Figure 9.2 User interface

contributes to the development of Korean corpora in a significant way by constructing enormous corpora with a unified type and system (Kim, Kang, & Hong, 2007; Lee, Jang, & Seo, 2009). Lee et al. (2009) developed a Korean learner corpus with annotation for particle error detection by investigating errors made by heritage and non-heritage speakers of Korean. The authors conclude that the learner corpus can be linked to specific feedback on the usage of Korean particles. This can especially benefit heritage speakers of Korean, who generate unexpected low-level errors, such as particles, as they usually bypass lower-level courses due to their level of oral fluency.

Spell checkers, online dictionaries, and social media for vocabulary teaching

Ma (2017) proposed a framework to comprehend the mediating role of technologies on vocabulary learning. The framework is based on three perspectives: 1) the role of computer technologies, 2) technology-mediated lexical applications, and 3) the incidental or intentional approaches to vocabulary acquisition. First, the role of computer as tutor can guide and evaluate students' vocabulary learning as well as facilitate students' learning and performance (Chen & Chung, 2008). For example, based on natural language processing, the Korean grammar and spell checker developed by Nam, Kim, and Kwon (2001) detects and corrects the misused derivative and compound nouns as well as syntactic and semantic errors in Korean sentences. The spell checker analyzes the nature of the error and connects learners to relevant learning materials and practice questions so the learner can actively engage in their learning (Nam et al., 2001).

Second, lexical tools or applications can promote the possibility of incidental and intentional learning, as demonstrated by online dictionary apps or lexical concordances. Hwang (2020), for example, developed an online dictionary for content-based Korean language instruction. The online dictionary provides the meaning of academic vocabulary as well as academic texts related to lexical items for students to use in in their autonomous and independent learning.

Lastly, intentional and incidental learning of vocabulary influences how a particular technology is chosen or implemented in teaching contexts. Methods of learning words with deliberate attempts are known as intentional learning (Hung, 2015). The general rationale for intentional vocabulary learning is grounded in Schmidt's (1990) noticing hypothesis. It is maintained that for learning to occur, learners must consciously notice L2 features in the input and pay deliberate efforts to form-meaning connections of vocabulary items. Spiri (2008) found that students who studied vocabulary with online flashcards outperformed those who studied with the printed word lists. Similarly, Hung (2015) investigated intentional vocabulary learning using digital flashcards and underscored the value of learning vocabulary with digital flashcards.

In KSL settings, technology use was more geared toward intentional vocabulary learning. When learning incidentally, technology is mainly used as a tool to provide an environment for learning. That is, when learners read online texts, their primary goal is to understand the text. Learners might look up unknown lexical items via e-dictionaries, hyperlinks, and so forth and incidentally acquire some new items (Hulstijn, 2005). Some KSL researchers experimented this approach with the social media platforms Twitter and Instagram. In a study of educational effect of social media on Korean education, Park (2012) used Twitter for three weeks in an intermediate-level university Korean class in Korea. Students were asked to follow a Twitter account of a native Korean speaker, and to then orally present their findings regarding the speaker's tweets. They were also tasked with selecting expressions and sentences that they liked from the tweets and retweet them with an explanation of why they selected those tweets. Data collected from a vocabulary knowledge scale (VKS) survey and interview showed that students were able to interact with their classmates through Twitter and notice various new vocabulary and expressions used by native speakers. However, incidental learning of vocabulary failed to occur. Such failure was due to the nature of tweets (i.e., thoughts expressed in short sentences and vocabulary used out of context); Twitter users communicate their thoughts through a variety of colloquialisms and rarely repeat the same lexical items to enable learning to happen. Similarly, Ahn and Shim (2018) exposed students to authentic input by uploading video clips containing target grammar and expressions on Instagram. These studies showed that using social media for grammar and vocabulary teaching could promote interaction and motivate students to learn Korean outside the classroom. Whether the use of these tools would lead to incidental learning is yet to be established, suggesting that understanding of the platform and designing appropriate activities are crucial.

Technologies for teaching and learning reading

The range of new technologies for L2 reading has grown rapidly (Liaw & English, 2017). An important aspect of second language reading is that it must extend beyond the classroom; students need to read materials outside the classroom to attain a sufficient amount of input and practice. The challenge for second language teachers is therefore how to promote reading practices through the use of scaffolds such as online glosses, social media, and interesting materials on the Web. In the digital age, various instructional technologies have been integrated to engage L2 readers in autonomous and independent reading.

SLA theories and application of technology to L2 reading: cognitive

To apply technology to L2 reading, researchers have adopted several SLA theories, including cognitive, psycholinguistic, and sociocultural theories (Chapelle, 2009). Cognitive theory on noticing, working memory, automatization of word recognition, and activating schemata has offered theoretical foundations for many studies on how reading comprehension is affected by online or multimedia reading annotations, such as online dictionaries and reading annotations (Liaw & English, 2017). Sugai (2013) developed a reading support tool for the Korean language using automatic morphological analysis technology. The tool processes Korean text using the open-source software MeCab for morphological analysis and an online dictionary to provide information about the text in terms of the learning level of words used in the text and its hanja notation, as shown in Figure 9.3. The tool is linked to Naver's dictionary, and when a learner clicks a word

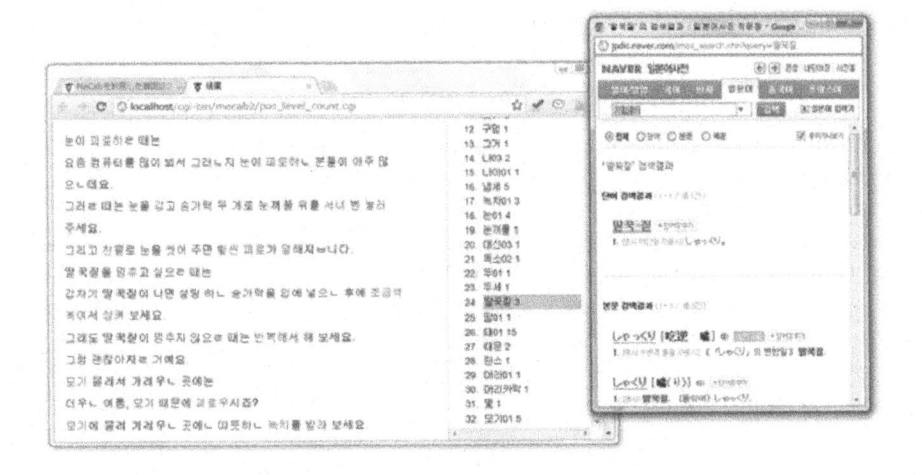

Figure 9.3 Screen capture of the tool

in the text, it shows the part of speech, word frequency, and word level. The tool, which is available on the internet, was initially developed to help Japanese learners of Korean but can assist any Korean reader with both the bottom-up and top-down process of reading comprehension.

Researchers have also applied Mayer's cognitive theory of multimedia learning (CTML) to Korean L2 reading studies. CTML maintains that meaningful learning occurs when students interact with words and pictures, organize them into coherent pictorial and verbal models, and integrate them with prior knowledge (Liaw & English, 2017). An example of CTML is the study by Park and Nicola (2010). The researchers developed a multimedia-based lesson to increase students' abilities to comprehend Korean literature in an upper-level KSL class. The lesson consisted of the following: a pre-reading activity, presentation of literary texts with interactive activities, a post-reading activity using multimedia, comprehension questions, and finally a writing activity. The lesson was found to provide opportunities for learners to interact with the texts and peers, foster comprehension of a literature text, and improve a learner-centered approach for the use of literature in KSL education. Figure 9.4 shows a screenshot of the multimedia-based Korean literature lesson.

SLA theories and application of technology to L2 reading: psycholinguistic

To understand how L2 reading behaviors are influenced by new technologies, another theoretical framework is provided by metacognitive approaches (Liaw & English, 2017). Research has compared reading strategies using text-based contexts and online environments (Genc, 2011), strategies used by EFL learners compared to L1 learners during online reading (Omar, 2014), and decision-making processes used as L2 learners engage in online reading (Park, Yang, & Hsieh, 2014). With eye-tracking technology, Kim and Kang (2016) found speed-reading training to be effective for individual learners in terms of fixation duration (time of gaze to process written information) and the average saccade amplitude (movement of the eyeball to understand written information). In analyzing the reading process of Korean learners across different proficiency levels, Im, Min, and Cho (2017) incorporated EEG (electroencephalogram; a test that detects electrical activity in one's brain during an activity) and eye-tracking technologies to tap into Korean learners' fixation time and number as well as saccade time and number. The results showed that beginner learners displayed meaningless eye fixation (indicative of a lack of reading comprehension) and, compared to intermediate and advanced learners, high levels of stress, which is shown in one's brain wave during reading.

SLA theories and application of technology to L2 reading: sociocultural

More recently, researchers have adopted sociocultural theories (which view learners as active constructors) to study technologies and L2 development (Liaw & English, 2017). From a sociocultural point of view, reading is not an individual skill to be mastered alone but, rather, a social skill requiring active participation and interaction among learners (Lantolf, 2000). In support of this view, developers have created web-based tools to facilitate collaborative reading, projects, and reading comprehension. Some studies have investigated how sociocultural background influences L2 learners' use of web-based tools for collaborative reading and reading comprehension (Gao, 2013). Other studies have explored the use of technology for collaborative reading projects. For example, in an attempt to teach Korean sijo in a more engaging and effective way, Kim (2015) incorporated Voicethread, a Web 2.0 voice-sharing application that enables learners to maintain conversations using visual and aural aids, such as images, text, and videos. Kim concluded that Voicethread could make poetry class digitally enriched,

Instructional technology in KSL settings

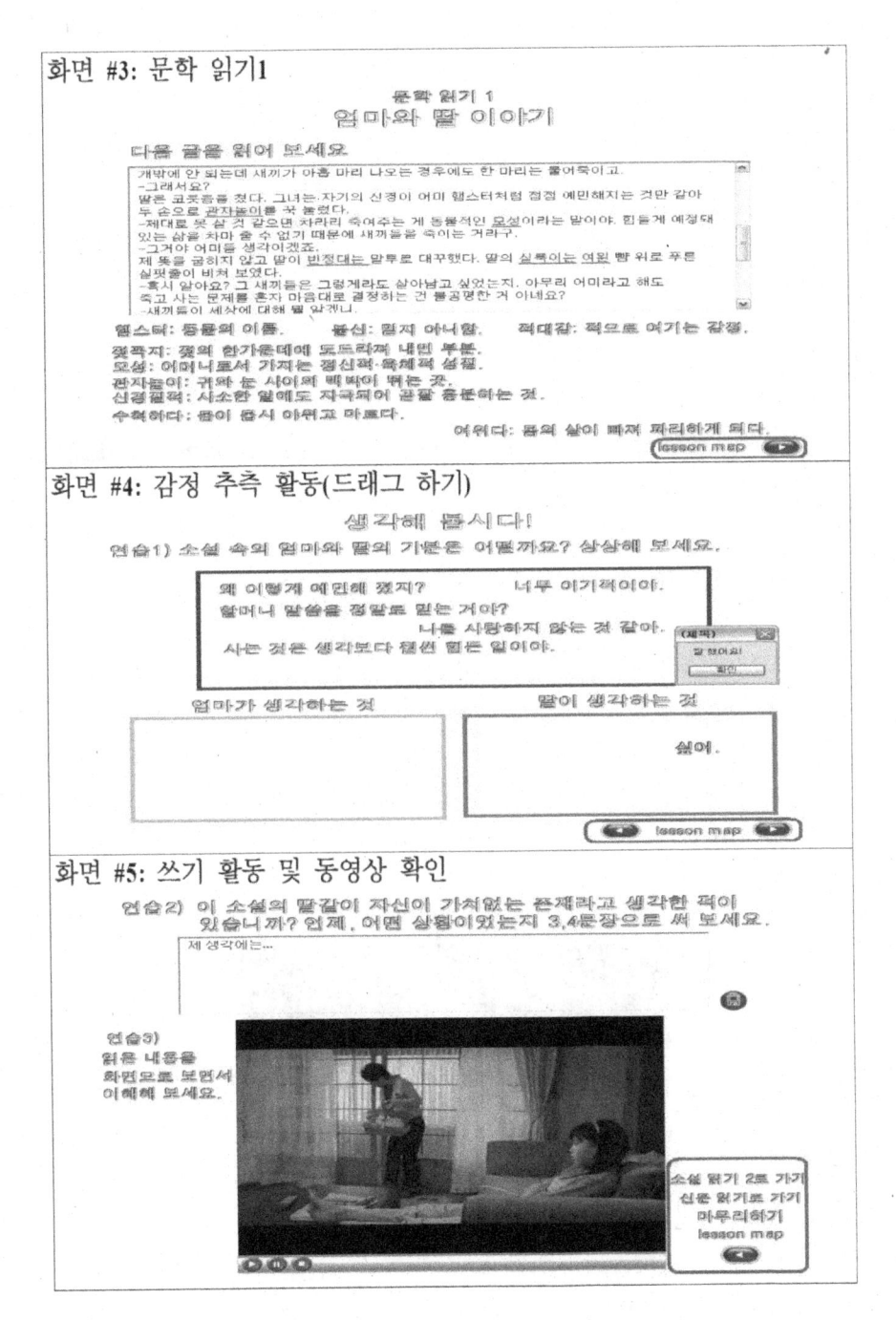

Figure 9.4 Screenshot of the multimedia-based Korean literature lesson

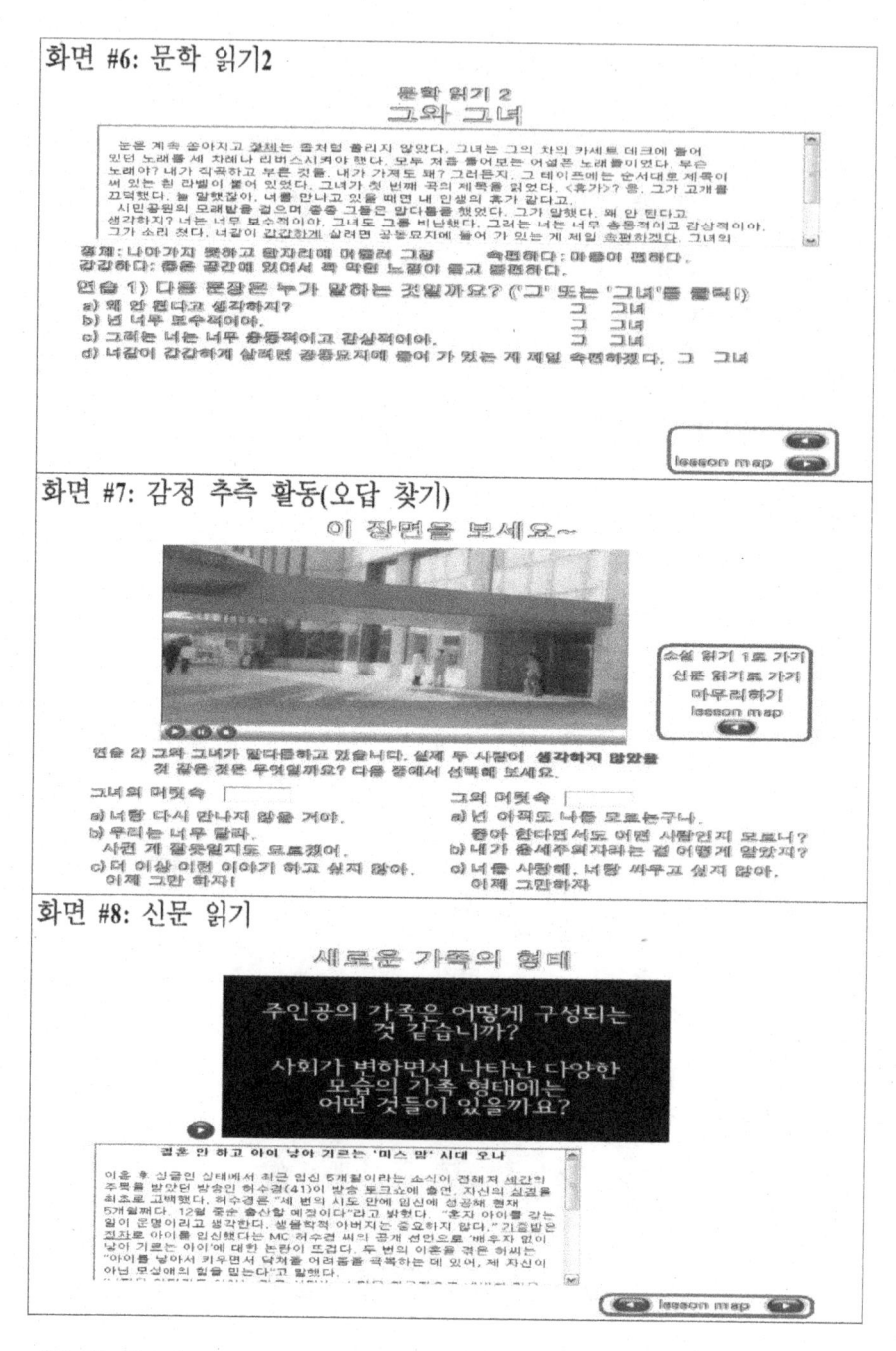

Figure 9.4 Continued

collaborative, and interactive, all of which help students understand sijo while improving their speaking and writing skills. Additionally, digital storytelling has been incorporated in support of higher-order thinking skills and literacy development. Park (2014) incorporated collaborative digital storytelling where Korean language learners work together to create a narrative and then reflect on their stories.

A review of the literature shows that SLA theories offer theory-based development of CALL materials and pedagogical approaches to L2 reading in KSL settings. Reading in a digital age is having an enormous impact on L2 reading instruction (Ma, 2017). Technologies and Web resources can support successful L2 reading, but at the same time it can also lead to distracted minds and information overload (Godwin-Jones, 2010). With the abundance of tools and resources, educators, more than ever before, must strive to keep up with the ever-evolving technologies and develop new visions for literacy.

Technologies for teaching and learning writing

Writing practices today are being reshaped by new technologies. For example, high school students may be asked to go beyond traditional writing tasks to put together PowerPoint slides, collages, or blogs. College students might continue to write research papers but also need to construct multimodal compositions that include text and visuals (Li, Dursun, & Hegelheimer, 2017). In this context, one of the goals of a typical L2 writing class is to equip learners with necessary writing skills to respond to the changing nature of writing. Technologies affecting today's writing practices provide a variety of tools for the teaching of second or foreign language writing. Among the wealth of tools, those commonly used in KSL settings include Web 2.0 applications and computer-mediated communication (CMC).

Web 2.0 tools

Web 2.0 tools include a variety of social networking sites, such as Facebook and Twitter, as well as blogs and wikis (Li et al., 2017). For L2 learners, these tools offer unprecedented opportunities to experiment with their language in a more authentic setting than the language classroom. In KSL settings, these websites are especially well suited for language classes where they can compensate for lack of time devoted to writing activities. One Web 2.0 writing tool, for example, is Padlet. Roh and Kim (2019) investigated its use in university Korean classes through a team-based, project-oriented writing activity. The study found that writing activities through Padlet helped Korean L2 learners incorporate in writing vocabulary and grammar that they learned in class. The activities allowed students to monitor their language progress in a more engaging way, which ultimately boosted their confidence in writing. Similarly, Kwon (2012) implemented Facebook-integrated writing activities in a university-level Korean class in Singapore. Consisting of three stages, students in a face-to-face class participated in a pre-writing activity, such as brainstorming and discussion; they then posted answers to the writing tasks on Facebook, and finally commented on others' postings. Using a survey, the study found that the students were able to increase their perceived writing ability as well as reading and speaking ability. Students positively perceived the use of Facebook as a platform for peer and instructor feedback. The Facebook-based activities in fact promoted interaction among learners and enhanced students' interest and motivation.

Computer-mediated communication (CMC)

In the late 1990s, with the advent a more stable internet and the widespread use of personal computers, some teachers and researchers explored the possibilities of CMC among students primarily through asynchronous (ACMC) email and synchronous (SCMC) chat (Heift & Chapelle, 2013). CMC was also implemented in the KFL classroom for various purposes (Cho & Carey, 2003; Lee, 2005). Shim (2003) implemented ACMC using Nicenet (www.nicenet.org) and Blackboard as a beginner-level university Korean class. The objective was to help students practice typing skills, to provide an atmosphere in which students could interact and negotiate meaning, and to enhance electronic literacy in Korean. Results from students' chat scripts and surveys showed that CMC helped promote interaction between students and provided opportunities for increased reading and writing activities in class. However, the asynchronous nature of interaction and students' lack of linguistic resources (i.e., beginning level of students) prevented learners from having extended negotiation of meaning.

CMC technologies gave rise to numerous telecollaborative exchanges (Belz, 2002; O'Dowd & Ritter, 2006; Ware & Kramsch, 2005). One example is the eTandem framework, which has been defined as online "language learning in which two of different native languages work together to help each other learn the other language" (Cziko, 2004, p. 25). Using this framework, Yang (2018) connected Korean language learners with English language learners through online chatting and personal blog writing. In the eTandem exchange, each pair exchanged feedback on one another's L2 writing and participated in group work where all the students took part in online discussions. The study revealed that students have different perceptions of paired and grouped CMC discussions, with them viewing paired CMC as being more effective in terms of developing their writing skills and receiving feedback from their peers.

For the technologies designed for writing to be effective, it is vital that there be learner training and instructor's active guidance and feedback (Li et al., 2017). Teachers should play an active role as learners engage in interaction through Web 2.0 tools and CMC activities. Merely assigning students to work with these tools may not naturally lead to any improvement in writing. To help students benefit from these tools, educators need to use empirical data to come up with a well-structured pedagogical plan.

Technologies for teaching and learning speaking

Students today need not rely solely on classroom activities to engage in speaking activities. They can exchange text, audio, and video in a variety of formats outside the classroom. As a result of this trend, there has been a reshaping of how L2 speaking is taught.

Theoretical frameworks

Theoretically, the use of CALL to promote L2 speaking is framed by some of the crucial ideas that are developed from L2 acquisition theory (Blake, 2017). One of the theories fundamental to CALL is Vygotsky's (1962) notion of zone of proximal development (ZPD) in sociocultural theory (Lantolf & Stephen, 2007). The main thrust of this notion is that two or more individuals working together can produce more accurate and elaborated L2 utterances. Another theory is the noticing hypothesis maintained by L2 researchers known as interactionalists (Blake, 2017). The noticing hypothesis maintains that learners need to first notice linguistic features of the input they are exposed to, and these features are likely to serve as "intake" for learning (Schmidt, 1990). Interactionalists also emphasize the "negotiation of meaning," a process that learners engage in while interacting with one another (Gass, 1997; Long, 1991; Pica, 1994). Accordingly, CALL pedagogy for speaking is situated within these frameworks and attempt to provide students with enough opportunities to collaborate with other speakers.

CALL learning environments for L2 speaking

One of the most common CALL activities for speaking is tutorial CALL and CMC, which can be further divided into ACMC and SCMC. Tutorial CALL enables learners to engage in different forms of self-directed practice. Usually carried out through text chat, ACMC provides an additional practice to face-to-face conversation which for many foreign language learners could otherwise induce anxiety. Evidence from ACMC research has shown that the written medium offers students chances to reflect on linguistic form while promoting participation in discussion (Chun, 1994). On the other hand, SCMC stimulates learners to produce more utterances with the spontaneous turn-taking behavior and negotiation of meaning displayed in face-to-face conversations (Abrams, 2003). This would suggest that CMC would be advantageous in promoting language learning (Blake, 2000). Besides the difference shown in ACMC and SCMC, researchers have found that interaction and negotiation of meaning in CMC interaction is affected by the following: participant type (e.g., interaction between non-native speakers [NNS/NNS] or native speakers and non-native speakers [NS/NNS]), task types (e.g., jigsaw task and information-gap tasks), and technology type (text chat and voice or videoconferencing; Blake, 2000; Doughty & Pica, 1986; Pica, 1994). These learning variables are outlined next.

Tutorial CALL

In the past, tutorial CALL programs have been given the unflattering name of "drill and kill," with the intention of pointing out the lack of any feedback (Blake, 2017). However, automatic speech recognition (ASR) systems call on students to carry out specific tasks, such as practicing pronunciation, repeating short sentences, and, if the L2 pronunciation of the target word or phrases deviates too much from statistical norms, restating utterances (Ehsani & Knodt, 1998). Thus, as Swain supported (2000), advanced tutorial CALL provides an excellent source of feedback along the lines of forced output (Swain, 2000). ASR capabilities are used in several commercially available programs such as Tell Me More, Dragon Naturally Speaking, and, more recently, RosettaStone. In KSL settings, You (2000) developed the Korean conversation program called K Buddy. Its objective is to provide a near-spontaneous and interactive environment for practice. The two high-tech engineering tools of voice recognition and cognitive-functional used in K-buddy accelerate the processing speed of the voice inputs and speech synthesis, thus improving the accuracy of the computer response to the learner's utterance. To be more specific, these two engines process learners' voice responses to a prompt and the program, in turn, finds matching output for the given utterance. K-buddy serves as a good example of how early CALL technology has been employed to connect newly developed technology to improve a program's interactivity.

Asynchronous CALL storytelling

Learners can be multimedia storytellers by using digital storyboard applications such as Book Creator, Little Bird Tales, My Story, Story Creator, and so forth, or using images, PowerPoint slides, and their own videos. Digital storytelling (DST) allows learners to become creative storytellers through the traditional processes of choosing a topic, writing a script, and developing an interesting story, after which it is combined with recorded audio, video clips, or music (Robin, 2008). In the process, learners receive feedback from teachers and their peers, reflect on their language, and use appropriate L2 usage. This approach not only facilitates their L2 speaking, but also brings learner empowerment and agency, as they become creators of L2 texts through their active creation (Blake, 2013). Park (2014) investigated the uses of collaborative storytelling in a virtual world where students can utilize immersive images and audio functions provided there. Cho (2013) implemented DST at all levels of Korean class from beginning to advanced class with varying levels of topics and technologies. By making a presentation and interacting with peers through the project, learners were able to practice various communication modes (interpersonal, interpretive, and presentational) and be exposed to authentic input by interviewing a native speaker or researching online. As a tool for oral presentation in KSL settings, educators also use Voicethread (Kang, 2017; Kim, 2015; Roh & Kim, 2019).

Synchronous CMC

Starting with asynchronous textual exchanges, CMC has a long history (Blake, 2017). The main drive for earlier CMC studies was to demonstrate that asynchronous written CMC provides L2 students with abundant opportunities to engage in negotiation of meaning and generate feedback in ways similar to what had already been found in face-to-face interactions (Abrams, 2003; Blake, 2000; Warschauer, 1996). Kern (1995) found many similarities between L2 oral speech patterns and ACMC textual writing, which is why SCMC textual exchanges are included in the discussion of L2 speaking. Other studies investigated the use of SCMC for the teaching of pragmatics, as SCMC embodies several factors, such as input, interaction, simulation, and multimodality, that are recognized as key to pragmatic learning (Taguchi, 2011). Kim and Brown (2014) found that CMC provides learners opportunities to broaden their discourse practice in a way that would not be available without the access of CMC, thus facilitating the learning of Korean address forms.

Gradually, textual CMC began to include voice-over IP sound (VoIP), a way of offering speakers two channels to communicate (Blake, 2017). Cho and Carey (2001) implemented an asynchronous voice forum called Wimba in their university-level Korean classes to encourage voice discussion and to provide appropriate feedback on speaking and pronunciation.

VoIP soon gave way to synchronous audio and synchronous video. In KSL settings, videoconferencing has been widely adopted to promote intercultural interaction between Korean-learning students and English-learning students (Lee & Song, 2019; Lim & Lee, 2015; Lim & Pyun, 2019). Various videoconferencing tools, such as Adobe Connect, Skype, and KakaoTalk, provide affordable platforms for successful videoconferencing projects. Using Skype, Lim and Pyun (2019) found that students who were initially nervous about interacting with their partners, found the activity fun and exhilarating. The students were able to closely interact with their partners through videos and find many similarities between them. The results of the study also suggested that videoconferencing provides students with opportunities to produce speaking outside their comfort zone and to raise awareness of pragmatic competence in the use of politeness forms. Lim and Lee (2015) highlighted the importance of learner reciprocity (i.e., both participants in the exchange should invest an equal amount of time and effort for mutual benefit) and the monitoring role of the instructor to promote reciprocity for a successful videoconferencing project.

The different CALL learning environments for L2 speaking described here show that the instructor has a rich array of choices to stimulate more and better L2 production. Given that the same learning environment can result in different outcomes depending on task types, participation types, and technology, instructors trying to maximize L2 learning need to adapt tasks and tools to each group of the students.

Technologies for teaching and learning culture and intercultural competence

One of the challenges of teaching language is exploring the relationship of language and culture (Sykes, 2017). Although linguistic accuracy is necessary for language learners to communicate effectively, when language "is used in contexts of communication, it is bound up with culture in multiple and complex ways" (Kramsch & Widdowson, 1998, p. 3). Thus, teaching of culture and intercultural competence has been one of the most important goals in foreign language classrooms (Hall, 2013).

Culture projects using CALL

Traditionally, culture learning in the classroom has been decontextualized and has borne minimal resemblance to actual communication scenarios. Over the years, CALL researchers have explored the potential of computer technology to support the teaching of culture and intercultural competence. Through technology, the limitations of the classroom can be overcome through the use of web-based tools to bring authentic texts and real intercultural communication experiences into the classroom (Byram, 1997). Web 2.0 technologies can also facilitate online practices that allow a classroom to connect with the world. Using audio-visual technologies and courseware (e.g., Blackboard), Roh (2011) established the cultural video project (CVP). In the CVP, students watched authentic culture videos from TV and other media, reflected on them, and completed a discussion online. The study showed that the CVP was well received, for different reasons, by both heritage and non-heritage learners. It demonstrated the value of culture projects in terms of increased learning motivation and cultural awareness. Similarly, Byon (2007) used various activities, such as a media-comparison activity, to raise awareness of Korean and American culture. Through the activity, students were asked to compare American cultural images displayed in Korean media with Korean cultural images projected in American media. The study found that students were able to gain a better understanding of their own culture and have a more open-minded attitude toward the target culture. Jee (2015) implemented a culture project using Facebook as a platform for asynchronous discussion and exchanges on culture. The students consisted of three groups with different cultural backgrounds (i.e., American students, Korean-American students, and Korean students), which provided them with broad perspectives on each other's cultural norms, attitudes, and behaviors.

Telecollaboration

One of the key elements of intercultural competence is the ability to communicate effectively and appropriately in intercultural situations based on cultural knowledge, open-minded attitudes, and appropriate behavioral intentions (Song, 2020). This has given rise to an effort in L2 classrooms to provide students with opportunities, through telecollaboration, to interact with people from different cultures through in-person interactions.

Telecollaborative projects were widely adopted in various forms with various tools. Some studies connected learners through an asynchronous mode (Cho & Carey, 2001), while the others incorporated synchronous interactive modes of conversing in real time through text, audio, and video (Choi, 2020; Lee & Song, 2019; Lim & Lee, 2015; Lim & Pyun, 2019), as well as a combination of the two (Jee & Byun, 2016; Yang, 2018). As for tools, a range of them have been adopted, including mobile-based chat applications such as WhatsApp (Choi, 2020), KakaoTalk (Jee & Byun, 2016; Lee & Song, 2019), Google Talk (Yang, 2018), Facebook Messenger (Jee & Byun, 2016), as well as the videoconferencing tool Skype (Lim & Lee, 2015; Lim & Pyun, 2019). Although most of the studies focused on the linguistic and cultural gains of the interactions, some researchers investigated methodological decisions, such as grouping types and task designs, which may have a potential impact on students' learning outcomes.

Lee and Song (2020) examined major implementation issues related to telecollaboration, including group composition (one-on-one vs. multiple-and-multiple) and task design (student-selected topics vs. teacher-assigned topics). The results revealed that a one-on-one relationship promoted a higher level of intimacy, thus providing an ideal environment for linguistic and emotional support in learning Korean. On the other hand, multiple-to-multiple communications seemed to be more beneficial for learning about different perspectives on the target cultures. Similarly, in a study that incorporated various modes, including paired e-mail exchange, paired online chat, and group discussion, Yang (2018) found that students preferred paired telecollaboration for linguistic gains, as the learners could receive linguistic feedback from their partners.

Another thing that should be taken into consideration in telecollaboration is the crucial role of instructor as a project designer, facilitator, tech consultant, and intercultural partner (Lim & Lee, 2015). Through telecollaboration, learners could correct any negative stereotypes that they held with regard to the target culture (Itakura, 2004), but if cultural clashes occur between speakers of different cultures, telecollaboration could, without the teachers' guidance, cause or confirm negative stereotypes of the target culture (Belz, 2005). Merely assigning students to participate in intercultural interaction may not lead to intercultural and linguistic gains (O'Dowd, 2003). To help students benefit from these exchanges, educators should consider a well-structured plan with the teacher playing an active role.

Distance learning/blended learning with technology

In L2 learning as well as general education, researchers are giving more attention to distance learning and blended learning. The number of students taking at least one distance learning course has recently increased, and as of 2016, online distance learning comprised 31% of all higher education (Allen & Seaman, 2017). Of classes delivered at the level of higher education, blended-learning makes up 70% (Kelly, 2017). This section provides an overview of research on the development of online and blended learning, focusing on the areas of inquiry and important considerations.

Distance learning

Distance learning is defined as teachers and learners being physically separated such that the "bulk of the learning takes place in non-co-presence" (Lamy, 2013, p. 144) and the technology that is used to mediate the process (White, 2017). Distance learning was once regarded by many as a marginal enterprise but is now widely adopted around the world as a well-established means to extend access and opportunities to language learners. A number of different models of distance language teaching have been identified, showing distinctions between traditional and emerging paradigms (White, 2006). For example, in the traditional distance language teaching model, the focus is on the development of course materials for independent study, with an emphasis on learning the target language through texts and tasks. Instruction has relied on one-way technologies to foster L2 acquisition with a lesser focus on speaking skills. Although it was not only for distance learners but also for those who take classes face-to-face, some Korean programs in North America provided self-developed Korean learning materials for L2 learners. The online materials included audio and video clips, texts, and visual images to make materials more attractive and to facilitate Korean learning (Jeon, 2004).

Emerging paradigms for distance language teaching focus on providing an interactive environment with more immediate opportunities for engagement and feedback from instructors and peers (White, 2017). One of the most famous examples of this paradigm is massive open online course (MOOC). Some of the famous platforms for MOOC are Udacity, Coursera, and Edx, which offer more than 500 classes in various fields with more than 700 million enrolled learners (Jang, Kim, & Yeo, 2019). Most of the Korean MOOC studies have focused on the design and implementation process with an emphasis on technology and pedagogical practices used (Jang et al., 2019; Kim & Kim, 2016; Kim, 2018). Jang and colleagues (2019) designed and implemented a beginning online class in China. The class consisted of lectures on pronunciation, grammar, reading, a TOPIK exam, and activities such as read-aloud and online discussions. One of the features of this MOOC class was its interactivity with the learners. Through online discussions, learners were able to actively participate in their learning by asking questions about the lecture and the language and solving the problems together in a form of collaboration. This online class was well received by over 70,000 learners in more than 400 universities in China, with the students showing a high level of satisfaction in terms of content, instructor feedback, and online discussion. Although MOOC Korean classes extend access to and learning opportunities for Korean, certain concerns still arise. These include the validity of assessments in MOOC, the amount of time and effort put into making MOOC classes, and the learning effectiveness of MOOC classes compared to traditional face-to-face classes.

Other studies investigated "presence" in online classes based on the community of inquiry (COI) model (Garrison, Anderson, & Archer, 1999). The COI framework presupposes that for successful online learning to occur, there needs to be three types of presence – cognitive, social, and teaching presence (Garrison et al., 1999; Garrison & Arbaugh, 2007). The last of these, teaching presence, is viewed as learners' awareness that the teacher is present in the online course. This awareness is created by the teacher designing, facilitating, and directing the course to ensure personally meaningful and educationally valuable learning outcomes. Teaching presence is considered critical in building the other components and is closely associated with learning success in online environments (Garrison & Arbaugh, 2007). In a study that compared teachers' perceived teaching presence between online and offline Korean classes, Han and Ahn (2020) found that teachers felt the level of teaching presence differed in an online class from an offline class. Unsurprisingly, the teaching presence level in the online class felt lower in terms of active interaction with the students, rapport, immediate feedback, and encouragement of students' learning. The result suggests that teachers of the online class have a more difficult time understanding students' progress, which makes it hard to provide appropriate feedback and encouragement. The study corroborates previous findings that it is challenging for teachers to design and implement a foreign language class online, while meeting the students' needs and expectations.

Blended learning/flipped learning

In its most general terms, blended learning is referred to as a combination of face-to-face classroom meetings and computer-mediated learning (Graham, 2006). More specifically, blended learning is often described as classes where face-to-face and online activities are planned and integrated in a meaningful way for L2 learning and where online activities replace a portion of face-to-face instruction (Picciano, 2009). Many scholars also refer to blended learning as hybrid learning (Grgurovic, 2017). Some of the applications of blended learning classes include online assessment, online discussion forums, uploading learning materials to a course website, and submission of course assignments online and so forth through a learning management system (e.g., Canvas) (Driscoll, 2002).

Another term used occasionally is flipped learning, a specific form of blended learning. Flipped learning is a pedagogical approach in which activities that traditionally take place inside the classroom take place outside the classroom. A simple description of a flipped classroom is one where a learner is asked to watch a lecture video complete with assignments before coming to class so that the class time can be devoted to important learning activities with their teachers and peers (Bergmann & Sams, 2012). Korean classes overseas suffer from a lack of instruction time and language exposure outside the classroom. Given this, flipped learning is considered as one of the ideal models that can overcome part of the difficulty of the current curriculum (Kim, 2020; Lee, 2020; Zhang & Kim, 2019).

Studies on blended and flipped learning are mainly divided, by the topic of investigation, into the following categories: 1) comparative studies of non-blended and blended classes, 2) teacher perceptions, 3) learner perceptions, and 4) course implementation.

The comparative studies compared the efficacy of blended learning to conventional face-to-face classes, that is, whether the learning gains were compromised when moving some instruction online (Grgurovic, 2017). Most of the comparative study found no significant difference between the students' performance in blended learning and non-blended class (i.e., traditional, conventional, or face-to-face classes) in terms of oral proficiency measures (Blake, Wilson, Cetto, & Pardo-Ballester, 2008), listening and reading (Young, 2008), and final course grades (Scida & Saury, 2006). In the KSL setting, Kim (2020) found that implementation of flipped learning resulted in an increase in academic performance over traditional classes in terms of listening and speaking skills.

Some studies investigated teacher perceptions of their readiness and interest and experience with teaching blended courses. Chenoweth, Ushida, and Murday (2006) and Comas-Quinn (2011) reported that novice teachers struggled in their first semester of teaching blended courses, as the teachers quickly realized that online language teaching required a different set of skills. There were many things the teachers had to juggle, including monitoring student progress, material selection for a new course format, and technological skills. Jang (2016) investigated levels of KSL teachers' interests, understanding, and readiness toward blended learning. The results showed significant differences between the overseas Korean teachers and the domestic Korean teachers. The former showed a slightly higher understanding, had more experience, and a more diverse use of blended learning. The study suggests that domestic Korean teachers could use more information, as well as instructional and administrative support.

Learner perceptions or attitudes toward blended or flipped learning were mostly studied via student surveys and interviews. Overall, studies found that learners were satisfied with the new teaching mode, as it promoted independent learning, provided more time during class so the most essential parts of the lessons are practiced and learned in class, and enhanced in-class engagement, as students came to class prepared (Ji & Yun, 2017; Zhang & Kim, 2019).

Many studies proposed learning models or lesson plans for Korean using flipped learning (Lee, 2020; Zhang & Kim, 2019) for various purposes, such as writing (Kim, 2017), speaking (Zhang & Kim, 2019), vocabulary (Bae, 2015), and grammar (Lee, 2015; Woo, 2017). Zhang and Kim (2019) provided a detailed flipped learning model, as shown in Figure 9.5. The study found that students learning Korean in China were satisfied with the flipped learning, as it provided more opportunities to practice Korean in class. Many consider that providing sufficient opportunity to practice is the biggest challenge in large-sized Korean classes in China. The findings also underscore the importance of learners communicating and interacting with one another and becoming engaged through pre- and post-class activities.

Emerging technology

Digital gaming

Until recently, relatively few in the field of SLA used gaming for L2 learning and teaching. This may have been because of limited resources, lack of SLA theoretical grounding, and usage being limited to computer lab settings (Jordan, 1992; Peterson, 2010). Over the past few decades, though, more casual and social games have become available, and with a flourishing of gaming culture and communities there now exists a large variety of discourse practices. The

Pre-class
동영상 시청 및 사전 과제 수행

In-class
학습 내용 점검(퀴즈)
↓
핵심내용 정리
↓
짝 활동 및 발표 활동 진행
↓
정리 및 마무리

Post-class
자기평가 및 동료평가
↓
말하기 녹음

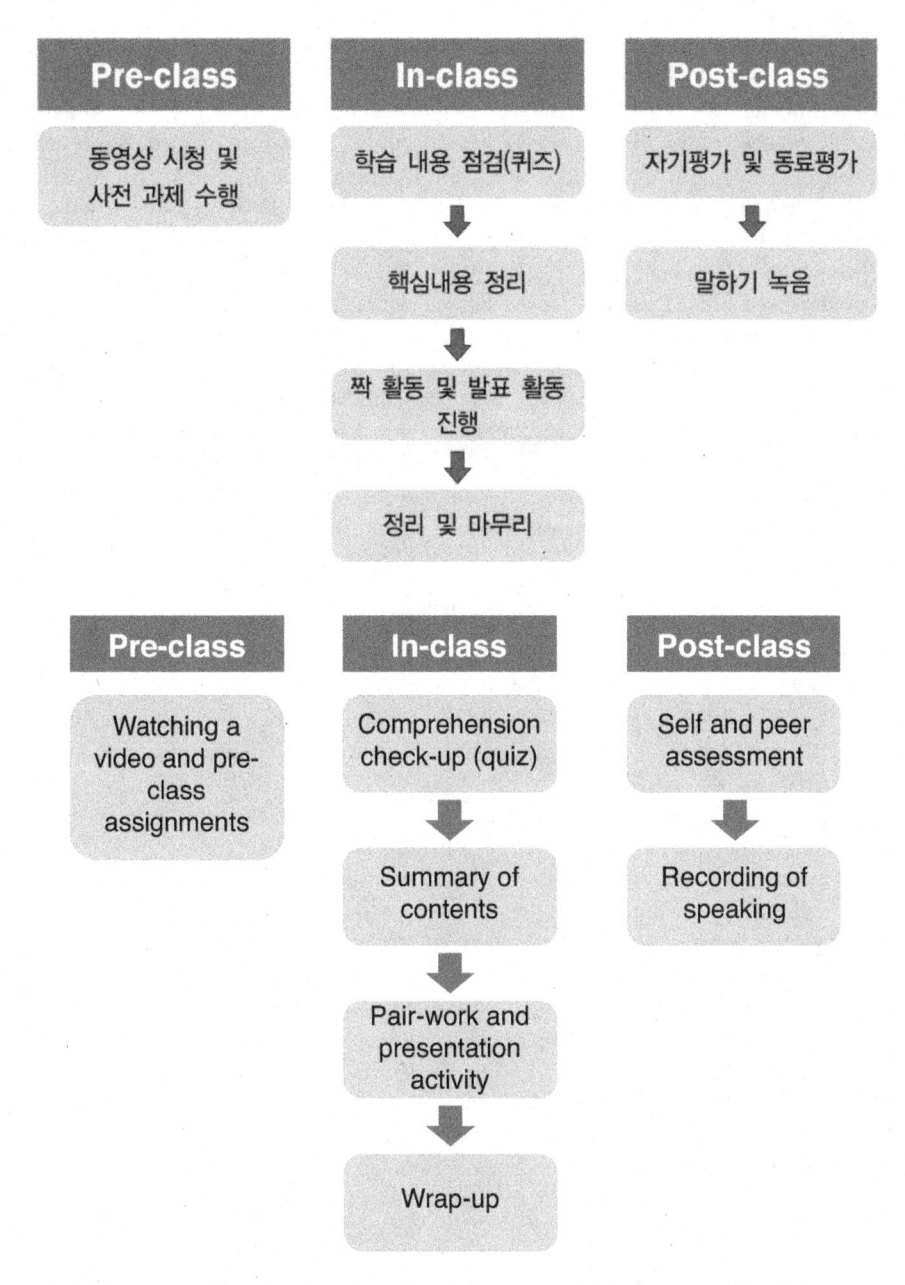

Pre-class
Watching a video and pre-class assignments

In-class
Comprehension check-up (quiz)
↓
Summary of contents
↓
Pair-work and presentation activity
↓
Wrap-up

Post-class
Self and peer assessment
↓
Recording of speaking

Figure 9.5 Korean speaking class based on flipped learning model in Korean and English

nature of these practices has become linguistically rich and more varied in genre and register (Reinhardt, 2017). Through interacting with digital games and other players, millions of players engage in a language-mediated activity, which can become a means to learning language informally (Chik, 2014). The qualities of game-mediated literacy practices and the capacity of games to direct focus on form and meaning have made L2 researchers reexamine the possibilities of using games for L2 learning. One of the early digital games specifically designed for L2 learning was simulated immersion environments (SIEs). In MIDDWorld Online and Practice

Spanish: Study Abroad games, players create avatars and engage in a variety of role-playing tasks similar to what they would experience in a study abroad situation (Muzzy Lane, 2014 cited in Reinhardt, 2017). These SIEs are designed for immersive, engaging, and authentic cultural experiences to reinforce language learning in the real-world context. More recently, online language-learning applications, such as DuoLingo, LingQ, and Livemocha, have emerged as game-based language-learning tools. While they might be effective in some ways, most have yet to be positively evaluated by CALL researchers due to their grammar-translation and memorization-based drill practices (Reinhardt, 2017).

Kwon and Woo (2013) proposed a digital game for Korean L2 learning based on game-based learning and Korean learning theory. Given that many Korean L2 learners are interested in Korean culture, K-Pop, drama, and films, the proposed game model includes such content as a base for listening, reading, speaking, and vocabulary activities. The learning is motivated through game character making, reward, mission control, and competition with other players, all of which are utilized in game-based learning. This pioneering model has yet to be implemented in L2 learning, and researchers have not investigated the effects of this game, making it hard to draw conclusions about how effective it is Korean L2 learning.

Virtual reality

Amid the rapid growth in the use of advanced technology for educational purposes, there are a variety of definitions for virtual reality (Feng, González, Amor, Lovreglio, & Cabrera-Guerrero, 2018). In basic terms, VR is defined as anything "inducing targeted behavior in an organism by using artificial sensory stimulation, while the organism has little or no awareness of the interference" (LaValle, 2016).

VR could be particularly beneficial for overseas Korean L2 learners who have limited opportunities to experience the target culture or to practice the target language. VR simulations can allow learners to have experiences that would otherwise be difficult or impossible, such as exploring a distant city or time period that they just encountered in a textbook. As such, these reproductions can boost motivation to learn about other cultures, cultivate curiosity, and may lead to deeper understanding than traditional learning modes due to their ability to replicate first-hand experience rather than relying on the learner's imagination (Li et al., 2017).

Two studies demonstrated a VR-implemented Korean lesson for Korean language and culture leaning (Choi, Cho, & Kim, 2020; Song, 2019). In Song's (2019) study, the researcher had students watch self-filmed VR videos containing naturally occurring conversations and famous tourist spots in Korea, which were used for language practice and discussions. Choi et al. (2020) used available VR videos on YouTube in a content-based, advanced Korean class. Both studies found the benefits of VR implementation curriculum in terms of 1) increased motivation and enjoyment and 2) presence (i.e., the feeling of being there, in this case, in Korea) through immersion, which are consistent with previous VR studies (Dede, Grotzer, Kamarainen, & Metcalf, 2017). The studies suggest that VR technology is becoming accessible; designers should use the research on how this technology impacts learning outcomes to inform their development of VR-embedded curriculum designs.

Mobile-based language learning (m-learning)

Mobile technologies have made a lifelong commitment to make language learning more feasible, accessible, and attractive. The personal nature of mobile tools is uniquely suited for language learning in a range of settings and for learners at all levels of proficiency (Kukulska-Hulme,

Lee, & Norris, 2017). Some of the benefits of m-learning include the following: 1) it is self-paced enabling learner autonomy; 2) it is ubiquitous and allows for mobility, overcoming the limitation of web-based learning, which is only available in specific learning settings; and 3) it provides a fun and motivating learning environment (Kukulska-Hulme & Shield, 2008). There is extensive literature on m-learning in the field of SLA, and many studies focus on specific guidance, such as how to teach language with mobile devices, what aspects of language can be taught, and what kinds of new competencies are needed (Kukulska-Hulme et al., 2017). This range of focus might arise from mobile devices' capacity to extend learning beyond the classroom setting, which could pose new challenges. That is, learners might encounter linguistically challenging situations through online applications or informal connections to target language speakers. Kukulska-Hulme (2013) maintained that language learners need to be re-skilled for m-learning in which learner autonomy is practiced. Many researchers regard learner autonomy as an ideal aim to educate learners who will be able to play an active role in their learning process and continue learning beyond the classroom.

In the case of KSL and m-learning, there are a number of mobile apps that are specifically designed for Korean language learning, and most studies analyzed these applications or proposed a lesson using these tools. Chu and Lee (2013) analyzed two mobile-based learning applications, Study Korean and L-Lingo, in terms of their learning goals, contents (i.e., the appropriate level of contents for language learners, organization, individualization of contents), and assessment (i.e., appropriate feedback for learning). They found that most available applications were for vocabulary learning, while the availability of applications for conversation, pronunciation, and grammar was still limited.

Future direction

The overview of CALL research reveals rich and valuable opportunities for Korean language learners, teachers, and researchers. For learners, there are many options for accessing the target language and culture, interacting with other learners and native speakers of Korean in virtual spaces, and obtaining abundant online resources. For KFL researchers and practitioners, various technologies could be a source of new experiments, applications, and research to understand the extent to which instructional technology can contribute to language learning.

Researchers in this area should consider several suggestions and issues. Given the changed landscape for L2 learning, one consideration is related to the professional knowledge required of language teachers. The primary goals for practitioners should be to first understand the technologies that sometimes mediate our daily interactions and second to consider appropriate instructional practices for the attendant changes in learning settings. A new generation of learners – digital natives – are joining Korean programs. These students are likely more familiar communicating with each other via texting, social media, Web 2.0 technologies, or in a networked world, rather than through traditional face-to-face conversation or print material. This shift calls for continued efforts and new directions for CALL researchers and practitioners where the focus is not comparing the efficacy of technology but the optimal pedagogical approach when the use of technology is becoming not just part of learners' expectations but required skills in the 21st century.

One possible area for future research is to examine how learning occurs through technology. Most of the studies reviewed here focused on the practical applications of various technologies in class and examined students' perceptions of the new technology. Other studies looked at the finished product or final outcomes without examining the process of learning. Future research should closely examine how learning occurs in new environments and in what ways the use of technology leads to actual learning gains.

Another area for further research is the use of technology for feedback. Many studies have explored peer feedback in CMC, telecollaboration, and videoconferencing settings for other languages. However, there are few studies on the use of technology for peer or instructor feedback in KSL settings. L2 learners can incidentally focus on language form during CMC exchanges with their peers. Through such incidents, learners can question their language use or correct themselves or others. Automatic writing evaluation (AWE), which is developed specifically for analysis and feedback for writers, can also be a useful tool for Korean L2 writing.

One last area for future research is the impact of blended or distance learning or best practices based on solid theoretical grounds. The global outbreak of COVID-19 has changed people's lives to a great extent, and this includes the teaching and learning of foreign languages. Distance or blended learning will undoubtedly continue to evolve by using new technologies and new learning models. In introducing any learning environments, it is essential to consider questions related to assessment, psychological issues (i.e., students questioning whether distance or blended learning can be enough), and pedagogical issues (i.e., activities suited for delivery mode). Future studies should delve into these issues and consider the constraints on language learners as they seek to adapt to new learning environments and learn to benefit from them.

Note

This work was supported by the Seed Program for Korean Studies through the Ministry of Education of the Republic of Korea and the Korean Studies Promotion Service of the Academy of Korean Studies (AKS-2020-INC-2230002).

References

Abrams, Z. I. (2003). The effect of synchronous and asynchronous CMC on oral performance in German. *The Modern Language Journal, 87*(2), 157–167.
Ahn, J., & Shim, Y. (2018). Exploring the instructional use of instagram for Korean language learning. *Journal of Korean Language Education, 29*(4), 65–92.
Allen, I. E., & Seaman, J. (2017). *Digital compass learning: Distance education enrollment report 2017*. Babson Survey Research Group.
Bae, D. (2015). A case study of the flipped learning classes at the university. *Urimal* (41), 179–202.
Bax, S. (2003). CALL: Past, present and future. *System, 31*(1), 13–28.
Belz, J. A. (2002). Social dimensions of telecollaborative foreign language study. *Language Learning & Technology, 6*(1), 60–81.
Belz, J. A. (2005). Intercultural questioning, discovery and tension in Internet-mediated language learning partnerships. *Language and Intercultural Communication, 5*(1), 3–39.
Bergmann, J., & Sams, A. (2012). Before you flip, consider this. *Phi Delta Kappan, 94*(2), 25–25.
Blake, R. (2000). Computer mediated communication: A window on L2 Spanish interlanguage. *Language Learning & Technology, 4*(1), 111–125.
Blake, R. J. (2013). *Brave new digital classroom: Technology and foreign language learning*. Washington, DC: Georgetown University Press.
Blake, R. J. (2017). Technologies for teaching and learning L2 speaking. In C. Chapelle & S. Sauro (Eds.), *The handbook of technology and second language teaching and learning* (pp. 107–117). Hoboken, NJ: Wiley-Blackwell.
Blake, R., Wilson, N. L., Cetto, M., & Pardo-Ballester, C. (2008). Measuring oral proficiency in distance, face-to-face, and blended classrooms. *Language Learning & Technology, 12*(3), 114.
Byon, A. S. (2007). Process-driven culture learning in American KFL classroom settings. *Applied Language Learning, 17*(2), 73–90.
Byram, M. (1997). *Teaching and assessing intercultural communicative competence*. Clevedon, UK: Multilingual Matters.

Chapelle, C. A. (2009). The relationship between second language acquisition theory and computer-assisted language learning. *The Modern Language Journal, 93*, 741–753.

Chen, C.-M., & Chung, C.-J. (2008). Personalized mobile English vocabulary learning system based on item response theory and learning memory cycle. *Computers & Education, 51*(2), 624–645.

Chenoweth, N. A., Ushida, E., & Murday, K. (2006). Student learning in hybrid French and Spanish courses: An overview of language online. *CALICO Journal*, 115–146.

Chik, A. (2014). Digital gaming and language learning: Autonomy and community. *Language Learning & Technology, 18*(2), 85–100.

Cho, H. (2013). Use of digital storytelling in KFL classrooms: Integrating digital storytelling into standard-based curriculum. In *Paper presented at the 23rd international conference on Korean language education*. The International Association for Korean Language Education, 615–625. Retrieved from http://kiss.kstudy.com/search/detail_page.asp?key=3159074.

Cho, I. (2000). Integrating technology into Korean language education: Teaching today's students for tomorrow's society *The Korean Language in America, 5*, 57–69.

Cho, I. J. (2014). A case study of utilizing Twitter and Moodle for teaching of communication strategies. *Journal of Korean Language Education, 25*(1), 203–234.

Cho, S. P., & Carey, S. (2001). Increasing Korean oral fluency using an electronic bulletin board and Wimba-based voiced chat. *The Korean Language in America, 6*, 115–128.

Cho, S. P., & Carey, S. (2003). To participate or not in an intercultural seminar via global computer-mediated communication. *The Korean Language in America, 8*, 221–232.

Choi, H. J., Cho, S.-H., & Kim, T. (2020). Reshaping advanced level KFL curriculum: Immersive cultural experience and interaction in virtual reality (VR) environments. In *Paper presented at the The 30th international conference on Korean language education*. Korea University, Korea.

Choi, O. H. (2020). Digitally connected Korean education: Reflections on an e-tandem language learning project in a UK university. In *Paper presented at the The 30th international conference on Korean language education*. Korea University, Korea.

Chu, K., & Lee, S. (2013). Analysis of smartphon applications for Korean vocabulary learning. In *Paper presented at the 23rd international conference on Korean language education*, Korea University, Korea.

Chun, D. M. (1994). Using computer networking to facilitate the acquisition of interactive competence. *System, 22*(1), 17–31.

Comas-Quinn, A. (2011). Learning to teach online or learning to become an online teacher: An exploration of teachers' experiences in a blended learning course. *ReCALL, 23*(3), 218–232.

Cziko, G. A. (2004). Electronic tandem language learning (eTandem): A third approach to second language learning for the 21st century. *CALICO Journal*, 25–39.

Da, J., & Zheng, Y. (2018). Technology and the teaching and learning of Chinese as a foreign language. In *The Routledge handbook of chinese second language acquisition* (pp. 432–447). Oxon and New York: Routledge.

Dede, C., Grotzer, T. A., Kamarainen, A., & Metcalf, S. J. (2017). Virtual reality as an immersive medium for authentic simulations. In *Virtual, augmented, and mixed realities in education* (pp. 133–156). Singapore: Springer.

Dickinson, M., Eom, S., Kang, Y., Lee, C. M., & Sachs, R. (2008). A balancing act: How can intelligent computer-generated feedback be provided in learner-to-learner interactions? *Computer Assisted Language Learning, 21*(4), 369–382.

Doughty, C., & Pica, T. (1986). "Information gap" tasks: Do they facilitate second language acquisition? *TESOL Quarterly, 20*(2), 305–325.

Driscoll, M. (2002). Blended learning: Let's get beyond the hype. *E-learning, 1*(4), 1–4.

Ehsani, F., & Knodt, E. (1998). Speech technology in computer-aided language learning: Strengths and limitations of a new CALL paradigm. *Language Learning & Technology, 2*(1), 54–73.

Feng, Z., González, V. A., Amor, R., Lovreglio, R., & Cabrera-Guerrero, G. (2018). Immersive virtual reality serious games for evacuation training and research: A systematic literature review. *Computers & Education, 127*, 252–266.

Gao, F. (2013). A case study of using a social annotation tool to support collaboratively learning. *The Internet and Higher Education, 17*, 76–83.

Garrison, D. R., Anderson, T., & Archer, W. (1999). Critical inquiry in a text-based environment: Computer conferencing in higher education. *The Internet and Higher Education, 2*(2–3), 87–105.

Garrison, D. R., & Arbaugh, J. B. (2007). Researching the community of inquiry framework: Review, issues, and future directions. *The Internet and Higher Education, 10*(3), 157–172.

Gass, S. M. (1997). *Input, interaction, and the second language learner*. Mahwah, NJ: Lawrance Erlbaum Associates.

Genc, H. (2011). Paper and screen: Reading strategies used by low-proficient EFL learners. *Sino-US English Teaching, 8*(10), 648–658.

Godwin-Jones, R. (2010). Literacies and technologies revisited. *Language Learning & Technology, 14*(3), 2–9.

Godwin-Jones, R. (2013). The technological imperative in teaching and learning less commonly taught languages. *Language Learning & Technology, 17*(1), 7–19.

Graham, C. R. (2006). Blended learning systems. In C. Bonk & C. Graham (Eds.), *The handbook of blended learning: Global perspectives, local designs* (pp. 3–21). San Francisco, CA: Pfeifer.

Grgurovic, M. (2017). Blended language learning: Research and practice. In C. Chapelle & S. Sauro (Eds.), *The handbook of technology and second language teaching and learning* (pp. 149–168). Hoboken, NJ: Wiley-Blackwell.

Hall, J. K. (2013). *Teaching and researching: Language and culture*. London: Pearson Education.

Han, H., & Ahn, J. M. (2020). Comparing teaching presence in an online and offline Korean class. In *Paper presented at the 30th international conference of Korean language education*. Korea University, Korea.

Hart, R. S. (1995). The Illinois PLATO foreign languages project. *CALICO Journal, 12*(4), 15–37.

Heift, T., & Chapelle, C. A. (2013). Language learning through technology. In S. M. Gass, Mackey, A. (Ed.), *The Routledge handbook of second language acquisition* (pp. 573–588). Oxon and New York: Routledge.

Heift, T., & Vyatkina, N. (2017). Technologies for teaching and learning L2 Grammar. In C. A. Chapelle & S. Sauro (Eds.), *The handbook of technology and second language teaching and learning* (pp. 26–44). Hoboken, NJ: Wiley-Blackwell.

Hubbard, P., & Siskin, C. B. (2004). Another look at tutorial CALL. *ReCALL, 16*(2), 448–461.

Huilin Zhang, H. S. (2019). An analysis of research trends in Korean education using video media. *Journal of Korean Language Education, 30*(4), 161–191.

Hulstijn, J. H. (2005). Theoretical and empirical issues in the study of implicit and explicit second-language learning: Introduction. *Studies in Second Language Acquisition, 27*(2), 129–140.

Hung, H.-T. (2015). Intentional vocabulary learning using digital flashcards. *English Language Teaching, 8*(10), 107–112.

Hwang, S.-E. (2020). A study on the academic vocabulary education for content-based Korean language education: A basic study for online dictionary development. *Journal of the Korea Society of Computer and Information, 25*(2), 67–74.

Im, J. N., Min, S. N., & Cho, S. M. (2017). Analysis of reading process with Korean learner using EEG and eye tracking. *Journal of the Ergonomics Society of Korea, 36*(6), 717–727.

Itakura, H. (2004). Changing cultural stereotypes through e-mail assisted foreign language learning. *System, 32*(1), 37–51.

Jang, M. (2016). A study on Korean language teacher's concerns about blended learning. *Journal of Korean Language Education, 27*(3), 289–321.

Jang, Y.-M., Kim, H.-S., & Yeo, C.-W. (2019). Implementing MOOC in Korean classroom: Beginning Korean class. In *Paper presented at the 29th international conference on Korean language education*. Korea University, Korea.

Jee, M. J. (2015). A case study of a cultura-inspired project for the teaching of culture. *Korean Language Education Research, 50*(5), 114–146.

Jee, M. J., & Byun, J. H. (2016). An intercultural exchange project between KFL and EFL students. *Foreign Languages Education, 23*(2), 107–136.

Jeon, J. (2004). On-site study of online Korean courses: Current analysis of online Korean courses. *The Korean Language in America, 9*, 210–224.

Ji, E., & Yun, Y. (2017). Efficacy of flipped classroom in language learning. In *Paper presented at the 27th international conference on Korean language education*. Kyung Hee University, Korea.

Jin, S. (2015). Using Facebook to promote Korean EFL learners' intercultural competence. *Language Learning & Technology, 19*(3), 38–51.

Jordan, G. (1992). Exploiting computer-based simulations for language-learning purposes. *Simulation & Gaming, 23*(1), 88–98.

Kang, L. (2017). Using voicethread as a tool for presentation: Procedures and implementation. In *Paper presented at the 27th international conference on Korean language education*. Seoul. The International Association for Korean Language Education, 221–231.

Kelly, R. (2017). Survey: Blended learning on the rice. *Campus Technology*. Retrieved from https://campustechnology.com/articles/2017/09/20/survey-blended-learning-on-the-rise.aspx

Kern, R. G. (1995). Restructuring classroom interaction with networked computers: Effects on quantity and characteristics of language production. *The Modern Language Journal, 79*(4), 457–476.

Kim, A. (2020). The effects of flipped learning on Korean language learners' academic performance. *Journal of Korean Language Education, 31*(3), 77–98.

Kim, E. Y. A., & Brown, L. (2014). Negotiating pragmatic competence in computer mediated communication: The case of Korean address terms. *CALICO Journal, 31*(3), 264–282.

Kim, H., & Kang, S. (2016). Effects of speed reading training for Korean learners on fixation and saccade-utilizing eye-tracking. *Journal of Korean Language Education, 27*(3), 23–48.

Kim, H.-G., Kang, B.-M., & Hong, J. (2007). 21st century Sejong Corpora (to be) completed. *The Korean Language in America, 12*, 31–42.

Kim, N. (1994). The current status and issues of Korean education in Los Angeles, U.S.A. *Korean Language Education, 5*, 262–270.

Kim, S. (2017). A study on using flipped learning in Korean language classroom. *Journal of Education and Culture, 23*(1), 529–550.

Kim, S.-S., & Kim, S.-J. (2016). A case study of developing Korean language education model in MOOC: Global MOOC and K-MOOC. *Korean Language Education, 44*, 85–130.

Kim, T. (2015). Bringing 14th century masterpieces to life by VoiceThread. *The Korean Language in America, 19*(1), 136–148.

Kim, W.-C. M. (1987). The colloquial Korean interactive videodisc project. *CALICO Journal, 4*(4), 71.

Kim, Y. (1994). Language education programs for minorities in Canada: Issues for the effective Korean language education. *Korean Language Education*, (5), 285–292.

Kim, Y. (1995). Computer-room demonstration at DLI: Teaching Korean through interactive videodisc (IVD)/computer. *The Korean Language in America, 1*, 265–268.

Kim, Y. (2018). The development and practice of Korean language for K-MOOC (Korean massive open online courses): A case of '한국어를 부탁해' intermediate level. *Korean Language Education, 44*, 85–130.

Kramsch, C., & Widdowson, H. (1998). *Language and culture*. Oxford: Oxford University Press.

Krashen, S. D. (1981). *Second language acquisition and second language learning*. Englewood Cliffs, NJ: Prentice-Hall International.

Kukulska-Hulme, A. (2013). *Re-skilling language learners for a mobile world*. Monterey: The International Research Foundation for English Language Education (TIRF).

Kukulska-Hulme, A., Lee, H., & Norris, L. (2017). Mobile learning revolution: Implications for language pedagogy. In C. Chapelle & S. Sauro (Eds.), *The handbook of technology and second language teaching and learning* (pp. 217–233). Hoboken, NJ: Wiley-Blackwell.

Kukulska-Hulme, A., & Shield, L. (2008). An overview of mobile assisted language learning: From content delivery to supported collaboration and interaction. *ReCALL, 20*(3), 271–289.

Kwon, C.-S., & Woo, T. (2013). A research on gamification methodology for Korean language education. *Journal of Korea Game Society, 13*(1), 61–74.

Kwon, J. A. (2012). The application of Facebook to Korean elementary class. *Journal of Korean Language Education, 23*(4), 1–29.

Lamy, M.-N. (2013). Distance CALL online. In M. Thomas, H. Reinders, & M. Warschauer (Eds.), *Contemporary computer-assisted language learning* (pp. 141–158). London: Continuum.

Lantolf, J. P. (2000). *Sociocultural theory and second language learning* (Vol. 78). Oxford: Oxford University Press.

Lantolf, J., & Stephen, L. T. (2007). Sociocultural theory and second language learning. In B. VanPattern & J. Williams (Eds.), *Theories in second language acquisition* (pp. 201–224). Mahwah, NJ: Lawrence Erlbaum.

LaValle, S. (2016). *Virtual reality*. Cambridge: Cambridge University Press.

Lee, D.-E. (2005). A study of improving Korean learners' pragmatic competence: Using computer-mediated communication. *Hangeul*, (268), 165–187.

Lee, J. (2020). Designing and implementing a flipped learning model for the 'Introduction to Korean language education' course based on the revised Bloom's taxonomy. *Journal of Korean Language Education, 31*(1), 77–103.

Lee, J., & Song, J. (2019). Developing intercultural competence through study abroad, telecollaboration, and on-campus language study. *Language Learning & Technology, 23*(3), 178–198.

Lee, J., & Song, J. (2020). The impact of group composition and task design on foreign language learners' interactions in mobile-based intercultural exchanges. *ReCALL, 32*(1), 63–84.

Lee, S.-H. (2015). Teaching of Korean grammar using flipped learning-focus on the Korean grammar class as a liberal arts subject. *Korean Language and Culture Education Society, 11*(2), 221–262.

Lee, S.-H., Jang, S. B., & Seo, S.-K. (2009). Annotation of Korean learner corpora for particle error detection. *CALICO Journal, 26*(3), 529.

Levy, M. (1997). *Computer-assisted language learning: Context and conceptualization*. Oxford: Oxford University Press.

Li, Z., Dursun, A., & Hegelheimer, V. (2017). Technology and L2 writing. In C. Chapelle & S. Sauro (Eds.), *The handbook of technology and second language teaching and learning* (pp. 77–92). Hoboken, NJ: Wiley-Blackwell.

Liaw, M. L., & English, K. (2017). Technologies for teaching and learning L2 reading. In C. A. Chapelle & S. Sauro (Eds.), *The handbook of technology and second language teaching and learning* (pp. 62–76). Hoboken, NJ: Wiley-Blackwell.

Lim, B.-J., & Lee, H.-J. (2015). Videoconferencing for Korean language education: Synchronous online interactions between learners of Korean and English beyond the classroom. *Korean Language Education, 26*, 1–28.

Lim, B.-J., & Pyun, D. O. (2019). Korean foreign language learning: Videoconferencing with native speakers. In Wang & Winstead (Eds.), *Handbook of research on foreign language education in the digital age* (pp. 253–276). Hersey, PA: IGI Global.

Long, M. H. (1991). *Focus on form: A design feature in language teaching methodology*. Amsterdam and Philadelphia: John Benjamins Publishing Company.

Ma, Q. (2017). Technologies for teaching and learning L2 vocabulary. In C. A. Chapelle & S. Sauro (Eds.), *The handbook of technology and second language teaching and learning* (pp. 45–61). Hoboken, NJ: Wiley-Blackwell.

Muzzy Lane Software. (2014). MiddWorld Online. Retrieved January 9, 2017, from http://muzzylane.com/project/mil.

Nam, H.-S., Kim, K.-Y., & Kwon, H.-C. (2001). Improving a Korean spell/grammar checker for the web-based language learning system. *The Korean Society for Cognitive Science, 12*(3), 1–18.

O'Dowd, R. (2003). Understanding the" other side": Intercultural learning in a Spanish-English e-mail exchange. *Language Learning & Technology, 7*(2), 118–144.

O'Dowd, R., & Ritter, M. (2006). Understanding and working with'failed communication'in telecollaborative exchanges. *CALICO Journal*, 623–642.

Omar, N. A. (2014). Online metacognitive reading strategies use by postgraduate Libyan EFL students. *International Journal of Humanities and Social Sciences, 8*(7), 2289–2292.

Otto, S. E. (2017). From past to present: A hundred years of technology for L2 learning. In C. A. Chapelle & S. Sauro (Eds.), *The handbook of technology and second language teaching and learning* (pp. 10–25). Hoboken, NJ: Wiley-Blackwell.

Park, E. S. (2012). The educational effect of Twitter on Korean education. *Journal of Korean Language Education, 23*(2), 115–141.

Park, H. (2014). Collaborative digital storytelling through sharing tool in second life. *Journal of Education and Human Development, 3*(2), 511–525.

Park, H., & Nicola, F. (2010). Development of a multimedia based Korean language literature lesson. *Journal of Korean Language Education, 21*(4), 119–152.

Park, J., Yang, J., & Hsieh, Y. C. (2014). University level second language readers' online reading and comprehension strategies. *Language Learning & Technology, 18*(3), 148–172.

Peterson, M. (2010). Computerized games and simulations in computer-assisted language learning: A meta-analysis of research. *Simulation & Gaming, 41*(1), 72–93.

Pica, T. (1994). Research on negotiation: What does it reveal about second-language learning conditions, processes, and outcomes? *Language Learning, 44*(3), 493–527.

Picciano, A. G. (2009). Blending with purpose: The multimodal model. *Journal of Asynchronous Learning Networks, 13*(1), 7–18.

Reinhardt, J. (2017). Digital gaming in L2 teaching and learning. In C. Chapelle & S. Sauro (Eds.), *The handbook of technology and second language teaching and learning* (pp. 202–216). Hoboken, NJ: Wiley-Blackwell.

Robin, B. R. (2008). Digital storytelling: A powerful technology tool for the 21st century classroom. *Theory into Practice, 47*(3), 220–228.

Roh, J. (2011). The development of the cultural video project and its impact on Korean learning. *The Korean Language in America, 16*, 73–100.

Roh, J., & Kim, T. (2019). Fostering learner autonomy through CALL and MALL in a Korean class: A case study. *Journal of Interactive Learning Research, 30*(2), 215–254.

Rubin, J., Ediger, A., Coffin, E., Van Handle, D., & Whiskeyman, A. (1990). Survey of interactive language discs. *CALICO Journal, 7*(3), 31–56.

Sanders, R., & Sanders, A. (1995). History of an AI Spy Game: Spion. *CALICO Journal, 12*(4), 114–127.

Schmidt, R. W. (1990). The role of consciousness in second language learning. *Applied Linguistics, 11*(2), 129–158.

Scida, E. E., & Saury, R. E. (2006). Hybrid courses and their impact on student and classroom performance: A case study at the University of Virginia. *CALICO Journal*, 517–531.

Seo, S.-K. (2005). Informatization and use of Korean language data. *The Review of Korean Studies*, 8–4.

Shim, Y.-S. (2003). The use of asynchronous CMC in a beginning Korean class. *The Korean Language in America, 8*, 199–220.

Song, J. (2019). Enhancing intercultural competence with 360-degree virtual reality videos. *The Korean Language in America, 23*(1), 85–98.

Song, J. (2020). The effects of a short-term study abroad program on developing students' intercultural competence and oral proficiency. *Linguistic Research, 37*, 1–29.

Spiri, J. (2008). Online study of frequency list vocabulary with the WordChamp website. *Reflections on English Language Teaching, 7*(1), 21–36.

Stevens, V. (1989). *A direction for CALL: From behavioristic to humanistic courseware*. La Jolla, CA: Athelstan.

Sugai, Y. (2013). The development of a reading support tool for the Korean language using automatic morphological analysis technology. *Journal of Korean Language Education, 24*(3), 139–159.

Swain, M. (2000). The output hypothesis and beyond: Mediating acquisition through collaborative dialogue. In J. Lantolf (Ed.), *Sociocultural theory and second language learning* (pp. 97–114). Oxford: Oxford University Press.

Sykes, J. (2017). Technologies for teaching and learning intercultural competence and interlanguage pragmatics. In C. Chapelle & S. Sauro (Eds.), *The handbook of technology and second language teaching and learning* (pp. 119–133). Hoboken, NJ: Wiley-Blackwell.

Taguchi, N. (2011). Teaching pragmatics: Trends and issues. *Annual Review of Applied Linguistics, 31*(1), 289–310.

Vygotsky, L. (1962). *Language and thought*. Cambridge, MA: MIT Press.

Ware, P. D., & Kramsch, C. (2005). Toward an intercultural stance: Teaching German and English through telecollaboration. *The Modern Language Journal, 89*(2), 190–205.

Warschauer, M. (1996). Computer-assisted language learning: An introduction. In S. Fotos (Ed.), *Multimedia language teaching* (pp. 3–20). Tokyo: Logos International.

White, C. (2006). Distance learning of foreign languages. *Language Teaching, 39*(4), 247–264.

White, C. J. (2017). Distance language teaching with technology. In C. Chapelle & S. Sauro (Eds.), *The handbook of technology and second language teaching and learning* (pp. 134–148). Hoboken, NJ: Wiley-Blackwell.

Woo, Y.-H. (2017). A study on flipped learning-based Korean elementary grammar teaching model development and its effect – Centered on Korean leaners in university of China mainland. *Teaching Korean as a Foreign Language, 46*, 53–83.

Yang, S. J. (2018). Language learners' perceptions of having two interactional contexts in eTandem. *Language Learning & Technology, 22*(1), 42–51.

Yoshida, H., Tani, S., Uchida, T., Masui, J., & Nakayama, A. (2014). Effects of online cooperative learning on motivation in learning Korean as a foreign language. *International Journal of Information and Education Technology, 4*(6), 473.

You, S.-H. (2000). K-buddy: A near-spontaneour and an interactive Korean conversation program. *The Korean Language in America, 5*, 105–114.

Young, D. J. (2008). An empirical investigation of the effects of blended learning on student outcomes in a redesigned intensive Spanish course. *CALICO Journal, 26*(1), 160.

Yun, W., Yoon, K., Park, S., Lee, J., Cho, S., Kang, D., . . . & Kim, J. (2015). The Korean corpus of spontaneous speech. *Phonetics and Speech Sciences, 7*(2), 103–109.

Zhang, H., & Kim, J. S. (2019). Teaching speaking using flipped learning for Chinese Korean larners of Korean. *Journal of Korean Language Education, 30*(1), 187–207.

10
CULTURE IN KOREAN LANGUAGE TEACHING
Focusing on a dynamic view of culture

Kyung-Eun Yoon

Introduction

Language is intricately related to culture, and researchers and practitioners generally agree that language learning also involves culture learning. Thus, it is vital for a language curriculum to incorporate culture teaching. This chapter presents an overview of previous studies on teaching culture, especially in the discipline of teaching Korean as a second/foreign language (KSL). It gives an overview of how prior studies define culture in the context of language teaching and how such definitions apply to Korean language teaching. This chapter then surveys particular aspects of the Korean language related to teaching and learning culture, which was investigated in previous research. It also examines pedagogical suggestions prior studies have made regarding teaching techniques, selecting and utilizing useful materials, and designing curriculum. Then, it addresses challenges faced by Korean teachers in teaching culture. Lastly, it discusses pedagogical implications for future developments.

Definitions of culture in language teaching

Culture is a complex concept, and there have been many attempts to define it in many disciplines. In the field of foreign language pedagogy, scholars have examined a variety of aspects of culture in relation to language teaching (e.g., Brown & Park, 2020; Kramsch, 1993, 2013, 2014a, 2014b; Pennycook, 2006; Walker, 2000). Kramsch (2013) summarizes that there are two coexisting ways of looking at culture in the field of language teaching: modernist and postmodernist perspectives. In a modernist perspective, she observes that culture is often seen as tied to identifiable speech communities or nations. That is, a humanistic concept of culture (big C culture) which is a general knowledge of the literature, and the arts is considered to be national culture within a state and promoted by the state and its institutions as national assets. On the other hand, regarding culture of everyday life (little c culture), such as ways of behaving, eating, talking, and believing, there is a conventional assumption that one nation or speech community has one culture. Language teaching and learning therefore focus on native speakers' typical, sometimes stereotypical, behavior and customs which are the most prominent to foreign eyes.

In a postmodernist perspective, "the old-fashioned national community has given way to multiple, real or imagined, multidimensional, and dynamic communities based on common interest and practices" (Kramsch, 2013, p. 67). She states that postmodernists view culture as a dynamic discursive process in which the meaning of events emerges through interaction with others and social reality is constructed minute by minute. However, she argues, a postmodern definition of culture should also entail the historicity of local national speech communities as well as the subjectivity of speakers and writers who participate in the discursive practices. Since there is a tension between the need to identify, explain, and categorize people and events according to modern objective criteria and the desire to take into account the postmodern subjectivity and historicity, teaching culture is noted as a difficult task in foreign language study.

In the Korean context as well, there have been debates between the two perspectives on viewing culture across disciplines. Some scholars show their perspectives considering Korean culture to be associated with traditional elements and values from the old time, such as the Choson period (e.g., Lie, 2012). Other scholars criticize such ethno-national perspectives (e.g., Fedorenko, 2018; Han, 2003; Yoon, forthcoming). Han (2003, pp. 7–8) argues:

[T]here might not be such a thing as Korean culture or Korean character per se. What has often been called Korean culture or Korean character is but a result of the generalization or selection of certain traits from the very diverse cultural and personality features of Koreans of different classes, ages, sexes, times, and places. Adding a modifier and talking about "traditional" Korean culture further begs the question of "tradition" and "modern" and simply presupposed the existence of a primordial Korean culture. By trying to identify "traditional" Korean culture, the timelessness or immutability of the national culture is assumed and the existence of a national culture is naturalized, i.e., made to be taken for granted. The idea of a national culture also presupposed the homogeneity and integration of people. Differences between regions, classes, historical periods, and ethnic groups are all ignored in the notion of a national culture. Diversity, conflict, contestation and change are largely ignored in the pursuit of a national essence or archetype. Also ignored is the interaction and mutual influence among the cultures.

In relation to teaching the Korean language and culture, Kim (2002) observes that approaches to teaching culture focus on big C culture, such as traditional cultural practices and products and do not pay much attention to little c culture. Byon (2004) also notes that KSL studies are largely content driven in teaching culture, which means that they deal with how to teach knowledge of culture through literature or media productions. Findings of a more recent study by Lee (2019) show the prevailing modernist view of culture in KSL research as well. Lee's study comprehensively surveys previous research on culture teaching in Korean language classrooms both in Korea and outside Korea. She examines approaches and contents of culture teaching discussed in many prior studies based on different types of learner groups in and outside of Korea. She identifies three major learner groups in Korea, namely, marriage-based immigrants, children from multicultural families, and study abroad students from other countries, and finds that many studies (e.g., Cho & Lee, 2018; Ryu & Kim, 2017; Won, 2008) commonly point out the importance of cultivating multiculturalism with mutual respect instead of unilaterally teaching Korean culture to the learners. She also notes that various studies provide lists of cultural elements or items to teach to KSL learners, for example, how to use public transportation, restaurants, etc., historical heritage, traditional performances, value systems, and customary behavior (Yoo, 2011). These observations show the prevalence of modernist, ethno-national perspectives on culture in the area of teaching Korean language and culture.

From a different perspective, Brown and Park (2020) point out the danger of assuming that culture is something determined and fixed and all native speakers have identical knowledge of it, which can easily lead to stereotyping. Their perspective coincides with Kramsch (2013, 2014a). On the one hand, they note that "seeing culture as performative does not mean that everything about culture is relative, subjective, and with no clear boundary," and acknowledge that "[t]here still *is* something that we can refer to as Korean culture" (pp. 83–84). On the other hand, however, they ultimately view culture as something that is dynamic, actively performed during social interaction, and thus socially constructed. They explain that individuals have different ideas of what Korean culture entails and they "actively 'perform' Korean culture through partaking in recognizable and recognized cultural practices such as eating Korean food, drinking soju, performing 제사 (*ceysa*) 'ancestor memorial ceremony,' singing karaoke, and using honorific language" (p. 83). In sum, culture is not something related to innate human abilities but is something that is "socially structured and transmitted through social learning" (p. 84). Following this perspective, this chapter proposes to look into how Korean cultural values are embedded and reflected in the Korean language and how such discursive language practices are taken into consideration in teaching culture in KSL settings.

Korean linguistic expressions and communicative acts examined in previous research

This section surveys what particular aspects have been investigated in previous research in relation to the Korean language and culture. More specifically, this section examines Korean linguistic expressions and communicative acts which are highly related to culture.

Linguistic expressions

Sohn (2001) states that the function of performing politeness is universal across languages and cultures and each language has its own linguistic devices for the practices. According to him, "the particular sociolinguistic rules and conventions of politeness language use in a linguistic community are . . . filtered by the underlying cultural perspectives such as social norms of behavior, value orientations, and cultural assumption" (p. 27). Brown and Park (2020) also assert that morphological and syntactic aspects of a language inherently reflect the social reality in which the language is used and that language learning involves social learning, which indicates that "language is also cultural" (p. 84). Following this perspective, many scholars in the area of teaching the Korean language and culture have examined the interplay between linguistic expressions and cultural practices. More specifically, they have paid special attention to honorifics and speech levels in Korean as linguistic devices inextricably interwoven with culture.

Honorifics

Korean honorifics can be seen as "cultural scripts about social relationships and associated communicative norms" (Yoon, 2004, p. 189), and they are "a central part of social deixis or indexicality" (Brown, 2011, p. 19). Traditionally, Korean honorifics are explained based on fixed semantic values of deference or formality (Hwang, 1990; Sohn, 1986). However, these traditional accounts have been criticized because they cannot account for the varied and complex usage of honorifics and speech styles in natural conversations. Brown (2015a) points out another issue with the traditional views in that they assume a one-to-one relationship between honorific expressions and their semantic values without considering the fact that indexical forms, such as honorifics, may have multiple expressive and social meanings attached to them. As alternative expressive meanings of Korean honorifics, Brown (2013a) observes that they are sometimes utilized to convey sarcasm or impoliteness, which shows that honorifics are not deferential in an absolute sense. Sarcastic honorifics are found to occur mostly when the addressee is an intimate of similar or subordinate rank. When they are used with non-intimates or strangers in which the use of honorifics is the unmarked norm, the speaker is found to choose super-high honorifics or mix honorifics with non-honorific or other face-threatening expressions in order to express sarcasm.

Brown (2015a) explicates a variety of affective meanings and social meanings communicated through Korean honorifics. For example, he explains that an honorific ending (-요, *yo*) makes the speech more personal, friendly, and emotionally involved, while another honorific ending (-습니다, *-supnita*) indexes affective meanings, such as stances of factuality, impartiality, and emotional distance. Dropping honorifics can convey a range of other affective meanings. That is, using non-honorifics such as the intimate speech style (-아/어, *-a/e*) or the plain style (-다, *-ta*), or omitting referent honorifics when addressing a superior or stranger can express affective stances of anger or scorn. Brown also explains the social meanings attached to the use of honorifics in terms of creating a social identity. He notes that the use of honorifics properly following the socially normative convention can create an identity of someone who is polite and well-educated in the Korean society. He also observes an identity of the service staff constructed through the overuse the honorific marker (-(으)시, *-(u)si*), which would be perceived as polite and appropriate by customers but as inappropriate and ignorant of the grammatical workings by prescriptive language authorities. He additionally argues that the use of honorifics is tied up with gender, the polite style (-요, *-yo*) associated with female speech and the deferential (-습니다, *-supnita*) with male speech. He maintains that the association of the deferential with masculinity and the polite form with femininity is closely connected to social expectations with regard to gender roles and behavior based on the social expectations of men to hold formal positions in the society, to provide factual knowledge, and to be emotionally removed in contrast with those of women to have informal and personal roles and to talk and behave based on their emotions. In sum, Brown's studies show that Korean honorifics have numerous functions for affective expressions and social meanings as opposed to just conveying deference to the interlocutor.

The complexity of the honorific system often causes difficulty for Korean language learners and sometimes even for native speakers. In a study by Lee, Huh, and O'Grady (2017) which investigates the impact of the relationship among the speaker, the hearer, and the referent to the use of honorifics, they find that different generations of native speakers deal with the complexity of Korean honorifics in different ways. For example, the older participants in their 60s to 80s and the younger participants ranging in age from 19 to 30 demonstrate different perceptions of the hearer-oriented theory and 압존법 (*apconpep*), the traditional proscription against the honorific use when the hearer has higher status than the referent. The older participants do not hesitate to accept referent honorification when the hearer, but not the speaker, outranks the referent of the subject, which runs against 압존법 (*apconpep*), whereas the younger participants manifest their hesitation and uncertainty about it. That is, the senior participants show a strong preference for paying no attention to the complicated traditional honorific rule of 압존법 (*apconpep*) anymore, while the younger participants still show their sensitivity to the status of both speaker and the hearer relative to the referent of the subject. As another generational difference, this study notes that the younger participants overuse the honorific suffix (-(으)시, *-(u)si*) even when the referent is inanimate and therefore honorification is not applicable. The study interprets the overuse of the honorific suffix as its extended use as a general politeness marker, but at the same time as a confusion that younger speakers experience due to the complexity of the honorific system.

It is then to be expected that understanding the honorific system is naturally difficult for Korean language learners. Wang (2019) investigates Korean language learners' understanding of the honorific system and finds that the learners experience difficulty in similar aspects of the honorific system, not much impacted by their proficiency level, native language background, or length of residence in Korea. Their difficulty is first found in referent/object honorifics, which are sometimes realized through special sets of honorific nouns, verbs, and nominative markers. It is compared to addressee/subject honorifics, which are understood relatively more easily by the learners. Wang provides a possible explanation of the difficulty, noting that it might be due to the various honorific lexical items which have complicated differences with similar items (e.g., 드리다 [*tulita*] vs. 주다 [*cwuta*], 모시다 [*mosita*] vs. 데리다 [*teylita*]) and due to the complexity in the matching subject sometimes with the honorific suffix (-(으)시, -*(u)si*) or sometimes without it. Another challenging area is found to be the addressee honorifics in close relationships (e.g., 해드릴까?, *hay-tuli-lkka?*), which is mostly realized through speech styles in the sentence endings. In comparison, the learners demonstrate better understanding of the use of honorifics and speech styles in relationships involving high-low status. Based on the results, Wang argues that the solidarity factor associated with social distance in the relationship is challenging to the Korean learners when choosing proper honorifics due to the complexity of the solidarity factor, whereas the power factor in hierarchical relationships is relatively easier to understand.

Speech styles

In the honorific system, speech styles have garnered special attention from researchers due to their highly social and cultural aspects. They are highly social and cultural because their primary function is to mark the social relationship between the speaker and the hearer (Brown, 2015a). Two honorific styles, the deferential (-습니다, -*supnita*) and the polite (-요, -*yo*) forms, have been the focus of much research regarding their social, cultural, and pragmatic functions. In the traditional views, the two honorific styles were considered to be determined by factors such as the degree of politeness (e.g., Lukoff, 1982), formality (e.g., Seong, 1985), or gender (e.g., Sohn, 1999). However, more recent studies have noted that shifting between these two styles often occurs in the same discourse between the same speakers, and hence a choice between the two styles cannot be simply explained by such factors. They have accordingly attempted to explain the differences regarding various pragmatic, interactional meanings and functions (Brown, 2015b; Kim & Suh, 2007; Park, 2014; Strauss & Eun, 2005; Yoon, 2014). For example, Strauss and Eun (2005) distinguish the functions of the two styles based on the cognitive and/or experiential domains of the speaker and the interlocutor. They explain that the deferential form indexes the speaker's stance of positioning the interlocutor as outside the sphere of the speaker's cognitive and/or experiential domains, and therefore it frames the discourse as detached, objective, and authoritative. On the other hand, they find that the polite form indexes the speaker's stance of positioning the interlocutor as inside the sphere, and hence a stance of inclusion. They conclude that the deferential form creates bounded distance between the speaker and the addressee whereas the polite form establishes and/or reinforces common ground between the two parties. Brown's later study (2015b) analyzes the deferential form as a resource for indexing a formal presentational stance and/or performing actions that are public and ritualistic as opposed to the polite form for a more casual and affective stance. Yoon (2014) also draws a distinction between the deferential and the polite forms and notes that the deferential is used in ritualized presentation, information delivery, or an announcement, whereas the polite form indicates a soft affective stance.

While the aforementioned studies use data from TV shows, Kim and Suh (2007) and Park (2014) analyze data in a different setting, that is, pedagogical discourse. Kim and Suh (2007) find that shifting speech styles function as linguistic resources for teachers signaling boundaries of pedagogical activities. The shift from the polite form to the non-polite form (-아/어, -a/e) in the teacher's talk to young learners is contextually motivated by the need to address classroom management tasks of dealing with individual students, such as disciplining, advising, encouraging, etc. The shift to the deferential form occurs when the teacher highlights key instructional elements and/or marks a boundary in pedagogical activities. Park (2014) finds that another form of the deferential speech style is used to mark a boundary in pedagogical activities in classroom discourse and to reinforce the teacher's role. Based on analyzing the use of the -(으)ㅂ시다 (-(u)psita) form, her study notes that the teachers employ the form to establish clear transitions between different activities or different stages within the same activity. She argues that the power-laden tone of the deferential form becomes a resource for drawing students' attention and achieving the desired student behavior, which also reinforces the teacher's identity as the one who is in charge of the pedagogical activities in class.

In sum, Korean honorifics and speech levels have been the focus of many studies in the field of Korean language and culture since they play an important role in establishing and managing social relationships and implementing and embedding communicative, social, and cultural norms in language use.

Communicative acts

While much research has focused on linguistic expressions, such as the honorific system and speech styles in investigating the interplay between the Korean language and culture, some studies have examined particular communicative acts regarding the linguistic and cultural practices, such acts as apologies, requests, and complaints, which Brown and Levinson (1987) characterize as face-threatening acts. The Korean concepts of face are explained, by Byon (2006), as having two aspects: one is the need to abide by norms in Korean culture, and the other is the need to express one's moral sense regarding their social role and status. The aforementioned communicative acts closely involve cultural norms and social positions in their practices.

Apologies

Sohn (2001) explains Korean apologies by comparing them with the apology strategies in English which Olshtain and Cohen (1983) identify: formulaic expression of apology, acknowledgment of responsibility, explanation, offer of repair, and promise of nonrecurrence. He argues that while the English strategies are generally applicable to Korean, Korean apologies have significant differences, such as the use of honorifics, politeness-indicating sentence enders, etc. He also discusses how two formulaic apology expressions in Korean, 미안하- (*mianha-*) and 죄송하- (*coysongha-*), are different from each other in terms of the power and distance factor in the relationships and the degree of seriousness of the infraction. Byon (2005) also analyzes the semantic formulae for apologies in Korean. Based on 50 native speakers' responses to a discourse completion task, he identifies 12 strategies, including an opting-out strategy (proceeding with conversation without an apologetic remark) and 11 apology formulae (accepting the blame, expressing regret, offer of apology, minimizing, querying preconditions, blaming someone else, expressing embarrassment, explanation, expressing concern, promise of forbearance, and offer of repair). The comparison between these native speakers' strategies and the apology act performed by American learners of Korean as a foreign language reveals that Korean speakers demonstrate their strong orientation to the power factor, while the Korean learners are more influenced by the distance variable. Byon (2005) asserts that the result reflects the relatively more collectivistic, hierarchical, and formalistic aspects of Korean culture compared to American culture, which is in agreement with Sohn's argument (2001) that Korean communication patterns, such as apology strategies, are governed by their relatively hierarchical and collectivistic value orientations in their cultural perspectives.

Requests

Requesting in Korean has gathered the most attention among communicative acts from researchers in the field of Korean language and culture. Since indirectness is often considered to be a characteristic of the Korean language (Sohn, 1986), many studies have centered on the relationship between indirectness and politeness in Korean requests. For example, in a study investigating 12 office workers' performance of requests in role-plays in a workplace setting, Rue, Zhang, and Shin (2007) find that indirect strategies are preferred, especially when the addressees are superiors and equal work members rather than juniors. Based on the finding, they conclude that the main factor for Korean request strategies is power relationship.

However, many other studies have observed that indirectness does not necessarily correlate with politeness in Korean. Byon (2006) examines the role of linguistic indirectness and politeness in Korean requests and notes that the primary resource for indicating politeness in Korean requests is the honorific rather than indirect strategies. For example, in a particular setting of making a request to a professor, the most frequently used strategy in a discourse completion task by the 50 college-student participants is "basic directive" (e.g., 교수님, 써 주십시오, 네?, *kyoswu-nim, ss-e cwu-si-psio, ney?* ['Professor, please write (a letter) for me, yes?']), rather than an indirect strategy, such as "ellipsis" (e.g., 선생님, 써 주시면 안 될까 해서요, *sensayngnim, ss-cwu-si-myen an toy-lkka-hay-se-yo* ['Professor, (I was) wondering if you can write me (a letter, so I came here to see you).']) (Byon, 2006, pp. 262–263). He explains that the politeness level in the direct requests is still appropriate due to proper use of honorific elements. According to him, the participants' use of direct request strategies does not engender a negative impression because of the expected social role of the addressee, which is to write a recommendation letter and to take care of students' academic affairs as a professor. Therefore, the directness level is influenced by sociocultural constraints, such as role and place in particular situations, and the politeness level is managed through elaborate use of the honorifics in Korean.

In a similar vein, Yu (2004, 2011) notes that Korean politeness is primarily expressed through the honorific system not through the level of indirectness and that participants' particular interrelationships in specific situations should be taken into consideration to assess politeness. Yu (2004) finds that Korean speakers employ more direct and explicit request forms in close relationships, more so than English speakers, and that such direct-request strategies are considered to be politer than indirect ones in Korean. Yu (2011), based on an analysis of a discourse completion task completed by 95 college students and a task of rating indirectness done by 81 college students, confirms that direct request strategies in Korean can be considered polite in certain contexts. She observes that the conventional indirect strategies are not significantly correlated with politeness, while certain direct strategies are perceived as polite in Korean. The participants' perception of politeness seems to depend on the use of honorifics rather than the level of indirectness. For example, they consider a directive imperative format to be politer if it is used with a deferential ending (e.g., 선생님, 책 좀 빌려주십시오, *sensaying-nim, chayk com pilly-ecwu-si-psio* ['Teacher, please do me a favor of lending the book.']) than an interrogative with a non-deferential -요 (e.g., 선생님, 책 좀 빌려주실래요?, *sensaying-nim, chayk com pilly-ecwu-si-llay-yo?* ['Teacher, would you like to do me a favor of lending the book?']).

Examining a different type of data, spontaneous interaction, Kim (2020) also observes that a direct imperative format is not avoided but dominantly used to make here-and-now requests, which requires the recipient to immediately comply. The difference between indirect strategies, such as interrogative requests and imperative forms, is found in the specific sequential and interactional context for the requested action. For example, whereas interrogative requests are usually employed when the requester launches a new activity in which the requestee is not yet involved, once the requester and the requestee are committed to and engaged in the same activity, the requester makes the request utilizing an imperative format as seen in the following excerpt.

(1) [Kim, 2020, pp. 377–378, Excerpt 2]
(In a TV show, the host (H) makes two requests in lines 1 and 3 to a guest's son who is sitting in the audience.)

    1 H: 아들 잠깐만 내려오실래요?
              atul camkkanman naylyeo-si-llay-yo?
              "Son, would you come down for a second?"
    2 S: 네.
              ney.
              "Yes."
    3 H: 옆에 있는 인형도 갖고 오세요.
              yeph-ey iss-nun inhyeng-to kacko o-sey-yo.
              "Also bring down the plush doll next to you."
    4 S: (S walks down to the main stage holding his doll in his hand.)

Kim explains that since the host does not know yet whether the recipient will or can comply, the request in line 1 is formulated utilizing an interrogative format. When the request is accepted in line 2, the host constructs the second request using an imperative format, and it is not considered to be impolite, although the participants do not have a close relationship. Kim asserts that imperatives are readily used in Korean requests, even when the speakers have distant relationships.

In sum, numerous studies have shown that politeness in Korean requests depends on linguistic choices, such as honorifics, and various social and interactional factors, such as the social relationship between the speakers, the anticipated social role, and the sequential context interaction.

Complaints

Another communicative act which has been investigated regarding the interplay between Korean language and culture is complaining. In her study explicating discursive patterns of complaining in Korean with data culled from a variety of naturally occurring oral and written discourse, Yoon (2021) examines practices of negotiating and constructing sociocultural norms, social identities, and relations. Yoon notes that since complaining is based on a failure of the target behavior to meet the complainant's certain expectation or a violation of a sociocultural norm, the complainant constructs the moral reprehensibility through the practices of complaining. As an example, the wife's complaint in line 2 in the following excerpt points out the insufficient amount of the fruit and demands her husband peel more for their guests, and it thereby suggests a cultural norm that the hosting party of a social gathering should provide a sufficient amount of food to the guests. The complainee challenges and counter-complains against the original complainant, but he shows the same orientation to the norm in his response, saying that he will prepare more.

(2) [Yoon, 2021, p. 82 (8)]
(Yun, the wife, and Suh, her husband, are hosting a pizza gathering for their three close friends.)

    1   (1.5)/ (Yun sees Suh put some peeled fruit onto a plate.)
    2   Yun: 에게: 더 깎어:
                    eykey: te kkakk-e:
                    "*Eykey:* peel mo:re!"
    3   Suh: 더 깎을 거야:
                    te kkakk-ul ke-ya:
                    "(I) WILL peel mo:re!"

While sociocultural norms are co-constructed through complaining, as seen in excerpt 2, they are sometimes challenged and contested, too. In the following excerpt from a conversation among friends at a dinner gathering, a participant, Joo, challenges a sociocultural norm which was previously brought up. In the preceding talk, Joo suggested that Young buy a nice rice cooker, but Young said that she would not buy one because she would not get married soon. Such a response by Young has brought up a norm in Korean culture that single women buy nice appliances when they are getting married. Then Joo, who is a single woman who has purchased an expensive rice cooker, complains about and challenges Young's stance in line 1.

(3) [Simplified from Yoon, 2021, p. 76 (3)]

    1   Joo: 야 결혼 안 하면 맛있는 거 먹으면 안 돼?
                    ya kyelhon an ha-myen masiss-nun ke mek-umyen an tway?
                    "Hey if not married, can (we) not eat delicious food?"
    2   Young: 미안해 s:: ((laugh))
                    mianhay s:: ((laugh))
                    "(I) am sorry s:: (laugh)"

Joo's complaint contests the norm brought up by Young and presents another kind of normative orientation that anybody, whether married or not or planning to get married, can buy nice appliances for their own selves. Young's response with an apology displays that she agrees with the newly presented norm through the complaint. Based on these findings, Yoon claims that sociocultural norms are not fixed or static entities but something dynamically negotiated and embodied in concrete shapes by social participants.

Yoon's study also finds that participants embody various social identities and negotiate whether or not they are operating according to the norm in the social group through the complaining activity. For example, the preceding excerpt (2) demonstrates that both participants claim that they are trying to be hospitable hosts via their complaints to each other. In some cases, participants complain to each other to strengthen solidarity within a social group that they belong to together. Yoon presents an example in which high school girls gathering at a party call a friend who is not attending and complain about her absence. The complaint in this particular setting manifests the complainers' care about the complainee's absence and hence the importance of the complainee as a member in their group. In turn, the complainee counter-complains that the other members did not notify her properly about the party. This counter-complaint also exhibits that she cares about the gathering of the group. The complaints from both parties show the speakers' desire that the addressees should feel wanted and appreciated as important members of the group. While complaining is often considered to be a "face-threatening act," which can be harmful to social relationships (Brown & Levinson, 1987), Yoon's study shows that it can be utilized as a positive politeness strategy which can create and strengthen social solidarity as well.

Pedagogical suggestions presented in previous research

This section surveys studies which make explicit pedagogical suggestions for teaching culture in Korean language classes.

Early suggestions

Sohn (2001) asserts that cultural aspects of language, such as politeness routines, should be taught explicitly rather than just fostering learners' awareness. He argues that since raising awareness is time consuming and fragmentary, complex aspects of culturally loaded speech acts should be taught systematically and intensively for the correct and effective use in learners' language. He states that techniques for teaching speech acts proposed by SLA scholars, such as Olshtain and Cohen (1991) and Dunham (1992), can be applicable to teaching Korean politeness routines. They are presented in the following.

(4) [Olshtain and Cohen, 1991, quoted from Sohn, 2001, p. 34]

    1   Diagnostic assessment
    2   Model dialogue
    3   The evaluation of a situation
    4   Role-play activities
    5   Feedback and discussion

(5) [Dunham, 1992, techniques for teaching complimenting quoted from Sohn, 2001, p. 34]

    1   Reviewing how it is done in the native culture
    2   Reviewing how it is done in the United States
    3   Vocabulary phrase list
    4   Student practice
    5   Role playing in pairs
    6   Teacher role play with students in front of the class
    7   Projects in which learners must compliment native speakers
    8   Students' oral reports to the class following their field experiences with native speakers
    9   Connecting techniques to lengthen conversation
    10   Paired interaction with complimenting and connecting techniques

Byon (2004, 2007a) also advocates explicit teaching of culture in the Korean language classroom. He makes the observation that cultural elements often become secondary to the main goal of teaching linguistic features in Korean due to the curriculum design although culture teaching is important. To teach culture skills, Byon (2004) suggests various teaching activities that can be used to foster open and positive attitudes toward Korean culture in a beginning-level Korean class in America, as demonstrated in the following.

(6) [Byon, 2004, pp. 18–23]

    1   Assessing students' attitudes

        i Background survey – To assess students' cultural backgrounds and interests, the levels of awareness regarding their own cultural backgrounds, and their attitudes regarding Korean culture.
        ii Four adjectives activity – To elicit stereotypes the students have and to identify the instructional needs – students comment with adjectives on what they know, like, and dislike about Korean culture.

    2   Understanding the relationship between culture and self-identity

        iii Pie activity – Students in groups draw pie charts which represent various aspects of American identities, compare them with other groups' pie charts, and discuss the role that culture plays in the formation of their cultural identities.
        iv Self-awareness activity 1 – To understand the relationship between cultural products and self-identity and to realize how difficult it is to formulate simple stereotypes about their own country – Students find cultural products, such as advertisements or clip art, that illustrate American culture and have group discussions on national stereotypes.
        v Self-awareness activity 2 – Students are provided with a list of American cultural phenomena, categorize them based on their own interpretations, examine aspects of their own surface culture, and try to recognize their own underlying cultural values.

    3   Decreasing stereotypical perceptions

        vi Media-comparison activity – Students compare American cultural images projected in the Korean media with Korean cultural images projected in the American media and evaluate how well or poorly the materials represent both cultures.
        vii Counter-stereotypes activity – Students are provided with visual images that run counter to common stereotypes of Korean and American cultures and share their reactions or impressions about the visual images.

In another study based on a process-driven perspective of culture teaching, Byon (2007a) examines a case of designing, implementing, and evaluating a semester-long culture portfolio project. The procedures for the project are as following.

(7) [Byon, 2007a, p. 6]

    1   In the beginning of the semester, the students completed a pre-project questionnaire in which they commented on their own definitions of culture and their previous experiences and/or images about the Korean culture and people.
    2   Based on their personal impressions of the Korean culture, they developed their own project hypothesis, which they set out to investigate throughout the portfolio project.
    3   To affirm or disprove their hypothesis, the students collected data through library research, online research, and/or informal interviews with Korean native speakers.

4 The students also kept records of what they felt and learned during the process.
5 In addition, they reported how their understanding of the target culture had expanded and how their stereotypes were reshaped over the semester.
6 They had to submit all the information gathered during the semester for a grade by the end of semester.
7 At the end of the term, they completed a post-project questionnaire regarding the project.

Based on the qualitative analysis of students' responses to the questionnaires and their classroom presentation as well as the researcher's notes during the process, Byon finds that the project helps the students gain insights into their own culture and the target culture. In the course of conducting the project, they become aware of their own cultural learning, recognize its impacts on learning the target culture, and modify their own stereotypical impressions of Korean culture and people. In sum, the portfolio project assists the students in developing open attitudes toward Korean culture, and the positive culture learning experience in return increases students' interest in studying the Korean language.

Suggestions for teaching materials

Teaching materials are considered to be very important in teaching culture, and many scholars have made suggestions of utilizing media materials in Korean language teaching as effective materials for teaching culture. First, Strauss (1999) advocates the use of television commercials as materials for discussions of culture as well as for authentic linguistic input related to cultural practices, such as speech levels and speech styles. On the one hand, TV commercials present overt cultural elements, such as types of food items, household scenes, and behavioral customs, such as bowing and typical hand gestures, which can be characteristic snippets of a foreign culture that may not be familiar to non-heritage learners. The advertisements also display covert cultural elements, such as social values, which can only be inferred by some recognizable patterns. Strauss provides examples of TV commercials and how to use them for cultural activities in addition to linguistic and sociolinguistic learning. In the activities, students can begin with noticing the difference between American and Korean culture based on a small sample of American and Korean commercials and then infer various cultural values in Korea on the basis of a larger collection. They can infer aspects of cultural values in terms of society and family and have discussions about the depictions of expected roles in the society, such as women and men or mother, father, and children in the families, and the like. She notes that teachers should make sure that students' inferences or observations do not become empty cultural stereotyping.

Cheon and Kim (2010) also consider TV advertisements to be useful materials for teaching culture in language class since advertisements, language, and culture are highly related with one another. To present pedagogical suggestions, they analyze numerous TV commercials regarding family or gender roles and explore how they reflect cultural values and how such values remain or change in the Korean society. Claiming that the use of advertisements can facilitate students' understanding of culture, especially for advanced learners, they provide a sample instructional format for a unit based on themes of family values and gender roles portrayed in Korean commercials. In this format, they list step-by-step guidelines for designing the lesson and implementing various activities and assessments.

Byon (2007b) is another study which explores possible instructional models and assessment tools utilizing TV media materials for teaching pragmatic elements of Korean related to culture. Focusing on two Korean speech levels, the polite (-요, -*yo*) and the deferential (-습니다, -*supnita*) forms, and the alternation between the two, he presents many sample activities and assessment materials using video clips of a TV morning talk show and a shopping channel show. He suggests multiple approaches to developing instructional activities, including deductive-oriented and inductive-oriented ones for teaching both receptive and productive language skills. As a practical example of activities for teaching productive skills, he proposes cloze-type exercises. With regard to assessment tools, he presents various formats to collect students' responses to the activities and their reflections of the learning procedure. The formats include (1) a one-sentence summary about their daily learning, (2) a minute paper for recording what they learned and still do not understand, and (3) feedback forms for rating different aspects of instruction from preparedness to particular types of instructional activities to teaching behavior, the purpose of which is to evaluate and enhance the efficiency of the activities. This study emphasizes the importance of metalinguistic factors in teaching as well as the importance of explicit instruction on Korean speech levels.

While Byon (2007b) focuses on honorific speech levels, Brown (2013b) pays attention to non-honorific (반말, *panmal*) speech styles in proposing the use of media materials for teaching them. He notes the limitations of traditional materials for teaching 반말 (*panmal*) and the usefulness of media materials as an authentic alternative. Building on some techniques suggested by Byon (2007b), Brown (2013b) presents a way of designing, implementing, and evaluating a series of instructional activities for teaching 반말 (*panmal*) to intermediate-level students. More specifically, Brown's study demonstrates an instructional design of a 100-minute session utilizing a clip from a Korean TV drama. The session is composed of four activities: (1) a task of working out the relationship of six characters in the clip, (2) a task of distinguishing non-honorific and honorific speech styles used by the characters and a discussion of why particular styles are chosen, (3) a task of recollecting the scene with pictures and matching the pictures with characters' lines from the script, and (4) a task of selecting proper styles between the plain (-다, -*ta*) and the intimate (-아/어, -*a/e*) styles for some parts in the script. This study further investigates the effectiveness of the teaching method based on students' feedback and finds generally positive results. The results support the usefulness of media materials and the necessity of explicit discussion of cultural aspects, such as family relations and gender roles, in teaching honorifics and non-honorifics in relation to the (im)politeness issue.

Suggestions for curriculum

Previous research suggests another direction for pedagogy by examining and presenting a curriculum for a whole semester. Kim (2005), for example, investigates the effectiveness of a content-based language instruction (CBI) model, particularly for Korean heritage students in a fifth-semester Korean class. She sees the benefit of CBI in that it can integrate a wide array of cultural topics and themes, such as history, social affairs, cultural products, and so on, which can be resources for fulfilling heritage students' desire to develop their cultural roots and a stronger sense of Korean identity. The curriculum for the class is based on topics in three broad areas: living tradition, literature, and social issues. Some subtopics are *kimchi*, *ondol*, a short story by Pak Wanso, *pansori*, old school ties, foreign guest workers, etc. Implemented activities include reading, recipe writing, presentations on favorite Korean cultural products and social issues, writing assignments, and so forth. The researcher uses ethnography of communication methodology to make observations of student participation and to evaluate language use and patterns of communication, such as speech events, speech functions, and discussion format in class. She reports that incorporating CBI facilitated an engaged and dynamic discussion and students' responses were positive about both the cultural content and the chances to read challenging texts and write about them.

Cheon (2012) also presents a CBI-based curriculum for culture teaching and learning. The curriculum proposed in her study is a theme-based one for designing two advanced-level courses taught at the Korean Language Flagship Center at the University of Hawai'i at Mānoa. First, she emphasizes the importance of developing authentic and student-centered textbooks and instructional materials and presents two textbooks, *Essentials of Korean Culture and Language* and *Culture of Korea*. The first one covers topics such as history, religion and philosophy, education system, language, literature, politics, economy, arts, science, and various social aspects, for two semesters of content learning and language improvement. The latter is used with selections of films whose content include historical background and contemporary social issues. The films can be basic texts as well as the starting point for class activities, and the textbook provides instructional content for readings, vocabulary lists, exercises, and questions for discussion, short essays, or further research. In addition to developing or selecting proper textbooks, she makes suggestions for designing syllabus and instructional strategies incorporating various activities for speaking, listening, reading, and writing skills and learning vocabulary and content. She also mentions the importance of emphasizing student learning outcomes in the syllabus for effective teaching and learning.

Challenges faced by Korean teachers in teaching culture

Kim (1997) notes challenges in teaching Korean culture. She first finds the difficulty in multi-disciplinary content which a culture course should cover. Since a culture course should cover most major cultural activities and accomplishments in history and the current state, the demands on the instructors are very high. They should have a proficient level of expertise in major areas of Korean cultural life and thus spend a tremendous amount of time and effort in conceptualizing, planning, and preparing, as well as actually teaching. Considering that Kim refers to culture courses which do not involve language teaching, it is evident that the workload for teaching culture in Korean language courses can be even more overwhelming.

The multifarious student composition, which Kim points out as another difficulty in culture courses, is a challenge that Korean language instructors, too, should face. Students bring different levels of motivation, preconception, and expectation to class based on their academic and personal interests and backgrounds. The differences between heritage students and non-heritage students are often noted as one of the major challenges in deciding the focus of instructional designs in Korean language courses. However, the challenge to teach is further complicated if we consider heterogeneity even within one group: For example, heritage students can be subdivided into those who have one parent of Korean descent, those who were born abroad, those who were born and spent their childhood in Korea, Korean adoptees, etc. The non-heritage students are also diverse in their ethnic and first-language backgrounds. It is therefore a great level of difficulty for language teachers to take into account such multifarious factors and accommodate students' diverse interests and needs for optimal learning.

Related to the issue of diversity of students in language courses, Kramsch (2014b) points out the advent of globalization as another factor which increases the level of challenge for teaching foreign languages and cultures. Globalization has diversified the backgrounds, interests, and needs of language-class students more than before, and therefore the students often speak different first languages, or even second or heritage languages. They also have various cultural backgrounds which have socialized them in varied ways and hence shaped their perspectives of appropriate behavior or social expectations differently. With the development of global communication technologies, young students go beyond the conventional forms of communication and show multimodal creativity by participating in multiple types of interactional activities using various online platforms. Then the target learners in the globalized era are multilingual and multicultural speakers, and as Kramsch quotes, teachers should help the students "operate between languages" and apply "translingual and transcultural competence" (MLA, 2007, p. 237). She suggests that it is no longer valid to assume that there is "a homogeneous C1 culture and an equally homogeneous C2 culture that each express themselves through their respective national language" (p. 252). She also argues that "[i]t is no longer sufficient to teach the L2 of some national monolingual native speaker attached to a homogeneous national C2 culture" (p. 249). The challenge which language teachers face with regard to this change is then to adapt to the reframed perspectives of culture and language use and readjust pedagogical approaches accordingly.

Future developments and implications for teaching Korean culture

The challenges discussed in the previous section can be an inspiration for future development of teaching culture in Korean language courses or conducting educational research on this topic. Since the educational context is multilingual and multicultural, the students themselves can be valuable instructional resources. Their experiences of growing up and receiving education in particular cultural settings, developing motivation to learn Korean language and culture, and interacting with others from different backgrounds, including Koreans, can be authentic discussion materials, targets of presentational or writing assignments, or data to be analyzed for pedagogical research. This direction in the language and culture pedagogy can be connected to the field of intercultural communication in which the notion of culture has shifted away from the culture-as-nation paradigm, and the focus of interpretation is on how participants make meaning of their sociocultural identities through interactions (Kramsch & Hua, 2016).

The diversified modes in everyday communication and in the media also have implications for teaching and research. In everyday communication, the variety of writing conventions have been increasing with the advent of instant messaging tools, such as Kakao Talk, or social networking services, such as Twitter, requiring short messages and involving language use with hashtags and memes. Most Korean TV programs or YouTube programs not only air oral discourse of the personalities but also provide captions as supplementary written texts on the screen. The multiplicity of modes involves a wide range of speech styles and writing styles in Korean used for different functions communicatively and socioculturally. The multimodality of communication can thus be the focus of attention in pedagogy and research. For example, media materials have been advocated as useful materials for language and culture teaching, and the newly developed multimodal media discourse can be helpful for teaching the complex aspects of Korean speech styles. Everyday language use in social media platforms can also be an easily accessible source of authentic teaching materials and research data.

In addition, the digital generation's active engagement in multimodal communication using various online platforms can be the source of new types of instructional activities for productive skills as well as receptive skills. Such activities can range from posting a tweet or a reply in Korean related to a trending issue on Twitter to making and posting a reaction video to a Korean TV show clip (e.g., a K-pop performance for a topic of entertainment, a K-drama for sociolinguistic or sociocultural topics, a documentary for historical or political topics). Such activities can be relatable to the everyday lives of students who are interested in contemporary Korean popular culture because many participants in the Korean Wave phenomenon, especially K-pop fans and consumers, actively participate in reproducing cultural content through reaction videos, dance cover videos, etc. and make it "doing" culture instead of just consuming (Yoon, forthcoming), and the students are likely to be familiar with the doing trend. The effectiveness of pedagogical activities engaging students in social media platforms can be investigated in future studies.

Conclusion

This chapter has provided an overview of the development of culture teaching and learning in Korean language classes thus far, the challenges in teaching culture, and implications for future developments. Korean educators' contributions to developing language and culture class have been remarkable. They have played multiple roles in culture teaching by selecting useful materials, designing and implementing instructional activities, and developing curriculum, and so on. The recent changes in global communication technologies and the meanings of communication, language, and culture are likely to give more multilayered challenges to Korean language teachers. It is hoped that the overview and further suggestions presented in this chapter could be of help to any teachers of Korean culture and/or language.

References

Brown, L. (2011). *Korean honorifics and politeness in second language learning*. Amsterdam and Philadelphia: John Benjamins Publishing Company.

Brown, L. (2013a). "Mind your own esteemed business": Sarcastic honorifics use and impoliteness in Korean TV dramas. *Journal of Politeness Research, 9*(2), 159–186.

Brown, L. (2013b). Teaching 'casual' and/or 'impolite' language through multimedia: The case of non-honorific *panmal* speech styles in Korean. *Language, Culture and Curriculum, 26*(1), 1–18.

Brown, L. (2015a). Expressive, social and gendered meaning of Korean honorifics. *Korean Linguistics, 17*(2), 242–266.

Brown, L. (2015b). Revisiting "polite" – *yo* and "deferential" – *supnita* speech style shifting in Korean from the viewpoint of indexicality. *Journal of Pragmatics, 79*, 43–59.

Brown, L., & Park, M. Y. (2020). Culture in language learning and teaching. In Y. Y. Cho (Ed.), *Teaching Korean as a foreign language: Theories and practices* (pp. 81–108). Oxon and New York: Routledge.

Brown, P., & Levinson, S. C. (1987). *Politeness: Some universals in language use*. Cambridge: Cambridge University Press.

Byon, A. S. (2004). Teaching culture skills to elementary KFL students. *The Korean Language in America, 9*, 15–30.

Byon, A. S. (2005). Apologizing in Korean: Cross-cultural analysis in classroom settings. *Korean Studies, 29*, 137–166.

Byon, A. S. (2006). The role of linguistic indirectness and honorifics in achieving linguistic politeness in Korean requests. *Journal of Politeness Research, 2*(2), 247–276.

Byon, A. S. (2007a). The use of culture portfolio project in a Korean culture classroom: Evaluating stereotypes and enhancing cross-cultural awareness. *Language, Culture and Curriculum, 20*(1), 1–19.

Byon, A. S. (2007b). Teaching the polite and the deferential speech levels, using media materials: Advanced KFL classroom settings. In D. Yoshimi & H. Wang (Eds.), *Selected papers from pragmatics in the CJK classroom: The state of the art* (pp. 21–64). Retrieved from http://nflrc.hawaii.edu/CJKProceedings.

Cheon, S. Y. (2012). Culture learning curriculum for advanced learners of Korean. *The Korean Language in America, 17*, 18–31.

Cheon, S. Y., & Kim, K. (2010). Teaching Korean culture with advertisements: Change and persistence in family values and gender roles. *The Korean Language in America, 15*, 1–22.

Cho, W., & Lee, S. (2018). The method of Korean culture textbook's unit composition for married female immigrants who have preschool children. *The Education of Korean Language and Culture, 12*(1), 127–147. (조위수 & 이승혜. (2018). 미취학 자녀 교육을 위한 여성결혼이민자 대상 한국 문화 교재 단원 구성 방안. 한국어문화교육, *12*(1), 127–147).

Dunham, P. (1992). Using compliments in the ESL classroom: An analysis of culture and gender. *Minne TESOL Journal, 10*, 75–85.

Fedorenko, O. (2018). The insiders and outsiders of Korean culture. *Acta Koreana, 21*(2), vii–xvi.

Han, K.-K. (2003). The anthropology of the discourse on the Koreanness of Koreans. *Korea Journal, 43*, 5–31.

Hwang, J.-R. (1990). "Deference" versus "politeness" in Korean speech. *International Journal of the Sociology of Language, 82*, 41–55.

Kim, H.-Y. (2005). Construction of language and culture in a content-based language class. *The Korean Language in America, 10*, 50–70.

Kim, K.-H., & Suh, K.-H. (2007). Style shift in Korean pedagogical discourse. *The Sociolinguistic Journal of Korea, 15*(2), 1–29.

Kim, M. S. (2020). Imperative requests in Korean interaction. In S. Iwasaki, S. Strauss, S. Fukuda, S.-A. Jun, S.-O. Sohn, & K. Zuraw (Eds.), *Japanese/Korean linguistics* (Vol. 26, pp. 373–386). Stanford, CA: CSLI, Stanford University.

Kim, Y. A. (2002). Korean language education and culture: The window of understanding multi-culture. In Y. Park (Ed.), *The status and issues of Korean language education (in the 21st century)* (pp. 473–506). Seoul: Hankook Publishing House. (김영아. (2002). 한국어 교육과 문화: 다문화 이해의 창. 박영순 편, *(21세기) 한국어교육학의 현황과 과제* (pp. 473–506). 서울: 한국문화사).

Kim, Y.-H. (1997). Teaching Korean culture: Its challenges and significance. *The Korean Language in America, 2*, 185–192.

Kramsch, C. (1993). *Context and culture in language teaching*. Oxford: Oxford University Press.

Kramsch, C. (2013). Culture in foreign language teaching. *Iranian Journal of Language Teaching Research, 1*(1), 57–78.

Kramsch, C. (2014a). Language and culture. *AILA Review, 27*, 30–55.

Kramsch, C. (2014b). The challenge of globalization for the teaching of foreign languages and cultures. *Electronic Journal of Foreign Language Teaching, 11*(2), 249–255.

Kramsch, C., & Hua, Z. (2016). Language, culture, and language teaching. In G. Hall (Ed.), *Routledge handbook of English language teaching* (pp. 38–50). Oxon and New York: Routledge.

Lee, M., Huh, S., & O'Grady, W. (2017). Korean subject honorifics: An experimental study. *Journal of Pragmatics, 117*, 58–71.

Lee, S. (2019). The status and issues of Korean culture education for Korean language education. *New Korean Language Life, 29*(1), 9–34. (이승연. (2019). 한국어교육을 위한 한국 문화 교육 연구의 현황과 과제. 새국어생활, *29*(1), 9–34).

Lie, J. (2012). What is the K in K-pop? South Korean popular music, the culture industry, and national identity. *Korea Observer, 43*(3), 339–364.

Lukoff, F. (1982). *An introductory course in Korean*. Seoul: Yonsei University Press.

MLA AdHoc Committee on Foreign Languages. (2007). Foreign language and higher education: New structures for a changed world. *Profession, 2007*, 234–245.

Olshtain, E., & Cohen, A. D. (1983). Apology: A speech act set. In N. Wolfson & E. Judd (Eds.), *Sociolinguistics and second language acquisition* (pp. 18–36). Rowley, MA: Newbury House.

Olshtain, E., & Cohen, A. D. (1991). Teaching speech act behavior to nonnative speakers. In M. Celce-Murcia (Ed.), *An introduction to teaching English as a second or foreign language* (pp. 154–165). Cambridge, MA: Newbury House/Harper Collins.

Park, M. Y. (2014). A study of the Korean sentence-ender -(u)psita: Implementing activity transitions in the KFL classroom. *Journal of Pragmatics, 68*, 25–39.

Pennycook, A. (2006). *Global Englishes and transcultural flows*. Oxon and New York: Routledge.

Rue, Y., Zhang, G., & Shin, K. (2007). Request strategies in Korean. In *5th biennial Korean studies association of Australasia conference* (pp. 112–119). Perth, Australia, 12–13 July 2007. Korean Studies Association of Australasia.

Ryu, H.-J., & Kim, K. H. (2017). A method on the development of textbooks on Korean culture for foreign undergraduate students. *Human Science, 67*, 61–88. (유현정 & 김경원. (2017). 학부 유학생을 위한 한국문화 교재 개발 방안. 인문과학, *67*, 61–88).

Seong, K.-C. (1985). *Research on contemporary honorifics*. Seoul: Kaymunsa. (성기철. (1985). 현대국어 대우법 연구. 개문사).

Sohn, H.-M. (1986). *Linguistic expeditions*. Seoul: Hanshin Publishing Company.

Sohn, H.-M. (1999). *The Korean language*. Cambridge: Cambridge University Press.

Sohn, H.-M. (2001). Teaching politeness routines in Korean. *The Korean Language in America, 6*, 25–35.

Strauss, S. (1999). Using television commercials as aids for teaching language, grammar, culture. *The Korean Language in America, 3*, 235–252.

Strauss, S., & Eun, J.-O. (2005). Indexicality and honorific speech level choice in Korean. *Linguistics, 43*(3), 611–651.

Walker, G. (2000). Performed culture: Learning to participate in another culture. In R. Lambert & E. Shohamy (Eds.), *Language policy and pedagogy: Essays in honor of Richard Lambert* (pp. 221–236). Amsterdam and Philadelphia: John Benjamins Publishing Company.

Wang, H.-S. (2019). Comprehension of the honorific system by learners of Korean. *The Korean Language in America, 23*(1), 53–84.

Won, J. (2008). Elementary Korean language education in multicultural era-focused on Korean language education approach for the children in multicultural families. *Korean Language Education Research, 32*, 269–303. (원진숙. (2008). 다문화 시대의 초등학교 국어과 교육 – 다문화 가정 자녀를 위한 한국어 교육 지원 방안을 중심으로. 국어교육학연구, *32*, 269–303).

Yoo, H. J. (2011). A study on developing Korean language teaching material for female immigrants. *Multicultural Contents Research, 10*, 29–48. (유해준. (2011). 여성결혼이민자를 위한 한국어 교재 구성 방안. 다문화콘텐츠연구, *10*, 29–48).

Yoon, K. J. (2004). Not just words: Korean social models and the use of honorifics. *Intercultural Pragmatics, 1*(2), 189–210.

Yoon, K.-E. (2021). *Complaining as a sociocultural activity: Examining how and why in Korean interaction*. Lanham, MD: Lexington Books.

Yoon, K.-E. (Forthcoming). Teaching varying perspectives of K-pop. In J. Dippman (Ed.), *Interdisciplinary approaches to teahing Korea in the undergraduate curriculum*. New York: SUNY Press.

Yoon, S.-S. (2014). Difference between the deferential and polite styles: In terms of their indexical meanings and discourse functions. *Language Information, 19*, 115–144.

Yu, K.-A. (2004). Explicitness for requests is a politer strategy than implicitness in Korean. *Discourse and Cognition, 11*(1), 173–194.

Yu, K.-A. (2011). Culture-specific concepts of politeness: Indirectness and politeness in English, Hebrew, and Korean requests. *Intercultural Pragmatics, 8*(3), 385–409.

11
KOREAN FOR SPECIFIC PURPOSES

Ji-Young Jung

Introduction

The purpose of this chapter is to provide a comprehensive overview of research on various fields of Korean for specific purposes (henceforth KSP) to date, discuss significant findings in each of the identified trends, and to offer useful suggestions for developing a viable and sustainable KSP curriculum. In recent years, there has been increasing recognition of the need to restructure and revamp foreign-language programs in post-secondary education. Speaking a foreign language undoubtedly plays a crucial role in developing practical communication skills to function competently in the global workforce. Besides, due to the increasing global connectedness aided by ever-advancing technology, newly created careers require in-depth cross-cultural and intercultural knowledge to deal with global issues, such as a global industry, geopolitical conflicts, global warming, and pandemics, to name just a few.

In this context, the role of foreign-language education has become even more critical in raising students' awareness of the need to expand and apply their foreign-language knowledge and skills outside and beyond the classroom. However, L2 Korean researchers and practitioners have only begun to explore new ways to attract students and prepare them to be specialized yet well-rounded users of the target language in the real world. For the last two decades, in U.S. higher education, Korean has enjoyed the most increase in student enrollment, while other foreign languages have experienced a gradual decline in student enrollment (MLA, 2016). In more recent years, Korean-language educators have been vocal about finding new ways to keep students invested in learning Korean before the heat of K-pop and the so-called Korean Wave die down. There have been various attempts to achieve this goal. For example, some researchers at large state universities suggest developing locally relevant language programs through community engagement, aligning courses tailored to local student demographics, and designing new curricula that connect college to career (Cho, Cho, Chun, Ko, & Lee, 2020). In this light, an overview of KSP research will serve as a useful resource that strategically prepares students to be as competitive as possible in the global world.

The chapter is structured as follows. The first section discusses the conceptualization and categorization of KSP based on those of languages for specific purposes (henceforth LSP). The following section sketches out research on Korean for occupational purposes, focusing on significant findings regarding learner needs and curriculum development. Then, maintaining the same foci, an overview of Korean for academic purposes is provided, followed by a brief discussion of assessment. Lastly, the chapter concludes with pedagogical implications and directions for future research on KSP as Korean as a foreign language (KFL, distinguished from KSL, Korean as a second language), which has relatively been scarce.

Conceptualizing KSP

KSP is generally defined as teaching and learning Korean as a second or foreign language to use Korean for a special purpose in a particular domain, as opposed to Korean for general purposes (henceforth KGP). Along with other foreign languages, KSP is often discussed as a branch of LSP, stemming from English for specific purposes (ESP). Therefore, LSP is the subsuming term used for various language variants learned to use in academic and professional settings distinguished from general language systems learned and taught in classrooms. KSP is categorized into Korean for academic purposes (henceforth KAP) and Korean for occupational purposes (henceforth KOP). KOP is further categorized into Korean for professional purposes for learners who are already working and developing skills that require specific linguistic competencies, and Korean for vocational purposes for those preparing for employment (Choi, 2018). In an attempt to address Korean learning occurring for practical applications in real-world situations, such as taking Korean to obtain academic skills to study a Korea-related subject, some researchers distinguish KAP from general Korean learning, such as taking Korean to meet the foreign language requirement at a college in the United States.[1] Figure 11.1 presents a visualized categorization of KSL/KFL.

Since Grosse and Voght's (1991) seminal study published in a special issue of the *Modern Language Journal*, many LSP researchers have actively engaged in various fields within wide-ranging analytic frameworks (Bowles, 2012). Unlike commonly taught languages like Spanish, however, KSP has hardly been discussed in the broader field of LSP. Systematic endeavors to

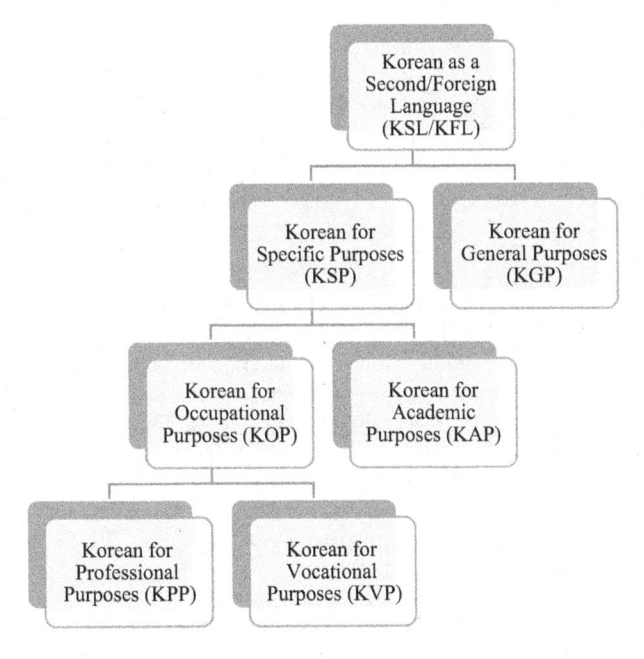

Figure 11.1 Categorization of KSL/KFL

understand KSP as a serious academic discipline are still in their infancy outside of Korea. Thus, only a handful of research published in English exists to date. Nevertheless, like all other branches of LSP, KSP shares one principal tenet with LSP: to teach and learn the target language for a specific purpose (Trace, 2015, p. 272). Then, what does 'specific' mean, specifically? Johns (2006) points to "specificity" (p. 684) as the defining tenet of any LSP in that the learner group in question must be differentiated from general learners of the target language in terms of motivations, learner characteristics, and classroom activities. The curriculum, syllabus, and pedagogical activities must be tailored to the learners' specific needs, proficiency levels, and, oftentimes, content knowledge in the specialized subject to some extent. For example, for learners of KSP for interpretation and translation, metalinguistic knowledge of Korean is critical for success, and thus they may require a more advanced level of proficiency than other disciplines. Also, a court interpreter working for Korean-speaking people in the United States will have to have basic knowledge about the U.S. legal system and, more importantly, the jargon used in the system. Most researchers and practitioners of LSP focus on teaching "special languages" (Swales, 2000, p. 60) – i.e., jargon or "technical vocabulary" (Douglas, 2000, p. 1) – and the specific rhetoric of the given genre in designing an LSP course. Therefore, it is "instrumental" (Brindley, 1989, p. 66) to identify learners' potential uses with the language to teach what the learners need to do with the 'special' language.

In addition to linguistic specificity, subject-specific skills and knowledge are also an integral part of LSP. LSP is interdisciplinary in nature, as learning LSP consequentially leads to gaining content or subject knowledge as well as general linguistic knowledge. Many business Korean courses, for example, aim to develop functional abilities required at the workplace, based on certain proficiency guidelines and typical workplace tasks. Such functional abilities center around context-dependent language use based on general knowledge about Korean society and culture and specific knowledge about the profession, such as stock trading. Knowledge in the content area is often a prerequisite in KSP as well. For example, a chef working in Korea is likely to be equipped with the necessary skills and knowledge in cooking and culinary culture but may not have the language needed to work in a Korean-speaking environment. For a diplomat, a scholar of Korean Studies, or a translator of Korean literature, a deeper understanding of Korean culture, history, and society will be equally instrumental. For this reason, the expertise and adequate training of the instructor become even more critical in KSP due to their direct impact on the learner's life.

In short, 'linguistic specificity' and 'subject specificity' are the two fundamental tenets of KSP, which categorically differentiate it from general Korean. Learning the domain-specific language is undoubtedly a founding tenet of KSP or LSP. Also, content knowledge central to the given field or profession is also a crucial component (Swales, 2000). Furthermore, some researchers point to the 'locality' of the target community as a significant component of KSP. Cho, Lee, and Wang (2021) convincingly argue for the need to strengthen the current KFL curriculum to address local challenges. For example, Rutgers University, located in an area densely populated with Koreans, has recently established a Korean–English translation and interpreting certification program to meet the increasing needs for Korean interpreters for Korean municipalities, such as courts, hospitals, and service agencies. The following three sections discuss how KSP curricula in different fields are designed and implemented in both KSL and KFL settings.

Korean for occupational purposes (KOP)

Business Korean

The most common practice and also the most actively studied area of KSP is business Korean. In Sánchez-López, Long, and Lafford's 2017 survey study with 150 LSP educators, *business* was the most preferred area of LSP research, followed by *culture* and *translation*, respectively (p. 19). In Long and Uscinski's survey (2012) with 183 foreign language departments, too, *business* is the most widely taught LSP course (44%), followed by *medicine* (12%). The term 'business Korean' is often used interchangeably with KOP, subsuming all language uses in a business setting in general. In today's global economy, it is unsurprising that business Korean courses have been widely established and offered in U.S. post-secondary education. The 2008 MLA brochure, which is designed to promote foreign languages to college students, underscored the connection between foreign-language learning and "improved career prospects," specifically in business:

> In business, any cross-cultural effort for corporation, sales, or negotiation will benefit from your experience of other languages and their communities. To be an effective professional, such as a doctor, lawyer, educator, artist, or scientist, communicating and investigating new knowledge in other languages as well as in English are essential in the increasingly international workplace. Exposure to another culture through its language will position you more favorably for success in your career, whatever career you may choose.
>
> *(MLA, 2008)*

Korean educators also recognized this renewed purpose of learning foreign languages that foreign-language learning is not only for personal enrichment but for professional development. Although Japanese has long been recognized for its importance in business and trade relations (Fryer, 2012, p. 124), business Korean has a relatively short history in LSP, and published research is heavily concentrated in South Korea. *Korean Language in America*, the first journal exclusively dedicated to Korean language education in North America, published several studies on business Korean about two decades ago. C. Kim (1998) predicted early on that East Asian languages, including Korean, would play a significant role in the global economy and proposed strategies for developing an intermediate-level business Korean course, including vocabulary pertinent to the selected topics, business writing skills, and discussions on cultural practices, such as conglomerates, current political and economic issues, and collectivism. Byon (2001) discussed the more fundamental issue of curriculum design. He suggested incorporating National Standards and a learner-centered approach based on a "theoretical and practical knowledge of systematic second language curriculum development" (p. 154). Lim (2002) offered more practical strategies in teaching business Korean. He found that using internet resources in completing course assignments was particularly useful for facilitating problem-solving skills in real-world situations (e.g., virtual stock market investment).

In South Korea as well, the vast majority of studies on KSP focus on business Korean. However, Korean language education for vocational purposes in the United States and that in Korea have a noticeable difference in the nature of the main learner group. In the United States, most KOP learners are college students taking a business Korean class out of personal interest rather than necessity. In contrast, in Korea, there are various learner groups learning KOP, including college students, company workers, simple laborers, and so on. Therefore, differentiated syllabi and materials are required to meet different needs of both learners who want to obtain a position related to Korea and those already working at a Korean company or a foreign company located in Korea (Jung, 2003).

For example, Lee's study (2008) on the then current state of KOP shows that the primary target of Korean language education for occupational purposes in Korea is simple laborers than professionals. Lee's argument is based on the South Korean Ministry of Justice's 2007 statistics on foreign workers. According to the data, simple laborers working in manufacturing and construction industries accounted for as much as 60% of the entire foreign worker population (as 'potential' learners of KOP). In contrast, only 4% accounted for professionals, including foreign-language educators, diplomats, and trade and business management workers. In addition, most Korean language education for foreign workers was conducted through training centers operated by civic groups and local governments for simple laborers and university- or company-associated language centers for professionals. Lee found that professionals were educated in higher quality than simple laborers because Korean language education for professionals was conducted through the consignment of foreign governments or institutions. Therefore, such learners were educated through a well-designed curriculum, selective textbooks, content, and tasks to meet their goals and needs fully. In contrast, language education for simple workers was characterized by a relatively generalized curriculum insufficient to meet their specific needs.

Analyzing business Korean

In terms of analytic focus, many studies on business Korean narrowly focus on lexical features (i.e., special vocabulary) and genre-specific features of written communication in analyzing business Korean. For example, Lee (2014) analyzed discursive characteristics and linguistic strategies used in e-mail requests. G. Kim (2011) focused on pragmatic failure found in e-mail requests and suggested the development of instructional content based on such problematic areas. Oh (2011) suggested that curriculum developers incorporate the canonical format of e-mail (e.g., title, signature, etc.) and sociocultural features underlying the linguistic practice in teaching business Korean.

There exist a handful of studies that incorporate a genre-based approach. For example, Hahm (2009) analyzed document formats and writing styles, which are frequently used in Korean business settings – e.g., 시말서 *simalse* 'a written apology,' 사직서 *sacikse* 'a resignation letter,' etc. – , and discussed their pedagogical applications. Ha and Lee (2013) conducted a genre analysis of 자기소개서 *cakisokayse* 'self-introduction letters' for foreign students who wish to work at Korean corporations. The researchers found that unfamiliar with this Korean-specific genre, even highly advanced learners had difficulty with employing effective strategies (e.g., narrating 성장 배경 *sengcang paykyeng* 'background of one's growth') to produce culturally appropriate letters.

Given that KSP is distinguished from KGP in terms of specificity, Ahn and Choe (2007) rightly point out that specific sets of language skills must be identified per different subfields of business Korean. For example, while reading and writing skills may be more important for office workers, listening and speaking skills are more important for tour guides and flight attendants. As discussed earlier, however, most existing studies on business Korean examine written communication. Yet, some studies on business Korean investigate spoken interactions occurring in a business setting. Jung and Cho (2011) pointed out that most studies on teaching business Korean overlooked its fluid and dynamic nature and only focused on linguistic features of written communication. Within a discourse analytic framework, the researchers analyzed mock interviews by advanced-level Korean students of a business Korean class at a large university. They found that the instructor's textbook-based, teacher-centered, and lexis-focused instruction was insufficient to perform the task. They further argued that it is vital to teach interactional competence, such as turn-taking and turn-holding strategies, to perform the task successfully.

It is interesting to note that the analytic focus in KSP has shifted analogously with that of LSP. Earlier studies focus on lexico-grammatical and genre-specific features, but more recent studies tend to describe spoken interactions in business Korean. Similarly, in LSP, an increasing number of studies utilize descriptive research data connecting to "instructable materials" (Bowles, 2012, p. 44). Bowles identified major trends in analyzing LSP as follows:

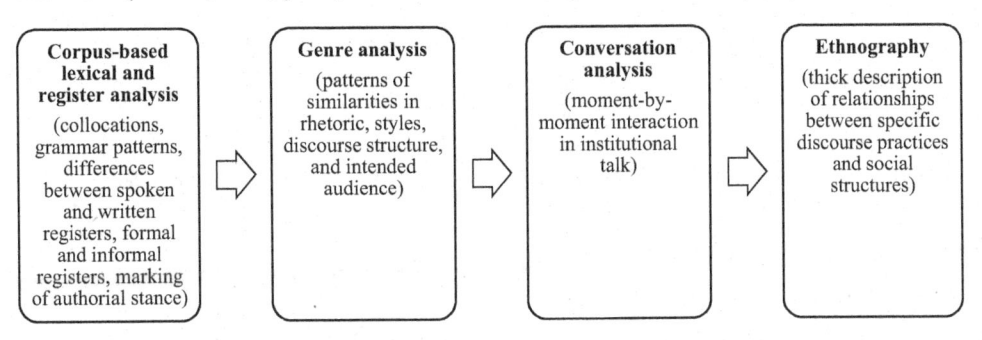

Corpus-based lexical and register analysis (collocations, grammar patterns, differences between spoken and written registers, formal and informal registers, marking of authorial stance)	⇨	Genre analysis (patterns of similarities in rhetoric, styles, discourse structure, and intended audience)	⇨	Conversation analysis (moment-by-moment interaction in institutional talk)	⇨	Ethnography (thick description of relationships between specific discourse practices and social structures)

Figure 11.2 Analyzing LSP (Bowles, 2012)

According to Bowles, "bottom-up corpus-driven methods" (p. 53) are more suitable for languages for academic purposes since the discourse communities and academic genres are less susceptible to change. To analyze workplace discourse, ethnographic and ethnomethodological methods (e.g., conversation analysis) are more useful because the corporate culture plays an instrumental role in determining the language use.

Business Korean curriculum

Designing and implementing an LSP curriculum is, by all means, not an easy task. Swales (2000) points to "weakness in institutional recognition" and "uncertain provision of professional training" (p. 68), among many structural difficulties in developing an LSP curriculum. In terms of curriculum design, however, there now exist many productive suggestions made by LSP researchers in various fields. Dudley-Evans and St. John (1998) put forward three primary characteristics of ESP as a vantage point for developing KSP curricula:

1 Design to meet the specific needs of learners
2 Utilize the methodology and activities particular to the field
3 Focus on language appropriate to those activities

Byon (2001) and Chun (2015) also view that conducting a needs analysis is the first step in developing a curriculum for business Korean. Lee (2003) conducted a needs assessment with 38 learners of business Korean. She found that, among a total of 25 skills, the learners identified the following as the most needed skills: (1) telephone and e-mail communication; (2) reading and writing documents, letters, and faxes; (3) negotiations; and (4) interviews.

In terms of methodology and activities, Jung and Cho (2011) suggested an integrated approach in designing a business Korean course, incorporating all linguistic, situational, interactional, and cultural dimensions in designing pedagogical activities. Kim (2019) considered content-based instruction (CBI) to be particularly useful in teaching intermediate-level KOP in that CBI incorporates both thematic and linguistic knowledge. According to the researcher, compared with task-based language teaching (TBLT), CBI has been under-utilized in KGP because CBI requires a minimum linguistic proficiency to fully understand the contents at hand. However, Kim's study demonstrates that not only do learners understand meanings through content, they also learn the linguistic forms and structure and sociocultural elements of the language in the process of understanding the meanings.

Kim (2012) offers a model for business Korean instruction designed according to different proficiency levels. In Kim's model, domain-specific skills are not yet introduced at the beginning level. Only at the intermediate level are simple business skills and relevant cultural elements taught. Essential workplace vocabulary and common business skills are introduced at the advanced level at which learners have acquired the general language knowledge required to perform the workplace-related tasks. Beyond the advanced level is an application stage in which learners actually apply the learned knowledge, skills, and technical vocabulary and skills to perform business tasks in a variety of public and formal settings of the profession.

According to Kim, Kang, Hong, Han, and Park (2018), most research on the development of materials for business Korean aims at the intermediate level or above. The researchers then point to the need to develop more textbooks that can be used for beginners who are foreign employees and managers working at local companies outside Korea. They developed a two-volume textbook series titled *Sejong Business Korean*, containing more oral/aural skills–oriented communications than literacy-oriented skills – e.g., introducing the company after reading a written introduction of the company, making a telephone order after reading order sheets, sharing an opinion after listening to a presentation on new product development, etc. However, it is hard to say that their textbook differs from existing business Korean textbooks in that the first volume assumes that its users come with the basic grammar and vocabulary covered in *Sejong Korean 1* and *2*, a textbook series for general Korean. Strictly speaking, therefore, their series for business Korean begins with an intermediate level. In the United States, the University of Pennsylvania is the only institution that offers different levels of business Korean courses: Business Communication in Korean for learners with intermediate-level language proficiency, Business Korean for advanced-level learners, and Advanced Business Korean beyond an advanced level. Analogous to Kim's model (2012), the Business Communication in Korean course introduces essential cultural elements and simple business skills, while the Business Korean course covers more content such as business trends and social changes affecting Korean business. The Advanced Business Korean course deals with highly advanced and complex business-management skills, mostly for business major students of Wharton School of Business, who are mostly native speakers of Korean. This course is taught by an expert in the field (usually a doctoral student at Wharton), and language instruction is rarely conducted (Cho, 2020).

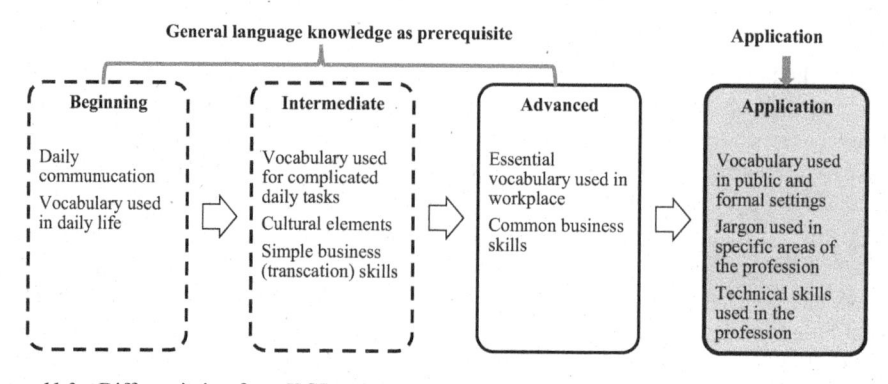

Figure 11.3 Differentiation from KGP to KSP (Kim, 2012, p. 11)

To summarize, scholarly interest and research in business Korean have consistently increased since the first published study appeared in the late 1990s in the United States and the early 2000s in South Korea. Early studies on business Korean were mostly concerned with reporting the then current state of business Korean education. In later studies, the development and analysis of instructional materials were the most frequent research topic, followed by curriculum and materials design. Jang (2020) analyzed 241 studies published in South Korea between 2001 and 2020 and found that, despite its steady progress, there is still a conspicuous lack of research on business Korean focusing on the development of teaching materials tailored to various occupational groups. Jang argues that, as foreign workers' occupations have become more diverse in Korea, it is urgent to develop materials and curricula that meet various occupational groups' needs.

Korean for interpretation and translation

As KSP learners continue to increase, the scope of KSP has widened to address diverse fields. Arguably, Korean for interpretation and translation (KIT) is the second most active area after business Korean, although trailing by far. This is probably because interpretation and translation skills can be widely used by Korean speakers in different disciplines, such as tour guides, literature translators, court interpreters, and medical translators. However, there has been relatively little interest in interpretation/translation programs in higher education because interpretation/translation requires language proficiency beyond an advanced level in both source and target language and professional understandings of the field. In addition, the misunderstanding that general Korean language learning to an advanced level will naturally lead to an ability to translate exacerbates the delay in the development of KIT education (Lee, 2012).

Several higher-education institutions offer KIT courses in the United States. For example, the World Languages and Literatures department of Boston University offers a literary translation course – LK470 Korean in Translation and Interpretation Workshop – for advanced learners. According to their course description, both printed and audiovisual texts (e.g., subtitles) are used for training alongside literary pieces. The Asian Languages and Cultures department of Rutgers, State University of New Jersey, offers the first certificate program in Korean translation, integrated into its undergraduate curriculum. Their certificate program requires 12 credits for completion, including KOR 320 Korean Translation: Introduction to Practical Translations, KOR 480 Korean Interpreting, and KOR 481 Korean Translation/Interpreting Internship. While Boston University and Rutgers University's KIT education cover general KIT, Georgia University offers a 40-hour certificate program for Korean medical interpreting for health care professionals, such as nurses, physicians, receptionists, laboratory technicians, etc.

Lederer (cited in Lee, 2012) posits four critical elements of foreign-language interpretation and translation: (1) "command of the source language," (2) "command of one's native language," (3) "command of the relevant world and background knowledge," and (4) "command of translating methodology" (p. 244). Furthermore, most educators would agree that KIT requires a comprehensive understanding of Korean society, culture, and history for genuinely successful learning. For these reasons, as Cho and Chun (2016) aptly point out, a KIT program plays a "centralizing" role at an institution because it integrates Korean studies (e.g., Korean literature, history, economics, politics, culture, etc.), Korean language learning, and technical training to obtain procedural knowledge (i.e., know-how).

Unfortunately, however, for the very same reasons, learning KIP presents some challenges for learners. Hong (2017) reports on the frustration experienced by foreign graduate students enrolled in a graduate school of interpretation and translation that learning to translate made them realize that they were, in fact, "alingual" (p. 160) without a mastery command in either language. For instance, simultaneous interpretation requires rigorous and a tremendous amount of training. According to Hong, interpreters also deal with a myriad of materials and written texts. Also, they often perform 'sight translation,' a form of interpretation that requires an ability to translate the text at hand immediately whether they have seen it before or not, based on familiarity with its genre and register, styles, organizational and sentence structures, and jargon, as well as knowledge of the underlying Korean culture and society. Therefore, it is true that 'perfect' bilinguals are generally considered to have an advantage over KFL learners because interference of their mother tongue is thoroughly avoided in the world of translators.

Korean for missionary purposes

Another prominent field of KOP known to be successful in terms of connection to career and high attainment is Korean for missionaries. Historically, it is not unreasonable to say that the first serious learners of KOP were missionaries. The first mission of missionaries is to learn and speak the language of those with whom they wanted to do missionary work and understand customs to connect with ordinary people. Even today, language ability is a key element of missionary work. For this reason, learners of Korean for missionary purposes are usually highly motivated and committed to achieving an advanced level of proficiency or above. Ko (2014) conducted an in-depth interview with three Catholic missionaries to investigate successful learning strategies. All three missionaries started to learn Korean at a university-affiliated language institute upon arrival in Korea. Since the formal education they received did not cover specific languages used to do their job, all of them used private tutoring at the same time. According to the interviews, the most urgent need was to acquire the ability to give a homily in Korean, which was also the most crucial part of their mission. They also used a textbook that included translations of religious texts, such as Catholic terms, gospel sentences, and prayers. One of the missionaries said that leaning Korean was imperative; in his own words:

> When you pray, you must first know God's words and prayers in the language of the country. You should pray in the language of the country even when you are alone. God's words are alive, and, of course, you know his words in Greek and Hebrew. However, since they are living words, they also become alive when translated into Korean. I'm sure God's words can give new light in a new culture and a new language.
> (p. 253)

An (2020) explored how teaching Korean for missionary work was perceived by preliminary protestant missionaries attending a Christian college in Korea. Over 90% of the students projected that it would be important to teach Korean, not for teaching the language *per se* but for successful missions. Such students even wished to become a certified Korean teacher to develop expertise and professional skills. In this context, Korean in their missionary work would be Korean for missionaries, although the language is not the direct medium of communication. Instead, it is an effective venue to connect with people, along with an open attitude and a sense of calling as a missionary.

As shown, Korean for missionaries carries several particularities differing from other disciplines of KSP. In recent years, in addition to evangelical propagation, overseas missionary work has well served to promote the Korean language and culture worldwide. Also, acquiring professional proficiency in Korean is not only a tool for professional success but for sharing personal faith and purpose of life. The mission statement of the Korean language program at Brigham Young University states explicitly that

> the program also supports the mission of Brigham Young University and its sponsoring institution, the Church of Jesus Christ of Latter-day Saints, by helping students develop academic skills and competencies in a faith-based setting which is also committed to the development of personal character and integrity.
>
> *(https://ane.byu.edu/korea/)*

As a messenger of the religious dogma and faith, it is crucial to develop a desirable character, religious views, and knowledge, which are expressed and shared through the use of Korean. For this reason, An (2020) suggests that Korean for missionary purposes be distinguished from and treated in parallel with KOP and KAP, rather than as a subdiscipline of KOP.

Korean for other specific occupations

This section discusses a small number of existing studies on Korean for various fields: diplomacy, tourism, military, and medicine. These studies mostly address the peculiarities of the given field, learners' corresponding needs, and effective interactional methods to meet such needs.

Korean for diplomacy

Due to the geopolitical significance of the Korean peninsula and the long-standing alliance between the United States and South Korea, Korean for diplomacy has drawn increasing attention in KSP. S. Kim (2007) notes that American diplomats and foreign service officers working in Korea may display an unusually high level of proficiency because they receive intensive training at the Foreign Service Institute (FSI) to achieve Level 3 on the Interagency Language Roundtable (ILR) scale, which denotes General Professional Proficiency in reading and speaking. In S. Kim's study, although most of these diplomats found their Korean proficiency was generally helpful in performing job-related tasks, they actually used Korean more frequently in informal spoken interactions, such as evening parties and receptions, to establish a good relationship with Korean people. This was because they were not as proficient as native speakers of Korean or professional interpreters to use Korean in high-stakes, official situations, such as diplomatic negotiations and public speeches.

Yoon (2015) also recognizes the importance of providing learners with opportunities to practice skills to manage intellectual conversations on current events and gain in-depth knowledge about Korean culture and society. Therefore, in designing a curriculum for Korean for diplomacy, she adopted both CBI and TBLT by incorporating media research to help learners develop information analysis and discussion skills, the topics of which included North Korean nuclear issues, the Korea–U.S. free trade agreement (FTA), and Northeast Asia and U.S. relations. Lee (2009) agrees that CBI is particularly useful in that dealing with the contents of diplomatic interests can be extremely motivating. According to Lee, it is important to teach speaking skills that can be practical for diplomats. Thus, teaching materials must include such tasks as public speech, negotiation, discussion, and interpretation, in addition to high-frequency diplomatic vocabulary, and rhetorically fixed expressions used for diplomacy and Korean language etiquette.

Korean for tourism

There is very little research on KSP for professional tourism. However, it is worth examining since, unlike other fields of Korean for vocational purposes, most of those who learn Korean for tourism seem to be true beginners. Sung (2015) proposed a KSP program for students at his institution, the largest community college in Hawai'i. He noticed the increasing need for a Korean-speaking workforce in the state, especially in the hospitality sector (e.g., hotels and resorts). Based on the results of a needs analysis, he identified three areas to be incorporated in the syllabus: introduction (romanization, introducing oneself, daily greetings, etc.), hotel check-in (numbers and counters, requesting guests' information, etc.), and directions (location words, giving directions, using hand gestures, etc.).

Seo (2020) pointed out that errors or misuse are commonly found in signs, signage, and menus for Korean tourists in Japan, ranging from simple orthographic and grammar errors to entirely incomprehensible or misleading information resulting from the use of the internet translation services or word-for-word translation of Japanese into Korean by private travel agencies. Examples included 새피부 만두 *sayphipwu mantwu* 'new human skin dumplings' for 'chicken skin dumplings,' 불타는 쓰레기 *pwulthanun ssuleyki* 'burning garbage' for 'burnable garbage,' and 허약하기 때문에 주의하십시오 *heyakhaki ttaymwuney cwuuyhasipsio* 'Be careful as your health is poor' for 'Be careful as it is fragile.' Seo attributed this to a lack of Korean-speaking agents in the field and called for a specialized curriculum fostering Korean-speaking Japanese professionals.

Korean for military

South Korea currently holds the world's ninth-largest military power, according to the U.S. News' 2020 Power Rankings, and the sixth according to the Global Firepower's 2020 Military Strength Ranking, based on such factors as manpower, types of combat equipment, possession of nuclear weapons, and diversity of weapons. As the nation's collaborations with foreign troops have increased, more foreign soldiers choose to learn Korean among many critical languages to national defense (Hyun, 2016). In the United States, the Defense Language Institute Foreign Language Center (DLIFLC) of the U.S. Department of Defense has long been providing systematic and intensive Korean-language training for U.S. soldiers. In South Korea, the Korea Defense Language Institute (KDLI) of the Joint Forces Military University was established in 2012 to promote global understandings and strategic competence for career military personnel and officers.

Hyun (2016) categorized learners of Korean at the KDLI into four groups according to their goals for learning Korean: international students who will join a military academy, major- and lieutenant colonel–level officers who will receive training in military science–related training, colonel-level or higher officers who are subject to training in security courses on military situations of the country and abroad, defense policies, military strategies, and lieutenant-level officers who will begin a master's program in military science. Hyun points out that since a large number of these learners learn Korean for their studies, Korean for the military is also categorized as KAP by some researchers (e.g., Park, 2008). However, according to Hyun, Korean for military most definitely differs from KAP or other KOP fields due to its focus on military terminology and military-specific culture. For example, as the military is a strictly hierarchical organization, it is critical to master different speech levels and their appropriate uses. In addition, vocabulary is graded differently (in terms of frequency of use) and used differently in the military, and abbreviations are frequently used. For example, the more frequent use of 탈모

thalmo in the military context will be 'taking off the hat,' rather than its primary meaning 'hair loss.' Also, 'hello' in a telephone conversation is 통신보안 *thongsinpoan* 'communication security,' not 여보세요 *yeposeyyo* 'hello.'

Indeed, learners of Korean for military, reminiscent of Korean for missionary, share similar dispositions, lifestyles, and values, which grants it a special place in KSP. However, despite the relative homogeneity of the learner group, teaching Korean for the military faces several challenges. As Song (2016) notes, learners' age range widely varies from the early 20s to the late 50s. Thus, it is highly challenging to carry out differentiated instruction in accordance with different educational levels, ranks, and life and learning experiences. Song further points to the fact that because learning takes place within the limited environment of the military, their Korean used in everyday life often falls behind their military Korean. Therefore, it is difficult to determine whether learners have reached the targeted proficiency level in a strict sense.

Korean for medicine

An increasing number of foreign medical staff come to Korea to train as Korea's health technology is arguably one of the best in the world, and domestic medical fields have been fast globalizing. Also, more and more tourists are visiting Korea, seeking high-quality medical treatments and services while vacationing. However, the fast-expanding Korean medical industry is not necessarily and always encouraging. Kim (2016) noted that poor communication between foreign patients, Korean medical staff, and hospital officials often results in misunderstandings, which in turn could lead to serious consequences. In this context, the role of international medical tour coordinators who speak both Korean and the patient's language has become more important in recent years. The Korean Ministry of Culture, Sports and Tourism (2013, cited in Kim, 2016) defines medical tour coordinators as those who play a key role in attracting medical tourism based on their medical knowledge and interpersonal and translation skills. They help their customers in many ways to receive high-quality medical services and enjoy their stay in Korea (e.g., airport reception, dining, sightseeing, etc.). They also assist Korean medical service providers so they can effectively take care of their customers. In doing so, it is language skills that the ministry suggests to be the essential and critical ability of professional medical tour coordinators for effective performance.

Kim (2016) identified 60 essential tasks expected to be performed by these coordinators, based on those described by the Korean Tourism Organization and Hyundai Medis, a consulting firm that conducts medical marketing, international medical staff training, attracting overseas patients, etc., and the guidelines for Korean test items of the qualification examination for medical tour coordinators designed by the Human Resources Development Service of Korea. Kim then conducted a survey with Korean medical staff, Korean administrative staff, and medical tour coordinators working in medical institutions. The researcher asked them which language skills they needed most and which of the 60 tasks were most important. All the respondents answered that they needed to improve listening and speaking skills more than reading and writing skills or technical and medical terminology. They also answered that their most important task was "to accurately communicate to Korean medical staff the patient's questions about symptoms, treatment methods, treatment plans, and side effects of drugs" (p. 24). Also, the response rate for "risk management" was relatively high, such as "delivering the contents of consultation with the patient accurately to the Korean medical staff when medical accidents occurred in the course of treatment" and "documenting in Korean the contents of counseling related to medical accidents" (p. 24).

Seo and Lee's study (2018) offered crucial elements incorporated into a curriculum for Saudi Arabian dentists for their successful training in Korea. First, the researchers listed the top 30 common symptoms of dental patients in Korean, including tooth decay, jaw joint disorder, snoring, swollen cheeks, etc. Also included was etiquette, which was a key to form friendly relationships and resolve conflict situations smoothly. In terms of culture, they pointed to the Korean hospital culture characterized by intensive working hours or fast work handling, and the general Korean culture where hierarchical, top-down relations are respected. Lastly, they included communication skills used in an initial examination and diagnosis, a re-examination and confirming improvement, and the ability to use language to form a rapport with patients to relieve their anxiety.

In sum, as has become evident from the KOP studies discussed so far that KOP shares two fundamental tenets that distinguish it from KGP regardless of the type of profession: linguistic specificity and subject specificity. KOP learners must possess a breadth of vocabulary and 'special' vocabulary used in their field. They also need to develop job-specific skills, both technical and interpersonal, for successful performance. Cultural knowledge, both general and workplace-specific, also plays a critical role in the way learners interact with Koreans. The discussion now turns to Korean for Academic Purposes (KAP), focusing on the language skills needed for academic success.

Korean for academic purposes (KAP)

Since the South Korean government launched the Study Korea Project in 2004 for the purpose of establishing Korea as an 'education hub' in Asia, the KAP learner population in Korea is fast growing (NIIED, National Institute for International Education). According to the Korean Educational Development Institute's educational statistics service, the number of international students in Korea was 142,205 as of April 2019, and over 60% of these students were enrolled in an academic degree program (Seo and Ahn, 2019). Accordingly, KAP is one of the most actively and fruitfully researched areas in KSL education. It is generally contended that, in the context of KSL, the term 'KAP learner' refers to (1) international students learning Korean to enter a college or a graduate school in Korea and (2) international students taking Korean at a college or a graduate school in Korea to obtain an academic degree in a particular academic field. In the context of KFL outside of Korea, KAP is generally conceptualized as learning Korean to acquire subject knowledge in order to understand the contents of their undergraduate or graduate studies through the medium of the Korean language. KAP is further categorized into Korean for general academic purposes and Korean for specific academic purposes, such as psychology, economics, and medicine. Figure 11.4 shows the categorization of KAP in KSP offered by Choe (2006, p. 282).

In contrast to KOP, in which learners' proficiency levels may vary widely according to the characteristics of and qualifications for the profession, KAP learners typically display an advanced level of proficiency or above. Furthermore, Choe and Yoon (2012) argue that, generally, the proficiency levels of Korean learners for 'specific' academic purposes tend to be even higher than those of general KAP. This is probably because specific academic disciplines deal with low-frequency, domain-specific jargon and expertise in content knowledge. KAP has been extensively studied in Korea for the last two decades. However, most of these studies focus on current instructional practices, including skill specifications and teaching materials. Therefore, instead of discussing various disciplines of KAP, as in the previous sections on KOP, this section discusses notable research trends in KAP: (1) learner needs, (2) curriculum design, and (3) assessment.

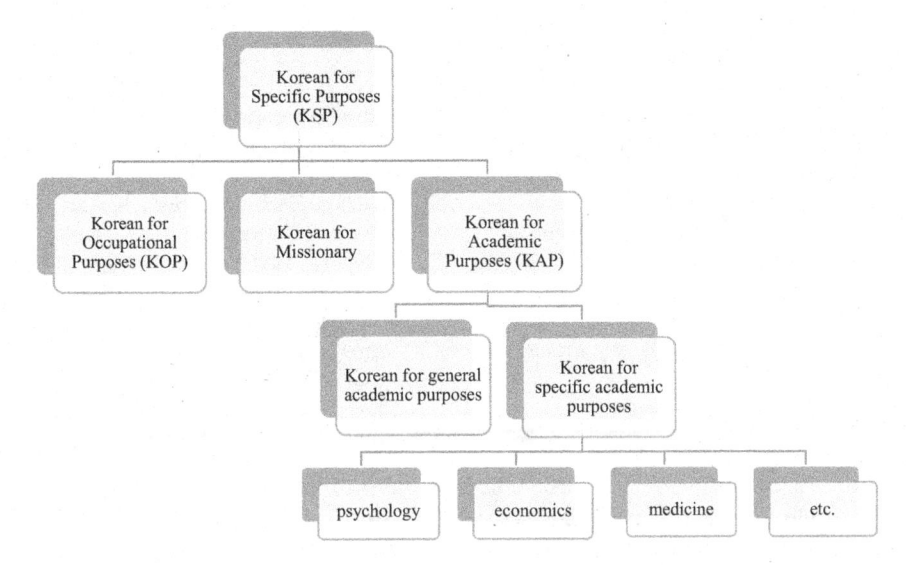

Figure 11.4 Categorization of KAP

Needs analysis of KAP learners

South Korea's Ministry of Education, Science and Technology recommends that the minimum language requirement for foreigners to be admitted to a Korean university be Level 4, roughly an advanced intermediate level, on the Test of Proficiency in Korean (TOPIK, comprising Levels 1–6) (Jung, 2016). It is only natural to assume that once learners are admitted to a college after meeting the general language requirement, the KAP curriculum should be designed around advanced-level linguistic and functional abilities – i.e., those corresponding to Levels 5 and 6 on TOPIK. Table 11.1 shows the descriptors of the linguistic competence of Levels 5 and 6 (www.topik.go.kr, emphasis added).

As the table shows, at Level 6, learners are expected to display near-native proficiency and functional ability in their field.

As Shin and Lee (2021) point out, TOPIK scores are widely used for high-stakes purposes, such as admission into academic programs and employment for companies. However, very little research has thus far been conducted and published for validating TOPIK as accurately measuring KAP skills matching the needs of KAP learners. In response to this imminent need to identify learning goals for KAP learners to design an effective KAP syllabus, some researchers set out to investigate learner needs. Jung (2016) surveyed 42 students enrolled in Level 5 and 6 classes at two university-affiliated language institutes. Park (2008) examined KAP programs offered at 14 universities in Korea. Both researchers reported that fundamental academic skills, such as presentation and discussion skills, must be included in the instructional agenda. In addition, Park noticed a lack of KAP courses for specific fields (as opposed to general KAP) to train students to gain the knowledge and skills required in their major.

In a similar vein, Kim et al. (2018) argued that in order for KAP to become "learning-oriented" rather than "teaching-oriented," and also "learner-centered" rather than "teacher-centered," it is urgent to (re)design textbooks to address the needs of learners more realistically (p. 127). The researchers conducted a survey with 218 learners enrolled in KAP courses offered at "S University" and 9 professors of these courses. Interestingly, most learners answered that they needed to acquire public speaking skills most, while only one professor answered that

Table 11.1 Linguistic competence at Levels 5 and 6 on TOPIK

Level 5	Level 6
• Able to perform linguistic functions to some degree that is necessary for research and work in professional fields • Able to understand and use the expressions related to even unfamiliar aspects of politics, economics, society, and culture • Able to use expressions properly, depending on formal, informal, and spoken/written contexts	• Able to perform linguistic functions necessary to the research and work in professional fields **relatively correctly and fluently** • Able to understand and use expressions related to even unfamiliar subjects of politics, economics, society, and culture • Able to experience **no difficulty in performing the functions or conveying the meaning**, although the proficiency has not reached full native speaker proficiency

speaking skills are important. Most professors believed that listening skills are essential to understanding lectures in major courses, which learners also identified to be necessary, followed by public speaking. Both students and professors listed writing as the most 'difficult' area. Students wished for more vocabulary explanations in the textbook, whereas professors wanted more multimedia materials to facilitate understanding of the content. Kim et al. (2018) evaluated that, overall, the materials used at S University served the purpose but did not fully meet the learners' needs.

It seems that KAP learners' needs differ according to their proficiency level. Kim (2018) asked 97 intermediate and 84 advanced learners of KAP to rate the importance of 34 academic language skills on a 6-point Likert scale. Advanced learners ranked higher than did intermediate learners in the following five areas: seminars/discussion, private study/reading, reference/library use, essays/reports, and examinations. Kim interpreted these results that advanced learners had a more potent "desire to gain self-directed learning skills in studying academic contents," "higher recognition of the importance of such study situations as reference/library use," and thus "a higher degree of engagement in the academic context" (p. 390).

Curriculum design

The number of international students studying for an academic degree in Korea has been increasing rapidly since 2000 (Cho, Lee, & Min, 2019). In Korea, the vast majority of learners enrolled in advanced Korean courses at college are, in fact, KAP learners. However, despite a large number of studies on KAP, there have been few systematic efforts to develop effective pedagogical interventions and content based on specific language skills that learners of KAP must acquire. This section discusses studies that examine a KAP curriculum and the specific skills necessary to make it successful.

Reading

To obtain knowledge in any discipline in higher education, the first step generally involves reading printed texts and understanding the content. In Jeon's study (2004, cited in Kim, 2020), reading is the most frequently used communication mode in the academic world. Reading proficiency, therefore, has been put forward by many KAP researchers as a key to academic success. Kim (2020) also viewed that reading is the focal point in differentiating KAP from KGP. The researcher examined how KAP reading was approached differently from KGP by comparing the KAP and KGP textbooks used by three major universities, Kyung Hee University, Seoul National University, and Yonsei University. The analytic focus was placed on topics, text types, and activities. The results showed that KAP textbooks dealt with more topics on humanities than KGP textbooks, while KGP textbooks mostly dealt with culture/arts, which are generally popular and accessible for lower-level learners. There were no significant differences in the text type; both used explanatory texts most frequently, although KAP textbooks used argumentative texts slightly more. Finally, as for reading activities, KGP textbooks centered on vocabulary, such as finding the correct vocabulary, expressions, or meaning of speech. In contrast, KAP textbooks showed a larger number of activities related to general academic skills, such as identifying the text type and structure, expressing an opinion, (dis)agreeing with/criticizing, and summarizing. In sum, the KAP textbooks were most clearly distinguished from KGP textbooks in activity types than in topics and text types.

Similarly, Jang (2017) analyzed topics, text types and structures, reading skills, and reading strategies used in nine KAP textbooks. The most prevalent topics included science (appeared in all nine textbooks, 100%), society (100%), economy/business (100%), culture (83%), and language (66%), and the least frequently treated topics were religion (33%) and politics (0%). As for the text type, argumentative (100%) and explanatory texts (100%) were the most prevalent types, followed by news articles (75%), novels (50%), and research papers (50%). As for reading skills, factual understanding comprised the largest portion (63%), followed by critical understanding (21%), inferred understanding (13%), and "sentimental" (i.e., psychological, attitudinal) understanding (3%). More importantly, Jang found that cognitive strategies, such as using linguistic clues and background knowledge, comprised 58%, while metacognitive strategies, such as evaluating and determining the text structure, comprised only 10%. Concerned with a lack of activities that facilitate inference and critical-thinking skills, Kim proposed to guide learners to use a broader range of topics and more metacognitive strategies to broaden the breadth and depth of their understanding of the contents.

Jang was not the first researcher who pointed out a lack of critical reading activities in KAP textbooks. Earlier, Park (2011) found that post-reading activities – i.e., comprehension questions – heavily focused on "literal reading," while "critical reading" was rarely used. Ku (2012) also argued that effective reading activities should be able to lead learners to the "creative understanding," in other words, making inferences, critiquing, and evaluating the text, beyond a simple understanding of the surface contents. She analyzed approximately 800 comprehension questions on 80 reading texts in 4 KAP textbooks, all of which were designed for advanced-level learners. Surprisingly, reading comprehension questions were heavily concentrated in questions on factual contents, comprising 89.6% of the data. Both inference and expansion questions asking learners to apply, analyze, evaluate, and recreate meanings constituted only 5.2%, respectively. Ku concluded that, in order to foster higher-order thinking skills, such as reasoning ability, critical-thinking ability, and creative-reading ability, it is vital to develop reading comprehension questions that can initiate reader–text and reader–reader "interaction" that allows learners to think about, talk about, and respond to the text.

Apparently, reading in an academic context differs from reading in an everyday context in its purpose. While everyday reading is intended for obtaining practical information on personal and general topics, reading scholarly texts on academic subjects is a genuinely purposeful activity aimed at intellectual growth in the given field. The ultimate goal of academic reading is to cultivate relevant knowledge through scholarly texts and to perform academic tasks based on it. Therefore, in designing academic reading activities, it is imperative to take into consideration strategic and high-level "study" skills, such as selecting relevant and useful information and critically evaluating the validity and academic value of the content (Jang, 2017).

Writing

Unlike learning Korean for general purposes centered on spoken communication, literacy holds a central place in KAP. Lee (2005) argues that academic writing is the most crucial component of KAP because the final assessment tool in advanced-level KAP classes typically takes the format of writing, such as essays. In this light, coupled with reading, writing skills are, undoubtedly, one of the deciding factors in successful KAP learning. Son and Jang's 2013 study revealed that, out of the 230 KAP studies they examined, 92 studies were writing-related research (40%). The researchers further found that KAP writing research was primarily concerned with teaching methods, textbook analysis, and analysis of learners' writing.

In particular, persuasive and argumentative writing has been shown by some researchers to foster the critical-thinking skills needed to tackle most academic tasks (Park, 2016). Park (2016) examined how critique is presented in 16 major textbooks for KAP. In the researcher's view, persuasive writing, like critiques, is the most prevalent genre in academia. However, most of the critical texts produced by learners tend to be merely a summary, rather than analysis or evaluation (Lee and Kang, cited in Park, 2016). Park found that as many as ten textbooks (63%) introduced writing tasks without specifying different genres to begin with, and even in six of the ten textbooks that did, there were no conformed guidelines for writing a critique. Furthermore, the topics were mostly in popular culture, like film and literature. According to the researcher, because the textbooks were designed for learners studying Korean for such purposes as entering a university or obtaining a degree, the topics and content should address a wider range of themes to address those commonly discussed in the college curriculum.

In terms of the methodology of teaching writing, Lee (2011) found that reading-to-write tasks differentiated from isolated reading and writing activities, are most effective in preparing learners to become efficient academic writers. According to Lee, this was because "source texts" provided learners with the prototypical discourse organizations, the rhetoric of academic writing, and opportunities to shape their ideas and standings toward the issue at hand.

As such, Kim (2007) proposes Project-Based Learning (PBL) as an effective way to equip KAP learners with integrative reading-and-writing skills needed for their studies. In a typical PBL class, learners select their own project topics, gather information, write reports, and present their project as the final assignment. In this sense, PBL enables comprehensive and integrated learning, incorporating all four language skills and both formal and informal language use. The learners in Kim's study were a total of 13 learners attending the Korean Language Center at Korea University, 8 of which were KAP learners, including graduate students majoring in Korean Studies, prospective undergraduate and graduate students, and prospective transferring students. Through analyzing the learners' work over two semesters, Kim found that PBL classes integrating writing with a formal presentation led to learner-centered and learner-driven learning, increased communication opportunities in various contexts, and improved formal writing and speaking skills.

Speaking

Discussion skills are also discussed as an important component of KAP. J. Y. Lee (2017) believes that the ability to organize discourse in a logical way is a critical component of academic discourse. The researcher analyzed debates on current events and controversial issues (e.g., filial piety contract, moving in together before marriage, etc.) found in six textbooks for KAP, focusing on the three rhetorical structures of debates in Korean: statement of one's standing, counterargument, and final remarks. Among these, for an effective counterargument,

J. Y. Lee viewed that it is vital to utilize genre-specific strategies to persuade others who have different opinions, for example, elaborating on the asserted standing and providing supporting details. The researcher identified an array of strategies and linguistic devices presented in the textbooks, including emphatic language use, softening refutation through partial agreement, and providing evidence or examples. Then, the researcher compared them with those used by native speakers of Korean in a TV show, *tvN's College Debate Battles*. The results showed that, although the textbooks and the native speakers used almost the same types of strategies, there were interesting discrepancies in their linguistic realizations. For example, native speakers often used strong expressions pointing out the fallacies of the other side's remarks, refuting after quoting the other's speech, and using rhetorical questions to claim the validity of one's remarks. In contrast, the textbooks never introduced such. In addition, while native speakers tailored their speech in accordance with the unfolding interaction, using informal styles as much as formal ones, the textbook discourse primarily suggested formal styles. J. Y. Lee concluded that studying the naturally occurring discourse of native speakers will be useful in developing practical and useful textbooks.

As shown in previous sections on reading and writing, for successful KAP learning, the development of cognitive skills is as crucial as communication skills (Lee, 2004). Kim (2015) noted the value of interviews as an integrated approach to learning KAP in that learners, as an interviewer or interviewee, come to practice all types of communication skills by asking and answering questions, listening to the recordings and reading the transcribed data, writing and reporting on the results. More importantly, utilizing interviews facilitates the development of skills for identification, analysis, categorization, prioritization, comparison, integration, deduction, reasoning, and evaluation, all of which are necessary for academic achievement. The learners in Kim's study indicated that, through interviews, they learned important academic skills such as logical thinking, producing Korean word documents and presentations slides, and making formal presentations. Furthermore, they came to understand the significant cultural differences between Koreans' ways of thinking and their own and learned how to collaborate and negotiate with others.

Listening

There are various academic activities required for content studies, such as seminars, assignments, discussions, and presentations. Some studies suggest that understanding lectures is the most critical function that directly affects academic performance, given that most classes are conducted through one-way lectures by professors in Korea (Y. Lee, 2016). College lectures include a large amount of specialized vocabulary related to the field, making it even more difficult for learners to understand, especially when they do not have sufficient and relevant background information. K. Lee (2016) argues that broadcast news is useful to prepare KAP learners for their majors because, through access to Korean politics, economy, society, and culture, they can obtain background knowledge about contemporary Korea. Other advantages of listening practice using broadcast news is that news anchors and reporters have relatively clear pronunciation and accurate grammar and vocabulary and that the sentence structures and expressions of news are similar to those of lectures and formal presentations that learners encounter all the time in college. The researcher further argues that the integrated task of listening to, briefing, and discussing the news is beneficial for developing essential skills required in college studies.

For this reason, some researchers believe that it is more effective to teach listening integrated with other language skills. Lee (2019) examined actual notetaking by foreign undergraduates, analyzed the factors affecting notetaking through in-depth interviews, and sought efficient ways to help them develop the "listening-to-lectures and notes-taking" skills. Based on the results, Lee concluded that "listening-to-lectures and notes-taking" is an important function that constitutes KAP proficiency, which can be developed and improved through instruction, rather than a language-learning strategy. In addition, in understanding lectures and taking notes, both the ability to grasp the essence and transcribe details are important. In Lee's view, "listening-to-lectures and notes-taking" must be included in the syllabus since they affect the learner's course grade and thus have a high-stakes consequence to the learner.

I. Lee's study (2016) is one of the rare studies that proposed KAP tasks integrating three language skills: reading, listening, and writing. The researcher examined KAP learners' performance in a task completed through three sequential stages: (1) skimming through the written text and making notes for important information; (2) predicting the audio to listen, listening to the audio, and making notes; and (3) comparing the written text and the audio, planning to write, organizing content, writing a summary, revising, and proofreading the summary. I. Lee found that learners with a higher level of general language proficiency better performed the task in presenting information; higher-level learners often used summary and paraphrasing, while lower-level learners mostly used quotes and declarative statements. An interesting observation was that most lower-level learners did not cite the source of information. These findings further imply that writing rules and ethical writing may also be subject to KAP instruction.

Culture of the community of practice (CoP)

In addition to communication skills, it is equally important to recognize and learn cultural norms and codes of conduct observed in and shared by the given Community of Practice (CoP). For example, Lee (2011) underscored the importance of teaching writing ethics to international students in Korea. Lee noticed that, while KAP writing textbooks introduced guidelines for writing itself, campus life, and Korea-specific college culture, academic ethics were nowhere to be found. Specifically, Kim (2014) emphasized the importance of teaching e-mail writing to KAP learners. Although writing e-mail in a socioculturally appropriate manner is crucial in constructing and maintaining a good relationship with professors and other gatekeepers, it is not explicitly taught or naturally acquired as their linguistic proficiency improves.

Yoon (2020) argued for the need to develop a textbook on thesis writing for international graduate students in Korea. She found that the existing textbooks for KAP writing were all for undergraduate students. Also, since most of the examples appearing in textbooks were excerpts from academic journal articles, it was difficult for learners to identify the genre-specific characteristics of the thesis. Yoon went on to propose an instructional model containing step-by-step guidelines: (1) identifying the canonical structure of a thesis, including frequently used discourse markers; (2) studying a sample thesis; (3) evaluating a thesis; (4) writing a thesis, including a table of contents, introduction, references, etc.; (5) receiving and exchanging feedback; (6) revising; and (7) self-evaluation.

Kang (2019) proposed materials for teaching "living culture" to international college students to adapt to academic life and complete the coursework. Highlighted cultural elements were interpersonal relationships and essential norms and patterns of behavior that students must observe. She conducted a survey with 65 KAP learners, and, surprisingly, all the learners answered that they needed cultural education on college life in Korea. Based on the survey results, Kang proposed a syllabus thata included campus, food, leisure, history, festival, play culture, popular culture, and career education – e.g., 휴강 *hyukang* 'class cancelation,' 과방 *kwapang* 'room for students of the program,' 교실 예절 *kyosil yeycel* 'classroom etiquette,'

선후배 관계 *senhwupay kwankyey* 'senior–junior relationship,' 음주문화 *umcwumwunhwa* 'drinking culture,' and 취업준비 *chwiepcwunpi* 'preparation for employment.'

Conceptualizing KAP learners as members of a CoP entails beneficial opportunities for learners to understand the shared cultural norms and values they might not otherwise become aware of and consider to learn. It also helps the instructor create a learner-oriented and collaborative learning environment by allowing learners to share their own experiences and existing knowledge.

Assessment

Assessment is worth discussing because it is an indispensable component of a KAP curriculum. After all, learners in a KAP course usually receive grades based on their performance and achievement. In KAP, assessment is used to evaluate the learner's academic achievement and readiness for admission and determine his/her placement into a course. Assessment also serves as an essential tool for instructors because it helps them make informed decisions about their pedagogy. Arguably, there is no assessment method that is widely agreed upon in terms of reliability and validity, probably because what to test and how to test can vary to a great extent depending on numerous variables, such as learning objectives, learner characteristics, teaching materials, the instructor's philosophy, institutional policy, and so on. Ways of analyzing test results also generally vary along different dimensions, such as usage (formative vs. summative assessment) and test type (diagnostic vs. achievement assessment). Note that "even language experts disagree wildly about what a task or item is testing or how difficult it is" (Douglas, 2000, p. 253). However, there exist several studies that specify a particular set of tasks or situations in which the targeted skills are used.

First, there is a broad consensus that what is being tested must be connected to the learners' needs and learning objectives. For example, deriving from previous research on speaking assessment in KAP, Min and Lee (2016) identified constructs to be measured in KAP, including, among others, discourse, pragmatic and sociolinguistic ability, vocabulary and grammar, pronunciation and intonation, strategic competence, interactional competence, and thinking skills (p. 90). In a later study, Min et al. (2017) narrowed the scope and grouped these constructs to three functional abilities for assessing speaking ability in the order of cognitive load: narration (telling past experiences), explanation (comparing, describing, summarizing), and persuasion (stating and supporting opinion). The researchers then administered a pilot test to confirm the reliability and compatibility of their test. The results showed a significant correlation between the learners' TOPIK score and their performance on the pilot test, which, in their opinion, warranted the use of the test.

Kim and Pak (2014) developed a computer-based test consisting of a set of "tasks" to assess speaking and examined whether the task types were suitable for assessing KAP learners' speaking abilities. The researchers developed three tasks to test essential academic abilities to study at a Korean college: (1) listening to a lecture and talking about it, (2) presenting an opinion in a discussion, and (3) making a presentation. They included an additional task, reciting, to measure accuracy in pronunciation, although acknowledging the task's limitation in measuring speaking ability. The results showed that using only two of the four tasks could still discern different performance levels.

Persuasive speaking seems to be an integral part of academic success. However, articulating and supporting one's opinion and effectively making counterarguments is not an easy task. Lee (2016) offers a specification for testing persuasive speaking: linguistic ability (vocabulary, grammar, and pronunciation), discourse ability (content and organization), and sociolinguistic ability (register and politeness), based on the evaluation criteria of such standardized speaking tests as the ACTFL's Oral Proficiency Interview (OPI) and TOEFL Speaking.

As discussed earlier, attaining academic literacies requires a higher level of thinking skills and knowledge about the CoP, far more than the mere production of comprehensible language and source comprehension on the surface level. Therefore, KAP learners often experience tremendous challenges with articulating and organizing ideas in a written mode to succeed in their studies. Y. O. Lee (2017) identified the types of descriptive questions suitable for academic purposes, which enables evaluation of thinking skills as well, such as problem-solving, critiquing, and evaluating:

> Comparing/contrasting (finding pros and cons)
> Presenting opinion on the given topic
> Offering a solution (for a hypothetical situation)
> Persuasive writing (argumentative essays/debates)
> Storytelling
> Reading and re-writing/listening and writing (summarizing)
> Finding information
> Describing and predicting a graph/picture
> Imagining and writing (creative writing)
> Document writing in an appropriate form (resumé, personal statement, thesis proposal)
> Term papers (literature review, research paper, laboratory observation report)
> Summarizing news articles
> Writing thesis statements
> Analyzing and summarizing data
> Writing speculations/predictions
> Essays, movie critique, columns
> Public notices (event promotions, job announcements, notices of lost items)

The researcher then examined writing questions of the TOPIK and found that controlled and structured items, such as filling in the blanks and sentence construction using the given words, which were mostly intermediate-level questions, were not appropriate for academic purposes. Based on the results, the researcher proposed four types of process-oriented writing questions that could measure academic writing ability: (1) reading a written input and writing opinion based on the pros and cons identified by the reader; (2) reading a news article and writing a public service announcement based on the position expressed in the news article; (3) looking at a series of pictures and completing a story by predicting and inferencing, and writing why; and (4) reading a community campaign and categorizing information according to its types, such as significance, solution, and effects.

There are specific genres that occur prevalently in academia, and some researchers believe those genres must be included in the test construct. In particular, S.-S. Kim (2011) observed that KAP learners found it most difficult to write term papers in their major studies, especially with organizing the discourse in a logical manner. According to Kim, general purpose Korean language courses focus on reducing errors with sentence structures and vocabulary. KAP assessment, however, should focus on the functional ability to perform the given task to ensure the validity of the assessment. Kim (2013) agreed and developed a task that could adequately evaluate KAP learners' academic competence in writing term papers. The developed task consisted of four steps: (1) reading two contrasting opinion pieces on the same topic, (2) identifying the thesis statements, (3) planning the paper, and (4) writing one's own opinion, citing the input effectively. The test was administered to a total of 53 KAP learners, and their responses were rated by 9 raters, including instructors and writing coaches. Results showed that the lowest-scoring paper had neither logical structure nor critical analysis of the subject, let alone lexical accuracy and stylistic appropriateness. It also disregarded basic academic writing rules, such as paragraph indentation and citation. The researcher argued that KAP learners need to learn the writing rules of the academic genre first. Similarly, Jang and Park (2018) also found that professors mostly pointed out their students' lack of knowledge about source citation as the most problematic area in writing term papers.

Conclusion

In South Korea, the 2000s and 2010s witnessed an exponential increase in the number of learners and research interest in KSP as Korea's economic power and geopolitical significance continue to grow. However, as shown thus far, the scope and quantity of research on KSP differ markedly between KSL and KFL research. Findings of KSL research may be unapplicable and unsatisfactory to KFL researchers who desperately seek ways to establish a new KSP curriculum that will work and sustain in a KFL setting unique to English-speaking students. Nevertheless, KSL studies offer a good account of how KSP differs from KGP and how it should be implemented. To briefly recapitulate some of the significant findings discussed so far, a needs analysis seems to be the necessary first step in developing a KSP curriculum to address the learners' specific needs and goals. In designing a syllabus, both linguistic specificity and subject specificity must be taken into account. Linguistic specificity refers to lexical elements like technical language and jargon, and syntactic and phonological characteristics, which constitutes a particular register. Also, an integrated approach seems to be particularly useful in KSP education because it equips learners with functional abilities required in the given context. In assessing KSP, it is important to consider "authenticity" to measure the ability to function competently in the given situation. In other words, what is being tested should be "authentically representative of that situation" and appropriate language use in situ (Douglas, 2000, p. 7).

In North America, KSP has just begun to show its presence. A good number of institutions now offer business Korean, and we can also find some organized, institutional efforts to promote business Korean education. For example, with research funding from the U.S. Department of Education, the Center for International Business Education and Research at George Mason University has held annual workshops exclusively dedicated to promoting business Korean education to empower students in the global economy since 2010. The Korean Language Flagship Center at the University of Hawai'i has offered a comprehensive KSP program to produce Korean specialists in a variety of academic and professional fields since 2002, funded by the U.S. Department of Defense (http://koreanflagship.manoa.hawaii.edu/). The Department of East Asian Languages and Civilizations of Harvard University is in the process of establishing a KAP curriculum, not only to promote the advancement of students' language proficiency and enrich their knowledge of Korean studies but to "directly connect and link the language program to the specific content of Korean studies classes available at Harvard" (Kim, 2020). The Korean Language Program at Columbia University offers GR 8010 Advanced Korean in Mixed Script in alternate years for graduate students in Korean Studies who need to read and discuss classical Korean texts, including *hanja*, Chinese characters.

Developing and implementing a KSP curriculum, however, face several challenges. As Kim (2020) and many other Korean educators note, there is virtually no connection or collaboration between Korean language educators and Korean Studies experts, either within a department or across departments. For example, due to the specialty and exclusiveness of the field of medicine, it is not always accessible for Korean educators to approach an expert in the field and acquire the content knowledge or even help with the content knowledge. This further implicates hardship with faculty training and professional development. Even when there are institutional support and resources, such as in-house workshops and funding to attend specialist conferences, language teachers' working hours and responsibilities often extend beyond their designated teaching load, preventing them from investing in developing and maintaining a new curriculum.

Also, it is often unpractical to offer a KSP course other than 'less specific' Business Korean or Academic Korean in a college setting because student enrollment and hiring and retainment of the specialized instructor are not always guaranteed. Many KSP courses are taught by part-time instructors or graduate students of the major, who often have less than desirable teaching experience and training. Moreover, it is infeasible to tailor the curriculum to every specific characteristic and need of individual learners. For example, just looking at Korean for Interpretation and Translation (KIT), there may be considerable differences in syllabi, instructional approaches, materials, etc. depending on whether it is for legal interpretation, medical interpretation, or literature translation.

Last, very little research has been conducted on KSP within the KFL context, and, thus, very little is known about KSP learning and teaching. In KAP, for example, many learners are, in fact, KGP students enrolled in the highest-level Korean course of the program, without any 'specific' purpose of making use of their Korean in mind other than advancing their language proficiency. Confusion does exist among researchers as well. For example, Park (2008) voices his concern that it is futile to differentiate KSP, especially KAP, from KGP because the demands and needs of Korean language learners are continually fluctuating and changing depending on their situations and fast-changing social environments. Some confuse content-based courses (e.g., an advanced Korean course using literature) with KAP courses (e.g., an advanced language course to study Korean literature). The critical difference between the two lies in the fact that the former teaches language skills, which are generally transferable to any other areas, whereas the latter teaches skills that can be used only in the specific and predetermined area.

Despite these challenges, however, the chapter concludes on some positive notes by shedding light on future directions for KSP education. First of all, developing a KOP curriculum may contribute to maintaining student enrollment in Korean. During the last decade, there has been a noticeable demographic shift in the learner population. Due to the immense popularity of K-pop and Korea-related cultural products, non-heritage students account for an increasing proportion, especially in lower-level classes. However, with their ultimate attainment level typically being only an intermediate level, it is difficult to expect them to acquire sufficient proficiency to take a KSP course before graduation, not unless they start taking Korean from their freshman year. Incorporating KSP into the existing language curriculum may motivate students to start learning Korean early on by encouraging them to invest in Korean not just for fun but for a tangible, utilizable outcome. At the same time, KSP can also provide unique opportunities for heritage learners, whose linguistic resources and cultural literacy allow them to reach an advanced level in a relatively shorter time. In this respect, KSP courses will serve this new 'clientele' in Korean language education and support their life-long learning and use of Korean beyond the classroom.

Furthermore, research on KSP will increase recognition of KFL in the broader field of foreign language education by contributing to a broader and deeper research base for LSP. Most of the existing research consists of KSL studies published in Korean-language journals, and their research topics are still limited to the survey of current status, textbooks analysis, and syllabus construction. There is an urgent need for more theoretically grounded and empirically based KSP research, for better understandings of learning processes, factors affecting the learning process, acquisitional issues, and effective pedagogical interventions. Also, more research on KSP is called for to understand effective assessment methods to bridge a gap between what is taught in the classroom and what learners are expected to do in the real world, maintaining a balance between general language knowledge and specific language use.

Finally, KSP shares many benefits with CBI, a long- and well-established pedagogical approach, in that "the integration of language and content across disciplines" can indeed "elevate the value of language education in academia" (Park, Choi, & Ko, 2021, p. 36). KSP instruction is exceptionally beneficial for developing critical academic abilities, as well as an advanced level of language proficiency and content knowledge, by facilitating critical thinking, problem-solving, and collaborative skills. As Long (2017) points out, by decentralizing the literature focus in a foreign language department, establishing a KSP curriculum will lead to a more well-rounded Korean language program capable of addressing students' real-world needs. In just the same way, KSP well addresses "the need to prepare students by enabling them to gain high-level language and cross-cultural communication proficiency that will serve them both professionally and personally in the global environment of the twenty-first century" (Long, 2017, p. 1).

In sum, KSP offers exciting times and opportunities in KFL education and research. A well-motivated and carefully designed KSP curriculum has tremendous potential to transform the Korean language program to produce educated speakers of Korean who have "deep translingual and transcultural competence" (MLA, 2007). For this reason, KSP surely deserves a recognized place in KFL education.

Note

1 Park (2008) argues against the separate treatment of KAP from KGP in that learners' needs and goals often overlap, especially in a KSL setting (e.g., female immigrants learning Korean to communicate with their new family and to learn the particular dialect used by the family). In this chapter, KAP is discussed separately, and KSP for immigrants is excluded from discussion since most users of this edited book are KFL educators and researchers.

References

Ahn, M., & Choe, J.-S. (2007). Specific purpose language competence and its description. *Journal of Korean Language Education*, *18*(1), 201–228.

An, H. (2020). A study on the perception of professional missions through Korean education. *The Journal of Humanities and Social Science*, *11*(2), 2163–2176.

Bowles, H. (2012). Analyzing languages for specific purposes discourse. *The Modern Language Journal*, *96*(Focus Issue), 43–58.

Brindley, G. (1989). The role of needs analysis in adult ESL programme design. In R. K. Johnson (Ed.), *The second language curriculum* (pp. 63–78). Cambridge: Cambridge University Press.

Byon, A. S. (2001). Developing a business Korean course based on a systematic approach. *Korean Language in America*, *6*, 153–172.

Cho, H. (2020, October 24). *Fostering interdisciplinary connections: The case of business Korean curriculum development* [Virtual presentation]. Bridging Language and Content: Making Interdisciplinary Connections in Higher Education. Yale University. Retrieved from http://ceas.yale.edu/events.

Cho, H., Cho, Y. Y., Chun, H. C., Ko, K., & Lee, H. (2020). Meeting local challenges in KFL program building in the era of expansion. In *Workshop at the annual AATK conference*. Columbia University, Virtual Workshop, June 19, 2020.

Cho, Y. Y., & Chun, H. C. (2016). College-level Korean for Specific Purposes (KSP): A curriculum proposal for professional Korean. In *Proceedings of the annual conference of the International Association for Korean Language Education* (pp. 175–187). Seoul, Korea: IAKLE.

Cho, Y. Y., Lee, A., & Wang, H.-S. (2021). KFL program building and professional development. In Y. Y. Cho (Ed.), *Teaching Korean as a foreign language: Theories and practices* (pp. 169–193). Oxon and New York: Routledge.

Cho, Y., Lee, J., & Min, J. (2019). Analysis of research trends of Korean for academic purposes: Focusing on Korean as general education. *The Journal of General Education, 10*, 259–284.

Choe, J.-S. (2006). Curriculum development and assessment in Korean for academic purposes. *Bilingual Research, 31*, 277–314.

Choe, J.-S., & Yoon, J.-W. (2012). Actual condition and suggestions in Korean education for academic purposes through analysis of trends in education research. *Eomunyeongu, 74*, 131–156.

Choi, Y. (2018). Into the Dragons' Den: Practicing KFL business communication skills through project-based learning. *Korean Language in America, 22*(2), 190–200.

Chun, H. C. (2015). Developing business Korean curriculum for advanced learners in an American university. In J. Trace, T. Hudson, & J. D. Brown (Eds.), *Developing courses in languages for specific purposes* (pp. 89–100). (NetWork #69) [PDF document]. Honolulu: University of Hawai'i. Retrieved from http://hdl.handle.net/10125/14573.

Douglas, D. (2000). *Assessing languages for specific purposes*. New York: Cambridge University Press.

Dudley-Evans, T., & St. John, M. J. (1998). *Development in ESP: A multi-disciplinary approach*. Cambridge: Cambridge University Press.

Fryer, T. B. (2012). Languages for specific purposes business curriculum creation and implementation in the United States. *Modern Language Journal, 96*(Focus Issue), 122–139.

Grosse, C., & Voght, G. (1991). The evolution of language for specific purposes in the United States. *Modern Language Journal, 75*, 181–195.

Ha, S., & Lee, M.-H. (2013). Genre analysis of Korean self-introduction letter. *Language Facts and Perspectives, 32*, 173–199.

Hahm, I. K. (2009). Study of Korean business writing: Analysis of business documents and its application to Korean language education. *The Language and Culture, 5*(2), 249–266.

Hong, S. Y. (2017). Suggesting a teaching method for enhancing student interpreters' Korean. *Korean Journal of Rhetoric, 28*(4), 159–184.

Hyun, Y.-H. (2016). Current state and challenges of military Korean language education: Focusing on Korean language education for foreign forces in the Korea Defense Language Institute (KDLI). In *Proceedings of the International Association for Korean Language Education* (pp. 117–133). Seoul, Korea: IAKLE.

Jang, H. (2017). An analysis of contents of education in reading in textbooks for KAP. *Journal of Korean Language Education, 157*, 341–374.

Jang, K. (2020). A Study on the research trend of Korean language education for occupational purpose: Focusing on the language network analysis. *Language and Culture, 16*(2), 135–156.

Jang, M., & Park, J.-E. (2018). A Study on the report assessment patterns of international undergraduate students and instructors. *Journal of Korean Language Education, 29*(3), 293–324.

Johns, A. M. (2006). Languages for specific purposes: Pedagogy. In K. Brown (Ed.), *Encyclopedia of language and linguistics* (pp. 684–690). Amsterdam: Elsevier.

Jung, J.-Y., & Cho, Y. Y. (2011). An integrated approach to the teaching of business Korean. *Korean Language in America, 16*, 1–40.

Jung, M. (2003). A study for designing of syllabus of business Korean. *Journal of Korean Language Education, 14*(2), 403–421.

Jung, M.-J. (2016). Reconsideration of syllabus and level description of advanced Korean course for learners with general purposes: Based on needs analysis of Korean learners. *Journal of Ewha Korean Language and Literature, 39*, 137–159.

Kang, S. (2019). A Study on the development of campus life-based cultural educational materials for those learning the Korean language for academic purpose. *Journal of Literary Creative Writing, 18*(3), 203–252.

Kim, B. (2019). Content-based instruction in intermediate-level Korean for specific purposes. *Bilingual Research, 74*, 1–29.

Kim, C. (1998). Considering on curriculum and teaching methodology for intermediate business Korean. *Korean Language in America, 3*, 283–295.

Kim, D.-Y. (2020). A study on the differentiation between the general purpose Korean textbooks and the academic purpose Korean textbooks: Focusing on text topics, text types, reading activities. *Bilingual Research, 79*, 1–24.

Kim, G. (2011). *A study on the teaching and learning of e-mail requests in Korean: Focusing on the speech act of requests by advanced learners* [Unpublished master's thesis]. Seoul, South Korea: Seoul National University.

Kim, H. (2012). *Needs analysis for designing the curriculum for web-based business Korean – focusing on learner support function* [Unpublished MA thesis]. Ewha Womans University.

Kim, H. (2016). Need analysis for designing curriculum of Korean language for medical tourism. *Journal of Korean Language Education, 27*(4), 1–34.

Kim, H., Kang, S., Hong, Y., Han, S., & Park, S. (2018). Research of developing textbooks for business Korean in King Sejong Institute. *Journal of Korean Language Education, 29*(3), 83–115.

Kim, H.-S. H. (2020, October 24). *Building Korean for academic purposes into KFL curriculum* [Virtual presentation]. Bridging Language and Content: Making Interdisciplinary Connections in Higher Education. Yale University. Retrieved from http://ceas.yale.edu/events.

Kim, J.-E. (2018). Investigating the learning needs of second language learners in the context of Korean for academic purposes. *Studies in Foreign Language Education, 32*(4), 373–394.

Kim, J.-Y. (2007). A study on the project work integrating term-paper writing and presentation in advanced level KAP learners. *Journal of Korean Language Education, 18*(2), 49–79.

Kim, S. (2007). *A study on reading education in Korean for occupational purposes for diplomats: focusing on English-speaking diplomats* [Unpublished master's thesis]. Seoul, Korea: Korea University.

Kim, S., & Pak, D. (2014). A study of the type of speaking assessment tasks for Korean for academic purpose: Focused on the application of the multi facets rasch model and the generalizability theory. *Korean Education, 100*, 115–141.

Kim, S.-S. (2011). Analysis of error sources and estimation of reliability in an analytic evaluation on writing ability for academic purpose Korean by applying Generalizability Theory. *Journal of Korean Language Education, 22*(3), 29–48.

Kim, S.-S. (2013). A study on the evaluating the Korean writing proficiency for academic purpose: Focused on the report writing tasks. *Journal of Korean Language Education, 24*(2), 57–80.

Kim, Y. (2014). *A study on the teaching of e-mail writing for learners of Korean for academic purposes: Focusing on the use of politeness expressions* [Unpublished master's thesis]. Seoul, South Korea: Sejong University.

Kim, Y. (2015). A study on the method of Korean education for academic purposes using interview. *Minjok Yeonku, 64*(Special Issue), 24–44.

Ko, Y. (2014). A study on the Korean learning strategies of missionaries. *Journal of Learner-Centered Curriculum and Instruction, 14*(5), 231–259.

Ku, M.-J. (2012). A study of analysis of comprehension questions in teaching Korean reading: Focused on the comprehension questions in the Korean reading materials for academic purpose. *Korean Education, 92*, 495–522.

Lee, E.-H. (2019). Case study of 'lecture-listening and note-taking' as an integrated activity of listening and writing: On the notes of undergraduate foreign students. *Korean Language Research, 51*, 185–213.

Lee, H. Y. (2004). Research on course design of Korean for academic purposes. *Journal of Korean Language Education, 15*(1), 137–164.

Lee, I. (2016). KAP learners' performance on an integrated reading-listening-writing task. *Journal of Korean Language Education, 27*(4), 189–217.

Lee, J. (2005). *Syllabus development for Korean academic writing: On essay composition* [Unpublished doctoral dissertation]. Seoul, Korea: Korea University.

Lee, J. (2009). Assessing thinking skills for KAP Learners. *Journal of Korean Language Education, 20*(2), 175–201.

Lee, J. (2011). The study on reading-to-write task for KAP learners. *Journal of Korean Language Education, 22*(4), 83–108.

Lee, J. (2016). A study of the development of persuasive speaking assessment tool. *The Journal of Linguistic Science, 76*, 233–266.

Lee, J.-Y. (2017). A study on the debate expressions in the Korean language textbooks for academic purposes. *Studies in Foreign Language Education, 31*(3), 227–253.

Lee, K. (2016). A Study on academic Korean ability improvement based on news tasks. *Journal of Bangyo Language and Literature, 42*, 389–418.

Lee, M. (2012). A Study on the course design of KIT (Korean Interpretation and Translation) for foreigners. *Journal of Korean Language Education, 23*(4), 233–259.

Lee, M.-H. (2003). Research on Korean for occupational purposes: Examination of the current state of the education and the development of business Korean. *Journal of Korean Language Education, 14*(2), 227–256.

Lee, M.-H. (2008). The current state and issues of Korea's occupational Korean language education. *Journal of Korean Language Education, 19*(3), 321–347.

Lee, S. (2014). A study on e-mail writing training for learners of Korean for business purposes: Based on the analysis of e-mail requests in Korean. *The Linguistic Society of Korea, 6*, 1–9.

Lee, Y. (2009). The present state and challenges of Korean language education for diplomats. *International Society of Korean Language and Literature, 4*, 123–154.

Lee, Y. (2011). Direction of 'ethical writing' education for KAP learners. *Bilingual Research, 45*, 167–188.

Lee, Y. (2016). A study on the method of improving skills for academic Korean listening: Focus on using YouTube to improve skill in listening to lectures. *The Journal of Language and Literature, 67*, 333–372.

Lee, Y. O. (2017). A study of development for the types of questions in A-TOPIK: On the focus of the writing section. *Korean Education, 97*, 495–522.

Lim, B.-J. (2002). The use of the internet resources to teach business Korean. *Korean Language in America, 7*, 79–87.

Long, M. K. (2017). Introduction: LSP studies and the creation of translingual and transcultural competence. In M. K. Long (Ed.), *Languages for specific purposes: Trends in curriculum development* (pp. 1–11). Washington, DC: Georgetown University Press.

Long, M. K., & Uscinski, I. (2012). Evolution of languages for specific purposes programs in the United States: 1990–2011. *Modern Language Journal, 96*(Focus Issue), 173–189.

Min, B., Cho, S.-J., Hong, E., Park, H.-J., Kang, S.-H., . . . & Ahn, H. (2017). Developing a Korean speaking test for academic purposes. *Journal of Korean Language Education, 157*, 309–340.

Min, B., & Lee, S. (2016). Issues in the development of Korean speaking test for academic purpose. *Journal of Korean Language and Literature Education, 38*, 67–110.

Modern Language Association. (2007). *Foreign language and higher education: New structures for a changed world.* Retrieved October 30, 2020, from www.mla.org/Resources/Research/Surveys-Reports-and-Other-Documents/Teaching-Enrollments-and-Programs/Foreign-Languages-and-Higher-Education-New-Structures-for-a-Changed-World.

Modern Language Association. (2008). *Language study in the age of globalization: The college-level experience.* Retrieved October 11, 2020, from www.mla.org/content/download/2804/79570/ADFL%20 College%20Brochure.pdf.

Modern Language Association. (2016). *Enrollments in languages other than English in United States institutions of higher education.* Retrieved May 3, 2020, from www.mla.org/content/download/110154/2406932/2016-Enrollments-Final-Report.pdf.

Oh, K. S. (2011). The instruction of Korean language and culture in teaching email writing for advanced KFL Learners. *Urimal, 29*, 393–416.

Park, H.-H. (2011). A study of post-reading activities in Korean textbooks for the academic purpose. *Korean Education, 88*, 171–192.

Park, M.-J., Choi, B., & Ko, S. (2021). Pedagogical approaches and practices in teaching Korean. In Y. Y. Cho (Ed.), *Teaching Korean as a foreign language: Theories and practices* (pp. 24–53). Oxon and New York: Routledge.

Park, N. (2016). A study on writing critique in KAP textbooks. *The Journal of Literary Creative Writing, 15*(1), 239–265.

Park, S.-J. (2008). Analysis on the present condition of teaching Korean for academic purpose in domestic universities. *Journal of Korean Language Education, 19*(3), 169–200.

Sánchez-López, Long, M. K., & Lafford, B. A. (2017). New directions in LSP research in US higher education. In M. K. Long (Ed.), *Language for specific purposes: Trends in curriculum development* (pp. 13–34). Washington, DC: Georgetown University Press.

Seo, A.-R., & Ahn, K.-J. (2019). An analysis of the research trend of Korean writing education for academic purposes. *Studies in Foreign Language Education, 33*(4), 83–119.

Seo, J.-S., & Lee, J.-H. (2018). A study on domestic medical environment for Korean education for specific purposes of Saudi Arabia dental staff: Focused on the recognition of domestic dental medical staff. *Korean Thought and Culture, 92*, 305–333.

Seo, Y.-J. (2020). An error analysis of Korean tourism signage in Japan. *Journal of Korean Culture Industry, 20*(2), 11–21.

Shin, S.-Y., & Lee, H. S. (2021). Korean language assessment. In Y. Y. Cho (Ed.), *Teaching Korean as a foreign language: Theories and practices* (pp. 147–168). Oxon and New York: Routledge.

Son, D.-J., & Jang, M.-J. (2013). Trends in research of Korean writing education for academic purpose. *Journal of Language and Literature*, *56*, 431–457.

Song, K. (2016). Current state and challenge of military Korean language education: Focusing on Korean language education for foreign forces in the Korea Defense Language Institute (KDLI) – Discussion paper. In *Proceedings of the International Association for Korean Language Education* (pp. 134–135). Seoul, Korea: IAKLE.

Sung, J. B. (2015). Korean for specific purpose program for students of hospitality. In J. Trace, T. Hudson, & J. D. Brown (Eds.), *Developing courses in languages for specific purposes* (pp. 253–270). (NetWork #69) [PDF document]. Honolulu, HI: University of Hawai'i. Retrieved from http://hdl.handle.net/10125/14573.

Swales, J. M. (2000). Languages for specific purposes. *Annual Review of Applied Linguistics*, *20*, 59–76.

Trace, T. (2015). Looking ahead in language for specific purposes. In J. Trace, T. Hudson, & J. D. Brown (Eds.), *Developing courses in language for specific purposes* (pp. 196–211). Retrieved from http://hdl.handle.net/10125/14573.

Yoon, C. (2020). A proposal for designing a textbook on thesis writing for international students at Korean graduate schools. *Language and Culture*, *16*(3), 235–259.

Yoon, Y. (2015). Curriculum development of Korean language for diplomacy. In J. Trace, T. Hudson, & J. D. Brown (Eds.), *Developing courses in languages for specific purposes* (pp. 89–100). (NetWork #69) [PDF document]. Honolulu, HI: University of Hawai'i. Retrieved from http://hdl.handle.net/10125/14573.

12
CONTENT-BASED INSTRUCTION IN KSL SETTINGS

Sang-Keun Shin

Introduction

Content is not the main teaching goal in most foreign language classrooms. Language courses are organized around linguistic criteria, such as grammar and communicative functions, and material writers select content materials that are comprehensible and interesting to all learners regardless of their academic and cultural backgrounds. This approach is not an issue when the learners are at the beginning or intermediate level. However, in a Korean as a second language (KSL) setting that includes advanced-level learners with a specific career path, this conventional approach is limited because their Korean language needs are not being fully met. A student majoring in biology will believe, for instance, that reading about genes rather than popular culture or dispersed families is more fitting for her or his eventual language uses.

Content-based instruction (CBI) is a teaching method that concurrently conducts content and language instruction using content materials that correspond to the needs of students (Brinton, Snow, & Wesche, 2004; Stryker & Leaver, 1997). In CBI courses, content is a vehicle for language learning: students learn the target language as the by-product of content learning. Thus, language learning is not an end in itself but a means to an end.

A CBI Korean course for economics majors, Introduction to Economics, for example, helps students prepare for the language demands of academia by teaching academic language as well as economic theories. Specifically, as the students read the section on supply and demand in the course textbook, *Principles of Economics*, they learn about the economic model of supply and demand and practice their reading skills to understand the gist and detailed information in the academic texts. They take notes while listening to the instructor's lecture. They practice speaking while participating in presentations or class discussions and also ask questions about content materials. Lastly, the students engage in writing as they answer exercise questions and draft written assignments. They are also provided with ample opportunities to learn both general and discipline-specific academic vocabulary not only from the instructor's proactive teaching but also, incidentally, from being exposed to them. Grammar activities familiarize them with grammar structures that are typical of economics discourse, including using imperatives to express imaginary economic situations. Accordingly, students learn the target language in the context of studying their major. They are not taking a Korean language course to study economics in the future but to learn the Korean language throughout the process of studying economics. An optimal environment for language learning is created because students are involved in communicative activities in much the same way as real-life communication (Richards & Rodgers, 2014; Wesche & Skehan, 2002).

CBI programs, however, face many challenges: coordination with content instructors, recruiting and training language instructors with a certain level of content knowledge, the paucity of teaching materials, identifying and sequencing language elements to be taught, developing language activities tied to the content, severe time constraints, promoting its benefits to prospective students, etc. Despite these numerous challenges, CBI is regarded as an excellent teaching method that can meet learners' linguistic needs and increase their learning motivation.

The interest in CBI is increasing in Korean language programs (Cheon, 2007; Kang, 2012; Kim, 2005; Kim, 2017; Lee & Kim, 2008; Noji & Yuen, 2012; Park, Choi, & Ko, 2020; Shin & Kim, 2000; Wang, 2012). In 2012, an entire issue of *The Korean Language in America*, the flagship journal of the American Association of Teachers of Korean (AATK), was devoted to the topic of innovations in teaching advanced Korean. It featured several articles suggesting CBI as a curriculum that can satisfy the language needs of advanced learners. In 2014, the AATK held its 19th annual conference under the theme of 'Korean Language Teaching through Film and Literature: Creating Connections'.

Several Korean language education programs in US universities offer classes that combine Korean language study with content instruction on Korean culture, history, and society – mainly for heritage language learners. Meanwhile, interest in CBI is also increasing in Korea, primarily due to the changing demographics of the Korean language learner population. The number of foreign students in Korean universities has soared from 83,842 in 2010 to 160,165 in 2019. This dramatic increase indicates a dire need for Korean universities to open Korean courses for academic purposes (Korean Ministry of Education, 2019). This chapter first explores the definition and characteristics of CBI along with its strengths and weaknesses and then discusses the major CBI programs in the KSL setting. Finally, future directions for research and practice are presented.

Content-based instruction: theories and practices

Definition of content-based instruction

CBI is a teaching method that integrates content instruction and language instruction. Richards and Rodgers (2014) define CBI as "an approach to second language teaching in which teaching is organized around the content or information that students will acquire, rather than around a linguistic or other type of syllabus" (p. 204). In a similar vein, Brinton (2003) states that CBI refers to "the teaching of language through exposure to content that is interesting and relevant to learners" (p. 201). As these definitions imply, the CBI approach is considerably different from traditional approaches in which syllabi are built around linguistic structures or communicative functions. Unlike the traditional approach, CBI uses content as a springboard for language practice. Accordingly, content is selected first, and the language points are determined based on the selected content. Content learning is as important as the aim of language learning in CBI courses.

While the definition of CBI is succinct and clear, it is not clear at all where to draw the line between what is and what is not a CBI program. Content and language integration is translated into various formats to meet the needs of diverse learners across learning environments. It should be noted that CBI has been used in both a broad and narrow sense. In a broad sense, CBI is an umbrella term that refers to all programs in which content and language learning are integrated (Stoller & Fitzsimmons-Doolan, 2017). Met (1998), for example, classified CBI programs into several types depending on the extent to which content and language are integrated and placed them on a continuum from content-driven programs to language-driven programs. In addition to immersion programs (Met, 1998; Sohn & Merrill, 2008; Tedick, Jorgensen, & Geffert, 2001), CBI programs include the following: sustained-content language teaching (Pally, 2000); foreign language across the curriculum (FLAC) (Allen, Anderson, & Narváez, 1992; Crank & Loughrin-Sacco, 2001); the cognitive academic language learning approach (CALLA) (Chamot & O'Malley, 1986) and the genre-based approach (Morton, 2010; Wray & Lewis, 1996). Content language integrated learning (CLIL), which is widely implemented in secondary schools in Europe, is also often classified as a type of CBI because content subjects are taught and learned in a second language in CLIL classrooms (Cenoz, 2015).

Meanwhile, CBI in a narrow sense refers to a program that teaches language through content instruction and is intended for adult learners with a language proficiency above the threshold level and specific language learning purposes, such as career development and academic study. Therefore, programs in K–12 school setting, in which students learn several subjects in a target language, would not be categorized as CBI programs under the narrow definition of CBI. Immersion programs provide an environment that allows young learners who speak the same language to study multiple subjects, such as math, science, and history, in a target language. Because these programs often begin in kindergarten, their participants are often true beginners. CLIL is also similar to immersion because CLIL programs guide students to study several school subjects in a foreign language in secondary schools. While some researchers use the concepts CBI and CLIL interchangeably (Cenoz, Genesee, & Gorter, 2014), it cannot be treated as CBI in the narrow sense of the term.

Perhaps it is easier to tell which program is a CBI program by looking at the characteristics of non-CBI programs. In immersion or CLIL programs, subjects offered in the school curriculum are taught in the target language, whereas in CBI programs, content related to the learners' academic major or future career is selected and taught in the target language. Given that the regular curriculum is taught using the target language (L2) in immersion and CLIL classrooms, other classrooms in the same institution often conduct classes in the native language (L1). CBI is also distinguished from English medium instruction (EMI) because the latter involves major courses conducted in English without establishing specific language teaching goals. Language is neither taught nor assessed in EMI courses. In the narrow sense of a CBI course, on the other hand, language learning is just as important as content learning. This chapter deals with CBI in the narrow sense.

Models of CBI

There are various types of CBI courses, but such variety can be summarized in three prototype models: (1) adjunct, (2) sheltered, and (3) theme-based instruction courses. First, in the adjunct model, a content class and a language class are, respectively, offered at the same time and linked to each other. A content instructor teaches the major course, and a language instructor with a certain level of content knowledge provides language lessons, helping the students with challenging language elements. Cooperation between the two instructors is absolutely required because the language instructor must have a good understanding of what the learners found challenging in the major classes and what assignments were given to them as well as make sure that the two courses proceed at the same pace. Nevertheless, because the language instructor is not responsible for the learners' acquisition of content knowledge, this model is less burdensome to the language instructor than the sheltered instruction model. An example of adjunct courses is a summer program for freshmen students at the University of California, Los Angeles, in which English classes were linked to introductory courses for anthropology, computer science, geography, political science, psychology, and social science (Brinton, 1997; Brinton & Snow, 1988).

The second type of CBI is sheltered instruction courses – a model in which non-native learners are sheltered (or separated) from native-speaking students and are provided with linguistic scaffolding for content study. Sheltered courses are commonly taught by a content instructor. If there are not sufficiently large numbers of non-native students, content instructors often provide language support either before or after each content lecture. In sheltered instruction, without curtailing the core content, instructors provide linguistic accommodations to non-native students, such as explaining the learning content using shorter sentences, easier grammar, or simpler vocabulary than the original to make the content more approachable. The instructor constantly monitors student learning and adjusts class activities or assignments to accommodate their language needs. The instructor also covers linguistic elements frequently employed in the major (Brinton, 2003). Students feel less self-conscious when asking questions and are far more willing to seek help because sheltered courses are attended only by non-native students. An example of sheltered instruction is the introductory psychology course offered only to second language learners at the University of Ottawa, Canada (Burger, 1989). Language assistance was provided to students before or after class to help them understand the major content covered in the class.

The last model is theme-based instruction courses, which are organized around a theme that is of interest to the learners. In most cases, a language teacher oversees a theme-based course. A class consists of several topics that explore the theme from various perspectives. This model may be considered a weaker version of CBI because its content is not as discipline specific as that of the adjunct or sheltered model. However, it is the most widely adopted model because of its relative ease of implementation compared with the previous two models (Benesch, 1988; Stoller & Grabe, 1997). The language instructor in charge of this course still has the burden of developing teaching materials by analyzing the needs of students, deciding on a theme that satisfies their needs, and selecting a few topics linked to the theme. Courses such as Korean Proficiency through Film, offered at the University of Hawai'I, or Korean Modern History, offered at Duke University, are good examples of the theme-based model. Altogether, these three models are the most typical CBI models, but they are implemented in various ways depending on the nature and context of the program.

Strengths of CBI

Allowing learners to study the target language while learning the content relevant to their needs, CBI provides varied affordances to promote target language learning. First, language learning is more successful when language is used as a vehicle to understand content than when learning it for its own sake (Genesee, 1991; Richards & Rogers, 2014). CBI creates an optimal environment for language learning because it facilitates learners to use language to communicate real information about the content of their interest or discipline. Moreover, students are better equipped to apply what they have learned to real-life situations because classroom tasks mirror target language use tasks.

The motivation for learning Korean is also increased in CBI classrooms. Learners are motivated to learn a language when they feel that their use of the language fits their needs (Larsen-Freeman, 2000). CBI courses allow them to improve their Korean while carrying on with their major studies, and the opportunity to earn credits and take major classes while receiving assistance with Korean is an extremely attractive option. Eventually, their transition to regular mainstream classes will be facilitated because the academic language and academic skills they have acquired in CBI courses will definitely help them rapidly adjust to content courses.

Furthermore, language learning through content learning is appropriate for the cognitive level of adult learners. Adult learners have greater cognitive capabilities and conceptual complexity than young learners (Robinson, 2005). They need a learning approach that is different from that applied to young language learners enrolled in primary and secondary schools because they must use or might already be using Korean as L2 for academic and professional purposes. Making adult learners practice language with content suitable for young learners with attention only given to linguistic complexity would not be a desirable practice. Content-based instruction is an optimal teaching method for adult learners since they can learn Korean while performing cognitively demanding language tasks.

Finally, CBI provides a good opportunity to learn the academic language in the context of content learning. Learners in a regular language class will learn isolated language items, whereas learners in a CBI classroom will learn a language in a relevant and purposeful context. CBI enables learners to learn both content-obligatory language that meets discipline-specific language demands and content-compatible language that is difficult to learn in everyday life but can be acquired while studying in a classroom (Snow, Met, & Genesee, 1989). In CBI classrooms, learners are exposed to academic language and are also given ample opportunities to hone their academic study skills, such as notetaking, summarizing, and extracting key information from texts to understand academic content, and give presentations related to the academic content. They also practice various genres of writing required in their discipline. CBI helps them familiarize themselves with academic language and the rhetorical structure required in the content domain. The CBI approach can be especially helpful for heritage language learners who have relatively poor cognitive academic language proficiency compared to basic interpersonal communication skills (Cummins, 1984; Richards & Rodgers, 2014).

Caveats for CBI

Given that there is no teaching method that is suitable for all situations or teaching purposes (Kumaravadivelu, 2001; Nunan, 1991), several limitations or drawbacks must be considered when implementing CBI. First, one of the drawbacks of CBI is that language teaching may not take place systematically. CBI seeks to foster second language competence with relevant discipline-related content, and instructors often put their utmost priority on teaching the academic content, which may lead to their failure to systematically attend to language. A number of research results indicate that immersion programs and sheltered CBI programs often do not provide linguistic scaffolding but only teach content, which could result because most subject teachers have not been trained on how to help language learners. They often believe that an additional focus on language is beyond their expertise and responsibility. As Lyster (2007) points out, it would be unnecessary to open a CBI course unless language learning is as important as content learning. If acquiring knowledge in a specific discipline is the only goal, then major courses would suffice. To ensure that language learning takes place properly alongside content learning, overt and explicit attention to language is critical. It is a daunting task, however, to deal with discipline-specific language needs because there is an overall lack of research on ways to teach the content while accommodating the linguistic challenges of second language learners (Lightbown, 2014; Stoller & Grabe, 1997; Swain & Lapkin, 1989).

Another drawback of CBI in terms of language instruction is that students may be exposed to language expressions limited to those identified in a particular content domain. Language elements in content materials may not be recycled as systematically as in language teaching materials. Moreover, language instruction in CBI classrooms presents huge challenges to instructors. Instructors must select language items to be taught from the content materials, sequence them, and present them in conjunction with the content. In most cases, there are no guidelines about what to teach, how to teach, and in what order. In addition to vocabularies or expressions that students might find challenging, instructors must also consider discipline-specific language and academic language.

CBI courses rely heavily on authentic materials, and it is not always easy to find content materials suitable for the language level of students. Theme-based programs do not use published course textbooks, and it is time-consuming to find content materials that are appropriate for the learners' language level and that are suitable for their interests, course expectations, and cognitive needs.

Another problem with authentic materials is that there is an increased risk that CBI materials are not comprehensible input for language learners. In classes adopting the sheltered or adjunct CBI model, major course textbooks used for mainstream students should be used as the content materials, and these textbooks can be difficult for non-native speakers. Course materials produced for L1 speakers can be overwhelming even for advanced-level learners because the language is not controlled. Academic textbooks often present low-frequency words including jargon, and the text is neither simplified nor elaborated for L2 learners, as is often the case with language-learning materials. There is also a huge difference in the amount of input leaners must process. Usually, the reading passages in multi-skill course textbooks are no more than four to five pages long, but students are often required to read the whole chapter in CBI classrooms. Due to the drastic increase in the amount and difficulty of the input materials, students often feel overwhelmed and intimidated in the first few weeks of semester and consequently show increased anxiety levels (Cumming & Lyster, 2016; Wesche & Skehan, 2002).

Students' beliefs about language teaching and learning influence their perception of classroom activities and instructional settings (Cotterall, 1999), and CBI courses may not correspond to learners' beliefs about good language teaching. Because CBI courses cover content that can be cognitively demanding for students, a considerable portion of the class time is spent on studying the content, and students may get the impression that they are not properly learning the target language. Also, a CBI class has the risk of becoming a teacher-centered class as the length of the teacher's lecture increases. In some cases, L1 is used in some parts of the class to reduce the learners' language burden. However, the more L1 is used, the less time students are exposed to the target language.

Content-based instruction requires a substantial investment of time, energy, and resources by both teachers and programs. For adjunct or sheltered CBI classes, coordination is required between the language program and academic departments. It is not easy to seek cooperation from academic departments that do not see the benefits of developing a CBI course. In the case of theme-based CBI courses, the teacher must set a theme and develop materials for the classes. Therefore, various arrangements, including course releases, should be made at the program level. Furthermore, teacher education and continuing professional development opportunities are essential. In CBI classrooms, teachers wear two hats and thus need to move beyond their comfort zone: a content specialist who teaches the major subject and a language teacher who leads language learning. Even for an instructor who has a certain level of content knowledge, he or she may feel uncomfortable dealing with content with students pursuing that major (Cammarata, 2009; Kong, 2009). Teachers may also have difficulty accommodating the needs of language learners because they did not major in language teaching.

Notable examples of CBI-based Korean programs

The most commonly adopted CBI format in Korean language programs is using films or literary works in advanced-level classes. Introduced in Cheon (2007, 2012), the Korean Proficiency through Film course in the Korean program at the University of Hawai'i is a theme-based CBI course designed for learning Korean while studying Korean history, society, and culture, mainly with Korean films. Targeted for students who have taken the fourth-year advanced Korean language course, this course proceeds in different stages – from reviewing vocabulary, grammar, and content from previous classes to giving presentations, listening to lectures, reading short articles, and having group and wrapping-up discussions.

Wang (2012) suggested developing CBI courses that meet the demands of superior-level students, pointing out that most of the Korean language education programs are having trouble opening the fourth- and fifth-year classes due to a sharp drop in student enrollment after the third-year courses. She concluded that the theme-based CBI course was appropriate, noting that most of the programs running the fourth- and fifth-year Korean language courses use textbooks composed of various topics. She proposed a curriculum that extends over two semesters under the theme of 'conflict' and presented five stages of a teaching cycle consisting of warm ups, reading assigned materials, class discussion, studying vocabulary and expressions, and writing assignments. Lastly, she succinctly presented several challenges that need to be addressed by other Korean language education specialists who want to develop and run CBI courses.

The Korean language program at Duke University offers a theme-based curriculum, focusing on Korean culture, history, and society (Kim, 2011). From the second year, texts and assignments are gradually organized according to themes. For example, in the third year, the first-semester classes are organized around the topics of the evolution of *pansori* and the changes in food culture under the theme of tradition and modernity. The second-semester classes are based on four themes: housing and urban development, college entrance examination and academic cliques, military service and military culture, and migrant workers. The fourth-year classes deal with two major themes; the contemporary history of Korea and contemporary Korean literature. The contemporary Korean history class is limited in scope to the history of the 20th century and covers themes such as Japanese colonialism and colonial modernization, the Cold War and division of Korea, democratization, and industrialization. Content materials include history textbooks written in Korean, Korean history textbooks written in English, and films dealing with major historical situations. Before each class, students are required to read 4–5 pages of Korean text and 10–20 pages of English text as homework. They also engage in small group and whole class discussions on given topics based on the readings. Various language-learning opportunities are provided, including text summaries and film introductions, along with a term project.

The Korean Flagship program at the University of Hawai'i offers courses that combine Korean language learning with Korean culture learning (Cheon, 2012; Sohn, 2012). Despite their advanced-level proficiency, learners in the overseas program had trouble participating in class and understanding college lectures due to the lack of knowledge on Korean society, culture, and history. For these learners, Sohn and Cheon (2013) published a course textbook titled *Essentials of Korean Culture*, which covers various fields, such as Korean history, religion, philosophy, the educational system, language, literature, politics, economy, science and technology, performing arts, and sports.

Park (2018) developed an adjunct CBI course for Korean language learners majoring in engineering that concurrently implemented the Basic General Physics course and the Korean language classes that teach the vocabulary used in the course textbooks. To select the vocabulary to be taught, she first constructed a corpus with five textbooks. She then selected physics terms among the words extracted from the corpus based on the entries in the glossary of physics terms selected by the Physics Society of Korea. The final vocabulary words were selected after a content expert evaluated the importance of each content vocabulary. For each class session, the content instructor first explained the content in the textbook to the language instructor. The language teacher studied the material and then met with the content instructor and asked questions about any parts that were hard to understand. Subsequently, the teaching material for the language class was developed and reviewed by the content instructor for any errors and used for the Korean language class.

Future directions

Korean language education programs have so far focused on assisting true and false beginners to reach an advanced level, and these programs have achieved outstanding growth. Now, it is necessary to develop courses designed to foster superior-level speakers or for students learning Korean for special purposes. A few Korean language education programs in American universities offer fourth- and fifth-year classes for heritage learners as CBI courses. Most Korean language education programs affiliated with Korean universities offer superior-level courses under titles such as Research Class, Advanced Program, or Superior-Level Intensive Course. Still, more diverse courses must be developed. Specifically, Korean language courses must be created for marriage immigrants, students who want to further improve their Korean skills after taking advanced-level classes, international students who have come to study in a Korean university, and students who want to learn Korean for specific academic or career purposes (like those attending the Korean Flagship Overseas Program to become specialists on Korean security, diplomacy, or business). As discussed in this chapter, CBI is one of the best teaching methods for advanced- and superior-level learners.

The theme-based CBI is the easiest model applicable in the Korean language programs at universities' Asian language departments. This is because there is little need for language teachers to study the content, and they can implement the curriculum autonomously from the rest of the faculty. Even though a certain number of students must be secured to develop a curriculum that is tailored to their needs, there are often not many learners who can take the fourth- or fifth-year course. However, developing CBI courses might instead serve as a measure for securing students. As in the case of the French program at Ohio University (Vines, 1997), student demand may not be the driving force behind new course development, but course development may be the path to securing new Korean classes. When there was a drastic decrease in enrollment after students took beginner-level courses, this program was able to reverse the situation and successfully operate by developing six courses related to French journalism – targeting students majoring in journalism and telecommunications.

Meanwhile, adjunct CBI and sheltered CBI models seem appropriate for Korean language courses for international students offered in Korean universities. Adjunct and sheltered CBI courses cannot be implemented by a Korean language education program alone. Cooperation with a content department or college is essential. Korean programs need to make extensive effort to convince other program's academic staff, who often have little interest in language education and do not feel the need for an academic language intervention, about the benefits of CBI and to ensure their participation in the development of CBI courses.

To run CBI courses, it is essential to expand the role of Korean language teachers. Beyond the role of a teacher who facilitates students' Korean learning through student-centered activities, it is important to have them assume other roles as well, such as a curriculum developer who develops CBI courses that meet the needs of learners, a materials writer who creates textbooks and develops class materials, a researcher who identifies discipline-specific language demands, and a language tester who evaluates the outcome of CBI classes. Teachers also need to become CBI program advocates who will explain the necessity and excellence of CBI programs to content instructors. These Korean language teachers must also serve as consultants to content instructors, suggesting strategies and techniques for providing scaffolding for second language learners. It seems apparent that the whole process places a considerable burden on the teachers involved in CBI classes. Undoubtedly, they should be equipped with the necessary educational and professional background to successfully implement CBI courses, and thus professional development opportunities should be provided to both in-service and pre-service teachers.

As pointed out in the CBI drawbacks section, language instruction tends to be neglected in CBI (Stoller & Grabe, 1997). Many previous studies reported that teachers tend to focus more on content than on language in immersion and EMI classrooms. To make sure that this concern does not materialize in Korean language education programs, it is necessary to be more systematic in making plans for supporting the language development of learners (Bigelow, Dahlman, & Ranney, 2006; Genesee, 1991; Lyster, 2007).

To ensure that instructors and students do not neglect language learning, CBI courses must clearly specify language learning objectives as well as content objectives (Larsen-Freeman, 2000; Lyster, 2011). Even though learners are exposed to the target language through various authentic input in CBI classes, exposure alone does not guarantee successful second language acquisition. Students should be provided with opportunities to produce them for communication. Korean programs often implement theme-based CBI courses dealing with Korean culture, history, or society. Instructors in these courses must ensure that language learning is as important as content learning. These courses are designed to provide ample opportunities to use Korean while participating in classroom activities. Even so, it is imperative to check whether students have indeed used the target vocabulary or grammar. Students may participate in discussions and write essays without using the target expressions (Cumming & Lyster, 2016; Swain, 1988). There is also the risk of construct-underrepresentation when language achievement is not a component of summative assessment.

The language elements teachers should cover in CBI courses also need to go beyond the scope of difficult words or grammar. A CBI course for a specific discipline should first identify the language demands of the discipline and provide opportunities for practicing commonly used lexical chunks, sentence structures, move structures, or discourse modes along with discipline-specific terminologies and academic vocabulary.

CBI curriculum developers need to endeavor to improve the authenticity of the tasks given to learners. Tasks performed during class should mirror the tasks performed by people in the target domain, which pertain to "the real-world communicative uses to which learners will put the L2 beyond the classroom" (Long, 2016, p. 6). Instructors must therefore analyze target language use tasks – determining what kind of language use tasks are required, what assignments are given in the major courses, the indigenous criteria that are considered most important in the target discourse domain, and what the type of questions are presented on the exam – and teach students with tasks that best reflect the target domain.

Korean language programs often use films and TV dramas as a point of departure for content-based language instruction. Given that most students in the courses are not from film and media studies, instructors need to double-check whether the courses are tailored to their future language needs. Academic language must be taught proactively and intentionally because there is a limit to the incidental acquisition of academic language through frequent exposure. Korean programs must make space for deliberate language instruction. Language instruction in CBI programs should also conform to the principles of language teaching. Deductive vocabulary teaching involving L1 definitions and metalinguistic explanations does not correspond to the basic principles of language teaching. CBI should be learner-centered and adopt a communicative approach as its frame of reference.

Finally, one topic that has not been often addressed in the literature is assessment in CBI programs (Stoller & Grabe, 1997). Although it is argued that CBI has many advantages, there is a lack of research on whether CBI is more beneficial than – or at least as beneficial as – other teaching methods for learners' content and language learning. As attempted by Kim (2005), more research should examine the nature of learning affordances provided by CBI by analyzing the interactions that take place in CBI classrooms. The focus of the assessment should be reoriented from an 'assessment *of* learning' to an 'assessment *for* learning', and the results should be used both formatively to help facilitate student learning and summatively to evaluate student achievement.

As is the case with assessment procedures in other language teaching approaches, it is important to clearly define the construct to be measured because unsatisfactory performance can be attributed not only to a language problem but also to a content problem. The most essential question is whether to evaluate students' content knowledge, Korean language proficiency, or both. Brinton et al. (2004) suggest that language skills should be the focus in the theme-based model. They also suggest that content mastery should be evaluated in sheltered classes, whereas in the adjunct model, content mastery should be evaluated in content classes and language skills should be evaluated in language classes.

In theme-based and adjunct instructions, language skills must be evaluated; yet, it is hard to rule out the influence of content because assessment tasks are expected to revolve around the content covered in the class. For example, it would be a stretch to say that a writing test asking to compare and contrast the pros and cons of urban and rural life after a class on the law of supply and demand is highly content valid.

It does appear to be reasonable to evaluate content mastery in a sheltered CBI class, but it is not clear whether it is desirable to administer a test that is equivalent to an achievement assessment for a course targeted for native speakers (Short, 1993). Decisions must be made about whether to provide language accommodations, such as allowing extra time or the use of bilingual dictionaries or making linguistic modification.

Conclusion

Content-based instruction is drawing attention as an effective teaching method that can satisfy the needs of students who want to learn Korean for academic and professional purposes. CBI courses present a great challenge, and yet they are the optimal teaching model that can be introduced into superior-level courses or for academic purpose courses that are direly needed in Korean language programs. It may seem like there is not enough demand for them right now; however, the development of CBI courses could create new demand.

One of the ways to ensure the vigorous implementation of CBI courses in Korean language education is to publish or share success stories of CBI courses, which will serve as a springboard for other programs exploring the idea of CBI to take a leap. As Brinton et al. (2004) suggest, the creation of an ongoing materials bank, in which teachers deposit teaching materials, is imperative. Sharing resources will help teachers envision how they can implement CBI in their classrooms and empower them because they do not have to start from scratch. The fact that there is little mention of CBI being attempted in the field of Korean language education in research papers and handbooks on CBI evidently shows that there have been insufficient efforts to inform other Korean language education programs of the achievements from implementing CBI courses.

Although CBI is a teaching method with enormous potential, it is not a panacea (Paran, 2013; Richards & Rodgers, 2014). CBI courses require extensive preparation and thus put an undue strain on teachers' preparation time. Besides, language goals may not be taught in a systematic manner. However, when eventual language use is considered, it is obvious that the arbitrary separation of content and language does not reflect the needs of learners. There may be disagreements about which proficiency level is ideal for introducing the CBI models, but no one will disagree with the idea that the Korean language needs of the biology major differ from those of the history major. The configuration in which content and language are integrated will vary, but one thing is clear: the integration of language and content should not be a choice but an imperative.

References

Allen, W., Anderson, K., & Narváez, L. (1992). Foreign languages across the curriculum: The applied foreign language component. *Foreign Language Annals, 25*(1), 11–19.

Benesch, S. (Ed.). (1988). *Ending remediation: Linking ESL and content in higher education*. Washington, DC: TESOL.

Bigelow, M., Dahlman, A., & Ranney, S. (2006). Keeping the language focus in content-based ESL instruction through proactive curriculum-planning. *TESL Canada Journal, 24*(1), 40–58.

Brinton, D. M. (1997). The challenges of administering content-based programs. In M. A. Snow & D. M. Brinton (Eds.), *The content-based classroom: Perspectives on integrating language and content* (pp. 340–347). New York: Longman.

Brinton, D. M. (2003). Content-based instruction. In D. Nunan (Ed.), *Practical English language teaching* (pp. 199–224). New York: McGraw Hill.

Brinton, D. M., & Snow, M. A. (1988). The adjunct model of language instruction: An ideal ESP framework. In S. Benesch (Ed.), *Ending remediation: Linking ESL and content in higher education* (pp. 33–52). Washington, DC: Teachers of English to Speakers of Other Languages.

Brinton, D. M., Snow, M. A., & Wesche, M. B. (2004). *Content-based second language instruction*. Ann Arbor, MI: University of Michigan Press.

Burger, S. (1989). Content-based ESL in a sheltered psychology unit: Input, output and outcomes. *TESL Canada Journal, 6*, 45–49.

Cammarata, L. (2009). Negotiating curricular transitions: Foreign language teachers' learning experience with content-based instruction. *The Canadian Modern Language Review, 65*(4), 559–585.

Cenoz, J. (2015). Content-based instruction and content and language integrated learning: The same or different? *Language, Culture and Curriculum, 28*(1), 8–24.

Cenoz, J., Genesee, F., & Gorter, D. (2014). Critical analysis of CLIL: Taking stock and looking forward. *Applied Linguistics, 35*, 243–262.

Chamot, A. U., & O'Malley, J. M. (1986). *A cognitive academic language learning approach: An ESL content-based curriculum*. Washington, DC: National Clearinghouse for Bilingual Education.

Cheon, S. Y. (2007). Content-based language instruction through Korean film. *The Korean Language in America, 12*, 15–30.

Cheon, S. Y. (2012). Culture learning curriculum for advanced learners of Korean. *The Korean Language in America, 17*, 18–31.

Cotterall, S. (1999). Key variables in language learning: What do learners believe about them? *System, 27*, 493–513.

Crank, J. P., & Loughrin-Sacco, S. J. (2001). Foreign languages across the curriculum: A model for the delivery of professional language training. *Journal of Criminal Justice Education, 12*(1), 193–211.

Cummins, J. (1984). *Bilingualism and special education issues in assessment and pedagogy*. Clevedon, UK: Multilingual Matters.

Cumming, J., & Lyster, R. (2016). Integrating CBI into high school foreign language classrooms. In L. Cammarata (Ed.), *Content-based foreign language teaching: Curriculum and pedagogy for developing advanced thinking and literacy skills* (pp. 77–97). Oxon and New York: Routledge.

Genesee, F. (1991). Second language learning in school settings: Lessons from immersion. In A. G. Reynolds (Ed.), *Bilingualism, multiculturalism, and second language learning* (pp. 183–202). New York: Psychology Press.

Kang, S. (2012). Curricular design for content-based advanced North Korean dialect materials: Pedagogical principles and practical issues. *The Korean Language in America, 17*, 79–92.

Kim, H. Y. (2005). Construction of language and culture in a content-based language class. *The Korean Language in America, 10*, 50–70.

Kim, H. Y. (2011). Content-based language teaching: A model for bridging with Korean studies. In *Proceedings of the International Association for Korean Language Education 2011 Conference* (pp. 97–104). Seoul: IAKLE.

Kim, S. (2017). A survey on postsecondary Korean language programs in the United States. *Journal of the National Council of Less Commonly Taught Languages, 21*, 99–126.

Kong, S. (2009). Content-based instruction: What can we learn from content-trained teachers' and language-trained teachers' pedagogies? *The Canadian Modern Language Review, 66*, 229–263.

Korean Ministry of Education. (2019). *International student enrollment statistics at Korean Universities in 2019*. Sejong: Ministry of Education.

Kumaravadivelu, B. (2001). Toward a postmethod pedagogy. *TESOL Quarterly, 35*(4), 537–560.

Larsen-Freeman, D. (2000). *Techniques and principles in language teaching*. Oxford: Oxford University Press.

Lee, J. S., & Kim, H. Y. (2008). Heritage language learners' attitudes, motivations, and instructional needs: The case of postsecondary Korean language learners. In K. Kondo-Brown & J. D. Brown (Eds.), *Teaching Chinese, Japanese, and Korean heritage language students: Curriculum needs, materials, and assessment* (pp. 159–185). Oxon and New York: Routledge.

Lightbown, P. M. (2014). Making the minutes count in L2 teaching. *Language Awareness, 23*(1–2), 3–23.

Long, M. H. (2016). In defense of tasks and TBLT: Nonissues and real issues. *Annual Review of Applied Linguistics, 36*, 5–33.

Lyster, R. (2007). *Learning and teaching languages through content* (Vol. 10). Amsterdam and Philadelphia: John Benjamins Publishing Company.

Lyster, R. (2011). Content-based second language teaching. In E. Hinkel (Ed.), *Handbook of research in second language teaching and learning* (2nd ed., pp. 611–630). Oxon and New York: Routledge.

Met, M. (1998). Curriculum decision-making in content-based second language teaching. In J. Cenoz & F. Genesee (Eds.) *Beyond bilingualism: Multilingualism and multilingual education*. Clevedon, UK: Multilingual Matters.

Morton, T. (2010). Using a genre-based approach to integrating content and language in CLIL. *Language Use and Language Learning in CLIL Classrooms, 7*, 81–104.

Noji, F., & Yuen, S. A. K. (2012). Developing content-based curriculum: Aimed toward superior level of proficiency. *The Korean Language in America, 17*, 93–108.

Nunan, D. (1991). *Language teaching methodology: A textbook for teachers*. New York: Prentice Hall.

Pally, M. (Ed.). (2000). *Sustained-content teaching in academic ESL/EFL*. Boston, MA: Houghton Mifflin.

Paran, A. (2013). Review of Coyle, Hood and March, Content and language integrated learning. *ELT Journal, 67*(1), 137–140.

Park, J. (2018). *A study on the vocabulary education based on the adjunct language instruction for Korean language learners majoring in engineering in Korean colleges: Focusing on basic vocabulary of physics* [Unpublished doctoral dissertation]. Sookmyung Women's University, Seoul, Korea.

Park, M.-J., Choi, B., & Ko, S. (2020). Pedagogical approaches and practices in teaching Korean. In Y. Y. Cho (Ed.), *Teaching Korean as a foreign language: Theories and practices* (pp. 24–53). Oxon and New York: Routledge.

Richards, J. C., & Rodgers, T. S. (2014). *Approaches and methods in language teaching* (3rd ed.). Cambridge: Cambridge University Press.

Robinson, P. (2005). Aptitude and second language acquisition. *Annual Review of Applied Linguistics, 25*, 46–47.

Shin, S., & Kim, S. (2000). The introduction of content-based language teaching to college-level Korean program for heritage learners. *The Korean Language in America, 5*, 167–179.

Short, D. J. (1993). Assessing integrated language and content instruction. *TESOL Quarterly, 27*(4), 627–656.

Snow, M. A., Met, M., & Genesee, F. (1989). A conceptual framework for the integration of language and content in second/foreign language instruction. *TESOL Quarterly, 23*, 201–217.

Sohn, H. M. (2012). Korean flagship: A new frontier for advanced language study. *The Korean Language in America*, *17*, 3–17.

Sohn, H., & Cheon, S. Y. (Eds.) (2013). *Essentials of Korean culture*. Seoul, Korea: Korea University Press.

Sohn, S., & Merrill, C. (2008). The Korean/English dual language program in the Los Angeles unified school district. In D. M. Brinton, O. Kagan, & S. Bauckus (Eds.), *Heritage language education: A new field emerging* (pp. 269–288). Oxon and New York: Routledge.

Stoller, F. L., & Fitzsimmons-Doolan, S. (2017). Content-based Instruction. In N. Van Deusen-Scholl & S. May (Eds.), *Second and foreign language education: Encyclopedia of language and education* (3rd ed., pp. 71–84). Cham, Switzerland: Springer.

Stoller, F. L., & Grabe, W. (1997). A six-T's approach to content-based instruction. The content-based classroom: Perspectives on integrating language and content. In M. A. Snow & D. M. Brinton (Eds.), *The content-based classroom: Perspectives on integrating language and content* (pp. 78–94). White Plains, NY: Longman.

Stryker, S., & Leaver, B. (1997). *Content-based instruction in foreign language education*. Washington, DC: Georgetown University Press.

Swain, M., & Lapkin, S. (1989). Canadian immersion and adult second language teaching: What's the connection? *The Modern Language Journal*, *73*(2), 150–159.

Swain, M. (1988). Manipulating and complementing content teaching to maximize second language learning. *TESL Canada Journal*, *6*, 68–83.

Tedick, D. J., Jorgensen, K., & Geffert, T. (2001). Content-based language instruction: The foundation of language immersion education. *The Bridge: Research to Practice. ACIE Newsletter*, *4*, 1–8.

Vines, L. (1997). Content-based instruction in French for journalism students at Ohio University. In S. B. Stryker & B. L. Leaver (Eds.). *Content-based instruction in foreign language education: Models and methods* (pp. 119–140). Washington, DC: Georgetown University Press.

Wang, H. S. (2012). A proposal for advanced level Korean curriculum. *The Korean Language in America*, *17*, 109–127.

Wesche, M. B., & Skehan, P. (2002). Communicative, task-based, and content-based language instruction. In R. B. Kaplan (Ed.), *The Oxford handbook of applied linguistics* (pp. 207–228). Oxford: Oxford University Press.

Wray, D., & Lewis, M. (1996). An approach to writing non-fiction. *Reading*, *30*(2), 7–13.

13
COMMUNITY SERVICE-LEARNING IN KOREAN

Sung-Ock S. Sohn and Soyeon Kim

Introduction

Over the past two decades, an increasing number of higher institutes in North America have incorporated service-learning into academic contexts in a wide range of disciplines, such as intercultural communication, societal inequities, civic engagement in international and domestic contexts, etc. In particular, service-learning in language education is gaining power as institutions of higher education pay special attention to the learning outcomes of students who find and actually exercise solutions to the problems around them. However, the vast majority of those studies that have examined service-learning in relation to language education are limited to Spanish courses, with some degree in other languages, such as English, French, or Russian as a second language.

This chapter explicates the implementation and effects of community service-learning (SL) in the pedagogical context of Korean as a second/foreign language (KSL) at higher institutions in North America. In particular, we focus on the effects of SL in the Korean heritage language context because heritage language learning is different from foreign language learning in many important aspects (Kondo-Brown, 2008; Lee & Kim, 2008; Sohn & Shin, 2007; So, Sohn, & Kim, 2018). One of the most salient features among heritage leaners is a significant gap between high levels of oral/aural proficiency and limited cognitive academic language ability. Moreover, heritage learners bring a unique sociolinguistic profile to the class in terms of their exposure to the intercultural and social-cultural awareness in Korean. Given a large heritage enrollment in advanced Korean courses at higher education institutes in N. America, it is imperative to explore the effects of service-learning on the development of academic cognitive skills and intercultural awareness in Korean.

We address the following two research questions. First, how does service-learning help students in Korean classes make connections between their knowledge acquired from class setting and their use of the language in authentic settings? Second, in what ways does service-learning enhance Korean heritage language learners' sociocultural awareness and foster their cultural identity? By exploring these research questions, we hope to improve current understanding of the educational needs of college-level Korean heritage learners and the overall effects of service-learning in language education.

We present service-learning as an effective pedagogical tool for Korean language education by examining two case studies of undergraduate college Korean courses at two higher institutions in the United States (UCLA and UM). The first case focuses on the effects of service-learning in advanced Korean classes in which students from a Korean heritage background engage in different types of community services according to their interests and career goals. A total of 50 college students and 4 community partners located in the heart of Koreatown in Los Angeles participated in this service-learning project.

The second case involves an undergraduate service-learning seminar class in which students with advanced to superior proficiencies in Korean are trained on language pedagogy and, as a fieldwork component, offer a Korean class to the community for those who do not have access to a formal Korean class. While the community partners for the first case study are located in an area with many Korean-speaking immigrants, the community partner for the second case study is located in the Midwest, with very few people with Korean proficiency.

We hereby present some background on service-learning and how it is applied to language education, particularly in Korean. This is followed by an introduction of the characteristics of Korean heritage language learners and the justification for incorporating service-learning into Korean language courses.

Service-learning (SL)

SL is an innovative pedagogical approach in which students actively participate in civic engagement to enhance their academic curriculum and share in critical reflection throughout their service to community organizations. It is a course-based, credit-bearing educational experience. As such, SL is broadly identified as "academic service-learning, civic engagement, civic responsibility, school-based service-learning, course-based service-learning, community-based learning, field projects, internships, and community engaged learning" (Chong, 2014, p. 348).

As noted in the previous definition, SL is a form of experiential learning that involves the process of "learning through experience and reflection on doing" (Felicia, 2011).

SL is distinguished from volunteerism (e.g., community service) and an internship in the following two aspects: *reflection* and *reciprocity*. *Reflection* activities are a critical component of effective SL because learners' written reflections connect the service activities to the rich frontloading of the academic content and assessment (Bringle & Hatcher, 1996). While community service focuses on providing the needs of service recipients, SL incorporates service activities into the academic curriculum to address community needs and helps students learn through active engagement and reflection (Harkavy & Hartley, 2010; Jacoby, 2015). As a form of experiential education, SL occurs through a cycle of action and reflection as students seek to achieve real objectives for the community and deeper understanding and skills for themselves. It also offers opportunities for students to take initiative, make decisions, develop critical-thinking skills, and be accountable for the results.

Historical philosophies behind SL

SL, with its roots in the theories of experiential learning by the American philosopher and educator John Dewey (1933), has developed as "a teaching and learning strategy that integrates meaningful community service with instruction and reflection to enrich the learning experience, teach civic responsibility, and strengthen communities" (from the National Service Learning Clearinghouse, 2008). The National Service-Learning Clearinghouse (NSLC) supports the SL community in higher education, kindergarten through grade 12, community-based organizations, tribal programs, and all others interested in strengthening schools and communities using SL.[1]

As noted, the basic theory of SL is Dewey's educational philosophy, that is, the interaction of knowledge and skills with experience is key to learning. Unlike traditional educators that stressed rote learning, Dewey emphasized *learning by doing*. The philosophy behind SL represents the intersection of two traditional theories on educational goals: (1) the American commitment to service to promote feelings of concern, care, and responsibility for one's community; and (2) experiential education pedagogy. Students are challenged to carry out meaningful tasks beyond the classroom in authentic, unscripted, real-world contexts (Moreno & MacGregor-Mendoza, 2016). Many of the early pioneers of SL envisioned it as a means to foster social and institutional change through both community development and student empowerment, as well as a vehicle for career and leadership development (Stanton, Giles, & Cruz, 1999).

Academic SL at higher institutes integrates service activities with student learning outcomes. Students in a SL course engage in activities that address community priorities. It takes as its starting point the idea that students are capable of self-direction and are able to develop an independent, proactive approach to their studies. Students need to learn about their communities, identify the root causes of social problems in their community, and explore how to contribute to a solution through *reflection*. This approach aligns with the philosophy underlying SL that contains reflection, critical analysis, and synthesis. According to Dewey, experience by itself does not necessarily result in learning. Experience becomes educative when critical *reflective* thought creates new meaning and leads to growth and the ability to take informed actions. In addition to *reflections*, *reciprocity* between the community organization and students engaged in service promotes a sense of mutual responsibility. High-quality service-learning classes demonstrate *reciprocity* between the campus and the community, with each party giving and receiving (Bringle & Hatcher, 1996). With *reciprocity* and *reflection*, the SL activity enables students to collaborate with the community partners to create sustainable long-term solutions to complex problems.

SL and the standards for world language learning

With regard to language education, SL has played an important role in improving language proficiency and motivation for language use (Abbott & Lear, 2010; Lizardi-Rivera, 2005; Mullaney, 2005). SL fulfills a variety of the ACTFL World Readiness Standards for Learning Languages, particularly those related to *communities* among the five domains for language learning (known as the 5C's): *communication, cultures, connections, comparisons*, and *communities*. The *communities* goal has often been termed the 'lost C' among the five goal areas. Many teachers assume that the *communities* goal area cannot be implemented within the walls of a language classroom, and thus it receives the least attention among the 5C's (Cutshall, 2012). However, this view overlooks the vision of language as having real-world communicative use "in multilingual *communities* at home and around the world" (from the ACTFL *communities* standards).[2]

Communities is an important goal area for language learners because students are empowered and motivated when they connect language learning with their personal goals and interests, as noted in the ACTFL *communities* standards. The *communities* goal area stipulates two standards. The first emphasizes applied learning and focuses on language as "a tool for *communication* with speakers of the language through one's life: in schools, in the *community*, and abroad." The second standard focuses on personal enrichment and sees language as "an avenue to information and interpersonal relations."

SL offers students an opportunity to fulfill the aforementioned 5C's successfully. Students use language beyond the classroom to *communicate* for real purposes in diverse communities, understand multi*cultural* and global issues, *connect* with other disciplines through experiential learning, make *comparisons* with their own language and culture, and participate in multilingual *communities*. Research in SL language courses (e.g., Korean and Spanish) at UCLA also demonstrates students' successes in making *connections* between academic curricula and related social actions by taking a community SL class in the target language (Abbott & Lear, 2010; Kim & Sohn, 2016). The *communities* standards can be integrated not only in language classes but also in content areas in Korean studies (e.g., social science, history, literature, ethnomusicology, etc.) through SL activities.

Korean heritage language learners and SL

While a growing body of literature testifies to the effects of SL in a variety of disciplines, including language education, a vast majority of those studies focused on the impact of SL in European languages (e.g., French, Spanish, or Russian). A few scholarly articles have begun to address the application of SL with heritage language communities in the United States (e.g., Astin, Sax, & Avalos, 1999; Kim & Sohn, 2016; Leeman, Rabin, & Román-Mendoza, 2011; Lowther Pereira, 2015; Martínez, 2010; Moreno & MacGregor-Mendoza, 2016; Petrov, 2013; Rabin, 2011; Trujillo, 2009; Pereira, 2015). Among these, the *Heritage Language Journal* (Special Issue Vol. 13(3), 2016) provides groundbreaking research by exploring SL in a wide range of heritage language education, including Korean. It offers insight into the diverse ways in which SL can be interpreted and applied in a variety of heritage language settings.

Although different types of populations can be categorized as Korean heritage language learners, the most widely accepted categorization considers them "children of first-generation Korean immigrants who grow up hearing and speaking Korean to varying degrees in the home and community" (Lee & Shin, 2008, p. 2). Typical Korean heritage learners would be bilingual in Korean and English as young children but speak exclusively or mostly English to their parents after the age of five (Min, 2000; Shin, 2005; Shin & Milroy, 1999). Lee and Shin (2008) reported that "the rate of heritage language attrition among second generation Koreans is one of the highest among Asian Americans" (p. 8). As such, a major challenge facing the Korean community in the United States is ensuring intergenerational transmission of the Korean language.

Korean American children are given few opportunities to learn Korean at an early age, except for community-based weekend schools.[3] Due to the lack of recognition of these schools by public school systems in addition to a scarcity of well-designed teaching materials, students show very little motivation to attend weekend schools. Consequently, the vast majority of Korean heritage students begin formal heritage language education upon entering college.

UCLA has one of the largest Korean language programs in the United States, offering separate classes for heritage learners and non-heritage learners at the beginning level. The number of non-heritage students decreases as the level goes up, as the majority of students enrolled in advanced- and superior-level classes are Korean heritage learners. Heritage language students do not fit in traditional foreign language classes since their language behavior and needs are quite different from those of foreign language learners (Lee & Shin, 2008; Sohn & Shin, 2007). One of the most commonly observed linguistic features among Korean heritage language learners is a severe gap between oral/aural skills and their written literacy. Most of the heritage students are placed into advanced-level Korean classes because they display a high degree of fluency in spoken Korean. However, these classes emphasize grammar and written texts, thus inhibiting heritage language development.

Lack of needed interaction with native Korean speakers in an authentic setting is another factor that inhibits heritage language development. According to Cho (2015), the Korean language is not widely used within Korean immigrant families, particularly once the children start school. Her study shows that only 30.4% of the 260 second-generation Korean American high school students spoke Korean most of the time with their parents.

In addition to second-generation Korean Americans, there exists another large group of Korean heritage learners in Korean classes nationwide. This group came to America from South Korea for early study abroad (Abelmann, 2012; Lo, Abelmann, Kwon, & Okazaki, 2015).[4] These study-abroad students appear to possess native-like proficiency in daily spoken Korean. However, they display limited proficiency in abstract and academic topics since they had left Korea at a young age and thus missed opportunities to learn and use the language in formal academic settings. Korean American students who have acquired conversational fluency at home also lack knowledge of the speech styles required in formal professional settings. The advanced-level Korean SL courses analyzed in this study are designed to meet the academic needs of both groups of heritage learners.

In the following, we discuss two case studies on SL Korean courses, offered at the University of California, Los Angeles (UCLA) and the University of Michigan in Ann Arbor (U-M), respectively. The coauthors of this chapter were the instructors of these courses for each campus. The data for this study was analyzed using thematic analysis (Braun & Clarke, 2006). The responses to surveys and the students' reflective comments in their writing assignments were reviewed in such a way that a set of themes may be identified across participants and data sets.

Case study (1): University of California, Los Angeles

Setting and participants

In Fall 2014, the Korean program at UCLA implemented a new course called Korean with Service-Learning (Korean 106SL). There was an urgent need for a superior-level (fifth-year) Korean language course for Korean heritage learners. In addition, the Department of Asian Languages and Cultures at UCLA implemented a new undergraduate major in Asian Languages and Linguistics. Along with the new BA degree program, there was a strong demand for more upper-division courses in Korean. The new SL course was created to meet the aforementioned needs.

To enroll in K106SL, students were required to demonstrate a high-level proficiency in Korean by either passing a placement test or completing a prerequisite course. The SL class was 1.5 hours and held twice a week. In addition, students worked at a preapproved off-campus community site for a minimum of 20 hours during the quarter. In-class activities and discussions dealt with both linguistic knowledge, such as formal/informal speech styles in different social settings, and sociocultural issues pertaining to the work at the community sites.

The large Korean community in Los Angeles offered ample resources for SL to be incorporated into Korean language education. We expected that the SL course would expand a traditional Korean class and complement the course material by providing heritage students with authentic contexts to use the target language in a formal register. It was additionally anticipated that interacting with other Korean speakers in the community through SL would provide heritage students with enhanced awareness of their cultural background and identity.

The data for the case study at UCLA was collected over a span of three quarters (2014–2016), which included a total of 50 students and 4 community partners. All the students were from a Korean-heritage background, although there was a wide range of variations in their exposure to the Korean language and culture. The largest group consisted of students who were born in Korea and moved to the United States in their pre- or early teens. They either immigrated with their parents (i.e., the so-called 1.5 generation Korean Americans) or came as early study-abroad international students who had left Korea before they entered middle or high school. The second group of students was born in Korea and then moved to another country in Asia (e.g., China, Japan, Singapore) with parents before coming to the United States for college education. These students are usually multilingual, although their academic proficiency in Korean is limited. Lastly, each quarter we found a couple of students who graduated from high school in Korea and came to America for their college education. Although they displayed a high level of proficiency in Korean, we decided to accommodate these students in the course because the class assessment was done through the comprehensive evaluation of weekly journals, reflection papers, and a final project.

During the first week of the class, the director of the UCLA Center for Community Learning and the site coordinators from the community partners were invited to class to give guest lectures on SL and community-service activities. The four community partners were all located in the heart of Koreatown in Los Angeles.[5] Most students were matched with their preferred site unless their schedule conflicted with that site's schedule. While the four community partners had different missions, all participants were placed in contexts where they utilized and developed their heritage language skills through the integration of course readings and community services. The distribution of the SL students across the community sites and the service activities at each site are summarized in the following section.

Community sites and SL activities

The distribution of the SL students (total 50) across four community sites is as follows: Korean Cultural Center (28), Cardiology hospital (11), elementary school (2), and Koreatown Youth and Community Center (9).

The first community partner was the Korean Cultural Center (KCC), operated by the Korean government. KCC runs a Korean language program called the Sejong Institute. They offer evening classes ranging from introductory to advanced levels with an aggregate enrollment of 200–250 students who are predominantly non-Korean adults. The SL students (total 28) assisted instructors in adult Korean language classes. In addition, the UCLA students tutored non-Korean adult learners enrolled in Korean classes while serving as a conversation partner in Korean.

The second community partner was a local cardiology hospital. Most of the hospital's patients were first-generation elderly Korean immigrants who have very limited or no knowledge of English. SL students (total 11) offered translation from English to Korean and assisted administrative tasks. They also organized and digitized physicians' and nurse practitioners' notes. In addition, they assisted elderly patients with creating email accounts for a medical portal and filling out forms, and measured patients' weight, body temperature, and blood pressure.

The third community partner was a public elementary school with a Korean–English dual language program. The students enrolled in the dual language program included both English-speaking and Korean-speaking students, and they received content instruction in both languages (Sohn & Merrill, 2008).[6] The SL participants assisted bilingual teachers in Korean–English dual language programs. Also, they helped both Korean heritage and non-heritage children in the Korean class and worked with children for content subjects (e.g., math). Moreover, they played with children at a playground and assisted extracurricular activities.

The Koreatown Youth and Community Center (KYCC), a multi-service organization, served as the fourth community partner from the second quarter of the SL course at UCLA. As a non-profit organization, KYCC offers a wide range of services and programs in education, health, housing, and finance for immigrants (e.g., Hispanic and Korean) and economically disadvantaged youth and families. The SL activities at the KYCC include the following: assist low-income families in preparing income tax forms by providing basic information and arranging appointments with volunteer accountants; conduct surveys with small business owners in Koreatown; translate brochures for low-income families with children pertaining to education and health issues; participate as a teacher assistant at a preschool center for children of low-income families; assist teachers to develop activities for afterschool programs.

Findings

Impacts of SL on students

Research in SL demonstrates a positive influence on students' personal and social development as well as academic learning (Astin et al., 1999; Avineri, 2019; Kovarik, 2010). This section focuses on the impacts of SL on the participating students by analyzing their reflection assignments and the post-service survey. The following quotations, all taken from the first online journal collected in the third week of SL, illustrate the students' general initial reflections at their community sites.

> "I was nervous about the first encounter but was surprised to meet the kind hospitality of the hospital staff. I realized that most patients in this hospital were the elderly, and I thought this was an opportunity for me to get used to the use of the Korean honorific style."
>
> *(Participant at a local hospital)*

> "It was amazing and new to me that each student in the same class had different proficiency levels in English and Korean. The teacher managed the class with speed and order, switching between Korean and English according to the individual student's level. It was a truly astoundingly amazing scene."
>
> *(Participant at the Korean Cultural Center)*

> "I was disappointed at myself that I had thought too easily of this activity. I was confident about my Korean skills and had no doubt about my ability to teach them. However, when one student asked a question about the Korean particles, I wasn't able to explain well and thought that I had been too self-confident."
>
> *(Participant at the Korean Cultural Center)*

As the term progresses, the students appear to be more attentive to and analytical about the issues that emerge at the service site, as shown in their second set of journal entries:

> "It was interesting to note the nurse would use *banmal* (the casual style) [to a patient] in a reassuring tone all the while referring to her as *emenim* ('mother'). I think the nurses using *banmal* is purposeful. I think she does it to establish herself as an authority figure who has the power to reassure patients."
>
> *(Participant at a local hospital)*

> "What I've been recognizing at the site recently is the patient's use of the casual style. Although some patients used the honorific style to me, most of them used the casual style to me. Even though they may see me at their grandchildren's age, a hospital is a

public place and I'm someone who works there. Therefore, I think that basic respect is essential, if not the honorific terms . . . I will be more observant to find out their intentions [behind the use of the casual style]."

(Participant at a local hospital)

As noted, participating students in SL activities are dealing with the subtlety of sociolinguistic features in Korean. This demonstrates that SL offers an opportunity to learn the target language in authentic contexts. The fact that the Korean heritage learners in this study were students of diverse backgrounds (e.g., Korean American, early study-abroad international students.) speaks to the potential of SL as an effective pedagogical approach for a variety of heritage language learners.

Perceived positive impact

Regardless of the assigned community site, three themes emerged recurrently in the student reflections: (1) perceived positive impact on language and communication skills, (2) personal growth and enhanced self-esteem and self-respect to the heritage language and culture, and (3) positive impact on career choices. Their comments from reflective journals show details as to which aspect of their services contributed to their learning.

Some students, especially those who served by teaching Korean, pointed out that the SL experience helped them realize their own weaknesses in their Korean competence, as illustrated next.

> "The translation task was greatly helpful for me. I learned new Korean and English words, and my sentence construction ability also seemed to have improved."

> "I was able to learn what types of honorific forms are used in the service industry and how they can be used incorrectly."

> "Even though going to the service-learning each week was time-consuming, I found the experience beneficial to my Korean skills . . . I've also acquired skills to communicate with people in all range of ages from 20's all the way to 50's."

> "Teaching someone the Korean letters was a learning moment for myself at the same time."

Another group of students who served at a cardiology hospital was delighted to be of help to the community using their Korean–English bilingual abilities, as shown here:

> "When I got essay assignments from school, I would put more weight on quantity than quality just to meet the page requirements. However, I realized that I cannot accomplish these translation tasks with the attitude of 'filling in the pages' or 'just getting it over with.' So I made sincere efforts. It was rewarding and I was proud of myself that I could help the hospital staff and patients with my Korean skills."

Recurring comments in the reflection assignments and the survey showed that SL had a positive impact on students' personal growth. The participating students seem to have acquired interpersonal skills through exposure to diverse groups of people beyond their comfort zone, which they found personally beneficial, as shown here:

"To be approachable to the students, I took the initiative to start conversations with them and had to be more proactive than my usual passive self. In that sense, it was a very helpful experience to me."

Furthermore, the SL experience helped Korean heritage learners view their own heritage language and culture in a more positive light, as shown in the following reflection.

"There were students in the Korean Cultural Center who started to learn Korean because of the influence of the Korean wave, and some even wanted to study abroad in Korea. I was able to feel the great influence and value of the Korean wave and its ripple effect on the interest in the Korean language."

Since Korean heritage speakers comprised the majority of the SL participants for this study, the opportunity to serve local communities with their heritage language skill was an eye opener for many participants.

Overall, the students' reflections support the research results in SL. Students benefit through hands-on use of language skills and knowledge that makes a positive impact on their academic learning. Furthermore, the students' reflective journals indicate greater interpersonal development and leadership and communication skills.

Learning outcomes through final projects

While the reflective assignments and the student survey provided direct access to the students' reaction to SL, the final projects had the students go beyond reflection by turning their experiences into research questions and seeking answers to them. As a culmination of all the coursework and SL experiences over ten weeks, the final projects show the students' deeper understanding of some of the critical issues that were addressed in their reflective journals.

The final projects raised a variety of topics in Korean language and cultures: Korean language pedagogy, motivation for learning Korean; translation of medical terms and differing speech styles used among patients, nurses, and doctors at a local hospital (e.g., honorifics vs. non-honorifics); various health issues among elderly Korean immigrants; and sociocultural awareness of the Korean language and culture. The results of the final projects are summarized next.

Students who participated in service activities at KCC conducted group projects. One of the group projects examined motivation factors for Korean language learning. Using a large sample size of surveys and interviews, the group explored a possible difference in motivation factors between non-Korean adult learners at KCC and Korean heritage learners at UCLA. The results showed that adult learners at KCC displayed diverse motivation factors that range from business and politics to entertainment and culture. In contrast, the vast majority (75%) of the beginning Korean class students at UCLA indicated K-pop and music as their main reason for learning Korean.

Another group project at KCC examined difficulties of the Korean language acquisition among non-Korean adult learners. For instance, introductory Korean typically begins with the Korean alphabet and pronunciation. However, the project team found that the pronunciation of Korean sounds (e.g., consonants) is extremely difficult for non-Korean learners at KCC.

The project team concluded in the final paper that the SL experiences at KCC widened their perspectives of the challenges and issues facing non-heritage Korean learners. Previously, their view of English-speaking Korean learners was that they were interested only in K-pop;

however, after speaking to many non-Korean leaners at KCC and conducting the survey, they realized how diverse each student's motives were. A project participant remarks,

> "I have always taken for granted my bilingual background. I realized there is a large population of Korean Americans and non-Korean adults who desire to learn Korean. Through my experience, I have gained an approach to teaching Korean to a person with no Korean background."

In sum, the final projects at all four community sites addressed the students' service activities. By observing professionals (e.g., teachers, doctors, nurses, and accountants) working in their disciplines, the SL students gained an appreciation for the importance of acquiring a high-level proficiency in heritage language. Additionally, the involvement in language teaching at the local school and the KCC and providing service at the hospital enhanced Korean heritage learners' awareness of social responsibility, communication skills, the subtleties of the Korean speech styles (e.g., honorifics), and most importantly, confidence in their cultural identities. Finally, the service activities at KYCC fostered civic engagement and commitment to community needs.

Responses from the community partners

This section presents the results from the survey conducted on the community partners. When asked what they were most satisfied with in regard to the student services, both the SL coordinator and the instructor at KCC appreciated the students serving as teaching assistants before and during the Korean class, particularly one-on-one engagement with students at KCC. The cardiology hospital indicated that the students were helpful with both clerical duties and other tasks that involved direct interaction with patients. It is interesting to note that, even though a few students sometimes expressed in their reflections a desire to do more language-involved tasks than clerical duties, both types of help were equally appreciated on the part of the community partner.

All the respondents replied that the SL students had met their expectations, although the instructor at KCC had hoped the students would have gained a deeper understanding of the institute, such as its student diversity in terms of age and learning objectives. On the other hand, the coordinator at the hospital assessed the student services highly positively: "The students exceeded our expectations. Any skepticism that the clinic staff had was pushed aside with appreciation." Because the skills the students brought to the service sites were language focused, the hospital, where the main services require a different set of special skills (i.e., medical knowledge), might have had low expectations in terms of the extent to which the students could be of help for them.

Case study (2): University of Michigan

Setting and participants

For another example, the Korean Language Program at the University of Michigan (U-M KLP) created its first SL course in 2017. This course was conceived in response to demands from two entities: students of the home institution and the local community. Although the U-M KLP had been offering up to 400-level courses, there was no course regularly offered for students with high advanced- to superior-level Korean skills. At the same time, there was a growing demand from high school students in the neighboring communities, as Korean was not offered at their schools. Located in the Midwest, Michigan does not have Koreatown or Sejong Hakdang in which resources are aggregated and readily available for those who wish to learn Korean. The SL course was thus designed to provide U-M students with the opportunity to hone and utilize their Korean skills by offering a Korean class to high school students.

After the course was piloted for two years, the curriculum was revised substantially to expand the service options and make coordination more manageable. The biggest change in the new curriculum was the addition of an oral history project, in which students had an interview with an elderly Korean immigrant in the community and transcribed their oral history into a written document. This project was also initially conceived because of demand from the community. When a local Korean American family reached out to the U-M KLP in search of assistance with documenting their immigrant parents' stories and experiences for current and future generations who do not speak Korean, the U-M instructor turned the idea into an oral history project for the SL course. In the revised curriculum, as a result, the U-M students provided two types of services: the interview documentation service through the oral history project and a one-time special Korean class for beginning-level learners. The findings discussed here are based on the experiences from five semesters, the last of which used the revised curriculum.

The number and dynamics of the U-M students enrolled in the SL course varied each semester. While the majority were either heritage students or international students from Korea, the number of non-heritage students was on the slow rise. The exact distribution of the U-M students for each semester is provided in Table 13.1.

During the first four semesters, when the course was run as a pilot, the class was held in the following format. The U-M class met once a week for two hours, and the high school class taught by the U-M students met three times a week for one and a half hours each. The U-M students were divided into three groups so that each group would be assigned to teach once a week only. Before the high school class started, the U-M faculty connected with the administrator in the District of Ann Arbor Public Schools (AAPS) to register the class in their Community Resources (CR) program. The CR program enables the AAPS students to earn credit from courses outside of their own schools.

In the U-M instructors' weekly class meetings with the U-M students, the first several weeks were spent introducing the concept of SL and orienting the students to language teaching and teaching youth. For assignments, they observed actual language classes and reflected on their past experiences to discuss effective language learning and language teaching. Toward the end of the orientation period, they started making lesson plans in groups for the high school class they were going to teach in one or two weeks. Another important part of the weekly meeting was for each group to present a mock teaching demonstration based on their lesson plan. The

Table 13.1 Distribution of students enrolled in the U-M SL course

	International students	*Heritage students*	*Non-heritage students*	*Total*
Semester 1	3	4	-	7
Semester 2	6	3	-	9
Semester 3	1	2	-	3
Semester 4	1	4	1	6
Semester 5	1	3	2	6
Total	12	16	3	31

mock teaching presentation not only offered the opportunity to exchange feedback on the lesson plans, but it was also a time to coordinate different groups' instructions in such a way that the high school class could be co-taught seamlessly even though three groups rotated to teach one class. The number of high school students in the CR class was kept at six or seven throughout the two-year pilot period.

With the revised curriculum, U-M students still met once a week for two hours. The first half of the semester focused on understanding the concept of SL and building a thorough foundation on language pedagogy. Each week was devoted to an important topic in the field, such as theories and methodologies in second language acquisition, heritage language education, and language assessment. For a midterm project, students conducted an oral history interview in Korean with a first-generation elderly immigrant as a way to experience a form of SL. The second half of the semester used more hands-on activities to prepare the students for the upcoming teaching session they would be offering for beginning learners. Students designed a syllabus for a Korean class, wrote a lesson plan, and created teaching materials, utilizing the knowledge they gained from the first half of the semester. Both the interviewee for the midterm project and the beginning learners for the special teaching session were recruited and arranged by the instructor.

Findings

Impact on cultural identity and competence

One of the most notable effects of the SL experience was the positive impact it brought on the students' cultural identity and cultural competence. Whether it was Korean heritage students, Korean international students, or non-heritage students, or whether the SL project was teaching others Korean or conducting the oral history interview, this theme of cultural identity and cultural competence frequently emerged in their reflections.

Heritage students who taught high school students appreciated the opportunity as a moment to realize and feel proud of their identity as Koreans.

> "I had moved to the United States when I was just 9 years old from South Korea and had never had the chance to learn proper grammar for Korean. [. . .] [B]eing in seminar and then heading over to [the classroom] afterward to teach the six high school students Korean made me appreciate my background and cultural identity much more."

> "Watching the students talk about different K-Pop idols, or reciting sentences in Korean made me realize how expansive and diverse Korean has become. If these high school students in Ann Arbor, Michigan cared so much about Korean despite cultural differences, why shouldn't I? Watching the students working hard to perfect their Korean opened my eyes to how proud I should be to be a Korean."

> "Being in this class taught me how to be a better student and teacher. It also made me appreciate and value the fact that I am and always will be a proud Korean."

A comment from a heritage student, whose Korean proficiency was the lowest of all the students enrolled in five semesters, illustrates how his sense of identity and linguo-cultural competence as a Korean have changed over time through the service-learning experience.

"In the beginning, I was a little worried because I felt that I was in over my head. Compared to my classmates, I was the only one more comfortable speaking in English than Korean, and I also felt that there were cultural differences. *I was not as "Korean" as my classmates*, and I was worried that it would affect my ability to teach the high school students effectively. However, once we started, I saw how enjoyable the students made the whole experience. . . . *I believe that I've improved my own Korean to a degree*, and *I've learned to have a little more respect and pride in being Korean*. I learned that there are young students around the world interested and engaged in Korean language and culture."

(emphasis added)

Just as their heritage peers, international students from Korea also recounted the pride they felt watching the high school students striving to learn Korean. Interestingly, however, one of the most frequent keywords in their reflections was a "sense of responsibility." They emphasized that their passion and sense of responsibility to provide well-designed instructions grew over time as the semester progressed. It seemed that this sense of accountability stemmed from their feeling of entitlement and ownership over Korean language and culture. Unlike heritage students, they were rarely in doubt or questioned about their identity as Koreans. Therefore, while the heritage students frequently reflected on how the SL experience afforded them a reaffirmation and enhanced appreciation of their identity as Koreans, the international students put more emphasis on fulfilling their responsibility of providing proper instructions as someone who should be knowledgeable about their own language and culture.

Students' reflections on the oral history project also spoke to its impact on their cultural identity and competence. On their experience of interviewing a 69-year-old first-generation immigrant who moved to the United States in her late 30s, students commented on their increased knowledge about Korean history and culture. In addition, they found the interview experience meaningful in that they rarely had direct contact with older generations, let alone talking to them about the old days in Korea that they read about from books.

"I learned a lot about the Korean history and what it was like living in Korea in the past before I was born and lived there."

"Through the oral history project, I was able to hear various expressions related to the history and culture of Korea while gaining the experience of having a direct conversation with the elderly, which I would not normally experience."

"As I listened to [the interviewee's] childhood, I realized a little bit about how difficult it was to live in Korea in the old days. When I learned the history of Cheongyecheon, I heard that Korea was a very poor country in the past, but it was even more shocking to hear the story directly from people who lived those times."

It was not only the Korean heritage students who found the interviewee's stories relevant. A Bengali heritage student made a connection between the interviewee and her immigrant parents.

"My parents immigrated to the United States before I was born, and they talk a lot about old times. So when [the interviewee] talked about old memories, it was like talking to my parents."

On the other hand, another student who considered herself as not sharing any common background with the interviewee still thought the interview helped her strengthen (inter-)cultural awareness and competence.

> "Learning about the culture of someone from a completely different background from myself was a shaping experience."

In sum, the experience of serving the community with their Korean skills made the students connect to their cultural roots and establish a stronger understanding of the Korean culture.

Impact on linguistic competence and awareness

As documented in the SL literature and exemplified in the UCLA's case study, the SL component in language courses brings a positive effect on students' learning of the target language. This was true in the U-M's case as well. Although there was no proficiency test conducted before and after the SL experiences, students frequently commented on how the class discussions and the service experiences contributed to improving their Korean skills. More specifically, students' reflections on the oral history project showed that they made a conscious effort to use polite and honorific speech styles proper to the interview with an elderly speaker. They also picked up new words from the interviewee's speech that they thought were used by older generations.

> "I used to speak Korean at home all the time, but as I communicated with teachers and students in class, I think I practiced the honorific style a lot. The time when I felt this advantage the most was during the [oral history] interview. I don't speak respectfully at home, so it was great to be able to practice the parts I lacked while talking with [the interviewee]."

> "[The interview] was a little difficult because I had never done such an interview in Korean and I did not have enough experience talking to older people, but it was good nonetheless."

> "After talking on the phone for quite some time and listening to it again, I learned the vocabulary that [the interviewee] used, and also came to know words that are not often used by young people these days."

For most students, the experience of teaching Korean was an eye opener to realize that there is a complex operating system underlying the Korean language that they had acquired and used so naturally. Some students, particularly those who were assigned to teach grammar patterns to high school students, had a hard time explaining the patterns without having enough meta-linguistic knowledge themselves. Not surprisingly, it was often the non-heritage students who were able to give the clearest explanations when it came to teaching how the Korean language works. One of the non-heritage students was not only an advanced learner of Korean but was an experienced teacher of English and Latin. He precisely pointed out that the language his Korean peers used toward beginning-level learners could have been more effective if they had a better understanding of what is easy and difficult for learners of Korean.

> "Since I also took beginning Korean classes in the past, I was able to easily match the students' level. Since I have some teaching experience, it was not difficult for me

to teach on the last day, but it seemed to be very difficult for my classmates who had no teaching experience. For example, some of my classmates used respectful words politely and appropriately [at the teaching session], but to be honest, when I was learning beginning Korean, respectful words were very confusing, so in this case, I think it is better to just [use the polite ending]. Sometimes it is better to just use words that are easy for students to understand than correct words. Then communication goes well and students do not lose confidence."

The SL activities not only provided the students with immediate opportunities to utilize Korean in various authentic contexts, but they also had a positive impact on the affective factors for successful language learning, such as self-confidence and motivation. These traits are fundamental to building learner autonomy and achieving a long-term success.

"Through this class, I had many opportunities to practice speaking in Korean (e.g., the honorific style), which I am lacking a lot. There are still a lot of awkward and confusing parts, but I think I have gained more confidence than the beginning of this class."

A growing sign of increased learner autonomy was also noticed when some students, whose English proficiency was better than their Korean, voluntarily switched from writing their reflections in English to Korean. The following quote from a heritage student shows her excitement in realizing the advantage of being bilingual through the SL experience. The powerful realization she gained from the firsthand experience will give her the motivation to develop and maintain her language skills in the long run.

"[Taking this class] made me realize how thankful I should be to my parents for making me speak Korean at home when I was in California. Being bilingual, I learned, was one of the best traits anyone could ever have. Because of this class, I was able to use my knowledge and ability to speak Korean to teach [the high school students] a language that they actually wanted to learn about!"

SL is one of the most effective ways to practice John Dewey's philosophy of *learning by doing*. Through authentic and meaningful tasks involved in the SL projects, students had the opportunity to boost communicative competence and build a more systematic understanding of the Korean language.

Connection to the community

The last most noticeable comments in the students' reflections were about the experience of serving the community. As most of the students' previous volunteering experiences consisted of assisting Korean classes at Sunday schools or tutoring other subjects than Korean, they appreciated the opportunity to give back to the community in ways they had not experienced or imagined before. They also noted that the community was very welcoming and supportive of the SL projects.

"I found the interview process very interesting overall. It was a unique experience being able to engage with someone in the Ann Arbor community, that I wouldn't have known otherwise."

"Although this is my last semester at the university, this experience was the first of its kind throughout my journey as a college student. I've never had the opportunity to give back to the community and as I get ready to graduate, I can't help but think that this class has been a great way to end my undergraduate career here in Ann Arbor."

"I learned that the community is very welcoming towards these projects."

For instructors, the first steps of setting up a SL course, such as finding community partners, making contacts, and coordinating projects between students and the community participants, can be a daunting job. In the case of U-M, the pilot curriculum, in which students offered a semester-long Korean course for high school students, was very challenging at first because the instructors were essentially in charge of both the U-M course and the high school class. In addition, the high school class was a credit-bearing course with specific curriculum requirements by the AAPS district; therefore, the U-M students had less freedom in designing their lessons. Nevertheless, the instructors agreed with the students' reflections that the SL course provides unique opportunities benefiting both the students and the community with academic goals and outcomes. The revised curriculum was thus devised to adjust the workload and yet offer a wider range of services to the community.

The case study at U-M exemplifies a SL model that can be widely implemented in Korean programs even with a relatively small number of students and community partners. As online education rapidly grows, the possibility of connecting with international partners is also becoming a viable option for most institutions. At U-M, this SL course was so well-received by the students that three students took the course for two semesters. Working on different projects with different participants from the community, they did not "retake" the course in a traditional sense. Through varying SL activities, students realized how their Korean skills could be instrumental in giving back to the community while enhancing their communitive and cultural competence along the way.

Challenges and suggestion

While SL offers many benefits to both students and community organization, there are unique challenges in terms of communication with community partners, time commitment, community expectation, and ensuring student learning.

Communication with community partners

In implementing SL courses, identifying and developing partnerships with community organizations pose some challenges. Many institutions of higher education offer a list of community partners for SL (also called *community-engaged*) courses.[7] However, to build trust with community members takes time and effort. The faculty in charge of a SL course is expected to communicate with community partners throughout the quarter/semester. As such, it may be cumbersome to coordinate with multiple community partners in different disciplines. Moreover, there are occasional and unexpected changes in the supervising staff at a community site without any prior notification, leading to some confusion among the participants and faculty.

It would be ideal to have a single site supervisor at each community organization to coordinate service schedules and serve as a contact person for the students and faculty throughout the partnership. Additionally, although the faculty and the community partner agreed to the roles and responsibilities prior to the service activities, the community members sometimes assigned additional tasks to the participants, adding unexpected workload. Maintaining open and clear communication with community partners throughout students' service is vital to the success of SL. It is extremely important to develop a written manual for community partners. Also, it would be beneficial to select community members with ties to the campus and the faculty in charge of the SL course.

Community capacity and expectation

Another challenge is the limited number of students the community partners are willing to accommodate. For the Korean SL course at UCLA, while KYCC and KCC were able to support more than ten students each quarter, the local hospital accepted only several students for the service project due to the limited number of staff. Consequently, some participants who were interested in areas of health care could not have SL experiences at the hospital. To ensure that SL has a significant impact on a community, it is important to address each community partner's most urgent needs. Furthermore, it is important to ensure that the community partner knows precisely the capacities and limitations of the students and to set realistic expectations for SL.

Logistical support

While students participating in SL have a strong motivation and knowledge to complete the community-engaged course, logistic difficulties, such as scheduling and transportation to the community sites, posed quite a challenge, especially for the evening program at a community partner located near downtown Los Angeles. Most students did not have their own car, so they opted for public transportation. As a result, it took an entire day for their SL activities. In the future, it would be helpful to get support from campus vehicle services (e.g., a vanpool service).

Workload and assignment

Workload issues present another big challenge for the students as well as the faculty in charge of the SL course. Since SL courses incorporate off-campus activities on top of the students' regular classes, it may increase their workload significantly. Without reducing some of the existing requirements for the course, adding a SL component may prove to be burdensome. To ensure that students are progressing toward the project's learning and service goals, it is important to assign relevant readings and assess their progress through tests, reports, oral presentations, or other assignments.

The faculty in charge of the advanced Korean SL course also faced other challenges. For instance, it was difficult to provide reading materials pertaining to different service projects; while the participants who served as tutors at KCC had a strong interest in language pedagogy, those at the hospital showed a keen interest in material related to medicine. During the first two years of the SL class, the instructor compiled articles from diverse areas, including immigrants in America, language identity and multicultural society, speech styles in Korean, etc. However, it was still difficult to satisfy the varying needs of students who encountered various challenges throughout the service experiences. From the third year, the instructor selected a book titled *A Different Republic of Korea That Only Koreans Do Not Know* (Pastreich, 2013), written in Korean by an American scholar about South Korea's strengths and unique characteristics from a foreigner's perspective. Students' responses to the book were very positive since it deals with a wide range of topics, such as Korean pop music and cinema, history, and technology from a fresh and unique perspective.

In summary, despite the aforementioned challenges that need to be overcome, community-engaged teaching allows students, faculty, and communities to experience profound growth.

Pedagogical implication and conclusion

This study discussed the implementation and effects of SL in Korean by presenting two case studies of SL Korean courses at UCLA and the University of Michigan. The participating students consisted of advanced- and superior-level speakers of Korean with diverse academic majors and backgrounds (e.g., Korean Americans, early study-abroad international students). The two research goals of this study were: (1) to explore how SL helps students in Korean classes make connections between their knowledge from the class setting and their use of the language in authentic setting and (2) in what ways SL enhances Korean heritage language learners' sociocultural awareness and fosters their cultural identity.

The findings from two case studies show strong positive outcomes. Specifically, service participation has a positive effect on the student's self-efficacy, cultural identity, and civic engagement, as noted in the students' written reflections and survey results. In addition, service participation has a positive effect on the student's career choice in the service field. Upon the completion of the SL course, two participating students from UCLA received and accepted a job offer from the community sites where they have served.

Another benefit associated with course-based SL is the enhancement of academic literacy for Korean heritage learners. As noted earlier, heritage language learners exhibit unique sociolinguistic features in that there is a severe gap between their high levels of oral proficiency and limited academic literacy skills. SL activities at diverse communities offer a great opportunity for the Korean heritage participants to practice and develop academic, professional proficiency in Korean. Moreover, as noted in students' surveys from U-M, positive SL experience at communities enhances a cultural identity for Korean heritage speakers. This is extremely important for the participating student's interest in the academic course materials.

Finally, the positive result of the SL Korean program at U-M sheds light on the future implementation of SL courses at other higher education institutes in North America. Located in an area with a relatively small Korean community, the Korean program at U-M initiated a SL program by offering a Korean class at a local high school. Therefore, SL in Korean is feasible for other campuses that do not have a large Korean community available to them. It also sheds light on the possibility of implementing SL into a beginning Korean class, accommodating varying resources available in different institutions and communities.

In short, this pilot study presents the ways in which SL provides opportunities for college students to put their bilingual skills into authentic learning and serve the community at the same time. In the future, we expect that in addition to qualitative data, quantitative data drawn from diverse institutes would provide strong empirical evidence for the positive impact of the SL program in Korean.

Notes

1 For more details, see the link: https://youth.gov/federal-links/national-service-learning-clearinghouse.
2 For more details, see the ACTFL *embracing communities*.
3 There are a few schools, however, that offer a Korean–English dual-language program for K–12 students in the Los Angeles Unified School District. See Sohn and Merrill (2008) for the history, implementation, and students' academic achievement in the dual-language program.
4 The number of South Korean international students studying abroad in the United States has soared since the 1990s. According to the 2015 Open Doors Report on International Educational Exchange

(Institute of International Education, 2015), South Korea ranks third in places of origin (following China and India) for international students who enrolled in American colleges and post-colleges. California is the top host state for these international students. Many Korean parents also take into consideration the large Korean community in California when they send their children to America for early study abroad.

5 Koreatown in Los Angeles is populated by a large Korean community. According to the U.S. Census Bureau's American Community Survey estimates for 2012–2015, California has the highest number of Korean speakers (total 375,856) among all states. Los Angeles County alone has 183,717 speakers of Korean (U.S. Census Bureau, 2016).

6 The Los Angeles Unified School District (LAUSD) began the Korean dual-language program in 1992 in a kindergarten class of 30 students. As the only Korean–English dual language program for K–12 in the United States, the LAUSD serves more than 1,100 students annually in ten schools throughout the school district in Los Angeles.

7 At UCLA, the Academic Senate's Undergraduate Council approved a new, flexible, and expansive framework (formerly defined as a SL course). Students have the opportunity to actively connect the community-based experience with their academic learning through critical reflection.

References

Abbott, A., & Lear, D. (2010). The connections goal area in Spanish community service-learning: Possibilities and limitations. *Foreign Language Annals*, *43*(2), 231–245.

Abelmann, N. (2012). *The-intimate-university: Korean American students and the problems of segregation*. Durham, NC: Duke University Press.

ACTFL. (2014). *World-readiness standards for learning languages*. Actfl.org.

Astin, A. W., Sax, L. J., & Avalos, J. (1999). Long-term effects of volunteerism during the undergraduate years. *The Review of Higher Education*, *21*(2), 187–202.

Avineri, N. (2019). Nested interculturality: Dispositions and practices for navigating tensions in immersion experiences. In Daniela Martin & Elizabeth Smolcic (Eds.), *Redefining teaching competence through immersive programs* (pp. 37–64). New York: Springer International Publishing; Palgrave Macmillan.

Braun, V., & Clarke, V. (2006). Using thematic analysis in psychology. *Qualitative Research in Psychology*, *3*(2), 77–101.

Bringle, R. G., & Hatcher, J. A. (1996). Implementing service-learning in higher education. *Journal of Higher Education*, *67*(2), 221–239.

Cho, G. (2015). Perspectives vs. reality of heritage language development: Second-generation Korean-American high school students. *Multicultural Education*, *22*(2), 30–38.

Chong, C. S. (2014). Service-learning research: Definitional challenges and complexities. *Asia-Pacific Journal of Cooperative Education*, *15*(4), 347–358.

Cutshall, S. (2012). More than a decade of standards: Integrating "communities" in your language instruction. *The Language Educator*, November 2012.

Dewey, J. (1933). *How we think: A restatement of the relation of reflective thinking to the educative process*. Boston, MA: D.C. Heath & Co Publishers.

Felicia, P. (2011). *Handbook of research on improving learning and motivation through educational games: Multidisciplinary approaches*. Information Science Reference. Ireland: Waterford Institute of Technology.

Harkavy, I., & Hartley, M. (2010). Pursuing Franklin's dream: Philosophical and historical roots of service-learning. *American Journal of Community Psychology*, *46*, 418–427.

Institute of International Education. (2015). *Open Doors 2015 Report*. Retrieved from https://www.iie.org/Why-IIE/Announcements/2015/11/2015-11-16-Open-Doors-Data

Jacoby, B. (2015). *Service-learning essentials*. San Francisco, CA: Jossey-Bass.

Kim, S. Y., & Sohn, S. O. (2016). Service-learning, an integral part of heritage language education: A case study of an advanced-level Korean language class. *Heritage Language Journal*, *13*(3), 354–381.

Kondo-Brown, K. (2008). Issues and future agendas for teaching Chinese, Japanese, and Korean heritage students. In K. Kondo-Brown & J. D. Brown (Eds.), *Teaching Chinese, Japanese, and Korean heritage language students: Curriculum needs, materials, and assessment* (pp. 99–134). New York: Lawrence Erlbaum Associates.

Kovarik, M. (2010). The effect of service-learning on interdisciplinary learning and curriculum reinforcement, and its application to public school environments. *International Journal for the Scholarship of Teaching and Learning, 4*(1).

Lee, J. S., & Kim, H.-Y. (2008). Heritage language learners' attitudes, motivations and instructional needs: The case of postsecondary Korean language learners. In K. Kondo-Brown & J. D. Brown (Eds.), *Teaching Chinese, Japanese, and Korean heritage language students: Curriculum needs, materials, and assessment* (pp. 159–185). New York: Lawrence Erlbaum Associates.

Lee, J. S., & Shin, S. J. (2008). Korean heritage language education in the United States: The current states, opportunities, and possibilities. *Heritage Language Journal, 6*(2), 153–172. Retrieved from www.heritagelanguages.org

Leeman, J., Rabin, L., & Román-Mendoza, E. (2011). Critical pedagogy beyond the classroom walls: Community service-learning and Spanish heritage language education. *Heritage Language Journal, 8*(3), 1–22.

Lizardi-Rivera, C. (2005). Learning the basics of Spanish translation: Articulating a balance between theory and practice through community service. In E. Zlotkowski, J. Hellebrandt, & L. T. Varona (Eds.), *Construyendo puentes (Building bridges): Concepts and models for service-learning in Spanish (American Association for Higher Education series on service-learning in the disciplines)* (pp. 107–122). Sterling, VA: Stylus Publishing.

Lo, A., Abelmann, N., Kwon, S. A., & Okazaki, S. (2015). *South Korea's education exodus: The life and times of study abroad*. Seattle: University of Washington Press.

Martínez, G. (2010). Medical Spanish for heritage learners: A prescription to improve the health of Spanish-speaking communities. In S. V. Rivera-Mills & J. A. Trujillo (Eds.), *Building communities and making connections* (pp. 2–15). Newcastle upon Tyne: Cambridge Scholars Publishing.

Min, P. G. (2000). Korean American's language use. In S. L. McKay & S. C. Wong (Eds.), *New immigrants in the United States* (pp. 306–332). Cambridge: Cambridge University Press.

Moreno, G., & MacGregor-Mendoza, P. (2016). Connecting Spanish heritage language students with the community through service-learning. *Heritage Language Journal, 13*(3).

Mullaney, J. (2005). Service-learning and language-acquisition theory and practice. In E. Zlotkowski, J. Hellebrandt, & L. T. Varona (Eds.), *Construyendo puentes (Building bridges): Concepts and models for service-learning in Spanish (American Association for Higher Education series on service-learning in the disciplines)* (pp. 49–60). Sterling, VA: Stylus Publishing.

National Service-Learning Clearinghouse. (2008). *History of service-learning in higher education*. New York: National Service-Learning Clearinghouse.

Pastreich, E. (2013). *A different Republic of Korea that only Koreans do not know*. Seoul: 21 Century Books.

Pereira, L. K. (2015). Developing critical language awareness via service-learning for Spanish heritage speakers. *Heritage Language Journal, 12*(2), 159–185.

Petrov, L. A. (2013). A pilot study of service-learning in a Spanish heritage speaker course: Community engagement, identity, and language in the Chicago area. *Hispania, 96*(2), 310–327.

Rabin, L. M. (2011). The Culmore bilingual ESL and popular education project: Coming to consciousness on labor, literacy, and community. *Radical Teacher, 91*(1), 58–67.

Shin, S. J. (2005). *Developing in two languages: Korean children in America*. Clevedon, UK: Multilingual Matters.

Shin, S. J., & Milroy, L. (1999). Bilingual language acquisition by Korean schoolchildren in New York City. *Bilingualism: Language and Cognition, 2*(2), 147–167.

So, Y.-S., Sohn, S.-O., & Kim, J.-E. (2018). An analysis of Korean heritage learners' writing across different discourse types. *Heritage Language Journal, 15*(3), 319–340.

Sohn, S.-O., & Merrill, C. (2008). The Korean/English dual language program in the Los Angeles Unified School District. In D. Brinton, O. Kagan, & S. Bauckus (Eds.), *Heritage language education: A new field emerging* (pp. 269–287). Oxon and New York: Routledge.

Sohn, S.-O., & Shin, S.-G. (2007). True beginners, false beginners, and fake beginners: Placement challenges for Korean heritage speakers. *Foreign Language Annals, 40*(3), 353–364.

Stanton, T. K., Giles, Jr., D. E., & Cruz, N. (1999). *Service-Learning: A movement's pioneers reflect on its origins, practice and future*. San Francisco, CA: Jossey Bass.

Trujillo, J. A. (2009). Con todos: Using learning communities to promote intellectual and social engagement in the Spanish curriculum. In M. Lacorte & J. Leeman (Eds.), *Español en Estados Unidos y otros contextos de contacto: Sociolingüística, ideología y pedagogía* (pp. 369–395). Madrid: Iberoamericana.

U.S. Census Bureau. (2016). American Community Survey (ACS) 5-year estimates. Retrieved from https://www.census.gov/library/visualizations/interactive/acs-5year-datamap.html

PART III

Approaches to Korean as a second language

14
CORPUS-BASED RESEARCH AND KSL

Sun-Hee Lee

What is corpus linguistics and corpus-based research?

Advances in computing technology have revolutionized the ways in which linguists can approach their data. The term *corpus* (pl. *corpora*) is used to refer to electronic language data; that is, any collection of recorded instances of spoken or written language. The first modern corpus of English is the Brown University Standard Corpus of Present-Day American English (the Brown Corpus),[1] which was followed by the rapid development of corpora through the 1980s. In the field of second language research and pedagogy, the publication of the Collins COBUILD English Language Dictionary in 1987 was a landmark publication that signified the potential of adopting corpus-based methodology. Since then, corpus-based language studies and pedagogical resources have grown exponentially and extended the impact of corpus-based methodology in applied linguistics (Römer, 2009). As highlighted by Gabrielatos (2005), corpus research in English language learning and teaching has produced substantial and abundant outcomes (see Biber, Conrad, & Reppen, 1998, Hunston, 2002, McEnery & Wilson, 2001, Stubbs, 1996, etc.). In general, corpus research can be divided into two kinds: corpus-based vs. corpus-driven studies as categorized by Tognini-Bonelli (2001, pp. 84–85). Corpus-based studies typically use corpus data for exploring a theory or hypothesis while aiming to validate it, refute it, or refine it. In contrast, corpus-driven studies oppose using corpus analysis as a method and claim that the corpus itself embodies a theory of language and should be the sole source of linguistic hypotheses. Most corpus research has taken the corpus-based approach, although the dichotomic categorization of the corpus-based and corpus-driven approaches are somewhat controversial (see McEnery, Xiao, & Tono, 2006, pp. 8–11).

By accessing large bodies of digital text (corpora) and searching for linguistic patterns and frequency information related to phenomena of interest, it is possible to uncover complexities in naturally occurring data and explore broader issues. With corpora and related technology thriving since the 1980s, the necessity of learner corpora to language learning and teaching has been recognized as a primary subject. Learner corpora can be defined as an "electronic collection of natural or near-natural data produced by foreign or second language (L2) learners and assembled according to explicit design criteria" (Granger, Gilquin, & Meunier, 2015, p. 1). The past 35 years of corpus-based research including learner corpora and corpus tools has shown remarkable developments in the area of English as a second language (ESL), as noted by Römer (2011). In line with the pioneering studies of Johns's (1986) data-driven learning and John Sinclair's corpus project with the Collins COBUILD dictionary (Sinclair, 1987, 1991), the importance of corpus linguistics and resources in language learning and pedagogy (mostly English, though) has been undoubtedly visible. Since then, numerous studies have rigorously explored corpus-based methods in applied linguistics, including Biber et al. (1998), Ellis, Römer, and O'Donnell (2016); Granger, Dagneaux, and Meunier (2002), Hunston (2002), McEnery et al. (2006), McEnery and Wilson (2001), and Römer (2008), among many others. As Granger et al. (2002) highlight the interdependency of second language acquisition and learner language, the new research strand of learner corpus research (LCR) has emerged as the mainstream in ESL. However, in contrast with abundant corpus-based research in Korean linguistics that have surged over the past few decades, corpus-based approaches to Korean as a second language (KSL) have been restricted, mainly due to limited knowledge of Korean corpora and a lack of available tools to extract valid information for Korean learners. In addition, there has been a lack of Korean learner corpora (L2 learner data including both the written and the spoken) that are publicly accessible and computational resources.

This paper provides an overview of the key aspects of corpora and applications that can contribute to KSL research while examining practical usages and related issues with respect to L1 and L2 Korean corpora with open access and linguistic annotation. Design principles of corpora and corpus applications to research on second language and pedagogy will be presented in Section 2. Pedagogical applications of general corpora will be divided into two major aspects of applications: direct usages vs. indirect usages. In addition to general corpora, basics of specialized corpora, corpora for language for specific purposes (LSP), and learner corpora will be briefly introduced. Section 3 focuses on three kinds of Korean corpora: 1) the Sejong Corpus – a large size L1 corpus; 2) the KoLLA learner corpus, a small size L2 corpus developed for automatic detection of particle errors; and 3) the NIKL learner corpus, a large size L2 corpus with diverse learner backgrounds and comprehensive annotations. By examining these corpora, we aim to identify the current status of the corpus-based approach in KSL, highlight its potential with specific challenges, and promote some future tasks utilizing corpora (particularly, learner corpora) for improving pedagogical practice and investigating learner language.

Corpus applications to KSL

The advancement of corpus linguistics has transformed the field of linguistics over the past few decades. The utility and effectiveness of corpora and related resources had been thoroughly recognized in second language research with the publication of the first corpus-based dictionary for learners in 1987, the Collins COBUILD English Language Dictionary. Since then, corpus-based approaches have produced significant outcomes in L2 research and pedagogical resources while attracting an increasing number of practitioners, including applied linguists, language learners, and teachers. This section will focus on the influence of corpus applications in second language research and pedagogy and examine what kinds of corpus applications have been proposed and how they are applicable to KSL. Before discussing the impact of corpus applications to L2 research and teaching, we need to clarify some of the key concepts of corpora and examine the relationship between corpora and second language learning and teaching.

Corpus design: representativeness, balance, and sampling

In corpus design, the key notions include representativeness and balance. Representativeness is an essential feature of a corpus; Leech (1991) defines a corpus as representative of a language variety if the findings based on corpus contents can be generalized to the language variety. In other words, we can understand the notion of representativeness by asking a question: can all the linguistic properties that are found in the *Korea Times* corpus be generalizable to all Korean-language newspapers? The answer is no. The *Korean Times* corpus has its own linguistic properties, so we cannot conclude that the corpus represents all newspapers. Biber (1993, p. 243) defines representativeness as referring to the extent to which a sample includes the full range of variability in a population. According to him, the corpus is a sample of a language variety (i.e., population). McEnery et al. (2006) describe representativeness of corpora as determined by balance and sampling. Although the notion of balance is heavily based on intuition and best estimates with no reliable scientific measures, the balanced corpus covers a wide range of text categories that are supposed to be representative of the language variety. The British National Corpus (BNC) is generally accepted as a balanced corpus with its design criteria; written texts were chosen with the three criteria of domain, time, and medium, while spoken data was collected based on the two criteria of demographic and context-governed. The BNC model has been followed by the Korean National Sejong Corpus, which we will examine in Section 3.1. In general, corpus representativeness and balance are connected with sampling, which is an inevitable process to select a representative sample with the goal of reproducing the characteristics of the larger population.[2] According to McEnery et al. (2006), a text typology (such as books, periodicals, etc.) sets the basis of external criteria of the sampling method for the written texts, while demographic sampling (such as age group, sex, social status, and geographical region) and context-governed sampling (including context-based categories, such as meeting, lecture, business, academy, etc.) do so for the spoken data. It is notable that sampling a spoken corpus is remarkably challenging because of complexity of identifying the criteria for a population. However, it is crucial for a researcher to understand corpus representativeness and balance for achieving the research goal; these key concepts determine if a particular corpus is suitable for answering the given research questions.

Corpora and second language research

This research focuses on how the second/foreign language is learned by L2 speakers and explores the factors and patterns of the mechanisms of the second/foreign language learning. Corpus linguistics provides "a quantitative paradigm grounded in the empirical tradition of language analysis" (McEnery, Brezina, Gablasova, & Banerjee, 2019, p. 74). Large size compiled data sets (corpora) are used to extract patterns in language use. Therefore, corpus linguistics and language learning research share the common goals of identifying patterns and factors in L1 and L2 language use and utilizing them for linguistic analysis, teaching, and assessment. The L1 corpus studies have demonstrated discrepancies between real-world usages and introspection-based usages, as manifest in Sinclair (1997). Authentic patterns and linguistic descriptions from L1 facilitate L2 learning, teaching, and assessment. In parallel, identified patterns in L2 data facilitate exploring variables that affect language acquisition. L1 and L2 corpora have significant utility and dependency with respect to pedagogical purposes. L1 corpora (such as the British National Corpus, the Brown Corpus, and the LOB Corpus) have been rigorously used for accurate linguistic descriptions, dictionaries, and pedagogical grammar in language learning and teaching contexts (Chambers, 2015, pp. 445–446). In comparison with L1 corpora in language teaching, L2 learner corpora have been less exploited, whereas the advancement of learner corpus research (LCR) has become accelerated with technological progress. The representative English L2 corpora can be divided into written (International Corpus of Learner English, ICLE; Longman Leaner Corpus; Cambridge Learner Corpus) and spoken (Louvain International Database of Spoken English Interlanguage, LINDSEI – 1.5 million words; Trinity Lancaster Corpus – 4 million words).

Corpus applications

The application of the corpus-based research to language learning has been visibly promoted since the early 1990s. The growing number of journal articles and books on the topic of language teaching and corpora are the supporting evidence (Aston, 2001; Aston, Bernardini, & Stewart, 2004; Burnard & McEnery, 2000; Granger, 2009; Granger et al., 2002, 2015; Hunston, 2002; Kettemann & Marko, 2000; Meunier, 2012; Sinclair, 2004; Tono, 2003; Wichmann, Knowles, McEnery, & Fligelstone, 1997, among many). Leech (1997) points out that convergence of corpora and language teaching can be found in three aspects: 1) the direct use of corpora in teaching; 2) the indirect use of corpora in teaching; and 3) developing special corpora, including languages for specific purpose (LSP), L1 developmental corpora, and L2 learner corpora. The direct use of corpora refers to the hands-on use of corpus data by teachers and students. The indirect use of corpora includes utilizing corpora for reference, material development, and language testing. Although Leech (1997) seems not to pay much attention to the third category of special corpora, the practical necessity and significance of developing resources for domain specific language and learner language has been gradually recognized in second language learning and teaching. In particular, learner corpus studies have shown multi-disciplinary applications and emerged as one of the major disciplines dealing with learner data over the three decades. In this article, we will examine empirical applications of corpora that will benefit KSL research and pedagogy, with a focus on three applications of corpora: direct applications, indirect applications, and special corpora.

The direct and indirect applications of corpora include both the use of corpus tools and corpus method; corpus tools of data collection and software packages allow corpus access, and diverse corpus methods are used for corpus data analysis. Römer (2011) highlights these two pedagogical usages of corpora and presents different types of direct and indirect applications as follows.[3]

Direct corpus applications

Direct applications involve the access of the learner and the teacher to corpora via various tools, such as text editors or corpus analysis toolkits for concordancing and text analysis. Concordancing

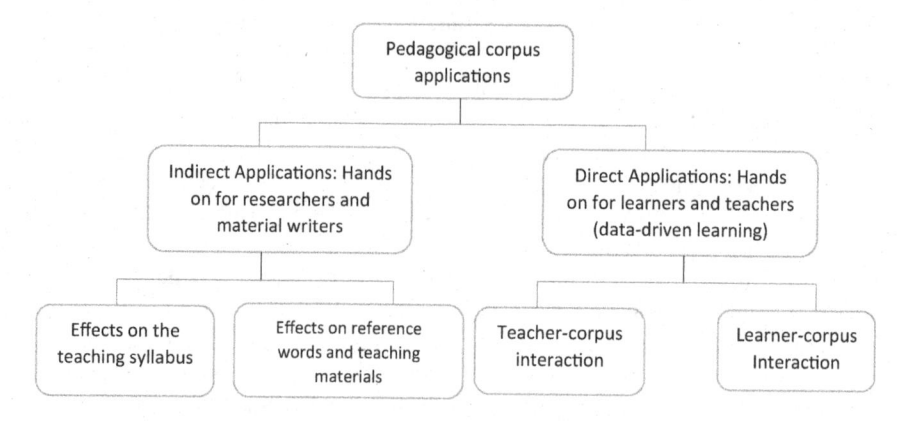

Figure 14.1 The use of corpora in second language learning and teaching (Römer, 2011, p. 207)

refers to listing each occurrence of a word or a pattern in a corpus with the surrounding words in the given context. A simple format of concordance is Key Word In Context (KWIC) in corpus linguistics, as shown in Figure 14.2. In ESL, direct use of corpora in learning grammar and vocabulary has been steadily promoted since the 1980s by Tim Johns (1986) at the University of Birmingham, who pioneered data-driven learning (DDL). He argued for confronting the learner with the data and making "the learner as a linguistic researcher." (Johns, 2002, p. 108). DDL approaches to learner-centered activities with corpora have made substantial progress along with the rapid development of English corpora and various corpus toolkits. While summarizing the representative DDL research over three decades, Römer (2011) presents practical tools and hands-on activities available online, including two significant language corpora – the Michigan Corpus of Spoken Academic English (MICASE) and the Michigan Corpus of Upper-Level Student Papers (MICUSP), which were developed at the English Language Institute at the University of Michigan (https://lsa.umich.edu/eli/language-resources/micase-micusp.html) – and Tom Cobb's Compleat Lexical Tutor, data-driven language learning on the web (www.lextutor.ca/).

In accordance with the technological advancement of corpus linguistics, there have been increasing needs of corpora and search tools in various fields of linguistics and applied linguistics. Among the researchers and practitioners who pursue utilizing corpus data, some of the most widely used corpus tools include Wordsmith tools and Sketch Engine. In addition, the new generation of free toolkits like AntConc, LancsBox, and CQPweb have shown remarkable developments in recent years. The toolkits facilitate user-friendly access to existing and one's own corpora and customizing the corpus analysis with various functionalities and data visualization for multiple languages. However, direct pedagogical corpus applications have been mainly focused on English along with corpus resources and tools concentrated on English data.

Indirect corpus applications

In contrast with direct use, indirect applications advocate for applying the corpus resources for course design and content of teaching materials (Hunston, 2002, p. 137). As Römer (2011)

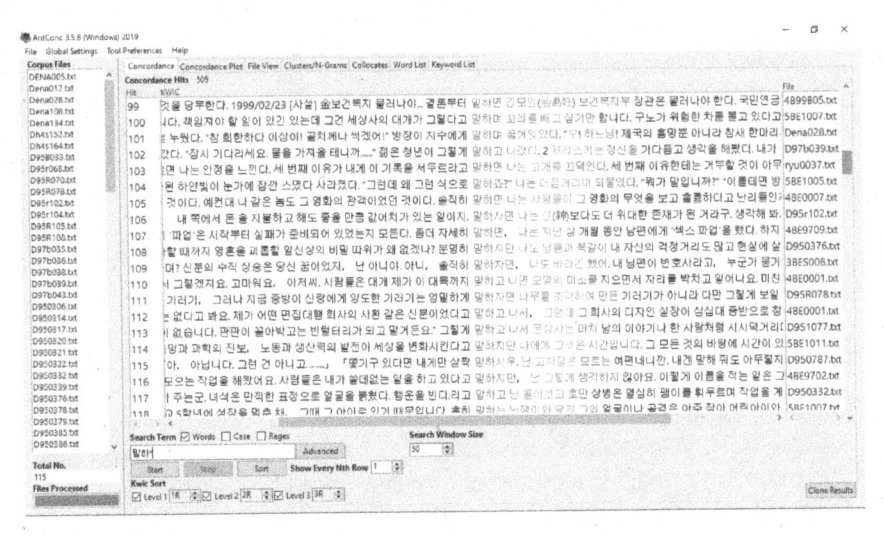

Figure 14.2 A KWIC sample of 말하- *malha*- 'to speak' extracted from the Sejong written corpus using a concodancer of AntConc 3.5.8 (a freeware corpus analysis toolkit for concordancing and text analysis).

points out, corpus studies identify prominent vocabulary and patterns that occur frequently in the target language that learners are likely to encounter in real-world contexts. The pioneering project of the COBUILD dictionary in pedagogically oriented lexicography has inspired numerous ESL studies focusing on lexical syllabi. A lexical syllabus was first proposed by Sinclair and Renouf (1988), and the first groundbreaking work was the Collins COBUILD English Course (CCEC) (Willis & Willis, 1989). Hunston (2002) claims that a lexical syllabus does not solely consist of frequent words but includes "all aspects of language, differing from a conventional syllabus only in that the central concept of organization is lexis." The notion of a lexical syllabus is parallel to Sinclair's (2000) lexical grammars that "build a grammar and lexis on an equal basis" (p. 191). Another exemplar outcome of corpus-based reference grammar is the Longman Grammar of Spoken and Written English (Biber, Johansson, Leech, Conrad, & Finegan, 1999). These lexical approaches to language teaching are noteworthy for KSL researchers and practitioners, although most of the studies have focused on English.

In addition to a lexical syllabus, the corpus-based materials include dictionaries and reference books. For Korean, the Yonsei Korean corpus was the first Korean corpus developed for compiling the *Yonsei Korean Dictionary* (1988) that covers 52,000 entries. There are other dictionaries: Yonsei Elementary *Korean Dictionary* (2002), *Korean Learner's Dictionary* (2006), *Korean Collocation Dictionary for Korean Language Education* (2007), *Korean Synonym Dictionary* (2012) and *Korean Usage Frequency of Basic Korean Vocabulary* (2014), and *Frequency Dictionary of Spoken Korean 1, 2* (2015). *The Korea University Korean Dictionary* (2009) was also compiled based on a corpus of 100 million *ecels* (a space-based word unit). The National Institute of Korean Language (NIKL) provides *The Standard Korean Language Dictionary* (2008), which is regularly updated through their website (https://stdict.korean.go.kr/), and lexical items listed in this dictionary are considered to be so-called standard Korean in school grammar. In addition, NIKL compiled the Korean Learner Dictionary with 52,229 lexical items listed and offers translated versions online in 11 different languages, including English, Japanese, Russian, Spanish, Mandarin, and Vietnamese (https://krdict.korean.go.kr/). Since most Korean learner dictionaries are written in Korean, these multilingual translated versions will be a practical help for learners with low proficiency. Another specialized corpus-based dictionary, *A Frequency Dictionary of Korean: Core Vocabulary for Leaners* (Lee, Jang, & Seo, 2016) provides the 5,000 most frequently used words. This dictionary is based on the Sejong National Corpora, comprised of 10 million words collected from different genres, and it provides the user with detailed information for each of the entries, including illustrative examples and English translations. Whereas dictionaries are a rich resource for language teaching and curriculum design, there are few reference materials providing grammatical patterns, teaching strategies, or testing or assessment tools for Korean. In consideration of surging publications of Korean corpora, one can expect to see more diverse reference materials of Korean with practical pedagogical applications in the near future.

Specialized corpora: LSP corpora and leaner corpora

Domain-specific language use and professional communication have been highlighted in language learning and teaching. Like general corpora, domain-specific corpora (e.g., from a particular field of expertise, such as business or academic research, or a narrowly defined group of speakers/writers, such as learners with a particular L1 or a certain level of proficiency) can be utilized for pedagogical purposes. Römer (2008) distinguishes three different types of specialized corpora: language for specific purposes (LSP), learner, and parallel or translation. Research in English for specific purposes (ESP), in particular, English for academic purposes

(EAP), has proven the effectiveness of corpora and corpus tools. In addition, knowledge of genre-specific features has been significantly explored by EAP researchers employing electronic corpora and tools; see Hyland's (1998) hedging and Hyland's (2005) meta discourse, Hunston and Francis's (1999) lexico-grammatical patterns, and Biber et al.'s (1998) and Ellis, Simpson-Vlach, Römer, O'Donnell, and Wulff's (2015) formulaic expressions, to name a few.

With the increasing number of Korean learners, Korean for academic purposes (KAP) studies have been growing rapidly within the area of KSL. As in EAP, KAP research benefits from corpora and corpus tools. Min (2010) identifies three distinct approaches to corpus application in KAP: a specific register-based approach for extracting academic vocabulary, a discourse analysis–based approach, and a function-based approach for academic reading and writing. Although these tasks are interconnected and can be more efficiently conducted by developing and sharing corpus resources, systematic development of academic corpora has not been paid attention in the field. In contrast, there is a wide range of written and spoken academic corpora in EAP, including the British Academic Written English (BAWE) corpus, the British Academic Spoken English (BASE) corpus, the Reading Academic Text (RAT) corpus, the Michigan Corpus of Upper-Level Student Papers (MICUSP), the Michigan Corpus of Academic Spoken English (MICASE), the TOEFL 2000 Spoken & Written Academic Language Corpus (T2K-SWAL), etc. It is noteworthy that the Korean National Sejong Corpus includes a raw corpus composed of 35% academic texts and 10% transcribed spoken Korean (Kim, 2006). In addition to the Sejong Corpus, there have been steady efforts to construct large size corpora for Korean language education, which have been sponsored by the National Institute of Korean Language since the early 2000s. These corpora have been developed for supporting specific projects, such as selecting basic vocabulary and lexical rating for Korean language education (Lee, 2017, 2018) or for developing the standard Korean curriculum (Kim, 2017, 2018).[4] Furthermore, in summer 2020, NIKL launched a new website, *Moduuy Corpus* (https://corpus.korean.go.kr/), for distributing corpus data constructed over the past 10 years, which includes 180 million *ecels* across 13 kinds of corpora (written corpus, spoken corpus, web corpus, morpheme tagged corpus, etc.). Although these resources allow easy access to various registers of academic papers, textbooks, newspapers, novels, etc., the usability of developed corpus data may not be as useful for international researchers and practitioners because data search and requests are handled only in Korean. While lacking the list and details of corpora, it is empirically difficult to identify the native corpora that can be used for second language learning and teaching. Furthermore, in consideration of corpus representativeness and balance, it is still necessary to develop the KAP corpus more systematically so that register and discourse analysis of KAP can be thoroughly explored.

With respect to L2 learner data, a new area of learner corpus research has emerged, connecting corpus linguistics with second language acquisition, learning, and teaching (Díaz-Negrillo & Thompson, 2013; Granger, 2011; Myles, 2015, among others). As McEnery et al. (2019) acknowledge, there are L2 learner corpus studies that are linked to numerous pre-computational studies. These manual analyses of naturally occurring language data and leaner errors make it difficult to identify a specific study as the beginning of LCR (p. 77). According to Gilquin (2015) argues that what distinguishes the learner corpus from the data used in earlier SLA studies is that it aims at representativeness of the L2. Although there were corpus-based studies of learner language on a small scale before LCR, the first emergence of learner corpus is the advent of the International Corpus of Learner English (ICLE, Granger et al., 2002–2009). McEnery et al. (2019) summarize three distinct properties of ICLE: scaled-up data collection, a machine-readable reusable resource with easily accessibility, and coverage of the L1 background of the L2 speakers. The last version of ICLE, released in 2009, comprised writings of upper-intermediate and advanced learners from 25 L1 backgrounds and 5.5 million words. In addition, the Louvain Corpus of Native English Essays (LOCNESS) was designed to facilitate comparison to L1 speaker data for ICLE. As for the spoken data, the Louvain International Database of Spoken English Interlanguage (LINDSEI) corpus provides 11 different L2 backgrounds in over 1 million words of transcribed data, with a companion corpus, the Louvain Corpus of Native English Conversation (LOCNEC), containing 124,935 words as part of transcribed interviews with 50 British English native speakers. The recent release of the Trinity Lancaster Corpus (TLC), which is the largest corpus of spoken L 2 English from 2,000 L2 backgrounds with 4.2 million words of oral examinations, undoubtedly extends the development of LCR by allowing substantial quantitative investigation of learner language (Gablasova, Brezina, & McEnery, 2019).

It is important to note that learner corpora can play a significant role by bridging corpus linguistics not only with SLA but with other areas of language testing and natural language processing. In Korean, there have been many corpus-based studies on a small scale, which is similar to the prior time period of English LCR. However, the importance of LCR has been keenly recognized in KSL studies with the exploding population learning Korean and there have been some innovative approaches to develop Korean learner corpora. Seo, Yoo, and Nam (2002) and Ko et al. (2004) have developed corpora for Korean language education, including a reference corpus collecting academic textbooks and a learner corpus collecting writings of Korean learners at six distinct levels. They have elaborated procedures and challenges of developing learner corpora and presented typology and scheme of error annotation. However, these learner corpora with error annotation have not been publicly released. With a lack of accessible learner corpora, most learner corpus studies have focused on particular types or learner errors or extracting pedagogical information by utilizing individual collected learner data and native corpora as comparison sets. Instead of scanning numerous studies of small sized corpora that were individually developed, we probe the details of Korean corpora with open access and appraise their usability for L2 learning and teaching in the next section.

Korean corpora for KSL

Kim (2019) examined 586 academic papers focusing on Korean corpora that have been published over the past 15 years using the Korea Citation Index. With a network analysis, she identified the academic discipline in which corpus applications are most actively used in Korea as Korean language education. The Sejong Corpus takes the central position in corpus-based Korean research. These findings also signify the importance of corpora in KSL. In this section, we examine accessible corpora and corpora tools for KSL, including the L1 Sejong Corpus and L2 learner corpora. In general, the Korean National Sejong Corpus has been the most widely used corpus in Korea language studies since the early 2000s. In addition to L2 learner corpora, an L1 general corpus can be used as a reference corpus that is used as a standard of comparison with L2 data. The Sejong Corpus can be also directly or indirectly used in the area of KSL. We will explore the properties and composition of the Sejong Corpus and its corpus toolkits in Section 3.1 and then discuss learner corpus resources for KSL in Section 3.2.

Sejong Corpus (2007)

The Sejong Corpus was constructed as the Korean National Corpus in the 21st-century Sejong Project funded by the Korean government between 1998 and 2007. The ten-year-long project aimed to develop Korean language informatics by developing a large-scale Korean corpus and related resources. The sub-corpora of the Sejong Corpus consist of two different kinds: the first

Table 14.1 Composition of the Sejong Corpus (general)

	Corpus type	Corpus size (ecels)
Written corpus	Raw	36,879,143
	Morpheme-tagged	10,066,722
	Semantic-tagged	9,071,054
	Parsed	433,839
Spoken corpus	Raw	805,646
	Morpheme-tagged	805,646

includes general corpora, including a raw corpus, morpheme-tagged corpus, semantic-tagged corpus, and parsed corpus; the second kind includes special corpora consisting of a corpus of transcribed colloquial discourse, a historical corpus, a corpus of international Korean, and a parallel corpus. The total size of the Sejong Corpus is known to be more than 200,320,000 *ecels*.[5] However, the publicly available Sejong Corpus is much smaller due to copyright issues, according to Hwang and Choi (2016). The following table shows the composition of the Sejong Corpus outcomes released in 2011, which are downloadable at *Enecengponanwunthe* (언어정보나눔터 https://ithub.korean.go.kr/) of the National Institute of Korean Language.

Although the released Sejong Corpus provides decently large L1 data, Hwang and Choi (2016) recommend the Sejong Balanced Corpus that was released in the early 2000s (with about 10,000,000 *ecels*, 90% written and 10% spoken data). This is because the corpus has been developed with reference to the British National Corpus and includes balanced registers. In addition to the corpus, a concordancer called *Hanmaru 2.0* is provided to search a particular form and collocation and to extract frequency from the Sejong Balanced Corpus. For a beginner's guide to using the Sejong Corpus and related tools, see Kim and Choi (2020), which provides basic information. In addition, the Sejong Project contains an electronic dictionary that includes 25,458 nominals, 15,181 verbs, 4,398 adjectives, and 4,320 adverbs. The grammatical information and concrete examples in the dictionary will be a useful resource for KSL learners and teachers.

Although the Sejong Project has provided empirical resources, including an L1 pedagogical corpus and such tools as concordancers and an electronic dictionary, the practical utility of the Sejong Corpus can be controversial because of the limited accessibility of the corpus data, a lack of balance and representativeness, and a lack of concrete information on the accuracy of tagging and analysis. Despite these issues, the Sejong Corpus will still serve as the major pedagogical L1 corpus for reflecting empirical language use of native speakers of Korean. In addition, the Sejong Corpus will serve as a reference corpus that will provide comprehensive information about the language for learner corpus research. As Leech (2002) emphasizes, a reference corpus is accepted as "a de facto standard for the language" and somehow it has to "represent the language." He explains that a reference corpus can be viewed for users as a standard of comparison to compare with some other variety of the language or some other languages (p. 3). He also claims that the representativeness of a reference corpus is determined by two factors: diversity, "a full sampling of the varieties of the language," and balance, "the subsamples or the subcorpora of different language varieties must in some sense be proportionate to their importance in the language" (p. 5). He also points out that the BNC Sampler Corpus, with only 1 million words of speech and 1 million words of writing, is better balanced than the whole BNC. In parallel, the Sejong Balanced Corpus, with about 10 million *ecels*, is expected to function better as a reference corpus than the final version of the Sejong Corpus released to the public.

Besides the Sejong Corpus, there are other open resources of corpora, including the KAIST raw corpus (70 million *ecels*, domains including novels, non-literature, articles, etc.), the KAIST morpho-syntactically annotated corpus (1 million *ecels*),[6] and the Exo-brain Corpora V. 5.0, which was developed by multiple institutions, including KAIST, the Electronics and Telecommunication Research Institute (ETRI), Ulsan University, etc., and is a corpus developed for natural-language processing (NLP) and speech-learning data.[7] These resources license open access and tagging guidelines, but the databases have been developed for feeding the machine-learning process of NLP projects. Therefore, the practical applicability of the corpora seems to be less promising, although there is still room for investigating their usability.

Learner corpus and its application for KSL

Another type of specialized corpora is the learner corpus. In this section, the definition of learner corpus and its related issues will be examined. In second language research, learner language and errors have been already identified as the major object of the study, and there have been numerous studies utilizing small (or larger) scale, paper-based corpora collecting learner language. With the advance of corpus linguistics, learner corpora have made remarkable progress by developing electronic collections of L2 data with explicit design criteria. Granger et al. (2015) points out two significant advantages: 1) scaled-up data in electronic format from a great number of learners enhance representativeness of corpora, and 2) the data can be easily accessible and analyzed with software tools equipped with multi-functionalities, i.e., part-of-speech tools and concordance programs specifying linguistic contexts, frequency, collocations, word clusters, keywords, and error analysis. Electronic learner corpora may add learner error annotation and analysis through error editors, which facilitates studies of automatic error detection and error correction in learner corpus research. To increase the usability of learner corpus for second language acquisition and language teaching and learning, it is crucial to understand the specific usages of learner corpus with error information related in these fields and explore how its usability can be improved through clear design criteria and systematic annotation system.

Usages of learner corpus and error annotation in KSL

In line with the advancement of corpus linguistics and computational tools, a new interdisciplinary strand of learner corpus research (LCR) has grown rapidly since the late 1980s. LCr has been progressing with strong theoretical and applicative potential and the potential to connect to the diverse fields of second language acquisition, language learning and teaching, NLP, etc. With the developing computational and statistical tools, LCR has become a crossroad of these fields. Although Korean has relatively fewer resources of learner corpora and tools at the current stage, a remarkable progress of Korean learner corpora is expected in the next decade with the growing interest in Korean language learning and expanding computational resources facilitating Korean corpus analysis.

Learner corpora are developed for a variety of reasons – to assist in pedagogical studies (e.g., Nesselhauf, 2004), to provide raw material for second language acquisition (SLA) research (e.g., Myles, 2005), to serve as testbeds for NLP systems (e.g., Ott & Ziai, 2010), and so on. Depending on specific goals, different aspects of learner language are focused. Thus, the design of learner corpora varies from project to project. However, explicit design criteria need to be clarified in the process of learner corpus build-up. Tono (2003) provides three major categories of design considerations for building learner corpora: 1) language-related criteria (e.g., mode, medium, genre, topic), 2) task-related criteria (e.g., data collection, elicitation), and 3) learner-related criteria (e.g., EFL or ESL, age, sex, mother tongue, overseas experience).

Table 14.2 Design considerations for building learner corpora

Types of feature language related	Task-related	Learner-related
Mode	Data collection	Internal-cognitive
[written/spoken]	[cross-sectional/	[age/cognitive style]
Genre	longitudinal]	Internal-affective
[letter/diary/essay]	Elicitation	[motivation/attitude]
Style	[spontaneous/prepared]	L1 background
[narration/argumentation]	Use of references	L2 environment
Topic	[dictionary/source text]	[ESL/EFL]/[level of school]
[general/leisure/etc.]	Time limitation	L2 proficiency
	[fixed/free/homework]	[standard test score]

Source: Tono, 2003, p. 800

As Tono (2003) emphasizes, one of the strengths of LCR is that the learner corpora can be shared with other researchers and can be carefully scrutinized by them. Thus, clear design criteria need to be systematically developed and publicized. Otherwise, the developed learner corpus will not be broadly used in the community. Granger (2004) elaborates two practical usages of learner corpora: contrastive interlanguage analysis (CIA), introduced by Granger (1998), and computer-aided error analysis (CEA: Dagneaux, Denness, & Granger, 1998). CIA involves the comparison of interlanguage (IL) data with L1 data and a comparison of different types of IL data of different L1 backgrounds. CEA is based on learner corpora with error annotation, which is based on a standardized system of error tags (p. 40). Both CIA and CEA have been major methodological practices of LCR and have contributed to developing resources for SLA or second language learning and teaching.[8] If learner corpora with a transparent and clear annotation is available, error studies become reproducible and replicable, which is aligned with the study of language acquisition processes (Lüdeling & Hirschmann, 2015). Therefore, systematic schemes and guidelines for error annotation plays a critical role in identifying and categorizing characteristics of learner language. With respect to error annotation tasks, Tono (2003) describes categorizing learner errors as a laborious and often fruitless job because there are various ways of classifying errors. While considering that different perspectives on error types may lead to very low inter-rater reliability, he highlights the importance of a generic error tagset in developing learner corpora. As specified by Lüdeling and Hirschman (2015), "learner corpora can be a valuable source of data for reproducible studies of language acquisition -but only if they are well designed, well described and publicly available. Corpus data must be interpreted and categorized to be useful" (p. 135).

Unannotated learner data can be used for exploring practical research questions related to learner profiles and to patterns and distributions of vocabulary and expressions. However, interpretation and categorization of learner data requires error annotation, which increases the value of leaner corpora. In addition to clear design criteria and error tagsets, it is important to recognize that error annotation is to present multilayered interpretations of the data with distinct levels of linguistic features, such as phonetic or phonological annotation, part-of-speech tagging, annotation of word chunks beyond word units, semantic/pragmatic annotation, etc. Thus, learner corpora need to provide multilayered standalone annotation layers that are independent from the raw data. This multilayered standoff architecture licenses the usability of learner corpus by keeping different interpretations of the same data. The existing systems for providing multilayered annotation include, for example, ANNIS (which stands for annotation of information structure, an open-source, cross-platform of Linux, Mac, and Windows; web browser-based search and visualization architecture; Krause & Zeldes, 2016)[9] and EXMARaLDA (extensible markup language for discourse annotation,[10] for working with oral corpora on a computer, including *Partitur-Editor*, a transcription and annotation tool; *Corpus-Manager*, a tool for managing corpora; and *EXAKT*, a query and analysis tool; www.exmaralda.org).

Korean learner corpora

In this section, two Korean learner corpora will be introduced: one is a small size corpus with particle error annotation developed for Korean learner language analysis (KoLLA, https://cl.indiana.edu/~kolla/), and the other is a large size learner corpus with error annotation released by the National Institute of Korean Language (https://kcorpus.korean.go.kr/ in Korean). Both learner corpora and related documentation are accessible online.

KoLLA AND ERROR ANNOTATION

The KoLLA project investigates data, annotation, and NLP tools for Korean particle usage among learners of Korean. A small corpus of 100 writing samples has been utilized to develop an automatic machine learning–based system for Korean particle-error detection. The package includes a raw corpus, an annotated corpus, an error tagset, and related papers. The raw corpus data is composed of 25 heritage beginners, 25 heritage intermediates, 25 foreign beginners, and 25 foreign intermediates. Despite its small size, the KoLLA corpus has proven to be substantially useful for defining the annotation scheme of particle errors and decisions that need to be made – largely orthogonal to NLP uses (Dickinson, Israel, & Lee, 2010, 2011) – to make it applicable for error analysis. Israel (2014) utilizes the annotated corpus as a crucial component of an evaluation set for the error detection system using machine learning. Along with serving as a sound test set for NLP, the KoLLA corpus provides a valuable resource for both pedagogical and corpus linguistics research fields through error annotation. The corpus features a multilayered annotation scheme that provides a step-by-step look at how the errors are annotated. The annotation scheme adheres to the principal of minimal interaction and remains as theory neutral as possible while still providing robust information about each particle in the corpus. To encode error annotation, the corpus annotation has been developed by using the EXMARaLDA that allows multilayered mark-ups. Lee, Dickinson, and Israel (2016) provide the KoLLA corpus design and error annotation scheme in detail.

In an annotation sample (Figure 14.3), annotation tiers include the original word tokens and corrected spacing and spelling errors. In addition to corrected spacing and spelling errors, two

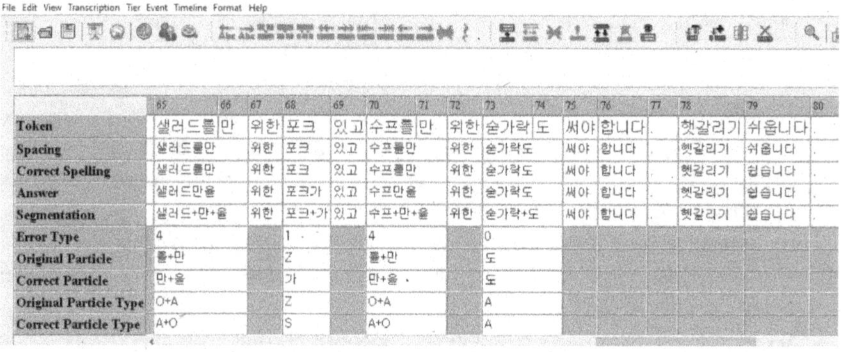

	65	66	67	68	69	70	71	72	73	74	75	76	77	78	79	80
Token	샐러드를	만	위한	포크	있고	수프를	만	위한	숟가락	도	써야	합니다	.	헷갈리기	쉬웁니다	.
Spacing	샐러드를만		위한	포크	있고	수프를만		위한	숟가락도		써야	합니다	.	헷갈리기	쉬웁니다	.
Correct Spelling	샐러드를만		위한	포크	있고	수프를만		위한	숟가락도		써야	합니다	.	헷갈리기	쉽습니다	.
Answer	샐러드만을		위한	포크가	있고	수프만을		위한	숟가락도		써야	합니다	.	헷갈리기	쉽습니다	.
Segmentation	샐러드+만+을		위한	포크+가	있고	수프+만+을		위한	숟가락+도		써야	합니다	.	헷갈리기	쉽습니다	.
Error Type	4			1		4			0							
Original Particle	를+만			Z		를+만			도							
Correct Particle	만+을			가		만+을			도							
Original Particle Type	O+A			Z		O+A			A							
Correct Particle Type	A+O			S		A+O			A							

Figure 14.3 An annotation sample using Partitur Editor of EXMARaLDA

other layers are added to facilitate automatic morpheme analysis and part-of-speech (POS) recognition: an answer layer and a segmentation layer. After the spacing and spelling errors are corrected, the corrected form(s) have been added in the answer layer, followed, in turn, by hand-tagged segmentation of correct forms. These separate answer and segmentation layers are designed for facilitating automatic error detection and correction. Although general POS tagging information can be incorporated on top of the corrected spacing and spelling forms, segmentation has been added only for the corrected forms of the related errors. This option is to expedite processing by focusing on specific errors, including particles and verb conjugation. Korean POS tagging corresponds to morpheme analysis due to linguistic properties of Korean as an agglutinative language. Therefore, POS tagging output includes derivational morphemes as well as inflectional morphemes, which may unnecessarily complicate our annotation. Instead of providing general POS annotation, POS information has been added in separate layers on the original error and correct forms, as in Figure 14.1, where the preprocessing components – including correct spacing, spelling, answer, and segmentation – appear on the top four tiers. After annotating preprocessing tiers to facilitate error detection and correction, specific error annotation can be added. Error annotation requires systematic classification of a linguistic category and related error types.

For developing leaner corpora with error annotation, it is crucial to recognize that annotation is not an end task in itself. We must consider its purpose. Error annotation needs to be better articulated to secure the quality of learner corpora. In addition to particle errors, different annotation tasks using the same learner corpus of KoLLA and its extension have been also explored: particle errors (Lee, Dickinson, & Israel, 2013; Israel, Dickinson, & Lee, 2013) and verbal conjugation errors (Jang & Lee, 2014). The solid annotation secures the quality and usability of learner data. Especially for error annotation, it is also necessary to outline the scope of errors: what types of errors occur, what types of morphosyntactic forms are involved in errors, how other words interact with the target forms and then to incorporate insights into annotation schemes. These issues are pertinent to the annotation of erroneous functional elements and argument dropping in morphologically rich languages, although many issues – e.g., the definition of grammaticality and handling multiple correct answers – face any learner language annotation. Given that other languages, such as Japanese and Arabic, face some of the same issues (e.g., Hanaoka, Mima, & Tsujii, 2010; Abuhakema, Faraj, Feldman, & Fitzpatrick, 2008), fleshing them out for error annotation and detection is useful beyond one particular language.

Lee, Dickinson et al. (2016) focus on the flexible definition of grammaticality depending on target analyses. They point out that certain grammatical patterns need to be annotated with a looser definition of grammaticality and that there are situations where more than one target form (answer) could be correct. Any form that makes the sentence grammatical will end up in the answer set. It may seem like there is usually a best answer, but there are no clear criteria for selecting one. Elaborating issues of grammaticality and multiple target forms are critical in "developing best practices for annotation and evaluation" of learner data (Tetreault, Filatova, & Chodorow, 2010).

Lastly, to gauge the reliability of the annotation, it is important to evaluate the consistence of annotation by measuring inter-annotator agreement rates in addition to developing gold standard guidelines and tagsets. Evaluation of error annotation is challenging because there are many possibly controversial decisions to make in error tagging, including target hypothesis and target error assignment (Lüdeling & Hirschmann, 2015). Lee, Dickinson et al. (2016) conclude that it is very difficult to achieve a high level of inter-annotator agreement in consideration of the complexity of annotation tasks with learner language. According to them, annotator agreement rates on error types (categories) seem to be much lower than on error tokens. Therefore, it is more practical for learner corpus researchers to secure solid annotation of error tokens first, to detect erroneous input and determine correct target forms. For developing learner corpora, it is noteworthy that error annotation with a well-developed scheme and specific guidelines is prerequisite for the quality of the learner corpora. In addition, learner corpus researchers may consider exploring more details on examples showing lower interannotator agreement ratios or higher error rates of annotation.

At present, there is very little work on annotated learner corpora for morphologically rich languages with open access and documentation. The corpus annotation in the KoLLA framework and its guidelines indicate the significant role of Korean learner corpora in KSL and the related fields.

NATIONAL INSTITUTE OF KOREAN LANGUAGE (NIKL) KOREAN LEARNER CORPUS WITH ERROR ANNOTATION

The Korean learner corpus and related resources have been under development with the supervision of NIKL, a government institution making language policy and sponsoring linguistic research (2015–2020). The NIKL learner corpus project aims to provide a large size corpus with error annotation for developing pedagogical materials and promoting learner language research.[11] It is also expected to be used for developing language learning and testing as well as Korean learner dictionaries. The corpus includes the written and the spoken learner data produced by Korean learners from Level 1 to Level 6 from 142 countries with 91 different L1 backgrounds. As of November 2020, the original unannotated corpus included 3.78 million *ecels* and 26,152 samples. Table 14.3 shows the composition of the corpus.

The corpus data were largely collected from three sources, including 18 Korean language institutions affiliated with Korean universities, 12 Korean immigrant educational institutions, and 33 educational institutions teaching Korean abroad, including 12 universities and 21 King Sejong Institutes. The corpus data were collected in collaboration with these institutions. The collected original data were digitized and transcribed by trained annotators, and morpheme tags were added using an automatic morpheme analyzer. Then, the error annotation was added to the morpheme-tagged corpus. Han et al. (2020) provides the details of the corpus design, annotation processing, and error analysis. More importantly, NIKL's website offers open access to the resources developed for Korean language education at https://kcenter.korean.go.kr/, which include project reports, standard language curriculums, and pedagogical resources. The NIKL's website for the Korean learner corpus allows searching lexical items and errors with statistical information, including learner background, at https://kcorpus.korean.go.kr/. They also provide learner corpora built between 2015 and 2020.

The NIKL corpus package includes a morpheme-tagged corpus. According to Kim (2017), the morpheme annotation of the NIKL corpus is based on the same annotation scheme as the Sejong National Corpus. It was also developed in conjunction with error annotation. It

Table 14.3 Composition of the NIKL Korean learner corpus

Corpus type	Written		Spoken		Total	
	ecels	# of samples	ecels	# of samples	ecels	# of samples
Raw	2,952,566	24,342	831,525	1,810	3,784,091	26,152
Morpheme-tagged	2,037,753	17,266	591,508	1,255	2,629,261	18,521
Error-annotated	462,325	4,149	331,049	75	793,374	4,903

is basically using the target hypothesis that the learner data can be analyzed the same way as native-speaker data or that the intended form of the instance can be inferred and tagged (Hirschmann, Doolittle, & Lüdeling, 2007; Rooy, 2015, p. 100). Since learner data contain errors, non-canonical forms, the annotation requires a solution of formulating the target hypothesis and the tagging of the presumed error-corrected forms. Although using the target hypothesis and annotation of the corrected forms may license more accurate retrieval of information from the corpus, there is controversy of the comparative fallacy among scholars with respect to the targeted annotation; the researchers may falsely assume that the target is what the learner was aiming at. In other words, there may be distance between the actual learner data and the target (Rooy, 2015, p. 102).[12]

The quality of annotations in the NIKL corpus might be contentious given a lack of the inter-annotator agreement ratio and the use of a less specific annotation scheme of four error types: addition, deletion, replacement, and malformation (including spelling errors). In addition, the Korean learner corpus does not allow multilayered annotation of errors with overlapping values across different levels. It also assumes one-to-one mapping for a learner error and an answer, but not multi-target forms, which are quite frequently observed in error annotation. Nonetheless, it is notable that the NIKL learner corpus is still under expansion and more resources are being added, which makes it difficult to provide a comprehensive evaluation of the corpus at this time. One clear advantage of the NIKL learner corpora is the availability of a large size raw corpus and annotated packages with search tools. To search keywords, errors, and distinct error types, and statistical results, etc., the NIKL website provides flexible search tools at https://kcorpus.korean.go.kr/ in Korean. More importantly, the raw learner corpus itself will function as a valuable resource for LCR researchers in the future. The whole data can be accessible by filling out the form online and making a formal request to NIKL.

Conclusion

Corpora and related tools have revolutionized linguistic description and analysis over the past few decades. Exponentially growing corpora and resources in ESL shed light on a new direction to applied linguistics and pedagogical studies in other languages. Rigorous studies connecting corpus linguistics and second language learning and teaching have demonstrated that corpora make it possible to provide more accurate linguistic descriptions and comparisons of native and learner language and make substantial contributions to improve research and pedagogical practices of second language learning and teaching. Adopting new methods and resources of corpora and tools in second language learning and teaching is demanding; it require learners and teachers to acquire new skills, such as extracting linguistic information of lexical usage, frequency, collocation, keywords, etc., and to analyze corpus information for developing pedagogical and research materials.

This article has focused on some of key aspects of corpora and introduced accessible corpora and tools for KSL. Although there has been consistent interest in applying corpus linguistic methods to identify and to develop research and pedagogical materials, most of the studies have focused on usages or frequency of lexical items or patterns based on a large size L1 Sejong Corpus or small size learner corpora that were individually constructed. With the limited availability of L1 and L2 corpora and tools, corpus linguistic approaches in KSL have not yet flourished as in ESL. However, by raising awareness of the practical impact and great potential of corpus linguistics in applied linguistics and second language learning and teaching, further expansion with research activities and pedagogical applications of corpora is predicted. The accessible L1 and L2 learner corpora mentioned in Section 3 are expected to function as grounding resources for further developments. The National Sejong Corpus and search tools are useful resources for developing pedagogical materials and identifying context-specific L1 usages. It is particularly promising to have the large size NIKL learner corpus with free access to raw learner data so that researchers and pedagogical practitioners can easily use them. There is still much to be done to integrate corpus-based methods and tools in KSL. The most pressing need is to compile leaner corpora with solid annotation schemes and guidelines and to provide annotation tools so that individual researchers and practitioners can easily access and flexibly manipulate them for their own purposes. This task requires more communication between corpus researchers and practitioners so that corpus-based resources can be effectively utilized in language learning and teaching. In addition, there need to be more applications using diverse types of corpora, including spoken data, longitudinal learner data, and specialized corpora targeting specific learner groups. It is also noteworthy that research outcomes and concordance tools of corpus-based ESL studies can be practical resources for exploring developments of corpus linguistics in KSL.

Notes

1. McEnery et al. (2006). Also, refer to Kučera and Francis (1967) and Francis and Kučera (1964).
2. More details of sampling have been discussed in McEnery et al.'s (2006) A2.5 (pp. 19–21).
3. Although Römer (2011) uses the term "pedagogical corpus applications," these applications cover resources of L2 research overall.
4. All the resources of Korean language education projects sponsored by NIKL are available at https://kcenter.korean.go.kr/.
5. Hong Yun-pyo (2009)
6. http://semanticweb.kaist.ac.kr/home/index.php/KAIST_Corpus.
7. http://aiopen.etri.re.kr/service_dataset.php.
8. Callies (2015) presents a critical assessment of these major practices in learner corpus analysis and present methodology.
9. https://corpus-tools.org/annis/.
10. https://exmaralda.org/en/about-exmaralda/.
11. To see the details of the design and issues related to the NIKL learner corpora, see Kim (2017) and Kang (2017).
12. Ragheb and Dickinson (2011) suggest that learner language annotation does not need to be target hypothesis based given three principles: all words must be tagged for POS and syntactic dependencies in addition to errors, textual evidence for assigning categories can be utilized instead of using inferences from the target, and multilayered annotation should be provided.

References

Abuhakema, G., Faraj, R., Feldman, A., & Fitzpatrick, E. (2008). Annotating an Arabic learner corpus for error. *Department of Linguistics Faculty Scholarship and Creative Works*. 10. Retrieved from https://digitalcommons.montclair.edu/linguistics-facpubs/10

Aston, G. (2001). Learning with corpora: An overview. In G. Aston (Ed.), *Learning with corpora* (pp. 7–45). Houston: Athelstan.

Aston, G., Bernardini, S., & Stewart, D. (2004). *Corpora and language learners*. Amsterdam and Philadelphia: John Benjamins Publishing Company.

Barlow, M. (2005). Computer-based analyses of learner language. In R. Ellis & G. Barkhuizen (Eds.), *Analyzing learner language* (pp. 335–369). Oxford, UK: Oxford University Press.

Biber, D. (1993). Representativeness in corpus design. *Literary and Linguistic Computing, 8*(4), 243–257.

Biber, D., Conrad, S., & Reppen, R. (1998). *Corpus linguistics: Investigating language structure and use*. Cambridge: Cambridge University Press.

Biber, D., Johansson, S., Leech, J., Conrad, S., & Finegan, E. (1999). *Longman grammar of spoken and written English*. London: Longman.

Burnard, L., & McEnery, T. (Eds.). (2000). *Rethinking language pedagogy from a corpus perspective: Papers from the third international conference on teaching and language corpora*. Frankfurt/Main: Peter Lang.

Callies, M. (2015). Using learner corpora in language testing and assessment: Current practice and future challenges. In E. Castello, K. Ackerley, & F. Coccetta (Eds.), *Studies in learner corpus linguistics: Research and applications for foreign language teaching and assessment* (pp. 21–35). Frankfurt/Main: Peter Lang.

Chambers, A. (2015). Integrating corpus consultation in language learning. *Language Learning and Technology*, 9(2), 111–125.

Dagneaux, E., Denness, S., & Granger, S. (1998). Computer-aided error analysis. *System*, 26(2), 163–174.

Díaz-Negrillo, A., & Thompson, P. (2013). Learner corpora: Looking towards the future. In A. Díaz-Negrillo, N. Ballier, & P. Thompson (Eds.), *Automatic treatment and analysis of learner corpus data* (pp. 9–30). Amsterdam and Philadelphia: John Benjamins Publishing Company.

Dickinson, M., Israel, R., & Lee, S. (2010). Building a Korean web corpus for analyzing learner language. In *Proceedings of the NAACL HLT 2010 sixth web as corpus workshop* (pp. 8–16). Association for Computational Linguistics.

Dickinson, M., Israel, R., & Lee, S. (2011). Developing methodology for Korean particle error detection. In *Proceedings of the 6th workshop on innovative use of NLP for building educational applications* (pp. 1419–1427). Association for Computational Linguistics. Retrieved from https://aclanthology.org/W11-1400.

Ellis, N. C., Römer, U., & O'Donnell, M. B. (2016). *Usage-based approaches to language acquisition and processing: Cognitive and corpus investigations*. New York: Wiley.

Ellis, N. C., Simpson-Vlach, R., Römer, U., O'Donnell, M. B., & Wulff, S. (2015). Learner corpora and formulaic language in second language acquisition research. In S. Granger, G. Gilquin, & F. Meunier (Eds.), *The Cambridge handbook of learner corpus research* (pp. 357–378). Cambridge, UK: Cambridge University Press.

Francis, W. N., & Kučera, H. (1964). *A standard corpus of present-day edited American English, for use with digital computers*. Providence, RI: Department of Linguistics, Brown University. Revised 1971. Revised and amplified 1979.

Frequency Dictionary of Spoken Korean 1, 2 (2015). Seoul: Hankuk Munhwa Sa.

Gablasova, D., Brezina, V., & McEnery, T. (2019). *The Trinity Lancaster corpus*: Applications in language teaching and materials development. In S. Götz & J. Mukherjee (Eds.), *Learner corpora and language teaching* (pp. 8–28). Amsterdam and Philadelphia: John Benjamins Publishing Company.

Gabrielatos, C. (2005). Corpora and language teaching: Just a fling, or wedding bells? *TESL-EJ*, 8(4), 1–37. Retrieved from www.tesl-ej.org/ej32/a1.html

Gilquin, G. (2015). From design to collection of learner corpora. In S. Granger, G. Gilquin, & F. Meunier (Eds.), *The Cambridge handbook of learner corpus research* (pp. 9–34). Cambridge: Cambridge Press. https://doi.org/10.1017/CBO9781139649414.002

Gilquin, G., & Granger, S. (2010). How can data-driven learning be used in language teaching?. In A. O'Keeffe & M. McCarthy (Eds.), *The Routledge handbook of corpus linguistics* (pp. 359–370). Oxon and New York: Routledge. Retrieved from http://hdl.handle.net/2078.1/75724.

Granger, S. (1998). The computer learner corpus: A versatile new source of data for SLA research. In S. Granger (Ed.), *Learner English on computer* (pp. 3–18). Oxon and New York: Routledge.

Granger, S. (2004). Computer learner corpus research: Current status and future prospects. In U. Connor & Th. A. Upton (Eds.), *Applied corpus linguistics: A multidimensional perspective* (pp. 123–145). Amsterdam: Rodopi.

Granger, S. (2009). The contribution of learner corpora to second language acquisition and foreign language teaching. In K. Aijmer (Ed.), *Corpora and language teaching* (pp. 13–332). Amsterdam and Philadelphia: John Benjamins Publishing Company. https://doi.org/10.1075/scl.33.04gra

Granger, S. (2011). How to use foreign and second language learner corpora. In A. Mackey & S. Gass (Eds.), *Research methods in second language acquisition: A practical guide* (pp. 7–29). Oxford, UK: Wiley-Blackwell. https://doi.org/10.1002/9781444347340.ch2

Granger, S., Dagneaux, E., & Meunier, F. (2002). *International corpus of learner English* [Handbook and CD-ROM]. Louvain-la-Neuve: Presses universitaires de Louvain.

Granger, S., Gilquin, G., & Meunier, F. (2015). Introduction: Learner corpus research – past, present and future. In S. Granger, G. Gilquin, & F. Meunier (Eds.), *The Cambridge handbook of learner corpus research* (pp. 2–5). Cambridge, UK: Cambridge University Press.

Han, S., Kim, S., Kim, J., Kim, I., Kim, H., An, K., . . . & Lee, Y. (2020). *The 2020 project report on the Korean learner corpora research and construction*. Seoul: National Institute of Korean Language.

Hanaoka, H., Mima, H., & Tsujii, J. (2010). A Japanese particle corpus built by example-based annotation. In *Proceedings of the seventh international conference on language resources and evaluation (LREC'10)* (pp. 17–23). Valletta, Malta: European Language Resources Association.

Hirschmann, H., Doolittle, S., & Lüdeling, A. (2007). Syntactic annotation of noncanonical linguistic structures. In M. Davies, P. Rayson, S. Hunston, & Danielsson (Eds.), *Proceedings of corpus linguistics* (pp. 27–30). Birmingham. Retrieved from http://edoc.hu-berlin.de/oa/conferences/reJbZHl3dKI9M/PDF/25hnJRhhYgJQY.pdf

Hong, Y. (2009). Outcomes and tasks of the 21st Century Sejong Project. *New Korean Life* (새국어생활), *19*(1), 5–33. National Institute of Korean Language.

Hunston, S. (2002). *Corpora in applied linguistics*. Cambridge: Cambridge University Press.

Hunston, S., & Francis, G. (1999). *Pattern grammar: A corpus-driven approach to the lexical grammar of English*. Amsterdam and Philadelphia: John Benjamins Publishing Company.

Hwang, Y., & Choi, J. (2016). Exploring the 21st Century Sejong Corpus – Utilizing the center for language information. *New Korean Life* (새국어 생활), *26*(2), 73–86. National Institute of Korean Language.

Hyland, K. (1998). *Hedging in scientific research articles*. Amsterdam and Philadelphia: John Benjamins Publishing Company. http://doi.org/10.1075/pbns.54.

Hyland, K. (2005). Stance and engagement: A model of interaction in academic discourse. *Discourse Studies*, *7*(2), 173–192. https://doi.org/10.1177/1461445605050365

Israel, R. (2014). *Building a Korean particle error detection system from the ground up* [Doctoral dissertation]. Linguistics Department. Indiana University.

Israel, R., Dickinson, M., & Lee, S. (2013). Detecting and correcting learner Korean particle omission errors. In *Proceedings of the 6th international conference on natural language processing* (IJCNLP-13) (pp. 1419–1427). Nagoya, Japan: Asian Federation of Natural Language Processing. Retrieved from https://aclanthology.org/I13-1.

Jang, C., & Lee, S. (2014). Annotating verb errors in Korean learner corpus. In *2014 Asia Pacific Corpus Linguistics Conference (APCLC)*. Hong Kong: Asia Pacific Corpus Linguistics Association.

Johns, T. (1986). Microconcord: A language -learner's research tool. *System*, *14*, 151–162.

Johns, T. (2002), Data-driven learning: The perpetual challenge. In B. Kettemann & G. Marko (Eds.), *Teaching and learning by doing corpus analysis* (pp. 107–117). Amsterdam, The Netherlands: Rodopi.

Kang, H. (2017). *A study on Korean learner's corpus*. Seoul: Sotong.

Kettemann, B., & Marko, G. (Eds.). (2002). Teaching and learning by doing corpus analysis. In *Proceedings of the fourth international conference on teaching and language corpora, Graz 19–24 July, 2000. Language and Computers*, 42. New York: Rodopi.

Kim, H. (2006). Korean national corpus in the 21st century Sejong project. In *Proceedings of the 13th NIJL international symposium* (pp. 49–54). National Institute for Japanese Language, Tokyo.

Kim, H. (2017). Factors and practice of Korean learner corpus annotation, *Baedalmal*, *61*, 149–173.

Kim, H. (2018). *Research and establishment of Korean Corpus in 2018*. Seoul: National Institute of Korean Language.

Kim, H. (2019). Trends and perspectives in corpus-based Korean language research. *Korean Linguistics*, *83*, 1–33. http://doi.org/10.20405/kl.2019.05.83.1

Kim, H., & Choi, J. (2020). *Basics of corpus construction – Guide for the beginners of Korean corpora*. Seoul: Kyungjin Publishing Co.

Ko, S., Kim, M., Kim J., Seo, S., Chung, H., & Han, S. (2004). *An analysis of Korean learner corpora and errors*. Seoul: Hanguk Publishing Co.

Korean Collocation Dictionary for Korean Language Education. (2007). Seoul: Communication Books Co.

Korean Synonym Dictionary. (2012). Seoul: Bak Yi Jeong Publisher.

Korean Usage Frequency of Basic Korean Vocabulary. (2014). Seoul: Hankuk Munhwa Sa.

Krause, T., & Zeldes, A. (2016). ANNIS3: A new architecture for generic corpus query and visualization. *Digital Scholarship in the Humanities*, *2016*(31). Retrieved from http://dsh.oxfordjournals.or g/content/31/1/11

Kučera, H., & Francis, W. (1967). *Computational analysis of presentday American English*. Providence, RI: Brown University Press.

Learner's Dictionary of Korean. (2006). Seoul: Shinwon Prime Publisher.

Lee, S. (2017, 2018) *Basic research for lexical grading and selection of basic vocabulary in Korean*. National Institute of Korean Language Report.

Lee, S., Dickinson, M., & Israel, R. (2013). Corpus-based error analysis of Korean particles. In S. Granger, G. Gilquin, & F. Meunier (Eds.), *Twenty years of learner corpus research. Looking back, moving ahead: Proceedings of the First Learner Corpus Research Conference (LCR 2011) Louvain-la-Neuve* (pp. 289–299). Louvain-la-Neuve, Belgium: Presses Universitaires de Louvain.

Lee, S., Dickinson, M., & Israel, R. (2016). Challenges of learner corpus annotation: Focusing on Korean learner language analysis (KoLLA) system. In *Language facts and perspectives* (Vol. 83, pp. 221–251). Seoul: Institute of Language and Information Studies.

Lee, S., Jang, S., & Seo, S. (2016). *A frequency dictionary of Korean: Core vocabulary for learners*. Oxon and New York: Routledge.

Leech, G. (1991). The state of the art in corpus linguistics. In K. Aijimer & B. Altenberg (Eds.), *English corpus linguistics: Studies in honour of Jan Svartvik*. London: Longman.

Leech, G. (1997). Teaching and language corpora: A convergence. In A. Wichmann, S. Fligelstone, T. McEnery, & G. Knowles (Eds.), *Teaching and language corpora* (pp. 1–23). London: Longman.

Leech, G. (2002). The importance of reference corpora. *Corpus lingüísticos. Presente y futuro*. Donostia: UZEI. Retrieved June 2013 from http://goo.gl/B9FK4

Lüdeling, A., & Hirschmann, H. (2015). Error annotation systems. In S. Granger, G. Gilquin, & F. Meunier (Eds.), *The Cambridge handbook of learner corpus research* (pp. 135–157). Cambridge, UK: Cambridge University Press.

McEnery, T., Brezina, V., Gablasova, D., & Banerjee, J. (2019). Corpus linguistics, learner corpora, and SLA: Employing technology to analyze language use. *Annual Review of Applied Linguistics*, 39, 74–92. https://doi.org/10.1017/s0267190519000096

McEnery, T., & Wilson, A. (2001). *Corpus linguistics*. Edinburgh: Edinburgh University Press.

McEnery, T., Xiao, R., & Tono, Y. (2006). *Corpus-based language studies: An advanced resource book*. London: Taylor & Francis.

Meunier, F. (2012). Learner corpora in the classroom: A useful and sustainable didactic resource. In L. Pedrazzini & A. Nava (Eds.), *Learning and teaching English: Insights from research* (pp. 211–228). Milan: Polymetrica.

Min, K. (2010). A study of corpus design for KAP teaching. *Language and Culture*, 6(1), 137–156.

Myles, F. (2005). Interlanguage corpora and second language acquisition research. *Second Language Research*, 21(4), 373–391.

Myles, F. (2015). Second language acquisition theory and learner corpus research. In S. Granger, G. Gilquin, & F. Meunier (Eds.), *The Cambridge handbook of learner corpus research* (pp. 309–331). Cambridge, UK: Cambridge University Press.

Nesselhauf, N. (2004). Learner corpora and their potential in language eteaching. In J. Sinclair (Ed.), *How to use corpora in language teaching* (pp. 125–152). Amsterdam and Philadelphia: John Benjamins Publishing Company.

Ott, N., & Ziai, R. (2010). Evaluating dependency parsing performance on German learner language. In *Proceedings of the ninth international workshop on treebanks and linguistic theories*. NEALT Proceedings Series (Vol. 9, pp. 175–186). Northern European Association for Language Technology (NEALT). Retrieved from http://omilia.uio.no/nealt/.

Ragheb, M., & Dickinson, M. (2011). Avoiding the comparative fallacy in the annotation of learner corpora. In *Selected proceedings of the 2010 second language research forum: Reconsidering SLA research, dimensions, and directions* (pp. 114–124). Cascadilla Proceedings Project, Somerville, MA.

Römer, U. (2008). Corpora and language teaching. In A. Lüdeling & M. Kytö (Eds.), *Corpus linguistics: An international handbook* (Vol. 1, pp. 112–130). HSK Series. Berlin: Mouton de Gruyter.

Römer, U. (2009). Corpus research and practice: What help do teachers need and what can we offer? In K. Aijmer (Ed.), *Corpora and language teaching* (pp. 83–98). Amsterdam and Philadelphia: John Benjamins Publishing Company.

Römer, U. (2011). Corpus research applications in second language teaching. *Annual Review of Applied Linguistics*, 31, 205–225. Cambridge University Press.

Rooy, B. (2015). Annotating learner corpora. In S. Granger, G. Gilquin, & F. Meunier (Eds.), *The Cambridge handbook of learner corpus research* (pp. 79–105). Cambridge, UK: Cambridge University Press.

Seo, S., Yoo, H., & Nam, Y. (2002). Korean learner's corpus and Korean education. *Korean Language Education*, 13(1), 127–156. The International Association for Korean Language Education.

Sinclair, J. (Ed.). (1987). *Looking up: An account of the COBUILD project in lexical computing*. London: Collins ELT.

Sinclair, J. (1991). *Corpus, concordance, and collocation*. Oxford: Oxford University Press.

Sinclair, J. (1997). Corpus evidence in language description. In A. Wichmann, S. Fligelstone, T. McEnery, & G. Knowles (Eds.), *Teaching and language corpora* (pp. 27–39). London: Longman.

Sinclair, J. (2000). Lexical grammar. *Naujoji Metodologija, 24,* 191–203.

Sinclair, J. (Ed.). (2004). *How to use corpora in language teaching.* Amsterdam and Philadelphia: John Benjamins Publishing Company.

Sinclair, J., & Renouf, A. (1988). A lexical syllabus for language learning. In R. Carter & M. McCarthy (Eds.), *Vocabulary in language teaching* (pp. 140–158). London: Longman.

The Standard Korean Language Dictionary. (2008). Seoul: National Institute of Korean Language.

Stubbs, M. (1996). *Text and corpus analysis: Computer-assisted studies of language and culture.* Oxford: Blackwell.

Tetreault, J., Filatova, E., & Chodorow, M. (2010). Rethinking grammatical error annotation and evaluation with the Amazon mechanical turk. In *Proceedings of the NAACL HLT 2010. fifth workshop on innovative use of NLP for building educational applications* (pp. 45–48). Los Angeles. Association for Computational Linguistics. Retrieved from https://aclanthology.org/W10-1000.

Tognini-Bonelli, E. (2001). *Corpus linguistics at work.* Amsterdam and Philadelphia: John Benjamins Publishing Company.

Tono, Y. (2003). Learner corpora: Design, development, and applications. In D. Archer, P. Rayson, A. Wilson, & T. McEnery (Eds.), *Proceedings of the corpus linguistics 2003 conference. UCREL technical paper* (Vol. 16, pp. 800–809). Lancaster University.

Wichmann, A., Knowles, G., McEnery, A., & Fligelstone, S. (Eds.). (1997). *Teaching and language corpora.* London: Longman.

Willis, D., & Willis, J. (1989). *Collins COBUILD English course.* London: HarperCollins.

Yonsei Elementary Korean Dictionary. (2002). Seoul: Dong-a Co.

Yonsei Korean Dictionary. (1999). Seoul: Dusan Dong-a Publishing Co.

15
CONVERSATION ANALYSIS FOR KSL

Teaching and learning sequence organization

Mary Shin Kim

Introduction

Almost all language courses start with the teaching and learning of the very basics of conversational practices, such as greetings, *how-are-you* inquiries, and asking and answering questions, yet acquiring the conversational skills to engage and interact competently in an ordinary conversation is still the most challenging aspect of learning a second or foreign language. One of the main reasons for this is that "what people think they do in conversation and what they actually do may be incongruent" (Huth & Taleghani-Nikazm, 2006, p. 63). There is a discrepancy between the way conversational practices and relevant linguistic forms are typically taught in language classrooms and how they are actually designed and utilized by participants in social interaction. Conversation analysis (CA) provides an empirical and concrete understanding of how conversation works, which can help us address areas that are lacking in the teaching of conversation (Wong & Waring, 2010).

This chapter provides an overview of what CA can offer for Korean as a second language (KSL) pedagogy. One of the key findings of CA is the importance of understanding the composition of an utterance, or more specifically a turn, and its position in a sequence (Schgeloff, 1993). Research on Korean CA has been steadily growing since the 1990s, when pioneering studies by K-H. Kim (1992, 1993, 1999) expanded our understanding of how Korean speakers engage and interact (Kim & Kim, 2015). This research has demonstrated not only the intricate interplay between grammar and interaction (how speakers deploy certain grammatical resources to formulate particular actions and how they are understood by others in interaction) but also the fundamental procedures and practices of interaction (how speakers construct and allocate turns and implement actions within turns in a certain order in the overall interactional structure). While traditional grammar-focused instruction emphasizes how phrases and utterances are composed, CA is concerned both with the composition of utterances and how they are positioned in the trajectories of the actions or activities in which the participants are engaged.

How position matters is easily illustrated by observing how a word is deployed in different positions in authentic interaction. Let's look at a set of forms commonly translated as *yes* or *yeah* and used for affirmative answers: polite *ney/yey* (interchangeable phonological variants) and casual *ung/e*. Natural conversational data show that these simple affirmative tokens can carry out a wide range of different actions beyond affirmative answers (Kim, 1993; Kim &

Suh, 1998; Kim, 1999; Pyun, 2009; Oh & Park, 2017; Pyun & Yoon, forthcoming).[1] Excerpts 1–3, from ordinary telephone calls, show how they are produced and understood by the participants of the interaction in different ways depending on position in a stretch of talk.

In Excerpt 1, both speakers deploy *ney/yey* (lines 3, 5, 6) but with differences in positions and actions.

Excerpt 1   KO_5683

1   B: 어 야: 이거 뭐 안기부에서 연락 오는 거 아니[죠? 하하하
         e ya: ike mwe ankipwu-eyse yenlak o-nun ke ani-cyo? hahaha
         "Uh, wow, I am not going to be contacted by the Korean CIA, right? Hahaha"

2   A: [아니에요.
                                                     aniey-yo.
                                                     "No."

3   B: 네:.
         ney:.

4   B: 별일 없으시구요?
         pyelil eps-usi-kwu-yo.
         "Everything is well (with you)?"

5   A: 예.=
         yey.=

6   B: =예.
         =yey.

Excerpt 2 shows another use of *ney* (line 2), which here elicits a specific response from the prior speaker.

Excerpt 2   KO_6002

1   B: 언니 자주 못 만나요?
         enni cacwu mos manna-yo?
         "You cannot meet her often?"

2   A: 네?
         ney?

3   B: 자주 못 만나요?
         cacwu mos manna-yo?
         "You cannot meet (her) often?"

4   A: 자주 못 뵙죠.
         cacwu mos poyp-cyo.
         "(I) cannot meet (her) often."

Excerpt 3 shows how a speaker produces first a single token (line 5) and then multiple tokens (line 10) of *e*. Such *multiple sayings* (e.g., *yes yes yes* or *no no no* under a single intonational contour; Stivers, 2004) are not simply an upgrade of a single token but occur at a particular position to address a larger course of ongoing action.

Excerpt 3   KO_5963

3   B: 어디서 해?= 어디서 빌려 와?
         eti-se hay?= eti-se pillye wa?
         "From where do (you) do it)? = From where do (you) rent?"

4   A: 그 Enterprise라구:,
         ku enterprise-la-kwu:,
         "A (place) called Enterprise,"

<u>5</u>   B: 어.
         e.

6   A: 그:: (.) 어디지?
         ku:: (.) eti-ci?
         "Tha::t (.) where is it?"

7   B: 동네?
         tongney?
         "(In your) neighborhood?"

8   A: 응 그니까 B U: 그 맥도날드 있지=
         ung kunikka B U: ku mayktonaltu iss-ci?
         "Yes, so you know the McDonald in B. U.="

9   A: =우리 (   ) [옛날에 썼던 데,]
         wuli   yeysnal-ey sse-ss-ten tey,
         "=the place we used to use (   )."

<u>10</u>   B: [어어어:.]
                              e e e:.

11   A: 거기 어디 있는 거야.
         keki eti iss-nun ke-ya.
         "It's somewhere there."

The differences in the uses of the affirmative tokens in these excerpts will be explained in the following sections as we discuss how turns-at-talk are organized in sequences and how a turn's sequential placement is critical in understanding the action implemented by the turn. The analysis will demonstrate how one word in distinct positions can carry out a variety of important actions.

Understanding the importance of an utterance's position in a sequence also explicates the difference between speech act theory and CA. Speech act theory mainly views an utterance as a reflection of a speaker's intention and focuses on mapping linguistic forms onto functions (Levinson, 1983). On the other hand, the CA perspective shows how actions are not constructed in isolation but formulated and implemented at a particular interactional juncture in a certain order and intersubjectively with other participants of the talk. What speakers actually do in conversation is made observable in CA through detailed transcription practices and the analysis of naturally occurring data (Schegloff, 2007; Clift, 2016).

This chapter addresses a growing need to incorporate empirical findings into language teaching. Based on empirical research on how Korean conversation works and how native speakers competently engage in socially organized activities, a number of recent studies have begun providing concrete KSL teaching materials and teaching techniques. The topics cover repair initiation, discourse markers, question design, assessments, reported talk, and action formation (Yoon, 2007; Kim, 2021a, 2022; Kim & Yoon, 2021). This chapter contributes an overview of sequencing practices in Korean interaction and calls for teaching L2 learners such practices. The following sections discuss in detail how sequences are organized and implemented and how they can be expanded in Korean conversation. Each section centers on excerpts from naturally occurring conversational data, which can be utilized as instructional materials.[2]

Adjacency pair: the unit of sequence organization

Sequence organization refers to how turns-at-talk are ordered and combined to implement a course of action (Schegloff, 2007, p. 9). The basic unit or building block of a sequence is an adjacency pair. An adjacency pair consists of two turns by different speakers adjacently placed, as in Excerpt 1. The first pair part (FPP) initiates some kind of action (e.g., greeting, question, request) and the second pair part (SPP) produces a responsive action to the prior turn (e.g., greeting, answer, granting/refusal).

Excerpt 1   KO_5683

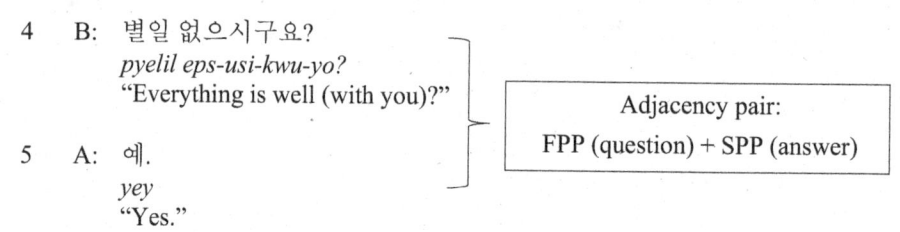

4   B: 별일 없으시구요?
            pyelil eps-usi-kwu-yo?
            "Everything is well (with you)?"

5   A: 예.
            yey
            "Yes."

Adjacency pair:
FPP (question) + SPP (answer)

B's question regarding A's well-being in line 4, formulated with the turn-final *ko* (also pronounced as *kwu*, as in line 4), is a declarative question (Kim, 2015a). This question design displays the speaker's strong epistemic certainty toward the proposition and makes a simple confirmation relevant in the next turn. The recipient provides the expected response in the next turn (line 5).

When the SPP, the relevant response, does not occur in the next turn, it will be treated as noticeably absent and become accountable, as seen in Excerpt 4. The conversation comes from a telephone talk between a child (C) and her mother's friend (A), referred to as *imo* "aunt" (line 7). After a short greeting and a *how are you* inquiry (not shown here), the aunt attempts to elicit the child's recognition of who she is (line 2).

Excerpt 4   KO_6773

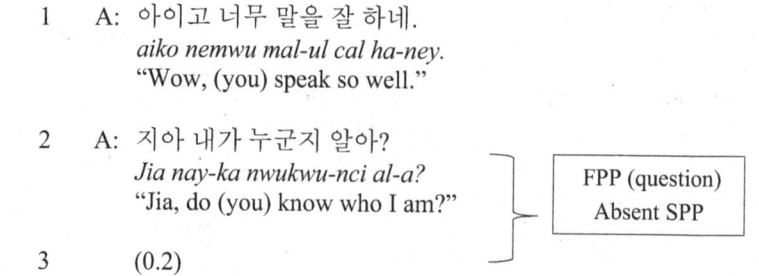

1   A: 아이고 너무 말을 잘 하네.
            aiko nemwu mal-ul cal ha-ney.
            "Wow, (you) speak so well."

2   A: 지아 내가 누군지 알아?
            Jia nay-ka nwukwu-nci al-a?
            "Jia, do (you) know who I am?"

3   (0.2)

FPP (question)
Absent SPP

4   C: ((makes unintelligible sound))

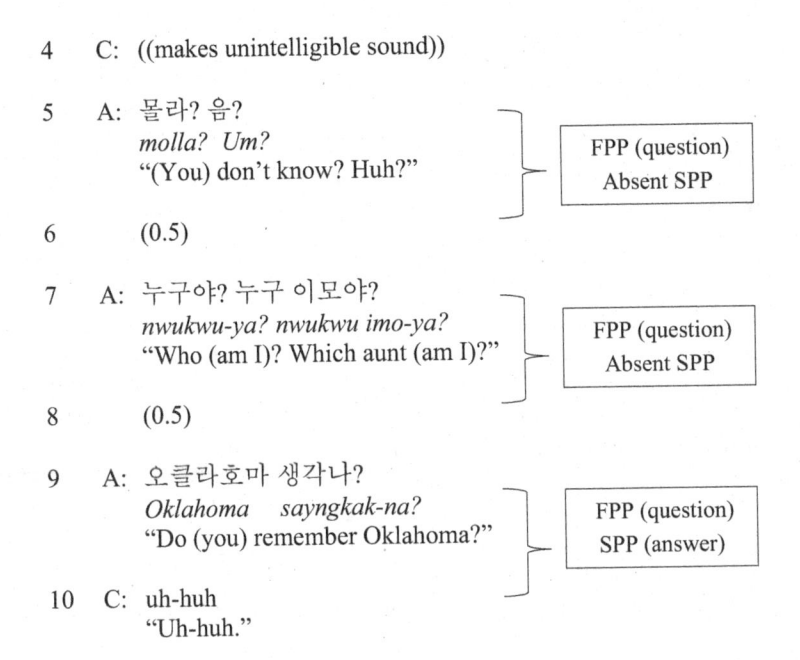

5   A: 몰라? 음?
    molla? Um?
    "(You) don't know? Huh?"   ⎫ FPP (question)
                                                 ⎬ Absent SPP
6   (0.5)   ⎭

7   A: 누구야? 누구 이모야?
    nwukwu-ya? nwukwu imo-ya?
    "Who (am I)? Which aunt (am I)?"   ⎫ FPP (question)
                                                 ⎬ Absent SPP
8   (0.5)   ⎭

9   A: 오클라호마 생각나?
    Oklahoma   sayngkak-na?
    "Do (you) remember Oklahoma?"   ⎫ FPP (question)
                                                 ⎬ SPP (answer)
10 C: uh-huh   ⎭
    "Uh-huh."

A's *yes/no* question of whether C knows A (line 2) makes a *yes* or *no* response immediately relevant and expectable. However, instead, there is a silence, and the child makes an unintelligible sound (lines 3–4); the SPP is missing. Accordingly, A further pursues an answer from C by reformulating the question (line 5). This subsequent question is not randomly formulated; it displays another important sequencing practice: preference organization (Schegloff, 2007). A preferred response promotes accomplishment of the activity in progress while a dispreferred response does not (e.g., the preferred response to an invitation would be to accept it while the dispreferred response would be to decline it). Here, Speaker A's initial question prefers a *yes* answer (establishing recognition between the two callers); however, as the child does not give the expected answer, the possibility that the child may not know A arises. Thus, the subsequent question is formulated as *molla?* ('(You) don't know?'). By redesigning her question, A reverses the preference so that the negative answer is now preferred (e.g., '(Right, I) don't know.').

As the recipient continues to not produce a conditionally relevant SPP, the questioner again redesigns the question, from a *yes/no* question to *wh* questions (line 7), and further tries to help the child retrieve her memory of the speaker (line 9). As clearly shown here, the absence of an SPP becomes so salient in the interaction, by breaking the contiguity between the FPP and the SPP, that it halts the progressivity of the talk.

Excerpts 1 and 4 are extracted from authentic interaction yet are very simple and should be easy for learners to understand and follow. Teachers can consider providing these two excerpts and having students identify the FPPs and SPPs. Without any prior knowledge or training in CA, students can easily observe how turns are systematically organized in pairs in a certain order. Even when the conditionally relevant responses do not follow, the interaction still operates under sequence organization (i.e., the questioner pursues an answer from the recipient by reformulating her questions).

As shown in the following table, a certain FPP action makes a certain SPP action relevant (Schegloff, 2007; Clift, 2016).

First pair part action	Second pair part action
Question	Answer
Summons	Answer
Request for information	Informative answer
Request for action	Grant/deny
Invitation	Accept/decline
Accusation	Admit/deny

Moreover, even among FPPs that implement a similar action, a certain design of the FPP makes a particular SPP relevant. For question-and-response sequences, depending on what actions the speaker implements in what position, the design of the question will vary, and the expected response will differ accordingly. For instance, the turn-final *ko* question in Excerpt 1 is optimized for an unproblematic, simple confirmation response (Heritage & Sorjonen, 1994). These are "little questions" that "get little answers" (Heritage & Raymond, 2012, p. 184). The question is designed for customarily confirming the other's well-being and does not have any further underlying agenda or purpose. In contrast, there are *yes/no* questions not designed for a simple *yes/no* response, as shown next.

Excerpt 5   Modified transcript, Kim (2015b, p. 769)

1   A: 아, 한국- 한국 (.) 스키 간 얘기 말고 뭐
            a, hankwuk hankwuk ski ka-n yayki malko mwe
            "Ah, Korea- Korea (.) instead of talking about (your) ski trip,"

2   (0.5)

3   A: 그 여자 친구 (.) 할머니 집에 데려갔다며::?
            ku yeca chinkwu halmeni cip-ey teylyeka-ss-tamye
            "I heard you took that girlfriend to grandmother's house, is it true?"

4   B: 아이 그때 엄마:랑 둘이 가려고 그랬어 나랑:.
            ai kuttay emma-lang twul-i ka-lyeko kulay-ss-e na-lang:
            "Well, I was going to go with my mom, the two of us to grandma's place."

5   A: [응].
            ung.
            "Uh huh"

6   B: [그랬]더니 엄마가:,
            kulay-ss-te-ni emma-ka:,
            "Then, my mom said,"

7   A: 어.
            e.
            "Uh huh"

The hearsay evidential marker *tamye* in line 3 makes a (dis)confirmation *yes* or *no* relevant in the next turn (Kim, 2011). However, this question is not designed for a simple confirmation. As seen in lines 1–3, A presses B to shift the topic of the talk from B's ski trip to B's visit to their grandmother's place with a girlfriend. The question is used to initiate a new topic, which makes an *expanded response* relevant (Lee, 2015). From line 4, B accordingly provides an expanded response as he explains how he ended up taking his girlfriend to meet their grandmother.

Excerpts 1 and 5 can be introduced to learners as teachers demonstrate that the composition of a question will vary depending on the action the speaker is implementing with it and in what sequential position it occurs in the unfolding interaction. In other words, a certain question design or type needs to be taught with the additional information of its action formation and its recurrent sequential positions so that learners have a concrete understanding of when and how to deploy them.

It is also important to raise learners' awareness of how interaction as it unfolds requires ongoing mutual monitoring and understanding of one another's talk and action. Although a certain FPP makes a certain SPP relevant, it may not always be followed by the projected SPP, and an alternative response may alter the trajectory of the ongoing interaction, as in Excerpt 6.

Excerpt 6   KO_5373

1   A: 은주 여기 미국에 온 거 알지?
           unjwu yeki mikwuk-ey o-n ke al-ci?
           "You know that Eunjoo came here to the United States, right?"

2   B: 정말?
           cengmal?
           "Really?"

3   A: 어 왔어.
           e wa-ss-e.
           "Yes, (she) came."

4   B: 어디 있어?
           eti iss-e?
           "Where is (she)?"

5   A: 지금 보스톤 쪽에
           cikum boston ccok-ey
           "Right now, (she) is in the Boston area."

A initiates talk about their mutual friend Eunjoo, who recently arrived in the United States. As shown in her pseudo tag question in line 1, she assumes B is a knowing recipient of the information she offers (i.e., of the friend's arrival), and so A expects a confirmation from B. However, as shown in line 2, this turns out to be news to B, who responds with a news-marking "Really?" This alternative SPP changes the direction of the sequence (eliciting A's confirmation of what she just said to inform B, now an unknowing recipient) and the projected interactional trajectory, which now shifts from A initiating a topic to A telling news. Accordingly, in the subsequent interaction, B requests further details of the news, and A provides the information (lines 4–5).

How the position of an utterance matters is well demonstrated by the question *X eti iss-e?* "Where is X?", which occurs in Excerpt 6 and in the following Excerpt 7. The question *eti iss-e?* in Excerpt 6 (line 4) occurs in first position, initiating a *wh* question asking for specific information (e.g., place). The same question in Excerpt 7 (line 3) occurs in second position as a response to the prior speaker's question in line 1.

Excerpt 7   Kim, 2015a, p. 69

<u>1</u>   S: 여기 애- 애기 낳아서 여기 계속 있었어?
         yeki ay- ayki nah-ase yeki kyeksok iss-ess-e?
         "Were you here the whole time after the baby- baby was born?"

2   (0.3)

<u>3</u>   H: 그럼 뭐 어딨어?
         kulem mwe eti-ss-e?
         "Then, where would (I be)?"

> Adjacency pair:
> question & response (rhetorical question)

In response to S's inquiry about whether H has been in the United States since his baby was born (line 1), H challenges the askability of S's question with a rhetorical question (line 3): there is no possibility that H would have been somewhere else. As the comparison of these two excerpts demonstrates, the same question placed in different positions implements different actions.

Jeong, Bae, and Ahn's (2021) study provides ample teaching materials and activities based on authentic interactional data for teaching these types of challenging rhetorical questions. The study shows how a current speaker displays a divergent stance toward the prior speaker's stance using rhetorical questions formulated with the interrogative suffix *nya* (e.g., *keki-kkaci encey ka-nya?* "When would (I) be able to make the time to go way out there?").

Sequence expansion

The base adjacency pair may be expanded before the FPP, after the SPP, and between the FPP and the SPP, as shown next. Each potential expansion position is recurrently occupied by particular types of sequences.

Schegloff (2007, p. 26)

⟵ Pre-expansion

A   First pair part

⟵ Insert-expansion

B   Second pair part

⟵ Post-expansion

Pre-expansion

The following excerpts show commonly observed pre-sequence types. Teachers can have learners identify the base sequence that implements the main action and further discuss what occurs before the main action in each excerpt.

Excerpt 8 Kim (2018, p. 342)

1 B: 하하[하하
       haha haha
       "hh hh hh"

2 A: [야 야 >야야야<
            ya ya   ya ya ya
            "Hey, hey, hey, hey, hey"   ⎫
                                                    ⎬ Pre-sequence:
3 B: 어.   ⎪ summons & answer
       e.   ⎭
       "Yeah."

4 A: 이름은 대지 말자.   ⎫
       ilum-un tay-ci mal-ca.   ⎬ Base sequence:
       "Let's not state our names."   ⎪ proposal + acceptance
                                                    ⎪
5 B: 어.   ⎭
       e.
       "Yeah."

6 A: 오케이.   ⎤ Sequence closure
       okheyi   ⎦
       "Okay."

Lines 2–3 show a generic summons-answer sequence (Schegloff, 2007, p. 48). Speaker A summons speaker B, who is engaged in a different activity (laughing), with a pseudo-address term *ya* "hey" before she proceeds with her main action in line 4 (proposing not to reveal their names during the recording they are making). With B's acceptance (line 5), A explicitly closes the sequence with *okheyi* "okay."

The following excerpt shows another instance of pre-expansion, but a different kind of type-specific pre-sequence. Before discussing Excerpt 9, have students first construct a dialogue with a partner asking for a favor (e.g., asking the partner to accompany them to a party or function). Then, students can compare how sequences are organized in their dialogue and in Excerpt 9 and further discuss how the different organizations affect the way speakers take turns and organize their actions.

Excerpt 9 Modified transcript of KO_6613

1 A: 내가 부탁이 하나 있는데 들어 줄래?
           nay-ka pwuthak-i hana iss-nuney tule cwu-llay?
           "I have a favor to ask, will you grant the request?"   ⎫
                                                                   ⎬ Preliminaries-to-
2 B: 뭔지 말해 봐.   ⎪ preliminaries
       mwe-nci malhay pwa.   ⎭
       "Tell me what it is about."

3 A: 4월 15일에 우리 학교에서 축제가 있거든.
   sa wel sip oil-ey wuli hakkyo-eyse chwukcey-ka iss-ketun.
   "On April 15, our school has a festival."

                   Preliminaries: background information

4 B: 응.
   ung.
   "Yes."

5 A: 근데 파트너하고 같이 가야 돼. 너가 와 줄 수 있나 해서.
   kuntey partner-hako kathi ka-ya tway. ne-ka wa cwu-l swu iss-na hay-se.
   "(You) have to go with a partner. (I) was wondering if you could come."

                   Base sequence: request + (grant/refuse)

   ....

As shown here, *I have a favor to ask* is not typically followed by a request for the favor but is a preliminary. There are two types of preliminaries (Schegloff, 2007, p. 44). The first, preliminaries-to-preliminaries (pre-pre), usually take the format of *Can I X?* (e.g., *Can I ask you a question?* or *Can I ask a favor?*), as seen in line 1, and are typically responded to with a go-ahead (promoting the progressivity of the action underway), as in line 2.

The second type of preliminary, which is the type in line 3, usually provides some background or preliminary information before producing the actual main action (the request). The practice of pre-pre not only projects the upcoming action but also allows the speaker to hold the turn, extend his/her talk, and minimize the recipient's contribution until the main action is produced.

Insert-expansion

Insert-expansion is an adjacency pair that occurs between the base FPP and the base SPP. Repair sequences are one of the routine sequence types in this position. As shown in Excerpt 10, line 2, here *ney?* does not serve as an affirmative answer but is doing something else: initiating repair to address an issue with hearing or understanding the preceding talk (Kim, 1993). Using the following excerpts (10–13), which show a range of different repair sequences, teachers can have students identify what the trouble source is, who initiates the repair and who makes the repair, and how repair ends and a repair sequence gets closed.

Excerpt 10 KO_6002

1 B: 언니 자주 못 만나요?
   enni cacwu mos manna-yo?
   "You cannot meet her often?"

2→ A: 네?
   ney?
   "Huh?"

         Insert sequence: repair sequence   Base sequence: question + answer

3→ B: 자주 못 만나요?
   cacwu mos manna-yo?
   "You cannot meet (her) often?"

4 A: 자주 못 뵙죠.
   cacwu mos poyp-cyo.
   "(I) cannot meet (her) often."

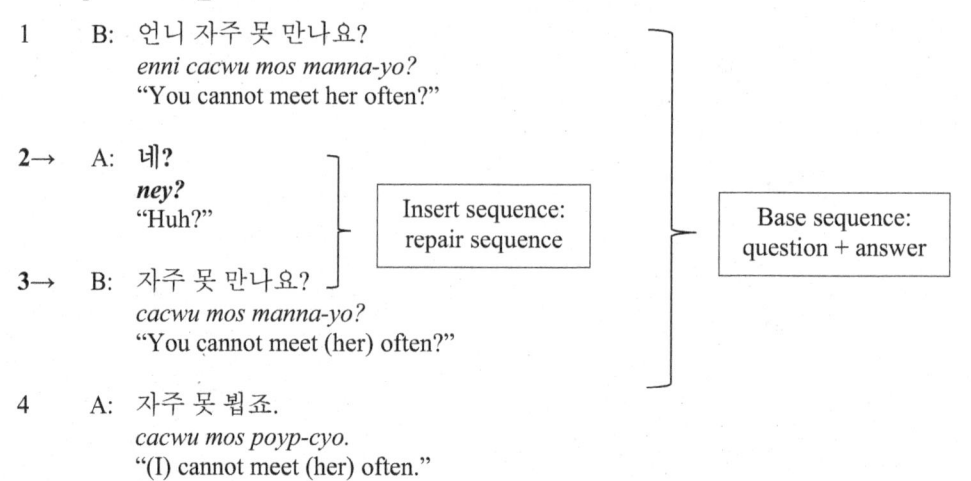

In ordinary conversation, speakers often encounter problems in hearing or understanding, and they have ways of indicating this to their recipient and potentially resolving the problem. This practice is referred to as other-initiation of repair (OIR; Schegloff, Jefferson, & Sacks, 1977). Studies of the organization of OIR, as well as of linguistic resources used to construct OIRs, have received sustained interest over the last few decades (Schegloff et al., 1977; Selting, 1996; Drew, 1997; Robinson, 2013). In line 2, *ney?* is more specifically an open-class repair initiator (e.g., *what?*, *huh?*), which does not specify the trouble source or the nature of the trouble (Drew, 1997). Accordingly, in the next turn, not knowing the specifics of the problem, Speaker B repeats the question. In response, A now provides the base SPP, the answer to B's question.

As seen here, the practice of OIR is not indicative of disfluency or incompetence but is, in fact, a sign of interactional competence. OIRs can show the speaker's and recipient's efforts to reach and maintain mutual understanding (Celce-Murcia, 2007; Wong, 2007). Despite the importance of the role of repair practices in interaction, they are generally not taught in language classrooms, and instructors often lack understanding of these practices (Nakamura, 2008).

An important matter to note is that OIR is not limited to talk. An examination of OIR practices across twenty-one languages (Enfield et al., 2013) showed that repair can be initiated or accompanied by visible behaviors, such as eyebrow-raising, gaze, and tilting of the head or body toward the speaker of the trouble source. Other studies have discovered systematic practices of OIR through embodiment and gaze, specifically a "freeze-look" response (Manrique, 2011) and a "head poke" (Seo & Koshik, 2010) toward the speaker of the trouble source. These studies all demonstrate that the precise position of these embodiments in interaction is what makes them understandable as OIR. They halt the progressivity of the interaction until the participants resolve the trouble source.

While the primary work of OIR is addressing a hearing or understanding problem, research has shown how OIR can also implement social actions in addition to, or other than, initiating repair (e.g., Schegloff, 1997). Some social actions with which OIR is involved include displaying surprise, disbelief, disaffiliation, and nonalignment (e.g., Drew, 1997; Wu, 2009). Prosodic cues (Selting, 1996) and question-intoned full repeats (Robinson & Kevoe-Feldman, 2010) have been identified as one of the key resources that contribute to the production and understanding of OIR in these ways. Kim and Kim (2014) illustrated another resource found in Korean: the addition of the subject particle *i/ka* and the object particle *(l)ul*. The study shows that the addition or deletion of these particles plays important roles in projecting the action of the OIR.

Extract 11 shows an instance of an OIR without the subject particle. The segment comes from a conversation between two friends talking about B's upcoming piano recital.

Excerpt 11   KO_5969

1   B: 그래서 내일 해. 하하
         kulayse nayil hay. haha
         "So, (the performance) is tomorrow. haha"

2   A: 잘 해라:.
         cal hay-la.
         "Do (your) best."

3   B: 응 잘 해야지.
         ung cal hay-ya-ci.
         "Yeah, (I) must do (my) best."

4   A: 피아노 잘 쳐?
       phiano cal chye?
       "Do (you) play piano well?"

5   B: 나?
       na?
       "Me?"

6   A: 어.
       e.
       "Yes."

7   (0.5)

8   B: 십 년 배웠다?   [십 년 넘-]
       sip nyen paywe-ss-ta. sip nyen nem-
       "(I) have studied for ten years. Past- ten years."

9   A: [우와.]
                        wuwa.
                        "Wow."

10 B: 다섯 살부터 배웠는데:,
       tases sal-pwuthe paywe-ss-nuntey:,
       "(I started) to learn from five years old, but:,"

11 A: 어.
       e.
       "Uh huh"

12 B: 십사 년 배운 거 만큼은 못 쳐. 하하
       sipsa nyen paywu-n ke mankhum-un mos chye. haha
       "(I) can't play as well as someone who has studied for fourteen years. haha"

The talk about B's upcoming performance seems to reach a closure as A wishes the best for B (lines 1–3). At this interactional juncture, A reopens the topic by asking B's level of piano skills (line 4). Note how B does not immediately answer the question, but initiates repair in line 5, seeking confirmation on whether A's question is regarding B, *na?* "Me?" This OIR is produced without a case particle (the subject particle *ka*), and in the subsequent turns, as soon as A confirms that the question is about B (line 6), the conversation that was on hold due to the repair is resumed; B moves on to answering A's question (lines 8, 10, 12). This shows that the speaker is using OIR to perform an understanding check to ensure correct understanding of the prior turn before responding to the question, rather than to carry out any negatively valenced action. Although they have been talking about B, the reason for the problem in understanding may be that A reopens the closing topic and does so with a question that is somewhat unexpected (i.e., asking someone who is about to give a piano recital about her piano skill level).

While examining this data, it is also important to note that A's *e* response in line 6 is different from A's *e* response in line 11 in terms of action and sequential position. In line 6, it occurs in second position as a *yes* answer to the repair initiation ("Me?" "Yes."); In line 11, it occurs in a different position while the other speaker's turn is continuing. From line 8, B is still in the midst of formulating her answer. After she discloses how long she has been playing, she continues to point out the contrast between the long years she has played and how well she actually plays. A's *e* in line 11 serves as a continuer, which displays that the speaker is yielding a turn and acknowledging that the other speaker's turn will continue (e.g., *uh huh, mm-hm*; Schegloff, 1982; Kim, 1999). Lee, Yoon, and Yoon (2017) offer several activities for teaching Korean response tokens, which include continuers.

On the other hand, the subject particle is consistently observed in OIRs when they are doing some other action, such as displaying disaffiliation or incipient disagreement (Kim & Kim, 2014), as in Excerpt 12. The excerpt comes from a face-to-face family talk where the father claims that everyone in their family has a prominent hooked nose (lines 1–2), and this claim triggers the members of the family to assess the shape of their noses.

Excerpt 12   Kim (2021b, p. 170)

1   Dad: 우리 (.) 집안에 코가, 좀 매부리코::가
             wuli (.) cipan-ey kho-ka, com maypwulikho::-ka

2   Dad: 좀 강하다구. = 굉장히 우성이야:.
             com kangha-ta-kwu. = koyngcanghi wuseng-i-ya:.
             "Our family noses are, we have the strong feature of hooked noses. It is really dominant."

3   (0.2)

4   Yun: 나는, [아닌데::]
             na-nun, [ani-ntey::]
             "But, I don't have it."

5   Dad: [거의::] 식구들이 다: [아주 특징이야.]
                    [keuy::] sikkwu-tul-i ta: [acwu thukcing-i-ya.]
                    "Almost all family members have the feature."

6   Mia: [너도 매부리야.]
                                           [ne-to maypwuli-ya.]
                                           "You have it too."

7   Dad: [다 매부리야.]
             [ta maypwuli-ya.]
             "(We) all have hooked noses."

8   Yun: [내가↑] ((shifts her gaze to Mia with her eyes wide))
             [nay-ka↑]
             "Me?"

9   Mia: 너도 있어. =요거. ((points at her own nose))
             ne-to iss-e. = yoke.
             "You have it too. This."

While listening to their father's claim, Yun, one of the daughters, displays disagreement, asserting that she does not have a hooked nose (line 4). However, the father upgrades his claim (lines 5, 7), and Yun's sister, Mia, disagrees with Yun by pointing out that Yun does have a hooked nose (line 6). Note how Yun responds in line 8 by initiating repair, "Me?", which she formulates with the subject particle *ka* (in contrast to Speaker B's choice of the zero particle in Excerpt 11, line 5). Yun's high pitch (marked with ↑), wide eyes, and direct gaze at Mia all display Yun's disbelief and disaffiliation with Mia's claim. This OIR is not simply addressing a hearing or understanding problem. This is further demonstrated in the way Mia responds to Yun's OIR. Unlike Speaker A's response to an OIR in Excerpt 11, line 6, Mia does not simply provide a confirmation *e* "yes" but reinforces her claim by verbally repeating the claim that Yun indeed has a hooked nose and by nonverbally pointing at her own nose to demonstrate her point (line 9).

Excerpts 11 and 12 can be utilized in class to discuss the two different formats of OIR and observe how the addition of the subject particle in initiating repair is not accidental. The speaker adds the particle to display the speaker's negatively valenced stance toward what was said or implied in a prior turn (Kim, 2021b).[3] Furthermore, the recipient's response demonstrates whether the speaker's repair initiation is carrying out a negatively valenced action rather than addressing a hearing or understanding problem.

Post-expansion

In general, preferred SPPs are closure-relevant, as in the summons-answer sequence in Excerpt 8, lines 2–3 and the repair sequence in Excerpt 11, lines 5–6. However, the sequence may get minimally expanded, as seen in Excerpt 1.

Excerpt 1   KO_5683

1   B: 어 야: 이거 뭐 안기부에서 연락 오는 거 아니[죠? 하하하
         e ya: ike mwe ankipwu-eyse yenlak o-nun ke ani-cyo? Hahaha
         "Uh, wow, I am not going to be contacted by the Korean CIA, right? Hahaha"

2   A: [아니에요.
                                                    aniey-yo.
                                                    "No."

3   B: 네:.
             ney:.

4   B: 별일 없으시구요?
         pyelil eps-usi-kwu-yo.
         "Everything is well (with you)?"

5   A: 예.=
         yey.=
         "Yes."

6   B: =예.
             =yey.

Each time, A answers B's questions (lines 1–2, 4–5), and B accepts A's response and closes the sequence with *ney* or *yey* in lines 3 and 6; both lines are turns in third position after the SPP; they are not the same as the affirmative answer *yey* in line 5, which occurs in second position as an SPP. The third-position *ney* is something equivalent to a third-position *okay* in English (Pyun & Yoon, forthcoming). Such turns are referred to as sequence-closing thirds (SCT), an additional turn beyond the SPP that accepts the prior action and closes the sequence (Schegloff, 2007, p. 119).

Sequences may also be expanded not minimally by a repair sequence, as with the repair sequence in Excerpt 13.

Excerpt 13   KO_5969

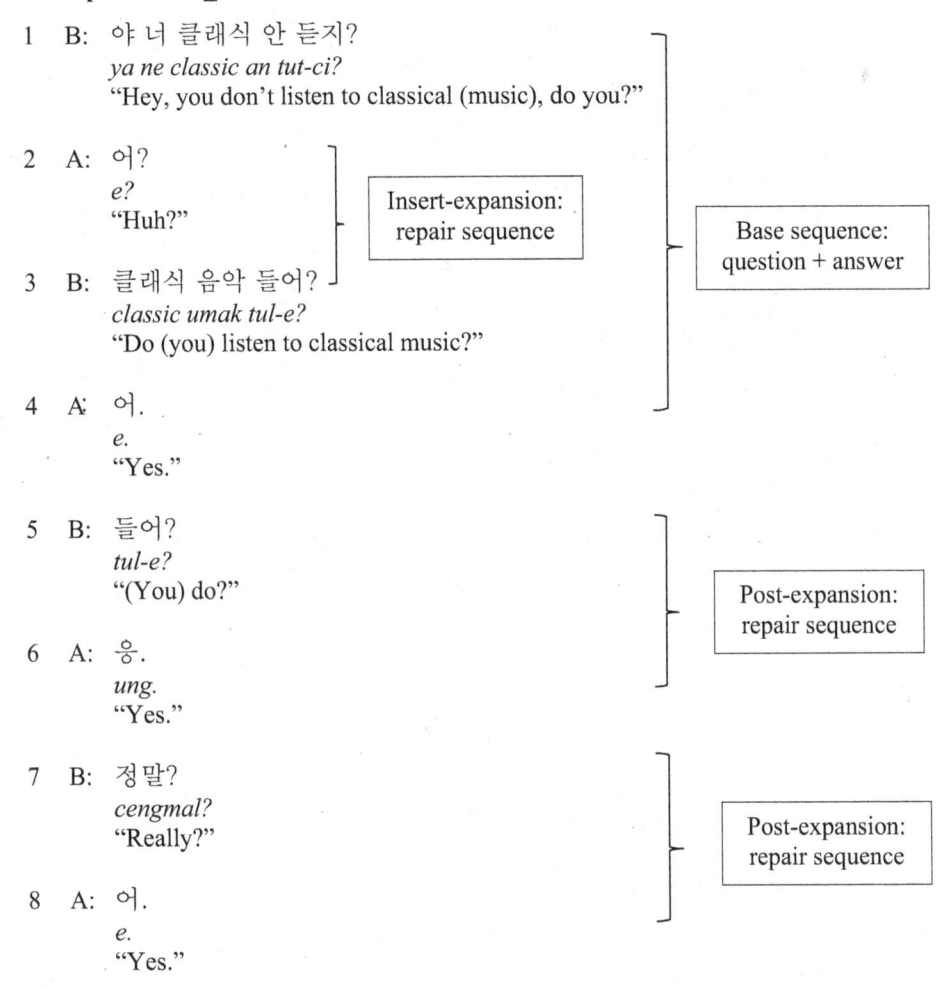

1 B: 야 너 클래식 안 듣지?
       ya ne classic an tut-ci?
       "Hey, you don't listen to classical (music), do you?"

2 A: 어?
       e?
       "Huh?"

3 B: 클래식 음악 들어?
       classic umak tul-e?
       "Do (you) listen to classical music?"

4 A: 어.
       e.
       "Yes."

5 B: 들어?
       tul-e?
       "(You) do?"

6 A: 응.
       ung.
       "Yes."

7 B: 정말?
       cengmal?
       "Really?"

8 A: 어.
       e.
       "Yes."

Lines 1–4 form the Base sequence: question + answer. Lines 2–3 are an Insert-expansion: repair sequence. Lines 5–6 and 7–8 are Post-expansion: repair sequences.

The base sequence, question and answer (lines 1, 4), not only gets expanded in the middle by an OIR sequence (lines 2–3) but also gets post-expanded. After the main SPP (line 4), two additional repair sequences follow (lines 5–8). As Schegloff (2007) notes, post-expansion sequences are often disagreement-implicated repair sequences. The speaker displays incipient disagreement, disbelief, or news-marking toward the prior speaker's response.

We have seen how sequences are systematically organized by adjacency pairs and how sequences can also be expanded at various points of the interaction for certain practices (e.g., repair practices), actions (e.g., asking for a favor), or activities (e.g., storytelling). We have also seen how the same linguistic resource (e.g., *ney/yey* "yes, yeah") can implement different actions and practices depending on the sequential position, which again demonstrates the importance of understanding the sequence organization that underlies interaction. Excerpt 14 (a longer sequence that includes Excerpt 3) shows how even the same token occurs in a different format (uttered once or multiple times under a single intonational contour, e.g., *yes yes yes*) depending on its sequential position and actions.

Excerpt 14   KO_5963

1 A: 그래가지고 월 화 수 삼 일만 하는데
      kulaykaciko wel hwa swu sam il-man ha-nuntey

2 A: 그것도 빌려 오고 갖다 주고 내가 다 하지.
      kukes-to pillye o-ko kac-ta cwu-ko nay-ka ta ha-ci.
      "So, (we rent the car) for three days, Monday, Tuesday, Wednesday only, and picking up (the car) and returning (the car), I do all of that."

3 B: 어디서 해?= 어디서 빌려 와?
      eti-se hay?= eti-se pillye wa?
      "From where do (you do it)? = From where do (you) rent?"

4 A: 그 Enterprise라구:,
      ku enterprise-la-kwu:,
      "A (place) called Enterprise,"

5 B: 어.
      e.

6 A: 그:: (.) 어디지?
      ku:: (.) eti-ci?
      "Tha::t (.) where is it?"

7 B: 동네?
      tongney?
      "(In your) neighborhood?"

8 A: 응 그니까 B U: 그 맥도날드 있지=
      ung kunikka B U: ku mayktonaltu iss-ci
      "Yes, so you know the McDonald in B. U:="

9 A: =우리 (   ) [옛날에 썼던 데,]
      wuli   yeysnal-ey sse-ss-ten tey,
      "=the place we used to use (   ),"

10 B: [어어어:.]
                      e e e:.

11 A: 거기 어디 있는 거야.
      keki eti iss-nun ke-ya.
      "It's somewhere there."

12 B: 응.
      ung.
      "Yeah."

13 A: 그래가지고 그런 거 내가 하지.
      kulaykaciko kulen ke nay-ka ha-ci.
      "So, those things, I do them."

The focus of the analysis is from line 4, where A begins to answer B's inquiry regarding where A rents the car (line 3). A's response, "A (place) called Enterprise," sufficiently answers the question (line 4), and B displays acknowledgement and no problem understanding the response with *e* "yeah" in third position in line 5. However, A continues, providing a very detailed account of exactly where the Enterprise rental car company is located in her neighborhood (lines 6, 8–9). B's response to this elaborated information in line 10 shows a contrast with her initial response in line 5. Unlike her earlier single use of *e*, serving as an acknowledgment token, B repeats *e* three times under one single intonational contour in line 10. This is an example of what Stivers (2004) called *multiple sayings*, a speaker repeating a word, phrase, or sentence multiple times under a single intonation contour, such as *yes yes yes*, *no no no*, or *wait wait wait*. According to Stivers, multiple sayings are not simply an upgrade on a single token but serve a discrete action at a particular interactional juncture. Multiple sayings, as shown in line 10, address not only the just-prior unit of talk but the larger preceding course of action, which the prior turns and talk embody. Thus, here, B does not simply convey that she recognizes the location but displays her stance that Speaker A has persisted unnecessarily in the prior course of action by providing over-extensive elaboration on the exact location in multiple stages (e.g., word search, line 6; eliciting B's memory of A's neighborhood, lines 8–9). As Stivers noted, multiple sayings often occur in overlap with prior talk, just as seen here in lines 9–10, as the speaker is doing the additional work of conveying that the other speaker's ongoing talk is unwarranted and unnecessary, thereby proposing that the course of action need not be continued. Accordingly, A wraps up the elaboration (line 11, "It's somewhere there") and resumes the main point of her talk, tying it back to her prior talk in line 1 with the discourse marker *kulaykaciko* "so" (line 13).

By exposing learners to this type of authentic conversational data and carefully selected excerpts, teachers can raise learners' awareness and understanding of the underlying structures of conversation – sequence organization, preference organization, turn-taking organization – and identify a wide range of actions and practices speakers implement through these organizations. As discussed throughout the chapter, excerpts from naturally occurring conversational data can be utilized effectively in class so students themselves can identify how sequences are organized and how actions and activities are implemented through sequencing practices. Teachers can also use the excerpts to create short exercises to understand the variable designs of utterances and turns depending on their action and sequential position in the interaction. Teachers can also show the beginning of a sequence or talk with a brief explanation of the context and the target action or activity in progress and have students complete the conversation with a peer as a pair activity (e.g., role play). It is important to provide simple yet concrete guidelines for understanding the focus of the talk and interaction (e.g., certain action formations, practices, activities, sequencing practices, or alternative turn designs). Such activities will provide students the chance to engage in more authentic activity types derived from concrete sequential and interactional contexts. Each pair can (re)perform their conversation, and teachers can provide the actual excerpt to further discuss alternative responses. It is also important to draw students' attention to how alternative responses may change the interactional trajectory of the talk and action in progress. Such activities and practices can help learners build awareness and develop the ability to jointly participate in interaction by monitoring and adapting to others' talk and actions, reciprocally maintaining shared understanding and accomplishing actions with other participants of the talk.

Conclusion

This chapter presents a conversation analytic account of how speakers manage their talk and actions through sequence organization in Korean interaction. Traditional instruction focuses on the structure of sentences, that is, the lexical, morphological, syntactic, phonological, and phonetic composition of sentences. CA-informed instruction (Clift, 2016, p. 32) additionally looks at the infrastructure of interaction: not just what a turn is composed of but how the turn is placed in the trajectories of the actions or activities in which the participants are engaged in their interaction.

Drawing on findings from prior CA research and offering a close analysis of naturally occurring Korean conversation excerpts, the chapter provides a detailed, situated picture of how turns-at-talk are composed to implement a certain action in a particular position and how these actions are systematically ordered and sustained through sequencing practices in Korean interaction. It also illustrates how sequences can be constructed and expanded and how each type of sequence or sequence expansion is tied to routine practices (e.g., repair, pre-pre, topic initiation, sequence closure).

The examination of how simple affirmative tokens (*ney/yey* and *e/ung*) are used across different sequential positions for discrete actions (e.g., affirmative answer, sequence-closing third, open class repair initiator, continuer, multiple sayings) clearly illustrates how critical it is to understand the importance of composition and position in interaction. CA has much to offer KSL pedagogy, as it derives from empirical research, takes an emic perspective, and makes the interaction of participants publicly intelligible and observable.

The chapter also discusses designing exercises and activities through which KSL learners can engage in real-life interactions and foster their conversational skills and interactional competence.

Notes

1 Rather than investigating the functions of affirmative tokens, this chapter illustrates the importance of an utterance's position by using affirmative tokens as examples. The extensive functions of the Korean affirmative tokens are discussed in other studies. (Kim, 1993; Kim & Suh, 1998; Kim, 1999; Pyun, 2009; Oh & Park, 2017; Pyun & Yoon, forthcoming).
2 The data originates from the Linguistic Data Consortium Korean Corpus of Telephone Conversations, which consists of a total of 100 different sets of ordinary telephone calls between native Korean speakers across different gender and age groups (Han et al., 2003).
3 Kim's study (2021b) illustrates the Korean speakers' routine practice of deploying the subject particle *ka* in negatively valanced questions that display incipient disagreement, express disbelief, or make a challenge or complaint. The study discusses how the subject particle contributes in formulating the negatively valanced questions.

References

Celce-Murcia, M. (2007). Rethinking the role of communicative competence in language teaching. In E. Alcon Soler & M. P. Safont Jorda (Eds.), *The intercultural language use and language learning* (pp. 41–58). Dordrecht: Springer.

Clift, E. (2016). *Conversation analysis*. Cambridge: Cambridge University Press.

Drew, P. (1997). 'Open' class repair initiators in response to sequential sources of troubles in conversation. *Journal of Pragmatics*, 28(1), 69–101.

Enfield, N., Dingemanse, M., Baranova, J., Blythe, J., Brown, P., Dirksmeyer, T., . . . & Torreira, F. (2013). Huh? What? – A first survey in twenty-one languages. In M. Hayashi, G. Raymond, & J. Sidnell (Eds.), *Conversational repair and human understanding* (pp. 343–380). Cambridge: Cambridge University Press.

Han, N.-R., Ko, E.-S., Graff, D., Strassel, S., Martey, N., Kim, M., . . . & Zipperlen, G. (2003). *Korean telephone conversations complete set LDC2003S07*. Web Download. Philadelphia, PA: Linguistic Data Consortium.

Heritage, J., & Raymond, G. (2012). Navigating epistemic landscapes: Acquiescence, agency and resistance in responses to polar questions. In J. De Ruiter (Ed.), *Questions: Formal, functional and interactional perspectives* (pp. 179–192). Language Culture and Cognition Series. Cambridge: Cambridge University Press.

Heritage, J., & Sorjonen, M. L. (1994). Constituting and maintaining activities across sequences: And-prefacing as a feature of question design. *Language in Society, 23*, 1–29.

Huth, T., & Taleghani-Nikazm, C. (2006). How can insights from conversation analysis be directly applied to teaching L2 pragmatics? *Language Teaching Research, 10*, 53–79.

Jeong, S., Bae, E. Y., & Ahn, J. (2021). Conversation analysis-informed instruction of -*nya* and -*ni* as stance alignment markers. *Korean Language in America, 24*(1), 3–29.

Kim, K.-H. (1992). *Wh-clefts and left-dislocation in English conversation with reference to topicality in Korean* [PhD dissertation]. UCLA.

Kim, K.-H. (1993). Other-initiated repair sequences in Korean conversation as interactional resources. In S. Choi (Ed.), *Japanese Korean linguistics* (Vol. 3, pp. 3–18). Stanford, CA: Center for Study of Language and Information.

Kim, K.-H. (1999). Phrasal unit boundaries and organization of turns and sequences in Korean conversation. *Human Studies, 22*(2–4), 425–446.

Kim, K.-H., & Suh, K.-H. (1998). Confirmation sequences as interactional resources in Korean language proficiency interviews. In R. Young & A. W. He (Eds.), *Talking and testing: Discourse approaches to the assessment of oral proficiency* (pp. 297–332). Amsterdam and Philadelphia: John Benjamins Publishing Company.

Kim, M. S. (2011). Negotiating epistemic rights to information in Korean conversation: An examination of the Korean evidential marker -*tamye*. *Discourse Studies, 13*(4), 435–459.

Kim, M. S. (2015a). A distinct declarative question design in Korean conversation: An examination of turn-final *ko* questions. *Journal of Pragmatics, 79*, 60–78.

Kim, M. S. (2015b). Reconstructing misinterpretation and misrepresentation through represented talk in Korean conversation. *Text and Talk, 35*(6), 759–787.

Kim, M. S. (2018). The Korean vocative interjection *ya* 'hey' beyond its summoning action. In S. Fukuda, M. S. Kim, & M. Park (Eds.), *Japanese/Korean linguistics* (Vol. 25, pp. 341–354). Stanford, CA: Center for Study of Language and Information, Stanford University.

Kim, M. S. (Ed.). (2021a). Special issue: Conversation analysis for Korean language pedagogy. *The Korean Language in America, 24*(1).

Kim, M. S. (2021b). Negatively valenced questions with the Korean subject particle *ka*: Interactional practices for managing discrepancies in knowledge, understanding, or expectations. *Journal of Pragmatics, 176*, 164–185.

Kim, M. S. (2022). Interactional competence in the Korean language. In S. Cho & J. Whitman (Eds.), *The Cambridge handbook of Korean language and linguistics* (pp. 800–831). Cambridge: Cambridge University Press.

Kim, M. S., & Kim, H. S. (2014). Initiating repair with and without particles: Alternative formats of other-initiation of repair in Korean conversation. *Research on Language and Social Interaction, 47*(4), 331–352.

Kim, M. S., & Yoon, K. E. (2021). Language in use. In Y. Y. Cho (Ed.), *Teaching Korean as a foreign language: Theories and practices* (pp. 54–80). Oxon and New York: Routledge.

Kim, S. H., & Kim, K.-H. (2015). Conversation analysis. In L. Brown & J. H. Yeon (Eds.), *The handbook of Korean linguistics* (pp. 271–286) West Sussex, UK: Wiley-Blackwell.

Lee, H. S., Yoon, K.-E., & Yoon, S.-S. (2017). Teaching listener responses to KFL students. *The Korean Language in America, 21*(2), 250–261.

Lee, S. H. (2015). Two forms of affirmative responses to polar questions. *Discourse Processes, 52*, 21–46.

Levinson, S. C. (1983). *Pragmatics*. Cambridge: Cambridge University Press.

Manrique, E. (2011). *Other-repair initiators in Argentine sign language: Handling seeing and understanding difficulties in face-to-face interaction* [MA thesis]. Radboud University, Nijmegen.

Nakamura, I. (2008). Understanding how teacher and student talk with each other: Anexploration of how "repair" displays the co-management of talk-in-interaction. *Language Teaching Research, 12*(2), 265–283.

Oh, S.-Y., & Park, Y.-Y. (2017). Interactional uses of acknowledgment tokens: '*ung*' and '*e*' as responses to multi-unit turns in Korean conversation. In G. Raymond, G. H. Lerner & J. Heritage (Eds.),

Enabling human conduct: Studies of talk-in-interaction in honor of Emanuel A. Schegloff (pp. 145–166). Amsterdam and Philadelphia: John Benjamins Publishing Company.

Pyun, D. O. (2009). A corpus-based analysis of Korean 'Yes' words *yey*, *ney*, and *ung*: A pedagogical perspective. *The Korean Language in America, 14*, 25–46.

Pyun, D. O., & Yoon, K.-E. (Forthcoming). Discourse functions of Korean 'yes' words. *Korean Linguistics*.

Robinson, J. D. (2013). Epistemics, action formation, and other-initiation of repair: The case of partial questioning repeats. In M. Hayashi, G. Raymond, & J. Sidnell (Eds.), *Conversational repair and human understanding* (pp. 261–292). Cambridge, UK: Cambridge University Press.

Robinson, J. D., & Kevoe-Feldman, H. (2010). Using full repeats to initiate repair on others' questions. *Research on Language and Social Interaction, 43*(3), 232–259.

Schegloff, E. A. (1982). Discourse as an interactional achievement: Some uses of 'uh huh' and other things that come between sentences. In D. Tannen (Ed.), *Analyzing discourse: Text and talk* (pp. 71–93). Georgetown University Round Table on Languages and Linguistics. Washington, DC: Georgetown University Press.

Schgeloff, E. A. (1993). Reflections on quantification in the study of conversation. *Research on Language and Social Interaction, 26*(1), 99–128.

Schegloff, E. A. (1997). Practices and actions: Boundary cases of other-initiated repair. *Discourse Processes, 23*, 499–545.

Schegloff, E. A. (2007). *Sequence organization in interaction: A primer in conversation analysis*. Cambridge: Cambridge University Press.

Schegloff, E. A., Jefferson, G., & Sacks, H. (1977). The preference for self-correction in the organization of repair in conversation. *Language, 53*, 361–382.

Selting, M. (1996). Prosody as an activity-type distinctive cue in conversation: The case of so- called 'astonished' questions in repair initiation. In E. Couper-Kuhlen & M. Selting (Eds.), *Prosody in conversation* (pp. 231–270). Cambridge: Cambridge University Press.

Seo, M. S., & Koshik, R. (2010). A conversation analytic study of gestures that engender repair in ESL conversational tutoring. *Journal of Pragmatics, 42*, 2219–2239.

Stivers, T. (2004). "No no no" and other types of multiple sayings in social interaction. *Human Communication Research, 30*(2), 260–293.

Wong, J. (2007). Answering my call: A look at telephone closings. In H. Bowles & P. Seedhouse (Eds.), *Conversation analysis and language for specific purposes* (pp. 272–304). Bern: Peter Lang.

Wong, J., & Waring, H. Z. (2010). *Conversation analysis and second language pedagogy: A guide for ESL/ELF teachers*. Oxon and New York: Routledge.

Wu, R. J. (2009). Repetition in the initiation of repair. In J. Sidnell (Ed.), *Conversation analysis: Comparative perspectives* (pp. 31–59). Cambridge, UK: Cambridge University Press.

Yoon, K. E. (2007). Application of conversation analysis to teaching Korean language and culture. *The Korean Language in America, 12*, 126–144.

APPENDIX
Conversation-analytic transcript symbols

.	Falling intonation
?	Rising intonation
,	Continuing intonation
(.)	Micropause
(n)	Numbers in parentheses indicated silence, represented in tenths of a second
:	Lengthened syllable
–	Sudden cut off
=	The second utterance is latched onto the first one, i.e., no gap between the two utterances
hh	Laughter
(hh)	Laughter within word boundaries
w<u>o</u>rd	Underlining indicates some form of stress or emphasis
WOrd	Upper case indicates loud talk
>word<	Word uttered at a faster pace
↑	The following word is said with a raised pitch or voice
(( ))	Transcriber's comments
(word)	Word in doubt
[	The beginning of overlapping
]	The end of overlapping

16
THE INTERSECTION OF DISCOURSE, GRAMMAR, REGISTER, PRAGMATICS, AND CULTURE[1]

Susan Strauss and Jongoh Eun

Introduction

Despite decades of applied linguistics research, practitioners in L2 pedagogy continue to rely heavily on textbooks using non-authentic language samples to illustrate the structure and uses of decontextualized bits of "grammar." Such materials are often based on invented dialogues and arbitrary vocabulary and grammar patterns that lend themselves to mechanical applications for students to master.

Moving away from textbook-central language samples and decontextualized grammatical constructions, this chapter provides an overview for the collection and close observation of authentic discourse data, with a view to apply novel perspectives and theoretical applications to Korean language pedagogy. Using a combined database of 140 online reviews of hotels (40) and food establishments (100), we demonstrate the types of close observation and focused attention to various types of linguistic forms and general analytic categories that could serve both teachers and students of high-intermediate to advanced language. The general nature of the online review is inherently rich with wide arrays of subjective evaluations, including expressions of feelings/emotions (affective stance marking), conjectures and expressions of (un)certainty (epistemic stance marking), and a multiplicity of context-specific lexical items and expressions that are potentially far more colorful, exciting, descriptive, and contextually accurate than many of the textbook language samples introduced to students at all levels of learning.

The examination of parallel instances of genre-based entries allows for the comparison and contrast of these spates of discourse from multiple points of view and at multiple levels of analysis, from the broadest distinctive categories to the most minute: genre, subgenre (narrative), lexical items and grammatical constructions for general reference and description, lexical items and grammatical constructions for highly specific reference and description, speech levels and honorifics, sentence-ending particles, evidentials, semantic/pragmatic discernment of near synonyms, and so forth. The parallel nature of these specific discourse samples builds a foundation for the discovery of linguistic patterns, particularly in the pragmatically sensitive domain of opinion giving within these narrative excerpts, where positive and negative

DOI: 10.4324/9781003034704-19

evaluations are crucial to each entry. The chapter is designed to illustrate how parallel discourse and the types of juxtaposition that such parallelism establishes can be used for awareness- and consciousness-raising activities for educators, materials designers, and students in the creation of innovative, interactive, and discourse-based materials (Leow, 2006; Rosa & Leow, 2004; Schmidt, 1993, 1995; *inter alia*).

Literature review: textbooks, authentic texts, discourse, genre, and register

Value and drawbacks of textbooks – authenticity, linguistic richness

The ubiquity of the textbook as primary resource for linguistic input in the foreign and second language curricula rests largely in the fact that language textbooks are designed and structured to introduce seemingly "natural" spates of oral and written discourse and interaction, progressing incrementally from the most simple of sentence structures and the most basic of vocabulary items to more complex ones. Quite generally, and across the board for most, if not all, languages, language textbooks can be characterized as follows: They provide repetition and recycling of high-frequency patterns in the target language; they isolate and recirculate key grammatical and interactional structures, introduced sequentially from the purportedly more basic to the more complex; and they provide exemplars of communicatively relevant expressions and sentence structures, interlacing target grammar patterns, discourse markers, and vocabulary, within predominantly, if not entirely invented dialogues, letters, expository texts, essays, and other communicative events (Olson, 1980; Simonsen, 2019; Zyzik & Polio, 2017;

Crucially, textbook language tends to follow a progression of perceived simplicity or difficulty, adapted to meet or gently surpass the literacy level of the users and their ability to comprehend, reproduce, and appropriate the target lexico-grammatical structures and entries in the target language. However, because of the preponderance of adapted language samples and a number of other criticisms (e.g., low likelihood of real-world applicability of linguistic exemplars in interactional settings), textbook language has been deemed unnatural, contrived, stilted, "sanitized," and lacking in realistic, situated sociocultural features of context (Gilmore, 2007; Glison, 2012; Glison & Donato, 2017; McCarthy & Carter, 1994, 1995).

In response to such drawbacks, the field of applied linguistics and second language pedagogy has undergone a number of transformations, including the infusion of policy and planning discourse pertaining to "authentic texts" in best practices design, materials development, and assessment standards (ACTFL, 2012, 2013; Gilmore, 2004, 2007, 2011; Glison, 2012; Glison & Donato, 2017; McCarthy & Carter, 1994, 1995; Pinner, 2019; Simonsen, 2019).

The concept of "text authenticity" has pervaded L2 research since at least the mid-1980s (Breen, 1985; Lee, 1995; Widdowson, 1980; among many others), and while the definitions and characteristics of the term differ according to need, usage, and context, its value in the arena of second language learning and teaching remains immense.

Following Glison and Donato's (2017, p. 65) discussion of high-leverage teaching practices (HLTP), we adopt the concept of "authentic texts" as texts produced "*by* and *for* monolingual, bilingual, or multilingual users of the TL and various other cultural groups." According to the HLTP framework, the thoughtful integration of well-chosen authentic texts into the L2 curriculum and classroom can provide high-quality conceptual knowledge of target language features in ways that unsupplemented textbook language cannot. Further, the use of authentic texts 1) establishes a foundation for instructors to promote students' discovery of meaning (both semantic and sociocultural) through problem solving, comparison, contrast, and the identification of systematic patterns of language use in discourse; 2) provides the discursive content and context amenable to the teaching of grammar as essentially conceptual, combining lexico-syntactic and semantic features of language with pragmatics and sociocultural meaning (Strauss, Feiz, and Xiang, 2018); and 3) presents linguistic content and context as representative of sociocultural interaction, register, and genre, paving the way for a multiplicity of richly complex communicative tasks and within interpersonal, interpretive, and presentational modes.

Discourse: genre (macro), subgenre/structure (meso), register (micro), and pedagogy

Throughout this chapter, we illustrate how the use of "authentic texts" as discourse and the application of simple discourse analysis can be incorporated into high-intermediate, advanced-level materials design for Korean. We proceed from the socio-culturally defined concept of *genre* as:

> [a] metaphorical frame of discourse, . . . shaped and constrained by socio-cultural conventions of practice, and re-shaped and re-created through discourse and social practice. Genres exhibit culturally recognizable discursive patterns for the conveyance of essential propositional content to some form of audience or hearer (imagined or real), within a particular context, with a view to accomplish a particular communicative purpose.
>
> *(Strauss & Feiz, 2014, p. 52)*

Genres are the very essence of discourse, the very ways we make broad sense of all communicative acts. It is through genre that members of sociocultural communities understand these "typified acts of communication" (Hyland, 2018, p. 1) as a lecture, a news report, a recipe, a book review, an opinion essay. And it is the genre coupled with its micro-level components of *register* that enable us to distinguish lectures from sermons, recipes from science experiments, book reviews from literary promotions, and research articles from opinion pieces, since each genre typically differs from the other in terms of its essential elements of audience, context, and purpose, as well as its distinctive sets of lexical items and grammatical constructions (Strauss & Feiz, 2014).

For this project, the online review is the macro-level discourse genre, i.e., the "typified communicative" means through which users of a product or service or clients of a business establishment evaluate that product or service and describe their experiences with that establishment and its offerings. In the case of our datasets, these online reviews are most often expressed through the subgenre of the *narrative* in which the writers provide detailed and highly subjective story snippets that combine to praise, criticize, extol, thank, complain about, and applaud various details about the product, food, service, ambience, and personnel (Ochs, 2004; Ochs & Capps, 1996, *inter alia*). We appeal to the analytic lenses of macro (the online review in general), meso (review narrative), and micro (the lexical items, grammatical constructions, and [in]formality levels, i.e., register) of the discourse.

If the macro- and meso-level structures of genre are the "what" of discourse, then the micro-level components of *register* are the "how" (Strauss & Feiz, 2014, p. 72). Register includes the discursive components of word choice, context- or area-specific lexicons, grammatical features, and communicative style (e.g., colloquial/informal [lower register] vs. academic/technical/formal [higher register]). *Registers* suffuse genres with their multifaceted ways of referring to people, things, ideas, and events; of addressing those entities; of describing them; of expressing stances, emotions, and opinions in relation to them.

Through the combined macro- and meso-lenses of *genre* and *narrative*, and the micro-lens of register, we demonstrate the process of compiling two mini corpora of different but related sets of online reviews. We provide a range of possible suggestions for how Korean language instructors might conduct their own analysis of the discourse data, develop sets of pedagogical materials based on those data and their findings, and then, depending upon their preferences and institutional expectations, design discourse-central research-based projects to further our understanding of the topics at hand and to contribute to the growing field of Korean applied linguistics.

Given the complexity and richness of the discourse samples in terms of high-specificity nouns, verbs, and descriptors that are interwoven into each narrative of personal experience, the materials designed from these datasets lend themselves well to application in high-intermediate to advanced language classrooms and curricula. The data are replete with socioculturally sensitive interactional choices of grammar in terms of keenly subjective scene setting, temporal reference, sensory descriptions, affective and epistemic stance marking, among other components. Further, this discourse analytic-pedagogical approach also lends itself seamlessly to language for specific purposes pedagogy (Hamp-Lyons, 2011; Hyland, 2004, 2018; Paltridge, 2014; Paltridge & Starfield, 2014, *inter* alia). The goals of such pedagogies are for learners to not only be able to identify the broader scope of genre but also to accurately pinpoint the relevant clusters of linguistic features, from basic reference types for things, people, and ideas to the more robustly complex ways of expressing ideas, opinions, sensory/affective reactions, with a view to participate in using the language at high levels of proficiency.

Unlike textbook language samples, which are typically driven by grammar patterns, discourse markers, and vocabulary (a form-first type of approach), discourse-based materials development is driven from a genre-/discourse-first approach. In contrast to the neat and orderly form-first framework (Figure 16.1), discourse-based samples can appear messy, indiscriminate, and complex. It is through macro-, meso-, and micro-level organization strategies and the observation of patterns that the discourse-first approach can be made orderly, manageable, and amenable to pedagogical materials development (Figure 16.2).

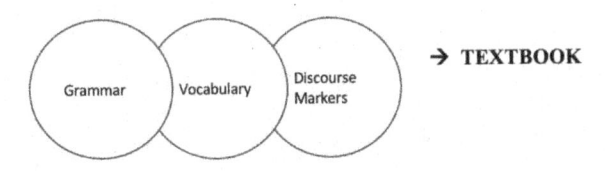

Figure 16.1 Form-first approach

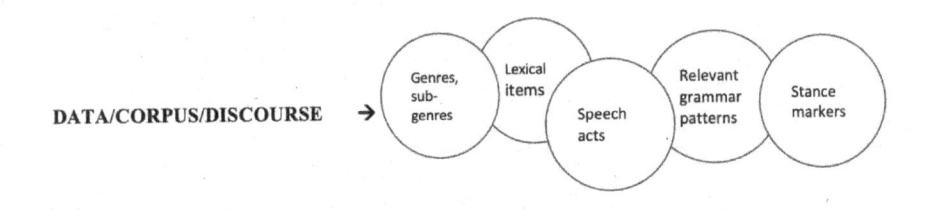

Figure 16.2 Discourse-first approach

As represented in the graphic, textbooks are driven by decontextualized grammar patterns, vocabulary, and discourse markers, which are then illustrated in invented dialogues and prose. Form takes precedence over discourse. Invented discourse is the medium through which forms are practiced, combined, substituted, and repeated.

Conversely, corpus- or discourse-driven materials begin with the data. The first step involves deliberate and purposeful data selection, moving from the category of genre to subgenre and register. This allows for analysis and the concomitant progressive subcategorization of forms and expressions into general context lexical items, specific/technical lexical items, affective stance markers, epistemic stance markers, expressions that intensify or mitigate an opinion or observation, temporal expressions, (non)honorifics, speech acts (complaint, praise, thanking, promise), near synonyms, context-situated serial verb constructions, and so-forth.

Data and methodology

For the purpose of this study, we compiled a dataset of two mini corpora of discourse-based online reviews related to travel, food, and hospitality. The dataset is replete with robust, context-central lexical items and pragmatic inventories that pertain to each setting, including relevant nouns, adjectives, adverbs, and verbs, in addition to evaluation and opinion giving, the whole of which can easily be adapted for wide-range use in a language classroom. Moreover, each entry is a comprehensive whole, with a discernible beginning, a discernible end, and a proportion of discourse that is of manageable length for review, practice, and analysis.

The two corpora are: 1) Trip Advisor, Korea, narrowed to a small subset of posts about two five-star hotels: Shilla (Korean) and Marriott (Western), and two locations each, Seoul and Jeju Island, and 2) MangoPlate, narrowed to a small subset of posts about five cuisine types and eateries (Korean, Japanese, Chinese, Western, and World Cuisine).[2]

For the Trip Advisor entries, we collected the ten most recent reviews, from July 20, 2020, moving backward in time to October 2019. Our rationale for selecting five-star brands was to capture a range of expressions that relate to class, luxury, and high expectations. We selected one brand representative of Western luxury hotels (Marriott) and one brand for Korean luxury hotels (Shilla). Further, we established potential contrasts within this mini corpus by selecting an urban business location (Seoul) and a tourist location (Jeju).

The MangoPlate (MP) entries are based on the first five major cuisine types/eatery styles in the MP search filter: Korean, Japanese, Chinese, Western, and World Cuisine (Figure 16.3). We did not include reviews for the last three categories of the filter, i.e., buffets, cafés, and bars,

Figure 16.3 MangoPlate search filter

due to the over-specificity of eatery style. The latter categories are marked in the figure with an "X." The Western category (양식) includes American food (e.g., burgers, steak, sandwiches), Italian, French and fusion styles, which combine European cuisines with other cuisine styles, earlier than other types, such as Mexican or Thai food (even British or German are considered world foods). World cuisine (세계 음식) food includes all other types, such as Vietnamese, Thai, Mexican, and Arabic. The variety of cuisine types allows for a wide range of food names (both Korean and international) as well as a more diverse range of taste terms and descriptors for dishes that might be less familiar to the Korean palate, and thus engender a wider range of taste- and texture-related expressions.

We collected the ten most recent entries for both the highest-rated and lowest-rated posts for each cuisine type, again, beginning on July 20, 2020, and moving backward in time. Table 16.1 provides a summary of the datasets used for this study.

For the Trip Advisor data, we excluded posts that made explicit or implicit reference to COVID-19 in an effort to: 1) keep the points of comparison consistent and focused on the hotel, its amenities, service, and so forth, and 2) enhance the timelessness of the data samples and to avoid confounding issues of (dis)comfort and (in)convenience with external factors and pressures. We also excluded posts that evaluated only the hotel restaurants or buffets (e.g., Flavors at Marriott Seoul), and not the accommodations. For all data (Trip Advisor and MangoPlate), we only included reviews that were five sentences or more in length, determined by punctuation, where each sentence was marked by a full stop.

We treated each dataset (Trip Advisor and MangoPlate) as repositories of vocabulary, grammar, and pragmatics, especially with respect to contextually situated narrative discourse on the one hand and evaluation-laden discourse on the other. As such, we reviewed all posts and established a framework for discourse-based use of these exemplars, as follows:

- Context-specific registers
    - vocabulary for hotels and restaurants: nouns, verbs, descriptors.
    - productive affixes, e.g., -류 'kind,' -집 'house,' -장 'sauce,' and 생- 'raw.'

Table 16.1 Summary of data: Trip Advisor (TrAd) and MangoPlate (MP)

		Seoul	Jeju	Total Reviews	Total Words
Trip Advisor					
	Marriott	10	10	20	
	Shilla	10	10	20	
TrAd Totals		20	20	40	**4,198**
		Highest Rating (4.8)	*Lowest Rating (4.0–4.3)*		
MangoPlate					
	Korean	10	10	20	
	Japanese	10	10	20	
	Chinese	10	10	20	
	Western	10	10	20	
	World	10	10	20	
MP Totals		50	50	100	10,067

- Discourse-grounded grammatical patterns:
  - affective stance markers and emotion terms, subcategorized according to positive/negative feelings:
    - positive emotions: 만족(하다)[3] 'satisfied,' 편안하다 'comfortable,' 편하다 'comfortable, easy,' 감동 'moved, touched,' 감사하다 'thankful'
    - negative emotions: 아쉽다 'disappointed,' 불편(하다) 'uncomfortable,' 걱정 'worry,' 답답하다 'stuffy, stifling'
  - epistemic stance markers and evidentials:
    - 당연히 'of course, naturally,' 솔직히 'frankly,' 아마 'maybe,' -것 같다 'it seems, I think,' 생각(하다) 'I think,' 기대(하다) 'I expect'
  - adverbial intensification and mitigation, subcategorized according to positive assessment/negative assessments:
    - intensifiers (e.g., 'very,' 'really'): 너무, 정말, 아주, 매우, 진짜, 참, 무척
    - mitigators: 좀 'a little,' 조금 'a little,' 약간 'slightly,' 살짝 'slightly'
  - expressions of taste and sensory perception (beyond basic expressions like: 달다 'sweet,' 짜다 'salty,' 맵다 'spicy')
    - 비리다 'fishy, smelly,' 비리게 느껴지다 'feel fishy,' 톡쏘는 맛 'pungent, tangy,' 상큼한 소스, 'crisp/refreshing sauce,' 침이 고이다, 'mouth is watering'
  - expressions that reflect varying formality levels (beyond sentence enders and honorific affixes):

    - delicious; tasty 맛있다   neutral

레알 짱 맛있다	more colloquial 'real good taste'
냠냠	colloquial yummy
맛이 훌륭하다	more formal 'tastes excellent'

    - really, very   정말, 아주   neutral

참, 엄청, 진짜	more colloquial
매우	more formal

    - uncomfortable 불편하다   neutral

찜찜하다	more colloquial

    - angry   화가 나다   neutral

대노하다	more formal

For each of these categories (and others), we conducted frequency counts and more fine-grained analysis of semantic features, e.g., positive stance, negative stance; however, due to the more practical and applied purpose of this paper, we do not include those tables here (see Strauss and Eun [in preparation] for a more in-depth and detailed discussion of the corpus-based analysis).

In addition to the previous features of discourse, we attend to the following constructions for potential use in materials development and linguistic "noticings" for intermediate to advanced-level pedagogical focus:

- Productive context-based nominal affixes (see Section 4.3.1)
- Serial verb constructions (see Section 4.3.2)
- Near synonyms (see Section 4.3.3)
- Idiomatic/colorful ways of expressing food appreciation and evaluation (see Section 4.3.4)
- Speech level alternations and (non)honorifics: (see Section 4.3.5)
    - Honorific sentence enders:

Deferential form	V-ㅂ니다/-습니다
Polite form	V-어/아 - 요

    - Non-honorific sentence enders:

Plain form	V-다
Nominalizations	-ㅁ/음

These categories, patterns, and individual lexico-grammatical features are illustrated in detail in Section 4, together with two sample reviews from each mini corpus.

Illustration of a discourse-first perspective

Throughout this section, we illustrate the manifold ways in which authentic texts and their discursive features can be "mined" and incorporated into a variety of activities for language learners designed to: provide rich and engaging linguistic content that promotes semantic and sociocultural meaning discovery; motivate students to immerse themselves in authentic texts and push past their comfort zones in the areas of linguistic comprehension and production; to experience first-hand the creative, playful ways authentic texts become the medium for richly constructed language, used by speakers and writers to narrate, praise, complain, assess, evaluate, and opine.

Section 4.1 introduces the discourse sample of two hotel reviews, together with a select list of context-specific lexical items, followed by two samples from MangoPlate and a select list of context-specific lexical items. Section 4.2 presents an abridged, skeletal analysis of the narrative at the meso level, together with a handful of micro-level elements that could be attended to by instructors and language learners for awareness-raising activities. Focused attention on specific elements within each narrative can lead teachers toward these high-leverage teaching practices through discourse-central meaning discovery, involving comparison, contrast, and semantic/pragmatic problem solving. Section 4.3 includes a selection of patterns that we refer to as "noticings." The term "noticings" refers to those bits of discourse, language, and grammar that cluster systematically within the discourse that can be culled for explanatory, illustrative, and elaborative purposes. Specifically, we address productive affixes from the MangoPlate data, serial verb constructions related to food prep and eating, near synonyms and other expressions with seemingly parallel meanings, idiomatic and colorful ways of expressing and describing food.

Discourse samples: Trip Advisor – Marriott and Shilla hotels

This section provides two discourse samples from the mini corpora, followed by a sample list of vocabulary and lexical items that could constitute a starting point for working with these data samples in a pedagogical context. The samples begin with the Trip Advisor mini corpus, followed by a vocabulary table and then two samples from MangoPlate, also followed by its vocabulary table.

(1) Shilla Hotel, Seoul

Rating: 5/5	Best
최고	It was an old hotel, but it was cleaner and better maintained than any other new hotel. I was assigned a Premier Double Room. As soon as I stepped into the room, I was impressed with the spaciousness and the clean/tidy carpet. The carpets and fabric sofas were all kept very clean, and the bedding was also comfortable, so I was able to sleep really well. Also, the bathtub was large and deep, so it was comfortable to take a half-body bath. The hotel lobby also had a stylish green interior and a bright and comfortable atmosphere overall. Above all, I really enjoyed getting up in the morning and walking the promenade inside the Shilla Hotel.
오래된 호텔이지만 어느 신설호텔보다도 더 깔끔하고 유지보수가 매우 잘 되어있는 호텔이었어요. 프리미어 더블룸으로 배정받았는데 객실 들어서자마자 넓은 공간과 너무나 깔끔한 카펫이 인상적이었어요. 카펫이나 페브릭 소파 모두 매우 청결하게 관리가 되어있었고 침구역시 편안해서 숙면할수 있었습니다. 욕조도 깊고 커서 반신욕하기에 편안했어요. 호텔 로비 역시 그린 인테리어가 세련되고 전체적으로 화사하고 편안한 분위기였네요. 무엇보다 아침에 일어나 신라호텔 안에 있는 산책로를 걷는 일이 무척 즐거웠습니다.	

(2) Marriott Hotel, Seoul

Rating 5/5	Delicious and happy Marriott stay with room service and breakfast buffet
룸서비스와조식부페로맛있고행복했던메리엇스테이	I booked 2 weekend nights for Friday and Saturday to use the 1-night-free coupon for Marriott members for 2 consecutive nights. Recently, my husband and I were both very exhausted from frequent business trips and work that lasted from the early mornings to late at night, so this time, we decided to eat, sleep, and swim only at the hotel. We ordered room service for dinner on our check-in day and dinner the next day, and it was really good. I immediately felt that the quality of all the ingredients was really good, and the food itself was so excellent that for *tteokgalbi* (Grilled Short Rib Patties), we even said that JW Marriott, not Damyang, is the top *tteokgalbi* house! In particular, I was grateful that the staff who brought room service responded so kindly and made us so comfortable. Since we live in Seoul, and even close to the hotel, we felt that it was a little fun to have room service meals while staying at the hotel. And we were happy with the service and food, so I think I'll visit again during the times that I'm too tired to travel. Thank you, Park Yohan Hotelier for your excellent service ☺
클럽 메리어트 회원에게 제공되는 2박 연박시 1박 무료 숙박권을 사용할 겸, 주말 금토 2박을 예약했어요. 최근에 잦은 출장과 새벽, 밤샘으로 이어지는 일 때문에 저와 남편 둘다 많이 지쳐 있던 터라, 이번엔 오롯이 호텔에서 먹고 자고 수영하고 쉬기로 마음 먹었고 체크인한 날 저녁도, 그 다음날의 저녁도 룸서비스를 주문해서 방에서 편히 먹었는데 정말 좋았어요. 모든 식재료의 질이 정말 좋다는게 바로 느껴졌고, 음식 자체의 조리도 훌륭해서 떡갈비 같은 경우에는 담양이 아니라 JW 메리엇이 떡갈비 맛집이다! 라고 얘기했을 정도? 특히나 룸서비스를 가져다 주신 담당 직원분께서 정말 친절하고 편안하게 응대해주셔서 감사했습니다. 집이 서울이고, 심지어 호텔에서 가까운데 살고 있어서 호텔에서 머무르며 룸서비스로 식사를 해결한다는게 약간 재밌다고도 느껴졌는데 서비스와 음식 모두 만족스러워서 다음에도 여행을 떠나기에도 피곤한 시기엔 또 방문할거 같아요. 훌륭한 서비스 해주신 박요한 호텔리어님 감사합니다 ^-^	

Intersection

Hotel lexicon: vocabulary table

From the original 10,067-word mini corpus, we identified 232 lexical items that relate to the hotel and hospitality register. From there, we pared down the list to the top 50, as shown in Table 16.2.

Lexical items selected here range from the more general descriptors and nouns related to the hotel ranking, e.g., 5-star hotel (5성급 호텔), to the building itself, e.g., main entrance (현관) and 1st floor reception (desk)/lobby (1층 리셉션/로비), and to the specific room and room amenities, e.g., room number 1401 (1401호), toiletries (욕실용품), and hand towel (화장실수건). Additional useful vocabulary includes those expressions related to room reservations (예약[하다]) and cancellations (취소[하다]); rates (요금); length of stay, e.g., 2 nights (2박); no vacancy (만실), among others.

A number of lexical items are simply *hangulized* English words, e.g., veranda/balcony (베란다), check-in counter (체크인카운트), front desk (프론트), penalty (페널티), and pool (풀, in addition to its Sino-Korean counterpart, 수영장).

And, finally, the corpus reveals a number of highly context-specific neologisms, like:

호캉스 – the portmanteau word combining hotel 호텔 + the French word '바캉스,' 돌기념여행 'travel celebrating a baby's first birthday' literally meaning 'travel

Table 16.2 Fifty representative lexical items from TrAd

Korean	English	Korean	English
5성급 호텔	5-star hotel	1인당	per person
시설	facility	상품	package
편의시설	amenities	객실안내	room information
현관	front door, main entrance	룸변경	room change
1층 리셉션/로비	1st floor lobby	투숙일	staying dates
체크인하는곳	check-in desk	투숙하다, 숙박하다, 머무르다, 묵다	to stay
수영장/풀	swimming pool	투숙일	dates of stay
야외/실내수영장/풀	outdoor/indoor pool	투숙목적	purpose of stay
짐	luggage	돌기념여행	Travel to celebrate a baby's first birthday
1401호	Room #1401	호캉스	hotel vacation: 호텔 + 바캉스
객실	guest room	태교여행	travel for pregnant women
침구/베딩	bedding	고객	customer
침실	bedroom	투숙객	hotel guest
욕실	bathroom	관광객	tourist
화장실수건	hand towel	손님	guest
대형타월	bath towel	직원	staff
욕실용품	toiletries	직원분	staff (honorific)
예약(하다)	reservation (reserve)	벨직원	bell staff
취소(하다)	cancellation (cancel)	프론트	front desk
성수기	high season	체크인카운트	check-in counter
만실	no vacancy	엘리베이터	elevator
2박	two nights	짐관련한핸들링	luggage service
가격	price	베란다	balcony, veranda
요금	rate	매니져님	manager (honorific)
잘관리되다	to be well maintained	페널티	penalty

commemorating the first birthday,' and 태교여행 – designating a special travel characteristic that relates to pregnant women (or future mom), literally 'before giving birth.'

The vocabulary items from Table 16.2 in and of themselves could be useful for Korean language students on multiple levels: 1) for personal use to coordinate their own travel arrangements, 2) to describe past and/or future travels and/or read about the travel of others, and 3) for linguistic and grammatical growth crucial for students of Korean for specific purposes, as robust repositories of vocabulary and basic grammar relating to the industry of hotel management, hospitality, and leisure.

MangoPlate samples and lexical items

(3) 감성타코 (Mexican)

괜찮다 May 2018	**Okay** May 2018
애매한 시간대인 3시에 갔는데도 손님 꽉 차네요.	Even though I went (there) at 3:00, which is not lunch or dinner time, it was full of customers.
가장 잘 나간다는 3.8만원짜리 파히타 먹었습니다.	I ate a 38,000 won fajita that is a bestseller.
맛있습니다. 맛은 부정 못하겠어요.	It's delicious. I can't deny it.
새우, 고기, 소스 전부 훌륭했어요.	The shrimp, meat, and sauce were all excellent.
타코 한입 먹을때마다 기분이 좋아졌습니다.	Every bite of the taco (lit. every time I bit the taco) made me feel great.
다만 음식 주문하고나올 때까지 거의 30분을 기다렸던거 같습니다.	However, I think I waited for about 30 minutes until the food came out.
먼저 빨리 나온 생맥주는 김이 빠지고 있었습니다..	The draft beer, which came out first, was turning flat.
거기에 애초에 적게 나온 또띠아 더 달라고 했는데 까먹었나 싶을 정도로 안나오더군요.	On top of that, I asked for more tortillas, which were not enough in the first place, but they never came out, so I thought they (the staff) forgot.
기다리다 짜증나서 그냥 고기 먹어치우고 나왔습니다.	I got annoyed from waiting so long, so I just finished the meat and left the restaurant.
타코집인데 타코는 즐기다 만 기분이네요.	It's a taco house, but I feel like I just half-enjoyed the tacos there.
분위기와 맛은 주변에 추천해줄만큼 좋았지만	The atmosphere and flavor were good enough to recommend the place to others, but I think this kind of service probably should be improved.
이런 서비스 부분은 개선해야하지 않을지?	
음식 조리에 공들이느라 오래 걸리는 걸까요 ㅎㅎㅎ;	Maybe it took long because they spent so much time cooking? ☺☺☺

(4) 노란상소갈비 (Korean)

맛있다 July 2020	Delicious July 2020
야들야들 맛있는 소갈비	Soft and delicious beef ribs
생갈비 정갈비 다 맛있어요.	The unmarinated and Suwon-style ribs are all delicious.
정갈비가 조금 더 달달해요.	The Suwon-style ribs are a little sweeter.
생갈비는 정석적인 맛.	The unmarinated ribs have a typical taste.
밑반찬 중 두부가 특히 맛있었어요.	Among the side dishes, the tofu was especially delicious.
양파 소스도 무난하고 괜찮아요 . . .	The onion sauce is also nice . . .

(Continued)

Intersection

(Continued)

... 한우도 아닌 게 비싸다.	... It's expensive even though it's not Korean beef.
그래도 이만한 퀄리티에 괜찮다.	Still, the food is good for this level of quality.
이런 의견이었어요.	This is my opinion.
재방문 의사는 반반이에요.	My intent to revisit is half and half (I may or may not go back).

MangoPlate lexicon: vocabulary table

In the original mini corpus of 4,198 words, we culled a list of 739 food-related terms and expressions: meal names, utensils and place settings, restaurant and cuisine types, dish names, ingredients (food and seasoning names), food-preparation terms, taste terms, and myriad ways of reacting to and evaluating foods and flavors – both positively and negatively, along a continuum from slight to moderate to extreme. We first organized the 739 lexical items and expressions into broad categories, such as type of food establishment and cuisine, atmosphere and seating options, utensils and dishware, meal names, dish names (and how served), personnel references, customer references, taste terms, food-preparation terms, and expressions that evaluate and react to food and flavors.

We excluded the more common lexical items like meat (고기), chopsticks (젓가락), store (가게), and spicy taste (매운 맛) since these are likely well known to higher-proficiency students. We further excluded *hangulized* expressions for non-Korean foods like sushi (스시), taco (타코), quesadilla (퀘사디아), quinoa (퀴노아), and salad bowl (샐러드보울), as, while potentially interesting on the surface, they reflect no more than mechanical transliteration of international foods into Korean script. Table 16.3 provides an encapsulation of 50 of these terms and expressions.

Again, we included common expressions for dining, including place settings and food names, e.g., soft tofu (순두부), firm tofu (단단한 두부), black mushroom (목이버섯), and shiitake mushroom (표고버섯). We also included lexical items referring to both clientele and establishment employees, e.g., party of 2 – guest plus one person (동반 1인), single guest (혼자 오신 분들), head chef (담당 셰프님), owner (사장님), as well as taste terms – relating to both taste and texture: appetizing taste [umami], (감칠맛), fishy (비리다), chewy [i.e., for noodles = al dente] (쫄깃하다), refreshing (상쾌하다).

Table 16.3 Fifty representative lexical items from MP

Korean	English	Korean	English
단품	single dish	소양념갈비2인분	marinated beef ribs, for 2 people
찬/밑반찬	side dishes	담당셰프님	head chef (hon.)
기본찬	basic side dishes	동반 1인	party of 2 (guest plus one person)
전채	appetizer	혼자오신분들	single guest (hon.)
디저트/후식	dessert	사장님	boss, owner (hon.)
음료	beverage	예약석	reserved seating

(*Continued*)

Table 16.3 (Continued)

Korean	English	Korean	English
간식	between meals snack	접시를치우다	to clear the dishes (from the table when diners are finished)
분위기	atmosphere	배달시키다	to have food delivered
식기	tableware	여러번리필해먹다	to eat with many refills
물수건	wet towel (for hands)	바짝익히다	to cook well
한우	Korean beef	굽다	to bake; grill
닭고기	chicken	비벼먹다	to mix and eat
치킨	(fried) chicken	계란을얹어서먹다	to add egg on top
순두부	soft tofu	바삭한치킨	crispy fried chicken
단단한두부	firm tofu	쫄깃하다	to be chewy (al dente)
군고구마	baked sweet potato	상쾌하다	to be refreshing
목이버섯	black mushroom	아삭한샐러드	crunchy salad
표고버섯	shiitake mushroom	신선하다	to be fresh
양념	seasoning	녹진한빵	soft and sticky buns/bread
조미김	seasoned seaweed	싱겁다, 밍밍하다, 심심하다, 슴슴하다	to be bland (4 expressions)
수타면	handmade noodles	톡쏘는맛	pungent taste/flavor
쌀국수	rice noodle	금방눅눅해지다	to get soggy quickly
통새우	whole shrimp	감칠맛	umami, appetizing
활고등어	live mackerel	비리다	to be fishy
참치	tuna	비리게느껴지다	to feel fishy

Meso-level analysis sample: narrative

Next are two slightly annotated review samples: One from Marriott (Trip Advisor), repeated text from example (1), and one from 감성타코 (MangoPlate), repeated text from example (3). The Trip Advisor review is a positive, praising one, with positive descriptors and positive stance marking throughout. The MangoPlate review is more mixed – containing some positive, praising commentary interspersed with negative, complaint commentary. Each review relates squarely and in minute detail to the location and quality of the respective poster's experience.

It is beyond the scope of the present chapter to annotate and identify a more comprehensive set of discursive and lexico-grammatical features. However, we do present a skeletal analysis of the narrative at the meso level, pointing out qualities of the opening and closing lines of each review (typically taking the form of a final assessment), together with a handful of micro-level elements that could be attended to by instructors and language learners for practical pedagogical application as well as awareness-raising activities. These include temporal adverbials, positive and negative emotion terms, additive adverbials, and speech-level sentence enders. The list of what we have annotated in each sample appears after excerpt (6). *Note the general structure and content of each review:*

(5) slightly annotated version of Example (1), Shilla, Seoul

최고	**Best**
오래된 호텔**이지만** 어느 신설호텔보다도 더 깔끔하고 유지보수가 매우 잘 되어있는 호텔이었어요. 프리미어 더블룸으로 배정받았는데 객실 들어서자마자 넓은 공간과 너무나 깔끔한 카펫이 인상적이었어요. 카펫이나 페브릭 소파 모두 매우 청결하게 관리가 되어있었고 침구역시 편안해서 <u>숙면할수 있었습니다</u>. 욕조도 깊고 커서 반신욕하기에 편안했어요. 호텔 로비 역시 그린 인테리어가 세련되고 전체적으로 화사하고 편안한 분위기였**네**요. 무엇보다 아침에 일어나 신라호텔 안에 있는 산책로를 걷는 일이 <u>무척 즐거웠습니다</u>.	It was **an old hotel, but** it was cleaner and better maintained than any other new hotel. I was assigned a Premier Double Room. **As soon as** I stepped into the room, I was **impressed** with the spaciousness and the clean/tidy carpet. Carpets and fabric sofas were all kept very clean, and the bedding was also **comfortable, <u>so I was able to sleep really well.</u>** The bathtub was large and deep, so it was comfortable to take a half-body bath. The hotel lobby also had a stylish green interior and a **bright and comfortable atmosphere overall**. Above all, I <u>**really enjoyed**</u> getting up in the morning and walking the promenade inside the Shilla Hotel.

(6) slightly annotated version of Example (3) 감성타코

괜찮다 May 2018	**Okay** May 2018
애매한 시간대인 **3시에 갔는데도** 손님 꽉 차**네**요. 가장 잘 나간다는 3.8만원짜리 파히타 <u>먹었습니다</u>.	**Even though I went (there) at 3:00,** which is not lunch or dinner time, it was full of customers. I **<u>ate</u>** a 38,000 won fajita that is a bestseller.
<u>맛있습니다</u>. 맛은 부정 못하겠어요. 새우, 고기, 소스 전부 훌륭했어요. **타코 한입 먹을때마다** 기분이 <u>좋아졌습니다</u>.	It's <u>**delicious**</u>. I can't deny it. The shrimp, meat, and sauce were all excellent. **Every bite of the taco** made me feel **<u>great.</u>**
다만 음식 주문하고 나올 때까지 거의 30분을 기다렸던<u>거 같습니다</u>. 먼저 빨리 나온 생맥주는 김이 <u>**빠지고 있었습니다**</u>. 거기에 애초에 적게 나온 또띠아 더 달라고 했는데 까먹었나 싶을 정도로 안나오더군요. **기다리다 짜증나서** 그냥 고기 먹어치우고 나왔습니다. 타코집인데 타코는 **즐기다 만 기분이네요**.	However, <u>**I think**</u> I waited for about 30 minutes until the food came out. The draft beer, which came out first, was <u>**turning flat**</u>. **On top of that**, I asked for more tortillas, which were not enough in the first place, but they never came out, so I thought they (the staff) forgot. **I got annoyed from waiting so long**, so I just finished the meat and left the restaurant. It's a taco house, **but I feel like I just half-enjoyed the tacos there**.
분위기와 맛은 주변에 추천해줄만큼 좋았지만 이런 서비스 부분은 개선해야하지 않을지? 음식 조리에 공들이느라 오래 걸리는 걸까요 ㅎㅎㅎ;	The atmosphere and flavor were good enough to recommend the place to others, but I think this kind of service probably should be improved. Maybe it took long because they spent so much time cooking? ☺☺☺

- OPENING LINE = one to two lines of scene setting (both establish a contrast)

  오래된 호텔**이지만**   'the hotel is old **but**....'
  3시에 갔는**데도**   '**Even though** I went (there) at 3:00....'

- Poster's actions and reactions – emotion terms as related to temporal adverbials, e.g., 'as soon as I' 'every time I....'

  - 객실 들어서**자마자** 넓은 공간과 **너무나** 깔끔한 카펫이 <u>인상적이었어요</u>.
  '**As soon as** I stepped into the room, **I was impressed** with the *spaciousness* and the *very clean/tidy carpet*.'
  타코한입먹을때**마다** <u>기분이좋아졌습니다</u>.
  '**Every time** I bit into a taco, **I felt great**.'

  Other emotion terms:
  - 무척 즐거웠습니다   'I **enjoyed** ... very much'
  - 기다리다 짜증나서   'I got **annoyed** from waiting so long....'
    타코는 즐기다 만 기분이네요.   'I feel like I just half-**enjoyed** the taco....'

- Epistemic stance markers/evidentials

  ...편안한 분위기였**네요**   '...(the hotel lobby ... also) had a comfortable atmosphere.'

  ...손님 꽉 차**네요**   '...it was full of customers'
  ...까먹었나 **싶을 정도로** 안나오**더군요**.   '...but they never came out, so I thought they (the staff) forgot.'

- Speech-level alternations – deferential, polite, plain (not in examples (5) or (6))

  애매한 시간대인 3시에 갔는데도 손님 꽉 <u>차네요</u>.
  가장 잘 나간다는 3.8만원짜리 파히타 <u>먹었습니다</u>.
  <u>맛있습니다</u>. 맛은 부정 못하겠어요.
  새우, 고기, 소스 <u>전부 훌륭했어요</u>.
  타코 한입 먹을때마다 기분이 <u>좋아졌습니다</u>.

  'Even though I went (there) at 3:00, which is not lunch or dinner time, it was full of customers. **I ate** a 38,000 won fajita that is a bestseller.
  It's delicious. I can't deny it.
  The shrimp, meat, and sauce <u>were all excellent</u>.
  Every bite of the taco (lit. every time I bit the taco) **made me feel great**.'

- Additive adverbials
  - 무엇보다   'above all'
  - 거기에 애초에   'on top of that'

- FINAL ASSESSMENTS
  - 무엇보다 아침에 일어나 신라호텔 안에 있는 산책로를 걷는 일이 무척 즐거웠습니다.

    'Above all, I really enjoyed getting up in the morning and walking the promenade inside the Shilla Hotel.'

  - 분위기와 맛은 주변에 추천해줄만큼 좋았지만 이런 서비스 부분은 개선해야하지 않을지? 음식 조리에 공들이느라 오래 걸리는 걸까요 ㅎㅎㅎ

'The atmosphere and flavor were good enough to recommend the place to others, but I think this kind of service probably should be improved. Maybe it took long because they spent so much time cooking? ☺ ☺ ☺'

Noticings

This section addresses a handful of the patterned discursive features that were systematically clustered across a number of different reviews. Specifically, we address four productive affixes from the MangoPlate mini corpus (-류, -집, -장, and 생-), serial verb constructions related to food prep and eating, idiomatic and creatively descriptive ways that posters refer to consuming larger quantities of food, and a set of four near synonyms from each of the two mini corpora.

Productive affixes relating to food types and food establishments

Table 16.4 presents a non-exhaustive representation of the discourse and grammar patterns from the MangoPlate corpus that reflect a variety of productive suffixes and prefixes, e.g., -류, -집, -장, and 생-.

The patterns identified here are both context and topic specific, as well as being productively formed to express food- and restaurant-related aspects. This includes the creatively formed expression 맛집, lit. 'flavor house,' as a way to refer to a restaurant as a "must-eat establishment."

Table 16.4 Productive suffixes and prefixes from the MP mini corpus

Productive nominal suffix modifiers: MangoPlate	
-류 kinds – collective noun	
식사류	kinds of meals
채소류	kinds of vegetables
젤라또류	kinds of gelato
견과류	kinds of nuts
-집 type of restaurant (lit. house)	
고기집	meat house (barbeque house)
국수집	noodle house
중국집	Chinese restaurant
딤섬집	Dim sum house
만두집	dumpling house
타코집	Taco house
맛집	"must-eat" house
-장 sauce	
간장	soy sauce
양념장	seasoned sauce
쌈장	sauce for wraps
춘장	sauce – black bean paste
된장	miso
Productive nominal prefix modifiers	
생-	raw, uncooked, fresh
생당근	uncooked carrot
생갈비	unmarinated ribs
생와사비	raw wasabi
생크림	whipping cream (lit. fresh cream)

Table 16.5 Serial verb constructions – actions before eating

비벼먹다	mix and eat
계란을얹어서먹다	add egg on top and eat
찍어먹다	dip (in sauce) and eat
부어먹다	pour (the sauce) and eat
소금에찍어먹다	dip in salt and eat
직접구워먹다	grill (the meat) yourself and eat

Table 16.6 Idiomatic/colorful ways of expressing food appreciation and evaluation

부드럽게술술넘어가는면	noodles that are swallowed smoothly
쌀알이너무많이깨져있다	grains of rice have too many cracks
씹는맛이아쉽다	chewing taste is not good
침이고이다	one's mouth waters
자꾸손이가다	can't stop eating (lit. my hand keeps going)
배터지게먹었다	I ate so much (lit. until my belly popped)
끊임없이들어갈것같은맛	a taste like I can eat without stopping

Serial verb constructions related to actions done before eating

In this section, we provide a non-exhaustive list of typical serial verbs that appeared in the MangoPlate mini corpus related to specific actions that are done before eating. These are illustrated in Table 16.5.

This handful of parallel grammatical expressions, i.e., serial verbs, indicates the dual process of taking one action prior to consuming the food. In that sense, the patterns make salient specific aspects of actions that are tightly related to how it is that Koreans consume certain dishes. That is, the actions of mixing, adding egg, dipping (into salt or sauce), and grilling prior to actually placing the food in one's mouth are foregrounded and transformed into an integral part of the cultural act of eating.

Idiomatic and colorful ways of expressing appreciation and evaluation of food

The patterns noted in Table 16.6 represent a mere glimpse into the richly descriptive ways that posters on MangoPlate expressed their praise, criticism, appreciation, and evaluation of the various elements of their dining experience. These highly personalized and subjective constructions reach far beyond the contrived samples provided in textbooks, which typically center on the basic taste terms and very basic, often stance-neutral types of descriptors.

Near synonyms and seemingly subtle meaning distinctions

In the 140-review combined mini corpora of Trip Advisor and MangoPlate posts, we noted no fewer than four so-called near synonyms for context-specific vocabulary. In the case of Trip Advisor, there were four individual expressions, all of which translate into English as "to stay." However, as noted in the right column, each lexical item differs from the other in terms of register (formality level), Sino Korean vs. Native Korean, and the actions that are saliently in focus for each expression.

Table 16.7 Near synonyms from TrAd and MP

Near synonyms: TrAd

투숙하다	to stay	to check into (a hotel); high register Sino Korean
숙박하다	to stay	lit. to sleep and stay; high register Sino Korean
머무르다	to stay	focuses on staying; to stop over Native Korean
묵다	to stay	focuses on sleeping at a place Native Korean

Near synonyms: MP

싱겁다	to be bland	weak seasoning
밍밍하다	to be bland	something feels missing or needs to be added for the right taste
심심하다	to be bland	not salty enough
슴슴하다	to be bland	Jeollabukdo Province dialect

Similarly, four expressions in the MangoPlate mini corpus all translate into English as "to be bland." However, as pointed out in the more detailed explanatory column on the right, each expression differs in terms of a more subtle feature, e.g., weakness, some element of flavor that is sensed to be lacking (including sufficient salt), or in terms of a dialectal difference. Again, these types of expressions emerged through a close analysis of the mini corpora and serve to illustrate with clear precision that some expressions in one language do not necessarily have translatable counterparts in another.

Speech-level alternations

Beyond the sample areas of structure and lexico-grammatical focus, such mini narratives of personal experience also lend themselves well to an analysis of the various speech levels used within this discourse, specifically deferential, polite, and plain. In addition to these three basic speech-level alternations, we also include the sentence-ending nominalizer -ㅁ/음, which fits neatly into the multiple stances (objective, subjective, emphatic, authoritative, etc.) that posters take and express by virtue of this unique set of grammatical conventions.

Deferential

From Seoul Shilla
남산뷰를 선택했는데, 방은 깨끗하고 창 밖으로 남산과 야외수영장이 시원하게 보여 **좋았습니다**. 저녁에는 일몰도 이쁘게 **볼 수 있었습니다**.
*namsanpyulul senthaykhayssnuntey, pangun kkaykkushako chang pakkulo namsankwa yaoyswuyengcangi siwenhakey poye **cohasssupnita**. cenyekeynun ilmolto ippukey **pol swu issesssupnita**.*

'I chose the Namsan View; **it was good** because the room was clean, and I could see Namsan and the outdoor swimming pool unobstructed out the window. **I was able to see** a pretty sunset in the evening, too.'

Polite

From Seoul Shilla
방에서쉬느라수영장이용은못해봤는데다음에꼭다시와서이용해보고 **싶네요**
*pangeyse swinula swuyengcang iyongun moshaypwassnuntey taumey kkok tasi wase iyonghaypoko **siphneyyo***
'I haven't used the swimming pool because I rested in the room, but **I want to** come again next time and be sure to use it.'

Plain (-다)

From Jeju Shilla
정원이 참 **잘 꾸며져있다**. 산책하기도 **좋다**.
*cengweni cham **cal kkwumyecyeissta**. sanchaykhakito **cohta**.*
'The garden **is well decorated**. It's also **good** for taking a walk.'

Nominalized ending

Nominalized ending - ㅁ/음
제주신라 좋은 호텔**임**. 그런데 너무 **낡았음**.
*ceycwusinla cohun hotheylim . kulentey nemwu **nalkassum**.*
'Jeju Shilla, **it's** a good hotel. But **it's** too old.'
지난번에는등푸른생선이살짝비렸었는데이번에는그런게 **없었음**.
*cinanpeneynun tungphwulunsayngseni salccak pilyessessnuntey ipeneynun kulenkey **epsessum***
'Last time, the blue-colored fish was a little fishy, but this time **I didn't taste** anything like that.'

From Seoul Shilla
음식 : 대한민국 3대 호텔 신라인데, 스텐다드 즉 국내 정상호텔의 표준의 **맛임**. 신라에 없으면 다른곳도 없고 신라가 맛없으면 다른 곳도 당연히 **맛없음**.
*umsik : tayhanminkwuk 3tay hotheyl sinlaintey, sutheyntatu cuk kwuknay cengsanghotheyluy phyocwunuy **masim**. sinlaey epsumyen talunkosto epsko sinlaka masepsumyen talun kosto tangyenhi **masepsum**.*
'Food: It's a top three Hotel Shilla in ROK, and it's a standard; in other words, **it's a** national top-notch hotel's standard **taste**. If you can't find something at Shilla, you can't find it anywhere else; if Shilla is not tasty, other places **are not tasty**, of course.'

Conclusion and implications

Through the perspective of discourse analysis (mini corpus, genre, and register), we have demonstrated multiple ways in which a discourse-first perspective can be implemented at the high-intermediate to advanced level of Korean language pedagogy, including an application to the development of teaching and learning materials by using "authentic texts."

The discourse-based approach to these authentic texts demonstrated here involves pattern discovery, especially with respect to context- and topic-specific lexical items (including word borrowings from other languages and neologisms), affective and epistemic stance, adjectives and emotion terms, opinion giving, and narrative. Each review is a mini narrative in and of itself, with a discernible opening and a discernible closing, and each contains a robust inventory of lexico-grammatical items that can be culled for future use in the development of pedagogical materials. Awareness raising and linguistic noticing are key elements to this approach.

Further, because of the context specificity of each mini corpus, the data are also easily applicable to the area of language for specific purposes, with an intended audience of students in the domain of tourism, restaurant and hotel management, and leisure studies.

Notes

1 The contents of this chapter were developed under grant #P229A180009 from the U.S. Department of Education to the Center for Advanced Language Proficiency Education and Research. However, those contents do not necessarily represent the policy of the department, and you should not assume endorsement by the federal government.
2 Trip Advisor, the world's largest travel platform, was founded in 2000, as a resource for worldwide travelers in planning and booking their trips; available in 49 markets and 28 languages (TA, Korea). MangoPlate, established in 2013, was the brainchild of "its four co-founders who love food, . . . to be a service that recommends restaurants based on honest reviews and accurate information" (MangoPlate website).
3 For the Korean discourse data samples, because of the sheer number of exemplars and the table- and list-based representations, we have chosen to indicate only the original *hangul* plus English translations or near equivalents, without including the Romanized versions, in the interest of space and word limits. We do provide Romanization for the final set of excerpts in Section 4.3.5 for the benefit of those readers who may not be familiar with Korean or the *hangul* alphabet.

References

ACTFL. (2012). Authentic texts. *ACTFL proficiency guidelines 2012 glosssary*. Retrieved from www.acfl.org/publications/guidelines-and-manuals/actfl-proficiency-guidelines-2012/glossary.
ACTFL. (2013). *Program standards for the preparation of foreign language teachers*. Retrieved from www.actful.org/sites/default/files/CAEP/ACTFLProgramStandards2013.pdf.
Breen, M. P. (1985). Authenticity in the language classroom. *Applied Linguistics*, *6*(1), 60–70.
Gilmore, A. (2004). A comparison of textbook and authentic interactions. *ELT Journal*, *58*(4), 363–374.
Gilmore, A. (2007). Authentic materials and authenticity in foreign language learning. *Language Teaching*, *40*, 97–118.
Gilmore, A. (2011). "I prefer not text:" Developing Japanese learners' communicative competence with authentic materials. *Language Learning*, *61*(3), 786–819.
Glison, E. W. (2012). National standards research into practice. *Language Teaching*, *45*(4), 515–526.
Glison, E. W., & Donato, R. (2017). *Enacting the work of language instruction: High-leverage teaching practices*. Alexandria, VA: American Council on the Teaching of Foreign Languages.
Hamp-Lyons, L. (2011). What is EAP. In E. Hinkle (Ed.), *Handbook of second language research* (Vol. II). Oxon and New York: Routledge.
https://tripadvisor.mediaroom.com/us-about-us. Retrieved September 20, 2020.
https://www.tripadvisor.co.kr. Retrieved September 20, 2020.
Hyland, K. (2004). *Genre and second language writing*. Ann Arbor, MI: University of Michigan Press.
Hyland, K. (2018). Genre and discourse analysis in language for specific purposes. In C. Chapelle (Ed.), *The encyclopedia of applied linguistics*. Oxford: John Wiley & Sons, Ltd.
Lee, W. Y. (1995). Authenticity revisited: Text authenticity and learner authenticity. *ELT Journal*, *49*(4), 323–328.
Leow, R. P. (2006). The role of awareness in L2 development: Theory, research, and pedagogy. *Indonesian Journal of English Language Teaching*, *2*(2), 1–15. Retrieved from www.mangoplate.com/en/company
McCarthy, M., & Carter, R. (1994). *Language as discourse*. Harlo, Essex: Longman.
McCarthy, M., & Carter, R. (1995). Spoken grammar: What is it and how can we teach it? *ELT Journal*, *49*(3), 207–218.
Ochs, E. (2004). Narrative lessons. In A. Duranti (Ed.), *A companion to linguistic anthropology* (pp. 269–289). Oxford: Wiley.

Ochs, E., & Capps, L. (1996). Narrating the self. *Annual Review of Anthropology, 25,* 19–43.

Olson, D. R. (1980). On the language and authority of textbooks. *Journal of Communication,* 186–196.

Paltridge, B. (2014). Genre and English for specific purposes. In B. Paltridge & S. Starfield (Eds.), *The handbook for English for specific purposes.* Oxford: Wiley Blackwell.

Paltridge, B., & Starfield, S. (2014). *The handbook for English for specific purposes.* Oxford: Wiley Blackwell.

Pinner, R. (2019). *Authenticity and teacher-student motivational synergy: A narrative of language teaching.* Oxon and New York: Routledge.

Rosa, E., & Leow, R. P. (2004). Awareness, different learning conditions, and L2 development. *Applied Psycholinguistics, 25*(2), 269–292.

Schmidt, R. (1993). Awareness and second language acquisition. *Annual Review of Applied Linguistics, 13,* 206–226.

Schmidt, R. (1995). Consciousness and foreign language learning: A tutorial on the role of attention and awareness in learning. In R. Schmidt (Ed.), *Attention and awareness in foreign language learning* (Technical Report #9) (pp. 1–63). Honolulu, HI: University of Hawai'i, Second Language Teaching & Curriculum Center.

Simonsen, R. (2019). An analysis of the problematic discourse surrounding "authentic texts". *Hispania, 102*(2), 245–258.

Strauss, S., & Eun, J. (in preparation). Discourse-first teaching materials for high-intermediate, low-advanced language pedagogy: A corpus-based analysis.

Strauss, S., & Feiz, P. (2014). *Discourse analysis: Putting our worlds into words.* Oxon and New York: Routledge.

Strauss, S., Feiz, P., & Xiang, X. (2018). *Grammar, meaning, and concepts: A discourse-based approach to English grammar.* Oxon and New York: Routledge.

Widdowson, H. G. (1980). The authenticity of language data. In H. G. Widdowson (Ed.), *Explorations in applied linguistics.* Oxford: Oxford University Press.

Zyzik, E., & Polio, C. (2017). *Authentic materials myths: Applying second language research to language teaching.* Ann Arbor, MI: University of Michigan Press.

17
ERROR ANALYSIS

Seong-Chul Shin

Introduction

Researchers of Korean as a second language (KSL) have been able to devote their efforts to examining students' proficiency development and its patterns in the acquisition of KSL. In an effort to better understand language acquisition of KSL in general, the learner language and the developmental patterns in particular, there have been a significant number of error analysis (EA) studies undertaken in KSL. These studies examine learner Korean, provide substantial linguistic and pedagogical explanations, and/or demonstrate teaching strategies based on experimental evidence. Both linguistically and pedagogically, it is necessary to look at language production of second language learners of Korean because it helps to establish a better understanding of the systematic features in their language, to provide insights into the learning of KSL, and to work with KSL instructors to devise appropriate corrective measures.

While studying L2 speakers' errors, researchers of EA identify and categorise errors, then utilise these findings in a number of ways. Researchers attempt to identify areas of particular difficulty to second language learners, classify errors in terms of their type and frequency, provide possible interpretations and explanations for the cause of those problematic features by utilising descriptive and contrastive linguistic techniques, undertake an in-depth examination of 'common errors' (George, 1972) that carry language-specific features in order to determine their linguistic conditions or restrictions, and explore the pedagogical implications of their findings for effective instruction.

Over the past thirty years or more, a number of researchers in KSL have investigated errors made by learners of Korean (e.g. Cho, I. J., 2006; Han, S.-M., 2014; Jang, S. B., 2019; Jeon, Y., 2011; Joo, A. & Shin, S.-C., 2016; Kang, H.-H. & Jo, M.-J., 2003; Kim, C.-S. & Nam, K.-C., 2002; Kim, J.-S., 2002; Kim, M.-O., 2002; Ko, S.-J., 2002; Lee, J.-H., 2003; Lee, M. W., 2020; Min, Y., 2008; Ranjan & Kim, H.-J., 2016; Shin, S.-C., 2017; Sohn, H.-M., 1986; Wang, H.-S., 1995; Yang, S.-Y., 2013). There is now a somewhat better understanding of the problematic areas that need special attention, which helps practising instructors confront such areas with greater confidence. We also have a better knowledge of the nature of the errors produced by learners of Korean. By studying errors, we can provide both instructors and linguists with information about common trends in the production of given error items of KSL learners, which in turn indicates the areas where the instructors need to pay more attention. Such investigations can provide information for the future development and improvement of the materials and pedagogy in the second language.

The descriptions and discussion that follow are organised into eight sections. The first two sections briefly discuss the concept of 'error' in second language analysis and why learner errors are significant in the second language learning process. It discusses a distinction between systematic faults and unsystematic faults, as well as the functions of a learner error in the process of second language learning and acquisition. The next section briefly discusses how EA research has developed, outlining the early developments in the 1970s, its merits and limitations, as well as the developments of Korean EA research. It is then followed by a section that discusses methodological approaches of EA research, detailing three key steps – collection, description, and explanation of errors. Then the three sections that follow describe what EA research has actually discovered about KSL, focusing on three key linguistic areas: orthographic, lexical, and grammatical. Each of the sections presents types of errors, provides explanations of possible sources or causes of the errors, and discusses pedagogical implications of frequent errors in second language teaching. The chapter ends with a section that briefly discusses the future direction of Korean EA studies.

What is 'error'?

First language (L1 – the primary language of learners) speakers of a language are assumed to possess a perfect internalised knowledge of the systems of their mother tongue, yet they also produce utterances which are judged inappropriate, unacceptable, or ungrammatical by fellow L1 speakers to varying degrees of seriousness. Therefore, it is necessary to make a distinction between types of 'faults', often categorised by three terms, namely: errors, mistakes, and lapses.

Corder (1981) makes a distinction between 'errors' as systematic and competence-based, and 'mistakes' as unsystematic and performance-based. Corder (1981, p. 10) maintains that the term *error* should refer to "the systematic errors of the learner from which we are able to reconstruct his knowledge of the language to date, i.e. his *transitional competence*." According to Corder (1975), an error is a systematic sign that the learner has not mastered the rules and code of the target language (TL) due to an incomplete knowledge of the language's system, which comes as a result of L2 learning. Mistakes, on the other hand, are unsystematic faults which both L1 and L2 users of a language make by incorrectly utilising the rules or system that they are aware of and which even L2 learners themselves can correct with some degree of confidence. Lapses, as opposed to mistakes, are slips of the tongue which all speakers of L1 and L2 make from time to time as a result of various performance factors and are often ignored by the teacher for practical reasons, like minimising interruptions. Since errors are systematic and result from the learner's unawareness of the rules, they are much more serious than mistakes (James, 1998). By contrast, lapses are not serious enough to require a corrective action. In EA, therefore, the systematic nature of errors is meaningful and important for an investigation. As noted by Ellis (1994), however, there are considerable difficulties in determining what is a learner's error and what is a mistake. Therefore, it is important to ensure whether a deviant form consistently – twice or more – appears as the same kind of deviance in the same sentence or paragraph. A deviant form regarded as a mistake needs to be excluded from the error counting when it appears as an isolated fault – that is, its correct form is used in the other parts of the same sentence or in the neighbouring sentences. Forms which appear to be deviant from the norm in the second language learning process occur at various linguistic levels: orthographic, morphological, lexical, grammatical, and pragmatic. These deviant forms, or 'errors', result from the learner's incomplete knowledge of the TL.

Why are learner errors significant?

L2 learners inevitably produce errors in the process of learning their TL, whether the language is as a second, foreign, or heritage language. Making errors is a common and natural phenomenon and is inevitable in the language learning process. What is important is not the occurrence of errors themselves so much as the roles they may serve. Errors may in fact be regarded as a positive process of learning. One of the most practical ways to understand the learner's second language acquisition (SLA) is through the study of learner errors (Ellis, 1994). Learner errors are not simply a representation of problems but a source of action for teachers, researchers, and students themselves.

Errors are significant in that they reveal information about the learner's achievements, provide evidence of the language learning process, and can be utilised as devices for language learning (Corder, 1981). The first function is a practical one. Errors enable language instructors to diagnose the areas of difficulty and thus assess the learner's stage of learning. The second function is a theoretical one, concerning the methodology of investigating the second language learning process. Errors provide insight into how the learners learn the language and what strategies they use to learn. In other words, learners' errors provide SLA researchers with evidence of how the acquisition of the second language has been processed by analysing the developmental patterns of errors. The third function is a combination of both, where a learner constructs and reconstructs a set of hypotheses to discover the system of the TL. The making of errors, therefore, is indispensable in discovering the nature of the TL being learned. Errors thus serve as devices for learners to test their hypotheses and discover the rules of the TL. Therefore, they are a fundamental component of the second language learning process and have significant pedagogical implications for teaching and learning.

Development of EA research

Enthusiastic debate on EA studies has gradually diminished in European languages. The most extensive research on EA in ESL and European languages was conducted in the 1970s, then declined due to its weaknesses in procedures and limitations in scope. There were some signs of it making a comeback in the late 80s and 90s (e.g. Taylor, 1986; Lennon, 1991; James, 1998). EA has continued with a desire to improve pedagogy and with the rise of learning demand for non-European languages, such as Korean.

There are a few main approaches which have been widely utilised for analysing learner errors in L2 production, including contrastive analysis (CA) and EA. Each of the approaches has its own merits and limitations. CA looks exclusively at the contrastive characteristics of the learners' L1 and TL, and this is a serious deficiency since relying on the linguistic differences between L1 and TL cannot provide a methodology for investigating learner language (Corder, 1981; Larsen-Freeman & Long, 1991; Wardhaugh, 1983). To supplant the weaknesses of CA and to improve pedagogy through the study of errors (Dulay, Burt, & Krashen, 1982; Ellis, 1994; James, 1980), EA became the principal methodology used for investigating learner language and the process of language learning. Language instructors are constantly concerned about the errors made by their students and how they can improve language teaching. EA became a new method of studying errors in SLA research in the 1970s (Ellis, 1994; James, 1998). During this period, EA was closely associated with the work of Corder (e.g. 1971, 1974, 1981), whose contributions are still widely referred to. Though losing popularity due to perceived weaknesses (Corder, 1981; Dulay & Burt, 1974; Dulay et al., 1982; Ellis, 1994), SLA research through EA continued into the 1980s and beyond.

EA research essentially concerns the learner language itself and the learner's current L2 competence and accommodates a range of error sources. They could be interference errors from L1, intralingual errors reflecting the general characteristics of L2, communicative performance errors that result from processing problems or using strategies such as circumlocution, or induced errors that are led by the instruction or teaching materials the learners have received. However, EA also has a number of limitations, mainly because of its methodological procedures and scope. Ellis (1994) points out a few of these problems, including the method of data collection, the distinction between errors and mistakes, and the difficulties of reconstructing the TL version.

When it comes to Korean, EA research reflects the blooming era of the history of teaching of Korean as a foreign or second language over the past thirty or more years. EA became a recognised area of KSL research in the 1990s, a development that came with the establishment, expansion, and/or consolidation of KSL programmes in many universities in Korea and abroad. A significant number of EA studies in Korean have been conducted from the mid-1990s to 2000s, then continuously up until the 2010s. Researchers were engaged in EA research in an attempt to discover more about L2 (Korean) acquisition and to improve pedagogy. Much EA research output on KSL were based on errors produced by Japanese and English speakers learning Korean in Korea or the USA. EA research has now widened its scope, reflecting the diversified learner base, to further include Chinese and South-East Asian language speakers, and most recently to Eurasian learners.

Methodological approaches in EA research

EA has managed to provide a methodological approach for investigating learner language and a theoretical framework for explaining the roles of errors in the process of second language acquisition. Corder (1981, pp. 21–25) suggested three key steps for EA research – identification of errors, description of errors, and explanation of errors – and two additional steps that should be completed before and after the key steps – collection of samples and evaluation of errors. These five steps constitute a general framework for EA studies. Among the five steps, explanation for the cause of errors is regarded as the most important stage, as it deals with how and why errors are made, giving insights into how a learner learns their second language (i.e. the process of SLA).

Collection of errors

EA research utilises both oral and written data for analysis, but written data is more frequently used due to the ease of data collection and analysis. Research utilising written data focuses on two classes of textual data: *free composition*, where learners express spontaneous ideas and intentions, like free composition, essay, and *reformulation* (Corder, 1981), where they attempt to reconstruct the ideas and intentions of other people, like with translations.

Free-composition data is generally preferred, but it is not easy to obtain. As an alternative, EA research uses two kinds of elicitation: clinical and experimental (ibid., p. 29). Clinical elicitation requires the learner to produce any voluntary data orally or in writing, while experimental methods use special tools to elicit data concerning specific linguistic items. In the process of data collection special caution needs to be taken to ensure that sampling is restricted to *errors* while eliminating *mistakes* from the analysis.

Description of errors

For the description of errors, there have been a number of studies identifying various error types. These studies have developed frameworks of error classification according to the linguistic level of description and the systematicity (e.g. Corder, 1981; Dulay et al., 1982; Richards, 1971b; Ellis, 1994; Lee, J.-H., 2003; Shin, S.-C., 2017; Sohn, H.-M., 1986; Wang, H.-S., 1995). Some are superficial and others are more systematic. For example, Corder (1975, 1981) suggests a matrix for error categorisation according to phenomena (omission, addition, and substitution), according to linguistic levels (orthography, syntax, and vocabulary), and according to systems (e.g. vowel or consonant systems). Dulay et al. (1982) suggest four categories of error (omission, addition, misinformation, and misordering). Ellis (1994, pp. 54–57) claims that the framework based on phenomena may have the advantage because it can give pedagogic information (e.g. the error item and frequency), but it provides little insight into how an L2 is learnt. A framework based on systematicity, like Corder's (1974), has an advantage in that it can provide explanations for the learner's behaviour in L2 contexts, but it may be difficult to utilise the framework, as it requires the researcher to individually interview the learners involved in the study, which can number from hundreds to thousands. Lennon (1991) proposes two new dimensions of error: domain and extent. 'Domain' refers to the breadth of context (word, phrase, clause, sentence, or discourse), while 'extent' refers to the size of the linguistic unit (morpheme, word, phrase, clause, or sentence).

The classification of errors involves an analysis of errors according to linguistic categories (e.g. syntax), according to systems within each category (e.g. particles or conjunctions), and according to phenomena (e.g. substitutions). Such taxonomies allow for a quantitative analysis of errors, a categorisation and detailed description of specific types. Error patterns can vary depending on several factors, such as the nature of the task, the linguistic level or area, the profile of learners, and the method of analysis.

For the description of Korean data, there are a few studies discussing methodological issues with, for example, error identification, classification and categorisation (e.g. Lee, J.-H., 2002; Park, S.-Y., 2007; Suk, J.-Y. & Ahn, K.-H., 2003). The methodological discrepancy should be understandable, though, when considering several factors, such as the focus of the research, the linguistic level, data-elicitation methods, and the profile of participants.

As for English L1 learners, Sohn, H.-M. (1986) uses six linguistic levels and categories: orthography, lexicon (nouns, verbs, etc.), morphology (modifier endings, *l*-related, suffix, copula-related, etc.), syntax (word order, case markers and delimiters, tense, negation, conjunction, etc.), sociolinguistics, and pragmatics. Lee, J.-H. (2002) provides a cross-sectional error categorisation according to the cause and 'end-results' (i.e. errors), that accounts for both the origin of the error and the type of error produced. The framework suggests three types of error sources (influence of the mother tongue, influence of the target language, and training), along with three ways of classifying end-results: by category (pronunciation, grammar, vocabulary, etc.), by phenomenon (substitution, omission, addition), and by the degree of error (whole/global, partial/local).

Explanation of errors

After identifying and describing errors, the next step is to attempt to explain them. Explanation is regarded to be the most important stage for EA research, as it involves the processes of SLA (Corder, 1981; Ellis, 1994; Taylor, 1986). Corder (1981, p. 24) maintains that this stage is the "ultimate object of error analysis" and should be "psycholinguistic", as it attempts to account for how and why the error was made by identifying their cause.

There have been several studies which identify the sources of errors and explain why the errors were made. For instance, Richards (1971a, 1971b) identifies three sources of errors: interference (interlingual) from L1, intralingual effect of learning, and 'transfer of training' and learning strategies (developmental). Stenson (1983) distinguishes another source of error:

induced. Interlingual errors, which are generally referred to as 'transfer' errors, occur when the learner applies their first language's structure to the target language. Intralingual errors, on the other hand, reflect the complex characteristics of the target language and arise when the learner fails to fully comprehend conditions under which its rules and restrictions apply. Overgeneralisation is a good example of such an error type. Interlingual and intralingual errors are often further subdivided. For example, Lott (1983, p. 259) identifies three interlingual categories: overextension of analogy, transfer of structure, and interlingual/intralingual errors. Richards (1971a) distinguishes four intralingual categories: overgeneralisation, ignorance of rule restrictions, incomplete application of rules, and false concepts. Meanwhile, induced errors (Stenson, 1983; Ellis, 1994) are errors deriving from inappropriate instruction or instructional materials the learner has received.

In addition, some studies have identified psycholinguistic sources. For example, Richards (1971a) refers to developmental errors that occur when the learner falsely hypothesises rules and concepts on the basis of earlier learning experiences, reflecting the stage of their language development. James (1998) identifies communication strategy errors that arise when the learner attempts to use an approximate form of the required word or an indirect expression called a 'circumlocution'. Although the terms used in various studies may be different, the methods for determining the source of error are similar and are largely applicable to different linguistic levels, with some specific modifications. Some studies report that interlingual transfer errors are overall more common and frequent than intralingual errors (e.g. Shin, S.-C., 2017; Sohn, H.-M., 1986), while others (e.g. Wang, H.-S., 1995; Yang, S.-Y., 2013; Zhang, W. & Kim, J. Y., 2019) find a higher proportion of intralingual and developmental errors in learners only at a particular level. This discrepancy in the source of errors is quite understandable because findings will be influenced by a range of factors, such as the task(s) used to elicit the samples, the linguistic level or area being investigated, and the profile of subjects. Even within the same or similar conditions, findings can be different according to the focus and methodology of the analysis and the researcher's interpretation of the findings.

The sections that follow will look into common learner errors in spelling, lexicon, and grammar, as they are essential components of second language learning or acquisition. A sound understanding of the nature and pattern of the errors should form the basis for adequate linguistic explanations and pedagogical strategies to deal with the problematic areas at different levels.

Orthographic errors

Orthographic errors refer to misspellings or spelling errors. Orthography or spelling is uncompromising. Levels of tolerance or acceptability given in grammar or lexis does not apply to orthography, as no approximations are allowed in spelling (James, Scholfield, Garrett, & Griffiths, 1993). There are only two options to evaluate in spelling: correct or incorrect. Identifying orthographic errors requires a decision-making process which distinguishes between orthographic and other levels of errors, i.e., lexical, morphological, and syntactic.

Bebout (1985) reports that there are areas of greater difficulty in spelling for second language learners and that there are areas of intrinsic orthographic difficulty, regardless of the learner groups. The fact that there are comparative and intrinsic areas of difficulty signifies that there are different causes of errors according to the group, thus requiring different pedagogical spelling strategies to rectify the problems. James et al. (1993) categorises the types of errors into three, namely, L1 interference, non-interference, and dual (or multiple) origin. The three types of errors can be further subcategorised into, for example, phoneme-to-grapheme, lexical cognate, overgeneralisations, and homophone confusion. James et al. (ibid.) claim that there is a strong L1 influence on L2 production in spelling and that it is possible to avoid or reduce the orthographic errors by identifying the potential problematic areas through contrastive analysis (CA).

When it comes to Korean orthography, there are many elements that can confuse second language learners. Choo and O'Grady (2003, pp. 3–4) identify 'threshold' challenges to be met by English L1-KSL learners, including "a number of speech sounds that have no direct counterpart in English" and "the pronunciation of particular Korean sounds [that] can vary enormously depending on the context in which they occur." Although a considerable proportion of errors produced by KSL learners are in spelling, studies of misspellings in KSL are only a few (e.g. Joo, A. & Shin, S.-C., 2016; Kim, J.-S., 2007; Kim, M.-O., 2001; Min, Y., 2008; Shin, S.-C., 2017; Sohn, H.-M., 1986). Among them, H.-M. Sohn (1986) observed four types of orthographic errors: graphic mismatch, phonemic transcription, wrong pronunciation, and wrong graphic association of sound features. He claims that many of the error types are attributable to three types of confusion between the allophonic Korean consonants, between single and double nasals and laterals, and between some vowel sounds. He concludes that phonological interference from L1 (English) is the strongest factor in this confusion.

Kim, M.-O. (2001) categorises spelling errors into four patterns: pronunciation-related consonant and vowel errors, phonology-related addition or omission errors, grammar-related phoneme-to-grapheme errors, and miscellaneous errors. The most frequent error types found in her study include consonant confusions between *ss* and *s* (ㅆ and ㅅ), *n* and *ng* (ㄴ and ㅇ), *k* and *kk* (ㄱ and ㄲ), and between *c* and *ch* or *cc* (ㅈ and ㅊ or ㅉ). Kim, M.-O. (2001) also identified frequent vowel confusions between *ey*-[e] and *ay*-[ɛ] (ㅔ and ㅐ), *e*-[ə] and *o*-[o] (ㅓ and ㅗ), and between *o*-[o] and *wu*-[u] (ㅗ and ㅜ). A study by Joo, A. and Shin, S.-C. (2016) found that Korean heritage language (KHL) learners have some similarities to KSL learners in orthographic skills, with some distinctive differences. The study identified sixty-seven error types, with the most frequent spelling errors caused by the failure to differentiate the usage of *ay* and *ey* (ㅐ and ㅔ), followed by the substitution of *ye* for *e* (ㅕ and ㅓ), and *oy* for *way* (ㅚ and ㅙ). They maintain that such errors occurred mainly due to phonemic transcription caused by the heritage speakers' lack of morpho-phonemic knowledge and wrong graphic association of sound features caused by both interlingual and intralingual interference. Shin, S.-C. (2017) found five patterns of error types in English L1 learners, including mismatch in three-series consonants, mismatch in vowels sounds, misuse of nasals and laterals, and omission and addition of *h* (ㅎ). He argues that interlingual factors, such as the mismatch in sound quality between the two languages, are a significant cause for the confusion of the three-series consonants, like *c* and *ch* or *cc* (ㅈ and ㅊ or ㅉ), and some vowel pairs, like *ey*-[e] and *ay*-[ɛ] (ㅔ and ㅐ). Intralingual factors, such as the perceived phonetic closeness between Korean sounds and their variation in casual speech, are also identified as sources of orthographic errors.

Identification of orthographic errors

The analysis of Korean orthographic errors should focus on grapheme-related errors that concern vowel and consonant misspellings. It is an individual letter representing a phoneme, such as *c* (ㅈ) in *ca.ta* (자다) 'sleep', *ch* (ㅊ) in *cha.ta* (차다) 'be cold', and *cc* (ㅉ) in *cca.ta* (짜다) 'be salty'. This way, orthographic errors are distinguished from morphology-related errors, which are related to word forms (e.g. *chin.kwu.kwa* [친구과] for *chin.kwu.wa* [친구와] 'with a friend'), lexical errors related to 'meaning' (e.g. *cak.ta* [작다] for *cek.ta* [적다] 'be small in size' for 'be small in number'), and syntactic errors related to the functions of grammatical items (e.g. *hwa.lul.nayss.un.tey.to* [화를 냈은데도] for *hwa.lul.nayss.nun.tey.to* [화를 냈는데도]'even if [I] got angry'). EA of orthographic errors usually does not include misspellings related to content words and their meanings, as they are separately dealt with under lexical errors. Misspellings related to morphological and syntactic usage are not treated as orthographic errors either, as they are usually dealt with as grammatical errors.

Frequent orthographic error types

EA studies based on Korean show some common frequent orthographic error types, and they include the following substitution error types: (a) substitution between *c* and *ch* (ㅈ and ㅊ); (b) substitution between *e* and *o* (ㅓ and ㅗ); and (c) substitution between *ay* and *ey* (ㅐ and ㅔ). In the *c* and *ch* (ㅈ and ㅊ) substitutions, the *c* for *ch* (ㅈ for ㅊ) is reported to be more frequent than the reverse. Examples for these three types include: (a) *c* for *ch*: 아짐 *a.cim* (> 아침 *a.chim*) 'morning'; (b) *ch* for *c*: 차가용 *cha.ka.yong* (> 자가용 *ca.ka.yong*) 'family car'; (c) *o* for *e*: 본호 *pon.ho* (>번호 *pen.ho*) 'number'; (d) *e* for *o*: 일번 *il.pen* (> 일본 *il.pon*) Japan; (e) *ey* for *ay*: 담베 *tam.pey* (> 담배 *tam.pay*) 'cigarette'; and (f) *ay* for *ey*: 가개 *ka.kay* (> 가게 *ka.key*) 'shop'.

Other frequent errors are reported to come from the substitutions of three-series consonants involving the lenis, aspirated, and tensed series of stops (i.e. labial, alveolar, palatal, and velar stops) and *s*-series, with varying degrees of frequency. Frequent three-series consonant errors include the following types: (a) *t–th–tt* (ㄷㅌ-ㄸ) (1) *t* for *tt*: 다라가요 *ta.la.ka.yo* (> 따라가요 *tta.la.ka.yo*) 'follow'; (2) *t* for *th*: 보동 *po.tong* (>보통 *po.thong*) 'usually'; and (3) *tt* for *t*: 절때 *cel.ttay* (>절대 *cel.tay*) 'absolutely'; (b) *p–ph–pp* (ㅂ-ㅍ-ㅃ) (1) *p* for *ph*: 비우면 *pi.wu.myen* (>피우면 *phi.wu.myen*) 'if one smokes'; (2) *ph* for *p*: 복잦해서 *pok.caph.hay.se* (> 복잡해서 *pok.cap.hay.se*) 'because (sth) is complex'; and (3) *p* for *pp*: 나바요 *na.pa.yo* (> 나빠요 *na.ppa.yo*) '(sb/sth) is bad'; (c) *k–kh–kk* (ㄱ-ㅋ-ㄲ) (1) *k* for *kk*: 어머님게 *e.me.nim.key* (> 어머님께 *e.me.nim.kkey*) 'to mother'; and (2) *kk* for *k*: 조끔 *co.kkum* (> 조금 *co.kum*) 'a little/some'; and (d) *s–ss* (ㅅ-ㅆ) (1) *s* for *ss*: 날시 *nal.si* (> 날씨 *nal.ssi*) 'weather'; and (2) *ss* for *s*: 5씨 *ta.ses.ssi* (> 5시 *ta.ses si*) 5 o'clock.

Another group of errors results from the substitution, addition, or omission of nasal *n* or *ng* (ㄴ or ㅇ) and lateral *l* (ㄹ). The nasal and lateral errors include the following types: (a) nasal (1) *ng* for *n*: 정공 *ceng.kong* (> 전공 *cen.kong*) 'major study'; (2) *n.n* for *.n*: 전녁 *cen.nyek* (> 저녁 *ce.nyek*) 'evening'; and (3) *n* for *ng*: 관고 *kwan.ko* (> 광고 *kwang.ko*) 'advertisement'; (b) lateral *l*-related (1) *.l* for *l.l*: 다라요 (*ta.la.yo* (> 달라요 *tal.la.yo*) '(sb/sth) is different'; (2) *l.l* for *.l*: 일름 *il.lum* (> 이름 *i.lum*) 'name'; and (3) *.l* for *l.*: 아라요 *a.la.yo* (> 알아요 *al.a.yo*) '(sb) knows'.

In vowels and diphthongs (glides), additional frequent errors are often observed from substitutions between *wu* and *o* (ㅜ and ㅗ), *a* and *e* (ㅏ and ㅔ), *way* and *oy* (ㅙ and ㅚ), and *u* and *wu* (ㅡ and ㅜ). Examples of such substitutions include: (a) *wu* for *o*: 과묵 *kwa.mwuk* (> 과목 *kwa.mok*) 'subject'; (b) *o* for *wu*: 아이보터 *a.i.po.the* (> 아이부터 *a.i.pwu.the*) 'from children'; (c) *a* for *e*: 경함 *kyeng.ham* (> 경험 *kyeng.hem*) 'experience'; (d) *e* for *a*: 더음주 *te.um.cwu* (> 다음 주 *ta.um cwu*) 'next week'; (e) *way* for *oy*: 안돼는*an.tway.nun* (> 안 되는*an toy.nun*) 'not allowed'; (f) *oy* for *way*: 안 되서 *an.toy.se* (> 안 돼서 *an tway.se*) '(sth) wasn't done/working'; (g) *u* for *wu*: 얼글 *el.kul* (>얼굴 *el.kwul*) 'face'; and (h) *wu* for *u*: 무순 *mwu.swun* (>무슨 *mwu.sun*) 'what sort of'.

In addition to these types, studies also report some other error types with less frequency and perhaps less gravity of importance, including the *h*-related (ㅎ) addition or omission: (a) ø for *h*: 바꾸지 안았 *pa.kkwu.ci an.ass* (> 바꾸지 않았 *pa.kkwu.ci anh.ass*) 'have not changed'; and

(b) *h* for ø: 설학산 *sel.hak.san* (>설악산 *sel.ak.san*) 'Mt Selak'. Other miscellaneous types of errors can be observed in substitutions between vowels and its diphthong (glide) form, such as *ey* and *yey* (ㅔ and ㅖ). It is also worth noting ill-formed transliterations of loan words form part of some orthographic errors, although they are sporadic and not usually treated as the primary concern of orthographic errors.

Possible causes of orthographic errors

Three-series consonant spellings involve differentiating the sound value of lenis, aspirated, and tensed consonants. Therefore, the failure to do so is largely attributable to the confusion between their sound features. The confusion is due to the perceived presence or absence of [aspirated] and that of [tense], thus error types such as *c* for *ch* (ㅈ for ㅊ) or *ch* for *c* (ㅊ for ㅈ), *p* for *ph* (ㅂ for ㅍ), and *t* for *th* (ㄷ for ㅌ) are concerned with the aspiration or the degree of aspiration, while types of errors such as *t* for *tt* (ㄷ for ㄸ), *k* for *kk* (ㄱ for ㄲ), *s* for *ss* (ㅅ for ㅆ) are concerned with tense. In Korean, there is a clear distinction in sound quality between *p*-, *t*-, *k*-, *c*-, and *s*-series: *p–ph–pp* (ㅂ-ㅍ-ㅃ), *t–th–tt* (ㄷ-ㅌ-ㄸ), *k–kh–kk* (ㄱ-ㅋ-ㄲ), *c–ch–cc* (ㅈ-ㅊ-ㅉ), and *s–ss* (ㅅ-ㅆ). The lenis, aspirated, and tense stops all appear at the beginning of a syllable, thus the patterns of misspellings in each of the three series of Korean consonants are attributable to the confusion among the three phonemic sound qualities in Korean. This appears to be caused by phonological mismatches between Korean and English (and other languages). Spelling, however, is not just a matter of distinguishing one sound from another, but more importantly it is a matter of knowing how to spell the word correctly.

Confusion also arises in differentiating whether a sound is aspirated or not, and this confusion is clearly revealed in the Korean aspirated *ch* (ㅊ) and the slightly aspirated *c* (ㅈ). It is because there is a certain degree of aspiration in some sounds that are defined as unaspirated in phonology (Kim-Renaud, 1997). In other words, the matter may be not whether it is aspirated, but rather the degree of aspiration, which seems to particularly be the case in *c* and *ch* (ㅈ and ㅊ). In fact, the unaspirated stops, *p*-[p], *t*-[t], *c*-[c], and *k*-[k], are all considered to carry a certain degree of the aspirate feature, which makes it difficult for learners of Korean to distinguish between the aspirated stops and the lenis stops.

The confusion of replacing *ey* with *ay* (ㅔ with ㅐ) or *ay* with *ey* (ㅐ with ㅔ) is primarily attributable to the mismatch in sound features between Korean and the approximate sounds of the learner's L1, but the habitual tendency of both Korean L1 and L2 speakers to follow easiness in pronunciation is also related to the frequent erratic productions in written form (Choo, M. & O'Grady, W., 2003). For example, Korean L1 speakers often pronounce *ay*-[ɛ] as *ey*-[e] in *nam.may* 'brother and sister', *tam.pay* 'cigarette', and *si.nay* 'city, town', and the non-sensical transcriptions *nam.mey*, *tam.pey*, and *si.ney* are considered to be closer to the actual utterance of the Korean L1 speakers. In fact, the distinction between *ey* and *ay* has almost disappeared in contemporary Korean, and most Korean L1 speakers, particularly among young adults, pronounce the two sounds almost identically, as a sound closer to *ey*-[e] (Martin, 1992). It is also worth noting that the sound quality of Korean *ay* does not precisely match with that of English [æ] (Sohn, H.-M., 1986, 1999). Such a mismatch in sound quality between Korean /ay/ and an approximate sound, as well as the sound distinction lost between them, would contribute to the cause of confusions and lead to the written production of errors since the learner would have a wrong graphic association of two sound features in their mind.

As for the *ay* for *ey* (ㅐ for ㅔ) type of error, it could be due to confusions between the approximate sounds/symbols or due to graphic mismatch where the learner knows how to pronounce and yet uses approximate, i.e., wrong, spellings. The confusion between Korean *o* and *e* (ㅗ and ㅓ) are largely due to the mismatch in sound qualities between Korean and English. Learners often perceive the short and monotonous Korean *o* as *e*-[ə] without knowing the difference in sound quality between English *o* and Korean *o* (Sohn, H.-M., 1986). Other pairs of errors, such as *way* and *oy* (ㅙ and ㅚ) and *ey* and *yey* (ㅔ and ㅖ), are also attributable to the perceived phonetic closeness of the pairs. It is hard to distinguish *oy* from *way*, and even Korean L1 speakers have trouble differentiating the sound qualities; thus in actual use the pronunciation of the pairs is perceived as being almost identical (Choo, M. & O'Grady, W., 2003). A similar explanation can be made in the pair of *yey* and *ey*, where the glide *y* sound in the diphthong *yey* is dropped after a consonant, as in [si.ke] for 시계 *si.kyey* 'watch'.

The confusion in the use of nasal *m*, *n*, and *ng* (ㅁ, ㄴ and ㅇ) and lateral *l* (ㄹ) are caused largely due to the pronunciation of the nasal and lateral consonants, which undergo a change caused by nasalisation and lateralisation. Thus, KSL learners tend to transcribe the nasal and lateral sounds phonetically. Among active nasal error types, the *ng* for *n* (ㅇ for ㄴ) type is often reported. It is due to the fact that the alveolar *n* is pronounced as velar [ŋ] before a velar consonant, as if it were *ng* when it is followed by, for example, *k*, *kh*, or *kk* (e.g. 항국 *hang. kwuk* for 한국 *han.kwuk* 'Korea'). The substitution is also facilitated under the influence of the same or similar neighbouring nasal sounds, as in 광광 *kwang.kwang* for 관광 *kwan.kwang* 'tour' or simply made by repeating the neighbouring 'ng' sound as in 공웡 *kong.weng* for 공원 *kong.wen* 'park'. The opposite case, i.e., *n* for *ng* (ㄴ for ㅇ) is largely due to the perceived similarity of *n* and *ng* in pronunciation, where *ng* is perceived as *n* by KSL learners, as seen in 준궁말 *cwun.kwung.mal* for 중국말 *cwung.kwuk.mal* 'Chinese language'.

The use of double nasals shown in such error types as *n.n* for *.n* is due to the shift of the pronunciation of 'n' between syllables, as seen in *a.cwu.men.ni* (아주먼니) for *a.cwu.me.ni* (아주머니) 'middle-aged woman'. Also, in nasalisation, consonant sounds *t*, *th*, *c*, *ch*, *s*, and *ss* have the same pronunciation of *t* when in the coda of a syllable, which then takes on the nasal pronunciation of *n* when followed by the nasal sound. This phenomena is found in 믿는다 *mit. nun.ta* → 민는다 *min.nun.ta* 'believe', 몇년 *myech.nyen* → 몃년 *myet.nyen* → 면년 *myen. nyen* 'how many years', 맞네요 *mac.ney.yo* → 맡네요 *mat.ney.yo* → 만네요 *man.ney.yo* 'it fits!', and 옛날 *yeys.nal* → 옛날 *yeyt.nal* → 옌날 *yeyn.nal* 'old days'. Such an adjustment could produce doubly spelled nasals.

In the meantime, lateral *l* (ㄹ) is often the subject of a singly or doubly spelled transcription when it comes between syllables. This also is largely due to the spelling based on pronunciation or the application (or re-application) of the English degeminisation rule. The opposite case is also well observed. It is largely influenced by the preceding or following lateral *l*, but they might also be affected by other factors, such as speech habit, as wrong utterances are occasionally observed in Korean L1 speakers' speech. Other types where the position of lateral *l* is switched, thus relocated to the syllabic initial or final of the adjacent syllable, are due mainly to the transcription based on phonetic syllabification or wrong syllabification.

The omission or addition of *h* (ㅎ) is often caused by the adjustments by the intersonorant *h*-deletion and -aspiration and by the learner's lack of understanding about the usage of some lexical items, such as the difference between the negative marker 안 *an* 'not' and the predicative 않 *anh* 'not in the state of'. Many *h* omissions are related to the *h*-weakening before, after, or between nasals (e.g. 미안압니다 *mi.an.am.ni.da* for 미안합니다 *mi.an.ham.ni.da* '[I] am sorry'; 여앵 *ye.ayng* for 여행 *ye.hayng* 'travel'), and *h*-deletion at the end of a verb stem in front of a verb sound (e.g. 조아요 *co.a.yo* for 좋아요 *coh.a.yo* 'It's good'; 마나요 *ma.na.yo* for 많아요 *manh.a.yo* 'there's a lot'), while some omissions are influenced by *h*-aspiration, where *h* is 'absorbed into the neighbouring sound, causing aspiration' when it occurs before and after a lenis consonant (e.g. [co.tha] for 좋다 coh.ta 'It's good'; [ki.lə.chi.man] for 그렇지만 ku.leh.ci.man 'but'; [pɛ.khwa.cəm] for 백화점 payk.hwa.cem 'department store') (Choo, M. & O'Grady, W., 2003).

Pedagogical implications of orthographic errors

It is often daunting for KSL learners to distinctly perceive and produce a sound/spelling on the basis of the degree of aspiration, the tenseness, or the sound qualities. This often occurs when the sound of the concerned Korean vowel or consonant does not exactly match with any of the vowels or consonants of the learner's L1. Orthography is not just a matter of spelling or pronunciation, it is also a matter of meaning. As a syllable/word consists of sound, meaning, and symbol, it is both effective and necessary to apply these three concepts to spellings, particularly for reinforcement and remedial purposes. It is important to provide learners with not only phonological explanations about sound features together with orthographic identification but also a semantic factor which shows the meaning of a syllable, thus highlighting the difference between spellings or pronunciations in question.

Another point relates to the 'visual' aspects as opposed to 'oral' aspects. KSL learners often experience difficulties in differentiating not only the sounds but also the shapes of the Hankul alphabet, due to their 'visual' similarities. This usually occurs among the three-series consonants and vowels in the same or close articulation level, such as *ay/ey* (ㅐ/ㅔ), *yay/yey* (ㅒ/ㅖ), and *way/oy/wey* (ㅙ/ㅚ/ㅞ). Such confusion reflects the morphophonemic principles of Hankul. Instead of a linear demonstration of the Hankul alphabet and a simplistic correction of misspellings, it is therefore necessary to give both 'visual' and 'oral' demonstrations to help learners understand the sound/symbol distinction better and increase their attention in the use of the alphabet as well.

Apart from the previous points, spellings based on pronunciation are largely affected by sound-shift phenomena. Sound shifts occur across a syllable boundary in Korean and seem to be particularly relevant when consonants are followed by vowels and when consonants are followed by other consonants across syllables. The three phenomena of resyllabification, palatalisation, and nasal *n* addition, which occur when consonants meet vowels, and consonant assimilation and tensification, which occur when consonants meet other consonants across syllables, are all found to be closely related to KSL spelling errors (NIKL, 2005). Such complex sound shifts need to be given more attention for instructional input. Also, whether it is for ordinary teaching or remedial teaching, it will be useful to devise pedagogically effective learning and teaching strategies encompassing sound, symbol, and meaning.

Lexical errors

James (1998) provides five reasons for undertaking lexical EA, including that learners often equate a language with its vocabulary, and lexical errors are the most frequent error category for some learners. In James (ibid.), lexical errors are fit broadly into two categories: formal and semantic. Formal errors refer to form-related categories, such as formal misselection, misformation, and distortions, while semantic errors refer to meaning-related categories, such as confusion of sense relation and collocation errors. Each of the categories are further subcategorised into, for example, borrowing, coinage, omission, misselection, use of a more general or too specific term, use of the wrong near-synonym, and arbitrary combination. The source of these errors is either interlingual or intralingual, i.e., formal misselection and misformation errors can be categorised as either interlingual or intralingual and distortions as intralingual, while confusion of sense relations is intralingual and collocational errors are either intralingual or interlingual.

When understanding Korean L2 lexical errors, it is helpful to consider some attributes of the Korean lexicon, where Sino-Korean (SK) words cover approximately 60% of the Korean vocabulary, with the remaining components being made up by native Korean (NK) words, affixes, and loan words (Sohn, H.-M., 1999). In the process of using Korean vocabulary, constructing a word or compound words, therefore, it is observed that KSL learners often produce SK or NK collocational errors as well as selection or mismatching errors. There are a good number of studies on lexical errors in Korean, including Kim, J.-S. (2007), Kim, M.-O. (2003), Lee, J.-H. (2008), Min, Y. (2008), Shin, S.-C. (2017), Shin, S.-C. and Joo, A. (2015), Sohn, H.-M. (1986), Wang, H.-S. (1995), and Zhang and Kim, J. Y. (2019).

Linguists have adopted and developed different frameworks for the categorisations of lexical errors, which include and exclude error types such as errors caused by confusion of similar meaning, errors caused by formal similarity in the TL, lexical shift/code-switch, collocation/idiomaticity, overgeneralisation, literal translation, and redundancy (e.g. Shin, S.-C., 2017; Shin, S.-C. & Joo, A., 2015; Sohn, H.-M., 1986; Wang, H.-S., 1995). In terms of the cause of lexical errors, Sohn, H.-M. (1986) reveals that the lexical errors are caused by wrong choices of words, interference from English, poor knowledge about semantic restrictions, and overgeneralisation. Wang, H.-S. (1995) discovers that the most frequent lexical errors are lexical shift/code-switch, followed by confusion of similar meaning and overgeneralisation. In the meantime, Shin, S.-C. and Joo, A. (2015), who examined heritage speakers' lexical errors, conclude that heritage students have a strong tendency to write the way they speak and that their lexical competence heavily relies on their oral competence. This aspect supports Montrul (2010), who suggests that the vocabulary span of heritage language learners is generally related to the home or childhood vocabulary, which remains limited during their schooling process in the dominant language. Shin, S.-C. (2017) finds that the incorrect choice of words caused a high percentage of errors in his study.

Types of lexical errors

EA studies on Korean lexical errors also focus on content words for lexical error analysis and categorise lexical errors into several types. These include errors of semantic similarity (e.g. 자식 *ca.sik* 'one's own children' vs. 아이들 *a.i.tul* 'children in general/boys and girls'), errors of lexical misselection (e.g. 휴일 *hyu.il* '[public] holiday' vs. 휴가 *hyu.ka* '[employees'] recreational holidays') and errors of overgeneralisation (e.g. 집비 *cip.pi* 'house' + 'expense' vs. 집세 *cip.sey* '[house] rent'. Other types include errors of literal translation (e.g. 친구 만들- *chin.ku man.tul-* '[literally] make friends' vs. 친구 사귀- *chin.gu sa.kwi-* 'get acquainted with friends'), errors of formal similarity (잊어버렸- *ic.e.pe.lyess-* 'completely forgot' vs. 잃어버렸- *ilh.e.pe.lyess-* 'lost'), errors of redundancy (e.g. 상사 회사 *sang.sa hoy.sa*, 'trading firm company' vs. 상사 *sang.sa*, 'trading company'), and errors of idiomatic collocation (e.g. 식사 *sik.sa* 요리하- *yo.li.ha-* 'cook [a meal]' vs. 식사 *sik.sa* 준비하- *cwun.pi.ha-* 'prepare [a meal']).

Possible sources and causes of lexical errors

Common categorisations of the source of lexical errors may be theoretically legitimate but arbitrary in practice since there are few errors or error types that have a single cause. These classifications then can be subjective to the judgement of the researcher. The general developmental pattern is that interlingual transfer from L1 is dominant at the early stages of L2 learning, and more errors come from intralingual sources as the learning advances (Brown, 1980; Shin, S.-C., 2017; Sohn, H.-M., 1986; Wang, H.-S., 1995).

Some lexical errors are caused by occasional or consistent confusion due to semantic similarities. Such errors are related to the learner's lack of knowledge of the conceptual differences between semantically related words, rather than resulting from random choice or complete ignorance of the meanings. Some other forms in this category contain pairs of words with similarity in meaning and sound (e.g. 비판 *pi.phan* 'criticism, judgement' vs. 비난 *pi.nan* 'criticism, denunciation' and 비평 *pi.phyeng* 'criticism, review'). Some errors of semantic similarity are caused by the confusion between time-related nouns (e.g. 시 *si* 'o'clock' and 시간 *si.kan* 'period of time', 시간 *si.kan* and 시절 *si.cel* 'season'). Still other errors caused by semantic similarity include some lexical items in collocation (e.g. 관광인 *kwan.kwang.in* 'tourism person' instead of 관광객 *kwan.kwang.kayk* 'tourist'). In addition to noun errors, there are also several types of verb errors of semantic similarity. Such types involve the wrong use of words expressing quantity (e.g. for 인구 *in.kwu* 'population': 작다 *cak.ta* 'small' in height, size > 적다 *cek.ta* 'small' in number/quantity), the overuse of one of the two competing verbs with similar meaning (e.g. 대중교통수단 *tay.cwung.kyo.thong.swu.tan* 'means of public transport': 써야 *sse.ya* 'use' > 이용해야 *i.yong.hay.ya* 'should make good use of') or subtle differences in meaning (e.g. 거절하- *ke.cel.ha-* 'refuse, reject, decline' vs. 거부하- *ke.pwu.ha-* 'refuse, reject, deny'). The difficulties with these kinds of subtle semantic differences are not just perceived by KSL learners but also by Korean L1 speakers, who have an unconscious knowledge of how to use them but find it difficult to pinpoint the difference. Similarly, verbs such as 변하- *pyen.ha-* 'change/undergo a change', 변경하- *pyen.kyeng.ha-* 'alter', 변화하- *pyen.hwa.ha-*, 'change/make a change', 바뀌- *pa.kkwi-* 'be changed' appear to be identical in meaning. They are often interchangeable in everyday use but carry different semantic boundaries and contextual restrictions.

In errors of lexical misselection, learners wrongly select vocabulary (e.g. 교제 *kyo.cey* 'social intercourse' for '[trading] company' and 연설 *yen.sel* 'public speech' for '[mailing] address'). They are due to wrong selection from dictionary entries or closely related to the wrong choice of non-contextual or nonsensical items. If KSL learners consult a dictionary for the Korean equivalents, they may find such words listed as one of the primary meanings. Additionally, there is another typical misselection, i.e., the existential adjective 있다 *iss.ta* 'exist, stay, have' in place of the copula 이다 *-i.ta* 'be'. Confusion between the copula 이다 *i.ta* and the existential verb 있다 *iss.ta* is common and attributable to three factors: (a) both share one semantic component – 'to be'; (b) the existential verb carries a complex conceptual interpretation – existence, location, and possession, with the confusion mostly caused by the transfer of its possessive meaning 'have/own'; and (c) both sounds are similar in actual utterances. This type of error is particularly common among English L1 speakers due to L1 transfer.

Lexical overgeneralisation occurs when learners create a deviant lexical item based on their earlier learning and insufficient knowledge of the target language. It is related to semantic association, involving a lexical item whose semantic component has a broad association with the appropriate item in the given context. Induced factors could also be involved in the production of such errors. Other groups of overgeneralisations are observed in the construction of time phrases (e.g. 이년 *i.nyen* for 올해/금년 *ol.hay/kum.nyen* 'this year'), and in word coinage (e.g. 농사 마을 *nong.sa ma.ul* 'farming + village' for 농촌 *nong.chon* '[farming] country'). These errors occur when learners create a deviant set expression on the basis of the individual lexical item they learned in previous KSL classes. It is also observed in Sino-Korean numeral collocation (e.g. 10날 *sip.nal* (> 10일 *sip.il*) '10 days') and is related to the two numeral systems in Korean (i.e. Native Korean and Sino-Korean). Which numeral system is utilised depends on the counters following the numeral. When overgeneralising, classifiers and numerals are overapplied, resulting in the wrong combination of numerals with 'day', 'month', and 'year'. Overgeneralisation, however, is a positive evidence, as it is produced as part of the learner's genuine effort, in most cases, to test and expand their knowledge on the basis of earlier learning and also forms part of their communication strategies (Corder, 1981; Richards, 1971a; Shin, S.-C., 2017; Wang, H.-S., 1995).

Literal translation comes from strong interference from learner's L1, since errors are made utilising the literal meaning of their L1 version or to the way the words or phrases are expressed in L1. A common type of such lexical errors among English L1 speakers is caused by the literal translation of 'to make' in expressions such as 'make a noise' and 'make friends' or of 'to play', which is diversified into a number of expressions in Korean according to the collocated words (e.g. humans/animals/toys – 놀다 *nol.ta*; sports of ball games – 하다 *ha.ta* [e.g. basketball]; sports that involve hitting a ball – 치다 *chi.ta* [e.g. tennis]; and musical instruments – 치다 *chi.ta* 'to hit' [e.g. piano], 불다 *pwul.ta* 'to blow' [e.g. flute], 켜다 *khye.ta* 'to saw' [e.g. violin]). These and other types of errors caused by literal translation are mostly due to strong interference from the learners' L1 (i.e. English), and they are negative transfer errors (Ellis, 1994).

Some lexical errors are attributable to confusion in their formal similarities. Such errors often result from confusion between sensory adjectives and corresponding verbs (e.g. 애기를 좋아서 *ay.ki.lul coh.a.se* 'as babies are good' [>좋아해서 *coh.a.hay.se* 'as (I) like babies']). Sensory or psycho-emotive adjectives, such as 좋다 *coh.ta*, 'good', 싫다 *silh.ta* 'unpleasant', and 슬프다 *sul.phu.ta* 'sad', are changed to transitive verbs when they are used to express one's internal feelings. Some types in this subcategory are also based on both formal and semantic similarities (e.g. 습관 *sup.kwan* 'habit' vs. 관습 *kwan.sup* 'custom'). These incorrect or inappropriate uses of words are primarily due to the orthographic (or phonetic) similarity, but the confusions seem to be assisted by semantic similarities.

Another subcategory comprises errors caused only by formal similarities without any semantic association (e.g. 지내- *ci.nay-* 'get along' for 지나- *ci.na-* 'have passed'). Errors caused by a combination of formal and semantic factors are observed even in Korean L1 speakers' utterances, as observed in such an erroneous use as 잊어버리- *ic.e.pe.li-* 'have forgotten' to mean 잃어버리- *ilh.e.pe.li-* 'have lost' or vice versa, both of which indicate 'something gone'. Thus, the primary cause of these kinds of errors is related to similarity in both form and sound, and in some cases similarity in form, sound, and meaning.

Learners also tend to add words unnecessarily, repeat what is mentioned, or paraphrase, unaware of the repetition or redundancy. This can be the case where words are unnecessarily added (e.g. 어른 사람 *e.lun sa.lam* 'adult person' instead of 어른 *e.lun* 'adult'), a preceding lexical item is unnecessarily repeated or words or phrases are unnecessarily paraphrased or explained instead of giving concise expressions (e.g. 밥 먹는 자리 *pap mek.nun ca.li* 'a place to eat meal' for 식탁 *sik.thak* 'a meal table'). Most of these errors of unnecessary addition, repetition, and circumlocution are developmental (Richards, 1971a; Wang, H.-S., 1995), and the cause is mainly attributable to the semantic knowledge about the definition and usage of a lexical item, with some cases being related to interference from L1, confusion, or syntactic influences.

In idiomatic expressions, no part can be replaced if the intended idiomatic meaning is to be maintained. Learners, however, tend to produce non-idiomatic expressions without knowing the idiomaticity of the expressions they intend to use. Many of these errors are caused by the violation of a collocation rule or the wrong selection, e.g., 식사 *sik.sa* – 요리하- *yo.li.ha-* 'cook a meal' for 식사 *sik.sa* – 준비하- *cwun.pi.ha-* 'prepare a meal'. While interlingual interference may appear to be the cause of these collocation errors, they could result from the complexity of the TL (i.e. Korean), which requires particular sets of lexical items or expressions. This indicates that intralingual factors are the most likely source of errors of idiomatic collocation.

Occasionally, learners produce sentences where part[s] are missing or the full form of a lexical item is oversimplified. Such missing words or forms are often attributable to interlingual transfer factors, where parts of some phrases can be or are often omitted in casual L1 speaking contexts. Examples are found in the omission of dependent nouns in Sino-Korean phrases (e.g. 9부터 5까지 *9.pwu.the 5.kka.ci* for 9시 부터 5시 까지 *9.si pwu.the 5.si kka.ci* 'from 9 o'clock to 5 o'clock'), in compound nouns and set phrases where part of the phrase is omitted and most of these omissions are derivational suffixes or dependent nouns (e.g. -지 *-ci* 'place' in 여행지 *ye.hayng.ci* 'tourist place', -비 *-pi* 'cost/fee' in 생활비 *sayng.hwal.pi* 'cost of living'), and in set phrases or idiomatic expressions (e.g. 택시 *thayk.si* 'taxi' instead of 택시 요금 *tayk.si yo.kum* 'taxi fares', 전화 *cen.hwa* 'phone' instead of 전화번호 *cen.hwa.pen. ho* 'phone number'). Some of the omissions here seem to be due to interference, and some others are attributable to insufficient knowledge or confusion factors. Learners may believe one part of the compound words would be enough without knowing that they are incomplete and inappropriate in parallel Korean contexts. Omission of lexical items are also found in counting classifiers in set phrases, and they seem to be due to the lack of learners' lexicon or lack of understanding about the Korean counting classifier rule, 'noun + numeral + counter'.

Apart from these categories, code-switching or code-shifting is also often observed in second language contexts. Learners occasionally borrow L1 codes to replace L2 lexical components, and they are transcribed in L2 letters (e.g. 사커 *sa.khe* > 축구 *chwuk.kwu* 'soccer', 익사이팅하- *ik.sa.i.thing.ha-* > 아주 재미있- *a.cwu cay.mi.iss-* 'to be exciting',) or written in L1 spellings (e.g. 패닉하- *panic ha-* > 당황하- *tang.hwang.ha-* 'to panic', law학교 *law. hak.kyo* > 법대 *pep.tay* 'law school'). These errors are often produced when learners lack the vocabulary in their L2. Generally, it is reasonable to suggest that the key lexical difficulty in KSL lies in learners' confusion or incompetence to distinguish two or more competing lexical items which share semantic and/or formal components.

Pedagogical implications of lexical errors

Lexical EA needs to be given more attention, as lexis now plays an increasingly important role in language learning (James, 1998). For instructors, there is a need to devise pedagogically effective learning and teaching strategies that prevent fossilisation of certain errors in students' lexical developments (Kang, H.-H., 2005). Students need to understand how a lexical item is used in various Korean contexts, how the usage of the Korean lexis is different from that of the L1 'equivalent', and what semantic restrictions a lexical item has. This is particularly relevant for vocabulary with similar and multiple meanings.

A large proportion of lexical errors reported in Korean EA studies are cases where learners have failed to distinguish semantic differences and unnecessarily add, overapply, or omit words. Studies of lexical errors in Korean (e.g. Kang, M., 2014; Shin, S.-C., 2017; Wang, H.-S., 1995) maintain that a large number of lexical errors are caused by confusion or ignorance of similar meanings, erratic one-to-one lexical matches between L1 and the TL (i.e. Korean), and contextually inappropriate use of words found in dictionaries. The frequent consultation of dictionaries is a particularly concerning source of errors, with a number of studies (e.g. Kang, H.-H., 2000; Park, E., 2008; Shin, H.-S., 1998) pointing out the inadequacy of dictionaries for KSL learners and the need for more adequate and accurate learner dictionaries, which should be linguistically adequate, learner friendly, and pedagogically well informed. As a practical approach to minimise lexical errors in general, there should be more instructional efforts that present the usage and examples of the problematic lexical items that are attributable to semantic and formal similarities, as well as curriculum planning for the development of teaching materials for reinforcement or remedial purposes.

Grammatical errors

There have been a large number of EA studies that examine grammatical errors made by learners of English (to name a few, Amiri & Puteh, 2017; Arani, 1986; Dulay & Burt, 1973; Jain, 1974; Hamzah, 2012; Kambal, 1980; Lott, 1983; Tang & Ng, 1995). Researchers have developed a wide range of classifications and explanations of grammatical errors. Classifications have included broad descriptions of the types of errors (e.g. Arani, 1986; Dulay & Burt, 1973; Jain, 1974; and Kambal, 1980), while others have utilised specific categories of smaller parts of grammar (e.g. Amiri & Puteh, 2017; Hamzah, 2012; Tang & Ng, 1995). Overall, the studies of ESL/EFL grammatical errors report certain problematic areas that presented common and consistent difficulties to learners of English regardless of their language background, and these areas include tense, auxiliary, and the use of articles, prepositions, and plurals.

In Korean, a good number of studies of grammatical errors are based on the data produced by KSL learners in Korea, many of which comprise English and Japanese L1 speakers (e.g. Cho, I. J., 2005, 2006; Jang, S. B., 2019; Kim, C.-S. & Nam, K.-C., 2002; Kim, Y.-M., 1994; and Shin, S.-C., 2017). Research later expanded to include learners of other linguistic backgrounds like Chinese, Spanish, and Vietnamese (e.g. Chen, J. & Lee, J.-H., 2020; Choi, S.-W., 2010; Kang, H.-H. & Jo, M.-J., 2003; Kim, J.-S., 2007; Kim, M.-O., 1994; Lee, H., 2018; Lee, K.-B., 2014; Rhee, S.-C., Kim, J. & Chang, J.-W., 2007; Shin, S.-C., 2010). Some studies compare the overall features of grammatical errors made by various L1 speakers learning Korean in Korea (e.g. Che, O., 1997; Kim, M.-O., 2002, 2003; Lee, J.-H., 2003), and some other studies focus on a particular area of the grammatical domain (e.g. Ahn, J.-H., 2002; Cho, I. J., 2005, 2006; Choi, S.-W., 2010; Kim, Y.-J., 2006; Kim, Y.-M., 2000; Lee, E.-K., 1999; Lee, J.-H., 2001). Many recent studies examine errors produced by Chinese learners (e.g. Chen, J. & Lee, J.-H., 2020; Han, S.-M., 2014; Lee, K.-B., 2014; Lee, S., 2013; Li, W. & Han, S. K., 2020). The Korean data reveals some common features in certain grammatical categories, such as case particles and conjunctors, in terms of the frequency and the cause of the error.

Categories of grammatical errors

EA studies on Korean report that a large portion of grammatical errors in Korean come from case particles, accounting for around half of the total grammatical errors, with some case particles more problematic for learners than others. The case particle and delimiter errors identified by studies include those involving nominative, accusative, locative-static, topic-contrast, locative-dynamic, genitive, connective, goal, dative, and directive. Among these, five particles – nominative, accusative, locative-static, topic, and locative-dynamic – account for the majority of identified case particle errors, with nominative particles being far more problematic than the others (Cho, I. J., 2006; Han, S.-M., 2014; Jang, S. B., 2019; Kim, C.-S. & Nam, K.-C., 2002; Shin, S.-C., 2017).

Sohn, H.-M. (1986) categorises grammatical errors of English-speaking learners into two domains with subcategorisations: morphology (e.g. modifier endings and copula-related) and syntax (e.g. case markers, tense, and conjunction), while Lee, J.-H. (2003) categorises frequent grammatical errors, such as case particles and conjunctive endings, and cross-classifies them by phenomena, i.e., substitution, omission, and addition. Studies of KSL errors report certain areas of Korean grammar that are consistently problematic to KSL learners irrespective of their L1 and in some cases the length of Korean language learning. The areas of difficulty include case particles, conjunctive suffixes, tense-aspect, and sentence-enders.

Types of grammatical errors

Statistical studies (e.g. Jang, S. B., 2019; Kim, M.-O., 2002; Ko, S.-J., 2002; Shin, S.-C., 2017) indicate that, irrespective of the learning stage and learner backgrounds, case particles with consistently high error occurrence are likely to produce the most common errors in KSL, with varying degrees of percentage value. With case particle errors, studies show that substitution makes up a large portion of case particle errors, followed by omission and addition. Substitution errors are found to be quite common in main case particle categories.

It is observed that a larger portion of substitution errors come from the substitution of: nominative *-i/ka* (-이/가) by accusative *-ul/lul* (-을/를); locative-dynamic *-eyse* (-에서) by locative-static *-ey* (-에); locative-static *-ey* (-에) by locative-dynamic *-eyse*(-에서); accusative *-ul/lul* (-을/를) by nominative *-i/ka* (-이/가); and topic *-un/nun* (-은/는) by nominative *-ey* (-에). There seem to be three areas that confuse learners, especially English L1 learners: (a) nominative and accusative particles, (b) locative-static and locative-dynamic particles, and (c) nominative and topic particles. The difficulty of distinguishing between nominative and topic particles, which is often perceived to be the most problematic by many KSL learners, is not necessarily reflected in EA statistics. High frequency does not always represent high difficulty, and error occurrence is not just affected by a certain linguistic difficulty of a grammatical item but by a variety of pedagogical and psychological factors, such as performance tasks, teaching input, and training (Ellis, 1994; Jain, 1974). Also, learners might use avoidance or omission strategies by utilising the characteristics of the Korean language, which allows sentence construction without any subject in certain contexts where it is assumed or unnecessary.

The second category is conjunctor errors, which follow a similar pattern to case particles, where most conjunctor errors result from substitution (e.g. Kim, J.-S., 2002; Lee, J.-H., 2003; Shin, S.-C., 2017), followed by omission. The frequent conjunctor errors are related to five conjunctive suffixes: the cause-effect suffixes *-ese/ase* (-어서/아서) 'so, and then, as' and *-(u)nikka* (– (으)니까) 'as, since, because'; the conditional suffixes *-(u)myen* (-(으)면)'if, when' and *-aya/eya* (-아야/어야) 'only if'; the background information provider suffixes *-(u)ntey/-nuntey* (-(으)ㄴ데/는데) 'and, but, while'; the sequentiality suffix *-ko* (-고) 'and, and also'; and the intentive suffixes *-(u)le* (-(으)러)'to, in order to' and *-(u)lyeko* (-(으)려고) 'to, in order to'.

Studies report that one of the most frequent substitution errors in conjunctors come from the confusion between the two cause-effect suffixes, *-ese/ase* (-어서/아서) and *-(u)nikka* (-(으)니까). These two causals have been one of the key areas that have been shown to present significant difficulty for KSL learners. Other substitutions of the causal suffix *-ese/ase* (-어서/아서) include substitution with the background information provider – *(u)ntey/nuntey* (-(으)ㄴ데/는데) and the sequentiality suffix *-ko* (-고). Also, the sequential conjunctor *-ko* (-고) is often substituted by the connective case particle *-hako* (-하고) or *-kwa/wa* (-과/와) and by the cause-effect (sequential) *-ese/ase* (-어서/아서) as well. Substitutions by the connective case particle *-hako* (-하고) 'and' also seem to reflect this trend. This may be because the particle *-hako* (-하고) (which is used as the connective meaning 'and' and the comitative meaning 'with' and is always preceded by a noun) is usually introduced and taught earlier than the conjunctor *-hako*

(-하고) 'and' (which is used to connect verbs). Also, some learners tend to confuse the *-ha* (-하) 'do' verbs plus the conjunctor *-ko* (-고) with the connective particle *-hako* (-하고) 'and'. The background information provider suffix *-(u)ntey/nuntey* (-(으)ㄴ데/는데) is substituted mostly by the causal suffix *-ese/ase* (-어서/아서) or *–(u)nikka* (-(으)니까). The opposite case (i.e. the substitution of the background suffix for the causal suffix) is also fairly frequent, which means that confusions between these two conjunctive suffixes are equally significant. The substitution of the conditional suffixes *–(u)myen* (– (으)면) includes the replacements with the causal suffixes *-ese/ase* (-어서/아서), as in 급한 일이 생겨서 *kup.han il.i sayng.kye.se* (>생기면 *sayng.ki.myen*) 저에게 도와줍니다 *ce.ey.key to.wa.cwup.ni.ta* '(sb) helps me, *if* an urgent matter *arises*'. And occasionally the concessive suffixes *-ato/eto* (-아도/어도). Additionally, there is also considerable confusion between the conditional suffix *-(u)myen* (– (으)면) 'if' and the intentive-conditional suffix, *-(u)lyemyen* (-(으)려면) 'if (one) intends to', which is the combination of the intentive suffix *-(u)lye* (– (으)려) 'intend to' and the conditional suffix *-(u)myen* (– (으)면). There are other substitutions in each category of conjunctors as well, but they seem to be only marginal and sporadic.

The third category is errors of sentence-enders. Substitutions in sentence-enders mainly come from: (a) the plain-level verbal declarative sentence-ender *-n.ta* (-ㄴ다) that is substituted with its pair *-nun.ta* (-는다) (e.g. 가려고 하는다 *ka.lye.ko ha.nun.ta* > 가려고 한다 *ka.lye.ko han.ta* 'intend to go', 좋아하는다 *coh.a.ha.nun.ta* > 좋아한다 *coh.a.han.ta* 'like'); and (b) a declarative predicate which is substituted by an adjective + copula (e.g. 지루한이에요 *ci.lwu.han.i.ey.yo* > 지루해요 *ci.lwu.hay.yo* 'It's boring'), verb stem + copula (e.g. 느끼이에요 *nu.kki.i.ey.yo* > 느껴요 *nu.kkye.yo* '[sb] feel') or adjective + declarative (e.g. 입예요 *ip.yey.yo* (> 입어요 *ip.e.yo*) '[sb] put [sth] on'). Another subtype of substitution is made by replacing the intentive conjecture suffix *-keyss* (-겠) + declarative ender with the prospective modal suffix *-(u)l* (-(으)ㄹ) + declarative ender (e.g. 좋은 추억이 남겠어요 *coh.un chwu.ek.i nam.kyess.e.yo* > 남을 거예요 *nam.ul ke.yey.yo* 'a good memory will probably remain'). The modal suffixes *-(u)l* (-(으)ㄹ) and *-keyss* (-겠) are one of the grammatical areas that the KSL learners often get confused about, as the two modal elements need some delicate differentiation and in-depth understanding. Another notable type of substitution is found in the construction of noun + existential verb or noun + declarative ender for the noun + *-ha* (-하) declarative ender clause (e.g. 후회있어요 *hwu.hoy.iss.e.yo* > 후회해요 *hwu.hoy.hay.yo*' [sb] regret'). Apart from these substitution types, there are some other sporadic error types, including such substitution pairs as: (a) the auxiliary opinion – *n/-un/-nun kes kath.ta* (ㄴ/은/는 것 같다) and the auxiliary observation *-n/-un/-nun.ka pota* (-ㄴ/은/는가 보다); (b) the polite-level declarative ender *-eyo/-ayo* (-어요/아요); (c) the plain-level declarative ender *-n.ta/-nun.ta* (-ㄴ다/는다); and (d) the deferential-level declarative ender *-p/-sup.ni.ta* (-ㅂ/습니다).

Types of additions in sentence-enders include the following three grammatical elements, namely, the addition of the plain-level declarative indicative suffix *-nun/-n* (-는/ㄴ) (e.g. 공부하고 싶는다 *kong.pwu.ha.ko siph.nun.ta* > 공부하고 싶다 *kong.pwu.ha.ko siph.ta* 'wish to study'), the addition of the copula stem *-i* (-이) (e.g. 뭐이니? *mwe.i.ni?* > 뭐니? *mwe.ni?* 'what is it?') or the existential adjective stem *-iss* (-있) (e.g. 많있습니다 *manh.iss.sup.ni.ta* > 많습니다 *manh.sup.ni.ta* 'there are many'), and the addition of the subject honorific suffix *-(u)si* (-(으)시) (e.g. 힘이 들으세요 *him.i tul.u.sey.yo* > 힘이 들어요 *him.i tul.e.yo* 'is hard'). It is observed that learners tend to overly apply the plain-level declarative indicative suffix *-nun* (-는) or *-n* (-ㄴ) to the adjective and past constructions, where the indicative suffix forms are zero (nil) in all polite-level expressions, plain-level adjective constructions and predicate constructions with a past/perfect or modal suffix *-ess/ass* (-었/았) and *-keyss* (-겠).

Tense-related errors in Korean are significant in their impact on the context. Understandably, most tense-aspect errors are substitution errors, with substitution from the non-past tense to the past tense and vice versa. Cases in which the non-past tense is substituted by the past tense are often observed in clauses with some particular conjunctive suffixes, including the event-oriented causal *-ese/-ase* (-어서/아서) (e.g. 늦게 잤어서 *nuc.key cass.e.se* > 늦게 자서 *nuc.key ca.se* 'as [sb] went to bed late'), the temporal sequential *-ko(na)se* (-고(나)서) (e.g. K와 싸웠고 나서 (K).wa *ssa.wess.ko na.se* > 싸우고 나서 *ssa.wu.ko na.se* 'after a fight with K'), the temporal interruptive *-ta(ka)* (-다(가)) (e.g. 회사에 다녔다가 *hoy.sa.ey ta.nyess.ta.ka* > 다니다가 *ta.ni.ta.ka* 'was working for a company, and then'), the speaker-oriented causal *-(u) nikka* (-(으)니까) (e.g. 쉬었으니까 *swi.ess.u.ni.kka* > 쉬니까 *swi.ni.kka* 'as [sb] took a rest'), the prospective time clause *-(u)l ttay* (-(으)ㄹ 때) (e.g. 어학당에 다녔을 때 *e.hak. tang.ey ta.nyess.ul ttay* > 다닐 때 *ta.nil ttay* 'as [sb] was attending a language school'), and the temporal sequential *-ese/-ase* (-어서/아서) in a propositive construction (e.g. 준비했어 *cwun.pi.hayss.e* > 준비해서 *cwun.pi.hay.se* 'prepare ... and'). Also, there are some other conjunctive coordinating or subordinating suffixes, such as *-ko* (-고) 'and, and also', *-ca(maca)* (-자(마자)) 'as soon as', *-ko(se)* (-고(서)) 'after, and then', *-ta(ka)* (-다(가)) 'do and then', *-(u)le* (-(으)러) 'in order to', and *-(u)myense* (-(으)면서) 'while', that affect the tense-aspect in a sentence. They do not normally accommodate the past-tense suffix *-ess/-ass* (-어서/아서) in an embedded clause within a past-tense sentence. The occurrence of the past-tense suffix in embedded clauses may cause ungrammaticality depending on the presence or absence of temporality (sequence, overlap, or transference) of conjunctive suffixes (Sohn, S.-O. S., 1992). When conjunctive suffixes convey a 'value of temporal ordering', the past tense form *-ess/ass* (-었/았) does not occur in embedded clauses but only in matrix clauses, thus the tense in temporal conjunctive clauses becomes the 'null form'. There are also several non-temporal conjunctive suffixes in Korean as well, including *-ko* (-고) 'and, and also', *-kena* (-거나) 'or', *-ciman* (-지만) 'but', *-eto/ado* (-어도/아도) 'even if', *-(u)myense* (-(으)면서) 'although', *-(u)nikka* (-(으)니까) 'because', and *-untey/-nuntey/-ntey* (-은데/는데/ㄴ데) 'and, but, while'. Clauses with these suffixes normally require the past-tense form in the embedded constructions.

Possible causes of case particle errors

The substitution of an accusative particle for a nominative particle is closely related to the use of the following grammatical items or sentence constructions: adjectival verb sentences (existential, descriptive, transitive sensory or psychoemotive, necessity, and copular negative verbs), intransitive sentences (common, locomotive, inchoative, processive, and passive verbs), and other specific constructions (relative clauses, multiple-subject sentences, quoted clauses, defective nouns, and negative adjective *-ci anh* (-지 않) 'be not' constructions). Many of the substitutions are caused by distinctive grammatical features where a predicate functions, semantically, like a transitive verb that takes an object, and it involves grammatical difference between the learner's L1 (i.e. English) and their TL (i.e. Korean). Specifically, the substitution is associated with the syntactic behaviour of several linguistic elements.

First, the cause of the nominative particle substitution is associated with existential verbs. Some learners are unaware that when existential verbs are used to express possession, the subject nominal functions as the object with its nominative particle remaining intact. Also, part of the confusion appears to be caused by the transfer of the English (i.e. learners' L1) verb 'have', which needs an object in English but is normally interpreted as one of the existential verbs in Korean that do not normally require an object and accusative particles. Second, the misinterpretation of the case for the noun referred to by descriptive adjectives causes the nominative particle substitutions. Learners tend to mistakenly interpret a complement in the descriptive sentences as an object. This is also due to a lack of knowledge of the sentence construction of 'X + adjectival verbs', where X is the subject and thus needs nominative particles. Third, the substitution of an accusative particle for a nominative particle is caused by the misinterpretation of the noun preceding intransitive verbs. Some substitutions in this category are caused by confusion of the similarity in form between the intransitive and its corresponding transitive verbs (e.g. N + -이/가 끝나다 -i/ka kkuth.na.ta '(N) finish' vs. N + -를/을 끝내다 -lul/-ul kkuth.nay.ta 'finish [N]').

Fourth, transitive sensory or psychoemotive adjectives, such as 싫다 *silh.ta* 'be disagreeable, dislike' and 부럽다 *pwu.lep.ta* 'be envious, envy', cause confusion in the choice of a particle for the object. There are two kinds of sensory/psychoemotive adjectives that need to be considered. One is intransitive sensory adjectives such as 기쁘다 *ki.ppu.ta*, 'be happy' and 슬프다 *sul.phu.ta* 'be sad', and the other is transitive sensory adjectives such as 좋다 *coh.ta* 'be good, like' and 부럽다 *pwu.lep.ta* 'be envious, envy'. Each of these has a corresponding verb: 기뻐하다 *ki.ppe.ha.ta* 'feel happy', 슬퍼하다 *sul.phe.ha.ta* 'feel sad', 좋아하다 *coh.a.ha.ta* 'like', and 부러워하다 *pwu.le.we.ha.ta* 'envy'. The structure which causes greater confusion in relation to the use of a case particle is a transitive-sensory adjective structure in which the object is in the nominative case, not the accusative.

Fifth, sentences containing inchoative verbs such as 되다 *toy.ta* 'become', 지다 *ci.ta* 'get, become', affect the occurrence of the substitution errors in the nominative particle. This is the case where learners are unaware that in inchoative sentences a subject and a complement are both in the nominative case. Sixth, adjectives that denote necessity are responsible for another type of substitution error in the nominative particle. In a sentence where the subject is marked by dative *-ey.key/han.they/kkey* (-에게/한테/께), the nominal referred to by the necessity adjectives functions as an object but is marked with a nominative particle. The confusion in this type is also related to negative transfer from the learners' L1 (i.e. English), which is often induced by presenting such construction as 'X needs Y'. Overall, the triggering constructions and verb types, including existential/possessive and intransitive constructions, account for the major cause for substitutions of the nominative particle by the accusative particle.

As for the substitution of accusative *-ul/lul* (-을/를) by nominative *-i/ka* (-이/가), the majority of the substitutions of this type occur when the subject is dropped and the accusative case is replaced with the nominative case (e.g. 한국 문화가 *han.kwuk mwun.hwa.ka* > 한국 문화를 더 배우기 위해 *han.kwuk mwun.hwa.lul te pay.wu.ki wi.hay* 'in order to learn more about Korean culture'). Many of these errors come from the misperception of the object as the subject or confusion between them. In Korean, which is referred to as a situation- or verb-oriented language, it is usual to speak and write with the subject being omitted in the contexts where the speaker or the reference is already understood by the hearer or the reader. In fact, pro-drop (e.g. I, you, they) is one of the characteristic phenomena of Korean, but KSL learners tend to mistreat the object as the subject in the sentence. Whether the substitution is due to a momentary confusion or an insufficient knowledge about the sentence construction, the subject drops seem to contribute to the failure of the distinction between subjects and objects, thus replacing the accusative case with the nominative case.

A second grammatical factor is related to the typical confusion between the psychological adjectives and the corresponding verbs, e.g., 좋다 *coh.ta* 'be good, like' and its verb form 좋아하다 *coh.a.ha.ta* 'like'. Some learners substitute the accusative particle with the nominative particle in sensory constructions that contain a transitive sensory verb, e.g., 좋아하다 *coh.a.ha.ta* 'like', which needs an object, thus an object particle. The confusion factor present between the sensory adjectives and their verb forms seem to play a certain role in the substitution, but the omission of the subject might also contribute to the confusion because learners perceive the nominal appearing at the beginning of a sentence as the subject, thus giving the nominative particle.

Other constructions include imperative sentences. When a formal or informal request is made, it is natural or necessary to omit the subject, which may lead learners to wrongly interpret the object as the subject, thus using the nominative particle instead of the accusative particle. The substitution is also observed in passive constructions where the substitution is made with confusion in the mental process of changing an active transitive sentence to a passive intransitive sentence. Lexical passive verbs are combined with verbal nouns to form compound passive verbs (e.g. 거절(을) 당하다 *ke.cel.(ul) tang.ha.ta* 'be refused'). There are a number of passive verbs in Korean, and if such verbs are transitive verbs, the accusative particle is needed to be added to the noun that comes with it (e.g. 존경(을) 받다 *con.kyeng.(ul) pat.ta* 'be respected', 꾸중(을) 듣다 *kkwu.cwung.(ul) tut.ta* 'be scolded'). In general, the substitution of the accusative particle by the nominative particle is directly or indirectly related to the change or omission of the subject, and this is compared with the opposite substitution (i.e. accusative for nominative) in that its cause is more related to the predicates – adjectives and verbs.

Studies show that substitutions of the locative-dynamic particle by the locative-static particle is one of the most frequent types and is unidirectional. The use of locative particles is primarily determined by the nature of the verb (i.e. static or dynamic) as well as its relation with the noun phrase in a sentence (Jin, D.-Y., 2005). From a learner's point of view, the nature of dynamicity of the verb may become clearer when it comes with an object word in SOV-type sentences, but not all SOV sentences mention the object. Some verbs, such as 자다 *ca.ta* 'sleep' and 쉬다 *swi.ta* 'rest', are a little ambiguous to learners because of their dynamicity and their intransitive nature. Therefore, the nature of a verb and the nature of sentence construction (e.g. presence or absence of an object) could also add to confusion in perceiving the dynamicity of a verb in a sentence. This explanation, however, is too simplistic for a variety of other peculiar usages of the pair particles to demonstrate the complex usage of the two locative particles and various pragmatic factors, such as distance, location, background, and the nature of the referral (Park, D.-S., 2000, 2019).

There are also pedagogical and psycholinguistic factors related to this type of substitution. The locative-static particle is introduced in KFL course materials and taught in classes usually earlier than the locative-dynamic particle to avoid confusion, as a pedagogical strategy or by chance. In such a learning context, it is inevitable that KSL learners have more time and training in learning the locative-static particle than the locative-dynamic particle, which means they become more familiar with the use of the static particle. Second, the function of -*ey* (-에), which is used as locative-static, dative, and goal particles, is wider than that of -*ey.se* (-에서), which is used as locative-dynamic and source ('from') particles. If learners tend to rely on the more familiar form, it is almost certain that the wider appearance of the identical form will play a role in the choice of the locative-static particle in place of the locative-dynamic particle. Third, the locative-static particle is shorter than the locative-dynamic particle, and this might lead less confident learners to choose the 'shorter' one (Lee, E.-K., 2003).

The opposite case, which is the substitution of the locative-static particle by the locative-dynamic particle also has a number of grammatical factors, including the misinterpretation of existential and descriptive verbs into dynamic verbs, e.g., 서울에서 *se.wul.ey.se* > 서울에 교통이 복잡하- *se.wul.ey kyo.thong.i pok.cap.ha-* 'the traffic is complex in Seoul'; the use of the time indicator -*ey* (-에) 'at, in, on'; and the locative-goal particle -*ey* (-에) 'to'. In addition to these common sources, some other substitutions are made in relation to locomotive, processive, and locational verbs. Some learners tend to violate the usage in which locomotive verbs require the directional particle -lo/u.lo (-로/으로) 'to, for' or the locative-goal particle – ey (에) 'to' to express the destination or the arrival point of a movement. Processive verbs also require the locative-goal particle -ey (-에) to express the goal. An act of placing something, e.g. 넣다, 놓다, 두다 neh.ta, noh.ta, twu.ta 'place something in/at/on' requires the locative-goal -ey (-에) to express the place for the object. All these verbs require the locative-goal particle ey (-에). The substitution is also related to the passive construction (e.g. 바닷가에서 pa.tas.ka.ey.se > 바닷가에 위치해 있었다 pa.tas.ka.ey wi.chi.hay iss.ess.ta. '[sth] is located at the seaside'). The state of being located in a place operates like an existential or descriptive verb and thus requires the locative-static particle -에 -ey to express the location.

Regarding substitutions of topic -un/nun (-은/는) by nominative -i/ka (-이/가), it is often observed that learners have a great deal of difficulty in understanding and differentiating these two particles, but in the contexts where free writing or speaking tasks are given, some learners tend to utilise strategies (e.g. avoidance, omission) to avoid possible errors that might be caused by using the particles, particularly when they are uncertain about the differences between them. The two pairs of particles are normally considered to have more complex usage (Sohn, H.-M., 1999) and are often observed 'competing' with each other in the utterance of L2 learners of Korean. The characteristic differences between the topic particle and the nominative particle are referred to by linguists in four ways: general introduction vs. exclusiveness, generic vs. specific, contrast vs. neutral and old information vs. new information. Among these features, the contrastive meaning of the topic particle and the exclusive meaning of the nominative particle are considered the most problematic or very difficult to distinguish. Confusion arises when it is used with its neutral meaning, and thus the noun phrase in the nominative case is unstressed. The individual acceptability may vary depending on how it is contextualised and how it is uttered or emphasised. At a pedagogical level, however, these features themselves may cause confusion or become intangible ideas for both learners and instructors.

Apart from the main substitutions, there are a couple of other case particle substitutions that are worth noting: topic by accusative and nominative by topic. The substitution of the topic particle by the accusative particle is made largely by misinterpreting the subject as the object of the copula, the complement, or the adjectival verb in the sentence. The necessity of the topic particle instead of the nominative particle in the subject case is determined from the context rather than the individual sentence. Many KSL students tend to misinterpret existential and intransitive verbs as transitive verbs, thus misconstruing the subject as the object of such a verb or a complement in the sentence. This kind of misinterpretation is related not only to knowledge about the basic grammatical functions of subject, object, verb, and complement but also to the differences between Korean and the learner's L1.

Pedagogical implications of grammatical errors

The main pedagogical implications of EA lie in the design of remedial syllabuses or materials, and the design of pedagogical grammars. Given that a number of studies have found similarities between L1 and L2 acquisition, particularly in the acquisition of syntactic structures (Larsen-Freeman & Long, 1991), instructors should be able to elaborate on the teaching order and the developmental sequence in KSL syllabus and teaching materials by utilising the information obtained from the learner's approximate system. In designing materials for individual linguistic items, it will be necessary to pay more attention to the main areas of difficulty in remedial drills than areas with fewer problems. The writing of pedagogical grammars must also reflect the language-learning strategies and processes that have been discovered from the learner's interlanguage data. The main challenge here is threefold: how to present the learner simple, clear, and complete information; how to effectively present the linguistic materials to the learner; and how to enable the learner to practise the grammatical elements effectively.

The very fact that more than half of the total grammatical errors come from case particles invites fundamental pedagogical questions such as 'Are particles learnable and teachable?', 'Are students taught about particles adequately?', 'Will explicit explanations about particles produce better results?', and 'How efficient and adequate are teaching methods or materials?' Long (1983) suggests that explicit grammar instruction enables learners to learn fast and achieve a higher level of L2 grammatical accuracy. Pienemann (1986) suggests that grammar instruction is successful only when learners are ready to acquire a grammatical feature as implicit knowledge, while Ellis (1993) maintains that grammar teaching should be directed at raising learners' consciousness about how the TL grammar works rather than practice. In KSL as well, studies such as Lee, H.-Y. (1998), Kim, N. (2002), and Paik, P.-J. (2001) stress the importance and necessity of grammar instruction and maintain that without grammar instruction, it is almost impossible to expect second language learners to communicate at an advanced level.

The difficulty learners face in grammar is centred around insufficient knowledge about what is acceptable, what is applicable, what particles and suffixes to choose in a given situation, and how this differs in other situations. Also, there are not only certain patterns in substitutions in the main grammatical error categories but also certain 'triggers' in most types that assist the occurrence of such substitution errors. The main types of substitution and the grammatical elements that operate as triggers are quite typical, consistent, and can be categorised in most cases, which means they can be utilised in planning or developing a course and course materials in such a way that learners might be able to minimise the production of the same errors. It is important to achieve this without losing the purpose of language learning and the interest of the students. The findings of EA studies also reinforce the importance of making provisions, where possible, for a remedial class targeting the whole or specific individual learner groups.

Future directions of Korean EA studies

With an improved data-collection method and a comprehensive error-categorisation system, future research should be able to provide grounds to better account for learners' production of errors. There is also a need for a parallel longitudinal study that deals with the error patterns, error types, and error occurrence of one or more learner groups, which will provide a better understanding of the process of learners' acquisition of L2 Korean. Also, to have a better understanding of the common errors, it will be useful to undertake a comparative study to investigate errors produced by learners of different linguistic backgrounds. EA researchers may further explore related topics, such as whether there is an 'absolute difficulty' among the grammatical items. It is also important and useful to investigate the acceptability of an idiosyncratic or deviant item perceived by various groups. Answers from such further research will provide significant grounds to make more adequate generalisations about students' L2 development in Korean.

References

Ahn, J.-H. (2002). A study of the [reason] connectives for the international Korean language education. *Journal of Korean Language Education, 2*, 159–180.

Amiri, F., & Puteh, M. (2017). Error analysis in academic writing: A case of international postgraduate students in Malaysia. *Advances in Language and Literary Studies, 8*(4), 141–145.

Arani, M. T. (1986). *Error analysis: The types and causes of the major structural errors made by Iranian university students when writing expository and imaginative prose* [Unpublished doctoral dissertation]. State University of New York at Buffalo.
Bebout, L. (1985). An error analysis of misspellings made by learners of English as a first and as a second language. *Journal of Psycholinguistic Research, 14*(6), 569–593.
Brown, H. D. (1980). *Principles of language learning and teaching*. Englewood Cliffs, NJ: Prentice Hall.
Che, O. (1997). *An analytic study of errors made by KFL learners* [MA in Korean Studies thesis]. Ewha Womans University.
Chen, J., & Lee, J.-H. (2020). Particle omission errors by Chinese learners of Korean: An error analysis of written learner corpus. *Teaching Korean as a Foreign Language, 58*, 317–349.
Cho, I. J. (2005). Errors of English-speaking learners of Korean: Inanimate subjects with transitive verbs. *Journal of Korean Language Education, 16*(3), 331–352.
Cho, I. J. (2006). Comparative linguistic analysis of subject and object case marking errors by English-speaking learners of Korean. *Journal of Korean Language Education, 17*(3), 281–299.
Choi, S.-W. (2010). An analysis of substitution errors in Korean adnominal ending form-focused on Chinese learner. *Teaching Korean as a Foreign Language, 35*, 157–185.
Choo, M., & O'Grady, W. (2003). *The sounds of Korean: A pronunciation guide*. Honolulu, HI: University of Hawai'i Press.
Corder, S. P. (1971). *Idiosyncratic dialects and error analysis*. Reprinted in Corder, S. P. (1981). *Error analysis and interlanguage*. Oxford: Oxford University Press.
Corder, S. P. (1974). Error analysis. In J. P. B. Allen & S. P. Corder (Eds.), *Techniques in applied linguistics* (pp. 122–131). Oxford: Oxford University Press.
Corder, S. P. (1975). Error analysis, interlanguage and second language acquisition. *Language Teaching and Linguistics Abstracts, 8*, 201–218.
Corder, S. P. (1981). *Error analysis and interlanguage*. Oxford: Oxford University Press.
Dulay, H., & Burt, M. (1973). Should we teach children syntax?. *Language Learning, 32*, 245–258.
Dulay, H., & Burt, M. (1974). Errors and strategies in child second language acquisition. *TESOL Quarterly, 8*, 129–136.
Dulay, H., Burt, M., & Krashen, S. (1982). *Language two*. Oxford: Oxford University Press.
Ellis, R. (1993). The structural syllabus and second language acquisition. *TESOL Quarterly, 27*(1), 91–113.
Ellis, R. (1994). *The study of second language acquisition*. Oxford: Oxford University Press.
George, H. V. (1972). *Common errors in language learning: Insights from English*. Rowley, MA: Newbury House.
Hamzah, H. (2012). An analysis of the written errors produced by freshmen students in English writing. *Lingua Didaktika, 6*(1), 17–25.
Han, S.-M. (2014). An analysis of errors in the discourse of Korean language learners – Focusing on the usage of particles. *Journal of Korean Language Education, 25*(3), 281–310.
Jain, M. P. (1974). Error analysis: Source, cause and significance. In J. Richards (Ed.), *Error analysis: Perspectives on second language acquisition* (pp. 189–215). London: Longman.
James, C. (1980). *Contrastive analysis*. London: Longman.
James, C. (1998). *Errors in language learning and use*. London: Longman.
James, C., Scholfield, P., Garrett, P., & Griffiths, Y. (1993). Welsh bilinguals' English spelling: An error analysis. *Journal of Multilingual and Multicultural Development, 14*(4), 287–306.
Jang, S. B. (2019). A quantitative study on particle errors of English-speaking Korean language learners. *Language Facts and Perspectives, 47*, 25–57.
Jeon, Y. (2011). Analysis of errors in the usage of Korean grammatical particles by female marriage-based immigrants. *Journal of Korean Language Education, 22*(4), 27–62.
Jin, D.-Y. (2005). Ssuki kyoyukuy kyoswu haksup (Teaching of [KFL] writing). In IAKLE (Ed.), *Hankwukekyoyuklon (KFL teaching methodology)* (Vol. 3). Seoul: Hankwukmwunhwasa.
Joo, A., & Shin, S.-C. (2016). Characteristic features of English-L1 KHL learner orthographic errors. *Journal of Korean Language Education, 27*(English edition), 1–36.
Kambal, M. A. A. (1980). *An analysis of Khartoum University students' composition errors with implications from remedial English in the context of Arabicization* [Unpublished doctoral dissertation]. The University of Texas at Austin.
Kang, H.-H. (2000). Oykwukinul wihan hankwuke sacenkwa malmwungchi [A Korean dictionary and language corpus]. *Korean Journal of Applied Linguistics, 16*(1), 99–117.

Kang, H.-H. (2005). Ilpanewa kwuke sacen [Ordinary words and Korean dictionary]. In IAKLE (Ed.), *Hankwukekyoyuklon (KFL teaching methodology)* (Vol. 2). Seoul: Hankwukmwunhwasa.

Kang, H.-H., & Jo, M.-J. (2003). Analysis of errors in sentence-ending, particles, tense-aspects, causative forms by Korean-learning Spanish native speakers. *Journal of Korean Language Education, 14*(2), 1–23.

Kang, M. (2014). An analysis of lexical errors of Korean language learners: Some American college learners' case. *Journal of Pan-Pacific Association of Applied Linguistics, 18*(2), 93–110.

Kim, C.-S., & Nam, K.-C. (2002). An analysis of errors in using Korean particles by native speakers of English. *Journal of Korean Language Education, 13*(1), 27–45.

Kim, J.-S. (2002). A study of Korean language learners' errors in connective endings. *Journal of Korean Language Education, 13*(2), 87–109.

Kim, J.-S. (2007). A study of errors in Korean compositions by Vietnamese students. *Journal of Korean Language Education, 18*(1), 49–71.

Kim, M.-O. (1994). An analysis of errors found in the learning of Korean. *Journal of Korean Language Education, 5*, 233–244.

Kim, M.-O. (2001). A study of spelling errors in writing. *Teaching Korean as a Foreign Language, 25–26*, 331–359.

Kim, M.-O. (2002). A statistical analysis of errors by Korean language learners. *Teaching Korean as a Foreign Language, 27*, 495–541.

Kim, M.-O. (2003). A statistical analysis of lexical errors by Korean language learners. *Journal of Korean Language Education, 14*(3), 31–52.

Kim, N. (2002). The importance of grammar in Korean language teaching. *Teaching Korean as a Foreign Language, 27*, 119–139.

Kim, Y.-J. (2006). Error analysis in the uses of particles and verb endings of advanced Korean-learning English speakers. *Teaching Korean as a Foreign Language, 31*, 129–152.

Kim, Y.-M. (1994). *Olyupwunsekul thonghan hyohyulcekin hankwuke cakmwun cito pangan yenkwu [Teaching Korean a second language with special reference to composition]* [Unpublished MA in Korean language & literature thesis]. Hankook University of Foreign Studies.

Kim, Y.-M. (2000). *Haksupca malmwungchilul iyonghan hankwuke haksupca olyu pwunsek yenkwu [A study of error analysis of Korean learners by using 'learner corpus']* [Unpublished MEd in KFL thesis]. Yonsei University.

Kim-Renaud, Y.-K. (Ed.). (1997). *The Korean alphabet: Its history and structure*. Honolulu, HI: University of Hawai'i Press.

Ko, S.-J. (2002). Error analysis of postposition in learner corpus. *Teaching Korean as a Foreign Language, 27*, 543–570.

Larsen-Freeman, D., & Long, M. H. (1991). *An introduction to second language acquisition research*. London: Longman.

Lee, E.-K. (1999). *Hankwuke haksupcauy cosa sayongey natanan olyu pwunsek [Error analysis of postposition used by learners of Korean]* [Unpublished MA in Korean language and literature thesis]. Yonsei University.

Lee, E.-K. (2003). Hankwuke haksupcauy cosa olyu pwunsek [Error analysis on case particles produced by learners of Korean]. In S.-K. Seo (Ed.), *Hankwuke kyoyukkwa haksup sacen [Teaching of Korean and a learner dictionary]*. Seoul: Hankwukmwunhwasa.

Lee, H. (1998). Mwunpep kyoswuuy wenliwa silcey [Theory and practice in grammar instruction]. *Bilingual Research, 15*, 411–438.

Lee, H. (2018). An analysis of error types in Korean nasalization-focusing on Chinese and Japanese learners. *Language Facts and Perspectives, 45*, 229–249.

Lee, J.-I. (2001). A study on tense errors found in KFL learners' compositions. *Bilingual Research, 18*, 259–275.

Lee, J.-H. (2002). A study of error determination criteria and classification in Korean. *Journal of Korean Language Education, 13*(1), 175–197.

Lee, J.-H. (2003). *Hankwuke haksupcauy olyu yenkwu (A study on errors produced by KFL learners)*. Seoul: Pakiceng.

Lee, J.-H. (2008). Error analysis of Chinese learners of Korean: Focused on analysis of the source of content-word errors. *Journal of Korean Language Education, 19*(3), 403–425.

Lee, K.-B. (2014). An analysis of errors in using Korean '-(l)/eul' by native speakers of Chinese. *Teaching Korean as a Foreign Language, 41*, 171–192.

Lee, M. W. (2020). An analysis of Korean language learners' errors by proficiency: Focus on statistical analysis using the multinominal logistic regression model. *Journal of Korean Language Education, 31*(2), 143–169.

Lee, S. (2013). An analysis of characteristics of '-ess' errors in Chinese-speaking Korean language learners. *Teaching Korean as a Foreign Language, 39,* 137–163.

Lennon, P. (1991). Error: Some problems of definition, identification and distinction. *Applied Linguistics, 12*(2), 180–196.

Li, W., & Han, S. K. (2020). A study on the errors made by native Chinese speakers with Korean prefinal endings. *Journal of Korean Language Education, 31*(2), 107–141.

Long, M. H. (1983). Does second language instruction make a difference? A review of the research. *TESOL Quarterly, 17*(3), 359–382.

Lott, D. (1983). Analysing and counteracting interference errors. *English Language Teaching Journal, 37,* 256–261.

Martin, S. (1992). *A reference grammar of Korean.* Rutland, VT: Tuttle.

Min, Y. (2008). An analysis of Chinese learners' errors caused by negative transfer. *Journal of Korean Language Education, 19*(1), 55–75.

Montrul, S. (2010). Current issues in heritage language acquisition. *Annual Review of Applied Linguistics, 30,* 3–23.

NIKL (The National Institute of the Korean Language). (2005). *Oykwukinul wihan hankwuke mwunpep [Korean grammar for foreigners]* (Vol. 1). Seoul: Communication Books.

Paik, P.-J. (2001). Oykwukeloseuy hankwuke kyoyukmwunpep [Instructional grammar in Korean as a foreign language]. *Journal of Korean Language Education, 12*(2), 415–445.

Park, D.-S. (2000). The two locative case markers in Korean. In Y. Chang (Ed.), *Korea between tradition and modernity* (pp. 384–398). Canada: University of British Columbia, Institute of Asian Research.

Park, D.-S. (2019). A semantic approach to the two locative markers -ey and -eyse in Korean. *Korean Language & Literature Education, 29,* 143–174.

Park, E. (2008). Examination of Korean language errors in Korean-Vietnamese dictionary. *Journal of Korean Language Education, 19*(3), 237–263.

Park, S.-Y. (2007). A study on constructing Korean [language] learners' error corpus and some problems. *Language Facts and Perspectives, 21,* 83–113.

Pienemann, M. (1986). Is language teachable? Psychological experiments and hypotheses. *Australian Working Papers in Language Development, 1*(3).

Ranjan, R. K., & Kim, H.-J. (2016). Research analysis of errors of beginner level Korean language learners of India. *Journal of Korean Language Education, 27*(2), 25–50.

Rhee, S.-C., Kim, J., & Chang, J.-W. (2007). An analysis of errors produced by English, Chinese and Japanese native speakers with a focus on Korean phonological rules. *Journal of Korean Language Education, 18*(1), 365–399.

Richards, J. C. (1971a). A non-contrastive approach to error analysis. Reprinted in J. C. Richards (Ed.). (1974), *Error analysis: Perspectives on second language acquisition* (pp. 172–188). London: Longman.

Richards, J. C. (1971b). Error analysis and second language strategies. *Language Sciences, 17,* 12–22.

Shin, H.-S. (1998). Hankwuke ehwikyoyukkwa uymi sacen [Vocabulary teaching in Korean and a dictionary of lexicon]. *Journal of Korean Language Education, 9*(2), 85–103.

Shin, S.-C. (2010). Grammatical errors in Chinese KFL learners' compositions and teaching implications. *Teaching Korean as a Foreign Language, 35,* 75–100.

Shin, S.-C. (2017). *Understanding L2 Korean learner errors: Description, explanation and implications.* Seoul: Sotong Publishing Co.

Shin, S.-C., & Joo, A. (2015). Lexical errors in Korean-Australian heritage learners' compositions. *Journal of Korean Language Education, 26*(English edition), 129–162.

Sohn, H.-M. (1986). Patterns of American students' composition errors in Korean. In H.-M. Sohn (Ed.), *Linguistic expeditions* (pp. 487–528). Seoul: Hanshin Publishing Co.

Sohn, H.-M. (1999). *The Korean language.* Cambridge: Cambridge University Press.

Sohn, S.-O. S. (1992). Speaker-oriented and even-oriented causals: A comparative analysis of -nikka and -ese. *Korean Linguistics – Journal of the International Circle of Korean Linguistics, 7,* 73–83.

Stenson, N. (1983). Induced errors. In B. Robinett & J. Schachter (Eds.), *Second language learning: Contrastive analysis, error analysis and related aspects* (pp. 256–271). Ann Arbor, MI: University of Michigan.

Suk, J.-Y., & Ahn, K.-H. (2003). Some problems with error analysis of learner Korean. *Journal of Korean Language Education, 14*(3), 189–215.

Tang, E., & Ng, C. (1995). A study on the use of connectives in ESL students' writing. *Perspectives* (City University of Hong Kong, Hong Kong), *7*(2), 105–121.

Taylor, G. (1986). Errors and explanations. *Applied Linguistics* (Oxford University Press), *7*(2), 144–166.

Wang, H.-S. (1995). Yengehwacauy hankwuke cakmwuney natanan ehwisang olyu pwunsek [An analysis of lexical errors in the Korean compositions produced by English speakers]. *Bilingual Research, 12*, 383–399.

Wardhaugh, R. (1983). The contrastive analysis hypothesis. In B. Robinett & J. Schachter (Eds.), *Second language learning: Contrastive analysis, error analysis and related aspects* (pp. 6–14). Ann Arbor, MI: University of Michigan.

Yang, S.-Y. (2013). The analysis of the Turkish learner's errors of honorific expressions in Korean writing. *Journal of Korean Language Education, 24*(2), 205–231.

Zhang, W., & Kim, J. Y. (2019). Analysis of Chinese students' spoken lexical errors in Korean. *Language Facts and Perspectives, 48*, 255–281.

18
SOCIAL INTERACTIONS IN KSL SETTINGS

Hakyoon Lee

Introduction

Social interaction is considered an empirical strand within the data-driven field of sociolinguistics and is used as means to understand people's behavior and social norms. The studies on social interactions have focused on investigating people's everyday communication (Fitch & Sanders, 2005), and social interactions have been investigated in interdisciplinary fields including communication studies, linguistic anthropology, social psychology, applied linguistics, and sociology. In their handbook on language and social interactions, Fitch and Sanders (2005) explore how language and social interactions are implemented in the academic subfields with diverse approaches: pragmatics, conversation analysis, language and social psychology, discourse analysis, anthropology, and technology.

Sanders (2005) notes the value of examining how people succeed in making meaning in what they say, observing that it is more likely that they successfully say things coherently by producing their utterances in a particular way. Moreover, these practices are co-constructed, meaning that nothing in an interaction is solely up to the speaker. This collaborative construction implies that the meaningfulness of an utterance depends on both how the speaker uses certain forms and contents and what the hearer makes of the utterance. Different fields can focus on the social state between the speaker and the hearer, the sequential organizations, stereotypes, or cultural identities. These different perspectives contribute to distinguishing functionalities of different types of interactions or utterances.

Despite its importance as the essential human activity, social interaction has not been much explored in the field of Korean as a second language (KSL). It is imperative to discuss social interaction because there are various elements that play a critical role in people's successful interactions with others. KSL educators and researchers need to know more about learners' social interaction, interactional types, and strategies both in and outside language classrooms to better understand the nature of learners' language use and learning. As the venues of the learners' language learning and use have become more diverse and dynamic, it is important to explore how the learners actually use language in interactions to holistically understand their learning motivations and needs.

Accordingly, this chapter first explores the definition of language and social interactions and then summarizes earlier studies on social interactions, particularly emphasizing the development of interactional competence. In addition, social interactions in the field of language socialization and its relation to other constructs will be reviewed before discussing social interactions in the Korean as foreign/second language contexts. Finally, pedagogical implications and potential direction of future research will be discussed.

What is language in social interaction?

Language is a mode of communication or a vehicle to transmit information, including ideas, thoughts, and feelings, to one another. Philosophers and social scientists consider metaphor as a means to describe the communicative function of language (Reddy, 1979). This metaphor is grounded in the commonsensical notion that, through speech, one person conveys information through the means of words, initiating communication. Instead of a referential approach to meaning, language is viewed as a medium of organized social activities and language performatives (Austin, 1962). The humans "do" the social world, which is a more dynamic and activist approach. According to Young (1999), besides diverse research areas including language and society (how social and political issues affect language use in a society), language variation (varied language use across different speakers and contexts), and language and culture (how a particular culture is related to a certain language), sociolinguistic investigations of language and social interactions have focused on how language is used in face-to-face interactions.

Social interactions are among the most commonly used notions in understanding human behaviors and communications. Social structures are constructed by people's contact with each other and vice versa. For example, communication norms and power relations (e.g., how to communicate appropriately in a certain context) in diverse social contexts, including workplaces and classrooms, are created through social interactions. Schegloff (1992) notes that interactions are the primitive site of human society. "Social interactions make it possible to inform, contest, create, ratify, refute, and ascribe among other things power, class, gender, ethnicity, and culture" (Jenks, 2014, p. 7). Thus, when people perform a variety of social actions, interactions work to facilitate this process. "(Interaction) is the fundamental resource through which the business of all societies is managed, their cultures are transmitted, the identities of their participants are affirmed, and their social structures are reproduced" (Heritage, 2001, p. 47). In terms of analysis, social interactions are examined in depth to see how social structures emerge. For example, the goals of the analysis of social interactions are how interactants construct their social and cultural identities (Brandt & Jenks, 2011), negotiate perspectives (Goodwin & Goodwin, 1990), and establish gender identities (Stokoe & Smithson, 2001).

Previous studies examine communication through a social-interaction lens that analyzes social practices and actions that people carry out and perform, and the findings are data driven or situated within the interactions. In addition, an understanding of social interactions has been used to inform language education (Wong, 2002), medical interaction (Gülich, 2003), and workplace support (Baker, Emmison, & Firth, 2005). The later part of this chapter consists of various contexts and social-interaction occurrences.

Social interaction in earlier studies: L2 interaction and interactional competence

Interactions are essential to social life, and interactional activities consist of non-institutional (greeting, joking, etc.) and institutional (doctor–patient interaction, workplace, etc.) events. When we interact, we use an "immense stock of sedimented social knowledge" (Hanks, 1996,

p. 238), which makes sense of the ways we speak in locally situated and culturally framed communications. In earlier studies, the notion of social interaction is used to understand empirical findings related to classroom discourses. A classroom is viewed as a social and linguistic context where second language acquisition occurs, and the interactional features, including teacher and student clarification or comprehension, are considered crucial for the second language acquisition process. Scholars believe that the types of classroom activities, such as decision-making or information exchange tasks, can influence (un)equal arrangement of interaction in the classroom (Pica, T., 1987).

Socially grounded investigations of L2 interactions have also focused on linguistic and cultural resources that learners draw from for their interactions. Interactional competence (IC) is grounded on the field of linguistic anthropology (Hymes, 1962, 1972). Hymes (1962) conceptualized language as a context-embedded social action, and he challenges generativists' accounts of linguistic competence and internal principles of the structural elements in a language system (Chomsky, 1965, 1996). He proposed "ethnography of speaking" to emphasize the socially constituted knowledge shared by group members to engage in their communities. Canale and Swain (1980) implemented Hymes's notion of communicative competence for language learning. By applying four elements – grammatical, sociolinguistic, strategic, and discourse competence – they developed an educational curriculum and evaluation.

Interactional competence is the ability to engage in interactions and accomplish meaningful social actions. This is also related to the management of social identities in diverse communication contexts; Hall and Doehler (2011) explained interactional competence as follows:

> IC, that is the context-specific constellations of expectations and dispositions about our social worlds that we draw on to investigate our way throughout interaction with others, implies the ability to mutually coordinate our actions. It includes knowledge of social-context-specific communicative events or activity types, their typical goals and trajectories of actions by which the goals are realized and the conventional behaviors by which participant roles and role relationships are accomplished.
>
> *(pp. 1–2)*

IC also includes the ability to recognize context-specific patterns and both linguistic and non-linguistic resources used to accomplish a range of actions.

Drawing on Hymes (1972), the dynamic understanding of IC and sociocultural understanding of interactions were on the rise in the 1990s. For example, Hall (1993, 1995, 1999) investigated interactive practices in language classroom contexts, which she defines as "socio-culturally conventionalized configurations of face-to-face interaction by which and within which group members communicate" (Hall, 1993, p. 146). She developed a framework to examine the communicative conventions constructed by the members in their social groups. Later, this model became developed by Young (2013) by proposing six elements: 1) rhetorical script, 2) register, 3) strategies for taking turns, 4) topic management, 5) participants' role and patterns of participation, and 6) boundary-signaling devices (e.g., transition).

Communicative competence was also accepted in the field of interlanguage pragmatics, which investigated different pragmatic language usage in diverse social contexts (Blum-Kulka, House, & Kasper, 1989; Kasper & Blum-Kulka, 1993). These attempts added a new dimension of communicative competence. However, the limitation of these approaches was also discussed in the later studies (McNamara & Roever, 2006; Young, 1999) in that communicative competence is considered static and focuses only on speaking ability and not the competence for interaction.

Sociocultural theory

One of the current approaches to second language acquisition (SLA) is to emphasize the social dimensions of language learning in diverse interactional ways. The sociocultural approach, for example, focuses on people's social and cognitive process in the contexts of various cultural activities and interactions (Lantolf, Poehner, & Swain, 2018; Lantolf, Thorne, & Poehner, 2015; Storch, 2017; Zuengler & Miller, 2006).

Vygotsky's (1986) sociocultural theory is one of the frameworks that SLA research is based on. Viewing development as a process that is socially mediated, Vygotsky considered social interaction as the fundamental element in cognitive development, and community plays a key role in meaning making. As Lantolf and Beckett's (2009) study and Lantolf et al.'s (2018) edited volume lay out, the central concepts of Vygotsky's sociocultural theory are zones of proximal development, private speech, internalization, mediation, and dynamic assessment. Learning occurs through social interaction with someone who is more skillful than the learner in the learner's zone of proximal development (ZPD). This zone is defined as the gap between what the learner can do alone and what the learner can do with the help of someone else. Through this collaborative dialogue, the learner understands, internalizes, and uses the information to regulate one's performance.

Studies focus on specific concepts within the sociocultural theory: private speech (de Guerrero, 2005; McCafferty, 2008; Swain, 2006), private speech and regulation (Ant´on & DiCamilla, 1998; Appel & Lantolf, 1994; Brooks & Donato, 1994; Centeno-Cort´es & Jim´enez-Jim´enez, 2004; Choi & Lantolf, 2008; Frawley & Lantolf, 1985; Lee, 2008; McCafferty, 1992), private speech and internalization (Pavlenko, 1997; Smith, 2007), the ZPD (Aljaafreh & Lantolf, 1994; Dunn & Lantolf, 1998; Kinginger, 2002; Nassaji & Swain, 2000; Ohta, 2000; Swain & Lapkin, 2002; van Lier, 2004), the ZPD and regulation (de Guerrero, & Villamil, 2000; DiCamilla & Ant´on, 1997; Donato, 1994; Thorne, 2003), and dynamic assessment (Lantolf & Poehner, 2004).

Brooks and Donato (1994) and Ohta (2000) discussed the use of private speech in collaborative tasks in L2 learning. Brooks and Donato (1994) focused on two-way information gap tasks and discussed the different functions of language in these tasks and how private speech helps with focusing on language resources. Ohta (2000) longitudinally examined an L2 classroom and explained how students use private speech to internalize the target language during the task. Donato (1994) also investigated learners' scaffolding in peer interactions and discussed how they mediate each other in their zones of proximal development, and De Guerrero and Villamil (2000) looked into L2 learners' scaffolding in peer revision in a writing class, revealing how interactions shaped the revision processes. L2 studies that focus on ZPD (Aljaafreh & Lantolf, 1994; Swain & Lapkin, 2002; Thorne, 2003) cover the negotiation of corrective feedback between learners and an expert (Aljaafreh & Lantolf, 1994), collaborative dialogues that reveal learners' ZPD allowing them to move forward with their learning (Swain & Lapkin, 2002), and the engagement in internet-mediated communication (Thorne, 2003).

In KSL, there are a few studies investigating diverse linguistic features in Korean by using sociocultural theory. Brown (2013) investigates Korean language learners' attitudes toward and uses of *oppa* (meaning older brother). The learners who used this term perceived it more positively in terms of affection. While being aware of the gender imbalance in the connotations of the term *oppa*, all participants except one used this term in limited contexts. Even without explicit instructions, less proficient learners can identify the connotations behind *oppa*. The author suggests that explicit instruction can provide a deeper sociohistorical context of the term.

The context of computer-mediated communication in classes has also been examined. Kim and Brown (2014) investigate how Korean language learners use address terms in computer-mediated communication to negotiate identities. An analysis of interactions and retrospective interviews suggests that, due to their low proficiency, they did not possess complete pragmatic competence in address terms. Nevertheless, computer-mediated communication and the use of address terms allowed these learners of Korean to switch their identities from learners to language users.

Kang and Pyun (2013) investigate L2 writing processes in regard to mediation strategies. Two Korean language learners' interviews, think-aloud protocols, and stimulated recall were collected. The analysis shows how the learner's situated context is relevant to writing strategies and mediation tools that one prefers. Learners' motivation, goals for L2 learning, and L2 proficiency were relevant factors. The learner with a career orientation used diverse strategies more frequently. The learner with a higher proficiency was better equipped to use mediating tools. Thus, it is important for teachers to understand students' sociocultural backgrounds in order to understand the students' use of strategies. Though there are several studies investigating Korean language learning within the sociocultural framework, we still need more diverse research on different types of learners considering most of the KSL studies were conducted in the language classes in college as well as diverse extra-institutional contexts. In the following section, social interaction in language socialization research will be discussed.

Social interaction and key constructs

Interaction is considered crucial in the studies that emphasize social aspects of language learning and language-use contexts. How social experience is being theorized in SLA research cannot be discussed without examining people's interactions. In this section, the major constructs related to social interaction in the scope of language socialization, the social-interactionist approach, and community of practices will be discussed.

The topics for language socialization are immense since any linguistic feature used by native speakers in daily interaction with novices may be studied as a potential socializing tool. As language socialization research's primary goal is to link the microanalytic examination of discourse to more general ethnographic accounts of the target language, researchers have focused on investigating natural conversational data between an expert and a novice (e.g., between parents and infants or children in the L1 home setting, or between teachers and students in the L1 or L2 school setting).

Since language socialization research emphasizes the importance of cross-linguistic studies, various languages have been examined (Byon, 2000). The topics include communicative style (Clancy, 1986), affective stance (Clancy, 1999; Suzuki, 1999), interactional routines (Nakamura, 1996), social relationship (Ervin-Tripp, 1988), status difference (Platt, 1986), language socialization through particular linguistic features (Cook, 1990, 1997; Platt, 1986; Suzuki, 1999), L1 socialization in a school setting (Cook, 1999), and L2 socialization in school settings (Kanagy, 1999; Ohta, 1994, 1999; Poole, 1992; Yoshimi, 1999). Watson-Gegeo and Nielsen (2003) explain the theory and method of language socialization, cognitive issues, and methodological strategies in language socialization. Further, they discuss the implications that language socialization can bring to SLA.

Language socialization (LS) research considers multiple levels of social dimensions, and it may be helpful to understand DFG. Recently, Duff (2019) reviewed Douglas Fir Group (DFG hereafter, 2016), which conceptualized factors influencing SLA through different macro (societal factors), meso (identity), andmicro (interaction or social action) levels and the interconnectedness of these three levels to understand the multifaceted nature of language learning and teaching. DFG (2016) placed language learning in real-world contexts rather than in the individual learners' minds. L2 learning is an ongoing process starting from the micro level in which each individual engages with others in multilingual contexts. The recurring contexts contribute to the establishment of multilingual repertoires. The contexts that the individuals are situated in are shaped at the meso level, such as institutions and communities. These communities and institutions are marked by economic or cultural conditions. Thus, they influence the types of social experiences that individuals can or cannot access. The macro level consists of ideological structures, including belief systems and values. These ideological structures shape and are shaped by the meso and micro levels. The three levels are mutually dependent.

This framework suggests two goals in language learning and teaching. First, it is important for the researchers and teachers to expand learners' multilingual repertoires so they can participate in a variety of social activities. Also, fostering learners' awareness of the meanings of the social actions as well as the dynamics of the actions is important. Achieving these goals entails the discussions of speech communities (Gumperz, 1968), discourse communities (Swales, 1990, pp. 21–32), and communities of practice (Lave & Wenger, 1991).

Duff (2019) explains the multiscale model and mentions, "both power and identity are negotiated and enacted or performed in social interactions at micro-interactional levels as well as in larger circulating discourses and institutional structures" (p. 9). With this view, an action, interaction, or event needs to be understood in relation to its broader sociocultural discourses and their contexts. For example, the diverse social interaction patterns were investigated in light of focal linguistic forms and practices (Burdelski & Howard, 2019; Duranti, Ochs, & Schieffelin, 2012).

The social-interactionist approach considers interactions situated in a certain context and brings various types of inputs and outputs as well as corrections, which are relevant to language development (Duff, 2019). One of the important concepts in LS is indexicality (Ochs & Schieffelin, 2017; Silverstein, 2003), which refers to the case when linguistic forms or cultural practices have salient meaning in a certain social context. "They point to (e.g., index) and may reproduce or transform structures and relationships beyond immediate interaction" (Duff, 2019, p. 12). This shows that LS research investigates selective linguistic signs or other elements of social and cultural significance, such as the notions of membership, affective stance, belonging, and participation. These notions are well explicated within the community of practice (CoP).

Participation and practice from CoP help to frame the process of how language learners and users become members of communities by taking part in various activities through a language medium. First, the notion of participation is defined in Wenger (1998) as follows:

> I will use the term participation to describe the social experience of living in the world in terms of membership in social communities and active involvement in social enterprises. Participation in this sense is both personal and social. It is a complex process that combines doing, talking, thinking, feeling, and belonging. It involves our whole person, including our bodies, minds, emotions, and social relations with the world.
> *(pp. 55–56)*

Participation is an active process. It does not refer to a simple act of engaging with people but an "encompassing procedure" of active involvement in the practice of communities and identity construction for individual participants – not only "what we do" but also "who we are" and "how we interpret what we do" (Wenger, 1998, p. 4). For example, the relations between parents and children or between workers and their boss are seen as mutually coconstructed. In addition, participation is much broader than engagement in practice. Participation is not something that can be turned on or turned off, but one's participation influences their experience and is not limited to particular contexts of their engagement.

Similarly, language learners or users interact in the group in a mutual way. They recognize the mutuality of their participation, and in this respect their participation becomes a source of shared identity. The findings from the CoP research present that participation is part of who they are, and it goes beyond specific activities in a community.

According to Wenger (1998), *practices* can be defined as social activities through interactions, views, and attitudes that members understand to be a way of participating in a community. Wenger's definition of practice within the framework of communities of practice is a helpful tool to understand the relation between individual doings and social ways of understanding individuals' practice. In particular, shared doings and shared understanding in Wenger's concepts are related to the shared sense of one's own or others' identities within the frames of a particular group that exist because the members have common interests and aims (Wenger, 1998). In this respect, shared practices are indicators of belonging and resources in building social relations. Community is more than a collection of people and practices, which is more than shared behaviors or shared ways of doing things through speech.

Wenger (1998) also explains the relations between participation and belonging. By proposing three different modes of belonging – engagement (involvement in negotiating meaning), imagination (creating images of the world and finding the connections through time and space from our experience), and alignment (coordinating the practice to fit to broader enterprises) – he describes a method of identity expansion through space and time in different ways. Joint enterprises are created and maintained through the shared and negotiable resource of practices. For example, in the interaction, the language learners' use of local words in their story structures is often repetitive and ritualized. These features frequently come into their interaction, and the participants make use of them as shared resources. Social participation entails meaning, practice, community, and identity and goes beyond the concept of simply "doing"; instead, as it is constructed within a CoP framework, the *practice* is "doing" within a particular historical and social context, and it offers structure and meaning to what they do (Wenger, 1998). This concept of "social practice" or "social interaction" thus offers us a way of understanding socially situated activities and grasping the complexity of the people's positionings. Based on these key constructs of CoP, how social interaction has been examined in diverse social contexts will be discussed in the following section.

Social interaction in diverse contexts

Family interaction

As a first locus of social interaction, a family is a significant context of language use and language socialization (Duff, 2015). Which language to learn as well as its maintenance and use (Hirsch & Lee, 2018) are crucial issues to a multilingual family. Family interaction has been investigated as a way of understanding how parents facilitate children's language and cognitive development (Blum-Kulka, 1997). In particular, interaction in immigrant families in a bilingual context has been shown to support development and maintenance of children's home language. These studies claim that parent–child interaction presents the immigrant parents' beliefs and planning for their children's language learning and use. In particular, the parents use different strategies to support their American-born children's development and maintenance of the home language. The parents' language use is the primary element in achieving children's bilingualism in immigrant contexts (Houwer, 2007; Kang, 2013). Kasuya (1998) has investigated the daily interaction found in English–Japanese families, where one parent's dominant language is English and the other parent's language is Japanese. Parents who speak different languages can play a significant role in language maintenance. Their discourse strategies can be a way in which children learn to make language decisions.

Aside from a small number of studies (Kang, 2013; Song, 2016b; Suh, 2020) that analyze the actual family interactions at home, the majority of the studies in this field employ questionnaires and qualitative interviews as the methodology in examining family interaction. However, recently, Wei and Hua (2019) called attention to the lack of mundane moments in family interactions. It is imperative to have more studies on family members' daily interactions in a wider range of contexts and diverse family types.

Korean American families are the sites where we can observe how family interactions are constructed. Studies on Korean–American bilingual families and their language use at home can contribute to the current efforts to bridge the two research domains of societal language policy and family interaction research paradigms (Cho, 2018; Cho, Song, & Lee, 2018; Kang, 2013; Song, 2012, 2019a; Song, 2016a, 2016b; Suh, 2020). Some strategies in interaction, including intervention (e.g., immediate feedback) and language use (e.g., consistent use of Korean and borrowing English expressions), are also suggested by empirical investigations of Korean American families (Kang, 2013). Other studies focus on interaction at home by analyzing specific linguistic features found in family interaction. For instance, Song's (2016b) study investigates the nature of translanguaging practices in Korean bilingual children and their families in home literacy events. Her findings highlight that translanguaging serves as a resource to clarify, negotiate, and coconstruct subtle meanings. For example, the parents often pronounced English words with Korean phonemes (pronouncing them in a way that the Korean oral language affords) or trans-enunciated to clearly convey meanings.

Song (2019a) investigated code-switching and language socialization at home in the case of a Korean–English bilingual child's language practices. She investigates the changes in tones of voice and speech acts in the child's code-switching. The finding shows this transformation is impacted by the child's different stances and persona in different languages.

Clancy (1989) conducted cross-linguistic research on child language acquisition and investigated the language socialization of two young Korean children's learning of *wh*-questions. This study analyzed the interactive and pragmatic functions of *wh*-questions within the model of language socialization. The findings of this study present linguistic forms and functions as a tool to transmit social knowledge, which is interrelated to the role of culture, family, and interactions in the family.

In another study, Suh (2020) investigates language socialization practice by analyzing the use of directives and honorifics in their interaction. The author presents three Korean American families' use of honorifics as a discourse strategy for signaling politeness and negotiation. In addition to parent–child interaction examined in Suh (2020), Cho (2018) investigated Korean siblings' interaction and language socialization process. A seven-year-old Korean–English bilingual girl and her three-year-old sister's interaction was observed over the year and analyzed through a language socialization perspective. In their interaction, the Korean family hierarchy and asymmetrical changes in power were found. This study highlights the bidirectionality of sibling socialization processes and their bilingual and bicultural development through the interaction. The findings of this study challenge the Piagetian and Vygotskian perspectives that an asymmetry of knowledge exists, but authority does not lead to ideal learning (Tudge & Rogoff, 1989). Overall, the in-depth analyses of the family interactions show that authority, ideology, and family culture play a crucial role in the development of children's bi/multilingualism.

Classroom interactions

Though a language classroom is the most widely discussed context for analyzing learners' social interaction, the scope of investigation of social interaction has been somewhat limited to teachers' and students' face-to-face communication (Kim & Lee, 2010; Young, 1999). Zuengler and Cole (2005) provide a comprehensive review of second-language socialization in educational settings (Duff, 1996, 2002; Duff & Early, 1999; Harklau, 2003; He, 2003; Kanagy, 1999; Moore, 1999; Watson-Gegeo, 1992). In particular, Sert (2015) devotes a chapter to social interaction and L2 classrooms. L2 classroom discourse is seen as a representation of socio-interactional practices in which teaching and learning a new language is portrayed through the use of language-in-interaction. According to Kim and Lee (2010), in the past, sociolinguistic issues and social interaction in the classroom had not been much explored in the KSL curriculum. Previous studies on social interaction in the classroom have focused on the effectiveness of instruction and sociolinguistic knowledge, such as honorifics, address terms, and dialects. Park (2012) examines teachers' use of intimate style when interacting with their students in KSL classrooms. This intimate style of interaction is said to create a feeling of solidarity. It also provides learners a chance to be exposed to this particular style.

Park (2016) suggests the importance of the teacher's rapport building in Korean within a foreign language classroom. This study examines the teacher's strategic language use for the purpose of rapport building in the language classroom, and the conversation analysis of classroom interaction demonstrates that the teacher shifts and negotiates different footings, such as formal or informal frames, to build a positive learning environment. Thorough analysis of interaction in the classroom as a social space ascertains the importance of the teacher's role in the language classroom.

Byon (2006) analyzes teacher–student interactions in two American college-level KSL classes in light of language socialization perspectives. The findings of this study illustrate that teacher– student interactions are consistent with hierarchism (Byon, 2004; Sohn, 1986), which is one of the major cognitive value orientations of Korean culture. The result of this study contrasts with English as a second language settings (Poole, 1992) in which English teachers try to lessen the status differences between themselves and students. Byon (2000) scrutinized politeness markers, -*yo* polite ending in the Korean classes with sociolinguistic perspectives. Analyzing the teacher–student's spontaneous conversations with a special focus on teacher-talk, the paper argues that "-*yo*" is the socialization tool, which can help the students acknowledge the social meanings of the marker and the different patterns in the Korean language.

More recently, Ahn (2020) investigated preschoolers' uses of honorifics and analyzed children's peer conflict in the interaction. The indexical meanings of honorifics, including authoritative and affective stances were analyzed. This study shows that the participating children creatively and strategically use honorifics to negotiate and achieve their interactional goals.

In addition to the research on teachers' or students' use of particular linguistic features, classroom research with instructional perspectives, particularly collaborative classroom tasks, need to be considered. For example, Kim and McDonough (2008) investigated Korean as a second language (KSL) learners' ways of resolving linguistic issues during collaboration with interlocutors from different proficiency levels. The findings of this study show that the collaborative dialogue with advanced interlocutors contained significantly more lexical language-related episodes (LREs) and correctly resolved LREs. In terms of their patterns of interaction, the learners showed different pair dynamics when collaborating with interlocutors from different proficiency levels. Similarly, Kim, Lee, and Kim (2017) illustrate Korean heritage learners and non-heritage learners' interactions during the collaborative writing tasks in the KSL classroom. This study finds that both groups developed their receptive and productive knowledge of Korean honorifics over time and developed a positive attitude toward the collaborative tasks through interaction.

The learners' interaction in advanced-level classes was also examined. Lee-Smith (2019), in her community-based classroom project designed for learning outside of the language classroom, introduced the Junior-and-Mentor project. She outlined the advantages of integrating communities and language instructions. This project focuses on the significance of community-based learning. In the next section, I will turn to research on social interactions in more diverse Korean communities.

Korean communities: schools and churches

The majority of the studies on heritage language education and classroom interaction are theoretically grounded on language socialization. Community-based heritage language schools have been constructively explored to learn and teach culturally and linguistically appropriate norms in classroom interactions (Byon, 2004; He, 2003; Lo, 2009; Poole, 1992). These studies highlight the complexities in learners' identity construction and negotiation as heritage language learners as well as the intricate process of teaching and learning cultural norms in the classroom.

There have been several studies emphasizing that the medium of instruction from the school impacts the students' language selection and interactional styles. This became a salient issue in predominantly bilingual or multilingual contexts. Arai, Ogoshi, Sun, and Li (2020) recently investigated the language use of Koreans in China. Through a language socialization lens, the participants' language choices were dissimilar between different regions. The findings of this study show that Koreans in China used a diverse range of language in their interactions depending on regions and genders.

Song (2019b) investigated a Korean teacher's use of the Korean pronoun, *wuli* meaning "we" in her heritage language classroom and examined stances evoked by the teacher's language use. From a language socialization perspective, this study shows that the use of *wuli* has several social functions: evoking a stance of solidarity between the teacher and students, mitigating face-threatening acts of imperatives and encouraging the students' active engagement. The findings demonstrate that the teacher's contrasting stances socialize the students into pedagogically and culturally appropriate practices. In other Korean heritage school contexts in the United States, Kim and Lee (2010) explored children's (pre-K) naming practices and how this practice reflects the process of developing a sense of self. This study highlights the importance of researching young children's interaction and linguistic practices in that observations of the children's naming practices tells us about their self-conception development and ways of negotiation.

Similar to Lo (2009), who investigated "respect" as an interactional achievement in the context of a Korean-American heritage language school, Byon (2003) examined the politeness of Korean and the teachers' use of *-yo*, a Korean polite ending marker. This study views teacher's talk as a socializing tool, and the findings suggest that teachers' use of *-yo* does not indicate politeness toward their students. It explicitly and implicitly teaches the meaning of *-yo* to the students, and they are socialized to express respect to a person who is higher in (social) status or in public contexts. Furthermore, heritage language learners' code-switching and code-mixing practices in the context of Korean Sunday school were researched (Shin, 2010). Among the interactional functions of code-switching, its role as a contextualization cue (Gumperz, 1982), signaling the changing of footing and directives in the interaction were found to be prominent indicators.

Furthermore, the relationship between social interactions and identities was analyzed. Korean–English bilinguals' ways of shaping their ethnic identities through interactions was investigated in Yun (2008). She examines children's naturally occurring interaction in a Korean church meeting and examines role play within the framework of language socialization. Her study demonstrates how the children's linguistic features were pragmatically used to set up the context of role play and to jointly construct their identities by analyzing the specific linguistic features, such as metacommunicative verbs, deictic, and code-switching. Park (2011, 2013) investigates ethnic churches in Canada. For the church to play a role in preserving the heritage language among the Korean immigrant youths, it needs to maintain a close partnership with students, teachers, and pastors. The students maintain their heritage language through interaction and participation in activities. In addition, No (2011) investigated the Korean immigrant children's language socialization in two languages in the school contexts. This descriptive case study explores Korean immigrant children in the United States both in a Korean language school and a local public school. Through analyzing the participants' language use and interaction, this study highlights the contrast between learning English in an American school culture and learning heritage language and culture in a Korean community school. Similarly, Cho (2016) investigates how Korean–English bilingual children's language socialization occurs differently in informal (church Sunday School) and formal academic contexts (public school), and how the constructions of multilingual competencies and identities through active involvement in one another's socialization process are built. The findings of this study parallel Toohey (1998), who argues the importance of peer interaction and communication for children's development and socialization in school. In her study, various types of cooperation were found, such as asking questions, giving compliments, and providing constructive comments, which eventually led to teaching each other socially appropriate behaviors.

In sum, though the various studies have different research foci, these studies within the language socialization framework focus on Korean–English interactions in Korean communities, Korean language schools, and Korean churches. These studies explore different linguistic features (e.g., *wuli*, code-switching), different age groups (beginning from pre-K), and different practices (e.g., naming, role play) to show the importance of investigating social interaction of bi/multilingual speakers. These speakers are mostly second-generation Korean Americans within particular ethnic or cultural communities, and culture plays a key role in influencing their interactions and reconfiguring language ideologies.

Pedagogical implication and future direction

Examining the learners' interaction closely is not only to understand what the learners learn but also how they learn and use languages they learned. Despite the variety of approaches to social interaction in different fields, the fundamental importance of investigating social interaction is to view language learners as language users who utilize different linguistic and cultural resources to effectively communicate. This will help us create a holistic way of understanding language learners and their language use in diverse social contexts.

As DFG (2016) conceptualized language learning, interaction or social action are a micro-level phenomenon, which can be connected to learners' identities and further be extended to the ideological structure or societal factors. Understanding social interaction helps us understand a multifaceted and multiscaled nature of language use and teaching. Analyzing interaction also contributes to our understanding of the particular types of language learners (e.g., heritage language learners) or learning contexts (e.g., study abroad contexts).

Increasing mobility has brought diverse cultural, linguistic, and educational experiences and resources to language learners in diverse contexts, and many of them have dissimilar backgrounds in terms of motivation and linguistic/cultural practices. In consideration of this situation, the investigation of language learning and use through their social interaction is a way of understanding the learners, their language learning and maintenance, and their wide-ranging needs.

In Wang's (2003) study on synthesizing the previous KSL studies, interaction is only considered within the field of sociolinguistics, discourse, and pragmatics: the main topics are how to learn and teach (authentic) conversation (Park, 1997); how to teach interactive features with sociopragmatic features in Korean (e.g., *ney*, Yuen, 2001), particularly honorifics (Byon, 2000); how to develop interactive teaching methods; and teachers' discourse patterns (Lee, 2002). As seen in these studies, data-driven empirical studies focusing solely on interaction are still scarce in the field of KSL contexts. I would highlight that social interaction research topics have been extensively investigated in previous/existing L2 social interaction studies but have not been examined in the KSL field yet.

More empirical studies on social interaction in KSL studies are needed, and the investigation can be extended both to the diverse populations and distinct contexts. For example, despite the importance of researching social interaction in study abroad (Nam, 2018), except for Lee, Kim, and Choi (2020), the cases of learners of Korean are underexplored. Previous study abroad (SA) studies explored how L2 students interact within their SA environments (Duff, 2007; Hwang, 2009; Tanaka, 2007; Tanaka & Ellis, 2003; Yang & Kim, 2011), but most of them investigated how learners of English socialize into their CoP at a local level in the host country.

As the language learners' background and motivation becomes diverse, learners of Korean as their third or additional language and their social interactions need to receive more attention. Moreover, more diverse and underexplored social contexts, such as workplaces or medical contexts, should be attentively examined to observe how learners of Korean achieve their daily interactional goals. Since the traditional language socialization theory reminds us that a person who is a novice in one situation can be an expert in another situation (Ochs & Schieffelin, 2012), it is crucial to understand context-by-context social interaction.

In particular, due to the growing number of K–12 schools adopting Korean as their language subject or the increasing number of dual-language immersion programs in the United States, further investigations on how the social interaction both in institutional contexts and outside educational contexts occurs and how it constitutes and promotes the language learning and use are needed. Furthermore, the unique and specific characteristics of the social interactions in Korean, which include the honorifics that mark the interlocutors' power and solidarity (Sohn, 2001), which are less likely to happen in other languages and cultures, should receive more attention. In this sense, cross-linguistic and cross-cultural investigation of social interaction is necessary. Lastly, given the increasing importance of language learning and use in an online context, more attention to social interaction and language learning and use in the virtual world, such as interactions in chat rooms and social media, is timely and fundamental to understand how KSL learners construct their social reality in virtual contexts.

References

Ahn, J. (2020). Honorifics and peer conflict in Korean children's language socialization. *Linguistics and Education, 59*, 100736. https://doi.org/10.1016/j.linged.2019.05.002

Aljaafreh, A., & Lantolf, J. P. (1994). Negative feedback as regulation and second language learning in the zone of proximal development. *The Modern Language Journal, 78*, 465–483.

Antón, M., & DiCamilla, F. J. (1998). Socio-cognitive functions of L1 collaborative interaction in the L2 classroom. *The Canadian Modern Language Review, 54*, 314–342.

Appel, G., & Lantolf, J. P. (1994). Speaking as mediation: A study of L1 and L2 text recall tasks. *The Modern Language Journal, 78*, 437–452.

Arai, Y., Ogoshi, N., Sun, L., & Li, D. (2020). A sociolinguistic study of Koreans in China: The 'language socialization' of Koreans in China. アジア・アフリカの言語と言語学 *[Asian and African Languages and Linguistics], 14*, 29–44.

Austin, J. (1962). *How to do things with words*. Cambridge, MA: Harvard University Press.

Baker, C. D., Emmison, M., & Firth, A. (Eds.). (2005). *Calling for help: Language and social interaction in telephone helplines*. Amsterdam and Philadelphia: John Benjamins Publishing Company.

Blum-Kulka, S. (1997). *Dinner talk: Cultural patterns of sociability and socialization in family discourse*. Mahwah, NJ: Erlbaum.

Blum-Kulka, S., House, J., & Kasper, G. (Eds.). (1989). *Cross-cultural pragmatics: Requests and apologies*. Orwood, NJ: Albex.

Brandt, A., & Jenks, C. (2011). 'Is it okay to eat a dog in Korea . . . like China?': Assumptions of national food-eating practices in intercultural interaction. *Language and Intercultural Communication, 11*(1), 41–58.

Brooks, F. B., & Donato, R. (1994). Vygotskyan approaches to understanding foreign language learner discourse during communicative tasks. *Hispania, 77*, 262–274.

Brown, L. (2013). "Oppa, Hold My Purse:" A sociocultural study of identity and indexicality in the perception and use of Oppa 'older brother' by second language learners. *The Korean Language in America, 18*, 1–22.

Burdelski, M., & Howard, K. M. (Eds.). (2019). *Language socialization in classrooms: Culture, interaction and language development*. Cambridge: Cambridge University Press.

Byon, A. S. (2000). The analysis of yo 'the politeness marker in Korean': From language socialization point of view. *The Korean Language in America, 4*, 125–140.

Byon, A. S. (2003). Language socialisation and Korean as a heritage language: A study of Hawaiian classrooms. *Language Culture and Curriculum, 16*(3), 269–283.

Byon, A. S. (2004). Learning linguistic politeness. *Applied Language Learning, 14*(1), 37–62.

Byon, A. S. (2006). Language socialization in Korean-as-a-foreign-language classrooms. *Bilingual Research Journal, 30*(2), 265–291. https://doi.org/10.1080/15235882.2006.10162877

Canale, M., & Swain, M. (1980). Theoretical bases of communicative approaches to second language teaching and testing. *Applied Linguistics, 1*, 1–47.

Centeno-Cortés, B., & Jiménez-Jiménez, A. (2004). Problem-solving tasks in a foreign language: The importance of the L1 in private verbal thinking. *International Journal of Applied Linguistics, 14*, 7–35.

Cho, H. (2016). Formal and informal academic language socialization of a bilingual child. *International Journal of Bilingual Education and Bilingualism, 19*(4), 387–407. https://doi.org/10.1080/13670050.2014.993303

Cho, H. (2018). Korean–English bilingual sibling interactions and socialization. *Linguistics and Education, 45*, 31–39.

Cho, H., Song, K., & Lee, J.-Y. (2018). Korean immigrant parents' involvement in children's biliteracy development in the U.S. context. In G. Onchwari & J. Keengwe (Eds.), *Handbook of research on pedagogies and cultural considerations for young English language learners* (pp. 344–359). Hershey, PA: IGI Global. https://doi.org/10.4018/978-1-5225-3955-1

Choi, S., & Lantolf, J. P. (2008). Representation and embodiment of meaning in L2 communication: Motion events in the speech and gesture of advanced L2 Korean and L2 English speakers. *Studies in Second Language Acquisition, 30*, 191–224.

Chomsky, N. (1965). *Aspects of the theory of syntax*. Cambridge, MA: MIT Press.

Chomsky, N. (1996). *World orders, old and new*. New York: Columbia University Press.

Clancy, P. M. (1986). The acquisition of communicative style in Japanese. In B. Schieffelin & E. Ochs (Eds.), *Language socialization across cultures* (pp. 213–250). Cambridge: Cambridge University Press.

Clancy, P. M. (1989). A case study in language socialization: Korean wh-questions. *Discourse Processes, 12*(2), 169–191. https://doi.org/10.1080/01638538909544725

Clancy, P. M. (1999). The socialization of affect in Japanese mother-child conversation. *Journal of Pragmatics, 31*, 1397–1421.

Cook, H. M. (1990). The role of the Japanese sentence-final particle no in the socialization of children. *Multilingua, 9*, 377–395.

Cook, H. M. (1997). The role of the Japanese masu form in caregiver–child conversation. *Journal of Pragmatics, 28*, 695–718.

Cook, H. M. (1999). Situational meanings of Japanese social deixis: The mixed use of the masu and plain forms. *Journal of Linguistic Anthropology, 8*(1–2), 87–110.

de Guerrero, M. C. M. (2005). *Inner speech-L2: Thinking words in a second language*. New York: Springer.

de Guerrero, M. C. M., & Villamil, O. (2000). Activating the ZPD: Mutual scaffolding in L2 peer revision. *The Modern Language Journal, 84*, 51–68.

DiCamilla, F. J., & Antón, M. (1997). The function of repetition in the collaborative discourse of L2 learners: A Vygotskian perspective. *The Canadian Modern Language Review, 53*, 609–633.

Donato, R. (1994). Collective scaffolding in second language learning. In J. P. Lantolf & G. Appel (Eds.), *Vygotskian approaches to second language research* (pp 33–56). Norwood, NJ: Ablex.

Douglas Fir Group. (2016). A transdisciplinary framework for SLA in a multilingual world. *Modern Language Journal, 100*(Supplement 2016), 19–47.

Duff, P. A. (1996). Different languages, different practices: Socialization of discourse competence in dual-language school classrooms in Hungary. In K. M. Bailey & D. Nunan (Eds.), *Voices from the classroom: Qualitative research in second language education* (pp. 407–433). Cambridge, UK: Cambridge University Press.

Duff, P. A. (2002). The discursive co-construction of knowledge, identity and difference: An ethnography of communication in the high school mainstream. *Applied Linguistics, 23*(3), 289–322.

Duff, P. A. (2007). Second language socialization as sociocultural theory: Insights and issues. *Language Teaching, 40*(4), 309–319.

Duff, P. A. (2015). Transnationalism, multilingualism, and identity. *Annual Review of Applied Linguistics, 35*, 57–80.

Duff, P. A. (2019). Social dimensions and processes in second language acquisition: Multilingual socialization in transnational contexts. *The Modern Language Journal, 19*, 2–22.

Duff, P. A., & Early, M. (1999, March). Language socialization in perspective: Classroom discourse in high school humanities courses. In *Paper presented at the American Association for Applied Linguistics conference*. Stanford, CT.

Dunn, W., & Lantolf, J. P. (1998). Vygotsky's zone of proximal development and Krashen's i + 1: Incommensurable constructs; incommensurable theories. *Language Learning, 48*, 411–442.

Duranti, A., Ochs, E., & Schieffelin, B. (Eds.). (2012). *The handbook of language socialization*. Malden, MA: Wiley-Blackwell.

Ervin-Tripp, S. (1988). The learning of social style marking and honorifics. In *Paper presented at the honorifics conference*. Portland, OR.

Fitch, K. L., & Sanders, R. E. (2005). *Handbook of language and social interaction*. Mahwah, NJ: Lawrence Erlbaum.

Frawley, W., & Lantolf, J. P. (1985). Second language discourse: A Vygotskyan perspective. *Applied Linguistics, 6*, 19–44.

Goodwin, C., & Goodwin, M. H. (1990). Interstitial argument. In A. Grimshaw (Eds.), *Conflict talk* (pp. 85–117). Cambridge: Cambridge University Press.

Gülich, E. (2003). Conversational techniques used in transferring knowledge between medical experts and non-experts. *Discourse Studies, 5*(2), 235–263.

Gumperz, J. J. (1968). Types of speech community. *Readings in the Sociology of Language, 460*, 472.

Gumperz, J. J. (1982). *Discourse strategies*. Cambridge: Cambridge University Press.

Hall, J. K. (1993). The role of oral practices in the accomplishment of our everyday lives: The sociocultural dimension of interaction with implications for the learning of another language. *Applied Linguistics, 14*(2), 145–166. https://doi.org/10.1093/applin/14.2.145

Hall, J. K. (1995). "Aw, man, where you goin'?": Classroom interaction and the development of l2 interactional competence. *Issues in Applied Linguistics, 6*(2), 37–62.

Hall, J. K. (1999). A prosaics of interaction: The development of interactional competence in another language. In E. Hinkel (Ed.), *Culture in second language teaching and learning*. Cambridge: Cambridge University Press.

Hall, J. K., & Doehler, P. (2011). L2 interactional competence and development. In J. K. Hall, J. Hellermann, & S. P. Doehler (Eds.), *L2 Interactional competence and development* (pp. 1–15). Clevedon, UK: Multilingual Matters.

Hanks, W. (1996). *Language and communicative practices*. Boulder: Westview Press.

Harklau, L. (2003). Representational practices and multi-modal communication in US high schools: Implications for adolescent immigrants. In R. Bayley & S. Schecter (Eds.), *Language socialization in bilingual and multilingual societies* (pp. 83–97). Clevedon, UK: Multilingual Matters.

He, A. W. (2003). Novices and their speech roles in Chinese heritage language classes. In R. Bayley & S. Schecter (Eds.), *Language socialization in bilingual and multilingual societies* (pp. 128–146). Clevedon, UK: Multilingual Matters.

Heritage, J. (2001). Goffman, Garfinkel, and conversation analysis. In M. Wetherall, S. Taylor, & S. J. Yates (Eds.), *Discourse theory and practice* (pp. 47–56). London: Sage.

Hirsch, T., & Lee, J. S. (2018). Understanding the complexities of transnational family language policy. *Journal of Multilingual and Multicultural Development*, *39*(10), 882–894.

Houwer, A. D. (2007). Parental language input patterns and children's bilingual use. *Applied Psycholinguistics*, *28*(3), 411–424.

Hwang, S. (2009). A comparative study of English learning contexts home and abroad: Are there any communicative situations?. *Korean Journal of English Language and Linguistics*, *9*, 31–59.

Hymes, D. (1962). The ethnography of speaking. In T. Gladwin & W. C. Sturtevant (Eds.), *Anthropology and human behavior*. Washington, DC: Anthropology Society of Washington.

Hymes, D. (1972). Models of the interaction of language and social life. In J. J. Gumperz & D. Hymes (Eds.), *Directions in sociolinguistics: The ethnography of communication* (pp. 35–71). New York: Holt, Rinehart, & Winston.

Jenks, C. J. (2014). *Social interaction in second language chat rooms*. Edinburgh: Edinburgh University Press.

Kanagy, R. (1999). The socialization of Japanese immersion kindergartners through interactional routines. *Journal of Pragmatics*, *31*, 1467–1492.

Kang, H.-S. (2013). Korean-immigrant parents' support of their American-born children's development and maintenance of the home language. *Early Childhood Education Journal*, *41*, 431–438.

Kang, Y.-S., & Pyun, D. O. (2013). Mediation strategies in L2 writing processes: A case study of two Korean language learners, Language, *Culture and Curriculum*, *26*(1), 52–67.

Kasper, G., & Blum-Kulka, S. (Eds.). (1993). *Interlanguage pragmatics*. New York: Oxford University Press.

Kasuya, H. (1998). Determinants of language choice in bilingual children: The role of input. *International Journal of Bilingualism*, *2*(3), 327–346.

Kim, E. Y. A., & Brown, L. (2014). Negotiating pragmatic competence in computer mediated communication: The case of Korean address terms. *CALICO Journal*, *31*(3), 264–284.

Kim, J., & Lee, K. (2010). "What's your name?": Names, Naming practices, and contextualized selves of young Korean American children. *Journal of Research in Childhood Education*, *25*, 211–227.

Kim, M., Lee, H., & Kim, Y. (2017). Learning of Korean honorifics through collaborative tasks: Comparing heritage and non-heritage speakers. In N. Taguchi & Y. Kim (Eds.), *Pragmatics from a task-based language teaching perspective*. TBLT Series. Amsterdam and Philadelphia: John Benjamins Publishing Company.

Kim, Y., & McDonough, K. (2008). The effect of interlocutor proficiency on the collaborative dialogue between Korean as a second language learners. *Language Teaching Research*, *12*(2), 211–234.

Kinginger, C. (2002). Defining the zone of proximal development in US foreign language education, *Applied Linguistics*, *23*, 240–261.

Lantolf, J. P., & Beckett, T. G. (2009). Sociocultural theory and second language acquisition. *Language Teaching*, *42*(4), 459–475.

Lantolf, J. P., & Poehner, M. E. (2004). Dynamic assessment of L2 development: Bringing the past into the future. *Journal of Applied Linguistics*, *1*, 49–72.

Lantolf, J. P., Poehner, M. E., & Swain, M. (Eds.). (2018). *The Routledge handbook of sociocultural theory and second language development*. Oxon and New York: Routledge.

Lantolf, J., Thorne, S. L., & Poehner, M. (2015). Sociocultural theory and second language development. In B. van Patten & J. Williams (Eds.), *Theories in second language acquisition* (pp. 207–226). Oxon and New York: Routledge.

Lave, J., & Wenger, E. (1991). *Situated learning: Legitimate peripheral participation*. Cambridge: Cambridge University Press.

Lee, D.-E. (2002). A Study of the language of evaluation: An analysis of Korean language teachers' discourse patterns. *The Korean Language in America*, *7*, 223–238.

Lee, H., Kim, Y., & Choi, B. (2020). "Koreans studying Korean in Korea?": Study abroad and identities in the case of 1.5 generation of Korean-American students. *Applied Linguistics Review*.

Lee, J. (2008). Gesture and private speech in second language acquisition. *Studies in Second Language Acquisition*, *30*, 169–190.

Lee-Smith, A. (2019). Linking language learning with community: A community-based learning project for advanced Korean courses. *The Korean Language in America*, *22*(2), 167–189.

Lo, A. (2009). Lessons about respect and affect in a Korean heritage language school. *Linguistics and Education*, *20*, 217–234.

McCafferty, S. G. (1992). The use of private speech by adult second language learners: A cross-cultural study. *The Modern Language Journal*, *76*, 179–189.

McCafferty, S. G. (2008). Material foundations for second language acquisition: Gesture, metaphor, and internalization. In S. G. McCaffery & G. Stam (Eds.), *Gesture: Second language acquisition and classroom research* (pp 47–65). Oxon and New York: Routledge.

McNamara, T., & Roever, C. (2006). *Language testing: The social dimension*. Malden, MA: Blackwell.

Moore, L. C. (1999). Language socialization research and French language education in Africa: A Cameroonian case study. *Canadian Modern Language Review*, *56*(2), 329–350.

Nakamura, K. (1996). The use of polite language by Japanese preschool children. In D. I. Slobin, J. Gerhardt, A. Kyratzis, & Guo, J. (Eds.), *Social interaction, social context, and language: Essays in honor of Susan Ervin-Tripp* (pp. 235–250). Mahwah, NJ: Lawrence Erlbaum Associates.

Nam, M. (2018). Study-abroad experiences of two South Korean undergraduate students in an English-speaking and a non-English-speaking country. *The Asia-Pacific Education Researcher*, *27*(3), 177–185. https://doi.org/10.1007/s40299-018-0376-3

Nassaji, H., & Swain, M. (2000). A Vygotskian perspective on corrective feedback in L2: The effect of random versus negotiated help on the learning of English articles. *Language Awareness*, *1*, 34–52.

No, S.-H. (2011). *Language socialization in two languages, schoolings, and cultures: A descriptive qualitative case study of Korean immigrant children* [Doctoral dissertation, University of Iowa]. https://doi.org/10.17077/etd.5j3m9apx.

Ochs, E., & Schieffelin, B. B. (2012). The theory of language socialization. In A. Duranti, E. Ochs, & B. B. Schieffelin (Eds.), *The handbook of language socialization* (pp. 1–21). West Sussex: Blackwell.

Ochs, E., & Schieffelin, B. B. (2017). Language socialization: An historical overview. In P. Duff & S. May (Eds.), *Language socialization: Encyclopedia of language and education* (3rd ed., pp. 3–16). Cham, Switzerland: Springer.

Ohta, A. S. (1994). Socializing the expression of affect: An overview of affective particle use in the Japanese as a foreign language classroom. *Applied Linguistics*, *5*, 303–325.

Ohta, A. S. (1999). Interactional routines and the socialization of interactional style in adult learners of Japanese. *Journal of Pragmatics*, *31*, 1493–1512.

Ohta, A. S. (2000). Rethinking interaction in SLA: Developmentally appropriate assistance in the zone of proximal development and the acquisition of L2 grammar. In J. P. Lantolf (Ed.), *Sociocultural theory and second language learning* (pp. 51–78). Oxford: Oxford University Press.

Park, M. Y. (2012). Teachers' use of the intimate speech style in the Korean language classroom. *The Korean Language in America*, *17*, 55–83.

Park, M. Y. (2016). Integrating rapport-building into language instruction: A study of Korean foreign language classes. *Classroom Discourse*, *7*(2), 109–130. https://doi.org/10.1080/19463014.2015.1116103

Park, S. M. (2011). The role of ethnic religious community institutions in the intergenerational transmission of Korean among immigrant students in Montreal. *Language, Culture and Curriculum*, *24*(2), 195–206.

Park, S. M. (2013). Maintenance of Korean as a heritage language: A case study of one Korean ethnic church in Canada. *Korean Journal of Applied Linguistics*, *29*(4), 139–170.

Park, Y.-Y. (1997). Teaching authentic conversation: How to incorporate discourse into teaching. *The Korean Language in America*, *2*, 27–37.

Pavlenko, A. (1997). *Bilingualism and cognition* [Ph.D. dissertation], Cornell University.

Pica, T. (1987). Second language acquisition, social interaction, and the classroom. *Applied Linguistics*, *8*(1), 3–21. https://doi.org/10.1093/applin/8.1.3

Platt, M. (1986). Social norms and lexical acquisition: A study of deictic verbs in Samoan child language. In B. Schieffelin & E. Ochs (Eds.), *Language socialization across cultures* (pp. 127–152). Cambridge: Cambridge University Press.

Poole, D. (1992). Language socialization in the second language classroom. *Language Learning*, *42*(4), 593–616.

Reddy, M. J. (1979). The conduit metaphor: A cast of frame conflict in our language about language. In A. Ortony (Ed.), *Metaphor and thought* (pp. 284–324). Cambridge: Cambridge University Press.

Sanders, R. E. (2005). Introduction: LSI as subject matter and as multidisciplinary confederation. In K. L. Fitch & R. E. Sanders (Eds.), *Handbook of language and social interaction* (pp 1–14). Mahwah, NJ: Lawrence Erlbaum.

Schegloff, E. A. (1992). Repair after next turn: The last structurally provided for place for the defense of intersubjectivity in conversation. *American Journal of Sociology*, *95*(5), 1295–1345.

Sert, O. (2015). *Social interaction and L2 classroom discourse*. Edinburgh: Edinburgh University Press.

Shin, S. (2010). The functions of code-switching in a Korean Sunday school. *Heritage Language Journal*, *7*(1), 91–116.

Silverstein, M. (2003). Indexical order and the dialectics of sociolinguistic life. *Language and Communication*, *23*, 193–229.

Smith, H. (2007). The social and private worlds of speech: Speech for inter- and intra-mental activity. *The Modern Language Journal*, *91*, 341–356.

Sohn, H.-M. (1986). *Linguistic expeditions*. Seoul, Korea: Hanshin.

Sohn, H.-M. (2001). *The Korean language*. Cambridge: Cambridge University Press.

Song, J. (2012). The struggle over class, identity, and language: A case study of South Korean transnational families. *Journal of Sociolinguistics*, *16*(2), 201–217.

Song, J. (2019a). Language socialization and code-switching: A case study of a Korean – English bilingual child in a Korean transnational family. *International Journal of Bilingual Education and Bilingualism*, *22*(2), 91–106. https://doi.org/10.1080/13670050.2016.1231165

Song, J. (2019b). Wuli and stance in a Korean heritage language classroom: A language socialization perspective. *Linguistics and Education*, *51*, 12–19.

Song, K. (2016a). Nurturing young children's biliteracy development: A Korean family's hybrid literacy practices at home. *Language Arts*, *93*(5), 341–353.

Song, K. (2016b). "Okay I will say in Korean and then in American": Translanguaging practices in bilingual homes. *Journal of Early Childhood Literacy*, *16*(1), 84–106.

Stokoe, E. H., & Smithson, J. (2001). Making gender relevant: Conversation analysis and gender categories in interaction. *Discourse & Society*, *12*(2), 243–269.

Storch, N. (2017). Sociocultural theory in the L2classroom. In S. Loewen & M. Sato (Eds.), *The Routledge handbook of instructed second language acquisition* (pp. 69–83). Oxon and New York: Routledge.

Suh, S. (2020). An examination of the language socialization practices Korean American families through honorifics. *Bilingual Research Journal*, *43*(1), 6–31. https://doi.org/10.1080/15235882.2020.1713922

Suzuki, R. (1999). Language socialization through morphology: The affective suffix -CHAU in Japanese. *Journal of Pragmatics*, *31*(11), 1423–1441.

Swain, M. (2006). Verbal protocols: What does it mean for research to use speaking as a data collection tool? In M. Chaloub-Deville, C. A. Chapelle, & P. Duff (Eds.), *Inference and generalizability in applied linguistics: Multiple research perspectives* (pp. 97–113). Amsterdam and Philadelphia: John Benjamins Publishing Company.

Swain, M., & Lapkin, S. (2002). Talking it through: Two French immersion learners' response to reformulation. *International Journal of Educational Research*, *37*, 285–304.

Swales, J. M. (1990). *Genre analysis: English in academic and research settings*. New York: Cambridge University Press.

Tanaka, K. (2007). Japanese students' contacts with English outside the classroom during study abroad. *New Zealand Studies in Applied Linguistics*, *13*, 36–54.

Tanaka, K., & Ellis, R. (2003). Study-abroad, language proficiency, and learner beliefs about language learning. *JALT Journal*, *25*(1), 63–84.

Thorne, S. L. (2003). Artifacts and cultures-of-use in intercultural communication. *Language Teaching and Technology*, *7*, 38–67.

Toohey, K. (1998). 'Breaking them up, taking them away': ESL students in grade 1. *TESOL Quarterly*, *32*(1), 61–84. https://doi.org/10.2307/3587902

Tudge, J. R., & Rogoff, B. (1989). Peer influences on cognitive development: Piagetian and Vygotskian perspectives. In M. H. Bornstein, & J. S. Brunner (Eds.), *Interaction in human development* (pp. 17–40). Hillsdale, NJ: Erlbaum.

van Lier, L. (2004). *The ecology and semiotics of language learning: A sociocultural perspective.* Boston, MA: Kluwer.
Vygotsky, L. S. (1986). *Language and thought.* Cambridge, MA: MIT Press.
Wang, H.-S. (2003). A review of research as Korean as a foreign language. *The Korean Language in America, 8,* 7–35.
Watson-Gegeo, K. A. (1992). Think explanation in the ethnographic study of child socialization: A longitudinal study of the problem of schooling for Kwara'ae (Solomon Islands) children. In W. A. Corsaro & P. J. Miller (Eds.), *Interpretive approaches to children's socialization* (pp. 51–66). San Francisco, CA: Jossey-Bass Publisher.
Watson-Gegeo, K. A., & Nielsen, S. (2003). Language socialization in SLA. In C. J. Doughty & M. H. Long (Eds.), *The handbook of second language acquisition* (pp. 154–177). Malden, MA: Blackwell Publishing.
Wei, L., & Hua, Z. (2019). Imagination as a key factor in LMLS in transnational families. *International Journal of Sociology of Language, 255,* 73–107.
Wenger, E. (1998). *Communities of practice: Learning, meaning and identity.* New York: Cambridge University Press.
Wong, J. (2002). Applying conversation analysis in applied linguistics: Evaluation dialogue in English as a second language textbooks. *International Review of Applied Linguistics, 40,* 37–60.
Yang, J. S., & Kim, T. Y. (2011). Sociocultural analysis of second language learner beliefs: A qualitative case study of two study-abroad ESL learners. *System, 39,* 325–334.
Yoshimi, D. R. (1999). L1 language socialization as a variable in the use of ne by L2 learners of Japanese. *Journal of Pragmatics, 31*(11), 1513–1525.
Young, R. F. (1999). Sociolinguistic approaches to SLA. *Annual Review of Applied Linguistics, 19,* 105–132.
Young, R. F. (2013). Learning to talk the talk and walk the walk: Interactional competence in academic spoken English. *Ibérica, 25,* 15–38.
Yuen, S.-A. K. (2001). Socio-pragmatic functions of the interactive sentence ender -ney from the politeness perspective. *The Korean Language in America, 6,* 337–356.
Yun, S. (2008). Role-play and language socialization among bilingual Korean children in the United States. *Simulation & Gaming, 39*(2), 240–252. https://doi.org/10.1177/1046878107310614
Zuengler, J., & Cole, K. M. (2005). Language socialization and second language learning. In E. Hinkel (Ed.), *Handbook of research in second language teaching and learning* (pp. 301–316). Mahwah, NJ: Lawrence Erlbaum Associates, Publishers.
Zuengler, J., & Miller, E. R. (2006). Cognitive and sociocultural perspectives: Two parallel SLA worlds? *TESOL Quarterly, 40*(1), 35–58.

19
NATIONAL STANDARDS AND KOREAN AS A SECOND LANGUAGE[1]

Young-mee Yu Cho

Introduction

The history of second language (SL) teaching can be traced back to ancient Greece and Rome, if not further back in human history (Wheeler, 2013), and for the past two millennia language educators have incessantly tried to design more effective methods and approaches than those of previous generations. The early 1980s witnessed a significant shift in the field that continues to influence SL practices today. This newly emerging communicative language teaching (CLT) abandoned the centuries-old grammar translation method and the behaviorist audiolingual method and was built on modern linguistics, which conceptualized the language as a rule-governed cognitive system and language acquisition as the expansion of linguistic competence. The emphasis was not on the acquisition of language structure per se but on the social use of language, grounded in the spoken language. The SL learner strives for "real-life" communication, for which social interaction in and outside the classroom is most valued. It was then no accident that the ever-globalizing world of the 1990s called for achieving fluency and efficiency by breaking down language skills into speaking, listening, reading, and writing in SL education.

In the social milieu of the mid-1990s, when the excitement of CLT reached the national and international stage, the attempts of the previous decade crystallized into a set of standards that would transcend local practices and articulate a common set of goals and guidelines across all foreign language (FL) education. These initiatives also coincided with the time when the field of FL education in North America emerged as an independent academic discipline capitalizing on several decades of expanded classroom teaching and accumulated research findings. "The National Standards in Foreign Language Education Project," initially funded by the U.S. Department of Education and the National Endowment for the Humanities, was a collaborative effort between the American Council on the Teaching of Foreign Language (ACTFL) and many associations of FL teachers. As an individual membership organization founded in 1967 with more than 13,000 language teachers and administrators at all levels of instruction, ACTFL often plays the leadership role of implementing FL needs and visions, including proficiency guidelines, the Oral Proficiency Interview (OPI), performance descriptors, and can-do statements (Kang et al., 2000). The first set of ten languages that developed the National Standards in the 1990s were French, German, Italian, Spanish, Portuguese, classical languages (Latin and Greek), Russian, Chinese, and Japanese.

In 2012 the second set of language standards for Arabic, Korean, and Scandinavian languages were developed, followed by American Sign Language and Hindi in the latest *World-Readiness Standards for Learning Languages* (*National Standards*, henceforth) in 2015.[2] *National Standards* is an expanded version of the *Standards for Foreign Language Learning: Preparing for the 21st Century* (1996, 1999, 2006). *Standards for Korean Language Learning* (*Korean Standards*, henceforth), modeled on the *Standards for Foreign Language Learning: Preparing for the 21st Century* (2006), was a collaboration between the American Association of Teachers of Korean (AATK) and K–12 Korean teachers and administrators.[3] Under the guidance of the Foreign Language Standards Project Collaborative, 17 teachers (7 K–12 and 10 college teachers) worked on the document for 3 years,[4] which was enthusiastically endorsed by 45 reviewers in North America, Korea, Europe, and Oceania. It is not an overstatement to say that *Korean Standards* marks a milestone in Korean language education by placing KSL in the proper context of FL education in North America and beyond.

This chapter provides an overview of *Korean Standards*: its characteristics, its impact on the KSL field since its publication, and its pedagogical implications for the future. The chapter is organized as follows. Section 2 lays out the role *Korean Standards* have played in the development of the KSL field and standards-based curriculum. Section 3 identifies three areas of standards-based KSL education: teaching materials and the two goal areas of *Connections* and *Communities*. Section 4 touches on remaining issues and limitations, along with a few suggestions regarding future directions.

Korean Standards and KSL education

Characteristics of Korean Standards

Korean Standards follow the same blueprint as other FLs in its plan for the extended sequence of study for the full K–16 range. *National Standards* are a road map consisting of a set of content and performance standards, spanning levels K through 16. The following grade levels are grouped to lay out concrete expectations and learning outcomes: K–4, 5–8, 9–12, and 13–16. For the incremental progress of language proficiency, *progress indicators* are clearly specified as guidelines and for assessment for each stage. The following three goals of *Korean Standards* are quite analogous to those laid out for the first ten languages: (1) providing a unified set of visions, aims, and expectations for all parties concerned; (2) helping learners achieve and maintain high levels of competency in areas of the Korean language and culture; and (3) gaining understanding of Korean in relation to other languages and cultures.

However, achieving these goals for learners of all linguistic and cultural backgrounds requires another set of detailed curricula implementation. Moreover, KSL education is unique in that it has to deal with the complex pedagogical and curricular issues of learner diversity, mainly involving heritage and non-heritage learners, and multilingual transnational students. At the beginning stage of Korean language education in North America, students were predominantly heritage learners. During the past decade, however, the trend has shifted so dramatically that heritage learners no longer make up the majority of the KL class, especially at the elementary level. For heritage learners who still constitute an important portion of college-level Korean classes, their first exposure to formal and academic Korean language instruction often begins at the college level, and their motivation for learning the language is also quite different from that of other types of learners. In addition, non-heritage learners are not a group of homogeneous monolingual English speakers from similar cultural backgrounds. In that respect, it is crucial to identify "the specific goals and needs surrounding these diverse language learners and ultimately for the establishment of common goals for Korean language learners of all backgrounds" (*Korean Standards*, p. 524).

As shown in Figure 19.1, each of the five interlocking standards represents a domain inherently associated with language learning, known as the five Cs: *communication* (communicate in languages other than English), *cultures* (gain knowledge and skills to interact with cultural competence), *connections* (connect with other disciplines and acquire information), *comparisons* (develop insight into the nature of language and culture), and *communities* (participate in multilingual communities at home and around the world).

National Standards espouse a philosophy of FL education that, under the goal of *communication*, integrates the traditional four skills (listening, speaking, reading, and writing) and incorporates the contexts or modes of communication (interpersonal, interpretive, and presentational). *Communication* is considered a social act through which various social actions are instantiated. This is the first and foremost goal of SL education at any level. Each designated level stipulates the so-called *sample progress indicators* to inform the learner of "what social actions and linguistic features should be acquired in the level in question. A special emphasis is placed on the honorific forms and the context-sensitive 'speech styles' of the Korean language" (*Korean Standards*, p. 532). Language inherently attends to the speaker's relationships to the addressee and to the referent, which requires students even in the beginning level to learn how to encode the socio-cultural relationships in linguistically appropriate ways. As Korean linguistic structures (honorifics, sentence enders, and other pragmatic aspects) code social actions and situations, mapping linguistic features with social situations is one of the most essential components of acquisition. Thus, each *sample progress indicator* makes explicit reference to critical differentiation with regard to the communication setting of a linguistic act: formal vs. informal and written vs. spoken.

With regard to the second and fourth goals of *cultures* and *comparisons*, again special considerations were needed for students to understand the unique perspectives of Korean culture and the distinguishing characteristics of the language, which are vastly different from Western culture and the English language (as well as the diverse L1s students bring to class). Due to its long and complicated history, understanding Korean culture should be multilayered so that

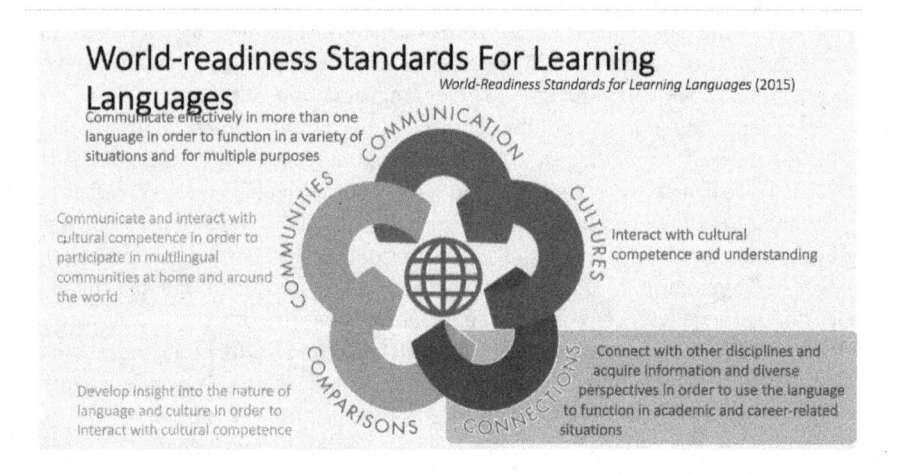

Figure 19.1 World-readiness Standards for Learning Languages

the curriculum includes traditional and contemporary Korean culture on the one hand and commonalities and differences between North and South Korean societies on the other. The *comparisons* goal is to "gain a comparative and critical perspective by examining historical and contemporary products, concepts, patterns of behavior, and social trends in the context of millennia-old East Asia" (*Korean Standards*, p. 545). For linguistic comparisons with other languages, the differences are too numerous to list, but the following four are highlighted: (1) the stratified lexicon of Native, Sino-Korean, and loan words; (2) the elaborate system of case particles and verb endings; (3) syntactic features of word order and its relative freedom; (4) pragmatic features of ellipsis; and (5) subject and addressee honorific patterns.

The two pillars of the five Cs' goal statements and *progress indicators* for each stage of language acquisition constitute a blueprint for designing a coherent curriculum. To demonstrate how these rather abstract and general guidelines could be implemented in the actual classroom, a set of learning scenarios were developed in the form of extended activities to facilitate future developments of standards-based curricula, as exemplified in (1) below. While some of the scenarios seem to have a shorter shelf life than others, this concrete activity-building experience had a positive effect on several curriculum-building efforts to come. These sample scenarios extrapolate the application of standards guidelines to teachers at different grade levels.

(4) Learning Scenarios (*Korean Standards*, pp. 552–570)

- Level K–4:

    Korean Lunar New Year
    Folktales and Counting Animals
    Mapping Skills

- Level 5–8:

    Singing Songs, Learning Language
    Paper Folding: Hanbok
    Daily Schedules
    Korean B-Boy Performance and *P'ungmullori*

- Level 9–12:

    Advertisement Poster
    Visit to Korean Stores
    Holidays: *Ch'usok* and Thanksgiving
    Noraebang
    Interview with Local Korean School Directors/Principals

- Level 13–16:

    Marriage Customs in Korea
    Analysis of Newspaper Cartoon, "An Editorial Without Text"
    Advertisement, Media, and Consumerism
    Korean's Perspective on Reunification

Korean Standards *for K–16 education*

National Standards is a clearly articulated road map, equipped with content and performance standards for an idealized K–16 FL program. They cover the entire span of public education and are based on three core philosophical assumptions: (1) competence in more than one language is an educational goal, (2) all students can be successful language learners, and (3) language and culture education are part of the core curriculum. The most recent instantiation of *National Standards* has played a critical role for the FL profession and has had a significant impact on curriculum development for more than two decades. *National Standards* in FL education affected the development of standards-based instruction, focusing more on what language students learn and what they can do with their comprehension and ability. The term "standards-based" in education refers to instructional practice, assessment, and academic reporting that are based on academic expectations in a grade level, a given course, or an entire curriculum. It aims to ensure that learners are acquiring the knowledge and skills they are expected to achieve in the given standards to success in school, higher education, and careers as they progress through their education (Magnan, Murphy, & Sahakyan, 2014; Magnan, 2017).

Since their publications, *National Standards* have impacted language teaching, curricula, and course design in unequivocally positive ways through the K–16 levels. FL educators and researchers view *National Standards* as "a common yardstick" for a shared pedagogical framework and learning outcomes assessment (Bärenfänger & Tschirner, 2008). They brought about critical changes in how language instructors are prepared and how languages are taught and learned. The five Cs goal areas provide a new conception of goals that had not been available before. The central role and major contributions of *National Standards* include providing language teachers a compelling rationale for curriculum development (ACTFL, 2015). The goals have served not only as guidelines in the instructional setting but also as a framework for curricular development. In its latest version, *National Standards* provide an updated and ambitious road map to guide language learners to be part of local and global communities in the 21st century. *National Standards* have facilitated the development of teaching materials for both commonly taught and less commonly taught languages in North America. Investigating the influence and benefits of standards, ACTFL conducted an extensive survey (2011 Standards Impact Survey) and revealed the extent to which the standards have impacted world language professionals (ACTFL, 2011). Survey results showed 89% of 2,000+ participants teaching in the K–12 levels indicated a familiarity with the standards, while 72% of the respondents indicated that they actually attempted to incorporate *National Standards* for their FL teaching.

The impact of *Korean Standards* for KSL education in North America has been as noticeable, as in other languages. They have served as a blueprint for the implementation of the extended sequence of study for the full K–16 range. However, in the past three decades the focus of Korean language and culture education in America has been on higher education (Kim, 2017), and consequently less attention has been paid to K–12 schools. Figure 19.2 shows the number of Korean language users in the United States by state. California has the highest number of Korean language users, with 33.5% of the total one million users, followed by New York, with 9.3%, and New Jersey, with 7.1%. Bergen County in New Jersey has the highest concentration of Korean residents per capita of any U.S. county, and Palisades Park is the most heavily Korean municipality in the country. Naturally, these statistics have a big implication on the current state of KSL education in K–12 schools.

With a growing number of Korean language learners in K–12, especially in high school, it has become more important than ever to connect primary to secondary and secondary to university programs for better articulation across the entire educational span. It will be a while before we see the full sequencing from K to 16 in the KSL landscape as laid out in the *Korean Standards*. The guidelines are primarily designed to ensure the effective transition from primary to secondary and secondary to postsecondary levels. However, K–12 programs are not widely available across North America and are much more restricted by the parameters of each

States	# of users	%	States	# of users	%
California	370062	33.5	Florida	20936	1.9
New York	103229	9.3	Hawaii	18116	1.6
New Jersey	78100	7.1	Massachusetts	16298	1.5
Texas	56688	5.1	Michigan	15605	1.4
Virginia	54623	4.9	Colorado	15095	1.4
Washington	47892	4.3	North Carolina	14761	1.3
Georgia	45221	4.1	Ohio	11394	1.0
Illinois	44848	4.1	Nevada	10969	1.0
Maryland	37819	3.4	Oregon	10115	0.9
Pennsylvania	29158	2.6	Arizona	9942	0.9

Figure 19.2 Number of Korean language users in the United States[5]

state and local school district. However, KSL at the high school level has been steadily growing to more than 100 schools in 2016, compared with 60 schools in 2007, while it is still limited at the earlier K–8 level. According to the Foundation for Korean Language and Culture in USA, 114 K–12 schools offer Korean language as of August 2018, as shown in Figure 19.3.[6] Around 50 schools are located in California, 22 in New York, and 8 in New Jersey, with 75% concentrated in three states, a natural reflection of Korean American demographics. Besides the top three states, Texas and Washington rank next, each with six K–12 schools. Around half of these schools are high schools (49%: 56 out of 114), followed by elementary schools (24%: 27 out of 114) and middle schools (16%: 18 out of 114).[7] In addition, 16 states (AZ, CA, CO, GA, HI, IL, KY, MD, MI, MN, NY, NJ, OH, TX, VA, WA) provide Korean language instruction at the primary and secondary levels.

Even though the current state of affairs regarding K–12 Korean language education is not as robust as that at the tertiary level (Cho, 2021), it is encouraging to note several recent studies that suggest improvements. Cheon (2017), for example, addresses the lack of coordination between a small number of public K–12 Korean programs and more than 1,400 Korean community schools, and suggests enhanced teacher-training workshops as a way to pool the available resources together. The K–12 level is an important feeder system to the university programs where KSL is flourishing at all levels of instruction, so there should be meaningful interactions between the two components in the education system by building unity and strengthening communication between the two components in the education ladder. Both learners and teachers are mutually connected through teacher certification, teacher training, testing (such as the SAT II in Korean and placement tests), and shared teaching materials. For instance, K–12 public schools often hire Korean teachers who are certified by either obtaining university degrees or individually obtaining credits in the required fields from local universities (e.g., Stonybrook University, Rutgers University).

As an illustration of how *Korean Standards* brought about a closer K–16 articulation, let us examine the case of the Rutgers Korean Teacher Program that was explicitly designed on the basis of the standards guidelines specified (Chun & Cho, 2018). While complying with *Korean Standards*, as a program in a state university that trains K–12 Korean teachers, it is imperative to take into consideration the New Jersey school system on organization, teaching, and assessment. While the standards-based curriculum ensures the alignment with recent nationwide

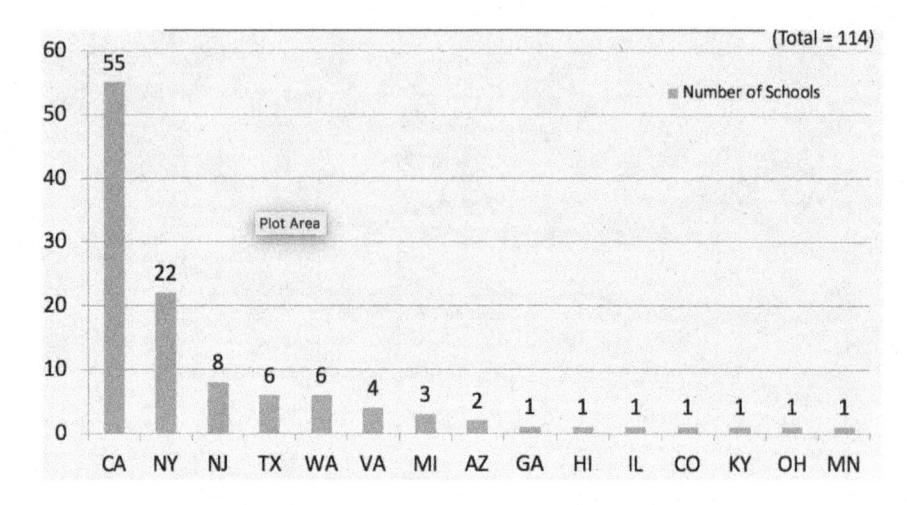

Figure 19.3 K–12 schools offering Korean in the United States (2015–2016)[8]

developments in KSL pedagogy (in particular, how to integrate KSL-specific linguistic and cultural aspects in curriculum design), local guidelines prepare teachers to be on par with other FL teachers in the state. In addition to *Korean Standards*, it is helpful for K–12 teachers to be acquainted with the "Program Standards for the Preparation of Foreign Language Teachers" (ACTFL, 2015), as listed in (2), and the *Teacher Effectiveness for Language Learning* (TELL, 2014) Project that covers seven areas: collaboration, environment, the learning experience, learning tools, planning, performance and feedback, and professionalism. Without doubt, contextualizing KSL pedagogy in the overall FL field brings a higher degree of professionalism into the teacher-training process.

(2) *Content and Supporting Standards for Program Standards* (ACTFL)

- Standard 1: Language proficiency (interpersonal, interpretive, presentational)
- Standard 2: Cultures, linguistics, literatures, and concepts from other disciplines
- Standard 3: Language acquisition theories and the knowledge of students and their needs
- Standard 4: Integration of standards in planning, classroom practice, and use of instructional resources
- Standard 5: Assessment of languages and cultures – impact on student learning
- Standard 6: Professional development, advocacy, and ethics

Just as the impact of *National Standards* was palpable on the consciousness of FL professionals, Korean language educators and researchers were calling for the need for a Korean-specific framework to incorporate standards-based instruction and assessment in their classroom (Sohn, 2000; Kwon, 2003; Kang & Lim, 2004). Finally, with the publication of *Korean Standards* (2009), it was possible to develop level-specific curricula in K–12. For example, Kwon (2003) proposed to develop standards-based Korean language Instruction in New York City public high schools.

What has happened in FL education in K–12 is in fact a reflection of the national trend of the past decade for advocating "Common Core State Standards" that focus on complex uses of language and literacy. In fact, 46 states in the United States recently adopted "Common Core

State Standards" that describe what students should know and be able to do in each subject in each grade from kindergarten through high school. Since 2010, a number of states have adopted the same standards for English and math that ensure students reach the same education goals regardless of location and ultimately prepare students for success in the workplace and in college. The U.S. states used to set their own academic standards, which could vary widely, and the shift to common standards was intended to ensure uniform academic rigor across the nation.

Korean Standards *for Korean as a heritage language (KHL)*

For the past several years *Korean Standards* have actively facilitated new curriculum development and the improvement of existing programs. As has been strongly recommended in Sohn, Jeong, and Park (2013, p. 754), *Korean Standards* should be adopted as "a model for nationally accepted curricular goals and standards that address four objectives" of promoting a pedagogical vision, instructional resources, accountability across levels, and cognitive continuity for students that spans the entire K–16 level. *Korean Standards* indeed have provided organizing principles in the core areas of KSL of curriculum, textbook, classroom instruction, and assessment. By establishing the common goals for KSL learners of all backgrounds, they specifically acknowledge the complex challenges of educating a mixed group of heritage and non-heritage learners in the same curriculum. They also have great potential for the large Korean heritage language community in North America; as a guide for language maintenance, they could provide a missing link in connecting Korean as a heritage language (KHL) curricula with formal K–16 programs. There are more than 1,400 Korean community schools through the United States (The Overseas Koreans Foundation)[9] with more than 10,000 students. Unfortunately, there is little coordination between Korean community schools and the formal educational sector of K–16 institutions, and we have yet to see concerted efforts to enhance KSL/KHL instruction in the standards framework (Sohn, Huh, & Choi, 2007).

Though probably not as disconnected as the two sectors of community-based KHL education and the academic K–16 institutions, there is room for improvement within the formal educational setting. While HL education made up much of formal instruction at the beginning stage of KSL programs across North America, for the past decade non-heritage learners and international students from diverse cultures and language backgrounds have been rapidly increasing across the continent. In many universities, non-heritage learners are no longer the majority of the class, in particular at the introductory level. However, in K–12 levels, about 80% of the students are heritage students with a wide spectrum of Korean language proficiency who have not experienced much formal instruction in Korean. It is true that *Korean Standards* were designed with a substantial percentage of heritage learners in mind. Several unique characteristics were noted so that the students could acquire sensitivity to the social meanings of certain language forms, such as honorifics, and be given age-appropriate reading materials for vocabulary building and literacy development (*Korean Standards*, p. 528).

Standards-based curriculum development

The publication of *Korean Standards*, the first major project undertaken by the AATK, was immediately met by a growing demand for curricular development. It made the most sense to address the area of highest need and to focus on the curriculum that has potential for the broadest impact – that is, producing a coherent and comprehensive college-level curriculum based on *Korean Standards*. The special issue of the *Korean Language in America* (vol. 19, no. 2,

2015), entitled *College Korean Curriculum Inspired by National Standards for Korean* (*College Korean Curriculum*, henceforth), is a result of the coordinated efforts by 25 KSL faculty members from 20 universities in the United States.

The document begins with the curricula overview and framework. The overview is a progress map of learning objectives defined by the five Cs on the one hand and layered level by level along the ACTFL proficiency guidelines on the other. For ease of reference for college KSL teachers, the proficiency guidelines roughly correspond to years of instruction in university settings but more accurately cover from novice to advanced high. It spans seven levels – six consecutive levels and the heritage level that straddles the first and the second levels, reflecting a common practice in most collegiate heritage curricula of covering two years of non-heritage curriculum in one year. The five Cs learning objectives are a customized and expanded version of objectives introduced in *Korean Standards*. The learning objectives covering K–16 had to be modified significantly to fit the interests and needs of the four-year postsecondary KSL education. In each subcategory of the five Cs, level-appropriate goals are spelled out, as exemplified in (3). The first goal, *communication*, includes three modes – interpersonal, interpretive, and presentational – each of which requires distinct objectives to aim for. The second goal, *cultures*, has two subgoals of practices and products, while the fourth goal, *Comparisons*, deals with linguistic and cultural objectives.

(3) Objectives (*College Korean Curriculum*, 2015, pp. 155–175)

Level 1: Communication-Interpersonal

- Students use and respond to simple speech acts, such as greetings, leave takings, giving thanks, and self-introductions.
- Students engage in simple, routine conversations on topics necessary for survival.
- Students respond to direct questions and requests for information in highly predictable situations.

Level 1: Communication-Interpretive

- Students understand key words and formulaic phrases in highly predictable and contextualized texts.
- Students understand short texts in familiar contexts by use of background knowledge and extralinguistic support.
- Students interpret gestures and other visual cues to understand the communicative intent.

Level 1: Communication-Presentational

- Students supply basic information on simple forms and documents.
- Students convey very simple messages with practiced materials.
- Students create simple sentences on a very familiar topic by recombining learned vocabulary and structures.

Level 3: Cultures-Practices

- Students discuss Korean cultural practices related to traditional and contemporary forms of special rites, such as weddings and funerals.
- Students recognize contributions from Korean cultures in areas such as art, music, film, fashion, or science.

Level 3: Cultures-Products

- Students understand the significance of Korean cultural products that reflect daily life, such as food, clothing, dwelling, and leisure activities.
- Students read materials about internationally known Korean artists, musicians, and athletes and analyze the types of global influences of Korean culture.

Level 3: Connections

- Students expand their knowledge of other subject areas through Korean, such as geography, environmental science, and politics.
- Students present simple reports on topics being studied in other courses and activities, such as music, art, travel, and study-abroad experience.

Level 4: Comparisons-Language

- Students demonstrate an understanding of different registers and tones (e.g., casualness, distance, courtesy, disapproval) rendered by different speech styles and lexical choices.

Level 4: Comparisons-Culture

- Students analyze Korean cultural perspectives regarding familial and generational relationships manifested in respect for elders, importance of birth order, family responsibilities and duties, and filial obligations in comparison with their own cultural perspectives.

Heritage Level: Communities

- Students communicate on a personal level with speakers of the Korean language via a variety of media.
- Students participate in a school or community celebration that involves Korea or Korean culture.
- Students interview members of the Korean community regarding topics of personal interest, community, or the world.
- Students participate in a career exploration or school-to-work project that requires intermediate proficiency in Korean.

Once a set of learning objectives were defined for each level in terms of the five Cs, the curricular framework was set up for each of the seven levels. Although it was a full-fledged curriculum based on a spiral model, it was designed as a modular format to meet the diverse needs and interests of students and to flexibly apply to various instructional settings and conditions. In addition to a set of guidelines, each unit was a comprehensive template that included lists of sample texts, audiovisual materials, instructional activities, classroom tasks, and student project ideas. Special attention was paid to acknowledge and reinforce heritage learners' receptive skills on the one hand and to develop productive skills on the other.

This 300-page-long *College Korean Curriculum* is comprehensive yet flexible enough to be immediately put to use in revising an existing curriculum by incorporating the standards guidelines as well as in designing a new course. At the end of the document, three standards-based Level 3 syllabi are provided by the University of Pennsylvania, University of Pittsburgh, and University of Maryland at Baltimore City, designed with different goals and diverse activities but all while following the standards guidelines. In addition, three sample learning scenarios are presented to demonstrate the use of standards-based activities in the classroom:

(1) marriage (The University of North Georgia), (2) dating (New York University), and (3) travel (Duke University). These examples incorporating concrete themes suggest some of the many ways to organize content and create meaningful activities.

In any curriculum-design effort everyone in the field acknowledges that assessment and student performance should be the first component to consider (McTighe & Wiggins, 2005), and researchers have recently explored the influences of implementing *National Standards* for language programs, in particular for assessment and language learning (Cox, Malone, & Winke, 2018). However, not much attention has been paid to the development of assessment tools in the standards-based instructional framework in the KSL field. As one of the few attempts to use *National Standards* for assessment, Kim (2020b) suggests the following two ways to bring academic content to the curriculum: (1) by means of curriculum evaluation through *National Standards* (in particular, identify linguistic skill areas and identify content areas to fill) and (2) by conducting an academic content survey with Korean Studies professors and identifying goals for Korean majors. She advocates for calibrating upper-level courses (the third-, fourth-, and fifth-year Korean courses) to achieve the *connections* goal, and utilizes *National Standards* objectives as "can-do statements" as evaluation methods to assess students and the curriculum. She recalibrated the six levels posited in *College Korean Curriculum* as a four-level system that could apply to a university Korean program: Levels 1 and 2 (second-year level), Levels 2 and 3 (third-year level), Levels 3, 4, and 5 (fourth-year level), and Levels 4, 5, and 6 (fifth-year level). Such customized modifications indicate the extent to which the frontline of KSL education in North America is currently adopting a standards-based approach.

Beyond the use of *Korean Standards* in identifying linguistic skill areas, KSL practitioners have also tried to find ways to prepare learners to become culturally competent in Korean and to assess the development of cultural competence in the Korean language classroom. Traditional approaches to the teaching of culture often treated culture as an afterthought, often introduced separately from the language components. Even when culture is systematically integrated into KSL curricula, it was tied to written texts in the printed medium, centering around the decoding and encoding of cultural information presented in the textbook.[10]

Three areas of standards-based KSL education

Standards-based teaching materials

With the growing geopolitical, economic, and cultural significance of South Korea, the recognition of the Korean language has risen globally in the last two decades. The Korean language is the seventh-most-commonly spoken language in the United States (U.S. Census Bureau, n.d.)[11] and is currently one of the 14 critical languages (along with Arabic, Chinese, Japanese, and Russian),[12] as designated by the Department of Defense. Moreover, KHL in particular is recognized as an indispensable national resource, as heritage learners are most likely to reach advanced levels of proficiency after formal education.

However, the linguistic and cultural abilities of heritage learners differ from those of traditional learners, as they come to class with prior exposure to the target language to varying degrees. These learners often tend to be more proficient in aural and oral skills than in their literacy skills. In addition, their linguistic repertoire is highly limited in terms of genre and register in that their language use is almost exclusively restricted to everyday conversational contexts at home (often dubbed pejoratively as "kitchen Korean") and colloquial uses of Korean. Finally, the motivations of heritage learners notably differ from those of non-heritage learners in that these motivations are more personal than instrumental. Therefore, heritage learners often take Korean courses to better communicate with their family members, explore their Korean identity, and connect with their heritage community by learning more about Korean culture and society – hence an increasing need for a textbook tailored to address the different needs of Korean heritage students. *Korean Standards* indeed sparked interest in curricular design and pedagogical research both at the secondary and tertiary levels of KSL education. For the college level, *College Korean Curriculum* mentioned in the previous section worked as a catalyst for further developments in teaching materials. Kim (2020a, p. 118) advocates the fine-tuning of heritage language (HL) curriculum by determining the HL-specific linguistic goals and optimizing HL acquisition. For instance, she mentions, "rather than focusing on the interpersonal skills, it is important to identify aspects of the Communication modes that HL learners lack and need, such as reading (interpretive) and writing/formal speaking (presentational) skills."

The two volumes of *Integrated Korean: Accelerated* (Cho, Jung, & Ha, 2020) comprise the first textbook specifically designed with *Korean Standards* in mind for heritage learners. Currently, many Korean programs that offer a separate heritage track or an intensive course often simply cram four volumes of existing textbooks (designed for non-heritage learners) into two semesters, rather than targeting the specific linguistic and cultural needs of Korean heritage learners. *Integrated Korean: Accelerated* is designed to bring efficiency and relevancy in order to restructure and advance heritage learners' existing language in a structured way through a curriculum informed by recent HL research. Each volume contains seven chapters, which are designed to be completed in one semester (60–75 contact hours). Volume 1 presents thematically organized topics, starting with familiar topics related to oneself and one's closest heritage community, such as family, close friends, daily routines, schoolwork, on-campus activities, social life, pastimes, dining out, and shopping. Volume 2 advances to more formal topics that incorporate cultural aspects (for the goal of *cultures*) and community beyond family and friends, such as travel, transportation, housing, holidays, lifestyles, career, history, geographic regions, and Korean people in Korea and around the world. Students and teachers are able to approach key topics with multilevel communicative classroom activities (for the goal of *communication*) and reading materials with standards-based tasks and projects (for the goals of *comparisons* and *connections*) that not only address the specific language needs and prior knowledge of heritage learners but also advocate for heritage learners to have meaningful participation in the local and worldwide Korean community, close and beyond (for the goal of *Communities*).

Based on several decades of teaching KHL, the survey results, and extensive feedback from practitioners in the field, this textbook incorporates the following elements to differentiate it from traditional textbooks for college Korean programs, as listed in (4).

(4) *Integrated Korean: Accelerated* (2020)

- More authentic conversations and texts: highlights real-life language use rather than artificial "foreigner talk."
- More formal contexts: both volumes contain communicative tasks that are designed to help students gain competence in both informal and formal contexts.
- More cultural contents: includes cross-cultural comparisons and sociolinguistic issues to enhance intercultural competence.
- Modular approach to vocabulary learning: in addition to "core" vocabulary, useful vocabulary is provided on the same topic for those who need expansion.
- Multilevel reading tasks: to address multilevel and multifaceted learners, two versions of the same reading text are given in the first volume of the textbook, and

- sufficient reading materials are included for those learners who need more exposure to written language in terms of literacy and vocabulary development.
- Multiliteracies approach incorporates a variety of authentic materials (poems, ads, cartoons, documentaries, folktales, articles, etc.).
- Structured tasks: all writing and presentation tasks are structured and scaffolded to include the target grammar and vocabulary.
- Formal language use: presents the formal counterparts of the colloquial expressions and slang frequently used by heritage learners.
- Motivated by error analysis: to prevent frequent errors made by heritage learners, pragmatically ambiguous structures are presented side by side and distinguished by contexts (e.g., 눕고 있다 *nwup-ko iss-ta* vs. 누워 있다 *nwuwue iss-ta* 'lie down'; -에 *-ey* vs. –(으—로 *-(u)lo* 'to'; -아/어서 *-a/ese* vs. –(으)—까 *-(u)nikka* 'because', -하고 *-hako* vs. 그리고 *kuliko* 'and').
- Task-based approach: collaborative language learning is facilitated through various interpersonal and group-based tasks.
- Standards-based curriculum: incorporates all of the five Cs (communication, cultures, connections, comparisons, and communities).
- Integrated Performance Assessment (IPA): all tasks are designed backwards for effective assessment and formative feedback in all three modes of communication (interpretive, interpersonal, and presentational), which are connected with each other in a cyclic manner.
- Topical approach: chapters are organized following ACTFL's guidelines for oral proficiency (e.g., familiar to unfamiliar topics, community to societal topics, and concrete to abstract topics).

In addition to the textbook mentioned earlier, a total revision of an upper-level *Integrated Korean: High Advanced* 1 & 2 (University of Hawthei'i Press) is currently underway, in an attempt to meet the guidelines specified in Level 5 of "College Korean Curriculum Inspired by National Standards for Korean" (2015, p. 341). The curriculum comprises four big topics of (1) society, (2) education, (3) economics, and (4) Korean language, under which the following learning goals are set up.

(5) Level 5 Curriculum: Topics & Learning Goals

1.1 Changes in Family

- Understand issues related to family and marriage in traditional and contemporary Korea and discuss different ideas and perspectives presented in actual cases and data.

1.2 Prejudice and Discrimination

- Identify various types of discrimination in Korea, discuss their cultural and historical backgrounds, and exchange opinions about possible solutions.

1.3 Regional Culture and Identity

- Learn about linguistic and cultural traits of different regions and analyze regional identity in relation to the historical and political development of contemporary Korea.

1.4 Schools and Networking

- Identify and understand the culture of educational networking in Korea and discuss the related issues and its social and historical backgrounds.

2.1 Education Policy in Korea

- Understand and discuss issues of the Korean education system, compare them with those of one's own country, and present suggestions to resolve education-related issues.

2.2 Issues in School

- Identify and analyze various youth- and school-related issues in Korea and one's own country, compare with one's experiences, and propose possible solutions.

3.1 Consumer Culture

- Identify, analyze, and discuss issues related to consumer culture, materialism, and "lookism" in contemporary Korea and other societies.

3.2 Information Technology

- Describe practices in using the Internet, social media, and technology; analyze and discuss related issues in contemporary Korea and other societies.

3.3 Cultural Industry

- Discuss various cultural products, including popular culture, and explore strategies to present them in the context of the global economy.

4.1 *Han'gŭl* and Korean Language

- Understand and analyze characteristics of the Korean language and its writing system, in comparison with other languages and in the context of historical development.

4.2 Changes in Korean Language

- Identify and learn about Korean dialects and linguistic changes in contemporary Korea, compare them with those of other languages, and discuss emerging usages and expressions.

As *College Korean Curriculum* provides a clear standards-based methodology, it, in turn, naturally leads to the development and publication of teaching modules that implement the curricular specifications of the framework, as exemplified by recent KHL and advanced-level textbooks discussed earlier.

Connections

Korean Standards and the subsequent publication of *College Korean Curriculum* have greatly contributed to streamlining KSL pedagogy toward the five Cs. Over the past ten years, *communication* and *cultures* have been actively addressed, resulting in tangible advancements, while occasional attempts have been made to integrate *comparisons* and *communities* as part of KSL curricula (Brown, 2018; Lee-Smith, 2018). *Connections* (with other disciplines), however, is the least developed among the five Cs due to the inherent open-endedness of the goal itself (Cutshall, 2012). As in (6), the *connections* goal consists of two subparts:

(6) *Connections*

- Standard 3.1: Students reinforce and further their knowledge of other disciplines through the Korean language.
- Standard 3.2: Students acquire information and recognize the distinctive viewpoints that are only available through the Korean language and culture (*Korean Standards*, pp. 542–544).

The *connections* goal already assumes the students' use of Korean communication skills (developed under the *communication* goal) and the cultural understanding (developed under the *cultures* goal) within a community (specified under the *communities* goal) in their academic/personal progress of extending their knowledge into new disciplines. Because KSL teachers are expected to create opportunities for interdisciplinary experiences in areas of the curriculum beyond the traditional KSL classroom, it is particularly challenging to incorporate the range of activities that are connected to other disciplines and to prove the essential role of the target language in acquiring information. Language teachers and content teachers work together to connect the FL curriculum with other disciplines of students' academic lives and to enrich their personal lives. These conscious attempts at creating connections should flow from other domains into the KSL classroom and vice versa, adding unique insights to the overall educational experience with a synthetic effect. In this section, we propose one such connections-based curriculum in a university in the United States that builds a two-way bridge between multiple disciplines and KSL education, following recent focus on the merging of language and literary/cultural content in advanced-level FL teaching in collegiate contexts (Paesani & Allen, 2012; Kramsch, 2006).

Recently, KSL teachers have begun to envision an integrated approach to bridge the divide between language and content in multiple levels. KSL courses are no longer assumed as a "service" program that fulfills the ultimate goals of Korean studies. Building linguistic proficiency is not a separate endeavor. A KSL curriculum could go beyond the usual practice of incorporating simple cultural components in KSL instruction. We can build a curriculum where Korean Studies courses employ primary materials in literature, history, and cinema, and KSL courses make organic connections to content courses offered in the same program. The workshop "Bridging Language and Content: Making Interdisciplinary Connections in Higher Education," held at Yale University on October 24, 2020, focused on advanced Korean curriculum in the three areas of program development, content development, and course development. This workshop indicates a growing interest in a connections-based approach that will enable the learner to connect with other disciplines and acquire critical perspectives through the use of the language in academic and career-related contexts.

An interesting attempt in implementing the *connections* goal in language curriculum is reported in the article "Citizen Sociolinguistics: Making Connection in the Foreign Language Classroom" (Jung & Lee, 2018). In the project, advanced-level students carried out a sociolinguistic exploration on language use in open-source media and presented their own interpretation on issues such as Konglish, neologism, and gendered speech. The experiment illustrates how a connections-based instruction helps students develop informed perspectives and ultimately fosters learners' critical-thinking skills through the use of the target language.

Creating *connections* between language and content is expected to be a focal point in advanced KSL curriculum in the near future. KSL teachers have also paid attention to content-based instruction (CBI) as a way of integrating the study of content and language, both in K–12 dual-immersion programs (Howard, Sugarman, Christian, Lindholm-Leary, & Rogers, 2007) and in colleges (Cheon, 2007; Kim, 2005; Shin & Kim, 2000). Park, Choi, and Ko (2021) evaluate Shin and Kim's course at UCLA, Cheon's at University of Hawai'i, and Kim's advanced heritage course at Duke University as theme-based CBI attempts to create a more natural, comprehensive, and motivating learning environment where learning goals are clearly articulated beyond proficiency improvement and the role of the target language is better defined. These courses, however, are not CBI models in its purest sense; they are KSL courses whose syllabi are organized around certain themes. They slightly shifted the focus from language acquisition to content, but the primary goal cannot be described as the acquisition of the subject matter through the Korean language. While it might be difficult to implement an entirely CBI curriculum in a KSL program, CBI inspires the teachers to reflect on the balance between language and content, choose content that meets the students' needs, employ authentic texts and activities, and promote student engagement. The connections-based curriculum has the potential to build on CBI, when couched in the cultures and languages across curriculum (CLAC) model (Cho & Chun, 2020). A truly integrated model of language and content goes beyond incorporating content in a language course or incorporating language in a content course because it espouses two-way synthetic integration between multiple disciplines and KSL education.

Communities

While all five Cs in *National Standards* are equally important and should be incorporated equally into a standards-based curriculum, the last three Cs (*comparisons*, *connections*, and *communities*) have not been explored in equal parts as the first two Cs (*communication* and *cultures*). The *communities* goal is defined as the learner's ability to "communicate and interact with cultural competence in order to participate in multilingual communities at home and around the world" (*Korean Standards*, p. 549). The two subgoals are as follows: (1) School and Global Communities: learners use the language both within and the beyond the classroom to interact and collaborate in their community and the globalized world, and (2) Lifelong Learning: learners set goals and reflect on their progress in using languages for enjoyment, enrichment, and advancement.

Although not explicitly framed in standards-based instruction, there has been a growing interest in community-based service learning. Kim and Sohn (2016) report on a UCLA course, "Advanced Korean with Service-Learning," where 50 Korean HL students work for 20 hours at 4 community partners in Koreatown: the Korean Cultural Center (for assisting language instructors), a cardiology hospital (for assisting English to Korean translation), Korean–English dual-language elementary schools (for assisting teachers), and Koreatown Youth and Community Center (for assisting low-income Korean American families). The authors conclude that service-learning provided an invaluable opportunity for hands-on experience using the Korean language as well as for students' reflection on linguistic and sociocultural issues.

Another recent example is the launching of the Korean-English Translation Certification Program at Rutgers, The State University of New Jersey.[13] The need for Korean translation/interpreting has increased in the United States, especially in states with large Korean populations. Throughout New Jersey, Korean (1%) is the third-most-spoken language at home, after English (70.3%) and Spanish (15.3%).[14] The program focuses on providing bilingual students with opportunities for systematic learning and deeper understanding of the translation process and ethics. It places the acquisition of practical skills to address local problems within a globalized intercultural framework.

One of the capstone courses for the program, *KOR481 Korean Translation/Interpreting Internship*, is designed to provide the student with an opportunity to translate/interpret in the real world for people with intercultural intermediation needs. Each student is assigned to an agency or organization that provides legal, medical, or social services and serves "on duty" for three hours per week. Once a week the students will meet, in class or online in alternate weeks, to share their experiences with each other and learn practical skills through lectures and guest speakers. The learning objectives are listed here:

(7) Learning Objectives (*KOR481*)

- Strengthen the instrumental and professional competences of translation
- Become familiar with the deontological and ethical codes as translator/interpreter
- Reflect on the translator's own vision and role in society
- Identify and develop one's strength in types of interpreting to pursue suitable job opportunities
- Be exposed to ways to establish oneself as an independent or freelance translator/interpreter
- Learn to perform basic administrative tasks, such as the production of translation estimates, orders, invoices, etc.
- Investigate different national and international certifications and how to prepare for them
- Prepare curricular vitae focused on different professional profiles; create a database of references for professional translators.

It is worth acknowledging an innovative project that engaged the KSL programs in three universities (Princeton, Emory, and Yale University) (Lee-Smith, Suh, & Choi, 2017). The three community-based projects are: (1) Senior and Youths (SAY), where KSL learners conducted weekly one-on-one Skype calls with Korean seniors to practice conversational Korean; (2) the Student-run Campus Tour in Korean, a collaborative effort between the language class and the university community visitor center to create a written brochure in Korean to be used for campus tours; and (3) the Linguistic Landscape Project, where participants produced a digital storytelling product based on the usage of Korean and the resulting linguistic landscape of the local suburban areas. In addition, Lee-Smith (2018) introduces the Junior and Mentor (JAM) project, where undergraduate students were matched with international Korean graduate student mentors based on "their career interests, majors, or areas of specialty" (p. 167). These endeavors illustrate to what extent a variety of collaborative projects utilizing today's multimodal technology can strengthen the *communities* goal of *Korean Standards* and open the door to many possibilities reaching beyond the classroom into the entire university, local Korean American communities, and global Korean-speaking communities.

Future directions

From the discussions in Sections 2 and 3, it is clear that *Korean Standards* serve as a basis of language instruction, curriculum, and performance evaluation. They cover not only content (what language learners need to know and do) and performance (how well language learners need to perform) but also assessment (how accurately and fluently language learners perform).

However, there are several remaining issues that need further attention. As Sohn (2000) suggests, Korean language professionals need to examine whether samples of student performances meet a standard and develop reliable performance assessment tools. In an effort to use valid progress indicators, J. Lee (2013) argues for the revision of progress indicators in *Korean Standards*. For instance, Standard 4.1 requires students to demonstrate their understanding of the nature of language by comparing the Korean language and their own. After collecting and analyzing 240 composition assignments from 49 students in the advanced-level Korean class, many of the current indicators for grades 12–16, such as awareness of various written styles, degree of formality, and speech-level choices, should be reassigned to lower grade levels. In addition, it is suggested that new indicators, such as the punctuation system, use of advanced-level appropriate lexical items, and composition style should be added to *Korean Standards*.

As *National Standards* set the clear criteria to assess learners' understanding and performance, standards-based assessment enables teachers to use language learners' assessment outcomes to give more meaningful feedback to learners and to identify programs' strengths and weaknesses. Assessment data also can indicate the extent to which language learners are prepared to achieve personal and professional goals. The ACTFL Proficiency Guidelines (ACTFL, 2012) have served as a framework for proficiency-based instruction and assessment in the field of foreign language education. The ACTFL proficiency guidelines are one of the well-adopted proficiency standards and are widely used to assess learners' proficiency gains. The guidelines are standardized into different proficiency levels, ranging from novice to intermediate to advanced to superior to distinguished. A standardized assessment, the ACTFL Oral Proficiency Interview (OPI), is often used to measure learners' speaking proficiency based on the proficiency standards. Later, the Integrated Performance Assessment (IPA, Adair-Hauck, Glisan, & Troyan, 2013) model was introduced to measure the learners' ongoing progresses of integrated skills of reading, listening, speaking, and writing. Within Korean language education, *Korean Standards* have been well adapted for Korean language curricular development and assessment over the decades. Many researchers (Cho, Chung, & Peterson, 2006; Kang & Lim, 2004) proposed to incorporate *National Standards* and use the proficiency guidelines for standardized Korean curricular design and performance assessment.

Teacher preparation standards for the National Council on the Accreditation of Teacher Education (NCATE) are derived from National Standards. FL education programs in universities address challenges to promote content knowledge and proficiency from the standards framework (Phillips & Abbott, 2011). The impact of the standards movement on teacher education is obvious in terms of requirements on the teacher licensure tests in many states. Teacher candidates are mandated to obtain an official ACTFL OPI test score of advanced low or intermediate high (ACTFL & CAEP, 2015; Wilbur, 2007) for K–12 certification. In addition, many states now require preservice teachers to demonstrate their ability to prepare, teach, and assess standards-based instruction (Cox et al., 2018). A body of current research has examined how standards have influenced language teacher education, such as minimum proficiency levels for teacher certification, curricular changes in language teacher education (Glisan, Swender, & Surface, 2013; Troyan & Kaplan, 2015), and important content knowledge on the teacher licensure tests (Kissau & Algozzine, 2017). As for the relationship between teacher professional development and *National Standards* since their creation, the 2011 ACTFL Decades of Standards Survey (ACTFL, 2011) demonstrated that 95% of professional development efforts considered *National Standards* and that 74% of language teachers participating in these workshops or seminars changed their instructions or implemented new pedagogies to align more with *National Standards*. In the context of KSL teacher education, S. W. Lee (2013) collected K–12 Korean teachers' opinions on teacher education and identified that the most pressing need was to develop concrete standards-based curricula. Although various topics regarding the impact of *National Standards* on teacher education and professional development have been investigated, most of the research data have come from qualitative studies or case studies with fewer than 30 teacher candidates and are still in a rudimentary phase. Nationwide longitudinal studies are needed to better understand the impact of standards-based instruction on the field of foreign language education as well as teacher education.

Despite the overall positive impact on FL educators and research, the following concerns remain. As discussed in Section 3, the *communication* and *cultures* goals have been overemphasized in instruction. When *National Standards* reached the decade mark, Phillips and Abbott (2011) assessed the influence and impact on FL/SL research, language teaching and learning, curriculum, and assessment. Teacher survey data indicated that language teachers are more likely to focus on *communication* (79%) and *cultures* (22%), while they have not promoted *connections* (11%) and *communities* (8%) as much in their teaching. In addition to the overemphasis on *communication* and *cultures*, Magnan (2017) has listed other concerns: (1) a tendency to consider the goal areas individually rather than in their interrelationship, (2) the narrow view of the standards' constructs, (3) the non-specification of needed fluency associated with the standards goals, and (4) the limited number of related performance-assessment tools. Recognizing these concerns, teachers and researchers continue to work on minor revisions and improvements with the hope of making *National Standards* more relevant to less commonly taught languages (LCTLs) and to college-level language teaching and learning.

As discussed in the introduction, *National Standards* was very much a cultural product of the structuralist language policies of the 1990s and the 2000s, when Communicative Language Teaching (CLT) was still *the* dominant ideology in FL education. The more critical poststructuralist era brought about completely different approaches to language teaching, represented by SL identities (Block, 2007), symbolic competence (Kramsch, 2006, 2009), multiliteracies (The New London Group, 1996; Allen & Paesani, 2010), and translanguaging (Garcia & Wei, 2014). These new revolutionary frameworks reconceptualize FL education as fostering dynamic critical thinking skills and deeper comprehension of the text and the world, a radical departure from CLT's emphasis on the learner's step-by-step development toward the predefined goal of communicative competency. What these new theories have in common is privileging fluid and uniquely individualistic language practices of multilingual speakers. Inasmuch as the *raison d'être* of *National Standards* is to impose a set of external standards on all aspects of FL learning, there awaits a radical rethinking to reconcile these two opposing pursuits.

Notes

1 We adopt the general term KSL, rather than KFL, to refer to Korean learning in all contexts other than Korean L1 education to native speakers, following the common SLA practice that rejects the distinction between FL and SL.
2 www.actfl.org/resources/world-readiness-standards-learning-languagesRetrieved on July 10, 2020. The document includes 15 languages: American Sign Language, Chinese, French, Hindi, Japanese, Portuguese, Scandinavian languages, Arabic, classical languages (Latin and Greek), German, Italian, Korean, Russian, Spanish, and Yoruba.
3 The AATK, established in 1994 and currently with over 300 members, is the only representative organization for Korean teachers of all levels and institutions in North America.
4 The names of the 17 participating institutions are as follows: Charter School for Better Learning, Lowell High School, La Canada High School, Illinois State Board of Education, MS 142 (Bronx), New Hope Academy, Keppel Elementary School, Defense Language Institute, Binghamton University, Duke University, Indiana University, Princeton University, Rutgers University, Sogang University, University of Chicago, University of Hawai'i, and Pennsylvania State University.

5 2012–2016 ACS (American Community Survey) five-year PUMS (Public Use Microdata Sample) data, Unites States Census Bureau (https://factfinder.census.gov/faces/tableservices/jsf/pages/productview.xhtml?pid=ACS_16_5YR_B16001&prodType=table)
6 www.klacUSA.org. Retrieved on August 3, 2020. The Foundation for Korean Language and Culture in USA (formerly known as the Foundation for SAT II Korean) is a main source of information on K–12 KSL education. It is "a private, non-profit organization whose primary mission is to promote Korean language and cultural education in American elementary, middle and high schools throughout the United States."
7 Among 114 schools, 13 are listed as either Elementary–Middle School, Middle–High School, or Elementary–High School.
8 한국어진흥재단 (Foundation for Korean Language and Culture in USA): www.klacusa.org/bbs/board.php?bo_table=page401.
9 www.mofa.go.kr/eng/wpge/m_5722/contents.do.
10 One attempt to develop a standards-based assessment tool in culture education is found in Jung, Ha, Cho, and Chung (2018), where intercultural communicative competence is measured by applying ACTFL's Integrated Performance Assessment and can-do statements in tandem.
11 www.census.gov/history/www/through_the_decades/overview/2010_overview_1.html.
12 The U.S. government considers the following 15 languages as critically important for diplomacy, trade, and national security: Arabic, Azerbaijani, Bangla, Chinese, Hindi, Indonesian, Japanese, Korean, Persian, Portuguese, Punjabi, Russian, Swahili, Turkish, and Urdu (www. https://clscholarship.org/languages).
13 For more information, see https://asianstudies.rutgers.edu/academics/undergraduate/the-korean-english-translation-interpreting-certificate-program.
14 www/nj.us/health/chs/hnj2020/documents/demog/pdf.

References

ACTFL. (2011). *A decade of foreign language standards: A survey*. Alexandria, VA: ACTFL.
ACTFL. (2012). *ACTFL proficiency guidelines 2012*. Alexandria, VA: ACTFL.
ACTFL. (2015). *World-readiness standards for learning languages*. Alexandria, VA: ACTFL.
ACTFL and CAEP. (2015). *ACTFL/CAEP program standards for the preparation of foreign language teachers*. Alexandria, VA: ACTFL.
Adair-Hauck, B., Glisan, E. W., & Troyan, F. J. (2013). *Implementing the integrated performance assessment in the 21st century classroom: A teacher's guide for improving student performance*. Alexandria, VA: ACTFL.
Allen, H. W., & Paesani, K. (2010). Exploring the feasibility of a pedagogy of multiliteracies in introductory foreign language courses. *L2 Journal, 2*, 119–142.
Bärenfänger, O., & Tschirner, E. (2008). Language educational policy and the language learning quality management: The Common European Framework of Reference. *Foreign Language Annals, 41*, 81–101.
Block, D. (2007). *Second language identities*. London: Continuum.
Brown, L. (2018). Contributions and future directions of College Korean Curriculum inspired by National Standards for Korean (2015). *The Korean Language in America, 22*(1), 71–74.
Cheon, S.-Y. (2007). Content-based language instruction through Korean film. *The Korean Language in America, 12*, 15–30.
Cheon, S.-Y. (2017). The design, implementation and evaluation of Korean K-12 teacher training workshops. *Journal of Less Commonly Taught Languages, 21*, 145–165.
Cho, S., Chung, I., & Peterson, M. (2006). Korean as a world language. *The Korean Language in America, 11*, 1–16.
Cho, Y. (2021). *Teaching Korean as a foreign language: Theories and practices*. Oxon and New York: Routledge.
Cho, Y., & Chun, H. (2020). Curricular co-creations and the connections goal in KFL. In *Paper presented at The International Association of Korean Language Education Annual Conference Meeting*, Seoul, Korea.
Cho, Y., Jung, J., & Ha, J. (2020). *Integrated Korean: Accelerated* (Vol. 1 & 2). Honolulu, HI: University of Hawai'i Press.
Chun, H., & Cho, Y. (2018). Building a locally relevant curriculum for Korean language teachers. *The Korean Language in America, 22*(1), 46–70.

College Korean Curriculum Inspired by National Standards for Korean. (2015). Special Issue. *The Korean Language in America, 19*(2).

Cox, T. L., Malone, M. E., & Winke, P. (2018). Future directions in assessment: Influences of standards and implications for language learning. *Foreign Language Annals, 51*(1), 104–115.

Cutshall, S. (2012). More than a decade of standards: Integrating 'connections' in your language instruction. *The Language Educator*, August, 32–38.

Garcia, O., & Wei, L. (2014). *Translanguaging: Language, bilingualism and education*. London: Palgrave Macmillan.

Glisan, E. W., Swender, E., & Surface, E. A. (2013). Oral proficiency standards and foreign language teacher candidates: Current findings and future research directions. *Foreign Language Annals, 46*, 264–289.

Howard, E., Sugarman, J., Christian, D., Lindholm-Leary, K., & Rogers, D. (2007). *Guiding principles for dual language education* (2nd ed.) Washington, DC: Center for Applied Linguistics.

Jung, J., Ha, J., Cho, Y., & Chung, H. (2018). *Cultivating intercultural competence through a pedagogy of multiliteracies*. AATK Workshop Panel. University of Toronto, June 21–23.

Jung, J., & Lee, E. (2018). Citizen sociolinguistics: Making connections in the foreign language classroom. *The Korean Language in America, 22*, 1–24.

Kang, S., & Kim, M. (2000). Assessing levels of proficiency in Korean. *The Korean Language in America, 4*, 211–222.

Kang, S., & Lim, B. (2004). Implications of ILR/ACTFL proficiency guidelines and text typology in teaching and testing college level Korean. *The Korean Language in America, 9*, 126–143.

Kim, H.-S. (2020a). Korean heritage language learning. In Y. Cho (Ed.), *Teaching Korean as a foreign language: Theories and practices* (pp. 109–126). Oxon: Routledge.

Kim, H.-S. (2020b). Building Korean for academic purposes into the KFL curriculum. In *Workshop on bridging language and content in higher education*. Yale University, October 24, 2020.

Kim, H.-Y. (2005). Construction of language and culture in a content-based language class. *The Korean Language in America, 10*, 50–70.

Kim, S. (2017). A survey on postsecondary Korean language programs in the United States. *Journal of Less Commonly Taught Languages, 21*, 99–126.

Kim, S., & Sohn, S. (2016). Service learning, an integral part of heritage language learners. *Heritage Language Journal, 10*(1), 17–35.

Kissau, S., & Algozzine, B. (2017). Effective foreign language teaching: Broadening the concept of content knowledge. *Foreign Language Annals, 50*, 114–134.

Korean National Standards Task Force. (2012). *Standards for Korean language learning*. Alexandria, VA: ACTFL Publications.

Kramsch, C. (2006). From communicative competence to symbolic competence. *The Modern Language Journal, 90*(2), 249–252.

Kramsch, C. (2009). *The multilingual subject*. Oxford: Oxford University Press.

Kwon, H. (2003). Standards-based Korean language instruction in New York City public high schools. *The Korean Language in America, 8*, 337–344.

Lee, J. (2013). Suggestions for the revision of indicators for Standards for Korean Language Learning. In S.-O. Sohn, S. Cho, & S.-H. You (Eds.), *Studies in Korean linguistics and language pedagogy: Festschrift for Ho-min Sohn* (pp. 522–551). Seoul: Korea University Press.

Lee, S. W. (2013). The present situation and issues of Korean language education at K-12 schools in the USA. *Journal of Korean Language Education, 24*(3), 187–120.

Lee-Smith, A. (2018). Linking language learning with community: A community-based learning project for advanced Korean courses. *The Korean Language in America, 22*(2), 167–189.

Lee-Smith, A., Suh, J., & Choi, B. (2017). Revitalizing 'communities' of the 5C's: Community-based language learning projects. In *The 22nd AATK annual conference and professional development workshop*. University of Southern California, Los Angeles, CA.

Magnan, S. S. (2017). The role of the national standards in second/foreign language education. In N. Van Deusen-Scholl & S. May (Eds.), *Second and foreign language education: Encyclopedia of language and education* (3rd ed.). Cham: Springer.

Magnan, S., Murphy, D., & Sahakyan, N. (2014). Goals of collegiate learners and the standards for foreign language learning. *The Modern Language Journal, 98*. Supplement.

McTighe, J., & Wiggins, G. (2005). *Understanding by design*. Alexandria, VA: ASCD.

National Standards in Foreign Language Education Project. (1996, 1999, 2006). *Standards for foreign language learning in the 21st century (SFFLL)* (1st, 2nd & 3rd eds.). Lawrence, KS: Allen Press.

The New London Group. (1996). A pedagogy of multiliteracies: Designing social futures. *Harvard Educational Review, 66*(1), 60–93.

Paesani, K., & Allen, H. W. (2012). Beyond the language-content divide: A review of research on advanced collegiate foreign language teaching and learning. *Foreign Language Annals, 45,* 54–75.

Park, M.-J., Choi, B., & Ko, S. (2021). Pedagogical approaches and practices in teaching Korean. In Y. Y. Cho (Ed.), *Teaching Korean as a foreign language: Theories and practices* (pp. 24–53). New York: Rutledge.

Phillips, J. K., & Abbott, M. (2011). *A decade of foreign language standards: Impact, influence, and future directions.* Survey results. Alexandria, VA: ACTFL.

Shin, S., & Kim, S. (2000). The introduction of content-based language teaching to college-level Korean program for heritage learners. *The Korean Language in America, 5,* 167–179.

Sohn, H., Huh, S., & Choi, Y. (2007). Needs analysis of Korean community schools in Hawaii. In *Proceedings of the 17th international conference on Korean language education* (pp. 587–603). The International Association of Korean Language Education.

Sohn, H.-M. (2000). Curricular goals and content standards for K-16 Korean language learning. *The Korean Language in America, 5,* 3–16.

Sohn, H.-M., Jeong, H.-J., & Park, M. (2013). Toward K-16 articulation for advanced Korean language learning. In H.-M. Sohn (Ed.), *Topics in Korean language and linguistics* (pp. 747–761). Seoul: Korea University Press.

Tell Project. (2014). *Teacher effectiveness for language learning.* Retrieved from www.TELLproject.org

Troyan, F. J., & Kaplan, C. S. (2015). The functions of reflection in high-stakes assessment of world language teacher candidates. *Foreign Language Annals, 48,* 372–393.

U.S. Census Bureau. (n.d.). *American community survey 5-year estimates, 2012. Language most commonly spoken at home.* U.S. Department of Commerce. Retrieved from https://data.census.gov/cedsci/table?q=language&tid=ACSST1Y2019.S1601

Wheeler, G. (2013). *Language teaching through the ages.* Routledge Research in Education 93. Oxon and New York: Routledge.

Wilbur, M. L. (2007). How foreign language teachers get taught: Methods of teaching the methods course. *Foreign Language Annals, 40,* 79–101.

20
USAGE-BASED APPROACH TO GRAMMAR IN KOREAN LANGUAGE TEACHING AND LEARNING

Hyo Sang Lee

Introduction

Even as virtually all language instructors pursue communicative language teaching (CLT), task-based language teaching (TBLT), and performance-based language teaching (PBLT), grammar is still an indispensable part of language instruction and language learning. Many instructors and learners alike feel that learning grammar is essential to learning a language. What both instructors and language learners often find wanting, though, is a good grammar description or resources from which they can find information that helps them understand a particular grammar point. The most accessible grammar description of a language to instructors and learners is usually the textbook used in a language class. Too often, however, the grammar description provided in language textbooks is too simple, often not detailed enough to help the readers understand the use or uses of a particular grammatical form or structure in question. More resourceful instructors and advanced students may seek reference grammars, or descriptive linguistic books; included among the most well-known Korean language grammar books of such are K. Lee (1993), Lee and Ramsey (2000), Martin (1992), NIKL (2005), Sohn (1999), and Yeon and Brown (2011). These linguistic books may provide detailed linguistic analysis on Korean grammar, but they may be too theoretical, abstract, and technical for ordinary language instructors and learners, and, more crucially, rather too generalized, giving an overall or representative meaning or function of a grammatical form or construction. It is often the case that grammatical descriptions given in language textbooks, reference grammar books, and linguistic analyses are confusing, misleading, and even imprecise. Not uncommonly, they do not seem to conform to how native speakers actually speak in ordinary conversations. This is largely attributed to the kind of data the descriptions and analyses are based on. The Korean language data used in these linguistic books are mostly examples made up through the linguists' introspection, not based on authentic discourse or conversation, with little if any attention paid to individual usages, and thus lacking crucial semantic-pragmatic and contextual as well as sociocultural information that is more useful or even more needed for language teaching and learning. Much generalized and rule-based linguistic descriptions of grammar do not reflect how native speakers actually speak and often do not provide information on how and why a certain grammatical form or structure is used in a particular conversational context.

This chapter will examine grammatical descriptions given in the major Korean language textbooks and evaluate their validity in terms of whether they truthfully and sufficiently reflect the usages and usage patterns of Korean. It will be illustrated that the grammar descriptions needed for language teaching and learning must be usage-based, rather than prescriptive rule-based.

What is grammar?

The term "grammar" can refer to two things: (i) the speaker's or speakers' knowledge of a language that enables them to speak the language and (ii) the analysis or description of such knowledge that is assumed to indwell in the speakers' mind, as found in language textbooks, reference grammars, and linguistic analyses.

The object of linguistic analyses is supposed to be giving a precise description of and account for the knowledge of a language the native speakers have to speak the language. There are three possible ways to get access to the speaker's knowledge of a particular language.

1. Intuition-based via introspection
2. Experiment-based, as in psycholinguistics
3. Usage-based

The most common grammatical descriptions and linguistic analyses available for language instructors and learners are intuition-based. The data used in those intuition-based grammatical descriptions and linguistic analyses are obtained mostly through introspection by the investigator/researcher, relying on the researcher's intuition on grammaticality judgment. The examples given in these intuition-based grammar descriptions and analyses are mostly sentence-oriented and out of context.

Psycholinguistic data are obtained through experiments that are used to single out a factor in linguistic processes and/or production (e.g., Kwon, Kluender, Kutas, & Polinsky, 2013). The problem with these experimental data is that the experiment settings are not natural communication settings, and the language data are mostly processed or produced in isolation with little context. Like the language data obtained through the investigator's introspection, the kind of language data used and obtained in psycholinguistic experiments are not quite the ones which native speakers would produce in natural settings.

Starting in the 1970s, a small number of functional linguists, such as Chafe (1970), Givón (1979), Halliday and Hasaan (1976), etc., began in their linguistic investigation to look at language use and real discourse, that is, language tokens actually produced by the speakers of a language.[1]

The linguistic analyses that are based on discourse and language use expanded further in the works of Hopper, Thompson, DuBois, and Bybee in the 80s and 90s and synthesized into a usage-based model of language (Bybee, 2006, 2010; Bybee & Beckner, 2010; Langacker, 1988, 2000). The usage-based model of language is an attempt to get access to the speaker's knowledge of language via investigating actual language uses in communication, as it is assumed that "grammar is the cognitive organization of one's experience with language." (Bybee, 2006, p. 711). According to the usage-based model of language, grammar is formed or "grounded in concrete usage events or utterances" (Langacker, 1987, as quoted in Behrens [2009]), as the speakers respond to their "experience of language events they encounter, categorizing and sorting for identity, similarity, and difference" and "creating and developing exemplars" (Bybee, 2006).

The main tenets of the usage-based theory of language can be represented as follows:

1. Language is an adaptive system, which reacts to environments, i.e., communicative contexts, needs, and goals, which the speaker's cognition is subject to respond to (Bybee & Beckner, 2010, pp. 852–823).
2. "High token frequency leads to entrenchment by leaving strong memory traces, whereas type variation leads to abstraction" (Behrens, 2009, p. 99), as repeated uses lead to chunking, automatization, and categorization (Bybee & Beckner, 2010). DuBois's (1985) moto of the ecology of grammar, "Grammars code best what speakers do most," sums it up well.
3. Grammar is "emergent, never fixed but moving toward a structure" (Hopper, 1987) and evolving (Bybee et al., 1993).
4. Grammar is being shaped constantly, and language change is ongoing, as frequent and repeated uses create and develop new exemplars through grammaticalization (Bybee & Beckner, 2010; Heine et al., 1991; Hopper & Traugott, 1993/2003). Old and new constructions become competing, which brings synchronic variations. As such, searching for an account for diachronic and synchronic regularities is an important aspect of the usage-based theory of language.
5. Usage-based theory of language "looks to evidence from usage for the understanding of the cognitive organization of language" (Bybee & Beckner, 2010, p. 827) and thus examines bodies of naturally occurring languages, rather than based on intuition and introspection (Bybee, 2006).

The usage-based theory of language seeks to provide description and explanation of what and how speakers produce in language and of why they speak in the ways they do. If grammar is the knowledge of a language that enables a speaker to speak the language, the access to it and its description must be usage-based, that is, through examining what the native speakers actually say in communication, not on made-up sentences the investigators assume to be grammatical or acceptable out of contexts.

Why usage-based grammar in language teaching and learning?

As mentioned, the main purpose of learning a language is to be able to communicate with the speakers of the language. To do so, the learners need to understand what the speakers of the language say and to produce what the speakers of the language can understand. For that purpose, learners need to know not just a set of grammatical rules that enable them to produce forms of a language that are grammatical, but also how and why they are used to convey what the speakers intend to convey.

The so-called standard grammars presented in language textbooks and linguistic analyses are mostly based on linguistic analyses done on examples made out of contexts and tend to deal with linguistic structures and devices that have already long been stabilized, as if they are rigidly fixed rules. Since they mostly represent context-neutral meanings, they often do not capture the ways they are adjusted and even give rise to new forms to fit various communicative contexts and to fulfill communicative needs at hand.

The speakers develop new usages and new structures to meet various communicative goals and concerns; that is, grammars constantly evolve as the speakers make adjustments of their existing knowledge to what they encounter in a variety of communicative contexts and settings. The standard grammars do not refer to these ongoing changes and variations thereof departing from old usages and old structure. Accordingly, L1 acquisition does not stop at one's childhood, but continues throughout one's lifetime, as speakers constantly create and develop not only new usages of a linguistic structure but also new structures to maximize expressivity and the effectiveness of communication. Children acquire a language initially by being exposed to adults' language but continue to develop their language as they encounter new usages and new structure. Behrens (2009) states that "language structure can be learned from language use," as the speakers recognize structures that are frequently used in specific contexts, which "leads to entrenchment" (p. 399) of the pairing of the structures and the communicative contexts they are used in.

Grounded in the usage-based theory of language discussed earlier, the literature in L2 studies notes that there are similarities and differences between the L1 and L2 acquisition. The most crucial similarity between the two is that in both, learning takes place from the actual use of the target language, that is, through interaction and communication. Given its importance, the literature advocating the usage-based approach to L2 teaching and learning put emphasis on the idea of learning through language use and the importance of form-meaning/function connection that the learners need to be exposed to in natural communication contexts (Behrens, 2009; Verspoor & Hong, 2013; Wulff & Ellis, 2018).

What learners of a second language often encounter is that the native speakers of the language produce utterances that do not conform to or are not comprehensible with the grammar they learned from the textbooks and in class. Furthermore, it is often the case that what they themselves produce may be grammatically correct but sounds unnatural or even awkward in a given context. This is largely due to the grammar descriptions presented in the textbooks and by the instructors providing only standardized and fixed context-neutral representative meanings, without giving context-sensitive discourse-pragmatic information on a given linguistic form or structure; that is, what a linguistic form or structure actually does in communication and why it is used in the contexts it is used. What language textbooks must present then, is how native speakers speak in actual communication and the precise description of form-meaning/function connections in specific communicative contexts and settings.

In the following, it will be illustrated that typical grammar descriptions available to the instructors and the learners of Korean do not reflect actual uses of the Korean language, that is, what the speakers of Korean actually say in communication, and that textbooks and linguistic analyses either provide misinformation or do not even address what actually happens in the Korean language contemporarily.

Grammar description in Korean language textbooks

As stated, grammar descriptions in Korean language textbooks and linguistic analyses are mostly based on examples, often out of context, made up out of the linguists' introspection, not much on what the native speakers actually say in communication. In this section, it will be showcased how grammatical descriptions are misrepresented or misleading in representative Korean language textbooks and pedagogical grammar books.

Spoken language not represented properly

As Lee (2005) points out, spoken language has not been investigated much in Korean linguistics, and consequently Korean language textbooks do not sufficiently reflect most naturally spoken language, relying heavily on "standard grammar" posited and authorized by Korean grammarians.[2] Conversations in the textbooks often do not represent authentic Korean, as they are arbitrarily made up based on the grammar items laid out in a lesson design. The conversations presented in such a way are apt to be unnatural or even awkward. For example, almost all Korean language textbooks treat as "optional" not marking a nominal overtly with a case particle, such as the subject particle -*i/ka* [이/가] and the object particle -*ul/lul* [을/를], as if marking a nominal with such a case particle is considered the norm. Textbooks provide little if any information on when leaving out a case particle is possible, beyond a brief note that it is frequently "omitted" in conversation – see Appendix 1. Consider the following excerpt from a major Korean language textbook:[3]

(1) [Integrated Korean: Beginning 1 (3rd edition), Lesson 2]

    1   Lisa: 지금 뭐 해요?
                       cikum mwe hay-yo?
                       "What are you doing now?"
    2   Sophia: 한국어를 공부해요.
                       hankwuke-***lul*** *kongpu-hay-yo.*
                       "I am studying Korean."
    3   오늘 한국어 시험을 봐요.
                       *onul hankwuke sihem-**ul** pwa-yo.*
                       I have [lit. take] a Korean exam today.
    4   그리고, 내일은 한국 역사 시험을 봐요.
                       *kuliko, nayil hankwuk yeksa sihem-**ul** pwa-yo.*
                       "And tomorrow I have a Korean history exam."

This dialogue introduces the object case particle -*ul/lul* [을/를]. For the context of this dialogue, however, 'Korean [한국어]' in 'studying Korean' in line 2 with the overt object particle actually sounds awkward and would be more natural without it. On the other hand, the object nominals 'Korean exam' in line 3 and 'Korean history exam' in line 4 are appropriately marked with the object particle.[4] That is, having or leaving out a case particle is actually not optional but purposely used to carry different pragmatic functions. Shin (1982) and Lee and Thompson (1989) propose that sharedness or familiarity of an activity among the interlocutors is the key factor for leaving out the object particle; either a referent is part of an activity that is ordinary or expectable or an idea that has been entertained in a given context. Sophia's studying Korean in the previous example is something expectable to Lisa, as she should be familiar with Sophia's school work and routines, but her 'taking a Korean exam' today and 'taking a Korean history exam tomorrow' are specific activities the information of which would not have been shared previously with Lisa. Familiar activities include daily routines, such as eating breakfast, drinking coffee, taking courses at school, etc., and a reference to these routines is made without the overt case particle as well, as in the following example:

(2) A: 커피 자주 드세요?
           Khephi cacwu tusey-yo.
           "Do you drink coffee often?"
     B: 네, 자주 마셔요.
           ney, cacwu masye-yo.
           "Yeah, I often do.

Lee (2005) also points out that the majority of Korean language textbooks do not deal with a spoken language phenomenon such as the uses of *kuntey/kulentey* [근데/그런데] and -*e/a kaciko* 'having taken' [어/아 가지고] in the colloquial language. *Kuntey/kulentey* is a conjunction that is used in a variety of contexts, largely in the context of changing a subject matter as well as making a contrast. Most of the Korean language textbooks examined in

Lee (2005), however, only recognize its function of changing a subject matter while introducing *kulehciman* as a representative contrastive conjunction. As a matter of fact, however, *kuntey/ kulentey* is the most commonly used conjunction in ordinary conversation that is used in the context of making a contrast in the sense of 'but'; Park (1997, 1999) reports that *kuntey/ kulentey* is the main conjunction to marking contrast, occurring 107 times in her conversational data of 200 minutes in length, while *kulehciman* occurs only twice.

– *E/A kaciko* [어/아 가지고], only used in colloquial language, is a newly developed construction replacing the sequential development-marking clausal connective *-ese/ase* [어서/아서]; both *-ese/ase* and *-e/a kaciko* can indicate either a sequence of closely tied activities, such as 'going to a library and studying [there]' and 'getting up [out of bed] and taking a shower,' or a cause/reason-effect/consequence relation, such as 'having a car accident and so being late for a class.' Even though *-e/a kaciko* occurs much more frequently than another clausal connective *-nikka* [니까] (Kim, 2000), which also marks a sequence of events and a cause/reason, it is introduced only in a few textbooks, while *-nikka* is introduced in almost all textbooks (Kim, 2000; Lee, 2005).

Another spoken language phenomenon poorly represented in Korean language textbooks is *kuleh-* [그렇-] 'do so' replacing *ha-* [하-] 'do' along with the omission of the complementizer *-ko* [고] in the indirect discourse construction *-ko ha-* [고 하-] and in the expression of intention or planning *-lyeko ha-* [-려고 하-]. See the following example for how indirect discourse construction is represented in a Korean language textbook:

(3) [Ewha Korean(이화 한국어) 3권 4과]

1 A: 연극반에서 가을 정기 공연을 위한 준비 모임이 있**다고** 하는데,
*Yenkuk-pan-eyse kaul cengki kongyen-ul wiha-n cwunpi moim-i iss-ta-**ko** ha-nuntey*,
알고 있어요?
al-ko iss-e-yo?
"**It is said that** there will be a preparatory meeting for the fall performance of the theater group, and do you know [that]?"

2 B: 아니오. 언제 한다**고 해**요?
*anio. encey ha-n-ta-**ko** hay-yo?*
"No. When **do they say** is the meeting?"

3 A: 다음 주 월요일 수업 후에 연습실로 모이라**고 했**어요.
*taum cwu welyoil swuep hwu-ey yensup-sil-lo moi-la-**ko** hay-ss-e-yo.*
"I was **told to** gather at the practice room after the class next Monday."

4 그리고 오늘 준호 선배도 만났는데
kuliko onul Joonho senpay-to manna-ss-nuntey
연극반 캠프도 같이 가자**고 했**어요.
*yenkuk-pan khaymphu-to kathi ka-ca-**ko** hayss-e-yo.*
"And, I ran into Junho, and (**he**) **said** we all go to the theatre group camp."

5 마이클씨는 어때요? 갈 수 있어요?
Michael-ssi-nun ettay-yo? Ka-l swu iss-e-yo?
"What about you, Michael? Can you go?"

6 B: 그럼요, 저도 간다고 **전해** 주세요.
*kulem-yo, ce-to ka-n-ta-**ko** cenhay cwu-sey-yo.*
"Of course. Please **tell (him)** that I am going, too."

In all Korean language textbooks, the indirect discourse construction is represented as *-ko ha-* [고 하-], where *ha-ta* 'to do' is used as a general verb of saying and *-ko* is a complementizer that connects the quoted proposition and the verb of saying. In colloquial speech, however, *-ko ha-* is replaced with *(-ko) kuleh-* [(고) 그렇-]. The previous dialogue would sound much more natural in the following:

(3') [Ewha Korean(이화 한국어) 3, Lesson 4 modified]

1 A: 연극반에서 가을 정기 공연을 위한 준비 모임이 있다 **그러**던데,
        Yenkuk-pan-eyse kaul cengki kongyen-ul wiha-n cwunpi moim-i iss-ta **kule**-*te-ntey,*
        알고 있어요?
        al-ko iss-e-yo?
        "**It is said** there will be a preparatory meeting for the fall performance of the theater group. Do you know?"
2 B: 아니오. 언제 한**대**요?
        anio. encey ha-n-t ay -yo?
        "No. When **did they say** is the meeting?"
3 A: 다음 주 월요일 수업 후에 연습실로 모이라 **그러**던데요.
        taum cwu welyoil swuep hwu-ey yensup-sil-lo moi-la **kule** *-te-ntey-yo.*
        'I was **told to** gather at the practice room after the class next Monday.'
4   그리고 오늘 준호 선배도 만났는데
        kuliko onul Joonho senpay-to manna-ss-nuntey
        연극반 캠프도 같이 가자 **그러**던데요.
        yenkuk-pan khaymphu-to kathi ka-ca kule-te-ntey-yo.
        "And, I ran into Junho, and **he said** we all go to the theatre group camp."
5   마이클씨는 어때요? 갈 수 있어요?
        Michael-ssi-nun ettay-yo? Ka-l swu iss-e-yo?
        "What about you, Michael? Can you go?"
6. B: 그럼요, 저도 간다**고 전해** 주세요.
        kulem-yo, ce-to ka-n-ta-ko cenhay cwu-sey-yo.
        "Of course. Please **tell (him)** that I am going, too."

Note that in the modified version in (3'), *kuleh-* [그렇-] is used without the complementizer *-ko* [고] instead of *-ko ha-* [고 하-].

This phenomenon is not an isolated one, as the same phenomenon occurs with the expression of intention/planning or imminent future, *-lye-ko ha-* [려고 하-].

(4) [Integrated Korean: Intermediate 1, Lesson 2]
    A: 비가 오**려고 하**네요.
        pi-ka o-lye-ko ha -ney-yo.
        "It's **about to** rain."
    B: 어제부터 날씨가 흐렸지요?
        ecey-pwuthe nalssi-ka hulyess-ci-yo?
        "It's been cloudy since yesterday, hasn't it?"

Colloquially, A's utterance would be more natural with *Pi-ka o-lla(-kwu) kule -ney-yo* [비가 올라(구) **그러**네요], where *ha-* [하-] is replaced with *kuleh-* [그러-] with the complementizer *-ko* [고] optionally used, and *o-lye-* [오려-] is phonologically altered as *o-lla* [올라] and *-ko* [고] if used as *-kwu* [-구].[5] Virtually all the textbooks do not address this colloquial phenomenon except for Integrated Korean. Learners need to know this, though, so that they can understand it when they encounter native speakers speaking this way and also if they would like to sound more like native speakers rather than speaking textbook Korean.

One of the grammar items that is so misrepresented in Korean language textbooks is *an-i-* [아니-], the negation construction of the equational Copula *-i-* [-이-]. The Copula construction *-i-* [-이-], which is realized in various forms, *-i-ta* [-이-다], *-(i-)p-ni-ta* [-입니다], *-i-ey-yo /yeyo* [-이에요/예요], and *-(i-)ya* [-(이)야], depending on the speech style, is introduced very early in all Korean language textbooks, and most of the textbooks also introduce along with it the negation of the construction, *an-i-* [안+이 > 아니]. As seen in Appendix 2, most of the textbooks examined emphasize the presence of the subject particle *-i/ka* [-이/가] on the complement nominal preceding the construction, with just a few textbooks noting that the subject particle is "optional," and present dialogues or examples like the following;

(5) [An excerpt from Integrated Korean: Beginning 1, Lesson 1]

마이클: 소피아 씨는 <u>한국 사람</u>**이에요**?   *Sophia ssi-nun hankwuk salam-**i-ey-yo** ?*   "**Are** you <u>a Korean</u>, Sophia?"   소피아: 아니요, <u>한국 사람</u>**이 아니에요**.   *ani-yo, hankwuk salam-**i an-i-ey-yo** .*   "No, I **am not** <u>a Korean</u>."   중국 사람**이에요**.   *Cwungkwuk salam-**i-ey-yo**.*   "I **am** <u>a Chinese</u>."

(6) [Sogang Korean (서강 한국어) 2A, Lesson 1]

안나: 이게 코지 씨 책이에요?   *i-key Koji ssi chayk-**i-ey-yo** ?*   "**Is** this Koji's book?"   유석: 아니요, <u>코지 씨 책</u>**이 아니에요**. 소라 씨 책이에요.   *Ani-yo, <u>Koji ssi chayk</u>-**i an-i-ey-yo** . Sora ssi chayk-i-ey-yo.*   "No, it **is not** <u>Koji's book</u>. It is Sora's book."

These examples are problematic in two respects. First, the conversational contexts are not ones in which the negative copula construction may occur. The negative copula construction occurs when the speaker denies what the interlocutor is assumed to think or an idea that is assumed to be entertained in the immediately preceding context; it is not used in a fact-checking context as in these examples. Second, even in a proper context where the negative Copula construction may be used, it is more natural without the subject particle. A more natural context where the negative Copula construction is used is given here:

(7) [Modified from (6)]
    안나: 어, 코지 씨가 <u>책</u>을 두고 갔네요.
        e, Koji ssi-ka <u>chayk</u>-ul twu-ko ka-ss-ney-yo.
        "Oh, Koji left (his) <u>book</u>."
    유석: 그거 <u>코지 씨 책</u> **아닌데요**.
        *ku-ke <u>Koji ssi chayk</u> **an-i-ntey-yo**.*
        "That's **not** Koji's book."
    그거 소라 씨 책이**에요**.
        *ku-ke <u>Sora ssi chayk</u>-**i-ey-yo** .*
        "That's <u>Sora's</u>."

In this example, Anna wrongfully assumes that a book someone left is Koji's. Yuseok points out that her assumption is mistaken. In this context, it is the most natural that no subject particle -*i* [-이] is attached to the nominal for Koji's book [코지 씨 책]; a possessor of the book is invoked in Anna's utterance and thus said to be shared by or familiar to Yuseok because Anna's assumption of the book being Koji's is in the mind of Yuseok when he denies it; hence no overt case particle – see the earlier discussion on the case particles and their omission.

The negative equational construction is correctly presented in the following example from a Korean language textbook.

(8) [Sogang Korean (서강 한국어) 2A, Lesson 1, p. 4]

1	제니(Jenny):	현철 씨, 연락처 좀 가르쳐 주세요.
		Hyeoncheol ssi, yenlak-che com kaluchye cwu-se-yo.
		"Hyeoncheol, could you give me your contact information?"
2	현철(Hyeoncheol):	네, 전화번호를 가르쳐 드릴게요.
		ney, cenhwa-penho kaluchye tuli-lkey-yo.
		"Sure, let me give you my phone number."
3	제니:	잠깐만요. 이름을 이렇게 쓰세요?
		camkkan-man-yo. ilum-ul ilehkey ssu-sey-yo?
		"Just a second. Do you write your name this way?"
4	현철:	아니요, '철'은 '**지읒**'**이 아니에요**.
		*ani-yo, 'chel'-un 'ciuc'-**i an-i-ey-yo**.*
		"No, 'Cheol' **is not** with ㅈ."
		'**치읓**'**이에요**.
		'*chiuch*'-***i-ey-yo***.
		"**It is** with ㅊ."
		제가 써 드릴게요.
		cey-ka sse tuli-lkey-yo.
		"Let me write it for you."
5	제니:	감사합니다.
		kamsa-ha-pni-ta.
		"Thank you."

In this example, Jenny spells the part of Hyeoncheol's name with ㅈ (read as 지읒) and asks Hyeoncheol in line 3 if what she wrote is correct. In line 4, Hyeoncheol corrects Jenny's error that it is not ㅈ, but ㅊ (read as 치읓). Note that in this context, the nominal with the subject particle -*i* [-이] is appropriate.

The problem with the Korean language textbooks in presenting the negative copula construction is that they are insensitive to proper conversational contexts it occurs, and to its linguistic form that occurs in conversation. Oddly, Integrated Korean notes that "[i]n conversation, the particle -*i/ka* is often omitted," but still inappropriately adds the particle in the model dialogue as seen in (5).

Two constructions interchangeable?

Korean language textbooks are often not so much sensitive to subtle pragmatic nuances and differences with two different constructions. None is more illustrative than the way Korean language textbooks deal with the two forms of negation, the short form of negation (SFN) and the long form of negation (LFN). The SFN is made by putting the negation adverb *an* [안] before a predicate, whereas the LFN is made with the predicate being marked by -*ci* [-지] and followed by a negative pro-verb *anh-* [않-], which itself consists of the negation adverb *an* [안] conflated with a general verb *ha-* [-하].

Whether the SFN and the LFN have the same or different meaning has long been controversial. The arguments put forward are lexical, syntactic, or semantic, but the issue is still unsettled, except being noted that the LFN is more formal than the SFN (Sohn, 1999). Having no clear conclusion, Korean language textbooks, as seen in Appendix 3, either do not mention anything about the meaning of the two negation constructions or treat them as having no meaning difference and thus being interchangeable. The following are some samples of how the LFN is introduced:

(9) [Yonsei 100 Hour Korean (연세대100시간 한국어), Lesson 5, p. 37]

영준:	부모님께 매일 전화합니까? *pwumo-nim-kkey mayil cenhwa-ha-pni-kka?* "Do you call your parents every day?"
수지:	아니요, 매일 전화하지 않습니다. *ani-yo, mayil cenhwa-ha-ci anh -sup-ni-ta.* "No, I do **not** call (them) every day." 가끔 합니다. *Kakkum ha-p-ni-ta.* "(I) call (them) once in a while."

(10) [Speaking Korean for Beginners, Lesson 4, p. 45]

톰 스미스:	어머니는 직장에 다니세요? *emeni-nun cikcang-e tani-sey-yo?* "Does your mother work?"
조영민:	아니요, 어머니는 직장에 다니시지 않아요. *ani-yo, ememni-nun cikcang-ey tani-si-ci anh -a-yo.* "No, my mom does **not** work."

(11) [Beautiful Korean (재미있는 한국어) 2, Lesson 9, p. 179]

가:	수미 씨, 어제 전화했어요? *Swumi ssi, ecey cenhwa-hayss-e-yo?* "Swumi, did you call (me) yesterday?"
나:	아니요, 저는 전화하지 않았는데요. *ani-yo, ce-nun cenhwa-ha-ci anh -ass-nuntey-yo.* "No, I did **not** call (you)."

All these examples present a mini dialogue where the focus is on whether some action occurs or not, as a matter of fact-finding. The dialogues with the LFN are awkward at best, however, because in these contexts, the SFN would be appropriate.

On the other hand, the following mini dialogue is presented with the LFN in a proper context:

(12) [Elementary Korean, Lesson 12, p. 321]

A:	언니는 요즘 뭐 해요? *enni-nun yocum mwe hay-yo?* "What is your older sister doing these days?"
B:	인제는 우리하고 같이 살지 않아요. *incey-nun wuli-hako kathi sal-ci anh -a-yo.* "She now does **not** live with me any longer."

In this dialogue, A's question does not focus on whether B's sister lives with B or not; rather, B's sister living with B is presupposed. B's denial in her response makes reference to that presupposed proposition in A's question, in which case the LFN is appropriate.

Recent researches on the two forms of negation (Lee, 2015a, 2019; Kang, 2019) show that the difference is not a matter of formality because both forms of negation occur in formal as well as informal discourse – although it is true that the LFN occurs more frequently in formal discourse, but they are actually used in different contexts. Lee (2015a) underscores that the LFN used in a question is a biased one in which the speaker positively leans toward or at least bears in mind the propositional content entertained or presupposed in the preceding context. For example,

(13) [K&H: K is putting on a pair of shorts H gave him.]

1 K: . . . 들어가는데?
tule ka-nuntey?
". . . It goes in [I think]."

2 H: . . . (1.0) **안** 맞을걸.
an *mac-ulkel*.
". . . I do**n't** think it will **fit** you."

3 K: . . . (1.0) 왜?
way?
". . . Why?"

4→ . . . 니가 나보다 크**지 않**나?
*ni-ka na-pota khu-**ci anh** -na*?
". . . Aren't you **bigger** than me?"

5→ . . . (2.0) 너 허리 나보다 크**지 않**아?
*ne heli na-pota khu-**ci anh** -e*?
". . . Aren't you **bigger** around the waist than me?"

6 K: . . . (6.0) 어휴,
ehyu,
". . . Gee ,"

7 . . . (2.5) 이거
i-ke
". . . this thing . . ."

8 H: . . . 맞[니?
mac-ni?
". . . Does it fit?"

9→ K: [이거 너무 야하**지** <h **않**어 h>?
i-ke nemwu yaha-ci anh-e?
"Is**n't** this too showy?"

In this conversation excerpt between two close friends, K is trying to put on a pair of shorts H gave him. Since K is much taller than H, H thinks his shorts may not fit K, as expressed in line 2 where the SFN is used. But K, assuming H is bigger around the waist, challenges H's assertion, by raising questions in line 3 and 4 in a way of seeking confirmation of his assessment from H, for which the LFN is used. In line 9, K realizes that H's shorts are too showy and seeks an agreement from H, using the LFN. In all of them, K is biased, leaning toward the propositional content in question, "H is bigger than him around the waist" in line 5, and "It looks too showy with H's shorts" in line 9. In these contexts, it is the propositional content of the speaker's bias that is marked with -*ci* [지] and is put in a negative question to seek an agreement from the interlocutor. The LFN in these contexts has an effect of saying "I believe such and such is the case, and isn't it?" In this context, the SFN would not properly convey the speaker's bias. Kang (2019) also illustrates, investigating the uses of the two forms of negation in TV debate programs, which are formal, that the SFN tends to be used in fact-checking contexts, whereas the LFN tends to be used in seeking agreement or rhetorical questions in making a biased assertion.

Lee (2015a) also demonstrates that the two forms of negation trigger different response patterns. In English, the affirmative/negative response tokens, *yes* or *no*, to yes/no questions match the actuality of the events in question, regardless of whether the question itself is in the affirmative or negative. In Korean, it is generally assumed that the affirmative/negative response tokens, *ney* [네] or *yey* [예] and *ani(yo)* [아니(요)], respectively, indicate whether the response matches the question in format (Kwon, 2012, p. 405; NIKL, 2005, p. 252; Yu et al., 2018, pp. 544–545). That is, if the question itself is in the negative, the affirmative response token *Ney* [네] or *Yey* [예] is used when the response is also in the negative as in line 4 of (14), and the negative response token *ani-yo* [아니요] is used when the response is in the positive.

(14) [Lee (2015a)]

1	A:	아침 <u>먹어요</u>?
		achim <u>mek-e-yo</u>?
		"Do you <u>eat</u> breakfast?"
2	B:	**아니요**, (아침) <u>**안** 먹어요</u>.
		ani-yo, (achim) <u>an mek-e-yo</u>.
		"**No**, I <u>don't eat</u> (breakfast)."
3	A:	(아침) <u>**안** 먹어요</u>?
		*(achim) <u>**an** mek-e-yo</u>?*
		"You <u>**don't** eat</u> (breakfast)?"
4→	B:	네, <u>**안** 먹어요</u>.
		*ney, <u>**an** mek-e-yo</u>.*
		"No, I don't."
5	C:	B 씨, <u>아침 먹**지 않**아요</u>?
		*B ssi, <u>achim mek-**ci anh** -a-yo</u>?*
		"B, don't you eat breakfast [because I saw you do]?"
6	B:	**아니요, 안** <u>먹어요</u>.
		Ani-yo, an <u>mek-e-yo</u>.
		"No, I don't."

Note that the responses in line 2 and 4 are both translated as "No, I don't" in English with the negative response token. In Korean, the negative response token *aniyo* [아니(요)] is used in line 2 in response to the positive question, but the affirmative response token *ney* [네] is used in line 4 when the response to the question in the SFN is also in the negative.

The response token to a negative question in the LFN, however, does not follow the standard grammar pattern of response tokens. Let's say there is the third speaker C in this made-up dialogue, who has seen B eating breakfast before. In this context, C would ask "Don't you eat breakfast?" for which the LFN would be used in Korean as in line 5, having in mind his awareness of B's eating breakfast. In this case, the negative response token *ani-yo* [아니-요] would be used, denying C's affirmative bias, as in line 6, contrary to the standard grammar description mentioned earlier, which dictates that the affirmative response token *ney* [네] be used because the format in the question and that in the response are the same – both are in the negative. Another example from a real Facebook posting is given here:

(15) [Facebook posting: Given the final scoreboard of an LPGA competition showing the top five players are all Korean][6]

    1   Choi: 이건 뭐 . . . 거의 양궁 분위기네요.
                     i-ke-n mwe . . . keuy yangkung pwunwiki-ney-yo.
                     "This is what? It's almost like in archery."
    2   Lee: 양궁보다 더 하**지 않**아요?
                     *<u>yangkwung-pota te **ha-ci anh** -a-yo</u>?*
                     "Is**n't** it <u>much more than in archery</u>?"
    3   Choi: 예.
                     yey.
                     "Yes."

In this Facebook posting exchange, Choi compares in line 1 the Korean women golfers' dominance in LPGA to that in archery. In line 2, Lee asserts that it is even more so than in archery, posing a rhetorical negative question with the LFN. In line 3, Choi responds with the affirmative response token *Yey* [예], which means he agrees with H, namely, it is more so than in archery. The standard grammar description would expect the negative response token *aniyo* [아니요], because Choi's response, which is positive, does not match the form of Lee's question, which is in negation. What the response tokens in Korean respond to is not the formal structure of the question but what propositional content is assumed to be in the interlocutor's mind, whether it is biased or simply entertained. The fact that questions in the SFN and the LFN trigger different patterns of response tokens indicates that they refer to different premises, contrary to the standard grammar's description that the two negation constructions have the same meaning.

The response patterns of the two negation constructions display "slippage" between standard ideas about grammaticality and the facts presented by natural data (Scheibman, 2001, as quoted in Bybee and Hopper [2001]). It is evident that textbook descriptions and standard grammar assumed in many linguistic analyses on the two forms of negation in Korean are not based on their actual uses.

Newly developing patterns manifesting synchronic variations

Language constantly changes, and changes are ongoing. Speakers develop a new usage of a linguistic form or construction, as repeatedly occurring contextual meanings via context-induced reinterpretation, conversational implicatures, and invited inference become associated with the form and the associations become entrenched (Heine et al., 1991; Hopper & Traugott, 1993/2003; Traugott, 1982, 1989, 2018; Traugott & Dasher, 2002; Traugott & König, 1991). For example,

(16) [Traugott and König (1991, pp. 194–195)]

    a   *I have done quite a bit of writing since we last met. (temporal)*
    b   *Since Susan left him, John has been very miserable (temporal/causal)*
    c   *Since you are not coming with me, I will have to go alone. (causal)*

Since in English is originally a temporal expression, as in (a). *Since* in example (b) can be interpreted as being used in a temporal sense as well, but due to the nature of the two events, a causal sense may be invoked. Eventually, it develops a causal meaning without any temporal sense, as in (c).

A similar semantic extension process can be found with clausal connective -*nikka* [니까] in Korean, as illustrated in Lee (2000):

(17) [Lee, 2000, p. 273)]

a 철수가 선물을 주**니까** 웬 선물인가 하구 쳐다만 봐.
   Cheolswu-*ka senmwul-ul cwu-**nikka** weyn senmwul-i-nka ha-kwu chyeta-man pwa*.
   "**When** Cheolswu gave her a present, she just looked at it, wondering what the present was for." [sequential]

b 내가 인사하**니까** 자기두 고개를 까딱 하더라구.
   *nay-ka insa-ha-**nikka** caki-twu kokay-lul kkattak ha-te-lakwu*.
   "**As** I greeted him, he reacted with his head nodding." [sequential and weak inferable cause]

c 철수가 선물을 주**니까** 좋아서 죽어
   Cheolswu-*ka senmwul-ul cu-**nikka** coh-ase cwuk-e*.
   "**As** Cheolswu gave her a gift, she was so delighted to death." [sequential and sensible cause]

d 인제 배를 광주리에 다 쏟아 놨**으니까** 또 올라가서 따는 거야.
   *incey pay-lul kwangkwuli-ey ta ssot-a nwa-ss-**unikka** tto olla ka-se tta-nun ke-ya*.
   "**Now that** he has poured out pears into the basket, he climbs up [the tree], and picks again." [sequential, but strongly causal]

e 내일은 길이 복잡할테니까 오늘 갔다 오는 게 나아.
   *nayil-un kil-i pokcapha-l they-**nikka** onul ka-ss-ta o-nun key na-a*.
   "**Since** there will be a lot of traffic tomorrow, it's better to go now." [no sequential, only causal]

Just like *since* in English, -*nikka* [-니까] in Korean has two usages, marking a sequentially unfolding of events observed by the speaker and setting a rhetorical ground for argumentation (Lukoff & Nam, 1982), that is, why the speaker says the subsequent.

Clausal connective -*ese/ase* [어서/아서] has developed two usages as well, marking sequential development and causal relation as seen here:

(18) a <u>민수</u>가 책을 집**어서** 수지한테 주었다.

   Minswu-*ka chayk-ul cip-**ese** Suji-hanthey cwu-ess-ta*.
   "Minswu picked up a book **and** gave it to Suji."

b 아침에 늦게 일어**나서** 수업에 늦게 갔다.
   *achim-ey nuc-key ilena-**se** swuep-ey nuc-ke ka-ss-ta*.
   "<u>I</u> got up late in the morning, **and (so)** went to the class late."

c <u>민수</u>가 떠나**서** <u>수지</u>가 요즘 기분이 안 좋다.
   Minswu-*ka ttena-**se** Swuji-ka yocum kipwun-i an coh-ta*.
   "**Because** <u>Minswu</u> left, <u>Swuji</u> doesn't feel good these days."

d 내일 <u>비</u>가 오겠어서 오늘 빨래를 했어요.
   nayil <u>pi</u>-ka o-keyss-ese onul ppallay-lul hayss-e-yo.
   "**Because** <u>it</u> would <u>rain</u> tomorrow, (<u>I</u>) did the laundry today."

Developing a meaning of logical sequence, such as causal relation or laying out a rhetorical ground from a meaning of temporal sequence, is a natural process of grammaticalization, which proceeds from more concrete concept to abstract concept (Heine et al., 1991). A temporal sequence can naturally be extended to a cause-effect or reason-consequence relation, given proper contexts, as the causing event and the caused event tend to take place in sequence. When a new usage gets developed, speakers do not recognize it as a separate grammatical form at first. As the new usage gets extended and expands its application to wider contexts, the new usage picks up new grammatical features. In the case of *-nikka*, for example, when it is used to express a temporal sequence, only the main clause gets a temporal marking because the preceding event and the following event are considered to be within the same temporal frame. When *-nikka* conveys a causal meaning, however, the two events are considered to be separate events in separate temporal frames, hence getting a separate temporal marking, as in examples (17d) and (17e).

In the case of *-ese/ase* as well, when it is used to express a temporal sequence, the subject of each clause must be the same actor, and the two events must be sequentially ordered, as in examples (18a) and (18b). When they have gained the causal meaning, not only the subject of each clause can be different as in examples (18c) and (18d), but also, they do not have to be sequentially ordered in the timeline, as in (18d). As for the temporal marking in the sentence, the standard grammar dictates that no temporal marking is allowed in the preceding clause, regardless of whether it expresses a temporal sequence or a causal relation (Integrated Korean: Beginning 2 [3rd ed.] 2020, p. 72; NIKL Korean Language Teaching and Learning Online Consultation Site [국립국어원 한국어교수학습샘터]),[7] It is not that difficult, however, to come across an instance of the use of *-ese/ase* in colloquial speech with a separate temporal marking, as in:

(19) [Soccer community posting][8]

시즌전체를놓고봤을때
Sicun cenchey-lul noh-ko pwass-ul ttay
중요한 경기는 아니**었어서** 괜찮다고 봅니다.
*cwungyoha-n kyengki-nun an-i-**ess-ese** kwaynchanh-ta-ko po-p-ni-ta.*
"Because it **was** not an important [soccer] game when you look at the whole season, I see it as not much of a problem."

Lee (2018) reports that the frequency of the use of *-ese/ase* [어서] with the past tense marker *-ess/ass-* [-었/았-], i.e., *-ess/ass-ese* [-었/았-어서] has gradually increased for the recent 10-year period. It occurs most frequently with the verb *mek-* [먹-] 'eat' in the internet blogs he examined between the year 2006 and 2017; there were 65 instances *-ess-ese* with *mek-* in 2006, and the frequency had increased to 6,440 in 2017. Lee (2018), although he did not exclude a possibility of potential language change, seems to see the phenomenon as mistakes or errors committed by the speakers/writers due to the lack of knowledge on grammatical rules and regulations or unintentional errors that occur in speaking or in internet environments, such as mobile communication. Such a view is an oversight, however, because it is a natural phenomenon of language change that a new usage begins to pick up a new grammatical feature as it expands its use and begins to be recognized as an independent usage departing from its source. The separate temporal marking is a sign that the speakers begin to conceptualize the event structure and frame differently and that the two events, once considered to be within a single temporal frame when they were viewed as a temporally sequential development, are now recognized as separate events that have a causal relation, the same phenomenon that has already happened with *-nikka*, as seen earlier.

These synchronic variations, i.e., a single linguistic form developing a new usage and gaining new grammatical features thereby, as well as developing a new linguistic construction for a same function as in the case of *-e kaciko* replacing *-ese/ase*, all are natural consequences of language change, more specifically grammaticalization. These changes are ongoing as they are getting more and more spread, starting in the colloquial language. Korean language instructors must be aware of these phenomena and the grammar descriptions in textbooks, and reference grammars must make reference to the phenomena such that the learners at least recognize them and avoid any misunderstanding or confusion in comprehension that may be incurred due to the discrepancy between their knowledge learned in the textbooks and in class and what they encounter in actual communication.

Researchers in Korean linguistics have recently begun to pay more attention to spoken language, and one of the phenomena that have been brought attention to is a new usage of -(*u*)*lkey* [-(으)ㄹ게] (Ahn, 2016; Bak, 2013; Huh, 2011; Lee & No, 2003; Park, 2016; Seo, 2017; Yoon, 2006). -(*U*)*lkey* [(으)ㄹ게] is known as expressing the speaker's volitional will, including promise as a way of accommodating or being considerate to the interlocutor's need (Bak, 2013; Cho, Lee, Schulz, Sohn, & Sohn, 2000, p. 123/2020, p. 148; Huh, 2011; Lee, 2004; Lee & No, 2003). For example,

(20) [Leah's letter 8, Lee (1991, p. 515)]

1 오빤 이 몸이 없어지니깐 재미가 없나 보지?
   oppa-n i mom-i eps-e-ci-nikka-n caymi-ka eps-na po-ci?
   "You don't seem to have any fun after this body disappeared, do you?"
2 편지로라도 cheer up 시켜 **줄게**.
   *Phyenci-lo-lato cheer up si-khye **cwu-lkey***.
   "**Let me** try to cheer you up even if it's just a letter."

(21) [Integrated Korean: Beginning 2 (3rd ed., 2020)]

1 A: 지금 시간 있으세요?
       cikum sikan-i iss-usey-yo?
       "Do you have time now?"
2 B: 지금 좀 바쁜데요.
       cikum com pappu-ntey-yo.
       "I'm a little busy now, so . . ."
3 A: 그럼, 이따가 다시 올게요.
       kulem, ittaka tasi o-lkey-yo.
       "Then, I'll come again later."

One of the contexts where -(*u*)*lkey* is used is when the speaker feels like having to ask the interlocutor to excuse his or her own action (Lee & No, 2003; Yoon, 2006; Huh, 2011; Bak, 2013), as in:

(22) [Bak (2013, p. 266)]

저 이만 자러 **들어갈게**요.
*ce iman cale **tuleka-lkey**-yo*.
"Please excuse me for going to bed now."

This usage is now extended to asking the interlocutor to excuse the speaker's polite request for the interlocutor's action rather than the speaker's own action (Bak, 2013; Park, 2016; Ahn, 2016), as seen here:

(23) [After a hairdresser demonstrates a hairdo][9]

빅픽처3 EP23_멋쟁이 신사 지나가실게요.
Big Picture 3 EP23_*mescayngi sinsa cina-ka-si-lkey-yo*.
"Let the dandy gentleman pass through."

(24) [Promoting some colleges for specialty majors]¹⁰
잠시만요! 이 대학들 좀 보고 가**실게**요!
*camsi-man-yo! i tayhak-tul com po-ko ka-si-**ilkey** -yo!*
"Just a moment! Please take a look at these colleges."

Bak (2013) characterizes this new usage as an extension from the speaker's volition of his/her own action to the speaker's volition on the interlocutor's action. Note that in this new usage, *-(u)lkey* [-(으)ㄹ게] is combined with the honorific suffix *-(u)si-* [-(으)시-] to pay respect to the listener since the action is to be carried by the listener.

Noticing its widespread usage, many Korean speakers, native or learners, inquire if this usage is a correct one. The National Institute of Korean Language (NIKL)'s online consultation site discourages the usage to the learners as "ungrammatical" because *-(u)lkey* is supposed to indicate the speaker's volitional will of his or her own action.¹¹

Learners need to be informed of this phenomenon, however, because they encounter native speaker's utterances of this kind quite frequently. Besides, just like in the case of *-ess-ese* [-었-어서], this new usage is not in error. The new usage of *-(u)lkey* [-(으)ㄹ게] may not conform to the standard grammar but is an instance of language change at its initial stage, a case of inter-subjectification (Traugott & Dasher, 2002) in which a meaning related to the speaker's subjective stance gets extended to factors related to the interlocutor. Therefore, these new practices, as they are spreading, should not be treated as errors on the part of the speaker or being ungrammatical.

Changes in part of speech

A word can be used in one way or another in terms of its part of speech. An English word *point*, for example, can be either a verb, as in "John points to the sky," or a noun, as in "John has a point." Likewise, *Khu-ta* [크-다] in Korean can be an adjective, as in *na-nun khi-ka **khu-ta*** [나는 키가 **크다**] 'I am **tall**,' or a verb, as in *namca-tul-un pothong kotung-hakkyo ttay khi-ka **khu-n-ta*** [남자들은 보통 고등학교 때 키가 **큰다**] 'Males **grow** a lot in high school.' Note that when *khu-ta* is used as a verb, it takes *-n-* [-ㄴ-] or *-nun-* [-는-], the non-past imperfective temporal marker (Lee, 1991), which renders the present time reference, while it does not take the temporal marker when it is used as an adjective. The part of speech of a word should be categorical and cannot be ambiguous in a given usage. Contrary to this standard idea, there are a small number of predicates in Korean that cannot be defined as one way or another in terms of part of speech; for example, *mac-ta* [맞-다] 'to get hit on the target, to be correct, right,' *almac-ta* [알맞-다] 'to be appropriate,' and *uski-ta* [웃기-다] 'to make someone laugh, funny, hilarious.' In Korean dictionaries, *mac-ta* [맞다] 'to get hit on the target, to be correct, right' and *uski-ta* [웃기-다] 'to make someone laugh, funny, hilarious' are defined as a verb, and *almac-ta* [알맞-다] 'to be appropriate' as an adjective. The problem is that the way the speakers use these predicates is unclear and confusing.

In Korean, one can tell whether a predicate is a verb or an adjective in two ways. One way is to see whether in the plain speech style it takes the non-past imperfective *-n-* [ㄴ] or *-nun-* [는], depending on whether the stem ends in a vowel or a consonant, respectively; as mentioned, only verbs take the temporal marking, not adjectives:

(25) Non-past Imperfective Marking in the Plain Style

    a   나는 키가 **크다/작다**.
          na-nun khi-la khu-ta/cak-ta.
          "I am **tall/short**."

b 남자들은 보통 고등학교 때 키가 **큰다**.
   *namca-tul-un pothong kotunghakkyo ttay khi-ka **khu-n-ta***.
   "Males **grow** a lot in high school."
c 나는 매일 아침을 **먹는다**.
   *na-nun mayil achim-ul **mek-nun-ta***.
   "I **eat** breakfast every day."

The other way is to see which noun-modifying form it takes. As seen in (26), verbs take *-nu-n* [느-ㄴ > 는] in the present time reference and *-un* [은] after a consonant or *-n* [ㄴ] after a vowel in the past time reference, whereas adjectives take *-un* [은] or *-n* [ㄴ],[12] regardless of the time reference.

(26) Non-past Imperfective Marking in the Noun-Modifying Constructions

   a 지금 **먹는** 빵은 어제 **먹은** 빵보다 **더 좋은** 빵이다.
      *cikum **mek-nu-n** ppang-un ecey **mek-un** ppang-pota te **coh-un** ppang-i-ta*.
      "<u>The bread</u> I **am eating** now is **better** [bread] than <u>the bread</u> I **ate** yesterday."
   b 어제 **산** 빵은 **비싼** 빵이었다.
      *ecey **sa-n** ppang-un **pissa-n** ppang-i-ess-ta*.
      "<u>The bread</u> I **bought** yesterday **was expensive** <u>bread</u>."

Even though Korean dictionaries define *mac-ta* [맞다] as a verb, which makes sense when it means 'to get hit on the target,' as in 나는 비가 오면 밖으로 뛰어 나가 비를 맞는다 'When it rains, I run out to the outside and **get rained on**,' its grammatical behavior is not so definitive when it denotes adjectival meanings such as 'be correct, be right.' It behaves like an adjective, not taking the non-past imperfective temporal marking *-n/nun* [-ㄴ/는] in the plain style, as in (27a). In the noun-modifying construction, however, it behaves like a verb, taking *-nu-n* [-는] instead of *–(u)n* [-(으)ㄴ], as in (27b):

(27) 맞다 'to be right, correct'

   a 지소미아는 종료하는 게 **맞다**/***맞는다**.
      *GSOMIA-nun conglyo-ha-nu-n ke **mac-ta**/*mac-**nun**-ta*.
      "It **is right** to terminate GSOMIA."
   b 이 문제는 **맞는**/***맞은** 답이 없다.
      *i mwuncey-nun **mac-nu-n** tap-i eps-ta/***mac-un** tap-i eps-ta*.
      "For this question, there is no **correct** answer."

Almac-ta [알맞다] 'to be appropriate' behaves slightly differently from *mac-ta* [맞다] 'to be correct, right.' While it behaves like an adjective in the plain speech style, it shows individual variations in the noun-modifying construction:

(28) 알맞다
   a 빈칸에 **알맞은** 말을 채우세요.
      *pi-n khan-ey **almac-un** mal-ul chaywu-sey-yo*.
      "Fill in the blank with an **appropriate** word."
   b 가격대비 훌륭한 와인들과 그에 알맞는 타파스까지![13]
      *kakyek taypi hwulyungha-n wine-tul-kwa ku-ey **almac-nu-n** Tapas-kkaci*.
      "Enjoy the wine that's excellent for its price and even <u>Tapas</u> that's **suitable** for it."

In (28a), it is used as if it is an adjective without the non-past imperfective *-nu-*, whereas in (28b), it is used as if it is a verb, taking *-nu-*, hence *-nu-n* [-는].

The National Institute of Korean Language deems *almac-nun* [알맞-는] to be ungrammatical in its online consultation site,[14] but many ordinary language users seem ignorant of the standard grammar.

What's happening here is that both *mac-ta* [맞다] 'to be correct, right' and *almac-ta* [알맞다] 'to be appropriate' were originally verbs but developed adjectival meanings and are undergoing a category change thereby into adjectives as they behave like adjectives in the plain speech style. They differ, however, in the stage of the change or the degree to which the change has advanced. It should be noted that noun-modifying constructions are more conservative and resistant to language change in general and tend to maintain an old system – see Lee (2015b) for the synchronic variations of temporal markings in Korean. *Mac-ta* [맞다] still maintains the verbal grammatical feature of temporal marking in the noun-modifying constructions, even when it denotes an adjectival meaning, because the categorical change from verb to adjective has not penetrated the historically conservative noun-modifying constructions. The categorial change from a verb to an adjective is more advanced in the case of *almac-ta* [알맞다] 'to be appropriate,' as the change began to penetrate the noun-modifying constructions, manifesting individual variations.[15]

Uski-ta [웃기다] 'to make someone laugh/entertained' is a causative verb that consists of the verb *us-* [웃-] 'laugh' and the causative morpheme *-ki-* [기], but the meaning is extended to mean 'hilarious, entertaining, funny, laughably absurd,' as in:

(29) 웃기다 'to make someone laugh'

    a   '무한도전' 박명수,
        'Mwuhan-tocen' Park Myungsu,
        웃기지못한다는이야기들을때스트레스[16]
        us-ki-ci mos-ha-n -ta-nun iyak tul-ul ttay suthuleysu
        "Park Myeongsu" in *Muhantojeon*, 'I get stressed when I hear that I don't **make people laugh**.'"

    b   근데 아무리 생각해도 미러링 되게 **웃긴다**.[17]
        *Kuntey amwuli sayngkakhay-to mileling toykye **us-ki-n-ta***.
        "By the way, no matter how you think of it, mirroring is so **funny** [lit. making (me) laugh]."

    c   **웃기는** 이야기:
        us-ki-nu-n iyaki:
        엄선된 6,000 여개의 **웃기는** 이야기와 사진을 모았습니다.[18]
        *Emsentoy-n 6,000 ye kay-uy **us-ki-nu-n** iyaki-wa sacin-ul mo-ass-sup-ni-ta*.
        "A funny story: over 6,000 carefully selected **funny** [lit. making (people) laugh] stories and photos are collected."

In these examples, *us-ki-* [웃기-] is used as a verb taking the non-past imperfective *-n-* [-ㄴ-] in the plain style and *-nu-* [-느-] in the noun-modifying construction (Lee, H. S., 1993).

Recently, started among younger speakers, *uski-ta* [웃기다] increasingly behaves more like an adjective, when it denotes adjectival meanings such as "be hilarious, entertaining, funny, or laughably absurd"; not taking the temporal marking *-n/nun-* [-ㄴ/는-] in the plain style, and *-nu-* [-느-] in the noun-modifying constructions, as in:

(30) 웃기다 'to be hilarious, funny, entertaining'

신민아 "실제 성격? 아는 사람들이 '되게 **웃기다**'고 한다."[19]
Shin Minah "*silcey sengkyel? a-nun salam-tul-i 'toekyey **us-ki-ta**'-ko ha-n-ta*."
"Shin Minah 'Her real personality? Those who know her say she is so **funny**.'"
세상에서가장 **웃긴** 이야기[20]
*seysang-eyse kacang **us-ki-n** iyaki*.
"The **funniest** story in the world."

The categorial change of *uski-ta* [웃기다] 'to make someone laugh/entertained' from a verb to an adjective seems to have begun quite recently, as it manifests individual variations both in the plain style and in noun-modifying constructions.

Again, the National Institute of Korean Language responds to inquiries from people in its online consultation site that *uski-ta* [웃기다] must be a verb, deeming its recent usage among ordinary speakers to be inappropriate.[21] The fact that there are individual variations in the use of the expression among the speakers indicate that the change is recent and ongoing. The new usage and the new grammatical feature manifested thereby should not be deemed as ungrammatical or due to the speaker's error. Korean language learners should be informed of the new usage as they frequently encounter the native speaker's practices deviating from the standard grammar.

Conclusion

The main purpose of learning a language is to be able to communicate with the speakers of the language, and the goal of language instruction is to enable the learners to understand what the speakers say and to produce language that can be comprehensible to the interlocutors. It is a cliché now that what the learners need to acquire is not just linguistic competence but communicative competence (Hymes, 1966), including what Kramsch (1986) terms interactional competence. Communicative competence in a language requires not only the knowledge on the linguistic structure, commonly called grammar (including vocabulary) of the language, but also the ways the speakers use it in communication and interact with each other. What's called "grammar" is commonly understood as a set of fixed rules that produce sentences and utterances that are deemed "grammatical." This static view of grammar or language in general, described and analyzed mostly based on language data made up via the investigators' introspection out of context, ignores or overlooks an important fundamental aspect of language that grammar in fact is formed and acquired through the language in use. Speakers create a new usage of a linguistic expression and a new structure to fulfill their communicative needs and goals. Repeatedly occurring patterns are entrenched in the speaker's cognition and form new exemplars, which compete with existing exemplars, synchronically creating variations and eventually result in language change. This dynamic view of language is theorized as a usage-based approach to language, as presented in Bybee (2006).

Both L1 speakers and L2 learners of a language constantly encounter the ever-evolving language and get adjusted to it. In the context of L2 learning, what the learners need to be instructed and learn is not the fixed set of rules, often prescribed as standard grammar, but what the native speakers do with their language in actual use, that is, usage-based grammar, which language textbooks and grammar books do not provide. In this chapter, it is illustrated that what is described in Korean language textbooks and grammar books often do not conform to what the Korean speakers actually do in using the language, some of which is even deemed "ungrammatical" by Korean language experts and authorities such as the National Institute of Korean Language. Model dialogues and examples presented to explain a certain grammar point, which are based on the so-called standard grammar, are often unnatural or even awkward. If the goal of language instruction is to enable the learners to be able to communicate with the speakers of the language, the material presented in the textbooks and grammar books must be usage-based, reflecting what the speakers actually do in communication, not what linguists and grammarians think are grammatical or correct.

A potential challenge for this could be how far along grammatical description in textbooks and grammar instructions should go in order to inform the learners of the ways native speakers speak. This is all the more why textbooks and course material should utilize authentic material, rather than relying on textbook writers' or instructors' intuition and introspection. A systematic description of usage-based grammar of course requires more attention to be paid to the usages of linguistic expressions and more research on them.

Notes

1 Using actual discourse and focusing on language use in communication has predecessors in sociolinguistics and anthropological linguistics, as the works in Hymes (1964) and Labov (1966), and also in Prague school linguists, such as Mathesius (1928/1964), Firbas (1964), etc.
2 "Standard grammar" in Korean is dictated and prescribed by the National Institute of Korean Language, a government agency dealing with Korean language and language policy.
3 The Korean language textbooks examined here are listed in the appendices.
4 It would be much more natural to say in line 3: 오늘 한국어 시험이 있어요. 'There is a Korean exam today.'
5 In colloquial language, -ko [고], if used, is often pronounced as -ku [구], particularly among the speakers of the Seoul dialect. The phonological variation between o [ㅗ] and u [ㅜ] is common in function words as the additive particle -to/tu [-도/두] 'too, also,' and the conjunctive connector -ko/ku [-고/구] as in kuliko [그리고] 'and.'
6 www.facebook.com/photo.php?fbid=10153214420565539&set=a.10152046849685539.107374 1830.747200538&type=1&theater.
7 https://kcenter.korean.go.kr/search/searchDetail.do?id=752#restriction.
8 www.juventus.kr/football/5377290.
9 www.vlive.tv/video/125889/playlist/123037.
10 https://ukp.ac.kr/archives/158071.
11 www.korean.go.kr/front/onlineQna/onlineQnaView.do?mn_id=216&qna_seq=59230.
12 Although the form of the non-past time reference temporal marking in the plain speech style and that of the noun-modifying form in the present time reference is similar, the noun-modifying form -nun [는] actually contains the non-past time reference temporal marking, combined with the attributive form -(u)n [(으)ㄴ], that is, -nu+n [느+(으)ㄴ]. The similarity is due to the phonological change that has taken place in the plain style (Huh, 1987). The noun-modifying form -(u)n [(으)ㄴ] that is attached to a verb – giving a past time reference and to an adjective does not contain any temporal marking (Lee, 1993).
13 www.tripadvisor.fr/LocationPhotoDirectLink-g664891-d1797249-i245550349-A_Petisqueira-Macau.html.
14 www.korean.go.kr/front/onlineQna/onlineQnaView.do?mn_id=84&qna_seq=151535&pageIndex=12.
15 It is interesting to note that while almac-ta [알맞다] 'to be appropriate, suitable' is listed as an adjective, and mac-ta [맞다] as a verb in the dictionaries, it is only recently that the National Institute of Korean Language acknowledges that mac-ta [맞다] can be either a verb or an adjective, criticizing that dictionaries have been wrong: https://korean.go.kr/front/onlineQna/onlineQnaView.do?mn_id=216&qna_seq=179980&pageIndex=1.
16 www.hankyung.com/life/article/201602271637H.
17 http://bbs.ruliweb.com/community/board/300143/read/30851875.
18 https://play.google.com/store/apps/details?id=com.crony.storybook&hl=ko.
19 www.chosun.com/entertainments/entertain_photo/2020/09/23/WQBZE25J6IEQMMJKPHMQP2GALA/.

20 http://blog.daum.net/ahahha21c/16461290.
21 www.korean.go.kr/front/onlineQna/onlineQnaView.do?mn_id=216&qna_seq=95890.

References

Ahn, J. (2016). A study on the function and formation process of the final sentence ending {-silgeyo}. *Discourse and Cognition, 24*(1), 47–67 (안주호. (2016). 종결어미 {-(으)실게요}의 기능과 형성과정. 담화와 인지, 24(1), 47–67).

Bak, J.-Y. (2013). The metonymic extension of Korean endings including modal meaning 'intention.' *Journal of Korean Linguistics, 68*, 253–288 (박재연. (2013). 한국어 의도 관련 어미의 환유적 의미 확장, 국어학, 68, 253–288).

Behrens, H. (2009). Usage-based and emergent approaches to language acquisition. *Linguistics, 47*(2), 383–411.

Bybee, J. (2006). From usage to grammar: The mind's response to repetition. *Language, 82*(4), 711–733.

Bybee, J. (2010). *Language, usage, and cognition*. Cambridge: Cambridge University Press.

Bybee, J., & Beckner, C. (2010). Usage-based theory. In B. Heine & H. Narrog (Eds.), *Oxford handbook of linguistic analysis* (pp. 827–855). Oxford: Oxford University Press.

Bybee, J., & Hopper, P. (2001). *Frequency and the emergence of linguistic structure*. Amsterdam and Philadelphia: John Benjamins Publishing Company.

Bybee, J., Perkins, R. D., & Paguliuca, W. (1993). *The evolution of grammar: Tense, aspect, and modality in the languages of the world*. Chicago: The University of Chicago Press.

Chafe, W. (1970). *Meaning and the structure of language*. Chicago: The University of Chicago Press.

Cho, Y., Lee, H. S., Schulz, C., Sohn, H.-M., & Sohn, S.-O. (2000). *Integrated Korean: Beginning* (Vol. 2). Honolulu, HI: University of Hawai'i Press.

DuBois, J. W. (1985). Competing motivations. In J. Haiman (Ed.), *Iconicity in syntax* (Vol. 343–365). Amsterdam and Philadelphia: John Benjamins Publishing Company.

Firbas, J. (1964). On defining the theme in functional sentence analysis. *Travaux Linguistique de Prague, 1*, 267–280.

Givón, T. (1979). *On understanding grammar*. New York: Academic Press.

Halliday, M. A. K., & Hasan, R. (1976). *Cohesion in English*. London: Longman.

Heine, B., Claudi, U., & Hünnemeyer, F. (1991). *Grammaticalization: A conceptual framework*. Chicago: University of Chicago Press.

Hopper, P. (1987). Emergent grammar. *BLS, 13*, 139–157.

Hopper, P., & Traugott, E. (1993/2003). *Grammaticalization*. Cambridge: Cambridge University Press.

Huh, K.-H. (2011). A study on the meaning of '-eulge' and '-eulrae.' *Language and Culture, 7*, 215–233. The Korean Language and Culture Education Society (허경행. (2011). '-을게'와 '-을래'의 의미 – '수용'과 '거부'의 관점에서. 언어와 문화 7, 215–233. 한국어문화교육학회).

Huh, W. (1987). *The history of temporal systems in Korean*. Seoul: Saem Munhwa-sa (허웅. (1987). 국어 때매김법의 변천사. 샘문화사).

Hymes, D. (Ed.). (1964). *Language in culture and society*. New York: Harper & Row.

Hymes, D. (1966). Two types of linguistic relativity. In W. Bright (Ed.), *Sociolinguistics* (pp. 114–158). The Hague: Mouton.

Kang, S. (2019). When and how to utilize two types of negation for asking questions in TV interview. In *Paper presented at the 24th annual conference and professional development workshop of AATK*. University of Minnesota, June 18–20, 2010.

Kim, M. (2000). What you did not learn in the classroom but what you will hear frequently in real conversation. *Korean Language in America, 5*, 317–329. AATK.

Kramsch, C. (1986). From language proficiency to interactional competence. *Modern Language Journal, 70*, 366–372.

Kwon, J. (2012). *A theory of Korean grammar*. Seoul: Taehak-Sa (권재일. (2012). 한국어 문법론. 태학사).

Kwon, N., Kluender, R., Kutas, M., & Polinsky, M. (2013). Subject/object processing asymmetries in Korean relative clauses: Evidence from ERP data. *Language, 89*(3), 537–585. Linguistic Society of America.

Labov, W. (1966). *The social stratification of (r) in New York City department stores*. Washington, DC: Center for Applied Linguistics.

Langacker, R. (1987). *Foundation of cognitive grammar: Theoretical prerequisites* (Vol. 1). Stanford, CA: Stanford University Press.

Langacker, R. (1988). Usage-based model. In B. Rudzka-Ostyn (Ed.), *Topics in cognitive linguistics* (pp. 127–161). Amsterdam and Philadelphia: John Benjamins Publishing Company.

Langacker, R. (2000). A dynamic usage-based Model. In M. Barlow & S. Kemmer (Eds.), *Usage-based models of language* (pp. 1–63). Stanford, CA: CSLI.

Lee, H. S. (1991). *Tense, aspect, and modality: A discourse-pragmatic analysis of verbal affixes in korean from a typological perspective* [UCLA doctoral dissertation].

Lee, H. S. (1993). The temporal system of noun-modifying (attributive) clauses in Korean from a typological perspective. *Studies in Language, 17*(1), 75–110.

Lee, H. S. (2000). Grammatic(al)ization and a panchronic view of grammar. In K. Lee (Eds.), *Cognitive linguistics* (pp. 255–298). Seoul: Hankook Munhwa-sa (이효상. (2000). 문법화 이론의 이해. 인지언어학 (이기동 편저), 255–298. 한국문화사).

Lee, H. S. (2005). Problems and issues in teaching grammar and Korean language textbooks. *The Journal of Korean Language Education, 16*, 241–268. Korean Language Education Research Institute, Seoul National University (이효상. (2005). 외국어로서의 한국어 교재와 문법 교육의 문제점. 국어교육연구 16, 241–268. 서울대학교 국어연구소).

Lee, H. S. (2015a). The long form vs. the short form of negation revisited: With the implication on teaching and learning of Korean as a foreign language. In *Paper presented at the 19th international conference on Korean Linguistics*. University of Chicago, July 24–26, 2015.

Lee, H. S. (2015b). Tense and aspect. In L. Brown & J. Yeon (Eds.), *The handbook of Korean linguistics* (pp. 232–248). Malden: Wiley-Blackwell.

Lee, H. S. (2019). *Usage-based grammar and the validity of grammatical description*. Keynote lecture given at the Winter Conference of the Linguistic Society of Korea, December 7, 2019.

Lee, H. S., & Thompson, S. A. (1989). A discourse account of the Korean accusative particle. *Studies in Language, 13*(1), 106–128.

Lee, I., & Ramsey, R. S. (2000). *The Korean language*. Albany: State University of New York Press.

Lee, J.-H. (2004). *A study on meaning system of Korean sentence-enders* [Ph.D. dissertation]. Yonsei University (이종희. (2004). 국어 종결어미의 의미체계연구. 연세대학교 박사학위 논문).

Lee, K. (1993). *A Korean grammar on semantic-pragmatic principles*. Seoul: Hankook Munhwa-sa.

Lee, Y.-J. (2018). A study on conjunctive ending "-a/eoseo" and temporal expressions-focused on the ungrammatical expression "-at/eoseoseo". *The Korean Language and Literature, 77*, 1–21 (이영준. (2018). 연결어미 '-아/어서'와 .-'-았/었어서' 표현을 중심으로-. 우리말글 77, 1–21).

Lee, Y. J., & No, J. N. (2003). A study on Korean modal expressions: Focused on 'conjecture' and 'volition.' *Korean Language Education, 14*(1), 173–209. The International Association for Korean Language Education (이윤진, 노지니. (2003). 한국어 교육에서의 양태 표현 연구: '추측'과 '의지'를 중심으로. 한국어 교육 14(1), 173–209. 한국어문교육학회.)

Lukoff, F., & Nam, K. (1982). Constructions in *-nikka* and *-ese* as logical formulations. In the Linguistic Society of Korea (Ed.), *Linguistics in the morning calm* (pp. 559–583). Seoul: Hanshin Publishing Company.

Martin, S. E. (1992). *Reference grammar of Korean: A complete guide to the grammar and history of the Korean language*. Rutland, VT: Tuttle Publishing.

Mathesius, V. (1928). On linguistic characterology, with illustrations from modern English. *Actes du Premier Congrès International Linguistes* 3 *à La Have*, 56–63. Reprinted in J. Vachek (Ed.). (1964). *A Prague school reader in linguistics* (pp. 59–67). Bloomington, IN: Indiana University Press.

National Institute of Korean Language (NIKL). (2005). *Korean grammar for foreigners* (Vols. 1 & 2). Seoul: Communication Books (국립국어원. (2005). 외국인을 위한 한국어 문법1 & 2. 커뮤니케이션북스).

Park, M. (2016). A study on "-*eusilgeyo*" under the use of directives speech act: Focusing on research-service circumstance. *Korean Semantics, 51*, 137–154 (박미은. (2016). 지시 화행에 사용되는 "-(으)실게요" 연구 -서비스 제공 상황을 중심으로. 한국어 의미학 51, 137–154).

Park, Y.-Y. (1997). *A cross-linguistic study of the use of contrastive connectives in English, Korean, and Japanese conversation* [Ph.D. dissertation]. UCLA.

Park, Y.-Y. (1999). The Korean connective *-nuntey* in conversational discourse. *Journal of Pragmatics, 31*, 191–218.

Scheibman, J. (2001). Local patterns of subjectivity in person and verb type in American English conversation. In Bybee & P. Hopper (Eds.), *Frequency and the emergence of linguistic structure* (pp. 61–90). Amsterdam and Philadelphia: John Benjamins Publishing Company.

Seo, M.-J. (2017). A linguistic analysis on '-*silgeyo*: An interpretation of erroneous expressions from the perspective of ecology of language. *Cogito, 81*, 397–420 (서민정. (2017). '-실게요' 사용에 대한 언어학적 분석: 오류 표현에 대한 언어생태학적 해석을 위하여. 코기토, 81, 397–420).

Shin, H.-S. (1982). A study of meaning of the object particle /-lul/. *The Korean Journal of Linguistics*, *1*(1), 118–139. The Linguistic Society of Korea (신현숙. (1982). "목적격 표지 /-를/의 의미연구," 「언어」 7(1), 118–139. 한국언어학회.)

Sohn, H.-M. (1999). *The Korean language*. Cambridge: Cambridge University Press.

Traugott, E. C. (1982). From propositional to textual and expressive meanings: Some semantic-pragmatic aspects of grammaticalization. In W. P. Lehmann & M. Yakov (Eds.), *Perspectives on historical linguistics* (pp. 245–271). Amsterdam and Philadelphia: John Benjamins Publishing Company.

Traugott, E. C. (1989). On the rise of epistemic meaning in English: An example of subjectification in semantic change. *Language*, *65*. 31–55.

Traugott, E. C. (2018). Rethinking the role of invited inferencing in change from the perspective of interactional texts. *Open Linguistics*, *4*, 19–34.

Traugott, E. C., & Dasher, Ri. B. (2002). *Regularity in semantic change*. Cambridge Studies in Linguistics 97. Cambridge: Cambridge University Press.

Traugott, E. C., & König, E. (1991). The semantics-pragmatics of grammaticalization revisited. In E. C. Traugott & B. Heine (Eds.), *Approaches to grammaticalization* (Vol. 1, pp. 189–218). Amsterdam and Philadelphia: John Benjamins Publishing Company.

Verspoor, M. H., & Hong, N. R. P. (2013). A dynamic usage-based approach to communicative language teaching. *European Journal of Applied Linguistics*, *1*(1), 22–54.

Wulff, S., & Ellis, N. C. (2018). Usage-based approach to second language acquisition. In D. Miller, F. Bayram, J. Rothman, & L. Serratrice (Eds.), *Bilingual cognition and language* (pp. 37–56). Amsterdam and Philadelphia: John Benjamins Publishing Company.

Yeon, J., & Brown, L. (2011). *Korean: A comprehensive grammar*. Oxon and New York: Routledge.

Yoon, E. K. (2006). A study on modality in Korean – Modal endings '-*eulge*. *The Language and Culture*, *2*(2), 41–63. The Korean Language and Culture Education Society (윤은경. (2006). 한국어 양태 표현 연구. 언어와 문화, *2*, 41–63. 한국언어문화교육학회).

Yu, H.-K., Han, J. Y., Kim, H.-B., Lee, J.-T., Kim, S.-K., Kang, H.-H., Koo, B.-K., Lee, B.-G., Hwang, H.-S., & Lee, J.-H. (2018). *Standard grammar of Korean*. Seoul: Jipmoondang (유현경, 한재영, 김홍범, 이정택, 김성규, 강현화, 구본관, 이병규, 황화상, 이진호. (2018). 한국어 표준 문법. 집문당).

APPENDIX 1
Non-occurrence of case particles

Textbooks	Lesson	Description
Korean through English	1권, 18과	It is optional in **conversation**.
Integrated Korean	Beginning 1 (2nd edition), 3과, 87쪽	In **conversation**, ... particles are frequently omitted.
고려대학교재미있는한국어	1권, 2과, 52쪽	It is often omitted in **daily conversation**.
Active Korean	1권, 145쪽	Object particles are often omitted in **spoken Korean**.
서강한국어	1권, 92쪽	In **colloquial speech** the object marker can sometimes be omitted.
Elementary Korean (King & Yeon)	7과, 105	In **spoken Korean**, either subject or object particle may drop out.
외국인을 위한 한국어 문법 1 (국립국어원)	414쪽	The object particle is often omitted in ordinary conversation.

APPENDIX 2
Negation of predicate nominals -i-ta [이-다]

Textbooks	Lesson	Description
100시간 한국	초급1, 1과, 9쪽	The negative of the copula – 이다 is – 이/가 아니다.
Sogang Korean	2A, 1과, 19쪽	'An-i-ta' is the negative form of '-i-ta.' **The marker '-i/ka' must be used** together with '아니다,' whereas the marker '-i/ka' does not need to be used with '-i-ta' because a noun is directly connected with '-ye-yo/-i-e-yo.'
Beautiful Korean	1–1, 7과, 63쪽	-가/이 아닙니다: '-가/이 아닙니다' is a negative form of 'noun+입니다'.
College Korean	2과, 31쪽	Negative BE verb 아니다 'not to be," "it is not ...": Unlike 이다, **아니다 requires the subject marker** for the complement noun before it.
Elementary Korean (King & Yeon)	Elementary, 5과, 65쪽	The copula is made negative by the word 아니, followed generally by the abbreviated form that is normal after vowels: 아니에요. The noun expression before the negative (but not before the affirmative) copula may, **optionally**, appear as a subject, i.e., it may have the particle 이~가 after it.
Integrated Korean	Beginning 1, 1과, 50–1쪽	Negative equational expressions: N1은/는 N2이/가 아니에요: The negative counterpart of [N1은/는 N2이에요/예요] is [N1은/는 N2이/가 아니에요], where N2 is followed by the particle 이/가 (G2.1).... In conversation, **the particle** 이/가 **is often omitted** (G3.4).
경희대한국어	초급 1, 7과, 58쪽 156쪽	(명사)이/가 아닙니다 Noun+이/가 아니다: In the polite style, the negation of 이다 is 이/가 아닙니다. In the informal style, it is 이/가 아니에요.

APPENDIX 3

Two forms of negation

Textbooks	Lesson	Description
말이트이는한국어	I, 5과, 38쪽	안+V: No grammar explanation
	I, 7과, 58쪽	~지 않다: No grammar explanation
100시간 한국	1, 제5과, 45쪽	The auxiliary verb '-지 않다' or an adverb '안' compound with an action verb or descriptive verb to indicate that a subject's action or state is negative.
서강한국어	1B, L2, 32쪽	'-지 않다' is used to make a negation. There is **no difference in meaning** between the form '안 verb/adjective' and the form 'verb/adjective stem -지 않다'.
아름다운한국어	1–2, 9과, 98쪽	"'-지 않다' is a longer negative form than '안+verb', the short negative form. Both **carries the same meaning**, but '-지 않다' is often used in written texts or formal speech as it sounds more formal."
재미있는한국어	2, 9과, 176쪽	-지 않다 is attached to a verb or adjective stem, changing the predicate sentence or interrogative sentence into a negative sentence, as 안 does. -지 않다 and 안 are used to make a negative statement or show that you do not want to do a certain thing.
Active Korean	1, 5과, 78쪽	The negating adverb '안' comes before a verb or an adjective and marks negation.
College Korean	8과, p. 84쪽	안: no description on its use or meaning.
	13과, 146쪽	Vstem+지 않다: no description on its use or meaning.
Elementary Korean (King & Yeon)	Elementary, Lesson 12, 222쪽	"The long negative differs from the short negative . . . only in that it is a phrase rather than a single word; **the meaning of each corresponding form is the same**."

(Continued)

(Continued)

Textbooks	Lesson	Description
Integrated Korean	**Beginning 2**, 14과, 225쪽	"In general, the long form of the negative ~지 않다, and the short form, 안+verb or adjective are used **interchangeably**, although the long form sounds slightly more formal. The long form is much more frequently used in writing than is the short form."
경희대한국어	초급 1, 16과, 102, 103쪽	In Korean, there is both a short form and a long form to express negation (p. 162).
Speaking Korean for Beginners	Lesson 4, Listen, 48쪽	"This pattern [~지 않다], attached to the verb or adjective stem, makes a negation." => No introduction of 안.

PART IV

Individual differences and social factors

21
INDIVIDUAL LEARNER DIFFERENCES IN LEARNING KOREAN AS A SECOND LANGUAGE

Danielle Ooyoung Pyun and Andrew Sangpil Byon

Introduction

Individual learner differences have been a topic of considerable importance in the field of second language acquisition (SLA) and foreign language pedagogy, as they can help explain why some learners are more successful in learning than others. While there are countless studies addressing the role of individual learner variables in learning English or European languages as a second/foreign language (L2), relatively few studies have investigated their effects on learning Korean as a second/foreign language (KSL).[1]

Past studies suggested that individual learner variables exert considerable influence on learning less commonly taught languages (LCTLs), such as Korean, Japanese, and Arabic (Elkhafaifi, 2005; Pyun, Kim, Cho, & Lee, 2014; Saito, Garza, & Horwitz, 1999). Saito, Garza, and Horwitz (1999), in their cross-linguistic study of L2 Spanish, Russian, and Japanese, put forward the idea that the more distant the L2 script is from L1 (first language), the more reading anxiety the learner is likely to experience. A similar implication was raised by Elkhafaifi (2005), who examined L2 Arabic learners' anxiety and their achievement scores. He presumed that the learners of LCTLs like Arabic would experience greater anxiety than those of commonly taught languages and, for the case of Arabic, possibly due to the unfamiliar writing or phonological system. Pyun et al. (2014), who investigated US college learners' affective states in learning Korean as a foreign language, speculated that the distance between L1 English and L2 Korean, such as differences in word order, morphological structure, and the sound system, could put an additional burden on L1 English learners compared to when they learn more commonly taught languages like Spanish and French.

These studies indicate that individual learner variables, such as affective factors, play a significant role in learning LCTLs or languages of greater difficulty to L1 English speakers. According to the chart of language difficulty rankings created by the Foreign Services Institute (Foreign Services Institute), Arabic, Chinese, Japanese, and Korean are placed under Category IV languages, which are labeled as languages exceptionally difficult for native English speakers, requiring approximately four times as much time as in learning Category I languages (e.g., Spanish, French, and Italian) to reach professional working proficiency. Category IV languages are considered "truly foreign," as they are noncognate with the English language, and their cultures are markedly remote from Western cultures (Christensen & Noda, 2002; Jorden & Walton, 1987, p. 111).

Given the importance of individual learner variables to the understanding of performance and achievements of LCTLs, the present chapter attempts to overview findings from KSL research published in English and Korean. Our discussion will focus on a few individual learner variables that have been investigated in the field of KSL, which are motivation, anxiety, and linguistic confidence. First, this chapter will examine central constructs of the individual learner variables under discussion along with the overview of notable works in SLA. Then, the chapter will review core issues and key findings from the previous literature of KSL. Finally, the chapter will discuss pedagogical implications and suggested areas for further research.

Individual learner differences

Classification of individual learner variables into a coherent picture is by no means an easy task. Terms referring to learner variables are not consistent, let alone that their constructs often overlap in conceptualizations, which makes it difficult to synthesize them. Some of the commonly acknowledged variables of learner differences are language aptitude, motivation, attitudes/beliefs, language-learning strategies, learner age, and affective and personality factors, such as anxiety, self-esteem, and risk-taking.

In an attempt to outline a framework of investigating L2 individual differences, Ellis (2008) identified four sets of interrelated factors (see Figure 21.1). The first set concerns abilities, that is, "cognitive capabilities for language learning that are relatively immutable" (p. 644). The factors that come under this set are intelligence, working memory, and language aptitude. The second set has to do with propensities (i.e., "cognitive and affective qualities involving preparedness or orientation to language learning," p. 644). The factors of propensities are subject to change and development according to an individual's experience, level of proficiency, and

Category	Factors
1. Abilities	Intelligence
	Working memory
	Language aptitude
2. Propensities	Learning style
	Motivation
	Anxiety
	Personality
	Willingness to communicate
3. Learner cognitions about L2 learning	Learner beliefs
4. Learner actions	Learning strategies

Figure 21.1 Factors responsible for individual differences in L2 learning

Source: (from Ellis, 2008, p. 645)

social contexts (Ellis, 2008). The factors of the third category are the beliefs the learner holds toward target language learning. The strategies a learner employs (i.e., the actions the learner takes for successful learning) comprise the fourth category. Ellis, however, notes that it is not always clearly defined whether a factor belongs to ability or propensity. A learner's choice of learning strategies, together with the learner's abilities, propensities, and beliefs, can have an effect on L2 performance and learning outcomes and vice versa.

In this chapter, our discussion will focus on the second category of factors in Ellis's framework (2008). A comprehensive survey of individual learner variables investigated in L2 research to date is beyond the scope of this chapter. Our discussion will be limited to some individual learner differences, namely, motivation, anxiety, and self-appraisal of one's ability (e.g., linguistic self-confidence), and their impact on L2 Korean performance and achievement. These variables are not necessarily mutually exclusive but often interrelated; they will be discussed separately and jointly in order to highlight distinct points of each variable as well as to collectively evaluate and understand them.

Motivation

On the list of a number of individual learner variables, motivation is probably the most frequently mentioned one. Without motivation, the driving force for learning, it would be hard to sustain and achieve the desired L2 outcomes. Motivation is a multifaceted construct that involves both cognitive and affective characteristics. Its general meaning in L2 learning can be drawn from a couple of definitions or explanations offered by leading experts in L2 motivation: "the extent to which the individual works or strives to learn the language because of a desire to do so and the satisfaction experienced in this activity" (Gardner, 1985, p. 7); "an attribute of the individual describing the psychological qualities underlying behavior with respect to a particular task" (MacIntyre, MacMaster, & Baker, 2001, p. 463); "the direction and magnitude of human behavior, that is, the choice of a particular action (why), persistence (how long) and effort (how hard)" (Dörnyei, 2001, p. 5). Scholars of L2 motivation have attempted to identify the underlying components of the motivation construct. The socio-educational model of Gardner (1985) incorporates such dimensions as learners' interest in and attitudes toward the L2 and effort invested in the L2. Gardner's motivation theory can be measured by the Attitude/Motivation Test Battery (AMTB) (Gardner, 1985, pp. 177–184), which includes the following subscales and items: interests in foreign languages (e.g., I enjoy meeting and listening to people who speak other languages), attitudes toward learning the foreign language (e.g., I love learning French), motivational intensity (e.g., I can honestly say that I really try to learn French), and desire to learn the foreign language (e.g., If there were a French Club in my school, I would be most interested in joining).

Gardner (1985, 2001) also made the widely known distinction between two types of motivational origination: *integrative motivation*, which is associated with the learner's desire to be connected to the culture and speakers of the language (e.g., genuine interest, enjoyment), and *instrumental motivation*, which stems from external factors or pressures (e.g., fulfilling academic requirements, career prospects). Many previous studies employed this distinction between integrativeness and instrumentality to explore their influence on L2 achievement. A good number of studies have found that integrative motivation exerts more positive influence on L2 learning than instrumental motivation (e.g., Dörnyei, 2001; Hernández, 2006; Masgoret & Gardner, 2003; Yang, 2003). In Hernández's (2006) study, for example, integrative motivation was found to be a significant predictor of students' scores on an oral proficiency interview as well as for students' determination to continue studying the L2 beyond the college requirement. Other studies, on the other hand, offered a view challenging the superiority of integrative motivation over instrumental motivation (e.g., Crookes & Schmidt, 1989). While the framework of these two types of motivation has served as a useful and usable guide for assessing students' behaviors and achievement in L2 learning, it is generally acknowledged that learners' motivation cannot be clearly dichotomized into integrativeness and instrumentality, as the two are often interconnected and work in synergy. In addition, a learner's situated context is believed to play a substantial role in motivational orientations. In an environment where the foreign language is a mandatory subject at school or used as an important index for admissions or employment, such as L2 English scores being used for job qualification in Korea, instrumental motivation is likely to be dominant regardless of one's desire to integrate into the target culture. In many cases, the two orientations are not easily separated from each other but tied together to some or a greater degree.

The approaches to and framework of L2 motivation were further developed and extended in the 1990s with more or alternative criteria added, thereby shedding new light on the parameters of motivation (e.g., Dörnyei, 1994; Oxford & Shearin, 1994; Tremblay & Gardner, 1995). Dörnyei (1994), for instance, offered a more education-centered and L2 classroom-relevant approach to motivation, which consists of three different levels: the *language level*, the *learner level*, and the *learning situation level* (pp. 279–282). The *language level* involves various aspects of the L2 that motivate the learner to learn, such as the L2's culture, community, and usefulness (e.g., integrative motivation, instrumental motivation). The *learner level* consists of two major components: (1) the need for achievement and (2) self-confidence. The third level, the *learning situation level*, relates to three areas: (1) course-specific motivation (e.g., whether the course content is relevant and interesting), (2) teacher-specific motivation (e.g., whether the teacher is empathic, inviting, and facilitative), and (3) group-specific motivation (e.g., whether the class promotes group goals, group cohesion, and a cooperative atmosphere).

Later, Dörnyei (2005, 2009) proposed a new model of L2 learning motivation, the L2 Motivational Self System. This model stemmed from psychological theories of the self and previous findings on L2 motivation. In a context where there are no or few L2 speaking communities into which a learner can integrate, it is relatively difficult to assess integrative motivation. Therefore, Dörnyei and his associate (Dörnyei, 2005, 2009; Dörnyei & Csizér, 2002) expanded the notion of integrativeness to include the learner's identification processes and concept of possible selves. According to the model (Dörnyei, 2005, 2009), a learner's motivational behavior is largely driven by three components: the *ideal L2 self*, the *ought-to L2 self*, and the *L2 learning experience*. A learner can be motivated by the ideal L2 self that he/she aspires or envisions to be as well as the ought-to L2 self that he/she feels pressured to possess in order to avoid negative consequences or to meet others' expectations. In addition, motivation can be affected by a learner's situated learning environment, such as his/her attitudes toward the teacher, peers, and curriculum.

Xie (2014) made use of the L2 motivational self-system by investigating the L2 self of beginning-level heritage and non-heritage leaners of Chinese. The results indicated that the ideal L2 self was a significant predictor of both heritage and non-heritage learners' motivational strength. Further, heritage learners' ought-to L2 self was found to be strongly influenced by their family; the Chinese heritage learners' ought-to L2 self was driven by their intention to meet the expectation of the people surrounding them. Based on the findings, Xie concluded that the L2 motivational self system is an effective means of understanding motivational variations and differences among learners.

Taken together, an individual's motivation is a dynamic process and is subject to both internal and external influences, from a learner's determination to exert control over his/her actions to the social context/environment the learner acts on and interacts with.

L2 anxiety

Language anxiety is "a distinct complex of self-perceptions, beliefs, feelings, and behaviors related to classroom language learning arising from the uniqueness of the language learning process" (Horwitz, Horwitz, & Cope, 1986, p. 128). It is "the feeling of tension and apprehension specifically associated with second language (L2) contexts, including speaking, listening, and learning" (MacIntyre & Gardner, 1994, p. 284). That is to say, language anxiety is situation specific and unique to foreign/second language learning, distinguished from a general personality trait (Hortwitz et al., 1986).

The causes of language anxiety can be varied. Learners may experience anxiety when they feel they are less proficient than their peers. They may feel apprehensive at the fear of "losing oneself" or "reduced personality" (Ellis, 2008, pp. 692–693). As conceptual foundations of foreign language anxiety, Horwitz et al. (1986) identified three components: communication apprehension, test anxiety, and fear of negative evaluation. They stated that foreign language anxiety is related to the difficulty of understanding the L2, difficulty making oneself understood in the L2 in which one has limited facility, fear of failure on the test, and being conscious about others' evaluations (Horwitz et al., 1986). The three underlying components are reflected in the questionnaire they devised, the Foreign Language Classroom Anxiety Scale (FLCAS). The scale consists of 33 items, examples of which are: "It frightens me when I don't understand what the teacher is saying in the foreign language," "I start to panic when I have to speak without preparation in language class," "I don't worry about making mistakes in language class," and "I feel very self-conscious about speaking the foreign language in front of other students" (pp. 129–130).

Subsequent studies attempted to examine the influence of anxiety on language performance and achievement. Anxiety can have both facilitating and debilitating effects on the process of language learning. Spielmann and Radnofsky's (2001) qualitative study, for example, discussed the positive role of tension in L2 learning. An optimal level of tension can stimulate learners' intellectual abilities and can motivate them to strive to achieve their L2 selves (Spielmann & Radnofsky, 2001). On the other hand, a great majority of studies on language anxiety addressed its detrimental effects on L2 performance (e.g., Aida, 1994; Horwitz et al., 1986; Horwitz & Young, 1991; Gardner & MacIntyre, 1993; Philips, 1992; Pyun et al., 2014; Saito & Samimy, 1996). In a study by Philips (1992), language anxiety had a moderately negative impact on L2 French students' oral exam grades. In a similar vein, Aida (1994) reported a moderate negative correlation between anxiety and L2 Japanese learners' final course grades. In Saito and Samimy's (1996) investigation of American learners of Japanese, language class anxiety was found to be the best predictor of achievements for their intermediate and advanced-level learners. In their study, language anxiety was significantly correlated with class risk-taking, implying that the more anxious a learner is, the less likely he/she is to take linguistic risks.

The state of apprehension seems to be intensified in a situation eliciting oral presentations or spontaneous utterances in the L2 (Frantzen & Megnan, 2005; Horwitz et al., 1986). However, not only listening and speaking but also reading and writing activities can provoke anxiety. Saito et al. (1999) reported that students do experience anxiety in processing the text. Those with greater reading anxiety earned significantly lower grades than their classmates with lower reading anxiety. Particularly, American learners of Japanese exhibited a higher level of reading anxiety than their counterparts learning Spanish and Russian due to "the unfamiliar and complex orthographic system" of Japanese (p. 215).

As one of the compounding variables accounting for foreign language anxiety, Sparks and Ganschow (2007) pointed to individuals' native language–learning skills. In their longitudinal investigation of US foreign language learners over a 10-year period, they found that students with higher levels of anxiety (measured by FLCAS) had significantly lower scores on the measures of oral and written native-language skills. They suggested that L1 learning skill is closely related to one's subsequent foreign language aptitude and foreign language anxiety; "anxiety is a consequence of weak language skills rather than a cause of poor performance in foreign language classes" (Ganschow & Sparks, 1996; Sparks & Ganschow, 2007, p. 279). This implies that a learner's high level of anxiety can be reduced when his/her language-learning skills are enhanced.

In general, previous studies suggest that anxiety is associated, to some or a greater extent, with students' behaviors, attitudes, and performance. Students who suffer from language anxiety tend to be less willing to participate in the L2 (MacIntyre & Gardner, 1991), tend to take less linguistic risks (Saito & Samimy, 1996), and tend to perform poorly in the classroom or on exams compared to their less anxious peers (Aida, 1994; Gardner & MacIntyre, 1993; Horwitz et al., 1986; Horwitz & Young, 1991; Philips, 1992; Saito & Samimy, 1996). L2 anxiety is also negatively related to language-learning motivation (Dörnyei, 2005) and one's perceived self-ability (Clément, Gardner, & Smythe, 1980; Kitano, 2001). Furthermore, it can negatively affect retention in foreign language courses (Bailey, Onwuegbuzie, & Daley, 2003).

Perception and appraisal of one's L2 ability

Variables concerning a learner's appraisal of his or her ability can affect the learner's L2 motivation, goal-setting, and resulting achievements. Among such variables are self-confidence and self-efficacy.

In the context of L2 learning, self-confidence, which is a dimension of self-concept, consists of two aspects, (1) an individual's positive evaluation of L2 competence (cognitive component) and (2) a state of low anxiety (affective component) (Clément, Dörnyei, & Noels, 1994; Clément & Kruidenier, 1985). Clément and his associates argued that self-confidence is the core determinant of a learner's attitude and efforts put in toward L2 learning. Their findings showed that students with little anxiety were more satisfied with their L2 performance and positively evaluated their L2 proficiency, which in turn motivated them to learn the L2 more. Accordingly, Clément et al. (1994) identified self-confidence as one of the major components of L2 motivation. An example of the measures of self-confidence is the one created by Gardner, Tremblay, and Masgoret (1997). It includes (1) items assessing a learner's confidence in four language skills (e.g., "I feel comfortable conducting myself in French almost any time"), (2) items differentiating self-confidence from one's achievement or proficiency (e.g., "I may not be completely fluent in French, but I feel confident speaking it," "Even when I make mistakes speaking French, I still feel sure of myself while trying to communicate"), and (3) items assessing one's self-confidence compared to others of the same level (e.g., "I am as confident using French as other people who know as much French as I do").

A notion similar to self-confidence is self-efficacy belief, which refers to "an individual's judgment of his or her ability to perform a specific action" (Dörnyei, 1994, p. 277). Psychologist Bandura (1986) defines self-efficacy as "people's judgments of their capabilities to organize and execute courses of action required to attain designated types of performances." While self-confidence is used in a rather broader sense, self-efficacy is a more cognitively oriented belief used in reference to carrying out a specific task or attaining a specific goal (e.g., giving a final presentation in the L2, earning a satisfactory course grade) (Dörnyei, 1994). It is said that a learner with a secure sense of self-efficacy is less discouraged in the face of obstacles or failure but makes perseverant efforts to achieve the set goals (Bandura, 1986, Dörnyei, 1994).

In the event of failure, self-efficacious students tend to attribute it to their insufficient knowledge or effort and thus continue to strive for success (Dörnyei, 1994; Hsieh & Kang, 2010). Self-efficacy can be developed and strengthened by various experiences, such as the learner's past accomplishments, observation of his/her peers, as well as reinforcement, encouragement, and positive evaluation from others (Dörnyei, 1994; Schunk, 1991).

Previous studies involving learners' self-appraisal of their ability showed its negative relationship with anxiety and positive correlation with achievement. In a study investigating the sources of college Japanese learners' anxiety, Kitano (2001) found that students who perceived their Japanese ability as lower than that of their classmates suffered from higher levels of anxiety. Gardner et al. (1997), who examined the relationships among individual learner variables based on the data collected from university students of French, observed a significantly positive correlation between self-confidence and French achievement. Along the same lines, Mills, Pajares, and Herron (2007) reported on the positive influence of L2 self-efficacy beliefs on the academic performance of college intermediate French learners. In their study, the measure of self-efficacy was on self-regulated learning (i.e., one's perceived ability to self-monitor progress and employ appropriate strategies to achieve the goal). The results indicated that self-efficacy for self-regulation was a significant predictor of students' success in French measured by their final grades. The positive contribution of self-efficacy beliefs to L2 achievement was also echoed by Hsieh and Kang (2010), who analyzed self-efficacy ratings of ninth-grade Korean EFL (English as a foreign language) students. Their analysis revealed that self-efficacy was a significant predictor of learners' English test scores. They further found that students with higher levels of self-efficacy attributed their test outcomes to more internal factors (e.g., factors that are within their control, such as effort put into preparing for the test) than those with lower levels of self-efficacy.

Overall, these studies suggest that a learner's perceived confidence, regardless of the learners' actual level of proficiency or ability, can profoundly affect their learning behaviors and academic achievement. Students who hold positive views about their capability are willing to undertake challenges, exhibit lower anxiety levels, persevere through adversity, and attribute learning outcomes to personal control factors, all of which contribute to higher achievement.

Individual learner differences in learning Korean as a second/foreign language

Like many other studies of individual learner differences in SLA, KSL scholars have attempted to measure L2 Korean learners' individual leaner variables and relate them to Korean learning capabilities or outcomes. Of the KSL studies reviewed in this chapter, approximately two-thirds were published in English and the remaining one-third in Korean.

Korean motivation

A strand of KSL motivation research has explored what motivates students to enroll in Korean classes and learn Korean as a second/foreign language. For example, Yang (2003) investigated motivational orientations of US college students enrolled in Korean, Chinese, and Japanese courses. Among 341 participants, 135 (39.6%) were KFL learners. In her questionnaire study, motivational orientations were classified into seven subgroups: integrative, instrumental, heritage-related, travel, interest, school-related, and language use. The highest mean was reported for *interest* motivational orientation (e.g., personal interest, curiosity, and the pursuit of intellectual challenge), followed by an integrated motivational orientation. Between Korean heritage and non-heritage learners, the average motivation score of heritage learners was significantly higher than that of non-heritage learners. However, on the *interest* motivational orientation, non-heritage learners' scores were higher than that of heritage learners. Overall, the data indicated that KFL learners chose to take Korean classes out of integrative motivation, reflecting their genuine interest in the Korean language and culture.

J. Lee and H. Kim's study (2008), on the other hand, focused on heritage learners' motivation. Their study was carried out with Korean heritage learners enrolled in two US universities. The data were collected through a survey of 111 Korean heritage students, as well as an interview with 10 Korean heritage students. Among the questionnaire items were 16 that examined motivational orientations inquiring about reasons for learning Korean (e.g., "I learn Korean to fulfill a graduation requirement," "I learn Korean because it is the language of my family heritage"). Through a principal component analysis of the 16 items, 4 major sources of motivation were identified: 2 were of instrumental orientation (school-related motivations and career-related motivations), and the other 2 were of integrative orientation (personal fulfillment–related motivations, heritage ties–related motivations). The highest mean score was observed in the heritage-ties motivation and the lowest in school-related motivation. No significant correlation was found between motivational orientations and Korean proficiency levels. The results indicated that most heritage learners of Korean in their study were motivated to learn Korean out of their desire to communicate with their family, to connect to Korean community, and to understand and appreciate their cultural roots and heritage. That is, integrative motivation played a far more significant role than instrumental motivation among Korean heritage learners.

Another survey research of motivation was conducted by Jee (2015) with 92 students enrolled in US college Korean courses. The survey contained items of motivational orientation adopted from the Attitude/Motivation Test Battery (AMTB). The results showed that students exhibited moderately high motivation. There was no significant difference in scores between integrative motivation and instrumental motivation, but instead the two were significantly correlated to each other, implying that students were not only motivated by their social-emotional wish to interact with Korean speakers and community but also equally motivated by practical and utilitarian benefits of knowing and using Korean.

The experience of a Korean community school in L2 Korean motivation is not negligible, according to Huh and Choi (2015). There are about 960 Korean community schools in the United States as of 2014, where the majority of students are Korean heritage children (Huh & Choi, 2015). In Huh and Choi's study, 106 Korean college learners were divided into two groups: those who have attended Korean community schools before entering college (KCS, N=19) and those who have not (non-KCS, N=87). The non-KCS participants were further divided into heritage non-KCS (N=41) and non-heritage non-KCS students (N=46). The KCS and non-KCS groups showed significant differences in motivation, attitudes, and proficiency. The placement test results indicated that KCS students were placed into significantly higher levels than non-KCS students, whereas no significant difference was found between heritage non-KCS and non-heritage non-KCS students. In addition, the KCS group expressed stronger motivation than the non-KCS group in both integrative and instrumental orientations. This study points out the significant role of Korean community schools in Korean education and its positive long-term effects on Korean learners' proficiency and motivation. Earlier exposure to Korean through Korean community schools can not only lead to better proficiency but may also significantly influence learners' motivational intensity.

Unlike the studies conducted in the United States, those administered in Korea often include participants of various L1 backgrounds. Kwon and S.-Y. Lee (2005), for example, carried out an in-depth interview with L1 Thai, L1 Chinese, and L1 Japanese learners of Korean (a total of 18 participants). Their qualitative analysis of the data revealed four emerging themes relating to L2 Korean motivation: (1) Korea-related jobs, (2) interest in Korea and Korean culture, (3) relationship with Koreans (e.g., a Korean spouse, Korean friends), and (4) religious purpose (e.g., missionary). They also found that learners with specific career goals scored higher in midterm and final exams. On the other hand, Shon and Jeon's (2011) study compared motivational differences according to participants' L1 and gender. Among 797 participants, including L1 English, L1 Chinese, and L1 Japanese learners of Korean, L1 English learners' motivation was significantly higher than that of L1 Chinese and L1 Japanese learners in both integrative and instrumental orientations. The higher motivational scores of L1 English speakers may be due to the wider cultural gap between Korean and English (compared to Korean–Chinese and Korean–Japanese), which can arouse more interest in the L2 and its culture. In terms of gender, male students demonstrated higher instrumental motivation than female students, suggesting that male learners learning Korean in Korea have a stronger desire to use Korean to expand career opportunities compared to their female counterparts.

In more recent studies, interest in Korean popular culture has emerged as a significant motivator for learning Korean as a foreign language. In their factor analysis of the data collected from 80 college Korean learners in Singapore, Chan and Chi (2010) found five major factors explaining students' Korean learning motivation, which were pop culture, career, achievement, academic exchange, and foreign languages and cultures. Among them, pop culture accounted for the biggest proportion of the total variance. I. Lee (2018), on the other hand, used qualitative data to investigate the effects of contact with Korean popular culture on L2 Korean motivation. In her interview with 17 college American non-heritage learners of Korean, 16 responded that their initial motivation to learn Korean was driven by their interest in Korean popular culture, which they first encountered through friends, acquaintances, or social media. A similar finding was reported by Wang and Pyun (2020), who examined the role of "Hallyu" (a term referring to the global popularity of Korean popular culture) in L2 Korean learning. Among 180 US college students of Korean, 36% of the participants responded that they consumed Korean popular culture (pop music, dramas, and films) frequently. About half of the participants (55%) responded that their interest in Korean popular culture was one of the main reasons for taking Korean classes. In particular, female non-heritage learners' motivation was most strongly tied to interest in Korean popular culture compared to their heritage and male counterparts.

Shin's study (2020) also points out Korean popular entertainment culture in connection to students' motivation to learn Korean. His study was conducted with participants enrolled in community-based non-award Korean courses in Australia. The 105 participants were of various backgrounds, including business managers, public servants, and members of interracial families. The survey questionnaire measured reasons for learning Korean, learning styles, and learning experiences. The results showed that, in general, participants were motivated to learn conversational/spoken Korean for such purposes as traveling to Korea, socializing with Koreans, and understanding Korean entertainment media. Regarding outside-classroom Korean learning activities, a great majority of the participants (98 out of 105) responded that they watch Korean TV/dramas/shows or listen to K-pop music. Based on the results, Shin suggested that the curriculum of community-based non-award Korean programs should be centered around speaking and listening skills as well as enjoyable classroom activities, particularly utilizing Korean popular entertainment media.

Another study conducted in the Australian setting (Fraschini, 2020) had 44 middle and high school students of Korean as participants. Informed by Dörnyei's theory of the L2

Motivational Self System (2005, 2009), Fraschini examined participants' envisioned language self, based on their responses to 47 statements. The statements were all phrased starting with "I can see myself. . .," such as "I can see myself working in Korea" and "I can see myself enjoying Korean popular culture such as music, films, TV etc." The data identified three major viewpoints of participants' L2 Korean self, while the three seem interrelated. The first point of view was related to the consumption and enjoyment of Korean popular culture. The second viewpoint was associated with their desire to expand their knowledge of foreign languages/cultures and the third viewpoint with their vision to become a fluent Korean speaker possibly living in Korea. Fraschini's study reveals that contemporary Korean popular culture plays a significant motivational role, particularly for adolescent learners.

A second strand of KSL motivation research aimed at understanding and explaining the relationship between motivation and other variables, such as anxiety, age, learning strategies, and achievement. Pyun (2013) investigated college KFL learners' attitudes toward task-based language learning in relation to four learner variables, namely, integrated motivation, instrumental motivation, anxiety, and self-efficacy. The results indicated that approximately half of the participants (54%) were both integratively and instrumentally motivated. The correlation analysis indicated that students' attitudes toward task-based language learning were positively associated with integrated motivation but not with instrumental motivation, implying that students with higher integrative motivation favored task-based language learning more. A significant correlation was also found between integrative and instrumental motivation, a finding similar to that of Jee's study (2015).

In Jee's study (2018b) on Korean heritage speakers in Australia, the motivation factor was examined with their age of immigration (AI). The participants, 76 adult Korean heritage speakers with Korean literacy, were divided into 4 groups based on their onset age of exposure to English: (1) a simultaneous bilingual group (AI 0–4), (2) an early childhood bilingual group (AI 5–8), (3) a late childhood bilingual group (AI 9–12), and (4) an adolescent bilingual group (AI 13–15). The analysis of participants' responses to the AMTB revealed that the late childhood bilingual group (AI 9–12) held the most positive attitudes toward learning Korean as well as the highest levels of both integrative and instrumental motivations. This group also reported the most frequent use of Korean at home. Jee speculated that the amount of exposure to Korean and the frequent use of Korean with family members at home contribute to boosting positive attitudes and motivation toward learning Korean.

K. R. Kim (2010), on the other hand, examined the motivation of learners of Korean for academic purposes (KAP) along with their reading strategies. The participants were 33 students enrolled in undergraduate or graduate degree programs in Korean universities, and their proficiency levels were Level 5 or above on the TOPIK (Test of Proficiency in Korean) scale. In terms of motivation, the instrumental orientation score (M=4.70) was higher than the integrated one (M=4.00), which is reflective of their primary goal of obtaining an academic degree in Korea in various fields (e.g., economics, journalism, social welfare). However, both instrumental and integrated orientations were positively correlated with metacognitive reading strategies, suggesting the efficacy of both types of motivation.

Another study (Jeon, 2015) of KAP focused on writing motivation of KAP learners, as writing skills are particularly emphasized in academic fields. Of 228 participants, 139 were learners studying in Korea and 98 were learners in China. Examples of the survey items he used are "I find writing in Korean interesting" and "I will make efforts to improve my Korean writing skills." The results indicated that the overseas group (KAP learners in China) showed a higher motivation level than the domestic group (KAP learners in Korea). In both groups, relatively lower scores were obtained for the items relating to sharing their writing with other people, such as fellows, teachers, and the general public. The author suggests making writing a more interactive and multichannel experience (e.g., sharing writing with others) rather than leaving it as a solely individual task.

L2 Korean anxiety, linguistic confidence, and self-efficacy beliefs

Anxiety and perceived confidence in one's ability are closely related, as a learner's confidence in L2 ability often reflects his/her state of low anxiety (Clément et al., 1994; Clément & Kruidenier, 1985). Studies of L2 Korean anxiety to date have examined learners' apprehension related to specific language skills (e.g., speaking, reading) or its relationship with other learner variables, such as linguistic confidence, self-efficacy beliefs, and achievement.

Among the studies discussing L2 Korean anxiety in specific language skills or performance are Pyun and Shim (2012), Pyun et al. (2014), Kim and Damron (2015), and Jee (2018a). Pyun and Shim (2012) examined whether L2 Korean learners' attitudes toward performance-based instruction and assessment were influenced by their levels of anxiety. Participants were 56 college students enrolled in beginning and intermediate-level Korean courses in the United States. They received performance-based instruction and assessment in which tasks and prompts used were designed to elicit students' oral communication skills. After receiving the performance-based approach for one school term, the participants completed a questionnaire measuring their anxiety in oral performance and their satisfaction with the performance-based approach. About one-third of the participants (34%) reported experiencing high anxiety, another third (29%) reported a moderate level of anxiety, and the remaining third (37%) reported low anxiety. A significant negative correlation was detected between anxiety and learners' satisfaction with the performance assessment, indicating that learners with greater amount of L2 speaking anxiety were less satisfied with the performance-based assessment.

Similarly, a study by Pyun et al. with 104 US college students of first-year Korean classes showed a significantly negative correlation between L2 speaking anxiety and students' oral achievement. On items of speaking anxiety, about 37% of the respondents expressed suffering from higher levels of anxiety, 38% reported moderate anxiety, and 25% reported lower levels of anxiety, a result roughly in line with that of Pyun and Shim (2012). In Pyun et al.'s study, anxiety was also negatively correlated with linguistic self-confidence. Students who felt more anxious about speaking Korean perceived themselves as less competent in using Korean, and vice versa. In addition, students with higher levels of anxiety reported making less frequent risk-taking attempts in their Korean class than their classmates with lower levels of anxiety. In summary, their data suggest that students who felt less apprehensive about using Korean rated higher on their linguistic self-confidence in Korean as well as displayed more frequent risk-taking attempts in class, and in turn earned higher oral achievement scores.

Quantitative research conducted in Korea often involves a large number of participants, as researchers can easily access a sizable population of L2 Korean learners. An example is the study by Oh and J. Kim (2019), which analyzed Korean learners' anxiety and its impact on achievement based on the data of 934 students enrolled in Korean language institutes in Korea. The results showed that the highest level of anxiety learners experienced was fear of interactive communication followed by fear of negative reaction, fear of evaluation and grades, and fear associated with class environment. As in the study by Pyun et al., a negative correlation was found between anxiety and achievement.

Kim and Damron (2015), on the other hand, looked at reading anxiety of L2 Korean learners. They analyzed 100 American college students' responses on the measures of the Foreign Language Classroom Anxiety Scale (FLCAS) and the Foreign Language Reading Anxiety

Scale (FLRAS) along with their reading performance scores. Of the participants, 19 were from first-year Korean, 19 from second-year Korean, 38 from third-year Korean, and 24 from fourth-year Korean. The results showed that first-year learners exhibited higher reading anxiety than learners of other levels. This is understandable considering that first-year students encounter for the first time the unfamiliar writing system of Korean, which can cause increases in reading anxiety. Among the FLRAS items, the highest mean score was on the item "I am worried about all the new symbols I have to learn in order to read Korean" (M=4.51 out of 5). The correlation between FLCAS and FLRAS was significant, meaning that students who feel more nervous in the classroom are likely to experience greater reading anxiety. On the other hand, there was no negative effect of reading anxiety on reading performance. Instead, a moderately positive correlation was observed between reading anxiety and reading comprehension scores of second-year Korean learners. This suggests that while students do experience reading anxiety to varying degrees, reading anxiety does not necessarily lead to poor performance in reading. Instead, a certain degree of reading anxiety can even exert positive influence on reading performance for some students.

Jee's study in 2012 is another example showing that anxiety does not always hinder or negatively influence a learner's learning outcomes. Jee compared three groups of KFL learners on their anxiety levels using the FLCAS: first-year Korean learners, second-year Korean learners, and accelerated first-year Korean heritage learners. Students of second-year Korean and accelerated first-year Korean rated higher on the anxiety scale than those of first-year Korean. Increased difficulty in tasks and assignments of higher levels was attributed to the increase in learners' anxiety levels. In addition, unexpectedly, there was a positive correlation between anxiety and course grades, that is, the higher the anxiety, the higher the achievement scores. She explained that it was possibly due to the fact that the final grades involved a small percentage of oral skills, which is typically regarded as most anxiety provoking. Similar results were observed in her later study (2014a), which investigated first-year KFL students' anxiety (using the FLCAS) over a period of two semesters. Their anxiety scores were higher during the second semester. Also, those who achieved higher during the first semester were found to experience greater anxiety during the second semester. It appears that varying degrees of apprehension and stress can be both conducive and inhibitory to learning depending on learners, proficiency levels, and learning contexts.

In the case of Jee's study in 2018a, anxiety was examined across four language skills (speaking, listening, reading, and writing). One hundred ten college learners of Korean in Australia participated in a questionnaire, measuring five areas of anxiety: (1) general foreign language anxiety, 33 items from the FLCAS; (2) speaking anxiety, 12 items adopted from Pae (2013); (3) listening anxiety, 33 items from J. Kim (2000); (4) reading anxiety, 20 items from Saito et al. (1999); and (5) writing anxiety, 22 items from Cheng (2004). The results indicated that the students exhibited a moderate level of general foreign language anxiety. The highest level of anxiety was found in speaking and the lowest in reading. Significant correlations were found between general foreign language anxiety and four skill-based anxieties. The regression analysis indicated that L2 Korean speaking anxiety was the strongest significant predictor of general foreign language anxiety, while L2 Korean reading anxiety was not a significant predictor of foreign language anxiety. Furthermore, based on closer examination of student responses, Jee identified four major sources of foreign language anxiety, which were "test anxiety," "speaking apprehension," "worrying about lack of knowledge," and "worrying about being left behind" (p. 36). Her findings suggest that KFL learners' speaking anxiety accounts for the greatest proportion of overall L2 Korean anxiety while their reading anxiety explains a marginal portion of it.

A couple of studies focused on Korean heritage learners' anxiety (Jee, 2014b, 2016; Kim, S., 2010). S. Kim's study, which involved a rather small number of participants (18 college Korean heritage learners) found a significant negative correlation between students' foreign language classroom anxiety and their achievement in the second-year Korean writing course. It can be inferred that, just like speaking, writing is a skill requiring production of the L2, which can arouse learners' L2 anxiety. Furthermore, writing and spelling abilities have been identified as the weakest areas of Korean heritage learners' competence (Kim, E. J., 2006; Pyun & Lee-Smith, 2011). Thus, it is reasonable to assume that writing can cause some heritage learners feelings of discomfort or apprehension.

In her 2014b study, Jee examined changes in Korean heritage learners' levels of anxiety over a period of two semesters. Participants were 16 Korean heritage learners enrolled in heritage-track intensive Korean courses in the United States. Measurements used were three types of anxiety scales: the FLCAS, the FLRAS, and the writing anxiety test (WAT). In the first semester, students showed relatively low foreign language classroom anxiety, slightly low level of reading anxiety, and a moderately level of writing anxiety. Their anxiety scores on all three measures were slightly reduced in the second semester, but not significantly. All three anxiety scores were negatively correlated with their achievement scores (speaking, reading, and writing test grades). The first semester anxiety scores were highly correlated with the second semester anxiety scores, suggesting that students who felt nervous continued to feel so in the following semester. Similar findings were noted in her 2016 study, which was conducted with 61 Korean heritage students in a US university. The same three anxiety scales were used. Korean heritage learners reported lower levels of foreign language anxiety and reading anxiety, whereas they expressed a slightly higher level of writing anxiety. Negative correlations were observed between all three types of anxiety and student achievement grades. She also compared heritage learners' anxiety scores against their perceived cultural identity. Those who identified themselves as Korean displayed significantly lower levels of anxiety as well as had significantly higher grades than those who perceived themselves as American. This finding leads to the speculation that heritage learners' self-perceived identity may be linked to their motivation to learn or maintain Korean, which in turn helps them build confidence in Korean while at the same time lowering their anxiety. The result that heritage students' writing anxiety was higher than speaking and reading anxieties in both studies (2014, 2016) is aligned with the general tendency that writing is heritage learners' least competent skill.

Previous claims of the close linkage between L2 anxiety and perceived self-confidence in the L2 (e.g., Clément et al., 1994; Clément & Kruidenier, 1985) have been supported in KSL studies. In Pyun et al.'s (2014) study of American KFL learners, anxiety was negatively correlated with linguistic self-confidence. Students who felt more anxious about speaking Korean perceived themselves as less competent in using Korean, and vice versa. In Jee's (2019) study, self-efficacy belief was discussed in relation to foreign language anxiety. Forty-one Australian KFL learners of intermediate Korean completed anxiety scales and a self-efficacy scale. The results indicated that among four language skills, the highest anxiety score was found in speaking and the highest self-efficacy score in listening. A negative correlation between self-efficacy and anxiety was also confirmed in the task-based KFL classroom. In Pyun's (2013) study of students' attitudes toward task-based language learning, the self-efficacy variable showed significant correlations with all other variables, namely, anxiety, motivation, and attitude toward task-based language learning. Students with higher self-efficacy belief reported feeling less anxious about in-class task performance, possessing stronger L2 Korean motivation and having positive attitudes toward task-based instruction. Overall, the results of these studies suggest that self-efficacious students experience lower levels of anxiety.

The close connection between anxiety and self-confidence was also affirmed among L2 Korean learners in Korea. Shon and Jeon (2011) reported on 797 learners enrolled in Korean language programs at a Korean university. Not only did they find a negative correlation between anxiety and self-confidence, they also found gender differences. Compared to female students of Korean, male students showed a significantly low mean score for anxiety and a significantly high mean score for self-confidence, indicating that gender may play a substantial role in these two variables.

H. Lee and Park's (2017) study is worth mentioning as it focused on listening comprehension anxiety and its relationship with self-efficacy belief. The study had 95 Thai college students majoring or minoring in Korean in Thailand as participants. Listening comprehension anxiety was measured using the items modified from Vogely (1998), whereas self-efficacy belief was measured based on the items from Kassem (2015). The results showed that self-efficacy belief had a significant negative correlation with listening anxiety. In addition, a regression analysis revealed that self-efficacy belief was the only significant predictor of participants' listening comprehension ability. To increase listening self-efficacy belief, the authors suggested providing more listening input via TV media and helping learners to interact with Koreans in spoken communication.

As was the case in H. Lee and Park (2017), two other studies support that learners with high self-efficacy are also high achievers. They are Shon, Jeon, and Hwang (2012) and C.-J. Kim and Kang (2016), which were both conducted with Korean learners in Korea. Shon et al. (2012) used a self-efficacy scale consisting of 26 items that were modified from A. Y. Kim (2002). It was revealed that students with a stronger sense of self-efficacy attributed their source of problems to themselves (i.e., internal factors rather than external factors) and obtained higher achievement scores.

In the same line of research, C.-J. Kim and Kang (2016) investigated the influence of self-efficacy on achievement and team effectiveness based on a survey conducted with 160 Korean learners enrolled in a college KSL program in Korea. The participants' proficiency levels varied from beginning to advanced. Their self-efficacy measure was devised based on the items developed by Pintrich and De Groot (1990). The correlation analyses indicated that self-efficacy belief was positively associated with achievement scores (measured by midterm and final exams) as well as attitudes toward students' classes as a team. They further found that self-efficacious students were more willing to share their knowledge and collaborate with their fellows, which positively contributed to the team effectiveness. Their study suggests the notable influence of self-efficacy not only on learning outcomes but also on group cohesion and cooperative learning.

As ways to boost students' self-efficacy beliefs, Shon and Jeon (2013) suggest offering attainable, learner-centered, and performance-based tasks as well as a goal-oriented approach. They argue that through self-regulated autonomous learning with specific and attainable goals set, students can explicitly recognize their progress in learning, which leads to greater improvement in their self-efficacy belief.

Implications and suggestions

KSL studies of motivation and anxiety have yielded varied and sometimes conflicting results and conclusions, reflecting the dynamic, context-dependent, and evolving nature of learner variables. Nonetheless some emerging trends and implications can be drawn.

One thing that seems to be certain among college or adult KSL learners is the presence of strong integrative motivation. They choose to learn Korean out of sheer interest in Korean language and culture and desire to come closer to the target community. Whether they are instrumentally oriented as well or not, their integrative orientation seems to constitute the foundation of their motivation. This is particularly so in KFL settings, such as the United States and Australia. It is very unlikely for American college learners to choose to take Korean out of external pressure or just to fulfill a foreign language requirement, in which case they would rather choose more commonly taught foreign languages, such as Spanish and French. Such commonly taught foreign languages are much easier to learn for L1 English speakers, and many students already have prior experience with them. Taking on the challenge of learning a foreign language quite distant from their L1 is unlikely without genuine interest and enthusiasm.

Over the years, KSL studies have seen more diversification in learners' motivational orientations. In an earlier study (Yang, 2003), it was noted that students' integrative orientation was significantly higher than instrumental orientation. In a later study (Jee, 2015), substantial increase was observed in instrumental motivation. Many students were both integratively and instrumentally motivated, showing a positive correlation between the two motivational orientations. This implies that not only did students wish to integrate themselves into Korean culture, they also had in mind the potential benefit of knowing Korean for career or business opportunities. We speculate that this is in part related to South Korea's growing economic prosperity and its more visible role in global society over the past two decades.

Another example of diversification in motivational orientations has to do with the growing interest in Korean popular culture. The global popularity of Korean popular culture referred to as *Hallyu* or the Korean Wave have fueled a Korean language boom worldwide. Students' interest in Korean pop music, TV dramas, and films has sparked their curiosity in Korea and its language, which resulted in new establishment or expansion of Korean programs in many countries, including the United States. Interest in Korean popular culture, thus, has become one of the major sources of KSL motivation, as demonstrated in studies by Chan and Chi (2010), Fraschini (2020), and Wang and Pyun (2020).

Another notable tendency is the motivational variation between heritage and non-heritage learners of Korean. The most prevalent source of heritage learners' motivation was to facilitate communication with their family and to connect with their Korean community, which suggests that Korean heritage students consider speaking Korean a significant part of their Korean American identity. In Wang and Pyun's (2020) study, Hallyu-driven motivation was strong among non-heritage learners, while it was weak among heritage learners, adding a difference in motivational orientations between heritage and non-heritage learners of Korean.

Findings from KSL anxiety studies are mostly in line with many of the previous claims made in SLA research. Among four language skills, speaking seems most closely associated with inducing nervousness and apprehension (Jee, 2018a; Pyun & Shim, 2012; Pyun et al., 2014), which lends support to the view that the state of anxiety can be escalated in a situation requiring oral production or improvisation in the L2 (Frantzen & Megnan, 2005; Horwitz et al., 1986). It was also noted that some learners of Korean experience a substantial degree of reading anxiety, particularly at the beginning stage of learning when they are less experienced with the Korean writing system (Kim & Damron, 2015), although the level of reading anxiety tends to be much lower than that of speaking (Jee, 2018a). It is reasonable to assume that an unfamiliar writing system can cause more discomfort and anxiety than a more familiar writing system (e.g., the Roman alphabet to L1 English speakers), as discussed in previous studies on L2 Arabic and L2 Japanese (Elkhafaifi, 2005; Saito et al., 1999). In the case of Korean heritage learners, writing was found to be more anxiety-inducing than speaking (Jee, 2016). It seems so because Korean heritage learners generally possess good listening comprehension skills and speaking fluency on everyday topics and relatively weaker writing and orthography skills.

As for the impact of anxiety on classroom performance or achievement, findings are rather inconclusive. Anxiety was found to negatively affect students' performance and achievement in Korean in some studies (Kim, S., 2010; Jee, 2014b, 2016; Pyun et al., 2014; Oh & Kim, J., 2019), whereas a positive correlation was reported in other studies (Jee, 2012, 2014a; Kim & Damron, 2015). As Spielmann and Radnofsky (2001) noted, a certain degree of tension and apprehension can encourage learners to put forth more effort in their learning, which contributes to higher achievement. After all, L2 anxiety is an understandable emotion, the manifestation of an individual's adaptive reaction to the challenge of learning a foreign/second language. Thus, it should not be regarded as an inherently negative state of emotion. The degree of the impact of anxiety may also vary according to the types, components, and formats of the exams/tests used to measure students' performance and achievement. In fact, a number of factors likely come into play when it comes to the relationship between anxiety and L2 Korean achievement.

The connection or overlap between anxiety and self-confidence was discussed in several KSL studies. All of them confirmed a negative correlation between anxiety and self-appraisal of one's ability (Jee, 2019; Lee, H. & Park, 2017; Pyun et al., 2014; Pyun, 2013; Shon & Jeon, 2011). Perceiving one's L2 capability as being low generally means that the individual is anxious and afraid of taking risks, making mistakes, and trying out novel expressions, which are all indispensable parts of language learning. Students need to be made aware that errors are natural, inevitable, and valuable parts of the language-learning process and should be encouraged to learn from trial and error.

The finding that learners with higher self-efficacy belief achieved more (Kim, C.-J. & Kang, 2016; Lee, H. & Park, 2017; Shon et al., 2012) highlights the need to increase learners' self-efficacy. Previous research suggests that self-confidence and self-efficacy beliefs can be enhanced through positive thinking, rewarding experiences, and frequent experiences of accomplishment (Pajares & Urdan, 2006). To increase learners' self-efficacy, teachers of Korean can help students to start with setting up small, attainable, and individualized goals; to carry out the goals successfully; and to gradually expand their goals to achieve more and higher. Through such a process, students can build more self-confidence in the L2, can cope better with L2 challenges, and can become less discouraged in the face of failure or imperfection.

KSL studies of individual learner differences thus far have focused on limited areas, mostly motivation, anxiety, self-confidence, and self-efficacy. Other general factors of individual differences that warrant future research include aptitude, learning styles, and personality. Language aptitude, a learner's natural ability to learn a language, may influence learning. Language aptitude can explain to some degree differences in performance among learners, particularly when it comes to a foreign language that is considerably distant from the L1, which requires more cognitive endeavors. The two most widely used instruments of language aptitude are the Modern Language Aptitude Test (MLAT) (Carroll & Sapon, 1959/2002) and the Pimsleur Language Aptitude Battery (PLAB) (Pimsleur, 1966). There are studies demonstrating a positive relationship between components of language aptitude and L2 outcomes (e.g., Harley & Hart, 1997; Hummel, 2009). Therefore, to what extent and in what particular dimension (such as phonological processing, grammatical sensitivity, and memory) individual variations in language aptitude can predict Korean proficiency is worthy of investigation.

Learning styles concern individuals' preferences in approaching tasks (e.g., holistic-analytic, verbal-imagery, inductive-deductive, etc.), which are differentiated from individuals' (cognitive) abilities (such as language aptitude) (i.e., how well an individual can learn). Previous research in SLA has found a weak relationship between learning styles and L2 achievement (Ehrman & Oxford, 1995). Data about KSL learners' various learning styles can inform and guide teachers' actions, practices, and material development.

The personality factor (e.g., introverted vs. extroverted, tolerance of ambiguity, etc.) may also affect L2 Korean learning. For example, one dimension of the personality factor is risk-taking, which can be of particular relevance to oral skills.

Finally, KSL studies of individual differences so far were predominantly conducted in college settings and mostly based on survey instruments. Future research may involve L2 Korean learners of various age groups to expand the existing literature. In addition, there are areas and details that survey questionnaires cannot fully answer or assess. Future studies may utilize other or combined methods to supplement previous KSL findings on individual learner differences.

Note

1 In this chapter, the term KSL is used in a broad sense to include both Korean as a second language (KSL) and Korean as a foreign language (KFL). However, when needed to specify a Korean as a foreign language context, KFL was used.

References

Aida, Y. (1994). Examination of Horwitz, Horwitz, and Cope's construct of foreign language anxiety: The case of students of Japanese. *Modern Language Journal, 78*, 155–167.
Bailey, P., Onwuegbuzie, A., & Daley, C. (2003). Foreign language anxiety and student attrition. *Academic Exchange*, Summer, 304–308.
Bandura, A. (1986). *Social foundations of thought and action: A social cognitive theory*. Englewood Cliffs, NJ: Prentice Hall.
Carroll, J., & Sapon, S. (1959/2002). *Modern language aptitude test: Form A*. New York: The Psychological Corporation.
Chan, W. M., & Chi, S. W. (2010). A study of the learning goals of university students of Korean as a foreign language. *Electronic Journal of Foreign Language Teaching, 7*(1), 125–140.
Cheng, Y. (2004). A measure of second language writing anxiety: Scale development and preliminary validation. *Journal of Second Language Writing, 13*(4), 313–335.
Christensen, M. B., & Noda, M. (2002). *A performance-based pedagogy for communicating in cultures*. Columbus, OH: National East Asian Languages Resource Center.
Clément, R., Dörnyei, Z., & Noels, K. A. (1994). Motivation, self-confidence, and group cohesion in the foreign language classroom. *Language Learning, 44*, 417–448.
Clément, R., Gardner, R. C., & Smythe, P. C. (1980). Social and individual factors in second language acquisition. *Canadian Journal of Behavioural Science, 12*, 293–302.
Clément, R., & Kruidenier, B. G. (1985). Aptitude, attitude and motivation in second language proficiency: A test of Clément's model. *Journal of Language and Social Psychology, 4*, 21–37.
Crookes, G., & Schmidt, R. (1989). Motivation: Reopening the research agenda. *University of Hawaii Working Papers in ESL, 5*, 217–256.
Dörnyei, Z. (1994). Motivation and motivating in the foreign language classroom. *Modern Language Journal, 78*, 273–284.
Dörnyei, Z. (2001). *Teaching and researching motivation*. Harlow, UK: Longman.
Dörnyei, Z. (2005). *The psychology of the language learner: Individual differences in second language acquisition*. Mahwah, NJ: Lawrence Erlbaum.
Dörnyei, Z. (2009). The L2 motivational self system. In Z. Dörnyei & E. Ushioda (Eds.), *Motivation, language identity and the L2 self* (pp. 9–42). Clevedon, UK: Multilingual Matters.
Dörnyei, Z., & Csizér, K. (2002). Some dynamics of language attitudes and motivation: Results of a longitudinal nationwide survey. *Applied Linguistics, 23*, 421–462.
Ehrman, M., & Oxford, R. (1995). Cognition plus: Correlates of language learning success. *The Modern Language Journal, 79*, 67–89.

Elkhafaifi, H. (2005). Listening comprehension and anxiety in the Arabic language classroom. *Modern Language Journal, 89*(2), 505–513.
Ellis, R. (2008). *The study of second language acquisition* (2nd ed.). Oxford: Oxford University Press.
Foreign Services Institute. FSI's experience with language learning. Retrieved from www.state.gov/foreign-language-training/
Frantzen, D., & Magnan, S. S. (2005). Anxiety and the true beginner-false beginner dynamic in beginning French and Spanish classes. *Foreign Language Annals, 38*, 171–190.
Fraschini, N. (2020). 'Because Korean is cool': Adolescent learners' vision, motivation, and the study of the Korean language. *Journal of Korean Language Education, 31*(English Edition), 37–74.
Ganschow, L., & Sparks, R. (1996). Foreign language anxiety among high school women. *Modern Language Journal, 80*, 199–212.
Gardner, R. C. (1985). *Social psychology and second language learning: The role of attitudes and motivation*. London: Edward Arnold.
Gardner, R. C. (2001). Integrative motivation and second language acquisition. In Z. Dörnyei & R. W. Schmidt (Eds.), *Motivation and second language acquisition* (pp. 1–19). Honolulu, HI: University of Hawai'i Press, Second Language Teaching and Curriculum Center.
Gardner, R. C., & MacIntyre, P. D. (1993). A student's contribution to second language acquisition. Part II: Affective variables. *Language Teaching, 26*, 1–11.
Gardner, R. C., Tremblay, P. F., & Masgoret, A.-M. (1997). Towards a full model of second language learning: An empirical investigation. *The Modern Language Journal, 81*, 344–362.
Harley, B., & Hart, D. (1997). Language aptitude and second language proficiency in classroom learners of different starting ages. *Studies in Second Language Acquisition, 19*, 379–400.
Hernández, T. A. (2006). Integrative motivation as a predictor of success in the intermediate foreign language classroom. *Foreign Language Annals, 39*, 605–617.
Horwitz, E. K., & Young, D. J. (1991). *Language anxiety: From theory and research to classroom implications*. Englewood Cliffs, NJ: Prentice-Hall.
Horwitz, E. K., Horwitz, M. B., & Cope, J. (1986). Foreign language classroom anxiety. *Modern Language Journal, 70*, 125–132.
Hsieh, P.-H., & Kang, H.-S. (2010). Attribution and self-efficacy and their interrelationship in the Korean EFL context. *Language Learning, 60*, 606–627.
Huh, S., & Choi, Y. H. (2015). Lasting effects of the Korean community schools on American college students' Korean language proficiency, motivation, and attitudes. *Journal of Korean Language Education, 26*(3), 287–318.
Hummel, K. M. (2009). Aptitude, phonological memory, and second language proficiency in nonnovice adult learners. *Applied Psycholinguistics, 30*, 225–249.
Jee, M. J. (2012). Effects of language anxiety on three levels of classes of Korean as a foreign language. *Journal of Korean Language Education, 23*(2), 467–487.
Jee, M. J. (2014a). Affective factors in Korean as a foreign language: Anxiety and beliefs. *Language, Culture and Curriculum, 27*(2), 182–195.
Jee, M. J. (2014b). Korean heritage language learners anxiety: Any changes over a year? *Korean Language Education Research, 49*(4), 111–138.
Jee, M. J. (2015). A study of language learner motivation: Learners of Korean as a foreign language. *Journal of Korean Language Education, 26*(2), 213–238.
Jee, M. J. (2016). Exploring Korean heritage language learners' anxiety: 'we are not afraid of Korean!'. *Journal of Multilingual and Multicultural Development, 37*(1), 56–74.
Jee, M. J. (2018a). Four skill-based foreign language anxieties: Learners of Korean in Australia. *Linguistic Research, 35*(Special issue), 23–45.
Jee, M. J. (2018b). Heritage language proficiency in relation to attitudes, motivation, and age at immigration: A case of Korean-Australians. *Language, Culture and Curriculum, 31*(1), 70–93.
Jee, M. J. (2019). Foreign language anxiety and self-efficacy: Intermediate Korean as a foreign language learners. *Language Research, 55*(2), 431–456.
Jeon, H.-G. (2015). The study on the motivational factor in the writing of KAP learners. *Journal of Korean Language Education, 27*(1), 157–183.
Jorden, E. H., & Walton, A. R. (1987). Truly foreign languages: Instructional challenges. *Annals of the American Academy of Political and Social Science, 490*, 110–124.
Kassem, H. M. (2015). The relationship between listening strategies used by Egyptian EFL college sophomores and their listening comprehension and self-efficacy. *English Language Teaching, 8*(2), 153–169.

Kim, A. Y. (2002). Development of standardized student motivation scales, *Journal of Educational Evaluation, 15*, 157–184.

Kim, C.-J., & Kang, S. H. (2016). The influence of self-efficacy on academic achievement and team effectiveness: A focus on the mediating effect of scaffolding through knowledge sharing activities. *Journal of Korean Language Education, 27*(2), 1–23.

Kim, E. J. (2006). Heritage language maintenance by Korean-American college students. In K. Kondo-Brown (Ed.), *Heritage language development: Focus on East Asian immigrants* (pp. 175–208). Amsterdam and Philadelphia: John Benjamins Publishing Company.

Kim, J. (2000). *Foreign language listening anxiety: A study of Korean students learning English* [Unpublished doctoral dissertation]. University of Texas at Austin.

Kim, K. R. (2010). A study on relationship between Korean language learners' language learning strategies, motivational factors and reading comprehension quotient. *Journal of Korean Language Education, 21*(4), 25–50.

Kim, S. (2010). Korean heritage learners' affect and performance. *Studies in Foreign Language Education, 24*(1), 243–267.

Kim, Y. J., & Damron, J. (2015). Foreign language reading anxiety: Korean as a foreign language in the United States. *Journal of the National Council of Less Commonly Taught Languages, 17*, 23–55.

Kitano, K. (2001). Anxiety in the college Japanese classroom. *Modern Language Journal, 85*, 549–566.

Kwon, M.-K., & Lee, S.-Y. (2005). Korean as a second language learners' motivation and learning achievement: From the viewpoint of adult learning. *Journal of Korean Language Education, 16*(3), 1–28.

Lee, H., & Park, J. (2017). The correlation among Korean listening comprehension ability, listening self-efficacy, listening strategy, listening comprehension anxiety, and listening exposure time for Thai Korean learners. *Journal of Korean Language Education, 28*(3), 85–104.

Lee, I. (2018). Effects of contact with Korean popular culture on KFL learners' motivation. *The Korean Language in America, 22*(1), 25–45.

Lee, J., & Kim, H. (2008). Heritage language learners' attitudes, motivations, and instructional needs: The case of post-secondary Korean language learners. In K. Kondo-Brown & J. D. Brown (Eds.), *Teaching Chinese, Japanese, and Korean heritage students: Curriculum, needs, materials, and assessment* (pp. 159–185). New York: Lawrence Erlbaum Associates.

MacIntyre, P. D., & Gardner, R. C. (1994). The subtle effects of language anxiety on cognitive processing in the second language. *Language Learning, 44*, 283–305.

MacIntyre, P. D., MacMaster, K., & Baker, S. C. (2001). The convergence of multiple models of motivation for second language learning: Gardner, Pintrich, Kuhl, and McCroskey. In Z. Dörnyei & R. Schmidt (Eds.), *Motivation and second language acquisition* (pp. 461–492). Honolulu, HI: University of Hawai'i Press.

MacIntyre, P., & Gardner, R. (1991). Methods and results in the study of anxiety and language learning: A review of the literature. *Language Learning, 41*, 85–117.

Masgoret, A. M., & Gardner, R. C. (2003). Attitudes, motivation, and second language learning: A meta-analysis of studies conducted by Gardner and associates. *Language Learning, 53*, 167–210.

Mills, N., Pajares, F., & Herron, C. (2007). Self-efficacy of college intermediate French students: Relation to achievement and motivation. *Language Learning, 57*, 417–442.

Oh, S., & Kim, J. (2019). Analysis of correlation between learning anxiety and achievement test of Korean learners. *Journal of Korean Language Education, 30*(3), 83–103.

Oxford, R., & Shearin, J. (1994). Language learning motivation: Expanding the theoretical framework. *Modern Language Journal, 78*, 12–28.

Pae, T.-I. (2013). Skill-based L2 anxieties revisited: Their intra-relations and the inter-relations with general foreign language anxiety. *Applied Linguistics, 34*, 232–252.

Pajares, F., & Urdan, T. (2006). *Self-efficacy beliefs of adolescents*. Greenwich, CT: Information Age Publishing.

Phillips, E. M. (1992). The effects of language anxiety on student oral test performance and attitudes. *The Modern Language Journal, 76*, 14–26.

Pimsluer, P. (1966). *Pimsleur language aptitude battery (PLAB)*. New York: Harcourt Brace Jovanovich.

Pintrich, P. R., & De Groot, E. V. (1990). Motivational and self-regulated learning components of classroom academic performance. *Journal of Educational Psychology, 82*(1), 33–56.

Pyun, D. O. (2013). Attitudes toward task-based language learning: A study of college Korean learners. *Foreign Language Annals, 46(1)*, 108–121.

Pyun, D. O., Kim, J. S., Cho, H. Y., & Lee, J. H. (2014). Impact of affective variables on Korean as a foreign language learners' oral achievement. *System, 47*, 53–63.

Pyun, D. O., & Lee-Smith, A. (2011). Reducing Korean heritage-learners' orthographic errors: The contribution of on-line and in-class dictation and form-focused instruction. *Language, Culture and Curriculum, 24*(2), 141–158.

Pyun, D. O., & Shim, J. (2012). Learner attitudes towards performance based assessments in the L2 Korean classroom. In A. Byon & D. Pyun (Eds.), *Teaching and learning Korean as a foreign language: A collection of empirical studies*. Columbus, OH: Foreign Language Publications, The Ohio State University.

Saito, Y., & Samimy, K. K. (1996). Foreign language anxiety and language performance: A study of learner anxiety in beginning, intermediate, and advanced-level college students of Japanese. *Foreign Language Annals, 29*, 239–251.

Saito, Y., Garza, T., & Horwitz, E. (1999). Foreign language reading anxiety. *Modern Language Journal, 83*, 202–218.

Schunk, D. H. (1991). Self-efficacy and academic motivation. *Educational Psychologist, 26*, 207–232.

Shin, S.-C. (2020). Korean language learning in socio-educational settings in Sydney: Motivation, learning-styles and learning experiences. *Teaching Korean as a Foreign Language, 58*, 351–381.

Shon, S., & Jeon, N. (2011). A study of language learning motivation of Korean language learners. *Journal of Korean Language Education, 22*(3), 133–152.

Shon, S., & Jeon, N. (2013). A study of achievement goal orientation and self-efficacy among Korean language learners. *Journal of Korean Language Education, 24*(2), 181–203.

Shon, S., Jeon, N., & Hwang, C.-I. (2012). The relationship among attribution tendency, self- efficacy and academic achievement of students learning the Korean language. *Journal of Korean Language Education, 23*(2), 171–189.

Sparks, R. L., & Ganschow, L. (2007). Is the foreign language classroom anxiety scale measuring anxiety or language skills? *Foreign Language Annals, 40*, 260–287.

Spielmann, G., & Radnofsky, M. (2001). Learning language under tension: New directions from a qualitative study. *Modern Language Journal, 8*, 259–278.

Tremblay, P. F., & Gardner, R. C. (1995). Expanding the motivation construct in language learning. *Modern Language Journal, 79*, 505–518.

Vogely, A. J. (1998). Listening comprehension anxiety: Student sources and solutions. *Foreign Language Annals, 31*, 61–80.

Wang, H.-S., & Pyun, D. O. (2020). "Hallyu" and Korean language learning: Gender and ethnicity factors. *The Korean Language in America, 24*(2), 30–59.

Xie, Y. (2014). L2 self of beginning-level heritage and nonheritage postsecondary learners of Chinese. *Foreign Language Annals, 47*, 189–203.

Yang, J. S. R. (2003). Motivational orientations and selected learner variables of East Asian language learners in the United States. *Foreign Language Annals, 36*, 44–56.

22
KOREAN AS A HERITAGE LANGUAGE

Samantha Harris and Jin Sook Lee

Introduction

The demand for Korean language education worldwide has undeniably increased in recent years. In 2016 the Modern Language Association reported that Korean was the 11th most studied language in American higher education institutions, with increased enrollment among both heritage language (HL) track learners and foreign language (FL) track learners by 14% in three years despite an overall decline in FL course enrollment (Looney & Lusin, 2018). Also, in 2019, applications for the Test of Proficiency in Korean (TOPIK) reached its record high of 370,000 (Kwak, 2020). In response to this surging interest, the South Korean Ministry of Culture has allocated record funding – 89.4 billion won ($75.3 million) – to invigorate Korean language education around the world starting in 2021 (Jung, 2020). In contrast to the burgeoning commercial enterprise of teaching and learning Korean as a foreign language (KFL), community-, heritage-, and family-based Korean language education has received little such enthusiasm.

Although there are a handful of K–12 schools that offer Korean instruction either as a world language or via dual-language immersion, in the United States, the general lack of in-school opportunities to foster Korean as a heritage language (KHL) for children forces Korean families to rely on out-of-school instructional spaces, such as Saturday Schools, language camps, church-based HL classes, and after-school supplemental classes, all of which have received minimal public or academic investment and financial support (Lee & Chen-Wu, 2021; Lee & Wright, 2014). Yet, the pressures to speak only English have permeated even these cultural spaces as children bring with them hegemonic ideologies from mainstream spaces where English is prioritized (Choi, Lee, & Oh, 2016). Furthermore, like many immigrant families in the United States, Korean parents may also internalize hegemonic myths about bilingualism and prioritize their children's acquisition of English over Korean (Choi et al., 2016; Lee & Jeong, 2013), and the lack of societal recognition for the importance of maintaining HLs has been found to deter motivation to learn and develop their HL among youth (Lee, 2002). These accumulating circumstances all contribute to the swift rate of HL attrition within the Korean American population, wherein proficiency in Korean is typically lost by the second generation (Au & Oh, 2009; Cho & Krashen, 1998; Lee & Shin, 2008).

Research has shown that there are extensive academic, socioemotional, and psychological benefits that accompany HL maintenance. For instance, studies have found that students with proficiency in their HL developed stronger cognitive, meta-cognitive, and socio-affective strategies (Lee, 2002); reported higher GPAs and standardized test scores (Jang & Brutt-Griffler, 2019; Portes & Hao, 1998; Wright, 2015); and experienced more educational achievement than their monolingual peers (Bankston & Zhou, 1995; García-Vázquez, Vázquez, López, & Ward, 1997; Lee, 2002). Moreover, those who are fluent in their HL are also more likely to feel secure in their ethnic identity (Lee & Suarez, 2009; Oh & Fuligni, 2010) and to have strong relationships and satisfactory communication with family when compared with their monolingual counterparts (Oh & Fuligni, 2010; Tannenbaum, 2005; Tannenbaum & Berkovich, 2005). Thus, educating parents, community members, and educators to acknowledge HL as a cognitive, societal, and personal asset is critical to successful maintenance efforts (Shin, 2013; Shin & Lee, 2013). However, HL speakers not only have the potential to benefit from these advantages but also have unique linguistic and socioemotional needs (Brecht & Ingold, 2002; Kondo-Brown, 2005; Lee, 2005). For this reason, in U.S. secondary and postsecondary settings, language instruction is often provided in two separate tracks for HL and FL (Kondo-Brown, 2005). As we continue to recognize and respond to the unique characteristics of HL learners and their needs, there foremost needs to be a renewed consideration of what it means to be a HL learner or speaker of Korean.

Although linguistic proficiency and ethnolinguistic affiliation have generally been the main criteria to distinguish between HL and non-HL learners (Cho, Cho, & Tse, 1997; Kondo-Brown, 2003, 2005; Lee, 2002, 2005; Peyton, Ranard, & McGinnis, 2001; Valdés, 1997; Wiley, 2001), previous definitions no longer fully capture the growing diversity among those that identify as being a HL speaker. For example, KHL learners may come from homes where Korean is not spoken by both parents, or their Korean proficiency may be near native-like due to their frequent transpacific moves between the United States and Korea. As such, HL maintenance efforts and research should continue to revisit and be intentional and critical about choosing a definition for KHL learners and speakers so that it is broad enough to include a variety of lived experiences and identities but narrow enough to distinguish them from FL learners and speakers.

In this chapter, we will review the evolution of the term "heritage language" and examine how it has influenced KHL research and education. We do so in a way that rejects native-speaker norms and deficit views of HL speakers. Instead, based on studies that document the language practices of KHL speakers that express their unique linguistic identities, we argue for the legitimacy of linguistic repertoires that evolve in response to community-/family-based forms of bi/multilingualism. We also revisit the expanding profiles of KHL learners to reflect the increasingly heterogeneous motivations and backgrounds of self-identified HL learners and speakers. Finally, in light of the diversity of KHL learners, we propose some directions for Korean language education pedagogy and research that is inclusive, necessary, and timely in our current context.

Defining HL learners and speakers

A fundamental challenge in the realm of HL education and research has been how to define what a HL is in relation to what is considered a second, foreign, or native language. Variability in language proficiency and identity has continued to complicate the linguistic and institutional criteria for who qualifies as a HL learner. Despite the general consensus that there are clear differences between HL and FL learners (Kondo-Brown, 2005), the specifics of what distinguishes the learning and use of one's HL compared to other types of language users are still debatable, especially in the context of the growing heterogeneity of the HL population. Hence, the question remains: should a language be defined as "heritage" based on the learner's linguistic proficiency, exposure to the language, ethnolinguistic affiliation, motivation, identity, or all of the above?

Fishman (2001) proposed that HLs are LOTEs (languages other than English) with which learners have some familial attachment. Shortly thereafter, Van Deusen-Scholl (2003) put forth a complementary vision of HL learners as "a heterogeneous group ranging from fluent native speakers to non-speakers who may be generations removed, but who may feel culturally connected to a language" (p. 222). However, she makes a distinction between heritage learners who have "achieved some degree of proficiency in the home language and/or have been raised with strong cultural connections" and "learners with a heritage motivation" who may be seeking to "reconnect with their family's heritage through language, even though the linguistic evidence of that connection may have been lost for generations" (p. 222). For the heritage learner group, differences in *proficiency* would dictate specific pedagogical implications; for the learners with a heritage motivation group, the differences in *motivation*, which range and shift across time and contexts, would also require appropriate pedagogical responses (He, 2006; Lee, 2002; Lee & Shin, 2008). According to Yang (2003), most students in Korean foreign language classes are second-generation Korean Americans, that is, HL learners who are seeking an opportunity to (re)learn Korean, but in recent years there has been an increase in KFL learners due to the influence of Hallyu Korean popular culture (e.g., K-pop, K-dramas) and the desire to communicate with Korean-speaking peers (Chan & Chi, 2010; Stotirova, 2014). Their motivation stems from both integrative and instrumental reasons, but the ways in which their language-learning paths play out are different, particularly due to their prior exposure in Korean proficiency (Kondo-Brown, 2005).

So, if proficiency is taken into account, by what measure and standard should the boundary between FL learners and HL learners be determined? For example, research that focuses on linguistic differences (e.g., grammars, phonology) between HL and FL learners takes a conservative approach, basing HL speakership on three main qualifiers. A HL learner is characterized as an early bilingual who 1) has exposure to and proficiency in their HL and a majority language (L2) from a young age, 2) switches in dominance from the HL to the L2 usually after schooling begins, and/or 3) does not acquire native-like proficiency in all domains of language (Benmamoun, Montrul, & Polinsky, 2013). Studies of KHL speakers' linguistic differences have adopted this narrow definition of HL learners (e.g., Kim, O'Grady, & Schwartz, 2018; Park-Johnson, 2019); yet, while it is valuable for investigating differences in linguistic production, the first requirement excludes an entire group of learners who may have no proficiency in the HL but have familial/ethnolinguistic affiliation to the language that can still distinguish their learning from FL learners. The second requirement excludes the numerous HL learners that have developed only receptive skills. Receptive proficiency or comprehension in some spaces is delegitimized and seen as having no proficiency; however, these receptive skills can be strong enough even in the absence of productive skills to set such HL learners apart from beginner and even intermediate-level FL learners (Valdés, 2005). Moreover, because the third requirement assumes some level of expected proficiency or ultimate attainment, to determine if acquisition of language is complete, it assumes a baseline by which it can be measured. Commonly that baseline is the standard language and monolingual native speaker (Canagarajah; 1999; Cook, 2016). However, this criterion assumes that bilingual HL speakers' linguistic systems can be the same as a monolingual speaker's system, which is unfounded. It also ignores the social context of language learning and use where the HL is used in contact with the dominant language and culture; it denies agency to the speakers who use their HL in innovative ways that differ from the standard variety, and the resulting bilingualism should not be delegitimized simply because of its structural difference (Kupisch & Rothman, 2018; Lee & Shin, 2008; Pascual y Cabo & Rothman, 2012; Shin & Lee, 2013).

Striking a balance between the social and linguistic characteristics of HL learners, Valdés (2005) offered a now widely cited definition that includes those who 1) have been "raised in a home where a non-English language is spoken," 2) "may speak or merely understand" their home language, and 3) therefore "may be, to some degree, bilingual" (p. 412). This view of HL opens up possibilities for a funds-of-knowledge, asset-based approach to HL education and research that does not overlook the role of investment and motivation and may be particularly salient for members of the Korean diaspora who feel a strong sense of connection to Korean culture and language in a transnational setting. It captures the profiles of a large portion of Korean American learners, yet it is not comprehensive; it assumes that learners have some exposure to and/or familiarity with Korean language or culture. However, there are learners for whom this is not true, yet their ancestral connection to the language and culture is enough to foster motivation and investments in language learning in ways that set them apart from FL learners. (Cho et al., 1997; Kondo-Brown, 2003, 2005; Lee, 2002; 2005; Peyton et al., 2001; Valdés, 1997; Wiley, 2001). Toward a more inclusive definition, Lee and Shin (2008) defined Korean HL learners as "those who have an ethnolinguistic affiliation to the Korean heritage, but may have a broad range of proficiency from high to none in Korean oral or literacy skills" (p. 154). However, in light of the current context, this definition may also be somewhat limiting. In the next section, we build on this definition to highlight the expanding boundaries of who constitutes Korean as a HL learner that reflect the fluidity of linguistic, cultural, and geographic border crossings that technology and global citizenship has enabled.

Profiling KHL learners and speakers

Korean is the HL of approximately 7 million Koreans living in Central Asia, China, Japan, Russia, and the United States (Lewis, 2009; World Bank, 2009). In the United States, those of Korean descent comprise the fifth-largest Asian group (1.7 million) (U.S. Census Bureau, 2010).

As mentioned, the typical profile of KHL learners and speakers within HL scholarship has been centered on children of Korean immigrants and assume that HL speakers grow up in homes with exposure to spoken Korean and therefore may have higher levels of oral proficiency but limited or no literacy skills. However, this is just a partial image, especially as we enter an era of third- and fourth-generation Korean Americans. The Korean American community is diverse, with a growing population of KHL learners or speakers that may not be exposed to Korean on a daily basis. HL researchers and educators have thus begun to recognize the need to be more inclusive when conducting research and designing language programs meant specifically to serve HL learners. Yet relatively few studies have investigated HL learning among a broader range of KHL learners or speakers; that is, very little discussion has focused on their lived experiences and specific challenges that learners and speakers face in their HL development and maintenance efforts or how other aspects of their diverse identities play a role in their relationships to their HL and their HL community.

Primarily, K–16 is the population that is most targeted in research and talked about in KHL circles, although across existing studies, motivation to learn the HL may persist throughout adulthood. For example, adults may have more agency to seek out and enroll in language-learning opportunities, but at the same time experience challenges in finding opportunities and the time to do so. There have been several efforts to revitalize Korean among young adult, second-generation Korean Americans as a result of increased interaction with Korean youth coming to the United States for education, the popularity of Korean pop culture, and Korean online communities (Kim, 2010), but adult (re)learners have different needs that have been rarely addressed. More research on adult learners in terms of their needs, access, and learning styles and a better understanding of how early childhood exposure to their HLs may affect their language-development process (see Oh, Au, Jun, & Lee, 2019) are needed. In the meantime, educators can tap into technology-based solutions that fit adult lifestyles and schedules and provide access to age-appropriate content that serve the needs of this population.

Moreover, often excluded from the normative profile of KHL are individuals who have mixed ethnic and/or racial ancestry. "Multi-" and "mixed heritage" are used as umbrella terms for many subcategories of identities held by individuals who come from two or more cultural, ethnic, and/or racial groups. As language learners, mixed-heritage individuals are commonly framed to be more closely resembling FL learners (Kondo-Brown, 2005; Shin, S.J., 2010; Yang, 2003). For such individuals, this might mean disrupting race-based expectations of who is and is not a KHL speaker. Based on the few studies that have been conducted on this population, findings are similar: mixed-heritage individuals feel excluded from their HL communities, and even if they are capable of visibly passing, linguistic differences can expose their ethnic or racial difference and contribute to their othering (Caldas, 2008; Mu, 2016; Noro, 2009; Potowski, 2016; Shin, S.J., 2010). In moments where their authenticity as a group member is challenged, mixed-heritage HL speakers have been shown to draw on their linguistic knowledge and skills as a way to authenticate their ethnic or racial identity (Bailey, 2000; Potowski, 2016; Shin, S. J., 2010).

However, it is important to note that speech production may also be read through the lens of hegemonic, raciolinguistic ideologies; in other words, listeners will hear language in certain ways that align with their ideologies of race and language and phenotype that may lead to acts of linguistic discrimination or microaggressions (Rosa & Flores, 2017). For example, mixed-race Koreans have historically faced discrimination from the community as a result of stigma and anti-Blackness that emerged out of war-time miscegenation and American occupation of South Korea (Harris & Lee, 2021; Kim, 2016). In her dissertation, Kim (2016) explores the experiences of biracial Korean Americans in U.S. university HL classes. She found that her participants mostly were concerned with HL development as a means to communicate with their extended family and as a way to authenticate their Korean identity. Her study showed that KHL classes were not available in their K–12 educational system, and many turned to the Korean church or other community-based HL programs, where they reported having negative learning experiences. Her participants were aware of their differing racial positionings in relation to their local Korean communities. Further research is required to understand these social dynamics in order to better address their specific needs and move beyond instruction that simply recognizes the multicultural identity of its students to instruction that instills critical awareness among community members and empowers learners with strategies to find their voice and position in the community. That is, pedagogically, more research with these groups may inform KHL educators about issues of racism, colorism, and anti-Blackness in the Korean community whose learners – whether monoracial or mixed – exist and move through the world as racial minorities.

Korean-born adoptees also represent a significant HL group. Korean American adoptees have reported experiences of exclusion from Korean American communities; especially feeling marginalized in interactions because of the cultural differences and perceived connection to Korean culture (Higgins & Stoker, 2011). Again, while scholarship on this group is still limited, there have been a number of public efforts to support Korean American adoptees' access to heritage culture and language learning. For instance, in 2019, K America Foundation started fundraising to create a summer camp for youth of Korean heritage, with specific attention to programming for transracial adoptees (Kraker, 2019). Their mission echoes the important studies on Korean American adoptees that point to the need for differentiated instruction for adoptees and their adoptive families. This includes not assuming students have some prior exposure to or knowledge of Korean language and culture and creating appropriate learning objectives based on students' linguistic backgrounds and goals (Shin, 2013). For example, educators may need to provide supplemental material and opportunities to practice the HL (e.g., private tutoring, online activities) for families who do not have local access to Korean cultural spaces and resources (Shin, 2013).

Profiles of KHL learners may also include third-plus generation Korean immigrants, children of transnational or "wild geese" families and children of military and other families that grow up in Korea but may not be of Korean descent. In addition, there is a growing number of non-Korean students that are being educated in Korean/English dual-language immersion programs. These students may identify themselves as Korean speakers and may connect with the language and culture more intimately than a FL speaker would with the target language. For such students, Korean becomes a part of their linguistic and academic identity not by inheritance but by personal choice and agency (see Jarmel & Schneider, 2009). Additionally, while there may be shared experiences with KHL speakers linguistically and culturally, their paths may diverge in other ways to contribute to differing forms of privilege and/or oppression as speakers of Korean. For example, experiences of white individuals living in Korea should not be compared to experiences of Korean Americans. Their presence in Asia is largely a result of the histories of U.S. imperialism and military occupation and global capitalism. That is, they exist in bubbles of privilege and can elect to assimilate to the local populations, and their proficiency in Korean can only uphold their status, while Korean American HL speakers are generally seen as outsiders in the United States and in Korea. Thus, HL learners with such circumstantial differences may have different motivations for learning and maintaining KHL, inconsistent access to language education, and varied ability to stay connected to Korean culture, which will likely affect their HL trajectories (Lee & Shin, 2008). Yet not much is known about these differentiated profiles of KHL speakers and their HL experiences.

In addition, we have no knowledge of research that explores the ways in which KHL programs (re)produce heteronormative and/or cisnormative ideologies and how that may affect the language-learning trajectories of queer Korean American youth. In an *LAist* article about religion and politics in the Korean American community (see Schrank, 2020), queer activist scholar and Korean American immigrant Ju Hui Judy Han explained how "a typical Korean American experience is actually growing up in a church-dominated community life," how few Korean churches are gay friendly, and how "when [LGBT Korean Americans] leave the church, they also often leave the Korean American community stuff in general because the church is such a big part of it." This reality has serious consequences for KHL learning, most of which exists in the Korean church, where, in some cases, religious content is part of the language curriculum (Lee & Shin, 2008; Shin & Lee, 2013). If queer Korean Americans are pushed out of these spaces, they would not only lose access to their culture but opportunities to develop or maintain their multilingualism. This is not a referendum on the Korean church, but it is a clear signal that more work needs to be done in the way of a community-based HL instruction in religious spaces and also on the language experiences of HL learners and speakers with identities that have been marginalized even within the HL community, such as queer identities (see Cashman & Trujillo, 2018 for research on Queering Spanish as a HL). Therefore, researchers and educators must take the initiative to bring the stories of these KHL learners to the forefront to ensure that HL pedagogical practices are able to respond to their socioemotional needs as well as resist and undo any heteronormative and cisnormative ideologies or implicit biases that may exist in the classroom. Knowledge about their backgrounds and needs will help develop effective instruction and foster a welcoming and inclusive KHL learning environment that will lead to sustained HL maintenance opportunities for all learners.

In sum, we must avoid repeated patterns of marginalization of those that do not fit the normative profile of KHL learners and speakers where they have felt shut out from their HL classroom and/or then from their communities, ultimately culminating in continued KHL attrition. For varying reasons, HL speakers with non-normative profiles have had limited access to formal HL education (Pascual y Cabo & Rothman, 2012) and as we move forward, researchers and educators should be more aware of, inclusive of, and responsive to the diversity in classrooms. Thus, to capture this diversity, we combine previous definitions of HL learners and speakers as those who have an ethnic, cultural, geographical, ancestral, and/or linguistic connection to the HL; may fluctuate in their receptive and productive proficiency and literacy in the HL, ranging from no skills to total fluency; and have varied instructional and interactional experiences in the HL. We acknowledge that is an evolving definition that will need continual refinement, especially in terms of their unique language practices that mark their HL identities. Next, we present the findings from studies that have examined the language practices of KHL speakers.

Language practices of KHL speakers

Among first-generation Korean immigrants, Korean is used extensively due to strong affiliations with Korean organizations and churches and Korean ethnic media. In contrast, studies report that second-generation Koreans do not use as much Korean as their immigrant parents, and attrition rates are high (Kim, 2010; Min, 2000). For those with some proficiency, despite being English dominant, they tend to use more Korean than English with parents and other Korean adults, while the reverse is true with siblings and friends, who are Korean proficient (Lee, 2002). Moreover, KHL speakers tend to be stronger in receptive skills than their productive skills and in many cases, may only have receptive skills in Korean and not given full recognition for the important linguistic skills they do possess. That is, rather than being positioned as agentive users of language who make strategic decisions about their language use or as possessing a complex/legitimate bilingual comprehension system (Chung, 2006), they have been framed as "semilingual" (Kim, 2001) or having "incomplete grammar" (Montrul, 2008). It is also rare that they rely on Korean alone when communicating with other KHL speakers; they employ a number of language-mixing strategies, like code-switching, to varying degrees and for varying purposes (Lee, 2002; Shin, S. Y., 2010; Kim & Lim, 2007; Shin & Milroy, 2000). Although code-switching and -mixing have often been assumed to be a compensatory strategy to fill the gaps of not knowing either language adequately rather than as a dexterous linguistic skill to mark solidarity and self-expression (Shin & Milroy, 2000), more recent studies are recognizing such practices as creative language play among multilinguals (Cheng, 2020; Chung, 2006; Martínez, 2013; Orellana & Rodriguez-Minkoff, 2016; Rampton, 2014; Song, 2009; Thomas, 2019).

Such deeply rooted deficit perspectives are prevalent in qualitative studies of KHL speakers that document day-to-day interactions, which have been shown to have very real-world consequences for the speaker. For instance, when Korean Americans are phenotypically perceived as native speakers (i.e., if they "look" like a native speaker of Korean), they are consequently expected to have native-like fluency (Agha, 2005; Lee, 2005), causing much frustration for those who are not proficient, as they are made to feel like failures or disappointments to their communities (Flores & Rosa, 2015; Higgins & Stoker, 2011). Similarly, when KHL learners come to class possessing features of regional dialects in their lexicon and pronunciation accents they may have learned from their parents, it may clash with the "standard" dialect that is taught (Jo, 2001; Lee & Shin, 2008). Their linguistic production is evaluated through the lens of Korean ideologies of language status that associate non-standard phonological and morphological distinctions with someone who is rural, backwards, old-fashioned, immature, and/or unintelligent (Song, 2010). Moreover, the ultimate goal of linguistic attainment for HL speakers in educational institutions has been "standard," native-like speech. Thus, HL speakers' unique phonological, morphological, syntactic, semantic, or pragmatic linguistic practices that are often the result of language contact between the language of the broader mainstream community (majority) language and their HL or remnants of their linguistic inheritance from their parents or grandparents are seen as incorrect, insufficient, or not native enough. However, such linguistic practices, which include code-switching/translanguaging, often operate as identity markers that mark them not as foreign or native speakers but as KHL speakers. They can be used by speakers and listeners to police the boundaries of Korean ethnic belonging and also contribute to new forms of authentic Korean speakership, hence demonstrating creative language play. The following studies show the creative ways KHL speakers engage their complete linguistic repertoire to accomplish specific communicative goals via rule-governed ways of speaking and creative ways of combining their linguistic systems.

As defined by García (2009), "translanguaging is the act performed by bilinguals of accessing different linguistic features or various modes of what are described as autonomous languages, in order to maximize communicative potential" (p. 140). In a study of KHL first graders' translanguaging practices, Lee and García (2020) found that children translanguage in response to their interlocutors' language choice, to fill in for words they could not translate/did not know, and to indicate their own language preference, but also to demonstrate and recognize their own and others' Korean and/or bilingual identities. Lee and García highlighted the pedagogical significance of these findings by proposing that educators and parents encourage and enable students to respond to instruction and assessments in any language they are able to.

Translanguaging also provides some pedagogical opportunities within formal HL instruction. In a dissertation that investigates ideologies of language and identity that circulate in community-based KHL schools, Lee (2019) observed translanguaging practices of teachers and students in the KHL classroom. He found that both teachers and students translanguage to achieve a language-learning goal and by doing so create more student engagement by allowing students to co-construct learning opportunities, build on each other's conversations, and engage in creative language play. His findings point to the need for KHL educators to not limit KHL education by employing a one-language policy as well as the benefit of allowing KHL learners (and teachers) to rely on their non-Korean linguistic resources to access Korean language-learning opportunities.

Song (2009) examined the ways in which KHL children navigated linguistic and cultural ideologies in different spaces and relied on their different linguistic codes to actively contribute to their own sociocultural positioning within their different communities. Relying on ethnographic data (i.e., observations and interviews), Song found that despite parents' socialization efforts, children made their own choices through improvised practices and invented new ways of using address terms. Strategies included anglicizing older peers' first names and omitting Korean kinship terms. These practices were consistent and intentional; that is, they were not mistakes or negative transfers from their other language(s). The children were aware that their language was not consistent with native-speaker norms, and they still chose their own forms, in some cases, to construct a "status-neutral social relationship" and in others to socially distance themselves from the subject. This demonstrates that KHL speakers' unique linguistic practices are not the result of a deficient acquisition of their HL. Rather, KHL speakers are engaging in, as Song puts it, "new hybrid practices in collaboration with one another, [and] redefining their social relationships through the dynamic means of language" (p. 228). S. Y. Shin (2010) had similar findings from her investigation of context-specific code-switching, specifically examining how KHL speakers code-switch within their Korean church. The strategies she observed included using kinship and referential titles to refer to elders to maintain politeness and invoke an authoritative voice when using directives as a mitigating strategy to signal a close relationship with a listener when it was time to have an uncomfortable or potentially face-threatening conversation. However, she also discovered that their decisions about language often involved the fulfillment of other specific functions – in particular to instantiate their Korean identities and ethnic solidarity. Her findings are important not only for understanding the strategic ways KHL speakers play with language but also for how this language play contributes to the maintenance of community and ethnic boundaries, which reflect and shape ideas about membership and belonging particularly within the Korean church – a site of cultural and linguistic socialization that becomes important when considering non-traditional KHL learners.

Despite the deficit ideologies that circulate about language mixing, combining Korean and English is common enough that this linguistic practice has been dubbed "Konglish" (Hadikin, 2005; Kim, 2001; Nam, 2010). According to Lawrence (2012)

> Konglish, Chinglish and Janglish are potential contact vernaculars developing as a creative mix between English and the local language. . . . They are "potential" in that they are not considered languages, but subsections of languages. They are "contact" in that they result from the contact of English and local languages. They are "creative" in that they are not static, but dynamic with new elements appearing and some disappearing over time. They are a "mix" in that elements of English are mixed with elements of the local language, or changed, or recombined with other elements of English in unique ways.
>
> *(p. 73)*

Although the term "Konglish" has mainly been used in reference to the mixing of Korean into English, studies as well as speakers themselves have also used this term in reference to KHL's language practices (see, for instance, Beausoleil, 2008; Cheng, 2020; Lee, 2002; Min, 2000). For example, Lee (2019) asked KHL participants to define "Konglish." For most, the definitions and descriptions of "Konglish" revealed an internalization of prescriptive, monoglossic ideologies and the view of language mixing as problematic and erroneous. However, they were also aware of some advantages that it provided as a tool for communicating and learning, but perhaps most importantly as a shared repertoire of Korean Americans. It was made evident that a certain type of "Konglish" exists as an in-group code created by KHL speakers and is used to create and identify membership in the larger KHL community.

Reyes (2016) observed how KHL speakers would engage in various forms of language play, including "Konglish," to establish such boundaries of group memberships. Amongst themselves, they would engage in linguistic performances that allowed them to embody or voice recognizable Korean figures, such as the "pleading Korean child," "authoritative Korean adult," "Korean immigrant fob," and "ideal Korean American." For these KHL students, use of their HL was not just about making up for missing vocabulary or speaking "in secret" amongst non-speakers of Korean. As Reyes puts it, "Korean use was about . . . harnessing the various ways to be recognizably Korean for purposes that seemed primarily meaningful to the students themselves" (p. 316). To accomplish this, these speakers had to be experts not only in linguistic norms but also in the cultural imagined figures. By embodying these figures, they were (re) creating the ideologies about Korean personhood.

For some scholars, the language practices of KHL speakers are unique enough that they have begun to ask if they constitute their own ethnolect of Korean. For example, Cheng (2020) conducted interviews with Korean Americans in California and argued for the potential emergence of a Korean ethnolect. He found that "Korean Americans are metalinguistically aware of a Korean American accent, and that their usage of Korean, English, and this Korean ethnolect is influenced mostly by their personal sense of ethnic identity and their connection to large Korean communities" (p. 51). While he was able to identify some linguistic differences (e.g., pronunciation of back vowels) and influences from Korean phonology on English that are different from English-only peers, Cheng called for more research on the acoustic qualities of Korean Americans' language practices to determine if it does indeed qualify as its own ethnolect. Additionally, more research should look at other aspects, such as morphology, syntax, semantics, and pragmatics, to assess the validity of a Korean ethnolect as well as examine the language practices of Korean Americans living in concentrated Korean ethnoburbs or should at the very least consider Koreatowns in places other than Los Angeles and California to determine its generalizability. Altogether, these studies point to HL practices not as insufficient duplicates of native-like speech, but a language in its own right that serves its own functions and constructs its own rules.

This review only represents a fraction of the existing KHL and certainly more innovative and insightful research is yet to come (see Chang & Weiss-Cowie, 2020; Jeon, 2020; Lo, 2009; Shin, 2016; Sohn & Park, 2003; Song, 2019; Suh, 2020). KHL learners as a whole do not uniformly possess or lack linguistic proficiency or intensity of socioemotional connection to the Korean language, nor do they all strictly follow these linguistic patterns. We are not claiming that there is no room or need for the HL to become more developed; rather, we are shedding light on the fact that there are unique characteristics of speech that KHL speakers possess that need to be acknowledged and validated rather than simply replaced by native-speaker standards and forms. Learners need to be trained to know what, when, where, and why certain language codes are deemed appropriate and necessary. This should be one of the goals of KHL education.

Pedagogical and research implications

Given the growing diversity of KHL learners and speakers, a reevaluation of the goals of Korean as a HL education is in order. Should KHL instruction continue to center on the development of "standard-like" Korean language and promote learners' connection to Korean cultural norms, traditions, and values or be reimagined as a space where diverse identities are supported and validated, for example? We argue for the transformative potential of KHL education to 1) recognize and validate the heterogeneity of language practices and unique linguistic identities of KHL learners and speakers, 2) utilize KHL programs to develop a social justice content-based pedagogical approach, and 3) integrate the use of technology to broaden innovative instructional access to wider populations of KHL learners and connect KHL learners in ways that strengthen the community of speakers.

To realize this transformative potential, the most important step is the need for educators and curriculum developers to be aware of and responsive to this growing diversity in terms of meeting the linguistic and socioemotional needs of students. Educators must not assume a "typical" background among their KHL learners. They must educate themselves about the various points and depths of contact their students have had with Korean to be able to respond to the socioemotional and linguistic needs of an increasingly diverse group of KHL learners. This includes 1) sensitivity to othering (e.g., avoiding blanket assumptions and microaggressions) of students who may have diverse backgrounds, 2) awareness of ideologies and implicit biases that they as well as their students may hold, and 3) careful and critical teaching practices that do not position linguistic practices of KHL students as not meeting the standards of native-speaker or academic norms. For all students, there should be a validation of unique registers and language practices that they possess as well as opportunities for them to reassess their ideologies and biases.

We are not suggesting that the standard variety of Korean not be taught. What we are proposing is the acknowledgement by teachers that opens up the space for KHL learners to recognize that their "Konglish" or "Korean ethnolect" is a part of their full linguistic repertoire and has legitimate communicative purposes. The study of pragmatics and the development of pragmatic competence must be built into the KHL curriculum. This would require a better understanding of the full linguistic repertoire of HL speakers and a discontinuation of blanketly upholding native speakers' language practices and standard varieties as the ultimate goal (Cook, 1999, 2016). In other words, educators will need to know about the language practices of KHL speakers and the different ways in which Korean is used among youth via social and digital media, for example, to distinguish between forms and usages that represent different varieties and registers from the textbook-like standards versus those that are marked within the community of speakers. Moreover, KHL speakers must be aware of their own language practices. Teachers do not step into the classroom free of their own language varieties, accents, or identities. The unique linguistic and cultural backgrounds they bring to the classroom can be used as a tool for co-learning (see Lee [2019] for examples of KHL teachers' translanguaging practices). Toward this end, KHL teachers and learners should be trained to be mini ethnographers of their own linguistic practices to learn what is considered appropriate for whom, when, where, how, and why as opposed to insisting on a "right way to speak" so that all KHL speakers can make informed decisions about their language use. In other words, they need to develop language and cultural competence in a way that recognizes their individual connections to the language and culture that may be different given the different KHL learners' individual differences and experiences.

KHL educators should also consider ways to directly engage with social justice and antiracist efforts in the Korean community and for the Korean community. KHL speakers are, by definition, members of a linguistic, ethnic, and racial minority group and are therefore subject to racism and marginalization. For example, they can internalize stereotypes like "FOB" or the "model minority" (Pyke & Dang, 2003), experience language policing (Yam, 2017) or increased hostility and violence in the face of rising anti-Asian sentiment (see Intarasuan, 2020; Ho, 2021; Li & Nicholson, 2021). Thus, HL education and research should not simply engage with questions of input, proficiency, or authenticity, but should take a social justice approach that intentionally interrogates systems of power in relation to HL learning and its contexts (Ortega, 2020). A social justice orientation toward HL learning connects the learner to their minoritized community and examines the ways in which oppression and privilege influence language learning (Ortega, 2020). In other words, KHL education should have a higher-order goal of multicultural or antiracist education, where KHL learners have a safe space to explore issues about diversity, identity, racism, and social justice with others who may share a familiar background or experiences.

Connecting KHL to such educational goals locates language education in a more authentic learning context; that is, language learning not just for the sake of proficiency development but, rather, proficiency is developed through content learning that has an authentic purpose of making a difference in the community. A content-based approach that includes critical pedagogy and social justice orientation could include how KHL speakers are positioned as Asian Americans and linguistic minorities in the world as well as action-based approaches to resisting this ideological positioning. There is a lot of work to be done in undoing raciolinguistic ideologies in the community, hence a social justice content-based approach to KHL education may be one way to address issues of discrimination and racism that are relevant to the KHL community. Empowering KHL students as experts of language and its social power would not only help KHL learners to have a more critical awareness and positive development of their cultural identities but would also enhance their agency within and beyond the classroom (Leeman, Rabin, & Román-Mendoza, 2012; Ortega, 2020; Shin, 2016).

Finally, educators and researchers need to be in tune with emerging new ways that technology can be used to support KHL learners. For example, for adult (re)learners who may have already experienced some language attrition, online and asynchronous learning may be more suitable for their already busy lifestyles. Also, for KHL learners living in rural parts of the United States, where HL educational programs may not be available, online options might give access to these much-needed spaces. Technology enables KHL learners to connect globally and develop synergy amongst themselves as a legitimate and important community of speakers. That is, technology can be creatively employed to afford more opportunities to engage in different kinds of language use with different kinds of speakers as well as gain access to more diverse instructional resources that can support their learning. It is already being employed as a way to create a shared community space for "non-traditional" HL learners; for instance, the Facebook groups "HalfKorean.com," with more than 3,000 members, and "Korean & Black," with more than 1,000 members, house their own diverse membership for individuals who are racially mixed, adoptees, parents of mixed Korean Americans, spouses, etc. The transformative potential for KHL education has already gained momentum; what we lack is a more systematic way to disseminate and share information and resources that can advance the goals of KHL education.

In sum, we need to better understand the relationship of ethnolinguistic affiliation and prior linguistic proficiency on students' instructional needs and their acquisition, which is a question that continues to await further research (Lee & Shin, 2008). Future studies may want to also examine the continued experiences throughout K–12 years (e.g., longitudinal, ethnographic studies) and beyond into late adulthood as well as the proficiency-identity connection of mixed-race KHL speakers or Korean adoptees. Lastly, research that captures the diverse, yet systematic ways in which KHL is used across different contexts (e.g., KHL classrooms, returnee trips to Korea, homes where parents may not speak the HL), including developmental patterns and the perceptions of hearers toward different HL speakers and dialects will yield important information that can shape not only our pedagogical practices but our fundamental understanding of the connections between identity and language. Like all living languages, the dynamic and evolving nature of KHL learners and their linguistic repertoires represent the rich and complex web of the experiences of KHL speakers.

Following the examples of the Korean Heritage language Speaker Research Study (www.facebook.com/koreanheritagespeakers/) conducted by researchers at Cal State Long Beach, which uses an open base survey via Facebook to collect examples of language practices among KHL speakers, or researchers that use open-source media, such as reality shows or talk shows, to capture the discourse practices of KHL speakers (Kang, 2009), we are hopeful that through such creative ways of data collection the empirical evidence to further support the validity and our appreciation for KHL practices and our understanding about the human capacity for language will continue to grow.

Reference

Agha, A. (2005). Voice, footing, enregisterment. *Journal of Linguistic Anthropology, 15*(1), 38–59.
Au, T. K., & Oh, J. S. (2009). Korean as a heritage language. In C. Lee, G. B. Simpson, & Y. Kim (Eds.), *Handbook of East Asian psycholinguistics* (pp. 268–275). London: Cambridge University Press.
Bailey, B. (2000). Language and negotiation of ethnic/racial identity among Dominican Americans. *Language in Society, 29*(4), 555–582.
Bankston III, C. L., & Zhou, M. (1995). Effects of minority-language literacy on the academic achievement of Vietnamese youths in New Orleans. *Sociology of Education*, 1–17.
Beausoleil, A. (2008). *Understanding heritage and ethnic identity development through study abroad: The case of South Korea* [Doctoral dissertation]. University of California Santa Barbara.
Benmamoun, E., Montrul, S., & Polinsky, M. (2013). Heritage languages and their speakers: Opportunities and challenges for linguistics. *Theoretical Linguistics, 39*(3–4), 129–181.
Brecht, R. D., & Ingold, C. W. (2002). *Tapping a national resource: Heritage languages in the United States*. Washington, DC: Eric Clearinghouse on Languages and Linguistics.
Caldas, S. J. (2008). Changing bilingual self-perceptions from early adolescence to early adulthood: Empirical evidence from a mixed-method case study. *Applied Linguistics, 29*(2), 290–311.
Canagarajah, A. S. (1999). Interrogating the "native speaker fallacy": Non-linguistic roots, non-pedagogical results. In G. Braine (Ed.), *Non-native educators in English language teaching* (pp. 77–92). Mahwah, NJ: Lawrence Erlbaum Associates.
Cashman, H., & Trujillo, J. A. (2018). Queering Spanish as a Heritage language. In K. Potowski (Ed.), *The Routledge handbook of Spanish as a heritage language* (pp. 124–141). New York: Routledge.
Chan, W. M., & Chi, S. W. (2010). A study of the learning goals of university students of Korean as a foreign language. *Electronic Journal of Foreign Language Teaching, 7*(1), 125–140.
Chang, S. E., & Weiss-Cowie, S. (2020). Hyper-articulation effects in Korean glides by heritage language learners. *International Journal of Bilingualism*, 1–18.
Cheng, A. (2020). *Accent and ideology among bilingual Korean Americans* [Doctoral dissertation]. University of California, Berkeley. Retrieved from https://escholarship.org/uc/item/8n53c9z5
Cho, G., Cho, K. S., & Tse, L. (1997). Why ethnic minorities want to develop their heritage language: The case of Korean-Americans. *Language, Culture and Curriculum, 10*(2), 106–112.
Cho, G., & Krashen, S. (1998). The negative consequences of heritage language loss and why we should care. In S. Krashen, L. Tse, & J. McQuillan (Eds.), *Heritage language development* (pp. 31–39). Culver City, CA: Language Education Associates.
Choi, J. Y., Lee, J. S., & Oh, J. S. (2016). Examining the oral language competency of children from Korean immigrant families in English-only and dual language immersion schools. *Journal of Early Childhood Research, 16*(1), 32–51.
Chung, H. H. (2006). Code switching as a communicative strategy: A case study of Korean–English bilinguals. *Bilingual Research Journal, 30*(2), 293–307.
Cook, V. (1999). Going beyond the native speaker in language teaching. *TESOL Quarterly, 33*(2), 185–209.
Cook, V. (2016). Where is the native speaker now?. *TESOL Quarterly, 50*(1), 186–189.
Fishman, J. A. (2001). 300-plus years of heritage language education in the United States. In J. K. Peyton, D. A. Ranard, & S. McGinnis (Eds.), *Heritage languages in America: Preserving a national resource* (pp. 81–98). Washington, DC, and McHenry, IL: Delta Systems/Center for Applied Linguistics.
Flores, N., & Rosa, J. (2015). Undoing appropriateness: Raciolinguistic ideologies and language diversity in education. *Harvard Educational Review, 85*(2), 149–171.
García, O. (2009). Education, multilingualism and translanguaging in the 21st century. In A. Mohanty, M. Panda, R. Phillipson, & T. Skutnabb-Kangas (Eds.), *Multilingual education for social justice: Globalising the local* (pp. 128–145). New Delhi: Orient Blackswan (former Orient Longman).
García-Vázquez, E., Vázquez, L. A., López, I. C., & Ward, W. (1997). Language proficiency and academic success: Relationships between proficiency in two languages and achievement among Mexican American students. *Bilingual Research Journal, 21*(4), 395–408.

Hadikin, G. S. (2005). *World Englishes and Konglish: What is Konglish and what are local attitudes to it.* London: Institute of Education, University of London.

Harris, S., & Lee, J. S. (2021). Korean-speaking spaces: heritage language learning and community access for mixed-race Korean Americans. *International Journal of Multilingualism*, 1–29.

He, A. W. (2006). Toward an identity theory of the development of Chinese as a heritage language. *Heritage Language Journal*, *4*(1), 1–28.

Higgins, C., & Stoker, K. (2011). Language learning as a site for belonging: A narrative analysis of Korean adoptee-returnees. *International Journal of Bilingual Education and Bilingualism*, *14*(4), 399–412.

Ho, J. (2021). Anti-Asian racism, Black Lives Matter, and COVID-19. *Japan Forum*, *33*(1), 148–159. https://doi.org/10.1080/09555803.2020.1821749

Intarasuan, K. (2020, June 19). NYC man called racial slur, told Asians don't belong in racist attack caught on video. *NBC New York*. Retrieved from www.nbcnewyork.com/news/local/nyc-man-called-racial-slur-told-asians-dont-belong-in-racist-attack-caught-on-video/2472697/

Jang, E., & Brutt-Griffler, J. (2019). Language as a bridge to higher education: A large-scale empirical study of heritage language proficiency on language minority students' academic success. *Journal of Multilingual and Multicultural Development*, *40*(4), 322–337.

Jarmel, M., & Schneider, K. (Directors). (2009). *Speaking in tongues* [Video file]. Retrieved from www.patchworksfilms.net/speaking-in-tongues

Jeon, A. (2020). "I had the best of both worlds": Transnational sense of belonging-Second-generation Korean Americans' heritage language learning journey. *Language and Education*, 1–13.

Jo, H. Y. (2001). 'Heritage' language learning and ethnic identity: Korean Americans' struggle with language authorities. *Language Culture and Curriculum*, *14*(1), 26–41.

Jung, S. H. (2020, September, 2). Record funding allocated to popularizing Korean language. *The Chosun Ilbo*. Retrieved from http://english.chosun.com/site/data/html_dir/2020/09/02/2020090201649.html

Kang, N. W. (2009). A study on the Korean heritage speaker's word recognition: Analyzing "Korean word speed quiz" of KBS Broadcasted materials. *Kul-eo-gyo-yuk yeon-ku* (24), 269–308.

Kim, H. A. (2016). *Biracial identity development: Narratives of biracial Korean American university students in heritage language classes* [Doctoral Dissertation]. University of Washington.

Kim, H. S. H. (2001). Issues of heritage learners in Korean language classes. *Korean Language in America*, 257–274.

Kim, J. Y. (2010). The phonological effect of single-word insertion by Korean heritage speakers: Vowel epenthesis in word-final position. *Eon-eo*, *35*(1), 49–70.

Kim, K., O'Grady, W., & Schwartz, B. D. (2018). Case in heritage Korean. *Linguistic Approaches to Bilingualism*, *8*(2), 252–282.

Kim, S. Y., & Lim, J. (2007). Errors and strategies observed in "Korean Heritage Learners" L2 writing. *Oe-kuk-eo-kyo-yuk*, *14*(4), 93–112.

Kondo-Brown, K. (2003). Heritage language instruction for post-secondary students from immigrant backgrounds. *Heritage Language Journal*, *1*(1), 1–25.

Kondo-Brown, K. (2005). Differences in language skills: Heritage language learner subgroups and foreign language learners. *The Modern Language Journal*, *89*(4), 563–581.

Kraker, D. (2019, May 14). 'To know what it is to be Korean': Foundation to build cultural center in Ely. *MPR News*. Retrieved from www.mprnews.org/story/2019/05/14/minneapolis-couple-eyes-ely-for-new-korean-culture-center

Kupisch, T., & Rothman, J. (2018). Terminology matters! Why difference is not incompleteness and how early child bilinguals are heritage speakers. *International Journal of Bilingualism*, *22*(5), 564–582.

Kwak, Y. S. (2020, September 2). The hallyu effect: Culture ministry vows to vitalize Korean language education. *The Korea Times*. Retrieved from www.koreatimes.co.kr/www/art/2020/09/398_295360.html

Lawrence, C. B. (2012). The Korean English linguistic landscape. *World Englishes*, *31*(1), 70–92.

Lee, C., & García, G. E. (2020). Unpacking the oral translanguaging practices of Korean-American first graders. *Bilingual Research Journal*, *43*(1), 32–49.

Lee, J. S. (2002). The Korean language in America: The role of cultural identity in heritage language learning. *Language Culture and Curriculum*, *15*(2), 117–133.

Lee, J. S. (2005). Through the learners' eyes: Reconceptualizing the heritage and non-heritage learner of the less commonly taught languages. *Foreign Language Annals*, *38*(4), 554–563.

Lee, J. S., & Chen-Wu, H. (2021). Community-organized heritage language programs: Weekend schools, after-school programs, and beyond. In M. Polinsky & S. Montrul (Eds.), *The Cambridge handbook of heritage languages and linguistics*. Cambridge: Cambridge University Press.

Lee, J. S., & Jeong, E. (2013). Korean–English dual language immersion: Perspectives of students, parents and teachers. *Language, Culture and Curriculum, 26*(1), 89–107.

Lee, J. S., & Shin, S. J. (2008). Korean heritage language education in the United States: The current state, opportunities, and possibilities. *Heritage Language Journal, 6*(2), 1–20.

Lee, J. S., & Suarez, D. (2009). A synthesis of the roles of heritage languages in the lives of children of immigrants: What educators need to know. In T. Wiley, J. S. Lee, & R. Rumberger (Eds.), *The education of language minority immigrants in the United States* (pp. 136–171). Clevedon, UK: Multilingual Matters.

Lee, J. S., & Wright, W. E. (2014). The rediscovery of heritage and community language education in the United States. *Review of Research in Education, 38*(1), 137–165.

Lee, S. (2019). *Speaking Korean in America: An ethnographic study of a community-based Korean heritage language school* [Doctoral dissertation]. University of Pennsylvania Publicly Accessible Penn Dissertations no. 3570. Retrieved from https://repository.upenn.edu/edissertations/3570.

Leeman, J., Rabin, L., & Román-Mendoza, E. (2012). Identity and social activism in critical heritage language education. *Modern Language Journal, 95*(4), 481–495.

Lewis, P. (Ed.). (2009). *Ethnologue: Languages of the world* (16th ed.). Dallas, TX: SIL International Online. Retrieved from www.ethnologue.com/show_language.asp?code=kor

Li, Y., & Nicholson Jr, H. L. (2021). When "model minorities" become "yellow peril" – Othering and the racialization of Asian Americans in the COVID-19 pandemic. *Sociology Compass, 15*(2), e12849.

Lo, A. (2009). Evidentiality and morality in a Korean heritage language school. In A. Reyes & A. Lo (Eds.), *Beyond yellow English: Toward a linguistic anthropology of Asian Pacific America* (pp. 63–83). New York: Oxford University Press.

Looney, D., & Lusin, N. (2018, February). *Enrollments in languages other than English in United States institutions of higher education, Summer 2016 and Fall 2016: Preliminary report*. Modern Language Association.

Martínez, R. (2013). Reading the world in Spanglish: Hybrid language practices and ideological contestation in a sixth-grade English language arts classroom. *Linguistics and Education, 24*(3), 276–288.

Min, P. G. (2000). Korean Americans' language use. In S. L. McKay & S. C. Wong (Eds.), *New immigrants in the United States: Readings for second language educators* (pp. 306–322). Cambridge, UK: Cambridge University Press.

Montrul, S. (2008). *Incomplete acquisition in bilingualism: Re-examining the age factor*. Amsterdam and Philadelphia: John Benjamins Publishing Company.

Mu, G. M. (2016). Looking Chinese and learning Chinese as a heritage language: The role of habitus. *Journal of Language, Identity and Education, 15*(5), 293–305.

Nam, H. (2010). Konglish, Korean L2 learners' unique interlanguage: Its definition, categories and lexical entries. *Eung-yong-eon-eo-hag, 26*(4), 275–308.

Noro, H. (2009). The role of Japanese as a heritage language in constructing ethnic identity among Hapa Japanese Canadian children. *Journal of Multilingual and Multicultural Development, 30*(1), 1–18.

Oh, J. S., & Fuligni, A. J. (2010). The role of heritage language development in the ethnic identity and family relationships of adolescents from immigrant backgrounds. *Social Development, 19*(1), 202–220.

Oh, J., Au, T. K.-F., Jun, S.-A., & Lee, R. M. (2019). Childhood Language memory in adult heritage language (re)learners. In M. S. Schmid & B. Köpke (Eds.), *The Oxford handbook of language attrition* (pp. 481–492). Oxford: Oxford University Press.

Orellana, M., & Rodriguez-Minkoff, A. (2016). Cultivating linguistic flexibility in contexts of superdiversity. *International Journal of the Sociology of Language, 2016*(241), 125–150.

Ortega, L. (2020). The study of heritage language development from a bilingualism and social justice perspective. *Language Learning, 70*, 15–53.

Park-Johnson, S. K. (2019). Case ellipsis: Acquisition of variability by young heritage speakers of Korean. *International Multilingual Research Journal, 13*(1), 15–31.

Pascual y Cabo, D., & Rothman, J. (2012). The (Il)logical problem of heritage speaker bilingualism and incomplete acquisition. *Applied Linguistics, 33*, 450–455.

Peyton, J. K., Ranard, D. A., & McGinnis, S. (2001). *Heritage languages in America: Preserving a national resource*. McHenry, IL: Delta Systems Company Inc.

Portes, A., & Hao, L. (1998). E pluribus unum: Bilingualism and loss of language in the second generation. *Sociology of Education*, 269–294.

Potowski, K. (2016). *IntraLatino language and identity: MexiRican Spanish* (Vol. 43). Amsterdam and Philadelphia: John Benjamins Publishing Company.

Pyke, K., & Dang, T. (2003). "FOB" and "whitewashed": Identity and internalized racism among second generation Asian Americans. *Qualitative Sociology*, *26*(2), 147–172.

Rampton, B. (2014). *Crossings: Language and ethnicity among adolescents*. New York: Routledge.

Reyes, A. (2016). The voicing of Asian American figures: Korean linguistic styles in an Asian American cram school. In H. S. Alim, J. R. Rickford & A. F. Ball (Eds.), *Raciolinguistics: How language shapes our ideas about race* (pp. 309–326). Oxford: Oxford University Press.

Rosa, J., & Flores, N. (2017). Unsettling race and language: Toward a raciolinguistic perspective. *Language in Society*, *46*(5), 621–647.

Schrank, A. (2020, June 22). Meet the queer activist scholar taking on the Korean American Christian right. *LAist: HomeLAnd*. Retrieved from https://laist.com/projects/2020/homeland/profiles/south-korea/

Shin, J. (2016). Hyphenated identities of Korean heritage language learners: Marginalization, colonial discourses and internalized whiteness. *Journal of Language, Identity & Education*, *15*(1), 32–43.

Shin, S. J. (2010). "What about me? I'm not like Chinese but i'm not like American": Heritage-Language learning and identity of mixed-heritage adults. *Journal of Language, Identity, and Education*, *9*(3), 203–219.

Shin, S. J. (2013). Transforming culture and identity: Transnational adoptive families and heritage language learning. *Language, Culture and Curriculum*, *26*(2), 161–178.

Shin, S. J., & Lee, J. S. (2013). Expanding capacity, opportunity, and desire to learn Korean as a heritage language. *Heritage Language Journal*, *10*(3), 64–73.

Shin, S. J., & Milroy, L. (2000). Conversational codeswitching among Korean-English bilingual children. *International Journal of Bilingualism*, *4*(3), 351–383.

Shin, S. Y. (2010). The functions of code-switching in a Korean Sunday school. *Heritage Language Journal*, *7*(1), 91–116.

Sohn, S. O., & Park, M. J. (2003). Indirect quotations in Korean conversations. In P. Clancy (Ed.), *Japanese/Korean linguistics* (pp. 105–118). Chicago: University of Chicago Press.

Song, J. (2009). Bilingual creativity and self-negotiation: Korean American children's language socialization into Korean address terms. In A. Reyes & A. Lo (Eds.), *Beyond Yellow English: Toward a linguistic anthropology of Asian Pacific America* (pp. 213–232). Oxford: Oxford University Press.

Song, J. (2010). Language ideology and identity in transnational space: Globalization, migration, and bilingualism among Korean families in the USA. *International Journal of Bilingual Education and Bilingualism*, *13*(1), 23–42.

Song, J. (2019). Wuli and stance in a Korean heritage language classroom: A language socialization perspective. *Linguistics and Education*, *51*, 12–19.

Sotirova, I. (2014). Hallyu and students' motivation in studying Korean. The global impact of South Korean popular culture. *Hallyu Unbound*, 70–80.

Suh, S. (2020). An examination of the language socialization practices of three Korean American families through honorifics. *Bilingual Research Journal*, *43*(1), 6–31.

Tannenbaum, M. (2005). Viewing family relations through a linguistic lens: Symbolic aspects of language maintenance in immigrant families. *The Journal of Family Communication*, *5*(3), 229–252.

Tannenbaum, M., & Berkovich, M. (2005). Family relations and language maintenance: Implications for language educational policies. *Language Policy*, *4*(3), 287–309.

Thomas, E. (2019). *Mexican American English: Substrate influence and the birth of an ethnolect*. Studies in English Language. Cambridge: Cambridge University Press.

U.S. Census Bureau. (2010). *2010 census summary file 1*. Retrieved from http://2010.census.gov/news/press-kits.summary-file-1.html.

Valdés, G. (1997). The teaching of Spanish to bilingual Spanish-speaking students: Outstanding issues and unan- swered questions. In M. C. Colombi & F. X. Alarcon (Eds.), *Laensenanea del espanol a hispanohablantes: Praxis y teoria [The education of Spanish to Spanish speakers: Practice and theory]* (pp. 93–101). Boston, MA: Houghton Mifflin.

Valdés, G. (2005). Bilingualism, heritage language learners, and SLA research: Opportunities lost or seized? *Modern Language Journal*, *89*, 410–426.

Van Deusen-Scholl, N. (2003). Toward a definition of heritage language: Sociopolitical and pedagogical considerations. *Journal of Language, Identity, and Education*, *2*(3), 211–230.

Wiley, T. (2001). On defining heritage languages and their speakers. In J. Peyton, D. Ranard, & S. McGinnis (Eds.), *Heritage languages in America: Preserving a national resource* (pp. 29–36). Washington, DC, and McHenry, IL: Center for Applied Linguistics and Delta Systems.

World Bank. (2009). *World development indicators: Total population 2009*. Retrieved from http://data.worldbank.org/indicator/SP.POP.TOTL?cid=GPD_1

Wright, W. E. (2015). *Foundations for teaching English language learners: Research, theory, policy, and practice*. Philadelphia, PA: Caslon Publishing.

Yam, K. (2017, December, 12). Starbucks customer demands Asian student stop speaking Korean. *HuffPost*. Retrieved from www.huffpost.com/entry/racist-starbucks-customer-korean-student_n_5a3911eae4b0c65287ac3a9a

Yang, J. S. R. (2003). Motivational orientation of Korean learners and ethnic identity development of heritage learners. *The Korean Language in America, 8*, 295–314.

23
LANGUAGE IDEOLOGIES AND IDENTITY FORMATION AMONG KSL LEARNERS

Mi Yung Park

Introduction

This chapter aims to provide readers with a comprehensive overview of the core issues and major findings in the study of language ideologies and identity formation among KSL learners. One aspect of identity that is especially relevant is linguistic identity, defined by Block (2007) as "the assumed and/or attributed relationship between one's sense of self and a means of communication" (p. 40). Learning a new language involves not only acquiring a set of linguistic skills but also adopting new ways of thinking, speaking, behaving, and being. This has significant consequences for the learners' identities and identity construction, which can affect their learning trajectories in powerful ways (Norton, 2013; Pavlenko & Blackledge, 2004). Learner trajectories are also influenced by language ideologies. Individual learners come to language learning with pre-existing attitudes and beliefs about language, which are influenced by broader social and cultural norms and ideologies. Through the process of learning and using a new language, they will encounter new language ideologies and further develop their own attitudes and beliefs about language. These language ideologies, both their own and those of others, impact and shape learners' identities, as well as their motivations, goals, and investment in language learning.

I have organized the chapter by first discussing key concepts related to identity, language ideologies, and language learning. I then review studies according to three identity categories that have been particularly salient in language ideology and identity research: (a) heritage language learners, (b) study abroad learners, and (c) immigrant learners. Particular focus will be placed on how these different groups of Korean language learners develop, negotiate, and resist language ideologies and construct their identities in the situated contexts of families, institutions, and the broader society. After reviewing relevant research done on each group, I discuss the pedagogical implications of the findings. I end the chapter by identifying some of the future directions I believe language ideology and identity research should take in advancing this important area of study.

Identity, language ideologies, and language learning

Interest in second language identity in the field of applied linguistics emerged with a shift from a predominantly (psycho)linguistic approach, which views learning as a cognitive process happening within the individual, to one which attends to the social dimensions of language learning. Viewed as inseparable from the individual learner's cognitive and emotional functioning, these social dimensions help capture a more comprehensive understanding of the dynamic processes involved in learning a language. Although she was not the first to examine identity issues, contemporary approaches to identity and second language learning are frequently traced to Bonny Norton's research on five immigrant women learning English in Canada (e.g., Norton, 2000; Norton Peirce, 1995). With a focus on the social nature of language learning, Norton argued for the role of identity in understanding the relationship between the language learner and the larger social context. Norton (2013) described identity as "how a person understands his or her relationship to the world, how that relationship is constructed across time and space, and how the person understands possibilities for the future" (p. 45). This conceptualization highlights the fluid and multifaceted nature of identity, showing the possibility of constructing identities not only in past and present contexts, but also within a future, imagined community. Based on her case study, Norton claimed that when learners invest in learning a new language, they do so with the understanding that knowing and speaking the language will offer them favorable identity options in the future.

Norton's notion of identity and the SLA field generally owe much to poststructuralist feminist scholar Chris Weedon's (1997) conceptualization of identity as a discursively produced construct. Using the term "subjectivity" instead of "identity," Weedon defined it as "the conscious and unconscious thoughts and emotions of the individual, her sense of herself, and her ways of understanding her relation to the world" (p. 32). In contrast to the structuralist view of identity as an individual's fixed and coherent core, Weedon viewed subjectivity as "precarious, contradictory and in process, constantly being reconstituted in discourse each time we think or speak" (p. 32). From this perspective, identity is dynamic, multiple, conflicting, changing, and even negotiable across time and space.

Highlighting the complexity of learner identity, many scholars have examined the role of identity negotiation in language learning (e.g., Kanno, 2003; McKay & Wong, 1996; Morita, 2004). Identity negotiation refers to the processes through which language learners constantly construct, negotiate, and reconstruct their identity in relation to different language ideologies, power relations, and the learners' perceptions of themselves and others (Pavlenko & Blackledge, 2004). Emphasizing the dynamic, complex, and fragmented nature of identity, Pavlenko and Blackledge (2004) proposed that there are three types: imposed, assumed, and negotiable. Imposed identities are not negotiable at a particular time and place. Assumed identities are also not negotiated, but unlike an imposed identity, they are accepted by individuals. Negotiable identities are those which are contested or resisted by individuals. Here, Kanno's (2003) study of Japanese bilingual university students who spent their adolescent years in Canada may be illustrative. In their Canadian high school, they were viewed as incompetent non-native English speakers, an identity imposed upon them by the host society. After returning to Japan, they aligned themselves with the prevalent discourse of English being a global language and international experience being inherently positive, assuming a positive identity in line with these assumed traits. Positioning and repositioning themselves in relation to surrounding discourses, they came to negotiate and construct their identities as empowered bilingual individuals.

More broadly, Blommaert (2005) suggested two types of identities: inhabited and ascribed. Inhabited identity is "a self-constructed and self-performed identity . . . through which people claim allegiance to a group" (p. 253), whereas ascribed identity is "attributed to someone by others" (p. 251). Language learners can experience emotional conflict and feelings of social exclusion when there is a discrepancy between their inhabited and ascribed identities, as shown in Park's (2017, 2019a, 2019b, 2020) studies on the experiences of Southeast Asian women living in Korea. Migrating to Korea, learning and speaking Korean, marrying Korean men, living in Korean families, and raising Korean children, they claimed inhabited identities as legitimate and successfully integrated members of Korean society. However, they were frequently ascribed identities as illegitimate speakers of Korean, incompetent mothers, and only marginally members of the society.

With language as "the locus of social organization, power, individual consciousness, and a form of symbolic capital" (Piller & Pavlenko, 2007, p. 492), language learners' identity formation is viewed as a site of struggle (Norton, 2013). Although they may wish to become legitimate speakers of the target language, it is not always easy for learners to gain entry into the target language community and take up their desired subject position. Certain language forms and practices are considered legitimate in educational and professional settings, for example, whereas others are not. Who can be counted as a "legitimate" speaker varies under specific social conditions and in relation to language ideologies existing in a particular context at a particular time. Becoming a legitimate speaker of a language is determined by the successful acquisition of a certain set of behaviors and characteristics, generally those shared by the members of the particular discourse community to which the learner wishes to belong. In the context of discourse communities, "discourse" is defined as "a socially accepted association among ways of using language, other symbolic expressions, and 'artifacts', of thinking, feeling, believing, valuing and acting that can be used to identify oneself as a member of a socially meaningful group" (Gee, 1996, p. 131).

Although identities are often constrained by social contexts, individual learners exercise their agency to construct, negotiate, and take up desirable identities. Lantolf and Pavlenko (2001) emphasized the socio-historic nature of agency, viewing it as "a relationship that is constantly co-constructed and renegotiated with those around the individual and with the society at large," rather than "a 'property' of a particular individual" (p. 148). Pavlenko (2004) in turn claimed that individuals are constantly seeking "new social and linguistic resources which allow them to resist identities that position them in undesirable ways, produce new identities, and assign alternative meanings to the links between identities and linguistic varieties" (p. 27). Thus, according to Norton and McKinney (2011), learners "who struggle to speak from one identity position can reframe their relationship with their interlocutors and reclaim alternative, more powerful identities from which to speak" (p. 74). Nevertheless, it must be acknowledged that an individual's ability to claim preferred identities depends on the available resources or strategies (Pavlenko, 2004).

It is also important to point out that identities are closely linked to language ideologies. According to Silverstein (1979), language ideologies are "any sets of beliefs about language articulated by the users as a rationalization or justification of perceived language structure and use" (p. 193). Because language ideologies are associated with norms and expectations regarding language use, they assign indexical meanings to specific linguistic forms and languages, which can consequently shape individual speakers' relationships with different languages. Pavlenko and Blackledge (2004) noted that language ideologies can "guide ways in which individuals use linguistic resources to index their identities and to evaluate the use of linguistic resources by others" (p. 14). Language use is therefore intertwined with language ideologies and self-perceived identities. While they include individuals' beliefs and feelings about language, language ideologies are also embedded in the larger discourses that shape beliefs and values at institutional, national, and global levels (Blackledge, 2005). A society's dominant ideologies and sociocultural norms influence individual speakers' attitudes toward language; thus, language ideologies are "constructed from the sociocultural experience of the speaker" (Kroskrity, 2004, p. 496). However, individuals may absorb, negotiate, or challenge ideological messages they receive from their families, peer groups, schools, communities, religious institutions, media, and so on, making language ideologies multiple, dynamic, and contested (Piller, 2015).

Identity and language ideologies in KSL research

A growing body of language research has explored the multilayered and socially situated nature of individuals' identities, challenging simplistic identity categories (e.g., the native vs. non-native dichotomy) and revealing how individuals develop their identities and language ideologies in different social contexts for specific goals. Much of the research reviewed next examines how particular factors, including ethnicity, race, gender, and sexual orientation, influence language development, learning, and use. The complexity of learner identity recognized in the previous studies has advanced and broadened the second language scholarship in many positive ways. In this section, I discuss three learner populations of particular interest to KSL identity and language ideology research in recent years: (a) heritage language learners, (b) study abroad learners, and (c) immigrant learners, with a focus on marriage-migrants and North Korean refugees. Based on the findings, I offer implications for teaching practices and further development of language programs for each learner population.

Heritage language learners

This section discusses language ideologies and identity construction among HL learners; that is, learners, of any proficiency level, who have an ethnolinguistic affiliation with the language they are learning (Valdés, 2001; Van Deusen-Scholl, 2003). HL and identity have been investigated extensively in the field of Korean language education. The majority of the studies have focused on the relationship between ethnic or cultural identity and Korean language proficiency, analyzing data gathered from surveys and questionnaires completed by a diverse range of HL speakers (e.g., Cho, 2000; Choi, 2015; Kang & Kim, 2012; Lee, 2002). The general findings of these studies indicate that HL proficiency and ethnic identity are positively correlated. For example, by analyzing questionnaire responses from 114 1.5-generation and second-generation Korean-American adults (aged 18–30), Cho (2000) found a strong relationship between self-evaluated Korean proficiency and ethnic identity, suggesting that those who developed their HL had a stronger ethnic identity and more interactions with HL speakers. Drawing on questionnaire data from a total of 181 first-, 1.5-, and second-generation Koreans, Choi's (2015) study also found that self-rated HL proficiency and ethnic identity were interrelated. Those who identified as Korean tended to demonstrate higher HL proficiency, while those who identified as American or claimed a hyphenated identity as Korean American had higher competency in English. Similar findings were reported in Lee's (2002) study, which examined questionnaire responses from a group of 40 Korean American university students. This study was also noteworthy in that the students who had higher proficiency in Korean identified themselves as more bicultural, which suggests that the maintenance of HLs is essential for promoting biculturalism.

Other studies (Kang & Kim, 2012; Kim, 2006) that have examined the connection between HL learners' actual HL proficiency (e.g., test scores) and ethnic identity support the findings of the studies that relied on participants' self-assessed HL proficiency. A mixed-method study by Kim (2006) analyzed survey data collected from 120 Korean American university students and found a positive correlation between actual HL proficiency and ethnic-group identification. Kang and Kim's (2012) investigation of adult Korean Americans' actual and perceived

HL proficiency in relation to their ethnic identity also observed a strong association between actual and self-assessed HL skills and ethnic identity. Korean HL speakers with stronger ties to their ethnic group and heritage culture exhibited better HL competence, especially in speaking skills.

Previous studies have found that reasons for learning Korean as an HL may differ from reasons for studying Korean as a foreign or second language. A number of studies have documented that the primary reasons for a majority of HL learners to take Korean language classes were to re-connect with their heritage culture and to construct their identity as Koreans (Higgins & Stoker, 2011; Jo, 2001; Kim, 2006; Lee, 2002; Lee & Kim, 2007; Park & Sarkar, 2007; Song, 2010). For instance, drawing on survey and interview data gathered from 111 university students, Lee and Kim (2007) examined the motivational orientation of Korean HL learners. The results indicated that an integrative orientation played a more important role in their desire to learn the HL than did an instrumental orientation. This tendency was consistent across different proficiency levels. Both low and high proficiency students identified most strongly with heritage-related motivational reasons ($M = 4.10$) and least strongly with school-related motivational reasons ($M = 2.21$). Lee and Kim concluded that the HL served as "the main connector to their roots and their family and an expressor of who they are as a cultural being" (p. 168).

In addition to associating the Korean language with ethnic identity and cultural roots, some Korean immigrants regard it as social and economic capital. In studies of Korean immigrant mothers' efforts to maintain their children's HL, Jang (2020) and Kwon (2017) found that the mothers tended to view HL proficiency as a positive asset that could open up "career options" for their children in the future. Song (2010) examined language ideology and identity construction among Korean immigrants and early study abroad sojourners in the United States and argued that the growing number of Koreans and increased economic value of the Korean language in the United States have broadened Koreans' views of the HL and changed their language ideologies concerning Korean; for them, the language has become not only a marker of ethnolinguistic identity but "a marketable commodity" (p. 39). Song argued that the language's rising status was contributing to a growing trend of learning Korean among immigrant Koreans.

However, having positive personal or familial language ideologies regarding the HL is not sufficient for maintaining and developing the HL when it is a minority language in a majority-language context. Research demonstrates that immigrant parents' language ideologies interact with institutional-level language ideologies, which usually negatively impact immigrant children's HL use in educational settings. For example, Jang (2020) explored the language ideologies of Korean immigrant mothers whose children were enrolled in early childhood education (ECE) programs in Canada. They tended to hold pluralist ideologies driven by their desire to help their children simultaneously integrate into the mainstream society and develop their ethnic identity as Koreans. And while they regarded the HL as crucial for preserving their cultural heritage and family relationships, this ideology was often challenged by the English monolingual ideologies of educators who discouraged the children from speaking their HL. Kitchen's (2014) study on Korean-born adolescents in a New Zealand high school also reported on their Korean identity and HL use not being legitimized or promoted in the classroom, despite the students viewing both languages as essential in their school life. Kitchen argued that teachers must help establish supportive learning environments so that bilingual students can utilize their linguistic resources and build their multilingual identities.

Recognizing identity as an integral part of HL use and learning, a number of qualitative studies have examined Korean HL speakers' identities. These studies have observed the links between identity and the ways speakers use their HL. Kang (2013) explored the fluid nature of Korean American HL learners' ethnic identities by observing their language practices. The HL learners used their HL and English for different purposes: Korean was associated with their kinship, childhood memories, and home food, whereas English was their primary means of communication. They also used linguistic devices, such as pronouns (*them* vs. *us*), to position themselves and their ethnic identities, moving between the two worlds of Americanness and Koreanness depending on the situation. More recently, Kim (2020) found that the Korean language served as a resource for Korean American HL speakers to construct a "third space" ethnic identity. The HL speakers in her study reported that, while speaking in English, they expressed themselves "in Korean ways," being "very blunt," which they considered to be a Korean thing, or integrating contemporary Korean slang words into English. Working with 1.5-generation Korean immigrants in New Zealand, Park (2021b) illustrated how they mixed Korean and English with siblings and friends, a practice they perceived as being part of a shared "Kowi" (Korean-Kiwi) identity. For example, they reported inserting Korean words (e.g., *taptaphay* 'frustrated, stuffy, restricted, repressed' and *engttwunghay* 'strange, weird, quirky, unpredictable, random') into English to express specific feelings, as these words have multiple meanings and do not have exact equivalents in English. In short, HL speakers draw on and combine both sides of their linguistic repertoires to convey their unique individual voices and ethnic identities.

Research shows that identity influences HL speakers' investment, or lack thereof, in HL learning and use. Park (2011) looked at the social experiences of three Korean American university students in Hawai'i who were enrolled in an advanced Korean language course. The study found their investment in the HL to be dependent on their identities and the (imagined) communities they wished to join. One participant, Sora, chose not to speak to older Korean immigrants, as her desire was to model her speech on a group of native Korean youths. Another participant, Taehi, distanced herself from first-generation Korean immigrants and international students who maintained hierarchical linguistic and cultural practices, including the use of honorifics, and instead identified herself with younger, second-generation Koreans who shared similar cultural values. Investigating 1.5-generation Korean immigrants' language use in New Zealand workplaces, Park (2021a) claimed that the participants' investment in HL use and maintenance was strongly tied to gaining membership as Koreans in their ethnolinguistic community. Having constructed their identities as members of the diaspora, they did not regard native-like Korean fluency or advanced literacy skills as necessary or contributing to their socioeconomic capital. Consequently, they showed a lack of investment in further HL development.

Two subsets of HL learners with highly complex identities are Korean adoptees and mixed-heritage diasporic Koreans, especially when they return to Korea. In a study of four Korean-born, US-raised "adoptee-returnees" residing in Seoul, Higgins and Stoker (2011) showed that they struggled to build a sense of belonging in Korean society. Given their ethnic and racial identity, locals expected them to adhere to Korean linguistic and social norms. Unable to accommodate these expectations, the adoptee-returnees were frustrated by not gaining membership in their country of birth. To overcome feelings of social exclusion, they sometimes constructed hybrid identities, using labels such as "overseas Korean" or "an adoptee who is a member of the society," claiming both their Koreanness and their displacement. An HL speaker's construction of a hybrid identity was also explored in Park's (2019c) research on a mixed-heritage university student, Gina, for whom HL learning had a transformative effect. Growing up as a monolingual English speaker in New Zealand with a European-background father and Korean mother, Gina decided to learn the HL and study abroad in Korea to build a stronger bond with her mother. In the course of her HL learning experience, she shifted her self-identification from "very New Zealander" to "half Korean, half New Zealander," claiming her "Koreanness" without needing to possess native-level HL proficiency.

The findings discussed earlier offer implications for HL education. First, previous research has illuminated that HL learners struggle to adhere to social and linguistic norms in interactions with fluent Korean speakers, both in diasporic contexts and in the heritage nation. The language spoken by Korean HL speakers is often viewed as divergent from monolingual norms, which can have a significant impact on their identities as well as their HL learning and use. In educational settings, instead of trying to minimize linguistic variation, HL teachers need to value and make use of heritage speakers' multilingual repertoires. Second, as a desire to connect to the culture is one of HL learners' main motivations, HL teachers need to integrate sufficient cultural components into the curriculum, reflecting HL learners' dynamic transnational experiences and acknowledging the complexities of their cultural hybridity as diasporic subjects. It is important to develop effective teaching materials that meet HL students' needs and interests, keeping in mind that the messages conveyed in the materials can directly impact students' identities and perceptions of Korean culture. According to Sun and Kwon (2020), the textbooks issued by the Korean government that are widely used for children in overseas Korean HL schools foster the ideology of monoculturalism, through oversimplified statements and "traditional" images of people. Specifically, the construction of an "us," a collective Korean identity, legitimizes static and stereotypical ideas about what counts as legitimately or truly Korean. Arguing that these fixed views of culture, language, and identity can marginalize HL learners in both the immigrant home and the host societies, Sun and Kwon stressed the urgent need to develop HL textbooks that reflect the complex identities of learners in multicultural contexts. At the university level, it is vital to design an HL literacy curriculum that focuses on aspects of Korean culture relevant to learners' everyday lives. Based on their own curriculum developed for advanced Korean HL learners at an American university, Choi and Yi (2012) demonstrated that the use of pop culture texts and media (e.g., television dramas, films) helped them create an effective forum for discussions on Korean sociocultural issues. This culture-based curriculum enabled the students to gain deeper understanding of their heritage culture and its position in the world and reexamine and strengthen their ethnic identities.

Study abroad learners

Identity-related experiences and conflicts are particularly salient in study abroad contexts, making identity a particular topic of interest in the field (Block, 2007). Studying abroad is a border-crossing experience that places students into a new cultural and linguistic setting and immerses them in the target language. This new environment often engenders identity challenges (Tullock, 2018). As Block (2007) noted, "when individuals move across geographical and psychological borders, immersing themselves in new sociocultural environments, they find that their sense of identity is destabilized and that they enter a period of struggle to reach a balance" (p. 864). While the cross-cultural transition can be productive for language learning, it also can be problematic for learners as they struggle to adapt to new discourses and social and cultural norms in the host society. A small yet growing body of literature has investigated the complex relationship between identity and language learning among study abroad students in Korea. These studies have focused on the "foreigner identity" of study abroad students in Seoul and how this foreigner identity (e.g., exchange student) affects their language learning.

Within the limited research in this area, Brown (2013) examined the use of honorific forms in Korean by four male advanced-level Korean learners of different nationalities studying in

Seoul. Korean social hierarchies require differing levels of honorific speech depending on a range of factors, including age, class, and social position, with *panmal* (non-honorific speech) being reserved for intimate personal relationships or for addressing social inferiors. One British participant, Richard, who was positioned as a "cute" younger brother, utilized his foreigner identity as an advantage, as it situated him outside the strict hierarchical boundaries of Korean society that govern who speaks in what speech style and to whom. This allowed him to use *panmal* without social repercussions and in fact to establish intimate relationships. Conversely, another participant, Patrick, from Austria, resisted being positioned as an outsider through strictly adhering to Korean norms, including honorifics, thereby claiming an "identity of equal status to Korean native speakers" (p. 292) and being offended by Koreans who treated him differently and used *panmal* even though he was older than them. In the case of a heritage learner, Daniel, he faced different expectations from community members due to cultural and ethnic ties; unlike the other participants, he was expected to adopt native-like patterns of language use. His Western preference for egalitarian language use clashed with the identity imposed on him as an ethnic Korean who should know and adhere to native-speaker norms. The findings demonstrated that the identities imposed by the host society impacted the study abroad students' language development. In the cases of Richard and Patrick, it limited their exposure to native-speaker norms of language use, which hindered their acquisition of advanced sociopragmatic knowledge; for both Patrick and Daniel, it limited their ability to develop and assert their own linguistic identities within the target language.

Sexual and gender identity can also influence study abroad students' experiences and interactions with local people in the host community. This is illustrated in Brown's (2016) study of Julie, a 50+-year-old Caucasian lesbian learner of Korean who studied in Seoul for six weeks. Julie's narrative demonstrated that she struggled to gain access to the target language community and establish a comfortable sense of identity due to societal hostility to her sexual orientation. These struggles were worsened by her experience in her Korean class, where she was socially marginalized as an older student and expected to interact and work with another older student, whom she described as a "sexist" and "narcissistic" 65-year-old European male. She exercised her agency to overcome these struggles by sitting away from that student and redefining her identity as a "cool old person" (p. 821).

Ethnicity, which is an important dimension of identity, plays a crucial role in Korean HL learners' experiences abroad. Lee, Kim, and Choi (2020) examined two 1.5-generation Korean American students and their study abroad experiences in Korea. Having been born in Korea and emigrated at a young age, they viewed themselves as distinct from both second-generation Korean Americans and native Koreans, and constructed "in-between" identities for themselves. Their study abroad experiences helped them claim an ethnic identity and gain cultural awareness and membership in Korean society through expanding their social networks. Park's (2019c) study of Gina, the mixed-heritage Korean New Zealander university student who studied abroad, illuminated the ways her mixed identity as half Korean both facilitated and hampered her opportunities to use the HL in Korea. Her ethnic background enabled her to transition into Korean society, socialize with local people, and build a sense of belonging. However, her identity as a Korean heritage speaker made her feel burdened to perform better than non-heritage learners. Her high expectations and language anxiety often kept her from speaking up in class and hindered her enjoyment of the learning process.

Brown's (2021) study exploring the language choices of an advanced Caucasian female learner of Korean who spent six months studying in Seoul contributes to an emerging line of research on language ideologies and identity construction in Korean study abroad. Her initial goal had been to speak only Korean while studying abroad, but it proved difficult for her to establish Korean-speaking interactions and construct an identity as a Korean speaker due to prevalent language ideologies favoring the use of English. Being an American English native speaker, she was often perceived through an imposed identity as a chance to practice English. However, socializing with other international students in Korean helped her reconsider her initial desired outcomes for studying abroad and develop her identity as a "translingual speaker competent in both English and Korean" (p. 146).

The results of this body of research have implications for study abroad programs. As this review indicates, one of the biggest obstacles for study abroad students is that, as outsiders, they are not necessarily expected to develop a high level of proficiency in the target language or exhibit the same linguistic behavior as native speakers. Further, they may not have sufficient opportunities to engage in meaningful interactions with people in the host society. The realities of study abroad often conflict with the discourse of immersion, which describes the experience of living in a homogenous community with constant and abundant speaking opportunities. It is therefore important to help raise students' awareness of the actual linguistic and cultural diversity that exists within a given language community. Developing a more multilingual and multicultural orientation will in turn help students define learning outcomes for study abroad that are both desirable and feasible, leading to greater enjoyment of the experience.

This research also shows identity's powerful role in shaping both the quality and the outcomes of study abroad experiences, which also has pedagogical implications. To support and guide learners' identity development and transformation, space for reflective activities and processing before, during, and after a program needs to be created. Before departure, while students explore their study abroad options, it would be desirable for language teachers and study abroad advisors to encourage them to learn about the host country and city of the program, including social and cultural norms, language ideologies, and local practices. This process will help students navigate how aspects of their identity may be perceived and treated in another cultural context and to be prepared for it. During the program, a portfolio that includes self-reflection journals and essays can be integrated into the study abroad curriculum. A variation of this would be to use digital storytelling in which students focus on selected experiences and provide a narrated slideshow in the target language, accompanied by an appropriate soundtrack. Reflection during and after their time overseas can help students critically process what they have experienced, encourage and monitor their identity development in relation to the host country context, and provide an important outlet when students encounter difficult situations. Additionally, study abroad programs should provide a forum for students to share their study abroad experiences and identity-related issues with other study abroad learners, offering both groups the possibility of new and diverse sources of support and information in their processes of identity (re)construction.

Immigrant learners

With globalization, Korean society has experienced increasing ethnic diversity and accompanying social issues. Many of these issues are related to the acculturation or assimilation of immigrants into the linguistic and cultural environment. In the following two subsections, I will examine language learning and identity construction among two immigrant populations in Korea: women who come to Korea from other countries for marriage with Koreans, and refugees from North Korea. In each subsection, I will start with some essential background information for understanding the context of the specific issues under discussion, including the government's policies and Korean language programs specifically designed for each group.

I will then discuss the key findings from the previous research and wrap up by offering suggestions for immigrant language programs.

Marriage-migrant women

An influx of marriage-migrants has led the government to create a new family model called the "multicultural family" (*damunhwa gajeong*), defined as a family with one Korean national and one foreign spouse. In 2008, the Korean government enacted the Support for Multicultural Families Act, which led to the establishment of over 170 multicultural family support centers throughout the country (Ahn, 2013). The centers provide various programs and services tailored to the needs of female marriage-migrants, including Korean language and culture programs and interpretation and translation services. Whereas migrant workers are considered temporary sojourners who will eventually need to return to their home country, marriage-migrants are viewed as potential Korean citizens, given their role in both the biological and cultural reproduction of the nation. Accordingly, the government's policies and social integration programs for marriage-migrants fall within a "patriarchal family-oriented welfare model," which aims to enable the women to successfully manage their families and households (Kim, 2011, p. 214). For this reason, Korean language programs designed for foreign brides have stressed "traditional women's roles as housekeepers, good daughters-in-law, wives and mothers – highlighting only submissive roles" (Lee, 2014, p. 306).

The Korean government implemented stricter language requirements for marriage-migrants beginning in April 2014, with the intention of addressing interlingual couples' communication problems. To apply for a spousal visa, marriage-migrants now have to pass Level 1 of the Test of Proficiency in Korean (TOPIK), an examination administered by Korea's National Institute for International Education. Level 1 requires a vocabulary of around 800 words necessary to perform basic language functions, such as introducing oneself, ordering, purchasing, and understanding and speaking on personal and familiar topics (TOPIK, 2018). Upon arrival in Korea, foreign brides are required to take Korean language classes designed specifically for them. These classes focus on teaching the women phrases and expressions used in family settings to manage everyday domestic tasks (Kim, 2010; Lee, 2014). The Korean government has also developed textbooks specifically for female marriage-migrants, which cover topics relevant to the gender-defined roles assigned to them, such as family relations, cooking, and shopping (Kim, 2008, 2010). The majority of the policies and programs are geared toward assimilating the foreign brides into Korean society; there are few to no resources for educating Korean spouses and in-laws about the languages or cultures of their new members. Thus, despite the language requirements and language programs, marriage-migrants tend to experience a number of linguistic and cultural problems.

A small yet growing body of research has explored the lived experiences of marriage-migrant women in Korea with a focus on their identity, ideologies, and Korean language learning. The scant research on this group has concentrated on the sociolinguistic challenges the women encounter in communicating with local Koreans. Park's (2017) study of Southeast Asian marriage-migrants in a rural city in North Gyeongsang Province showed that they were positioned with an imposed identity as incompetent L2 speakers on account of their lack of sociolinguistic competence. The women faced pressure nonetheless to strictly observe Korean sociolinguistic and cultural norms both within the household and in the workplace. One of the participants, Jeong, reported being reprimanded by an older colleague because of her lack of awareness concerning the differences between honorific and non-honorific registers. Having learned Korean in the home, she was more familiar with non-honorific registers used in intimate settings. By using *panmal* with her older colleagues, she failed to convey the proper respect required within Korea's social hierarchy, which led to misunderstandings and conflicts in the workplace.

Moreover, it has been documented that Southeast Asian marriage-migrant women experience linguistic discrimination when they speak a non-standard Korean dialect, a common situation, as most marriage-migrants settle in rural areas. Park's (2020) study demonstrated that speaking the Gyeongsang dialect, which they acquired in the homes they married into, caused a sense of marginalization, especially in the workplace. Consequent feelings of anxiety and inferiority about their way of speaking prevented them from forming healthy, pluralistic language ideologies. Instead, they tended to view standard Korean, or "Seoul speech," as a symbol of prestige required to gain membership in mainstream Korean society. They actively invested in mastering standard Korean as a way to resist linguistic discrimination and to establish their identities as legitimate Korean speakers, drawing on various strategies, such as enrolling in formal Korean courses, choosing specific media offerings (e.g., news programs), and reconstructing their immediate linguistic environment to have more exposure to standard Korean.

Gender is also a factor in marriage-migrants' second language learning. Park's (2019b) research investigated the impact of gender roles and ideologies on these women's Korean language learning and use in the hierarchical Korean context. With Korea's gender hierarchy, prevalent negative stereotypes of marriage-migrants (e.g., money-seeking opportunists), and their limited Korean skills, these women were positioned as "unskilled mothers" who were unable to provide adequate educational support to their children, resulting in feelings of not belonging. Rigid gender ideologies acted as a constraint on the participants' language use, restricting their ability to socialize and expand their social networks, which resulted in a lack of opportunities for meaningful contact and intercultural communication with Koreans. Nevertheless, their identity as mothers of multicultural children emerged as a key factor in their decisions to pursue Korean language competence, which they saw as required to protect their children from potential discrimination at school and in Korean society at large.

The findings offer valuable implications for second language teachers and curriculum developers who work with marriage-migrants. Given the stereotypes and multiple marginalizations experienced by these women, better efforts could be made to develop immigrants' place in wider Korean society by recognizing and appreciating their multiple identities and the rich resources they bring to the nation. Second language programs designed for immigrant women continue to emphasize their domestic roles (Lee, 2014) and fail to support the women's identities and growth as full citizens. More systematic efforts should be made to help them enhance their ability to speak Korean effectively and appropriately in various social and professional contexts beyond the domestic domain and support them in transitioning to employment and further education and training. Korean language programs could offer different tracks for immigrants with different needs, including business Korean, academic Korean, and university preparation classes for those who plan to pursue higher education. With proper education and professional training, immigrants can participate and gain membership in their desired academic and professional communities.

Furthermore, some marriage-migrant women seem to have internalized the hegemonic standard language ideology under which regional dialects are regarded as less prestigious than standard Korean. Accepting this ideology and encountering the negative perceptions of others toward their regional dialect leads to a desire to shift to standard Korean, often at the expense of the regional dialect. An awareness of the importance of linguistic and cultural diversity on the part of the host society could do much to address marriage-migrants' linguistic marginalization and identity construction. In the language program classroom, it would be desirable for language teachers to promote flexible language ideologies that view dialect use as a resource rather than a disadvantage and to support immigrant women's ability to communicate effectively in multiple varieties of Korean. For example, bidialectal teachers who are competent in using both the regional dialect and standard Korean in educational settings could help the women build their self-esteem in relation to their language use and identity. Legitimatizing the use of multiple varieties of Korean could motivate the learners to view their linguistic repertoires as valuable resources and engage in more holistic bidialectal practices, which could potentially empower them in home- and work-related situations as well.

Finally, language programs for marriage-migrants should go beyond developing only linguistic skills. Language teachers can serve as cultural mediators and transformers by providing their students with strategies for handling challenging interactions and discrimination. Explicit instruction in responding to negative stereotypes could help them improve their communication skills and empower them to participate confidently in intercultural interactions. In particular, the women should be supported in learning how to challenge assumptions about not just their own but any group of people and to help lead non-judgmental communication. The more Koreans learn about the real facts of immigration and the actual experiences of individual migrants, the more likely it is that the negative group stereotypes prevalent in the society will eventually break down.

North Korean refugees

The studies discussed in the previous section demonstrate that language ideologies and identities developed in specific societal contexts are deeply intertwined with migrants' language use in new and different contexts. North Koreans in South Korea provide another unique context: immigrants with a shared ethnicity but distinct varieties of the same language. In this section, I will discuss language ideologies and identity construction among North Korean refugees in South Korea.

Despite shared ethnicity and support from the South Korean government, many North Koreans find it challenging to acculturate to South Korean society (Kim, 2016). Specifically, North Korean refugees encounter a language barrier in South Korea. These communication difficulties have been reported by media as one of the biggest obstacles to the social adaptation of North Korean refugees (BBC News, 2019; The Korea Times, 2017). The Southern and Northern varieties of Korean share the Korean alphabet and are mutually intelligible. However, there are noticeable linguistic differences, including in spelling and pronunciation (Song, 2005). North Korean refugees encounter "ridicule due to the stigma that South Korean society places on North Korean accents," as shown in popular South Korean comedy shows (Lee, Han, & Hyun, 2016, p. 293). Comedians sometimes parody Northern pronunciation and use old-fashioned North Korean words not used in the South for humorous effect.

The biggest language difference is the use of Sino-Korean words and English loanwords (Lee, 2016). South Korean has changed vastly thanks to exposure to foreign cultures and technology, whereas North Korean has evolved very little since the national division following World War II. In North Korea, the use of Chinese characters and Sino-Korean words and phrases was abandoned, and most of the loanwords from English, Japanese, and Russian were converted into "pure" Korean (Song, 2015). Language ideologies and education in North Korea foster purism, which does not favor language borrowing or mixing. In South Korea, English is viewed as a symbol of affluence, prestige, and upward mobility, and English loanwords are part of every South Korean's linguistic repertoire. North Koreans, meanwhile, learn English only as a school subject and do not use it in their daily lives. For this reason, many

English loanwords are not intelligible to North Koreans (Song, 2005). Instead of the English loanwords and transliterations that are commonplace in the South, North Koreans favor literal descriptions using Korean root words. Thus, for instance, while "remote control" and "skin toner" are rendered as *limokhen* (a contracted form of *remote control*) and *sukhin* in the South, North Koreans call them *maktayki* 'bar' and *salkyelmwul* 'skin water' (Park, 2021c).

The South Korean government attempts to ease North Korean refugees' transition to the new linguistic environment by providing a language-support program (Ministry of Unification, 2019). The Resettlement Support Center for North Korean Refugees, commonly known as Hanawon, has offered this language-support program since 1999 as a mandatory part of South Korea's refugee resettlement program. Hanawon, established by the Ministry of Unification, helps newly arrived North Korean refugees settle into South Korean society by providing them with a three-month-long educational program (Ministry of Unification, 2019). As of 2019, the educational program (400 hours in total) comprises five components: (a) emotional stability and health (31 hours), (b) understanding South Korean society (119 hours), (c) career counseling and vocational training (166 hours), (d) initial resettlement support (57 hours), and (e) life planning (27 hours). The program aims to help refugees from North Korea "regain emotional stability, overcome cultural differences, and become socially and economically independent" (Park, 2021c, p. 2). The language-support program includes 41 hours of the "understanding South Korean society" component, comprising approximately 34% of that component's hours and 10% of the whole educational program. It covers South Korean standard pronunciation, differences in the Northern and Southern varieties of Korean, loanwords, and basic English.

Despite the mandatory language-support program, North Koreans still face hurdles in dealing with the language differences, and communication difficulties are exacerbated by South Koreans' negative reactions to North Korean accents. Lee (2016) found that the greatest challenges for North Korean refugees were pronunciation differences, loanwords from English, and Sino-Korean words. She argued that the current language-support program provided by the South Korean government was insufficient to meet the needs of the refugees and that it should be revised, considering refugees' linguistic background, to better address the challenges they encounter. Another study, by Lee et al. (2016), observed that some North Koreans try to change their accent, as North Korean accents are both easily distinguished by South Korean users and stigmatized in the South because of the political tension between the two countries. According to a language awareness survey conducted by South Korea's National Institute of Korean Language in 2016, over 40% of North Korean defectors in South Korea (N = 305) reported having experienced mistreatment and marginalization as a result of their accent (National Institute of Korean Language, 2016).

A growing body of literature has examined North Korean refugees' identity construction and language ideologies toward the two varieties of Korean. For example, in a study of the multilingual practices and ideologies of North Korean refugee students at South Korean universities, Lee et al. (2016) found that the students used a South Korean variety as a primary language to gain acceptance into South Korean society, while speaking their North Korean variety only with other North Koreans. Even in groups where only one South Korean was present, they chose to use the Southern variety in order not to be identified as North Korean. Drawing on audio-recorded data collected from student meetings, Lee and Ahn (2016) explored how university students from North Korea constructed their identities and interacted with South Korean students. The patterns of their communication indicated that the North Koreans tended to agree with their South Korean peers, avoided discussing topics related to North Korea, and tried to hide their North Korean accents, reflecting their peripheral position in South Korean society. Salo and Dufva (2018) analyzed two North Korean refugees' multilingual practices and the emotions they attached to each of their language varieties. Although the two participants both viewed South Korean as a prestigious variety, they held different attitudes toward North Korean. Whereas one participant, Dora, embraced and accepted the two varieties of Korean as part of her linguistic repertoire, the other, Bona, strove to eradicate her North Korean accent. Their different language ideologies were manifested in the strategies they employed to integrate into South Korean society. Bona invested in gaining a standard South Korean accent through attending a speech clinic and observing other people's speech styles, while Dona tried to learn more about her friends' interests (e.g., South Korean celebrities) in order to become part of her new community.

Park's (2021c) study looking at identity and language ideologies among North Korean refugees in Seoul illustrated that their values and beliefs, cultivated in North Korea, conflicted with the new ideologies they encountered in South Korea, especially in terms of the use of English loanwords. Drawing on interviews with North Korean refugees, this study found that they suffered from stigmatization because of their socially marked North Korean accents, which led them to internalize a hierarchical view of the two varieties of Korean and to strive to speak like South Koreans. However, some of the participants repositioned themselves and their linguistic and cultural resources through imagining their futures as desirable and useful cultural and linguistic bridges in a reunified Korea and the possibilities therein. Challenging the inferior identities imposed on them by the mainstream society, they constructed their imagined identities as valuable assets after reunification. In doing so, they used their bidialectal and bicultural skills to positively differentiate themselves from South Koreans and empower themselves.

The findings of these studies offer implications for refugee language-support programs. The research demonstrates that North Korean refugees feel pressured to assimilate and hide their background for fear of discrimination, which not only threatens their identities but suppresses the nation's linguistic and cultural diversity. It is crucial for refugee educators to deepen their knowledge of the social prejudice and other challenges refugees encounter in their adaptation process and to realize the significant impact these challenges can have on refugees' identities. Many refugees struggle to develop their desired linguistic identities and their sense of belonging within the host society. Understanding their unique experiences, struggles, and needs is the first step toward facilitating their smooth integration. Furthermore, the host society's recognition of linguistic and cultural diversity is vital in addressing the refugees' linguistic stigmatization. Rather than prioritizing assimilation and treating North Korean refugees' culture, language, and identities as sources of interference in that process, South Korean society would be enriched by acknowledging and embracing the differences. Refugee educators need to develop appropriate classroom activities that celebrate diverse backgrounds and build on refugees' existing linguistic repertoires while adding the ability to communicate in a new variety. By promoting flexible and plural language ideologies in the classroom and viewing the use of the two varieties as a resource rather than a disadvantage, teachers could support refugees' engagement in the bidialectal and bicultural practices that are part of their daily lives. If refugees' hybrid language use was legitimized and valued in this way, destructive feelings of linguistic insecurity and inauthenticity could be mitigated. Refugees also need to be supported to gain critical awareness of the power differences inherent in language use, challenge dominant ideologies, and negotiate diverse norms for communication. When they can confidently and comfortably draw on their multiple languages, ideologies, and identities to their advantage, they can construct more empowered identities, which can contribute to their successful acculturation. Lastly, North Korean immigrants trained in language education should be encouraged to teach in refugee language-support programs. This practice would provide space for North Korean refugees to utilize their bidialectal and bicultural resources as useful members of South

Korean society, as they are better able to understand other refugees' experiences and positively influence their learning and identity construction, serving as mentors and models.

Suggestions for future research

In this section, I identify several aspects of identity and language ideology research that I feel need further consideration. I first address the need for studying diverse learner populations in order to understand and conceptualize the multifaceted and multilayered identities of KSL learners. For example, the majority of the previous literature on Korean HL identity has concentrated on a fairly restricted group of HL speakers, usually in North American contexts: 1.5- and second-generation adult HL learners whose parents both grew up in Korea and speak Korean as their dominant language at home (e.g., Kang & Kim, 2012; Kim, 2006; Lee, 2002; Lee & Kim, 2007). However, an increasing number of Korean HL learners come from families where Korean is not spoken regularly (Lee & Shin, 2008). These learners largely comprise three groups: people who were born in Korea but adopted overseas by foreign families, third- or fourth-generation Koreans whose families are not proficient in the language of their ancestral home, and mixed-heritage learners whose parents each speak a different native language. Therefore, it is important for researchers to examine the motivations and needs of these understudied HL learners and how they experience the process of constructing their identity and learning their HL.

Similarly, studies on immigrant identity in Korea have focused on the experiences of a limited number of marriage-migrant women from Southeast Asia (e.g., Vietnam, Cambodia, the Philippines) who resided in North Gyeongsang Province and spoke a regional dialect. The Southeast Asian women in these studies may not be representative of all migrant women in their position, let alone the wide variety of other migrants resident in Korea. Therefore, future research should extend this line of research by comparing immigrants of different ethnicities, linguistic and socioeconomic backgrounds, and educational levels, including those who are based in urban areas who learn standard Korean. It would also be interesting to compare the experiences of Southeast Asian immigrants with those of immigrants from East Asia (e.g., Chinese, Japanese), who likely encounter fewer negative stereotypes as their linguistic and cultural backgrounds have higher status in Korean society. This would help document and understand the heterogeneity of immigrant women's language-learning experiences and identities, avoiding stereotypical portrayals of these women.

Second, language ideology and identity research better captures the complexity of identity construction when it integrates more holistic perspectives into the analysis and diversifies its research methods. Much of the prior relevant research consists of qualitative case studies based on interview data. While interviews provide a powerful tool for gaining an understanding of how learners perceive their experiences as well as themselves as agents of their own learning, they should not be treated as simple reports. It is crucial for researchers to approach interview data as discursive constructions created in complex ongoing sense-making processes and to pay attention to how research participants use language to make sense of their experiences and take up one's own particular position during an interview. Pavlenko (2002) pointed out that the largest group of identity studies is focused on exploring research participants' "subject reality" (Pavlenko, 2007, p. 165) in their narratives through thematic or content analysis, often neglecting to look at the interplay between context, content, and form. Considering the discursive and linguistic elements involved in a narrative can contribute to our understanding of the myriad micro-processes, practices, and activities that make up a narrative. In addition, in studying identity and language ideologies, it would be worthwhile to take a longitudinal approach. For example, when examining attitudes held by immigrant parents and children toward HL maintenance and development, this method would enable a better understanding of how and whether ideologies change, especially as the children enter the school system, and in what ways both generations' ideologies might affect the younger generations' HL use.

Another area that future research must address is the need to connect theories related to identity and language ideologies with pedagogical practices. While the importance of language learners' identities has been recognized in the literature, little research has looked at how theories of second language learning, identity, and language ideologies can be translated into teaching. Some previous studies have demonstrated that teachers play an important role in developing students' identities (e.g., Jang, 2020; Kitchen, 2014), which, however, carries risks. As Norton (2010) pointed out: "Despite the best intentions, classroom practice can recreate subordinate student identities, thereby limiting students' access not only to language learning opportunities, but to other more powerful identities" (p. 361). To prevent making the classroom a site for reproducing essentialist discourses and ascribing institutionally imposed identities on language learners, which can lead to marginalization or resistance, more pedagogical research needs to be conducted. These research efforts should be geared toward documenting effective practical activities, behaviors, and forms of communication that validate students' multifaceted identities, foster their identity construction, and empower individuals to take up new and preferred identities.

Lastly, a related concern is the matter of teacher education for Korean language teachers. Future research needs to examine the actual needs of teacher education in relation to student identity and language ideologies and to explore possible curricula and materials appropriate for teacher education programs of this kind. It is increasingly acknowledged that the learning and development of language teachers includes more than learning subject matter, theories of second language teaching and learning, and pedagogical skills. Learning to teach involves developing understanding of one's own identities as well as the students' identities, language ideologies, and experiences. More research is needed on how to integrate identity work into teacher education programs to help teachers implement pedagogical strategies that facilitate positive identities in all their students.

Conclusion

I end the chapter by urging continued and focused investigation of how the body of knowledge and findings from language ideology and identity research can be translated into accessible and actionable forms for educators and policymakers so they can engage in practices that can transform the classroom, communities, and society at large. A shift in the conceptualization of second language learning from a predominantly psycholinguistic process to a social one has changed the ways in which we understand language- and identity-related experiences among diverse KSL learners who are often marginalized within particular sociocultural contexts. Through creating synergy between research and practice, we can help minimize the incongruence between KSL learners' imposed identities and their desired identities and facilitate the cultivation of their positive identities and agency in the language they are learning.

References

Ahn, J.-H. (2013). Global migration and the racial project in transition: Institutionalizing racial difference through the discourse of multiculturalism in South Korea. *Journal of Multicultural Discourses, 8*(1), 29–47.

BBC News. (2019). *Crossing divides: Two Koreas divided by a fractured language*. Retrieved December 15, 2019, from www.bbc.com/news/world-asia-47440041

Block, D. (2007). *Second language identities*. London: Continuum.
Blommaert, J. (2005). *Discourse*. Cambridge: Cambridge University Press.
Brown, L. (2013). Identity and honorifics use in Korean study abroad. In C. Kinginger (Ed.), *Social and cultural aspects of language learning in study abroad* (pp. 269–298). Amsterdam and Philadelphia: John Benjamins Publishing Company.
Brown, L. (2016). An activity-theoretic study of agency and identity in the study abroad experiences of a lesbian nontraditional learner of Korean. *Applied Linguistics, 37*(6), 808–827.
Brown, L. (2021). "Sorry, I don't speak any English": An activity-theoretic account of language choice in study abroad in South Korea. In W. Diao & E. Trentman (Eds.), *The multilingual turn for study abroad* (pp. 145–169). Clevedon, UK: Multilingual Matters.
Cho, G. (2000). The role of heritage language in social interactions and relationships: Reflections from a language minority group. *Bilingual Research Journal, 24*, 369–384.
Choi, J. K. (2015). Identity and language: Korean speaking Korean, Korean-American speaking Korean and English? *Language and Intercultural Communication, 15*(2), 240–266.
Choi, J., & Yi, Y. (2012). The use and role of pop culture in heritage language learning: A study of advanced learners of Korean. *Foreign Language Annals, 45*(1), 110–129.
Gee, J. P. (1996). *Sociolinguistics and literacies: Ideology in discourses* (2nd ed.). London: Taylor & Francis.
Higgins, C., & Stoker, K. (2011). Language learning as a site for belonging: A narrative analysis of Korean adoptee-returnees. *International Journal of Bilingual Education and Bilingualism, 14*(4), 399–412.
Jang, S. Y. (2020). The pluralist language ideology of Korean immigrant mothers and the English-only principle in early childhood education programs. *Language and Education, 34*(1), 66–80.
Jo, H.-Y. (2001). "Heritage" language learning and ethnic identity: Korean Americans' struggle with language authorities. *Language, Culture and Curriculum, 14*(1), 26–41.
Kang, H.-S. (2013). Korean American college students' language practices and identity positioning: "Not Korean, but not American". *Journal of Language, Identity & Education, 12*(4), 248–261.
Kang, H.-S., & Kim, I.-S. (2012). Perceived and actual competence and ethnic identity in heritage language learning: A case study of Korean-American college students. *International Journal of Bilingual Education and Bilingualism, 15*(3), 279–294.
Kanno, Y. (2003). *Negotiating bilingual and bicultural identities: Japanese returnees between two worlds*. Mahwah, NJ: Lawrence Erlbaum.
Kim, E. J. (2006). Heritage language maintenance by Korean-American college students. In K. Kondo-Brown (Ed.), *Heritage language development: Focus on East Asian immigrants* (pp. 175–208). Amsterdam and Philadelphia: John Benjamins Publishing Company.
Kim, H. M. (2011). The emergence of the "multicultural family" and genderized citizenship in South Korea. In K.-S. Chang & B. S. Turner (Eds.), *Contested citizenship in East Asia: Developmental politics, national unity, and globalization* (pp. 203–217). Oxon and New York: Routledge.
Kim, M. (2008). *Gendering marriage emigration and fragmented citizenship formation: "Korean" wives, daughters-in-law, and mothers from the Philippines* [PhD dissertation]. State University of New York, Albany.
Kim, M. (2010). Gender and international marriage migration. *Sociology Compass, 4*(9), 718–731.
Kim, M. (2016). A North Korean defector's journey through the identity-transformation process. *Journal of Language, Identity & Education, 15*(1), 3–16.
Kim, Y.-K. (2020). Third space, new ethnic identities, and possible selves in the imagined communities: A case of Korean heritage language speakers. *Journal of Language, Identity & Education*. https://doi.org/10.1080/15348458.2020.1832493
Kitchen, M. (2014). Korean students' stories from an Aotearoa New Zealand high school: Perceived affordances of English and Korean language use. *Language and Education, 28*(6), 552–567.
The Korea Times. (2017). *Helping North Korean defectors overcome the language gap*. Retrieved December 15, 2019, from www.koreatimes.co.kr/www/nation/2019/07/181_232888.html
Kroskrity, P. V. (2004). Language ideologies. In A. Duranti (Ed.), *A companion to linguistic anthropology* (pp. 496–517). Malden, MA: Blackwell.
Kwon, J. (2017). Immigrant mothers' beliefs and transnational strategies for their children's heritage language maintenance. *Language and Education, 31*(6), 495–508.
Lantolf, J., & Pavlenko, A. (2001). (S)econd (L)anguage (A)ctivity Theory: Understanding second language learners as people. In M. Breen (Ed.), *Learner contributions to language learning: New directions in research* (pp. 141–158). London: Longman.

Lee, H., Kim, Y., & Choi, B. (2020). Study abroad, language usage, and the development of multilingual identities: The case of 1.5 generation Korean-American students. *Applied Linguistics Review*. https://doi.org/10.1515/applirev-2019-0049

Lee, H.-K. (2014). The role of multicultural families in South Korean immigration policy. In E. Ochiai & K. Aoyama (Eds.), *Asian women and intimate work* (pp. 289–312). Leiden: Brill.

Lee, J. S. (2002). The Korean language in America: The role of cultural identity in heritage language learning. *Language, Culture and Curriculum*, *15*(2), 117–133.

Lee, J. S., & Kim, H. (2007). Attitudes, motivation and instructional needs of heritage language learners. In K. Kondo-Brown & J. D. Brown (Eds.), *Teaching Chinese, Japanese, and Korean heritage students: Curriculum, needs, materials, and assessment* (pp. 159–185). Mahwah, NJ: Lawrence Erlbaum.

Lee, J. S., & Shin, S. J. (2008). Korean heritage language education in the United States: The current state, opportunities, and possibilities. *Heritage Language Journal*, *6*(2), 1–20.

Lee, M. W. (2016). Micro language planning for refugee resettlement language support programs: The case of North Korean refugees in South Korea. *Asia-Pacific Education Researcher*, *25*(5–6), 743–752.

Lee, M. W., & Ahn, S.-H. (2016). Relocation in space, language, and identity: Dislocated North Korean undergraduates in South Korean universities. *Language and Communication*, *47*, 43–52.

Lee, M. W., Han, M.-S., & Hyun, E. R. (2016). Multilingual practices and ideologies of refugees in the neoliberal era: The case of North Korean refugee students in South Korea. *Language Awareness*, *25*(4), 290–304.

McKay, S., & Wong, S. (1996). Multiple discourses, multiple identities: Investment and agency in second-language learning among Chinese adolescent immigrant students. *Harvard Educational Review*, *66*(3), 577–608.

Ministry of Unification. (2019). *North Korean defectors' recent status*. Retrieved July 15, 2019, from www.unikorea.go.kr/unikorea/business/NKDefectorsPolicy/status/lately/

Morita, N. (2004). Negotiating participation and identity in second language academic communities. *TESOL Quarterly*, *38*, 573–603.

National Institute of Korean Language. (2016). *2016 survey on language awareness of North and South Korea*. Retrieved July 10, 2019, from www.korean.go.kr/front/reportData/reportDataView.do?mn_id=207&report_seq=886&pageIndex=2

Norton Peirce, B. (1995). Social identity, investment, and language learning. *TESOL Quarterly*, *29*(1), 9–31.

Norton, B. (2000). *Identity and language learning: Gender, ethnicity and educational change*. Harlow, UK: Longman.

Norton, B. (2010). Language and identity. In N. Hornberger & S. McKay (Eds.), *Sociolinguistics and language education* (pp. 349–369). Buffalo, NY: Multilingual Matters.

Norton, B. (2013). *Identity and language learning: Extending the conversation* (2nd ed.). Clevedon, UK: Multilingual Matters.

Norton, B., & McKinney, C. (2011). Identity and second language acquisition. In D. Atkinson (Ed.), *Alternative approaches to second language acquisition* (pp. 73–94). Oxon and New York: Routledge.

Park, M. Y. (2011). Identity and agency among heritage language learners. In K. Davis (Ed.), *Critical qualitative research in second language studies: Agency and advocacy* (pp. 171–207). Charlotte, NC: Information Age.

Park, M. Y. (2017). Resisting linguistic and ethnic marginalization: Voices of Southeast Asian marriage-migrant women in Korea. *Language and Intercultural Communication*, *17*(2), 118–134.

Park, M. Y. (2019a). Developing bilingualism in a largely monolingual society: Southeast Asian marriage migrants and multicultural families in South Korea. In F. Fozdar & R. Zarine (Eds.), *Mixed race in Asia: Past, present and future* (pp. 67–81). Oxon and New York: Routledge.

Park, M. Y. (2019b). Gender ideologies and Korean language learning: Experiences of Southeast Asian migrant women in South Korea. In K. Horner & J. Dailey-O'Cain (Eds.), *Multilingualism, (im)mobilities and spaces of belonging* (pp. 197–215). Clevedon, UK: Multilingual Matters.

Park, M. Y. (2019c). "I feel more Korean now": Heritage language learning and identity transformation of a mixed-heritage Korean New Zealander. In V. Anderson & H. Johnson (Eds.), *Migration, education and translation: Cross-disciplinary perspectives on human mobility and cultural encounters in education settings* (pp. 59–72). Oxon and New York: Routledge.

Park, M. Y. (2020). "I want to learn Seoul speech!": Language ideologies and practices among rural marriage-migrants in South Korea. *International Journal of Bilingual Education and Bilingualism*, *23*(2), 227–240.

Park, M. Y. (2021a). Heritage language use in the workplace: 1.5-generation Korean immigrants in New Zealand. *International Multilingual Research Journal*. https://doi.org/10.1080/19313152.2021.1904347

Park, M. Y. (2021b). Language ideologies, heritage language use, and identity construction among 1.5-generation Korean immigrants in New Zealand. *International Journal of Bilingual Education and Bilingualism*. https://doi.org/10.1080/13670050.2021.1913988

Park, M. Y. (2021c). Language ideologies and identity construction among North Korean refugees in South Korea. *Language Awareness*. https://doi.org/10.1080/09658416.2020.1867563

Park, S. M., & Sarkar, M. (2007). Parents' attitudes toward heritage language maintenance for their children and their efforts to help their children maintain the heritage language: A case study of Korean-Canadian immigrants. *Language, Culture and Curriculum, 20*(3), 223–235.

Pavlenko, A. (2002). Narrative study: Whose story is it anyway? *TESOL Quarterly, 36*(2), 213–218.

Pavlenko, A. (2004). "The making of an American": Negotiation of identities at the turn of the twentieth century. In A. Pavlenko & A. Blackledge (Eds.), *Negotiation of identities in multilingual contexts* (pp. 34–67). Clevedon, UK: Multilingual Matters.

Pavlenko, A. (2007). Autobiographic narratives as data in applied linguistics. *Applied Linguistics, 28*(2), 163–188.

Pavlenko, A., & Blackledge, A. (2004). *Negotiation of identities in multilingual contexts*. Clevedon, UK: Multilingual Matters.

Piller, I. (2015). Language ideologies. In K. Tracy, C. Ilie, & T. Sandel (Eds.), *The international encyclopedia of language and social interaction* (pp. 917–927). Chichester, UK: Wiley Blackwell.

Piller, I., & Pavlenko, A. (2007). Globalization, gender, and multilingualism. In H. Decke-Cornill & L. Volkmann (Eds.), *Gender studies and foreign language teaching* (pp. 15–30). Tübingen: Narr.

Salo, N. N. P., & Dufva, H. D. (2018). Words and images of multilingualism: A case study of two North Korean refugees. *Applied Linguistics Review, 9*(2), 421–448.

Silverstein, M. (1979). Language structure and linguistic ideology. In P. R. Clyne (Ed.), *The elements: A parasession on linguistic units and levels* (pp. 193–247). Chicago: Chicago Linguistic Society.

Song, J. (2010). Language ideology and identity in transnational space: Globalization, migration, and bilingualism among Korean families in the USA. *International Journal of Bilingual Education and Bilingualism, 13*(1), 23–42.

Song, J. J. (2005). *The Korean language: Structure, use and context*. Oxon and New York: Routledge.

Song, J. J. (2015). Language policies in North and South Korea. In L. Brown & J. Yeon (Eds.), *The handbook of Korean linguistics* (pp. 477–491). Oxford: Wiley Blackwell.

Sun, W., & Kwon, J. (2020). Representation of monoculturalism in Chinese and Korean heritage language textbooks for immigrant children. *Language, Culture and Curriculum, 33*(4), 402–416.

TOPIK. (2018). *Introduction*. Retrieved from www.topik.go.kr/usr/cmm/subLocation.do?menuSeq=2210101#none

Tullock, B. (2018). Identity and study abroad. In C. Sanz & A. Morales-Front (Eds.), *The Routledge handbook of study abroad research and practice* (pp. 262–274). Oxon and New York: Routledge.

Valdés, G. (2001). Heritage language students: Profiles and possibilities. In J. K. Peyton, D. A. Ranard, & S. McGinnis (Eds.), *Heritage languages in America: Preserving a national resource* (pp. 37–77). Washington, DC: Center for Applied Linguistics.

Van Deusen-Scholl, N. (2003). Toward a definition of heritage language: Sociopolitical and pedagogical considerations. *Journal of Language, Identity, & Education, 2*(3), 211–230.

Weedon, C. (1997). *Feminist practice and poststructuralist theory*. Oxford: Blackwell.

24
INSTRUCTOR INDIVIDUAL CHARACTERISTICS IN A KSL/KFL SETTING
A research perspective

Hye-Sook Wang

Introduction

The three main components of a learning context are the learners, the teachers/instructors, and the learning content (i.e., materials). Various factors affect learning outcomes in each of these components, including classroom environments and others. Among these components much more focus has been placed on learners and learning materials, resulting in less attention paid to the teacher variable in Korean as a second language (KSL) or Korean as a foreign language (KFL), partly because of an advocacy for 'learner-centered learning' that has gained enormous popularity since the advent of the 'communicative language teaching and learning.' Research seems to reflect this trend, and the interest in teachers is more frequently discussed in relation to teacher training programs, rather than their individual characteristics and how they affect the learners' learning outcomes. According to Kang (2017), among the most recent review study on Korean language education articles and theses published since 2000, only 3.8% of the entire publication was on Korean language teachers, reflecting the reality that teachers were rather peripheral.

Given the substantial progress and development that the field of KSL/KFL has seen both in terms of increase in student enrollment in Korean classes in colleges and universities in America and elsewhere in the world and the 'not-so-short' history of KSL/KFL as an independent academic discipline, it is imperative to critically assess the state of current research on instructors in order to set new research agendas for the field to move forward. While it is encouraging that studies on teachers have been gradually on the rise and the subtopics have been diversified since 2000, this is an area that needs a serious look. With this background, this chapter will a) review previous studies conducted on the individual characteristics of college Korean language teachers in Korea and America, b) discuss the current status of research focusing on core issues and key findings of this topic, and c) provide direction and suggestions for future research.

Review of related literature on instructors and instructor characteristics in KSL/KFL

Studies on research trends on Korean instructors

KSL context

Several studies have reviewed research trends on teachers in KSL (e.g., Jang et al., 2014; Kang, 2011, 2014; Kim, 2019; Kim & Park, 2019; Lee, 2011). Kang's (2011, 2014) and Lee's (2011) reviews offered a general trend on all aspects of teachers, while Kim (2019) specifically focused on studies conducted on non-native instructors; Kim and Park (2019) specifically on studies conducted on teacher talk/utterances; and Jang, Jung, Kim, and Lee (2014) specifically on feedback studies. In a KFL context, two reviews were done. Wang (2003) reviewed articles published in the *Korean Language in America*, which is the official journal of the American Association of Teachers of Korean (AATK) from 1994 up to 2002, and Choi, Jung, and Chun (2020) reviewed studies broadly related to Korean language education, published both in Korea and in America up to 2019. Neither study, however, focused on teachers specifically.

Kang's (2011) review covered studies from 2000 to 2010 on teachers, learners, and teachers and learners in KSL. She reported that among the total of 134 identified, 24 (17.9%) were on teachers, 96 (71.6%) were on learners, and 14 (10.4%) were on teachers and learners. When those 24 studies on teachers were broken down, 14 (58.3%) studies were on teacher talk, teacher feedback, teaching method, and teaching strategies, and 6 (25%) studies were on the role of the teacher or characteristics. Only four (16.7%) studies were conducted on teacher factors such as psychological adaptation, teacher efficacy, communications across cultures, and teachers' self-assessment. According to Kang (2014), studies investigating teacher education issues take 36%, feedback-related research takes 34%, followed by studies on teacher-related factors (20%) and those on teachers' roles/qualifications (10%). Lee (2011), on the other hand, reviewed those studies published between 1991, when the first paper on teacher education was published, and 2011. Out of a total of 87 papers (i.e., 46 journal publications and 41 degree theses), those on teacher education (e.g., teacher training/education) were 44 (50.6%); those on teacher qualifications (e.g., teacher's role, teaching techniques) were 23 (26.4%); and those on teacher-related policy (e.g., assessment, working conditions) were 11 (12.6%).

While the aforementioned three review studies covered all aspects of Korean language teachers broadly, review studies on subtopics of Korean teachers also began to emerge in recent years. For instance, Kim and Park (2019) analyzed studies conducted specifically on teacher talk/utterances published up to 2018 and identified 105 articles. The authors noted that studies on the so-called teacher talk began to appear in 1998 and showed a substantial increase around 2012/2013. Subtopics were divided into linguistic characteristics of teacher talk (6), teachers' use of learners' native language (7), teacher talk/utterances during the classroom interactions (28), teachers' scaffolding (7), error correction/feedback (36), and questions and answers (21). The study showed a trend that indicated a heavy focus on teachers' correction/feedback and their classroom interaction within the teacher-talk research. On the other hand, Kim (2019) reviewed research on non-native instructors. Unlike in the USA, in most Asian countries, including China, Mongolia, and Sri Lanka, there are substantially more non-native Korean instructors teaching Korean than native Korean instructors. Thirty-two studies that Kim identified (i.e., 15 journal articles, 17 degree theses) consist of those on teacher utterance (3), instructor factors (8), teacher education (9), teacher role (7), and teacher perception (5), which paints a somewhat different picture than Kim and Park (2019).

Table 24.1 Research Trend by Research Topic/Theme on Instructors

Topics	Categories
Teacher utterance	Utterance errors, instructional language (e.g., learners' native language vs. target language), etc.
Teacher-related factors	Teacher anxiety, efficacy, teacher identity, etc.
Teachers' educational background and training	Teacher education curriculum, teacher certification system, etc.
Teacher role	Teachers' role, team teaching, etc.
Teacher perception	Teachers' self-perception, teachers' perception of learners, etc.

Source: Consolidated Kang, 2014 & Kim, 2019

Each review used slightly different classification methods, but they generally analyzed studies with respect to publication dates in order to see a trend over time, research type/publication venue (i.e., journal articles vs. degree theses), methodology (i.e., quantitative, qualitative, mixed), and topic/theme to a varying degree. As the topic area can be wide-ranging, the above table is provided integrating two previous studies.

A number of points can be made from these research trend review studies in KSL. First, studies on Korean language instructors were significantly fewer than other topics in Korean language education research. Second, among the topics associated with instructors, teacher talk/utterances and teacher feedback received the most attention from the researchers, whereas the teachers' individual characteristics have received the least attention. Third, there appears to be an increased interest in non-native Korean instructors in recent years.

KFL context

In a KFL setting, two papers mentioned earlier reviewed a general research trend in Korean language teaching up until 2002 (Wang, 2003) and 2019 (Choi et al.,(2020). Wang (2003) noted that only three papers (Byon, 1999; Kang, 2002; Lee, 2002) out of all the papers included in the seven volumes of *Korean Language in America* examined teacher-related issues: Kang on the effects of the use of Korean and English in KFL classrooms of non-heritage learners, Lee on Korean language teachers' discourse patterns, and Byon on teachers' use of politeness marker 'yo.'

On the other hand, Choi et al. (2020) is a much bigger-scale review encompassing both KSL and KFL. The authors noted two general tendencies as a result of their review. One is that studies exclusively focusing on KFL pedagogy began to appear between 2006 and 2010 in major journals on foreign language education in America, which include *Foreign Language Annals (FLA)*; *Modern Language Journal (MLA)*; *Heritage Language Journal (HLJ)*; and *Language, Culture and Curriculum (LCC)*. The other is that articles published in *Korean Language in America* comprise almost half of the entire data (46.9%) they collected, acknowledging a central role that KLA plays as a venue for delivering research in KFL in America. Despite the role it plays, it is alarming that very few papers were published about instructors in general and instructor characteristics in particular. The same can be said for Choi et al. (2020) in which the final database included 524 studies (including 29 doctoral dissertations) in 35 journals (i.e., 21 major journals published in North America and the UK, as well as 14 journals published in South Korea), all of which focused exclusively on a KFL context for learners of Korean whose native language is English. This review does not provide statistics on research on teachers specifically because the categorization method they used assigned only one primary topic to each study and the teacher was not one of the categories. However, the study reveals that the three most actively researched topics between 1995 and 2019 were pedagogical approaches and practices, Korean as a heritage language, and learner language and language processing. The role of the teacher was not one of them.

For the purpose of the current review, an attempt was made to review most of, if not all, those studies published in major KSL journals in Korea (i.e., *Bilingual Research*, *Journal of Korean Language Education*, *Teaching Korean as a Foreign Language*, *The Language and Culture*) and major journals in the field of foreign/second language education in America (i.e., *Korean Language in America*; *Language, Culture, and Curriculum*; *Foreign Language Annals*; *Journal of Less Commonly Taught Languages*; and *Modern Language Journal*). As for the LCTL journal, which exclusively publishes studies on less commonly taught languages, unlike other journals mentioned, there were ten articles in total published on the topic of Korea or Korean specifically. From 2004, when the journal was first launched, to 2019, only two articles were on teachers.

When discussing instructor characteristics, in a series of studies in the context of teaching Spanish as a foreign language, Gurzynski-Weiss (2013, 2017, 2019) suggested that the research on instructor characteristics falls into three main topics – instructor's native/non-native language background, instructor's years of teaching experience, and instructor's training and/or educational background, although other characteristics, such as instructor's engagement with research, research specialty, working memory, and gender, are also cited as relevant areas to be investigated. In the following, I will review and discuss studies on these topics first followed by other teacher-related topics.

Instructor's native/non-native language background

Instructor's native/non-native language background might not play a huge role in a KFL context, as it does in Spanish or perhaps in other languages, because the overwhelming majority of Korean language instructors are native speakers of Korean. Given the status of Spanish in America as the most widely spoken and taught foreign language, there should be as many American teachers as teachers of Spanish ethnicity. Unlike Spanish, Korean is still considered a less-commonly taught language that is also very difficult for non-natives to acquire the native-speaker level of proficiency required to teach. Furthermore, Korean teachers are much less in demand, as the number of colleges and universities offering Korean language courses is still relatively small despite its growing number in recent years. Only a few studies have examined this.

Whether teachers use learners' target language or learners' native language in classroom instruction and to what extent (i.e., the amount) they use learners' native language if they did, and what effects the language they use have on learning are all important questions often debated among foreign language teachers. Varying views and research findings exist.

Damron (2009) analyzed student evaluations of native and non-native KFL teachers, who are teaching assistants and part-time teachers, to examine their strengths and weaknesses perceived by students during a time span of three years, from 2005 to 2008. A total of 632 evaluations were analyzed for an analysis of variants (ANOVA). Three groups of TAs were compared with respect to their native language and gender: native Korean-speaking females, native Korean-speaking males, and non-native males. Since there was not a sufficient number of non-native female teachers to form a group, they were not included.

The study reported several notable differences among the groups. First, native Korean-speaking female TAs were rated the lowest of all groups, and non-native male TAs rated the highest of all groups. Native (Korean) female TAs tended to teach using a lecture format, while non-native male TAs tended to teach using a discussion format. It was also shown that native TAs had difficulty adapting to the language level of the students and that non-native TAs exhibited a more visible enthusiasm for Korean culture than other groups. Second, the most salient differences between groups were displayed in the ratings of the amount students had learned, the TAs' preparedness, the TAs' active involvement in students' learning, the TAs' enthusiasm, and the TAs' tardiness. The study concluded that "differences in ratings are based on both teaching patterns associated with each group of TAs and student response bias that favors non-native male speakers" (p. 73). Causes for student bias conjectured in the study include 'othering' females and natives, TA selection procedures, and trends in evaluating TAs based on language level. While this study used TAs rather than regular teachers as the subject of the study, it is a rare study dealing with a substantially large number of subjects compiled over an extended period of time, making nativeness and gender the focus of the investigation.

The teachers' perception of classroom language use was examined in Ahn (2017a). Based on the interviews with 8 teachers and surveys collected from 117 teachers, Ahn looked at whether the teachers' language background (i.e., native vs. non-native) and location of the instruction taking place (i.e., domestically in Korea vs. overseas) made any difference. The findings were that a) teachers generally believed that using L3 (a foreign language, neither learners' native language nor target language) was more effective in the beginner level and they reduced the use of L3 as the level went up, and b) the use of a foreign language was not determined by external factors but by the teachers themselves. Even when the teachers' language background and teaching environment were similar, the use of a foreign language differed according to the teachers, making them the willful decision-makers.

Based on classroom observations of eight teachers over two semesters twice for each teacher, Kang (2002) tested a hypothesis as to whether the teachers' use of more Korean (i.e., learners' target language) than English (i.e., learners' native language) or exclusive use of Korean in a classroom setting would improve the non-heritage learners' Korean language proficiency. A questionnaire seeking the teachers' beliefs and attitudes regarding the use of English in the Korean classroom supplemented the observation data. Students' proficiency scores and their evaluations of the teachers' use of the target language were compared in order to check the correlations between the English/Korean use and the learners' proficiency improvement measured by the proficiency tests. Kang reported that there was a wide range of views in the use of Korean by the teachers and that most teachers agreed that the more Korean was used, the more motivated their students became, a result that was not surprising.

Unlike previous studies, Han (2012) analyzed linguistic errors that appeared in the discourse of non-native trainees who finished a Korean language teacher-training program, based on ten recorded Korean classes. It reported that among a total of 498 verbal errors identified, pronunciation errors appeared most frequently (79.7%), followed by grammatical errors (15.9%), while vocabulary and expression errors and pragmatic errors appeared far less frequently, at only 2.2% each. As for nonverbal aspects, problems in gesture, facial expression, posture, and staring/gazing were observed in two teachers' behaviors, and intonation problems were observed in most of the teachers' discourse. It is regrettable that this study compared TAs rather than regular instructors for the obvious reason – the lack of non-native Korean language instructors, like Damron's study (2009) mentioned earlier. The fact that the overwhelming majority of the errors, at nearly 80%, were made in pronunciation is worthy of attention, suggesting that a teacher-training program needs to take this into consideration in its curriculum planning.

While these studies shed light on different aspects of instructors' native or non-native language background, in general, the language proficiency of non-native Korean language teachers does not appear to be a major concern in KSL/KFL in Korea and America for the reason stated earlier, although the situations in other countries might be different. There is a very small number of non-native Korean language teachers teaching in institutions in America and Korea. Korean being a Category IV language makes it hard for learners to attain native-like proficiency in Korean in order to become a Korean instructor if they are not native speakers. In some Asian countries in which staff shortage is serious, learners are hired as TAs (e.g., *Donga Daily* article), but this is rather uncommon in U.S. institutions. However, if/when demand exceeds supply, utilizing non-native teachers will be an option to consider, and their proficiency in Korean will need to be looked into more seriously. In fact, non-native Korean language instructors can offer a unique and invaluable perspective to teaching that native instructors might not be able to. They used to be Korean language learners themselves at some point in their career, and this could make significant differences, especially in terms of learners' affective factors.

Discussed also in the context of non-native Korean language teachers' proficiency is the language medium for instruction. Studies conducted to date on the language use of the instructors in the classroom centered around how useful it would be to use the learners' native language, when using learners' native language would be most effective or learning conducive, and how the learners perceive it. The usefulness may depend on the instructional context and the 'target language only' view/practice can be relaxed (e.g., Choi, 2009), as some studies (e.g., Shin, 2009) reported that learners at all levels wanted the instructors to use learners' native language more. As we have seen, the decision appears to be ultimately the instructors'. More future research will certainly help us gain a better sense of this issue.

In a KSL setting, courses are taught almost exclusively in the target language, Korean, regardless of the proficiency level of the students, whereas in a KFL setting, both Korean and the learners' native language are used. More flexibility is exercised in a KFL setting than in a KSL setting in which teachers are more strictly governed by the programs or schools. The teachers' belief plays an important role in their decision. More target language input will be beneficial is what seems to be many teachers' belief, but what is really beneficial is not just the amount of input but the kind of input called 'comprehensible input' that would lead to meaningful output. Furthermore, learners' affective state (i.e., anxiety and fear) needs to be taken into account in the decision, especially at the beginner level, to make sure the benefits of the 'target language only' classroom are bigger than the cost.

Instructors' years of teaching experience

Instructors' years of teaching experience is a major criterion that is frequently used in the discussion of teachers for various aspects of inquiry. Different approaches are taken for pre-service and in-service teacher-training programs, and their development is specifically geared toward seasoned teachers and novice teachers, as their needs are different. Instructors' years of teaching experience, usually labeled as novice teachers vs. experienced teachers, and its impact on teaching have received some attention from researchers, although this topic has been more frequently studied in the context of teacher-training programs and investigated in conjunction with other variables, such as the instructors' educational background.

Several studies (e.g., Ahn & Kim, 2011; Choi, 2010; Lee, 2002; Lee, H., 2013; Won, 2009) reviewed in this chapter indeed found that instructors' years of teaching experience to be an important variable. For instance, Lee (2002) investigated Korean language teachers' discourse patterns on student assessment, making their teaching experience a main objective of investigation. The study compared the patterns from both groups of experienced teachers and inexperienced/less experienced teachers, with a special focus on how conflicts are expressed and managed using an interactional sociolinguistic approach. She found out that experienced teachers maintained their assessment through stories from stratified experiences to specific contexts. On the other hand, inexperienced teachers presented their opinions by hypothetically forming their judgments on the level of accomplishment that is expected to be achieved during the entire learning process based on their current assessment. The author claimed that the assessment through discussion among the teachers, together with assessing students' Korean language proficiency via tests, was expected to improve the effects of Korean language learning because it underscored each individual learner's distinctive and learner-specific characteristics.

H. Lee (2013) also compared the teachers' rating tendency in assessing the students' speaking ability with a special focus on pronunciation according to the raters' teaching experience and their major for the purpose of testing the impacts of these variables on their rating behavior with 20 Korean language teachers. It was found that a) teachers with less experience (i.e., fewer than five years) were stricter in rating than those with more experience, and b) teachers who majored in phonology were stricter in rating, especially for accuracy, among the four groups (i.e., teachers who majored in Korean phonology, teachers who majored in other subfields of Korean language, teachers who majored in Korean language education, and teachers who majored in foreign language) compared. Similarly, Won (2009) found out that both teachers' educational background and years of teaching experience (six years as the dividing line) were significant in her study to the extent that more experienced teachers were not only able to analyze foreign culture more positively but also were more open to foreign culture when she tested the effects of these two variables on teachers' intercultural competence.

The underlying assumption in the inquiry of teachers' years of experience is that experienced teachers would be and/or should be more effective in teaching, fostering better learning outcomes in learners. Some studies supported such assumption. However, the question remains as to how exactly or in what specific ways teachers' years of teaching experience influence learning and, more importantly, how this can be measured. As we have seen in the review, three years is the threshold in some studies, while in other studies the number differs to five or six years. Here, Kini and Podolsky's (2016) claim, which is based on the review of 30 studies, that the teaching effectiveness rose sharply in the first few years of teachers' careers, provides some insight. However, this issue might be more complex than straightforward, as Irvine (2018) warned. Irvine (2018) discussed the interrelationship between teaching experience and teaching effectiveness from a policymaking perspective and concluded that "decisions based on assumptions that the relationship between experience and effectiveness is direct and linear are simplistic and lead to less than optimal policy" because the relationship is "complex, nuanced, and nonlinear" (p. 1). While there is no doubt that instructors' teaching experience is an important variable to look into in teacher-related research, again more research is needed given the complexity of this variable.

Instructor's training and/or educational background

Instructors' training and/or educational background might have significant effects on learners' learning of Korean. Not only before they gain any experience but also in the duration of their teaching career, teachers' academic training and educational background play a critical role in their teaching. Wang (2014), the only study that attempted to report the results of the current state of Korean language teachers in U.S. higher education from a governance perspective, discussed the findings in the broad context of Korean language teaching. In this study, two sets of data collected from the members of the AATK in 2006 and 2012 through detailed survey questionnaires were compared with respect to the teachers' personal profile and status (e.g., gender, age, current position, frequency of renewal, year of Korean language teaching, highest degree earned, field of specialization, current salary range) and their perceived job satisfaction (e.g., satisfaction for instructional duties, other non-instructional aspects, workload, working environment, job security, salary, and status of the Korean program). The findings pertinent to teachers' profiles suggested that the majority of the respondents reported that they attended some kind of workshop regularly in their workplace or through academic organizations that they were affiliated with.

As Wang (2014) also reported, Korean language teachers teaching in American higher education institutions have diverse educational backgrounds; some have MAs, while others have PhDs or EdDs as their terminal degrees. Their specialty also varies; some have a degree in Korean Studies, while others have degrees in second language acquisition, applied linguistics, or theoretical linguistics. However, whether or not and/or what impact such differences in their educational background have on their teaching has rarely, if ever, been investigated to date. Ongoing professional training might have a larger effect on the teachers' performance than their educational background does, but this needs to be empirically tested.

With a slightly different focus, Ahn (2017b) examined the impact of Korean language teachers' foreign language learning experience on their life as teachers as well as on their teaching in the classroom. Interviews with eight teachers – two teachers each by their native language (i.e., Korean native vs. non-Korean native) and their location of employment (i.e., domestic in Korea vs. overseas) – showed how teachers' foreign language learning experience positively affected their teaching in such a way that it helped them a) better understand the challenges their students face and b) reflect on their teaching styles and strategies. The study concluded by emphasizing the necessity and importance of Korean language instructors having a foreign language learning experience.

Another recent study on this topic is Kim and Kim (2020). In this qualitative study, the authors compared two teachers and analyzed how their different foreign language learning experiences affected their practices in classroom by looking into the oral corrective feedback the teachers provided to the students. As a data source, journals written by both teachers and students, class recordings, and interviews with the teachers were used. The results showed that one teacher who learned his/her foreign language focusing on written language emphasized students' vocabulary expansion and accurate grammar learning, whereas another teacher whose foreign language learning oriented more toward oral language underscored speaking activities, such as role play and application of dialogues to relevant situations. Kim and Kim concluded that teachers' foreign language learning experiences not only influence their teaching practices but also affect the motivations of their becoming a Korean language teacher as well as the beliefs they hold as a teacher. A strong implication of this study is that foreign language learning experience can be an important qualification for Korean language teachers.

Instructors' gender

Perhaps due to a small number of male instructors in the field of KSL/KFL, instructors' sex/gender factor has rarely been examined and thus is apparently one of the least investigated characteristics in the field. One notable study that examined teachers' language use in the KSL classroom from the lens of gender is Kwak (2004). The study investigated gender-preferential language from lexical, syntactical, and phonemic/phonological characteristics, using data collected from classes of beginning and intermediate level (2 Beginning, 1 Intermediate) taught by three male teachers and three female teachers in three different institutions for the span of one month. The study found some gender preferential features, especially in interjections and sentence-ending intonation. As for interjections, Korean male teachers tended to use 'ja' (자), 'ah' (아), and 'nae' (네), while Korean female teachers tended to use 'ye' (예) and 'eo' (어) in a typical classroom. However, both male and female teachers often used the '-a/eo(yeo) eyo' (-아/어(여)요) form more often than the '-upnita' (-ㅂ/습니다) form as politeness expressions. With respect to intonation at the end of a sentence or when using ending boundary tones in sentences, female teachers used rising intonations more often than males did in their teaching.

This study was path-breaking in that it brought the gender variable into the realm of Korean language teacher investigations. Given the overwhelming majority of Korean language teachers both in Korea and America being female, such a female-dominant teaching environment might have discouraged this type of research due to the anticipated challenges of collecting a substantial amount of comparable data from males, which would enable a comparison between the male and female groups.

Another study that took gender into consideration in relation to teachers with a different focus is Yoon and Kwak (2017), which investigated listeners' perception of femininity of male Korean teachers. The findings suggest that listeners' backgrounds (e.g., teacher vs. non-teacher, teachers with teaching experience of fewer than two years vs. those with more than four years, speakers of the Seoul dialect vs. the Gyeongsang dialect vs. the Jolla dialect) affect the listeners' perception of the speech of male teachers. While this study took more of a sociolinguistic approach than a language-education approach and its focus was on the listeners' perception rather than on the effects of gender on teaching, it still offers some insights to the field, especially because the gender variable has not been actively researched in a KSL/KFL context.

Sunderland's (2000a, 2000b) review article on gender in second or foreign language education acknowledges that gender is not a category that might be salient for teachers and that classroom interaction is the most salient area in relation to gender for teachers. Feery (2008) also notes that "neither a singular field of research relating specifically to gender and SLA nor a theory of gender and SLA exist as yet" (p. 42) while still acknowledging a gradual emergence of the research on this topic. There have been studies investigating teachers' perceptions of the role and importance of gender in second or foreign language classroom in SLA literature, but it would be safe to say that the focus mostly has been on learners' gender (e.g., who is more motivated, who achieves more, who receives more attention from the teachers, whether or not learners are treated differently from their teachers by gender, etc.) in relation to their learning. However, this is not even the case in KSL/KFL, and there is all the more reason for more research that places gender as a main variable.

Other instructor-related studies

'Good teachers' study

Teachers' teaching effectiveness is measured by a variety of factors, and one of them is how they are viewed as teachers and how their teaching is perceived by the students they teach. Learners' perception of 'good' Korean language teachers as well as teachers' perception of 'good' Korean language teachers were investigated in a couple of studies. Kang (2010) identified the characteristics of 'good' Korean language teachers perceived by Korean language learners by analyzing 84 essays written by learners who had been studying in one of the Korean language institutes in Korea for longer than a year. The study reported that in addition to the teacher's knowledge and teaching skills, teachers' personality and attitude also matter.

On the other hand, Ahn (2015), who took a qualitative approach based on in-depth interviews with four teachers teaching in French universities, described the qualifications of 'good' teachers from the perspective of the teachers themselves through their narratives. The study discussed each of the 13 categories that were identified in two major factors – personal and professional. Personal factors included the teachers' major, degree, personality, foreign language learning experience, cultural adaptability, and individual circumstances. Professional factors included years of teaching experience, classroom management skills, class preparation, relationship with students, and knowledge of the Korean language and pedagogies. Ahn suggested that each of these items needs to be further investigated in the context of sociocultural backgrounds of where Korean language education is taking place as well as Korean language teachers' professional expertise and perception.

Taking a different approach from Ahn (2015) both in terms of participants and data-collection methodology, Lee (2018) attempted to characterize qualities of 'effective' Korean language instructors teaching in U.S. colleges, based on a survey collected from 190 learners of Korean. The study put forth a number of interesting findings. First, students considered teachers' mastery of the target language to be more important than teachers' nativeness. Second, students found it more important for teachers to understand students' different cultural backgrounds than to understand American culture. Third, students found teachers who provided good feedback and clear criteria were effective. Fourth, students agreed upon the importance of teaching Korean in their target language (i.e., Korean) as an instructional medium, but they disagreed on the effectiveness of the 'teaching only in Korean' approach. Finally, students perceived that Korean teachers were more approachable, understanding, patient, and better at creating a bond with students compared to teachers of other subjects.

Studies on instructors' roles

Korean language instructors can and are expected to play multiple roles in delivering instruction; as scaffolder, facilitator, feedback provider, performance evaluator, class manager, and the like. Several studies placed teachers' roles at the center of their investigation. Jin (2002) was interested in the teacher's behaviors in interactions with the students in action. She investigated teacher–student interactions in a third-year Korean classroom in which there were seven students. The study focused on the teacher's role in these interactions specifically using a scaffolding framework: modeling, monitoring students' utterances, and allocating student turns. This study provided some meaningful information as to how teachers and students interact through a qualitative method (i.e., micro-level analysis) and stressed the significance of teacher scaffolding in classroom interactions. However, the study did not compare how different characteristics of different teachers affected their interaction with students.

Subsequently, Jin (2004) looked into the situations in which communication breakdowns occur between the teacher and students in classroom interactions and how the teachers negotiate the meaning through a discourse analysis method. Two classes from each level (1st–3rd) for two hours for each level were recorded and analyzed, with a focus on teacher–student dialogues as to how classes progressed when teaching grammar and vocabulary. Three major types of problems were identified, and they were conversation avoidance, message-delivering failure, and additional information request. These problems were further divided into 12 categories, including student unresponsiveness, preposterous response, incorrect sentence construction, incomplete sentence construction, a response using student's native language, repetition of teacher-initiated utterance, using a rising intonation of sentence ending, request for elaboration, request for clarification, indirect elicitation expressing lack of understanding, partial repetition, and explicit expressions of misunderstanding. This study is illuminating in that it helps us learn more about instructors' management of the class when faced with a challenge.

The role of Korean language teachers as both a scaffolder and facilitator is also the topic of investigation for Jeong and Pak (2009) with a slightly different focus. They examined teachers' scaffolding behaviors and characteristics that would facilitate learners' modified output for 13 learners at the beginner level whose proficiency level was so low that their output was limited. For this the authors analyzed the interactional process between the teacher and the learners, using a qualitative method of analyzing classroom discourse. The study looked at four types of scaffolding (i.e., corrective feedback, direction/conversation maintenance, demonstration, and reduction in degree of freedom/task simplification) that were further subdivided into 14 different types. It was found that corrective feedback and verbal and nonverbal cues were deemed to be most effective for helping learners produce modified input.

One of the important roles instructors play in teaching is providing feedback to students, and two studies are reviewed here specifically on this topic. Han (2001a) analyzed the types of instructors' feedback spoken in the classroom using the conversation analysis approach. The data consisted of 20 intermediate-level classrooms taught by 20 teachers in different institutions in Korea. The study also described the characteristics of feedback types and techniques. Types of feedback identified in the data included evaluation, correction, reinforcement, confirmation, explanation, affective reaction by way of interactive encouragement, and nonverbal response. The study concluded that a) many teachers lacked appropriate feedback skills, showing a lack of understanding of the pedagogical functions of each type of feedback, and b) the explanation type of feedback occurred more frequently than other types of feedback. Similarly, Jin (2005), another study on teachers' corrective feedback, analyzed teachers' feedback and learners' uptake in two intermediate-level classrooms, the relationship between feedback type and learner uptake, different types of feedback provided, and which type was most likely to lead to better learning. The findings pointed to the fact that implicit feedback types, such as clarification request, elicitation, or repetition, were likely to lead to an uptake, citing elicitation as the most effective.

While both Han (2001a) and Jin (2005) were conducted in a KSL context, Ko (2011) was conducted in a KFL context. Unlike these two studies focused on feedback types in oral feedback, Ko (2011) investigated teachers' written feedback practices on students' writings by comparing those of KFL instructors with those of ESL instructors. One hundred fifty-three KFL/ESL college instructors in North America were surveyed online using a questionnaire. The study reported that a major difference between the two groups was found in issues chosen for feedback. KFL instructors offered more feedback regarding language-related issues at the local level, rather than writing-related issues at the global level, than ESL instructors did. Moreover, KFL instructors tended to be consistently concerned with local issues even in the multiple-draft process, whereas ESL instructors changed their focus of feedback from global issues in earlier drafts to local issues in later drafts. The author suggested that these differences might be due to instructors' training, cultural factors, student proficiency, and learner needs. Ensuing studies with an exclusive focus on KFL instructors may bring about why they exhibited such tendency.

Studies on teacher talk

How teachers talk in the classroom as an instructor and classroom manager has been another topic for teacher-related research. This includes types of teacher talk, teachers' use of foreigner talk, problems with utterances teachers make, and questions teachers ask and the functions of those questions. Han (2001b) analyzed the types of teacher talk when they initiated/elicited the interaction based on the functions of the utterances and described the characteristics of teacher talk. The results demonstrated that there were three types of teachers' initiation talk – elicitation, statement on procedures, and instruction. Teachers used an overwhelming number of enumeration questions unrelated to class objectives, and they did not offer sufficient time for students to respond to their initiation utterances. The study concluded that it is important for teachers to understand the functions of each utterance and develop proper skills to use them in the right contexts.

M. Lee (2013) examined Korean language teachers' use of so-called foreigner talk in the classroom with respect to its types (both verbal and nonverbal) and functions, using video-recorded classroom instructions. Foreigner talk in language classes, as Lee defined, refers to a teacher's speech that is modified for smooth communication with the learners, whose most salient characteristic is simplification and modification (e.g., control the speed of the utterances; use simple vocabulary and syntax). Teachers' utterances were largely divided into content-related utterances and class management–related utterances. The results showed that teachers used simple words and formal expressions, short sentences and ungrammatical forms. They also controlled the speed of their utterances and exaggerated intonation and pronunciation. When it was looked at in relation to class content, this foreigner talk was more actively utilized in utterances related to managing the class than delivering class content. It was also found that the way foreigner talk was used was affected by the proficiency level of the learners, but the study confirmed that a teacher variable had a larger influence in foreigner talk than a level factor.

Another study by Kim (2007) audio recorded 2–3 level classes in four different institutions (two classes for each), with the research goal of finding out problems with teacher utterances qualitatively. The study analyzed the amount of teachers' utterances and described various problems that emerged in the data. It reported that teachers' utterances took up 66% of all the utterances, indicating that teachers talk a lot. First, teachers corrected learners' utterances but did not provide learners with opportunities to re-utter. Second, the teachers' explanations might help learners understand the materials, but this limited the time for learners to practice their language. Problems with teachers' utterances for each stage of the classroom talk was also revealed, and teachers used too many open-ended questions at the transition from the introductory stage to the next stage, making it hard for learners to participate. Even during the practice and application stages, teachers frequently intervened or interrupted learners' utterances, stripping the chance for their utterances.

Unlike Han (2001b), which looked at the types of teacher talk, and Kim (2007), which focused on the amount of teacher talk, Park (2003) was interested in the pattern and function of the questions that Korean language instructors asked. It looked at questions asked by a teacher inducing learners' responses in a classroom setting. As commonly accepted in the literature, one of the most frequently used techniques by teachers in classroom interactions is a question-and-answer format. In this study, the teachers' questions were categorized into 'learning content–related questions,' which were further divided into echoic questions and epistemic questions, and 'learning progress–related questions,' which were further divided into social relation questions, procedure progression questions, and attention-calling questions. Echoic questions are asked for ensuring understanding and requesting explanation. Epistemic questions are asked for presenting and rechecking. The goal of this study appears to be presenting various types and functions of instructors' questions, rather than providing analytical results.

Despite the few studies on teacher talk reviewed earlier, speech acts (e.g., requesting, apologizing, complimenting/praising, etc.) used by teachers in a classroom setting is one area that has been almost completely ignored in the study of instructors in KSL/KFL. One recent study by Kim (2020) examined the patterns of praise that teachers offered to their students. A recording of a total of 750 minutes of actual Korean classes at the intermediate and advanced levels was analyzed with respect to a) how frequently, b) toward whom (i.e., individual, group, entire class), c) about what, and d) using what language expressions of praise were offered. It turned out that five participating teachers gave praises 308 times in 15 Korean classes, averaging 14–20 times in one class. Teachers praised students most frequently in grammar classes and least frequently in speaking classes. Praises were offered most frequently to individual, then to class, and then to groups. The overwhelming majority of praises were offered for recognizing learning outcomes and relating to learning processes, which accounted for over 98% of the praises. Praises for students' personality, abilities, or attitudes were minimal. The language used in performing the function of praise included 그렇다/맞다 (to be correct), 잘 하다 (to do well), 좋다 (to be good), and 괜찮다 (to be okay), showing a lack of linguistic diversity. Like the author noted, this study contributes to our understanding of positive feedback study (i.e., praises are a type of positive feedback) and expands the research horizon to the under-researched area of teacher utterances.

Unlike those studies that focused on a few aspects specifically, Choi (2010) examined various aspects of Korean language teachers combined. This study investigated the correlation between Korean language teachers' communication styles/types and teaching behaviors as well as their general characteristics, such as gender, years of teaching experiences, qualifications-credentials, majors, and personality types. The study classified Korean language teachers' communication styles into a) the scholar type, b) the social butterfly type, and c) the private academy instructor type. As for Korean language teachers' personality characteristics, the study used the well-known MBTI model (the Myers-Briggs Type Indicator is "an introspective self-report questionnaire indicating differing psychological preferences in how people perceive the world and make decisions," according to Wikipedia). Findings showed that, as for personal characteristics, those teachers who had two to four years of teaching experience showed the highest correlation; as for personality characteristics, the majority of Korean teachers were the Sensing (S), Thinking (T), and Judging (J) type. With respect to communication styles, 62% of the subjects turned out to be the scholarly type, while 32% were the reflective type. Only 6% showed the private academy instructor type. In correlation between communication type and teaching behavior, the scholarly type teachers showed the most effective cognitive behavior, whereas the social butterfly type teachers showed the most effective affective behavior. Among teachers' general characteristics (i.e., gender, teaching experiences, qualifications, major, personality characteristics) and its correlation to teaching behavior, the years of teaching experience displayed the highest correlation in relation to both communication types and teaching behaviors.

Studies on instructor efficacy

Although few, studies on teacher efficacy (i.e., teachers' subjective perception of their influence on the learners' learning) for Korean language teachers bring invaluable insights to this discussion on instructors. Ahn and Kim (2011) tested Korean language teachers' sense of self-efficacy for seven items/variables that turned out to be meaningful in a pilot survey of 20 teachers. Those seven items (i.e., Korean teaching experience, retraining experience, status, number of students they teach, Korean language teacher certificate, motivations for becoming Korean language teacher, salary) were tested for 162 in-service teachers in the main study. The survey contained 24 items in 3 categories of efficacy related to teaching strategies, efficacy related to classroom management, and efficacy related to student participation, having 8 items for each category. Among the three efficacies inquired, teaching strategies showed the highest efficacy. Among the seven teacher-related variables tested, only teaching experience, the number of students taught, and their salary showed meaningful correlations statistically.

Teachers' self-efficacy through writing assessments was looked into by Lee (2014). Three research questions the study attempted to answer were a) how teachers' self-efficacy on writing was manifested, b) what the characteristics of teachers' assessment of writing were, and c) if teachers' self-efficacy was related to their assessment characteristics. The study administered a writing self-efficacy survey that consisted of 17 items to 39 teachers who were divided into 3 groups based on their teaching experience (i.e., those with fewer than two years, those between two and five years, and those with more than five years) with the assumption that teaching experience might have an impact on teachers' self-efficacy. The participants were also asked to assess ten essays written by students. The study reported that there were noticeable differences between the group of teachers with fewer than two years of experience and the two groups of teachers with more than two years of experience. More specifically, the three groups differed regarding a) their strictness in applying evaluation criteria and b) the suitable consistency they exhibited. It concluded that the teachers' writing assessment self-efficacy was correlated to/ mutually affected by assessment ability.

Teachers' level of intercultural or cross-cultural awareness and/or competence is an area that caught researchers' attention somewhat later well into the new century. Both Ko (2008) and Won (2009) placed Korean language teachers' intercultural and cross-cultural competence at the center of their inquiry while acknowledging the importance of a close connection between language and culture as well as lack of attention paid to this topic in the field. Four factors were identified through factor analysis in Won's (2009) study, and they were a) individual attitude toward foreign culture, b) competence to analyze and knowledge of foreign culture, c) openness to foreign culture, and d) the ability to adapt in a global environment. The instructors' years of teaching experience (i.e., those who had more than six years of teaching experience vs. those who had fewer than six years of teaching experience) as well as the instructor's education level were found to affect instructors' knowledge of and ability to analyze a foreign culture positively. In addition, those with more teaching experience were clearly more open to a foreign culture than those with less teaching experience. Ko (2008) emphasized the role of teachers from an intercultural communication perspective in the Korean language classrooms. The study underscored intercultural sensitivity and flexibility that teachers need to develop for better communication with learners as well as effective teaching. This study is more theoretical than empirical, suggesting the role of teachers in connection to cultural contexts (i.e., high-context culture vs. low-context culture) when learners' native culture and their target culture are very different.

Summary and suggestions for future research

Research on instructors in general and those on instructor characteristics and their effects on learning in KSL/KFL in particular has been quite limited. Furthermore, the majority of studies reviewed in this chapter were written in the context of KSL and published in Korea. Those published in America in the context of KFL were surprisingly few. For instance, there were few to no studies focusing on Korean language instructors or Korean language instructor characteristics among the approximately 80 papers appearing under the subject heading of 'Korean language teacher characteristics' for the journal *Korean Language in America* and another approximately 80 papers under the same heading for the journal *Language, Culture, and Curriculum*. Given the instructors' role and place in the Korean language learning context, the current state of research on teachers is rather alarming.

This review revealed where a research gap exists regarding instructor characteristics in KSL/KFL, and it guides us to offer some suggestions for future research. Previous review articles cited in this chapter (e.g., Kang, 2014; Kim, 2019; Lee, 2011) supported the urgent need for more research focusing on instructors, especially instructor qualifications and characteristics. Despite a broad spectrum of issues regarding teacher characteristics, the scarcity of research on this topic raises a question as to why. It might have to do with the complexity and ambiguity of measuring these characteristics rather than a lack of interest in them (Ahn & Kim, 2011, p. 110). Operationalizing instructor characteristics in an explicit manner (Gurzynski-Weiss, 2013, p. 543) is a necessary but daunting task that would require serious thinking and theorizing. Grounding this type of research in second language acquisition (SLA) theory and establishing a causal relationship between instructor characteristics and SLA as suggested in Gurzynski-Weiss (2013, pp. 540–543) is another impediment. As such, more groundwork is called for.

Challenges with data collection are assumed to be another major obstacle for more studies on instructors in general and instructor characteristics in particular, as this presupposes agreement and cooperation from participating teachers. Opening up one's classroom is a prerequisite for classroom-based empirical studies, and finding ways to make this process more accessible need to be ensured. In a KFL setting, junior or less-experienced instructors are observed by senior or more-experienced colleagues on a regular basis, a practice regularized on the institutional level, and the data from this visit could serve as the baseline data.

Diversification of research methodology is cited as a suggestion for future research. As shown in Lee (2011), more than half of the papers (52%) that were reviewed were theoretical research. Among empirical research, quantitative research took up 36%, while qualitative research was only 12%. Among quantitative research, 90% used surveys, while only 10% were empirical research. Qualitative research was observational research. According to Kim (2019), 67% of the studies that were reviewed used a survey questionnaire as the main data-elicitation method. Other studies used qualitative data (i.e., audio or video recordings of classroom interactions), but the number is small. Quantitative studies, on the other hand, tended to use descriptive statistics and/or a reliance on frequency analysis without robust statistical analysis, although some studies in recent years offer correlation analysis and variance analysis. Moreover, although classroom-based research is crucial in deepening our understanding of learning effects, empirical studies in a classroom setting has been apparently lacking despite a gradual increase, and they are strongly desired.

While virtually no research is available to make a reference to KSL/KFL to date, a longitudinal study that measures the relationship between teacher talk and learners' proficiency gains over an extended period of time would be a valuable addition to the body of literature. Most studies done so far used data collected at one point in time, and thus little is known as to whether or how teachers' use of learners' native language or target language affect the learners in the long term. Many teachers are unaware of how much (amount) they talk or how (manner) they talk in their classrooms unless they critically review their classroom behaviors. Empirical studies that compare teachers' talk before and after they listen to their own talk would shed some light on the actual effects of instructors' talk. A serious lack of longitudinal studies in KFL/KSL might have to do with a productivity over diversity/quality mentality in academia, and this needs to be reevaluated.

Expanding the research scope in terms of topic, especially including those that have been neglected so far, is another area of concern. For example, instructors' engagement with research activities and their research specialty needs to be looked into. Research is an indispensable and integral part of teaching, as teachers are informed of the best practices from active research. This not only includes instructors' direct engagement with research as investigators but also their indirect engagement as readers of research. The working environment in KSL/KFL most likely affects the level of instructors' engagement in addition to their personal interests, but studies on this aspect are almost nonexistent.

There is an urgency for research on fostering the diversity and inclusivity of Korean language instructors. Given the current climate of language learning/teaching in an increasingly globalized world in which various beliefs and experiences of instructors are to be represented, respected, and appreciated, this would be of tremendous importance, yet little to none has been done about this in the field. Diversity can include gender, race, ethnicity, and other attributes, yet the community of Korean language instructors has been and still is quite homogeneous in terms of these attributes, overwhelmingly dominated by female instructors who are native Korean speakers. Neither learners' gender nor teachers' gender on the effects of students' learning have been taken up for research in KSL and KFL alike, unlike other languages, including Japanese, which has seen some major effort very recently in this respect (see Mori & Hasegawa, 2020).

Conclusion

In this chapter, I reviewed extant literature on Korean language teachers more broadly and their characteristics in KSL/KFL more specifically that are published in major journals in Korea as well as in America over the past two decades. However, this review is selective and partial rather than comprehensive, which is a limitation of this review. Unarguably, our understanding of Korean teachers in the field appears to be quite limited from a research perspective, represented not only by its quantity but also by the range of subtopics investigated to date. In particular, there is a tendency for teacher utterances and teacher feedback to be relatively well researched, whereas instructor gender is not. There is still so much to learn despite an increased attention to teachers more recently.

Understanding our learners the best we can is of utmost importance in our teaching practices, but understanding ourselves as instructors is equally important to maximizing the learning effect of our students. The field needs to extend its research scope to include more teacher-related factors, especially the various characteristics of Korean language instructors and to bring empirical evidence as to how their characteristics affect the learners' learning outcomes. Considering the unique and important role each plays in a teaching/learning context, a balanced research effort among three components of teachers, learners, and content materials would be desirable and thus is strongly recommended.

References

Ahn, J. (2015). Teachers' narratives on factors of 'good' Korean language teachers: Focused on Universities in France. *Journal of Korean Language Education*, 26(4), 101–132.

Ahn, J. (2017a). A study on using foreign language in the Korean classroom: Focused on teachers' linguistic background and educational environment. *Bilingual Research*, 67, 193–228.

Ahn, J. (2017b). The influence of foreign language learning experiences of Korean Teachers: Focusing on interview analysis. *Korean Language Education Research*, 39, 189–224.

Ahn, J., & Kim, J. (2011). A study on Korean language teachers' sense of efficacy. *Bilingual Research*, 45, 109–132.

Byon, A. (1999). The analysis of 'yo' the politeness marker in Korean: From language socialization point of view. *The Korean Language in America, 4*, 125–140.

Choi, G. J. (2009). An attitude survey on using the learner's native language in the Korean language classroom. *The Language and Culture, 5*(1), 219–244.

Choi, H. J., Jung, J.-Y., & Chun, H. C. (2020). Annotated bibliography on KFL pedagogy. In Young-mee Yu Cho (Ed.), *Teaching Korean as a foreign language: Theories and practices* (pp. 195–256). Oxon and New York: Routledge.

Choi, H. S. (2010). A study of correlation between communication types of the Korean teacher and teaching behavior. *Education Culture Research, 16*(3), 205–234.

Damron, J. (2009). An analysis of student evaluations of native and non-native Korean foreign language teachers. *Journal of Less Commonly Taught Languages, 7*, 73–92.

Feery, K. (2008). Current perspectives on the role of gender in second language acquisition research. *ITB Journal, 9*(1), 32–51.

Gurzynski-Weiss, L. (2013). Instructor characteristics and classroom-based SLA of Spanish. In K. Geeslin (Ed.). *The handbook of Spanish second language acquisition* (pp. 530–546). Hoboken, NJ: John Wiley & Sons.

Gurzynski-Weiss, L. (2017). Instructor individual characteristics and L2 interaction. In *Expanding individual difference research in the interaction approach: Investigating learners, instructors, and other interlocutors* (pp. 152–172). Amsterdam and Philadelphia: John Benjamins Publishing Company.

Gurzynski-Weiss, L. (2019). L2 instructor individual characteristics. In *The Routledge handbook of instructed second language acquisition* (pp. 451–467). Oxon and New York: Routledge.

Han, S. M. (2001a). A study on the analysis of types of feedback in the Korean language classroom. *Teaching Korean as a Foreign Language, 25–26*, 453–505.

Han, S. M. (2001b). A study on the teacher talk in teaching Korean as a foreign language: An analysis of types of teacher talk in the initiative category based on interactional function. *Journal of Korean Language Education, 12*(2), 223–253.

Han, S. M. (2012). An error analysis on non-native Korean language teachers' classroom discourse: Focusing on the discourse of trainees who finished a Korean language teacher training program. *The Language and Culture, 8*(3), 325–349.

Irvine, J. (2018). Relationship between teaching experience and teacher effectiveness: Implications for policy decisions. *Journal of Instructional Pedagogies, 22*, 1–19.

Jang, H., Jung, W., Kim, S. Y., & Lee, S. (2014). A study on the research trends of feedback studies in Korean language education. *Bilingual Research, 56*, 313–339.

Jeong, M. H., & Pak, D. H. (2009). The study of teachers' scaffolding for learners' modified output. *Bilingual Research, 41*, 361–394.

Jin, J. H. (2002). An analysis of the role of the teacher in classroom interaction based on the framework of scaffolding. *Journal of Korean Language Education, 13*(1), 243–264.

Jin, J. H. (2004). Types of communication problems that occur during teacher-student interactions in the Korean language classroom. *Journal of Korean Language Education, 15*(3), 255–276.

Jin, J. H. (2005). Corrective feedback and learner uptake in Korean classroom. *Bilingual Research, 28*, 371–390.

Kang, S. (2002). The effect of the use of Korean and English in KFL classrooms of non-heritage learners. *Korean Language in America, 7*, 25–38.

Kang, S. H. (2010). The characteristics of a 'good' Korean teacher perceived by Korean learners. *Journal of Korean Language Education, 21*(1), 1–27.

Kang, S. H. (2011). An analysis of previous research on Korean teachers and learners in Korean language education. *Bilingual Research, 47*, 687–712.

Kang, S. H. (2014). An analysis of previous research on Korean teachers and learners in Korean language education research. *Bilingual Research, 56*, 1–29.

Kang, S. H. (2017). Korean academic research domains identified by analyzing prior Korean language education research. *New Korean Language Education, 110*, 12–146.

Kim, G. (2019). An analysis of trends in non-native Korean teachers' research. *Korean Language Education Research, 43*, 1–31.

Kim, J. W. (2007). A study of teachers' utterances in the Korean class. *Bilingual Research, 34*, 27–47.

Kim, K., & Kim, Y. J. (2020). A qualitative study on the influence of Korean teachers' foreign language learning experiences on teacher practices. *Teaching Korean as a Foreign Language, 59*, 1–28.

Kim, S. (2020). A study on the patterns of teacher praise in Korean class. *Teaching Korean as a Foreign Language, 59*, 29–64.

Kim, S. H., & Park, J. H. (2019). An analysis of teacher speech research trends in Korean language education. *Journal of CheongRam Korean Language Education, 70*, 7–42.

Kini, T., & Podolsky, A. (2016). *Does teaching experience increase teacher effectiveness? A review of the research*. Palo Alto, CA: Learning Policy Institute.

Ko, K. (2008). The roles of Korean language teachers from the intercultural communication perspectives. *The Language and Culture, 4*(3), 1–20.

Ko, K. R. (2011). Grammar versus content: KFL/ESL teachers' trends in feedback on college student writing. *Korean Language in America, 16*(1), 41–72.

Kwak, B. M. (2004). Gender differences in the Korean teacher's classroom language. *Journal of Korean Language Education, 15*(2), 23–50.

Lee, D. E. (2002). On evaluative discourse: Evidence from Korean language teacher's talk. *Journal of Korean Language Education, 13*(2), 181–204.

Lee, H. (2013). A study of raters' rating patterns on a pronunciation criteria in speaking assessment: Focusing on rater experience and major. *Teaching Korea as a Foreign Language, 39*, 213–245.

Lee, I. H. (2014). Assessment self-efficacy and evaluation characteristics of Korean language teachers in writing assessment. *Bilingual Research, 56*, 231–266.

Lee, I. H. (2018). Characteristics of an effective language teacher as perceived by learners of Korean in the US. *Bilingual Research, 72*, 221–253.

Lee, J. H. (2011). A review on the recent Korean language teacher education research in Korea. *Bilingual Research, 47*, 713–733.

Lee, M. H. (2013). The study on functions of language types in foreigner talk used by Korean teachers. *Bilingual Research, 53*, 151–182.

Mori, J., & Hasegawa, A. (2020). Diversity, inclusion, and professionalism in Japanese language education: Introduction to the special section. *Japanese Language and Literature, 54*(2), 253–266.

Park, S. O. (2003). A study on the pattern and function of the questions of a Korean language teacher who teaches Korean as a foreign language. *Discourse Research, 5*, 371–399.

Shin, S. C. (2009). Language instructors' use of learners' L1 and L2 in classroom: Perceptions by students and teachers of Korean. *Language Fact and Perspective, 24*, 157–186.

Sunderland, J. (2000a). Issues of language and gender in second and foreign language education. *Language Teaching, 33*(4), 203–223.

Sunderland, J. (2000b). New understandings of gender and language classroom research: Texts, teacher talk and student talk. *Language Teaching Research, 4*(2), 149–173.

Wang, H. S. (2003). A review of research as Korean as a foreign language. *Korean Language in America, 8*, 7–35.

Wang, H. S. (2014). Korean language teachers in higher education in N. America: Profile, status, and more. *Journal of Less Commonly Taught Languages, 16*, 147–187.

Won, M. (2009). The exploratory study of factors of cross-cultural competence of Korean language instructors. *Journal of Korean Language Education, 20*(2), 85–105.

Yoon, E. K., & Kwak, S. W. (2017). A sociolinguistic approach to the speech style of male Korean language teachers. *Language and Linguistics, 75*, 125–152.

PART V

Assessment

25
KSL ASSESSMENT
The TOPIK, achievement tests, and research trends

Chungsook Kim, Jung Hee Lee, Danielle Ooyoung Pyun, and Andrew Sangpil Byon

Introduction

Language assessment is a complex process involving discretionary decisions, such as what areas to assess, what methods to use, and how to increase the validity and reliability of the assessment. Various kinds of KSL (Korean as a second language) assessments are administered to track student learning and progress, including a proficiency test intended to measure a learner's actual command of the language in real life independent of what language training he/she has received, an achievement test used to evaluate how successfully a learner has mastered assigned course content and materials, a placement test designed to assess a learner's prior knowledge of the language and determine an appropriate level for him/her within the institution's curriculum, and a diagnostic test conducted to identify a learner's specific areas of strengths and weaknesses in language skills so as to understand which particular areas he/she needs more improvement on. As these tests serve different goals and purposes, they vary widely in content, format, scope, testing tools, and difficulty level. Particularly, a range of variations exist in achievement tests and placement tests according to each institution's beliefs, mission, and resources.

Assessment methods and content can create a significant washback effect on students' learning and instructional practices as well as on pedagogical approaches and curricula. For example, the implementation of the Test of Proficiency in Korean (TOPIK) in 1997 significantly affected the design and construction of the textbooks and curricula of KSL institutions in Korea. As TOPIK became a credible test recognized by the South Korean government (e.g., in obtaining a South Korea work visa) and Korean universities (e.g., in foreign students' admission to Korean universities), it has been serving as the proficiency guidelines for KSL. Accordingly, many South Korean KSL institutions started to arrange and organize their curricular content in line with, or at least related to, what is measured through TOPIK.

In previous studies of KSL assessments, little has been reported on placement tests and diagnostic tests. In this chapter, therefore, we will focus on the discussion of (a) TOPIK, the most widely used KSL proficiency test, (b) current practices of achievement tests amongst KSL institutions in Korea, and (c) previous research on KSL assessment. Studies of KSL assessment discussed in this chapter were searched through the Research Information Sharing

Service (RISS), an academic research search system operated by the Korea Education and Research Information Service. Therefore, it should be noted that most of them are the ones published in South Korea.

KSL assessments

Korean proficiency test:[1] the Test of Proficiency in Korean (TOPIK)[2]

According to the official TOPIK website, the aim of TOPIK is "to set a Korean language learning path for those who do not speak Korean as their native tongue, and to promote the Korean language by officially evaluating their Korean language proficiency." A good majority of TOPIK takers nowadays are those who intend to use Korean to study at a Korean university or to find employment in Korea. The assessment system and method of TOPIK were first developed based on the study by H. Kim et al. (1996, 1997). Its first test was held in 1997 and, as of 2021, the test is offered 6 times a year in over 81 countries around the world. As a Korean government–recognized test, TOPIK is administered by the National Institute for International Education (NIIED) under the Ministry of Education. After Article 34–7 of the Higher Education Act was newly established in 2020, which included the implementation of the Korean Language Proficiency Test, the status and authority of TOPIK has become even more elevated.

For the past 25 years of administration, TOPIK has undergone two restructurings and has improved significantly both in quantity and quality after conducting it over 75 times. No change, however, has been made in the nature and purpose of the test. When the South Korean Ministry of Justice introduced the visiting employment system in March 2007, TOPIK added another track, Business TOPIK (B-TOPIK), to measure the Korean proficiency of overseas Koreans who wish to work in Korea. Business TOPIK was offered a total of 8 times, from the 11th test in 2007 to the 19th test in 2010.

From the beginning of the implementation until now, TOPIK has adopted a rating system in which the test results are displayed in proficiency levels 1–6. For the first to ninth TOPIK tests (1997–2005), the six proficiency levels were determined using six different level-specific tests (one for each level). From the 10th to 34th tests (2006–2014), the six levels were evaluated through three different levels of tests (i.e., beginner, intermediate, and advanced). This change was informed by Kim et al.'s research in 2004. Yet another change was made in 2014 from the 35th test. Based on the research by Cho et al. (2013), TOPIK started to offer two different levels of tests to assign six proficiency levels: TOPIK I (the basic level) and TOPIK II (the intermediate and advanced levels combined). These changes were motivated to improve the practicality of test making and administration as the number of KSL learners and TOPIK takers has significantly increased since the mid-2000s.

Currently, TOPIK I consists of listening and reading sections, whereas TOPIK II is composed of listening, writing, and reading sections. In the 1st to 34th tests, the following areas were evaluated for all proficiency levels: vocabulary, grammar, writing, listening, and reading. However, from the 35th test, the vocabulary and grammar parts were excluded to achieve a more integrated and contextualized assessment. In addition, the writing part was also excluded in TOPIK I to reduce the burden on beginner-level examinees. The current TOPIK does not include the speaking part, which is a crucial component of L2 proficiency. In that regard, it can be said that TOPIK does not yet adequately ensure the integrity as a comprehensive proficiency test.

For TOPIK's question types, multiple choice is used for listening and reading, and supply-type questions are used for writing. Prior to the 34th test, writing was evaluated mostly using multiple-choice questions, but from the 35th test, the entire writing section was changed to narrative/essay questions. This change was made to assess the examinee's ability to perform real-life tasks, thereby improving the validity of TOPIK befitting its name as a proficiency test.

The passing scores of TOPIK are based on the total scores achieved. The format and the range of passing scores for each proficiency level are provided in Table 25.1. For example, in the case of TOPIK I, if 80–139 points are earned out of 200 points, level 1 is given, and level 2 is given if 120 points or more are achieved.

For the 1st to 34th tests, there was a minimum score requirement for each section. Even if the average score exceeded the passing criteria, a pass was not given if the score for each section did not reach the minimum score required by the level. However, from 2014, TOPIK was revised to the current format, eliminating the minimum score requirement for each language skill. While it is important to achieve a balance among language skills, this revision was intended not to penalize those who have a weakness in certain language skills and to assess the overall ability to communicate in Korean. Table 25.2 presents the TOPIK proficiency scale and performance descriptors for each level.

TOPIK is currently carried out asynchronously in 81 countries around the world using the same questions. This can make TOPIK vulnerable to security risks. Geographic dispersion and time zone differences pose a challenge to maintaining the integrity of the exam. To remedy this issue, starting from 2007 (the 11th test), TOPIK test developers changed the sequence of about 30% of the questions to create two versions, Version A (for non-Asian regions) and Version B (for Asian regions). From the 50th test, given the large number of test takers in Asian regions, Version B was further divided into two versions by arranging test items differently. In addition, for the writing section, 80% of the writing prompts differ between Version A and Version B. Nonetheless, as TOPIK is becoming more popular and widely used, more thorough and effective policies and procedures need to be in place to ensure test security and confidentiality.

At present, TOPIK is offered as a paper-based test (PBT). Research and efforts are in progress to offer an internet-based test (IBT) as well. For the past five years, the National Institute of International Education has conducted a study on the TOPIK speaking section, which underwent a preliminary assessment in 2020 and a pilot administration in 2021. The speaking section is scheduled to be added in an IBT format in 2022. This will allow examinees in countries with internet infrastructure to take it online.

TOPIK results hold for two years from the date of the announcement of the results. TOPIK scores are used for various purposes, such as to be admitted to Korean universities, to apply

Table 25.1 The format and range of passing scores for each proficiency level in TOPIK

Test type	Sections	Item type	Number of items	Range of score	Passing scores
TOPIK I	Listening (40 mins.)	Multiple choice	30	0–100	0–79 (Fail)
					80–139 (Level 1)
	Reading (60 mins.)	Multiple choice	40	0–100	140–200 (Level 2)
TOPIK II	Listening (60 mins.)	Multiple choice	50	0–100	0–119 (Fail)
					120–149 (Level 3)
	Writing (50 mins.)	Supply type	4	0–100	150–189 (Level 4)
					190–229 (Level 5)
	Reading (70 mins.)	Multiple choice	50	0–100	230–300 (Level 6)

Source: From NIIED (2014), www.topik.go.kr

Table 25.2 TOPIK proficiency scale

Test type	Level	Descriptions
TOPIK I	Level 1	• Able to carry out basic conversations related to daily surviving skills, such as self-introduction, purchasing, ordering food, etc., and able to understand the contents related to very personal and familiar subjects, such as himself/herself, family, hobbies, weather, and the like. • Able to create simple sentences based on a basic vocabulary of approximately 800 words and possess understanding of basic grammar. • Able to understand and compose simple and useful sentences related to everyday life.
	Level 2	• Able to carry out simple conversations related to daily routines, such as making phone calls and asking favors, as well as using public facilities in daily life. • Able to use about 1,500 to 2,000 vocabulary words and understand personal and familiar subjects in a certain order, such as paragraphing. • Able to use formal and informal expressions accordingly, respective to the situation.
TOPIK II	Level 3	• Able to carry out daily routine, with fair use of public facilities, and able to socialize without significant difficulty. • Able to express or understand social subjects familiar to oneself, as well as specific subjects, based on paragraph. • Able to understand and differentiate written language and spoken language based on their distinctive basic characteristics.
	Level 4	• Able to use various public facilities, socialize, and carry out some degree of ordinary work. • Able to understand easy parts in news broadcasts and newspapers. • Able to understand and use the expressions related to social and abstract subjects relatively correctly and fluently. • Able to understand social and cultural subjects, based on the understanding of Korean culture and frequently used idiomatic expressions.
	Level 5	• Able to perform linguistic function to some degree, which is necessary for research and work in professional fields. • Able to understand and use the expressions related to even unfamiliar aspects of politics, economics, society, and culture. • Able to use the expression properly, depending on formal, informal, and spoken/written context.
	Level 6	• Able to perform linguistic functions necessary to the research and work in professional fields relatively correctly and fluently. • Able to understand and use the expressions related to even unfamiliar subjects of politics, economics, society, and culture. • Able to experience no difficulty in performing the functions or conveying the meaning, although the proficiency has not reached full native-speaker proficiency.

Source: From NIIED (2014), www.topik.go.kr

for South Korean government scholarships, to obtain a work visa or marriage visa, to obtain permanent residency in Korea, for foreign-trained doctors to apply for domestic licenses, and for foreigners to acquire Korean language teacher certificates.

The number of TOPIK candidates was only 2,692 in its first test, but it has experienced rapid growth, reaching 375,871 in 2019.[3] At the beginning of TOPIK implementation, the number of beginner-level test takers was the largest, followed by intermediate- and advanced-level examinees, but from 2004 (the 8th test), intermediate-level test takers were the largest in number, followed by beginner-and advanced-level candidates. From 2008 (the 12th test), advanced-level test takers outnumbered that of beginning-level examinees. From the 35th exam, the intermediate- and advanced-level tests were combined as TOPIK II, so it is not possible to accurately grasp the distribution of intermediate- and advanced-level applicants. However, in light of the test results, it can be inferred that the distribution of applicants still remains unchanged, that is, in the order of intermediate level, advanced level, and beginner level. This distribution means that the Korean learners' overall proficiency has substantially increased compared to those from late 1990s and early 2000s. This can also be taken to imply that L2 Korean learners are not learning Korean temporarily, but many are engaged in continuous learning for academic or vocational purposes and aim for reaching working or professional-level proficiency (Korea Institute for Curriculum and Education, 2010, p. 48). Meanwhile, the number of beginner-level candidates, which has been proportionally decreasing compared to that of intermediate- and advanced-level candidates from the late 2000s, is on the rise again since 2015, which can be interpreted as an indication of a new group of Korean learners and examinees. It is believed that *Hallyu*-motivated (*Hallyu* referring to the Korean Wave or global popularity of South Korean popular culture) Korean learners, King Sejong Institute learners,[4] and secondary school learners of L2 Korean, which all began to surge in the 2010s, have contributed to this increase of beginner-level applicants.

In summary, TOPIK had a significant impact on KSL education by not only serving as a proficiency test but also guiding the direction of KSL teaching and learning toward desired proficiency and serving as a reference standard for curriculum design and development. Based on the analyses and suggestions made in previous studies, TOPIK went through revisions and restructurings.[5] Efforts have been made by KSL scholars and test administrators to create a virtuous cycle of curriculum, instruction, and assessment. However, there is still much room to improve the reliability, validity, and practicality of the test, as well as to enhance the security of the testing process.

KSL achievement tests

The number of university-affiliated KSL institutions significantly increased from the 2000s, along with the influx of foreign students who came to study at Korean universities. Currently, though different in size and scale, most universities have established and are operating a KSL institute or center. While they develop and administer their own achievement tests, research on the content and methods of their achievement assessment is relatively scarce.

Among the studies of achievement tests administered within KSL institutions are Jee (2005a), Choi (2006), Hur (2018), Y. H. Kim (2019), and C. Kim (2021). Jee (2005a) examined achievement tests of four university KSL institutes on their test areas, methods, topics, and pass/fail regulations. Based on the results, she addressed the following points as shortcomings: accuracy valued much highly than overall communicative fluency, a heavy dependence on the paper-based evaluation, test development by those who lack subject-matter knowledge, and the predominant use of discrete point tests over integrative tests. After surveying four institutions on their test types, test frequency, assessment areas, rating criteria, and standards/requirements for advancement and program completion, Choi (2006) suggested that (a) performance-based assessment should be incorporated in order to authentically measure students' communicative ability and (b) more research be devoted to the rating criteria for speaking and writing. Y. Kim (2019), on the other hand, investigated the elements of Korean oral achievement tests and suggested that (a) empirically tested assessment manuals be established, (b) specific assessment guidelines be offered, and (c) the feedback and assessment results for students be made more explicit and detailed.

C. Kim (2021) carried out an extensive survey of the institutional system of achievement tests with nine university-based KSL institutes located in Seoul and other regions, including Daejeon, Gwangju, Busan, and Daegu. The key findings of her study are outlined in what follows. The nine institutions are indicated in alphabet letters A to I in place of their names.

The system and characteristics of achievement tests

At all nine institutions surveyed, each semester consisted of 10 weeks and 200 hours. The course levels they offer varied, from six levels (seven institutions) to five levels (one institution) and four levels (one institution). Overall, their achievement tests were used to measure not only the learners' skills and knowledge of the instructional content but also students' ability to apply them to various contexts and situations (seven out of eight institutions). In that regard, many of their achievement tests showed some characteristics of proficiency assessment. Only one institution responded that their achievement tests solely focused on what was introduced through instruction and learning materials. The approximate ratio of test items assessing learned content versus application capability was 7:3 for four institutions, 6:4 for one institution, and 5:5 for three institutions.

As shown in Table 25.3, most institutions were using midterm and final exams to measure students' achievement. Some institutions incorporated other components as well, including quizzes, daily performance, participation/attendance, and alternative assessment. The midterm and final exams accounted for 30–100% of students' achievement scores. In seven institutions, the percentage of midterm and final exams exceeded 70% of the total course grade, indicating that the two exams occupied a significant proportion of the achievement scores. In calculating

Table 25.3 Percentage for each component of achievement assessment

Institute	Levels	Midterm exam	Final exam	Alternative assessment	Attendance daily performance	Others
A	Levels 1–6	40	50	-	-	10 (online lecture participation)
B	Levels 1–4	25	50	-	-	25 (quizzes)
	Levels 5–6	50	50	-	-	-
C	Levels 1–6	30	30	20 (productive skills)	20	20 (quizzes; receptive skills)
D	Levels 1–3	30	30	-	40	-
	Levels 4–5	15	15	30	40	-
E	Levels 1–6	30	40	-	20	10 (quizzes)
F	Levels 1–6	40	40	-	20	-
G	Levels 1–4	40	40	-	20	-
H	Levels 1–5	45	45	-	10	-
	Level 6	30	30	20	20	-
I	Levels 1–6	50	50	-	-	-

Source: Kim, C., 2021, p. 238

the final course grade, two institutions solely depended on midterm and final exams, whereas six institutions utilized other assignments or activities as well. Other assignments or activities included quizzes, such as end-of-lesson quizzes (three institutions), and alternative forms of assessment, such as presentations, discussions, and portfolios (three institutions). In six institutions, the same evaluation method was used across all levels. The remaining three institutions made use of varying evaluation methods according to levels: in two institutions, the proportion of alternative assessment and daily performance was higher in the intermediate and advanced levels; in one institution, quizzes were frequently provided at the beginner and intermediate levels, while they were not provided at the advanced level.

The areas of achievement assessment are displayed in Table 25.4. The assessment areas were divided into four linguistic skills in most institutions. In three institutions, vocabulary and grammar were set as a separate area of evaluation. The passing score to advance to the next level or complete the program varied from 50 to 82 points: on average, scores were somewhere between 60 and 70 points.

Test development, administration, and result notification

All nine institutions responded that they utilize their existing database of test items or assessment tasks. When newly developing test items/prompts, three institutions responded that they create scoring rubrics or guidelines that accompany the test item/prompt to maximize rater reliability. Four other institutions reported that they leave test rating to individual instructors without specific guidelines.

In three institutions, a KSL assessment expert was in charge of developing test items, whereas in six institutions regular instructors were taking turns to create test items. It was reported that speaking and writing tests, consisting of open-ended or essay-type questions, were conducted and graded mostly by classroom instructors. In some institutions, to ensure objective grading, tests were administered by or in collaboration with another instructor.

As for open-ended, essay-type questions, most institutions relied on analytic scoring: seven institutions used the analytic scoring method, one institution used a combination of analytic scoring (for writing) and holistic scoring (for speaking), and the remaining institution used the holistic scoring. Several advantages associated with analytic scoring help explain this phenomenon, such as: raters can look at a set of criteria for a language sample and the set criteria can

Table 25.4 Areas of achievement tests

Institute	Levels	Listening	Reading	Speaking	Writing	Vocabulary and grammar
A	1–6	O	O	O	O	O
B	1–6	-	O	-	O	O
C	1–6	O	O	O	O	-
D	1–5	O	O	O	O	-
E	1–3	O	O	O	O	-
	4–5	-	O	O	O	O
	6	-	-	-	-	-
F	1–6	O	O	O	O	-
G	1–4	O	O	O	O	-
H	1–6	O	O	O	O	-
I	1–6	O	O	O	O	-

Source: Kim, C., 2021, p. 236

contribute to increasing rater reliability. In part, it could also have been influenced by TOPIK, which adopted analytical scoring for its writing section.

When presenting the evaluation results to learners, most institutions were providing scores or grades only. Five institutions offered test results in the form of scores/grades for each skill area, and two institutions provided descriptive feedback in addition to scores/grades. The descriptive feedback, however, was very general, such as 'excellent job' or 'more effort is needed,' without specific and elaborate comments. Only the remaining two institutions reported that they deliver a paragraph-length narrative evaluation for each skill area along with the score/grade.

Post-exam item analysis, which is important to uphold the test validity and to revisit instructional content and practices, was rarely conducted. Only two institutions responded that they review test items after each examination. Their review, however, was limited to a general overview of the items without specific analyses on the distribution, discrimination, and validity of individual items.

Strengthening and improving achievement tests

On survey items asking about institutional efforts to improve their achievement tests for the past 10 years, most institutions positively responded. Two institutions stated that their achievement tests have significantly improved. Five institutions responded to it as slightly improved. One institution rated it as neutral, while the remaining institution reported a lack of effort. Table 25.5 shows the institutional efforts to improve achievement tests over the past 10 years.

When asked about the needs that demand immediate attention and action, the following things were addressed (see Table 25.6).

While KSL institutions have made big strides to improve their achievement assessment, there are still tasks and challenges that need to be addressed. For an achievement test to be

Table 25.5 Institutional efforts to improve achievement tests for the past 10 years

Institution	Efforts for improvement
A	• Building an assessment framework • Reviewing and revising instruction and curriculum based on the results of achievement assessment
B	(No response)
C	• Increasing the weight of performance assessment for writing and speaking skills at the advanced level • Setting minimum requirements for a pass grade
D	• Adjusting proportions of question types and assessment types
E	• Increased use of authentic real-life materials and assessment of students' learning based on those materials • Rating by two different instructors (speaking); scoring by more than one instructor (writing)
F	• Establishing a more professional and systematic assessment system through research
G	• Creating assessment guidelines and frameworks; Sharing scoring rubrics and criteria among instructors
H	• Test items developed and created by the ones who have expertise on the subject matter and item development
I	• Articulating assessment standards and guidelines for speaking and writing skills; adding a step of reviewing test items

Source: Kim, C., 2021, pp. 247–248

Table 25.6 Urgent needs in achievement assessment that demand immediate attention

Institution	Urgent needs
A	• Revisiting assessment standards and criteria for speaking and writing skills • Adding various forms of assessment in addition to midterm and final exams
B	(No response)
C	• Adding supply items for reading and listening exams • Increasing the proportion of assessment measuring productive skills
D	• Refining test items • Refining scoring rubrics for speaking and writing
E	• Teacher training on test development • Teacher training on test rating
F	• Creating a test item bank to produce multiple versions of tests • Improving the program and curriculum based on assessment results
G	• Instructors' participation in assessment workshops • Establishing core assessment constructs
H	• Providing a systematic procedure for test development • Institutional investment in professional development
I	• Developing a test item bank • Providing a valid measure of communicative speaking ability

Source: Kim, C., 2021, p. 248

valid and reliable, it should represent course content and expectations as well as be reflective of individual students' learned knowledge and accomplishment. To help teachers prepare and design high-quality achievement tests, hands-on teacher training workshops should be made available and maintained. There were four institutions offering teacher-training workshops occasionally to their instructors, but they were not necessarily focused on assessment. More efforts are warranted to expand and strengthen institutional support for professional development programs on assessment.

Research trends in Korean as a second/foreign language (KSL) assessments

In this section, we will look into the research trends in KSL assessment by providing a general overview of studies published in the last four decades. Using RISS, we were able to locate a total of 676 KSL assessment studies published in Korea (i.e., 419 journal articles and 275 dissertations). We will delineate research trends from two perspectives: (a) per period of time and (b) per language skill area.

KSL assessment research trends by era

As the washback effect of TOPIK has been quite substantial, we will divide the era into the following four periods: The first period is from 1983, when there was no nationally accredited assessment tool for KSL learners, to 1996, the year before TOPIK was first offered nationwide. The second period is from 1997 to 2005, during which TOPIK was implemented incrementally with a modest increase in its number of test takers every year. The third period is from 2006 to 2013, during which the number of TOPIK test takers increased dramatically, and this in turn brought forth a need for continual enhancement of the test to meet a growing demand of test takers from varying backgrounds. The fourth period is from 2014 to the present, during which revised versions of TOPIK have been developed and implemented.

The first era (1983–1996)

During this period, only a limited number of university-affiliated Korean language institutes offered KSL education, and KSL assessments were done locally within these individual institutes. In addition, there was no government-sponsored and accredited standardized test for KSL learners. The field of KSL was in its infancy, and so was research on KSL assessments. The number of studies published in academia that addressed KSL assessment was small. However, there was a growing awareness regarding the need to develop a formal assessment tool for different KSL skills, such as listening, reading, writing, vocabulary, and grammar (Noh, 1983). A limited number of studies introduced the instances of overseas KSL assessment tools or materials, such as ILR (the Interagency Language Roundtable) of Foreign Service Institute (FSI) in the United States and the American Council on the Teaching of Foreign Languages (ACTFL) guidelines, and discussed their implications to KSL (e.g., Kim, H. S. et al., 1996; Kim, J.-S. & Won, 1993; Noh, 1983; Won, 1992). Despite such a limited number of KSL assessment studies having been published, it was during this time that there was a growing awareness regarding the need to develop standardized KSL tests, and their development was underway.

The second era (1997–2005)

The second period is characterized by the implementation of TOPIK in 1997, its impact on KSL education, and the increasing demand for Korean assessment abroad. The six proficiency levels of TOPIK and its rating system significantly influenced the curriculum of KSL institutes. It was during this period that most Korean language education institutes organized their curricula into six levels. In addition, foreign countries began to adopt Korean as part of their college admission tests.

The number of KSL assessment studies published during this period was approximately 53 studies (41 journal articles and 12 dissertations). The research topics of these studies can be grouped into three categories: The first group concerns TOPIK, the second group focuses on Korean proficiency evaluations conducted outside Korea, and the third group addresses issues related to assessing speaking ability.

The implementation of TOPIK sparked interest from the field of education and KSL, producing studies on the TOPIK itself. H. S. Kim (1997), one of the leading authorities of the TOPIK, defined the objective of TOPIK as "the standard certification test for Korean Proficiency Assessment" that could be used to assess the Korean ability of foreign KSL learners as well as Korean heritage learners, who intended to use the test scores for college entrance or employment.

A number of studies examined and raised concerns about various aspects of TOPIK: how grammar, writing, reading, and listening were assessed and rated (Kim, C., Choi, E. K., & Kim, Y. J., 2005a); how to set passing grades or acceptance scores (Min, B. G., 2005); and regarding the content, question types, and validity issues related to vocabulary and grammar tests (Cho, H., 2000; Lee, 2005). Some studies pointed out its weaknesses, such as the writing part mainly consisting of multiple-choice questions and the lack of a speaking part (Kim, J. S., 1998; Lee, G. S., 2000; Seo, 2005). They also suggested that test developers include more positive social and cultural topics and incorporate a computerized testing format. To increase the quality of TOPIK, H. Lee (2004) asserted that KSL scholars and test developers should construct a graded list of vocabulary and grammar as well as a list of topics and genres of Korean texts.

Meanwhile, some universities launched graduate degree programs in teaching Korean as a second language in mid or late 1990s. Since then, master's theses on teaching Korean as a second language have been published. Many of these master's theses echoed the criticisms raised in previous studies: the question types/formats of the writing section of TOPIK were mostly multiple-choice questions; more open-ended supply-type test questions needed to be incorporated in the test; the validity of the grammar and vocabulary areas needed to be reexamined; and whether the type of questions in the reading and listening areas were appropriate needed to be evaluated.

The second group concerns the KSL assessment conducted abroad. In the 1990s, Korean was adopted as one of the foreign languages for college entrance exams abroad. For instance, Korean was included as part of a university entrance exam in Australia in 1994, and Korean was taken as one of the SAT II tests (a college entrance exam) in the United States. In 2002, Korean was included in the Japanese college entrance exam. Accordingly, there was an increased awareness and interest among Korean language educators and researchers, both domestic and abroad, regarding the Korean assessment tools used abroad. Reflecting these welcomed changes, a number of studies were published regarding KSL curriculum and Korean language assessments tools used abroad: in Russia (Vercholyak & Kaplan, 2002), Thailand (Pippidhana, 2002), China (Mao, C. M., 2002), and Australia (Kim, Y., 2005). For example, H. Kang (1999) and S. O. Sohn (2002) analyzed the format, contents, and difficulty levels of sample SAT II Korean test questions. J. Lee (2005) examined the type, difficulty level, and content patterns of Korean questions in the Japanese college entrance exam.

The third group is about the development of speaking assessment tools. The aspect of TOPIK that has received the most criticism was the absence of a speaking component in its content. A number of studies echoed this concern, asserting the importance of developing assessment tools that could measure the speaking skills of Korean language learners (e.g., Kang, S. H., 2005; Kim, Choi, & Kim, 2005b).

The third era (2006–2013)

The third period is characterized by the drastic increase in the number of TOPIK test takers, reflecting the fast-growing interest in Korean language education around the world. During this time, the original TOPIK version continued to undergo scrutiny to better serve and meet the growing demands of the expanding number of test takers. For example, the original six types for six levels were revised and simplified to three types with six levels. During this time, the number of KSL assessment studies was approximately 206 (116 journal articles and 90 theses). When compared to the number of studies published in the previous periods, it was substantially more, and such growing figures indicated that assessment had become a crucial component in the KSL field.

The research topics of assessment studies in this period can be grouped into four categories: (a) the evaluation and revision of TOPIK, (b) assessment for learners of Korean for academic purposes (KAP) or occupational purposes, (c) assessment for speaking ability, and (d) assessment for test takers from multicultural families.

Since its first implementation in 1997, TOPIK questions were available to the public, and this made it possible for researchers to scrutinize past test items. Approximately 100 studies (out of 206) published in this period analyzed the criterion for setting standards for Korean proficiency tests, difficulty analysis, and content validity. These studies investigated the validity and reliability of testing items and conducted the content analysis of various types of test items, such as idiomatic expressions, four Chinese character idioms, Chinese characters, synonyms, and polysemy. These studies often compared their results with KSL textbooks used in major Korean language institutes. The findings of these studies offered valuable insights to KSL teachers, curriculum developers, and researchers regarding how, what, and to what extent what they teach correlates with what TOPIK aims to assess. Moreover, between 2007 and 2010, a number of studies investigated more specific types of TOPIK, such as EPS-TOPIK (for overseas Koreans who intended to get an employment visa in Korea), and B-TOPIK (for foreign workers).

The second group includes those studies that concerned the development of KSL assessment tools for KAP international students. There was a general consensus regarding the need to set a common scale for KAP and the development of a basic academic proficiency assessment tool that corresponds to the European common reference criteria and the rating scale of ALTE (Association of Language Testers in Europe) (e.g., Choe, J. S., 2006). In addition, a number of studies looked into different skills sets involved in the KAP assessment: academic purpose listening (Ahn, M. R., 2007), speaking (Han, S. M., 2009), reading (Ahn, M. R., 2008), writing skills (Kim, S. S., 2011b; Kim, S. S., 2013; Kim, M. K., 2012; Kim, M. K., 2013), and critical-thinking skills (Lee, J., 2009b).

The third group of studies was about speaking evaluation. C. Kim, Lee, Lee, and Choi (2007) and Jeon et al. (2007) asserted that there was an urgency for the development of standardized speaking assessment. J. T. Kim (2008) suggested standardized guidelines for creating items for assessing speaking ability and exam graders' training programs to strengthen inter-rater reliability. As for speaking evaluation methods, Han et al. (2009) proposed a CBT (computer-based test) method utilizing interviews. Several studies (e.g., Shin, J. Y., 2008; Kim, J. E., 2012; Lee, H., 2013) discussed the importance of testing pronunciation, speech, and other phonological factors. K. S. Kim, Lee, & Kang (2010), and S. Y. Lee (2013) analyzed the speaking assessment patterns, evaluation criteria, grading policies, and factors related to grading procedures, implemented at individual Korean language institutes. H. S. Jee (2006) and H. J. Kang (2013) raised the importance of interactional competence and task-performance competence as two important elements and explored the application of web-based speaking tests.

The fourth group of studies concerned assessments for KSL learners from multicultural family backgrounds. With the increasing number of immigrants entering the country, various policies and facilities for immigrants have developed, and it has resulted in a growing interest in these learners' language proficiency assessments (e.g., Kim, J. S., 2011; Cho, N. M. & Nam, M. H., 2013; Cho et al., 2013). Various opinions were expressed regarding whether the current TOPIK was appropriate for this particular group of KSL test takers (e.g., Kim, S. H., 2011; Park, M. Y., 2012).

The fourth era (2014–present)

This is the period when the TOPIK was expanded to be offered six times a year in Korea and up to four times a year overseas, as the number of international students enrolling in academic degree programs in Korea was surging. We retrieved a total of 298 studies on KSL assessment for this period (153 research articles and 144 academic theses/dissertations). Research topics during this period were generally similar to those of the third period: (a) studies on the TOPIK (Shim, 2014; Yi, 2014), (b) studies on KAP assessment, (c) studies on oral proficiency, and (d) studies on assessment tools for children and youth.

First, there were 114 studies related to the TOPIK. Two of them analyzed the vocabulary and grammar in the TOPIK and proposed the content of educational material for a specific L1 (first language) group (Yi, 2014; Chu, M. M., 2015). As for the TOPIK listening section, several studies have looked at discourse contexts, authenticity of listening scripts, and authenticity of audio clips (e.g., Han & Yang, 2014; Kim, J. M., 2016). Also published were studies proposing oral assessment and discussing oral assessment standards (Lee, H. Y. & Lee, H., 2015; Jung, W. K., 2015). Special attention was paid to the quality and quantity of the TOPIK, including studies analyzing the quality and difficulty level of test items (Chang, 2014; Ham & Kim, 2014; Kim, J. M., 2016; Shin, 2016). In addition, several studies compared the TOPIK to other foreign language proficiency tests, such as the ACTFL OPI (Oral Proficiency Interview) in the United States, the JLPT (Japanese Language Proficiency Test) in Japan, the HSK (*Hanyu Shuiping Kaoshi* or Chinese Proficiency Test) in China, and the DELE (*The Diplomas de Español como Lengua Extranjera* or Diplomas of Spanish as a Foreign language) in Spain (Na, 2017; Ha & Kaneko, 2020; Wang, 2016; Kim, D. H., 2020). Among language skill areas, research on reading was the largest (e.g., Park, J. J., 2015; Shin, 2016; Jang, 2017), which seems to be related to the increase in the number of learners for academic purposes and the increased enrollment of international students at Korean universities. We also noticed that quite a few studies addressed and analyzed item 53 in the TOPIK writing, which asks an examinee to describe a given picture (e.g., Lee, M. H., 2017; Kim, G. S., 2019). Other topics included the characteristics of rating writing, teachers' or learners' perception of TOPIK writing, and suggestions for TOPIK writing questions (Lee, E. H., 2015; Jang, M. J., 2018; Jeong, 2020). Among the dissertations published during this period, 74 were studies examining the TOPIK, of which about 10 provided a comparative analysis between Sino-Korean words and Chinese words (e.g., Kim, S. H., 2018; Kim, J. N., 2020). This seems to indicate that the number of Chinese international students has steadily increased, and their knowledge of vocabulary became important in obtaining TOPIK Level 3, which is often required to enter a Korean university. In addition to linguistic skills, E. H. Park (2016) suggested including items assessing a learner's L2 cultural competence in the TOPIK. Lee, Ahn, and Lee (2019), who investigated the research trend of KSL assessment through semantic network analysis, found that the key word with the highest frequency was 'TOPIK,' confirming its pivotal position in KSL assessment.

Second, another group of studies concerned the development of Korean assessment for academic purposes (e.g., Kim, S. K. & Park, D. H. 2014; Nam, 2017; Park, S. H., 2019). Unlike previous KAP assessment studies, most of the KAP assessment studies published during this period were related to oral assessment. More than half of KAP assessment studies dealt with the development of task types and evaluation plans/tools for oral assessment. This contrasts with the previous period, where KAP assessment research focused much on writing. It may be thanks to the KAP oral assessment tool developed by B. G. Min et al. (2015), a foundational work upon which further studies were conducted. Other studies of KAP assessment included research on rater training and writing evaluation methods (Lee, E. H., 2015; Kim, H. J., 2019) and development of reading assessment tools and listening assessment tools (Jang, M. J., 2018; Lee, C., 2019).

Third, as for oral assessment research, while studies of the previous period by and large focused on the development of assessment tools, studies of this period touched on a wide range of topics. For example, based on mock oral interviews, a few studies examined issues in rating oral performance or discussed topics and questions for speaking (e.g., Won & Kim, 2017; Won & Hwang, 2018). Other studies included: studies on the necessity of introducing CBT (Kim, K. S., 2017; Eom, 2018), studies on elements of oral assessment (Won & Hwang, 2018; You, 2019), a study on core components for assessing pragmatic competence (Lee, J. H., 2019), and a study on learners' oral performance errors (Kang, S. H., 2016).

Fourth, another set of studies explored assessment for immigrants and migrant workers. Kang (2020) pointed out that while there are immigrants of various backgrounds in Korea, studies mostly focused on assessment for marriage immigrants and migrant workers. A few other studies discussed how to evaluate Korean proficiency of young KSL learners, such as children entering the country and studying in Korean public schools (e.g., Hong, 2015). Hong (2015) suggested diagnostic assessment as a suitable and helpful tool for assessing such children.

In summary, the prominent feature of this period is that research topics have diversified with increasing interest in Korean proficiency assessment. The topics that have not been much dealt with in the previous eras but substantially discussed during this era include teacher evaluation, comprehensive literacy education, and performance-based assessment. Particularly, there have been quite a few studies on performance-based assessment (E. H. Lee, 2015; S. H. Kim, 2019). This not only reflects the current trend of the learner-centered, task-oriented approach, one of the central philosophies of KSL education, but also shows KSL educators' continuous attempts for a seamless integration of learning goals, instruction, and assessment.

KSL assessment research by language skills

Among the four central language skills, a great majority of studies so far have dealt with assessment of speaking and writing. Table 25.7 is a summary of KSL assessment studies on specific domains of language skills, which were obtained through RISS.

Studies of speaking skill are the largest in number, those of writing skill are second largest, followed by those of reading and listening. In terms of micro-skills, those on vocabulary, grammar, and culture occupy a great portion. In the case of cultural competence, most studies focused on how to evaluate a learner's knowledge of target culture. C. W. Kim (2007), for example, subcategorized cultural competence assessment into five areas – namely, viewpoints of the target language and its use, knowledge of properties of expressions, understanding culture-loaded texts, communication strategies, and sensitivity to macro-discourses – and called for a more systematic alignment of culture instruction, learning, and assessment. Some studies suggested literary texts as an effective tool to evaluate learners' cultural knowledge and cultural awareness (N. E. Park, 2019; Shin, 2009). J. H. Lee (2019), on the other hand, discussed contextual and discourse factors to consider in assessing pragmatic competence and further offered types of assessment tasks. Based on the analysis of the TOPIK, Kang and Y. K. Kim (2016) classified assessment criteria into linguistic, non-linguistic, and prosodic aspects, and suggested components of pragmatic competence (e.g., pragmalinguistic and sociopragmatic aspects).

Listening

Much of KSL listening assessment research concerned the proficiency measure of listening ability and the authenticity of listening passages. An earlier study by Kang et al. discussed the

Table 25.7 KSL assessment studies on specific domains of language skills

Macro-skills	Journal articles	Dissertation or thesis	Total	Micro-skills	Journal articles	Dissertation or thesis	Total
Listening	14	18	32	Vocabulary	12	27	39
Speaking	57	44	101	Grammar	11	16	27
Listening and speaking	2	1	3	Vocabulary and grammar	4	7	11
Listening and reading	2	2	4				
Reading	26	26	52	Pronunciation	9	1	10
Writing	49	47	96	Culture	11	1	12
Reading and writing	1	1	2	Pragmatics	3	0	3

goals, elements, and directions of listening assessment and exemplified types of assessment questions (Kang, Lee, Lee, & Jeong, 1999). Subsequent studies examined the authenticity of the audio recordings used in listening tests (Kim, J. M., 2016; Lim, Cho, & Lee, 2018; Park, M. S., 2008). J. M. Kim (2016), for instance, critically analyzed the audio recordings of the TOPIK listening section and found that (a) the utterances were not adjusted according to the type and difficulty of the discourse and (b) the speed of the utterances was only 40–70% of the natural real-life speech rate. M. S. Park (2008) argued that many audio clips in TOPIK and KSL textbooks lacked reactive tokens, such as 'yeah,' 'uh-huh,' and 'exactly,' and showed unnatural turn-taking as well as too controlled topic shifts. Lim et al. (2018) also pointed out the elements that deteriorate the authenticity of listening clips, which included lengthy modifying phrases, lack of cohesion, and phrases/expressions that were not reflective of the place where the conversation takes place.

Another group of studies on listening assessment focused on listening strategies such as learners' strategies according to the types of listening texts, effective ways to comprehend the listening passage within a limited amount of time, and the need for strategy training (Jin, Y. J., 2013; Kang, S. N., 2016; Woo, J. H., 2019).

In listening questions, options can be given by either voice or text. J. H. Kim and Oh (2017) found that test takers find it most difficult to grasp detailed information when options are presented by voice in the target language. They suggested that presentation of options can be adjusted according to the types of questions. Based on a survey of graduate KSL learners, Lee and Han (2018) found that the use of pictures as clues was positively received. They further recommended that the pictures used in the assessment be simple, clear, and realistic. Jeong, Park, and Lee (2018), on the other hand, suggested that the clues leading to the correct answer should not appear within one sentence or a few words in the passage but should be scattered in several places to encourage test takers to infer the answer from the entire passage.

Speaking

The topics of previous research on KSL speaking assessment include the necessity of developing a valid speaking assessment tool, factors comprising speaking ability, and assessment criteria for speaking (e.g., Won, 1992; Kim & Won, 1993; Kong, 1993; Jee, 2005b; Kang, 2005; Jeon et al., 2007; Kim, C. et al., 2007; Won & Hwang, 2018; Kang, 2019). For example, as an important part of speaking proficiency, Jee (2005b) highlighted interactive strategies such as management of turn-taking and turn transition, and speakers' co-construction of the discourse. A few scholars reviewed ACTFL proficiency guidelines to help establish the evaluation criteria for Korean speaking ability (Won, 1992; Kim, J. S. & Won, 1993; Kong, 1993).

A part of speaking ability is pronunciation, which is linked to several factors, such as fluency (speed), stress, intonation, and aspects of phonological variation. In Yang and Jeong's study (2017), all of these factors were found to be positively correlated with pronunciation scores. In particular, the highest correlation coefficient was observed in suprasegmentals, which suggests that in classroom instruction closer attention needs be paid to suprasegmental features, such as stress and intonation.

Based on the analysis of learners' spoken data, Kang (2019) emphasized the importance of sociolinguistic ability as part of speaking competence. She suggested that when designing a test, test developers should make use of a title that can appropriately refer to the relationship between speakers and should provide enough background information on the context where the interaction takes place.

Next, there are studies on rater or inter-rater reliability. Quite a few studies analyzed the raters' scoring tendency using a multifacet Rasch model or raters' reliability according to the scoring rubrics (Cho & Yang, 2018; Kim & Kim, 2017; Kim & Kim, 2018; Kim & Won, 2018; Lee, H., 2018; Won & Kim, 2017). For instance, S. S. Kim and K. K. Kim (2011) suggested that in order to reduce the difficulty in rating speaking and to increase inter-rater reliability, pilot data should be collected, pilot scoring should be conducted, and then specific rating guidelines should be created at the stage of item development.

A few studies addressed the assessment of speaking Korean for academic purposes (KAP). Hong et al. (2016) stressed the need for speaking assessment tools for international students in Korea. Min et al. (2017) summarized the constructs of speaking proficiency into four categories: content, organization, vocabulary and grammar, and pronunciation and fluency. They argued that KAP assessment should evaluate students' ability to produce narrative discourse, informative discourse, and persuasive discourse.

The introduction of CBT and IBT (internet-based tests) and the procedure of scoring the responses on the Web were also discussed in several studies. Among them are a study comparing the face-to-face interview with the computer-based interview (Kim, K. S., 2017) and a study modeling a CBT design based on test takers' perception of the OPIc (Oral Proficiency Interview-Computer) (Eom, 2018).

Regarding oral achievement tests, Choi (2017) analyzed test questions and evaluation criteria used in KSL institutions in Korea. He found that in many tests the test validity was not sufficiently met as the tests lacked evaluation criteria and detailed achievement goals (Choi, 2017). After providing performance-based assessment along with constructive feedback afterwards, Cho (2006) found its positive washback effect on learning in fostering students' speaking ability. B. H. Kim (2010) explored the potential of portfolios in a discussion-based class and found that a portfolio is an effective vehicle for evaluating the ongoing progress of students' oral development as well as for providing meaningful teacher or peer feedback.

Reading

A good number of studies of reading assessment examined the reading items or the difficulty level of reading passages in the TOPIK, which include: a study that analyzed the reading questions to examine the difficulty level, discriminative power, and the content validity of the items (Jeong, 2012; Park, J. J., 2015); a study reviewing TOPIK II reading items based on information literacy skills categories (Park, S. J., 2015); and a study analyzing the types of reading items in the TOPIK in comparison with those of other foreign language evaluations (Jung, 2013). For instance, Jung (2013) suggested that TOPIK reading items should include questions related to the reader's ability to identify the main idea, understand vocabulary and sentences, and summarize the passage.

The next group of studies are those related to text analysis. Researchers examined the genre, subject, function, and semantic structures of reading passages (Shim, 2014; Mou, 2015; Du, 2019). For example, Jung (2010), who analyzed the test difficulty of the TOPIK reading passages according to syntactic characteristics, found that the difficulty gap was considerably big between beginner and intermediate levels, whereas it was not clearly noticeable between intermediate and advanced levels. J. Y. Kim (2017), on the other hand, examined the test difficulty based on sentence length and sentence structure. In Jang's study (2012), factors contributing to a text's difficulty level were classified into three groups: vocabulary-related factors, sentence-related factors, and structure-related factors. Among the three, she suggested that structure-related factors have the greatest influence on the difficulty level, followed by sentence-related factors and vocabulary-related factors.

As in listening assessment, a number of studies of reading assessment have dealt with learners' reading strategies. To study in a degree program at Korean universities, KSL students have to pass a certain level of TOPIK required by the university (e.g., Level 3). Having Chinese learners of Korean in mind, Chen (2013) and Lu (2018) offered various reading strategies according to different types of reading items. Another reading strategy–related research is the one by J. H. Kim (2020), where she offered specific reading strategies for the TOPIK and recommended reference books for self-directed reading.

Along with writing, reading is a core literacy skill that is essential for academic performance. However, few studies have looked at assessment of reading ability in the context of KAP. Ahn (2007) presented types of questions that can be used in KAP reading and writing assessments. Two other studies by Jang (2017, 2018) proposed ways to evaluate academic Korean reading ability based on the Construction-Integration (CI) model, where Jang illustrated how to evaluate students' comprehension of the main ideas and supporting details.

Writing

Similar to speaking assessment, the research topics of reading assessment focused on rating methods, rating standards, and securing of rater reliability (e.g., Kim, C., 2010; Kim, S. S., 2011a; Lee, I. H., 2012). For example, C. Kim (2010) compared analytic and holistic scorings and found that the reliability of analytic scoring was higher than that of holistic scoring. She counted the following as advantages of analytic scoring: it is easier to discriminate and rank learners' writing skills; it is easier to detect which areas of writing skills the learner particularly lacks. By comparing raters' scores using a multifacet Rasch model, Y. S. Lee (2014) discussed how to identify raters' scoring patterns, detect scoring errors, reduce the gap between the highest and lowest scores, and induce a more reliable scoring.

Regarding Korean writing for academic purposes, M. K. Kim (2012) suggested several types of writing questions (e.g., describing pictures, paraphrasing, and writing opinions after reading) that are appropriate for assessing KAP learners' knowledge of abstract vocabulary and various writing registers, as well as their ability to express thought logically and critically. To increase the authenticity of KAP writing assessment, Ahn (2008) and Ge (2018) advocated an integrated evaluation of reading and writing skills.

In addition, there were studies on the writing section of TOPIK. An earlier study by Seo (2003) pointed out that multiple-choice items for the writing skill cannot appropriately evaluate a learner's ability to articulate or organize his/her thoughts, and multiple-choice writing questions hardly differ from grammar questions. While multiple choice was eliminated from the TOPIK writing section in 2014, there is still some need for further improvement. Oh (2015) pointed out that TOPIK writing prompts were quite limited in number, topics were not diverse, and the difficulty level between intermediate and advanced levels was not distinct. On the other hand, G. S. Kim (2019) suggested that instructions on TOPIK writing prompts need to be clear, with key information provided. She further proposed that when providing visual cues, they should be unambiguous and should be given with concise information (Kim, G. S., 2019).

Suggestions and future directions

We have overviewed the TOPIK, current practices of KSL achievement tests, and previous studies on KSL assessment. In this section, we provide suggestions and recommendations for future actions and research.

While TOPIK is widely recognized in Korea and many Asian countries, its visibility and public awareness still remain limited in Europe and the United States. In part, it is because European and U.S. institutions are not familiar with the proficiency standards and levels of TOPIK (i.e., proficiency standards for each of the six levels). Particularly, little is known about how the TOPIK scale compares to those of the CEFR (Common European Framework of Reference for Languages) and ACTFL (American Council on the Teaching of Foreign Languages) proficiency guidelines, which are predominantly used in Europe and the United States, respectively. For detailed descriptions of the CEFR levels and ACTFL scale, readers may refer to the Council of Europe (2011) and the ACTFL proficiency guidelines (ACTFL, 2012). The alignment between CEFR and ACTFL ratings has been officially established and is available at ACTFL (2015). Future research may look at and empirically examine how the TOPIK scale can be compared to or aligned with either the ACTFL or CEFR scale. While the TOPIK, CEFR, and ACTFL scales may not exactly match or align with one another due to variations in test constructs and different types of test items, discussion on their potential correspondences will yield a greater understanding and knowledge of the TOPIK worldwide.

For achievement assessment to be more systematic, valid, and reliable, several points should be paid attention to. First, the means of KSL achievement assessment need to be diversified. Many current institutions measure students' achievement mainly through formal tests, such as quizzes, midterms, and final exams. As J. Lee (2009a) suggests, sole dependence on quantitative or result-oriented evaluation should be refrained. Instead, institutions should incorporate more process-oriented and performance-based assessment based on in- or outside class tasks and activities. Also recommended are hands-on projects or tasks/assignments that require creative or critical thinking rather than rote memorization. To observe students' needs, motivation, and attitudes as well as evaluate their ability to apply learned knowledge to new problems or situations, more alternative forms of assessment should be utilized, including e-portfolios, journal entries, and audio/video recordings.

Second, most institutions currently provide students with achievement results with scores/grades only. Such score/grade information alone does not allow students to identify or understand their strengths and weaknesses. The evaluative feedback should be more specific and elaborate so students can be reassured about their strengths and accomplishments or can know about the elements/areas they need to work on. The evaluative feedback should be given in an ongoing and timely manner while the content of the assignment or test is still fresh to students. The feedback can also offer directions or actionable recommendations so students can take necessary steps toward achieving expected goals.

Third, more expertise needs to be added to the current practices of achievement assessment. Concrete and transparent evaluation criteria should be constructed and communicated to students, let alone they be aligned with and reflective of expected learning outcomes. Test items or assessment tasks should be designed in a way that students can build on what they have learned. In addition, tests should be validated for effectiveness through item analyses (e.g., the percentage of students who answered the item correctly; the item's power to discriminate among students at lower or higher levels of achievement). Furthermore, institutions should provide instructors with more regular opportunities of educational and professional development.

As for research development of KSL assessment, active discussions have been held on what to use as components of evaluation and how to improve the validity and reliability of evaluation means. In particular, research on TOPIK and assessments for KAP learners has been prolific and influential. One observation we have made is that much of KSL assessment research concerned proficiency measures, particularly the TOPIK. As widely known, assessment can have a large washback effect on teaching and learning. In fact, the implementation of the TOPIK has resulted in creating a somewhat narrow and uniform curriculum across many KSL institutions in Korea. Recently, there are even institutions whose curriculum solely centers on TOPIK. This kind of skewed practice will lead to excessive standardization of KSL curricula, which consequently will fail to address and meet the diverse and changing needs of learners. For a more balanced approach to and research of assessment, increased attention should be paid to other types of evaluation, including achievement assessment, diagnostic assessment, and various kinds of alternative assessment.

Notes

1 In addition to TOPIK, the Korean Proficiency Test conducted in Korea includes the Employment Permit System TOPIK (EPS-TOPIK). This test is conducted by the Ministry of Labor, Human Resources Development Service of Korea, for the purpose of assessing foreign job seekers' Korean language ability and their potential to adapt into Korean society.

   The test consists of listening and reading sections and measures the applicant's knowledge of the Korean language, Korean culture, and occupational safety and health regulations. However, as this test is designed to recruit and select workers in the industrial field, it measures a very limited level of Korean language proficiency and thus lacks the characteristics of L2 proficiency measures. Therefore, EPS-TOPIK is not discussed in this paper.
2 Earlier, until the 9th test, this Korean proficiency test was called the Korean Proficiency Test (KPT) and then was changed to TOPIK (Test of Proficiency in Korean), starting from the 10th test.
3 The number of applicants in 2020 was 218,869, which was a significant decrease compared to the previous year, but this is believed to be a temporary phenomenon caused by the COVID-19 pandemic.
4 King Sejong Institute is a public Korean language institution established by the South Korean government to promote Korean language and culture overseas. As of June 2020, there are 213 King Sejong institutes in 76 countries.
5 For details on the TOPIK system, assessment methods, countries where TOPIK was administered, general information about applicants, and test results from 1997 to 2016, refer to C. Kim (2017).

References

ACTFL. (2012). *ACTFL proficiency guidelines 2012*. Alexandria, VA: American Council on the Teaching of Foreign Languages. Retrieved from www.actfl.org/sites/default/files/guidelines/ACTFLProficiencyGuidelines2012.pdf

ACTFL. (2015). *Assigning CEFR ratings to ACTFL assessments*. Alexandria, VA: American Council on the Teaching of Foreign Languages. Retrieved from www.actfl.org/sites/default/files/reports/Assigning_CEFR_Ratings_To_ACTFL_Assessments.pdf

Ahn, M. R. (2007). Assessing academic listening. *Bilingual Research, 34*, 247–270.

Ahn, M. R. (2008). Assessing reading and writing for academic purposes using descriptors of language competence in Korean. *Foreign Languages Education, 15*(1), 521–544.

Chang, E. A. (2014). A study of analyzing the quality of items on the Test of Proficiency in Korean (TOPIK) using item response theory. *Journal of Korean Language Education, 25*(4), 219–247.

Chen, R. (2013). *Research on reading strategy for Chinese learner: Centered on test of proficiency in Korean (TOPIK)* [Unpublished MA thesis]. Kyung Hee University.

Cho, A. R. (2006). *A comparative study on washback effect of Korean speaking* [Unpublished MA thesis]. Ewha Womans University.

Cho, H. R., Lee, M. H., Shin, S. K., Choi, E. G., Han, S. W., Lee, Y. S., . . . & Kim, Y. R. (2013). 한국어능력시험 체제개편에 따른 평가틀 제작 및 표준 문항 개발 *[Production of evaluation framework and development of standard items according to the reorganization of TOPIK]*. Seoul, Korea: National Institute for International Education.

Cho, H. Y. (2000). A study on testing vocabulary of KPT. *Korean Language Education, 101*, 1–20.

Cho, N. M., & Nam, M. H. (2013). Development and validation of Korean language skill test for multicultural students – With focus on writing skill test. *The Linguistic Science Society, 67*, 287–314.

Cho, Y. J., & Yang, M. H. (2018). A study on raters' reliability and consistency observed in Korean speaking tests. *Journal of Speech Communication, 40*, 105–128.

Choe, J. S. (2006). Curriculum development and assessment in Korean for academic purposes. *Bilingual Research, 31*, 227–313.

Choi, E. G. (2006). The practice and task of the Korean language testing. *Korean Language Education, 17*(2), 289–319.

Choi, S. Y. (2017). *A study on content validity of speaking assessment from Korean language education institution in university settings* [Unpublished MA thesis]. Paichai University.

Chu, M. M. (2015). *The study on the Korean verb '보다' used in the intermediate textbooks and TOPIK* [Unpublished MA thesis]. Hoseo University.

Council of Europe. (2011). *Common European Framework of Reference for languages: Learning, teaching, assessment*. Strasbourg: Council of Europe. Retrieved from www.coe.int/t/dg4/linguistic/source/framework_en.pdf

Du, Y. T. (2019). *A study of TOPIK II reading text: Focused on function, topic and structure* [Unpublished MA thesis]. Yonsei University.

Eom, S. W. (2018). 컴퓨터를 활용한 한국어 말하기 평가 도구 개발을 위한 기초 연구 *[A study for the development of Korean speaking assessment tools using computers]* [Unpublished MA thesis]. Korea University.

Ge, Y. (2018). 학문 목적 한국어 읽기·쓰기 통합 평가 문항 유형 개발 연구 *[A study on the development of item types in the integrated evaluation of Korean reading for academic purposes]* [Unpublished MA thesis]. Korea University.

Ha, C., & Kaneko, R. (2020). Comparative analysis of cultural factors in TOPIK and JLPT reading text. *The Language and Culture, 16*(1), 349–375.

Ham, J. S., & Kim, M. G. (2014). Critical appraisal on setting difficulty of reading area in TOPIK -On the focus of intermediated level between the 25th and the 27th. *Hanminjok Emunhak, 66*, 145–185.

Han, H. R., & Yang, J. S. (2014). 한국어능력시험 듣기 담화의 상황 맥락 연구 [A study on the situational context of listening discourse in TOPIK]. *Bilingual Research, 55*, 457–485.

Han, S. M. (2009). A study on Korean speech proficiency test for academic purpose: Focusing on pre-college courses. *Journal of Korean Language Education, 20*(1), 207–238.

Hong, E. S., Park, H. J., Cho, S. J., Min, B. G., Ahn, H. K., Oh, Y. L., & Kang, S. H. (2016). The needs analysis of Korean speaking test for academic purposes. *Journal of Korean Language Education, 27*(4), 243–268.

Hong, J. M. (2015). A study on the KSL diagnosis test tool-focusing on the analysis of content validity and improvement measures. *Journal of CheongRam Korean Language Education, 53*, 301–326.

Hur, Y. K. (2018). 한국어 성취도 평가의 문항 분석 및 실제 연구: 지필 평가를 중심으로 *[A study on item analysis of Korean achievement test: Focusing on paper-based evaluation]* [Unpublished doctoral dissertation]. Hansung University.

Jang, M. J. (2017). A study of using Delphi survey on constructive factors of Korean reading ability evaluation for academic purposes. *Journal of Korean Language Education, 18*(4), 149–179.

Jang, M. J. (2018). *A study on construction-integration (CI) model-based assessment of Korean reading proficiency for the learners for academic purpose* [Unpublished doctoral dissertation]. Kyung Hee University.

Jang, M. K. (2012). 담화 구조를 활용한 한국어 읽기 텍스트의 난이도 평가 방안 연구 [A study on the difficulty levels of Korean reading texts using discourse structures] 국제한국어교육학회 춘계학술발표논문집 *[Proceeding of the 2012 Fall Annual Conference of International Korean Language Education]*, 224–269.

Jee, H. S. (2005a). 국내 한국어 교육기관의 평가 체제 발전 방향 연구 [A study on the development direction of the assessment system of Korean language education institutes in Korea]. 국제한국어교육학회 [International Association of Korean Language Education] (Eds.), 한국어교육론 1 *[Korean language pedagogy 1]* (pp. 399–418). Seoul, Korea: Hanguk Pulishing Co.

Jee, H. S. (2005b). Understanding the test construct of Korean oral ability through a discourse analysis of Korean achievement interview tests. *Korean Language Education Research, 16*, 79–104.

Jee, H. S. (2006). The error analysis of spoken grammar in Korean interview tests. *Journal of Korean Language Education, 17*(3), 301–323.

Jeon, N. Y., Han, S. M., Yoon, E. M., Hong, Y. H., Bae, M. K., Jung, H. J., ... & Yang, S. H. (2007). A research on the development of a testing tool for the assessment of speaking proficiency in Korean. *Teaching Korean as a Foreign Language, 32*, 259–338.

Jeong, J. O. (2012). *The analysis on validity in the reading section of test of proficiency Korean, TOPIK: Centering on the 21st to the 25th intermediate level tests* [Unpublished MA thesis]. Sangmyung University.

Jeong, S. H., Park, J. W., & Lee, M. H. (2018). A Study on the direction for the construction of the listening test transcripts-focused on clues affecting difficulties. *Journal of Korean Culture, 42*, 173–212.

Jeong, Y. N. (2020). 중급 한국어 쓰기 교재의 설명문 쓰기 개선 방향에 대한 연구 : *TOPIK II 53번 문항 분석을 중심으로 = 구성-통합 모형을 기반으로 한 학문 목적 한국어 읽기 능력 평가 방안 연구 [A study on the enhancement of expository writing items in intermediate Korean writing textbooks: Focusing on the item #53 TOPIKII]* [Unpublished MA thesis]. Dongshin University

Jin, Y. J. (2013). 듣기 텍스트 유형에 따른 듣기 전략 연구 : 한국어능력시험 듣기 문항 대상으로 *[A study on listening strategies according to the type of listening text: Targeting the listening items of the Korean Proficiency Test]* [Unpublished MA thesis]. Korea University.

Jung, E. J. (2010). *A study on syntactic difficulty of reading texts in TOPIK* [Unpublished MA thesis]. Hankuk University of Foreign Studies.

Jung, S. B. (2013). *A study for the improvement of TOPIK reading questions: Focusing on the comparison of the types of advanced question in TOPIK, HSK, and JLPT* [Unpublished MA thesis]. Honam University.

Jung, W. K. (2015). Introduction of the proposed evaluation speaking test of proficiency in Korean-focusing on the assessment of speaking ACTFL-OPI. *Hansung-Eomunhak, 34*, 465–497.

Kang, H. H. (1999). An analysis of Korean language test in SAT 2: Using the 1998 official sample test. *Journal of Korean Language Education, 19*(2), 117–134.

Kang, H. J. (2013). <한국어 쓰기에서의 교사 논평과 동료 논평 양상 비교>의 토론문 [Discussion on "The comparison of teachers' and colleagues' comments regarding Korean writings"]. 국제한국어교육학회 춘계학술발표논문집 *[Proceeding of the 2013 Fall Annual Conference of International Korean Language Education]*, 224–269.

Kang, H. J. (2019). A study on sociolinguistic competence as a construct of Korean speaking test. *Journal of Korean Language Education, 30*(2), 1–23.

Kang, M. S., Lee, M. H., Lee, J. H., & Jeong, H. J. (1999). A method on Korean listening proficiency test. *Journal of Korean Language Education, 10*(2), 47–94.

Kang, S. H. (2005). A study on the development of evaluation instruments for speaking skills of advanced level learners of the Korean language. *Teaching Korean as a Foreign Language, 30*, 1–21.

Kang, S. H. (2016). A study of the constant errors in criterion referenced examinations of Korean speaking. *Bilingual Research, 63*, 1–22.

Kang, S. J. (2020). Exploration on the direction of development of the research for Korean assessment of immigrants. *Journal of Education & Culture, 26*(2), 887–911.

Kang, S. J., & Kim, Y. K. (2016). A Study of establishing an assessment framework for pragmatic competence through resetting content categories in TOPIK. *Language Information, 22*, 5–40.

Kang, S. N. (2016). *A research study on the teaching and learning methods and the application of test-taking strategies according to the different types of TOPIK listening section problem types* [Unpublished MA thesis]. The Graduate School of Jeonju University.

Kim, B. H. (2010). 한국어 말하기 포트폴리오 평가 방안 연구 : 고급 학습자 대상의 토론하기를 중심으로 *[A study on Korean speaking portfolio method: Focusing on discussion for advanced learners]* [Unpublished MA thesis]. Korea University Graduate School of Education.

Kim, C. (2010). A study on the assessment of writing proficiency in Korean: Focus on the result of comprehensive and analytic scoring. *Bilingual Research, 43*, 81–99.

Kim, C., Jeong, K. H., Cho, E. G., Kim, Y. J., & Kwak, S. Y. (2004). 한국어능력시험의 등급 부여 방식 및 평가 문항 유형 개선 방안 연구 *(A study on the improvement of assessment item types and grading patterns of TOPIK)*. Seoul, Korea: Korea Institute for Curriculum and Education.

Kim, C. (2021). A study on the achievement assessment of Korean language education institutions in Korea. *Journal of Korean Culture, 52*, 229–256.

Kim, C. S., Choi, E. K., & Kim, Y. J. (2005a). Suggestions for the test of proficiency in Korean (TOPIK): Evaluation and division of levels. *Journal of Korean Language Education, 16*(1), 77–98.

Kim, C. S., Choi, E. G., & Kim, Y. J. (2005b). A study on improvement plans for the test of proficiency in Korean (TOPIK) (II)-focusing on types of test items. *Journal of Korean Language Education, 16*(2), 91–108.

Kim, C. S., Lee, D. E., Lee, Y. K., & Choi, E. J. (2007). Primary research on the development of the standard Korean speaking evaluation. *Hanminjok Emunhak, 51*, 227–258.

Kim, C. S., & Won, J. S. (1993). Recent trends of bilingual studies: Studies for the establishment of evaluation standard in Korean language speaking ability. *Bilingual Research, 10*(1), 24–33.

Kim, C. W. (2007). Cultural literacy test in Korean education as a foreign language. *Journal of Korean Language Education, 18*(2), 81–114.

Kim, D. H. (2020). 한국어능력시험(TOPIK)과 스페인어능력시험(DELE)의 읽기 문항 비교 분석 *[The comparison of reading items of TOPIK and DELE]* [Unpublished MA thesis]. The Graduate School of Yonsei University.

Kim, G. S. (2019). The task analysis on the writing question No.53 in the TOPIK and the improvement measures. *Korean Education, 119*, 375–403.

Kim, H. J. (2019). Fundamental research of argumentative writing evaluation for the future Korean learners with academic purposes. *Bilingual Research, 75*, 55–79.

Kim, H. S., Park, Y. S., Paik, P. J., Yoon, H. W., Seo, S. K., Kim, C., & Lee, D. (1996). 한국어 능력 검정 제도의 실시를 위한 기본 연구에 관한 최종보고서 *[Final report on basic research for implementation of TOPIK]*. Ministry of Education of Korea.

Kim, H. S., Yoon, H. W., Seo, S. K., Hwang, J. H., Won, J., Cho, H. R., & Chin, K. H. (1997). 한국어 능력 평가 제도의 기본 모형 개발에 관한 최종보고서 *[Final report on the development of a basic model of TOPIK]*. Seoul, Korea: Ministry of Education of Korea.

Kim, J. E. (2012). Teachers' recognition and assessment on phonetical and phonological factors in Korean language learners' oral presentation. *Journal of Korean Language Education, 23*(4), 65–90.

Kim, J. H. (2020). *Analysis of reading part in TOPIK I · II A study on self-directed TOPIK reading learning strategy* [Unpublished MA thesis]. The Graduate School of Korea University.

Kim, J. H., & Oh, S. K. (2017). A study on the presentation modes of answer options in Korean listening questions. *Journal of The Society of Korean Language and Literature, 79*, 205–229.

Kim, J. M. (2016). An analysis on the authenticity of audio material in TOPIK II listening comprehension examination. *Journal of Korean Language and Culture, 59*, 167–189.

Kim, J. N. (2020). 한국어능력시험을 위한 의미 기반 한자어 교육 연구: 『세종한국어를 중심으로 *[A study on semantic-based Chinese character education for TOPIK: Focusing on Sejong Korean]* [Unpublished MA thesis]. The Graduate School of Hankuk University of Foreign Studies.

Kim, J. S. (1998). The development and the analysis of Korean proficiency test. *Bilingual Research, 15*(1), 123–140.

Kim, J. S. (2011). Teaching Korean as a second language for admission of universities-comparing of SAT Subject Test: Korean with listening to international baccalaureate Korean B. *Poetics & Linguistics, 20*, 81–102.

Kim, J. T. (2008). A test development model and its validation procedure of Korean speaking tests. *The Language and Culture, 4*(3), 47–76.

Kim, J. Y. (2017). *Analysis research of the level of difficulty of reading text in Korean proficiency test: Centered on sentence length and sentence structure* [Unpublished MA thesis]. The Graduate School of Education of Ewha Womans University.

Kim, J. Y., & Won, M. J. (2018). Analysis of scoring bias in Korean speaking test. *Bilingual Research, 70*, 59–83.

Kim, K. S. (2017). *A comparative study of the psychometric properties between computer-based format and face-to-face interview format of the Korean speaking test* [Unpublished doctoral dissertation]. The Graduate School of Yonsei University.

Kim, K. S., Lee, G. M., & Kang, S. H. (2010). Analysis of error sources and estimation of reliability in a Korean speaking achievement test by applying generalizability theory. *Journal of Korean Language Education, 21*(4), 51–75.

Kim, M. K. (2012). A study of evaluation types for the academic TOPIK – On the focus of the writing section. *The Journal of Korean Arts Education Research, 20*, 103–139.

Kim, M. K. (2013). Proposal of the assessment types of writing proficiency in Korean language for academic purpose. *The Journal of Korean Arts Education Research, 22*, 373–389.

Kim, N. M., & Kim, Y. J. (2017). Scoring reliability verification of L2 Korean speaking fluency assessment: Use of many-faceted Rash Model. *Journal of Linguistic Studies, 45*, 483–524.

Kim, N. M., & Kim, Y. J. (2018). Investigating the correlation of constructs in speaking fluency assessment of L2 Korean intermediate learners. *Korean Semantics, 59*, 87–108.

Kim, S. H. (2011). 읽기폭 검사를 통한 한국어 읽기 능력 측정 연구: 여성 결혼 이민자를 대상으로 *[A study on the measurement of Korean reading ability through the reading width test: Targeting female married immigrants]* [Unpublished MA thesis]. The Graduate School of Hankuk University of Foreign Studies.

Kim, S. H. (2018). *The study on education method for expanding Korean vocabulary using semantic transparency and word formation of Chinese character: An aspect of the korean vocabulary of the TOPIK (Test of Proficiency in Korea) for elementary and intermediate learners* [Unpublished MA thesis]. The Graduate School of Gyeongin National University of Education.

Kim, S. H. (2019). *A study on reliability of Korean learner's writing performance assessment* [Unpublished MA thesis]. The Graduate School of Kyung Hee University.

Kim, S. K., & Park, D. H. (2014). A study of the type of speaking assessment tasks for Korean for academic purpose-focused on the application of the many facets Rasch Model and the Generalizability theory. *Korean Education, 100*, 115–141.

Kim, S. S. (2011a). Analysis of error sources and estimation of reliability in an analytic evaluation on writing ability for academic purpose Korean by applying generalizability theory. *Journal of Korean Language Education, 22*(3), 29–48.

Kim, S. S. (2011b). *Development of an analytic rating scale and a test of its validity in the basic writing ability evaluation for Korean academic purposes* [Unpublished doctoral dissertation]. The Graduate School of Yonsei University.

Kim, S. S., & Kim, K. K. (2011). A Study on the relationship between predicted and communicative functions in Korean speaking test. *Korean Linguistics, 52*, 25–50.

Kim, Y. A. (2005). Korean language performance assessment and fairness. *Journal of Korean Language Education, 16*(3), 1–18.

Kim, Y. H. (2019). *A study on the evaluation methods of Korean speaking achievement: Focusing on core evaluation constructs settings* [Unpublished doctoral dissertation]. The Graduate School of Korea University.

Kong, I. J. (1993). 한국어 숙달 지침과 말하기 능력 측정에 대하여 [About Korean language proficiency guidelines and speaking ability measurement]. *Gyoyug Han-Geul, 6*, 91–118.

Korea Institute for Curriculum and Education. (2010). 한국어능력시험 15년사 *(15 years of TOPIK)*. Seoul, Korea: Korea Institute for Curriculum and Education.

Lee, C. (2019). *A study on the ability of Chinese learners to understand Korean implicature* [Unpublished MA thesis]. The Graduate School of Soongsil University.

Lee, E. H. (2015). Study on the estimation of reliability of writing performance assessments in Korean as a second language. *Korean Language Education, 149*, 241–277.

Lee, E. K. (2005). Research of the evaluating grammar on the KPT. *Grammar Education, 3*, 199–231.

Lee, G. S. (2000). The study of the 3rd and 4th Korean Proficiency Tests' vocabulary evaluation. *Studies of Humanities, 4*, 249–268.

Lee, H. (2018). Study of raters' rating patterns on a pronunciation criteria in speaking assessment-focusing on rater experience and major. *Teaching Korean as a Foreign Language, 39*, 213–245.

Lee, H. Y. (2004). The current state of examination of Korean language and its improvement: The current situation and improvement plan of Korean Proficiency Test. *Korean Language Education Research, 20*, 197–235.

Lee, H. Y., & Lee, H. (2015). A basic study on the development of grading scale description in Korean speaking assessment-focusing on the functional phase of speech sample analysis ssing discourse analysis. *Journal of Studies in Language, 31*(2), 451–478.

Lee, I. H. (2012). 한국어 쓰기 평가의 채점 방식에 따른 채점자 신뢰도 연구: 종합적 채점 및 분석적 채점을 중심으로 *[A study on scorer reliability according to the scoring method of Korean writing assessment: Focusing on comprehensive scoring and analytical scoring]* [Unpublished MA thesis]. The Graduate School of Korea University.

Lee, J. (2009a). *The principles and practices of performance assessment for Korean language education* [Unpublished doctoral dissertation]. The Graduate School of Korea University.

Lee, J. (2009b). Assessing thinking skills for KAP learners. *Journal of Korean Language Education, 20*(2), 175–201.

Lee, J. (2019). A study on designing sub-components of Korean pragmatic competence assessment. *Journal of Korean Language Education, 30*(2), 283–310.

Lee, J. H. (2005). A study on Korean language test in center test. *Journal of Korean Language Education, 16*(3), 253–274.

Lee, J. H., & Han, Y. J. (2018). A study on assessment measures of Korean proficiency using test questions with picture cues – Based on the recognition analysis survey of test items with picture cues in the TOPIK exam. *Journal of The Society of Korean Language and Literature, 83*, 176–201.

Lee, J. H., Ahn, S. H., & Lee, S. J. (2019). A study on research trends of language testing on Korean language education using semantic network analysis. In *The 29th international conference on Korean language education* (pp. 304–311). Seoul, Korea: The International Association for Korean Language Education.

Lee, M. H. (2017). 한국어 학습자의 토픽 (TOPIK) 쓰기 오류 양상 -53번 설명문 쓰기 중심으로 [TOPIK writing errors Korean learners-focusing on writing comments No. 53]. *Journal of the International Network for Korean Language and Culture, 14*(2), 231–254.

Lee, S. Y. (2013). A study on segmentation of evaluation-criteria in achievement test of Korean speaking. *The Studies of Korean Language and Literature, 45*, 27–55.

Lee, Y. S. (2014). A validation of the scoring of KFL writing assessment based on the many-facet Rasch measurement model. *Foreign Languages Education, 21*(3), 355–375.

Lim, T. W., Cho, K. S., & Lee, Y. G. (2018). The study of authenticity in TOPIK listening items. *Studies of Humanities, 56*, 477–508.

Lu, C. Y. (2018). *A study on the teaching method about the reading strategy of TOPIK II by the types of questions on reading: For intermediate Chinese background learners* [Unpublished MA thesis]. The Graduate School of Sejong University.

Mao, C. M. (2002). A study on the phase of evaluation about the teaching Korean in China. *Journal of Korean Language Education, 10*, 449–463.

Min, B. G. (2005). Suggestions for improving the management of test of proficiency in Korean (TOPIK). *Journal of Korean Language Education, 16*(3), 137–162.

Min, B. G., Cho, S. J., Hong, E. S., Park, H. J., Kang, S. H., Lee, S. J., ... & Ahn, H. K. (2017). Developing a Korean speaking test for academic purposes. *The Education of Korean Language, 157*, 309–340.

Min, B. H., Kang, S. H., Cho, S. J., Hong, E. S., Park, H. J., & Ahn, H. K. (2015). 학문 목적 한국어 말하기 평가 도구 개발 및 타당화 연구 *[Development and validation of Korean speaking assessment tools for academic purposes]*. NRF KRM (Korean Research Memory).

Mou, Y. Z. (2015). *A study of TOPIK advanced reading text: Focused on function, structure and topic* [Unpublished MA thesis]. The Graduate School of Yonsei University.

Na, E. Y. (2017). Study on the relationship between achievement test and ACTFL OPI-focused on the CLS Korean program learners. *The Journal of Humanities and Social Science, 8*(6), 247–259.

Nam, S. H. (2017). Developing Korean speaking assessment questions for KAP learners through task analysis. *Language and Culture, 13*(1), 137–169.

National Institute for International Education. (2014). *Test of proficiency in Korean*. Retrieved from www.topik.go.kr

Noh, D. K. (1983). Tests and measurements of Korean as a second language. *Bilingual Research, 1*(1), 139–170.

Oh, J. H. (2015). 한국어능력시험 '쓰기' 평가의 문제점 및 개선 방안 [Problems and improvement plans for the Korean language proficiency writing test]. 한국말글학 *[Hangungmalkwulhak], 32*, 77–98.

Park, E. H. (2016). Cultural competence in Korean education and development of cultural competence test tools on beginning level. *Journal of the International Network for Korean Language and Culture, 13*(3), 145–168.

Park, J. J. (2015). A study of analyzing the quality of reading items on TOPIK. *Journal of Reading Research, 34*, 147–170.

Park, M. S. (2008). A study of authenticity of the text of Korean listening comprehension test. *Journal of Korean Language Education, 19*(1), 93–112.

Park, M. Y. (2012). A study on the Korean listening test of migrant woman. *Korean Language and Literature, 52*, 5–29.

Park, N. E. (2019). *A study on the use of literary education in Korean education: Focusing on the cultural adaptation of TOPIK advanced level learners* [Unpublished MA thesis]. Graduate School of Duksung Women's University.

Park, S. H. (2019). Investigating the validity of the TOPIK for academic uses: Based on an argument-based framework. *Journal of Korean Language Education, 30*(3), 21–49.

Park, S. J. (2015). Analysis on TOPIK reading items for information literacy. *Studies of Korean & Chinese Humanities, 48*, 291–309.

Pippidhana, B. (2002). Evaluation method of Korean language for Thai students. *Journal of Korean Language Education, 10*, 321–341.

Seo, H. J. (2005). 한국어능력시험 쓰기 영역 문항 개발에 관한 연구 [A study on the development of questions in the writing area of the Korean proficiency test]. 고황논집 *[Gho Hwang Non Jib], 36*, 34–65.

Seo, Y. N. (2003). 한국어능력시험 쓰기 평가 개선방안 연구: 4회, 5회, 6회 문제 분석을 중심으로 *[A study on the improvement plan for the writing evaluation on the Korean Proficiency Test: Focusing on the analysis of the 4th, 5th, and 6th questions]* [Unpublished MA thesis]. The Graduate School of Kyung Hee University.

Shim, M. H. (2014). *Analysis of advanced reading section passages of TOPIK: Focused on genre and topic* [Unpublished MA thesis]. The Graduate School of Education Yonsei University.

Shin, J. H. (2016). Text difficulty of readings on the TOPIK: Focusing on reading texts in TOPIK Ⅱ. *Bilingual Research, 62*, 29–48.

Shin, J. Y. (2008). Phoneme and syllable frequencies of Korean based on the analysis of spontaneous speech data. *Communication Sciences and Disorders, 13*(2), 193–215.

Shin, Y. K. (2009). Literary text in Korean cultural literacy evaluation as a foreign language. *Journal of Korean Society of Literary Education, 29*, 131–156.

Sohn, S. O. (2002). 미국에서의 한국어 교육 평가: SAT Ⅱ 한국어와 응시자들의 사회 언어적 배경을 중심으로 [Evaluation of Korean language education in the US: Focusing on SAT II Korean and the sociolinguistic background of test takers]. *Journal of Korean Language Education, 10*, 383–402.

Vercholyak, V., & Kaplan, T. Y. (2002). The present situation of evaluation method of Korean language teaching in Russian universities: By the example of higher college of Korean studies, Far Eastern State University. *Journal of Korean Language Education, 10*, 275–289, Korean Language Education Research Institute.

Wang, D. (2016). Foreign language testing in China: Literature review of research on English, Japanese, and Korean tests, 2002–2013. 한국(조선)어교육연구 *[Hanguk Joseoneo kyoyuk yeonku], 11*, 260–293.

Won, J. S. (1992). 한국어 말하기 능력 평가 기준 설정을 위한 연구 [A study on the development of criteria for evaluating Korean speaking ability]. 한국어문교육 *[Korean Literature and Language Education], 6*, 101–133.

Won, M. J., & Hwang, J. Y. (2018). Korean speaking test as a language competence test. *Eo-Mun-Lon-Chong, 75*, 45–78.

Won, M. J., & Kim, J. Y. (2017). A study on the grading tendencies of the Korean speaking performance test development. *Teaching Korean as a Foreign Language, 47*, 169–192.

Woo, J. H. (2019). *A study on listening strategies of Chinese learners of Korean according to the different types of listening text: Focused on TOPIK listening text* [Unpublished MA thesis]. The Graduate School of Hanyang University.

Yang, S. H., & Jeong, M. H. (2017). Correlation analysis of linguistic factors in non-native Korean speech and proficiency evaluation. *Phonetics and Speech Sciences, 9*(3), 49–56.

Yi, K. Y. (2014). A study for expanding the horizons of lexical competence assessment. *Korean Semantics, 44*, 171–197.

You, J. H. (2019). TOPIK 말하기 평가 구인으로서의 음절 말화 속도에 대한 연구: 음성인식 기술을 활용하여 *[A study on syllable speech speed as a construct for TOPIK speaking assessment: Using speech recognition technology]* [Unpublished MA thesis]. The Graduate School of Yonsei University.

26
INTEGRATED PERFORMANCE ASSESSMENT AND KSL

Sahie Kang

Introduction

Integrated Performance Assessment (IPA) has been gaining attention over the last few decades and is regarded as a pioneering form of summative assessment in second and foreign languages, including Korean. It was designed and initiated at the end of the twentieth century by the taskforce of the American Council on the Teaching of Foreign Language (ACTFL) for the purpose of not only measuring students' in-class language-performance progress but also for the purpose of guiding them toward proficiency outcomes. Additionally, it has had an impact on classroom assessment practices in the field of second language.

IPAs are organized around a series of purposefully designed tasks centered on the communication goal, one of the learning goals of the 5Cs: communication, culture, comparison, connection, and community, in accordance with the National Standards for Language Learners (The National Standards Collaborative Board, 2015). These allow learners to perform interpretive, interpersonal, and presentational tasks under one theme and receive immediate feedback on each task performance, using rubrics that are created based on ACTFL proficiency and performance descriptors (ACTFL, 2012a, 2012b). These tasks are designed using authentic contexts or topics one would likely encounter in the target language environment.

As in many diagnostic and performance-based assessments, the IPA entails a three-step process in cyclic mode: 1) students first take an assessment; 2) the teacher provides feedback on student performances; and 3) students take additional assessments, followed by teacher feedback. The process is expected to help students grow in their performance skills in the target language during and after the implementation, as in the following diagram. The purpose of using such performance assessments is to link them with learning. In other words, the IPA expects that learning is taking place not simply for the sake of learning but for the sake of applying it to interactions with others outside the classroom (Schenck, 2019, pp. 107–108).

An IPA begins with an overview that describes the context and purpose of the series of realistic communicative tasks. This overview provides a framework for the assessment and presents how three communicative tasks are integrated cyclically leading up to the culminating task, oral or written presentational product, as the diagram displays (see Appendix A for an example of an IPA overview). In addition, each communicative task is assessed based on various criteria indicating different aspects of performances, as summarized next

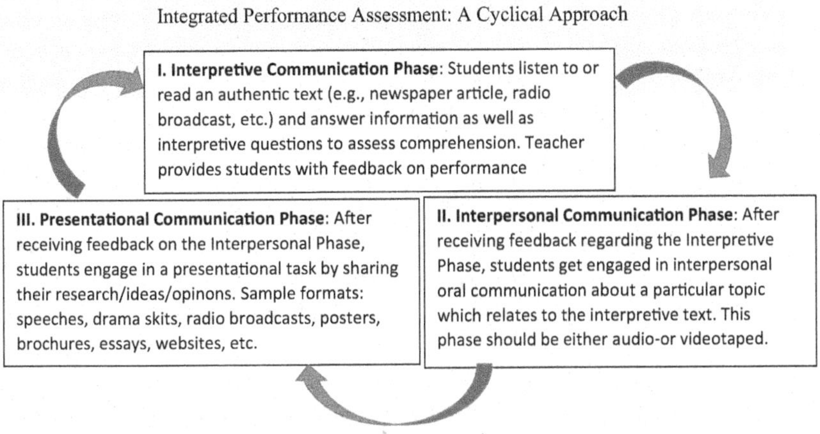

Integrated Performance Assessment: A Cyclical Approach

I. Interpretive Communication Phase: Students listen to or read an authentic text (e.g., newspaper article, radio broadcast, etc.) and answer information as well as interpretive questions to assess comprehension. Teacher provides students with feedback on performance

III. Presentational Communication Phase: After receiving feedback on the Interpersonal Phase, students engage in a presentational task by sharing their research/ideas/opinons. Sample formats: speeches, drama skits, radio broadcasts, posters, brochures, essays, websites, etc.

II. Interpersonal Communication Phase: After receiving feedback regarding the Interpretive Phase, students get engaged in interpersonal oral communication about a particular topic which relates to the interpretive text. This phase should be either audio-or videotaped.

Figure 26.1 Integrated performance assessment

Source: GlisanAdair-Hauck, Koda, Sandrock, and Swender (2003, p. 18); Adair-Hauck, Glisan, and Troyan (2013, p. 10)

Table 26.1 Criteria for three communicative tasks of IPA rubrics

[1]*Interpretive tasks*	*Interpersonal tasks*	*Presentational tasks*
Literal comprehension:	Language function	Language function
Word recognition	Text type	Text type
Main idea		
Supporting details detection		
Interpretive comprehension:	Communication strategies	Impact
Organizational features	Comprehensibility	Comprehensibility
Guessing meaning from context	Language control	Language control
Inferences (between the lines)		
Author's perspective		
Cultural perspective		

Source: Adair-Hauck et al. (2013, pp. 12–16)[2]

(see Appendix B for detailed descriptions of these criteria in IPA rubrics for use in scoring tasks across three modes of communication).

While proficiency tests such as the Oral Proficiency Interview (OPI), based on ACTFL proficiency guidelines (ACTFL, 2012a), have had a large impact on curriculum design and instruction over the last several decades, they are not necessarily optimal assessment tools to measure learners' weekly progress within a semester-long course. They measure the wide range of speakers' real-life use of language abilities described in each proficiency level, rather than learned performance skills within a short time frame. On the other hand, IPAs are designed to be used during instruction, not as separate stand-alone tests but as tools to measure students' performances connected with ongoing learning (Sandrock, 2010). Research on IPAs reports benefits to both learners and teachers, who have testified specifically to their positive washback effect, which helps teachers and students engage in real-life communication.

This chapter reviews research that focuses on various aspects of IPAs. Research findings report that learners' performances in different communication modes do not necessarily progress evenly as their metacognitive awareness regarding their own process of language learning increases. IPA fills this need for a performance-based assessment that measures learners' progress in meeting both proficiency and World-Readiness Standards; additionally, teachers indicate that IPA has a washback effect on instruction and curricular design. Yet precious little research reports on the effectiveness of feedback based on the rubrics, an essential feature of the IPA that helps learners advance to higher levels on the proficiency scale; fortunately, the field of KSL is paying more attention to IPA nowadays. After reviewing the research detailing these effects in the second language and Korean as a second language fields, the chapter suggests further empirical research in KSL. It then discusses pedagogical implications of the nature of student learning outcomes, as well as the purposeful design of curricula and assessment in Korean as a second language which fosters the attainment of measurable student learning outcomes.

IPA research in L2 settings

The history of IPA

IPA was originally designed as a result of the Integrated Performance Assessment Design Project, a three-year research initiative established by ACTFL in 1997–2000 and sponsored by the U.S. Department of Education International Research and Studies Program. During the three-year grant, the project team designed the IPA and delivered professional development to participating teachers at six different sites. Then the IPA was piloted by forty different language teachers and over one thousand students of Chinese, French, German, Italian, Latin, and Spanish. The actual pilot tests used, as well as the implementations following teachers' and students' positive feedback on the IPA's usefulness and feasibility, are compiled in Adair-Hauck et al. (2013). The Center for Advanced Research on Language Acquisition (CARLA, 2009) at the University of Minnesota has also collected a rich resource of IPAs.

The primary goal of the project was to develop an integrated performance skills assessment prototype that would measure students' progress toward the World Readiness Standards for Foreign Language Learning (The National Standards Collaborative Board, 2015). A secondary goal of the project was to use the assessment prototype as a catalyst for curricular and pedagogical reform.

Learners

Research findings during the early implementation of IPAs present positive perceptions of IPAs by students and teachers, despite some challenges. Earlier research on IPAs attempted to measure their effectiveness by looking at how well students would perform in three different communication modes, how their learning and classroom activities were connected with such assessments, and whether these assessments actually helped students understand their own learning in different stages. At the same time, some research on teachers' perspectives focused on how IPAs impacted teachers' classroom practices and attitudes.

Glisan, Uribe, and Adair-Hauck (2007) investigate how postsecondary students exceed, meet, and do not meet communication expectations across the three modes of communication, while also examining the extent to which secondary and postsecondary language study influences their performances. The results show that students perform best on presentational tasks, most likely because this has been the predominant mode in many language classrooms. In contrast, student performance in the interpersonal mode did not quite meet the same expectations as in presentational mode, possibly due to the challenges of teaching spontaneous fact-to-face communication. Ultimately, the interpretive mode turns out to be the most challenging for students; they do not meet expectations, possibly due to a lack of adequate exposure to authentic language listening strategies in many classrooms with more traditional approaches. Since this is the first instance of a video text being used, (given that the early IPA projects used only printed texts,) such an outcome seems to confirm that students have not received enough exposure to authentic listening in classrooms.

The study also reports that there was a positive correlation between years of language study in middle school and performance in the interpersonal mode, while there was a surprising negative correlation between years of language study in high school and performance across the three modes of communication. The authors' explanation on such opposing outcomes is that many middle school programs in the United States tend to be communicative and interactive, focusing on novice-level language development, whereas some high school programs may have instructional and curricular lacunae in assisting students to meet the performance standards for focusing on traditional grammar-based instruction. Students' language background questionnaires support such an explanation.

Similarly, Davin, Troyan, Donato, and Hellman (2011) examines the performance of Grade 4 and 5 students of Spanish on the IPA across three communication tasks during implementation. This study of IPAs in an Early Foreign Language Learning program shows that, of the three communicative tasks, early language students' performances rated the lowest on the interpretive task, as have the postsecondary students, as described in Glisan et al. (2007). Both studies discuss how low ratings in interpretive tasks perhaps stem from the students' lack of exposure to authentic spoken texts, which generally include a higher concentration of unfamiliar vocabulary. Davin et al. (2011) also explains that novice-level authentic materials are hard to find, and young learners need more opportunities to interpret appropriate authentic texts with supportive feedback from the teacher.

Additionally, a student post-IPA survey shows that these young learners exhibit metacognitive awareness of their own process of language learning in interpretive and presentational tasks. Young learners understand the connection between classroom activities and the IPA in which they can identify knowledge and experiences to progress to a higher level. Another interesting outcome of the post-IPA survey is that multilingual students tend to perform better in interpersonal tasks than monolingual students, most likely because they have already developed strategies in dealing with unknown languages.

These two studies report that students in both contexts respond quite positively to the IPA in post-IPA surveys, and they enjoy the opportunity to interact orally with their classmates in the interpersonal task. It is interesting to note that students in the elementary school program performed well in interpersonal mode, while the postsecondary students did not. This is because the majority of class time in most elementary school language programs is focused on oral communication, as it is in most middle school programs.

Gabriela C. Zapata (2016) reports on postsecondary students' perceptions on IPA implementation based on the opinions of 1,236 novice, intermediate low, and intermediate mid Spanish students. Students generally offer positive opinions of IPAs, although these opinions vary somewhat depending on participants' proficiency levels, previous assessment experiences, reasons for taking Spanish, and the characteristics of the students' individual instructors and classes.

The findings confirm university students' overall approval of the implementation of IPA and their ability to see the connection between classroom learning and assessment in Spanish classes across the three levels of instruction. However, this study also presents student comments that raise important issues about the instructional aspects that may have influenced their perceptions and which could affect IPA implementation. In other words, student concerns with instructors' lack of knowledge or commitment in implementing an innovation like IPA implies that there may exist issues of instructor attitudes regarding the implementation process. It is obvious that learners in classes taught by instructors who embrace the curricular change expressed their experience in very positive terms, noting the benefits in the IPA models. In contrast, in classes where instructors are not willing or capable of integrating innovation into instruction, learners perceive the disconnect between classroom instruction and assessment. This result clearly suggests the need for regular professional development and classroom observations, followed by more individualized instructor guidance.

Students with a lower level of proficiency requesting more exposure to authentic listening and interpretations echo the findings of Glisan et al. (2007) and Davin et al. (2011), who posit that learners need to be exposed to more authentic spoken texts, particularly in the interpretive mode. Also, student rejection of the IPA comes from their fear of academic failure under the new assessment because such students enroll in these courses with the intention of fulfilling language requirements, rather than learning the language. It is important to clearly communicate with students the outcome expectations, as well as the IPA's relationship to grades, to avoid confusion and rejection based on misunderstanding of the purpose and basic principles of IPA. Most importantly, the study validates the IPA approach as an effective pedagogical tool that links learning, assessment, and the use of the target language in real-world tasks.

Instructors

The research discussed so far examines the benefits and effectiveness of IPA on student performances and perceptions. More recently, some studies examine instructor attitudes and practices in successful IPA implementation, as well as the impact of designating instructors with the main role in designing, administering, and implementing the IPA.

Martel and Bailey (2016) investigates instructor attitudes toward summative IPAs, which were institutionalized by an administrator as midterm and final examinations in a postsecondary intensive summer language program. Findings include positive and negative attitudes toward standardizing implementation procedures, using the IPA rubrics and assigning grades, and the sustainability of the innovation in the program. Instructor attitudes are generally positive on the standardization of assessment procedures through implementation of IPAs across four different language programs. However, they are consistently more negative regarding the use of rubrics for their complexity and for possible inflation of course grades.

Data indicate that some instructors' rejections to IPAs entail logistical concerns in addition to the aforementioned pedagogical implications. In other words, instructors' negative attitudes may come from the top-down decisions on IPA implementation and the associated additional workload, despite the fact that the program's past instructional approaches and instructors' pedagogical styles are generally aligned with the basic principles of the IPA. It is interesting to note that such negative attitudes appear even when instructors are given extra time in preparation of draft IPAs, flexibility in making decisions on specific aspects of implementation, and training on IPA through professional development opportunities. These points raise some alarm regarding the effectiveness of the various strategies for managing educational innovations and suggest that the IPA innovation may be more successfully institutionalized by involving both administrative and instructor decision-making in various steps throughout the process. Additionally, instructors have expressed concerns surrounding the lack of IPA models for postsecondary learners, which underscore the urgent need to develop more postsecondary IPAs based on themes tapping the intellectual capacities of the adult learner.

Eddy and Bustamante (2020) explore collaboration between student teachers and cooperating teachers by looking into their experiences of implementing Spanish IPAs in world language teacher education programs at two postsecondary education institutions. By examining the perceptions of nine student teachers (ST), seven cooperating teachers (CTs), and the university field supervisor (UFS), using data from interviews, focus groups, and classroom observations, this study suggests that minimizing or closing the gap between the ST and CT through collaborative professional development will enhance successful implementation of IPA.

The findings from these two colleges indicate that the ST's preparation and the CT's familiarity with the IPA are not necessarily well connected, showing disparate relationships between familiarity, implementation, and impact on pedagogical beliefs, and these disparities suggest the need for professional development. Data show that there is a discrepancy between ST familiarity and that of CTs due to different requirements in teacher certification of two groups. In other words, the CT group enters the workforce without IPA implementation experience, whereas STs are required to implement the interpretive mode and at least one other mode of communication and to provide feedback for all three modes during student teaching. In addition, the STs must justify subsequent instructional decisions with research-based practices.

The data also reveal that lack of IPA familiarity by CTs is a hindrance to ST implementation of the IPA; however, in classrooms where CTs are familiar, they are more amenable to its use. The intervention of the UFS, as a trusted figure to CTs, is key to minimizing such gaps, by helping the CTs understand the purpose of IPA and encouraging them to be more amenable to buying-in by explaining the integration of culture and thematic context throughout the IPA, as well as the importance of target language instruction. On the other hand, STs feel that professional development on IPA for CTs is imperative, and even suggest that STs themselves could provide said development to CTs. The researchers note that this reciprocal learning approach suggested by STs is interesting because STs are generally perceived as the recipients of such professional development. At the same time, a packet from the certification program, and a webinar, are currently in development at the request of CTs, as a direct result of this research, which explores collaborative models between method instructors and CTs to further close the gap between new teacher candidates and in-service teachers.

Kissau and Adams (2016) report that IPAs provide elementary, secondary, and postsecondary instructors with the opportunity to align standards-based foreign language instruction with assessment practices. It is interesting to note that data from teacher and student interviews show that teachers' beliefs are not reflected in their practices.

In spite of teachers' stated commitment to the IPA approach, and students' impressive understanding of the assessment of the three communicative modes, the research findings indicate that the teachers did not implement a balanced assessment system that addresses all modes of communication equally. Since the teachers emphasize the assessment of interpretive reading and presentational writing and pay comparatively less attention to the assessment of interpretive listening and interpersonal and presentational speaking, it is obvious that the students' language development is also quite unbalanced. Further, the teachers' assessment practices frequently do not reflect their beliefs in a strong emphasis on developing interpretive listening and interpersonal speaking in introductory language classrooms. In other words, both quantitative and qualitative data indicate that these skills were assessed less frequently than other skills. Similarly, although teachers comment that presentational writing is the most challenging skill and should be introduced later, it actually represents almost one-third of all Level I assessments and as much as 55% of assessments in the Spanish I class.

The research also indicates that assessment practices are far from standardized, with observed variation in practices among teachers. The findings also support the earlier work by

Adair-Hauck, Glisan, Koda, Swender, and Sandrock (2006), which suggests that difficulties in finding age-appropriate authentic resources may result in teachers of novice language learners avoiding frequent assessment of their students' interpretive listening skills.

These findings highlight the logistical challenges related to time, space, lack of instructional resources, and lack of familiarity with various assessment strategies. They also set the stage for a second cycle in the process, involving continued department-wide professional development, collaborative work to develop new assessments and rubrics, implementation of those new assessments, continued data-gathering, and thoughtful self-analysis. As made evident in this study, the decision to adopt an IPA protocol represents a deep philosophical and pedagogical change.

Washback effect

As one of the goals of designing IPA is "to use the assessment to prompt curricular and instructional reform," Adair-Hauck et al. (2006) report that IPA has had a "washback effect" on teachers' classroom instruction. While implementing IPA, teachers also modify classroom instructions to enhance student performance by integrating three modes of communication on a regular basis, by designing more standards-based learning tasks using authentic materials and by measuring student performance and progress using standards-based rubrics. The findings indicate this washback effect by examining teachers' instructional practices during and after implementation of IPAs on instructional design and practice.

More recently, Martel (2019) explores the washback effect of IPA on instructors in an intensive summer language program at the tertiary level. The participants share ways in which the IPA has influenced their overall instructional practices, including what they chose to teach, how they taught it, the rate at which they taught it, their attitudes toward testing, their knowledge about language teaching and learning, their approach to preparing for teaching, and their feelings about their instruction. Overall, the findings indicate a positive washback of the IPA from the participants' perspectives, and the researcher points out that IPA can indeed "inform and improve the curriculum, teaching and learning practices beyond the test" (Adair-Hauck et al., 2013, p. 103) at postsecondary language programs.

The perspectives captured in this study are in agreement with many of those from Adair-Hauck et al. (2006). The participants in both studies feel generally good about the changes to their practices and thinking, which fall largely in line with the Standards. Participants in both studies have also experienced a similar consciousness-raising effect of the IPA, notably in setting forth intentions to add certain types of activities to their pedagogical repertoires. In terms of challenges, participants in both studies state that it has been difficult to convert the rubrics into letter grades. As a result, the researcher suggests that the creators of the IPA framework design feedback strategies.

Using washback as its principal lens, the present study captures evidence of positive washback of the IPA on teachers in the local summer language program, demonstrating that the IPA can be used to foster reform at the tertiary level, manifested in increased standards-based instruction. Furthermore, the study recommends longitudinal designs for studying the washback effect of the IPA to observe and reveal whether influences of the IPA on teachers' practices and cognitions endure over the long term and/or change over time, or even across instructional contexts. Thus, data collection should be done first, before IPA implementation; then during and after IPA implementation, it would be imperative to make sure actual changes or reforms take place.

Feedback and technology integration

The IPA model provides opportunities for students to demonstrate their ability to communicate around a specific theme across these three modes of communication while constantly having opportunities to receive feedback and improve. One core feature of the IPA, a feature that is also key to any formative assessment, is its emphasis on a "cyclical approach" to assessment, which combines continuous modeling, practice, performance, and feedback.[3] A "feedback loop," a key component of the framework, helps provide continuous feedback to learners throughout the assessment process (Glisan et al., 2003; Adair-Hauck, B., 2003, 2011; Adair-Hauck et al., 2013). For example, before they move on to the next task, students would receive feedback from the teacher on their performance with the first, interpretive, task. After completing the second task, the interpersonal task, they again receive feedback before continuing on to complete the IPA cycle with the presentational task. The presentational task provides more opportunities for feedback as students are engaged, in preparing for the task, and after they complete the task.

Adair-Hauck et al. (2013) stress that the feedback loop will be more beneficial and productive if the teacher provides cognitively challenging co-constructive feedback rather than explicit feedback. Since explicit feedback provides models for desired performance, where suggested improvements are based on those models, it does not allow for student participation (Wiggins, 1998). On the other hand, co-constructive feedback leads students to participate in a dialogic and bidirectional process through the teacher's assisting questions and cognitive probes, so they can self-assess, self-reflect, and self-regulate. Adair-Hauck et al. (2013) provide examples of co-constructive feedback samples in contrast to a model with explicit feedback.

Adair-Hauck and Troyan (2013) present a descriptive and co-constructive approach to feedback related to performance in the interpersonal mode of communication in the IPA. This study describes and analyzes the discursive features of effective IPA feedback, in which the teacher encourages the student, as a co-constructor, to do self-reflection and self-assessment following the different assessment criteria of the rubric. To this end, critical discourse analysis of a feedback session between a teacher and a student is presented. An example of an analysis of the teacher's questions shows that using the plural pronoun "we" instead of "I" or "us" instead of "me" signifies inclusiveness of the learner in the process of reflection or feedback.

Also, the co-constructive approach is descriptive, in contrast to evaluative or judgmental feedback, which research has shown to have little impact on performance (Wiggins, 1998, 2004). This study discusses how this type of descriptive feedback on detailed criteria, using "assisting questions" instead of "directives" or "commands," is more meaningful to learners and can lead to improved performances through self-reflection and self-assessment.

The feedback in IPA provides useful information to both the teacher and the learners regarding the kinds of authentic tasks the learners can perform across the three modes of communication and what the learners need to do to improve their language performance. Some instructors may initially be hesitant to implement IPA with a feedback loop because it takes more time than other approaches to assessment. For this project in Adair-Hauck and Troyan (2013), the teacher sometimes conducted feedback sessions in dyads while the other students were working on their IPA presentational tasks. This also suggests that peer feedback can offer valuable and efficient ways to implement the feedback loop after students become more familiar with IPA rubrics and more comfortable with self-assessment.

While the language used for feedback in this study is English for a wider audience, researchers note that some of the participants in this study are in favor of using the target language in portions of a co-constructed feedback session. They also hope the IPA feedback in this study convinces researchers, teachers, and teacher-trainers of the cognitive, social, and linguistic benefits of a descriptive and co-constructed approach to assessment. The data reveal that, through the use of well-attuned assisting questions, there is awareness and consciousness raised on the part of both the learner and the teacher.

As language teaching currently transitions to more remote virtual options, some research looks into the integration of technology into IPA implementation. While proposing Technology-Enhanced Performance Assessment (TIPA) by incorporating online discussion forums into IPA, Abraham and Williams (2009) explore the use of online discussion forums as a component of an IPA within a language curriculum. The study first examines the linguistic, discursive, and interactional versatility of discussion forums and then highlights the advantages of integrating discussion forms into a proposed TIPA. The authors present two models for incorporating the discussion form into a TIPA: either the interpretive or the interpersonal mode of communication for a theme-based unit on ecology and the environment. An analysis of the discourse in these models also illustrates the linguistic affordances this online communication environment offers for signaling participants' stances and attitudes through the use of pronouns, verb tense, aspect, and mood. TIPA offers a framework that would allow students to participate in these online environments for academic, professional, or personal reasons, while the authors also recommended integrating TIPA with offline collaborative tasks.

IPA in KSL

To date, IPA has rarely been adopted and implemented in KSL, and so has little research been reported on IPA in a KSL setting. Since different research findings in other languages support the evidence that IPA can measure students' progress in meeting the standards during ongoing classroom settings while also demonstrating the washback effect on instructional design and practice, resulting in seamless connection between learning outcomes and assessment, it is a viable option for a performance assessment in any KSL program across age groups, levels, and various institutional settings. Encouragingly, the implementation of IPA has been initiated in some postsecondary Korean programs in the United States for the last few years, and a few research studies regarding it are presented.

Kang (2016, 2022) reports that student performances in IPAs in a higher-level Korean course show correlations with their final oral proficiency gains after implementing two different IPAs during an intensive eight-week postsecondary Korean summer program. Following the original design and research model of IPA in Adair-Hauck et al. (2013), the two sets of IPAs were implemented in the third and sixth weeks of instruction during the eight-week intensive advanced Korean classes. When the initial course orientation was given to students, two sets of IPAs were introduced to them as part of the official assessment tools of one of four content courses. The course title was "Language and Society in Two Koreas," in which eight different topical areas of South and North Korean society were handled using authentic media materials. The rationale behind the IPAs were explained to students with a sample at the beginning of the course. They also were presented with learning objectives as well as rubrics for interpretive, interpersonal, and presentational tasks and performances, and were encouraged to plan for their own language improvement based on them.

Student performances are similar to those reported in Glisan et al. (2007) in that they generally performed better in the presentational mode than in the interpersonal mode. Students also confirmed that while they have often given oral presentations as their class assignments, they have never had spontaneous interpersonal interactions with their peers in their prior Korean learning experiences. Additionally, all student performances in the interpretive reading met expectations, while two students did not meet expectations with the interpretive listening in IPA1. Please see Appendix C for Korean IPA1.

These two students meet the advanced-level expectations minimally in IPA2, yet their performances are slightly lower than ones in the presentational and interpersonal modes. These findings are parallel to the data shown in both Glisan et al. (2007) and Davin et al. (2011) in which students' lower performances in listening indicate a lack of sufficient exposure to listening texts with proper strategies in their prior language classes. Students also confirmed later that they did not have enough experience in listening to authentic passages in their prior Korean learning experiences.

Students do not perform as well on the interpersonal tasks as on the presentational tasks, as Glisan et al. (2007) also found. Again, this is likely because students were not given enough opportunities for spontaneous interactions with each other. The authors also conjecture that this may stem from students' interaction with non-native speakers, i.e., their peers. Unlike OPIs, in which they interact with native or near-native speaking testers, students were disadvantaged by IPA's interpersonal communication with non-native speakers, who naturally lack native speakers' communication strategies. Despite the differences between native and non-native interlocutors, there seem to be correlations between student performances with interpersonal communication skills and their final OPI outcomes. Although the sample is quite small, student results show that interpersonal performances might be able to predict the final OPI ratings slightly better than performances in other communication modes.

Additionally, the students' own comments attest that IPAs have helped them identify weaknesses and improve their own learning. Students find that IPAs are very challenging at the beginning, but activities such as classroom debates, short essay writings, and oral presentations help them do better the second time. Two students even comment that IPA tasks seem more realistic than many other classroom activities. The majority of students also comment that understanding detailed course learning objectives and the rationale for IPAs at the beginning of the assessment genuinely help them understand where they are in terms of language performance and in what areas they need improvement. At the same time, they comment that IPAs have helped them have more confidence, especially in taking the second assessment. Since rubrics are quite detailed and the professor's feedback is individualized, students do experience a little difficulty in following some feedback questions and in initially providing their own self-reflection.

More recently, there has been a slight increase in the number of studies on IPAs in the field of KSL, which have been introduced and presented in conferences in the United States and Korea (Huh, 2020; Pyun, 2019; Shin & Moon, 2019). While Pyun (2019) and Shin and Moon (2019) make a partial introduction of the IPA prototype to the field in Korea, Huh (2020) reports actual implementation of IPAs in a postsecondary Korean program, as well as some findings from post-IPA questionnaires to students.

Huh (2020) reports that implementing the IPA in an existing postsecondary Korean language program in a college was quite feasible and well-received by the students. Student surveys show that they favored the IPA tasks over the old format of performance tasks, such as role plays, because they are more interesting, creative, and less stressful for not memorizing or preparing. The paper also discusses challenges, some of which are mirrored in prior studies: difficulty in finding age-appropriate, authentic materials for the intermediate-level college learners of Korean; challenges with less engaging students, who are less willing to communicate with others in discussions during the interpersonal tasks; and IPA rubrics, which are not user-friendly and might not be suitable for Korean use.

Pedagogical implications and future directions

Since the IPA prototype was first introduced almost two decades ago, many researchers and practitioners have designed, implemented, researched, and made local adjustments to the original prototype. And research findings have shown that this performance assessment model actually helps measure students' ongoing performance progresses effectively, based on detailed three-mode rubrics, and this model also raises students' metacognitive awareness of their own language learning. At the same time, participating students and teachers recognize the usefulness of IPA in measuring actual language performance beyond linguistic knowledge of the language and in connecting assessment with instruction, as well as with course learning objectives.

Consequently, the IPA helps teachers recognize what may be lacking in their classroom practices when providing feedback and grading student performance, and then they are able to adjust their lesson design or syllabus by incorporating activities to help students perform well in the IPA. At the same time, some negative teachers' attitudes may stem from misunderstandings of the basic principles of IPA and/or logistical burdens requiring more work on their end. To avoid possible rejection of IPA, many researchers recommend that instructors be given adequate pre-service and ongoing professional opportunities, time for IPA development and implementation, and involvement in decision-making for implementation of IPAs to execute them successfully.

Likewise, the data from post-IPA surveys show that IPA helps students gain metacognitive awareness of their own learning and their needs for communicative approaches beyond learning grammar and vocabulary. Most students seem to grasp the purpose of implementing such innovations in assessment practices and view the implementation positively; as such, they demand that teachers provide more authentic language texts as well as authentic language practices in classrooms. At the same time, other students may exhibit negative attitudes due to fear of academic failure. Researchers recommend that instructors inform students of the principles and rationale behind IPA, along with rubrics and expected learning outcomes before its implementation. Thus, students can identify their strengths and weaknesses by understanding the curricular design and how their instruction, learning, and assessment are all connected.

Additionally, the research on student performance indicates that students need more uniform exposure across all three communication modes with authentic language texts, whether they are spoken or written, to develop their language skills in a balanced way.

Overall, most research findings support the original purpose and goals of creating the IPA prototype. Researchers have identified data from student performances and responses to post-IPA surveys that support the idea that the IPA prototype measures student progress toward World Readiness Standards for Language Learning (The National Standards Collaboravie Board, 2015), and IPA also influences curricular and instructional design and practices. In that sense, IPA's positive washback effects on instruction bring about curricular and instructional reform, which themselves lead toward improvement in student proficiency.

Despite IPA's positive washback effects, postsecondary classrooms may be slow to embrace the IPA model for various logistical issues. The problem is not that teachers are not in favor of this type of assessment, but that even teachers who believe in a standards-based communicative approach to teaching and assessment still face challenges, such as limited resources with additional workload and large class sizes that can make implementing this approach difficult.

In particular, IPA has rarely been adopted and implemented in KSL classrooms, so little research has been reported on IPA in a KSL setting. Since a number of postsecondary KSL programs and their instructors have recently attempted to implement IPA, KSL should soon catch up with various studies in relation to IPA to join not only the community of performance assessment trends but also the movement to link learning, assessment, and student outcomes in higher education.[4]

At this point, it is legitimate to raise questions on the validity and reliability of IPA as one of the major assessment tools measuring learners' language ability. In fact, both Phillips (1996) and Colton et al. (1997) already noted their alarm at the many potential challenges in identifying validity and reliability of various performance assessments, even before IPAs were introduced into the field. The following statements indicate the complexity of validity and reliability of any performance assessment, including IPA.

> The authors argue that since "performance assessments promise potential benefits for teaching and learning, it is important to accrue evidence of such positive consequences as well as evidence that adverse consequences are minimal." The primary adverse consequence that should be investigated is the potential negative impact on individuals or groups derived from sources of invalidity such as construct underrepresentation or construct-irrelevant variance. In the former case, individuals may be scoring low because the assessment is missing something that best represents the construct. In the latter case, individuals may score low because the measurement process contains something irrelevant that interferes with the student's ability to demonstrate proficiency.
>
> *(Phillips, 1996, p. 3)*

> Validity and reliability issues relating to performance assessments have been much discussed, but further research and technical development is needed. For example, reliability with performance assessments has frequently been relegated to solely the agreement among the raters scoring the assessments. Although this is certainly an important component, it is not sufficient to ensure a reliable assessment.
>
> *(Harris, 1997, p. 2)*

As such, while there have been criticisms on the validity and reliability of performance and proficiency tests for the last few decades, there have also been quite a few research findings that report on the validity and reliability of OPIs based on mass quantitative data analysis. In spite of this evidence, proficiency tests such as OPI and WPT (Writing Proficiency Test) have gained more attention and users in higher education institutions, as well as federal government agencies and private sectors, not only due to statistically proven validity and reliability but also because of these institutions' agreement and endorsement of the criteria and systems. Similarly, performance tests are gaining more attention by the majority of practitioners, so research on their validity and reliability has been in high demand, despite the challenges of data collection. Although IPA gives flexibility to classroom teachers to adjust or create new tests to meet their needs, IPA also has more standardized requirements and rubrics. Thus, it would be beneficial to see more quantitative and qualitative research within one or more institutions that share the same IPA designs.

The following are additional suggestions for possible research topics that require further attention in the field of KSL. Since one of the main purposes of IPA is to measure student performance as it correlates to ongoing learning, further study is needed on the correlations between IPA results and students' course outcomes. Additionally, studies on IPA implementation issues and positives across a wider range of KSL program types, ranging from elementary to secondary to postsecondary, would provide a strong foundation upon which to establish further implementation in different KSL programs.

KSL would also benefit from further research and study reporting on learner and instructor attitudes and perceptions toward IPA and its impact on effective implementation, just as similar studies have been done in other language programs. One of the key features of IPA is giving feedback to students after each communicative task using rubrics, and there are several questions that would interest teachers and researchers and merit further study: What kinds of feedback strategies and types are more effective in helping students meet learning objectives? How effective are rubrics and their respective criteria? Are rubrics practical? Are there correlations between IPA results based on its own rubrics and student proficiency outcomes?

There is a need for research on the relationship between the National Standards and the IPA: To what extent are the 5Cs of the National Standards actually reflected in the IPA? What are the ways to measure the other four Cs other than communication in IPA? Do students' performances develop equally or differently across the three modes of communication? Are the three communication modes related to or separate from each other? Do any of these three develop more fully than the other two communication modes? Or do they develop equally?

From a practical standpoint, one hopes that more IPAs are developed and implemented in Korean to provide the basis for any KSL research on IPA. Furthermore, any reports and success stories of the IPA implementation process can be shared with the KSL community to introduce to them the IPA's principles and benefits. To further explore the question of whether it is easier or harder to implement IPA at the lower versus higher levels of KSL instruction, some possible related topics to research include selecting level-appropriate authentic texts, developing and implementing IPA across levels (Levels 1–5), and additional challenges encountered in implementing IPA. Ultimately, a large and varied collection of various IPAs and related research would provide an immense resource and benefit to teachers, who would be able to use already-created IPAs in their classrooms, as well as gather inspiration from existing research.

Concluding remarks

Wiggins (2004) notes that language educators need to spend less time assessing students' learning using traditional measures and more time encouraging learners to perform in the language and assisting those performances through educative feedback.

While traditional tests focus on measuring the understanding of linguistic forms, IPA intends to assess students' ability to perform various communicative tasks using such linguistic forms in real-life contexts. IPA serves as an exemplary model in demonstrating not only how research and practice can be more closely brought into line but also how standards-based classroom instruction and assessment practices can meet to form a seamless connection (Clementi & Terrill, 2013).

Furthermore, using "backward design," (Wiggins & McTighe, 2005) in which assessments guide instruction stressing the essential role of feedback (i.e., feedback loop), the IPA fosters a close link between learning and assessment practices, unlike traditional, non-contextualized assessments. IPA's cyclic model with continuous feedback strengthens students' gradual progress in language use. Although the benefits and viability of the IPA have been attested across languages and institutional settings, to date, it has been rarely implemented in KSL classroom settings (Huh, 2020; Kang, 2016).

As KSL continues to join the mainstream of standards-based instruction and assessment, moving toward more performance-based assessment practices like IPA that align with the current trend is no longer optional. Various research findings in different languages already report its immediate washback effect in language curricular design and instruction. It holds much promise for the future as our profession in KSL continues to advance in standards-based instruction and assessment.

Notes

1. It should be noted that the IPA Interpretive Comprehension Guide Template is provided for students to complete the interpretive tasks, starting from literal comprehension to interpretive comprehension. Instructors can use the template to create their own comprehension task.
2. Each communicative mode contains several different criteria listed in the table here. Please see Adair-Hauck, Glisan, and Troyan (2013) for detailed descriptions of different criteria.
3. IPA is designed to be used as a summative assessment; however, it also has characteristics of formative assessment for giving feedback to help students progress to the next step.
4. Rifkin (2019) states that the performance and proficiency assessment are probably the most powerful assessment form that serve as a model for many other liberal arts disciplines in the development and use of their own discipline-specific performance benchmarks and the development and implementation of curricula that foster the attainment of measurable student learning outcomes.

References

Abraham, L. B., & Williams, L. (2009). The discussion forum as a component of a technology- enhanced Integrated Performance Assessment. *Electronic Discourse in Language Learning and Language Teaching*, 25, 319.

ACTFL. (2012a). *ACTFL proficiency guidelines 2012*. Alexandria, VA: American Council on the Teaching of Foreign Languages. Retrieved from www.actfl.org/sites/default/files/guidelines/ACTFLProficiencyGuidelines2012.pdf

ACTFL. (2012b). *Performance descriptors for language learners 2012*. Alexandria, VA: American Council on the Teaching of Foreign Languages.

Adair-Hauck, B. (2003). Providing responsive assistance using the IPA feedback loop. In E. W. Glisan, B. Adair-Hauck, K. Koda, S. P. Sandrock, & E. Swender (Eds.), *ACTFL integrated performance assessment* (pp. 11–15). Yonkers, NY: ACTFL.

Adair-Hauck, B. (2011, February). *The IPA feedback loop: Assisting questions that foster self-assessment, self-reflection and self- regulation*. Presentation for the New Jersey Department of Education (Title VI Grant). Trenton.

Adair-Hauck, B., Glisan, E. W., Koda, K., Swender, E. B., & Sandrock, P. (2006). The integrated performance assessment (IPA): Connecting assessment to instruction and learning. *Foreign Language Annals*, 39, 359–382.

Adair-Hauck, B., Glisan, E. W., & Troyan, F. (2013). *Implementing integrated performance assessment*. Alexandria, VA: American Council on the Teaching of Foreign Languages.

Adair-Hauck, B., & Troyan, F. J. (2013). A descriptive and co-constructive approach to Integrated Performance Assessment feedback. *Foreign Language Annals*, 46, 23–44.

CARLA, University of Minnesota, Integrated Performance Assessment. Retrieved from https://carla.umn.edu/assessment/vac/CreateUnit/p_2.html

Clementi, D., & Terrill, L. (2013). *The keys to planning for learning: Effective curriculum, unit, and lesson design*. Alexandria, VA: American Council on the Teaching of Foreign Languages.

Colton, D. A., Gao, X., Harris, D. J., Kolen, M. J., Wang, D. M., & Welch, C. J. (1997). *Reliability issues with performance assessments A collection of papers*. ACT Research Report Series, Iowa City, IA: ACT Inc.

Davin, K., Troyan, F. J., Donato, R., & Hellman, A. (2011). Research on the integrated performance assessment in an early foreign language learning program. *Foreign Language Annals*, 44, 605–625.

Eddy, J., & Bustamante, C. (2020). Closing the pre and in-service gap: Perceptions and implementation of the IPA during student teaching. *Foreign Language Annals*, 53, 634–656.

Glisan, E. W., Adair-Hauck, B., Koda, K., Sandrock, S. P., & Swender, E. (2003). *ACTFL integrated performance assessment*. Yonkers, NY: American Council on the Teaching of Foreign Languages.

Glisan, E. W., Uribe, D., & Adair-Hauck, B. (2007). Research on integrated performance assessment at the post-secondary level: Student performance across the modes of communication. *Canadian Modern Language Review*, 64(1), 39–67.

Harris, D. J. (1997). Using reliability to make decisions. In Colton et al. (Eds.), *Reliability issues with performance assessments: A collection of papers* (pp. 1–12). ACT Research Report Series. Iowa City, IA: ACT, Inc.

Huh, S. (2020). Implementation of the Integrated Performance Assessment (IPA) in U.S. post-secondary Korean language classrooms-focusing on learner's experiences, perceptions, and attitudes towards the IPA. *Journal of Korean Language Education, 31*(1), 241–272.

Kang, S. (2016). Linking assessment and learning via performance and proficiency assessment, *International Journal of Korean Language Education, 2*(2), 97–123.

Kang, S. (in press). Towards integrated performance assessment. In S. Cho & J. Whitman (Eds.), *The Cambridge handbook of Korean linguistics* (pp. 769–779). Cambridge: Cambridge University Press.

Kissau, S., & Adams, M. J. (2016). Instructional decision making and IPAs: Assessing the modes of communication. *Foreign Language Annals, 49*(1),105–123.

Martel, J. (2019). Washback of ACTFL's Integrated Performance Assessment in an intensive summer language program at the tertiary level. *Language Education & Assessment, 2*, 57–69.

Martel, J., & Bailey, K. M. (2016). Exploring the trajectory of an educational innovation: Instructors' attitudes toward IPA implementation in a postsecondary intensive summer language program. *Foreign Language Annals, 49*(3), 530–543.

The National Standards Collaborative Board. (2015). *World-readiness standards for learning languages*. Alexandria, VA: Author.

Phillips, G. W. (Ed.). (1996). *Technical issues in large-scale performance assessment*. Washington, DC: National Center for Education Statistics.

Pyun, D. (2019). Assessment of Korean oral achievement. In *Proceedings of the annual conference of the International Association of Korean Language Education* (pp. 680–686). Seoul: International Association of Korean Language Education.

Rifkin, B. (2019). The power of performance-based assessment: Languages as a model for the liberal arts enterprise. In P. Winke & S. M. Gass (Eds.), *Foreign language proficiency in higher education* (pp. 15–21). Boston, MA: Springer.

Sandrock, P. (2010). *The keys to assessing language performance: A teacher's manual for measuring student progress*. Alexandria, VA: American Council on the Teaching of Foreign Languages.

Schenck, S. M. (2019). Integrated performance assessments: A review of the literature and steps to move forward. *Spanish and Portuguese Review, 5*, 105–117.

Shin, H. Y., & Moon, J. (2019). An Integrated Performance Assessment (IPA) model by language proficiency for Korean classes. In *Proceedings of the annual conference of the International Association of Korean Language Education* (pp. 831–834). Seoul: International Association of Korean Language Education.

Wiggins, G. (1998). *Educative assessment*. San Francisco, CA: Jossey-Bass.

Wiggins, G. (2004). *More feedback on real tasks: Less evaluation based on audits only*. Retrieved from www.grantwiggins.org/documents/E&H.pdf

Wiggins, G., & McTighe, J. (2005). *Understanding by design* (Expanded 2nd ed.). Alexandria, VA: ASCD.

Zapata, G. C. (2016). University students' perceptions of Integrated Performance Assessment and the connection between classroom learning and assessment. *Foreign Language Annals, 49*(1), 93–104.

APPENDIX A
Sample IPA overview

Advanced level

'Role of open market in North Korea'

You have been studying recent changes in North Korea's markets, which are considered to be a sign of opening the closed economy and society of the country. You will listen to a related interview where North Korean defectors testified that North Korea is already transitioning to a market economy internally. In addition, you can do related research on your own and eventually will plan for a presentation to North Korean defector students in our weekly exchange program.

First, you will listen to an interview with young North Korean defectors regarding their experiences in North Korea's open market. Then, you will discuss with a partner its positive and negative impact on North Korean society, exploring the possible impact on South Korea as well as South and North Korean relationships. Finally, you will make a presentation on "Would North Korea open its doors in the near future?" or "What are things we can do to accelerate the opening of North Korea's doors?" during the weekly exchange program with North Korean students living in South Korea.

*Please note that Appendix C shows the sample Korean IPA following this overview.

APPENDIX B
IPA rubrics

(Adair-Hauck, Glisan, & Troyan, 2013, pp. 127–135).
Interpretive Mode Rubric–A continuum of performance*

Criteria	Exceeds Expectations	Meets Expectations		Does Not Meet Expectations
	Accomplished Comprehension (4)**	Strong Comprehension (3)	Minimal Comprehension (2)	Limited Comprehension (1)
LITERAL COMPREHENSION				
Word recognition	Identifies all key words appropriately within context of the text	Identifies majority of key words appropriately within context of the text	Identifies half of key words appropriately within context of the text	Identifies a few of key words appropriately within context of the text
Main idea detection	Identifies the complete main idea(s) of the text	Identifies the key parts of the main idea(s) of the text but misses some elements	Identifies some part of the main idea(s) of the text	May identify some ideas from the text but they do not represent the main idea(s)
Supporting detail detection	Identifies all supporting details in the text and accurately provides information from the text to explain these details	Identifies the majority of supporting details in the text and provides information from the text to explain some of these details	Identifies some supporting details in the text and may provide limited information from the text to explain these details. Or Identifies the majority of supporting details but is unable to provide information from the text to explain these details	Identifies a few supporting details in the text but may be unable to provide information from the text to explain these details

INTERPRETIVE COMPREHENSION

Category	(Strong)			(Weak)
Organizational features	Identifies the organizational feature(s) of the text and provides an appropriate rationale	Identifies the organizational feature(s) of the text; rationale misses some key points	Identifies in part the organizational feature(s) of the text; rationale may miss some key points. Or Identifies the organizational feature(s) but rationale is not provided.	Attempts to identify the organizational feature(s) of the text but is not successful
Guessing meaning from context	Infers meaning of unfamiliar words and phrases in the text. Inferences are accurate.	Infers meaning of unfamiliar words and phrases in the text. Most inferences are plausible, although some may not be accurate.	Infers meaning of unfamiliar words and phrases in the text. Most inferences are plausible, although many are not accurate.	Inferences of meaning of unfamiliar words and phrases are largely inaccurate or lacking.
Inferences (reading/listening/viewing between the lines)	Infers and interprets the text's meaning in a highly plausible manner	Infers and interprets the text's meaning in a partially complete and/or partially plausible manner	Makes a few plausible inferences regarding the text's meaning	Inferences and interpretations of the text's meaning are largely incomplete and/or not plausible
Author's perspective	Identifies the author's perspective and provides a detailed justification	Identifies the author's perspective and provides a justification	Identifies the author's perspective but justification is either inappropriate or incomplete	Unable to identify the author's perspective
Cultural perspectives	Identifies cultural perspectives/ norms accurately. Provides a detailed connection of cultural products/practices to perspectives.	Identifies some cultural perspectives/ norms accurately. Connects cultural products/ practices to perspectives.	Identifies cultural perspectives/ norms accurately. Provides a minimal connection of cultural products/practices to perspectives.	Identification of cultural perspectives/ norms is mostly superficial or lacking. And/or connection of cultural products/ practices to perspectives is superficial or lacking.

Evidence of Strength Examples of Where You Could Improve

*The Interpretive Rubric is designed to show the continuum of performance for both literal and interpretive comprehension for language learners regardless of language level. See *Implementing Integrated Performance Assessment*, Chapter 2 for suggestions on how to use this rubric to assign a score or grade.

Interpersonal Mode Rubric–Advanced Learner**

Criteria	Exceeds Expectations	Meets Expectations		Does Not Meet Expectations
	(4 points)*	Strong (3 points)	Minimal (2 points)	(1 point)
Language function Language tasks the speaker is able to handle in a consistent comfortable, sustained, and spontaneous manner	Narrates and describes fully and accurately in all major time frames. Can discuss some topics abstractly, especially those related to particular interests and expertise. May provide a structured argument to support opinions and may construct hypotheses.	Consistently and extensively narrates and describes in all major time frames by providing a full account. Participates actively in most informal and some formal conversations on a variety of concrete topics and topics relating to events of current, public, and personal interest. Can handle successfully and with ease on an unexpected turn of events or complication.	Consistently narrates and describes in all major time frames. Able to participate in most informal and some formal conversations on familiar topics, which may include current events, employment, and matters of public interest. Can handle appropriately an unexpected turn of events or complication.	Handles successfully uncomplicated tasks and social situations requiring exchange of basic information related to work, school, recreation, particular interests, and areas of competence. Narrates and describes in all major time frames, although not consistently.
Text type Quantity and organization of language discourse	Uses paragraph-length discourse and some extended discourse	Uses connected, paragraph-length discourse	Uses connected sentences and paragraph-length discourse	Uses mostly connected sentences and some paragraph-like discourse
Communication strategies Quality of engagement and interactivity, how one participates in conversation and advances it; strategies for negotiating meaning in the face of breakdown of communication	Converses with ease, confidence, and competence. Maintains, advances, and/or redirects conversation. Demonstrates confident use of communicative strategies, such as paraphrasing, circumlocution, and illustration.	Converses with ease and confidence. Maintains and advances conversation. Uses communicative strategies, such as rephrasing and circumlocution.	Maintains conversation. May use communicative strategies, such as rephrasing and circumlocution.	Converses with ease and confidence when dealing with routine tasks and social situations. May clarify by paraphrasing.
Comprehensibility Who can understand this person's language? Can this person be understood only by sympathetic listeners used to interacting with non-natives? Can a native speaker unaccustomed to non-native speech understand this speaker?	Is readily understood by native speakers unaccustomed to interacting with non-natives	Is readily understood by native speakers unaccustomed to interacting with non-natives	Is understood by native speakers, even those unaccustomed to interacting with non-natives, although this may require some repetition or restatement	Is generally understood by those unaccustomed to interacting with non-natives, although interference from another language may be evident and gaps in communication may occur.

Language control Grammatical accuracy, appropriate vocabulary, degree of fluency, sociolinguistic appropriateness	Demonstrates full control of aspect in narration in present, past, and future time. Uses precise vocabulary and intonation, great fluency, and ease of speech. Accuracy may break down when attempting to perform complex tasks associated with the superior level over a variety of topics.	Demonstrates good control of aspect in narrating in present, past, and future time. Has substantial fluency and extensive vocabulary. The quality and/or quantity of speech generally declines when attempting to perform functions or handle topics associated with the superior level.	Demonstrates minimal fluency and some control of aspect in narrating in present, past, and future time. Vocabulary may lack specificity. Speech decreases in quality and quantity when attempting to perform functions or handle topics associated with the superior level.	Demonstrates significant quality and quantity of intermediate-level language. When attempting to perform advanced-level tasks, there is breakdown in one or more of the following areas: the ability to narrate and describe, use of paragraph-length discourse, fluency, and breadth of vocabulary.

Evidence of Strength Examples of Where You Could Improve

*The scoring criteria for Interpersonal and Presentational Rubrics are aligned with both the performance domains in the ACTFL Performance Descriptors for Language Learners (2012a) and the assessment criteria in the ACTFL Proficiency Guidelines (2012b). Thus, the rubrics describe a range of performance across different levels, from novice to advanced. Please see Adair-Hauck, Glisan, and Troyan (2013, pp. 127–135) for all different level rubrics.

Presentational Rubric–Advanced Learner

Criteria	Exceeds Expectations	Meets Expectations		Does Not Meet Expectations
	(4 points)*	Strong (3 points)	Minimal (2 points)	(1 point)
Language function Language tasks the speaker/writer is able to handle in a consistent comfortable, sustained, and spontaneous manner	Narrates and describes fully and accurately in all major time frames. Can discuss some topics abstractly, especially those related to particular interests and expertise. May provide a structured argument to support opinions and may construct hypotheses.	Consistently and extensively narrates and describes in all major time frames by providing a full account. Able to communicate on a variety of concrete topics and topics relating to events of current, public, and personal interest.	Consistently narrates and describes in all major time frames. Able to communicate on familiar topics, which may include current events, employment, and matters of public interest.	Handles successfully uncomplicated tasks and social situations requiring exchange of basic information related to work, school, recreation, particular interests, and areas of competence. Narrates and describes in all major time frames, although not consistently.
Text type Quantity and organization of language discourse [continuum: word-phrase-sentence-connected sentences-paragraph-extended discourse]	Uses paragraph-length discourse and some extended discourse	Uses connected, paragraph-length discourse	Uses connected sentences and paragraph-length discourse	Uses mostly connected sentences and some paragraph-like discourse

(Continued)

(Continued)

Criteria	Exceeds Expectations (4 points)*	Meets Expectations Strong (3 points)	Minimal (2 points)	Does Not Meet Expectations (1 point)
Impact Clarity, organization, and depth of presentation; degree to which presentation maintains attention and interest of audience.	Presented in a clear and organized manner. Presentation illustrates originality, rich details, and an unexpected feature that captures interest and attention of audience.	Presented in a clear and organized manner. Presentation illustrates originality and features rich details, visuals, and/or organization of the text to maintain audience's attention and/or interest.	Presented in a clear and organized manner. Some effort to maintain audience's attention through visuals, organization of the text, and/or details.	Presentation may be either unclear or unorganized. Minimal to no effort to maintain audience's attention.
Comprehensibility Who can understand this person's language? Can this person be understood only by sympathetic listeners used to interacting with non-natives? Can a native speaker unaccustomed to non-native speech/writing understand this speaker/writer?	Is readily understood by native speakers unaccustomed to the speaking/writing of non-natives	Is readily understood by native speakers unaccustomed to the speaking/writing of non-natives	Is understood by native speakers, even those unaccustomed to the speaking/writing of non-natives, although this may require some additional effort	Is generally understood by those unaccustomed to the speaking/writing of non-natives, although interference from another language may be evident and gaps in comprehension may occur
Language control Grammatical accuracy, appropriate vocabulary, degree of fluency	Demonstrates full control of aspect in narration in present, past, and future time. Uses precise vocabulary and intonation, great fluency, and ease of speech. Accuracy may break down when attempting to perform complex tasks associated with the superior level over a variety of topics.	Demonstrates good control of aspect in narrating in present, past, and future time. Has substantial fluency and extensive vocabulary. The quality and/or quantity of language generally declines when attempting to perform functions or handle topics associated with the superior level.	Demonstrates minimal fluency and some control of aspect in narrating in present, past, and future time. Vocabulary may lack specificity. Language decreases in quality and quantity when attempting to perform functions or handle topics associated with the superior level.	Demonstrates significant quality and quantity of intermediate-level language. When attempting to perform advanced-level tasks, there is breakdown in one or more of the following areas: the ability to narrate and describe, use of paragraph-length discourse, fluency, and breadth of vocabulary.

Evidence of Strength Examples of Where You Could Improve

APPENDIX C
Sample Korean IPA (advanced learner)

1 독해/해석 과제: 7월 6일 월요일 11:00–12:00시, 끝난 후 워드파일을 '과제'에 올려 주세요. (캔버스의 '과제' 페이지에 올립니다.)
지금까지 공부한 북한의 "장마당"을 더 이해하기 위해서 주어진 인터뷰를 듣겠습니다. 첫번째 듣기자료는 최근 탈북한 두 사람이 장마당이 생기게 된 배경과 자기들의 경험을 이야기하고 있습니다. 자세히 듣고, "독해/해석 문제"들에 쓸 수 있는 만큼 답을 쓰십시오.

2.말하기 (토론 과제): 7월 8일 수요일 4교시 비대면 (토론을 녹음해서 캔버스의 과제 페이지에 올립니다.)
'해석과제'를 끝낸 후에 받은 피드백과 다른 매체에서 찾은 뉴스나 글들을 바탕으로 "북한의 대외개방이 가능한가"에 대한 토론을 준비하십시오. 수요일 4교시에 두명씩 짝이 되어 자신의 의견을 처음에 2–3분씩 이야기하고, 다른 사람의 의견을 듣습니다. 그 후, 서로의 의견에 동의하는지, 반대하는지, 그리고 왜 그런지를 근거를 들어서 다시 2–3분씩 토론하겠습니다. 토론중에 자신의 생각과 의견을 논리적으로 정확하게 표현해 주십시오. 토론은 전체 15분을 넘지 않아야 합니다. 토론을 녹음해서 캔버스의 과제: 수행능력 평가1에 올려 주세요.

2 발표 과제: 7월 10일 대면, 금요일 3교시 (발표전체를 줌으로 녹음합니다.)
지금까지 읽고, 듣고, 토론하고 피드백을 받은 내용을 바탕으로, "북한의 대외개방 가능한가," 또는 "북한의 대외개방을 위해 우리가 할 수 있는 일"이라는 주제로 3교시에 각자 발표 준비를 하겠습니다. 준비중에는 인터넷 자료들을 참고해도 좋고, 다른 학생들이나 선생님한테 질문해도 좋습니다. 금요일 3교시에 준비한 내용을 바탕으로 5분씩 각자 발표하겠습니다. 한 학생이 발표하는 동안 잘 듣고 관련된 질문을 반드시 한 개씩 해 주십시오.

27
INTERACTIONAL COMPETENCE IN KOREAN AND ITS ASSESSMENT

Hyo Sang Lee, Kyung-Eun Yoon, and Sang-Seok Yoon

Introduction

It is now a cliche to say that learning a language is not just learning its vocabulary and linguistic structure but should be more like learning its use in communication. Therefore, the goal of language instruction is to foster learners' communicative competence (Hymes, 1972). Communication is a social activity for which language is its primary tool and is thus interactional in nature (Gumperz, 1982). For this reason, Kramsch (1986) redefines communicative competence as interactional competence (IC) and emphasizes that language ability must ultimately be measured for IC, criticizing the proficiency-oriented practices represented in the ACTFL proficiency guidelines and Oral Proficiency Interview (OPI). Despite that virtually all language instructors aspire to a communicative approach, interactional components of language use are still not much in focus in language pedagogy, particularly in Korean language education.

Canale and Swain (1980) divide communicative competence into four subtypes: (i) grammatical competence or linguistic competence (knowledge on linguistic structure and vocabulary), (ii) sociolinguistic competence (knowledge on proper use of the language in various social settings and contexts, including who you speak to and about), (iii) discourse competence (knowledge on how to produce coherent and cohesive utterances and texts beyond the sentence level), and (iv) strategic competence (knowledge on how to monitor and modulate in collaboration and negotiation of "intended, perceived, and anticipated meanings" [Kramsch, 1986] to communicate successfully). Although Kramsch (1986) uses interactional competence to refer to overall language ability, IC in a literal sense encompasses Canale and Swain's sociolinguistic and strategic competence.

The concept of IC has been further developed by many scholars. He and Young (1998) attempt to define it in terms of how to best assess language learners' speaking ability, presenting a set of resources for learners to aptly bring to practices in the given interactional contexts to exhibit IC in their speech. The resources include knowledge of rhetorical scripts, a turn-taking system, topic management, and recognition of boundaries between various speech activities. They emphasize that IC is not a learner's knowledge within his/her individual realm but his/her ability to co-construct the interaction with another participant through interactive practices.

Conversation analysis (CA) has inspired scholars such as Kasper (2006) and Young (2008) to explicate the notion of IC further. Since CA research examines orderliness of conversation as the most basic mode of interaction or "primordial site of sociality" (Schegloff, 1986, p. 112), CA has vast implications for language teaching and learning. That is, findings of CA research on how actions are constructed through linguistic resources and how such actions are managed interactionally and sequentially provide more specific and systematic characteristics of IC. Adopting the CA approach into second language acquisition, Kasper (2006, p. 86) defines IC as the following abilities:

- to understand and produce social actions in their sequential contexts;
- to take turns at talk in an organized fashion;
- to format actions and turns, and construct epistemic and affective stances (Ochs, 1996) by drawing on different types of semiotic resources (linguistic, nonverbal, nonvocal), including register-specific resources;
- to repair problems in speaking, hearing, and understanding;
- to co-construct social and discursive identities through sequence organization, actions-in-interaction, and semiotic resources (Goffman, 1981; Zimmerman, 1998); and
- to recognize and produce boundaries between activities.

Similarly, Wong and Waring (2010) acknowledge the contribution of CA to language teaching and explicate interactional practices that compose IC as follows:

> Turn-taking practices lie at the base because a turn is the most elementary unit of conversation; two or more turns are connected in sequencing practices to accomplish social actions such as complimenting, complaining, or story-telling; sequences can then be brought together in overall structuring practices to organize a conversation, as in openings and closings; repair practices filter throughout the entire system by targeting problems of speaking, hearing, or understanding of the talk (p. 8).

Such descriptions of interactional practices are important in studies that advocate the integration of IC as a target construct in language assessment. Burch and Kley (2020) note a fundamental function of IC as achieving and maintaining intersubjectivity and thus argue for the incorporation of intersubjectivity as a ratable construct in language assessment. To assess how learners make publicly visible their understanding of each other through subsequent actions, they examine how learners construct their turns for the degree to which they build upon prior talk and display stances toward that talk in an observable fashion. The specific practices Burch and Kley use are as follows (pp. 28–29):

- Providing a conditionally relevant (Schegloff & Sacks, 1973) or "contingent" (Lam, 2018) next turn, as in a second-pair part in an adjacency pair (i.e., answering a question, responding to a request, et cetera);
- Initiating repair (either on one's own talk or on their interlocutor's prior talk);
- Providing responses that are not necessarily made conditionally relevant or are less constrained by adjacency. These types of responses, to varying degrees, display the participants' alignment and affiliation (Stivers, 2008) with each other. For instance,
  - Continuers (Schegloff, 1982) and minimal receipt tokens such as "mm" (Gardner, 2001) which pass up the floor and often do not display understanding or stance,

although these can be laminated through the use of intonational features or facial expressions.
- Minimal assessments such as "good" (Schegloff, 2007) or newsmarkers (Gardner, 2001) such as "really," which can display stance, although the strength of this stance is dependent upon the type and the intonational and embodied resources used.
- Non-minimal assessments, usually through longer turns which display a greater understanding or stance toward the prior talk and thus can show a degree of alignment with the ongoing action and affiliation and display 'substantive recipiency' (Lam, 2018; Waring, 2002).
- Non-minimal expansions (Schegloff, 2007), including questions that are tied to the previous talk, which display how the participant has understood the prior talk.

Roever and Kasper (2018) also emphasize the importance of assessing learners' IC and criticize a variety of commonly administered tests, noting that they do not address interactional components as key criteria of assessment. Even though the ACTFL proficiency guidelines (2012) make sporadic references to some interactional components,[1] Roever and Kasper (2018) point out that even tests such as IELTS Speaking or the ACTFL OPI, which use a face-to-face format, do "not emphasize the measurement of interactional abilities but uses the interaction primarily as an elicitation tool to obtain a ratable sample of spoken language" (p. 332), not to measure language use embedded in social interaction.

This chapter is to illustrate how those interactional features or practices are manifested in Korean (Section 2) and how L2 Korean learners in different proficiency levels manage them (Section 3) and to propose preliminary criteria for assessing learners' level-appropriate interactional competence (Section 4).

Interactional features in Korean from a conversation-analytic perspective

Communication is composed of a series of social actions that are conducted in orderly and sequential manners. As previously briefed, conversation analysis provides a set of conceptual tools with which these orderly and sequential social actions are identified and described. Let us explain these key concepts mentioned earlier with Korean examples.

First, an adjacency pair is a sequence of two relevant utterances that are produced by different speakers and ordered as a first part and a second part (Levinson, 1983). The two utterances are relevant because a particular first-pair part requires a particular second, e.g., a greeting requires a greeting, a question seeks for an answer, an offer or a suggestion makes an acceptance or rejection relevant as a second, stating an opinion is responded by an agreement or a disagreement, etc., as in the following examples:

Adjacency pair:

(1) [Suggestion and acceptance: Family lunch]

    A: 밥 먹자.
        pap mek-ca
        "Let's eat?"
    B: 음.
        um.
        "Okay."

(2) [Adjacency pair: Stating opinion and agreement: Office lunch]

    A: 불고기 같은 거는 달아야 맛있잖아
       pwulkoki kath-un ke-nun tal-aya masiss-canha-a
       "Things like *pwulkoki* are delicious only when they are sweet, right"
    B: 음:. 갈비도 그렇구.
       u:m. kalpi-to kuleh-kwu.
       "Yea:h. So is *kalpi*."

Certain adjacency pairs, such as Excerpt (1), or that of question and answer are clear examples that can be easily taught and learned at the beginning level. On the other hand, the relevance between the first-pair part and the second-pair part is not as explicit in other types of adjacency pairs, such as Excerpt (2), or that of stating opinion and agreement, which might be more difficult to learn at the beginning or intermediate level.

Repair is a term for a range of practices managing various types of troubles in producing self-utterances or understanding others' utterances in conversation (Schegloff, Jefferson, & Sacks, 1977). Excerpt (3) is an example of self-initiated self-repair through which a speaker solves a problem in searching for a word and producing it.

Self-repair:

(3) [Two friends]

    A: 그리구 그:거 있잖아. 뭐야 (.) 그 (.) 높은 거 아치.
       kulikwu **ku:-keiss-canh-a. mwe-ya** (.) *ku* (.) **noph-un ke achi**.
       "Also there is **tha:t thing**, you know. **What is it** (.) That (.) **the tall thing. The arch**."

The speaker is talking about her trip to St. Louis and trying to mention the famous arch. She could not come up with the target word, *achi* [아치] (arch), at first and therefore holds the place of the word in the first sentence with *ku:-ke* [그거] (that thing) and specifies it with *noph-un ke* [높은 거] (the tall thing) at the second attempt. Then, she completes repairing the two noun phrases with the searched-for word *achi* [아치] at the end of the utterance. This self-repair process involves multiple resources, such as a demonstrative phrase (*ku:-ke* [그거]), an explicit self-repair-initiating expression (*mwe-ya* [뭐야] [what is it or whatchamacallit]), a hesitation marker in a demonstrative format (*ku* [그] [that]), and multiple pauses. Of these resources, demonstratives are found to be frequently and systematically used as hesitation markers or placeholders for upcoming referents in repair practices in Korean (Yoon, 2003). The use of demonstratives as hesitation markers may be relatively easy to learn because their linguistic forms do not have systematic variations, while demonstratives as placeholders will be more difficult to learn due to the systematic variations of the linguistic forms.

Excerpt (4) shows a case of other-initiated repair (OIR) utilizing *u:m* [음:]? (Hu:h?). With the repair-initiator in line 2, B displays his trouble understanding A's previous utterance, and thereby A repeats his utterance again in line 3.

Other-initiated repair:

(4) [Friends' gathering]

    1 A: 아이 속 거북한데.
              ai sok kepwukha-ntey.
              "Ah I feel uncomfortable in my stomach."

2→ B: 음:?
       u:m?
       "Hu:h?"
       (1.0)
3   A: s: hh 속 거북한데(h).
       s:: hh sok kepwukha-ntey(h).
       "s: hh I feel uncomfortable in my stomach(h)."

The linguistic resource that is most utilized for OIR in Korean is the group of affirmative response tokens with a rising intonation, such as *e*? [어?], *um*? [음?], *ung*? [응?], *yey*? [예?], and *ney*? [네?] (Kim, 1999a; Yoon, 2010). Another type of OIR is *mwe*? [뭐? (what?)], whose function is not merely to ask for clarification of a trouble-source per se, but to display a disaffiliative stance toward the targeted utterance or the action as a whole (Kim, 1999a). Other practices for OIR in Korean include a question word (e.g., *nwukwu* [누구 (who)]), a question word with partial repeat of the trouble-source turn (*eti-eyse mek-e*? [어디에서 먹어? (Eat where?)]), and a quotative construction (*eti-eyse mek-ess-ta-ko*? [어디에서 먹었다고? (Where did you say you ate?)]).

Other-initiated repairs are often done through a repeat of the trouble source of the preceding utterance, as in the following example:

(5) [Excerpt from an interview of a heritage learner (JJ) by a native speaker]
1   IR: 취미는 뭐가 있나요?
         chwimi-nun mwe-ka iss-na-yo?
         "What hobby do you have?"
2→ JJ: 취미요?
         chwimi-yo ?
         "A hobby?"
3   IR: 네.
         ney.
         "Yeah."
4   JJ: 취미는 여러가지 있는데::
         chwimi-nun yele-kaci iss-nuntey::
         "I have several hobbies, bu::t,"

A continuer is a small token through which a listener indicates his/her understanding of the current speaker's talk in progress and signals the speaker to continue talking (Schegloff, 1982). Whereas a continuer typically occurs at sentential unit boundaries in English conversation, Korean speakers often produce continuers at phrasal unit boundaries (Kim, 1999b; Kim & Yoon, 2021), as shown in the following example:

Continuer:

(6) [Office lunch]
1   A: 파는 피자는,
         pha-nun phica-nun,
         "As for ((frozen)) pizzas they sell,"
2→ B: 음.
         um.
         "Uh huh."

3   A: 쫌 비싸면 비쌀 수록 낫긴 난 거 같아요.
         ccom pissa-myen pissa-l swulok nas-ki-n na-n ke kath-ayo.
         "It seems that they are indeed better if they are more expensive."

A minimal receipt token is a passive acknowledgment token through which a listener simply confirms their hearing of the prior turn (Gardner, 2001). While it is commonly done through "okay" in English, it is done through affirmative response expressions in Korean, such as *um* [음] or *yey* [예] (Pyun & Yoon, forthcoming), as in Excerpt (7).

Minimal receipt token/acknowledgment token:

(7) [Father–son conversation]

   1   A: 뭐 필요한 거 있으세요?
            mwe philyoha-n ke iss-usey-yo?
            "Is there anything you need?"
   2   B: 난 필요한 거 없어:.
            na-n philyoha-n ke eps-e:.
            "There is nothing I need."
   3→ A: 음.
            um.
            "Okay."

Another type of response token expressing listenership is a newsmark token (Gardner, 2001). It typically accompanies a change-of-state token, such as *oh* in English (Heritage, 1984), which is done through *a* [아] or affirmative response expressions often with vowel lengthening and a dynamic rising-falling intonation contour in Korean (Pyun & Yoon, forthcoming). Such a newsmark token can be considered to display a higher degree of listenership than a continuer and a minimal receipt/acknowledgment token as shown in Excerpt (7). Excerpt (8) shows an example of a change-of-state token *a* [아 (Oh)] combined with a more explicit newsmark expression, *kulay-ss-eyo?* [그랬어요? (Did they? [lit. Was it so?])].

Newsmark:

(8) [Friends' gathering]

   1   A: 그 건물에 있는 사람들이 다 시도했다가 다 실패했거든.
            ku kenmwul-ey iss-nun salam-tul-i ta sitohay-ss-taka ta silphayhay-ss-ketun.
            "Everyone in that building tried and all of them failed, you know."
   2→ B: 아 그랬어요?
            a kulay-ss-eyo?
            "Oh, did they?"

A continuer, an acknowledgement token, and a newsmark token have a function of providing alignment in conversation. Stivers, Mondada, and Steensig (2011) explain alignment as something the listener provides by "facilitating the proposed activity or sequence, accepting the presuppositions and terms of the proposed action or activity" (p. 21). Their explanation on alignment emphasizes that alignment is interactional cooperation regarding the structure of the talk, meaning it helps the ongoing talk to progress. Since a continuer and a newsmark token help the primary speaker's ongoing talk to proceed, they provide alignment. An acknowledgement token can also be considered to show a type of aligning function since it helps the sequence in progress continue to the next step. For example, an affirmative response token (*um*. [음.]) in Excerpt (7) is produced after the second-pair part in the question-answer adjacency pair. This affirmative response token in the third position not only acknowledges the answer but also proposes a closure of the sequence (Schegloff, 2007), so the participants can continue to the next sequence in talk.

In addition to alignment, Stivers et al. (2011) explain affiliation as another form of interactional cooperation. Whereas alignment is a support at the structural level, affiliation is "the affective level of cooperation" (p. 21), meaning that affiliative responses express support by showing the same evaluative stance and empathy toward the other speaker. An example of an affiliative action that can be done through a response token is an agreement. An agreement can be expressed through either a small response token or an extended turn or both. Korean response tokens performing agreement include affirmative response expressions (Pyun & Yoon, forthcoming) and "*mac-a-yo/kuleh-cy-o* [맞아요/그렇죠 (Right)]" (Lee, Yoon, & Yoon, 2017). In Excerpt (9), B produces *u:m.*, which would have been a sufficient action to express her agreement. However, B further extends her action of agreement by continuing to a more substantial utterance, "*kalpi-to kuleh-kwu*" [갈비도 그렇구 (So is *kalpi*)]. This additional utterance strengthens the degree of agreement and hence the degree of affiliation.

Agreement:

(9) [Office lunch]

    1   A: 불고기 같은 거는 달아야 맛있잖아
                  pwulkoki kath-un ke-nun tal-aya masiss-canha-a
                  "Things like *pwulkoki* are delicious only when they are sweet, right"
    2→ B: 음:. 갈비도 그렇구.
                  ***u:m.** kalpi-to kuleh-kwu.*
                  "**Yea:h.** So is *kalpi*."

Another action that can display an affiliative (or disaffiliative) stance[2] is an assessment. An assessment is an evaluative reaction to what is being talked about, and it can be done as a minimal assessment that can be performed through one adjective word typically combined with epistemic sentence-enders, such as *-ta* [-다], *-ney* [-네], and *-kwun(a)* [-구나] (Lee, 1993, Kim, 2004) or *-ci* [지] (Lee, 1999); e.g., *coh-ta/ney/kwun(a)*! [좋다/네/구나! (Nice!)]; *coh-keyss-ta/ney/kwun(a)*! [좋겠다/네/구나! ([It must be] Nice!)]; *coh-ass-keyss-ta/ney/kwun(a)*! [좋았겠다/네/구나! ([It must have been] Nice!)]; *mas-iss-ta/ney/kwun(a)*! [맛있다/네/구나! (Delicious!)]; *coh-ci*! [좋지! (Good [indeed, definitely, of course]!)]. For example,

Minimal assessment:

(10) [Family lunch]

    1   A: 우리가 있었던 데는 삼층짜리 아파트였어요.
                wuli-ka iss-ess-ten tey-nun sam-chung-ccali aphathu-y-ess-eyo.
                "The place where we stayed was a three-story apartment building."
    2→ B: °좋았겠다: 음::.°
                °***coh-ass-keyss-ta**: u::m*°
                "**It must've been ni:ce** yea::h."

Affiliative actions such as agreement and assessment can help the participants accomplish sociability and solidarity in interaction. An assessment can be performed through a longer turn, and such a non-minimal assessment shows a stance toward the prior talk more elaborately. It can display varied degrees of affiliation or disaffiliation, and it will be beneficial to teach such an elaborate action to learners as their levels become more advanced. For example,

Non-minimal assessment:

(11) [S & H, an excerpt modified from Lee (1993, p. 156): S & H have been talking about teaching assistants' salaries in Korea.]

    1 S: ∴ 그니까는,
               .. *ku-nikka-nun*,
               ".. So you see,"
    2   보너스 나오믄 육십만원 (그렇게 돼요).
               ponesu nao-mun yuk-sip-man-wen (kuleh-key tway-yo).
               "if you do get a bonus, it's about six hundred thousand won."
    3→H: 어이 되게 많이 나오네::!
               ei toy-key manhi nao-ney:: !
               "Wow, it pays a lot!"

In line 3, H reacts with a non-minimal assessment, "*ei toykey manhi nao-ney::!*" [어이 되게 많이 나오네:: (It pays a lot!)] to the higher-than-expected amount of teaching assistants' salary in Korea stated by S in lines 1 and 2.

It should be noted that a non-minimal assessment also expands the sequence of talk in progress. Another way to expand a conversational sequence is to ask a follow-up question that is tied to the previous talk and thereby to exhibit how the participant has understood the prior talk. For example, in Excerpt (12), the wife and the husband exchange the first-pair part of asking about the cost of repairing their car and the second-pair part of answering the question from line 1 to line 9. This adjacency-pair sequence is not closed but, rather, is expanded when the wife asks a follow-up question in line 10.

Non-minimal post expansion:

(12) [Family lunch]

    1   Wife: 얼마 나왔어 그래갖구?
                     elma nawa-ss-e kulay-kackwu?
                     "So, how much was it?"
    2   Hus: 원래 걔들이 에스티메이트 레잇을 줬을 때는:
                     wenlay kyay-tul-i eysuthimeyithu leyis-ul cwe-ss-ul ttay-nu:n
                     "When they first gave me the estimated rate,"
    3   Wife: 음.
                     um.
                     "Uh huh."
    4   Hus: <뭐가 백팔십불> 해서 백팔십 몇 불이구:,
                     <*mwe:-ka paykphalsip pwul*> *hay-se paykphalsip myech pwul-i-kwu:,*
                     "<Something was one hundred and eighty> dollars and so it was one hundred and something dolla:rs,"
    5   Wife: 응.
                     ung.
                     "Yeah,"

6	Hus:	그 담에 브레이크 하는 데:
		>*ku tam-ey< puleyikhu ha-nun tey:*
		">and then< for the bra:ke,"
7	Wife:	응.
		ung.
		"Yeah."
8	Hus:	구십구불.
		kwusipkwu pwul.
		"Ninety nine dollars."
9→	Wife:	브레이크를 왜 해?
		puleyikhu-lul way hay?
		"Why did they do the brake?"
10	Hus:	앞에 브레이크가 너무 닳아졌대[:.
		aph-ey puleykhu-ka nemwu talh-acy-ess-tay[:.
		"They said the front brake got worn out too mu:ch."
11	Wife:	[음:. 음.
		[*u:m. um.*
		"Yea:h yeah."
12	Hus:	그래가지고,
		kulay-kaciko,
		"Because of that,"
13	Wife:	음.
		um.
		"Yeah."
14	Hus:	그걸 갈아야 된다고 그러더라[구.
		kule-l kal-aya toy-ntako kule-te-lak[wu.
		"they said they should get it replaced."
15	Wife:	[음.
		[*um.*
		"Yeah."

Based on the key concepts explained earlier, the next section will discuss how IC has been dealt with in previous KSL research and why assessing IC is important in language teaching.

Why L2 Korean interactional competence in assessment?

Even though virtually all language instruction, including the contexts of Korean as a second or foreign language (KSL/KFL), pursues a communicative approach to foster communicative competence of learners, IC, which is an integral component of communicative competence, has not been paid much attention to in Korean language pedagogy until recently (Ha, 2020; Jeong, Bae, & Ahn, 2020; Kim, 2013, 2014, 2015, 2020, 2021; Kim & Yoon, 2021; Kim, this volume; Lee, 2016; Lee et al., 2017; Yoon, 2003, 2007, 2010; Yoon & Jeong, 2016). Learners may, as they advance, sophisticate their linguistic competence with expanded vocabulary and complex structures, discourse-pragmatic competence of producing utterances coherently and cohesively beyond the sentence level and understanding contextually more subtle and complex communicative actions, such as making polite requests, refusing an offer, expressing hope, etc. (Bardovi-Harlig, 2014; Kasper & Rose, 2001), and even some sociolinguistic competence, such as knowledge on speech styles and the use of honorifics. However, noticeably lacking in their conversation are interactional features that were illustrated in Section 2. Furthermore, assessment on learners' proficiency is heavily skewed toward measuring the production of linguistically accurate utterances, and little effort has been made to address learners' interactional competence in language assessment.

In this section, it will be illustrated how learners' conversations manifest interactional features to varying degrees depending on their proficiency level and, particularly, what interactional features are missing in their conversations.

Yoon (2007) points out that learners' language may be linguistically well-formed, but unnatural or even awkward in terms of interactional sequence, as seen in Excerpt (13).

(13) [Beginning learners' conversation: Making plans (Yoon, 2007)]

```
1    A:   이번 토요일 아침에 약속 있어요?
          i-pen thoyoil achim-ey yaksok iss-eyo?
          "Do you have plans for Saturday morning this week?"
2         친구들이랑 바닷가 갈래요?
          chinkwu-tul-ilang pataska ka-llay-yo?
          "Would you like to go to the beach with other friends?"
3    B:   미안해요.
          mianhay-yo.
4         이번 토요일은 안 되는데. 다음 주말에 같이 가요.
          i-pen thoyoil-un an toy-nuntey. taum cwumal-ey kathi ka-yo.
          "I'm sorry. This Saturday doesn't work for me. Let's go next weekend."
5    A:   그럼 몇 시에 갈까요?
          kulem myech si-ey ka-lkka-yo?
          "Then, what time shall we depart?"
6    B:   아침 8시 30분부터 5시까지 가요. 어디서 만날까요?
          achim 8 si 30 pwun-pwuthe 5 si-kkaci ka-yo. eti-se manna-lkka-yo?
          "Let's go from 8:30 am to 5 pm. Where shall we meet?"
7    A:   우리 집에서 만나요.
          wuli cip-eyse manna-yo.
          "Let's meet at my place."
8    B:   좋아요.
          coh-ayo.
          "Okay."
```

This is a dialogue of beginning-level learners who studied Korean for less than one year. What is noticeable in this conversation is that the learners hardly display any interactional features discussed in Section 2.

First, it is noted that the dialogue consists of a series of simple adjacency pairs and lacks expansions of the basic sequences that are useful for negotiation in making their plan. As Kim and Suh (1998) point out, beginner-level learners mainly orient to information and grammatical aspects, and the only social action they are conducting is exchange of information, with little process of negotiation on and modulation of the conveyed message. In line 1, for example, A asks if B has a plan in the morning of the upcoming Saturday before making a suggestion of going to the beach with friends. The question is a first-pair part in a pre-sequence (Levinson, 1983), which would commonly be produced as a separate sequence before continuing to the main sequence of actually making a suggestion. The pre-sequence is necessary to check the recipient's availability first, so the participants could avoid the interactional burden of making a suggestion and rejecting it. However, A does not consider such interactional aspects but continues in line 2 on to the main action of making a suggestion without listening to B's response. In lines 3 and 4, B straightly rejects A's suggestion and proposes an alternative time, "next weekend." In this process of B's deciding on an appointment time, B should ask whether A is available next weekend before making this new suggestion, but such a negotiation process does not take place.

Second, the learners in this excerpt do not exercise any repair when there are trouble sources in making their plan. For example, A's proposal for an outing in lines 1 and 2 contains multiple pieces of new information, that is, time and place all together in a single sequence. In a real situation, B would be caught off guard and need to take a measure to absorb the influx of information. A possible action that can be taken by B here may be to launch a repair initiator by repeating the trouble-source, *thoyoil* [토요일], as in "*thoyoil -ey-yo?*" [토요일에요? (On Saturday?)] to confirm her understanding or to produce a pre-rejection of the proposal. Instead, B rejects A's proposal straight in lines 3 and 4. B's proposal in line 4 poses another trouble source for their communication: "next weekend" consists of two days, and A should thus ask for a clarification whether B meant Saturday or Sunday by "weekend," but she just accepts the new proposal and asks the departure time in line 5. Further, B's response in line 6 does not respond with a departure time but with a duration of time for staying on the beach. Despite this interactional problem, A does not initiate repair for the clarification but simply accepts in line 7 the suggested time frame and meeting place.

Third, these learners do not utilize even minimal responsive tokens, such as continuers, change-of-state tokens, newsmark tokens, let alone assessments, alignments, acknowledgments, etc. When A suggests going to a beach with friends on Saturday in line 2, one could express her assessment on the event, such as "The beach? That would be fun." When B says Saturday is not good for her in line 4, A could acknowledge B's situation with a newsmark token like "*kulay-yo?*" [그래요? (Is that so?)]. Having set the time of the event, i.e., next weekend, one could also expand the conversation with a follow-up question on, say, weather, e.g., "Would the weather be good next weekend?" Such interactional features are completely missing.

Let us examine a dialogue between learners in their fourth semester, which displays more interactional features.

(14) [Fourth-semester learners' conversation, A & S: Vacation activities]

```
1    A:    S 씨 안녕하세요?
           S ssi annyengha-sey-yo?
           "S, how are you?"
2    S:    안녕하세요?
           annyengha-sey-yo?
           "How are you?"
3    A:    지난 겨울 방학에 뭐 했어요?
           cinan kyewul panghak-ey mwe hayss-e-yo?
           "What did you do during the last winter break?"
4    S:    지난 겨울 방학에 어 공부 해야 돼요,
           cinan kyewul panghak-ey e kongpuhay-ya-tway-yo,
           "During the last winter break, I uh have to study."
5          어 지금은:: 어 어려운 수업이 들었어요.
           e cikum-un:: e elyep-un swuep-i tul-ess-e-yo.
           "Uh, now:: uh I took a difficult class now."
```

6→	A:	음:.
		u:m.
		"I see."
7	S:	어: S씨는요?
		e: S ssi-nun-yo?
		"U:h what about you, S?"
8→	A:	어 저는 시카고-- 여자친구하고 같이 시카고에 갔어요.
		e ce-nun sikhako-- yeca chinkwu-hako kathi sikhako-ey ka-ss-eyo.
		"Well, I Chicago-- I went to Chicago with my girlfriend."
9		그런데 많은 어 사람들한테 음 ( ) 식당에 가야-- 가야 되는데
		kulentey manh-un e salam-tul-hanthey um ( ) siktang-ey ka-ya toy-nuntey
		"By the way, many people are supposed to go uh ( ) restaurant, but."
10		우리는 ( )에서 안 갔어요.
		uli-nun ( )-eyse an ka-ss-e-yo.
		"we did not go to ( ) restaurant."
11		근데 밀레니엄 팍에 갔고 맛있는 uhm 태국 식당에 먹었어요.
		kuntey Millennium Park-ey ka-ss-ko mas-iss-nun thaykuk siktang-ey mek-ess-e-yo.
		"Instead, we went to the Millennium Park, and ate at a delicious Thai restaurant."
12→	S:	아 네:
		a ney,
		"Oh, I see:"
13→		어 봄-- 아 다음 봄 학에:: (.) 봄 방학에 뭐 할 가요?
		e pom-- a taum pom hak-ey:: (.) pom panghak-ey mwe ha-l ka-yo?
		"Uh what are you going to do in sp-- ah next spring brea:: (.) spring break?"
14→	A:	네: 엄. 가족 같이 뉴올리언스에 아 여행 할 거예요.
		ney: em. kacok kathi New Orleans-ey a yehayng ha-l ke-yey-yo.
		"Yeah, uh I am going to travel to New Orleans with my family."
15		그런데 ( )에서 ( ) 술이 너무 마셨는데 저는 술 마셜
		kulentey ( )-eyse ( ) swul-i nemwu masy-ess-nuntey ce-nun sul masye-l
		"By the way, we drank a lot of alcohol at ( ), but I could not drink."
16		수 없어요. S 씨는요?
		swu eps-e-yo. S ssi-nun-yo?
		"What about you, S?"
17	S:	어: 저:는 뉴욕: 어: 에 가요.
		e: ce:-nun New Yo:rk e:-ey ka-yo.
		"Uh I am going to uh New York."
18		어 친구 만나고 아 클럽에 갈 거예요.
		e chinkwu manna-ko a khullep-ey ka-l ke-yey-yo.
		"Uh I am going to see a friend and uh going to a club."
19→	A:	어:. 뉴욕에서 뉴욕 피자를-- 뉴욕 피자를 먹어야 돼요.
		e:. New York-eyse New York phica-lul mek-eya tway-yo.
		"Mm. In New York, you should eat New York pizza."
20→	S:	아:, 어 뉴욕 피자 아-- (.) 안 (.) 먹어-- 안 봐요. (.) 봤어요
		a:, e New York phica a-- an mek-e-- pwa-yo. (.) pwass-e-yo.
		"O:h (I see), I have no-- not try-- tried uh New York pizza."
21→	A:	네. 아: 다시 암 사전거-- 자전거를 암 타도 돼요.
		ney. a: tasi sacenke-- cacenke-lul am tha-to tway-yo.
		"Mm. U:h you can uh ride uhm a vi-- bike again."

22   뉴욕에서 자전거를 타도 돼요.
        New York-eyse cacenke-lul tha-to tway-yo.
        "You can ride a bike in New York."
23→ S: 아: 네:.
        a: ney:.
        "Oh, I got it."

The conversation between these learners in their fourth semester also manifests the same simplistic question-and-answer format overall as the beginning-level learners in Excerpt (13). They also fail to deal with problems of talk in understanding each other through repair at the beginning of the dialogue. For example, S's response in lines 4 and 5 to A's question asking S what he did during the past winter break has multiple grammatical problems, especially with time adverbials and tenses in the sentence endings, which impede understanding of the message. Such a problem should be dealt with through repair. However, A does not initiate one, but instead produces an acknowledgement token (*u:m.* [음:.]) in line 6, and the two learners proceed to the next sequence. Interactionally, more active learners would utilize repair, as in the following example, where two participants successfully solve a problem in talk-in-interaction.

(15) [Fourth-semester learners' conversation: Z & S]

1   Z: S씨 여름 방학에 뭐 했어요?
         S ssi yelum panghak-ey mwe hay-ss-eyo?
         "S, what did you do during the summer break?"
2→ S: 여름방학? 겨울?
         yelum panghak? kyewul?
         "Summer break? Winter?"
3   Z: 아 겨울방학에.
         a kyewul panghak-ey.
         "Oh during the winter break."
4   S: 네 제 겨울 방학에 음 겨울 학기 있어서 런던에 갔어요
         ney cey kyewul panghak-ey um kyewul hakki iss-ese lenten-ey ka-ss-eyo.
         "Yeah, during my winter break uh I went to London because I had a winter semester."

Z asks S what she did during the summer break, but S points out in line 2 *yelum* [여름 (summer)] as a trouble source in the question because they are having the conversation after the winter break. After producing this repair initiator, S further provides her candidate understanding by presenting an alternative vocabulary item *kyewul* [겨울 (winter)], and Z confirms it and completes the repair in the next turn, "*a kyewul panghak-ey*" [아 겨울 방학에 (Oh, during the winter break)]. The failure by the learners in Excerpt (14) to utilize repair to handle the problem indicates these learners' low level of IC.

On the other hand, the learners in Excerpt (14) manifest a little more advanced interactional features than the beginners in Excerpt (13), despite their lack of ability of going beyond the simplistic question-and-answer format. They manage to utilize at least minimal response tokens, if at the minimum level throughout, such as short change-of-state tokens *a* [아] or *e* [어] in lines 12, 20, and 23, what Clancy, Thompson, Suzuki, and Tao (1996) call "resumptive openers"[3] *e* in line 8, and short acknowledgment tokens like *um* [음] (I see) in line 6 and *ney* [네] (I see) in lines 12, 14, 21, and 23, although their uses of such response tokens are mimicry reactions of native speakers rather than strategic social actions based on proper understanding of each type, and thus their functions are often unclear. In addition, A is also able to make comments in line 19 ("You should eat New York pizza in New York") and 21 ("You can ride a bike in New York.") in relation to S's prior utterance and initiate expanded sequences, which is an indication of a little more active participation.

The following example is also a dialogue between learners in the fourth semester, but interactively more advanced ones.

(16) [Fourth-semester learners' conversation, S & C: Vacation activities]

```
1    S:    음 (.) 그래서 겨울 방학에 뭐 했어요?
            um kulayse kyewul panghak-ey mwe hay-ss-e-yo?
            "Uh (.) so what did you do during the winter break?"
2    C:    아: (.) 처음에는 일 많이 했어요.
            a: (.) cheum-ey-nun il manhi hay-ss-e-yo.
            "Uh (.) I worked a lot in the beginning."
3          (.) 그 다음에 코스타리카에 갔어요.
            (.) ku taum-ey Costa Rica-ey ka-ss-e-yo.
            "(.) After that, I went to Costa Rica."
4→   S:    아 코스타리카 (.) 어땠어요?
            a Costa Rica (.) ettay-ss-e-yo?
            "Oh, Costa Rica, how was it?"
5    C:    너무 예쁜 나라예요.
            nemwu yeyppu-n nala-yey-yo.
            "It is really a beautiful country."
6→   S:    아::
            a::
            "Ah::"
7    C:    숲 많이 하고:
            swup manhi hako:
            "Many forests, a:nd"
8          바다 많이 있고:
            pata manhi iss-ko:
            "Lots of oceans, a:nd"
9          동물 많이 있어요.
            tongmwul manhi iss-e-yo.
            "there are many animals."
10→  S:    아::
            a::
            "Oh::"
11   C:    너는 뭐 했어요? 겨울 방학에?
            ne-nun mwe ha-ss-e-yo? kyewul panghak-ey?
            "What did you do during the winter break?"
12   S:    저는 겨울방학에 아: 캘리포니아에 갔어요.
            ce-nun kyewul panghak-ey a: California-ey ka-ss-e-yo.
            "I went to u:h California during the winter break."
13→  C:    오 캘리포니아 예뻐요
            o California yeypp-e-yo
            "Oh, California is pretty"
```

14   S: 네. 캘리포니아에서 요세미티에 아 등산했어요.
          ney. California-eyse Yosemite-ey a tungsan hay-ss-e-yo.
          "Yeah. I went uh hiking at Yosemite in California."

15→ C: 아:↑ 어땠어요?
          a:↑ ettay-ss-e-yo?
          "O:h↑, how was it?"

16   S: 너무 추워서 아 (.) 기분이 안 좋(h)아(h)요(h)
          nemwu chwuw-ese a (.) kipwun-i an coh(h)-a(h)-yo(h)
          "Because it is too cold, (.) I don't(h) feel(h) good(h)"

17→ C: 아 그래요?
          a kulay-yo?
          "Oh, is that so?"

18   그럼 봄 방학에 뭐 할 거예요?
          kulem pom panghak-ey mwe ha-l ke-yey-yo?
          "Then, what are you going to do in the spring break?"

19   S: 봄 방학에 아:: 저는 오하이오 스테이트 아: 갈 거예요.
          pom panghak-ey a:: ce-nun Ohio State a: ka-l ke-yey-yo.
          "In the spring break, u::h I am going to u:h Ohio."

20   친구: (.) 만나서 오하이오에 갈 거예요.
          chinkwu: (.) manna-se Ohio-ey ka-l ke-yey-yo.
          "I am going to Ohio to see my friend."

21→ C: 아::, 오하이오에 뭐 할 거예요? [친구랑?]
          a::, Ohio-ey mwe ha-l ke-yey-yo chinkwu-lang?
          "O::h (I see). What are you going to do in Ohio, with your friend?"

22   S: [아::] 그냥 친구를 만나-- 친구를 만나고, 아 영화 봐요?
          a:: kunyang chinkwu-lul manna-- chinkwu-lul manna-ko a yenghwa pwa-yo.
          "U::h just meeting a frie-- meeting a friend, and, uh, see a movie."

23→ C: 아 예:.
          a yey:.
          "Oh, I see."

24   오하이오는 조금 추워요
          Ohio-nun cokum chwuw-e-yo.
          "It's a bit cold in Ohio."

25→ S: 그래요?
          kula-yo?
          "Is that so?"

26   C: 네
          ney.
          "Yeah."

27→ S: 어::. 오하이오 못-- 못 가 봤어요.
          e:: Ohio mos-- mos ka pw-ass-e-yo.
          "Mm. I have not-- not been able to go to Ohio."

28→ C: 아:: (.) 아 한 번에 가 봤어요
          a:: (.) han pen-ey ka pw-ass-e-yo.
          "O::h, (.) uh I've been there once."

The conversational sequences in this example illustrate that these learners are able to utilize, in addition to change-of-state tokens and a minimal acknowledgement token seen in Excerpt

(14), various types of responses, including a case of assessment in line 13 (California is pretty) and an explicit newsmark, "*a kulay-yo?*" [그래요? (Is that so?)] in line 17. In addition, S and C produce a follow-up question "How was it?" in lines 4 and 15, respectively, and a reactive comment (Oh, I have not been able to go to Ohio) in line 27, which initiates a non-minimal expansion (Schegloff, 2007) to a new sequence tied to the previous talk and displays how the participant has understood the prior talk.

On the other hand, the speakers could still be more engaging by utilizing special sentence-enders, such as *-ta* and *-ney*, which index various epistemic stances (Ha, 2018; Kim, 2004; Lee, 1993). For example, S could insert her assessment in line 4, such as "*wa, choh-ass-keyss-ta!*" [와, 좋았겠다! (Wow, it must have been pleasant!)], using the sentence-ender *-ta* in reaction to C's statement in line 3 that she went to Costa Rica. Instead, S directly asks C how it was. Similarly, when S said that she went hiking at Yosemite in line 14, C could have given her reaction with the sentence-ender *-ney* [네] like "*aa, chaymiss-ess-keyss-**ta/ney** (-yo)!*" [재밌었겠다/네(요)! (It must have been fun!)]. Just like S in line 4, however, C again goes straight to ask how it was in line 15. In line 13, C gives an assessment that California is beautiful in reaction to S's preceding statement that she went to California during the winter break. An advanced or native speaker is likely to respond to such an assessment with a second assessment or an affiliative agreement by saying "*ney, cengmal yeyppu-te-lakwu-yo*" [네, 정말 예쁘더라구요 (Yeah, it was really beautiful)] or "*kuleh-cyo, yeyppu-cyo*" [그렇죠, 예쁘죠 (Yeah, it [certainly] is pretty)] with the sentence-ender *-ci* [지]. Instead, S simply goes on to say "Yeah, I went hiking at Yosemite" in line 14.

In the following example, it is illustrated that more-advanced learners in their sixth semester are able to use these sentence-enders in indicating their epistemic and affective stances.

(17) [Sixth-semester learners: J & A]

```
1      J:    어: 지난: 추수 감사절에: 뭐 하-- (.) 뭐 했어?
              e cinan chwuswu kamsacel-ey: mwe ha-- (.) mwe hay-ss-e?
              "Uh, what d-- (.) what did you do during the last Thanksgiving Day?"
2      A:    어 제가 그냥 일하::: (.) 일 했어요
              e cey-ka kunyang il-ha::: (.) il hay-ss-e-yo
              "Oh I just wo::rk (.) worked."
3            쉬는 날도 없어요
              swi-nun nal-to eps-e-yo
              "I don't even have a day of break."
4→     J:    오:::. 그렇구나::
              o:::. kuleh-kwun-a::
              "Oh, I see:::."
5            그 쇼핑은 안해?
              ku shopping-un an hay?
              "Like, aren't you going shopping?"
6→     A:    아 (.) 오: 맞다:: (hh) 쇼핑을 했어요::
              a (.) o: mac-ta:: (hh) syophing-ul hay-ss-e-yo::
              "Oh, yeah. (hh) I went sho::pping."
7            Black Friday 쇼핑을 했어요.
              Black Friday syophing-ul hay-ss-e-yo
              "I shopped on Black Friday."
```

8   J: 많이 샀어?
          manhi sa-ss-e?
          "Did you buy a lot?"
9   A: 아 오 많이 많이 샀어요::=
          a o manhi manhi sa-ss-e-yo::=
          "Uh yeah. I bought a lot."
10→ J: =좋겠다
          =coh-keyss-ta
          "It must be great."
11 A: =응 언니도 뭐 했어요?
          =ung enni-to mwe hay-ss-e-yo?
          "Yeah. What did you do?"
12 J: 나는:: 그냥 어 며칠 동안 집에서 그냥 공부하구 (.)
          na-nu::n kunyang e myechil tongan cip-eyse kunyang kongpwuha-kwu (.)
          "I:: just uh studied at home for a few days, and (.)"
13   어:: 쉬-- 쉬었어요
          e:: swi-- swi-ss-e-yo.
          "u::h res-- rested."
14   그럼 그리고 그:: 주말에 친구하고 시카고에 갔어.
          kulem kuliko ku:: cwumal-ey chinkwu-hako Chicago-ey ka-ss-e.
          "Then, and u::h I went to Chicago with a friend of mine."
          :
19 A: 아 어떤 음식을:: 먹었어요?
          a etten umsik-ul:: mek-ess-e-yo?
          "Ah what foo::d did you eat?"
20→ J: 아:: 맞다.
          a:: mac-ta .
          "Oh, yeah."
21   한국 음식 (.) 나 (.) 저 저희 많이 먹었어요.
          hankwuk umsik (.) na (.) ce cehi manh mek-ess-e-yo.
          "Korean food (.) I (.) we we ate a lot."
22→ A: 아 정말요?
          a cengmal-yo?
          "Oh really?"
23 J: 네=
          ney=
          "Yeah."
24→ A: =와
          =wa
          "Wow"
25 J   코리아타운에 가서:: 그 불고기를 먹었어
          Koreatown-ey ka-se:: ku pwulkoki-lul mek-ess-e
          "We went to Koreatown and:: we ate *pulkoki*."
26 A: 응? 시카고에서 코리아타운가 있어요?
          ung? Chicago-eyse Koreatown-ka iss-e-yo?
          "Huh? Is there Koreatown in Chicago?"
27 J: 네 있었는데
          ney, iss-ess-nuntey
          "Yeah, there was,"

28→ A: 정말?
         cengmal?
         "Really?"

33   언니는 크리스마스:: 어:: (1.5) 어떻게:: 보낼게요?
         enni-nun Christmas e:: (1.5) ettehkey ponay-lkey-yo?
         "How are you uh going (1.5) to spend Christmas?"

34 J: 아 제가 내 친구 내 친구 캐나다 한 명 있는데::
         a cey-ka nay chinkwu nay chinkwu khaynata han myeng iss-nuntey::
         "Ah, I have my friend a friend in Canada, and"

35   이 친구가 내년에 결혼 할 거니까::
         i chinkwu-ka naynyen-ey kyelhon ha-l ke-nikka::
         "since this friend is going to marry next year, so::"

36   나 아마 크리스마스 캐나다에 가서: 뭐
         na ama khulisumasu khaynata-ey ka-se: mwe
         "Maybe I will like go to Canada (in) Christmas, a:nd"

37   결혼:: 필요한 (.) 결혼:: 필요한 (.) 거 많이 많이 준비
         kyelho::n philyoha-n (.) kyelho::n philyoha-n (.) ke manhi manhi cwunpi
         "I, like, helped her with many things that need (.) need to be prepared for the wedding,"

38   도와줬구 뭐 웨딩 드레스도 뽑하고 뭐
         towa-cw-ess-kwu mwe weyting tuleysu-to ppopha-ko mwe
         "like selecting a wedding dress,"

39   이런 거 캐나다에 (.) 서 보내 (.) 보낼게요(h)
         ilen ke khaynata-ey(.)se ponay (.) ponay-lkey-yo(h)
         "I will spend time doing those things in Canada(h)"

40→ A: 아 그렇군요 재밌겠다.
         *a kuleh-**kwun**-yo caymi-ss-keyss-**ta** .*
         "Oh, I see. It would be fun."

52 J: 여행 계획 없어?
         yehayng kyeyhoyk eps-e?
         "Don't you have any travel plans?"

53 A: 어 여행을 가고 싶은데 돈을 많이 벌::: 벌고 (.)
         e yehayng-ul ka-ko siph-untey ton-ul manhi pe:::l pel-ko (.)
         "Uh I'd like to, but I [need to] ma:::ke make a lot of money, and (.)"

54   어 돈을-- 돈을 없어서 그냥 집에서:: 할 거::니까
         e ton-ul-- ton-ul eps-ese kunyang cip-eyse:: ha-l ke::-nikka
         "uh I don't have mon-- money, so I will just stay home."

55→ J: 어 아쉽네
         *e aswip-**ney***
         "Oh, that's too bad."

56 A: 응 완전 아쉽다.
         ung wancen aswip-ta.
         "Yeah, it is totally bad."

57 J: 으, (0.5) 그래-- 그래도 새해 복 많이 받아
         u, (0.5) kulay-- kulayto sayhay pok manhi pat-a
         "Uh, (0.5) even-- even so, Happy New Year!"

58   A: 네, 언니도.
           ney, enni-to
           "Yeah, you, too."

These advanced learners display more interactive participation, producing context-sensitive alignment and affiliative stance markings: e.g., an acknowledgment token "*kuleh-kwun-a*" [그렇구나] or "*kuleh-kwun-yo*" [그렇군요 ([I see] that is the case)] in lines 4 and 40; an alignment token like "*mac-ta*" [맞다 (That's right)] in lines 6 and 20; assessment tokens like "*coh-keyss-ta*" [좋겠다 (It must be pleasing)] in line 10, "*caymi-ss-keyss-ta*" [재밌겠다 (It must be fun)] in line 40, and "*aswip-ney*" [아쉽네 (That's too bad)] in line 55; and a newsmark token "*cengmal(-yo)?*" [정말(요)? (Really?)] in lines 22 and 28, etc. These learners not only use response tokens with little difficulty but also fairly fluently utilize a variety of sentence-enders that mark the speaker's various epistemic stances, e.g., *-ta* [다], *-ney* [네], *-kwuna* [구나], etc. (Ha, 2018; Kim, 2004; Lee, 1991, 1993).

With regard to sequential organization, it is observed that low-level learners tend to orient to exchanging information (Kim & Suh, 1998) and thus sticking to simple question-and-answer formats (Burch & Kley, 2020). Consequently, they are not only unable to utilize appropriate response tokens showing their epistemic stances, as seen in the earlier examples, but are also rarely able to initiate non-minimal expansion sequences tied to the previous talk, asking a follow-up question. In contrast, the sixth-semester learners in this excerpt seem to be able to manage expansion sequences quite successfully. Upon hearing A say that she just worked during the Thanksgiving break, J asks "Aren't you going shopping?" in line 5. In line 8 as well, J asks "Did you buy a lot?" upon hearing A say she shopped on Black Friday. In lines 19 and 26, too, A is able to expand the preceding sequences by asking relevant follow-up questions – "What food did you eat?" and "Is there a Koreatown in Chicago?" respectively – which also shows their ability to manage topic transitions naturally.

Advanced learners can also utilize non-minimal reactions indexing their epistemic stance as well as explicit other-initiation of repair.[4] For example,

(18) [An excerpt from an interview of an advanced heritage learner (JJ) by a native interviewer (IR)]

1   IR: 아, 어디에서 오셨어요?
           a, eti-eyse o-sy-ess-e-yo?
           "Ah, where did you come from?"
2   JJ: 캘리포니아
           California
           "California."
3   IR: 아:: 네::
           a ney.
           "Oh, I see."
4   미국에서 태어나셨어요?
           mikwuk-eyse thayena-sy-ess-e-yo?
           "Were you born in the States?"
5   JJ: 미국에서 (.) 제가 한 네 살 때 이민 갔거든요.
           mikwuk-eyse (.) cey-ka han ney sal ttay imin ka-ss-ketun-yo.
           "You see, I immigrated [to here] (.) when I was about four years old."
6   IR: 근데, 한국말 너무 잘 하세요.
           kuntey, hankwukmal nemwu cal ha-sey-yo.
           "But, you speak Korean so well."

7→	JJ:	잘하는 거 아니-- [((laugh))]
		cal ha-nun ke ani--[((laugh))]
		"Not doing well--"
8	IR:	[((laugh))]
9	JJ:	요즘, 영어도 못하고 한국말도 [못하고.]
		yocum yenge-to mos-ha-ko hankwukmal-to [*mos ha-ko.*]
		"These days, I don't speak English well, and neither do I speak Korean well."
10	IR:	[((laugh))]
11	IR:	한국어 어떻게 공부하셨어요?
		hankwuke ettehkhey kongpwuha-sy-ess-e-yo?
		"How did you study Korean?"
12→	JJ:	저요?
		ce-yo?
		"(Who,) me?"
13		그냥 뭐,
		kunyang mwe,
		"Just like,"
14		대학교에서 한국말 많이 배웠고요,
		tayhakkyo-eyse hankwukmal manhi payw-ess-ko-yo,
		"I learned Korean a lot in college,"
15		그 한국에서 뭐,
		ku hankwuk-eyse mwe,
		"uh, in Korea, like,"
16		이 삼 년 정도 있었거든요=
		i sam nyen cengto iss-ess-ketun-yo=
		"I was [in Korea] two or three years, you see."
17	IR:	=아:: 그러셨어요::
		=*a kule-sy-ess-e-yo?*
		"Oh, I see [lit. Oh, were you?]"
18	JJ:	네.
		ney.
		"Yeah."
19	IR:	취미는 뭐가 있나요?
		chwimi-nun mwe-ka iss-na-yo?
		"What hobby do you have?"
20→	JJ:	취미요?
		chwimi-yo?
		"A hobby?"
21	IR:	네.
		ney.
		"Yeah."
22	JJ:	취미는 여러가지 있는데::,
		chwimi-nun yeleh-kaci iss-nuntey::,
		"I have several ho::bbies,"
23		요즘 대학원생이라 너무 바빠서 그냥 뭐 책만 보고 있는데=
		yocum tahakwensayng-i-la nemwu papp-ase kunyang mwe chayk-man po-ko iss-nuntey,=
		"I am too busy because I am a graduate student, so I am just reading, but,"

```
24   IR:     =아::: [그러세요?
             =a::  [kule-sey-yo?
             "Oh, is that so?"
25→ JJ:      [독서가 취미라고 할 수 있겠죠.
             [tokse-ka chwimi-la-ko ha-l swu iss-keyss-cyo.
             "You can say reading is my hobby, I suppose."
```

In Excerpt (18), the advanced heritage learner is able to produce a non-minimal reaction of disaffiliation, as in line 7, denying the interviewer's compliment that he speaks Korean well. Lower-level learners either may not respond at all or may give a minimal expression, such as "*ani-ey-yo*" [아니에요] (No [I am not]). The advanced heritage interviewee also utilizes other-initiation of repair in lines 12 and 20. In line 25, this advanced learner also manages to use the sentence-ender of certainty, *-ci* (Lee, 1999), to index his epistemic stance in response to the interviewer's question about his hobby.

It is evident that L2 Korean learners do not command well those interactional features that are necessary to facilitate and move forward a conversation in an orderly fashion. This is mainly because, although communicative approach has been prevalent recently, linguistic competence is still the major focus of Korean language education, lacking in addressing interactional competence.

Noting on what L2 Korean learners lack in IC, there have been some suggestions on how to foster the learners' ability to command some of the interactional features, such as response tokens (RTs) and sentence-enders in appropriate conversational contexts. Lee and Choi (2017) point out that such expressions of requesting for clarification are not well dealt with in KFL textbooks and suggest exercises for dealing with the situations when they need to request for clarification. Yoon and Jeong (2016) suggest teaching active listenership using authentic video materials. Lee et al. (2017) also suggest KFL educators develop activities for raising awareness of RTs, modify textbook conversations with various RTs, teach discourse functions and positions of continuers, discourage students' unnatural use of L1 transfer, and educate various forms of *kule-* [그러-] (to be so), which has various discourse functions. They found that KFL learners could produce more RTs after they learned about discourse functions of RTs and did some activities analyzing RTs of their L1 and Korean by watching authentic video materials. Building upon Jeong's (2018) findings, Jeong et al. (2020) propose ways to implement a Korean language instruction of teaching those stance-marking functions of the interrogative suffixes *-na* [-나], *-(u)nka* [-(으)ㄴ가], *-nya* [-냐], and *-ni* [-니]; e.g., showing video or audio clips through which students recognize different alignment (i.e., converging or diverging) stances, and conducting a series of activities to have students respond to a variety of "stance-lead" utterances with different "stance-follow" utterances. To improve students' ability to use proper assessment sequences with some of the sentence-enders, Ha (2020) proposes discourse competition tasks and interactional activities for which students are explicitly instructed to use the sentence-enders that mark the speaker's specific affiliative stances.

What is needed, then, is how students' learning of these interactional features is assessed and their overall interactional competence is measured. In the next section, we will propose, based on the ways learners display interactional features as illustrated in this section, rough criteria by which interactional competence can be measured.

Assessing interactional competence in Korean

There has been criticism that standardized oral proficiency tests, such as the ACTFL OPI, TOEFL, and IELTS, pay little or limited attention to assessing learners' IC (Burch & Kley,

2020; Kramsch, 1986; Roever & Kasper, 2018). Kramsch (1986) rebukes that proficiency-oriented assessment methods simply emphasize accuracy and overlook "dynamic process of communication" (p. 368) through which intended or pragmatic meaning is monitored, negotiated, and regulated for successful communication. Similarly, Roever and Kasper (2018) point out that those standardized tests try to elicit ratable samples of spoken language for linguistic competences, such as pronunciation, grammar, and vocabulary, with limited attention to discourse aspects of language use in real interaction, which is a complicated process that can be built collaboratively while negotiating intended meanings with other interlocutor(s). Burch and Kley (2020) argue that the assessment of IC should be made foregrounded from the perspectives of intersubjectivity, not based on discrete competences.

Compared to linguistic competence, measuring learners' IC is more difficult. Interaction does not consist of isolated utterance but involves connected discourse (Huth, 2020). Therefore, IC can only be viewed in its sequential context, and a learner's IC should be assessed in interactions in a holistic and discursive way.

Recently, a growing number of studies show how IC appears differently depending on learners' levels and argue that one's IC can be an indicator of their communicative competence. For example, Lam (2018, p. 392) argues that "contingency on previous speaker contribution," i.e., a current speaker referring back to or topicalizing elements from a previous speaker's talk, is the core of IC. He analyzes L2 English conversations and argues that paraphrasing or reformulating the points of the previous speaker's talk (reformulation), accounting for one's (dis-)agreement (accounting) and developing the idea from the previous talk (extending) should be included in the assessment of students' IC.

As indicators of IC, Roever and Kasper (2018) focused on preliminaries that appear differently depending on the learner's level. The preliminaries include pre-sequences of various social acts (e.g., invitation, announcements, or requests) and prefaces in responding to such actions as disagreement or refusals. They found that as learners' levels increase, they could better organize socially expected sequences to create a condition to take the main action appropriately.

Similarly, Burch and Kley (2020) examined paired-speaking assessment tasks and analyzed how learners of German displayed their IC with turn-taking and repair. In their data, low-level learners could only show repeated question-and-answer pairs as seen in Excerpts (14) and (15), while advanced learners could collaboratively expand upon each other's talk. Advanced learners could further express their understanding of the previous talk while expressing epistemic and affective stances and orient to problems in understanding through repair processes.

Galaczi (2014) focused on specific aspects of IC, including developing topics, topic shifts, listener involvement and turn-taking strategies. She analyzed conversation data from different levels of ESL students focusing on topic extension, listener support moves and turn-taking management. She found that as learners' levels increase, they can expand other initiated topics more than their own topics, express more confirmation of comprehension than simple backchannels, and start a turn more naturally after a latch or overlap.

Youn (2015, 2020) argues that L2 pragmatics can be assessed through role play. She suggests comprehensive rating criteria for assessing IC that include three levels of interactional features: length of interaction, engaging with interaction, and sequential organizations. The length of interaction refers to the number of words per turn and number of turns in role-play situations. The engaging with interaction refers to rating criteria such as how smoothly L2 learners would initiate turns or transition from one to the next with few pauses, how L2 learners would display their understanding of prior turns through their own conduct, how L2 learners would recipient-design (i.e., tailor) their utterances to a given situation and/or interlocutor or whether adjacency pairs are recognized and completed across turns and speakers. The sequential organizations refer to a series of turns that are organized to produce social actions in interaction, that include turn-taking, adjacency pairs, and preference organization.

For Korean, Lee (2016) illustrates that L2 Korean learners in different levels deploy a different range of response tokens. Low-level learners only produce minimal response tokens that are rather instinctive reactions, such as *ah, uh, oh*, etc., or minimal acknowledgement tokens, such as *ney* [네] (I see), as seen in Excerpt (15). More-advanced learners are shown to utilize a wide variety of response tokens, including non-minimal response tokens, that are actively engaging and carry strategic social actions that indicate the speaker's epistemic and affective stances, such as alignment and affiliation.

Drawing on the aforementioned research and the ways learners display their interactional features in Section 3, we attempt here to propose a set of criteria for assessing Korean learners' IC. The key question that needs to be addressed in assessing learners' IC is: Do learners display the ability to understand and produce social actions in their sequential contexts? In other words, do they format actions and turns and construct epistemic and affective stances by doing the following?

1. Producing first-pair parts and/or second-pair parts in sequentially appropriate contexts:

    a. Producing a first-pair part of a new sequence when there is no next turn is conditionally relevant, such as a question in a question-answer sequence, e.g., "*cikum myech-si-yey-yo?*" [지금 몇 시예요? (What time is it now?)]

    b. Producing a second-pair part in an adjacency pair, e.g., an answer in a question-answer sequence, "*twu-si-yo*" [두 시요 (It's two o'clock]

2. Initiating repairs (either self- or other-repair) to address problems in speaking, hearing, or understanding of the talk;

3. Producing response tokens or other types of utterances in sequentially appropriate contexts to display their engaged listenership:

    a. producing a continuer to pass up their floor, e.g., *ney* [네], *yey* [예], *um* [음], *e* [어] (yes)

    b. producing acknowledgement tokens, such as *ney* [네], *yey* [예], *um* [음], and *e* [어] (yes); a newsmark, such as *a kulay-yo?* [아 그래요? (Oh, is that so?)]; minimal agreement, such as *mac-ayo* [맞아요] and *kuleh-cyo* [그렇죠] (That's right); minimal assessment, such as *wa* [와 (Wow)], *coh-keyss-ney-yo* [좋겠네요 (It must be good)], *celen* [저런 (Oh dear)], and *aikwu* [아이구 (Oh my)]

    c. collaboratively completing the other speaker's utterance

4. Initiating a non-minimal expansion sequence tied to the previous talk (e.g., asking a follow-up question, such as "*kulem ku-ke-n ettehkey ha-nun ke-yey-yo?*" [그럼 그건 어떻게 하는 거예요? (In that case, how do you do that?)]; and

5. Producing context-sensitive alignment and affiliative stance markings.

We suggest the following criteria for assessing interactional competence.

    Novice: producing second-pair parts in basic adjacency pairs, such as greetings, expressions of gratitude and apology, simple questions and answers; may produce minimal response tokens

    Intermediate: responding to the first-pair parts that typically invoke a second-pair part, such as greetings, questions, and requests; initiating simple adjacency pairs of questions and

answers; producing continuers and minimal acknowledgement and newsmark tokens; utilizing self-initiated repairs and simple other-initiated repairs, such as affirmative response tokens and repetition of simple words or phrases; producing minimal assessment; may manage elaborate other-initiated repair sequences; may produce non-minimal assessment/agreement and non-minimal post-expansion sequences to some degree
- Advanced: producing adjacency pairs proficiently, even when relevance to the prior talk is implicit; utilizing response tokens and elaborate other-repair sequences without difficulty; producing non-minimal assessment/agreement and non-minimal post-expansion sequences without difficulty; expressing context-sensitive alignment/disalignment and affiliative/disaffiliative stance to some degree
- Superior: producing non-minimal expansion sequence proficiently, expressing context-sensitive alignment/misalignment and affiliative/disaffiliative stance proficiently through conducting collaborative completion, approving or refuting the others' stances, etc.

It should be noted that this is a preliminary attempt to set up criteria to assess interactional competence. The criteria will need to be more refined based on more learners' data in a wider variety of proficiency levels. These suggested criteria will also need to be validated in real assessments, and more research needs to be done on the correlation between these criteria and the designated proficiency level, as done in Youn (2020) for English.

Conclusion

Language is the primary tool for communication, and the very goal of language instruction is for learners to foster their communicative competence. For successful communication, the speakers need to have knowledge not only of the vocabulary and linguistic structure of the language, but also of its use. Conversation is the primordial form of communication, consisting of a series of social actions that are interactional in nature. Therefore, IC is a crucial part, or even a defining aspect, of communicative competence (Kramsch, 1986). Current practices of language pedagogy take communicative approaches, but despite the indispensability of the interactional features for successful communication, they have not been paid much attention to in Korean language pedagogy until recently. Based on CA-based research, we have identified a number of interactional features that are crucial for orderly conversation and have examined how these interactional features are manifested in Korean conversations. The interactional features that have been examined here are systematic turn-taking in adjacency-pair formats, self- and other-initiated repairs that locate trouble sources in communication and seek resolution, various types of response tokens that facilitate smooth communication and exhibit active participation, expansion sequences such as follow-up questions, as well as context-sensitive epistemic and affective stances such as alignment and affiliation. It has been observed that L2 Korean learners manifest these interactional features to varying degrees depending on their proficiency levels. We have proposed a set of criteria for which L2 Korean learners' interactional competence can be assessed. We also propose that these criteria be included in existing testing, such as the ACTFL OPI guidelines, to more comprehensively assess learners' language ability.

The data used for this chapter are based on limited L2 Korean learners' data. We hope there will be more research analyzing conversations in a variety of social contexts from full ranges of proficiency levels of L2 Korean learners. We also hope that our proposed criteria will be further elaborated upon and applied in assessing learners' proficiency. We believe that further studies on assessment of L2 Korean learners' IC will provide more resources for language assessment and second language acquisition studies in general.

Notes

1 One of the reviewers pointed out that the ACTFL proficiency guidelines (2012) include:
"[Distinguished level speakers] can tailor language to a variety of audiences by adapting their speech and register in ways that are culturally authentic" (p. 4).
"Superior-level speakers employ a variety of interactive and discourse strategies, such as turn-taking. . . ." (p. 5).
"Advanced High speakers may demonstrate a well-developed ability to compensate for an imperfect grasp of some forms or for limitations in vocabulary by the confident use of communicative strategies, such as paraphrasing, circumlocution, and illustration. . . ." (p. 5).
"Intermediate Mid speakers tend to function reactively, for example, by responding to direct questions or requests for information. However, they are capable of asking a variety of questions when necessary to obtain simple information to satisfy basic needs, such as directions, prices, and services" (p. 7).
It should be noted that the previous statement on distinguished-level speakers refers to general sociolinguistic features, not strategic competence that is crucial to interactional competence. The statement regarding intermediate mid speakers addresses the basic question-and-answer format, which is only a limited component of interactional competence manifested in lower-level learners' language production. The reviewer also pointed out that ACTFL OPI role play provides "situated contexts." But by "the situated contexts" OPI role play does not mean to explicitly refer to interactional features in a comprehensive way, as we illustrate in this chapter.
2 Assessment can be a disaffiliative action if it conveys a different position from the prior speaker's evaluative stance.
3 Resumptive openers are non-lexical phrases like "mhm" and "ah" that appear at the beginning of a new speaker's turn with her or his full turn appearing after it (Clancy et al., 1996, p. 362).
4 Young and Lee (2004) found that Korean native speakers use a larger variety of reactive tokens compared to English native speakers.

References

American Council on the Teaching of Foreign Languages. (2012). *ACTFL proficiency guidelines 2012*. Retrieved from www.actfl.org/sites/default/files/guidelines/ACTFLProficiencyGuidelines2012.pdf
Bardovi-Harlig, K. (2014). Documenting interlanguage development. In Z.-H. Han & E. Tarone (Eds.), *Interlanguage 40 years later* (pp. 127–146). Amsterdam and Philadelphia: John Benjamins Publishing Company.
Burch, A. R., & Kley, K. (2020). Assessing interactional competence: The role of intersubjectivity in a paired-speaking assessment task. *Papers in Language Testing and Assessment, 9*(1), 25–63.
Canale, M., & Swain, M. (1980). Theoretical bases of communicative approaches to second language teaching and testing. *Applied Linguistics, 1*(1), 1–47.
Clancy, P. M., Thompson, S. A., Suzuki, R., & Tao, H. (1996). The conversational use of reactive tokens in English, Japanese, and Mandarin. *Journal of Pragmatics, 26*, 355–387.
Galaczi, E. D. (2014). Interactional competence across proficiency levels: How do learners manage interaction in paired speaking tests? *Applied Linguistics, 35*(5), 553–574.
Gardner, R. (2001). *When listeners talk: Response tokens and listener stance*. Amsterdam and Philadelphia: John Benjamins Publishing Company.
Goffman, E. (1981). *Forms of talk*. Oxford: Blackwell.
Gumperz, J. (1982). *Discourse strategies*. Studies in Interactional Sociolinguistics 1. Cambridge: Cambridge University Press.
Ha, K. (2018). *The social actions of the sentence-ending suffixes -ney, -ci, and -kwuna in Korean conversation* [Ph.D dissertation]. University of California, Los Angeles.
Ha, K. (2020). Assessment sequences in Korean conversation and their pedagogical applications. *Korean Language in America, 24*(1), 30–50.
He, A., & Young, R. (1998). Language proficiency interviews: A discourse approach. In R. Young & W. He (Eds.), *Talking and testing: Discourse approaches to the assessment of oral proficiency* (pp. 1–24). Amsterdam and Philadelphia: John Benjamins Publishing Company.
Heritage, J. (1984). *Garfinkel and ethnomethodology*. Cambridge, MA: Polity Press.
Huth, T. (2020). Testing interactional competence: Patterned yet dynamic aspects of L2 interaction. *Papers in Language Testing and Assessment, 9*(1), 1–24.

Hymes, D. H. (1972). On communicative competence. In J. B. Pride & J. Holmes (Eds.), *Sociolinguistics: Selected readings* (pp. 269–293). Harmondswarth, Middlesex: Penguin.

Jeong, S. (2018). *The discourse-pragmatic uses of the Korean interrogative sentence-enders -Na/-(u)Nka, and -Ni* [Ph.D dissertation]. University of California, Los Angeles.

Jeong, S., Bae, E. Y., & Ahn, J. (2020). Conversation analytic-informed instruction of -Nya and -Ni as stance alignment markers. *Korean Language in America, 23*(1), 3–29.

Kasper, G. (2006). Beyond repair: Conversation analysis as an approach to SLA. *AILA Review, 19*, 83–99.

Kasper, G., & Rose, K. (Eds.). (2001). *Pragmatics in language teaching*. Cambridge Applied Linguistics. Cambridge: Cambridge University Press.

Kim, K.-H. (1999a). Other-initiated repair sequences in Korean conversation: Types and functions. *Discourse and Cognition, 6*(2), 141–168.

Kim, K.-H. (1999b). Phrasal unit boundaries and organization of turns and sequences in Korean conversation. *Human Studies, 22*, 425–446.

Kim, K.-H. (2004). A conversational analysis of Korean sentence-ending modal suffixes -*ney*, -*kwun(a)*, and -*ta*: Noticing as a social action. *The Sociolinguistic Journal of Korea, 12*(1), 1–35.

Kim, K.-H. (2020). Topic marker Nun in conversation: Interactional practices and pedagogical implications. *The Korean Language in America, 24*(1), 51–82.

Kim, K.-H., & Suh, K.-H. (1998). Confirmation sequences as interactional resources in Korean language proficiency interviews. In A. He & R. Young (Eds.), *Talking and testing: Discourse approaches to the assessment of oral proficiency* (pp. 297–332). Amsterdam and Philadelphia: John Benjamins Publishing Company.

Kim, M. S. (2013). Answering questions about unquestionable in Korean conversation. *Journal of Pragmatics, 57*, 138–157. https://doi.org/10.1016/j.pragma.2013.08.004

Kim, M. S. (2014). Reported thought as a stance-taking device in Korean conversation. *Discourse Processes, 51*(3), 230–263. https://doi.org/10.1016/j.pragma.2013.08.004

Kim, M. S. (2015). Reconstructing misinterpretation and misrepresentation through represented talk in Korean conversation. *Text and Talk, 35*(6), 759–787. https://doi.org/10.1515/text-2015-0021

Kim, M. S. (2021). Interactional competence in Korean language In S. Cho & J. Whitman (Eds.), *The Cambridge handbook of Korean language and linguistics* (pp. 800–831). Cambridge: Cambridge University Press.

Kim, M. S. (This volume). Conversation analysis in KSL. In A. Byon & D. O. Pyun (Eds.), *Handbook of Korean language education*. Oxon and New York: Routledge.

Kim, M. S., & Yoon, K.-E. (2021). Language in use. In Y. Cho (Ed.), *Teaching Korean as a foreign language: Theories and practices* (pp. 54–80). Oxon and New York: Routledge.

Kramsch, C. (1986). From language proficiency to interactional competence. *Modern Language Journal, 70*, 366–372.

Lam, D. M. K. (2018). What counts as "responding"? Contingency on previous speaker contribution as a feature of interactional competence. *Language Testing, 35*, 377–401. https://doi.org/10.1177/0265532218758126

Lee, H., & Choi, Y.-H. (2017). Pardon me? Requests for clarification and pedagogical implications for KFL education. In *The 27th International Conference on Korean Language Education* (pp. 546–553). Seoul: International Association for Korean Language Education.

Lee, H. S. (1991). *Tense, aspec, and modality: A discourse pragmatic analysis of verbal affixes in Korean from a typological perspective* [Ph.D dissertation]. University of California, Los Angeles.

Lee, H. S. (1993). Cognitive constraints on expressing newly perceived information: With reference to epistemic modal suffixes in Korean. *Cognitive Linguistics, 4*(2), 135–167.

Lee, H. S. (1999). A discourse-pragmatic analysis of the Committal *ci* in Korean: A synthetic approach to the form-meaning relation. *Journal of Pragmatics, 31*, 243–275.

Lee, H. S. (2016). *Convergence of conversation analysis and Korean language education: Measuring interactional competence through learners' usage of reactive tokens*. Keynote Lecture given at the 18th International Conference of Korean Language Education, October 22, 2016. Seoul National University, Seoul, Korea.

Lee, H. S., Yoon, K.-E., & Yoon, S.-S. (2017). Teaching listener responses to KFL students. *Korean Language in America, 21*(2), 250–261.

Levinson, S. C. (1983). *Pragmatics*. Cambridge: Cambridge University Press.

Ochs, E. (1996). Linguistic resources for socializing humanity. In J. J. Gumperz & S. L. Levinson (Eds.), *Rethinking linguistic relativity* (pp. 407–437). New York: Cambridge University Press.

Pyun, D., & Yoon, K.-E. (Forthcoming). Discourse functions of Korean 'yes' words. *Korean Linguistics*.

Roever, C., & Kasper, G. (2018). Speaking in turns and sequences: Interactional competence as a target construct in testing speaking. *Language Testing, 35*(3), 331–355. https://doi.org/10.1177/0265532218758128

Schegloff, E. (1982). Discourse as an interactional achievement: Some uses of 'uh huh' and other things that come between sentences. In D. Tannen (Ed.), *Analyzing discourse: Text and talk* (pp. 71–93). Washington, DC: Georgetown University Press.

Schegloff, E. (1986). The routine as achievement. *Human Studies, 9*(2), 111–151.

Schegloff, E. (2007). Sequence-closing sequences. In *Sequence organization in interaction: A primer in conversation analysis* (pp. 181–194). Cambridge: Cambridge University Press.

Schegloff, E., Jefferson, G., & Sacks, H. (1977). The preference for self-correction in the organization of repair in conversation. *Language, 53*(2), 361–382.

Schegloff, E., & Sacks, H. (1973). Opening up closing. *Semiotica, 8*(4), 289–327.

Stivers, T. (2008). Stance, alignment, and affiliation during storytelling: When nodding is a token of affiliation. *Research on Language and Social Interaction, 41*(1), 31–57. https://doi.org/10.1080/08351810701691123

Stivers, T., Mondada, L., & Steensig, J. (2011). Knowledge, morality, and affiliation in social interaction. In T. Stivers, L. Mondada & J. Steensig (Eds.), *The morality of knowledge in conversation* (pp. 3–24). Cambridge: Cambridge University Press.

Waring, H. Z. (2002). Displaying substantive recipiency in seminar discussion. *Research on Language Sciences, 23*, 651–677.

Wong, J., & Waring, H. Z. (2010). *Conversation analysis and second language pedagogy: A guide for ESL/EFL teachers*. Oxon and New York: Routledge.

Yoon, K.-E. (2003). Demonstratives in Korean conversation as interactional resources. *Crossroads of Language, Interaction, and Culture, 5*, 67–91.

Yoon, K.-E. (2007). Application of conversation analysis to teaching Korean language and culture. *Korean Language in America, 12*, 126–143.

Yoon, K.-E. (2010). Questions and responses in Korean conversation. *Journal of Pragmatics, 42*, 2782–2798.

Yoon, S.-S., & Jeong, H. (2016). Teaching reactive tokens to KFL students using authentic language. In *Paper presented at the conference of the American Association of Teachers of Korea*. Emory University, Atlanta, GA, June 16–18, 2016.

Youn, S. J. (2015). Validity argument for assessing L2 pragmatics in interaction using mixed methods. *Language Testing, 32*, 199–225. https://doi.org/10.1177/0265532214557113

Youn, S. J. (2020). Interactional features of L2 pragmatic interaction in role-play speaking assessment. *TESOL, 54*(1), 291–233.

Young, R. (2008). Managing proposal sequences in role-play assessment: Validity evidence of interactional competence across levels. *Language Testing*. Advance Online Publication. http://doi/10.1177/0265532219860077

Young, R. F., & Lee, J. (2004). Identifying units in interaction: Reactive tokens in Korean and English conversations. *Journal of Sociolinguistics, 8*, 380–407.

Zimmerman, D. H. (1998). Identity, context and interaction. In C. Antaki & S. Widdicombe (Eds.), *Identities in talk* (pp. 87–106). London: Sage.

APPENDIX

Transcription conventions (adapted from Ochs, Schegloff, & Thompson, 1996, pp. 461–465)

Some segments are transcribed to the minimum as needed for the focus of our discussion.

[	The point at which overlapping talk starts
]	The point at which overlapping talk ends
=	If the two lines connected by the equal signs are produced: (i) by the same speaker, the continuous talk is broken up to accommodate the placement of overlapping talk; (ii) if they are produced by different speakers, the second follows the first with no discernable silence between them (i.e., "latched" to it).
(0.5)	The length of silence in tenths of a second
(.)	Micro-pause
word	Some form of stress or emphasis, either by increased loudness or higher pitch
WOrd	Especially loud talk
°word°	A passage of talk quieter than the surrounding talk
:::	The prolongation or stretching of the sound just preceding them
.	Falling, or final intonation
?	Rising intonation
,	Half-rising intonation
¿	Rising stronger than a comma but weaker than a question mark
_:	Inflected falling intonation contour
:_	Inflected rising intonation contour
↑↑	A passage of talk with higher pitch than the surrounding talk
><	Increase in tempo, as in a rush-through
<>	Markedly slow talk
<	"Jump-started," i.e., starting with a rush
—	A cut-off or self-interruption (modified to be distinguished from the morpheme boundary marker, -)
hhh	Audible outbreath
.hh	Audible inbreath
(hh)	Laughter within a word
(word)	Uncertainty of hearing on the transcriber's part
( )	Something being said but no hearing achieved
(( ))	Transcriber's remark

INDEX

academic language 208, 222, 226
accent 444, 446, 465–467
achievement test 493, 497–501, 510
acknowledgment token 545, 552, 554, 562
ACTFL proficiency guidelines 372, 381, 507, 510, 519, 540, 542, 564
action formation 280, 283
addition 323, 325–326, 328–329, 332, 335–336
address terms 55–56, 58, 60, 62, 112–114, 119, 123–125, 350, 444
adjacency pair 280, 284, 286, 291, 541–543, 546–549, 562–563
adjunct model 224, 231
adverbials 80, 304, 310, 312, 552
affective factors 249, 417, 478
affective stance 179–180, 298, 302, 304, 350–351, 354, 541, 555, 561–563
affiliation 287, 438–440, 541–542, 546–547, 562–563; *see also* affiliative stance
affiliative stance 558, 560, 562
affirmative tokens 277, 279, 294
agency 52, 60, 64, 161, 440, 456, 461, 469
agent 72–73, 79, 97
agreement 542–543, 546, 561–563
alignment 541–542, 545–546, 558, 560, 562–563
analytic scoring 499, 509
animacy 72–73, 76, 83
annotation scheme 268
anxiety 417–419, 421–423, 426–432; listening anxiety 428, 430; reading anxiety 427–429, 431; speaking anxiety 427–428; writing anxiety 428–429
apologies 56–57, 62–64, 181–182
aspect hypothesis 83
assessment 124–125, 486, 493–494, 541–542, 546, 548–550, 555, 558, 560–561, 563–564; CBI programs 231; minimal assessment 546–547, 562–563; non-minimal assessment 547, 563
Attitude/Motivation Test Battery (AMTB) 419, 424, 426
authentic contexts 60, 239, 242, 249; authentic setting 235, 238–239
authenticity 215, 230, 299
authentic materials 521; age-appropriate 524; level-appropriate 530; practices 528; texts 528
automatic speech recognition (ASR) 161

backward design 530
balance 259
blended learning 164–166
bottleneck hypothesis 82
British National Corpus (BNC) 259, 265
business Korean: analysis of 198–199; curriculum of 199–201; models for teaching 200; needs analysis of 199; subfields of 198; teaching of 196–198

case ellipsis 76, 82
case marking 89, 90, 97, 100
causative 79, 80, 404
change-of-state token 545, 550, 552, 554
Child Language Data Exchange System (CHILDES) 104
civic engagement 235–236, 244; civic responsibility 236
classroom interaction 354–355
cognitive academic language learning approach (CALLA) 224
cognitive theory of multimedia learning (CTML) 156
common errors 319, 335, 341
Common European Framework of Reference for Languages (CEFR) 510

communicative competence 348, 405, 540, 548, 561, 563
communicative function 222, 347
communicative language teaching (CLT) 364, 382, 386
community 235, 237–238, 371–373, 375–378, 379–380, 382, 424, 440–442; community-based learning 355; community-engaged learning 236; community needs 236; community partner(s) 236–237, 244; community service 236; community sites 240
community engagement 194
community of practice (CoP) 212–213, 351–352
competition model 69, 71, 79
complaints and complaining 181, 183–185
compliments 56–57, 124, 185, 356
computer-aided error analysis (CEA) 267
computer-assisted language learning (CALL) 149–152, 160–163
computer-based test (CBT) 213, 504–505
computer-mediated communication (CMC) 62, 136, 153, 159–162, 170, 350
concordancing 260–261
connections 237–238, 365–366, 373–379, 382
consonants 32–33; affricates 39–41; fricatives 41–43; stops 36–39
contaysmal 115, 123
content-based language instruction (CBI) 145, 188–189, 199–200, 222, 379
content language integrated learning (CLIL) 224
content-obligatory language 226
context-induced 398
context-specific 298, 303, 305, 307, 314, 348
continuer 289, 541, 544–545, 550, 560, 562–563
contrastive interlanguage analysis (CIA) 267
conversational implicature 398
conversation analysis (CA) 277, 279, 281, 294, 541–542
Copula construction, the 393–394; negative Copula, the 393–394; negative equational construction, the 394
corpus-driven 257; corpus (pl. corpora) 257; corpus-based 257
critical discourse analysis 525
cultural competence 146, 246, 250, 366, 374, 447, 506
cultural identity 235, 246–247, 252, 429, 457
culture 53, 56–57, 59–60, 111, 162–164, 196, 228, 243–248, 347, 365–366, 425, 439–440, 460; definitions of 176–178; modernist and postmodernist perspectives 176–177

data-driven learning (DDL) 261
degree of imposition 113
developmental errors 323–324, 332
diagnostic test 493
diagram-based instruction 18

dialect 315, 444, 464–465, 468, 481
digital storytelling (DST) 161–162
disaffiliative stance 544, 546, 563; *see also* affiliative stance
disagreement 289, 291, 542, 561; *see also* agreement
disalignment 563; *see also* alignment
discourse competence 348, 540
discourse-first approach/perspective 301, 305, 316
discourse hypothesis 83
discourse suffix 72, 81–82
distance 52, 113
distance learning 164
diversification 125, 437
diversity and inclusivity 488
domain-specific corpora 262
Douglas Fir Group (DFG) 350–351, 356
Dutch 36–37

ecology of grammar 388
effective Korean language teachers/instructors 481–482
emergent 388
epistemic stance 298, 301–302, 304, 312, 316, 558, 560
error 319–320, 322–330, 334–336, 338, 341; analysis 319, 323, 330, 333–335, 340–341; categorisation 323, 334, 341; cause of errors 319–320, 322–325, 327, 330, 332–334, 337–339; classification 322–323; description 320, 322; explanation 320, 322–323, 328–329, 334, 339, 341; occurrence 321, 335, 338, 341; patterns 321, 323–325, 327, 341; source of errors 323–324, 329–330, 333; types of errors 320, 324, 327, 332–334
error annotation 264, 266–271
eTandem 160
ethnic identity/affiliation 438–441, 445–446
ethnicity 60, 457, 461, 465
evidentials 298, 304, 312

face-threatening acts 181, 185
family interaction 352–353
feedback 518, 520, 527–528, 530; feedback loop 525; feedback strategies 524, 530; types 530
first pair part (FPP) 280–284, 286
Five Cs 366, 367–368, 372–373, 376–379, 518, 530
flipped learning 165
focus 75–76
foreign accent 46
Foreign Language Classroom Anxiety Scale (FLCAS) 421–422, 427–429
Foreign Language Reading Anxiety Scale (FLRAS) 427–429
foreigner talk 483
formality 300, 304, 314

formative assessment 525
form-first 301
fundamental differential hypothesis 84–85
fundamental frequency (f0) 33

gender ideologies 464
genre 298–299, 300–302, 316–318
genre-based approach 224
gesture 58
grammatical categories 335
grammatical competence 540; *see also* linguistic competence
grammatical errors 326, 334–335, 340–341
grammaticality 269
grammaticalization 388, 399, 400
grammatical roles 70, 74–75

heritage 365, 371–376, 379; heritage language 235, 238, 245; heritage language attrition 437, 443, 448; heritage language learners 235, 238–240, 242–244, 438–440, 457; heritage language motivation 437, 439–440, 442; heritage language pedagogy 444, 446–449; heritage language proficiency 437, 439–440, 443, 446, 448; heritage learners 60, 61–62
holistic scoring 499, 509
honorifics 51–64, 72, 78, 83, 78, 113, 178–180, 182, 188, 298, 302, 305, 307, 459–461; hearer honorifics *see* speech styles; indirectness and directness 182–183; referent honorifics 54–55, 61; subject honorifics 114
hybridity 460
hybrid learning 165

identity 60, 64; ascribed 455–456; assumed 455; cultural 457; ethnic 457–461; ethnolinguistic 458; hybrid 459; imposed 455, 462–463, 469; inhabited 455–456; learner 455, 457; linguistic 454, 461, 467; multilingual 458; negotiable 455; second language 454
image schema 17
image schema-based instruction 19
immersion 224, 226, 230
immigrant learners 454, 462
impoliteness 52, 57–58, 64
incidental learning 154
(in)definiteness 72–74, 76
indigenous criteria 230
indirect discourse 391
indirect/secondary perspective 70–71, 73, 75
individual learner variables 417–418, 423
induced errors 322, 324, 331, 338
insert-expansion 284, 286
integrated performance assessment (IPA) 518
Intelligent CALL (ICALL) 149, 152–153
intentional learning 154
interactional competence (IC) 348, 540–542, 548–549, 560–563

inter-annotator agreement 269, 271
interface hypothesis 81
interference 322–325, 330, 332–333
interlingual 323–325, 329
International Corpus of Learner English (ICLE) 259, 263
internet-based test (IBT) 495, 508
interpersonal mode 520–522, 526–527; interpersonal tasks 521, 525; speaking 523
interpretive mode 521, 523, 526
interpretive tasks 521, 525
inter-subjectification 402
intimacy 117
intralingual 322–325, 329–331

Japanese 37, 39, 42

kinship terms 56, 59, 62, 120
Konglish 445, 447
Korean adoptees 459
Korean American 238–239, 242, 245, 252
Korean as a second language (KSL) 222, 319–320, 322, 325, 328–331, 333–336, 338–341; KSL learners 112, 319, 325, 328–331, 333–336, 338–339
Korean communities 355–356
Korean ethnolect 446–447
Korean for academic purposes (KAP) 263, 426, 503–505, 508–509, 511; assessment of 213–215; community of practice 212–213; categorization of 206–207; listening 211–212; needs analysis of 207–208; reading 208–209; speaking 210–211; writing 210
Korean for missionary purposes 202–203
Korean for occupational purposes (KOP): diplomacy 203; medicine 205–206; military 204–205; tourism 204
Korean for specific purposes (KSP): categorization of 195–196; locality 196; tenets of 196
Korean language curricula 123–124
Korean Learner Language Analysis (KoLLA) corpus 258, 268
Korean Wave (*Hallyu*) 111, 425, 431, 497

L2 Motivational Self System 420, 426
language accommodation 231
language ideologies 454–458, 461–469; flexible language ideologies 465, 467; pluralistic language ideologies 464; standard language ideology 464
language-related episode (LREs) 136, 138, 141–142
language socialization 59–62, 350–352
learner corpus (pl. corpora) 257
learner corpus research 258, 266–267
learning objectives 372–373, 526–528, 530; learning outcomes 528

Index

less commonly taught languages (LCTLs) 382, 417–418
lexical categories 329
lexical errors 13, 25, 325–326, 329–331, 333–334
linear distance 90–91, 94, 104
linguistic categories 323
linguistic competence 540, 548, 560–561
linguistic confidence 418, 427
linguistic discrimination 464

macro, meso, micro 300–301, 305, 310
manner of articulation 32
marginalization 464, 466, 469
marriage-migrants 463–465, 468
massive open online course (MOOC) 164–165
media materials 187–188
metacognitive awareness 528
minimal receipt token 541, 545
mistakes 320, 322
mixed-heritage 459, 461, 468
Moduuy Corpus 263
monoculturalism 460
motivation 418–419, 422–426, 431–432; instrumental motivation 419, 424, 426, 431; integrative motivation 419, 423–424, 426, 430
multicultural family 463
multilayered mark-ups 268
multimodality 52–53, 63–64, 190
multimodal modulation hypothesis 122
multiple sayings 278, 293–294
Myers-Briggs Type Indicator (MBTI) model 485

National Institute of Korean Language (NIKL) corpus 270
National Standards 518, 530; World-Readiness Standards 520, 528
negation 393–398; long-form of negation (LFN), the 394–398; short-form of negation (SFN), the 394–398
newsmarker 542; newsmark token 545, 550, 555, 558, 562–563
nodding and bowing 121
non-heritage learners 60
non-honorific speech 460–461, 463
non-minimal expansion 542, 555, 558, 562–563; non-minimal post expansion 547, 563
nonverbal behaviour 52, 58–59
nonverbal honorifics 121
North Korean refugees 457, 465–467
noticings 304–305, 313
noun phrase accessibility hierarchy 82–83
null/zero pronoun 74–75, 82
number of foreigners learning Korean 112

object/affected 70–71, 73, 79
oblique/circumstantial 70–71, 73–74
omission 323, 325–326, 328–329, 333, 335, 339–340

Oral Proficiency Interview (OPI) 214, 364, 381, 505, 519, 540, 542, 560, 563–564
Oral Proficiency Interview-Computer (OPIc) 508
orthographic errors 324–327, 329
overgeneralisation 324, 330–332

pair dynamics 136, 141–142
panmal 115
peer interaction 129, 136, 349, 356
perceptual assimilation 34–37, 40, 42–44, 46
performance-based assessment 497, 506, 508, 510, 520
performance-based language teaching (PBLT) 386
phonation type 33
placement test 369, 424, 493
place of articulation 32, 39–40
politeness 51–64, 178, 182–183, 188
polysemous 11–16; core meaning 16
portfolio project 186
post-expansion 284, 290
postposition suffix 72, 81–82
power 52, 62–63, 113, 116–117, 180–182, 351, 357, 455
pragmalinguistic competence 59
pragmatics 51, 59, 63–64, 111–112, 303, 447
pre-expansion 284–285
preference organization 281, 293
presentational mode 520, 527; presentational tasks 520, 525, 527; speaking 523
proficiency test 493–495, 497, 503, 505, 529
prosody 52, 69
prototypicality 18

reference corpus 264–265
refugee language-support programs 467
refusals 56
register 14, 20, 124, 167, 202, 263, 298–303, 307, 314–316, 373–374, 447, 463
relational hierarchy 90, 103–104
relative clause 77–78, 82
relative clause frequency: adult L2 speech 104; child speech 104; maternal speech 104
relative clause types: direct object 90–94, 97, 102–103; indirect object 94–95, 97–99, 101–102; Korean *vs.* English 89–90; oblique 94–95, 100, 102–103; subject 90–94, 96–97, 101–102
reliability 493, 497, 503, 511, 529; inter-rater reliability 504, 508; rater reliability 499, 500, 508–509
remedial 329, 334, 340–341
repair 286–291, 541, 543–544, 547, 550, 552, 558, 560–563
representativeness 258–259
requests 56, 62–64, 182–183, 198
response token 544–546, 552, 558, 560, 562–563
resumptive openers 552, 564

risk-taking 418, 421, 427, 433
rubrics 520, 522, 526–528, 530
rule-based 386–387

scaffolding framework 482
second-pair part (SPP) 280–284, 286–287, 290–291, 541
Sejong Balanced Corpus 265
Sejong Corpus 258, 263, 264–266
self-confidence 419–420, 422–423, 427, 429–430, 432
self-efficacy 422–423, 426–427, 429–430, 432
semantic priming 13, 16
semantic transfer 13
sequence-closing third (SCT) 290, 294
sequence expansion 284, 294
sequence organization 277, 280–281, 291, 293
service learning 235–237; service-learning activities 240
shared syntax hypothesis 79, 80–81, 85
sheltered model 225
social exclusion 459
social interactionist approach 351
sociocultural awareness 235, 243, 252
sociolinguistic competence 540, 548
sociopragmatic competence 59
Spanish 36–37, 39
speech acts 56–57, 62–64, 185, 302, 372
speech styles 54–55, 57, 59, 61, 114–115, 178–181, 188
speech style shift 115–118
Standard Korean 464–465, 468
standards-based learning 524; instruction and assessment 530; standards-based rubrics 524
strategic competence 204, 213, 540, 564
structural prominence 94, 96, 103–104
study abroad 60, 126, 168, 177, 239, 357; study abroad learners 454, 458, 460–462; study abroad programs 462
subject/perspective 70–72, 75, 79
subject-prominent language 75
subset principle 80–81
substitution 35, 79, 102, 323, 325–326, 328, 335–341
summative assessment 518; summative IPAs 522
sustained-content language teaching 224
swearing 58
synchronous written corrective feedback (SWCF) 138

task: collaborative tasks 138, 141–143; individual task 138; task design 137; task engagement 135–138; task implementation 129, 135, 142; task performance 137–145; task repetition 142–144
task-based language teaching (TBLT) 129, 386
task-referenced language teaching (TRLT) 134–135
task-supported language teaching (TSLT) 134–135
teacher efficacy 474, 485–486
teacher/instructor individual characteristics: beliefs and attitudes 477–478; foreign language learning experience 480; gender 480; intercultural competence 479; native/non-native language background 476–477; personalities/characteristics 485, 487; role 482, 487; teaching effectiveness 481; training and educational background 478–480; years of teaching experience 478–479
teacher talk 354, 474, 483, 487
teacher training program 477–478
technology-enhanced 526; online discussion forum 526
telecollaboration 163–164
Test of Proficiency in Korean (TOPIK) 493–496, 501–511
textbooks 20, 61, 63, 123, 125–126, 189, 200, 209–212, 227–229, 299, 375, 386–394, 460
theme-based model 225, 231
theme/patient 73, 79
three-way contrast *see* phonation type
topic maker 74, 76, 81–82
topic-prominent language 75
transfer 80, 84, 323–324, 331–333, 337–338
translanguaging 444, 447
Trinity Lancaster Corpus 260

unaccusative 73, 79–80
unergative 73, 79–80
usage-based 386–389, 405–406

validity 493, 497, 502–503, 511, 529; test validity 500, 508
Vietnamese 41, 43
voice onset time (VOT) 33, 36, 39
Voicethread 156, 162
vowels 34, 43–44
Vygotsky's sociocultural theory 349

washback effect 501, 508, 511, 519–520, 524, 526, 528, 530
Web 2.0 150–151, 156, 159–160, 163, 169
wh-question 75, 84–85
word frequency 19
word order 90–92, 94, 96–97, 100, 104